Covenants Against Competition in Franchise Agreements

FOURTH EDITION

Michael R. Gray, Natalma M. McKnew,
and William W. Sentell, Editors

AMERICAN BAR ASSOCIATION
Forum on Franchising

Cover design by ABA Design

Printed in the United States of America.

26 25 24 23 5 4 3 2 1

A catalog record for this book is on file with the Library of Congress.

Contents

State Law Analysis

Canadian Province Analysis

Mexico Analysis

About the Editors

Michael R. Gray is a partner in Minneapolis office of Lathrop GPM. He brings 36 years of experience representing franchisors, companies, and individuals in trial, arbitration, and other civil proceedings throughout the United States. He is lead litigation counsel for several national franchise companies and has litigated, arbitrated, and mediated all manner of franchise, intellectual property, and business disputes in state and federal courts in over 38 states.

Mike has authored articles and presented materials on franchise and intellectual property topics for the American Bar Association Forum on Franchising, the International Franchise Association, the *Franchise Law Journal*, the Practising Law Institute, the University of St. Thomas, and the Business Law Institute. Mike is a contributing author to the *Franchise Desk Book* (W. Michael Garner, Editor); co-editor of *Covenants Against Competition in Franchise Agreements*, ABA Forum on Franchising (3d ed. 2012; 4th ed. 2022); and co-author of the chapter "Intellectual Property Issues in Franchising" for *The Intellectual Property Deskbook for the Business Lawyer* (4th ed. 2019) and many other presentations and publications.

Mike served for six years on the Governing Committee of the ABA Forum on Franchising where he was the Finance Officer from 2016 through 2019 and was Co-Chair of the 41st Annual Forum on Franchising in Nashville, Tennessee. Mike has been recognized by Chambers USA for Franchising; has been named as one of the "Best Lawyers in America" by Woodward/White, a "Super Lawyer" by Minnesota Law & Politics, and a "Legal Eagle" by Franchise Times; is listed in *The International Who's Who of Franchise Lawyers* and is a "Certified Franchise Executive" by the International Franchise Association. Mike is admitted to practice in Minnesota and Wisconsin as well as numerous federal district and appellate courts throughout the United States.

Natalma M. ("Tami") McKnew is a partner in Fox Rothschild, LLP, in Greenville, South Carolina. She has been in private practice since 1978 with Fox Rothschild or its predecessors Smith Moore Leatherwood and Leatherwood Walker Todd & Mann, P.C. She served as the latter's managing director for six years. She concentrates her practice in the areas of franchising, intellectual property, and antitrust, primarily in litigation. She is a member of the South Carolina Bar and is admitted to practice in all state and federal courts in South Carolina, the Fourth Circuit Court of Appeals, the Federal Circuit Court of Appeals, and the U.S. Supreme Court.

Tami served on the Forum's Governing Committee for six years and co-chaired the Forum's Annual Meeting in New Orleans. She frequently speaks on franchise, intellectual property, and antitrust issues. Tami co-edited the third edition of this publication, is a contributing author to the *Franchise Desk Book* (W. Michael Garner, editor) and an upcoming Forum franchisee reference book, co-authored *Annual*

Franchise and Distribution Law Developments 2008, and has authored numerous articles on franchising and trademark issues.

Tami received a master's degree from the University of California, Los Angeles and her law degree from the Northeastern University School of Law. She is included in *The Best Lawyers in America* and in South Carolina Super Lawyers among other professional recognitions. She has received various awards and recognitions for her work outside the law, including the "Women Making History" and "Heart in the Arts" awards. She is a founder of the Institute for Child Success and has served for almost two decades on the Boards of the United Way of Greenville County and the South Carolina chapter of The Nature Conservancy.

William W. Sentell is a partner with Akerman LLP in Houston. He focuses his practice on franchise dispute resolution and related corporate, regulatory, and compliance matters.

With more than 14 years of complex commercial litigation experience, including first- and second-chair trial and arbitration experience, William provides support and clear risk assessment in all phases of litigation. Avoiding risk in the area of franchise sales and managing relationships throughout the franchise lifecycle are practice focuses for William.

William speaks regularly about issues affecting the franchise community, including before the American Bar Association, International Franchise Association, and the Louisiana State Bar Association and at Tulane University and the University of New Orleans. His written work has appeared in the *Franchise Law Journal, The Franchise Lawyer, Franchising World, Modern Restaurant Management*, Franchising.com, and *Law Week Colorado*, among other publications. William has also contributed to the ABA's best-selling *Franchise Deskbook* (3rd ed.), and he is a member of the ABA Franchise Forum's Publications Committee.

Foreword

Among the many strengths of the Forum on Franchising are the topical relevance and high quality of our publications. No book reflects these qualities better than *Covenants Against Competition in Franchise Agreements*, now in its fourth edition. First published in 1992, *Covenants* is one of the longest-running publications of the Forum. Due to its important subject matter, it is no doubt one of the most widely used as well. It has been an invaluable resource for Forum members for the past 30 years. The fourth edition continues this tradition of excellence.

On behalf of the Forum, I first want to thank the editors whose hard work has brought this latest edition to fruition. Mike Gray and Tami McKnew continued their fine work as editors of the third edition with their efforts as editors for this book, and we are grateful that they agreed to serve again. William Sentell added his talents as a co-editor for the fourth edition, and his efforts helped to make this version the best one yet. I also want to recognize Peter Klarfeld, who served as editor for the first and second editions of this publication, and who laid the foundation for the editions that followed.

Next, I want to thank all the state chapter authors who prepared the essential content for the book. The chapter authors all are experienced practitioners in this subject area, and they ably explain the nuances of each state's relevant legal framework. We used Forum members for most chapters, which highlights the breadth of talent and experience among our members.

Finally, I want to recognize the Forum's Publications Chairs who nurtured and brought this book to life. Gary Batenhorst initiated efforts for this fourth edition, and Ben Reed saw it through to publication. We appreciate your efforts throughout the process.

I'm sure I speak for all Forum members in saying that I can't wait to put the fourth edition of *Covenants* to regular use in my practice!

Ron Coleman
Chair, Forum on Franchising

Foreword

Introduction

The legal principles affecting restrictive covenants are founded in English common law that is at least three centuries older than the modern franchise industry. Our colleague and editor of the first edition of *Covenants Against Competition in Franchising,* Peter Klarfeld, cited *Mitchell v. Reynolds,* 1 P. Wms. 181, 24 Eng. Rep. 347 (Q.B. 1711) as an early example of a non-compete in connection with the sale of a business. Three hundred years earlier in *Dyer's Case,* 2 Hen. V., fol. 5, sp. 26 (1414), the court refused to enforce a non-compete in an employment contract, as a restraint on trade. Over the next centuries, a limited exception was made based on geography, but it was not until the *Mitchell* decision that legal principles defining acceptable geographic and temporal terms were formed. From this common lineage, the legal principles underpinning restrictive covenants developed, in similar but often divergent directions.

In a federal system, the states and provinces are the arbiters of the analytical principles defining valid restrictive covenants. The common and statutory analytical framework varies from state to state and province to province, but the overarching objective of the analysis is the same: to balance the legitimate needs of the promisee employer or business seller against the effects of the restriction on the promisor and on competition. Each state's jurisprudence shares this objective, but there is no requirement, and indeed no inclination, to uniformity.

A de facto nearly universal approach to analyzing restrictive covenants is to assess whether the restriction is reasonable to all—does it address the legitimate interests of the promisee, does it reasonably restrict the promisor's activities, has the promisee received reasonable value for agreeing to the restriction, does the restriction allow the promisor reasonable access to future employment, and does it adversely affect the public interest? But the touchstone of reasonableness is variously interpreted by courts and legislatures. In most states, reasonableness requires an inquiry into the consideration for the covenant, the promisee's legitimate protectable interests, the geographic sweep of the covenant, the limitations on the promisee's activities, and the duration of the non-compete. But with the growth of worldwide internet-based businesses, instant communications, and businesses without physical locations, even the application of an established reasonableness assessment faces challenges.

Various forms of restrictive covenants, including non-compete, non-solicitation, and non-disclosure provisions, are common features of most franchise agreements. These provisions reflect the perceived need of the franchisor to protect the intellectual property that is imparted to the franchisee, the value of the franchisor's investment in the franchisee, the integrity of the entire franchise system, and harmony among franchisees. Franchisees, on the other hand, may view such provisions as rendering their investment in the franchise business valueless, inhibiting their right to leave the system and from continuing in their chosen field. Because restrictive covenants are baked into many, if not most, franchise agreements, the need for predictability for both franchisor and franchisee is high. The lack of uniformity or even predictability in the laws affecting non-competes is frustrating in an industry in which a core value is consistency. There is no safe harbor test by which to test the viability of a restrictive covenant. Instead, enforceability is determined on a state-by-state (or province-by-province) and case-by-case basis, arguably the most expensive and least efficient method of determining validity.

This fourth edition of *Covenants Against Competition in Franchise Agreements* focuses on the analytical framework for assessing the validity and enforceability of restrictive covenants in franchise agreements in North America. In the cases and statutes reported in this book, the practitioner will find the principles and challenges described above reflected in caselaw and statutes. In some instances, franchise-specific authority is absent, in which case, reference is made to general principles set forth in other analogous situations.

It is worth noting, however, that franchising presents unique considerations that do not easily analogize to other business relationships. There are at least three groups directly affected by a franchise agreement: the franchisor, the franchisee signing an agreement, and other franchisees in the system. Can a franchisor reasonably protect the other franchisees in the system from potential post-expiration or termination actions by an ex-franchisee? Can or should a court consider the other franchisees in its analysis? A franchise system is based on a bundle of intellectual property rights, potentially ranging from trade secrets to general know-how. How much of that bundle is reasonably protected in a non-compete or non-disclosure? Does the centrality of goodwill associated with the franchisor's trademark or service mark change the analysis? Should it? A franchisee buys a license to run a business, not the business itself. Is the non-compete thus assessed as if it appeared in a business purchase agreement, or in an employment agreement? Neither relationship is readily comparable to a franchise. What consideration should be made of the franchisee's investment in the business?

This book does not provide answers; rather, it provides the franchise lawyer a summary of the laws applicable to restrictive covenants as of the date of publication. Courts and legislatures can, and do, amend the laws from time to time. In the United States, pleas for a uniform federal system have arisen in the past, thus far without tangible results. However, there are no restraints on how or whether legislatures will enact or amend statutes affecting restrictive covenants, and there are few guardrails on courts as they continue to define and apply the basic tests of reasonableness. We trust we have provided a solid basis for further investigation.

We thank the authors of the entries. These are busy lawyers who generously give of their time to edify their colleagues. It has been our pleasure to work with them, some for the second time, as two of us (Tami McKnew and Michael Gray) edited the third edition. We also wish to thank Antonia Scholz, Chair of the Publications Committee, for her assistance in getting this publication to print. Finally, it has been our pleasure to work with William Sentell on this fourth edition. The fifth edition, when it is undertaken, will be under his direction. We wish him the best!

Michael R. Gray, Editor
Natalma M. ("Tami") McKnew, Editor
William W. Sentell, Editor

State Law Analysis

Alabama

*by Linda Friedman, Rudy Hill, and Andrew Tuggle**

1. Has the state addressed covenants against competition in the context of franchising?

- **Does the state have a franchising statute or regulations that address covenants against competition?**
- **Does the state have a covenants statute of general applicability that would encompass franchise covenants?**
- **Have the courts addressed covenants in the context of franchising either under a statute or under the state's common law?**

Alabama has a statute that generally addresses covenants against competition. Ala. Code §§ 8-1-190 through 197 (replacing prior section 8-1-1 effective January 1, 2016). Alabama does not have a general franchise statute or regulations that specifically address covenants against competition in the franchise context. Although Alabama does not have a general franchising statute, some industry-specific statutes apply to franchise and dealer agreements in particular industries. These statutes are addressed in section 10 below.

Although the new statute repealed prior section 8-1-1, it retains much of the language of that section and codifies much of the prior common law, including a declaration that

> this article expresses fundamental public policies of the State of Alabama. Therefore, this article shall govern and shall be applied instead of any foreign laws that might otherwise be applicable in those instances when the application of those foreign laws would violate a fundamental public policy expressed in this article.

Ala. Code § 8-1-197.

As discussed below, prior to 2016 restrictive covenants in a franchise agreement had been enforced as "partial restraints" that fell outside prior section 8-1-1. An argument might be made that restrictive covenants in franchise agreements that

*The authors are attorneys with the law firm of Bradley Arant Boult Cummings LLP. Linda Friedman is a retired partner in Birmingham, Alabama. Rudy Hill is a partner in the firm's Birmingham, Alabama, office, and Andrew Tuggle is an associate in the firm's Huntsville, Alabama, office.

were entered into before January 1, 2016, can be enforced as "partial restraints" under the prior caselaw. *See* Comment, ALA. CODE § 8-1-197 ("This act is not meant to void or cast doubt on agreements entered into prior to the effective date of this act."). However, according to an article written by four attorneys who were on the committee that drafted the legislation, including the attorney who chaired the committee, the new statute "will apply to actions filed on or after January 1, 2016." Will Hill Tankersley, Richard J. R. Raleigh, Jr., J. Casey Pipes & Adam K. Israel, *Alabama Enacts Major Revision of Alabama Code 8-1-1*, 76 ALA. LAW. 385, 389 (2015) [hereinafter *Tankersley*]. Still, "[t]here is no indication that the statute applies retroactively to agreements executed before that date." *McGriff Seibels & Williams, Inc. v. Sparks*, 2019 WL 4600051, at *12 (N.D. Ala. Sept. 23, 2019).

The Alabama Supreme Court has not addressed the application of the 2016 statute to franchise agreements. A close review of the statute suggests that prior caselaw is preserved only to the extent that the prior caselaw has been codified in the new statute.

For example, the comment to section 8-1-197 says "[t]his section is intended to codify current Alabama caselaw." Because this comment refers to "this section" rather than "this article," the comment appears to apply specifically to the section's declaration that the article expresses the state's fundamental public policy, rather than to all prior caselaw, such as caselaw involving franchise agreements. *See Tankersley, supra* (". . . the Act brings clarity to the proper application of Alabama's restrictive covenant law, rejecting some judicial applications that were based on the language of the statute (i.e., the 'total' vs. 'partial' restraint dichotomy)").

The current statute begins with language taken directly from repealed section 8-1-1:

> Every contract by which anyone is restrained from exercising a lawful profession, trade or business of any kind otherwise than as provided by this section is to that extent void.

ALA. CODE § 8-1-190(a).

Prior section 8-1-1 listed specific exceptions to the foregoing prohibition, as does current section 8-1-190. Although none of the exceptions in prior section 8-1-1 addressed covenants in franchise agreements, caselaw had upheld reasonably limited restrictive covenants in franchise agreements pursuant to a judicially created "partial restraints" exception to the statutory prohibition against restraints of trade. *Sylvan Learning Inc. v. Learning Solutions, Inc.*, 795 F. Supp. 2d 1284, 1294 (S.D. Ala. 2011) (applying Maryland law, after finding it not inconsistent with Alabama law, to enforce restrictive covenant in franchise agreement); *Sylvan Learning, Inc. v. Gulf Coast Educ., Inc.*, 2010 WL 3943643, at *2–3 (M.D. Ala. Oct. 6, 2010) (applying Maryland law to enforce franchise agreement's restrictive covenant, after finding it not in conflict with Alabama's fundamental public policy); *Gafnea v. Pasquale Food Co.*, 454 So. 2d 1366 (Ala. 1984) (prior section 8-1-1 held not to bar enforcement of post-term covenant prohibiting franchisee from competing in a five-mile radius from franchise premises for eighteen months after termination). Current section 8-1-190, similar to prior section 8-1-1, lists exceptions to the general prohibition, but the exceptions do not expressly mention franchise agreements nor the term "partial restraints." The statute, in section 8-1-190(b), sets forth the following six types of contracts that, "*[e]xcept as otherwise prohibited by law,*" are "allowed *to preserve a protectable interest,*" as defined by section 8-1-191 (emphasis added):

(1) non-hire agreements that limit a party's ability to hire an agent or employee of another party if that person holds a "position uniquely essential to the management, organization, or service of the business";
(2) exclusive dealing agreements (i.e., agreements "to limit commercial dealings" to the parties);
(3) agreements in which the seller of a business' good will agrees not to compete with the buyer or not to solicit the business' customers "within a specified geographic area so long as the buyer, or any entity deriving title to the good will . . . carries on a like business therein, subject to reasonable time and place restraints";
(4) & (5) employment agreements or other agreements that prohibit "an agent, servant, or employee of a commercial entity" from "engaging in a similar business" or that prohibit solicitation of the business' "current customers" of the commercial entity, subject to specified time limits and other conditions;
(6) agreements among partners, owners, or members of a commercial entity being dissolved not to carry on a similar commercial activity where the entity had been transacting business.

See ALA. CODE § 8-1-190(b)(1)–(6).

Notably, exceptions (1), (2), (3), and (6) to the general prohibition are rather narrow and do not appear to apply to the typical post-term non-competition or non-solicitation covenant in a franchise agreement that restrains the franchisee after the franchise ends, although these exceptions could theoretically apply to a franchise relationship under their rather narrow circumstances. The remaining exceptions, in subsections (4) and (5), clearly do not apply to a typical franchise because these exceptions expressly apply only to covenants between a commercial entity and its agent, servant, or employee. A franchisee is not considered an "agent" of the franchisor, and certainly is not its "employee" or "servant."

With respect to exception (1), it could be applied to franchises, but only with respect to no-hire covenants. Specifically, the first exception would allow a franchisor to preserve its "protectable interest" by prohibiting a franchisee from hiring an agent or employee of the franchisor if that person holds a "uniquely essential" position with the franchisor. The comment to section 8-1-190 explains that "[t]he term 'uniquely essential' . . . reflects the intent to limit use of the exception to circumstances in which the employee in question holds a position which is not only important to the business, but in which the agent, servant or employee's services would be very difficult to replicate."

With respect to exception (2), which permits parties to preserve a protectable interest by limiting "commercial dealings to each other," it would allow a franchise agreement to require that a franchisee and franchisor confine their dealings to each other during the term of the franchise, but it does not appear to allow a unilateral commitment that binds only the franchisee or franchisor. Moreover, exception (2) does not logically apply after the franchise ends and the parties stop dealing with each other.

With respect to exception (3), which permits the seller of good will of a business to agree with the buyer to refrain from competition with the business or from soliciting the business's customers, it would apply if a franchisee buys the good will of a franchised location, either from the franchisor or another party (in which case the franchisor or other selling party is restrained), or if a franchisee or other party sells its business's good will to a franchisor (in which case the franchisee or other selling party is restrained).

The six exceptions in section 8-1-190 represent an expansion of the statutorily permitted restrictive covenants set out in prior section 8-1-1, which listed as permitted exceptions employment agreements, sales of a business's good will, and agreements in connection with dissolving a business. The comment to section 8-1-190 explains that the new statute added other exceptions in order to codify certain exceptions recognized by caselaw. Specifically, the comment states, in pertinent part:

> This section preserves the current presumption previously found in Section 8-1-1 of the Code of Alabama, 1975 against contracts in restraint of trade. It also retains, in subsections (b)(3) and (b)(5), two exceptions from the previous statute. *Because other "partial restraints" have been recognized by the courts as not inconsistent with the general prohibition, this redraft codifies those exceptions.*

Comment, ALA. CODE § 8-1-190 (emphasis added).

According to the comment, section 8-1-190(b) was drafted to codify partial restraints that had been recognized by the courts as lawful. Yet, the 1984 decision by the Supreme Court in *Gafnea*, 454 So. 2d 1366, which upheld a post-term restrictive covenant in a franchise agreement as a "partial restraint," was not codified. Neither the statute nor the comment states that *all* restraints previously held to be lawful as partial restraints remain lawful. Therefore, a fair conclusion is that the holding in *Gafnea* is inconsistent with the current statute and that a restrictive covenant in a franchise agreement is prohibited unless it fits within one of the exceptions in section 8-1-190(b).[1]

Although the Alabama Supreme Court has not yet addressed the continued relevance of *Gafnea*, and the language of the statute appears not to cover the typical post-term covenant in a franchise agreement, one federal court followed *Gafnea* in interpreting current section 8-1-190. *Right at Home, LLC. v. Gaudet*, 2021 WL 308237 (D. Neb. Jan. 29, 2021) (applying Alabama law to franchise agreement despite agreement's choice of Nebraska law, and granting preliminary injunction to enforce

---

1. The authors note that section 8-1-193 states, "[I]f a contractually specified restraint is overly broad or unreasonable in its duration, a court may void the restraint in part and reform it to preserve the protectable interest or interests. If a contractually specified restraint does not fall within the limited exceptions set out in subsection (b) of Section 8-1-190, a court may void the restraint in its entirety." Because section 8-1-193 says that a court "*may*" rather than "shall" *void* a restraint not "within the limited exceptions" in section 8-1-190(b), does that mean that a court "may" *enforce* a restraint not listed at all in section 8-1-190(b), such as a post-termination restraint against competition in a franchise agreement that does not fit any of the six exceptions? Such a conclusion, however, would be inconsistent with the wording of section 8-1-190 as well as with the comment to that section. Rather, the second sentence in section 8-1-193 should be read as a clarification of the *first* sentence, which permits a court to blue-pencil a restraint that is overly broad or unreasonable in its duration. For example, an agreement in anticipation of dissolution of a business that prohibits the owners from carrying on a similar business anywhere in the world would "not fall within the limited exceptions set out in subsection (b)" if the business had not transacted business throughout the world, because subsection (b)(6) requires that such a restraint be confined to the "geographic area where business has been transacted." In that case, section 8-1-193 provides that the court may blue-pencil the restraint geographically, or the court "may void" it in its entirety.

a non-compete covenant prohibiting Alabama franchisees from engaging in the same services as the franchised business for eighteen months after termination of franchise within ten-mile radius from outer boundaries of franchise territory; the case was dismissed after entry of a stipulated permanent injunction that enforced the franchise agreement's restrictive covenants, among other provisions).

The Nebraska federal court in *Right at Home* determined that the franchise agreement, executed before the effective date of the current Alabama statute, was subject to the current statute. *Right at Home*, 2021 WL 308237, at *6 n.3. The court then reasoned that "the amended statute codifies the common law with respect to partial restraints of trade," yet failed to identify any provision in the statute that referred to "partial restraints" or that "codified" the type of covenant in the Right at Home franchise agreement. Oddly, in its review of the six types of agreements that are allowed by section 8-1-190(b) as exceptions to the general prohibition in section 8-1-190(a), the court cited the exception in section 8-1-190(b)(6) as the exception that "may more likely" apply. *Id.* at *7 n.4. That exception allows "partners, owners, or members" of a "commercial entity" to agree that, "upon dissolution" of the commercial entity, "none of them will carry on a similar commercial activity in the geographic area where the commercial activity has been transacted." ALA. CODE § 8-1-190(b)(6).

---

2. Have the courts articulated the "legitimate interests" of the franchisor that will support enforcement of a covenant against competition contained in a franchise agreement?

- **If so, what are they (e.g., protection of goodwill, protection of confidential information), and in what contexts did the issue arise?**
- **If not, what interests have been recognized in other contexts (e.g., employment agreements, the sale of business context)?**

Current section 8-1-190 provides that a "protectable interest" must exist for contracts specified in sections 8-1-190-1(b)(1)–(6) to be valid. Although the exceptions in section 8-1-190(b) do not appear to relate to the typical post-term covenant in a franchise agreement, in which the franchisee is prohibited from operating a competing business after the franchise terminates, the statute's definition of a protectable interest expressly refers to franchises.

Section 8-1-191 states that a "protectable interest includes all of the following:

(1) Trade secrets, as defined in Alabama Code section 8-27-2.
(2) Confidential information, including, but not limited to, pricing information and methodology; compensation; customer lists; customer data and information; mailing lists; prospective customer information; financial and investment information; management and marketing plans; business strategy, technique, and methodology; business models and data; processes and procedures; and company provided files, software, code, reports, documents, manuals, and forms used in the business that may not otherwise qualify as a trade secret but which are treated as confidential to the business entity, in whatever medium provided or preserved, such as in writing or stored electronically.

(3) Commercial relationships or contacts with specific prospective or existing customers, patients, vendors, or clients.
(4) *Customer, patient, vendor, or client good will associated with any of the following:*
   a. *An ongoing business, franchise,* commercial, or professional practice, or trade dress.
   b. A specific marketing or trade area.
(5) Specialized and unique training involving substantial business expenditure specifically directed to a particular agent, servant, or employee; provided that such training is specifically set forth in writing as the consideration for the restraint.

(Emphasis added.)

Section 8-1-191 must be read in conjunction with section 8-1-190, because the existence of a protectable interest does not render a covenant enforceable if it does not pass muster under section 8-1-190. As stated in section 1 of this chapter, section 8-1-190(b)(1) permits non-hire agreements, in which a party agrees not to hire an agent or employee of the other party if the person "holds a position uniquely essential to the management, organization or service of the business"; section 8-1-190(b)(2) permits exclusive dealing agreements; and section 8-1-190(b)(3) permits a seller of good will in a business to agree to refrain from competition with, or solicitation of current customers of, the business, as long as the buyer carries on a like business in the area. Each type of restrictive agreement must serve to preserve a protectable interest. Therefore, a franchise agreement presumably could prohibit a franchisee from hiring an employee or agent of the franchisor, during the franchise agreement's term and thereafter, if the person holds such a "uniquely essential" position. Also, a franchise agreement could impose an exclusive dealing restriction, although that type of covenant appears to require that both franchisor and franchisee agree to the exclusivity and, further, it would logically only apply *while the franchise is in effect*. And, if a franchisee or franchisor buys or sells the good will of a franchised business, the seller could agree to a reasonable and geographically restricted covenant so long as the buyer carries on a like business in the area.

The comment to section 8-1-191 refers to the sale of good will situation in connection with the sale of a franchise. In pertinent part, the comment says that "[r]estrictive covenants related to good will in franchise or other agreements that otherwise satisfy the requirements of this act are enforceable." Comment, Ala. Code § 8-1-191.

However, as discussed earlier in section 1 of this chapter, typical *post-term* restrictive covenants do not appear to fit any exception to the general prohibition in section 8-1-190. Before enactment of the current statute, the Alabama Supreme Court had recognized a franchisor's protectable interest that justified a post-term restrictive covenant. *Gafnea*, 454 So. 2d 1366. The *Gafnea* court explained:

> The covenant is necessary to afford fair protection to the parties' interests. The Gafneas have gained experience and built a clientele using the Pasquale reputation and the benefits of their franchise with Pasquale. Pasquale must be able to protect its franchise system by the minimal restrictions designed to prevent franchisees from taking unfair advantage of the benefits Pasquale provides. If Pasquale is forced to suffer this sort of drain on its established business, it may not be able to continue to market its franchise operations or its products and services, which would clearly

> be detrimental to other franchisees under contracts such as the one under which the Gafneas operated.

454 So. 2d. at 1369. *See also Sylvan Learning, Inc. v. Learning Solutions, Inc.*, 795 F. Supp. 2d 1284, 1301–02 (S.D. Ala. 2011) (applying Maryland law after finding it not in conflict with Alabama law; recognizing that protection from loss of customers and difficulties in attracting new franchisees to territory are important interests of franchisor); *Sylvan Learning, Inc. v. Gulf Coast Education, Inc.*, 2010 WL 3943643, at *4–6 (M.D. Ala. Oct. 6, 2010) (applying Maryland law after finding it not in conflict with Alabama law, and recognizing a franchisor's interest in protecting its goodwill and customer base; the dangers of "the potential for diversion of [the franchisor's] business to former franchisees"; and "the danger to a franchisor's network created by 'breakaway' franchises continuing to operate in violation of a non-compete agreement"). These cases, decided prior to the 2016 effective date of current section 8-1-190, were cited in 2021 by the U.S. District Court for the District of Nebraska that applied Alabama's current statute to a post-term restrictive covenant in a franchise agreement. *Right at Home*, 2021 WL 308237 (citing the "protectable interests" expressed in sections 8-1-191(a)(3) and (4)(a) in granting preliminary injunction, holding that the franchisor was likely to succeed on merits to enforce post-termination covenant prohibiting franchisees from being engaged in similar business for eighteen months within ten-mile radius from outer boundaries of franchise territory). As discussed earlier in section 1 of this chapter, however, the Nebraska court's decision does not square well with the statute's language or its comments.

---

3. What time limitations have courts recognized as reasonable in the franchise context?

- **If no franchise cases have been decided, what time limitations have been recognized in other contexts?**
- **How have they been related to the interests protected?**

Alabama's current statute codifies much of the caselaw prior to January 1, 2016 (when current section 8-1-190 *et seq.* became effective), and much of the prior caselaw is also preserved. However, the current statute does not contain a provision allowing a covenant that prohibits a franchisee from engaging in a competing business after the franchise ends. Rather, the statute generally declares that "[e]very contract by which anyone is restrained from exercising a lawful, profession, trade, or business of any kind otherwise than is provided by this section is to that extent void," and then specifies six types of agreements that are "allowed to preserve a protectable interest." Ala. Code § 8-1-190. As discussed previously in this chapter, the six types of "allowed" agreements do not describe the typical franchise-agreement covenant against post-termination competition.

Although three of the six types of agreements permitted by section 8-1-190(b) provide time limits that "are presumed to be reasonable," those three types of agreements do not describe the typical post-termination covenant not to compete. *See* §§ 8-1-190(b)(3) (agreement to sell business' good will; one-year restraint presumed reasonable), (b)(4) (agreement between an entity and its agent, servant, or employee prohibiting competition with the entity; two years presumed reasonable), (b)(5) (agreement between an entity and its agent, servant, or employee prohibiting solicitation of entity's current customers; eighteen-month restraint presumed reasonable).

Since the Alabama Supreme Court has not yet interpreted the current statute in the context of franchise agreements, it is worth noting that, prior to 2016 when the current statute became effective, the Alabama Supreme Court had enforced a covenant that restricted franchisee competition for eighteen months after termination of the franchise. *Gafnea v. Pasquale Food Co.*, 454 So. 2d 1366, 1369 (Ala. 1984); *see also Sylvan Learning, Inc. v. Learning Solutions, Inc.*, 795 F. Supp. 2d 1284 (S.D. Ala. 2011) (two-year restriction on competition in licensing agreement did not conflict with Alabama public policy); *Sylvan Learning, Inc. v. Gulf Coast Education, Inc.*, 2010 WL 3943643 (M.D. Ala. Oct. 6, 2010) (same). However, the decision in *Gafnea*, upholding a post-term restraint in a franchise agreement, is not codified in new section 8-1-190 and, as discussed earlier in this chapter, appears to no longer be authoritative. Nonetheless, the eighteen-month restriction period that *Gafnea* allowed is consistent with the time periods that the current statute considers reasonable for other types of restraints that are allowed to preserve a protectable interest.

---

4. What geographic limitations have courts recognized as reasonable in the franchise context?

- **How have they been related to the interests protected?**
- **Have courts recognized the legitimacy of protecting other franchisees from competition?**

Prior to enactment of Alabama's current statute, ALA. CODE § 8-1-190 *et seq.* (which became effective January 1, 2016), the Alabama Supreme Court enforced a post-termination covenant in a franchise agreement with a geographic restriction of five miles from the franchisee's location. *See Gafnea v. Pasquale Food Co.*, 454 So. 2d 1366 (Ala. 1984). The court deemed this area a "narrowly confined location" and found that the non-competition clause as a whole was not unreasonable. *Id.* at 1369. The court did not expressly analyze the geographic limitation in the agreement as it related to the protected interest of the franchisor. *See also Sylvan Learning, Inc. v. Learning Solutions, Inc.*, 795 F. Supp. 2d 1284, 1294, 1301–02 (S.D. Ala. 2011) (applying Maryland law as not in conflict with Alabama law to uphold non-compete restriction in a licensing agreement that barred competition for two years in the territory governed by the agreement and any area within five miles of the border of that territory, and recognizing the franchisor's interest in protecting itself from loss of customers and from difficulties attracting new franchisees to the territory); *Sylvan Learning, Inc. v. Gulf Coast Education, Inc.*, 2010 WL 3943643, at *3–6 (M.D. Ala. Oct. 6, 2010) (applying Maryland law as not in conflict with Alabama law to uphold non-compete restriction in a licensing agreement that barred competition for two years within a twenty-mile radius of any franchise in operation on the effective date).

Although the Alabama Supreme Court has not addressed the viability of *Gafnea* under the new statute, a careful reading of the statute leads to the conclusion that decisions issued before January 1, 2016, are preserved only to the extent they are consistent with the statute. None of the six types of "allowed" exceptions to the general prohibition against competitive restraints fits the fact situation in *Gafnea* or in the *Sylvan Learning* cases, nor, indeed, do they fit any typical post-term agreement that prohibits a franchisee from engaging in the same business, or soliciting former customers of the franchise, after the franchise ends.

Among the six types of "allowed" restraints, the one most readily applicable to a franchise is an "agreement between two or more persons or businesses or a person and a business to limit commercial dealings to each other." ALA. CODE § 8-1-190(b)(2). Accordingly, the statute would allow a franchisor and franchisee to agree to limit exclusive dealings to each other; this exception makes sense only so long as the parties are dealing with each other, as opposed to after the franchise ends. Also, this exception appears to require that both parties agree to deal exclusively with each other, thus binding the franchisor as well as the franchisee. Of course, if a franchisor agrees to deal exclusively with a franchisee, it will likely want to limit the exclusive dealing commitment to the franchisee's territory. This exception does not mention geographic limits to the exclusive dealing arrangement, leaving to future courts to consider geographic limits to an exclusive dealing arrangement.

Two exceptions that could apply to a franchise, although in very narrow circumstances, contain geographic restrictions. ALA. CODE § 8-1-190(b)(3) (agreement by seller of business's good will not to engage in similar business and not to solicit customers of the business "within a specified geographic area so long as the buyer . . . carries on a like business therein, subject to reasonable time and place restraints"); § 8-1-190(b)(6) (partners, owners, or members of a business, upon dissolution or in anticipation of dissolution of the entity, "may agree that none of them will carry on a similar commercial activity in the geographic area where the commercial activity has been transacted").

With respect to the sale of a business's good will, the statute merely refers to "a specified geographic area so long as the buyer . . . carries on a like business therein." ALA. CODE § 8-1-190(b)(3). Because the predecessor statute, section 8-1-1, contained a similar provision that allowed a restrictive covenant to protect the good will purchased by the buyer of the business, cases decided under prior section 8-1-1 may be instructive to future courts in applying section 8-1-190(b)(3). For example, under prior section 8-1-1, the Alabama Supreme Court upheld a non-competition covenant executed by the seller of a business's good will to the extent that it prohibited the seller from engaging in competitive activity anywhere in the United States and Canada where the seller had previously done business. *Kershaw v. Knox Kershaw, Inc.*, 523 So. 2d 351 (Ala. 1988). Accordingly, a nationwide or even broader geographic restriction, such as the one allowed in *Kershaw*, appears consistent with the current statute, but only so long as the buyer "carries on a like business therein." ALA. CODE § 8-1-190(b)(3).

In contrast to the *Kershaw* court's willingness to enforce a covenant outside Alabama's borders, a federal district court more recently took a different approach when confronted with a contractual restraint that applied, by its terms, to activities in Alabama and Georgia. *DJR Associates, LLC v. Hammonds*, 241 F. Supp. 3d 1208 (N.D. Ala. 2017) (granting preliminary injunction with respect to former employee's non-solicitation of former employer's Alabama customers, but not with respect to Georgia customers, reasoning that Alabama's section 8-1-190(b)(4) allowed enforcement, whereas enforcement was determined to conflict with the fundamental public policy of Georgia).

5. What limitations on activities have courts recognized as reasonable in the franchise context?

Alabama's current statute provides that agreements that restrain anyone from exercising a lawful profession, trade, or business "otherwise than is provided by this section [are] to that extent void." ALA. CODE § 8-1-190(a) (effective as of January 1, 2016). The statute then describes, in section 8-1-190(b), six types of agreements that are "allowed to preserve a protectable interest."

Courts in Alabama have not yet addressed application of the statute or its six "allowed" agreements in the context of a franchise relationship. Indeed, no reported decision in Alabama issued after enactment of the current statute has addressed the effect of the statute on prior caselaw that had upheld a franchise agreement's post-termination covenant against competition. *Gafnea v. Pasquale Food Co.*, 454 So. 2d 1366 (Ala. 1984) (upholding agreement that barred a former franchisee from engaging in "the same or similar business" as the one operated under the franchise agreement); *see also Sylvan Learning, Inc. v. Learning Solutions, Inc.*, 795 F. Supp. 2d 1284, 1302 (S.D. Ala. 2011) (granting preliminary injunction against former franchisee to prohibit use of franchisor's trademarks, phone numbers used while a franchisee, and contacts with customers solicited as a franchisee); *but see McGriff Seibels & Williams*, 2019 WL 4600051, at *12 ("There is no indication that the statute applies retroactively to agreements executed before that date."). As previously discussed, the holdings in *Gafnea* and *Sylvan Learning* do not fit the statutory exceptions.

6. Does the state recognize a difference between in-term and post-term covenants?

There are no published decisions that address the differences between in-term and post-term covenants under Alabama law. However, the statute expressly allows, "to preserve a protectable interest," exclusive dealing agreements in which the parties commit to "limit commercial dealings to each other." ALA. CODE § 8-1-190(b)(2). This provision would apply to in-term agreements in which the franchisor and franchisee agree to limit their dealings to each other. The remaining types of restraints allowed by the statute do not apply to the typical, general, post-term provision that prohibits a franchisee from engaging in the same line of business after the franchise ends.

7. Has the state allowed enforcement of covenants against non-signatories (e.g., family members, newly formed corporations)?

As a general rule, Alabama courts do not permit enforcement of non-competition covenants against non-signatories. *See Pinzone v. Papa's Wings, Inc.*, 72 So. 3d 620, 624–25 (Ala. Civ. App. 2010), *cert. denied* (Ala. 2011) ("A person who has not executed or signed the contract or covenant is not bound by the stipulation against engaging in business, and he may not be enjoined from competing with the covenantee.") (quoting *Russell v. Mullis*, 479 So. 2d 727, 729 (Ala. 1985) (quoting *Yost v. Patrick*, 245 Ala. 275, 280, 17 So. 2d 240, 244 (1944)). Although the statute did not expressly codify that rule in those terms, it does require that non-competition covenants "be reduced to writing [and] signed by all parties." ALA. CODE § 8-1-192. However, despite the statute and the earlier caselaw, some courts have enforced against non-signatories when enforcement was necessary to prevent circumvention of the covenant by a signatory.

In *Yost v. Patrick*, 17 So. 2d 240 (Ala. 1944), the Alabama Supreme Court held that a non-competition agreement signed by the principal shareholder individually and on behalf of the company sold was not binding on his son-in-law, who was a minority shareholder of the company. In *Yost*, it did not appear that the signatory was involved with the competitive activities of the non-signatory shareholder. Decisions of Alabama courts suggest that, to enforce a covenant against a non-signatory, there must be some evidence from which the court can reasonably conclude that the non-signatory is acting on behalf of the signatory or that the signatory is assisting in the competitive enterprise.

In *Tyler v. Eufaula Tribune Publishing Co.*, 500 So. 2d 1005 (Ala. 1986), the Alabama Supreme Court enforced a covenant against competition against non-signatories to an employment contract. Mrs. Tyler signed an employment contract that contained an agreement on her part not to engage in the same or a similar business within 50 miles for two years following termination of her employment. Her employer published a shoppers' guide and a newspaper. One month after she resigned, her husband and two children began publishing a shoppers' guide in a town less than 50 miles away. In affirming the trial court, the Alabama Supreme Court stated:

> The record evidences that Mrs. Tyler's husband and children had no experience in, or knowledge of, the publication of an advertisement newspaper, and the trial court was reasonable in concluding that the expertise required for the undertaking was provided exclusively by Mrs. Tyler [who was] bound by [her] employment contract with the Tribune Company. The court justifiably found that Mrs. Tyler's family was conducting a business in competition with the Tribune Company with the assistance and guidance of Mrs. Tyler.

Id. at 1008.

Some additional noteworthy decisions of Alabama courts address the liability of *signatories* under non-competition covenants. Strict judicial interpretation permitted a franchise owner to circumvent the spirit if not the letter of a covenant against competition in *Business Investment Group of Alabama, Inc. v. Cleveland*, 571 So. 2d 1021 (Ala. 1990). Cleveland signed a franchise agreement with Business Investment Group in 1984 and in 1985, with the approval of the franchisor, transferred his franchise to a corporation, Riverchase. The opinion suggests that Cleveland remained in control of Riverchase after he assigned the franchise to it. Cleveland was an officer and an employee of Riverchase. In 1987, Riverchase sold its assets to another corporation solely owned by Cleveland and his wife in a transaction that apparently did not include an assignment or assumption of the franchise agreement. Shortly thereafter, the franchisor sued Cleveland and Riverchase for damages resulting from a breach of a covenant against competition in the franchise agreement.

The Alabama Supreme Court affirmed the trial court's finding that Cleveland was no longer bound by the covenant against competition after its assignment to Riverchase. *Id.* at 1024. The court recited provisions of the non-competition covenant that triggered its operation "in the event of termination." *Id.* at 1023. The court also noted that provisions in the covenant that stated that the covenant would survive termination of the agreement did not mention assignment of the agreement. *Id.* at 1022–24. The court seemed to place significance on the fact that the franchisor elected to approve the assignment to Riverchase rather than to exercise its right of first refusal.

However, in an earlier case, *Files v. Schaible*, 445 So. 2d 257 (Ala. 1984), the court had no difficulty awarding damages for breach of a covenant against competition by the seller of a business who tried unsuccessfully to mask his ownership and control of a competing business. The seller argued he was merely an employee of the new business, and the covenant did not, by its terms, prohibit this employment. *Id.* at 261. A third party was listed as the owner on the lease and other documents, but the weight of the evidence suggested that the seller funded and directed the competing operation and that the third party was merely a front. *Id.*

Finally, in the corporate context, Alabama courts have addressed the ability of a surviving corporation to enforce non-compete agreements executed by a former corporate entity and employees of the former corporate entity. Enforceability depends on the nature of the corporate transaction. In *Clark Substations, LLC v. Ware*, 838 So. 2d 360 (Ala. 2002), the Alabama Supreme Court held that a corporation that purchases all of the assets of another corporation is not entitled to enforce non-compete agreements executed by the former corporation and its employees absent a valid assignment of specific contractual rights. *Id.* at 363–64. On the other hand, in *Sevier Insurance Agency, Inc. v. Willis Corroon Corp.*, 711 So. 2d 995 (Ala. 1998), *overruled on other grounds, Ex parte Howell Engineering & Surveying, Inc.*, 981 So. 2d 413 (Ala. 2006), the court held that a post-merger surviving corporation can enforce non-compete agreements executed by a predecessor corporation before the merger. *Id.* at 1000–01. *See also Pitney Bowes, Inc. v. Berney Office Solutions*, 823 So. 2d 659, 662 (Ala. 2001) ("The employee–employer exception to the voidness of non-compete agreements does not save a non-compete agreement unless the employee–employer relationship exists *at the time the agreement is executed.*").

8. Will the state modify, "blue-pencil," or otherwise reduce a covenant found to be overbroad?

The statute expressly gives courts the power to blue-pencil a non-competition covenant (or to void it entirely):

> If a contractually specified restraint is overly broad or unreasonable in its duration, a court may void the restraint in part and reform it to preserve the protectable interest or interests. If a contractually specified restraint does not fall within the limited exceptions set out in subsection (b) of Section 8-1-190, a court may void the restraint in its entirety.

ALA. CODE § 8-1-193.

Even before the statute was enacted, Alabama courts frequently modified overbroad or vague covenants and then enforced them to the extent reasonable. For example, several courts have reduced the geographic scope of covenants that were found to be overbroad. *See, e.g., King v. Head Start Family Hair Salons, Inc.*, 886 So. 2d 769, 772–73 (Ala. 2004) (limiting restriction that prevented former employee from working within two miles of any of thirty locations of her former employer's business to a two-mile radius around only the location at which she was last employed); *Daughtry v. Capital Gas Co.*, 229 So. 2d 480, 484 (Ala. 1969) (limiting geographic restriction from four counties to one county); *Nobles-Hamilton v. Thompson*, 883 So. 2d 1247, 1250–51 (Ala. Civ. App. 2003) (limiting non-competition covenant that lacked definite geographical limitation to radius of five miles around former employer's store).

More recently, Justice See discussed at length the court's power to blue-pencil covenants against competition in a specially concurring opinion in *Westwind Technologies, Inc. v. Jones*, 925 So. 2d 166 (Ala. 2005). He began by recognizing that "[i]t is clear from our caselaw that, if a covenant against competition is overbroad, it is within the power of the courts to narrow it." *Id.* at 173 (See, J., specially concurring) (citing *Kershaw*, 523 So. 2d 351, and *Daughtry*, 285 Ala. 89, 229 So. 2d 480). He then added that the courts' having that power does not mean they should always exercise it:

> [T]here also are times when there is good reason to strike down such a clause. An unreasonably broad noncompetition clause deprives the former employee and his prospective employer of guidance as to what employment is permissible. Therefore, both the former employee and the prospective employer run the substantial risk of litigation if the former employee is hired. For this reason, some courts refuse to enforce any part of an overbroad noncompetition clause unless the entire clause is reasonable.

Id. (See, J., specially concurring). At the conclusion of his analysis, and after a review of what *Corbin on Contracts* had to say about the issue, Justice See proposed a middle-of-the-road approach to blue-penciling: "The middle view, that a court should in general reform an overbroad noncompetition clause, but should refuse to do so when the clause demonstrably was not drafted in good faith, thus appears to offer a balanced response to the problem of overbreadth." *Id.* (See, J., specially concurring).

There are, however, no decisions of Alabama courts in which covenants have been modified in the franchise context. The willingness of courts to blue-pencil covenants against competition in the employment context suggests that they would do the same in the franchise context unless it appeared that the franchisor purposefully drafted the covenant to be overbroad or otherwise drafted the covenant in bad faith.

9. When does a non-compete period begin to run? Will courts equitably extend the term?

A covenant against competition typically begins to run according to its own terms, which is usually the date that the franchise or employment relationship terminates. *See, e.g.*, *Eastis v. Veterans Oil Co.*, 65 So. 3d 443, 445 (Ala. Civ. App. 2010). To the extent that ambiguity exists about when this period begins to run, courts will interpret that ambiguity against the drafter—i.e., against the franchisor or employer. *See, e.g.*, *Scale Reproductions, LLC v. Skinner*, Civil Action No. 07-191-CG-B, 2007 WL 3086033, at *3 (S.D. Ala. Oct. 19, 2007). The Alabama Supreme Court has upheld as enforceable a provision in a covenant against competition that provided that the expiration date of the covenant was to be extended by a day for each day that the covenant was breached. *See Knox Kershaw v. Kershaw*, 598 So. 2d 1372 (Ala. 1992).

10. Are there additional nuances or peculiarities about the state's treatment of covenants in the franchising context?

The statute codified a preference for the "fundamental public policies of the State of Alabama" expressed by the statute. ALA. CODE § 8-1-197. The statute, therefore

> shall govern and shall be applied instead of any foreign laws that might otherwise be applicable in those instances when the application of those foreign laws would violate a fundamental public policy expressed in [the statute].

Id.; *see also Sylvan Learning, Inc. v. Gulf Coast Education, Inc.*, 2010 WL 3943643, at *2 (M.D. Ala. Oct. 6, 2010) (citing *Cherry, Bekaert & Holland v. Brown*, 582 So. 2d 502, 506 (Ala. 1991)) (where the parties' contract provides that the laws of another state govern, Alabama law provides that the other state's law cannot be "'contrary to the fundamental public polices of the forum state' in order for the parties' choice of law to be given effect"). In *Gulf Coast Education*, the court determined that Maryland law, which was the law specified in the parties' license agreement, was "analogous to Alabama law." *Id.* at *3. The court then applied Maryland law to determine the enforceability of the agreement and granted a preliminary injunction against a former franchisee that had been terminated for failure to attend mandatory conferences. *Id.* at *4–9. *See also Movie Gallery U.S., LLC v. Greenshields*, 648 F. Supp. 2d 1252, 1269–70 (M.D. Ala. 2009) (upholding forum selection clause, which applied Montana law, to determine enforceability of covenant against competition because fundamental policies of Alabama law and Montana law were not in substantial conflict); *Curves International, Inc. v. Mosbarger*, 525 F. Supp. 2d 1310, 1312–13 (M.D. Ala. 2007) (declining to determine whether Texas law or Alabama law applied to interpret franchise agreement because "the laws of both [states] do not differ materially on the issues before the court"). *But see Benchmark Medical Holdings, Inc. v. Rehab Solutions, LLC*, 307 F. Supp. 2d 1249, 1260 (M.D. Ala. 2004) (applying Alabama law to determine whether covenant against competition was void as against public policy because "[i]f the covenant[] not to compete[] . . . [is] void under Alabama law, then [the fact that it is] valid under [another state's] law is irrelevant").

In Alabama, some industry-specific statutes apply to franchise and dealer agreements in particular industries. For example, the Motor Vehicle Franchise Act, ALA. CODE § 8-20-1 *et seq.*, prohibits "any manufacturer, factory branch, factory representative, distributor, or wholesaler, distributor branch, or distributor representative" from engaging in a list of "unfair and deceptive trade practices." *Id.* § 8-20-4. Indeed, the express purpose of the Act is "to regulate motor vehicle manufacturers, distributors, dealers, and their representatives and to regulate the dealings between manufacturers and distributors or wholesalers and their dealers in order to prevent fraud and other abuses upon the citizens of [Alabama]." ALA. CODE § 8-20-2(a).

Prohibited activities include imposing a non-compete covenant on the dealer during the term of the agreement, *id.* § 8-20-4(1)(e); unreasonably entering into another franchise with another dealer in the same area, *id.* § 8-20-4(3)(l); and owning or controlling another dealership, except in very limited circumstances, *id.*

§ 8-20-4(3)(s). Additionally, the act "shall not be modified or superseded by a choice of law clause." *Id.* § 8-20-14.

Other statutes regulate similar business relationships in other industries. *See, e.g., id.* § 28-8-1 *et seq.*; § 28-9-1 *et seq.* (alcoholic beverages); *id.* § 8-21B-1 *et seq.* (heavy equipment); *id.* § 8-21C-1 *et seq.* (recreational vehicles). Local laws may also provide county-specific regulations in certain industries. *See, e.g.*, Ala. Act 2008-461; Ala. Act 2008-462 (liquid goods in Baldwin and Mobile Counties); Ala. Act 1993-483 (wine in Mobile County). It is also worth noting that the Alabama Deceptive Trade Practices Act, ALA. CODE § 8-19-1 *et seq.*, expressly covers franchises. *See* ALA. CODE § 8-19-3(6) (the term "goods" includes "any franchise").

Some additional observations about covenants against competition under Alabama law include:

- The existence of a covenant against competition cannot be implied or proven with parol evidence. *Pinzone v. Papa's Wings, Inc.*, 72 So. 3d 620, 624–25 (Ala. Civ. App. 2010), *cert. denied* (Ala. 2011); *see also* ALA. CODE § 8-1-92 (signed writing requirement).
- A technical violation of a valid and enforceable covenant against competition with no proof of actual damages may support an award of nominal damages, but such an award is limited in amount. *Roberson v. C.P. Allen Construction Co.*, 50 So. 3d 471, 479–80 (Ala. Civ. App. 2010) (holding an award of $25,000 in nominal damages to be excessive).
- A trial court has jurisdiction to issue a preliminary injunction to enforce a covenant against competition pending arbitration. *Spinks v. Automation Personnel Service, Inc.*, 49 So. 3d 186, 190 (Ala. 2010).
- Proof that a covenant against competition has been breached is persuasive, but not dispositive, in establishing irreparable injury for purposes of obtaining a preliminary injunction. *Sylvan Learning, Inc. v. Learning Solutions, Inc.*, 795 F. Supp. 2d 1284, 1300 (S.D. Ala. 2011).
- The amount of security that an applicant for a preliminary injunction must post under Federal Rule of Civil Procedure 65(c) "'is a matter within the discretion of the trial court,'" *Learning Solutions*, 795 F. Supp. 2d at 1304 (quoting *BellSouth Telecommunications, Inc. v. MCImetro Access Transmission Service, LLC*, 425 F.3d 964, 970–71 (11th Cir. 2005)). The *Learning Solutions* court was willing to waive this requirement for a franchisor "[b]ecause of the high likelihood of success on the merits of [the franchisor's] claims," *id.*

Finally, section 8-1-190 broadly declares: "Every contract by which anyone is restrained from exercising a lawful profession, trade or business of any kind otherwise than is provided by this section is to that extent void." ALA. CODE § 8-1-190(a). The statute is not clear about its impact on covenants relating to the practice of a profession in a franchise setting. A "protectable interest" does include "[c]ustomer, *patient*, vendor, or *client* good will associated with . . . [a]n ongoing business, *franchise*, commercial, or *professional* practice." *Id.* at § 8-1-191(a)(4) (emphasis added). It might be reasonable, then, to expect that restrictive covenants would be enforceable to protect certain professional franchisees' interests in their relationships with clients or patients. *See Right at Home*, 2021 WL 308237, at *7 ("It makes no sense to protect those franchise interests while at the same time creating an impediment to enforcement of the valid agreements that are vehicles for doing so."). Further, the statute preserves "any professional exemption recognized by Alabama law." ALA. CODE § 8-1-196.

Nonetheless, a long line of decisions of Alabama courts has refused to enforce such restrictions signed by professionals. *See, e.g., Benchmark Medical Holdings, Inc. v. Barnes*, 328 F. Supp. 2d 1236 (M.D. Ala. 2004) (physical therapists); *Pierce v. Hand, Arendall, Bedsole, Greaves & Johnston*, 678 So. 2d 765 (Ala. 1996) (attorneys); *Cherry Bekaert & Holland v. Brown*, 582 So. 2d 502 (Ala. 1991) (certified public accountants); *Friddle v. Raymond*, 575 So. 2d 1038 (Ala. 1991) (veterinarians); *Salisbury v. Semple*, 565 So. 2d 234 (Ala. 1990) (physicians); *but see J.E. Hanger, Inc. v. Scussel*, 937 F. Supp. 1546, 1557 (M.D. Ala. 1996) ("[O]rthotists and prosthetists are not professionals as that term is defined under Alabama law."); *Alabama Board of Optometry v. Eagerton*, 393 So. 2d 1373, 1378 (Ala. 1981) ("[T]he practice of optometry is not to be considered as the practice of a learned profession."); *Dobbins v. Getz Exterminators*, 382 So. 2d 1135, 1137 (Ala. Civ. App. 1980) (pest exterminators are not professionals for purposes of then-current section 8-1-1). Alabama courts have not yet re-examined these holdings under the new statute, so the precedential status of these non-exceptions remains unclear.

Alaska

*by M. Scott Broadwell**

1. Has the state addressed covenants against competition in the context of franchising?

- **Does the state have a franchising statute or regulations that address covenants against competition?**
- **Does the state have a covenants statute of general applicability that would encompass franchise covenants?**
- **Have the courts addressed covenants in the context of franchising either under a statute or under the state's common law?**

Alaska has not addressed covenants against competition in franchise agreements, either through legislation, regulation, or caselaw. Nor does Alaska have a statute dealing with covenants against competition in general.

Alaska's antitrust statutes potentially could apply to a covenant against competition in a franchise agreement if the covenant restrains trade. ALASKA STAT. § 45.50.566 prohibits agreements not to use goods and services of a competitor if the agreement could substantially lessen competition.

> It is unlawful for a person to lease or make a sale or contract for sale of goods, wares, merchandise, machinery, supplies, or other commodities, or services, whether patented or unpatented, for use, consumption, enjoyment, or resale, or fix a price charged for it, or discount from, or rebate upon, that price, on the condition, agreement, or understanding that the lessee or purchaser will not use or deal in the goods, wares, merchandise, machinery, supplies, or other commodity or service of a competitor or competitors of the lessor or seller, if the effect of the lease, sale or contract for sale, or of the condition, agreement, or understanding may be substantially to lessen competition or tend to create a monopoly in any line of commerce.

Id.

*M. Scott Broadwell is an attorney in the Anchorage office of the law firm Davis Wright Tremaine, LLP.

However, there are no Alaska cases applying the antitrust statutes to covenants not to compete, and the Alaska Supreme Court has made clear that to demonstrate a prima facie case of restraint of trade, the plaintiff must prove the existence of an agreement among two or more persons with the intent to harm or restrain competition. *See Sisters of Providence v. A.A. Pain Clinic*, 81 P.3d 989, 1000 (Alaska 2003). This seems a difficult standard to meet in the context of a routine covenant not to compete. The Alaska Supreme Court has held that the state legislature intended the courts to look to federal cases interpreting the Sherman Act for guidance. *See West v. Whitney-Fidalgo Seafoods, Inc.*, 628 P.2d 10, 14 (Alaska 1981). While a discussion of federal standards is beyond the scope of this article, covenants not to compete are valid under the Sherman Act if (1) ancillary to the main business purpose of a lawful contract and (2) necessary to protect the covenantee's legitimate property interests. *Los Angeles Memorial Coliseum Commission v. N.F.L.*, 726 F.2d 1381, 1395 (9th Cir. 1981); *Lektro-Vend Corp. v. Vendo Co.*, 660 F.2d 255, 265 (7th Cir. 1981).

Alaska also has an unfair trade practices statute, which prohibits "[u]nfair methods of competition and unfair or deceptive acts or practices in the conduct of trade or commerce." Alaska Stat. § 45.50.471(a). The nonexclusive list of unfair acts in section 45.50.471(b) consists mainly of acts that harm consumers, but the Alaska Supreme Court has specifically held that the Act may apply in business-to-business transactions. *See Western Star Trucks, Inc. v. Big Iron Equipment Service, Inc.*, 101 P.3d 1047, 1054 (Alaska 2004). Again, however, no cases have applied the unfair trade practices act to covenants not to compete.

Alaska courts have not addressed covenants against competition in franchise agreements. The only caselaw dealing with covenants against competition has arisen in the sale-of-business and employment contexts. As noted below, the employment caselaw is not necessarily analogous.

Historically, Alaska courts have recognized that covenants not to compete contained in contracts for the sale of a business may be enforceable. *See Wenzell v. Ingrim*, 228 P.3d 103 (Alaska 2010) (acknowledging general rule that covenants not to compete ancillary to business sale are enforceable but adopting public policy exception and remanding for further consideration under that standard); *Aviation Associates, Ltd. v. Temsco Helicopters, Inc.*, 881 P.2d 1127 (Alaska 1994) (affirming a damages award to the purchaser of a business who sued the former owner for breach of a covenant not to compete); *National Bank of Alaska v. J.B.L. & K. of Alaska, Inc.*, 546 P.2d 579 (Alaska 1976) (affirming award for breach of covenant not to compete in sale of insurance business, but questioning calculation of damages); *Barber v. Northern Heating Oil, Inc.*, 447 P.2d 72, 73 (Alaska 1968) (affirming permanent injunction not to compete and reasoning that the weight of authority is that a showing of an actual loss of customers or of particularly pecuniary or inadequacy of the remedy at law need not be made where the buyer of a business seeks an injunction to restrain the seller who has executed a covenant not to compete). Interestingly, although the court had previously decided many cases involving covenants not to compete in the context of the sale of a business, the court in *Wenzell* regarded the issue of whether such a covenant could be enforced as an issue of first impression that had never been squarely addressed. "Irreparable injuries of the above type are presumed to result from a violation of the covenant not to compete." *Barber*, 447 P.2d. at 73. *See also Himschoot v. Dushi*, 953 P.2d 507, 510 n.2 (Alaska 1998) (rejecting lower court's interpretation that parties did not intend part of a covenant not to compete to be binding and enforceable). In either the employment or business sale context, covenants not to compete are subject to standard contract defenses, such as unconscionability, mistake, and waiver. *See, e.g., J.B.L. & K.*, 546 P.2d at 587 (analyzing claim of waiver).

The Alaska Supreme Court has indicated that some covenants not to compete in employment contracts are enforceable. *See Data Management, Inc. v. Greene*, 757 P.2d 62 (Alaska 1988) (reversing lower court's finding that non-compete provision was unenforceable and remanding for the trial court to determine whether the provision could be "reasonably altered" to make it enforceable); *cf. Metcalfe Investments, Inc. v. Garrison*, 919 P.2d 1356 (Alaska 1996) (reversing grant of summary judgment against employer who sued former employee for breach of non-compete agreement); *Wirum & Cash v. Cash*, 837 P.2d 692 (Alaska 1992) (enforcing non-compete provisions in partnership agreement).

In *Data Management*, the court reversed the trial court's holding that a non-compete provision was unenforceable in its entirety, and remanded for consideration whether the lower court could "reasonably alter[]" it to make it enforceable. The court quoted a lengthy passage from an Ohio case that explained the factors relevant to making an unenforceable covenant reasonable:

> Among the factors properly to be considered are: the absence or presence of limitations as to time and space; whether the employee represents the sole contact with the customer; whether the employee is possessed with confidential information or trade secrets; whether the covenant seeks to eliminate competition which would be unfair to the employer or merely seeks to eliminate ordinary competition; whether the covenant seeks to stifle the inherent skill and experience of the employee; whether the benefit to the employer is disproportional to the detriment to the employee; whether the covenant operates as a bar to the employee's sole means of support; whether the employee's talent which the employer seeks to suppress was actually developed during the period of employment; and whether the forbidden employment is merely incidental to the main employment.

Data Management, 757 P.2d at 65 (internal quotation marks and punctuation omitted) (quoting *Raimonde v. Van Vlerah*, 325 N.E.2d 544, 546–47 (Ohio 1975)). Although *Data Management* cited these factors as relevant to narrowing an overbroad covenant, the factors apply as well to the antecedent question of whether the covenant is reasonable. *See Wirum & Cash*, 837 P.2d at 709 (stating that "there is no showing that the [non-compete] clause here is 'unreasonable' given the factors to be considered" and citing *Data Management*). Thus covenants not to compete in employment or partnership contracts are subject to an initial, multifactor reasonableness analysis, at least if the reasonableness of the covenant is called into question.

The Alaska Supreme Court distinguishes between broad covenants against competition generally and more narrow covenants designed to prevent solicitation of customers or employees, which are reviewed less stringently. *Data Management*, for instance, involved a highly restrictive blanket on all competition with the employer, to which the panoply of reasonableness factors would apply. *See* 757 P.2d at 63 n.1. *Metcalfe Investments*, by contrast, involved a covenant that prohibited only the expropriation of the employer's information and customers. The court in *Metcalfe* held that the covenant there could be enforced regardless of durational or geographic limits, explaining, "The lack of a geographical limitation is irrelevant because the covenant was not a blanket prohibition on competition, but rather a selective restraint on doing business with people who were potential Metcalfe Investments customers at the time of her termination. Such restrictive covenants are subject to a less stringent test of reasonableness than blanket prohibitions of competition." *Metcalfe Investments*, 919 P.2d at 1361.

Given the scarcity of Alaska law on franchising, one necessarily has to look to the treatment of covenants against competition in other areas. One should not, however, rely too heavily on principles developed in the employment context for application in franchising or other business contexts. The Alaska Supreme Court has signaled that non-compete agreements in employment contracts are special in several respects. Non-compete agreements in employment contracts are regarded as more punitive because they broadly impact an individual's ability to earn a living. *See DeCristofaro v. Security National Bank*, 664 P.2d 167, 169 (Alaska 1983). Employment contracts often involve a different distribution of bargaining power than contracts between businesses. *See Aviation Associates, Ltd. v. Temsco Helicopters, Inc.*, 881 P.2d 1127, 1130 n.5 (Alaska 1994). Because of these differences, covenants not to compete in employment contracts are strictly construed, whereas similar covenants in contracts for the sale of businesses are not. *Cf. DeCristofaro*, 664 P.2d at 168–69 (stating that "noncompetition agreements are disfavored in the law as restraints upon trade and because they impose hardships on individuals seeking to earn a livelihood. They are, therefore, strictly construed.") *with Aviation Associates*, 881 P.2d at 1130 n.5 ("Our decisions have distinguished between covenants-not-to-compete which are ancillary to sales agreements and employer-employee covenants"; the former may be interpreted more liberally because "the parties presumably bargain from positions of equal bargaining power.") (quoting *Centorr-Vacuum Industries, Inc. v. Lavoie*, 609 A.2d 1213, 1215 (N.H. 1992)).

---

2. Have the courts articulated the "legitimate interests" of the franchisor that will support enforcement of a covenant against competition in a franchise agreement?

- **If so, what are they (e.g., protection of goodwill, protection of confidential information), and in what contexts did the issue arise?**
- **If not, what interests have been recognized in other contexts (e.g., employment agreements, the sale of business context)?**

There is no caselaw in Alaska on covenants against competition in franchise agreements, although these concepts have been addressed in other contexts. The Supreme Court has referred to the "legitimate interests" protected by such covenants in the employment area but has never offered much explanation. For example, in *Metcalfe Investments, Inc. v. Garrison*, 919 P.2d 1356 (Alaska 1996), the court referenced the employer's "interests in its customer lists," interests it found served by a covenant prohibiting a former employee from expropriating information and customers from the employer. *Id.* at 1362. In addition, some of the "reasonableness" factors listed in *Data Management, Inc. v. Greene*, 757 P.2d 62 (Alaska 1988) relate to employer interests, for example, those concerning an employee's knowledge of confidential information or trade secrets and the unfairness of competition to the employer. *Id.* at 65.

In *Wenzell v. Ingrim*, 228 P.3d 103 (Alaska 2010), the Alaska Supreme Court affirmed that covenants not to compete may be enforced in the context of a business sale and adopted a two-pronged public policy exception against the enforcement of overbroad covenants:

> According to the Restatement (Second) of Contracts, a covenant not to compete is unenforceable on grounds of public policy if it unreasonably restrains trade, either because: (a) the restraint is greater than is needed to protect the promisee's legitimate interest, or (b) the promisee's need is outweighed by the hardship to the promisor and the likely injury to the public. In the context of covenants not to compete ancillary to the sale of a business, the Restatement describes the "promisee's legitimate interest" as the "value of the goodwill that he has acquired" in the purchase of the business. When determining the enforceability of a covenant not to compete ancillary to the sale of a business, a court must therefore consider whether the restriction bargained for is no greater than is needed to protect the goodwill the purchaser has acquired in the business and, if so, whether the purchaser's need to protect that goodwill outweighs the hardship to the seller and likely injury to the public.

Id. at 110–111. The court did not have occasion, however, in *Wenzell* to apply these standards, as the case was remanded for further proceedings.

---

3. What time limitations have courts recognized as reasonable in the franchise context?

- **If no franchise cases have been decided, what time limitations have been recognized in other contexts?**
- **How have they been related to interests protected?**

There is no caselaw in Alaska on covenants against competition in franchise agreements, although these concepts have been addressed in other contexts. In *Data Management, Inc. v. Greene*, 757 P.2d 62 (Alaska 1988), one of the reasonableness factors is "the absence or presence of limitations as to time." *Id.* at 65 (reviewing five-year noncompete following termination of employment but remanding for further consideration and not deciding the permissibility of the five-year duration). Generally, the duration of broad restrictions on employment has been subject to greater scrutiny than covenants prohibiting solicitation of customers or employees, or covenants associated with the sale of a business, given the differing interests involved. In *Metcalfe Investments, Inc. v. Garrison*, 919 P.2d 1356, 1362 (Alaska 1996), the court held a non-solicitation agreement by a departing employee not to use the employer's customer lists enforceable notwithstanding the lack of a durational limit because the "limited scope of the activity restraint is narrowly drawn to protect Metcalfe Investment's interests in its customer lists." *Id.* at 1362. In *Wirum & Cash v. Cash*, 837 P.2d 692 (Alaska 1992), the court upheld a two-year non-solicitation agreement following a business partner's withdrawal from a partnership. In *Aviation Associates, Ltd. v. Temsco Helicopters, Inc.*, 881 P.2d 1127 (Alaska 1994), the court upheld a seven-year non-compete following the sale of a business. In *National Bank of Alaska v. J.B.L. & K. of Alaska, Inc.*, 546 P.2d 579 (Alaska 1976), the court upheld a 10 year non-compete following the sale of a business. In *Barber v. Northern Heating Oil, Inc.*, 447 P.2d 72 (Alaska 1968), the court upheld a covenant not to compete "in the area" following the sale of business; the case does not specify the duration of the covenant, although it is not unreasonable to conclude that the covenant was of unlimited duration. And most recently, while considering the validity of a fraud in the inducement claim, the court upheld a non-compete clause in an operating agreement that prohibited the signatories "from engaging in any similar business in Alaska for one year . . . ." *Alaska Interstate Const., LLC v. Pacific Diversified Investments, Inc.*, 279 P.3d 1156, 1174 (Alaska 2012).

Finally, it should be noted that in *Schluter v. Wadman*, 9 Alaska Reports 423 (Alaska Territorial Court 1939), the territorial court limited the application of a five-year covenant not to compete in the city of Anchorage following the sale of a painting business. However, the *Schluter* decision has never been cited with approval by the Alaska Supreme Court and appears to be a relic of territorial times.

4. What geographic limitations have courts recognized as reasonable in the franchise context?

- **How have they been related to the interests protected?**
- **Have courts recognized the legitimacy of protecting other franchises from competition?**

There is no caselaw in Alaska on covenants against competition in franchise agreements, although these concepts have been addressed in other contexts. In *Data Management, Inc. v. Greene*, 757 P.2d 62 (Alaska 1988), one of the reasonableness factors is "the absence or presence of limitations as to space." *Id.* at 65 (reviewing covenant not to compete in the state of Alaska following termination of employment, but remanding for further consideration and not deciding the permissibility of the statewide scope). Generally, the geographical scope of broad restrictions on employment has been subject to greater scrutiny than covenants prohibiting solicitation of customers or employees, or covenants associated with the sale of a business, given the differing interests involved. In *Metcalfe Investments, Inc. v. Garrison*, 919 P.2d 1356, 1362 (Alaska 1996), the court held a non-solicitation agreement by a departing employee not to use the employer's customer lists enforceable notwithstanding the lack of a geographic limit because the "limited scope of the activity restraint is narrowly drawn to protect Metcalfe Investment's interests in its customer lists." *Id.* at 1362.

In *Wirum & Cash v. Cash*, 837 P.2d 692 (Alaska 1992), the court upheld a two-year non-solicitation agreement of unlimited geographic scope following a business partner's withdrawal from a partnership. In *Aviation Associates, Ltd. v. Temsco Helicopters, Inc.*, 881 P.2d 1127 (Alaska 1994), the court upheld a seven-year non-compete "within all areas of Alaska south of Yakutat" following the sale of an air-taxi business. In *National Bank of Alaska v. J.B.L. & K. of Alaska, Inc.*, 546 P.2d 579 (Alaska 1976), the court upheld a 10-year agreement not to solicit customers or to compete on Kodiak Island following the sale of a business. In *Barber v. Northern Heating Oil, Inc.*, 447 P.2d 72 (Alaska 1968), the court upheld a covenant not to compete "in the area" following the sale of a business. Although not explicitly articulated, implicit in the court's analysis is that a noncompetition agreement may be unenforceable at least in part if its geographic scope is broader than reasonably necessary to protect the reasonable commercial interests of the party to whom the promise not to compete is made.

5. What limitations on activities have courts recognized as reasonable in the franchise context?

There is no caselaw on the breadth of activities that can be appropriately restrained in the franchise context. Cases in the sale-of-business and employment contexts have involved covenants of varying restrictiveness. At one extreme are blanket prohibitions on competing in a particular line of business. *See, e.g., Himschoot v. Dushi,* 953 P.2d 507 (Alaska 1998) (no competition in the taxi business); *Aviation Associates, Ltd. v. Temsco Helicopters, Inc.*, 881 P.2d 1127 (Alaska 1994) (no competition in the commercial air-taxi business); *Data Management, Inc. v. Greene*, 757 P.2d 62 (Alaska 1988) (no competition with employer); *DeCristofaro v. Security National Bank,* 664 P.2d 167 (Alaska 1983) (no competition in the banking business); *National Bank of Alaska v. J.B.L. & K. of Alaska, Inc.*, 546 P.2d 579 (Alaska 1976) (no competition in the insurance business); *Barber v. Northern Heating Oil, Inc.*, 447 P.2d 72 (Alaska 1968) (no competition in business similar to selling fuel oil).

At the other end of the spectrum are non-solicitation covenants narrowly tailored to prohibit only the covenantor's expropriation of customers or information from the covenantee. *See, e.g., Metcalfe Investments,, Inc. v. Garrison*, 919 P.2d 1356 (Alaska 1996); *Wirum & Cash v. Cash,* 837 P.2d 692 (Alaska 1992). As noted above, non-solicitation covenants may generally have a wider temporal and geographic scope than blanket restrictions on competition given the limited nature of activities being restricted.

6. Does the state recognize a difference between in-term and post-term covenants?

This issue has not been addressed by courts in Alaska.

7. Has the state allowed enforcement of covenants against non-signatories (e.g., family members, newly formed corporations)?

There are no cases in Alaska that address application of a covenant against competition to non-signatory family members. One case, *National Bank of Alaska v. J.B.L. & K. of Alaska, Inc.*, 546 P.2d 579 (Alaska 1976), involved the application of a non-compete agreement to the successors-in-interest of the signatories. The case does not apply anything beyond ordinary principles of successor liability and cannot support extension of a covenant to parties who are not legally considered successors to a signatory. *See also Savage Arms, Inc. v. Western Auto Supply Co.*, 18 P.3d 49 (Alaska 2000) (expanding corporate successor tort liability where there is a "continuity of enterprise" in a business acquisition asset sale, although the potential application of the "continuity of enterprise" doctrine to contract claims is unclear). And more recently the court held that the sole shareholder of a company that entered into an operating agreement was personally bound by a non-compete clause. *Alaska Interstate Const., LLC v. Pacific Diversified Investments, Inc.*, 279 P.3d 1156, 1175–76 (Alaska 2012). In that case, the sole shareholder had argued he was not personally bound since he had signed the operating agreement only in his capacity as president of the operator and not in his personal capacity. *Id.* at 1175. However, a jury found that the parties intended the sole shareholder to be bound and despite arguing fraudulent inducement, the shareholder failed to make a showing that he misapprehended the agreement or was induced to sign by any deception. *Id.* at 1176.

8. Will the state modify, "blue-pencil," or otherwise reduce a covenant found to be overbroad?

In *Data Management, Inc. v. Greene*, 757 P.2d 62 (Alaska 1988), the Alaska Supreme Court held that a trial court could modify an overly broad non-compete provision to make it enforceable. It adopted a "rule of reasonableness" whereby the trial court attempts to "reasonably" alter a provision to make it enforceable. *Data Management*, 757 P.2d at 64.

The rule of reasonableness "is to hold that if an overbroad covenant not to compete can be reasonably altered to render it enforceable, then the court shall do so unless it determines the covenant was not drafted in good faith." *Id.* at 64. A court modifying a provision in this manner tries to fashion "a contract reasonable between the parties, in accord with their intention at the time of contracting," and in accord with "all the factors comprising 'reasonableness' in the context of employee covenants." *Id.* at 65 (quoting *Raimonde v. Van Vlerah*, 325 N.E.2d 544, 546–47 (Ohio 1975)). The court quoted an extensive list of reasonableness factors from an Ohio case. *See id.*; *see also Metcalfe Investments, Inc. v. Garrison*, 919 P.2d 1356, 1361 (Alaska 1996) (reprising the holding in *Data Management* that "so long as an overly broad covenant not to compete was drafted in good faith, the court [can] make reasonable alterations to render it enforceable."). It is unclear from the court's recent decision in *Wenzell v. Ingrim*, 228 P.3d 103 (Alaska 2010) how the public policy exception to enforcement of an overbroad non-compete would be harmonized with the "rule of reason," or whether there is any incompatibility between the two concepts.

9. When does a non-compete period begin to run?

- **Will courts equitably extend the term?**

Alaska courts have not specifically addressed these issues in reported caselaw.

10. Are there additional nuances or peculiarities of the state's treatment of covenants in the franchising context?

Alaska law regarding covenants against competition has not been applied in the franchise context, and, thus, no nuances of application in that context have arisen.

Arizona

*by Christina M. Noyes**

1. Has the state addressed covenants against competition in the context of franchising?

- **Does the state have a franchising statute or regulations that address covenants against competition?**
- **Does the state have a covenants statute of general applicability that would encompass franchise covenants?**
- **Have the courts addressed covenants in the context of franchising either under a statute or under the state's common law?**

Arizona does not have a franchising statute or regulations of general applicability addressing covenants against competition.

The Arizona Vehicle Dealer Requirements and Restrictions Act prohibits a manufacturer from coercing a new motor vehicle dealer not to participate in other lines of motor vehicle businesses "unless justified by reasonable business considerations." Any provision in a franchise or distributorship agreement waiving compliance with any provision in this Act is void except that a person is permitted to enter into an agreement waiving any such provision or voluntarily settling legitimate disputes if the franchisee or distributor "receives separate and valid consideration at the time" that the waiver is executed. ARIZ. REV. STAT. ANN. § 28-4458.

Arizona's Uniform State Antitrust Act (USAA) prohibits unreasonable restraints of trade and can apply to covenants against competition if they are so restrictive that they are deemed unreasonable restraints on trade. ARIZ. REV. STAT. ANN. § 44-1402.

The USAA provides that "a contract . . . between two or more persons in restraint of . . . trade or commerce . . . is unlawful." Although, on its face, the USAA appears to require that any contract that has the effect of restraining trade in any respect is illegal, Arizona courts have followed the lead of federal court decisions under the Sherman Act and held that only unreasonable restraints of trade are prohibited. *Three Phoenix Co. v. Pace Industries, Inc.*, 135 Ariz. 113, 118–19, 659 P.2d 1258, 1263–64 (Ariz. 1983); *Tee Time Arrangers Inc. v. Visto Gold Partners, LLC*, 2008 WL 4149295, at *11 (Ct. App. 2008) (decision by a group to participate in a new discount golf card program with an exclusive participation clause was not an unreasonable

*Christina M. Noyes is a member of the firm of Gust Rosenfeld, P.L.C. in Phoenix, Arizona.

restraint of trade). However, there are no reported cases deciding that a restrictive covenant in a franchise agreement violated the USAA.

In Arizona, a limited number of cases have addressed a restrictive covenant in a franchise agreement under common law. *Snelling & Snelling, Inc. v. Dupay Enterprises, Inc.*, 125 Ariz. 362, 364–65, 609 P.2d 1062 (Ct. App. 1980); *Furniture Medic, L.P. v. Jantzen*, Bus. Franchise Guide (CCH) ¶ 12,749, 37,511–12 (D. Ariz. 2003) (unpublished); *Miller v Hehlen*, 209 Ariz. 462, 467–70, 104 P.3d 193 (Ct. App. 2005); *First Ascent Ventures, Inc. v. DLC Dermacare, LLC*, 2006 U.S. Dist. LEXIS 77945 (D. Ariz. 2006); *Fitness Together Franchise Corp. v. Higher Level Health and Fitness, Inc.*, 2009 WL 2753026, at *2 (D. Ariz. 2009) (unpublished opinion); *BU Holdings, LLC v. Hayn*, 2012 WL 13019170, at *6–10 (D. Ariz. 2012); *ReBath LLC v New England Bath Inc.*, Bus. Franchise Guide (CCH) ¶ 12,749 (D. Ariz. 2016). These cases are each discussed in more detail below.

Under Arizona common law, a covenant against competition will not be enforced if the restraint is greater in scope than necessary to protect the legitimate interests of the party seeking to enforce it, or if those interests are outweighed by hardship to the restricted party or public injury. The scope of a covenant is defined by its duration, geographic area, and the activity prohibited. There is no exact formula for weighing these three factors.

---

2. Have the courts articulated the "legitimate interests" of the franchisor that will support enforcement of a covenant against competition contained in a franchise agreement?

- **If so, what are they (e.g., protection of goodwill, protection of confidential information), and in what contexts did the issue arise?**
- **If not, what interests have been recognized in other contexts (e.g., employment agreements, the sale of business context)?**

In *Snelling & Snelling, Inc. v. Dupay Enterprises, Inc.*, 125 Ariz. 362, 609 P.2d 1062, 1064–65 (Ct. App. 1980), the court did not expressly address whether franchise covenants should be treated similarly to sale-of-business cases or employment cases—or uniquely. The court looked to the standards enunciated in Arizona business sale cases as its primary guide for the enforceability of a restrictive covenant in the franchise context. The court held that the three-year, 35-mile restrictive covenant was enforceable because it was reasonably necessary to protect the business interests (goodwill and customer contacts) of the franchisor. However, the court refused to enforce the restrictive covenant prohibiting competition within 35 miles of other Snelling franchise locations. That restriction was found overbroad because it was not limited to an area where the franchisee had established customer contacts and goodwill. *Snelling*, 609 P.2d at 1064–65.

In *ReBath LLC v. New England Bath Inc.*, Bus. Franchise Guide (CCH) ¶ 12,749 (D. Ariz. 2016), ReBath sought a preliminary injunction to enjoin a former franchisee from operating a competing bathroom remodeling business at the former franchised location. The court stated that a covenant not to compete is invalid unless it protects some legitimate interest and found that ReBath's restrictive covenant "likely is necessary" to protect ReBath's legitimate business interests, including its confidential information, trade secrets, and goodwill.

In *Fitness Together Franchise Corp. v. Higher Level Health and Fitness, Inc.*, 2009 WL 2753026 (D. Ariz. 2009) (unpublished opinion), the franchisor filed suit alleging that the former franchisees were continuing to offer "competitive personal fitness services," utilizing the franchise system and proprietary assets. The court granted a preliminary injunction enforcing the one-year, eight-mile restriction. However, the court compared the restriction sought against how the franchisor described its business method in the complaint and limited the injunction to "one-on-one personal fitness training" instead of a broader restriction on competitive personal fitness services. The court also prohibited the former franchisee from any unauthorized use of the franchisor's franchise system or proprietary assets and ordered the franchisee to return all confidential and proprietary information. *Id.* at *2.

In *First Ascent Ventures, Inc. v. DLC Dermacare, LLC*, 2006 U.S. Dist. LEXIS 77945 (D. Ariz. 2006), the district court for Arizona determined that Dermacare, an Arizona-based franchisor of skin-care clinics, was barred from enforcing its post-termination non-compete because of its "unclean hands." After operating for a year, Dermacare franchisees coordinated and attended a trade association meeting. Dermacare's principal disapproved of the meeting and the existence of an association without involvement by the franchisor. The principal then attempted to coerce the owners into signing highly restrictive amendments prohibiting the franchisees from contacting non-Colorado franchisees, threatened the franchisees with financial ruin if they fought back, refused to grant requests to use the local-area advertising fund monies paid by the franchisees, and cut off communications by the franchisor's personnel to the franchisees. *Id.* at *14–18.

After the franchise contracts were either terminated or rescinded, the franchisees continued to operate two skin-care clinics under a different name, but in the same location with the same phone number and offering the same services. The court found that the three-year, 30-mile non-compete provision was reasonable as to time and geographic territory, that the franchisees had breached the covenant, and that Dermacare had suffered irreparable harm and loss of goodwill. The court also found that the franchisor had suffered irreparable harm from the inability to establish a new franchisee in the former franchisee's territory, the loss of actual and potential customer data, and intangible damage to the franchise system. The court stated that in order to obtain an injunction against the franchisees, Dermacare must have acted fairly and without fraud or deceit in the controversy at issue because an injunction is an equitable remedy. The court found that Dermacare acted in bad faith, and its unclean hands prohibited it from enjoining the former franchisees from operating competing clinics. However, the franchisor's proprietary interests in its name, logos, marks, manuals, other confidential information, and telephone numbers were deemed worthy of protection by the court, which issued an injunction preventing the former franchisees from using these assets. *Id.*

The Arizona District Court in *Furniture Medic, L.P. v. Jantzen*, Bus. Franchise Guide (CCH) ¶ 12,749 (D. Ariz. 2003) (unpublished), found that a furniture repair franchisor would suffer irreparable harm to its established goodwill, name, and relationships with franchisees if the court did not enjoin the former franchisee from engaging in direct competition with Furniture Medic franchisees by continuing to operate a similar business under a different name in Maricopa County. The court noted that the failure to enforce the non-compete agreement could damage the franchise system if former franchisees could terminate their franchise agreements and "compete with impunity." Citing a New Jersey case, the district court stated that while the harm to the former franchisee is substantial, the harm to the franchisor is greater. *Id.* at 37,512.

In *In re Saban*, 30 B.R. 534, 539–41 (B.A.P. 9th Cir. 1983), U-Haul attempted to enforce a post-termination non-compete agreement against a former U-Haul dealer preventing the former dealer from engaging in a similar rental business within Maricopa County for the time period coterminous with an existing Yellow Pages telephone directory listing, plus one year. The court held that enforcing the non-compete agreement against engaging in any rental business offering similar rental equipment was reasonably necessary to protect U-Haul's business.

In *Noodles Development, L.P. v. Latham Noodles, LLC, et al.*, 2009 WL 2710137, at *3 (D. Ariz. 2009), the court determined that a franchisor was permitted to seek emergency injunctive relief on the franchisee's trademark and trade dress infringement to preserve the status quo until it could make a substantive determination on the merits of its claim through arbitration. This was because the franchise agreement stated only that the franchisor "had the right" to petition for a temporary or permanent injunction on the franchisee's use of the marks, violation of the confidentiality, and covenants not to compete. The franchise agreement contained a mandatory arbitration clause but did not permit the franchisor to seek a permanent injunction before obtaining an arbitration determination. After the individual defendants failed to pay the arbitration fees, the court permitted the case to be heard outside of arbitration.

In *Cramton v. Grabbagreen Franchising LLC*, 2019 WL 7048773 (D. Ariz. 2019), the franchisor argued that its former high-level employee and minority shareholder violated a confidentiality and non-compete agreement, and engaged in unfair competition, by joining Kahala Brands, Ltd., a competitor in the restaurant franchise industry. This allegation was a counterclaim to the employee's lawsuit that alleged multiple tort and contract claims related to her employment, ownership, and the sale of Grabbagreen's assets to Kahala. The noncompetition provision prohibited the employee from any association with any business creating, manufacturing, producing, or marketing "health fast food + juice." The judge found that the claim failed because the website printout submitted by the franchisor failed to establish that the brands controlled by Kahala were competitive with Grabbagreen or were located in the restricted five-mile territory, there was no evidence that the employee accessed her knowledge of Grabbagreen's confidential information or customer relationships, and there was no evidence that the employee interfered with the Kahala purchase. *Id.* at *2, *36–38.

The court in *ReBath, LLC v. HD Solutions LLC*, Bus. Franchise Guide (CCH) ¶ 16,534 (D. Ariz. 2019), evaluated the efforts a former franchisee had made to remove the ReBath name from online customer reviews on Facebook, Angie's List and Google to comply with a preliminary injunction. The court noted that after ReBath's filing, the former franchisee submitted a Google request with individual URLs for reviews and that this was an acceptable effort even though Google declined to act. The court declined to require the former franchisee to create new Facebook pages for the new franchisee entity or to disable the review feature stating that the franchisee can demonstrate compliance with the order without having to completely annul 12 years of internet presence. Instead, the court accepted the former franchisee's efforts to contact each Facebook individual to request changes as sufficient steps. The court declined to apply a financial sanction or to grant ReBath an award of profits but ordered the former franchisee to submit proofs of its request to Angie's List for removal or redaction of the customer reviews.

3. What time limitations have courts recognized as reasonable in the franchise context?

- **If no franchise cases have been decided, what time limitations have been recognized in other contexts?**
- **How have they been related to the interests protected?**

The reasonableness of time limitations in the franchise context has been addressed in several cases, and courts have enforced time frames from one year to three years. In *Snelling & Snelling, Inc. v. Dupay Enterprises, Inc.*, 125 Ariz. 362, 364–65, 609 P.2d 1062, 1065–65 (Ct. App. 1980), the court upheld a three-year restrictive covenant without discussing how the time period related to the franchisor's protectable interests in customer contacts and goodwill. In *First Ascent Ventures, Inc. v. DLC Dermacare, LLC*, 2006 U.S. Dist. LEXIS 77945, at *14–18 (D. Ariz. 2006), a three-year noncompetition covenant for a related entity unit and master regional franchisee was deemed reasonable.

The court in *Furniture Medic, L.P. v. Jantzen*, Bus. Franchise Guide (CCH) ¶ 12,749, 37,512 (D. Ariz. 2003) (unpublished), enjoined a former franchise from operating a competing business for two years but noted that the reasonableness of the time frame was never challenged by the franchisee. In *In re Fralc*, 2008 WL 1932311, at *2–5 (Bankr. D. Ariz. 2008), an arbitration decision enjoined the terminated franchisee from competing in the designated territory for a period of two years from the date of the award. In *In re Saban*, 30 B.R. 534, 539–40 (B.A.P. 9th Cir. 1983), the court enforced a restrictive covenant for the duration of the agent's existing telephone directory listing plus one year thereafter. (The covenant was ultimately held to be unenforceable because it applied only upon a termination of the contract for breach by the agent and was therefore unenforceable for public policy reasons as a penalty.)

In *Fitness Together Franchise Corp. v. Higher Level Health and Fitness, Inc.*, 2009 WL 2753026, at *1–2 (D. Ariz. 2009) (unpublished opinion), the court enforced a one-year restrictive covenant against the former franchisee without any discussion regarding protectable interests. The court specified that the restriction started from the date of termination, without addressing the eight months from the date of termination to the date of the court's decision in which the former franchisee was violating the non-compete agreement. In *ReBath LLC v New England Bath Inc.*, Bus. Franchise Guide (CCH) ¶ 12,749 (D. Ariz. 2016), the court found a one-year restriction to be reasonable in temporal scope.

4. What geographic limitations have courts recognized as reasonable in the franchise context?

- **How have they been related to the interests protected?**
- **Have courts recognized the legitimacy of protecting *other* franchisees from competition?**

A limited number of Arizona cases have addressed the reasonableness of geographic limitations in the franchise context. In *Snelling & Snelling, Inc. v. Dupay Enterprises, Inc.*, 125 Ariz. 362, 364–65, 609 P.2d 1062, 1064–65 (Ct. App. 1980), the court enforced a restrictive covenant prohibiting competition within 35 miles of the franchisee's former business to protect the franchisor's business interests (goodwill and customer contacts). However, the court refused to enforce the portion of the covenant prohibiting competition within 35 miles of other Snelling offices, finding that provision overbroad and not limited to the area where the franchisee had established customer contacts and goodwill. The issue of protection for other franchisees was not addressed.

The court in *ReBath LLC v New England Bath Inc.*, Bus. Franchise Guide (CCH) ¶ 12,749 (D. Ariz. 2016), found a geographic restriction of 50 miles from the franchised territory of Suffolk County to be reasonable in geographic scope and not overly broad, after the franchisor asserted that the 50-mile radius was necessary to protect its goodwill and customer base in the territory and surrounding area. In holding that the franchisor will suffer irreparable harm from the absence of a preliminary injunction, the court specifically noted that the franchisee had operated the same location for seven years and that an overnight switch may signal to customers a loss of faith in the ReBath brand, cause a loss of customers, and may make it more difficult to establish another franchisee in the territory.

In *First Ascent Ventures, Inc. v. DLC Dermacare, LLC*, 2006 U.S. Dist. LEXIS 77945 (D. Ariz. 2006), the court found a covenant not to compete reasonable when it prohibited related unit and master region franchisees from having any competitive business located in the designated franchise area or within 30 miles of any clinic in the system. The unit franchisee's territory was a specified territory around Cherry Creek, Colorado, and the master regional franchisee's territory was the state of Colorado. The court noted that the franchisor would suffer harm from the inability to establish a new franchisee in the former franchisee's territory with competition from the former franchisees as well as the franchisor's loss of its actual or potential customer base. *Id.* at *14–20.

In *Furniture Medic, L.P. v. Jantzen*, Bus. Franchise Guide (CCH) ¶ 12,749 (D. Ariz. 2003) (unpublished), the non-compete applied to an area extending one mile from the outer perimeter of the county in which the franchise business was operated, each county adjoining that county, and any county in which another Furniture Medic franchise operated in Arizona. The franchisor had franchisees in Maricopa, Pima, and Coconino Counties in the state. Enforcement as written would have prohibited the former franchisee from operating in almost every Arizona county. The franchisor sought only to enforce the geographic scope in Maricopa County and a one-mile perimeter around the county. The court found that Maricopa County was a reasonable geographic scope because the franchisee had advertised "valley-wide services." The court did not specify whether it was using Arizona or Tennessee law to evaluate the reasonableness of the geographic restriction. (The franchise agreement required application of Tennessee law.) *Id.* at 37,511–12.

In *Fitness Together Franchise Corp. v. Higher Health and Fitness*, 2009 WL 2753026, at *1–2 (D. Ariz. 2009) (unpublished opinion), the court enforced a non-compete agreement that prohibited specific fitness services within the former franchisee's territory or within an eight-mile radius around the territory. The court did not address whether it considered the geographic limitations to be related to any specific protectable interests. In *In re Saban*, 30 B.R. 534, 539–41 (B.A.P. 9th Cir. 1983), the court found a countywide restriction to be reasonable (although the covenant was ultimately held to be unenforceable because it applied only upon a termination of the contract for breach by the agent and was therefore unenforceable for public policy reasons as a penalty). In *In re Fralc*, 2008 WL 1932311, at *2–5 (Bankr. D. Ariz.

2008), an arbitration panel enjoined the terminated franchisee from competing in the designated territory in and around Tucson, Arizona, for a period of two years from the date of the award.

The court in *BU Holdings LLC v. Hayn*, 2012 WL 13019170, at *6–9 (D. Ariz. 2012) took a strict interpretation of the geographic terms of the noncompetition provision. The franchise agreement prohibited a former BOUNCEU franchisee from operating any indoor party facility within 25 miles "of any BOUNCEU Facility (whether or not franchised) then in operation, under construction or for which a franchise agreement has been executed." The former franchisee was the only Ohio franchise at the time of termination and continued operating in the same location. The court did not extend the provision to the former franchisee, holding that there was no BOUNCEU facility within 25 miles of the former franchisee's new business and the franchisor had not established a claim for breach of the non-compete clause.

5. What limitations on activities have courts recognized as reasonable in the franchise context?

In one of the limited number of franchise cases decided by Arizona courts, *Snelling & Snelling, Inc. v. Dupay Enterprises, Inc.*, 125 Ariz. 362, 364–65, 609 P.2d 1062, 1064–65 (Ct. App. 1980), the covenant against competition provided that the franchisee would not engage in a similar business. The court enforced the portion of the restriction that was limited to the geographic area where the franchisee had established customer contacts and goodwill.

In *ReBath LLC v New England Bath Inc.*, Bus. Franchise Guide (CCH) ¶ 12,749 (D. Ariz. 2016), the former franchisee operated both a kitchen and bathroom remodeling company. The court noted that the franchisor was not seeking to prohibit the kitchen component or any plumbing work that was not part of a typical bathroom remodel. The court found that prohibiting activity that competes with the business of selling, marketing, and installing bath, shower, and other bathroom remodel-related products and services was not overbroad.

The court in *Furniture Medic, L.P. v. Jantzen*, Bus. Franchise Guide (CCH) ¶ 12,749, 37,512 (D. Ariz. 2003) (unpublished) enjoined a former franchisee from owning, participating in, being employed by, consulting with, or having any interest in any other business in the furniture repair or restoration business in the county in which the former franchisee had operated its franchise business. The court evaluated the former franchisee's ongoing business and found that it was not different or distinguishable from the franchised business.

Without any discussion, in *First Ascent v. DLC Dermacare, LLC*, 2006 U.S. Dist. LEXIS 77945, at *14–20 (D. Ariz. 2006), the court found reasonable restrictive covenant prohibiting a unit and master region franchisee from owning, maintaining, or having any interest in a "competitive business" located or doing business within the designated franchise area or within 30 miles of a clinic in the system for a period of three years from the date of termination. However, the court declined to issue an injunction prohibiting the former unit franchisee from continuing to operate a skin clinic in the same location due to the franchisor's bad faith prior to termination.

In *Fitness Together Franchise Corp. v. Higher Health and Fitness*, 2009 WL 2753026, at *1–2 (D. Ariz. 2009) (unpublished opinion), the court enforced a permanent injunction only to the extent that the former franchisee's activities involved "one-on-one personal fitness training." The court specifically noted that the franchisor's complaint alleged that it had developed a unique and proprietary business method for the operation of businesses that offer one-on-one personal training. Because of this description, the court restricted only that particular business type. The former franchisee was also prohibited from unauthorized use of the franchisor's system or proprietary assets and was required to return any confidential or proprietary information.

6. Does the state recognize a difference between interim and post-term covenants?

This issue has not been addressed in the context of franchising. It has been addressed only in the limited context of whether an injunction can be issued to enforce a covenant against competition against a former employee. An Arizona statute prohibits the issuance of an injunction to prevent the breach of a contract, the performance of which would not be specifically enforced. ARIZ. REV. STAT. ANN. § 12-1802(5) (West 1994). In *Titus v. Superior Court, Maricopa County*, 91 Ariz. 18, 20–22, 368 P.2d 874, 876–78 (Ariz. 1962) (en banc), the court distinguished between a negative covenant applicable during the term of employment that would not be enforced (because its purpose would be to enforce indirectly a contract to render services) and a post-term covenant not to compete, which did not require any affirmative act by the former employee. Applying this rationale, a covenant by a disc jockey and news reporter not to be associated with any radio station within 50 miles of Phoenix for one year after the termination of his employment was enforced by the court.

7. Has the state allowed enforcement of covenants against non-signatories (e.g., family members, newly formed corporations)?

This issue has not been specifically addressed under Arizona law. However, in two cases where the former franchisee's individual owners formed new entities that started competing businesses, the courts did not excuse enforcement based on a newly formed entity after the franchisor filed suit against all parties. *ReBath, LLC v. HD Solutions LLC*, Bus. Franchise Guide (CCH) ¶ 16,534 (D. Ariz. 2019).

8. Will the state modify, "blue-pencil," or otherwise reduce a covenant found to be overbroad?

Arizona courts will "blue-pencil" (or perhaps more accurately "blue-line") restrictive covenants to eliminate grammatically severable, unreasonable provisions if it is clear from its terms that the contract was intended to be severable. The court will then enforce the lawful part and ignore the unlawful part. The court will not, however, add terms or otherwise rewrite an agreement. *Snelling & Snelling, Inc. v. Dupay Enterprises, Inc.*, 125 Ariz. 362, 364–65, 609 P.2d 1062, 1064–65 (Ct. App. 1980) (provision of covenant not to compete within 35 miles of franchisee's area enforceable, while separate provision not to compete within 35 miles of other Snelling offices stricken). *See also Valley Medical Specialists v. Farber*, 194 Ariz. 363, 372, 982 P.2d 1277, 1286 (Ariz. 1999) (en banc); *OLIVER/Pilcher Insurance, Inc. v. Daniels*, 148 Ariz. 530, 533, 715 P.2d 1218, 1221 (Ariz. 1986) (en banc); *Amex Distributing Co. v. Mascari*, 150 Ariz. 510, 519, 724 P.2d 596, 605 (Ct. App. 1986); *Compass Bank v. Hartley*, 430 F. Supp. 2d 973, 980 (D. Ariz. 2006). The court in *Farber* did express concern, however, about the in terrorem effect of overly broad covenants on departing employees should an employer create an ominous covenant knowing that, if challenged, the court would strike sufficient portions to make it enforceable. The court may also decline to issue a permanent injunction on provisions of a restrictive covenant if the franchisor has "unclean hands." *First Ascent v. DLC Dermacare, LLC*, 2006 U.S. Dist. LEXIS 77945, at *14–20 (D. Ariz. 2006). In *Furniture Medic, L.P. v. Jantzen*, Bus. Franchise Guide (CCH) ¶ 12,749, 37,512 (D. Ariz. 2003) (unpublished), the franchisor elected to enjoin a former franchisee's activities in only one of the territories in which the franchise agreement prohibited the franchisee from operating without mentioning any "blue-pencil" capabilities.

One federal case applying Arizona law has specifically evaluated the practice of using "step-down" provisions in noncompetition covenants in limited circumstances. These provisions include several scenarios of what may be found by the court to be reasonable. The step-down provision must be carefully crafted. If the provision is indefinite, inconsistent with underlying provisions, or not easily severable from the unreasonable provisions, then the covenant is invalid. *Compass Bank v. Hartley*, 430 F. Supp. 2d 973 (D. Ariz. 2006) (finding that a time and location range was saved by the step-down provisions for "2 years/18 mo./12 mo." as well as a geographical restriction from engaging in a competitive business within "50 miles (and if 50 miles is determined by the court to be overly broad, then 25 miles)," allowing the court to limit the duration to one-year and the scope to 25 miles). *Id.* at 976–77, 981.

9. When does a non-compete period begin to run?

➤ Will courts equitably extend the term?

The Arizona courts in the franchise cases discussed above have not evaluated the issue of when the non-compete period begins except to summarily restate the applicable contract provisions and require enforcement of the time period starting on the date of the court decision. The court in *ReBath LLC v New England Bath Inc.*, Bus. Franchise Guide (CCH) ¶ 12,749 (D. Ariz. 2016), enjoined the former franchisee from operating a competing bathroom remodeling business "until further notice of the Court, but lasting no longer than one year" from the court order. In *Furniture Medic, L.P. v. Jantzen*, Bus. Franchise Guide (CCH) ¶ 12,749, 37,511–12 (D. Ariz. 2003) (unpublished), a district court evaluating a franchise agreement with a Tennessee law provision and citing Tennessee caselaw stated that its equitable powers include "the power to make meaningful the non-competition agreement by making it effective from the date of issuance of any permanent injunction." The court enforced the full two-year non-compete period from the date of the order. In *Fitness Together*, the court's injunction issued in August 2009 was for only one year from the January 2009 date of termination, leaving only four months for the non-compete to run. The decision does not indicate whether the franchisor requested equitable tolling or even addressed the time disparity. 2009 WL 2753026, at *2.

In *Realty Executives Int'l, Inc. v. RE/EX Cal., Inc.*, 2011 WL 13185715 (D. Ariz. 2011), the court granted summary judgment to the former franchisees because the covenants were only in effect for two years. Realty Executives terminated its franchisee in March 2009. In April 2010, owners of the former franchisee started a new real estate franchise company and approached Realty Executives' franchisees in several states to persuade them to become their franchisees. The court found the issue of the alleged violations of the covenants to be moot in June 2011. The court did not address extending the time of the covenant for the additional year that the former franchisee was alleged to be violating the covenant. *Id.* at *6.

On this issue, an Arizona bankruptcy court questioned an arbitration decision that enjoined the franchisee from competing in the designated territory for a two-year period from the date of the arbitration award instead of the date of termination. The court indicated that it did not believe that it had the power to summarily revise the provision to begin at a different date. However, it remanded the issue of the non-compete starting date to the district court. There was no reported decision resolving the issue. *In re Fralc*, 2008 WL 1932311, at *2 (Bankr. D. Ariz. 2008).

---

10. Are there additional nuances or peculiarities of the state's treatment of covenants in the franchising context?

Because there are a limited number of cases involving franchising, the nuances and peculiarities under Arizona law are primarily discussed above. The district court's refusal to grant equitable relief due to the franchisor's "unclean hands" is one aspect that practitioners will want to evaluate before pursuing an injunction action. Practitioners will also wish to provide for clear step-down provisions in order to provide Arizona courts with the flexibility to enforce what it might find to be a reasonable covenant. One other issue that might arise in the franchising context is whether Arizona courts would refuse to enforce a non-compete that was enforceable under the laws of another state if such enforcement was against Arizona law. This issue has been mentioned in only one Arizona case. In *Snelling & Snelling, Inc. v. Dupay Enterprises, Inc.*, 125 Ariz. 362, 364, 609 P.2d 1062, 1064 (Ct. App. 1980), the parties agreed that Arizona law controlled on the issue of the covenant in question, although the contract specifically provided that it "be interpreted and governed by the laws of the commonwealth of Pennsylvania." The court stated that "regardless of whether Pennsylvania or Arizona law applies, the covenant not to compete must be reasonably limited in both time and territory." This statement implies that Arizona could refuse to enforce a provision that it deems to be unreasonable. *Snelling* and *In re Saban*, 30 B.R. 534, 539 (B.A.P. 9th Cir. 1983), are widely considered to be the controlling caselaw in Arizona, although *Snelling* is a Division Two case from Tucson. There has been no Arizona Supreme Court case on restrictive covenants in the franchise context.

Arkansas

*By Sarah Keith-Bolden**

1. Has the state addressed covenants against competition in the context of franchising?

- **Does the state have a franchising statute or regulations that address covenants against competition?**
- **Does the state have a covenants statute of general applicability that would encompass franchise covenants?**
- **Have the courts addressed covenants in the context of franchising either under a statute or under the state's common law?**

The Arkansas Franchise Practices Act, ARK. CODE ANN. § 4-72-201 *et seq.*, applies to certain franchise agreements entered into, renewed, or transferred after March 4, 1977, and regulates the termination, cancellation, sale, and transfer of franchises. The statute does not, however, apply to franchises subject to the Federal Trade Commission's franchise disclosure regulations, 16 C.F.R. 436.1 *et seq.*, or certain industry-specific Arkansas franchising statutes. ARK. CODE ANN. § 4-72-203. Arkansas also has a Farm Equipment Retailer Franchise Statute, ARK. CODE ANN. § 4-72-301 *et seq.*; a Petroleum Products Suppliers and Distributors Franchise Statute, ARK. CODE ANN. § 4-72-401 *et seq.* and ARK. CODE ANN. § 4-72-501 *et seq.*; and a Restaurant Franchise Statute, ARK. CODE ANN. § 4-72-601 *et seq.* None of these statutes addresses covenants against competition.

Arkansas does not have a general statute regarding covenants against competition. Section 4-75-101, which went into effect on July 22, 2015, addresses covenants not to compete that are ancillary to an employment relationship. This statute does not, however, apply to covenants not to compete that are ancillary to other contractual relationships, including franchise agreements. ARK. CODE ANN. § 4-75-101(h)(1). Existing common law standards continue to apply to these covenants. *Id.* The statute also exempts people who hold certain medical licenses. *Id.* at (j)(1).

*Sarah Keith-Bolden is a Member of Quattlebaum, Grooms & Tull, PLLC based in Little Rock, Arkansas.

Under Arkansas common law, covenants against competition are restraints on trade that are disfavored by courts. *Optical Partners, Inc. v. Dang*, 2011 Ark. 156, at 10, 381 S.W.3d 46, 53 (analyzing a covenant not to compete in a lease agreement between a business that sold eyeglasses and an optometrist). Courts will not enforce covenants against competition to protect a party against ordinary competition. *Dawson v. Temps Plus, Inc.*, 337 Ark. 247, 254, 987 S.W.2d 722, 726 (1999). An enforceable covenant not to compete must meet three requirements: (1) there must be a valid interest to protect; (2) the time limit contained in the covenant must be reasonable; and (3) the scope of the covenant must not be overly broad. *Mercy Health Sys. of Nw. Ark., Inc. v. Bicak*, 2011 Ark. App. 341, at 8, 383 S.W.3d 869, 874. For a covenant to be reasonable, the restriction on one party must be no greater than is reasonably necessary to secure the interest of the protected party and the scope of the covenant must not be so broad as to be injure a public interest. *Duffner v. Alberty*, 19 Ark. App. 137, 139, 718 S.W.2d 111, 112 (1986) (analyzing a covenant not to compete given by a doctor to his former medical group). Although covenants not to compete are disfavored, the burden is on the party challenging the validity of the covenant to show that it is unreasonable and contrary to public policy. *Dawson*, 337 Ark. at 254, 987 S.W.2d at 726. As with other contracts, an ambiguous covenant not to compete will be construed against the drafting party. *Wright Med. Group v. Darr*, 2010 WL 3168259 (E.D. Ark. Aug. 6, 2010) (noting that, where parties jointly draft an agreement, parole evidence regarding the parties' intentions might be admissible to explain the parties' intent).

The only case in which an Arkansas court has a addressed a covenant against competition in the franchising context is *Hobbs v. Pool*, 1987 WL 8004 (Ark. Ct. App. Mar. 18, 1987), an unreported case in which the Arkansas Court of Appeals followed the common law generally applicable to covenants against competition. In *Hobbs*, the franchisor of a catfish restaurant concept sued a franchisee after the franchisee stopped making royalty payments, changed the restaurant name, and continued operating a catfish restaurant in the same location. *Id.* at *1. The franchisee's covenant not to compete prohibited the franchisee from engaging in the business of catfish preparation within 100 miles of the franchised restaurant for a period of 12 months after termination of the franchise agreement. *Id.* at *2. The lower court found that the franchisor had a legitimate interest to protect and that a covenant not to compete was valid. *Id.*

On appeal, the franchisee argued that the terms of the covenant were unreasonable, unduly broad, and covered too large a geographical area. *Id.* Considering these arguments, the court cited general principles that apply to covenants against competition outside the franchise context, explaining that covenants not to compete are disfavored but the burden is on the party challenging the validity of the covenant to show that it is unreasonable and against public policy. *Id.* The court also noted that "a contract in restraint of trade ancillary to a sale or a business transaction, which is reasonably limited as to time and place, is not against public policy and is not invalid." *Id.* Turning to the circumstances of the case, the court reversed the lower court, finding that the 100-mile radius was "unnecessarily large," especially given that the franchisor was operating other catfish restaurants that competed with the franchisee within the 100-mile radius. *Id.* at *3. The court also concluded that the scope of the restriction was overly broad because it prohibited the franchisee from "engaging in the business of catfish preparation," which "could very easily be construed as encompassing the raising, processing or distribution of catfish." *Id.*

2. Have the courts articulated the "legitimate interests" of the franchisor that will support enforcement of a covenant against competition contained in a franchise agreement?

- **If so, what are they (e.g., protection of goodwill, protection of confidential information), and in what contexts did the issue arise?**
- **If not, what interests have been recognized in other contexts (e.g., employment agreements, the sale of business context)?**

In *Hobbs v. Pool*, the Arkansas Court of Appeals did not directly address the lower court's determination that the franchisor had a legitimate interest to protect through a covenant against competition. 1987 WL 8004 (Ark. Ct. App. Mar. 18, 1987). The court did, however, explain that "a contract in restraint of trade ancillary to a sale or a business transaction, which is reasonably limited as to time and place, is not against public policy and is not invalid." *Id.* at *2. By citing this rule before considering whether the scope of the covenant at issue was reasonable, the court implicitly acknowledged that a franchisor, like the purchaser of a business, may have a legitimate interest to protect through a covenant against competition. No other Arkansas court has addressed what constitutes a "legitimate interest" in the context of a franchise agreement.

In the context of the purchase of a business, Arkansas law upholds covenants against competition "to the extent reasonably necessary for the purchaser's protection." *Easley v. Sky, Inc.*, 15 Ark. App. 64, 67, 689 S.W.2d 356, 358 (1985). A purchaser has a legitimate interest in protecting the operation of the purchased business and in recouping its investment in the business. *Id.* at 67–68, 698 S.W.2d at 358–59 (discussing a purchaser's interest in preventing the seller from engaging in any activity that "could affect the operation" of the purchased business for a time period that allows the purchaser "to amortize a large part of its initial debt and recapture a substantial part of its investment"). Where the seller of a business "has the wherewithal to start a new business" and understands the nature of the business and "how profitable it could be," the purchaser has a legitimate interest to protect through a covenant against competition. *Dawson v. Temps Plus, Inc.*, 337 Ark. 247, 254, 987 S.W.2d 722, 726 (1999). "At a minimum, enforcement of a restrictive covenant requires that the parties have competing businesses as opposed to complementary businesses," so a party to a business transaction does not have a protectable interest in prohibiting the other party from engaging in activities that are "not in direct competition." *Optical Partners, Inc. v. Dang*, 2011 Ark. 156, at 12–13, 381 S.W.3d 46, 54.

Under common law, covenants not to compete in employment contracts are subject to stricter scrutiny than those connected with a sale of a business. *Dawson*, 337 Ark. at 254, 987 S.W.2d at 726. An employer does, however, have a legitimate interest in "preventing a former employee from appropriating its customers." *Freeman v. Brown Hiller, Inc.*, 102 Ark. App. 76, 81–82, 281 S.W.3d 749, 754. "When the covenant grows out of an employment or other associational relationship, the courts have found an interest sufficient to warrant enforcement of the covenant only in those cases where the covenantee provided special training or made available trade secrets, confidential business information, or customer lists, and then only if it is found that the associate was able to use the information so obtained to gain an unfair competitive advantage." *Mercy Health Sys. of Nw. Ark., Inc. v. Bicak*,

2011 Ark. App. 341, at 8, 383 S.W.3d at 874; *see also* ARK. CODE ANN. § 4-75-101(b) (outlining the scope of an employer's protectable business interest to include trade secrets, intellectual property, customer lists, goodwill with customers, knowledge of the employer's business practices, methods, profit margins, costs, other valuable and confidential business information, training and education, and other valuable employer data). Trade secrets that may be protected by covenants not to compete include secret plans, processes, tools, methods, or compounds. *Quality Liquid Feeds, Inc. v. Plunkett*, 89 Ark. App. 16, 199 S.W.3d 700 (2004).

3. What time limitations have courts recognized as reasonable in the franchise context?

- **If no franchise cases have been decided, what time limitations have been recognized in other contexts?**
- **How have they been related to the interests protected?**

In the sole Arkansas case to examine covenants not to compete in the franchise context, *Hobbs v. Pool*, 1987 WL 8004 (Ark. Ct. App. Mar. 18, 1987), the court held that the franchisee's covenant against competition was "unsupported by the evidence." The court did not, however, comment on the 12-month duration of the covenant but instead focused on the overbroad scope of the geographic restriction and prohibited activities.

Outside the franchise context, because covenants against competition are reviewed on a case-by-case basis, there is no bright-line limit on the duration of covenants not to compete. *See Optical Partners, Inc. v. Dang*, 2011 Ark. 156, at 11–12, 381 S.W.3d at 54 (explaining that the reasonableness of a covenant against competition must be "determined under the particular circumstances involved"). Under common law, the Arkansas Supreme Court has upheld covenants lasting 5 years, 10 years, and 20 years, and covenants with no stated time limit. *Dawson v. Temps Plus, Inc.*, 337 Ark. 247, 254, 987 S.W.2d 722, 726 (1999). A two-year post-employment restriction is presumptively reasonably under section 4-75-101.

4. What geographic limitations have courts recognized as reasonable in the franchise context?

- **How have they been related to the interests protected?**
- **Have courts recognized the legitimacy of protecting other franchisees from competition?**

In *Hobbs v. Pool*, 1987 WL 8004 (Ark. Ct. App. Mar. 18, 1987), the court applied the "general rule" that "the territory established in the covenant, in order to be reasonable, must be necessary for the protection of the promisee's interest" to a restrictive covenant ancillary to a franchise agreement. *Id.* at *3 (citing *Easley v. Sky, Inc.*, 15 Ark. App. 64, 67, 689 S.W.2d 356, 358 (1985)). As explained above, under the particular facts at issue, the court held that a post-termination covenant not to compete within a 100-mile radius of the franchise location was "unsupported by the evidence."

Hobbs is the only Arkansas case interpreting a covenant against competition ancillary to a franchise agreement, but Arkansas courts have considered geographic limitations in other contexts. To determine whether a geographic restraint is reasonable, Arkansas courts will consider "whether it is such only as to afford a fair protection to the interests of the party in whose favor it is given, and not so large as to interfere with the interests of the public." *Optical Partners, Inc. v. Dang*, 2011 Ark. 156, at 12, 381 S.W.3d 46, 54 (quoting *Evans Lab., Inc.*, 262 Ark. at 870, 562 S.W. at 464). Although a 100-mile radius was held unreasonable in *Hobbs*, the same radius is not unreasonable if it is closely tied to the protected party's interests. *Easley*, 15 Ark. App. at 68, 689 S.W.2d at 359 (upholding a 100-mile restriction ancillary to the sale of a gas station where the restriction was chosen because trucks refuel every 100 to 200 miles). The lack of a geographic restriction does not render a covenant against competition unreasonable if the covenant has other limitations that closely tailor it to the protected party's interests. *HRR Ark., Inc. v. River City Contractors, Inc.*, 350 Ark. 420, 430, 87 S.W.3d 232, 239 (2002) (citing a case in which the Arkansas Court of Appeals found a restrictive covenant reasonable where it did not contain a geographic restriction but only prohibited a salesperson from soliciting customers he was servicing at the time of his termination); *see also* Ark. Code Ann. § 4-75-101(c)(1) (providing that the lack of a geographic restriction in a covenant against competition ancillary to an employment relationship does not make the covenant overly broad if the covenant is appropriately limited in time and scope).

5. What limitations on activities have courts recognized as reasonable in the franchise context?

In *Hobbs v. Pool*, 1987 WL 8004 (Ark. Ct. App. Mar. 18, 1987), the court found a restriction that prohibited a former franchisee of a catfish restaurant from engaging in "catfish preparation" was unreasonable because it potentially covered activities, such as raising catfish, that were outside the scope contemplated by the parties to the agreement. In doing so, the court applied the general rule that, like other restrictions, activities prohibited by a covenant against competition must be narrowly tailored to the promisee's interest. *Easley v. Sky, Inc.*, 15 Ark. App. 64, 67, 689 S.W.2d 356, 358 (Ark. Ct. App. 1985). Under appropriate circumstances, however, a covenant against competition may prohibit activities that the protected party does not engage in but that nonetheless impact the protected party's interests. *Id.* at 67–68, 689 S.W.2d at 358–59 (finding that the seller of a convenience store that sold gasoline could be prohibited from working or distributing for an oil company because the seller could affect the operation of the sold business by engaging in these activities).

6. Does the state recognize a difference between in-term and post-term covenants?

There is no caselaw discussing the differences between in-term and post-termination covenants against competition.

7. Has the state allowed enforcement of covenants against non-signatories (e.g., family members, newly formed corporations)?

The Arkansas Supreme Court has acknowledged that a non-signatory to a non-compete agreement may be bound under certain circumstances where the non-signatory conspired to breach a contract or acted in concert with the signatory to do so. *Dawson v. Temps Plus, Inc.*, 337 Ark. 247, 987 S.W.2d 722 (1999).

8. Will the state modify, "blue-pencil," or otherwise reduce a covenant found to be overbroad?

"It has long been the rule, at least in Arkansas, that when a covenant not to compete overreaches, the court will not make a new contract for the parties." *Quality Liquid Feeds, Inc. v. Plunkett*, 89 Ark. App. 16, 20–21, 199 S.W.3d 700, 704 (2004); *see also Church Mut. Ins. Co. v. Copenhaver*, 2010 WL 2105623, at *4 (E.D. Ark. May 24, 2010) ("No matter how close a non-compete agreement is to being valid, Arkansas courts will not rewrite the contract."). This rule was applied in the context of a franchise agreement in *Hobbs v. Pool*, 1987 WL 8004 (Ark. Ct. App. Mar. 18, 1987), where the court found the restrictive covenant unreasonable and refused to enforce it because it (1) extended over too great a geographic area and (2) prohibited the franchisee not only from engaging in a catfish restaurant business but also from "engaging in any phase of 'catfish preparation.'" Because the covenant as written was overly broad, the court refused to enforce it, even though the former franchisee was operating the same restaurant, in the same location, as was covered by the franchise agreement.

In the context of employment relationships, however, ARK. CODE ANN. § 4-75-101 now specifically requires courts to reform an overbroad covenant entered into after July 22, 2015, to the extent necessary to make it enforceable. Courts applying Arkansas common law have also recently expressed a willingness to enforce severability and reformation provisions in noncompetition agreements. *Mounce v. Jeronimo Insulating*, LLC, 2021 Ark. App. 195, 625 S.W.3d 367 (holding that the circuit court had not blue-penciled the noncompete in question but also "hasten[ing] to add that the agreement itself contains a severability clause, so the parties agreed to permit reformation of this non-compete agreement to any extent necessary to make it enforceable under the law"); *Pitts v. Fire Extinguisher Sales & Svcs. of Ark. LLC*, 2021 WL 2547796 (E.D. Ark. May 13, 2021) (citing *Mounce* in holding that "even outside of Arkansas Code Section 4-75-101 (meaning where common law applies), courts can modify a noncompetition agreement where the parties expressly agreed to reformation and severability").

9. When does a non-compete period begin to run?

- **Will courts equitably extend the term?**

There is no dispositive rule on when the time period covered by covenants against competition begins to run in Arkansas.

10. Are there additional nuances or peculiarities of the state's treatment of covenants in the franchising context?

Arkansas courts will honor a choice-of-law provision "provided that the law selected is reasonably related to the transaction and does not violate a fundamental public policy of the state." *Guardian Fiberglass, Inc. v. Whit Davis Lumber Co.*, 509 F.3d 512, 515 (8th Cir. 2007) (applying Michigan law in determining a dealer's covenant not to compete was not enforceable due to the covenantee's lacking a legitimate business interest to protect).

California

*by Jonathan Solish **

1. Has the state addressed covenants against competition in the context of franchising?

- **Does the state have a franchising statute or regulations that address covenants against competition?**
- **Does the state have a covenants statute of general applicability that would encompass franchise covenants?**
- **Have the courts addressed covenants in the context of franchising either under a statute or under the state's common law?**

Although no statute specifically addresses covenants against competition in the franchise context, a statute of general applicability invalidates all covenants not to compete except those exempted by the statute. CAL. BUS. & PROF. CODE § 16600 *et seq.* (1976). Section 16600 states: "Except as provided in this chapter, every contract by which anyone is restrained from engaging in a lawful profession, trade or business of any kind is to that extent void." Non-compete agreements are allowed in conjunction with the sale of a business (§ 16601) or the dissolution of a partnership (§ 16602) or a limited liability company (§ 16602.5). Section 16601 is meant to protect purchasers of businesses in limited circumstances. *Hill Medical Group v. Wycoff,* 86 Cal. App. 4th 895, 901 (2001).

Section 16600 applies to "any sort of contract" including franchise agreements. *Comedy Club, Inc. v. Improv West Associates,* 553 F.3d 1277, 1290 (9th Cir. 2009); *Scott v. Snelling & Snelling,* 732 F. Supp. 1034, 1040–41 (N.D. Cal. 1990). *See also La Fortune v. Ebie,* 26 Cal. App. 3d 72, 76 (1972); *Dayton Time Lock Service, Inc. v. Silent Watchman Corp.,* 52 Cal. App. 3d 1, 6 (1975); *Great Harvest Franchising v. McKinley,* Bus. Franchise Guide (CCH) ¶ 11,260 (C.D. Cal. 1997). The franchisee's use of the franchisor's goodwill is not sufficient to bring the relationship within the statutory exception of section 16601. *Scott,* 732 F. Supp. at 1041. A sham transaction designed to bypass the statute is void and unenforceable. *Bosley Medical Group v. Abramson,* 161 Cal. App. 3d 284, 289 (1984).

*Mr. Solish is a partner in the Los Angeles office of Bryan Cave Leighton Paisner LLP and a California certified legal specialist in franchise and distribution law.

In *Comedy Club, Inc. v. Improv West Associates*, 553 F.3d 1277, 1292 (9th Cir. 2009), the court held that "an in-term covenant not to compete in a franchise-like agreement will be void if it forecloses competition in a substantial share of a business, trade or market." The court vacated an arbitrator's award that had enforced an in-term covenant against the operation of competing comedy clubs. Viewing the relationship of the parties as "in essence a franchise agreement," the court followed *Dayton Time Lock Service v. Silent Watchman Corp.*, 52 Cal. App. 3d 1, 6 (1975), where the court held that "in-term covenants may be proscribed when it is probable that performance of the contract will foreclose competition in a substantial share of the affected line of commerce." *See also Kelton v. Stravinski*, 138 Cal. App. 4th 941, 946 (2006) (affirming that *Dayton Time Lock* applies to franchise agreements).

In *Comedy Club*, enforcement would have foreclosed comedy club competition nationwide for more than 14 years, effectively foreclosing "competition in a substantial share of the market," and thus violated section 16600. *Comedy Club*, 553 F.3d at 1292. Rather than striking the entirety of the non-competition clause, the court limited the in-term covenant to counties where the licensee already was operating licensed comedy clubs.

Most recently, in *Ixchel Pharma, LLC v. Biogen, Inc.*, 9 Cal. 5th 1130, 1159 (2020), the California Supreme Court clarified that restraints on business operations and commercial dealings are subject to a reasonableness standard. The court explained that "[i]n context, section 16600 is best read not to render void per se all contractual restraints on business dealings, but rather to subject such restraints to a rule of reason." *Id.* at 1150. In *Ixchel*, defendant Forward entered into a settlement agreement with co-defendant Biogen requiring Forward to terminate its existing contracts with Ixchel and to not enter into any new contracts pertaining to the development of products with the active ingredient dimethyl fumarate. *Id.* at 1138–39. Ixchel argued that "*Edwards [v. Arthur Andersen*, 44 Cal. 4th 937, 189 P.3d 285 (2008)] conclusively held that section 16600 invalidated all restraints on trade for all contracts, no matter how reasonable," but the court explained that *Edwards* was limited to employee non-competition agreements and "the question of whether noncompetition agreements outside the employment context are per se invalid was not presented in *Edwards*." *Id.* at 1158. The court held that a rule of reason applies in determining the legality of provisions that prohibit a party from engaging in lawful trade or business. *Id.* at 1162–63. The court indicated that section 16600 should incorporate the same standard as the Cartwright Act, § 16700 *et seq.*, which asks whether an agreement promotes or suppresses competition by considering the circumstances, details, and logic of a restraint. *Id.* at 1159–60. Although *Ixchel* is not a franchise case, the court noted that exclusive dealing arrangements are often part of franchise agreements and may have a pro-competitive effect. *Id.* at 1160–1161.

After the Supreme Court's clarification, the Ninth Circuit affirmed the district court's finding that the agreement between Forward and Biogen was not an unreasonable restraint on trade. *Ixchel Pharma, LLC v. Biogen, Inc.*, 821 Fed. Appx. 897, 898 (9th Cir. 2020).

In a case decided after *Ixchel*, the court held that a rule of reason applies in assessing the validity of an exclusive dealing arrangement because the contract did not limit an individual's ability to engage in a profession, trade, or business. *Quidel Corporation v. Superior Court of San Diego County*, 57 Cal. App. 5th 155, 166–67 (2020). The proper inquiry asks whether (1) the agreement restrains trade more than promotes it, (2) the agreement is necessary to protect the respective parties in dealing with each other, or (3) the agreement forecloses a substantial share of the line of commerce. *Id.* at 171. In a footnote, the court declined to reach any conclusion as to whether a franchise agreement was comparable to other types of exclusive dealing arrangements. *Id.* at n.4.

The potential ramifications of *Ixchel* for franchising were analyzed in a Colorado case, where a California franchisee was sued for violating a restrictive covenant. In weighing the franchisee's claim that California's strong public policy against such covenants ought to negate a Colorado choice-of-law provision, the court in *Postnet Int'l Franchise Corp. v. Wu,* No. 1:20-cv-03790-DDD-SKC, 2021 BL 103675 (D. Colo. Feb. 19, 2021), held that after *Ixchel,* California's policy on restrictive covenants did not appear to diverge from Colorado's. The court acknowledged that California still had a strong public policy against restrictive covenants in the employment context, but that the rule of reason now applied in business relationships. The court concluded that "in-term covenants, in the franchise context, at least, are expressly not per se invalid under California law." *Id.* at *10. The court therefore applied Colorado law. Despite acknowledging the problems that might arise in failing to enforce a restrictive covenant, the court nonetheless declined to enjoin the former franchisee. Whether this analysis will be followed when California courts apply *Ixchel* to franchising remains to be seen, but the "clarification" of California law in *Ixchel* could signal a very significant sea change. *See also Bambu Franchising v. Nguyen,* 2021 WL 1839664, at *19–23 (N.D. Cal. May 7, 2021).

NARROW RESTRAINT EXCEPTION

Section 16600 prohibits contracts that prevent engaging in a trade, profession, or business. Some cases have held that it does not apply "where one is barred from pursuing only a small or limited part of a business, trade or profession. . . ." *Boughton v. Socony Mobil Oil Co.,* 231 Cal. App. 2d 188, 192 (1964). "[W]here one is barred from pursuing only a small or limited part of a business, trade or profession, the contract has been upheld as valid." *Id.* This has been referred to as the "narrow restraint" exception. *Walia v. Aetna Ins.,* 93 Cal. App. 4th 1213, 1222 (2001). *See also General Commercial Packaging, Inc. v. TPS Package Engineering, Inc.,* 126 F.3d 1131, 1135 (9th Cir. 1997) (upholding a covenant not to compete solely because it was limited to a narrow segment of the market). This exception was applied to franchising in *Great Harvest Franchising v. McKinley,* Bus. Franchise Guide (CCH) ¶ 11,260 (C.D. Cal. 1997) and *Great Harvest Franchising v. Artim,* Bus. Franchise Guide ¶ 11,259 (E.D. Cal. 1997), where courts held that former franchisees were not barred from pursuing a business just because they were barred from baking wholewheat bread.

In *Edwards v. Arthur Andersen LLP,* 44 Cal. 4th 937 (2008), the trial court had applied the "narrow restraint" exception, but the California Supreme Court held that there is no "narrow restraint" exception under California law. Had the legislature "intended for the statute to apply only to restraints that were unreasonable or overbroad, it could have included language to that effect. . . ." *Id.* at 951.

Since *Edwards,* various California courts have rejected the "narrow restraint" exception. *See e.g., Retirement Group v. Galante,* 176 Cal. App. 4th 1226, 1241 (2009); *Dowell v. Biosense Webster, Inc.,* 179 Cal. App. 4th 564, 574–75 (2009); *AMN Healthcare, Inc. v. Aya Healthcare Services, Inc.,* 28 Cal. App. 5th 923, 938–39 (2018) (not expressly rejecting it but doubting the continuing validity of *Loral Corp. v. Moyes,* 174 Cal.

App. 3d 268, 280 (1985), which had found an employee non-solicitation provision to be a narrow enough restraint, and holding that the employee non-solicitation provision was invalid as it restrained defendants even in a "narrow manner"). *See also Batts v. Bankers Life & Casualty Company*, 2015 WL 166869, at *4 (N.D. Cal. Jan. 13, 2015); *Lawrence Crane Enterprises, Inc. v. Abrams*, 2013 WL 12123997, at *3 (C.D. Cal. Jan. 28, 2013); *Couch v. Morgan Stanley & Co., Inc.*, 2015 WL 4716297, at *20 (E.D. Cal. Aug. 7, 2015).

However, some courts have declined to fully endorse or extend the narrow restraint prohibition from *Edwards*. *Golden v. California Emergency Physicians Medical Group*, 896 F.3d 1018, 1023–24 (9th Cir. 2018) (acknowledging *Edwards'* rejection of the narrow restraint exception and stressing that restraints will rarely fall outside of section 16600 but not precluding the possibility); *Barker v. Insight Global, LLC*, 2018 WL 3548911, at *8 (N.D. Cal. July 24, 2018) (finding the employee non-solicitation provision valid and distinguishing it from the customer non-solicitation provision in *Edwards*); *Vestis, LLC v. Caramel Sales, Ltd.*, 2019 WL 11542355, at *4 (C.D. Cal. Nov. 5, 2019) (finding an NDA not to be overly broad in light of the Ninth Circuit's clarification in *Golden*).

Since the California Supreme Court has recently limited the holdings in Edwards to the employment context, it remains to be seen how the narrow restraint exception may be treated in the context of franchising. *Ixchel Pharma, LLC v. Biogen, Inc.*, 9 Cal. 5th 1130, 1158–59 (2020).

TRADE SECRET EXCEPTION

Business & Professions Code section 16600 must be "construed in light of common law decisions on the same subject." *Centeno v. Roseville Community Hospital*, 107 Cal. App. 3d 62, 69 (1979). California courts have recognized a judicially created exception to section 16600, where trade secrets are involved. *Muggill v. Reuben H. Donnelley Corp.*, 62 Cal. 2d 239, 246 (1965) (section 16600 invalidates post-contract covenants not to compete "unless they are necessary to protect the employer's trade secrets"). *See also Gordon Termite Control v. Terrones*, 84 Cal. App. 3d 176, 178 (1978) ("Section 16600 of the Business and Professions Code . . . has been construed by the Supreme Court as invalidating contracts not to compete, except where their enforcement is necessary to protect the trade secrets of an employer"); *Fowler v. Varian Associates, Inc.*, 196 Cal. App. 3d 34, 44 (1987) ("agreements designed to protect an employer's proprietary information do not violate section 16600"); *Shipley Co., LLC v. Kozlowski*, 925 F. Supp. 28, 30 (D. Mass. 1996) (California Supreme Court has held that section 16600 invalidates non-competition clauses "unless they are necessary to protect the employer's trade secrets" (citing *Muggill*)); *Hollingsworth Solderless Terminal Co. v. Turley*, 622 F.2d 1324, 1338 (9th Cir. 1980); *Scott v. Snelling & Snelling*, 732 F. Supp. at 1043.

In *Edwards v. Arthur Andersen LLP*, 44 Cal. 4th 937 (2008), the California Supreme Court chose not to address "the applicability of the so-called trade secret exception to section 16600." *Id.* at 946, n.4. Given the "bright line" drawn by the *Edwards* court, the trade secret exception may be open to question, although the court did cite the *Muggill* case with apparent approval. Courts have continued to recognize a trade secret exception under California law. *See Asset Marketing Systems, Inc. v. Gagnon*, 542 F.3d 748, 758 (9th Cir. 2008) ("Under California law, non-competition agreements are unenforceable unless necessary to protect an employer's trade secret.");

Bank of America, N.A. v. Lee, 2008 WL 4351348, at *5, *6 (C.D. Cal. Sept. 22, 2008) ("The court concludes that 'trade secret exception' to § 16600 still applies.").

In *Scott v. Snelling & Snelling*, 732 F. Supp. at 1045, however, a franchisor was unable to prevent the entry of summary judgment against it because the court found an absence of trade secrets, as a matter of law. The franchisor was not allowed to take advantage of a subsequently enacted statute that might have designated customer lists to be trade secrets.

In *Juarez v. Jani-King of California, Inc.*, 2012 WL 177564, at *12 (9th Cir. Jan. 23, 2012), the court considered the application of the trade secret exception to a noncompetition agreement that prevented the plaintiffs from working as janitors for any other company during the term of the franchise and for some time after termination. The court denied the franchisor's summary judgment motion for lack of a showing that the covenant was necessary to protect trade secrets or proprietary information. The court also rejected the enforceability of the covenant under the more "lenient" standard from *Dayton*. *Id.*

Where a chiropractic licensing arrangement prohibited the solicitation of former clients for two years after the termination of the arrangement, there was no violation of section 16600, because the restriction was limited to the use of proprietary information. *Gatsinaris v. ART Corporate Solutions, Inc.*, 2015 WL 4208595, at *14 (C.D. Cal. July 10, 2015).

California has adopted the Uniform Trade Secrets Act, CAL. CIV. CODE § 3426 *et seq.*, providing that a trade secret is valuable information where reasonable efforts have been made to maintain secrecy. Generally, an employer will be able to restrain only conduct by a former employee "that would have been subject to judicial restraint under the law of unfair competition, absent the contract." *Metro Traffic Control, Inc. v. Shadow Traffic Network*, 22 Cal. App. 4th 853, 861 (1994). *See also Empire Steam Laundry v. Lozier*, 165 Cal. 89, 99 (1913) (unwarranted use of trade secrets is protected against even "in the absence of a stipulation to the contrary"); *Loral Corp. v. Moyes*, 174 Cal. App. 3d 268, 275 (1985) (same).

STATUTORY EXCEPTIONS

Sections 16601, 16602, and 16602.5, which set forth the exceptions to the general rule, are strictly construed. In *Golden State Linen Serv. v. Vidalin*, 69 Cal. App. 3d 1 (1979), a provision in the employment agreement of a route driver required him to sell his goodwill in the employer's business to the employer for one dollar on termination of employment. The court refused to enforce the covenant because goodwill can only be owned by the owner of a business and the employee never owned an interest in the business. *Id.* at 5.

Most franchise agreements recite that all goodwill in the franchised business belongs to the franchisor, not the franchisee. Notably, the franchise agreements in *Great Harvest Franchising v. McKinley*, Bus. Franchise Guide (CCH) ¶ 11,260 (C.D. Cal. 1997) and *Great Harvest Franchising v. Artim*, Bus. Franchise Guide ¶ 11,259 (E.D. Cal. 1997), provided that the franchisees had purchased the franchisor's goodwill, in an apparent attempt to invoke the protection of the exception in section 16601; despite this, neither court chose to consider that issue. Where the franchisor owns the goodwill of the franchised business, the franchisee, like an employee, has no goodwill to transfer, and section 16601 does not apply. *Scott v. Snelling & Snelling*, 732 F. Supp. 1034 (N.D. Cal. 1990).

2. Have the courts articulated the "legitimate interests" of the franchisor that will support enforcement of a covenant against competition contained in a franchise agreement?

- **If so, what are they (e.g., protection of goodwill, protection of confidential information), and in what contexts did the issue arise?**
- **If not, what interests have been recognized in other contexts (e.g., employment agreements, the sale of business context)?**

"Section 16600 presently sets out the general rule in California—covenants not to compete are void." *Hill Medical Group v. Wycoff*, 86 Cal. App. 4th 895, 902 (2001). Franchise agreements are not exempted from the statutory prohibition on non-competition agreements; therefore, even legitimate franchisor interests may not justify a non-competition agreement. However, given the California Supreme Court's recent clarification in *Ixchel Pharma, LLC v. Biogen, Inc.*, 9 Cal. 5th 1130, 1158–59 (2020), that restraints on business operations and commercial dealings are now subject to a reasonableness standard, and the court's apparent limitation of the per se invalidity of non-competition agreements to the employment context, it is uncertain how this analysis will be applied to the franchise business model.

The judicially created exemption protecting trade secrets may support the enforcement of a covenant against competition in the right circumstances. In *Scott*, the court determined that the franchisor had no trade secrets that warranted protection; in *Great Harvest Franchising v. McKinley*, Bus. Franchise Guide (CCH) ¶ 11,260 (C.D. Cal. 1997) and *Great Harvest Franchising v. Artim*, Bus. Franchise Guide ¶ 11,259 (E.D. Cal. 1997), the courts declined to address trade secrets arguments that had been presented, ruling on other grounds in each case. In *Juarez v. Jani-King of California, Inc.*, 2012 WL 177564, at *12 (9th Cir. Jan. 23, 2012), the court held that it was unclear whether the in-term and post-term covenants were warranted to protect trade secrets or proprietary information. However, in *Gatsinaris v. ART Corporate Solutions, Inc.*, 2015 WL 4208595, at *14 (C.D. Cal. July 10, 2015), the court held that the post-term covenant only restricted the ability to use proprietary information and thereby did not run afoul of section 16600.

In the context of an in-term covenant, the Ninth Circuit Court of Appeals held that a franchisor has a legitimate interest in protecting and maintaining its "trademark, trade name, and goodwill," but this interest must be balanced against a franchisee's right to operate its business in order to determine whether a covenant not to compete is valid under section 16600. *Comedy Club, Inc. v. Improv West Associates*, 553 F.3d 1277, 1293 (9th Cir. 2009).

3. What time limitations have courts recognized as reasonable in the franchise context?

- **If no franchise cases have been decided, what time limitations have been recognized in other contexts?**
- **How have they been related to the interests protected?**

Under California law, even strict temporal limitations in a covenant against competition will not save the covenant. *Bosley Medical Group v. Abramson*, 161 Cal. App. 3d 284, 288 (1984). *See also Scott v. Snelling & Snelling*, 732 F. Supp. at 1043–44, holding that California courts have not recognized "geographical and temporal restrictions on competition to be merely partial restrictions." The court in *Kolani v. Gluska*, 64 Cal. App. 4th 402, 406 (1998), held that a clause restricting competition for one year within a one-mile radius was void, refusing to reform the contract to make it lawful.

A clause restricting competition for two years within a ten-mile radius of any branded store was held to be void in *Sonoma Tires, Inc. v. Big O Tires*, LLC, 2013 WL 12173748, at *2, *7 (N.D. Cal. Jan. 22, 2013). A covenant not to compete must be limited to the time during which the covenantee, or his or her assignee, carries on a similar business within the specified territory. *Martinez v. Martinez*, 41 Cal. 2d 704, 711 (1954). A covenant that is not limited in time will be construed to cover the time allowed by law. *Mahlstedt v. Fugit*, 79 Cal. App. 2d 562, 568 (1947).

Even if a covenant is not invalidated under section 16600, it must also be reasonable in light of the particular circumstances. *Beatty Safeway Scafford, Inc. v. Skrable*, 180 Cal. App. 2d 650, 657 (1968). Thus, a five-year covenant was held to be enforceable in one case, *Laird v. Steinmann*, 97 Cal. App. 2d 781, 784 (1950), while a three-year covenant was held to be unreasonable in another case, *Beatty Safeway Scafford, Inc. v. Skrable*, 180 Cal. App. 2d 650, 657 (1968).

---

4. What geographic limitations have courts recognized as reasonable in the franchise context?

- **How have they been related to the interests protected?**
- **Have courts recognized the legitimacy of protecting other franchisees from competition?**

Even strict geographical limitations in a covenant against competition will not render a covenant enforceable. *Bosley Medical Group v. Abramson*, 161 Cal. App. 3d 284, 288 (1984). *See also Scott v. Snelling & Snelling*, 732 F. Supp. at 1043–44, holding that California courts have not recognized "geographical and temporal restrictions on competition to be merely partial restrictions." The court in *Kolani v. Gluska*, 64 Cal. App. 4th 402, 406 (1998), held that a clause restricting competition for one year within a one-mile radius was void, refusing to reform the contract to make it lawful. A clause restricting competition for two years within a ten-mile radius of any branded store was held to be void in *Sonoma Tires, Inc. v. Big O Tires, LLC*, 2013 WL 12173748, at *2, *7 (N.D. Cal. Jan. 22, 2013).

However, a Ninth Circuit Court of Appeals decision indicates that in-term covenants that are appropriately restricted to a reasonable geographic area are lawful under section 16600. *Comedy Club, Inc. v. Improv West Associates*, 553 F.3d 1277, 1293 (9th Cir. 2009). In *Comedy Club*, the court was confronted with a non-competition covenant that barred a licensee from operating any non-licensed comedy clubs within the contiguous United States for the duration of a trademark agreement with the licensor, which spanned over fourteen years. *Id.* at 1281. Although the non-competition covenant as drafted was void and in violation of section 16600, the court reformed the covenant by restricting its application solely to the counties where the licensee currently operated licensed comedy clubs. *Id.* at 1293. The court reasoned that such a geographic restriction was reasonable to protect both the licensor's interest in its trademark, trade name, and goodwill and the licensee's interest in conducting its business. *Id.* One out-of-state court has noted the "possible impact upon a national franchise system" where a franchisor is unable to enforce a contract term in California that franchisees elsewhere are required to observe. *Great Frame Up Systems, Inc. v. Jazayeri Enterprises, Inc.*, 789 F. Supp. 253, 256 n.5 (N.D. Ill. 1992). *See also International Business Machines Corp. v. Bajorek*, 191 F.3d 1033 (9th Cir. 1999) (concern expressed about the creation of two classes of IBM employees: those who live in California and those who live elsewhere).

5. What limitations on activities have courts recognized as reasonable in the franchise context?

In *Great Harvest Franchising v. McKinley*, Bus. Franchise Guide (CCH) ¶ 11,260 (C.D. Cal. 1997) and *Great Harvest Franchising v. Artim*, Bus. Franchise Guide ¶ 11,259 (E.D. Cal. 1997), courts upheld a post-term covenant not to compete in the sale of whole wheat bread products. Because the former franchisees could still bake other products, courts ruled that they were not prevented from engaging in an entire trade or profession and, thus, the non-competition provision did not (*Artim*) or, at least, might not (*McKinley*) violate section 16600. The court in *Scott v. Snelling & Snelling* acknowledged that the judicially created exception for the protection of trade secrets would apply to franchises, even though it held that there were no trade secrets worthy of protection in that particular case.

An in-term covenant preventing a licensee from operating non-licensed comedy clubs was reasonable only if limited to counties where the licensee was already operating *licensed* comedy clubs. *Comedy Club, Inc. v. Improv West Associates*, 553 F.3d 1277, 1293–94 (9th Cir. 2009).

6. Does the state recognize a difference between in-term and post-term covenants?

In-term covenants that do not prevent the practice of an entire profession, trade, or business are not void under California law. *Comedy Club, Inc. v. Improv West Associates*, 553 F.3d 1277, 1292 (9th Cir. 2009); *Dayton Time Lock Service, Inc. v. Silent Watchman Corp.*, 52 Cal. App. 3d 1, 6 (1975) (although post-term clauses violate antitrust laws, limitation imposed during the life of a franchise is valid so long as it does not foreclose competition in a substantial share of a business, trade, or market); *Great Frame Up Systems, Inc. v. Jazayeri Enterprises, Inc.*, 789 F. Supp. 253, 256 (N.D. Ill. 1992) (although finding "no California case which specifically addresses whether an in-term franchise restriction is valid under § 16600," in-term covenants were partial restraints and, thus, valid under California law).

As discussed above, in *Comedy Club* the Ninth Circuit vacated an arbitrator's award that enforced an in-term covenant because it foreclosed "competition in a substantial share of a business, trade or market." *Id.; see also Dayton Time Lock Service, Inc. v. Silent Watchman Corp.*, 52 Cal. App. 3d 1, 6 (1975). The covenant would have prevented competition across "the entire contiguous United States comedy club market" for fourteen years. The court modified the covenant so that the licensee could not operate a competing comedy club in any county where it already operated a licensed comedy club.

In *Sonoma Tires, Inc. v. Big O Tires, LLC*, 2013 WL 12173748, at *8 (N.D. Cal. Jan. 22, 2013), the court upheld an in-term covenant where there was ample competition in the retail industry, and the franchisee's two stores did not constitute a "substantial share" of the market. The court further noted that the covenant would not prevent the former franchisee from engaging in its entire profession, business, or trade because they could still open additional Big O stores.

7. Has the state allowed enforcement of covenants against non-signatories (e.g., family members, newly formed corporations)?

A person who is not a party to a covenant may not be restrained from competing, unless he or she is the alter ego of the covenantor or a mere instrumentality by means of which the covenantor seeks to break the agreement. *See Comedy Club, Inc. v. Improv West Associates*, 553 F.3d 1277, 1287 (9th Cir. 2009) (holding that enforcement of a covenant not to compete against non-party relatives and ex-spouses constitutes a violation of section 16600); *Fenton Material Co. v. Challet*, 49 Cal. App. 2d 410, 415 (1942). This rule applies to corporations as well as to individuals. *Id.* A stranger to a valid non-competition agreement may, however, be enjoined from aiding the covenantor to breach the agreement by employing him or her, being employed by him or her, or going into partnership with him or her. *Id.*

Where the franchise agreement made the franchisee responsible for the activities of immediate family members, the former franchisee was responsible for the post-term conduct of family members. *Bambu Franchising v. Nguyen*, 2021 WL 1839664, at *19–23 (N.D. Cal. May 7, 2021).

8. Will the state modify, "blue-pencil," or otherwise reduce a covenant found to be overbroad?

Business & Professions Code section 16600 provides that "every contract by which anyone is restrained from engaging in a lawful profession, trade, or business of any kind is to that extent void."

In *General Paint Corp. v. Seymour*, 124 Cal. App. 611, 618 (1932), the court held that the predecessor statute to section 16600 did "not say the entire contract is void," but only that the excess beyond its provisions was void. *See also Swenson v. File*, 3 Cal. 3d 389, 395 (1970), where the California Supreme Court reached the same result, holding that an over-inclusive covenant does "not invalidate that covenant in its entirety, for under section 16600 a contract in restraint of trade is only 'to that extent void.'" *See also Mahlstedt v. Fugit*, 79 Cal. App. 2d 562, 566 (1947) (court will construe provision "in such manner as to make it valid"). Courts will save a covenant, however, only "to the extent it falls within the limits permitted by statute." *Roberts v. Pfefer*, 13 Cal. App. 3d 93, 98 (1970).

In *Kolani v. Gluska*, 64 Cal. App. 4th 402, 406 (1998), a contract prohibited competition for one year within a one-mile radius, further providing that should a court find the term or area unfair, the court "shall fix such lesser term or area" necessary to make the clause lawful. The court held that reformation was available only where the parties had made a mistake. If an unlawful contract could be saved by a judicial rewriting, the policy of section 16600 would be undermined, and there would be no disincentive against the use of broad, illegal clauses.

In *Hill Medical Group v. Wycoff*, 86 Cal. App. 4th 895, 902 (2001), the court was asked to reform a non-competition clause to bring it into compliance with section 16600. Although noting that section 16600 only invalidates contracts restraining trade "to the extent void," the court declined to do so: "this is not a situation in which an otherwise valid covenant covers an unreasonably large geographical area or is unreasonably long in duration. Since there has been no compensation for goodwill, it is impossible to rewrite this void covenant. To rewrite the covenant would undermine California's public policy of open competition as embodied in section 16600" (citing *Kolani v. Gluska*).

The court in *Comedy Club Inc. v. Improv West Associates*, 553 F.3d 1277, 1293–94 (9th Cir. 2009), however, limited the terms of an in-term covenant to the counties where a licensee was already operating licensed locations, instead of striking the entire provision.

---

9. Are there additional nuances or peculiarities of the state's treatment of covenants in the franchising context?

California has a settled public policy in favor of open competition. *Howard v. Babcock*, 6 Cal. 4th 409, 416 (1993). Section 16600, therefore, states a strong public policy of the state of California. *KGB, Inc. v. Giannoulas* (1980), 104 Cal. App. 3d 844, 848; *Great Frame Up Systems, Inc. v. Jazayeri Enterprises, Inc.*, 789 F. Supp. 253, 255 (N.D. Ill. 1992); *D'Sa v. Playhut*, 85 Cal. App. 4th 927 (2001) (employer may not condition employment upon signing an agreement that contains an unenforceable covenant). Accordingly, if a contract to be performed in California is invalid under section 16600, California courts will refuse to enforce it even though the contract would have been valid under the law of another state designated in a choice-of-law clause. *Scott v. Snelling & Snelling*, 732 F. Supp. 1034, 1039–40 (N.D. Cal. 1990); *Hollingsworth Solderless Terminal Co. v. Turley*, 622 F.2d 1324, 1338 (9th Cir. 1980). *See also Gatsinaris v. ART Corporate Solutions, Inc.*, 2015 WL 4208595, at *12 (C.D. Cal. July 10, 2015) (noting that regardless of the language of the agreement, which included a Colorado choice-of-law provision but allowed the application of California law in the event of conflict, California public policy dictates that section 16600 applies to the contract); *Sonoma Tires, Inc. v. Big O Tires*, LLC, 2013 WL 12173748, at *6 (N.D. Cal. Jan. 22, 2013). A Tennessee court, however, declined to apply California law to a franchise covenant because the franchisee cited California's policy on covenants, but failed to address Tennessee law on the issue and failed to discuss whether that law was contrary to a fundamental policy of a state having a materially greater interest. *Servpro Indus., Inc. v. Woloski*, No. 3:17-cv-01433, 2019 WL 3552516 (M.D. Tenn. Aug. 5, 2019).

The policy is so strong that it has been applied to invalidate a contractual provision in a Maryland employment agreement, where a California employer wished to employ the employee who was not from California. *The Application Group, Inc. v. The Hunter Group, Inc.*, Trade Cas. (CCH) ¶ 72,076 (Cal. App. 2001). The court further upheld the trial court's finding that the inclusion of a covenant in a Maryland contract was an unfair business practice under California's Little FTC Act.

In *Mail Boxes, Etc., USA, Inc. v. Considine*, Trade Cas. (CCH) ¶ 73,000 (9th Cir. 2000), not for publication, the franchise agreement called for the application of California law, except where inconsistent with the laws of Washington. The court interpreted this "inelegant provision" as invalidating the covenant not to compete because Washington had no policy against the application of California law. In the absence of the choice-of-law provision, Washington would have enforced the covenant under a reasonableness test.

The California statute prohibiting post-termination restraints applied even to "reasonable" restraints. *See Bosley Medical Group v. Abramson*, 161 Cal. App. 3d 284, 288 (1984) ("the so-called rule of reasonableness was rejected by this state in 1872"); *Bayly, Martin & Fay, Inc. v. Pickard*, 780 P.2d 1168, 1172 n.9 (Okla. 1989) (California does not subscribe to rule of reason); *Campbell v. Board of Trustees*, 817 F.2d 499, 502 (9th Cir. 1987) (the statute does not except reasonable restraints on trade); *Scott v. Snelling & Snelling*, 732 F. Supp. at 1042–43 (California courts may apply a rule of reason to partial restraints); *Great Frame Up Systems, Inc. v. Jazayeri Enterprises, Inc.*, 789 F. Supp. at 256. However, after *Ixchel*, it remains to be seen whether courts will apply a rule of reason to post-termination restraints under certain circumstances.

In *Viner v. Sweet*, 117 Cal. App. 4th 1218 (2004), a lawyer not licensed to practice in California had a malpractice judgment entered against him because he was not familiar with section 16600 and included a purportedly unenforceable non-competition clause in a stock sale agreement.

Colorado

*by Heather Carson Perkins**

1. Has the state addressed covenants against competition in the context of franchising?

- **Does the state have a franchising statute or regulations that address covenants against competition?**
- **Does the state have a covenants statute of general applicability that would encompass franchise covenants?**
- **Have the courts addressed covenants in the context of franchising either under a statute or under the state's common law?**

Colorado has no franchising statute or franchising regulations addressing covenants against competition. Colorado does, however, have a statute that deals with covenants against competition generally. In 1973, the Colorado Legislature created a statutory presumption against the enforceability of non-compete agreements by amending Colorado Revised Statute § 8-2-113 (1973) to void all covenants that limit future employment, except those that relate to the sale of a business, protection of trade secrets, recovery of training expenses, or restraint of certain key personnel.

Section 8-2-113 provides in relevant part:

> (2) Any covenant not to compete which restricts the right of any person to receive compensation for performance of skilled or unskilled labor for any employer shall be void, but this subsection (2) shall not apply to:
>
> (a) Any contract for the purchase and sale of a business or the assets of a business;
>
> (b) Any contract for the protection of trade secrets;
>
> (c) Any contractual provision providing for recovery of the expense of educating and training an employee who has served an employer for a period of less than two years;
>
> (d) Executive and management personnel and officers and employees who constitute professional staff to executive and management personnel.

*Heather Carson Perkins is a partner at Faegre Drinker Biddle & Reath's Denver, Colorado, office. Brandee Caswell of the same firm authored the original chapter and contributed to the 2012 update.

Since its enactment, state and federal courts have issued a number of opinions interpreting and applying Colo. Rev. Stat. § 8-2-113 in the context of franchise relationships and have generally held that covenants not to compete in franchise agreements fit into one or more statutory exceptions to unenforceability. *See, e.g., Core Progression Franchise LLC v. O'Hare*, Civil Action No. 21-CV-0643-WJM-NYW, 2021 WL 1222768 (D. Colo. Apr. 4, 2021) (finding covenant fell within protection of trade secrets exception); *PostNet Int'l Franchise Corp. v. Wu*, No 1:20-cv-03790, 2021 WL 1037914 (D. Colo. Feb. 19, 2021) (finding covenant fell within protection of trade secrets and executive and management personnel exceptions); *Fitness Together Franchise, L.L.C. v. EM Fitness, L.L.C.*, Civil Action No. 1:20-cv-02757-DDD-STV, 2020 WL 6119470 (D. Colo. Oct. 16, 2020) (same); *Homewatch Int'l v. Navin*, 2017 WL 4163358, 2017 WL 4163358 (D. Colo. Sept. 20, 2017) (finding covenant fell within sale of business exception); *Big O Tires, LLC v. JDV, LLC*, No. 08-CV-1046-WYD, 2008 WL 4787619 (D. Colo. Oct. 31, 2008) (finding covenant fell within sale of business exception); *I Can't Believe It's Yogurt v. Gunn*, Bus. Franchise Guide (CCH) ¶ 11,197, 1997 WL 599391 (D. Colo. Apr. 15, 1997); *Keller Corp. v. Kelley*, 187 P.3d 1133 (Colo. App. 2008); *DBA Enters., Inc. v. Findlay*, 923 P.2d 298 (Colo. App. 1996) (applying sale of business exception in resale context); *Gold Messenger v. McGuay*, 937 P.2d 907 (Colo. App. 1997) (applying trade secret exception).

DBA Enterprises, Inc. v. Findlay, 923 P.2d 298 (Colo. App. 1996), was the first reported case involving a franchise agreement in a resale scenario for an established Lawn Doctor franchise, which provided lawn fertilization and core aeration services. The sellers agreed not to compete directly or indirectly within the geographic area described in the original franchise agreement between the sellers and Lawn Doctor, Inc. for a period of five years. Under the agreement, the sellers retained their lawn-mowing business and customers and they would no longer provide fertilization or core aeration services offered by Lawn Doctor but would continue providing mowing services.

Sellers eventually began providing competitive services to clients for free or contracted through third parties to provide the services. The buyers lost roughly half of the Lawn Doctor customers and ceased making payments to sellers. Buyers sued but did not seek injunctive relief. The trial court found that the sellers materially breached the covenant in a variety of ways and awarded damages to the purchasers. On appeal, the court found that the sale-of-business exception in section 8-2-113 applied so that the covenant was enforceable. The primary dispute on appeal thus related to how the trial court had calculated damages for the breaches and remanded to the trial court on the issue of damages, holding "[t]he purpose of the covenant is not to control the seller's future income, but to prevent the seller from soliciting the buyer's new customers and to protect the goodwill inherent in the purchase." *DBA Enterprises*, 923 P.2d at 302 (citing *Gibson v. Eberle*, 762 P.2d 777 (Colo. App. 1988); 6A Corbin, *Contracts* §§ 1385, 1387 (1962); and Williston, *Contracts* § 1636 (3d ed. 1972)).

In the next reported case, *Gold Messenger v. McGuay*, 937 P.2d 907 (Colo. App. 1997), the Colorado Court of Appeals directly addressed the statutory exception relating to trade secrets in the context of a franchise agreement. There, the franchisor of an advertising circular business sought and obtained a preliminary injunction prohibiting its franchisee and the franchisee's partner from publishing or distributing competing circulars. The franchisor had developed a comprehensive system for setting up and operating an advertising circular business. McGuay's life partner purchased a franchise and became a franchisee of the Gold Messenger advertising business. As a part of the agreement, the franchisee received an Operations and Procedures Manual detailing the operation of a successful Gold Messenger franchise. McGuay was present during the negotiations and signed a deposit check to secure the franchise but did not sign the franchise agreement itself.

The franchisor terminated the franchise agreement when the franchisee failed to make periodic royalty payments. Around the same time, McGuay began publishing a competing circular in the same distribution area of the franchisee's former territory. The franchisor sued McGuay and the franchisee, claiming the defendants breached the covenant not to compete and misappropriated trade secrets belonging to Gold Messenger under the Colorado Uniform Trade Secrets Act, COLO. REV. STAT. § 7-74-101 *et seq.* The district court entered an injunction against both the franchisee and McGuay, holding that the covenants were valid because the franchise agreement was akin to a contract for the sale of a business. *See* COLO. REV. STAT. § 82-113(2)(a). Only McGuay appealed the district court's ruling.

McGuay made three arguments on appeal. First, he argued the district court erred in holding the covenant valid because creating a franchise agreement does not constitute the sale of business under COLO. REV. STAT. § 8-2-113(2)(a). The court sidestepped this argument, noting that while the sale of existing business fit into the statutory exception, there was a question as to whether the exception would apply to the *creation* of a franchise. Second, McGuay argued that the covenant was not valid under the trade secret exception because the purpose of the covenant was not for the protection of trade secrets, and the Operations and Procedures Manual did not contain trade secrets. The court found that the agreement fell within the trade secret exception and was reasonably limited in scope to protect the trade secrets. Third, McGuay argued that even if the covenant were valid, he was not bound by it because he did not sign the franchise agreement. As discussed below, the court rejected this argument.

The Colorado Court of Appeals again addressed the purchase and sale of business exception to the statutory presumption in *Keller Corp. v. Kelley*, 187 P.3d 1133 (2008). This time, the court held that a covenant not to compete within a franchise agreement can be enforced by a franchisor against a former franchisee under the sale of business exception in COLO. REV. STAT. § 8-2-113(2)(a).

In *Keller*, defendant Kelley purchased an established Blind Man of America franchise selling and installing residential and commercial window coverings. At the same time, Kelley signed a franchise agreement with franchisor Keller Corporation. The franchise agreement included a covenant not to compete within a 50-mile radius of any of the franchisor's existing Colorado franchises for a period of three years after termination of the agreement. The agreement also prohibited Kelley from disclosing any of the franchisor's trade secrets. When the contract terminated, Kelley formed and operated a window-covering business in the same location called Accent Window Coverings.

The franchisor brought suit seeking injunctive relief and liquidated damages against Kelley along with unspecified actual damages from Accent Window Coverings for unfair competition. The trial court ignored the franchisor's claim that the agreement was for the purchase and sale of a business. Basing its order solely on the trade secrets exception, the court denied the request for a preliminary injunction. The franchisor appealed, asserting that the covenant not to compete fell within both statutory exceptions to unenforceability.

The court of appeals affirmed the trial court's finding that the trade secret exception did not apply under the circumstances. However, it remanded the franchisor's request for preliminary injunction for reconsideration in the context of a covenant "contained within a contract for the purchase and sale of a business." Even though the covenant not to compete was technically in the franchise agreement rather than in the contract with the selling third-party franchisee, the court reasoned that the sale of business exception could apply because Kelley entered into the franchise agreement as "part of the same transaction in which Kelley acquired a going business from the previous franchisees." The court further explained that the statutory exception for the purchase and sale of a business is not limited on its face to covenants that protect buyers; the exception can also protect a franchisor, particularly after the franchise term ends.

Although the court did not actually hold that the sale of business exception applies to a covenant within a franchise agreement established in a new territory, the court drew an analogy between the temporary sale of goodwill in a franchise agreement and the sale of a business. Such reasoning could be used by future courts or litigants to justify the enforceability of covenants not to compete in franchise agreements for sales to new franchisees. Finally, following *Gold Messenger*, the court noted that the transaction involved the sale of an established franchise and therefore declined to decide whether a sale to a new franchisee would constitute the sale of a "business" within the meaning of section 8-2-113(2)(a).

Since these seminal state court decisions, several federal court decisions have held that a covenant not to compete in a franchise agreement for a newly established territory fell within the scope of the sale-of-business exception to the statutory presumption against non-compete agreements under Colorado law. *See, e.g., Homewatch Int'l v. Navin*, 2017 WL 4163358, 2017 WL 4163358 (D. Colo. Sept. 20, 2017) (finding covenant fell within sale of business exception); *Big O Tires, LLC v. JDV, LLC*, No. 08-CV-1046-WYD, 2008 WL 4787619 (D. Colo. Oct. 31, 2008) (finding covenant fell within sale of business exception); *I Can't Believe It's Yogurt v. Gunn*, Bus. Franchise Guide (CCH) ¶ 11,197, 1997 WL 599391 (D. Colo. Apr. 15, 1997).

In addition, more recently, a federal judge has decided in two cases that a franchise owner qualified as "executive and management personnel" under the statute as "an independent contractor and owner of the franchise business. *PostNet Int'l Franchise Corp. v. Wu*, No 1:20-cv-03790, 2021 WL 1037914 (D. Colo. Feb. 19, 2021) (finding owner was executive and management personnel but declining to grant preliminary injunction); *Fitness Together Franchise, L.L.C. v. EM Fitness, L.L.C.*, Civil Action No. 1:20-cv-02757-DDD-STV, 2020 WL 6119470 (D. Colo. Oct. 16, 2020) (finding franchise owner to fall within executive and management personnel exception and granting injunction).

---

2. Have the courts articulated the "legitimate interests" of the franchisor that will support enforcement of a covenant against competition contained in a franchise agreement?

- **If so, what are they (e.g., protection of goodwill, protection of confidential information), and in what contexts did the issue arise?**
- **If not, what interests have been recognized in other contexts (e.g., employment agreements, the sale-of-business context)?**

Colorado's legislature defined the "legitimate interests" that will support enforcement of covenants against competition in the statute: (1) the purchase of a business, (2) contracts for the protection of trade secrets, (3) recovery of education and training expenses, and (4) protection from competition by executive and management personnel. COLO. REV. STAT. § 8-2-113(2). The legitimate interests of the franchisor, in particular, have been recognized in three of these categories.

In the sale-of-business context, the buying franchisee has a legitimate interest in protecting the value of the business it is purchasing from the previous franchisee. *See DBA Enterprises v. Findlay*, 923 P.2d 298, 302 (Colo. App. 1996). The buying franchisee has a legitimate interest in not having the franchisor compete with it within the franchisee's exclusive territory during the franchise term. *Keller Corp. v. Kelley*, 187 P3d 1133, 1138 (Colo. App. 2008).

Similarly, courts have analogized the creation of a franchisor to the sale of business; a franchisor has a legitimate interest in precluding the former franchisee from trading on the franchisor's goodwill or using the knowledge, training, and experience gained from the franchisor to compete against it. *Homewatch Int'l v. Navin*, 2017 WL 4163358, 2017 WL 4163358 (D. Colo. Sept. 20, 2017); *Big O Tires, LLC v. JDV, LLC*, No. 08-CV-1046-WYD, 2008 WL 4787619 (D. Colo. Oct. 31, 2008).

Franchisors also have a legitimate interest in protecting their trade secrets and confidential information. *See Core Progression Franchise LLC v. O'Hare*, Civil Action No. 21-CV-0643-WJM-NYW, 2021 WL 1222768 (D. Colo. Apr. 4, 2021); *PostNet Int'l Franchise Corp. v. Wu*, No 1:20-cv-03790, 2021 WL 1037914 (D. Colo. Feb. 19, 2021); *Fitness Together Franchise, L.L.C. v. EM Fitness, L.L.C.*, Civil Action No. 1:20-cv-02757-DDD-STV, 2020 WL 6119470 (D. Colo. Oct. 16, 2020); *Gold Messenger, Inc. v. McGuay*, 937 P.2d 907, 911 (Colo. App. 1997). By definition, the possession and/or use of such trade secret information provides "an opportunity to obtain an advantage over competitors who do not know or use it." *Management Recruiters of Boulder, Inc. v. Miller*, 762 P.2d 763, 765 (Colo. App. 1988). Under *Gold Messenger* and the cases following it, the franchisor has a legitimate interest in protecting the trade secrets conveyed or licensed to the franchisee as a part of the franchise agreement.

In *McGuay*, the court set forth two requirements for finding a covenant valid under the statutory trade secrets exception. First, the purpose of the covenant must be for the protection of trade secrets. Second, the covenant must be reasonably limited in scope to protect those trade secrets. The wording of the franchise agreement was the sole factor in the court's evaluation of both requirements. The court stated that "[I]t [was] evident from the preamble to the franchise agreement that the agreement was entered into with the express purpose of protecting trade secrets." *Gold Messenger*, 937 P.2d at 910. The preamble focused largely on the franchisor's ownership of certain techniques, know-how, and procedures used in the business of advertising circulars. It also stated that the franchisor had developed a unique system for operating the business, and the franchisee lacked such expertise and information. The covenant provided that the franchisee would not engage in:

> [a]ny other business which offers or sells any product or service (or component thereof) which comprises or may in the future comprise a part of the Franchisor's franchise system or which competes directly or indirectly with Franchisor's system, if such other business is located in or within fifty (50) miles of Franchisee's Territory, or within fifty (50) miles of any other Territory which is part of Franchisor's franchisee system.

Id.

In a relatively liberal reading of the language of the preamble in conjunction with the covenant, the court held that the covenant was designed for the protection of trade secrets. Specifically, the court noted, the covenant precluded the franchisee from using confidential information obtained through its franchise to compete with the franchisor or other franchisees.

A case from the U.S. District Court for the District of Colorado applying Colorado law provides a reminder that it is not sufficient to simply allege legitimate and protectable interests: the franchisor must also provide proof that irreparable harm to those interests will occur if the covenant is not enforced. *See Big O Tires, LLC v. Felix Bros., Inc.*, 724 F. Supp. 2d 1107 (D. Colo. 2010). In *Big O Tires*, the franchisee had three Big O Tires locations under three franchise agreements. One agreement expired, and the franchisee de-identified the location and continued to operate it as Budget Tires while operating the other two locations as Big O Tires. The franchisor sued to enforce the in-term covenants in the two remaining agreements and sought a preliminary injunction.

The court denied the motion, holding that while Big O identified legitimate interests supporting enforcement of the covenant not to compete, it failed to present evidence that the franchisee's operation of Budget Tires harmed those interests. Specifically, Big O Tires pointed to diversion of customers and access to proprietary information as legitimate interests protected by the non-compete. The court did not appear to take issue with these interests as being protected; rather, it held that Big O failed to adduce evidence to support the proposition that the franchisee was harming them. The court held, "[i]n short, Big O presents no evidence of any specific harm it is actually suffering, but simply identifies categories of harm it *could* theoretically suffer under a different set of circumstances." *Id.* at 1120.

Likewise, in *PostNet Int'l Franchise Corp. v. Wu*, No 1:20-cv-03790, 2021 WL 1037914 (D. Colo. Feb. 19, 2021), the court declined to grant a preliminary injunction where the franchisee flipped the signs and ran a directly competitive business from a new location, despite finding the covenant not to compete valid. The court held that the franchisor's claimed loss of a prospective franchisee could be remedied with money damages because the franchisor could calculate its loss from being unable to refranchise from its own records or information obtainable through discovery. The court likewise found that the evidence of customer confusion was "weak" because the former franchisee had not used franchisor branding and trademarks at his new store and the franchisor failed to offer evidence of customer poaching. Next, the court found that the franchisor failed to produce evidence that the former franchisee was misappropriating trade secrets, using protected client lists to poach franchisor customers or using knowledge gained from the franchisor to compete. The court credited the former franchisee's testimony that he was not and did not need to use the information in his new business.

And, while the court gave some credence to the franchisor's argument that declining to issue a preliminary injunction would send a message to other franchisees that they need not abide by valid covenants not to compete, the court noted that at the early stage where injunctive relief was disfavored, this is not sufficient to overcome the unusual circumstances of how the franchisee operated largely independently from the system. The court also noted that a franchisor could seek other remedies, such as money damages, that would deter franchisees from breaching contracts like any other business.

3. What time limitations have courts recognized as reasonable in the franchise context?

➤ **If no franchise cases have been decided, what time limitations have been recognized in other contexts?**

➤ **How have they been related to interests protected?**

The five-year covenant in *DBA Enterprises Inc. v. Findlay*, 923 P.2d 298 (Colo. App. 1996), was not challenged as unreasonable. Similarly, a three-year limitation went unchallenged in *Gold Messenger Inc. v. McGuay*, 937 P.2d 907 (Colo. App. 1997). In *Big O Tires, LLC v. JDV, LLC*, No. 08-CV-1046-WYD, 2008 WL 4787619 (D. Colo. Oct. 31, 2008), the court agreed with the franchisor that a two-year limitation was not unreasonable. *See also Core Progression Franchise LLC v. O'Hare*, Civil Action No. 21-CV-0643-WJM-NYW, 2021 WL 1222768 (D. Colo. Apr. 4, 2021) (one-year provision covering a 25-mile radius likely reasonable and enforceable); *Fitness Together Franchise, L.L.C. v. EM Fitness, L.L.C.*, Civil Action No. 1:20-cv-02757-DDD-STV, 2020 WL 6119470 (D. Colo. Oct. 16, 2020) (non-compete provision covering three-mile radius for one year likely reasonable and enforceable); *Homewatch Int'l v. Navin*, 2017 WL 4163358, 2017 WL 4163358 (D. Colo. Sept. 20, 2017) (upholding two-year restriction within 25-mile radius of franchised location).

4. What geographic limitations have courts recognized as reasonable in the franchise context?

➤ **How have they been related to the interests protected?**

➤ **Have courts recognized the legitimacy of protecting other franchisees from competition?**

There is no Colorado case setting a definitive geographic limitation. As with temporal limitations discussed above, in many cases, franchisees did not challenge the geographic limitation. Geographic limitations were not challenged in *Core Progression Franchise LLC v. O'Hare*, Civil Action No. 21-CV-0643-WJM-NYW, 2021 WL 1222768 (D. Colo. Apr. 4, 2021) (25-mile radius); *Fitness Together Franchise, L.L.C. v. EM Fitness, L.L.C.*, Civil Action No. 1:20-cv-02757-DDD-STV, 2020 WL 6119470 (D. Colo. Oct. 16, 2020) (three-mile radius); *Homewatch Int'l v. Navin*, 2017 WL 4163358, 2017 WL 4163358 (D. Colo. Sept. 20, 2017) (25-mile radius of franchised location); *DBA Enterprises Inc. v. Findlay*, 923 P.2d 298 (Colo. App. 1996) (not specified in case); *Gold Messenger, Inc. v. McGuay*, 937 P.2d 907 (Colo. App. 1997) (50 miles from any Gold Messenger franchise territories); or *Keller Corp. v. Kelley*, 187 P.3d 1133 (Colo. App. 2008). *See also Big O Tires, LLC v. JDV, LLC*, No. 08-CV-1046-WYD, 2008 WL 4787619 (D. Colo. Oct. 31, 2008) (upholding without discussion a restriction on the franchisee competing within a 10-mile radius of the franchise location).

In *Gold Messenger*, however, the geographic limitation is clear. The franchisee was prohibited from engaging in competition within 50 miles of any Gold Messenger franchise territory. Given that the franchisee's competitive activities were in the same area as its former franchise, the scope of the geographic limitation was not challenged in *Gold Messenger*. However, depending on the number of Gold Messenger franchises, the geographic limitation could have been vast and could conceivably grow from year to year. There are no reported Colorado cases allowing that broad a restriction, and courts outside of Colorado have declined to enforce covenants not to compete that would reach future, unknown territories. In *Keller Corp.* the covenant also restricted the franchisee from competing within a 50-mile radius of other Blind Man of America franchises, six of which existed in the state, resulting in a restricted geographic area that the trial court labeled "enormous."

One Colorado case has addressed the legitimacy of protecting other franchisees from competition, albeit in an employment context. In *Gulick v. A. Robert Strawn & Assocs.*, 477 P.2d 489, 490 (Colo. App. 1970), Strawn operated a franchised Snelling & Snelling employment agency in Denver. Gulick, an employee, entered into a written employment contract with Strawn that restricted Gulick from being employed by a competing business within a radius of 35 miles of Strawn's Snelling & Snelling office or within a radius of 35 miles of any city in which a Snelling & Snelling employment office was located. After Gulick left Strawn's employ, he associated himself with another employment agency in Denver, in violation of the restrictive covenants contained in his employment agreement.

The trial court concluded that enforcement of the restrictive covenant was justified on the facts before it, but noted that the territorial reach of the provision contained in the contract was too restrictive. The court decided that the restriction should be limited to the territory in which Gulick had established customer contacts during his employment. The court of appeals agreed that it would be unreasonable to assume, in the absence of any evidence, that Gulick established enough customer contacts outside the Denver metropolitan area to justify imposition of the restrictive covenant in its entirety. Accordingly, the court reduced the geographic reach of the covenant to within 10 miles of the boundaries of the city and county of Denver, where Gulick had established his customer base. *See also Wagner v. A & B Personnel Sys.*, 473 P.2d 179, 180 (Colo. App. 1970) (territorial restriction reduced from "within 50 miles of any city in which Agency is doing business to within 50 miles of Denver").

More recently, a federal court applying Colorado law held that a covenant not to compete limiting a franchisee and guarantor from operating a competing business within 5 miles of an existing Steak n Shake location or within 5 miles of the franchisee's prior authorized locations was properly limited and reasonable as to scope and duration. *Steak n Shake Enters., Inc. v. Globex Co., LLC*, 2013 WL 4718757, at *13 (D. Colo. Sept. 3, 2013). The franchisor's victory was dampened, however, because the district court limited the definition of "competing business" to the operation of a Steak n Shake restaurant, which allowed the franchisee to continue operating a restaurant so long as it was fully deidentified. This decision, and the subsequent order granting summary judgment to the franchisor, is a bit of an oddity in that the judge never mentions nor applies section 8-2-113 in the analysis of the covenant, but does cite Colorado cases in support of the analysis on the breach of covenant claims. There appears to have been some dispute between the parties as to whether the law of Indiana or Colorado applied, with the franchisee apparently preferring Indiana by the time the court took up the franchisor's motion for summary judgment. *Steak n Shake Enterprises, Inc. v Globex Co., LLC*, 110 F. Supp. 3d 1057, 1070 (D. Colo. 2015). The judge sidestepped the choice-of-law issue by concluding that the franchisee raised the choice-of-law argument without analysis and therefore waived it.

5. What limitations on activities have courts recognized as reasonable in the franchise context?

Aside from the cases discussed earlier, Colorado courts have not identified any additional limitations on activities that are reasonable in the franchise context.

6. Does the state recognize a difference between in-term and post-term covenants?

Colorado courts have not addressed whether recognition of a difference in enforceability between in-term and post-term covenants would be appropriate. However, *Keller Corp. v. Kelley*, 187 P.3d 1133 (Colo. App. 2008), noted that the party with the protectable interest may change from the franchisee, during the franchised term, to the franchisor after the term ends. In *Big O Tires v. Felix Bros*, Case No. 10-cv-00362, 2011 WL 6181448 (D. Colo. Dec. 13, 2011), the court declined to enforce an in-term covenant, but, as discussed above, that was because the court concluded that the franchisor had not carried its burden of proof, not because of any differences between in-term and post-term covenants.

7. Has the state allowed enforcement of covenants against non-signatories (e.g., family members, newly formed corporations)?

Yes. In *Gold Messenger Inc. v. McGuay*, 937 P.2d 907 (Colo. App. 1997), the court enforced the non-compete agreement against the franchisee's roommate and life partner, who did not sign the franchise agreement. The court held that a non-signatory is "bound by the covenant at least to the extent that he or she assists the covenantor to violate the covenant not to compete." *Id.* at 912. The court noted that the non-signatory assisted in running the franchise for two years and received training from the franchisor. In the competing business, the non-signatory was the owner of record but operated the new business in the same manner as the Gold Messenger franchise. *See also Fitness Together Franchise, L.L.C. v. EM Fitness, L.L.C.*, Civil Action No. 1:20-cv-02757-DDD-STV, 2020 WL 6119470 (D. Colo. Oct. 16, 2020); *Homewatch Int'l v. Navin*, 2017 WL 4163358, 2017 WL 4163358 (D. Colo. Sept. 20, 2017) (holding that while owner did not sign franchise agreement, she did sign a guaranty incorporated into the franchise agreement, which was sufficient for purposes of finding the franchisor likely to succeed on the merits.

In *Fitness Together Franchise, L.L.C. v. EM Fitness, L.L.C.*, Civil Action No. 1:20-cv-02757-DDD-STV, 2020 WL 6119470 (D. Colo. Oct. 16, 2020), defendant Mellinger operated three Fitness Together gyms in Ohio under three separate franchise agreements executed between 2011 and 2013 by Fitness Together Franchise and three separate limited liability companies owned by Mellinger. In 2020, Mellinger and Fitness Together agreed to terminate the franchise agreements pursuant to an agreement by which Mellinger agreed to discontinue operations at her three gyms and direct clients to other Fitness Together gyms. In exchange for a payment, Fitness Together agreed to reduce the duration of the covenant not to compete from two years to one, with other post-termination obligations remaining in place. During the negotiation of the agreement, Mellinger allegedly formed three LLCs (the "Axio Defendants") with the intent to open new gyms at the former franchise locations under the name Axio Fitness. Fitness Together provided substantial evidence connecting Mellinger and the entities that executed the franchise agreements with the Axio Defendants.

Fitness Together sued and sought a preliminary injunction. The Axio Defendants moved to dismiss for lack of personal jurisdiction, claiming that the forum-selection clauses in the franchise agreements did not bind them as non-signatories to the agreements. The court disagreed, finding that the Axio Defendants were bound by the forum-selection clauses in the franchise agreements, and therefore the covenants not to compete, by application of a number of doctrines. First, the court discussed the "closely related" doctrine, whereby "non-signatories to a contract are subject to its valid forum selection clause if they . . . are closely related to the contractual relationship." The court discussed conflicting authority in the Tenth Circuit and other jurisdictions and concluded that it need not resolve the debate because the doctrine appeared to be an umbrella term that "refers to a variety of common law doctrines courts used to bind non-signatories to contracts, including third-party beneficiaries, successors-in-interest, principles of signatory agents and alter egos." The court found by application of principles of equitable estoppel, successor liability, and agency principles, the Axio Defendants were bound and enjoined their operation of the new gyms along with the signatories to the agreements.

8. Will the state modify, "blue-pencil," or otherwise reduce a covenant found to be overbroad?

There is no reported Colorado franchise case in which a court "blue-penciled" a covenant not to compete found to be overbroad. However, a Colorado federal court applying Florida law (which it found to be not contrary to Colorado public policy) modified a 25-mile radius restriction around the territories of every other franchisee within a franchise system. The court found the restriction to be unreasonable given the proximity of other existing franchises. *Dry Cleaning To-Your-Door, Inc. v. Waltham Limited Liability Co.*, No. 07-CV-01483-WDM-MJW, 2007 WL 4557832, at *3 (D. Colo. Dec. 20, 2007). The court reduced the restriction to a five-mile radius around the former franchisee's territory because otherwise the restriction would effectively preclude the franchisee from competing on the front range "from Colorado Springs to north of Ft. Collins."

Outside of the franchise context, the Colorado Court of Appeals recently noted that "Colorado law provides little guidance as to when, and to what extent, trial courts may blue pencil unreasonable noncompete provisions." *23 LTD v. Herman*, 457 P.3d 754 (Colo. App. 2019). After surveying extra-jurisdictional approaches to blue-penciling and Colorado decisions, the court of appeals concluded that trial courts have the discretion to blue-pencil unenforceable provisions to some extent.

Colorado courts have modified covenants to reduce the scope of geographic restrictions because such an area was unnecessary to protect the legitimate needs of a covenantee. In *Barrows v. McMurtry Manufacturing*, 131 P. 430 (Colo. 1913), the court observed that a contract containing some unreasonable terms should be enforced "wherever it is possible to so divide it as to declare it binding over such territory as is necessary for the protection of the purchaser." *Id.* at 432. Colorado courts have not adhered strictly to this articulation of a blue-pencil rule but have reformed geographically overbroad covenants to make them reasonable. *Whittenberg v. Williams*, 135 P.2d 228 (Colo. 1943) (limiting contract specifying no territorial limitations to that portion of Colorado south of the northern boundary of the city and county of Denver and east of the Rocky Mountains); *Gulick v. A. Robert Strawn & Assocs.*, 477 P.2d 489 (Colo. App. 1970) (limiting contract that precluded competition within 35 miles of any city in which a Snelling & Snelling office is located to within 10 miles from the boundary of Denver); *Wagner v. A & B Personnel Sys.*, 473 P.2d 179, 180 (Colo. App. 1970) (limiting contract prohibiting competition within "fifty miles of any city in which agency was doing business" to within 50 miles of the agency's location in downtown Denver).

Colorado courts will not, however, automatically reform an overbroad covenant. In *National Graphics Co. v. Sharon Dilly*, 681 P.2d 546 (Colo. App. 1984), the Colorado Court of Appeals voided a covenant because it was silent as to both time and geographic limitation and thus unreasonable. The court rejected the plaintiff's argument that the trial court abused its discretion by failing to reform the agreement to supply the missing limitations of duration and geographic scope.

And in *23 LTD*, the court of appeals rejected the proposition that "contracting parties, by inclusion of language in a contract, may compel a court to blue pencil an agreement that violates the public policy of the state." 457 P.3d at 754. There, an employer contended that a severability section in the agreement with the former employee obligated the district court to blue-pencil the agreement to conform it to Colorado law. The court disagreed, holding that the court was not a party to the agreement, and the parties " have no power or authority to enlist the court as their agent" and "cannot contractually obligate a court to blue pencil noncompete provisions that it determines are unreasonable." *Id.* at 759. It is worth noting that the agreement's geographic and temporal restrictions were not at issue and, instead, the former employer sought to obligate the district court to blue-pencil an overly broad non-solicitation provision only.

9. When does a non-compete period begin to run?

➤ Will courts equitably extend the term?

Neither question has been answered in the franchise context. However, in analyzing the enforceability of non-solicitation provisions in employment agreements, the Colorado Court of Appeals has held that a post-termination non-solicitation provision expires at the time set forth in the provision itself and has declined to extend a covenant beyond the term specified in the parties' agreement. *Phoenix Capital, Inc. v. Dowell*, 176 P.3d 835, 843 (Colo. App. 2007) (citing *Amtel Corp. v. Vitesse Semiconductor Corp.*, 30 P.3d 789, 796 (Colo. App. 2001) (declining to extend injunction beyond the term set forth in non-solicitation clause in employment agreement)), *abrogated in part on other grounds by Ingold v. AIMCO/Bluffs, L.L.C. Apartments*, 159 P.2d 116, 124 (Colo. 2007). *See also Cont'l Credit Corp. v. Garcia*, No. 15-CV-1251-NYW, 2016 WL 614475 (D. Colo. Feb. 16, 2016) (where defendant signed non-compete provision with a corporation and then later transferred to a subsidiary, the "clock" on the non-compete provision did not restart when defendant moved, because each subsidiary was a distinct corporation).

In *Amtel Corp.*, an employer brought an action against three former employees and their new employer to enforce non-solicitation clauses in their employment agreements. The trial court entered the preliminary injunction against all defendants, even though the non-solicitation provisions had expired for two of the three former employees. In granting the injunction, the trial court held that she was extending the term of the non-solicitation provision for a year beyond the date of the ruling on the preliminary injunction motion "as a matter of equity" because the defendants had violated the agreement during its term and during the pendency of a temporary restraining order entered by the court. *Amtel Corp.*, 30 P.3d at 796.

The court of appeals concluded that the trial court had abused its discretion by extending the duration of the preliminary injunction beyond the one-year non-solicitation term set forth in the employment agreements. The court of appeals reasoned that:

> The purpose of an injunction is to prevent "future harm," not to penalize a defendant for past unauthorized actions. Harm that has already occurred cannot be remedied by an injunction. Injunctive relief based on a restrictive employment agreement must be coextensive with the terms of the contract.

Id. (citations omitted). The court of appeals concluded that the trial court was attempting to remedy the past harm caused by the defendants' competition during the term of the non-solicitation provision with future injunctive relief, which it held was error.

Given the holdings in *Amtel Corp.* and *Phoenix Capital* and the general statutory presumption against enforcement of covenants not to compete, it seems unlikely that a court would equitably extend a covenant not to compete in most cases. Thus, a franchisor is well advised to be vigilant with respect to a former franchisee's activities and take steps to seek enforcement of a covenant not to compete before it expires.

Left unanswered by *Amtel Corp.* and *Phoenix Capital* is the question of what a Colorado court would do if confronted with a covenant not to compete that, by its terms, either contains a provision requiring equitable tolling during any period of noncompliance or provides that the covenant does not commence running until the franchisee is in compliance. Although the non-compete provision in the franchise agreement in *Homewatch International, Inc. v. Navin* ran two years "commencing on the effective date of termination or expiration, or the date on which Franchisees ceases to conduct business, whichever is later," the enforceability of this language was not at issue. 2017 WL 4163358, at*2. *Amtel Corp.* and *Phoenix Capital* would not seem to foreclose the extension of a covenant through such language, but there is a risk that such a clause could be invalidated for indefiniteness or imposing a temporally unreasonable restriction.

10. Are there additional nuances or peculiarities of the state's treatment of covenants in the franchising context?

Although no reported Colorado state court case has clearly held that the sale-of-business exception applies to newly created franchises and franchise resales equally, several federal decisions have. *Homewatch Int'l v. Navin*, 2017 WL 4163358, 2017 WL 4163358 (D. Colo. Sept. 20, 2017); *Big O Tires, LLC v. JDV, LLC*, No. 08-CV-1046-WYD, 2008 WL 4787619 (D. Colo. Oct. 31, 2008); *I Can't Believe It's Yogurt v. Gunn*, Bus. Franchise Guide (CCH) ¶ 11,197, 1997 WL 599391 (D. Colo. Apr. 15,

1997). To fall within the trade secret exception, franchisors must carefully draft their restrictive covenants so that the covenant will be enforced as a contract for the protection of trade secrets. *Core Progression Franchise LLC v. O'Hare*, No. 21-CV-0643-WJM-NYW, 2021 WL 1222768 (D. Colo. Apr. 1, 2021); *DBA Enterprises Inc. v. Findlay*, 923 P.2d 298 (Colo. App. 1996); and *Gold Messenger Inc. v. McGuay*, 937 P.2d 907 (Colo. App. 1997). In addition, franchisors must take steps to ensure that the information they give to franchisees is deemed a trade secret under the criteria established by the Colorado Trade Secrets Act by taking steps to maintain the secrecy of their information and know-how. The Tenth Circuit has noted that including a confidentiality agreement within a franchise agreement can be probative of one factor in determining the existence of a trade secret: whether the holder has taken precautions to guard the secrecy. *Harvey Barnett, Inc. v. Shidler*, 338 F.3d 1125, 1132 (10th Cir. 2003) (applying Colorado law).

Although *Gold Messenger*, *Core Progression*, and *Fitness Together* are quite favorable to franchisors, the enforceability of restrictive covenants under the statutory trade secrets exception may not be as simple as these cases. Indeed, there are pitfalls for the unwary, as some Colorado decisions take a narrow view of the permissible scope of a covenant for the protection of trade secrets and even what constitutes a trade secret.

The Colorado Court of Appeals has held that "[a] noncompetition clause designed to protect trade secrets must be narrowly drafted to fit into the statutory exception." *Management Recruiters of Boulder v. Miller*, 762 P.2d 763 (Colo. App. 1998). Thus, an argument could be made that, under Colorado law, a covenant against competition is invalid to the extent that it restricts a franchisee beyond that which is required to protect the franchisor's trade secrets.

I Can't Believe It's Yogurt v. Gunn, Bus. Franchise Guide (CCH) ¶ 11,197, 1997 WL 599391 (D. Colo. Apr. 15, 1997) did not involve the sale of an existing franchise, but it was decided before *Gold Messenger* and therefore relied on *DBA Enterprises* by analogy. More important, however, the court held that the franchisee did not misappropriate the franchisor's trade secrets (a separate cause of action in Colorado) because the franchisor failed to prove the existence of trade secrets. The district court concluded that the information claimed to be trade secrets was not trade secrets because the information was generally known or readily ascertainable and because the franchisor had not taken adequate steps to guard the secrecy of the information. *Id.* at *23.

In another federal case, the district court took a very restrictive view of what constitutes a trade secret under Colorado law. In *Rivendell Forest Products Ltd. v. Georgia-Pacific Corp.*, 824 F. Supp. 961 (D. Colo. 1993), the district court determined that the plaintiff had no trade secrets as a matter of law. The alleged trade secret was "Quote Screen," a pricing software program for lumber. The district court concluded that the concepts and ideas required to create the software were either known or readily ascertainable and, therefore, were not trade secrets. Further, the court held that those ideas and concepts could be permissibly used to create a separate but similar software ("Quick Quote"). The decision was subsequently reversed by the Tenth Circuit. *See Rivendell Forest Products Ltd. v. Georgia-Pacific Corp.*, 28 F.3d 1042 (10th Cir. 1994). The Tenth Circuit held that the existence of a trade secret is a question of fact (*see Network Telecommunications, Inc. v. Boor-Crepeau*, 790 P.2d 901 (Colo. App. 1990)), and thus the district court erred in entering summary judgment in favor of the defendant. Despite its reversal, *Rivendell* demonstrates the reluctance of some courts to construe information as trade secrets.

Given that a franchisor will be required to show that it has provided trade secrets to its franchisee before a covenant will be upheld under existing cases construing the trade secrets exception, franchisors should take all available measures to maintain the confidentiality of their information and know-how. This includes (1) restricting access to the information, (2) obtaining a copyright for any manuals, (3) including express provisions in the franchise agreement that the franchisor has provided confidential information and know-how to the franchisee that the franchisee lacked, and (4) obtaining a written acknowledgment or agreement from the franchisee and the franchisee's principals that the information being provided constitutes trade secrets and the confidentiality of the information is not subject to contest. The presence of each of these factors allowed the court to uphold the covenant in *Gold Messenger*.

As a final note, courts applying Colorado law may consider whether a covenant not to compete governed by the law of another state is unenforceable because it is contrary to Colorado public policy even where the covenant would be upheld under the other state's law. *Dry Cleaning To-Your-Door, Inc. v. Waltham Limited Liability Co.*, No. 07-CV-01483-WDM-MJW, Bus. Franchise Guide (CCH) ¶ 76,044 2007 WL 4557832, at *2 (D. Colo. Dec. 20, 2007). The court noted that although Colorado law renders some covenants not to compete void, Colorado law provides exceptions for the purchase and sale of a business and to protect trade secrets. *Id.* Although the court did not discuss its reasoning, it concluded that Florida law was not contrary to Colorado public policy because Colorado law allows for enforcement of non-competes in certain instances, and went on to enforce the covenant. *See also Wells Fargo Ins. Servs. USA, Inc. v. McQuate*, 276 F. Supp. 3d 1089 (D. Colo. 2016) (holding Colorado law applied instead of West Virginia because Colorado had materially greater interest and public policy implications).

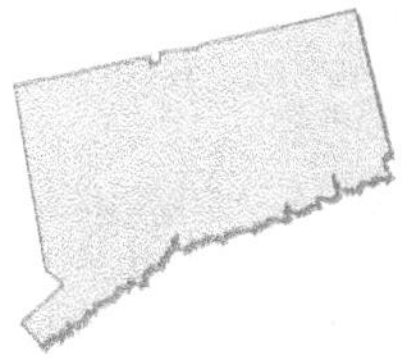

Connecticut

*by Karen T. Staib**

1. Has the state addressed covenants against competition in the context of franchising?

- **Does the state have a franchising statute or regulations that address covenants against competition?**
- **Does the state have a covenants statute of general applicability that would encompass franchise covenants?**
- **Have the courts addressed covenants in the context of franchising either under a statute or under the state's common law?**

Connecticut has a general franchising statute, the Connecticut Franchising Act, CONN. GEN. STAT. § 42-133e *et seq.*, but that statute does not address covenants against competition. The Connecticut Supreme Court has discussed the scope of the term "franchise" under the Connecticut Franchising Act. The test for determining whether there is a franchise relationship is whether the parties' conduct, in addition to their words, constitutes an agreement or arrangement; any actions constituting an agreement or arrangement, in turn, must be examined when determining whether a marketing plan or system is substantially prescribed. *Edmands v. CUNO, Inc.*, 277 Conn. 425, 439, 892 A.2d 938, 949 (2006). *Compare id.* (finding no franchise relationship between manufacturer and distributors) and *Getty Petroleum Marketing, Inc. v. Ahmad*, 253 Conn. 806, 812–20, 757 A.2d 494, 497–501 (2000) (finding no franchise between lessee of gasoline station and the lessor petroleum company, which owned the gasoline and bore the entrepreneurial risk; characterizing gas station lessee a "commissioned agent" rather than a franchisee under the Connecticut Franchising Act) *with Hartford Electrical Supply Co. v. Allen-Bradley*, 250 Conn. 334, 347–61, 736 A.2d 824, 832–39 (1999) (finding that a franchise relationship existed between a distributor and manufacturer). Connecticut also has a specialized petroleum franchising act, the Connecticut Gasoline Dealers Act, CONN. GEN. STAT. § 42-133j *et seq.* (CGDA), which limits what obligations can be imposed on a motor fuel dealer and imposes certain requirements on a franchisor relating to grounds and procedures for termination and nonrenewal. Although the CGDA does not

*Karen T. Staib is a partner in the Hartford, Connecticut, office of Shipman & Goodwin LLP. Sarah N. Niemiroski, an associate in the same firm, assisted with the preparation of this analysis.

directly address covenants not to compete, the statute does require payment for goodwill upon termination by the franchisor unless the franchisor both gives one year's notice of termination and agrees in writing not to enforce any non-compete covenant, subject to certain limited exceptions. *Id.* § 42-1331(b); *Bellmore v. Mobil Oil Corp.*, 783 F.2d 300, 305–06 (2d Cir. 1986).

Connecticut does not have a general covenants statute; instead, Connecticut courts apply the state's common law to restrictive covenants. In Connecticut, the law is settled that a restrictive covenant ancillary to a lawful contract is enforceable if the restraint on trade is reasonable. *Elida, Inc. v. Harmor Realty Corp.*, 177 Conn. 218, 225, 413 A.2d 1226, 1229 (1979). What is reasonable is a very fact-intensive inquiry. To be reasonable, the covenant not to compete should afford a "fair protection" to the interests of the party in whose favor the covenant runs, and it should not interfere with the public interest. *Scott v. General Iron Welding Co.*, 171 Conn. 132, 137, 368 A.2d 111, 114–15 (1976). The five factors Connecticut courts use to evaluate the validity and enforceability of a covenant not to compete, established in *Scott v. General Iron Welding Co.*, are:

(1) The length of time the restriction operates,
(2) The geographical area covered,
(3) The fairness of the protection afforded to the party imposing the restriction,
(4) The extent of the restraint on the employee's opportunity to pursue his or her occupation, and
(5) The extent of interference with the public's interest.

368 A.2d at 114–15; *see also Robert S. Weiss & Associates v. Wiederlight*, 208 Conn. 525, 529 n.2, 546 A.2d 216, 219 (Conn. 1988).

The *Scott* test is disjunctive rather than conjunctive, so that a finding of unreasonableness in any one of the criteria is enough to render the covenant unenforceable. *See also New Haven Tobacco Co. v. Perrelli*, 18 Conn. App. 531, 534, 559 A.2d 715, *cert. denied*, 212 Conn. 809, 564 A.2d 1071 (1989); *Van Dyck Printing Co. v. Dinicola*, 43 Conn. Super. Ct. 191, 648 A.2d 898, 902, *aff'd*, 231 Conn. 272, 648 A.2d 877 (1994) ("A restriction covering a large area might be reasonable if in effect for a brief time, while a restriction covering a small area might be reasonable for a longer time."). As recently as 2021, the Connecticut Appellate Court reaffirmed the *Scott* test and the body of well-settled principles applicable to determining the reasonableness and enforceability of restrictive covenant, in the employment context in *DeLeo v. Equale & Cirone, LLP*, 202 Conn. App. 650, 246 A.3d 988, 1004 (Conn. App. 2021).

In Connecticut, relatively few non-compete agreement cases have arisen in the context of franchise agreements. In *Sotheby's International Realty, Inc. v. Jones*, 2011 WL 1105806 (Conn. Super. Ct. Feb. 24, 2011), the parties entered into an agreement under which (1) the defendant acquired the plaintiff's Greenwich and Litchfield County real estate brokerage operations, (2) the plaintiff was barred from operating a real estate brokerage business in Greenwich and in a ten-mile radius area surrounding the plaintiff's Marbledale offices for a period of ten years ("restricted areas"), and (3) the parties entered into a franchise agreement under which the plaintiffs were authorized to operate the defendant's brokerage businesses in 21 offices outside the restricted areas for a period of 12 years, and the defendant agreed not to expand its operations outside the restricted areas during that period. *Id.* at *2–3. When a business minority-owned by the plaintiffs sought to enter the Greenwich market, the superior court granted a temporary injunction enforcing the non-compete agreement, concluding that the ten-year term of the agreement was not a violation of public policy and that the equities favored enforcement of the agreement. *Id.* at *4.

Money Mailer Franchise Corp. v. Wheeler, 2008 WL 4415942 (Conn. Super. Ct. Sept. 16, 2008) is another superior court case in which the court issued a temporary restraining order to enforce a non-compete agreement in the franchise context. In that case, two non-competes were involved. When the franchisee originally acquired the franchise, he agreed to refrain from competitive activities for two years in a 50-mile radius surrounding both his own franchise territory and that of each of the other franchisees. *Id.* at *1. Subsequently, upon selling the franchise to a third party, he contracted with the buyer not to compete for a period of three years in the latter's franchise zones and territories. The franchisee allegedly proceeded to violate both agreements by working the following year as an independent contractor for the buyer's direct competitor and by pursuing his previous franchise clients. The court concluded that the buyer and franchisor (as joint plaintiffs) were likely to prevail on the merits and that the equities were in their favor, including that the non-compete obligation was created in conjunction with the sale of the franchise. *Id.* at *4.

In *Carvel Corp. v. DePaola*, 2001 WL 528203, at *1, *13 (Conn. Super. Ct. Apr. 24, 2001), the superior court granted a franchisor a temporary restraining order where former franchisees continued to operate ice cream stores at former Carvel locations despite non-compete covenants in the franchise agreements. Although the court construed the covenants themselves under New York law (as provided for in the agreements), it relied on Connecticut law to analyze the imminent harm and balancing of the equities. *Id.* at *3–6, *10–13. The court explicitly identified the franchisor's need to protect and maintain the integrity of its franchise system as a valid justification for restraining the former franchisees. *Id.* at *11–12. Also in the franchise context, the U.S. District Court for the District of Connecticut applied Connecticut non-compete law in *Grease Monkey Int'l, Inc. v. Watkins*, 808 F. Supp. 111 (D. Conn. 1992) to enforce a restrictive covenant in a franchise agreement that prohibited the former franchisee of a fast-service automotive lubrication franchisor from engaging for two years in such a business within a 50-mile radius of his former franchise location, applying the *Scott* test. 808 F. Supp. at 118, 120.

A plethora of caselaw exists in Connecticut regarding the enforceability of restrictive covenants in the context of the employer-employee relationship, and the application of *Scott* factors in these factual contexts is instructive. The Connecticut Supreme Court has recognized the legitimate right of an employer to protect its business interests, stating in *Robert S. Weiss & Associates*, 546 A.2d 216:

> [w]hen the character of the business and the nature of employment are such that the employer requires protection for his established business against competitive activities by one who has become familiar with it through employment therein, restrictions are valid when they appear to be reasonably necessary for the fair protection of the employer's business or rights.

Id. at 221. To be binding, an agreement "must be partial and restricted in its operation in respect either to time or place . . . and must be reasonable." *Scott*, 368 A.2d at 114 (internal quotation marks omitted). Connecticut courts treat a non-compete covenant made in connection with the sale of a business as an asset of the purchased business. As such, the courts have found that to be a compelling factor favoring enforcement of these covenants, which is not a consideration regarding non-compete covenants made in connection with an employment contract. *See Mattis v. Lally*, 138 Conn. 51, 54–56, 82 A.2d 155, 156–57 (1951) (having sold his barbershop "together with all goodwill," seller should be held to restrictive covenant in sales agreement (no barbering in that town or within one mile of the old shop for five years) because "[t]o excuse him from the performance of his agreement would amount to returning to him a large part of what he has sold"); *see also Sagarino v. SCI Connecticut Funeral Services, Inc.*, 2000 WL 765260, at *2, *5–6 (Conn. Super. Ct. May 22, 2000) (enforcing non-compete covenant for 15 years in a 30-mile radius around funeral home sold, where the court found strong goodwill and "brand loyalty" built up in the Italian-American community and a nine-year average lag time for "return business"); *Hilb, Rogal & Ham Co. v. Palwich*, 1995 WL 914231, at *8 (Conn. Super. Ct. Feb. 16, 1995) (having transferred his former accounts as part of the sale of his insurance business and signed a non-compete for three years as to those accounts, an insurance salesman cannot "fairly be heard to claim a right to work them in direct contravention of the terms of the sale").

---

2. Have the courts articulated the "legitimate interests" of the franchisor that will support enforcement of a covenant against competition contained in a franchise agreement?

- **If so, what are they (e.g., protection of goodwill, protection of confidential information), and in what contexts did the issue arise?**
- **If not, what interests have been recognized in other contexts (e.g., employment agreements, the sale of business context)?**

Although no specific "legitimate interests" test has been articulated, Connecticut courts typically evaluate the interests to be protected when deciding whether a covenant is reasonable. This process often leads to the recognition of goodwill, as well as confidential, proprietary, and trade secret information, as protectable interests. *Money Mailer Franchise Corp.*, 2008 WL 4415942, at *2. Within the franchise context in *Grease Monkey Int'l*, the former franchisee, although terminated for default of payment, continued to use the franchisor's trademark, processes, materials, signs, manuals, name, and methods. *Id.* at 114. The district court enforced the two-year, 50-mile radius restriction against competition contained in the franchise agreement, concluding that "it was fair for [franchisor] GMI to attempt to protect its trademark and business practices, and to seek to maintain or establish relations with its present and potential customers." *Id.* at 120.

Similarly in *Carvel Corp.*, 2001 WL 528203, at *1, *13 (Conn. Super. Ct. Apr. 24, 2001), the superior court granted a franchisor a temporary restraining order where former franchisees continued to operate ice cream stores at former Carvel locations despite non-compete covenants in the franchise agreements prohibiting such activity within a two-mile radius for a three-year duration. Although the court construed the covenants themselves under New York law (as provided for in the agreements), it relied on Connecticut law to analyze the imminent harm and balancing of the equities. *Id.* at *3–6, *10–13. The court explicitly accepted the franchisor's need to protect and maintain the integrity of its franchise system as a valid justification for restraining the former franchisees, explaining that:

> Carvel has a legitimate interest in protecting its know-how, trade secrets, goodwill and the integrity of its franchise system. Thus, Carvel has a legitimate and reasonable interest in limiting the defendants' ability to operate a substantially similar, if not identical, ice cream shop offering substantially similar, if not identical, ice cream products in the same location as the former Carvel shops. Furthermore, the defendants' continued use of Carvel's proprietary information in a competing operation, without paying the franchise fees and other fees provided for by the agreements, tends to undermine the integrity of the franchise system.

Id. at *11–12.

In the employment context, courts also have recognized the protection of trade secrets, customer lists, and sales territories as legitimate interests. *See New Haven Tobacco Co. v. Perrelli*, 11 Conn. App. 636, 639, 528 A.2d 865, 867 (1987). Through investing time and money in building goodwill, an employer acquires "a proprietary right to his customers which he may protect for a reasonable time." *Id.* at 869, n.5. In the oft-cited *Scott v. General Iron Welding Co.*, 171 Conn. 132, 137, 368 A.2d 111, 114–15 (1976) case, the Connecticut Supreme Court affirmed the trial court's enforcement of a five-year, statewide restrictive covenant signed by a former management employee in a welding and metals manufacturing business in connection with a promotion. *Id.* at 116. The employer was entitled to protect its list of clients and other confidential information, the court explained, which the company had developed through years of effort. *Id.* Those principles were reaffirmed most recently by the Connecticut Appellate Court in *DeLeo*, which provides a thorough review of the factors applied under Connecticut law and the overall body of noncompete caselaw. 246 A.3d at 1003–06.

CT

3. What time limitations have courts recognized as reasonable in the franchise context?

- **If no franchise cases have been decided, what time limitations have been recognized in other contexts?**
- **How have they been related to interests protected?**

The time (and geographical) restrictions of a non-compete covenant must be reasonable, partial, and limited in scope for the covenant to be enforceable. *Grease Monkey Int'l, Inc.*, 808 F. Supp. at 119. Temporal and geographical restrictions are reviewed as intertwined considerations. "A restriction covering a large area might be reasonable if in effect for a brief time, while a restriction covering a small area might be reasonable for a longer time." *Van Dyck Printing*, 648 A.2d at 902.

Sotheby's International Realty, Inc. v. Jones, 2011 WL 1105806 (Conn. Super. Ct. Feb. 24, 2011) arose in the context of the plaintiff's acquisition of the defendant's real estate offices. *Id.* at *3–4. The parties agreed that (1) the defendant acquired the plaintiff's Greenwich and Litchfield County real estate brokerage operations; (2) the plaintiff was barred from operating a real estate brokerage business in Greenwich and in a ten-mile radius area surrounding the plaintiff's Marbledale offices for a period of ten years ("restricted areas"); and (3) the parties entered into a franchise agreement under which the plaintiffs were authorized to operate the defendant's brokerage businesses in 21 offices outside the restricted areas for a period of 12 years, and the defendant agreed not to expand its operations outside the restricted areas during that period. When the sellers proceeded to establish a real estate brokerage business in Greenwich, the court issued a temporary injunction enforcing the agreement, implicitly finding that the ten-year time frame did not violate public policy. *Id.* at *4.

Likewise in *Grease Monkey Int'l*, the district court enforced a restrictive covenant in a franchise agreement prohibiting the former franchisee of a quick-service automotive lubrication franchisor from engaging for two years in such a business within a 50-mile radius of his former franchise location. *Grease Monkey Int'l*, 808 F. Supp. at 118, 120. The franchisee did not object to the time restriction, and the court noted that the restraint was neither overbearing nor infinite. *Id.* at 120. Rather, the restraint was a fair attempt by the franchisor "to protect its trademark and business practices, and to seek to maintain or establish relations with its present and potential customers." *Id.*; *see also Money Mailer Franchise Corp.*, 2008 WL 4415942, at *5 (granting temporary restraining order to enforce two-year non-compete with a 50-mile radius).

Cases from outside the franchising context give further guidance regarding the contours of time and geographic scope limitations. In *DeLeo*, 246 A.3d 988, the Connecticut Appellate Court reviewed the reasonableness of a non-compete provision that imposed a five-year restriction on servicing clients represented by a Danbury, Connecticut–centered accounting firm. In addition to other grounds on which it upheld the trial court's determination of unreasonableness and therefore unenforceability, the court held that while there is no "default number of years that is uniformly reasonable," five years in these circumstances was longer than necessary to protect the accounting firm's interests. *Id.* at 1009. In *Scott v. General Iron Welding Co.*, 171 Conn. 132, 137, 368 A.2d 111 (1976), the Connecticut Supreme Court enforced a five-year statewide restriction barring a former management employee of a welding and metal-working company from working in a similar management position in any competing business. *Id.* at 114. The time restriction was deemed reasonable because the company had spent years acquiring its customers. *Id.*

Federal court rulings applying Connecticut law are consistent with these determinations. In *A.H. Harris & Sons, Inc. v. Maso*, 94 F. Supp. 3d 280 (D. Conn. 2015), the U.S. District Court for the District of Connecticut reviewed the contours of numerous cases in the employment context with respect to time limitations, noting that in many instances, a two-year term was found reasonable under Connecticut law. *Id.* at 294. Where it had not been, the court observed it was at least in part because the industry in which the covenant was imposed was one in which a shorter time frame was needed to protect interests, such as when a customer listing only lasted a period of months or the rapidly changing nature of the market. *Id.* Similarly, the U.S. District Court for the District of Connecticut deemed a non-compete provision reasonable where, among other factors, it prohibited a former employee of a recruiting/job placement firm from working at a competitor company in a similar capacity for period of one year, in *Entegee, Inc. v. Korwek*, 2015 WL 5202902, at *4–5 (D. Conn. Sept. 4, 2015).

Finally, even an indefinite time limitation can be permissible if not unreasonable when all factors are balanced together. In *Robert J. Reby & Co., Inc. v. Byrne*, 2006 WL 2089480 (Conn. Super. Ct. July 13, 2006), the superior court enforced a non-compete in spite of its indefinite duration because of the limited scope of the activity enjoined, which was to solicit or have contact with any current or former clients or defined leads of the employer financial services plaintiff entity, and did not prevent the departing employee from engaging in business within the industry generally. *Id.* at *1, *2. *See also Sagarino*, 2000 WL 765260, at *2, *5–6 (enforcing 15-year covenant not to compete within a 30-mile radius of family-run funeral home, where unique nature of business and its customer base required that buyer have opportunity to take advantage of goodwill it had purchased).

4. What geographic limitations have courts recognized as reasonable in the franchise context?

- **How have they been related to the interests protected?**
- **Have courts recognized the legitimacy of protecting *other* franchisees from competition?**

As with time restrictions, the geographical restrictions of a non-compete covenant must be reasonable, partial, and limited in scope for the covenant to be enforceable. *Grease Monkey Int'l*, 808 F. Supp. at 119. Temporal and geographical restrictions are reviewed as intertwined considerations: "[a] restriction covering a large area might be reasonable if in effect for a brief time, while a restriction covering a small area might be reasonable for a longer time." *Van Dyck Printing*, 648 A.2d at 902. In general, restrictive covenants in Connecticut "will be confined to a geographical area which is reasonable in view of the particular situation. A restrictive covenant which protects the employer in areas in which he does not do business or is unlikely to do business is unreasonable with respect to the area." *Trans-Clean Corp. v. Terrell*, 1998 WL 1424336, at *5–6 (Conn. Super. Ct. May 4, 1998) (finding covenant unreasonable, including because business selling its goodwill had operated almost entirely in Connecticut, whereas restrictive covenant against former owner protected buyer in wider area, including New York).

Starting with franchise cases, in *Grease Monkey Int'l*, the district court relied on the *Scott* test to assess the reasonableness of a restrictive covenant in a franchise agreement prohibiting the former franchisee of a quick-service automotive lubrication franchisor from engaging in such a business for two years within a 50-mile radius of his former franchise location. Although the court noted that 50 miles "seems somewhat broad," it nonetheless enforced the restriction, explaining that the covenant was a fair attempt by the franchisor "to protect its trademark and business practices, and to seek to maintain or establish relations with its present and potential customers." *Grease Monkey Int'l*, 808 F. Supp. at 120. Similarly, in *Money Mailer Franchise Corp. v. Wheeler*, 2008 WL 4415942 (Conn. Super. Ct. Sept. 16, 2008), the court enforced a franchise non-compete agreement barring the franchisee from operating within 50 miles of the territory of any other franchisee for two years after termination. *Id.* at *5.

Outside the franchise arena, the precedents within the employment context are instructive as to reasonable geographic scope. In *Scott v. General Iron Welding Co.*, 171 Conn. 132, 137, 368 A.2d 111(1976), the Connecticut Supreme Court enforced a five-year, statewide restriction barring a former management employee of a welding and metal-working company from working in a similar management position in any competing business. The court concluded that barring competition throughout the state was not unreasonable where the company did business with over 1,000 customers in up to 75 towns in the state. *Id.* at 114, 115.

Geographic areas should be reasonably drawn "to reflect an area where [the employer's] customer base is located." *New Country Motor Car Group, Inc. v. Vilca*, 2021 WL 4896153, at *4 (Conn. Super. Ct. Sept. 27, 2021) (a 30-mile geographical restriction on competition post-employment was upheld as reasonable where the business was a car dealership with a presence limited to certain counties in Connecticut). *See also Sabatassio v. Ranciato*, 2013 WL 2947896, at *4 (Conn. Super. Ct. May 24, 2013) (upholding one-year, ten-mile restrictive covenant in context of hair salon, noting that such terms have been upheld repeatedly in other cases). In *A.H. Harris & Sons*, the U.S. District Court for the District of Connecticut reviewed a restrictive covenant of two years and a 100-mile radius in the employment context and found it reasonable, because the former employer was still very active in that geographical market despite having closed an office in that region, which was one where the former employee had specifically done business. 94 F. Supp. 3d at 296–97.

A global scope was determined to be reasonable in a Connecticut Superior Court decision involving a Connecticut and New York City–based publisher and organizer of conferences for the digital advertising and marketing industry in *Friese v. Fadner Media Enterprises, LLC*, 2017 WL 1238436 (Conn. Super. Ct. Jan. 18, 2017). There, given the nature of the business involved, the court concluded that "plaintiff makes no convincing argument why a global prohibition against competing with [defendant's] global internet business is unreasonable." *Id.* at *6. A similar conclusion was reached in *Ineo, LLC v. Lenehan*, 2018 WL 1386221, at *7 (Conn. Super. Ct. Feb. 20, 2018), where the Connecticut Superior Court upheld a worldwide geographic scope to a restrictive covenant in the employment context where the business was involved in the movement and relocation of employees for large international corporations

In contrast, in *Prezio Health Inc. v. Schennk*, 2016 WL 1367726, at *4 (D. Conn. Apr. 6, 2016), the U.S. District Court for the District of Connecticut examined an employment agreement prohibiting a former employee from acting in any capacity for any company in competition with the former employer, and also prohibited solicitation of any "potential" customers within the "medical-surgical devices and equipment industry." The court determined that effectively to be an unlimited geographic scope that was unreasonable in the circumstances and would prevent the departing employee from pursing his occupation. *Id.*

---

5. What limitations on activities have courts recognized as reasonable in the franchise context?

In the handful of Connecticut cases scrutinizing restrictive covenants in franchise agreements, courts have enjoined former franchisees from continuing to operate substantially the same business from their former franchise locations. *See Grease Monkey Int'l, Inc. v. Watkins*, 808 F. Supp. 111, 118–20 (D. Conn. 1992) (enforcing covenant against operating similar business for two years within fifty-mile radius of former franchise location); *see also Sotheby's International Realty, Inc. v. Jones*, 2011 WL 1105806 (Conn. Super. Ct. Feb. 24, 2011) (enforcing ten-year agreement barring franchisee/seller from operating real estate brokerage business in Greenwich and within ten-mile radius of offices in Marbledale, Connecticut).

In *Money Mailer Franchise Corp.*, 2008 WL 4415942, the covenant at issue provided that upon termination, the franchisee of a direct-mail advertising business would refrain from engaging in any competitive activities within 50 miles of the territory of any other franchisee for two years. The court enforced the agreement (as well as a subsequent agreement between the franchisee and its purchaser), concluding that the subsequent purchaser was losing business and the intended purpose of the non-compete agreements was being frustrated by the former franchisee's ongoing efforts to solicit competitive business. *Id.* at *4. *See also Carvel Corp.*, 2001 WL 528203, at *1, *5 (enforcing three-year covenant prohibiting former franchisees from operating ice cream stores within two miles of their former franchise locations as reasonable under New York law, and finding injunctive relief warranted under Connecticut law based on analysis of imminent harm, adequate remedy at law, and balancing of equities); *Grease Monkey Int'l*, 808 F. Supp. at 118–20 (enforcing covenant against operating similar business for two years within 50-mile radius of former franchise location); *Sotheby's Int'l Realty*, 2011 WL 1105806 (enforcing at temporary restraining order stage a ten-year agreement barring franchisee/seller from operating real estate brokerage business in one entire town and within ten-mile radius of offices in other town).

In the employment context, the degree to which the departing employee's ability to pursue his or her livelihood, and the extent to which the protection for the former employer's business is tailored, are critical. For example, the U.S. District Court for the District of Connecticut found in *A.H. Harris & Sons, Inc. v. Maso*, 94 F. Supp. 3d 280 (D. Conn. 2015) that the extent of retrain on the departing employee's ability to pursue her occupation not to be unreasonably restrained where the employer was "not seeking to prevent [the former employee] from working in an only somewhat-related industry or for an employer with no solid connections to [its] business. *Id.* at 298. Instead, the plaintiff is seeking to enjoin [the former employee] from working with a direct competitor" that was also the only competitor specifically named in the restrictive covenant itself. *Id.* Similarly, in *Beacon Insurance & Inv. Group, LLC v. Panzo*, 2016 WL 4507389 (Conn. Super. Ct. July 25, 2016), the superior court considering the degree of interference with employees' employment enforced a restrictive covenant that prevented a former employee from working for two years in only one of the eight counties in the state, in part because the covenant did not force the defendant to "sacrifice his livelihood." *Id.* at *5.

Conversely, the U.S. District Court for the District of Connecticut held in *Sunbelt Rentals, Inc. v. McAndrews*, 2021 WL 3417958, at *5–6 (D. Conn. Aug. 5, 2021), that a restrictive covenant in an employment agreement was unreasonable where the geographic scope of 50 miles from any of plaintiff's stores regardless of whether defendant worked there, and further had no limitation whatsoever in terms of the nature of work he was prohibited from doing. As a result, the geographic restriction as applied to the "extremely broad definition of [the employer's] 'Business' . . . would result in precluding [Defendant] from working in the construction site matting industry even in geographic areas in which [the former employer] is not engaged in matting whatsoever." *Id.* Finally in *Walker Group, Inc. v. Hannaford*, 2021 WL 3722709 (Conn. Super. Ct. July 15, 2021), the superior court found a non-compete to be unenforceable because it determined that "the legally protectable interest includes preventing a former employee from exploiting client relationships developed on behalf of the former employer and exploiting any knowledge of the particular needs of the former employer's clients," but that here, the former employer was instead seeking to simply "prevent a competitor from hiring talented at-will employees by contractually prohibiting those employees from working for that competitor." *Id.* at *6.

6. Does the state recognize a difference between in-term and post-term covenants?

Because the vast majority of Connecticut cases dealing with non-compete covenants deal with post-term rather than in-term covenants, it is difficult to generalize about differences between the two. It appears, however, that Connecticut applies the same test to both. In *Elida, Inc. v. Harmor Realty Corp.*, 177 Conn. 218, 225, 413 A.2d 1226 (1979), the Connecticut Supreme Court held that the correct test to apply to a restrictive covenant in a mall lease that prevented the landlord from leasing space to another bakery was "the rule of reason by which the factfinder weighs all of the circumstances of the case in deciding whether a restrictive practice should be prohibited as imposing an unreasonable restraint on trade." The court reversed the lower court's decision that the restrictive covenant was a "per se" unreasonable restraint on trade and remanded the case for an examination of reasonableness, delineated as "limited in its operation with respect to time and place and afford[ing] no more than a fair and just protection to the interests of the party in whose favor it is to operate, without duly interfering with the public interest." *Id.* at 1230. It bears noting that the Connecticut Supreme Court in an unrelated case later upheld in relevant part the lower court's decision to enforce a restrictive covenant in the lessee bakery's mall lease preventing the bakery from operating as a restaurant. *Gino's Pizza v. Kaplan*, 193 Conn. 135, 475 A.2d 305 (1984). A restaurant lessee in the same mall sued the landlord for specific performance on its own lease, which provided that the landlord would not permit other restaurants in the complex. *Id.* at 306. The court did not undertake any analysis of the reasonableness of these restrictive covenants. *Id.*

In *PRF of Connecticut, Inc. v. Gosselin*, 1993 WL 512430 (Dec. 1, 1993), the superior court enforced a restrictive covenant contained in a purchase-option lease contract for an airport valet service; the covenant prohibited the family of the lessor/vendor from operating an airport valet service within a five-mile radius of the airport for five years from the date of the contract. The superior court analyzed the reasonableness under *Elida*, using the *Scott* factors. *Id.* at *4–5. The court characterized the lease contract with purchase option as a sale of a business, noting that the courts view covenants in the context of the sale of a business with "greater indulgence" than those in the employment context. *Id.*

7. Has the state allowed enforcement of covenants against non-signatories (e.g., family members, newly formed corporations)?

Connecticut courts have shown willingness to enforce covenants against non-signatories in certain circumstances. In *Sagarino v. SCI Connecticut Funeral Services, Inc.*, 2000 WL 765260 (Conn. Super. Ct. May 22, 2000), the superior court enforced a stringent non-compete agreement signed for a fee of $65,000 by a son, Sagarino, in conjunction with his mother's sale of the family funeral home to a corporation that wished to continue to operate the home under the family name. *Id.* at *2, *5–6. The court determined that the nature of the business (customer families would return every nine years on average), the funeral home's particular customer base (the Italian-American community they had been serving for years), and the personal nature of the services made it reasonable to hold Sagarino (the son) to the covenant in order to permit the buyer the opportunity to take advantage of the goodwill it had purchased. *Id.* at *5–7. The court rejected Sagarino's argument that, because he was not the seller, the covenant did not arise out of the sale of the business, stating:

> [I]t is well settled that an agreement not to compete will be considered to have been given in connection with the sale of a business even if the covenantor is not the seller, if the covenant was reasonably necessary for the protection of the goodwill of the business. If the covenantor was active in the management of or intimately involved with the business, as Sagarino was, the covenant will be considered to have been given in connection with the sale of the business.

Id. at *4.

Similarly, in *Custard Insurance Adjusters, Inc. v. Nardi*, 2000 WL 562318, at *56 (Conn. Super. Ct. Apr. 20, 2000), the superior court explicitly enforced a non-compete provision in an employment agreement against both the former employee who signed the agreement (Nardi) and a non-signatory, the competing new employer (Mark). The court enforced the covenant prohibiting Nardi from working within 50 miles of Orange, Connecticut, for two years (although the court reduced this to six months in light of the delay in adjudicating the case), and also enjoined both Nardi and Mark from servicing any clients Nardi took from the plaintiff, Custard. The court determined that Nardi had colluded with Mark to lure away Custard's employees and customers while still employed by Custard, and that this was a precondition of Nardi's future employment with Mark. It therefore found against Nardi for breach of contract, common-law breach of loyalty, tortious interference with business relationships, and violation of the Connecticut Unfair Trade Practices Act (CUTPA), CONN. GEN. STAT. § 42-110a *et seq.*, and against Mark for tortious interference and violation of CUTPA. *Id.* at *50–51.

8. Will the state modify, "blue-pencil," or otherwise reduce a covenant found to be overbroad?

Connecticut is considered a "blue-pencil" jurisdiction. That is, a Connecticut court generally will only strike—that is, blue-pencil—the specific provisions of a non-compete agreement that the court determines to be illegal or unreasonable, as opposed to rewriting an overly broad covenant. *Sylvan R. Shemitz Designs, Inc. v. Brown*, 2013 WL 6038263, at *9 (Conn. Super. Ct. Oct. 23, 2013). The Connecticut blue-pencil rule is restrictive in that the courts will sever an invalid provision only where the covenant is "in effect a combination of several distinct covenants," so that excising the unreasonable provision leaves a complete, enforceable agreement intact. *Industrial Technologies, Inc. v. Paumi*, 1997 WL 306723, at *3–4 (Conn. Super. Ct. May 28, 1997) (discussing differences between Connecticut's blue-pencil rule and the Massachusetts approach). In other words, the blue-pencil rule applies only "where the contract in terms specifies several distinct areas, so by erasing the description of one or more of these areas there is left the description of an area for which the restriction is reasonable." *Gartner Group Inc. v. Mewes*, 1992 WL 4766, at *4 (Conn. Super. Ct. Jan. 3, 1992); *see also Beit v. Beit*, 135 Conn. 195, 203, 63 A.2d 161, at 165 (1948) (collecting cases).

An example of how the blue-pencil rule is traditionally applied to save a non-compete agreement from unreasonableness is reflected in *Gartner Group*. 1992 WL

4766, at *4. There, the superior court used the blue-pencil rule, bolstered by a severability clause in the employment contract, to enforce an otherwise overly broad non-compete covenant. The covenant restricted a former employee from competing—or working for any company that competed—with any current or future product or service of the company. It applied anywhere the company did business during his tenure, including, but not limited to, Connecticut, Massachusetts, and New York (the company did work in many areas of the world) for one year. *Id.* at *3–5. The court restricted enforcement to any existing or potential customers of the company in Connecticut, Massachusetts, and New York. *Id.* at *5.

There are limits, however, to the types of provisions to which the blue-pencil rule can be applied. In *Beit*, a frequently cited older case, the Connecticut Supreme Court declined to enforce any portion of a restrictive covenant covering all of New London County, even though it might reasonably have been enforced only in the towns of New London and Norwich, because the agreement was "intended by the parties to be an entirety." 63 A.2d at 166. Similarly, in *Trans-Clean Corp. v. Terrell*, 1998 WL 1424336, at *5–6 (Conn. Super. Ct. May 4, 1998), the superior court found that an area spanning a 60-mile radius around the plaintiff's Stratford, Connecticut, home office was "indivisible" and, accordingly, declined to rewrite the agreement under the blue-pencil rule. *Id.* at *5–7; *see also Timenterial, Inc. v. Dagata*, 29 Conn. Supp. 180, 184–85, 277 A.2d 512, 514–15 (Conn. Super. Ct. 1971) (declining to either enforce or rewrite non-compete agreement that unreasonably barred salesman from practicing his trade in much of New England for one year following termination).

Some Connecticut courts have interpreted *Beit* to mean that a court has greater flexibility to rewrite an overly broad or unreasonable restrictive covenant where the parties have included language in the covenant itself empowering a court to modify its terms. In *Grayling Assocs. v. Villota*, 2004 WL 1784388, at *1 n.3, for example, the superior court modified the scope of the restrictive covenant from a 100-mile radius to the entire state of Connecticut with the exception of Fairfield County, because the contract "specifically permits the court to modify any position of the restrictive covenant to make it reasonable as opposed to invalid or unreasonable." *See also Group Concepts, Inc. v. Barberino*, 2004 WL 1050098, at *5 (Conn. Super. Ct. Apr. 16, 2004) (enforcing agreement where the "parties have agreed to enforce the entire covenant even if the court determines that a modification of its geographic scope is required"). However, in *Sylvan R. Shemitz Designs*, 2013 WL 6038263, at *9, the superior court declined to apply the blue-pencil rule to strike portions of the non-compete obligations. There, the court determined that the unreasonable provision, which "specifically prohibits any employment by a 'Specialized Lighting Business,' regardless of the importance of the position or its relatedness to those duties which the employee held with the plaintiff," rendered it impossible to use the blue-pencil rule "because the unreasonable provisions form the heart of the agreement." *Id.* (citations omitted).

Finally, as a procedural note, the superior court in *Saxe v. William Raveis Real Estate, Inc.*, 2018 WL 4199004, at *3 (Conn. Super. Ct. Aug. 24, 2018), held preliminarily that where a ten-mile geographic restriction on a former employee of a realtor was deemed unreasonable, the court noted it was willing to exercise its blue-pencil authority to limit the scope down to a reasonable geographic range, and ordered the parties to provide supplemental briefs on the issue, and a subsequent opportunity to be heard. *Id.*

9. When does a non-compete begin to run?

➤ Will courts equitably extend the term?

The question whether and when a court sitting in equity can extend the duration of a restrictive covenant in a contract as a remedy for a violation of the restrictive covenant has not been definitively answered in Connecticut. In *KX Industries, L.P. v. Saaski*, 1997 WL 583629 (Conn. Super. Ct. Aug. 29, 1997), the parties entered into an agreement that restricted the employee from obtaining competing employment for one year, commencing upon termination. The agreement further provided, however, that if the employee took such employment within a year from termination without providing adequate notice to the employer, the covenant would be tolled until such time as the former employer learned of the new employment. The court held this to be a reasonable restriction, notwithstanding the possibility that it could be enforced many years after termination, because the geographic restriction involved was extremely narrow. More recently in *VisionPoint, LLC v. Gish*, 2016 WL 8135540 (Conn. Super. Ct. Dec. 27, 2016), the superior court extended the start of the one-year time restriction in a former employee's covenant not to compete to the date of the court's decision on the application for temporary injunction, as the former employee began working in a manner that violated the covenant not to compete only days after leaving the plaintiff company. *Id.* at *7.

The fact that this issue has not been definitively resolved was underscored in *Aladdin Capital Holdings, LLC v. Donoyan*, 2011 WL 2293236 (D. Conn. June 8, 2011), *appeal dismissed as moot*, 438 F. App'x 14 (2d Cir. 2011), where the U.S. District Court for the District of Connecticut concluded that Connecticut most likely would adhere to the majority position barring equitable tolling if not expressly permitted by a restrictive covenant, even while conceding that several Connecticut courts have implicitly reached the opposite conclusion. *Id.* at *4.

10. Are there additional nuances or peculiarities of the state's treatment of covenants in the franchising context?

With respect to demonstrating the reasonableness or unreasonableness of a restrictive covenant under Connecticut law, the party contesting the covenant's reasonableness bears the burden of proof. *A.H. Harris & Sons*, 94 F. Supp. 3d at 288 (collecting cases); *Connecticut Bathworks Corp. v. Palmer*, 2003 WL 22006402, at *2 (Conn. Super. Ct. Aug. 1, 2003); *Merryfield Animal Hospital v. Mackay*, 2002 WL 31000298, at *3 (Conn. Super. Ct. July 31, 2002); *Riordan v. Barbosa*, 1999 WL 124335, at *3 (Mar. 1, 1999). At least one superior court case, *DelVecchio Reporting Servs., LLC v. Edwards*, 2017 WL 3623432 (Conn. Super. Ct. July 13, 2017), observed that Connecticut is in the minority in placing the burden on the challenging party. *Id.* at *5 (collecting cases).

Delaware

by Marla Hirshman Norton *

1. Has the state addressed covenants against competition in the context of franchising?

- **Does the state have a franchising statute or regulations that address covenants against competition?**
- **Does the state have a covenants statute of general applicability that would encompass franchise covenants?**
- **Have the courts addressed covenants in the context of franchising either under a statute or under the state's common law?**

The Delaware Franchise Security Law, 6 DEL. CODE §§ 2551–2556, deals mainly with unjust termination or nonrenewal and does not address non-competition covenants. The Delaware Motor Vehicle Franchising Practices Act, 6 DEL. CODE §§ 4901–4918, makes it unlawful to impose unreasonable restrictions on a motor vehicle dealership "relative to the sale, transfer, right to renew, termination, discipline, *noncompetition covenants*, site control (whether by sublease, collateral pledge of lease or otherwise), right of first refusal to purchase, option to purchase, compliance with subjective standards and assertion of legal or equitable rights [emphasis added]." 6 DEL. CODE § 4914(a). No other Delaware legislation or regulation is generally applicable to franchise relationships or speaks to non-competition covenants in the franchising context.

Similarly, no Delaware court has substantively addressed the principles applicable to a covenant not to compete in the context of a franchise relationship. The few instances in which Delaware courts have been asked to enforce a covenant against competition contained in a franchise agreement do not provide much guidance. *See La Bouttica, Ltd v. Clayton*, 1978 WL 4976 (Del. Ch. Aug. 28, 1978) (preliminary injunction denied); *Cheese Shop Int'l, Inc. v. Steele*, 1977 WL 5159, at *4 (Del. Ch. Apr. 19, 1977) (because franchisee remained bound by franchise agreement, validity of the non-competition provision was not ripe for consideration); *Caldwell Flexible Staffing, Inc. v. Mays*, 1976 WL 1716 (Del. Ch. Nov. 29, 1976) (former franchisee

*Marla H. Norton is an attorney with the law firm Bayard, P.A., in Wilmington, DE. Brynne MacDonnell, law clerk, of the same firm assisted Ms. Norton in the researching the materials for this analysis.

operating independently could not enforce non-competition agreements by signed former employees for the benefit of the franchisor and its Delaware franchisees).

The U.S. District Court for the District of Delaware, applying Pennsylvania law to a franchise agreement that selected Pennsylvania governing law, has noted, "Generally speaking in franchise law, courts favor enforcement of non-competition agreements and find irreparable harm when former franchisees violate such provisions." *Goddard Systems, Inc. v. Gondal*, C.A. No. 17-1003-CJB, slip op. at 59 (D. Del. Mar. 29, 2018) (Business Franchise Guide ¶ 16,167). But because the violation occurred "in a cabined time period in the past" during which the former franchisee assisted a successor of the business in transitioning to a non-franchised operation, absent evidence of likely future violations, there was no current irreparable harm to support an injunction. *Id.* Although it denied a motion for a preliminary injunction, the *Goddard* court expressly left open the possibility of monetary damages if the plaintiff could prove it had been harmed.

A covenant against competition implicates competing public policy considerations—Delaware's public policy favoring freedom of contract and the public policy considerations disfavor restraints on competition. *See Lyons Insurance Agency, Inc v. Wark*, 2020 WL 429114 (Del. Ch. Jan. 28, 2020). Thus, the Delaware Court of Chancery has stated that "Delaware courts do not mechanically enforce non-competes." *FP UC Holdings, LLC v. Hamilton*, 2020 WL 1492783 (Mar. 27, 2020). But the Delaware Court of Chancery has also recognized that "An agreement prohibiting 'ordinary competition' is enforced in Delaware so long as the agreement is not 'oppressive to the employee.'" *Cabella's v. Wellman*, 2018 WL 5309954, at *8 (Del. Ch. Oct. 26, 2018).

As a threshold matter, Delaware courts hold that a covenant not to compete is enforceable if it (1) meets general contract law requirements, (2) is reasonable in scope and duration, (3) advances a legitimate economic interest of the party enforcing the covenant, and (4) survives a balance of the equities. *Kan-Di-Ki, LLC v. Suer*, 2015 WL 4503210 (Del. Ch. July 22, 2015); *see Lyons Ins. Agency, Inc. v. Wilson*, 2018 WL 4677606 (Del. Ch. Apr. 29, 2018). General contract law requirements include offer and acceptance and consideration, *American Homepatient v. Collier*, 2006 WL 1134170, at *2 (Del Ch. Apr. 19, 2006), and absence of a material breach excusing performance, *Physiotherapy Corp. v. Moncure*, 2018 WL 1256492 (Del. Ch. Mar. 12, 2018) (employer's elimination of bonus plan that was a material inducement to employee's acceptance of employment relieved the employee of his restrictive covenant); *Take-A-Break Coffee Service, Inc. v. Grose*, 1990 WL 67392, at *3 (Del. Ch. May 14, 1990, *as rev.* May 30, 1990). In balancing the equities, Delaware courts will not enforce a non-competition covenant if it would impose an undue hardship on a former employee. *See Elite Cleaning Co., Inc. v. Capel*, 2006 WL 4782306 (Del. Ch. June 2, 2006) (where a restriction on gainful employment is involved, the sensitivity to the interests affected is heightened); *Bernard Personnel Consultants, Inc. v. Mazarella*, 1990 WL 124969, at *5 (Del. Ch. Aug. 28, 1990) (finding it unconscionable to require personnel agency employee with few assets and no car to choose between commuting to or relocating to an area outside the restricted region or foregoing employment for one year in the only occupation in which she has marketable skills).

Because an action to enforce a non-competition covenant is generally brought in the Delaware Court of Chancery, a court of equity, equitable principles will apply. When injunctive relief is sought, courts will require a plaintiff to establish (1) a likelihood (for a preliminary judgment) or actual (for a permanent injunction) success on the merits, (2) that a failure to grant an injunction will result in irreparable harm, and (3) that the balance of the equities favors injunctive relief. *See, e.g.*,

Vitalink Pharmacy Services, Inc. v, Grancare, Inc., 1997 WL 458494, at *5; *Revolution Retail Sus., LLC v. Sentinel Tech.*, 2015 WL 661, at 22 (Del. Ch. 2015). Delaware courts have recognized that each case is examined on its specific facts and circumstances, particularly in the employment context in which the livelihood of individuals is balanced against the commercial interests of the employer-based nature of the analysis. *McCann Surveyors, Inc. v. Evans*, 611 A.2d 1, 2 (Del. Ch. 1987). Thus, even where a legitimate interest may be present, a Delaware court may award a remedy such as a prohibition on solicitation of customers, rather than a total ban on working in the industry. *See, e.g., Take-A-Break Coffee Service v. Grose*, 1990 WL 67392 (Del. Ch. May 14, 1990, *as rev.* May 30, 1990) (distinguishing employer's legitimate interest in protecting itself against *unfair* competition as opposed to *all* competition). Due to the fact-intensive nature of the inquiry, most of the Delaware decisions addressing non-competition covenants are unreported.

---

2. Have the courts articulated the "legitimate interests" of the franchisor that will support enforcement of a covenant against competition contained in a franchise agreement?

- **If so, what are they (e.g., protection of goodwill, protection of confidential information), and in what contexts did the issue arise?**
- **If not, what interests have been recognized in other contexts (e.g., employment agreements, the sale of business context)?**

As noted above, the dearth of relevant caselaw provides little guidance regarding "legitimate interests" that are specific to a franchise relationship. In *La Bouttica, Ltd v. Clayton*, 1978 WL 4976, at *1 (Del. Ch. Aug. 28,1978), on a motion for a temporary restraining order, the court expressed skepticism that a franchisor licensing retail boutiques could establish irreparable harm from the former franchisee's operation of an independent women's clothing store where the merchandise did not bear the franchisor's label and the franchisor had no other locations in or near Delaware.

In employment cases, Delaware courts have acknowledged that "legitimate interests" include "protection of employer goodwill, and protection of employer confidential information from misuse." *Kan-Di-Ki, LLC v. Suer*, 2015 WL 4503210, at * 20 (Del. Ch. July 22, 2015). When a sales representative accepts employment with a competitor of the former employer, the employer's confidential information may include customer lists, pricing, trade secrets, and other proprietary information. *Sensus USA Inc., v. Franklin*, 2016 WL 1466488 (Apr. 14, 2016) (where employee had key knowledge about employer's technology; had held positions in business development and sales that involved cultivating client relationships; had worked with employer's largest customers; and knew its pricing, negotiation approach, and business strategy, barring him from working with a direct competitor protected employer's legitimate business interests). *Elite Cleaning Co., Inc. v. Capel*, 2006 WL 4782306 (Del. Ch. June 2, 2006) (recognizing a company's interest in preventing its employees from "cutting out the middleman" by directly soliciting and serving the company's customers). *But see KPMG Peat Marwick LLP v. Fernandez*, 709 A.2d 1160, 1165 (Del. Ch. 1998) (courts will scrutinize a provision preventing a former employee from competing for the business of clients of the former employer with whom the employee had no contact or relationship during the term of employment).

The fact that an employer devoted resources toward an employee's certification or membership in the certifying organization does not give the employer a legitimate interest in preventing that employee from capitalizing on those credentials in competition with the former employer. *RHIS, Inc. v. Boyce*, 2001 WL 1192203, at *6 (Del. Ch. Sept. 26, 2001) (holding that the employee and not the employer owns "both his membership in [the certifying body] and the right to exploit it commercially"); *see also Bernard Personnel Consultants, Inc. v. Mazarella*, 1990 WL 124969 (Del. Ch. Aug. 28, 1990) ("[a]n employee who achieves technical expertise or general knowledge while in the employ of another may thereafter use that knowledge in competition with his former employer, so long as he does not use or disclose protected trade secrets in the process.").

At least one Delaware case holds that "[t]he legitimate economic interests of an employer in restricting the substantially similar activities of an independent contractor will be more limited than they would be with respect to an employee." *Edix Media Group, Inc. v, Mahani*, 2006 WL 3742595 (Del. Ch. Dec. 12, 2006). The justification for the more rigorous scrutiny stems from the employer's reduced investment in the contractor, including lack of responsibility for payment of benefits, and reduced investment of firm-specific know-how. Accordingly, restricting an independent contractor from engaging in "substantially similar" activities is more likely to be "both inequitable to the contractor and against public policy." As such, to the extent that a provision in a non-competition agreement prohibiting a person who, as an independent contractor, sold advertising for the plaintiff's magazine and website geared toward enthusiasts of after-market automotive enhancements, following termination of the contract, from performance services peripheral to or unrelated to advertising to car enthusiasts failed to serve a legitimate economic interest.

DE

When a non-competition agreement arises in connection with the sale of a business, Delaware courts tend to give much more latitude to a buyer's restrictions against the seller competing, since the buyer has paid significant consideration to the seller to acquire the goodwill of the business. *See, e.g., Kan-Di-Ki, LLC v. Suer*, 2015 WL 4503210 (Del. Ch. July 22, 2015); *O'Leary v. Telecom Resources Service, LLC*, 2011 WL 379300 (Del. Super. Ct. 2011); *Concord Steel, Inc. v. Wilmington Steel Processing Co., Inc.*, 2009 WL 3161643 (Del. Ch. Sept. 30, 2009); *Tristate Courier and Carriage, Inc. v. Berryman*, 2004 WL 835886 (Del. Ch. Apr. 15, 2004).

3. What time limitations have courts recognized as reasonable in the franchise context?

- **If no franchise cases have been decided, what time limitations have been recognized in other contexts?**
- **How have they been related to the interests protected?**

As noted, since no Delaware case reaches the merits of a covenant against competition in a franchise context, no particular duration has been blessed in a franchise case. Indeed, the analysis in employment cases focuses more on the business sector in which the employer operates and the role of the employee. *Sensus USA Inc., v. Franklin*, 2016 WL 1466488, at *7 (Apr. 14, 2016) ("Delaware courts have consistently found that two-year restrictions on covenants not to compete are reasonable, especially in industries where business transactions take years to conclude.").

Delaware courts have recognized different durational restrictions as reasonable in the employment context depending on the facts of the particular case. For example, in the charter bus and tour bus industry, a three-year term was deemed unreasonable because "price is the most important factor in preserving a customer base" and over a three-year period, plans would change and customers would turn over. *Delaware Express Shuttle, Inc. v. Older*, 2002 WL 31458243, at * 14 (Del. Ch. Oct. 23, 2002). Restrictive covenants with a two-year term have generally been upheld. *See Weichert Co. v. Young*, 2007 WL 4372823 (Del. Ch. Dec. 7, 2007) (noting that the only instances in which a two-year duration were found unreasonable involved unskilled workers with no specialized training or goodwill that was valuable for less than two years); *American Homepatient, Inc. v. Collier*, 2006 WL 1134170 (Del. Ch. Apr. 19, 2006) (one-year duration was valid and enforceable). But a two-year period is not automatically enforced. In *RHIS, Inc. v. Boyce*, 2001 WL 19192203, at * 6–7 (Del. Ch. Sept. 26, 2001), the Delaware Court of Chancery found that, because realtors do not have exclusive relationships with home inspection companies and the plaintiff typically received three to four referrals per year from the typical realtor relationship, a two-year non-solicitation restriction was unreasonable and reduced the term to one year.

Delaware courts are more likely to enforce non-competition agreements with longer durations where a sale of a business is involved. *See Kan-Di-Ki, LLC v. Suer*, 2015 WL 4503210, at *52 (Del. Ch. July 22, 2015) (noting that restrictive covenants five years in length have been found reasonable as part of the sale of a business as a going concern); *O'Leary v. Telecom Res. Service, LLC*, 2011 WL 379300 (Del. Super. Ct. 2011) (finding that the four-year duration of the restrictive covenant was "particularly reasonable considering that it was part of the sale of a business"). In an older case that is still good law, the Delaware Supreme Court found a ten-year restriction to be reasonable. *Tull v. Turek*, 147 A.2d 658 (Del. 1958).

4. What geographic limitations have courts recognized as reasonable in the franchise context?

- **How have they been related to the interests protected?**
- **Have courts recognized the legitimacy of protecting other franchisees from competition?**

No reported Delaware decision addresses the issue of geographic reasonableness in a franchise context, although as noted above, in denying a motion for injunctive relief, the Court of Chancery in *La Bouttica, Ltd v. Clayton* made note of the absence of other nearby franchised locations. In an employment context, the focus is often on protecting an employer's goodwill in the market in which the employer has its customer base. *Delaware Express Shuttle v. Older*, 2002 WL 31458243, at *13 (Del. Ch. Oct. 23, 2002); *Norton Petrol. Corp. v. Cameron*, 1998 WL 118198, at *4 (Del. Ch. Mar. 5, 1998).

Lack of an express geographic limit is not necessarily fatal to enforceability of a restrictive covenant. Because the purpose of a geographic limitation is to protect an employer's goodwill in a given market, the reasonableness of a geographic scope "should not be judged merely in terms of geographic distances." *Delaware Express Shuttle v. Older*, 2002 WL 31458243, at *13 (Del. Ch. Oct. 23, 2002). Thus, a non-compete prohibiting direct competition or customer solicitation "inherently establish[es] a geographic limit that ultimately protects the legitimate economic interests of the employer and provide a reasonable and foreseeable basis for ascertaining the territorial scope of the covenant not to compete, even if no geographic limitation is expressly set forth in the agreement." *Id.; see also Lyons Insurance Agency Inc. v. Wilson*, 2018 WL 4677606, at *15 (Sept. 28, 2018) (a non-competition covenant with a reasonable temporal limitation, but no specific geographic scope, was not per se invalid because it prohibited activities competitive with those of the former employer and therefore protected legitimate economic interests).

Similar considerations will support a nationwide geographic scope if the time period and the breadth of the restriction are reasonably tailored to protect the employer's business. *See, e.g., Research and Trading Corp. v. Powell*, 468 A.2d 1301 (Del. Ch. 1983) (upholding a restrictive covenant prohibiting individuals from accepting employment at a business entity directly or indirectly in competition with employer in the sale of any products in the entire continental United States).

DE

In considering the geographic reach of a covenant not to compete, Delaware courts have enforced broader geographic restrictions in connection with the sale of a business. The Chancery Court in *FP UC Holdings, LLC v. Hamilton*, 2020 WL 1492783, at *7 (Del. Ch. Mar. 27, 2020), noted: "These broader restrictions make senses following the sale of a business. The buyer has just paid handsomely for the business and the broad non-compete clears the seller from the competitive space while the buyer strives to make the business he just bought successful." Similarly, the Chancery Court has noted in connection with the sale of a business "Delaware law does not impose a strict requirement that the area covered by the covenant map perfectly onto the geographical area of the plaintiff's business." *Kan-Di-Ki, LLC v. Suer*, 2015 WL 4503210, at *20 (Del. Ch. July 22, 2015) (enforcing a non-competition agreement that covered 23 states west of the Mississippi River, notwithstanding that at the time the contracts were executed, the plaintiff's operations were limited to Delaware and California, but it had affiliates doing business in six Midwest states and had since expanded into all but five of the covered states).

5. What limitations on activities have courts recognized as reasonable in the franchise context?

As noted, there are no cases directly addressing non-competition covenants in franchise relationships; therefore, no specific restrictive covenants have been upheld in the franchise context. However, Delaware courts have acknowledged the legitimacy of prohibitions on competing directly with an employer, soliciting customers or prospects of a former employer, or interference with customer relationships, confidentiality provisions and restrictions on contacting or soliciting customers of the former employer, as well as general prohibitions on setting up a competing business.

Delaware courts have enforced a three-year worldwide restriction covenant allocating markets for currency-sorting products by price point agreed to when the defendant, which had formed the plaintiff to develop and sell a product with premium features, spun off as part of a change in control. *Revolution Retail Systems LLC v. Sentinel Technologies Inc.*, 2015 WL 6611601 (Del. Ch. Oct. 30, 2015), *order clarified*

November 5, 2015. Where the former parent began to market a competitive product prior to the expiration of the restrictive covenants, the court relied on contractual affirmations that the restrictions were reasonable and necessary to protect the goodwill of the parties and that the parties would not have consummated the divestiture transaction (including certain technology licenses) without them.

A covenant prohibiting a former office manager of a realtor's office from solicitating employees and independent contractors of his former employer protects a valid interest in preserving its goodwill and protecting its relationship with its employees and the considerable resources it devoted to training them and helping them obtain their licenses. *Weichert Co. of Pennsylvania v. Young*, 2007 WL 4372823, at *4 (Del. Ch. Dec. 7, 2007).

Delaware courts will also scrutinize liquidated damages provisions in non-competition agreements and "will not enforce them if they function as coercive penalties." *Lyons Insurance Agency Inc. v. Wark*, 2020 WL 429114, at *4 (Del. Ch. Jan. 8, 2020) (where the former employer's customer's migration to the former employee's new employer was not attributable to a breach by the former employee of her non-solicitation covenant, the liquidated damages remedy did not support the employer's interest in preventing loss due to ex-employee competition; thus, the liquidated damages clause was unenforceable as a penalty). But a liquidated damages provision is enforceable if the actual damages are difficult to ascertain, the contract establishes "a good faith estimation" of forecast damages, and the damages are rationally related to the injury that resulted from a breach. *Delaware Bay Surgical Services, P.A. v. Swier*, 900 A.2d 646, 650–51 (Del. 2006) (citing *S. H. Deliveries, Inc. v. TriState Courier & Carriage*, 1997 WL 817883 (Del. Ch. May 21, 1997) and *Lee Builders, Inc. v. Wells*, 103 A.2d 918 (Del. Ch. 1954)).

6. Does the state recognize a difference between in-term and post-term covenants?

No reported Delaware case has directly addressed this issue. However, Delaware courts have upheld non-competition agreements that prohibit an employee from competing with the employer both during the time of employment and for a period of time following termination. *Badger Holding LLC v. Kirsch*, 2018 WL 4709563 (Del. Ch. Oct. 1, 2018) (a valid covenant may restrict competition during the term of the employee's employment and for two years after termination); *Research & Trading Corp. v Powell*, 468 A.2d 1301, 1305 (Del. Ch. 1983). The Delaware Chancery Court has enforced non-competition provisions in joint venture documents prohibiting a party from engaging in the business of the joint venture except through the joint venture during the term of the venture and for a period of one year thereafter. *Symbiont.io, Inc. v. Ipreo Holdings, LLC*, 2021 WL 3575709, at *26 (Del. Ch. Aug. 13, 2021); *see also eCommerce Industries, Inc. v. MWA Intelligence, Inc.*, 2013 WL 5621678, at *22–27 (Del. Ch. Oct. 4, 2013) (assessing whether the parties breached mutual non-compete provisions applicable during term of an exclusive license agreement). But the Delaware District Court in *Goddard Systems, Inc. v. Gondal*, C.A No. 17-1003-CJB (D. Del. Mar. 29, 2018) (Business Franchise Guide ¶ 16,167), expressly acknowledged that the Goddard School franchise agreement contained both in-term and post-term covenants and analyzed the alleged breaches of both, albeit under Pennsylvania law.

7. Has the state allowed enforcement of covenants against non-signatories (e.g., family members, newly formed corporations)?

While no Delaware case has addressed this issue directly in the franchise context, Delaware courts have refused to enforce a restrictive covenant against non-signatories to the franchise agreement containing the restrictive covenant. *See Caldwell Flexible Staffing, Inc. v. Mays*, 1976 WL 1716 (Del. Ch. Nov. 29, 1976) (franchisee who converted to independent business could not enforce restrictive covenants against former employees whose obligations under the restrictive covenants were to the prior franchise operation).

Delaware courts have issued orders granting injunctive relief against a former employee and the companies through which the former employee now conducts business. *See, e.g., Weichert Co. of Pennsylvania v. Young*, 2007 WL 4372823 (Del. Ch. Dec. 7, 2007) (injunctive relief extended to defendants Colonial Real Estate Services, LLC and Colonia Real Estate Group, LLC, through which defendant Young conducted his real estate business). The Delaware Court of Chancery has recognized that where a party to a restrictive covenant agrees that neither it nor its affiliates will engage in a competitive business, competing activities by an affiliate constitute a breach by the party bound by the agreement. *Symbiont.io Inv. v. Ipreo Holdings LLC*, 2021 WL 3575709, at *27 (Del. Ch. Aug. 13, 2021).

A competitor who solicits the key employee responsible for a customer relationship in order to help secure that client's business with knowledge that the employee is bound by a non-competition agreement and induces that key employee to induce his co-workers to join him may be found liable for tortious interference with contract and may be enjoined from performing services for that customer. *Hough Associates, Inc. v. Hill*, 2007 WL 148751 (Del. Ch. Jan. 17, 2007); *see also eCommerce Industries, Inc. v. MWA Intelligence, Inc.*, 2013 WL 5621678 (Del. Ch. Oct. 4, 2013) (sister company and a parent company found liable for tortious interference with contract and interference with prospective business advantage for aiding and abetting a breach by their affiliate).

DE

8. Will the state modify, "blue-pencil," or otherwise reduce a covenant found to be overbroad?

In recent years, the Delaware Court of Chancery has acknowledged that while it has "discretion to blue pencil an overly broad non-compete to make its restrictions more reasonable," as a court of equity, it also may exercise discretion "not to allow an employer to 'back away from an overly broad covenant by proposing to enforce it to a lesser extent than written.'" *FP UC Holdings, LLC v. Hamilton*, 2020 WL 1492783 (Del. Ch. Mar. 27, 2020) ("whether to blue pencil [a] non-compete is a fact-intensive question"). Thus, where a non-compete barred a licensed nurse practitioner from working in any capacity for an urgent care clinic anywhere the plaintiff ran clinics or proposed to operate, the Vice Chancellor denied a preliminary injunction, noting "serious doubts that the Court would be inclined to rewrite the clause to make it more reasonable as a matter of equity" even on a more developed factual record. In *Delaware Elevator, Inc. v. Williams*, while reluctantly enforcing a Maryland law-governed non-competition agreement, Vice Chancellor Laster expressed frustration with overbroad non-compete agreements, stating, "If an employer knows that the court will enforce a reasonable covenant as a fallback, the employer has every reason to start with an overbroad provision." 2011 WL 1005181, at *10 (Del. Ch. Mar. 16, 2011). Noting the lack of bargaining power and resources available to mid- to low-level employees, the Vice Chancellor stated, "These same concerns lead me to conclude that when a restrictive convent is unreasonable, the court should strike the provision in its entirety. [citations omitted] The threat of losing all protection gives employers an incentive to restrict themselves to reasonable clauses." *Id.*

As a court of equity, the Delaware Court of Chancery will under appropriate circumstances reduce an overly broad geographic restriction to make it reasonable under the circumstances. *See, e.g., Singh v. Batta Environmental Services*, 2003 WL 21309115, at *8 (Del. Ch. May 21, 2003) (geographic scope reduced from within 200 miles of any employer location to the state of Delaware, where 90 percent of the employer's customers were); *Norton Petroleum Corp. v. Cameron*, 1998 WL 118198, at *4 (Del. Ch. Mar. 5, 1998) (territory reduced from a 100-mile radius to a 20-mile radius, where the bulk of the former employer's customers were located, and prohibited defendant from selling only the products sold by the former employer, rather than all petroleum products); *Knowles-Zeswitz Music, Inc. v. Cara*, 260 A.2d 171 (Del. Ch. 1969) (geographic scope reduced from 100 miles from former place of employment or 25 miles from certain school districts to those school districts for which former employee was sole sales representative during final year of employment). Delaware courts have also demonstrated a willingness to impose a geographic limit in enforcing an agreement with a reasonable duration but no express geographic territory, especially where the agreement in question proscribes activities "in competition with" the employer's business rather than activities that are merely similar to the employer's business. *Lyons Insurance Agency, Inc., v. Wilson*, 2018 WL 4677606, at *5 (Del. Ch. Apr. 29, 2018) (citing *Delaware Express Shuttle, Inc. v. Older*, 2002 WL 31458243 (Del. Ch. Oct. 23, 2002)). In *Delaware Express Shuttle*, the court narrowed the unbounded geographic scope of the covenant at issue to the portions of New Castle County, Delaware, and neighboring Elkton, Maryland, in which the employer's customers were concentrated. 2002 WL 31458243, at *13.

Delaware courts have also reduced an excessive time period in a non-competition covenant. In *RHIS, Inc. v. Boyce*, 2001 WL 1192203 (Del. Ch. Sept. 26, 2001), the operator of a home-inspection business sued to enforce a covenant not to compete against a former employee that, among other things, prohibited the employee from soliciting business or referrals from his former employer's sources for a period of two years following termination. The court limited the durational time period of the covenant to one year, noting that clientele in the home-inspection industry is both non-exclusive and relatively fluid. *Id.* at *7.

9. When does a non-compete period begin to run? Will courts equitably extend the term?

Delaware courts will look to the contractual language to determine when the time period of a covenant not to compete begins to run. Where an employment agreement provides that the employee will not compete for a defined period of time following termination of employment, the non-compete period commences on the date the termination is effective. *Continental Warranty, Inc. v. Warner*, 108 F. Supp. 3d 256 (D. Del. 2015); *All Pro Maids, Inc. v. Layton*, 2004 WL 1878784 (Del. Ch. Aug. 9, 2004); *Norton Petroleum Corp. v. Cameron*, 1998 WL 118198 (Del. Ch. Mar. 5, 1998); *RHIS, Inc. v.*

Boyce, 2001 WL 1192203 (Del. Ch. Sept. 26, 2001). Beyond the employment context, a contractual provision restricting competition is generally effective when the contract takes effect. *See inTEAM Associates, LLC v. Heartland Payment Systems, Inc.*, 2016 WL 5660282 (Del. Ch. Sept. 30, 2016) (covenants not to compete ran for a period of five years following the closing date of an asset purchase agreement and co-marketing agreement); *O'Leary v. Telecom Resources Service, LLC*, 2011 WL 379300 (Del. Super. Ct. 2011) (covenant ran for a period of four years following the closing date of an asset purchase agreement); *Tristate Courier and Carriage, Inc. v. Berryman*, 2004 WL 835886 (Del. Ch. Apr. 15, 2004) (covenant ran for a period of two years following the closing date of a stock purchase agreement). If the duration of a covenant restricting competition is unclear, Delaware courts will examine the contractual language and conduct of the parties. In *Badger Holding LLC v. Kirsch*, the Court of Chancery found that a non-compete agreement embedded in a four-year employment contract was still binding on the employee after the expiration of four years because a supplementary stock contract contained a similar provision and because he "seamlessly" continued to be employed in the same position and on the same terms.

As a court of equity, the Court of Chancery may, given appropriate circumstances, equitably toll the running of the term for a period equal to the period during which the covenants were violated. *See, e.g., inTEAM Assocs. LLC v. Heartland Payment Systems Inc.*, 2016 WL 5660282, at *28 (Del. Ch. Sept. 30, 2016). In *inTEAM Assocs. LLC v. Heartland Payment Sys. Inc.*, because Heartland received only four and one half years of non-solicitation rather than the five for which it bargained, the Court of Chancery extended the non-solicitation term for six months beyond its original expiration. 2016 WL 5660282, at *28 (Del. Ch. Sept. 30, 2016). On appeal, the Delaware Supreme Court found that the Court of Chancery did not abuse its discretion by equitably extending the term of the non-competition agreement. *Heartland Payment Systems, LLC v. inTEAM Associates, LLC*, 171 A.3d 544, 547 (Del. 2017); *see also Norton Petroleum Corp. v. Cameron*, 1998 WL 118198, at *5 (Del. Ch. Mar. 5, 1998) (permanent injunction ran for three years from the date a temporary restraining order was issued); *but see KPMG Peat Marwick LLP v. Fernandez*, 709 A.2d 1160 (Del. Ch. 1998) (denying request to extend two-year term by an additional six months, finding insufficient evidence that the defendants acted in bad faith).

But Delaware courts will not equitably extend the term of a non-competition covenant after the contractual term has lapsed. *All Pro Maids, Inc. v. Layton*, 2004 WL 1878784, at *12 (Del. Ch. Aug. 9, 2004); *Tansey-Warner, Inc. v. Phelan*, 1999 WL 182578 (Del. Ch. Mar. 30, 1999).

The Delaware Court of Chancery will enforce a contractual provision tolling the non-compete period during the continuance of a breach. *See Concord Steel, Inc. v. Wilmington Steel Processing Co., Inc.*, 2009 WL 3161643, at *16 (Del. Ch. Sept. 30, 2009) (where contract provided that a party's breach would toll the running of non-compete period for as long as such breach continues; upon finding that a breach lasted 51 weeks, the court extended the duration of the covenant for that amount of time. *Id.*).

10. Are there additional nuances or peculiarities of the state's treatment of covenants in the franchising context?

There are no additional nuances or peculiarities that have been identified under Delaware law with respect to enforcement of covenants against competition in the franchise context.

In several recent Delaware cases, the courts have declined to enforce a Delaware governing law clause in the face of a strong public policy disfavoring noncompetition agreements in the jurisdiction whose law would otherwise control. *See, e.g., AG Resource Holdings, LLC v. Terral*, 2021 WL 486831 (Del. Ch. Feb 10, 2021) (granting a stay as to employment agreement claims pending resolution of Louisiana case but denying a motion to dismiss as to claims arising under a limited liability company agreement for a Delaware limited liability company, the internal affairs of which are governed by Delaware law); *Focus Fin. Partners, LLC v. Holsopple*¸ 241 A.3d 784 (Del. Ch. 2020); *Ascension Ins. Holdings, LLC v. Underwood*, 2015 WL 356002, at *2 (Del. Ch. Jan. 28, 2015) (noting that Delaware follows the RESTATEMENT (SECOND) OF CONFLICT OF LAWS). In *Ascension*, most of the contacts were with the state of California, where the contract would be void, except that the plaintiff was a Delaware limited liability company with its principal place of business and most of its operations in California. Accordingly, the interests of the State of California trumped Delaware's interest in supporting freedom of contract. *Id.* at *5.

Delaware law regulates covenants not to compete by certain professionals, namely physicians and attorneys. Section 2707 of the Delaware Code chapter governing contracts invalidates an "employment, partnership or corporate agreement between and/or among physicians" restricting a physician's right to practice medicine in a specified territory and for a defined time period after termination of employment or affiliation. 6 *Del. C.* § 2707. While a covenant purportedly preventing a physician from moving to a competing practice is void, a liquidated damages clause tied to the loss of business by the former practice is expressly permitted under Section 2707. *Id.; Saez v. Nephrology Associates*, 2019 WL 5207918, at *3 (Del. Super. Ct. Oct. 26, 2019). Section 2707 does not prohibit a restriction on a physician's ability to see patients "on the side" while employed. Where a doctor who practices medicine outside of Delaware is bound by a contract that selects Delaware law as the governing law, Delaware courts have suggested that Section 2707 is not implicated, finding it unlikely that the Delaware legislature intended Section 2707 to have extra-territorial application. *Bakotic v. Bako Pathology LP*, 2019 WL 6896465 (Del. Super. Ct. Dec. 11, 2019); *Dunn v. Fastmed Urgent Care, P.C.*, 2019 WL 66011724131010, at *14 (Del. Ch. Aug. 30,2019); (holding Section 2707 inapplicable because contract only prohibited the defendant from working as an executive and expressly permitted him to practice medicine).

Similarly, pursuant to the Delaware Lawyers' Rules of Professional Conduct ("DLRPC") prohibit it is unethical for a lawyer to offer or enter into (1) a partnership agreement, shareholders agreement or the equivalent that restricts the right of a lawyer to practice after termination of the relationship, except for an agreement relating to benefits on retirement, or (2) an agreement restricting a lawyer's right to practice as part of a settlement of a client controversy. DLRPC Rule 5.6.

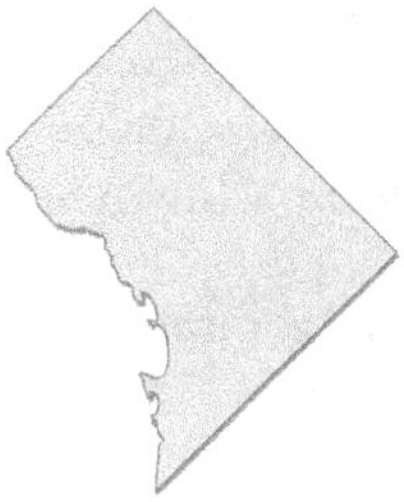

District of Columbia

*by Michael L. Sturm**

1. Has the District of Columbia addressed covenants against competition in the context of franchising?

- **Does the District of Columbia have a franchising statute or regulations that address covenants against competition?**
- **Does the District of Columbia have a covenants statute of general applicability that would encompass franchise covenants?**
- **Have the courts addressed covenants in the context of franchising either under a statute or under the District's common law?**

There is presently no statute in the District of Columbia that directly regulates the franchise relationship. In 1989, the District enacted a franchise relationship statute, but that statute did not address covenants against competition. District of Columbia Franchising Act of 1988, D.C. CODE ANN. § 29-1201 *et seq.* (1989). The statute was repealed in 1998 and has not been reinstated or replaced. *See* D.C. LAW 12-86 (1998).

Although there is no franchise-specific legislation, covenants not to compete have been the subject of intense legislative activity in the District of Columbia in recent years. In 2020, the D.C. City Council passed a broad ban on non-compete agreements, but the planned effective date of that legislation was repeatedly extended and ultimately it never took effect. *See* D.C. LAW 23-563 (2021). In July 2022, the D.C. Council passed the Non-Compete Clarification Emergency Amendment Act of 2022, D.C. CODE ANN. § 32-581.01 *et seq.* (2022). By its terms, this statute voids most covenants not to compete entered after October 1, 2022 with employees who make less than $150,000 annually in total compensation (adjusted for inflation). *Id.* § 32-581.02. Covenants with "highly compensated employees" are restricted but not banned. *Id.* § 32-581.03. Franchises are not directly addressed

*Mr. Sturm is a partner in the Washington, D.C. office of the law firm of Lathrop GPM LLP. He is a member of the District of Columbia bar. Mr. Sturm wishes to thank Cameron Johnson, an associate in the D.C. office of Lathrop GPM LLP, for his contributions to this chapter.

in the legislation, and the definitions of "employer" and "employee" would not naturally appear to encompass franchisors and franchisees, respectively. *See id.* § 32-581.01(7)(A)(i) (defining an "employee" in part as "an individual who performs work for pay in the District on behalf of an employer"). The legislation contains a specific exclusion for otherwise lawful non-compete provisions entered between a seller and a buyer in connection with the sale of a business. *See id.* § 32-581.01(15)AB).

It is unclear how, if at all, passage of the statute may affect future common law enforcement of covenants that fall outside its scope. Prior to the effective date of the originally proposed statute, one court rejected preemptive consideration of the statute to modify the District's existing common law. The court noted that the ban reflected in the new statute was not in effect "and, in any event, applies only to non-compete agreements formed after the law's effective date." *M3 USA Corp. v. Qamoum*, No. 20-2903 (RDM), 2021 WL 2292266, at *18 (D.D.C. June 4, 2021). Thus, according to the court, any alleged "'trend' [against enforcement of non-compete agreements] has . . . arrived too late to help [the defendants] in this case." *Id.* The statute as enacted is more nuanced and notably less hostile to non-compete agreements, removing the ban on non-compete agreements for highly compensated employees and recognizing that employers have a legitimate interest in protecting confidential and proprietary information. D.C. Code Ann. § 32-581.01(15)(B)(1). Still, it is possible that D.C. common law will evolve substantially in the coming years, and practitioners will need to consider both the direct applicability of the statute and the extent to which the common law may have changed. As a result of the passage of the statute, it is clear that many covenants that would have been upheld under the existing common law rules will no longer be valid if entered into after October 1, 2022.

While not focused on covenants against competition, the District of Columbia Antitrust Act of 1980, D.C. Code Ann. § 28-4501 *et seq.* (2001), generally prohibits "unreasonable restraints of trade and monopolistic acts." Committee on the Judiciary, Report on the District of Columbia Antitrust Act of 1980, Bill 3-107, at 1 (1980), *quoted in Ellis v. James V. Hurson Associates*, 565 A.2d 615, 618 n.12 (D.C. 1989). In addressing the enforceability of covenants against competition, however, District of Columbia courts have not given independent weight to this statutory provision, but have focused instead on common law principles. *See, e.g., Ellis*, 565 A.2d at 618 n.12 (noting origin of antitrust statute in common law restraint of trade principles).

There are few District of Columbia decisions addressing covenants against competition in the context of franchising. In a case involving the sale of two Five Guys franchised restaurants, the U.S. District Court for the District of Columbia held that a covenant that precluded the sellers from operating a competing restaurant within four blocks was not violated by the sellers' operation of a restaurant more than four blocks away. *B&H National Place, Inc. v. Beresford*, 850 F. Supp. 2d 251 (D.D.C. 2012). The court rejected any expansion of the contractual covenant beyond the geographic limit specified in the plain language. In dictum, the court also noted the principle in D.C. law that "non-compete agreements should be construed narrowly so as to be reasonable." *Id.* at 258 (citing *Deutsch v. Barsky*, 795 A.2d 669, 648–78 (D.C. 2002)). Because the conduct at issue fell outside the literal scope of the covenant, however, there was no occasion to consider whether the covenant would need to be narrowed in order to survive scrutiny.

2. Have the courts articulated the "legitimate interests" of the franchisor that will support enforcement of a covenant against competition contained in a franchise agreement?

- **If so, what are they (e.g., protection of goodwill, protection of confidential information), and in what contexts did the issue arise?**
- **If not, what interests have been recognized in other contexts (e.g., employment agreements, the sale of business context)?**

No District of Columbia court has directly addressed the interests of a franchisor that would support the enforcement of a franchisee's non-competition covenant. The decisions of the District of Columbia courts do, however, identify many of the types of interests that franchisors can assert to support the enforcement of an agreed covenant.

In a 1989 case involving a non-competition covenant in an employment contract, the District of Columbia Court of Appeals adopted the RESTATEMENT (SECOND) OF CONTRACTS formulation of the law governing covenants in restraint of trade, which states that a covenant against competition ancillary to an otherwise valid transaction or relationship is nevertheless invalid as an unreasonable restraint of trade if:

(a) the restraint is greater than is needed to protect the promisee's legitimate interest, or
(b) the promisee's need is outweighed by the hardship to the promisor and the likely injury to the public.

RESTATEMENT (SECOND) OF CONTRACTS § 188 (1981), *quoted in Ellis v. James V. Hurson Associates*, 565 A.2d 615, 618 (D.C. 1989). Subsequent decisions have confirmed the continuing applicability of these principles. *See Deutsch v. Barsky*, 795 A.2d 669, 674–76 (D.C. 2002) (reviewing the prior District of Columbia caselaw concerning covenants against competition and reaffirming the applicability of the RESTATEMENT principles); *Dyer v. Bilaal*, 983 A.2d 349, 359 n.10 (D.C. 2009) (summarily affirming enforceability of covenant and citing *Ellis* and *Deutsch*); *Robert Half Int'l Inc. v. Billingham*, 315 F. Supp. 2d 419, 430–31 (D.D.C. 2018) (upholding covenant and granting preliminary injunction, citing *Ellis* and *Deutsch*).

The RESTATEMENT specifically recognizes the employer's interest in preventing a former employee from soliciting the employer's customers as warranting protection. *See Ellis*, 565 A.2d at 619; *see also Robert Half*, 315 F. Supp. 3d at 430; *Morgan Stanley DW Inc. v. Rothe*, 150 F. Supp. 2d 67, 74 (D.D.C. 2001) (recognizing the employer's interest in "prevent[ing] potentially harmful interference with its crucial client base").

In addition to the employer's interest in protecting its client base and accounts, courts in the District of Columbia have also recognized an employer's interests in protecting (1) its trade secrets and confidential information, (2) its business or goodwill, (3) its investment in its employee, (4) the fruits of the employee's services during employment, and (5) the fiduciary duty of the employee to the employer. *Hospitality Staffing Solutions, LLC v. Reyes*, 736 F. Supp. 2d 192, 199 (D.D.C. 2010) ("restrictions . . . are limited in duration and appear to be limited to protecting [plaintiff's] business interests in the relevant market by preventing [defendant] from using [plaintiff's] information to attract employees or customers to a competitor"); *Mercer Management Consulting, Inc. v. Wilde*, 920 F. Supp. 219, 237 (D.D.C. 1996) (recognizing the employer's interest in "protect[ing] the investment [the employer] made in its employees, preserv[ing] the confidentiality of information gleaned in the course of employment [with the employer], and protect[ing] itself from its employees leaving and capitalizing on [the employer's] client base"). Notably, even the new statute excludes from its reach "[a]n otherwise lawful provision" that restricts the employee from disclosing the employer's confidential or proprietary information. D.C. CODE ANN. § 32-581.01(15)(B)(1).

In the franchise context, the franchisor has an interest in protecting not only its trade secrets, confidential information, and goodwill, but also the integrity of its business and brand. The franchisor's ability to recruit and retain franchisees depends on the extent to which the franchisor can maintain uniformity and control over its trademarks and system. Although the District of Columbia courts have not addressed the issue, this unique aspect of the franchise relationship suggests that franchise covenants against competition might be afforded somewhat more liberal treatment than similar covenants in the employment context. The District of Columbia courts historically have applied a liberal standard to covenants against competition given by the seller of a business. *See Cox v. Helvering*, 71 F.2d 987, 988 (D.C. Cir. 1934) (recognizing the buyer's interest in "the enjoyment of the fruits of the contract"). Consistent with this principle, the newly enacted statute does not prohibit "[a]n otherwise lawful provision contained within or executed contemporaneously with an agreement between the seller of a business and one or more buyers of that business wherein the seller agrees not to compete with the buyer's business." D.C. CODE ANN. § 32-581.01(15)(A).

Some District of Columbia courts also give weight to the fact of covenantor's prior agreement. As the U.S. District Court for the District of Columbia stated in enforcing an anti-solicitation provision:

> In what borders on a desperate attempt to justify the conduct at issue, the defendant maintains that "what [the plaintiff] is complaining of here is nothing more than standard industry practice." On the face of the present record, the defendant appears to advance the notion that standard industry practice in the financial services industry involves routinely breaching contracts. Hopefully, this is not the case. Instead, the court expects that when an employee signs a contract agreeing not to solicit his former clients for one year upon leaving his old firm, the employee will honor it.

Morgan Stanley DW Inc. v. Rothe, 150 F. Supp. 2d 67, 75–76 (D.D.C. 2001); *see also Dyer v. Bilaal*, 983 A.2d 349, 359 (D.C. 2009) (noting that "[i]t was [the bound party] who affirmatively offered" the provision claimed to be unenforceable). D.C. courts on occasion also have looked to covenants required by an employee's new employer in assessing the reasonableness of a covenant entered into with the prior employer. *Robert Half*, 315 F. Supp. 3d at 431 (citing more onerous terms of the new employer's non-compete provision as evidence of reasonableness of former employer's agreement).

---

3. What time limitations have courts recognized as reasonable in the franchise context? If no franchise cases have been decided, what time limitations have been recognized in other contexts?

- **How have they been related to the interests protected?**

No published decisions have addressed time limitations in covenants against competition in the franchise context.

In the context of the sale of a business, the courts have upheld time limits on competition by the seller for as long as the purchaser owns the purchased business, *Allison v. Seigle*, 79 F.2d 170, 171 (D.C. Cir. 1935) (per curiam); for ten years after the sale of the business, *Burton, Parsons & Co. v. Parsons*, 146 F. Supp. 114, 115 (D.D.C. 1956); and for four years after the sale of the business, *Citibank (S.D.), N.A. v. FDIC*, 857 F. Supp. 976, 978 (D.D.C. 1994). In the context of the dissolution of a "partnership" between two dentists, which the court essentially treated as the sale of a business interest, the District of Columbia Court of Appeals held that a mutual two-year restriction was not facially invalid. *Deutsch v. Barsky*, 795 A.2d 669, 676–77 (D.C. 2002) (remanding for further proceedings). The exception in the statutory ban for covenants ancillary to the sale of a business does not include a specific durational limit. D.C. CODE ANN. § 32-581.01(5)(B).

In the context of employment contracts, the courts generally have enforced limits on competition by employees during the term of employment and for periods of one to three years after termination of employment. *Robert Half Int'l Inc. v. Billingham*, 315 F. Supp. 2d 419, 430–31 (D.D.C. 2018) (collecting cases); *M3 USA Corp. v. Qamoum*, No. 20-2903 (RDM), 2021 WL 2292266, at *17 (D.D.C. June 4, 2021) (upholding one-year covenant and noting *Robert Half* discussion of covenants lasting one to three years after termination). Some earlier decisions enforced more lengthy covenants. *See Erikson v. Hawley*, 12 F.2d 491, 492 (D.C. Cir. 1926) (ten years after employment); *Meyer v. Wineburgh*, 110 F. Supp. 957, 959 (D.D.C. 1953) (five years after employment), *aff'd*, 221 F.2d 543 (D.C. Cir. 1955). One federal court held that a three-year post-employment covenant against competition was invalid, finding the length of the covenant unreasonable given that the parties were engaged in a business involving unskilled, manual labor and no significant trade secrets. *Chemical Fireproofing Corp. v. Krouse*, 155 F.2d 422, 423 (D.C. Cir. 1946). In the new statute, agreements with most highly compensated employees entered into on or after October 1, 2022 are limited to one year. D.C. CODE ANN. § 32-581.03(a)(1)(C)(i).

In the somewhat unusual context of a defendant who was accused of operating a mortgage foreclose-avoidance scam, the D.C. Court of Appeals confirmed the enforceability of the defendant's agreement not to engage in a certain business "in the future." *Dyer v. Bilaal*, 983 A.2d 349, 359 (D.C. 2009). In affirming this effectively perpetual duration covenant, the court noted that the defendant could continue to earn a living as a real estate investor and that the court was "confident that [the defendant's] inability to engage in sale/leaseback transactions will not negatively impact consumers in the market for home refinancing." 983 A.2d at 359 n.10. More recently, however, the U.S. District Court for the District of Columbia found that an effectively perpetual and geographically unlimited prohibition was unreasonable and unenforceable. *Meyer Group, Ltd. v. Rayborn*, No. 19-1945 (ABJ), 2020 WL 5763631, at *9 (D.D.C. Sept. 28, 2020) (finding covenant "invalid and unenforceable" because "[t]he plain language of the provision would effectively lock [the defendant] out of the real estate business indefinitely").

The U.S. District Court for the District of Columbia has outlined the test under District of Columbia law for determining the validity of temporal and geographic limitations on competition in employment and sale of business contracts as:

> [W]hether the restraint was any greater than was necessary to afford fair protection to the party in whose favor they were made, and not so extensive

> as to interfere with the interests of the public. . . . The very purpose of the contract and the surrounding circumstances suggest the measure of protection needed and furnish a standard by which the legality of the restraint may be tested.

Orbo Theatre Corp. v. Loew's, Inc., 156 F. Supp. 770, 777 (D.D.C. 1957), *aff'd*, 261 F.2d 380 (D.C. Cir. 1958). In more recent cases, however, the courts generally have not articulated the relationship between the time limits on non-competition deemed acceptable and the interest protected, except to state that the time limits must be "reasonable" in light of the facts of the case. *See Ellis v. James V. Hurson Associates*, 565 A.2d 615, 621 (D.C. 1989); *Smith, Bucklin & Associates, Inc. v. Sonntag*, 83 F.3d 476, 480 (D.C. Cir. 1996).

---

4. What geographic limitations have courts recognized as reasonable in the franchise context?

- **How have they been related to the interests protected?**
- **Have courts recognized the legitimacy of protecting other franchisees from competition?**

There have been no published decisions addressing the reasonableness of geographic limitations contained in covenants against competition in the franchise context. In *B&H National Place, Inc. v. Beresford*, 850 F. Supp. 2d 251 (D.D.C. 2012), the U.S. District Court for the District of Columbia considered an alleged breach of a covenant not to compete within a four-block radius given in connection with the sale of a Five Guys restaurant franchise, but the enforceability of the covenant was not disputed.

In the context of the sale of a business, the following geographic limitations on competition by the seller have been recognized as reasonable: within ten blocks of the business sold, *Allison v. Seigle*, 79 F.2d 170, 171 (D.C. Cir. 1935) (per curiam); within the District of Columbia, *Godfrey v. Roessle*, 5 App. D.C. 299 (1895); and anywhere in the United States, *Burton, Parsons & Co. v. Parsons*, 146 F. Supp. 114, 116 (D.D.C. 1956). In a decision involving the dissolution of a dental practice, the court held that a covenant with a five-mile radius was not facially invalid, but noted that reasonableness was a "fact intensive inquiry." *Deutsch v. Barsky*, 795 A.2d 669, 676–77 (D.C. 2002) (remanding for further proceedings).

In the context of an employment contract, the District of Columbia Court of Appeals, in *Ellis v. James V. Hurson Associates*, 565 A.2d 615, 620 (D.C. 1989), ruled that a geographic limitation was not necessarily required when the limitation sought to be enforced was on soliciting the employer's customers rather than on competing generally in the same business. This rule has been reaffirmed in subsequent decisions. *See M3 USA Corp. v. Qamoum*, No. 20-2903 (RDM), 2021 WL 2292266, at *17 (D.D.C. June 4, 2021) (finding that no geographic limitation was necessary on covenant prohibiting solicitation of former clients); *Hospitality Staffing Solutions, LLC v. Reyes*, 736 F. Supp. 2d 192, 198 (D.D.C. 2010) (approving antisolicitation covenant with no geographic restriction). On the other hand, a provision with no geographic limitation and that prohibited solicitation of any client or potential client of the employer was held to be overbroad and unenforceable. *Meyer Group, Ltd. v. Rayborn*, No. 19-1945 (ABJ), 2020 WL 5763631, at *9 (D.D.C. Sept. 28, 2020).

In other cases involving employment contracts, the federal courts applying D.C. law have upheld restrictions on competition within the District of Columbia, *Erikson v. Hawley*, 12 F.2d 491, 495 (D.C. Cir. 1926), within 50 miles of the offices with which the employee had been connected, *Robert Half Int'l Inc. v. Billingham*, 315 F. Supp. 2d 419, 430 (D.D.C. 2018), within 30 miles of any office with which the employee had been directly connected, *Meyer v. Wineburgh*, 110 F. Supp. 957, 957–58 (D.D.C. 1953); and within 100 miles of the District of Columbia, *Morgan Stanley DW Inc. v. Rothe*, 150 F. Supp. 2d 67, 74 (D.D.C. 2001).

In most cases, the only stated rationale for enforcing or not enforcing a particular geographic restriction on competition is the "reasonableness" of the restriction and the furtherance of some "legitimate business interest." *Robert Half Int'l Inc. v. Billingham*, 315 F. Supp. 3d 419, 430–31 (D.D.C. 2018). The courts have rarely discussed the relationship between the "reasonableness" and the particular interest assertedly protected by the covenant, although the covenant must be "reasonably tailored." *M3 USA Corp. v. Qamoum*, No. 20-2903 (RDM), 2021 WL 2292266, at *17 (D.D.C. June 4, 2021) (quoting *Smith, Bucklin & Associates, Inc. v. Sonntag*, 83 F.3d 476, 480 (D.C. Cir. 1996)).

5. What limitations on activities have courts recognized as reasonable in the franchise context?

The District of Columbia courts have not addressed the types of restrictions on activities that would be considered reasonable in the franchise context. More generally, courts in the District of Columbia have approved limitations on solicitation of the former employer's customers and employees, *M3 USA Corp. v. Qamoum*, No. 20-2903 (RDM), 2021 WL 2292266, at *17 (D.D.C. June 4, 2021), *Hospitality Staffing Solutions, LLC v. Reyes*, 736 F. Supp. 2d 192, 198 (D.D.C. 2010), *Mercer Management Consulting, Inc. v. Wilde*, 920 F. Supp. 219, 237 (D.D.C. 1996), *Morgan Stanley DW Inc. v. Rothe*, 150 F. Supp. 2d 67, 75–76 (D.D.C. 2001), restrictions on disclosure of confidential business information, *id.*, and more generally against competition, *Robert Half Int'l Inc. v. Billingham*, 315 F. Supp. 3d 419, 430–31 (D.D.C. 2018), *Ellis v. James V. Hurson Assocs.*, 565 A.2d 615, 618 (D.C. 1989).

6. Does the District of Columbia recognize a difference between in-term and post-term covenants?

There are no reported cases in which a District of Columbia court has refused to enforce an in-term covenant. In *Saul v. Thalis*, 156 F. Supp. 408, 411 (D.D.C. 1957), the court stated that the validity of a covenant restricting an employee from competing with an employer during a fixed term of employment "cannot be questioned so long as the employee remains in the employ of the employer." However, the court held that once the employment relationship ended prematurely, despite the fact that the parties had agreed that the covenant would remain in force, the covenant "no longer ha[d] validity, being unsupported by an existing employer-employee relationship or any special right or consideration," such as trade secrets, confidential knowledge, expert training, or fruits of employment. *Id.* at 412–13. In the context of a lease dispute, the D.C. Circuit held that an exclusive use provision was reasonable in the past because it was limited to the duration of the lease. *Red Sage Ltd. Partnership v. Despa Deutsche Sparkassen Immobilien-Anlage Gasellschaft MBH*, 254 F.3d 1120, 1132 (D.C. Cir. 2001). In so holding, the court contrasted the situation before it with a post-termination restriction on employment, which the court noted would be subject to heightened scrutiny under the RESTATEMENT principles applied under D.C. law. *Id.* (citing *Venture Holdings Ltd. v. Carr*, 673 A.2d 686, 689 (D.C. 1996)).

The recently enacted statute provides some textual basis for distinguishing between in-term and post-term covenants. D.C. CODE ANN. § 32-581.01(15)(B)(ii). However, it remains to be seen how strong a distinction will develop as the courts begin to enforce the statute.

7. Has the District of Columbia allowed enforcement of covenants against non-signatories (e.g., family members, newly formed corporations)?

There are no published decisions under District of Columbia law addressing the enforcement of a covenant against competition against a non-signatory in the franchise context.

In general, D.C. law provides that non-parties owe no contractual duty to contracting parties. *Charlton v. Mond*, 987 A.2d 436, 441 (D.C. 2010). In rejecting an attempt to hold a non-party liable for a violation of a non-disparagement provision in a settlement agreement, the U.S. District Court for the District of Columbia noted this principle and declined to follow the reasoning of an out-of-jurisdiction franchise case applying a covenant not to compete against a non-signatory spouse. *Guttenberg v. Emery*, 41 F. Supp. 3d 61, 69 (D.D.C. 2014) (distinguishing *McCart v. H&R Block, Inc.*, 470 N.E.2d 756, 762 (Ind. Ct. App. 1984)). While the district court in *Guttenberg* found that *McCart* was non-binding and contrary to the prevailing rule in the District of Columbia, the court also noted evidence in *McCart* that the non-signatory was acting collusively with the contracting party. 41 F. Supp. 3d at 69 n.4. *Guttenberg* does not appear to foreclose the possibility that, if such evidence were present, the general rule in the District of Columbia that non-signatories are not bound might be overcome.

Although not contractual, parties that intentionally induce a breach of a valid covenant may be liable under a theory of tortious interference and may be enjoined from such violations. *Robert Half Int'l Inc. v. Billingham*, 315 F. Supp. 3d 419, 430–31 (D.D.C. 2018) (granting preliminary injunction against new employer as well as against former employee who executed covenant). The court only briefly discussed the issue, however, because it noted that enjoining the employee as a practical matter would have the same effect. *Id.* at 435–36.

8. Will the District of Columbia modify, "blue-pencil," or otherwise reduce a covenant found to be overbroad?

In 2018, the District of Columbia Court of Appeals resolved this previously open issue and held that the doctrine of equitable reformation should be applied in the consideration of overbroad covenants not to compete. *Steiner v. American Friends of Lubavich (Chabad)*, 177 A.3d 1246, 1257 (D.C. 2018) ("We join the jurisdictions that have adopted the equitable reformation doctrine"). In so holding, the court noted that it had previously rejected the alternative of refusing to enforce overbroad covenants in their entirety. *Id.* (citing *Ellis v. James V. Hurson Associates*, 565 A.2d 615, 617 (D.C. 1989)). The court concluded that the alternative of "blue-penciling" overbroad covenants by removing objectionable language (but not modifying or adding language) was unduly "rigid and technical." *Id.* at 1258. Thus, the court permitted equitable reformation "where courts entertain judicial modification of unreasonable covenants." *Id.*

While the court of appeals in *Steiner* formally adopted the principle of equitable reformation, it noted a trend against reforming agreements that are unreasonable on their face, and suggested that it might be appropriate to limit reformation to situations in which the party seeking reformation had acted in good faith. *Id.* The court also recognized a general aversion to rewriting contracts or requiring courts to determine essential terms of the contract. *Id.* The court explained that it did not want to encourage drafting of overbroad agreements based upon the assumption that any overbroad provision would subsequently be reformed in the enforcement process. *Id.* at 1257 n.10. Finally, the court made clear that equitable reformation was not a mandate; as the court noted, "[t]he assertion of a legitimate interest does not automatically require the court to reform a covenant that was not drafted to properly protect that interest in the first place." *Id.* at 1259.

In a decision subsequent to *Steiner*, the U.S. District Court for the District of Columbia declined to engage in equitable reformation of an overbroad covenant. *Meyer Group, Ltd. v. Rayborn*, No. 19-1945 (ABJ), 2020 WL 5763631 (D.D.C. Sept. 28, 2020). In *Meyer*, the covenant at issue lacked any geographic or temporal limitations, and was also vague as to the conduct that was prohibited. In these circumstances, where the court essentially would have been required to draft the covenant from scratch, the court declined to exercise its equitable reformation power. *Id.* at *10.

9. When does a non-compete period begin to run? Will courts equitably extend the term?

District of Columbia courts have not addressed when a non-compete provision begins to run or whether the period can be equitably extended as a consequence of non-compliance.

10. Are there additional nuances or peculiarities of the District of Columbia's treatment of covenants in the franchising context?

D.C. law historically has provided little franchise-specific guidance, due to the relative paucity of decisions arising from franchise disputes. In the absence of clear authority, practitioners may wish to consider whether there is any informative Maryland law. D.C. courts "ordinarily turn to the common law of Maryland for guidance where there is no District of Columbia precedent on an issue." *George Washington Univ. v. Scott*, 711 A.2d 1257, 1260 n.5 (D.C. 1998). Additionally, the interpretation of the new statute, and the extent to which (if any) it is applied in the franchising context, will be important issues for franchise practitioners to consider.

Florida

*by Jason M. Murray**

1. Has the state addressed covenants against competition in the context of franchising?

- **Does the state have a franchising statute or regulations that address covenants against competition?**
- **Does the state have a covenants statute of general applicability that would encompass franchise covenants?**
- **Have the courts addressed covenants in the context of franchising either under a statute or under the state's common law?**

Courts and commentators alike widely refer to Florida Statute section 817.416 as the Florida Franchise Act despite the fact that the Florida Legislature did not use that title throughout the legislative process. The Florida Franchise Act sets the broad guidelines for the establishment of franchises and distributorships in Florida; however, it is not an all-encompassing regulation of franchise business relationships, and it does not address covenants against competition in the franchise context.

Under Florida law, the use of restrictive covenants and non-compete agreements is permitted as a legislatively created exception to the rule under the Florida Antitrust Act, which states that "every contract, combination, or conspiracy in restraint of trade or commerce in this state is unlawful." FLA. STAT. § 542.18 (2020). Because such agreements are specific exceptions to the legislative policy encouraging business competition, they can be analyzed only by reference to the statutes permitting the exceptions. As one Florida court has explained,

> Because the noncompetition statutes have been amended in 1990 and again in 1996, it bears mention that: "[P]ractitioners in Florida must pay close attention to i) the effective date of a particular restrictive covenant and ii) the effective date of any arguable subsequent amendment or ratification. There now are three sets of different rules governing the enforceability of restrictive covenants in Florida: a) Rules governing contracts effective prior to June 28, 1990; b) Rules governing contracts effective on or after June 28, 1990, but before July 1, 1996; and c) Rules governing contracts effective

---

*Jason M. Murray is a partner in the Miami Office of K&L Gates LLP.

on or after July 1, 1996. The rules governing contracts effective in each period are quite different, and practitioners will continue to find 'traps for the unwary' so long as contracts effective before July 1, 1996, continue in force."

American Residential Servs., Inc. v. EventTech. Servs., Inc., 715 So. 2d 1048, 1049 (Fla. Dist. Ct. App. 1998), quoting John A. Grant, Jr. & Thomas T. Steele, *Restrictive Covenants: Florida Returns to the Original "Unfair Competition" Approach for the 21st Century*, 70 Fla. B. J. 53, 55 (Nov. 1996).

Accordingly, agreements entered into before June 28, 1990, are subject to the old version of Florida Statute section 542.33 (before 1980 designated section 542.12); agreements entered into on or after June 28, 1990, and before July 1, 1996, are subject to the current version of section 542.33; and agreements entered into on or after July 1, 1996, are subject to the current section 542.335. Because of the potential for disagreements between franchisors and franchisees based on agreements entered into long ago, franchisors and their counsel must be familiar with the three statutory schemes and their significant differences.

Under the pre-1990 version of Florida Statute section 542.33, a covenant not to compete will be enforced if the contract is otherwise valid, the party seeking enforcement continues to carry on a like business, and the time and scope of the non-compete provisions are reasonable. Courts have interpreted this version of the statute as not permitting judicial inquiry into possible hardships upon defendants or the existence of legitimate business interests. The current version of section 542.33, on the other hand, broadened courts' discretion in determining the enforceability of non-compete and other restrictive covenants. Specifically, courts have construed the amended version of section 542.33 as calling for greater judicial inquiry and an increased burden on parties in establishing their right to enforce covenants not to compete. The current version of the statute, however, provides no guidelines to courts for the exercise of their discretion, nor does it set standards for the appropriate burden to place upon parties seeking to enforce non-compete agreements. Under the current version of section 542.33, actions seeking enforcement of covenants not to compete entered into between June 28, 1990, and July 1, 1996, have no real standards and are often inconsistent. Section 542.335, however, is a more comprehensive statutory scheme that sets out detailed guidelines and standards for the enforcement of covenants not to compete. This statute, which governs covenants not to compete entered into after July 1, 1996, sets out the relevant factors for courts to consider. The current section 542.335 is clearly more "pro-enforcement" of covenants not to compete because it expressly allows courts to modify or "blue-pencil," and thus preserve, overbroad covenants. To fully understand Florida's law governing covenants not to compete in the context of franchising, each of the three statutory schemes discussed above must be fully explored.

AGREEMENTS PRIOR TO JUNE 28, 1990

At common law, agreements that restricted competition and employment were disfavored by the courts. Grant & Steele, *supra,* at 53. In 1953, the Florida Legislature enacted Florida Statute section 542.12 (later amended and subsequently recodified as section 542.33), which for the first time explicitly authorized contractual restraints on competition. *Id.* The U.S. Court of Appeals for the Fifth Circuit construed the original version of Florida's non-compete statute in the context of franchising. In *Wilkinson v. Manpower, Inc.*, 531 F.2d 712 (5th Cir. 1976), a franchisor of a temporary-help service sought to enjoin its former franchisee from competing with the franchisor pursuant to a franchise agreement provision that prohibited competition for a period of two years within the licensed area covered by the franchise or any city in which the franchisor or its affiliate operated. The court of appeals ruled that the covenant was unenforceable under Florida law because it was not among the statutorily provided exceptions to the prohibition against contracts in restraint of trade, but it ultimately enforced the covenant not to compete because the agreement was governed by the laws of Wisconsin and not in conflict with Florida public policy.

The Florida Supreme Court, in *Capraro v. Lanier Bus. Products*, 466 So. 2d 212, 213 (Fla. 1985), noted that the normal remedy under section 542.33 for breach of a covenant not to compete is an injunction. The court also held that irreparable injury is presumed and does not have to be proven to obtain an injunction where a covenant not to compete is violated. *Id.*

Florida Statute section 542.33 was first applied in the franchise context by the U.S. District Court for the Western District of Missouri. In *Gold v. Holiday Rent-A-Car International, Inc.*, 627 F. Supp. 280, 281–82 (W.D. Mo. 1985), a franchisor/licensor brought an action against a former franchisee/licensee to enforce a covenant not to compete within a 75-mile radius of the franchise business for two years after termination of the license agreement. Citing section 542.33(2)(b), the *Gold* court held that Florida enforces covenants not to compete if reasonably limited as to time, area, and scope. *Id.* at 282. The court specifically found that the covenant not to compete in *Gold* met the standard and granted a preliminary injunction enjoining the franchisee/licensee from violating the covenant not to compete contained within the license agreement. *Id.* at 285.

The statute's vagueness, however, led to conflicting decisions and uncertainty in enforcement. Grant & Steele, *supra*, at 53. To understand the conflict, one needs to look no further than to two decisions of Florida's Second District Court of Appeal that staked out opposing views of the statute. Compare *Sarasota Beverage Co. v. Johnson*, 551 So. 2d 503 (Fla. Dist. Ct. App. 1989) (when analyzing enforceability of non-compete agreement, court may only determine whether the agreement is reasonable as to time and area, and rejecting the previously enunciated standard that courts were to balance all elements generally required for the issuance of injunction, including possible negative impact on the former employee as contrasted with the potential negative harm to the former employer), with *Hapney v. Central Garage, Inc.*, 579 So. 2d 127 (Fla. Dist. Ct. App.) (the party seeking enforcement of covenant not to compete must plead and prove a legitimate business interest, thus giving significant element of discretion to the trial court), *review denied*, 591 So. 2d 180 (Fla. 1991).

The Florida Supreme Court settled the debate between the *Sarasota Beverage* and *Hapney* decisions in *Gupton v. Village Key & Saw Shop, Inc.*, 656 So. 2d 475 (Fla. 1995). The court expressly disapproved *Hapney* to the extent that it held the 1990 amendments to section 542.33 were applicable retrospectively and reaffirmed that "under the 1989 version of the statute, the trial court's authority is limited to determining the reasonableness of time and geographic area limitations." *Id.* at 479, n.2. Accordingly, for non-compete and other restrictive covenants entered into before June 28, 1990, the trial court's discretion is strictly curtailed: if the contract is otherwise valid, the party seeking enforcement continues to carry on a like business, and the time and scope of the non-compete provisions are reasonable, the agreement will be enforced without need for showing a legitimate business interest to protect or any consideration of the defendant's possible hardships should enforcement be granted.

One Florida trial court has found the requirement that "the party seeking enforcement continues to carry on a like business in the area" inapplicable when a franchisor grants an exclusive territory. *Int'l Bartending Inst., Inc. v. Baird*, Bus. Franchise Guide (CCH) ¶ 10,222 (Fla. 13th Cir. Ct. 1993) (permitting breakaway franchisee to avoid non-compete provision on basis that franchisor was not carrying on like business in area of exclusive franchise territory would lead to absurd result and run counter to intention of statute; franchisor should not have to haphazardly set up new business just to enforce bargained-for restriction in valid franchise agreement). Another Florida court made it clear that Florida Statute section 542.33(2)(b) did not require use of the licensor's trademark or business format in the competing business. *Servpro Indus., Inc. v. Spohn*, 638 So. 2d 1001 (Fla. Dist. Ct. App. 1994). In *Servpro*, a franchisor of cleaning and restoration services business brought an action against former franchisees for violation of a non-compete agreement and failure to report and pay royalties. *Id.* at 1002. In overruling the trial court's granting of a directed verdict in favor of the franchisees, Florida's Fourth District Court of Appeal held:

> [T]he trial court erred when it ruled that the licensee must not only carry on a similar business but also use the licensor's trademark or identifiable business format to fit within this exception. Our reading of the statute does not support such an interpretation. The plain wording of the statute simply does not require that the trademark be used in order to violate a non-compete agreement.

FL

Id. The outcome in *Hapney*, however, is best explained by the fact that the court in that case was looking through the lens of the 1990 amendments to the statute, which had been recently enacted when the court made its decision. The *Hapney* court simply applied the amendments to the statute retrospectively.

AGREEMENTS AFTER JUNE 28, 1990, BUT BEFORE JULY 1, 1996

The Florida Legislature amended Florida Statute section 542.33 in 1990 in an apparent effort to correct the deficiencies of the prior law. The legislature added to the end of subsection 2(a) the following language:

> However, the court shall not enter an injunction contrary to the public health, safety, or welfare or in any case where the injunction enforces an unreasonable covenant not to compete or where there is no showing of irreparable injury. However, use of specific trade secrets, customer lists, or direct solicitation of existing customers shall be presumed to be an irreparable injury and may be specifically enjoined. In the event the seller of the goodwill of a business or a shareholder selling or otherwise disposing of all his shares in a corporation breaches an agreement to refrain from carrying on or engaging in a similar business, irreparable injury shall be presumed.

Fla. Stat. § 542.33(2)(a) (1991). Accordingly, the legislature granted more discretion to the courts when passing on non-compete agreements. Further, the amendment's addition of the language stating that the "use of specific trade secrets, customer lists, or direct solicitation of existing customers shall be presumed to be an irreparable injury" reduced one of the hurdles to obtaining injunctive relief. *Id.* The amendment did not alter the language applicable to licensors.

While the amendment might have sought to clarify the law regarding the enforcement of non-compete agreements, it probably has had the opposite effect.

Grant & Steele, *supra*, at 53–54. The "reasonableness" and "public health, safety or welfare" considerations may have broadened the trial court's discretion, but they failed to provide objective standards for the exercise of that discretion. *Id.* "This deficiency permitted the development of differing judicial views on how contractual restrictions upon competition should be evaluated and enforced, and that difference in viewpoints generated unclear, inconsistent, and oftentimes inexplicable results." *Id.* Consequently, actions to seek enforcement of non-compete agreements entered into between June 28, 1990, and July 1, 1996, which are subject to this "standardless" standard, are likely to be fraught with surprise and uncertainty.

In *Lovell Farms, Inc. v. Levy*, 641 So. 2d 103, 104 (Fla. Dist. Ct. App. 1994), the Third District Court of Appeal noted that the Florida Legislature amended section 542.33(2)(a) in 1990 with the intent of restricting the availability of injunctive relief and the existence of an irreparable injury. The *Lovell* court construed the legislature's intent in passing the amendment as calling for a greater burden on the part of employers in establishing their right to enforce a covenant not to compete. In the context of trade secrets, the court noted that the employer must establish the existence of a trade secret and must prove that the employee used the specific trade secret at his new place of employment. *Id.* at 105. Further, the *Lovell* court held that a court "must state its factual findings, specifying whether 1) the disputed information constitutes a trade secret, and 2) the former employee used the specific trade secret in his new place of employment." *Id.* If the court finds that the former employee used a specific trade secret in his new employment, the *Lovell* court held that then there is a presumption of irreparable injury. *Id.* Following these initial findings, the court must determine the reasonableness of the non-compete agreement's time and space restrictions. *Id.* If the restrictions are reasonable, then the non-compete covenant may be enforced by injunction. *Id.*

In *Globe Data Sys. v. Johnson*, 745 So. 2d 1101, 1103 (Fla. Dist. Ct. App. 1999), the Third District Court of Appeal also recognized that the 1990 amendment placed a greater burden on parties seeking to enforce covenants not to compete under Section 542.33. Specifically, the *Globe* court noted that "[u]nder this [new] version of section 542.33, irreparable injury is not normally presumed upon proof of breach of an agreement not to compete." *Id.* at 1103. The court did, however, recognize that the use of trade secrets, customer lists, or direct solicitation of existing customers is an exception to the new general rule and do give rise to a presumption of irreparable injury. *Id.* After a finding of irreparable harm, the court must examine the noncompetition agreement to determine its reasonableness. *Id.*

AGREEMENTS AFTER JULY 1, 1996

In 1996, the Florida Legislature created Florida Statute Section 542.335. The 1996 statute is more comprehensive than the prior statutes and was created to correct the inadequacies in the prior versions governing restrictive covenants that led to inconsistency in the application of the law. Grant & Steele, *supra*, at 53–56. Section 542.335 sets out the general rule that "enforcement of contracts that restrict or prohibit competition during or after the term of the restrictive covenants, so long as such contracts are reasonable in time, area, and line of business, is not prohibited." Fla. Stat. § 542.335(1) (2020); *see Proudfoot Consulting Co. v. Gordon*, 576 F.3d 1223 (11th Cir. 2009). The statute does not define "reasonable" in terms of area or line of business, but does set forth presumptions as to what constitutes a reasonable time. When a restrictive covenant imposes a time period in excess of the presumptions, there must be evidence in the record to rebut the presumption. *See Re/Max Int'l, Inc. v. Citimaxx Corp.*, No. 8:08-cv-2554-T-27TBM, 2009 WL 1883035, at *2 (M.D. Fla. June 30, 2009); *Balasco v. Gulf Auto Holding, Inc.*, 707 So.2d 858, 860 (Fla. Dist. Ct. App. 1998); *Flickenger v. R.J. Fitzgerald & Co.*, 732 So. 2d 33, 34 (Fla. Dist. Ct. App. 1999). Where there is no evidence to rebut the presumption of unreasonableness, the court will enforce the restriction only for the maximum time permitted by the statute. *Id.*

What constitutes a reasonable time, area or line of business restriction is not capable of a fixed definition—the facts of the case will determine what is reasonable. *See Health Care Fin. Enters., Inc. v. Levy*, 715 So. 2d 341, 343 (Fla. Dist. Ct. App. 1998). Accordingly, when drafting a restrictive covenant, it is possible that the drafting party may think the agreement is reasonable, but a court may ultimately find to the contrary. However, this will not void the covenant in its entirety. *Id.* If a time, area, or line-of-business provision is found overbroad, it will be modified by the court and enforced, not stricken. Additionally, a restrictive covenant or non-compete agreement that omits one of these terms remains enforceable—the court will supply the missing term. *See Env't Servs., Inc. v. Carter*, 9 So. 3d 1258, 1264 (Fla. Dist. Ct. App. 2009); *Sears Termite and Pest Control, Inc. v. Arnold*, 745 So. 2d 485, 486 (Fla. Dist. Ct. App. 1999).

Although it may seem academic, it bears repeating that all restrictive covenants and non-compete agreements under Section 542.335 must be in writing. "A court shall not enforce a restrictive covenant unless it is set forth in a writing signed by the person against whom enforcement is sought." Fla. Stat. § 542.335(1)(a) (2020). However, lack of a copy of the agreement may not be fatal to efforts to enforce a non-compete agreement. A court can allow a lost non-compete agreement and its terms to be proven according to the rules of evidence. *Env't Servs., Inc.*, 9 So. 3d at 1267.

In a return to the reasoning of the *Hapney* decision, the 1996 amendment requires that all restrictive covenants or non-compete agreements be supported by a "legitimate business interest." Fla. Stat. § 542.335(1)(b) (2020). Lack of support by a legitimate business interest renders these agreements unlawful, void, and unenforceable. *Delivery.com Franchising, LLC v. Moore*, 2020 WL 3410347, at *11 (S.D. Fla. June 19, 2020) report and recommendation adopted, No. 20-20766-CIV, 2020 WL 4464674 (S.D. Fla. July 14, 2020) (franchisor in business of delivery pick up services could not enforce non-compete against potential franchisee because business of pick up and food delivery did not require specialized skills or training, franchisor did not provide potential franchisee "with any unique training or procedure of the business," and franchisor had no actual presence in the geographic area subject to the covenant). *Id.* The burden is on the party seeking enforcement (i.e., a franchisor) to "plead and prove" the existence of the legitimate business interest. Fla. Stat. § 542.335(1)(b). This imposes a burden on the claimant of proper pleading in the petition or claim for relief, as well as an evidentiary burden to show the existence of the legitimate business interest.

In *Rauch, Weaver, Norfleet, Kurtz & Co. v. AJP Pine Island Warehouses, Inc.* 313 So. 3d 625, 627 (Fla. Dist. Ct. App. 2021), a broker sued a potential buyer for breach of confidentiality agreement. The broker did not cite to 542.335 in his complaint, nor did he plead that the agreement was necessary to protect a legitimate business interest. *Id.* at 628. Likewise, the potential seller did not raise any affirmative defenses related to the statute. *Id.* At the summary judgment stage, the potential buyer argued that the confidentiality agreement was void under Section 542.335. *Id.* Broker objected to this argument because it was never pled as an affirmative defense. *Id.* The trial court rejected broker's argument and the appellate court affirmed, holding that it was not potential buyer's burden to raise Section 542.335 as an affirmative defense, but, rather, broker's burden to plead and prove the existence of a legitimate business interest and that the restraint was reasonably necessary to protect a legitimate business interest. *Id.* at 630. This was true even though neither party cited to the statute at the pleading stage, because when a breach of contract action is based on the enforcement of a restrictive covenant, "the plaintiff must plead and prove additional elements in order to establish that the restrictive covenant is a valid restraint on trade." *Id.*

Contrary to *Int'l Bartending Inst., Inc. v. Baird*, Bus. Franchise Guide (CCH) ¶ 10, 222, Section 542.335(1)(g)(2) provides that "[i]n determining the enforceability of a restrictive covenant, a court may consider as a defense the fact that the [party] seeking enforcement no longer continues business in the area or line of business that is the subject of the action." Fla. Stat. § 542.335(1)(g)(2).

In *Pirtek USA LLC v. Whitehead*, Bus. Franchise Guide (CCH) ¶ 13,339 (S.D. Ala. Apr. 27, 2006), the court in interpreting Florida law held that the absence of the franchisor and any of its franchisees in the area that was subject of the action militated against a finding that the non-compete agreement was reasonably necessary to protect the established interests of the franchisor. Accordingly, the court in *Pirtek* found that the franchisor failed to establish that it had a legitimate business interest in protecting against competition in the area or territory of the former franchisee because it was not operating a franchise in the geographic area of the terminated franchise. *Id.; see also Pirtek USA LLC v. Richard Wilcox & Wilcox, LLC*, Bus. Franchise Guide (CCH) ¶ 13,368 (M.D. Fla. June 21, 2006) (franchisor failed to establish a legitimate business interest in action where franchisor made no effort to refranchise the territory and was not operating within at least 200 miles of territory).

Section 542.335 also sets forth a number of miscellaneous provisions that are significant. First, a rule of reasonable construction of restrictive covenants is mandated. Fla. Stat. § 542.335(1)(h) (2020). A court may not employ a rule of construction that requires the court to construe the restrictive covenant narrowly nor require that contract ambiguities be construed against the drafter. Accordingly, a franchisor that drafts a restrictive covenant or non-compete agreement is not forced to bear the burden of any ambiguities. Instead, the court must interpret the covenant in favor of providing reasonable protection to all of the franchisor's legitimate business interests. *Id.* Of course, this new requirement is not without its own potential set of difficulties. Because neither party is prejudiced if the contract contains an ambiguity, there is no motivating factor for the parties, particularly the drafter, to make the agreement as specific as possible. Whether this provision might actually invite ambiguity and pose a possible violation of public policy is an issue that remains to be explored.

As with the prior law, the court is authorized by Section 542.335 to provide temporary and permanent injunctive relief. Fla. Stat. § 542.335(1)(j) (2020). Further, "[t]he violation of an enforceable restrictive covenant creates a presumption of irreparable injury" to a franchisor seeking to enforce such an agreement with injunctive relief. *Id.* This broadens the presumption of irreparable injury as to non-compete agreements introduced in the 1990 amendment to franchise and licensing agreements as well.

A franchisor seeking an injunction, however, is required to post an appropriate bond, and no agreement waiving or limiting the amount of the injunction bond will be given effect. *Id.* However, one Florida court has expressly stated that the bond requirement may be waived by a contract entered into prior to the effective date of Florida Statute Section 542.335 because the statute applies prospectively. *Diaz v. John Adcock Insurance Agency, Inc.*, 729 So. 2d 465, 467 (Fla. Dist. Ct. App. 1999).

Finally, the court is empowered to award costs and attorney's fees to a prevailing party in an action to enforce, or challenge the enforcement of, a restrictive covenant, even in the absence of a contractual provision authorizing such an award. Fla. Stat. § 542.335(1)(k) (2020). No such attorney's fee provision existed in the prior statutes. A party seeking to recover attorney's fees under this section, however, still must plead entitlement in a claim for relief or answer. *See Aim Target Programs, Inc. v. Family Quest, Inc.*, 752 So. 2d 1270, 1271 (Fla. Dist. Ct. App. 2000). Otherwise, such claim is waived. *Id.*

As can be seen by the prior discussion, the law of non-compete agreements and restrictive covenants in Florida is complex. The time the agreement was executed determines which of three potential statutory schemes to apply. Franchisors and their counsel must take note of which scheme to apply when seeking to enforce a restrictive covenant.

2. Have the courts articulated the "legitimate interests" of the franchisor that will support enforcement of a covenant against competition contained in a franchise agreement?

FL

- **If so, what are they (e.g., protection of goodwill, protection of confidential information), and in what contexts did the issue arise?**
- **If not, what interests have been recognized in other contexts (e.g., employment agreements, the sale of business context)?**

AGREEMENTS PRIOR TO JUNE 28, 1990

Prior to 1990, Florida courts had not addressed the "legitimate interests" of a franchisor in enforcing a noncompetition agreement. The Supreme Court of Florida, however, explained in the employment context that Florida's non-compete statute was "designed to allow employers to prevent their employees and agents from learning their trade secrets, befriending their customers and then moving into competition with them." *Miller Mech., Inc. v. Ruth*, 300 So. 2d 11, 12 (Fla. 1974). As to both employers and licensors, the statute imposed the requirement that the employer or licensor continue to carry on a like business therein. *See* Fla. Stat. § 542.33 (1989). The court also explained that "[i]n determining the reasonableness of such an agreement, the courts employ a balancing test to weigh the employer's interest in preventing the competition against the oppressive effect on the employee." *Miller Mech., Inc.*, 300 So. 2d at 12.

AGREEMENTS AFTER JUNE 28, 1990 BUT BEFORE JULY 1, 1996

Significantly, the 1990 amendment to Section 542.33 added that in the sale of business or employment context, the "use of specific trade secrets, customer lists, or direct solicitation of existing customers shall be presumed to be an irreparable injury." Fla. Stat. § 542.33 (1991). In *Dyer v. Pioneer Concepts, Inc.*, 667 So. 2d 961, 963 (Fla. Dist. Ct. App. 1996), the Second District Court of Appeal held in the employment context that "the statute authorizes contracts in restraint of trade only to protect the employer's legitimate business interest." *Id.* In addition, the court went on to hold that "an employer's legitimate protectable interests are trade secrets and confidential business lists, records, and information; customer goodwill; and, to a limited extent, extraordinary or specialized training which the employer has provided." *Id.* at 963–64 (citing *Hapney*, 579 So. 2d at 131, *disapproved on other grounds by Gupton*, 656 So. 2d at 475). With respect to extraordinary or specialized training, the *Dyer* court held that training is classified as extraordinary when it exceeds "what is usual, regular, common, or customary in the industry in which the employee is employed." *Id.* at 964 (quoting *Hapney*, 579 So. 2d at 132).

AGREEMENTS AFTER JULY 1, 1996

The 1996 amendment expressly requires that all restrictive covenants or non-compete agreements be supported by a "legitimate business interest." Fla. Stat. § 542.335(1)(b) (2020). Lack of support by a legitimate business interest renders these agreements unlawful, void, and unenforceable. *Id.*; *see also Rauch*, 313 So. 3d. at 630. The burden is on the party seeking enforcement to "plead and prove" the existence of the legitimate business interest. Fla. Stat. § 542.335(1)(b) (2020); *see Proudfoot*, 576 F.3d at 1231. A "legitimate business interest" as defined by the statute includes, but is not limited to:

1. Trade secrets, as defined in Florida Statute Section 688.002(4).
2. Valuable confidential business or professional information that otherwise does not qualify as trade secrets.
3. Substantial relationships with specific prospective or existing customers, patients, or clients.
4. Customer, patient, or client goodwill associated with:
   a. An ongoing business or professional practice, by way of trade name, trademark, service mark, or "trade dress";
   b. A specific geographic location; or
   c. A specific marketing or trade area.
5. Extraordinary or specialized training.

Fla Stat. § 542.335(1)(b) (2020); *compare Ansaarie v. First Coast Cardiovascular Institute, P.A.*, 252 So. 3d 287, 290-91 (Fla. Dist. Ct. App. 2018) (in action against former physician employee, medical institute successfully pleaded and proved at least two legitimate business interests where the evidence showed that existing customers requested their files be transferred to former physician employee and the medical facility made substantial investments in developing customer base and customer goodwill within the restricted area), *with Evans v. Generic Solution Eng'g, LLC*, 178 So. 3d 114, 116 (Fla. Dist. Ct. App. 2015) ("the protection of former customers generally does not qualify as a legitimate business interest where no identifiable agreement exists with such customers establishing that they would return with future work" (quoting *Envtl. Servs.*, 9 So. 3d at 1261)).

It must be noted, however, that the examples listed at Section 542.335(1)(b) are non-exhaustive. *White v. Mederi Caretenders Visiting Servs. of Se. Fla., LLC*, 226 So. 3d 774, 786 (Fla. 2017) (noting that protection of referral sources, which is not an enumerated example within the statute, may be a legitimate business interest). Section 542.335 is a "context-dependent" statute, and whether an interest is a legitimate business interest" will be determined by the "context and proof adduced." *Id.*

While Florida Statute section 542.335(1)(b)(3) provides that a restrictive covenant can be supported by proof of a legitimate business interest in substantial relationships with specific prospective or existing customers, patients, or clients, the court in *S. Wine and Spirits of America v. Simpkins*, No. 10-21136-Civ, 2011 WL 124631, at *3 (S.D. Fla. Jan. 14, 2011), refused to extend the reach of Section 542.335(1)(b)(3) to cover prospective and existing relationships with suppliers. However, later the Second District Court of Appeal in *Surgery Center Holdings, Inc. v. Guirguis*, 2021 WL 2385411 (Fla. Dist. Ct. App. June 11, 2021) did acknowledge prospective business as a component of a legitimate business interest.

The factors identified in the statute often are present in franchisor-franchisee relationships. In *Peterbrooke Franchising of Am., LLC v. Mia. Chocolates, LLC*, 2016 WL 8787063, at *3 (S.D. Fla. June 29, 2016), a franchisor in the business of selling chocolate treats terminated its franchise agreement with a Miami-based franchisee for failure to install a mandatory POS system. *Id.* The former franchisee continued to operate a competing business at the same location. *Id.* The franchisor sued to enforce the franchise agreement's post-termination restrictive covenant. *Id.* at *3–4. The former franchisee argued that franchisor had no legitimate business interest because, with the absence of the former franchisee, it no longer had a presence in South Florida. *Id.* at *8. The court rejected this argument:

FL

> The evidentiary record supports a finding that [franchisor] has indeed established a legitimate business interest as it pertains to protecting the goodwill associated with [franchisor's] marks in the geographic region. [Franchisor] has undisputedly expended resources to promote the [franchisor's] brand in South Florida through advertising campaigns and promotional events. Moreover, Florida courts have held that covenants not to compete are reasonably necessary to protect a franchisor's legitimate business interest of re-entering the market formerly serviced by a terminated franchise.
>
> [. . .]
>
> Thus, a "breakaway" franchise like [former franchisee] should not be able to avoid enforcement of a restrictive covenant . . . on the grounds that [franchisor] is not doing business in the area.

Id. at *8–9; *see also PWG Franchising, LLC v. FTL Enters., Inc.*, No. 6:14-cv-2056-Orl-40TBS, 2015 WL 12684458, at *4 (M.D. Fla. Mar. 2, 2015) (franchisor had a legitimate business interest in protection of marks and goodwill, where, upon termination of franchise agreement, former franchisee continued to operate competing business at former franchise location and continued to use franchise designated email address for customer contact).

Accordingly, trade secrets and valuable confidential business information; substantial relationships with existing customers, patients, and clients; associated goodwill; and trademarks and service marks are all properly legitimate business interests a franchisor can seek to protect upon the termination of a franchise agreement. The existence of these enumerated factors provides greater guidance to the courts than the malleable "reasonableness" standard set out in the 1990 amendment.

The statute also requires that the restraint be reasonably necessary to protect the legitimate business interest justifying the restriction. Fla. Stat. § 542.335(1)(c) (2020). In other words, the relief granted should be no greater—and no less—than what is necessary to protect the business interest in dispute. Again, it is the burden of the party seeking enforcement to plead and prove the reasonable necessity. *Id.*; *see also Austin v. Mid State Fire Equip. of Cent. Fla., Inc.*, 727 So. 2d 1097, 1098 (Fla. Dist. Ct. App. 1999) (where former employee provided similar service work with competitor as he had for more than 16 years with numerous other employers, former employer could not enjoin former employee from working for competitor, but could only enforce covenant as to disclosure of knowledge of customer and pricing information obtained at former employer where such knowledge was unrelated to responsibilities of former employee's new job); *Exchange Intern., Inc. v. Vacation Ownership Relief, LLC*, No. 6:10-cv-1273-Orl-35DAB, 2010 WL 4983669, at *8 (M.D. Fla. Oct. 27, 2010) (former employer in the business of providing services to timeshare resellers could not enforce restrictive covenant against former employee currently in the business of selling new timeshares to new owners). Where a restriction seeks to provide more protection than is reasonably necessary to protect the complaining party's legitimate business interests, it will not be enforced.

---

3. What time limitations have courts recognized as reasonable in the franchise context?

- **If no franchise cases have been decided, what time limitations have been recognized in other contexts?**
- **How have they been related to interests protected?**

As noted earlier, a trial's court's authority under the pre-1990 version of Florida Statute section 542.33 is limited to determining the reasonableness of time and geographic area limitations. *Gupton*, 656 So. 2d at 479 n.2. Section 542.33(2)(b) provides for the enforcement of covenants not to compete in the licensor/licensee context if the covenant is reasonably limited as to time and area so long as the licensor, or any person deriving title from the licensor, continues to carry on a like business in the area. In *Gold*, 627 F. Supp. at 285, the court applied the Florida statute to hold that a two-year restrictive covenant met the standard and granted a preliminary injunction enjoining the franchisee/licensee from violating the covenant not to compete contained within the license agreement. *See also Labor Finders Int'l, Inc. v. Dove Enter., Inc.*, Bus. Franchise Guide (CCH) ¶ 11,723 (D.S.C. 1999) (holding that a post-termination covenant not to compete, as modified by the franchisor pursuant to the terms of the franchise agreement, was reasonable in duration under Florida law where the modified covenant only prohibited the franchisee for a period of two years from operating a similar business or servicing customers within the prohibited territory).

With respect to restrictive covenants sought to be enforced against a former franchisee under section 542.335, a duration of one year is presumptively reasonable, while a restriction of more than three years is presumptively unreasonable. Fla. Stat. § 542.335(1)(d)(2) (2020); *see also R.J. Gators Franchise Sys., Inc. v. MBC Restaurants, Inc.*, Bus. Franchise Guide (CCH) ¶ 13,204 (M.D. Fla. Nov. 9, 2005) (finding a restriction from operating a competing business within ten miles of the former franchise for a period of two years to be reasonable). When a restrictive covenant imposes a time period in excess of the presumption of reasonableness, there must be evidence in the record to rebut the presumption of unreasonableness. *See Re/*

Max Int'l, Inc., 2009 WL 1883035, at *2; *Balasco*, 707 So. 2d at 860; *Flickenger*, 732 So. 2d at 34. Where there is no evidence to rebut the presumption of unreasonableness, the court will enforce the restriction only for the maximum time permitted by the statute. *Id.*

4. What geographic limitations have courts recognized as reasonable in the franchise context?

- **How have they been related to the interests protected?**
- **Have courts recognized the legitimacy of protecting other franchisees from competition?**

As noted earlier, the pre-1990 Florida Statute section 542.33(2)(b) provides for enforcement of covenants not to compete in the licensor/licensee context if the covenant is reasonably limited as to time and area as long as the licensor, or any person deriving title from the licensor, continues to carry on a like business in the area. The court in *Gold*, 627 F. Supp. at 281–82, enforced a 75-mile radius restriction as a reasonable geographic restriction.

One Florida court found that a nationwide restriction on an employee's entering into competition with his former employer appeared reasonable. *Auto Club Affiliates, Inc. v. Donahey*, 281 So. 2d 239 (Fla. Dist. Ct. App.), *cert. denied*, 285 So. 2d 28 (Fla. 1973). The Second District Court of Appeal reversed a final judgment denying an injunction restraining a former employee from soliciting or attempting to do business in violation of a covenant not to compete. The primary objection to the covenant not to compete was that the territorial limitation, which extended throughout the United States, was too extensive. Applying the law of Indiana, the *Auto Club* court held that a nationwide restriction is not invalid *per se*. *Id.* at 241. The court pointed out that "[w]hat is reasonable depends upon the nature of the business, the employment and the situation of the parties." *Id.* In addition, the court noted that "the area in which competition is restricted must not be broader than is necessary to protect the employer's interests." *Id.* Accordingly, the *Auto Club* court further held that "[c]onsidering the nature of the business, a highly specialized field of insurance and the type of employment, nationwide selling, the restriction is not unreasonable." *Id.* at 244; *see also Marshall v. Gore*, 506 So. 2d 91 (Fla. Dist. Ct. App. 1987) (holding that the evidence was sufficient to warrant the nationwide scope of the geographical limitation contained within a covenant not to compete, and covenant would be enforced insofar as it precluded employee from engaging in any business that competed with employer in the development and marketing of specialized computer software).

In *Dyer*, 667 So. 2d at 965, an employer filed a cross-appeal contesting the fact that the trial court limited the injunction to only five counties when the agreement included a geographical restriction of "a radius of 100 miles of each of the Company's branch offices from which he has been employed by Company, conducted sales for the Company, or provided janitorial and maintenance or other services on behalf of Company." The Second District court held that the trial court must find that a non-compete covenant's geographical limitation is not reasonable on its face in order to address the reasonableness of the geographic limitation on its own. *Id.* at 965. If the covenant not to compete is reasonable on its face, the defendant has the burden to plead and prove that the restriction is unreasonable based on the facts of the case. *Id.* Because the geographic restriction was reasonable on its face and the defendant failed to present evidence showing that it was unreasonable under the facts of the case, the *Dyer* court held that the trial court abused its discretion in limiting the injunction to five counties and remanded the case for modification of the injunction to apply the geographical area contained in the non-competition agreement. *Id.* at 965–66.

Section 542.335 states that "enforcement of contracts that restrict or prohibit competition during or after the term of the restrictive covenants, so long as such contracts are reasonable in time, area, and line of business, is not prohibited." FLA. STAT. § 542.335(1) (2020). Although section 542.335 sets forth presumptions as to what constitutes a reasonable time restriction, it does not define "reasonable" in terms of area or line of business.

In *Snelling & Snelling Inc. v. Reynolds*, 140 F. Supp. 2d 1314, 1318 (M.D. Fla. 2001), the court enforced a ten-mile non-compete agreement against a Florida franchisee. Although the court ultimately enforced the Pennsylvania choice-of-law provision in the franchise agreement, the court held that the franchisor's ten-mile non-compete restriction was not contrary to Florida's public policy since it met Florida's statutory presumptions of reasonableness. *Id.*

The Southern District of Florida held that a post-termination non-compete provision in a franchise agreement restricting competition for one year "within an eight mile radius of the Franchised Location" or any franchisee was reasonable in time and scope, and thus enforceable against the defendants. *Winmark Corp. v. Brenoby Sports, Inc.*, 32 F. Supp. 3d 1206, 1219 (S.D. Fla. 2014). The court noted that similar time and geographic scope restrictions have been upheld under Florida law, as they enable a franchisor to have the time and ability to protect its other franchisees and re-license the territory. *Id.*

In *Medi-Weightloss*, the court held that a 25-mile restriction against a franchisee was reasonable under Florida law. *Medi-Weightloss Franchising USA, LLC v. Medi-Weightloss Clinic of Boca Raton, LLC*, 11-CV-2437, 2012 WL 260902, at *5 (M.D. Fla. Jan. 3, 2012). The franchise agreement "prohibited operation of a competitive business in any capacity" at or within a 25-mile radius of the franchised location or any franchisee for two years post-termination. *Id.* The Middle District of Florida held that the restrictive covenant was reasonable as to the geographic scope, noting that Florida courts have enforced geographical restrictions covering a radius of 75 miles. *Id.*

5. What limitations on activities have courts recognized as reasonable in the franchise context?

In *Gold*, 627 F. Supp. at 281–82, a franchisor/licensor brought an action against a former franchisee/licensee to enforce a covenant not to compete within a 75-mile radius of the franchise business for two years after termination of the license agreement. Citing Florida Statute section 542.33(2)(b), the *Gold* court held that Florida enforces covenants not to compete if reasonably limited as to time, area, and scope. *Id.* at 282. The court specifically found that the covenant not to compete in *Gold* met the standard and granted a preliminary injunction enjoining the franchisee/licensee from violating the covenant not to compete contained within the license agreement. *Id.* at 285. In addition, the court ordered the franchisee to perform the following acts: (1) execute all documents necessary to assign and transfer to the franchisor the balance of the lease of the premises and (2) transfer each and every phone number used by the franchisee in connection with the advertisement of the franchise as set out in the license agreement. *Id.*

Similarly, in *U.S. Lawns, Inc. v. Landscape Concepts of CT, LLC*, No. 6:16-cv-929-Orl-41DAB, 2016 WL 9526340, at *1 (M.D. Fla. Oct. 31, 2016), a franchisor in the business of landscape maintenance moved to enjoin a former franchisee from "diverting or attempting to divert any business, customers or prospective customers" of franchisor. The court found the two-year post-termination restrictive covenant to be reasonable because the covenant allowed former franchisee to "operate a landscape maintenance business so long as they service[d] customers other than those previously serviced, within the past twenty-four months, by [franchisor]." *Id.* at *6.

6. Does the state recognize a difference between in-term and post-term covenants?

Under the pre-1990 statute, Florida law did recognize a distinction between in-term and post-term covenants not to compete. In *Orthopedic Equip. Co. v. Streetman and Assocs., Inc.*, 390 So. 2d 134, 135 (Fla. Dist. Ct. App. 1980), the Fifth District Court of Appeal held that the "best efforts" clause in the contract was in effect an in-term covenant not to compete and, therefore, was not subject to the non-competition provisions of Florida Statute section 542.12, which was later recodified as Florida Statute section 542.33. The court thus enforced the in-term provision.

Section 542.335 sets out that "enforcement of contracts that restrict or prohibit competition during or after the term of the restrictive covenants, so long as such contracts are reasonable in time, area, and line of business, is not prohibited." FLA. STAT. § 542.335(1) (2020). In this respect, Florida law analyzes in-term covenants governed by section 542.335 in the same manner as post-term covenants. However, Florida law does provide for rebuttable presumptions of reasonableness for post-term restrictive covenants that do not apply to in-term restrictive covenants. *See* FLA. STAT. § 542.335(1)(d) (2020) (regarding post-term restrictive covenants not related to trade secrets); § 542.335(1)(e) (2020) (regarding post-term restrictive covenants related to trade secrets).

7. Has the state allowed enforcement of covenants against non-signatories (e.g., family members, newly formed corporations)?

One Florida court construed the original version of Florida's non-compete statute as it relates to third-party beneficiaries in the context of franchising. In *Manpower, Inc. of Milwaukee v. Olsten Permanent Agency*, 309 So. 2d 57, 57–58 (Fla. Dist. Ct. App. 1975), a franchisor of a temporary help services business along with two of its franchisees brought an action against a former employee of one of the franchisor's subsidiaries. The Second District Court of Appeal held that the franchisor could not enforce the covenant not to compete because it was not the former employee's employer when the covenant not to compete was signed and the former employer was not a party to the lawsuit. *Id.* at 58. In addition, the court held that the franchisee plaintiffs, which could be considered as third-party beneficiaries under traditional contract law, could not avail themselves of Florida Statute section 542.12 to enforce the covenant not to compete. *Id.* at 58–59.

The pre-1990 version of Florida Statute section 542.33, however, did extend to a successor employer seeking to enforce a covenant not to compete against a former employee whose employment contract had been obtained pursuant to express assignment provisions within the agreement. *Pino v. Spanish Broad. Sys. of Florida, Inc.*, 564 So. 2d 186, 189 (Fla. Dist. Ct. App.) (where employment contract containing covenant not to compete included provision permitting assignment, employee's covenant not to compete was assignable and, therefore, enforceable by company that purchased employee's original employer's business), *review dismissed*, 567 So. 2d 435 (Fla. 1990). Florida Statute section 542.335 provides that a restrictive covenant or non-compete agreement may be enforced by a third-party beneficiary or assignee of the agreement, but only as follows:

1. In the case of a third-party beneficiary, the restrictive covenant expressly identified the person as a third-party beneficiary of the contract and expressly stated that the restrictive covenant was intended for the benefit of such person.
2. In the case of an assignee or successor, the restrictive covenant expressly authorized enforcement by a party's assignee or successor.

FLA. STAT. § 542.335(1)(f). This provision mandates that where a third-party beneficiary is known at the time of contracting, the restrictive covenant must indicate that it was intended for the benefit of that specifically identified person to be enforced by them. As to successors and assignees, the statute seems less specific, requiring only that the restrictive covenant indicate that enforcement is authorized by a successor or assignee generally. No cases have been decided on this point, but the plain language of the agreement supports this reading. Accordingly, franchisors contemplating third-party beneficiary situations or assignment of restrictive covenants must be aware of this requirement and draft their agreements accordingly. The significance of this provision lies in its application to business transactions where franchises are bought and sold. Small single-franchise transactions to large franchising system acquisitions will all be affected. It is therefore critical that this provision be heeded, or assignees and third-party beneficiaries may find that restrictive covenants and non-compete agreements will not be enforceable by them.

Although a franchisor cannot technically enforce the terms of a written covenant not to compete against non-signatories, the franchisor can seek to enjoin non-signatories from conspiring with or aiding and abetting the franchisee in breaching the covenant. Under Florida law, "individuals and entities may be enjoined from aiding and abetting a covenantor in violating a covenant not to compete." *Dad's Properties, Inc. v. Lucas*, 545 So. 2d 926, 928 (Fla. Dist. Ct. App. 1989). In addition, an injunction may bind non-parties identified with parties in interest, in privity with them, represented by them, or subject to their control. *Id.* In *Dad's Properties*, it was clear that the wife of the covenantor and her controlled company were aiding and abetting the covenantor in the intentional violation of a valid covenant not to compete. The Second District Court of Appeal held:

> Because of their close relationship to the covenantors, Susan Lucas and Martus, Inc. may be enjoined or, to state it differently, an injunction would be effective against them. We cannot excuse appellees [Al Lucas and Al

> Lucas Enterprises, Inc.] from their promise not to compete because, technically, Mrs. Lucas and her corporation were not parties to the agreement. Mr. Lucas cannot be allowed to do indirectly, through his wife and her controlled corporation, that which he covenanted not to do himself.

Id. at 929. In *Layer*, Bus. Franchise Guide (CCH) ¶ 13,257, the court also found that a franchisor could enforce the terms of a written covenant not to compete against non-signatories deemed to be the assignees of a franchised business where franchisee indicated that he gave business to his wife. As in the *Dad's Properties*, it was clear in *Pirtek USA, LLC v. Layer* that the covenantor's wife and her controlled company were aiding and abetting the covenantor in the intentional violation of a valid covenant not to compete.

An injunction may also bind non-party competing businesses that hires employees who are a party to a non-compete agreement. *Office Depot, Inc. v. Impact Office Products, LLC*, No. 1:09-cv-2791, 2011 WL 4833117, at *19 (N.D. Oh. Oct. 12, 2011) (applying Florida law, enjoining current employer of former employee from soliciting or servicing former customers of former employer who were converted by former employee for a period of six months)

8. Will the state modify, "blue-pencil," or otherwise reduce a covenant found to be overbroad?

Under the law applicable to restrictive covenants and non-compete agreements entered into prior to July 1, 1996, a court will modify unreasonable restrictions and enforce them to the extent reasonable, the rationale being that voiding a restrictive covenant altogether would frustrate the intent of the legislature and the parties. *See Health Care Fin. Enters.*, 715 So. 2d at 342–43; *Miller Mech.*, 300 So. 2d at 12; *Flammer v. Patton*, 245 So. 2d 854 (Fla. 1971); *Orkin Exterminating Co. v. Martin*, 516 So. 2d 970, 971–72 (Fla. Dist. Ct. App. 1987). When the legislature created Florida Statute Section 542.335 in 1996, it specifically added that "[i]f a contractually specified restraint is overbroad, overlong, or otherwise not reasonably necessary to protect the legitimate business interest or interests, a court shall modify the restraint and grant only the relief reasonably necessary to protect such interest or interests." FLA. STAT. § 542.335(1)(c) (2020); *see Proudfoot*, 576 F.3d at 1231. Therefore, if a time, area, or line of business provision is found overbroad, it will be modified by the court and enforced, not stricken, regardless of when the agreement was entered into. A restrictive covenant or non-compete agreement that omits one of these terms remains enforceable. The court will supply the missing term. *See Env't Servs.*, 9 So. 3d at 1264; *Sears*, 745 So. 2d at 486. In modifying a non-compete agreement, the Florida Supreme Court has touted the trial courts' wide discretion to create a "context-dependent" solution. *White*, 226 So. 3d at 785.

In *Labor Finders*, Bus. Franchise Guide (CCH) ¶ 11,723, the court applied a Florida choice-of-law provision in a franchise agreement to a situation where the franchisor, pursuant to a contractual right to reduce the scope of the covenant not to compete, had modified the covenant not to compete following the expiration of the franchise agreement to reduce the scope of the stated restrictions. The court found that the contractual provision allowing the franchisor to unilaterally reduce the scope of a franchise agreement's non-competition provision was not void under Florida law. The court further held that the post-termination covenant not to compete, as modified by the franchisor pursuant to the terms of the franchise agreement, was reasonable in geographic scope and duration under Florida law.

---

9. When does a non-compete period begin to run?

➤ Will courts equitably extend the term?

There is no statutory or common law rule for when a covenant begins to run. Florida courts look first to the terms of the contract to govern the starting point and duration of such restrictive covenants. In *Marx v. Clear Channel Broad., Inc.*, 887 So. 2d 405, 406 (Fla. Dist. Ct. App. 2004), the Fourth District Court of Appeal noted that "[t]he general rule as to interpretation of noncompetition agreements is that such contracts will not be construed to extend beyond their proper import or further than language of the contract absolutely requires." If a restrictive covenant is triggered by a certain condition, courts seem to look closely to see that the condition was, in fact, satisfied.

Florida courts have held that post-termination non-compete restrictions contained in an agreement for a specific term expire once the agreement containing the restriction has been fully performed and the term of the written agreement expires. *See Zupnick v. All Fla. Paper, Inc.*, 997 So. 2d 1234, 1238 (Fla. Dist. Ct. App. 2008); *Sanz v. R.T. Aerospace Corp.*, 650 So. 2d 1057, 1059 (Fla. Dist. Ct. App. 1995). However, non-compete provisions survive the expiration of an agreement where (1) the contract expressly provides that its terms will continue after the contract's expiration and (2) the contract expressly provides that the non-compete clause will continue to be in effect following the expiration or termination of the agreement. *See St. John's Inv. Mgmt. Co. v. Albaneze*, 22 So. 3d 728, 732 (Fla. Dist. Ct. App. 2009); *Brenner v. Barco Chem. Div., Inc.*, 209 So. 2d 277, 278 (Fla. Dist. Ct. App. 1968).

Under the pre-1990 statute, Florida law recognized that courts could equitably extend the term of a valid covenant not to compete to give effect to the parties' non-competition agreement. In *Capelouto v. Orkin Exterminating Co.*, 183 So. 2d 532, 535 (Fla. 1966), the Florida Supreme Court affirmed the chancellor's decision to enjoin the activity of a former employee who had breached his covenant not to compete. The court reasoned that:

> [U]nder the contract the appellee-employer was entitled to have a period of two years during which the appellant-employee would not be in competition with it and in contact with its customers in the area involved. Inasmuch as the appellant had been in competition with the appellee continuously since his resignation, the chancellor must have determined that this was the only way to give the appellee its two competition-free years. We can find no fault with this theory or with the result of its application.

Id. at 534. The court's reasoning in *Capelouto* remains valid. In *Michele Pommier Models, Inc. v. Diel*, 886 So. 2d 993, 996 (Fla. Dist. Ct. App. 2004), the Third District Court of Appeal noted that "[i]t is well established that Florida caselaw permits a non-compete period to be equitably extended to allow for what was intended in the bargain." (citing *Capelouto*, 183 So. 2d at 535). Indeed, the federal court for the Southern District of Florida in *Cheney v. IPD Analytics, LLC*, No. 08-23-188-CIV, 2009 WL 1298405, at *3 (S.D. Fla. Apr. 16, 2009), also recognized that "Florida case law permits a non-compete period to be equitably extended to allow for what was intended in the bargain." (citing *Sunbelt Rentals, Inc. v. Dirienzo*, 487 F. Supp. 2d 1361, 1363 (S.D. Fla. 2007)); *see also Anakarli Boutique, Inc. v. Ortiz*, 152 So. 3d 107, 109 (Fla. Dist. Ct. App. 2014) (extending non-compete period where majority of period ran while former employer was appealing trial court's erroneous denial of injunction to enforce the same).

10. Are there additional nuances or peculiarities of the state's treatment of covenants in the franchising context?

Florida law regarding covenants not to compete entered into after July 1, 1996, is governed by a detailed statute that sets out the relevant factors for courts to consider. The statute's level of detail includes the presumptions as to reasonable geographic scope and time duration limitations. Such detail allows for greater certainty in enforcing such covenants. The analysis under section 542.335 also is more "pro-enforcement" than in many states because it expressly allows the court to "blue-pencil" and thus preserve overbroad covenants. In addition, certain defenses to enforcement have been limited by section 542.335.

First, a court "[s]hall not consider any individualized economic or other hardship that might be caused to the person against whom enforcement is sought." FLA. STAT. § 542.335(1)(g)(1) (2020). That is, the fact that enforcement of a restrictive covenant or non-compete agreement might have negative economic consequences for a franchisee should not be considered as a defense to enforcement by the court. This unambiguous language chosen by the legislature clearly eliminates what was, at least for a time, a consideration before the court when ruling on a non-compete agreement. *See Auto Club Affiliates*, 81 So. at 241 (employer must not deprive employee of a skill on which he or she depends for his or her livelihood); *Miller Mech.*, 300 So. 2d at 12 (balancing test must weigh employer's interest in preventing competition against oppressive effect on employee); *Gore*, 506 So. 2d at 92 (injunction enforcing non-compete agreement must not unduly restrict one's livelihood). It must be noted, however, that this defense remains viable under covenants not to compete entered into before July 1, 1996. Although in *Sarasota Beverage*, 551 So. 2d at 506, the Second District Court of Appeal declared the defense unavailable under the pre-1990 statute, no other court has ever expressly overruled it. Given the uncertain state of the prior law, it is possible that this defense could be successfully asserted.

In addition to abolishing the economic hardship defense for agreements after July 1, 1996, the new amendment instructs that the court "[m]ay consider as a defense the fact that the person seeking enforcement no longer continues in business in the area or line of business that is the subject of the action to enforce the restrictive covenant only if such discontinuance of business is not the result of a violation of the restriction." FLA. STAT. § 542.335(1)(g)(2) (2020). This represents a significant departure from the prior rule, where the franchisor ostensibly had to show that it continued to carry on a like business during the time and area of the restriction sought in order to obtain enforcement of the restriction. The scope of this pre-1996 requirement has never been fully examined in an appellate court decision. However, the Florida Circuit Court of the Thirteenth Judicial Circuit, Hillsborough County, addressed the issue in 1993, suggesting that the requirement is less than absolute under the prior law. *Int'l Bartending Inst.*, Bus. Franchise Guide (CCH)

¶ 10,222. Whether or not the franchisor continues business in the time and area of the former franchisee is only a consideration, not a total defense, as the prior statute might seem to suggest. The date on which the restrictive covenant was entered into will determine which rule to apply.

In re Printronics, 189 B.R. at 1000, addressed the enforcement of a non-compete agreement in the bankruptcy context. The bankruptcy court in that case held that a debtor/printing franchisee's rejection of its franchise agreement as an executory contract under federal bankruptcy law would not be equivalent to termination of the agreement and, therefore, would not preclude enforcement of a reasonable covenant not to compete contained in the agreement. *Id.* Additionally, the court held that the covenant not to compete was not a "claim" subject to discharge under federal bankruptcy law, as injunctive relief was the franchisor's exclusive remedy for future breaches of the covenant. *Id.* at 1002. The debtor/franchisee could only discharge prior breaches of the non-competition agreement. *Id.*

A Florida court has recently weighed in on the non-poaching clauses that have become a standard part of franchise agreements in the last decade. In the context of franchisor no-poach agreements, a trial court in the Southern District of Florida set aside the question of which standard should be applied to determine whether such agreements were unreasonable, and held that franchisee and franchisor should be treated as a single entity with a unity of interest and thus incapable of conspiring in violation of the first section of the Sherman Act. *Arrington v. Burger King Worldwide, Inc.*, 448 F. Supp. 3d 1322 (S.D. Fla. 2020). In *Arrington*, franchisee employees alleged that the franchisor's no-poach agreements were per se unlawful under the antitrust laws and amounted to an unreasonable restraint on trade. *Id.* at 1327. The court held that the franchisor's relationship with its franchisees was more akin to that of a corporate parent to a subsidiary, thus rendering treatment as a single entity under the antitrust laws. *Id.* at 1330. In making that determination, the *Arrington* court noted that both the franchisor's existence and success were "wholly dependent on systemwide uniformity." *Id.* at 1331. Accordingly, the court held that because franchisor could not conspire with franchisees, the no-poach agreement did not violate the Sherman Act. *Id.* at 1332 (citing *Williams v. I.B. Fischer Nevada*, 999 F.2d 445, 447 (9th Cir. 1993)). While the trial court ruled that the franchisor's no-poach agreement served as an agreement to internally implement a single, uniform policy, it nonetheless noted that a functional and fact-specific approach is necessary in determining whether a franchisor-franchisee relationship can run afoul of antitrust laws. *Id.* At time of publication, the case was on its way to argument before the Eleventh Circuit. While this case did not address no-poaching agreements in the context of Florida's restrictive covenant statutory scheme, it will likely be the first of many cases in the state to attack employee no-poach provisions made by franchisees.

Finally, it is worth noting that Florida caselaw supports a franchisee's enforcement of a "non-compete agreement" or "exclusivity provision" against a franchisor where an exclusive territory is provided to a franchisee. In *Gossard v. Adia Servs., Inc.*, 723 So. 2d 182 (Fla. 1998), the Florida Supreme Court answered the following question certified by the U.S. Court of Appeals for the Eleventh Circuit: "Whether Florida law recognizes a claim for tortious interference against a corporation which purchases as a subsidiary a corporation which has a pre-existing obligation not to compete against its franchisee, and subsequently purchases another subsidiary which is in direct competition with the franchisee?" The Florida Supreme Court provided the following factual summary:

> [W]e understand Gossard's claim to be based on the following assertions. Nursefinders and Gossard had an "agreement" that neither a parent nor affiliate of Nursefinders would provide similar health care services within Gossard's territory. Adia was aware of this "agreement" at the time it purchased Nursefinders. Adia then purchased Star-Med, a direct competitor of Gossard located in Gossard's territory. Consequently, Star-Med became Nursefinders' affiliate by virtue of their common parent, Adia. Therefore, by purchasing Star-Med, Adia knowingly caused Nursefinders to be in breach of its "promise" to Gossard that neither a parent nor affiliate of Nursefinders would provide similar health care services with Gossard's territory. Stated another way, because of Adia's purchase of Star-Med, Nursefinder had "no choice" but to be in violation of its franchise agreement with Gossard.

Gossard, 723 So. 2d at 184. Based on the facts presented, the Florida Supreme Court held that a prima facie case of tortious interference was established and answered the certified question in the affirmative.

Georgia

*by Ronald T. Coleman, Jr. and Paul R. Barsness**

1. Has the state addressed covenants against competition in the context of franchising?

- **Does the state have a franchising statute or regulations that address covenants against competition?**
- **Does the state have a covenants statute of general applicability that would encompass franchise covenants?**
- **Have the courts addressed covenants in the context of franchising either under a statute or under the state's common law?**

In 2011, Georgia adopted a new restrictive covenant statute, the Georgia Restrictive Covenants Act (GRCA), which made significant changes to the decades of common-law rules and decisions that had made Georgia widely known for its hostility toward enforcing non-competition and non-solicitation agreements, including in the franchise context. Georgia's new law has now been in effect for over ten years. It specifically addresses franchise agreements, provides clearer guidance to franchisors seeking to enforce contractual restrictive covenants, and gives courts broader discretion to modify and enforce covenants that unquestionably would be stricken under the prior common law. Although the GRCA has been in effect for over ten years, there is still limited caselaw, particularly from Georgia appellate courts, interpreting the statute.

The judicially created law as it existed before 2011 remains relevant, however, because it continues to apply to any contract entered into prior to the effective date of the new statute. Under prior law, the enforceability of even a relatively narrow restrictive covenant was often highly uncertain. Moreover, the lack of specific constitutional or statutory guidance under the old law meant that parties had to wade through a maze of fact-specific, and at times inconsistent, caselaw in an effort to evaluate the enforceability of a restrictive covenant.

Many of the cases discussed in this chapter involve employment agreements because Georgia law generally treats franchise agreements like employment

*Ronald T. Coleman, Jr. and Paul R. Barsness are partners with the law firm of Parker Hudson Rainer & Dobbs LLP in Atlanta, Georgia. They wish to acknowledge the contribution of Jared C. Miller, also a partner with the same firm, who co-authored this chapter for the third edition.

agreements under both the pre-2011 common law and the GRCA. Although the presumptively reasonable time period for restrictive covenants in the GRCA is greater for franchise agreements (three years) than employment agreements (two years), the term "employee" is defined to include franchisees, GA. CODE ANN. § 13-8-51(5)(D), and the statute otherwise generally applies to franchise agreements in the same manner as employment agreements.

AGREEMENTS ENTERED UNDER THE NEW LAW

For agreements entered into on or after May 11, 2011, the GRCA attempts to harmonize and codify preexisting caselaw with the goal to make enforcement of restrictive covenants more consistent and predictable. *See* GA. CODE ANN. § 13-8-50.

The GRCA applies only to certain types of specifically enumerated contracts including agreements between franchisors and franchisees, between distributors and manufacturers, and between employers and employees. GA. CODE ANN. § 13-8-52; *see also* GA. CODE ANN. § 13-8-51(5) (defining "employee" to include franchisees, distributors, and representatives in connection with franchise and distributorship agreements). In a reversal of Georgia's prior public policy disfavoring restrictive covenants, the Georgia General Assembly has now recognized the importance of reasonable restrictive covenants designed to protect legitimate business interests. *See* GA. CODE ANN. § 13-8-50 ("The General Assembly finds that reasonable restrictive covenants contained in employment and commercial contracts serve the legitimate purpose of protecting legitimate business interests and creating an environment that is favorable to attracting commercial enterprises to Georgia and keeping existing businesses within the state."); *see also* GA. CODE ANN. § 13-8-54 (courts shall construe restrictive covenants "in favor of providing reasonable protection to all legitimate business interests").

GA

Like Georgia's pre-2011 common law, the GRCA permits the enforcement of restrictive covenants that contain reasonable temporal and territorial restrictions and that prohibit a reasonable scope of activities. *See* GA. CODE ANN. § 13-8-53 ("[E]nforcement of contracts that restrict competition during the time of a restrictive covenant, as long as such restrictions are reasonable in time, geographic area, and scope of prohibited activities, shall be permitted."). The GRCA provides specific guidance regarding the factors to be considered in analyzing the enforceability of restrictive covenants, including certain presumptions relating to the traditional reasonableness factors of time, territory, and prohibited activities. Perhaps the most important feature of the GRCA, however, is that it permits courts to "blue-pencil" and modify overbroad restrictive covenants, rather than requiring courts to strike overbroad provisions in their entirety. These specifics are discussed in more detail in the following sections.

AGREEMENTS ENTERED PRIOR TO THE NEW LAW

Agreements entered into prior to May 11, 2011, are governed by the common law. The GRCA applies to contracts "entered into on and after May 11, 2011, and shall not apply in actions determining the enforceability of restrictive covenants entered into before such date." *Fortress Investment Group, LLC v. Holsinger*, 354 Ga. App. 405, 411 (2020).

Prior to its amendment in November 2010, the Georgia Constitution provided: "The General Assembly shall not have the power to authorize any contract or agreement which *may have the effect of or which is intended to have the effect of defeating or lessening competition*, or encouraging a monopoly, which are hereby declared to be unlawful and void." GA. CONST. art. III, § VI, para. V(c) (emphasis added). Georgia courts construed non-competition agreements and contractual restrictive covenants, including those in franchise agreements, to be contracts having "the effect of defeating or lessening competition." As a result, such covenants were generally disfavored in Georgia, and courts developed strict rules limiting their enforceability.

Georgia courts applied very strict scrutiny in reviewing restrictive covenants in franchise agreements under the pre-2011 law: "A non-competition covenant entered into in connection with a franchise or employment contract is enforceable, but only where it is strictly limited in time and territorial effect and is otherwise reasonable considering the business interest of the employer sought to be protected and the effect on the franchisee." *Allen v. Hub Cap Heaven, Inc.*, 225 Ga. App. 533, 538, 484 S.E.2d 259, 264 (1997); *see also Atlanta Bread Co.*, 285 Ga. at 589, 679 S.E.2d at 724; *Owens v. RMA Sales*, 183 Ga. App. 340, 341, 358 S.E.2d 897, 899 (1987); *Law v. Kwik-Kopy Corp.*, No. C85-2997A, 1986 U.S. Dist. LEXIS 28483, at *6 (N.D. Ga. Mar. 6, 1986); *Uni-Worth Enterprises, Inc. v. Wilson*, 244 Ga. 636, 638–39, 261 S.E.2d 572, 574 (1979). The strict scrutiny "reasonableness" test employed by Georgia courts under the old law requires a case-specific analysis. *Hub Cap Heaven*, 225 Ga. App. at 538, 484 S.E.2d at 264. Whether a particular restrictive covenant is reasonable is a question of law for determination by the court. *Ceramic & Metal Coatings Corp. v. Hizer*, 242 Ga. App. 391, 392, 529 S.E.2d 160, 162 (2000).

As a general matter, practitioners and franchisors evaluating the enforceability of restrictive covenants in Georgia under the pre-2011 law are well advised to carefully review Georgia's restrictions on enforcing covenants not to compete in the franchise *and* employment contexts. Georgia courts strongly disfavor such covenants and will enforce them only if they are narrowly drafted to comply with the limitations established by Georgia caselaw regarding time, scope, and geographic territory. Moreover, to the extent franchisors still have any franchisees operating under pre-2011 franchise agreements, franchisors should not consider having those franchisees execute new agreements or amendments to take advantage of the benefits contained in the GRCA.

---

2. Have the courts articulated the "legitimate interests" of the franchisor that will support enforcement of a covenant against competition contained in a franchise agreement?

- **If so, what are they (e.g., protection of goodwill, protection of confidential information), and in what contexts did the issue arise?**
- **If not, what interests have been recognized in other contexts (e.g., employment agreements, the sale of business context)?**

AGREEMENTS ENTERED UNDER THE NEW LAW

Georgia Code section 13-8-55 provides: "The person seeking enforcement of a restrictive covenant shall plead and prove the existence of one or more legitimate business reasons justifying the restrictive covenant." The term "legitimate business interest" is defined as including, but not limited to:

A. Trade secrets;

B. Valuable confidential information that otherwise does not qualify as a trade secret;

C. Substantial relationships with specific prospective or existing customers, patients, vendors, or clients;

D. Customer, patient, or client goodwill associated with an ongoing business or professional practice (including by way of a trade name, trade mark, service mark, or trade dress), a specific geographic location, or a specific marketing or trade area; and

E. Extraordinary or specialized training.

GA. CODE ANN. § 13-8-51(9). *See also Kennedy v. Shave Barber Co., LLC*, 348 Ga. App. 298, 305 (2018) (preventing loss of customer goodwill is legitimate interest); *Global Payments Inc. v. Green*, 484 F. Supp. 3d 1372 (M.D. Ga. 2020) (recognizing legitimate interest in client and partner relationships, goodwill, and confidential and trade secret information); *Heartland Payment Systs, LLC v. Stockwell*, 446 F. Supp. 3d 1275 (N.D. Ga. 2020) (protecting investment in developing skills of employee, protecting client relationships, and protecting confidential and/or trade secret information are legitimate business interests to support non-compete). Franchisors drafting covenants to comply with the GRCA should include recitals or other agreement provisions whereby the franchisee expressly recognizes these interests and the existence of these factors.

Protecting *former* clients or employees was not a legitimate business interest under the pre-GRCA common law and will not likely support a covenant under the GRCA. In *Martin v. Hauser, Inc.*, 2021 WL 1053637 (Ga. Bus. Ct. Mar. 5, 2021), the newly created State-Wide Business Court held that a covenant prohibiting the solicitation of entities who "were customers or clients of Company at . . . any time during the 18 months prior to [Plaintiff's] employment terminating" was overbroad in violation of section 13-8-53(b). The court noted that it was "well-established" prior to the GRCA that "there was no legitimate business interest in prohibiting the solicitation of former clients or customers." *Id.* at *10 (citing cases). According to the court, nothing in the GRCA reflects an intent "to abrogate this common sense principle." *Id.* The court used its blue-pencil authority under the GRCA to limit the clause to just customers or clients at the time of the employee's termination. *Id.* at *11.

AGREEMENTS ENTERED PRIOR TO THE NEW LAW

In the employment context, a restrictive covenant must be limited to the scope necessary to protect the legitimate interests of the employer. *Allen v. Hub Cap Heaven, Inc.*, 225 Ga. App. 533, 538, 484 S.E.2d 259, 264 (1997). Under Georgia's "reasonableness" test, courts consider the nature of the employer's business interest and the duties performed by the employee to determine whether the scope of a non-competition provision is overbroad. Georgia courts generally require that the scope of restricted activities must be limited to the type of activities that the employee performed for the former employer. Georgia courts have routinely invalidated restrictive covenants that prohibit an employee from working for a competitor "in any capacity." *Stultz v. Safety & Compliance Management, Inc.*, 285 Ga. App. 799, 802, 648 S.E.2d 129 (2007) (in context of employment agreement).

The few Georgia courts that have examined the nature of a franchisor's legitimate business interests focus on whether the franchisee was the "heart and soul" of the franchised business and whether the franchisee gained knowledge that the franchisor has a "reasonable stake in protecting." *Allen*, 225 Ga. App. at 538, 484 S.E.2d at 264 (citing *Watson v. Waffle House, Inc.*, 253 Ga. 671, 673, 324 S.E.2d 175, 178 (1985)). In *Allen*, the court of appeals treated the franchisor's interest as a threshold issue, finding that Hub Cap Heaven had a legitimate interest in protecting the knowledge it imparted to Allen and that Allen was the heart and soul of Allen's franchised business. Despite recognizing Hub Cap Heaven's legitimate interest in enforcing the covenant, the *Allen* court went on to hold that the covenant's duration was overbroad and thus unenforceable. In *Watson*, the court upheld a narrower covenant not to compete based, in part, on the defendant's access to proprietary information.

Because Georgia courts have held that franchise agreements are not analogous to agreements for the sale of businesses, the legitimate interest of the buyer of a business that it not face competition from the seller in the same business purchased from the seller is inapplicable. Focusing on the employment context, Georgia courts have identified the following as "legitimate interests" of the employer: (1) the employer's time and monetary investment in employees' skills and development, e.g., *Beckman v. Cox Broadcasting Corp.*, 250 Ga. 127, 296 S.E.2d 566 (1982); *Lighting Galleries, Inc. v. Drummond*, 247 Ga. App. 124, 126, 543 S.E.2d 419, 421 (2000) ("The employer has interests in protecting its investment in the development of the employee's skills and craft and in preventing the employee from taking unfair advantage of customer relationships he developed while working for the employer."); (2) customer relations and goodwill, e.g., *Howard Schultz & Associates v. Broniec*, 239 Ga. 181, 183, 236 S.E.2d 265, 268 (1977) ("a court will accept as prima facie valid a covenant related to the territory where the employee was employed as a legitimate protection of the employer's investment in customer relations and goodwill"); *Palmer & Cay of Georgia, Inc. v. Lockton Cos.*, 280 Ga. 479, 481, 629 S.E.2d 800, 803 (2006) (employer has "legitimate business interest to protect in preventing [Employees] from leaving and encouraging clients to leave with [them]"); *Murphree v. Yancey Brothers Co.*, 311 Ga. App. 744, 748, 716 S.E.2d 824, 827 (2011) (employer has "a protectable interest in the customer relationships its former employee established and/or nurtured while employed by the employer"); and (3) confidential information, e.g., *Johnson v. Lee*, 243 Ga. 864, 866, 257 S.E.2d 273, 275 (1979) (upholding covenant when employee took with him information "such as identities of present and potential customers, and details of bids entered for maintenance contracts"); *Lee v. Environmental Pest & Termite Control, Inc.*, 271 Ga. 371, 373, 516 S.E.2d 76, 78 (1999) ("When a duty has been imposed upon an employee pursuant to contract not to disclose confidential business information upon termination of employment, public policy is swung in favor of protecting these commercial intangibles and of preventing unfair methods of exploiting them in breach of duty.").

---

3. What time limitations have courts recognized as reasonable in the franchise context?

- **If no franchise cases have been decided, what time limitations have been recognized in other contexts?**
- **How have they been related to the interests protected?**

AGREEMENTS ENTERED UNDER THE NEW LAW

As a general matter, the GRCA allows the enforcement of any contract that restricts competition provided that the restrictions contained in the restrictive covenant are reasonable in time, geographic area, and scope of prohibited activities. GA. CODE ANN. § 13-8-53(a).

The GRCA offers parties specific guidance regarding the maximum time period for which a restriction is presumptively reasonable. Under the GRCA, for a restrictive covenant sought to be enforced against a current or former franchisee, distributor, dealer, lessee of property, or trademark licensee not involving the sale of a business or equity interest in a business or professional enterprise, "a court shall presume to be reasonable in time any restraint three years or less in duration and shall presume to be unreasonable in time any restraint more than three years in duration" following the date of termination of the business relationship. GA. CODE ANN. § 13-8-57(c).[1] Numerous cases have held that time periods within the statutory presumption are clearly enforceable. *See, e.g., U.S. Security Assocs., Inc. v. Schwartz*, 2019 WL 10303652, at *5 (N.D. Ga. Feb. 15, 2019). To date, there are no reported decisions where a court refused to enforce a time period less than the presumptively reasonable period.

These presumptions are rebuttable, but the statute does not explain what evidence might be persuasive to rebut them. *Martin v. Hauser, Inc.*, 2021 WL 1053637 (Ga. Bus. Ct. Mar. 5, 2021) is an example of a company's failure to rebut the statutory presumption of unreasonableness for a longer covenant. *Martin* was an employment case, so the shorter two-year time period applied instead of the three-year period for franchisees. The employment contract had a three-year restriction, which the court noted was presumptively unreasonable under the GRCA. The company's president testified that it could take two to three years to develop a client relationship but acknowledged that "acquisition rates vary considerably." *Id.* at *7. He could not explain why three years was chosen and also acknowledged that the three-year period was included in every employee's agreement regardless of their role or access to sensitive information. The court held that the testimony failed to rebut the presumption of unreasonableness but exercised its authority to modify the provision. Notably, rather than shorten the duration to the presumptively reasonable two-year period, the court modified the restriction to just one year. *Id.* at *9. Better drafting likely would have given the company another year of protection.

For restrictions during the term of an employment or business relationship, restrictions "equal to or measured by duration of the parties' business or commercial relationship" are considered presumptively reasonable, provided that the length of the post-term restriction complies with section 13-8-57. GA. CODE ANN. § 13-8-56(1).[2] Furthermore, the statute specifically provides that an in-term restrictive covenant, including one operating during the term of a franchise relationship,

GA

1. *Compare* GA. CODE ANN. § 13-8-57(b) (restrictive covenants against employees are presumptively reasonable if two years or less) *with* GA. CODE ANN. § 13-8-57(d) (restrictive covenants ancillary to the sale of a business or equity interest in a commercial enterprise are presumptively reasonable for the longer of five years or the period of time during which payments are being made as a result of such a sale).

2. Although it does not expressly reference franchise relationships, GA. CODE ANN. § 13-8-56(1) appears to apply to franchise relationships because it applies to "employment or *business* relationships." (emphasis added). *But cf.* GA. CODE ANN. § 13-8-56(4) (specifically referencing franchise relationships).

shall not be considered unreasonable because it lacks a specific limitation upon the duration of the restriction "so long as it promotes or protects the purpose or subject matter of the agreement or relationship or deters any potential conflict of interest." GA. CODE ANN. § 13-8-56(4).

With respect to agreements to refrain from soliciting the business of a former employer's customers (*see infra* Section 5), the new statute provides that, notwithstanding any other provision in the statute, parties may agree to such a provision "for a stated period of time following termination" provided that the other requirements for enforceability are satisfied. GA. CODE ANN. § 13-8-53(b).

AGREEMENTS ENTERED PRIOR TO THE NEW LAW

There is greater uncertainty with older agreements governed by the common law. Noncompetition clauses must be reasonably limited in duration. *See, e.g., Watson v. Waffle House, Inc.*, 253 Ga. 671, 324 S.E.2d 175 (1985); *Howard Schultz & Associates v. Broniec*, 239 Ga. 181, 236 S.E.2d 265 (1977) (contract for services by an independent contractor treated as employment contract); *Rakestraw v. Lanier*, 104 Ga. 188, 30 S.E. 735 (1898) (partnership). There is, however, no per se reasonable (or unreasonable) period. *Johnson v. Lee*, 243 Ga. 864, 866, 257 S.E.2d 273, 275 (1979).

Georgia courts have upheld as reasonable in the franchise context periods including one year, *Williams v. Shrimp Boat, Inc.*, 229 Ga. 300, 191 S.E.2d 50 (1972) (covenant barring competition in any county specified by the contract as having a franchise reasonable as to time and territory and otherwise valid, but agreement only referred to one unit); two years, *Watson, supra*; and three years, *Mansfield v. B. & W. Gas, Inc.*, 222 Ga. 259, 149 S.E.2d 482 (1966) (upholding non-competition provision in contract of independent contractor, labeled as "exclusive franchise" by court, prohibiting sale of butane or propane within ten-mile radius). But courts also have invalidated two-year covenants. *T.E. McCutcheon Enterprises, Inc. v. Snelling & Snelling, Inc.*, 232 Ga. 609, 212 S.E.2d 319 (1974) (non-competition covenant of two years within ten miles of franchise or one year within five miles of franchise or any other franchise was unenforceable); *Richard R Rita Personnel Services International v. Kot*, 229 Ga. 314, 315, 317, 191 S.E.2d 79 (1972) (two-year non-competition covenant in three metro-Atlanta counties or other territories where franchise has been granted was overbroad).

Periods held to be reasonable in the employment context are similar. *See, e.g., Beckman v. Cox Broadcasting Corp.*, 250 Ga. 127, 296 S.E.2d 566 (1982) (six months); *Puritan/Churchill Chemical Co. v. McDaniel*, 248 Ga. 850, 286 S.E.2d 297 (1982) (two years); *Palmer & Cay of Georgia, Inc. v. Lockton Cos.*, 284 Ga. App. 196, 199, 643 S.E.2d 746, 749 (2007) (two-year non-solicitation covenant limited to certain products); *McMurray v. Bateman*, 221 Ga. 240, 144 S.E.2d 345 (1965) (three years). The longest period upheld in a reported Georgia decision is five years. *See Johnson v. Lee, supra; Smith v. HBT, Inc.*, 213 Ga. App. 560, 445 S.E.2d 315 (1994); *see also Hicks v. Doors by Mike, Inc.*, 260 Ga. App. 407, 579 S.E.2d 833 (2003) (restrictive covenants covering five years and 50-mile geographical scope were enforceable in conjunction with sale of business, to which "much less scrutiny" applies).

Georgia courts generally refuse to enforce attempts by drafters of covenants to extend the time period covered by a covenant not to compete through tolling provisions that "stop the clock" during any violation of the covenant on the theory that such tolling provisions potentially extend the duration of such covenants indefinitely and are, therefore, unreasonable. *See infra* Section 9.

4. What geographic limitations have courts recognized as reasonable in the franchise context?

- **How have they been related to the interests protected?**
- **Have courts recognized the legitimacy of protecting other franchisees from competition?**

AGREEMENTS ENTERED UNDER THE NEW LAW

As a general matter, Georgia's new restrictive covenant statute allows the enforcement of any contract that restricts competition provided that the restrictions contained in the covenant are reasonable in time, geographic area, and scope of prohibited activities. GA. CODE ANN. § 13-8-53(a).

The GRCA authorizes a restriction based on "the territory where the employee is working at the time of termination" or similar language, so long as the person bound by the restraint "can reasonably determine the maximum reasonable scope of the restraint at the time of the termination." GA. CODE ANN. § 13-8-53(c)(2). It is advisable to parrot the language of the statute in the contract, and courts are freely enforcing contractual language similar to that in the statute such as "within the territory where Employee is working for Employer at the time of Employee's termination." *U.S. Security Assocs., Inc. v. Schwartz*, 2019 WL 10303652, at *5 (N.D. Ga. Feb. 15, 2019). This provision is designed to uphold restrictions described by reference to an employee's territory, rather than requiring an employer to have an employee sign a new contract every time the employee changes territories. Although the language of this section of the statute does not specifically reference the franchise context, it is reasonable to assume that this provision applies to both employment and franchise agreements.

GA

Moreover, territorial restrictions are sufficient when they "provide[] fair notice of the maximum reasonable scope of the restraint," even if the description is generalized or "could possibly be stated more narrowly to exclude extraneous matters." GA. CODE ANN. § 13-8-53(c)(1). The statute also permits parties to make a "good faith estimate" of the restricted geographic area that will apply at the time of termination, even if the estimate ultimately includes extraneous geographic areas. In the event such a restriction is overbroad, it will be construed to cover only the geographic areas in which the employee was actually involved within a reasonable time prior to termination rather than struck down entirely. *Id.*

The statute further provides that geographic restrictions, whether in-term or post term, are presumptively reasonable if they "include[] the areas in which the employer does business at any time during the parties' relationship, even if not known at the time of entry into the restrictive covenant," provided that: "(A) The total distance encompassed by the provisions of the covenant also is reasonable" and/or "(B) The agreement contains a list of particular competitors as prohibited employers for a limited period of time after the term of employment or a business or commercial relationship." GA. CODE ANN. § 13-8-56(2).[3] The statute specifically

---

3. Although it does not expressly reference franchise relationships, GA. CODE ANN. § 13-8-56(2) appears to apply to franchise relationships because it applies to "employment or *business* relationships." (emphasis added). *But cf.* GA. CODE ANN. § 13-8-56(4) (specifically referencing franchise relationships).

provides that an in-term restrictive covenant, including those operating during the term of a franchise relationship, shall not be considered unreasonable because it lacks a specific limitation as to geographic area "so long as it promotes or protects the purpose or subject matter of the agreement or relationship or deters any potential conflict of interest." GA. CODE ANN. § 13-8-56(4).

With respect to agreements to refrain from soliciting the business of a former employer's customers (*see infra* Section 5), the new statute provides that "[n]o express reference to geographic area . . . shall be required in order for the restraint to be enforceable" provided that the other requirements for enforceability are satisfied. GA. CODE ANN. § 13-8-53(b).

The statute further provides that a court shall not refuse to enforce a restrictive covenant merely because the party seeking enforcement has failed to prove that the covenant has been violated as to the entire geographic area of the covenant. GA. CODE ANN. § 13-8-56(3) (where party has presented evidence that covenant has been violated, but not "violated as to the entire scope of the prohibited activities of the person seeking enforcement or as to the entire geographic area of the covenant," a court shall not refuse to enforce the covenant solely on that basis).

The reasonableness of the restrictive covenant's geographic territory is one of the most litigated issues under the GRCA. Courts have the authority to modify or "blue-pencil" unreasonable restrictions, but the scope of that authority is a disputed issue (*see infra* Section 8), as is whether an employee non-solicitation clause requires a geographic territory.

Non-competition covenants require a geographic territory

While customer non-solicitation clauses are expressly exempted from the GRCA's requirement to have a geographic territory, non-competition covenants are not. A covenant that prohibits the acceptance of business from particular customers is a non-compete provision, rather than a non-solicit, and must satisfy the statutory requirements for a non-compete, including a geographic territory. *See DJR Assocs., LLC v. Hammonds*, 241 F. Supp. 3d 1208, 1229 (N.D. Ga. 2018) (holding that a provision prohibiting the acceptance of business must satisfy the requirements for a non-compete). There are a few cases invalidating restrictions because of the absence of a geographic territory. In *Carpetcare Multiservices, LLC v. Carle*, 347 Ga. App. 497 (2018), one of the few Georgia Court of Appeals decisions interpreting the GRCA, the contractual provision prohibited the individual from providing services to any customer with whom he had material contact. The court of appeals rejected the argument that limiting the "type of customer" that an individual could work with was a sufficient alternative to a geographic area. According to the court, because the covenant "did not contain any reference to a geographic area limitation," it was void and unenforceable. *Id.* at 500. The GRCA does contemplate client-based non-competition provisions, which may afford opportunities to protect areas beyond the territory where a specific employee worked, but they still require a reasonable territory to be enforceable. In *Gallagher Benefit Srvs, Inc. v. Campbell*, 2021 WL 1140204 (N.D. Ga. Mar. 24, 2021), the court enforced a client-based restriction throughout the entire United States, because the company was not a regional company and operated on a nationwide scale.

In *Chef Merito, Inc. v. Gonzalez*, 2020 WL 5548339 (N.D. Ga. Aug. 19, 2020), the size of the mileage restriction was left blank and the starting point ("present location of the Company") was uncertain. *See id.* at *7. The plaintiff was a California company with sales in North America, the Caribbean, Asia, and Europe, and the court held that the covenant was not entitled to a presumption of reasonableness because it lacked a geographic territory. *Id.*

Territorial references outside the specific restrictive covenant section may be insufficient if not properly incorporated. Although the Georgia Court of Appeals has not addressed this issue, a federal district court held that the mere fact an agreement specifies an employee's territory is not sufficient to satisfy the GRCA. *See Automotive Assurance Group v. Giddens*, 2020 WL 10056277 (N.D. Ga. Dec. 16, 2020). In *Giddens*, the agreement defined the territory where the individual would work ("Southern and Eastern States in the USA"), but this language was not part of the non-compete section. According to the court, "because the plain text of the non-compete covenant contains no geographic limitation (by reference or otherwise), it fails as a matter of Georgia law." *Id.* at *4. The court further stated that even if the territory definition from the other section was incorporated, it was not sufficiently precise to be enforceable. *Id.* at *5 (noting that the description failed to provide "boundary lines, specific state limitations, or any other details").

Companies may want to consider the use of multiple-tier, or "step down," provisions to describe the geographic territory. In *Cellairis Franchise, Inc. v. Duarte*, 2015 WL 6517487 (N.D. Ga. Oct. 21, 2015), the non-competition covenant in the franchise agreement had three tiers of protected territory: (1) at the franchisee's location, (2) within ten miles of that location, or (3) within ten miles of any employer location "in operation and existence as of the termination date." *Id.* at *6. The court enforced the covenant and held that the largest territory was reasonable to allow the plaintiff "to re-license territory and protect other franchisees." *Id.*

GA

Split of authority on whether an employee non-solicitation clause requires a geographic territory

The Georgia Court of Appeals has confirmed that employee non-solicitation clauses are governed by the GRCA, but has not provided guidance on the requirements. A split of authority has recently developed. In *Southern Felt Co., Inc. v. Konesky*, 2020 WL 5199269, at *8 (S.D. Ga. Aug. 31, 2020), a federal district court expressly rejected the argument that an employee non-solicitation clause requires a reasonable geographic territory, citing common-law decisions predating the GRCA. *See also Heartland Payment Systs, LLC v. Stockwell*, 446 F. Supp. 3d 1275 (N.D. Ga. 2020) (enforcing employee non-solicit that lacked a territorial restriction).

In a recent decision, however, the new Georgia State-Wide Business Court held that an employee non-solicitation covenant needs a reasonable geographic territory. *See Martin v. Hauser, Inc.*, 2021 WL 1053637 (Ga. Bus. Ct. Mar. 5, 2021). According to the court in *Martin*, section 13-8-53(a) states that *all* restrictive covenants must be reasonable in time, geographic area, and scope of prohibited activities. *Id.* at *12. Because the express exemption in section 13-8-53(b) refers to *customer* non-solicitation provisions, the court held that employee non-solicitation provisions are not subject to the exemption. *Id.*

AGREEMENTS ENTERED PRIOR TO THE NEW LAW

As noted in Section 1, Georgia courts require non-compete covenants to be limited to a reasonable territory. The territory within which activities are restricted must be reasonably limited and adequately identified. *See, e.g., Atlanta Bread Co. International, Inc. v. Lupton-Smith*, 285 Ga. 587, 591, 679 S.E.2d 722, 725 (2009).

Franchise cases in which geographic restrictions have been upheld as reasonable include *Zampatti v. Tradebank International Franchising Corp.*, 235 Ga. App. 333, 508 S.E.2d 750 (1998) (six-county territory); *Watson v. Waffle House, Inc.*, 253 Ga. 671, 324 S.E.2d 175 (1985) (five-mile radius); *Mansfield v. B. & W. Gas, Inc.*, 222 Ga. 259, 149 S.E.2d 482 (1966) (ten-mile radius); *Wood v. Bowers Battery & Spark Plug Co.*, 221 Ga. 215, 144 S.E.2d 101 (1965) (50-mile radius; distributorship was selling products throughout the restricted area).

If the geographic scope of the covenant is limited to the area of the restricted party's business activities under the franchise, the geographic limitation is generally prima facie reasonable because "a court will accept as prima facie valid a covenant related to the territory where the employee was employed as a legitimate protection of the employer's investment in customer relations and goodwill." *Reardigan*, 238 Ga. App. at 145, 518 S.E.2d at 147 (citing *Rollins Protective Services Co. v. Palermo*, 249 Ga. 138, 139–40, 287 S.E. 2d 546, 548–49 (1982)); *see also Howard Schultz & Associates*, 239 Ga. 181, 236 S.E.2d 265 (1977); *Sysco Food Services, Inc. v. Chupp*, 225 Ga. App. 584, 586, 484 S.E.2d 323, 325 (1997) (citing *W.R. Grace & Co. v. Mouyal*, 262 Ga. 464, 466, 422 S.E.2d 529, 532 (1992).

Under the common law, however, Georgia courts will not enforce restrictive covenants with geographic restrictions based solely on the areas in which the employer or franchisor conducts business. *See Wiley*, 258 Ga. 357, 370 S.E.2d 744. A restrictive covenant covering areas where the employer does business, but beyond the territory where the employee worked, generally will be deemed overbroad and thus invalid. *Peachtree Fayette Women's Specialists, LLC v. Turner*, 305 Ga. App. 60, 63–64, 669 S.E.2d 69, 72–73 (2010); *Dent Wizard International Corp. v. Brown*, 272 Ga. App. 553, 556, 612 S.E.2d 873, 876 (2005).

Moreover, in contrast to the GRCA's focus on the territory at the time of termination, the precise scope of the restraint must be fixed and determinable at the time the restrictive covenant agreement is signed to be enforceable under the common law. *See AGA, LLC v. Rubin*, 243 Ga. App. 772, 774, 533 S.E.2d 804, 806 (2000). Covenants that change in geographic scope based on where the employer might have an office at the time employment ceases are not enforceable. *Id.* For that reason, a territory provision that expands with the business of the employer or franchisor is not sufficiently definite and renders a non-competition covenant void. In *New Atlanta Ear, Nose & Throat Associates, P.C. v. Pratt*, 253 Ga. App. 681, 560 S.E.2d 268 (2002), a covenant not to compete in an employment agreement prohibited a physician from practicing medicine within an "8 mile radius of a 'Prohibited Office,'" and defined "Prohibited Offices" as any office in which the physician saw patients in the 18 months prior to the termination of the employment agreement. The court of appeals held this territorial restriction to be unenforceable because "a territorial restriction that cannot be determined until the date of the employee's termination is too indefinite to be enforced. [The employee must be] able to forecast with certainty the territorial extent of the duty owing." *New Atlanta Ear, Nose & Throat*, 253 Ga. App. at 685, 560 S.E.2d at 272. Note, however, that the court did hold that the fact that a territory could be *narrowed* during the term of the agreement does *not* render the non-compete provision unenforceable because it works to the employee's advantage.

A line of cases stands for the proposition that "if the scope of prohibited behavior is narrow enough (contacting those with whom the employee dealt while working for the employer), the covenant may be reasonable even if it has no territorial limitation or has a territorial limitation which is very broad." *See Azzouz v. Prime Pediatrics, P.C.*, 296 Ga. App. 602, 606, 675 S.E.2d 314, 319 (2009); *Chaichimansour v. Pets Are*

People Too, No. 2, Inc., 226 Ga. App. 69, 71, 485 S.E.2d 248, 250 (1997); *Palmer & Cay of Georgia, Inc. v. Lockton Cos.*, 273 Ga. App. 511, 514, 615 S.E.2d 752, 756 (2005) (two-year non-solicitation restriction without geographical restriction was enforceable). *But see Becham*, 2011 U.S. Dist. LEXIS 103841, at *20 ("With regard to non-solicitation or non-recruitment of employees, covenants that have no territorial restriction are unenforceable.") (citing *Hulcher Services, Inc. v. R.J. Corman Railroad Co.*, 247 Ga. App. 486, 491–92, 543 S.E.2d 461, 467 (2000) (*aff'd*, 2012, U.S. App. LEXIS, at *16).

It should be noted that the *Chaichimansour* court specifically disapproved two cases, *Vortex Protective Service, Inc. v. Dempsey*, 218 Ga. App. 763, 463 S.E.2d 67 (1995), and *Darugar v. Hodges*, 221 Ga. App. 227, 471 S.E.2d 33 (1996), that applied *W.R. Grace* to reach the opposite conclusion—prohibitions on competition with respect to customers or potential customers beyond those with whom the employee dealt during his employment will always be unreasonable, even if in a specified and otherwise reasonable geographic area. Thus, the narrower the scope of activity prohibited by a covenant not to compete, the broader the geographical territory encompassed by the covenant may be.

5. What limitations on activities have courts recognized as reasonable in the franchise context?

GA

AGREEMENTS ENTERED UNDER THE NEW LAW

As a general matter, the GRCA allows the enforcement of any contract that restricts competition provided that the restrictions contained in the restrictive covenant are reasonable in time, geographic area, and scope of prohibited activities. GA. CODE ANN. § 13-8-53(a).

The GRCA authorizes restrictions against "activities, products, or services that are the same as or similar to the activities, products, or services of the employer." GA. CODE ANN. § 13-8-53(c)(1). The statute also makes clear that, with respect to post-employment covenants entered into prior to termination, "any good faith estimate of the activities, products, or services, or geographic areas, that may be applicable at the time of termination" shall be sufficient "even if such estimate is capable of including or ultimately proves to include extraneous activities, products, or services, or geographic areas." *Id.* ("The postemployment covenant shall be construed ultimately to cover only so much of such estimate as relates to the activities actually conducted, the products or services actually offered, or the geographic areas actually involved within a reasonable period of time prior to termination.") Moreover, descriptions of restricted activities, products, and services are sufficient when they "provide[] fair notice of the maximum reasonable scope of the restraint," even if the description is generalized or "could possibly be stated more narrowly to exclude extraneous matters." *Id.* This language, though somewhat obtuse, is intended to avoid the problem under the old law that a slight or inadvertent overstatement of the restricted territory or prohibited activities would invalidate the entire covenant.

The GRCA provides a safe harbor for defining prohibited activities, stating that restrictions as to activities, products, or services shall be considered sufficiently described if the reference to activities, products, or services is qualified by the phrase "'of the type conducted, authorized, offered, or provided within two years prior to termination' or similar language containing the same or a lesser time period." GA. CODE ANN. § 13-8-53(c)(2). Courts have been fairly lenient in enforcing language so long as it makes some reference to prohibiting similar work. *See, e.g., U.S. Security Assocs., Inc. v. Schwartz*, 2019 WL 10303652, at *6 (N.D. Ga. Feb. 15, 2019).

The GRCA also appears to specifically permit competitive restrictions "measured by the business of the employer or other person or entity in whose favor the restrictive covenant is given," provided that courts may not refuse to enforce a restriction where the party seeking enforcement has established that a restriction was violated, but has not proven that the covenant has been violated with respect to the entire scope of prohibited activities or the entire restricted geographic area. GA. CODE ANN. § 13-8-56(3).[4]

The GRCA also distinguishes customer non-solicitation restrictions from non-competition restrictions. The GRCA provides that employees may agree in writing "to refrain, for a stated period of time following termination, from soliciting, or attempting to solicit directly or by assisting others, any business from any of such employer's customers, including actively seeking prospective customers, with whom the employee had material contact during his or her employment for purposes of providing products or services that are competitive with those provided by the employer's business." GA. CODE ANN. § 13-8-53(b). Parties are not required to include an express territorial limitation or to specifically identify the types of products or services considered to be competitive in order for a non-solicitation restraint to be reasonable. *Id.* Further, a non-solicitation restriction that prohibits "soliciting or attempting to solicit business from customers" or that uses similar language is considered adequate and shall be "narrowly construed to apply only to: (1) such of the employer's customers, including actively sought prospective customers, with whom the employee had material contact; and (2) products or services that are competitive with those provided by the employer's business."[5] *Id.*

Although section 13-8-53(b) does not expressly reference franchise agreements, the provision presumably applies to such agreements given that the term "employee" is defined to include franchisees, GA. CODE ANN. § 13-8-51(5)(D), and given the general applicability of the statute to franchise agreements. GA. CODE ANN. § 13-8-52(a)(5). There may, however, be some ambiguity given that section 13-8-53(b) also references "employment," which the statute in some cases references separately from franchise relationships.

Companies can prohibit the solicitation of vendors through a customer non-solicitation provision. *See Southern Felt Co., Inc. v. Konesky*, 2020 WL 5199269, at *6 (S.D. Ga. Aug. 31, 2020) (permitting the inclusion of vendors and contractors within customer non-solicit); *Interra Int'l, LLC v. Al Khafaji*, 2017 WL 4866266, at *12 (N.D. Ga. Mar. 21, 2017) (non-solicitation of vendors enforceable under GRCA). As noted in Section 4, a customer non-solicitation clause cannot prohibit the acceptance of unsolicited business without satisfying the separate requirements for a non-compete. Similarly, an employee non-solicitation covenant must be limited to the solicitation of employees. *See Southern Felt Co., Inc. v. Konesky*, 2020 WL 5199269, at *8 (S.D. Ga. Aug. 31, 2020)

---

4. Although it does not expressly reference franchise relationships, GA. CODE ANN. § 13-8-56(3) appears to apply to franchise relationships because it applies to "employment or *business* relationships." (emphasis added). *But see* GA. CODE ANN. § 13-8-56(4) (specifically referencing franchise relationships).

5. The terms "material contact" and "products or services" are defined by the statute. *See* GA. CODE ANN. §§ 13-8-51(10) and 13-8-51(13). The statue defines "activities, products, or services that are competitive with the activities, products, or services of an employer" to include activities, products, or services "that are the same as or similar to" the activities, products, or services of the employer. GA. CODE ANN. § 13-8-53(c)(1).

(clause sufficiently limited because it prohibited the solicitation of employees and was not a no-hire provision). The State-Wide Business Court, in *Martin v. Hauser, Inc.*, 2021 WL 1053637 (Ga. Bus. Ct. Mar. 5, 2021), invalidated a restriction that went beyond employee solicitation to prevent "interference" with employee relationships. According to the court, a broad provision to prohibit an individual from "interfering" with an employee's relationship with the company or one of its affiliates failed to give the individual fair notice of the scope of prohibited activity. *Id.* at *13.

Customer non-solicitation covenants must be limited to those with whom the individual had material contact, but employee non-solicitation clauses are not necessarily so limited. *See Southern Felt Co., Inc. v. Konesky*, 2020 WL 5199269, at *8 (S.D. Ga. Aug. 31, 2020) (enforcing restriction applied to all company employees, not just those with whom the individual had material contact). As noted in Section 4, though, employee non-solicitation provisions may require a geographic territory.

AGREEMENTS ENTERED PRIOR TO THE NEW LAW

Georgia courts generally require covenants not to compete to state with particularity the activities they prohibit. It is well established in the employment context that covenants that prohibit working for a competitor "in any capacity" are unenforceable. *See Fantastic Sams Salons Corp. v. Maxie Enterps., Inc.*, 2012 WL 210889, at *3 (M.D. Ga. Jan. 24, 2012) (franchise agreement that prohibits former franchisee from employment with competitor "in any capacity" unreasonable as matter of law).

GA

There is a recognized exception in the franchise context, but the standard can be difficult to meet. In *Watson v. Waffle House, Inc.*, 253 Ga. 671, 324 S.E.2d 175 (1985), the court enforced a covenant effectively preventing competition "in any capacity." The court observed that the franchisee was the "heart and soul" of the franchised restaurant, participated in "every facet of the business," and "gained knowledge which the [franchisor] has a reasonable stake in protecting." The court concluded that it was not unreasonable to enforce a covenant, which otherwise had reasonable business, territorial, and time elements, that prevented the franchisee from engaging in the restaurant or fast-food business. *Watson*, 253 Ga. at 673, 324 S.E.2d at 178. *But cf. Arnall Insurance Agency v. Arnall*, 196 Ga. App. 414, 396 S.E.3d 257 (1990) (for employee who had been a major player but not the "heart and soul" of the business, words "or otherwise" following list of proscribed activities were the functional equivalent of "in any capacity" and rendered the restrictive covenant unreasonable); *Gandolfo's Deli Boys, LLC v. Holman*, 490 F. Supp. 2d 1353, 1358 (N.D. Ga. 2007) ("[A] covenant that restricts a former franchisee from employment in a competing business 'in any capacity' is overbroad and will not be enforced."); *Fantastic Sam's Salons Corp. v. Maxie Enterprises, Inc.*, Case No. 3:11-CV-22 (CDL), 2012 U.S. Dist. LEXIS 8106, at *7–9 (M.D. Ga. Jan. 24, 2012) (covenant prohibiting franchisee from serving in "any . . . capacity in any business engaged in the sale or rental of products or services the same as or similar to those of the" franchisor was overbroad; distinguishing *Waffle House* because franchisor had not presented evidence that franchisee was the "heart and soul" of the business or that his participation involved "every facet of the business").

The analysis of whether the scope of activities restricted by a covenant is reasonable is a highly fact-specific inquiry. In *National Teen-Ager Co. v. Scarborough*, 254 Ga. 467, 330 S.E.2d 711 (1985), the court declared that "whether a given covenant falls into the prohibited 'in any capacity' category is not determinable solely from the face of the contract," but rather is a function of 'the particular factual setting to which it is applied.'" 254 Ga. at 469, 330 S.E.2d at 713 (quoting *Watson, supra*).

Further, in *Moore v. Preferred Research, Inc.*, 191 Ga. App. 26, 381 S.E.2d 72 (1989), the court upheld a covenant incorporating the term "related services" to define the proscribed activities. The agreement, ancillary to the transfer of licensed information, prohibited the licensee from competing with the licensor in a "similar business to that licensed and established under the license agreement." The court upheld the covenant because it found that the description of the "business" in the license agreement defined the prohibited activities with sufficient particularity, despite the presence of a "related services" clause in the description.

Fields v. Rainbow International Carpet Dyeing & Cleaning Co., 259 Ga. 375, 380 S.E.2d 693 (1989), involved a franchisor's termination of a franchisee's license to operate the franchise. The parties' license agreement contained a covenant not to compete that provided "for three (3) years after the termination hereof, [Franchisee] will not, . . . , directly or indirectly, as principal, agent, servant or otherwise, carry on or engage in the business [of Franchisor]." The court found this covenant fell into the "in any capacity" category and thus refused to enforce it.

It can be argued that a franchisee is by definition the "heart and soul" of the franchised business. Georgia courts, however, do not necessarily apply this rationale. For example, in *Hub Cap Heaven*, *supra*, the franchisee was arguably the "heart and soul" of the franchised business, but the court did not apply a more lenient analysis, as it did in *Waffle House*. Thus, there is little guidance on the scope of activities that Georgia courts will allow franchisors to prohibit.

As a conceptual matter, it also seems likely that franchisors may have wider latitude in restricting the post-term activities of a corporate franchisee than an individual franchisee, though it is unlikely that this theory would apply to the individual shareholders of the corporation. Georgia courts have not had the opportunity to address this position, but an argument can be made that a corporate franchisee formed specifically to own and operate a franchised business has no scope of activities other than those related to the franchised business.

6. Does the state recognize a difference between in-term and post-term covenants?

AGREEMENTS ENTERED UNDER THE NEW LAW

The GRCA specifically addresses in-term restrictive covenants, including those operating during the term of a franchise relationship, and allows broader restrictions for in-term covenants. So long as an in-term restriction promotes or protects the legitimate business purpose of the agreement, it is enforceable even if it lacks a particular activity or geographic limitation. Section 13-8-56(4) provides:

> Any restriction that operates during the term of an employment relationship, agency relationship, independent contractor relationship, partnership, franchise, distributorship, . . . or other ongoing business relationship shall not be considered unreasonable because it lacks any specific limitation upon scope of activity, duration, or geographic area so long as it promotes or protects the purpose or subject matter of the agreement or relationship or deters any potential conflict of interest.

Id.

AGREEMENTS ENTERED PRIOR TO THE NEW LAW

Under Georgia's pre-2011 caselaw, the same strict-scrutiny standard applicable to post-term covenants is used to analyze restrictive covenants operating during the term of the parties' relationship. In *Atlanta Bread*, the Georgia Supreme Court declined to adopt a lesser standard of scrutiny for in-term restrictive covenants in franchise or distributor agreements, and held that such provisions are subject to the same strict scrutiny as restrictive covenants applicable after the expiration of the contract. *Atlanta Bread Co. International, Inc. v. Lupton-Smith*, 285 Ga. 587, 590–91, 679 S.E.2d 722, 725 (2009) (holding in-term restrictive covenant unreasonable and unenforceable where it did not contain any territorial limitation and because the court was not authorized to "blue-pencil" the provision to render it enforceable). *See also Early v. MiMedx Group, Inc.*, 330 Ga. App. 652 (2015) (in-term and post-term restrictions subject to same level of scrutiny). Moreover, an overbroad in-term covenant will invalidate a post-term restrictive covenant, even if the post-term covenant is carefully drawn to meet Georgia's strict standards for such covenants.

---

7. Has the state allowed enforcement of covenants against non-signatories (e.g., family members, newly formed corporations)?

GA

Georgia courts have not addressed whether restrictive covenants in franchise agreements may be enforced against non-signatories. The Georgia Supreme Court has, however, held that restrictive covenants in employment agreements and agreements for the sale of businesses may not be enforced against non-signatories. It is likely that courts would treat non-compete covenants in franchise agreements similarly.

In *Bennett v. Kimsey*, 218 Ga. 470 S.E.2d 506 (1962), the defendant sold his partnership interest in an ornamental iron works business to the plaintiff. The agreement included a provision prohibiting the seller from engaging in that type of business within a 50-mile radius. Shortly thereafter, the seller began managing an ornamental iron works business that his brother claimed to own. The buyer sought to enjoin the seller and his brother from participating in the business. The lower court enjoined both individuals, but on appeal the Georgia Supreme Court reversed the lower court's decision as to the brother, noting that "[h]e was not a party to the restrictive covenant agreement, and there [was] no reason alleged which would prevent him from engaging in business in competition with the [buyer]." *Id.* at 475 S.E.2d at 510.

Likewise, in *Kessler v. Puritan Chemical Co.*, 213 Ga. 845, 102 S.E.2d 495 (1958), two employees entered into non-competition covenants with their employer. Shortly thereafter, they left the company and formed a competing business. The employer sued both employees, as well as their new corporation and one employee's spouse. The Georgia Supreme Court enforced the covenants against the employees but refused to enforce the covenants against the corporation or the spouse because neither were parties to the contracts containing the restrictive covenants. *Id.* at 846–47, 102 S.E.2d at 496. *See also Wallace Business Forms, Inc. v. Elmore*, 221 Ga. 223, 224, 144 S.E.2d 82, 83 (1965) (refusing to enforce restrictive covenant against non-signatory corporation); *Satilla Health Services, Inc. v. Bell*, 280 Ga. App. 123, 134 n.6, 633 S.E.2d 575, 583 n.6 (2006) ("Likewise, because the Doctors were not parties to the 2001 or 2002 Agreement, the non-competition covenant contained therein could not be enforced against them individually.").

Although restrictive covenants may not be enforced against non-signatories, non-signatories may still be liable for common-law torts associated with unfair competition. *See Bijou Salon & Spa, LLC v. Kensington Enterprises, Inc.*, 283 Ga. App. 857, 861, 643 S.E.2d 531, 534 (2007) (noting that "a third party may be [liable for unfair competition and tortious interference with business and contractual relations] in such a case where there is evidence that it maliciously aided and abetted the breach of restrictive covenants with knowledge thereof").

8. Will the state modify, "blue-pencil," or otherwise reduce a covenant found to be overbroad?

AGREEMENTS ENTERED UNDER THE NEW LAW

Perhaps the most significant change implemented by the GRCA is that it allows a court to modify a covenant that is otherwise overbroad and to enforce the modified covenant to the extent reasonable. Section 13-8-53(d) expressly authorizes modification of an otherwise void and unenforceable covenant. "Modification" is defined to include both severing that part of a restrictive covenant that would otherwise make the entire covenant unenforceable and "[e]nforcing the provisions of a restrictive covenant to the extent the provisions are reasonable." GA. CODE ANN. § 13-8-51(11). In modifying a restrictive covenant, a court should "grant only the relief reasonably necessary" to protect the legitimate business interests of the employer "and to achieve the original intent of the contracting parties to the extent possible." GA. CODE ANN. § 13-8-54(b).

Importantly, the statute provides that a court "may modify" an otherwise overbroad and unenforceable restrictive covenant, but it does not *require* a court to do so. *See Belt Power, LLC v. Reed*, 354 Ga. App. 289 (2020) (holding that trial court has discretion to refuse to blue-pencil a provision). The one exception to this discretionary authority is in the context of customer non-solicitation clauses, where the statutory language automatically modifies any broader language to prohibit only the solicitation of customers with whom the individual had "material contact." *See Southern Felt Co., Inc. v. Konesky*, 2020 WL 5199269, at *6 (S.D. Ga. Aug. 31, 2020) (covenant automatically narrowed to those customers with material contact). Otherwise, the statute does not provide guidance as to when a court should or should not blue-pencil an overbroad covenant.

Although the GRCA has been in effect since 2011, there are a limited number of decisions addressing the authority to modify overbroad restrictions. Most often, when the authority is used, it is to narrow the geographic territory. *See Kennedy v. Shave Barber Co., LLC*, 348 Ga. App. 298, 305 (2018) (affirming trial court's modification of a clause prohibiting competition within a three-mile radius from "any" business location to a three-mile radius from the company's location at the time of termination); *Acuity Brands, Inc. v. Bickley*, 2017 WL 1426800 (E.D. KY Mar. 31, 2017) (interpreting GRCA) (narrowing nationwide non-competition territory to the company's South Central Region, which included Texas, Oklahoma, Arkansas, Louisiana, Mississippi, and New Mexico); *Heartland Payment Systs., LLC v. Stockwell*, 446 F. Supp. 3d 1275 (N.D. Ga. 2020) (enforcing preliminary injunction because employer was only seeking to prevent competition in two states while the agreement provided for a nationwide restriction). In *Cunningham Lindsey U.S. LLC v. Box*, 2018 WL 6266554 (N.D. Ga. Oct. 23, 2018), a federal district court held that the phrase "within the territory of the office in which Employee is employed" was ambiguous because it could mean the physical location of the office (Atlanta, Georgia) or the region of clients assigned to the office. *Id.* at *8. The court used its blue-pencil authority to limit enforcement, for the purpose of the temporary restraining order, to clients located in Atlanta, Georgia, since both parties agreed that the territory at a minimum covered such clients. *Id.*

Some courts, however, have declined to exercise this discretionary authority. The most common instance is when a non-competition covenant lacks any geographic territory whatsoever. In such situations, courts often state that fixing such a deficiency requires the court to add materials terms that are improper. In *Chef Merito, Inc. v. Gonzalez*, 2020 WL 5548339 (N.D. Ga. Aug. 19, 2020), as outlined in Section 4, the geographic territory was unreasonable because the starting point for the restriction ("present location of the company") was uncertain and the mileage radius was left blank. The court rejected the argument that the territory could be narrowed to the regional sales routes covered by the two individuals. *Id.* at *7. ("The standard language of the agreement, which is drafted in terms of the 'present location of the company,' does not lend itself to the proposed revision based on regional sales routes.") "To make such a modification would be adding a material term which the Court cannot do." *Id.* (internal quotation omitted); *see also Wind Logistics Pro., LLC v. Universal Truckload, Inc.*, 2019 WL 4600055, at *10 (N.D. Ga. Sept. 23, 2019) (refusing to add a territory or list of competitors because it would add a material term).

GA

The GRCA states that a court cannot modify a restriction to make it more restrictive than originally drafted. Some courts have cited that language to refuse to create a territory when there is not one initially. *See Auto. Assurance Grp. v. Giddens*, 2020 WL 10056277, at *4 & n.4 (N.D. Ga. Dec. 16, 2020) ("Because the non-compete at issue contains *no* geographic limitation, the Court declines to modify the covenant, as adding any such limitation would be more restrictive with regard to Defendant Giddens than the original agreement drafted by AAG."); *Carpetcare Multiservices, LLC v. Carle*, 347 Ga. App. 497 (2018) (noting, without addressing, the trial court's conclusion that inserting a territory would be prohibited by the GRCA because it would be more restrictive than as originally drafted).[6] A company needing to enforce a restriction could counter this position by arguing that the lack of an express territory means the limitation, as drafted, is worldwide and insertion of a narrower territory as intended by the parties is not more restrictive than the clause as written.

Finally, one federal district court relied on pre-GRCA common law interpretations of blue-penciling authority to hold that the power is limited to striking overbroad terms. In *LifeBrite Laboratories, LLC v. Cooksey*, 2016 WL 7840217 (N.D. Ga. Dec. 9, 2016), the non-competition clause lacked a geographic territory. Noting the pre-GRCA caselaw held that the blue-pencil could strike, but not rewrite, contractual

6. As noted in Section 4, the Georgia Court of Appeals in *Carpetcare Multiservices, LLC v. Carle*, 347 Ga. App. 497 (2018) affirmed that a non-competition restriction lacking a geographic territory was void and a list of specific competitors would not serve as a substitute for a territory. The power of the trial court to potentially rectify the issue, however, was not before the court because the company did not appeal that issue. *Id.* at 499 & n.1. While the majority did not address the issue, the dissenting judge voiced his opinion that the trial court erred in concluding that it lacked the authority to limit the territory to the company's principal operating area. *Id.* at n.1.

language, the court held that it was bound by this limitation because statutes in derogation of the common law are narrowly construed, and further reasoned that nothing in the GRCA indicated a change in the common law approach "other than to allow it in more circumstances." *Id.* at *7.[7] The Georgia Court of Appeals has not addressed this issue, and all of the cases are in the employer-employee context. The court in *Cooksey* noted "the concern over the power imbalance between employers and employees in the employment contract is still present." *Id.* at *7. Thus, a franchisor may be able to argue that different bargaining power alleviates that concern. Moreover, as outlined at the start of this section, the definition of "modification" has two parts; one of which is the striking of unreasonable language. The second part—"[e]nforcing the provisions of a restrictive covenant to the extent the provisions are reasonable" (Ga. Code Ann. § 13-8-51(11))—would be superfluous if the authority were limited to striking unreasonable language. The State-Wide Business Court has expressly rejected the position that blue-penciling authority is limited to striking words and phrases. *See Martin v. Hauser, Inc.*, 2021 WL 1053637 (Ga. Bus. Ct. Mar. 5, 2021). Although the *Martin* court declined to modify the employee non-interference covenant that was both overbroad in scope and lacked a geographic territory, it rejected the argument that the blue-pencil was limited to striking provisions. *Id.* at n.11.

AGREEMENTS ENTERED PRIOR TO THE NEW LAW

Under pre-2011 Georgia law, Georgia courts would not "blue-pencil" overbroad non-competition covenants in employment or franchise agreements. *See Atlanta Bread Co. International, Inc. v. Lupton-Smith*, 285 Ga. 587, 591, 679 S.E.2d 722, 725 (2009); *Whimsical Expressions, Inc. v. Brown*, 275 Ga. App. 420, 423, 620 S.E.2d 635, 638 (2005); *Allen v. Hub Cap Heaven, Inc.*, 225 Ga. App. 533, 538, 484 S.E.2d 259, 264 (1997); *Watson v. Waffle House, Inc.*, 253 Ga. 671, 671–72, 324 S.E.2d 175, 177 (1985). If a restrictive covenant in an employment or franchise agreement is overbroad in any respect, Georgia courts will not strike the offending part or narrow it to enforce the covenant to a more limited extent; it is unenforceable in its entirety. An extension of this rule provides that where a non-competition or customer non-solicitation covenant in an employment or franchise agreement is unenforceable, other such restrictive covenant in the same agreement also is unenforceable even if the other covenant is reasonably limited in scope. *Riddle v. Geo-Hydro Engineers, Inc.*, 254 Ga. App. 119, 121, 561 S.E.2d 456, 458 (2002); *Becham v. Synthes (U.S.A.)*, Civ. Action No. 5:11-CV-73 (MTT), 2011 U.S. Dist. LEXIS 103841, at *19–20 (M.D. Ga. Sept. 14, 2011) (failure to include territorial limitation invalidated the entire non-competition covenant and also invalidated a separate non-solicitation of customers covenant)[8]

---

7. The court in *Cooksey* refused to modify the contract, but indicated it would have used its authority to impose an alternative geographic area if the contract contained a "step-down" provision. *See id.* at n.78 ("If the contract had included a 'step-down' provision, which provided an alternative geographic limitation, the court could have done so. But it will not provide new terms wholesale that the parties have not agreed to.").

8. Confidentiality or non-disclosure provisions contained in an agreement, however, are not automatically invalidated if a non-compete or non-solicitation provision in the same agreement is deemed unenforceable. *See Trujillo v. Great Southern Equipment Sales, LLC*, 289 Ga. App. 474, 479 n.8, 657 S.E.2d 581, 585 n.8 (2008) (invalidating non-competition clause because non-solicitation clause in same agreement was unenforceable, but noting that that finding "ha[d] no bearing on the issue of whether the agreement's confidentiality clause was unenforceable"); *see also Wiley v. Royal Cup, Inc.*, 258 Ga. 357, 359–60, 370 S.E.2d 744, 746 (1988).

(*aff'd* No. 11-14495, 2012 U.S. App. LEXIS 11225, at *16 (11th Cir. June 4, 2012) (unpublished).

This rule is different, however, for a restrictive covenant entered into in connection with the sale of a business. *Allen*, 225 Ga. App. at 538, 484 S.E.2d at 264; *Watson*, 253 Ga. at 671, 324 S.E.2d at 177; *White v. Fletcher/Mayo/Associates, Inc.*, 251 Ga. 203, 303 S.E.2d 746 (1983). Overbroad restrictive covenants determined to be incidental to the sale of a business may be blue-penciled. *Redmond v. Royal Ford, Inc.*, 244 Ga. 711, 261 S.E.2d 585 (1979). Georgia courts may blue-pencil a restrictive covenant entered into in connection with the sale of a business to enforce other valid terms if certain covenants in the agreement are unenforceable. *Allen*, 225 Ga. App. at 538, 484 S.E.2d at 264.

The rationale for the distinction is that "a contract of employment inherently involves parties of unequal bargaining power to the extent that the result is often a contract of adhesion." *Watson*, 253 Ga. at 672, 324 S.E.2d at 177. Georgia courts apply the same rule in the franchise context and refuse to blue-pencil or otherwise reduce unenforceable covenants in franchise agreements. *See, e.g.*, *Atlanta Bread Co.*, 285 Ga. at 591, 679 S.E.2d at 725; *Allen*, *supra*; *Watson*, *supra*; *Richard R Rita Personnel Services International v. Kot*, 229 Ga. 314, 191 S.E.2d 79 (1972).

9. When does a non-compete period begin to run?

GA

➤ Will courts equitably extend the term?

An enforceable non-competition covenant begins to run at the time set forth in the contract between the parties. Contractual tolling provisions generally are not enforceable.

The time periods contained in the GRCA within which a restrictive covenant is presumptively reasonable and greater than which a restriction is presumptively unreasonable are measured from the date of the termination of the business relationship between the parties. *See* GA. CODE ANN. §§ 13-8-57(b)–(c). The statute defines "termination" to mean "the termination of an employee's engagement with an employer, whether with or without cause, upon the initiative of either party." GA. CODE ANN. § 13-8-51(18).

Some drafters have attempted to extend the period covered by a covenant not to compete by including tolling provisions that "stop the clock" during any violation of the restrictive covenant. Before the GRCA Georgia courts refused to enforce such tolling language, finding that such provisions "potentially extend the duration of [such covenants] without limit and render [them] unreasonable and unenforceable on [their] face." *ALW Marketing Corp. v. McKinney*, 205 Ga. App. 184, 188, 421 S.E.2d 565 (1992); *see also Gandolfo's Deli Boys, LLC v. Holman*, 490 F. Supp. 2d 1353, 1359 (N.D. Ga. 2007) (tolling covenant was unenforceable even where it did not employ the use of the word "tolling"). The GRCA does not authorize tolling, and courts have held that tolling provisions in agreements subject to the GRCA are unenforceable, though a court can exercise its discretion and delete the offensive language. *See AWP, Inc. v. Henry*, 2020 WL 6876299, at *7 (N.D. Ga. Oct. 28, 2020) (holding that tolling provision was unenforceable, but could be removed under the GRCA); *Interra Int'l, LLC v. Al Khafaji*, 2017 WL 4866266, at *13 (N.D. Ga. Mar. 21, 2017) (same).

In a seemingly outlier case decided under the old law, *Paul Robinson, Inc. v. Haege*, 218 Ga. App. 578, 462 S.E.2d 396 (1995), the Georgia Court of Appeals considered the enforceability of a non-competition covenant that included a tolling provision under which, if the enforceability of the covenant were challenged in court and the employee was not enjoined from breaching the covenant but a court later found the covenant to be enforceable, the time period would be tolled during the pendency of the lawsuit until the appeal period expired. The tolling provision could be triggered only if the employee challenged the enforceability of the covenant during the term of the contract or the covenant. The court of appeals distinguished the case from *ALW Marketing* and found that the tolling provision was reasonable and enforceable. *Id.* at 479, 462 S.E.2d at 398 ("The tolling provisions in those cases were triggered by a covenant violation, which may extend indefinitely. In contrast, the tolling provision in this case can only be triggered if the enforceability of the covenant is challenged in a lawsuit instituted during either the term of the agreement or the one-year post-termination period when the covenant is in force.").

Further, Georgia courts will not allow post-term non-competition provisions to "hibernate" during the time between when a franchisee sells its franchise and the time that the franchise agreement would expire on its terms. The franchisor in *Allen v. Hub Cap Heaven* took such a position, arguing that the franchisee was bound by a one-year post-term non-competition agreement that began, by its terms, upon the expiration of the franchise agreement. *Allen v. Hub Cap Heaven*, 225 Ga. App. 533, 484 S.E.2d 259 (1997). The *Allen* court rejected this view, holding that because the franchisee sold its franchise in 1995, the covenant was either enforceable for one year beginning in 1995 and expiring in 1996—well before the case came to trial—or unenforceable due to overbreadth. The court rejected the franchisor's position that the one-year term should begin upon the original expiration date of the franchise agreement in 1998 because that construction would have extended the non-competition period for four years, rather than one year, rendering it unreasonable.

10. Are there additional nuances or peculiarities of the state's treatment of covenants in the franchising context?

Under Georgia law, restrictive covenants must be in writing, *Pope v. Kem Manufacturing Corp.*, 249 Ga. 868, 870, 295 S.E.2d 290, 292 (1982), and must be supported by consideration, *Thomas* v. *Coastal Industrial Services, Inc.*, 214 Ga. 832, 833, 108 S.E.2d 328, 329 (1959). Georgia's new statute does not squarely address this issue, except that section 13-8-53(b), which governs non-solicitation agreements, provides that an employee may agree "in writing" to certain non-solicitation covenants. Provisions requiring an individual to provide notice regarding competing activities are enforceable under the GRCA. *See Interra Int'l, LLC v. Al Khafaji*, 2017 WL 4866266, at *12 (N.D. Ga. Mar. 21, 2017) (holding that provision requiring individual to provide notice to former employer of any request by customer or vendor for products or services similar to those the former employer provides for a two year period is enforceable under the GRCA).

It is well established under Georgia's pre-2011 law that the reasonableness of a restrictive covenant is a question of law. *Koger Properties, Inc. v. Adams-Cates Co.*, 247 Ga. 68, 69, 274 S.E.2d 329, 331 (1981); *Stevenson v. Preferred Research, Inc.*, *supra*. But *cf. National Teen-Ager Co. v. Scarborough*, 254 Ga. 467, 469, 330 S.E.2d 711, 713 (1985) (reversing judgment on the pleadings in favor of franchisee on the grounds that "the three-element test of duration, territorial coverage, and scope of activity is best utilized not as an arbitrary rule but as a helpful tool in examining the reasonableness of *the particular factual setting to which it is applied*") (emphasis in original). Analysis of restrictive covenants under the GRCA, however, involves greater factual analysis and exercise of discretion by the trial court. *See, e.g.*, GA. CODE ANN. §§ 13-8-55 and 13-8-51(9). Appellate review of decisions made by trial courts under the new act therefore could be more limited, at least until Georgia appellate courts provide guidance regarding interpretation of key parts of the new act. Additionally, it is unlikely that a franchisor could avail itself of a more restrictive non-competition covenant contained in any agreement entered into along with a franchise agreement. Georgia courts have held that where a party, in conjunction with the same transaction, signs an employment agreement and a partnership agreement with the employer, the restrictive covenant in the employment agreement is subject to strict scrutiny. *See New Atlanta Ear, Nose & Throat Associates, P.C. v Pratt*, 253 Ga. App. 681, 560 S.E.2d 268 (2002). There is no reason to think that Georgia's new statute changes this analysis.

The GRCA provides that once a party seeking to enforce a restrictive covenant has established by prima facie evidence that the restraint complies with section 13-8-53, the party opposing enforcement has the burden of establishing that the restraint does not comply with the statute or is otherwise unreasonable. GA. CODE ANN. § 13-8-55. As discussed above, however, parties seeking to enforce restrictive covenants must meet greater proof requirements under the new law. *See, e.g.*, GA. CODE ANN. §§ 13-8-55 (person seeking enforcement "shall plead and prove the existence of one or more legitimate business reasons justifying the restrictive covenant"), 13-8-51(9) (defining the term "legitimate business interest").

GA

Under the GRCA, courts have much broader latitude to enforce non-solicitation restrictions than general non-competition restrictions. *See* GA. CODE ANN. § 13-8-53(b). Therefore, where a non-solicitation covenant offers sufficient protection to the franchisor, franchisors may want to consider using such provisions in their agreements with franchisees rather than non-competition restrictions.

Georgia's new statute authorizes courts to enforce restrictive covenants "by any appropriate and effective remedy available at law or equity," including injunctive relief. GA. CODE ANN. § 13-8-58(c).

Finally, an important litigation strategy issue to note is that, due to Georgia's strong public policy regarding restrictive covenants, Georgia courts will disregard contractual choice-of-law provisions selecting the law of another state where the other state's law would "contravene the public policy of Georgia against certain unlawful covenants not to compete." *Hulcher Services, Inc. v. R.J. Corman Railroad Co.*, 247 Ga. App. 486, 489, 543 S.E.2d 461, 465 (2000) (affirming invalidation of non-competition covenant under Georgia law and disregarding Texas choice-of-law provision); *Nasco, Inc. v. Gimbert*, 239 Ga. 675, 238 S.E.2d 368 (1977). With respect to franchise agreements, this rule effectively renders choice-of-law clauses unenforceable in restrictive covenant cases litigated in Georgia courts. *See Boone v. Corestaff Support Services, Inc.*, No. 1:11-CV-1175-RWS, 2011 U.S. Dist. LEXIS 85454, at *11 (N.D. Ga. Aug. 3, 2011) ("If a restrictive covenant is not enforceable under Georgia law, it is violative of Georgia's public policy and a choice-of-law provision choosing the law of a foreign jurisdiction may not be applied to enforce the covenant."). Therefore, choice of forum and state choice-of-law rules can be outcome determinative. For this reason, a franchisor seeking to enforce a non-competition covenant against a Georgia franchisee should consider filing first elsewhere if there are any concerns regarding the enforceability of the covenant under Georgia law.

Conversely, a Georgia franchisee wishing to avoid the application of a covenant not to compete should consider filing a declaratory judgment action to have a Georgia court determine whether the provision is enforceable under Georgia law. *See Enron Capital & Trade Resources Corp. v. Pokalsky*, 227 Ga. App. 727, 490 S.E.2d 136 (1997) (affirming injunction in declaratory judgment action filed by former employee enjoining former employer from enforcing restrictive covenant that was overbroad under Georgia law).

Since the enactment of the GRCA, some litigants have argued that because Georgia's new statute indicates a shift in Georgia's public policy, courts should determine whether to enforce contractual choice-of-law provisions in pre-2011 contracts by determining whether the restrictive covenants at issue violate Georgia public policy as reflected by Georgia's new statute. The Georgia Court of Appeals, however, rejected this position. *See Fortress Invest. Group, LLC v. Holsinger*, 354 Ga. App. 405 (2020) (holding that courts must assess whether there was a conflict between Georgia law and the law of another state at the time the agreement was effective; the fact that Georgia law is now consistent with that of another jurisdiction is irrelevant). A court may limit the scope of an injunction when restrictions operate outside of Georgia. *See DJR Assocs., LLC v. Hammonds*, 241 F. Supp. 3d 1208 (N.D. Ala. 2018) (because application of Alabama law conflicted with Georgia public policy, court enjoined certain activities in Alabama but refused to enjoin similar conduct in Georgia).

Hawaii

*by Martin E. Hsia**

1. Has the state addressed covenants against competition in the context of franchising?

- **Does the state have a franchising statute or regulations that address covenants against competition?**
- **Does the state have a covenants statute of general applicability that would encompass franchise covenants?**
- **Have the courts addressed covenants in the context of franchising either under a statute or under the state's common law?**

Hawaii's Franchise Investment Law governs franchise registration and disclosure issues. HAW. REV. STAT. § 482E-1 *et seq*. The statutes also regulate various aspects of the franchisor-franchisee relationship and contain broad language requiring good-faith dealing by the parties and prohibiting any "arbitrary standard of conduct" by a franchisor. *See* HAW. REV. STAT. § 482E-6. However, none of these relationship provisions directly pertain to covenants against competition.

Although it does not specifically address covenants in the franchise context, Hawaii's antitrust statute generally prohibits contracts in restraint of trade or commerce in the state, providing exemptions for certain forms of covenants against competition that may or may not be applicable in various franchising contexts.

HAW. REV. STAT. § 480-4 provides:

> Combinations in restraint of trade, price-fixing, and limitation of production prohibited:
>
> (a) Every contract, combination in the form of trust or otherwise, or conspiracy, in restraint of trade or commerce in the State, or in any section of this State is illegal.
>
> (b) [forbidding price fixing]
>
> (c) Notwithstanding the foregoing subsection (b) and without limiting the application of the foregoing subsection (a) it shall be lawful for a person to enter into any of the following restrictive covenants or

*Martin E. Hsia is a Partner at Cades Schutte LLP. in Honolulu. Text taken from the third edition was written by Scott F. March. Text taken from the second edition was written by W. Gregory Chuck.

agreements ancillary to a legitimate purpose not violative of this chapter, unless the effect thereof may be substantially to lessen competition or to tend to create a monopoly in any line of commerce in any section of the State:

(1) A covenant or agreement by the transferor of a business not to compete within a reasonable area and within a reasonable period of time in connection with the sale of the business;

(2) A covenant or agreement between partners not to compete with the partnership within a reasonable area and for a reasonable period of time upon the withdrawal of a partner from the partnership;

(3) A covenant or agreement of the lessee to be restricted in the use of the leased premises to certain business or agricultural uses, or covenant or agreement of the lessee to be restricted in the use of the leased premises to certain business uses and of the lessor to be restricted in the use of premises reasonably proximate to any such leased premises to certain business uses;

(4) A covenant or agreement by an employee or agent not to use the trade secrets of the employer or principal in competition with the employee's or agent's employer or principal, during the term of the agency or thereafter, or after the termination of employment, within such time as may be reasonably necessary for the protection of the employer or principal, without imposing undue hardship on the employee or agent.

(d) [voiding non-compete and nonsolicit clauses in employment contracts for employees of a technology business, which is defined as a trade or business that derives the majority of its gross income from the sale or license of products or services resulting from its software development or information technology development, or both]

On February 17, 2022, in *Prudential Locations, LLC v. Gagnon*, 2022 WL 482601, the Hawaii Supreme Court held that non-competition and non-solicitation clauses must be ancillary to a legitimate purpose that does not violate Chapter 480 of the Hawaii Revised Statutes, and that restricting competition is not a legitimate ancillary purpose. Although some of the parties appear to have been franchisees of major real estate brokerage franchises, their franchisee status did not appear to have any effect on the decision. The Hawaii Supreme Court said that Haw. Rev. Stat. § 480-4(a) prohibits contracts in restraint of trade or commerce in the state, and that Haw. Rev. Stat. § 480-4(c) "enumerates several types of restrictive covenants that may be lawfully entered into '*ancillary to a legitimate purpose* not violative of this chapter.'" (emphasis in original; footnote omitted). Referring to *Technicolor, Inc. v. Traeger*, 57 Haw. 113, 551 P.2d 163 (1976) (discussed below), the Hawaii Supreme Court then said that "We held the restrictive covenants and agreements enumerated under [HRS §] 480-4(c) were not meant to be exclusive in their respective fields. . . . We held that a restrictive covenant is not reasonable if: (i) it is greater than required for the protection of the person for whose benefit it is imposed; (ii) it imposes undue hardship on the person restricted; or (iii) its benefit to the covenantee is outweighed by injury to the public."

The Hawaii Supreme Court then referred to *7's Enterprises, Inc. v. Del Rosario*, 111 Haw. 484, 143 P.3d 23 (2006) (discussed below) and stated, "Even if a restrictive covenant otherwise satisfies the *Traeger* three-factor reasonableness test, it is unenforceable unless it is ancillary to a legitimate purpose not violative of Chapter 480."

The Hawaii Supreme Court then determined that the reasons cited by Prudential Locations were not ancillary to a legitimate purpose. Prudential Locations argued its legitimate purposes were to prevent Gagnon from (1) using proprietary information obtained as a sales coach, (2) forming a competing firm, and (3) "poaching" its agents. The Hawaii Supreme Court said that (1) the non-trade-secret confidential information that Prudential Locations asserts constitutes a protectible legitimate purpose was not actually "confidential" because others had access to the information who did not sign non-compete agreements, and Prudential Locations admitted that there were no trade secret violations; (2) preventing competition is not a legitimate ancillary purpose under HAW. REV. STAT. § 480-4(a) based on the plain language purpose to prohibit contracts in restraint of commerce or trade in the state; and (3) workforce stability and customer relationships can be legitimate ancillary interests for a non-solicitation agreement, but solicitation of employees required that Gagnon actively initiate contact with the solicited employees, and there was a genuine issue of material fact as to whether Gagnon actively solicited one employee.

In *Technicolor, Inc. v. Traeger*, 57 Haw. 113, 551 P.2d 163 (1976), the Hawaii Supreme Court affirmed the validity of a covenant against competition entered into between a photo-finishing business and its former regional vice president, Traeger. The trial court granted Technicolor summary judgment dismissing Traeger's claims that the non-competition covenant was an unreasonable restraint of trade in violation of HAW. REV. STAT. § 480-4 and that it violated Hawaii's unfair competition statute, HAW. REV. STAT. § 480-2 (1985).

HI

Although Traeger had access during his employment to Technicolor's customer list and pricing information, which Technicolor considered confidential, this fact apparently was not sufficient to bring the covenant within the exception provided in HAW. REV. STAT. § 480-4(c)(4) because it was unclear whether Traeger had access to any trade secrets. *Id.* at 166. The court found that the restrictive covenants and agreements enumerated in HAW. REV. STAT. § 480-4(c) were not meant to be the only permissible types of non-competition covenants in employment contracts. *Id.* at 170. Thus, it appears that if a restrictive covenant is not declared a per se violation under HAW. REV. STAT. § 480-4(b), the covenant will be subject to a "rule of reason" test similar to that applied by the federal courts in considering cases under Section 1 of the Sherman Act, 15 U.S.C. § 1. *Id.*

The covenant in *Traeger* prohibited the employee from competing with his employer or associating with any of his employer's competitors in the state of Hawaii for the term of his employment agreement and for three years thereafter. The court held that there was ample evidence to support the trial court's finding that this covenant was reasonable in geographical scope, length of time, and breadth of the restriction placed on the former employee's activity. *Id.* Under the analysis set out in that decision, a restrictive covenant will be deemed reasonable if (1) it is not greater than required for the protection of the person for whose benefit it is imposed, (2) it does not impose an undue hardship on the person restricted, and (3) its benefit to the covenantee is not outweighed by injury to the public resulting from enforcement. *Id.* This "reasonableness analysis" is to be done by the court as a matter of law, and not by a jury as matter of fact. *Id.* (citations omitted).

Subsequently, the U.S. District Court for the District of Hawaii upheld a two-year non-competition provision against salespersons selling business forms. In

UARCO Inc. v. Lam, 18 F. Supp. 2d 1116, 1121–22 (D. Haw. 1998), the court observed that both the terms and the duration of the non-compete provision were "less restrictive" than what had been deemed reasonable and upheld in *Traeger* and therefore enforced the non-competition provision against the two salesmen.

In *Merrill Lynch, Pierce, Fenner & Smith Inc. v. McClafferty*, 287 F. Supp. 2d 1244 (D. Haw. 2003), the U.S. District Court for the District of Hawaii determined that a prohibition on soliciting accounts to a new employer for one year after termination of employment was reasonable and issued a temporary restraining order.

In 2006, the Hawaii Supreme Court upheld another three-year non-competition provision in *7's Enterprises, Inc. v. Del Rosario*, 111 Haw. 484, 143 P.3d 23 (2006). Defendant Del Rosario was hired and trained by 7's Enterprises as a "briefer" (a salesperson who sells products, tours, and souvenirs to travel agencies). When Del Rosario resigned and formed a competing company, 7's Enterprises filed suit to enforce the terms of the non-competition provision of Del Rosario's employment agreement that precluded her from working or otherwise being employed as a briefer in the state of Hawaii for a period of three years post-employment. 7's Enterprises prevailed at trial, and Del Rosario appealed on the grounds (relevant here) that (1) Hawaii law does not recognize an employer's training to be a legitimate business interest that can be protected by a restrictive covenant and (2) three years was an unreasonable duration.

With respect to the issue of training, the trial court held that the purpose of the restrictive covenant in Del Rosario's agreement was to prevent a briefer from seeking employment elsewhere using the special training received while employed by 7's Enterprises and that the training provided and services performed by Del Rosario were unique. On appeal, the Hawaii Supreme Court found that the trial court's findings were not erroneous and "[h]ence, as a matter of law, we hold that training that provides skills beyond those of a general nature is a legitimate interest which may be considered in weighing the reasonableness of a noncompetition covenant, when combined with other factors weighing in favor of a protectable business interest such as trade secrets, confidential information, or special customer relationships." *Id.* at 32.

Regarding the duration of the restrictive covenant, the court cited *Traeger* and its holding that the overall reasonableness of a restrictive covenant in a post-employment context is determined by using the three-pronged "reasonableness analysis" discussed *supra*. The Del *Rosario* court applied a similar three-pronged test and found that a reasonable time limit must (1) be necessary in its full extent for the protection of the legitimate interests of the employer, (2) not be so long as to injure the employee by precluding the employee from his or her occupation and thus preventing the employee from earning a living, and (3) not be so long as to interfere with the interests of the general public by depriving it of the restricted party's industry or services. *Id.* at 36. Under such an analysis, the court in *Del Rosario* determined that the three-year time period was reasonable. *7's Enterprises, Inc. v. Del Rosario*, 111 Haw. 484, 143 P.3d 23, 37 (2006).

In *Standard Register Co. v. Keala*, 2015 WL 3604265 (D. Haw. 2015), the U.S. District Court for the District of Hawaii determined that, although the issue has not been settled by Hawaii courts yet, under Hawaii law, continuing at-will employment is, by itself, sufficient consideration for an otherwise reasonable non-competition agreement entered into during a term of employment.

In *Barranco v. 3D Systems Corporation*, 482 F. Supp. 3d 1090 (D. Haw. 2020), the U.S. District Court for the District of Hawaii, on remand from the Ninth Circuit, determined that the claimant under a non-compete counterclaim was not entitled to contractually agreed-upon equitable relief and, the claimant having previously admitted that it could not establish damages, granted the defendant judgment on that counterclaim.

2. Have the courts articulated the "legitimate interests" of the franchisor that will support enforcement of a covenant against competition contained in a franchise agreement?

- **If so, what are they (e.g., protection of goodwill, protection of confidential information), and in what contexts did the issue arise?**
- **If not, what interests have been recognized in other contexts (e.g., employment agreements, the sale of business context)?**

In *Prudential Locations, LLC v. Gagnon*, 2022 WL 482601, the Hawaii Supreme Court held that non-competition and non-solicitation clauses must be ancillary to a legitimate purpose that does not violate Chapter 480 of the Hawaii Revised Statutes, and that restricting competition is not a legitimate ancillary purpose. Referring to *Technicolor, Inc. v. Traeger*, 57 Haw. 113, 551 P.2d 163 (1976) (discussed above), the supreme court then said "We held 'the restrictive covenants and agreements enumerated under [HRS §] 480-4(c) were not meant to be exclusive in their respective fields. . . . We held that a restrictive covenant is not reasonable if: (i) it is greater than required for the protection of the person for whose benefit it is imposed; (ii) it imposes undue hardship on the person restricted; or (iii) its benefit to the covenantee is outweighed by injury to the public."

HI

The Hawaii Supreme Court then determined that the reasons cited by Prudential Locations were not ancillary to a legitimate purpose. Locations had argued its legitimate purposes were to prevent Gagnon from (1) using proprietary information obtained as a sales coach, (2) forming a competing firm, and (3) "poaching" its agents. The court said that (1) the non-trade-secret confidential information that Locations asserts constitutes a protectible legitimate purpose was not actually "confidential" because others had access to the information who did not sign non-compete agreements, and Locations did not dispute that there were no trade secret violations; (2) preventing competition is not a legitimate ancillary purpose under HAW. REV. STAT. § 480-4(a) based on the plain language purpose to prohibit contracts in restraint of commerce or trade in the state; and (3) workforce stability and customer relationships can be legitimate ancillary interests for a non-solicitation agreement, but solicitation of employees required that Gagnon actively initiate contact with the solicited employees, and there was a genuine issue of material fact as to whether Gagnon actively solicited one employee.

Thus, the court found that workforce stability and customer relationships were legitimate interests to support a non-solicitation agreement, but rejected preventing competition as a legitimate interest to support a noncompetition agreement, and determined that protecting non-trade secret confidential business information had not been factually established, without conceding that such protection would be a legitimate interest to support a non-competition agreement. Citing *7's Enterprises, Inc. v. Del Rosario*, 111 Hawai'i 484, 493, 143 P.3d 23, 32 (2006), the court held that specialized training, when combined with trade secrets, confidential information, or special customer relationships, also may be considered in weighing the reasonableness of a non-competition covenant.

Hawaii franchise statutes and regulations do not specifically address the issue of covenants against competition contained in franchise agreements. However, Hawaii's statute governing covenants of general applicability recognizes the legitimacy of interests to be reasonably protected in connection with, inter alia, a sale of a business, restricted uses in leases, and protection of trade secrets. *See* HAW. REV. STAT. § 480-4(c)(1)–(4) and analysis of the *Technicolor, Inc. v. Traeger*, 57 Haw. 113, 551 P.2d 163 (1976), and *7's Enterprises, Inc. v. Del Rosario*, 111 Haw. 484, 143 P.3d 23 (2006) cases, discussed *supra*.

---

3. What time limitations have courts recognized as reasonable in the franchise context?

- **If no franchise cases have been decided, what time limitations have been recognized in other contexts?**
- **How have they been related to the interests protected?**

In *Technicolor, Inc. v. Traeger*, 57 Haw. 113, 551 P.2d 163 (1976), a three-year post-employment restriction was not questioned. In *7's Enterprises, Inc. v. Del Rosario*, 111 Haw. 484, 143 P.3d 23 (2006), the court applied a three-pronged test to determine the reasonableness of a time limitation and concluded that the three-year post-employment restrictive covenant was reasonable. *Id.* at 37.

---

4. What geographic limitations have courts recognized as reasonable in the franchise context?

- **How have they been related to the interests protected?**
- **Have courts recognized the legitimacy of protecting other franchisees from competition?**

The court in *Technicolor, Inc. v. Traeger*, 57 Haw. 113, 551 P.2d 163 (1976), simply affirmed without further discussion the statewide geographical scope of the covenant at issue. Similarly, in *UARCO Inc. v. Lam*, 18 F. Supp. 2d 1116, 1121–22 (D. Haw. 1998), the court affirmed a statewide scope without analysis. In *7's Enterprises, Inc. v. Del Rosario*, 111 Haw. 484, 143 P.3d 23 (2006), the geographical scope of the restrictive covenant was limited to the island of Oahu and was not an issue at trial or on appeal. It can be inferred from the *Traeger* and *Lam* decisions that, at least where the former employee's activities and responsibilities were statewide, a covenant restricting competition in the entire state of Hawaii would be considered reasonable.

---

5. What limitations on activities have courts recognized as reasonable in the franchise context?

This issue has not been addressed under Hawaii law.

6. Does the state recognize a difference between in-term and post-term covenants?

There are no reported Hawaii cases dealing with in-term covenants against competition. The restrictive covenants in *Technicolor, Inc. v. Traeger*, 57 Haw. 113, 551 P.2d 163 (1976), *UARCO Inc. v. Lam*, 18 F. Supp. 2d 1116, 1121–22 (D. Haw. 1998), and *7's Enterprises, Inc. v. Del Rosario*, 111 Hawaii 484, 143 P.3d 23 (2006), all addressed post-term application.

7. Has the state allowed enforcement of covenants against non-signatories (e.g., family members, newly formed corporations)?

There are no reported Hawaii cases addressing enforcement of covenants against non-signatories. However, in the context of transfers of ownership of franchises, Hawaii's franchise statute provides that if a proposed transferee fails to agree in writing to be bound by all lawful obligations imposed by the franchise agreement, or fails to meet any of the franchisor's or sub-franchisor's reasonable qualifications or standards then in effect for a franchisee or sub-franchisor, then good cause exists to refuse a transfer of ownership. HAW. REV. STAT. § 482E-6(I). A covenant not to compete should comply with the requirements of section 480-4(c) and/or the rule of reason in the *Traeger* case as a "lawful obligation" or "reasonable qualification or standard," and must be for a legitimate ancillary purpose, per the holding in *Prudential Locations, LLC v. Gagnon*, 2022 WL 482601. HI

8. Will the state modify, "blue-pencil," or otherwise reduce a covenant found to be overbroad?

Because the covenant in *Technicolor, Inc. v. Traeger*, 57 Haw. 113, 551 P.2d 163 (1976), was deemed reasonable, the issue of whether the covenant would be rewritten to make it reasonable was not presented. In *7's Enterprises, Inc. v. Del Rosario*, 111 Hawaii 484, 143 P.3d 23 (2006), defendant Del Rosario requested that the appellate court modify the duration of the restrictive covenant from three years to two months. However, the court determined that three years was reasonable and upheld that duration. *Id.* at 36–37. It is unresolved whether a Hawaii court would blue-pencil or reduce a covenant found to be overbroad.

9. When does a non-compete period begin to run? Will courts equitably extend the term?

This issue has not been addressed under Hawaii law.

10. Are there additional nuances or peculiarities of the state's treatment of covenants in the franchising context?

There are none other than what has been discussed above.

Idaho

*by Michael R. Gray**

1. Has the state addressed covenants against competition in the context of franchising?

- **Does the state have a franchising statute or regulations that address covenants against competition?**
- **Does the state have a covenants statute of general applicability that would encompass franchise covenants?**
- **Have the courts addressed covenants in the context of franchising either under a statute or under the state's common law?**

There are no statutes or regulations that specifically address franchise covenants not to compete in Idaho.

Idaho's antitrust and consumer protection statutes, IDAHO CODE ANN. § 48-101 *et seq.* and § 48-601 *et seq.*, respectively, may impact covenants relating to franchise relationships. There are no reported cases addressing covenants not to compete under either the antitrust or consumer protection statutes.

In 2008, Idaho enacted IDAHO CODE ANN. § 44-2701 *et seq.*, that comprehensively deals with covenants against competition that protect the employer's legitimate business interests. "Legitimate business interests" under the statute include an employer's goodwill, technologies, intellectual property, business plans, business processes and methods of operation, customers, customer lists, customer contacts and referral sources, vendors and vendor contacts, financial and marketing information, and trade secrets. IDAHO CODE ANN. § 44-2702(2). This statute applies when agreed upon between an employer and key employees or key independent contractors. "Key employees" and "key independent contractors" include those employees or independent contractors who, by reason of the employer's investment of time, money, trust, exposure to the public, or exposure to technologies, intellectual property, business plan, business processes and methods of operation, customers, vendors, or other business relationships during the course of employment, have gained a high level of inside knowledge, influence, credibility, notoriety, fame, reputation, or public persona as a representative or spokesperson of

Michael R. Gray is a Partner in the Minneapolis office of Lathrop GPM, LLP. E. Scott Lee and Michael Gaffney of Beard St. Clair Gaffney in Idaho Falls, Idaho, contributed to the prior edition.

the employer and, as a result, have the ability to harm or threaten an employer's legitimate business interests. IDAHO CODE ANN. § 44-2702(1).

While not specifically directed at the franchise industry, any key employee or key independent contractor may be bound by the provisions of a non-compete provision under the parameters set forth in the statute. The statute expressly addresses the traditional components of non-compete agreements discussed *infra.* To date, there have been no reported cases interpreting this statute. However, the Idaho Supreme Court recently confirmed that the traditional analysis applies: "The reasonableness of a noncompete provision is generally assessed by examining three essential terms: (1) time; (2) territory; and (3) scope of restricted activities." *Taylor v. Taylor*, 504 P.3d 342, 350 (Idaho 2022).

Idaho's sole franchise restrictive covenant case is *Shakey's Inc. v. Martin*, 91 Idaho 758, 430 P.2d 504 (1967). In *Shakey's*, the Idaho Supreme Court upheld the enforcement of a one-year post-termination covenant not to compete found in the franchise agreement for a Shakey's pizza parlor. The covenant restricted competition within a 30-mile radius of any Shakey's franchised or licensed premise.

2. Have the courts articulated the "legitimate interests" of the franchisor that will support enforcement of a covenant against competition in a franchise agreement?

- **If so, what are they (e.g., protection of goodwill, protection of confidential information), and in what contexts did the issue arise?**
- **If not, what interests have been recognized in other contexts (e.g., employment agreements, the sale of business context)?**

In *Shakey's Inc. v. Martin*, 91 Idaho 758, 430 P.2d 504 (1967), a franchisee left the system and began operating a pizza parlor under a different name in the same location. The Idaho Supreme Court held that a franchisor has a "protectable business interest" in the franchise system itself because that is what the franchisor has to sell to any new franchisee. *Id.* at 509–10. The reasonableness of a non-compete provision, in turn, hinges on whether the provision extends only as far as is reasonably necessary to protect the legitimate business interest of the covenantee. *Bybee v. Isaac*, 145 Idaho 251, 257, 178 P.3d 616, 622 (2008).

In connection with the sale of a business, in *Vancil v. Anderson*, 71 Idaho 95, 227 P.2d 74 (1951), the court awarded damages for breach of a one-year covenant not to compete that covered the county in which the business was located. In *Ryska v. Anderson*, 70 Idaho 207, 214 P.2d 874 (1950), the court upheld a damages award for breach of a five-year covenant not to compete that covered the city where the business was located. The court stated that the measure of damages is lost profits.

In *Magic Lantern Production, Inc. v. Dolsot*, 126 Idaho 805, 892 P.2d 480 (1995), the Idaho Supreme Court, in refusing to enforce an oral covenant not to compete in connection with an agreement to build a mall with a cinema, intimated that even though an implicit restriction on geographic scope may be found by isolation from other similar markets, a restriction was not enforceable unless a duration was stated.

Idaho Court of Appeals cases have also enforced covenants not to compete entered into in connection with the sale of a business. In *Carr v. Carr*, 108 Idaho

684, 701 P.2d 304 (Ct. App. 1985), the court held that a spouse in a divorce proceeding could be compelled to execute a covenant not to compete contained in an agreement for the sale of community property. The covenant contained a five-year duration and a ten-mile territorial restriction. In *Dunn v. Ward*, 105 Idaho 354, 670 P.2d 59 (Ct. App. 1983), the court found that damages for the breach of a four-year covenant not to compete was the goodwill lost as a result of the breach. The value of the goodwill was the consideration for the restrictive covenant; when no separate consideration is in the purchase agreement, damages may be calculated according to lost profits.

In a case involving the sale of used equipment, the Idaho Court of Appeals held in *McCandless v. Carpenter*, 123 Idaho 386, 848 P.2d 444 (Ct. App. 1993), that a covenant not to compete must be supported by consideration, be ancillary to a lawful contract, and be reasonable and consistent with public policy. The court further held that covenants not to compete used primarily to limit competition or restrain the right to engage in a common calling are not enforceable. The court reiterated the categories of contracts in which there are legitimate interests to protect: employment contracts, contracts for the sale of businesses, partnership agreements, and principal-agent relationships.

Idaho courts have upheld covenants not to compete in employment agreements, but the courts scrutinize those covenants more closely than restrictive covenants related to the sale of a business. To the extent that the individual signing the non-compete provision is a key employee or independent contractor as defined by IDAHO CODE ANN. § 44-2701 *et seq.*, discussed *supra*, the caselaw will be effectively superseded by said statute. Where the employee is not determined to be a key employee or independent contractor, common law will still apply.

There are several Idaho Supreme Court cases concerning covenants not to compete entered into as part of an employment agreement. In *Insurance Associates Corp. v. Hansen*, 116 Idaho 948, 782 P.2d 1230 (1989), the court upheld a covenant not to compete for a period of two years as it related to customers of the insurance agency acquired during the former employee's employment.

In *Stipp v. Wallace Plating, Inc.*, 96 Idaho 5, 523 P.2d 822 (1974), the court upheld a covenant not to compete contained in an employment contract that resulted in the former employee losing his contribution to his pension plan. Because the loss of pension benefits was the only consequence of the finding of a breach, the court did not scrutinize the covenant as strictly as it would have had the covenant restricted the former employee's future employment opportunities. The court used an intermediate standard, set between that utilized with employment agreements and the "less restrictive standard" used with the sale of a business. *Id.* at 824. The court found the covenant not to compete reasonable, even though it did not contain territorial or time limitations.

In *Insurance Center, Inc. v. Taylor*, 94 Idaho 896, 499 P.2d 1252 (1972), the court refused to enforce a post-termination restrictive covenant because it lacked limitations of time, area, and scope. The court refused to enforce or modify the covenant because it was "so lacking in essential terms . . . that [it was] as a matter of law unenforceable." *Id.* at 1256.

In *Pinnacle Performance, Inc. v. Hessing*, 135 Idaho 364, 17 P.3d 308 (Ct. App. 2001), the court, in its most comprehensive analysis of restrictive covenants in the employment context, refused to enforce a two-year restrictive covenant that was geographically overbroad and did not specifically define the restricted "service." The court refused to adopt a rule that the absence of an express geographic limitation rendered a covenant not to compete per se unenforceable, instead ruling that the issue must be addressed on a case-by-case basis. *Id.* at 313–14.

In *Magic Valley Truck Brokers, Inc. v. Meyer*, 133 Idaho 110, 982 P.2d 945 (Ct. App. 1999), the court upheld a restrictive covenant applicable for one year within a 300-mile radius. *Id.* at 950.

In *Dick v. Geist*, 107 Idaho 931, 693 P.2d 1133 (Ct. App. 1985), the court refused to enforce a two-year post-termination covenant not to compete on public policy grounds where physicians would have been barred from providing neonatal intensive care in the county. The covenant not to compete covered a radius of 25 miles from the city in which the group was located. *Id.* at 1137.

In *Anderson v. Farm Bureau Mutual Ins. Co. of Idaho*, 112 Idaho 461, 732 P.2d 699 (Ct. App. 1987), an agent brought an action for wrongful termination. The contract provided that service bonus commissions would be severed if the agent competed inside the territory assigned to him within one year from the date of termination, and renewal commissions would be severed if the agent, within two years, worked in the state for any competitor of the company. *Id.* at 708. The court upheld the insurance company's right, based on the employment contract, to withhold renewal commissions and service bonus commissions. The court upheld the agreement because it was not a "restrictive covenant"; it did not prohibit competition, but merely imposed "contractual forfeitures." *Id.* at 708.

---

3. What time limitations have courts recognized as reasonable in the franchise context?

- **If no franchise cases have been decided, what time limitations have been recognized in other contexts?**
- **How have they been related to the interests protected?**

In *Shakey's Inc. v. Martin*, 91 Idaho 758, 430 P.2d 504 (1967), the Idaho Supreme Court upheld a one-year post-termination covenant not to compete contained in a franchise agreement without discussion of how the period related to the protectable interest. *Id.* at 509–10.

In a case involving copartners alleging breach of a settlement agreement between them, the court concluded that the non-compete provision in the settlement agreement was unenforceable because it contained no limitation on duration. "Regardless of what the agreement is called, the protectable business interest analysis is the same. In this case the noncompete contains no temporal limitation and is, therefore, unreasonable as a matter of law." *Taylor v. Taylor*, 504 P.3d 342, 351 (Idaho 2022).

The Idaho cases dealing with covenants not to compete in agreements relating to the sale of a business primarily address the measure of damages; they do not expressly address whether a certain time period is enforceable. However, the following periods have been implicitly approved: five years, *Carr v. Carr*, 108 Idaho 684, 701 P.2d 304 (Ct. App. 1985); *Ryska v. Anderson*, 70 Idaho 207, 214 P.2d 874 (1950); four years, *Dunn v. Ward*, 105 Idaho 354, 670 P.2d 59 (Ct. App. 1983); and one year, *Vancil v. Anderson*, 71 Idaho 95, 227 P.2d 74 (1951).

In the context of employment non-competition agreements, an 18-month restriction on competition is presumptively enforceable. Idaho Code Ann.

§ 44-2703(2). The following time periods have been enforced, or at least implicitly approved, with regard to restrictive covenants in the employment context: three years, *Marshall v. Covington*, 81 Idaho 199, 339 P.2d 504 (1959); two years, *Insurance Associates Corp. v. Hansen*, 116 Idaho 948, 782 P.2d 1230 (1986); *Anderson v. Farm Bureau Mutual Ins. Co. of Idaho*, 112 Idaho 461, 732 P.2d 699 (Ct. App. 1987); and one year, *Magic Valley Truck Brokers, Inc. v. Meyers*, 133 Idaho 110, 982 P.2d 945 (Ct. App. 1999).

Idaho cases have not explained how the "reasonableness" of a time restriction is analyzed.

---

4. What geographic limitations have courts recognized as reasonable in the franchise context?

- **How have they been related to the interests protected?**
- **Have courts recognized the legitimacy of protecting other franchisees from competition?**

In *Shakey's Inc. v. Martin*, 91 Idaho 758, 430 P.2d 504 (1967), the Idaho Supreme Court upheld a geographical restriction that consisted of a 30-mile radius from the franchised premise or 30 miles from any other franchised or licensed premises. *Id.* at 510.

In the context of the sale of a business, Idaho courts have upheld covenants not to compete with the following territorial restrictions: a ten-mile radius from the business establishment, *Carr v. Carr*, 108 Idaho 684, 701 P.2d 304 (Ct. App. 1985); the county in which the business was located, *Vancil v. Anderson*, 71 Idaho 95, 227 P.2d 74 (1951); and the city in which the restaurant was located, *Ryska v. Anderson*, 70 Idaho 207, 214 P.2d 874 (1950).

The territorial restrictions in covenants contained in employment agreements are subject to a high degree of scrutiny. *Stipp v. Wallace Plating, Inc.*, 96 Idaho 5, 523 P.2d 822 (1974). A limit of 25 miles from a medical clinic was enforced in *Marshall v. Covington*, 81 Idaho 199, 339 P.2d 504 (1959). A 300-mile radius was upheld in *Magic Valley Truck Brokers, Inc. v. Meyer*, 133 Idaho 110, 982 P.2d 945 (Ct. App. 1999).

Further, Idaho courts have upheld restrictions, or indicated they would uphold restrictions, where, instead of a geographic territory being restricted, a specific group of known persons or entities are named as off-limits to competition. *Insurance Associates Corp. v. Hansen*, 116 Idaho 948, 782 P.2d 1230 (1989); *Magic Lantern Productions, Inc. v. Dolsot*, 126 Idaho 805, 892 P.2d 480 (1995) (implicit restriction because of isolation from other competitors).

In the employment context, geographic limitations that are "restricted to the geographic areas in which the key employee or key independent contractor provided services or had a significant presence or influence" are presumptively enforceable. IDAHO CODE ANN. § 44-2704(3). A "key employee" is defined as including any employee who is among the highest-paid 5 percent of the employer's workforce or who has access to specialized information, data, intellectual property, and other proprietary information as related to the employer's "legitimate business interest," defined *supra*. This portion of the statue has not been construed in any reported cases.

5. What limitations on activities have courts recognized as reasonable in the franchise context?

There is no reported Idaho case discussing the limitations on activities that can be imposed on a franchisee in a covenant not to compete.

In the employment context, limitations on post-employment activities as to the type of employment or line of employment conducted by the key employee or key independent contractor while working for the employer are also presumptively enforceable. IDAHO CODE ANN. § 44-2704(4). This code provision has not been judicially construed.

6. Does the state recognize a difference between in-term and post-term covenants?

There is no reported Idaho case discussing a distinction between in-term and post-term covenants. All of the cases decided under Idaho law have concerned post-term covenants.

7. Has the state allowed enforcement of covenants against non-signatories (e.g., family members, newly formed corporations)?

No Idaho case has expressly enforced a covenant not to compete against a non-signatory. However, in *Carr v. Carr*, 108 Idaho 684, 701 P.2d 304 (Ct. App. 1985), the court held that it could compel a spouse to execute a covenant not to compete when selling the community property as part of a divorce proceeding. The court reasoned that the covenant would convey goodwill to the seller, and goodwill is a community property asset. *Id.* at 309–10.

8. Will the state modify, "blue-pencil," or otherwise reduce a covenant found to be overbroad?

No Idaho case has applied the "blue-pencil" rule in a franchise or sale of a business context. The rule has, however, been applied in employment cases. *Insurance Center v. Taylor*, 94 Idaho 896, 499 P.2d 1252 (1972); *Stipp v. Wallace*, 96 Idaho 5, 523 P.2d 822 (1984). In *Taylor*, however, the court required the covenant to contain essential terms before it could be modified by the court. 499 P.2d at 1256; *see also Pinnacle Performance, Inc. v. Hessing*, 135 Idaho 364, 17 P.3d 308 (Ct. App. 2001) (court refused to modify the provision but discussed when it could do so, leaving blue-penciling to the discretion of the court).

However, in the 2008 employment non-competition statute, IDAHO CODE ANN. § 44-2703 now requires the court to "blue-pencil" any employment non-competition agreement or covenant "as it shall determine necessary to reflect the intent of the parties and render it reasonable in light of the circumstances in which it was made and specifically enforce the agreement or covenant as limited or modified." This code provision has not been judicially construed.

9. When does a non-compete period begin to run? Will courts equitably extend the term?

Under IDAHO CODE ANN. § 44-4201 described *supra,* the non-compete period begins upon termination of the key employee or independent contractor. There is a rebuttable presumption that any time period up to 18 months is reasonable as to duration and may not be extended unless consideration, in addition to employment or continued employment, is given by the employer. The statute does not indicate whether mention of this additional consideration need be memorialized in the employment agreement. The plain language of IDAHO CODE ANN. § 44-4203 requires the court to "limit or modify" the agreement as the court determines necessary to reflect the intent of the parties and render it reasonable in light of the circumstances. While this presumably would be used to limit rather than enlarge the scope of the non-compete provision in the employment context, the plain language of the statute does not preclude the lengthening of a non-compete period in the event it is for a time period of less than 18 months for key employees and independent contractors.

In the sale of business context, the court in *MWI Veterinary Supply Co. v. Wotton,* 896 F. Supp. 2d 905, 912 (D. Idaho 2012) extended the non-compete agreement between the parties for one year based on the strong factual record before the court and the holding in *WGI Heavy Materials, Inc. v. Gorrill,* 2006 WL 6105887 (Id. 1st Jud. Dist. Apr. 21, 2006). (The court extended the preliminary injunction 76 days to reflect the time period between the date the defendant began competing in violation of the non-compete agreement and the date of the temporary restraining order.)

10. Are there additional nuances or peculiarities of the state's treatment of covenants in the franchising context?

Idaho law has not exhibited any additional nuances or peculiarities in its treatment of covenants against competition in the franchising context.

Illinois

by Ann H. MacDonald

1. Has the state addressed covenants against competition in the context of franchising?

- **Does the state have a franchising statute or regulations that address covenants against competition?**
- **Does the state have a covenants statute of general applicability that would encompass franchise covenants?**
- **Have the courts addressed covenants in the context of franchising either under a statute or under the state's common law?**

The Illinois Franchise Disclosure Act of 1987 (815 ILL. COMP. STAT. 705/1, *et seq.*) (IFDA) addresses covenants against competition in the context of franchise non-renewal. Under section 20(a) of the IFDA, it is a violation for a franchisor to refuse to renew the franchise of a franchised business located in the state without compensating the franchisee, either by repurchase or by other means, for the diminution in the value of the franchised business caused by expiration of the franchise where:

> [t]he franchisee is barred by the franchise agreement (or by the refusal of the franchisor at least 6 months prior to the expiration date of the franchise to waive any portion of the franchise agreement that prohibits the franchisee) from continuing to conduct substantially the same business under another trademark, service mark, trade name or commercial symbol in the same area subsequent to the expiration of the franchise; . . .

815 ILL. COMP. STAT. 705/20(a). There are no Illinois cases interpreting this section of the IFDA, though there are cases addressing corollary issues. *See, e.g.*, *JTH Tax LLC v. Natalie Grabowski, Supernat LLC*, Case No. 19-C-8123, 2020 WL 6203355, at *2 (N.D. Ill. Oct. 22, 2020) (suggesting in dicta that 815 ILL. COMP. STAT. 705/20(a) of the IFDA might apply to a franchisee's territory outside of Illinois if the parties have selected Illinois law to govern their agreement).

Illinois does not have a covenants statute of general applicability that would encompass franchise covenants.

*Ann H. MacDonald is a partner in the law firm ArentFox Schiff LLP. She thanks her colleagues Michael K. Molzberger and Mallory McMahon for their contributions to this chapter.

The Illinois Freedom to Work Act (IFWA), which was signed into law in 2016 and became effective on January 1, 2017, established thresholds for covenants not to compete between employers and employees and banned covenants not to compete for certain employees earning less than $13 an hour. Franchise covenants were not included in either the original law or the recent amendments to the statute, which took effect on January 1, 2022, and are not retroactive. *See* 820 ILCS 90/1 *et seq.* However, as discussed further below, Illinois courts have often analogized franchise agreements to employment agreements for purposes of evaluating covenants not to compete, so the statute and related caselaw may have persuasive impact on courts' consideration of franchise covenants.

The IFWA excludes from its definition of a "covenant not to compete" a covenant entered into by a person purchasing or selling the goodwill of a business or otherwise acquiring or disposing of an ownership interest. *See* 820 ILCS 90/5. The IFWA, as amended, prohibits employers from entering into covenants not to compete with any employee whose earnings do not exceed $75,000 per year and prohibits employers from entering into covenant not to solicit with any employee whose earnings do not exceed $45,000 per year. *See* 820 ILCS 90/10. The IFWA does not limit other types of restrictive covenants, such as confidentiality covenants. *See* 820 ILCS 90/5.

Notably, the IFWA also permits the attorney general to initiate or intervene in litigation if an employer adopts a pattern or practice that violates the statute (820 ILCS 90/30); provides for statutory, one-way fee-shifting to the employee under certain circumstances (820 ILCS 90/25); and mandates certain notice requirements so that employees are informed about their obligations (820 ILCS 90/20). Further, the IFWA, as amended, defines "adequate consideration" for employer-employee non-compete obligations. *See* 820 ILCS 90/5; *Fifield v. Premier Dealer Services, Inc.*, 2013 IL App. (1st) 120327, ¶ 19, 993 N.E.2d 938, 943.

Under the state's common law, Illinois courts will enforce covenants not to compete only where the covenant is ancillary to either a transaction (an otherwise valid contract) or a valid relationship, and where the covenant is reasonably necessary to protect the legitimate business interests of the party seeking enforcement. Whether a restrictive covenant is enforceable is a question of law. *Agrimerica, Inc. v. Mathes*, 199 Ill. App. 3d 435, 441, 557 N.E.2d 357 (1990); *Corroon & Black of Illinois, Inc. v. Magner*, 145 Ill. App. 3d 151, 162, 494 N.E.2d 785 (1986); *see also The Pampered Chef v. Alexanian*, 2011 U.S. Dist. LEXIS 75752, at *35 (N.D. Ill. 2011); *Roberge v. Qualitek International, Inc.*, 2002 U.S. Dist. LEXIS 1217, at *11 (N.D. Ill. 2002).

Although a covenant can attach to any transaction or valid relationship (*see Lawrence and Allen, Inc. v. Cambridge Human Resource Group, Inc.*, 292 Ill. App. 3d 131, 685 N.E.2d 434, 441 (Ill. 1997)), Illinois courts generally analogize the covenant at issue to one of two types: a covenant ancillary to an employment agreement or a covenant ancillary to an agreement for the sale of a business.

> In the sale of a business, the interest to be protected is the goodwill that is transferred. The interest of an employer, on the other hand, has been described as that of "retaining its present customers in circumstances where the employee's contacts and relationships with those customers engenders a substantial risk that the employee will be enabled to divert part of or all the employer's business to the employee's self-interest.

Eichmann v. National Hospital & Health Care Services, Inc., 308 Ill. App. 3d 337, 719 N.E.2d 1141, 1146 (1999), *appeal denied*, 724 N.E.2d 1267 (Ill. 2000); *see also Health*

Professionals, Ltd. v. Johnson, 229 Ill. App. 3d 1021, 1033, 274 Ill. Dec. 768, 780, 791 N.E. 2d 1179, 1191 (2003) (when considering agreements ancillary to the sale of businesses, the focus is on the protection of goodwill, and where it might reasonably be expected).

Although the standard of inquiry into each type of covenant is reasonableness, courts will look with more scrutiny at covenants ancillary to employment agreements than at those ancillary to the sale of a business.

No Illinois Supreme Court opinion has addressed covenants against competition in the franchise context. The Illinois Court of Appeals enforced an in-term covenant against a franchisee's competitive activities in *McDonald's System, Inc. v. Sandy's Inc.*, 45 Ill. App. 2d 57, 195 N.E.2d 22 (1963). The appellate court held that the franchisees had violated an in-term covenant not to engage in a similar business during the term of the franchise, and also violated a covenant prohibiting the franchisees from duplicating the franchise system or using it except at the franchise location. *Id.* at 31. The case was settled while an appeal to the Illinois Supreme Court was pending. Although the appellate court did not cite any Illinois authority for its holding, it did cite cases involving employment-restrictive covenants.

In *Liautaud v. Liautaud*, Jim Liautaud, the founder of the Jimmy John's sandwich shop franchise, sought to enforce a restrictive covenant against his cousin, who had been given access to Jimmy John's trade secrets for use in developing his own brand of sandwich shops in Madison, Wisconsin. *Liautaud v. Liautaud*, 221 F.3d 981, 986–87 (7th Cir. 2000). As a condition to that access, the defendant agreed to forever refrain from engaging in any "sub/club business" outside of Madison, Wisconsin. 221 F.3d at 984. Though the covenant was found to be ancillary to a gift transaction, the Seventh Circuit applied employment-like scrutiny to the restriction. 221 F.3d at 986–87 ("Although noncompetition agreements typically stem from an employment relationship or from the sale of a business, another valid transaction may support a covenant not to compete."). In affirming the U.S. District Court for the Central District of Illinois, the Seventh Circuit found that the restrictive covenant was unenforceable because it imposed restrictions greater than those necessary to protect the plaintiff's legitimate business interests, was oppressive to the defendant, and was harmful to the general public. *Id.* at 987–88 (noting that the agreement prevented the defendant from ever expanding "even if he develop[ed] his own recipes and business strategies").

No Illinois state court has ruled on a post-term restrictive covenant in the franchising context, but several federal district court cases have addressed the issue. Two unpublished opinions from the U.S. District Court for the Northern District of Illinois have addressed the issue on summary judgment motions, though both predate the Illinois Supreme Court's landmark decision in *Reliable Fire Equip. Co. v. Arredondo*, 2011 IL 111871, ¶ 43, 965 N.E.2d 393, 403, discussed *infra*, which rejected the proposition that goodwill, confidential information, and clientele are the only "legitimate interests," and overruled precedent embracing formulaic rules when assessing employment covenants not to compete.

In *Oil Express National Inc. v. P & F Express, Inc.*, Case No. 84-C-3110, 1985 WL 3586, 1985 U.S. Dist. LEXIS 14104 (N.D. Ill. 1985), the district court analyzed a restrictive covenant ancillary to a franchise agreement as though it were ancillary to an employment agreement. The court explained that Illinois courts will enforce a covenant not to compete only if it is reasonably necessary to protect an employer's legitimate business interests or to protect the employer from improper or unfair competition. The franchisor argued that the franchise agreement should be analogized to the sale of a business, but the district court disagreed:

> Like an employee, a franchisee is not selling the franchisor his goodwill, and therefore, franchisors should not be able to assert such an interest in their franchisees' covenants not to compete. Also like an employee, a franchisee is usually in a weaker bargaining position, and his hardship in not being able to pursue his profession after contract termination is equal to an employee's hardship. In short, a franchisee is like the franchisor's salesman. He can profit from his sales relationship with the franchisor by stealing his franchisor's existing clientele or his trade secrets; therefore, the same principles that apply to covenants restricting employees from such theft should apply to franchisees.

Id., 1985 WL 3586, at *3, n.2.

The *Oil Express* view of covenants in franchise agreements was also adopted by the district court in *Servpro Industries v. Schmidt*, Case No. 94-C-5866, 1997 WL 158316, 1997 U.S. Dist. LEXIS 4013 (N.D. Ill. 1997), where the court said that there are three business interests that can be protected by a covenant not to compete: goodwill, clientele, and confidential information. However, the court held that goodwill is generally not one of the legitimate interests that may be asserted by a franchisor in justifying a covenant not to compete, because such covenants are generally found in contracts for the sale of a business. *Id.*, 1997 WL 158316, at *8, 1997 U.S. Dist. LEXIS 4013, at *29 (citing *Oil Express National Inc. v. P & F Express, Inc.*, 1985 WL 3586, at *3, n.2). Consequently, the franchisor was left with only two interests to assert: preserving customers for its franchisees and preserving its trade secrets. The district court found that the franchisor did not have an interest in its customers that could be protected by a covenant not to compete and did not prove that the former franchisee was using the franchisor's trade secrets in its current operation. *Id.*, 1997 WL 158316, at *9, 1997 U.S. Dist. LEXIS 4013, at *31.

The Northern District of Illinois has also enforced a post-termination covenant against a franchisee by issuance of a permanent injunction. In *Meineke Discount Muffler Shops, Inc. v. Smith*, Bus. Franchise Guide (CCH) ¶ 9930 (N.D. Ill. 1991), the court permanently enjoined former franchisees from engaging in any business that is the same as, similar to, or competitive with any Meineke shop for a period of one year within 20 miles of the shop operated by the former franchisees. The court's order did not reference a contract clause specifically justifying the injunction or any legal authority for its holding. Similarly, in *My Favorite Muffin, Too, Inc. v. Wu*, the court permanently enjoined a former franchisee from using plaintiff franchisor's trademarks or service marks, and from operating the same type of business "within a twenty-five-mile radius of the subject location." Case No. 00-C-7820, 2002 WL 826483, at *5 (N.D. Ill. Apr. 30, 2002).

However, when the franchisor of the Fantastic Sam's system failed to demonstrate irreparable harm, this same court refused to issue a preliminary injunction. *E.B.N. Enterprises, Inc. v. C.L. Creative Images, Inc.*, 2011 WL 1131313, 2011 U.S. Dist. LEXIS 32829 (N.D. Ill. 2011). In *E.B.N. Enterprises, Inc.*, a former Fantastic Sam's franchisee continued to operate a salon under a different name after terminating the franchise arrangement. *Id.* at 2011 WL 1131313, at *2, 2011 U.S. Dist. LEXIS 32829, at *4. The franchisor argued that its irreparable injury is presumed from a breach of the non-competition provision of the franchise agreement. *Id.* at 2011 WL 1131313, at *3, 2011 U.S. Dist. LEXIS 32829, at *8. The court, however, found that the rulings supporting such presumption were at least partially based on evidence that former franchisees' continued operations were improperly using proprietary or unique elements of the franchisors' business, and that no evidence was presented here to support the claim that the defendant was improperly using Fantastic Sam's propriety elements. *Id.* With respect to E.B.N. Enterprises, Inc.'s contention that its former franchisee was improperly using its confidential method of operations, the court noted that knowledge of the system came from the franchisee owner's prior experience as an employee at a Fantastic Sam's salon rather than as a result of her signing of the franchise agreement. The court concluded that E.B.N. Enterprises, Inc. failed to identify any elements of its "system" and failed to show that its former franchisee was using anything other than "generally sound business practices and hair styling techniques" in her new business. *Id.* at 2011 WL 1131313, at *3, 2011 U.S. Dist. LEXIS 32829, at *9. With respect to the claim that the former franchisee was improperly trading on the goodwill of Fantastic Sam's, the court found that E.B.N. Enterprises, Inc. failed to show any evidence that the defendant's customers sought salon features unique to Fantastic Sam's and therefore did not improperly trade upon its goodwill. *Id.* at 2011 WL 1131313, at *4, 2011 U.S. Dist. LEXIS 32829, at *9–10.

While most courts applying Illinois law in the franchise context have applied the employment analogy, the U.S. Bankruptcy Court for the Central District of Illinois upheld a covenant in the franchise context using a different analytical approach. *In re KBAR, Inc.*, 96 B.R. 158 (Bankr. C.D. Ill. 1988). In *KBAR*, the court analogized the covenant in a franchise agreement that involved a service franchise, as well as distribution and use of the franchisor's supplies, to that of a licensor-licensee restrictive covenant, and applied the following standard to the covenant contained in a Hardee's franchise agreement: "[W]hether the restriction is reasonable or 'necessary in its full extent for the protection' of the one party 'and at the same time not oppressive' to the other party or 'injurious to the interests of the general public.'" 96 B.R. at 160 (quoting *In re Talmage*, 758 F.2d 162, 165 (6th Cir. 1985) (stating that Illinois applied a different standard for employer-employee restrictive covenants than for licensor-licensee agreements between independent business entities)). The licensor-licensee standard is akin to the sale-of-business standard. *But see Morrison Metalweld Process Corp. v. Valent*, 97 Ill. App. 3d 373, 422 N.E.2d 1034, 1039 (1981) (applying the stricter employee/employer standard to a non-solicitation covenant in a license agreement).

IL

Illinois state courts have addressed covenants against competition in the related contexts of independent contractors and dealership arrangements using what appears to be the employer-employee standard. In *O'Hare-Midway Limousine Service, Inc. v. Quick*, 37 Ill. App. 3d 554, 346 N.E.2d 3 (1976), a three-year, post-term covenant prohibiting the provision of livery service within 50 miles of O'Hare airport or Midway airport was enforced against a livery driver whose relationship with the livery service was characterized as that of an independent contractor. *See also Eichmann v. National Hospital & Health Care Services, Inc.*, 308 Ill. App. 3d 337. In *U-Haul Company of Central Illinois, Inc. v. Hindahl*, 90 Ill. App. 3d 572, 413 N.E.2d 187 (1980), an Illinois appellate court affirmed the issuance of a preliminary injunction enforcing a post-termination covenant against competition for one year, encompassing one county, against former U-Haul dealers who continued to conduct a similar business. *But see Budget Rent A Car Corp. v. Harvey Kidd Auto*, 249 F. Supp. 2d 1048, 1050 (N.D. Ill. 2003) (distinguishing *U-Haul*, where former dealer retained phone numbers listed in Yellow Pages under the U-Haul name and thus had the ability to divert business from U-Haul, from the case at bar, and denying temporary restraining order, where former dealer's telephone number was maintained by Budget, would divert potential customers to nearby alternate Budget dealer and where repeat customers were already contacted by Budget to divert them to Budget-owned lots).

In sum, Illinois law appears to follow the majority view in assessing restrictive covenants that, while a franchise agreement is neither an employment contract nor a contract for the sale of a business, it is more akin to a contract of employment. *See* Annotation, *Validity and Construction of Restrictive Covenant Not to Compete Ancillary to Franchise Agreement*, 50 A.L.R.3d 746 (1973) (citing *McDonald's System* and *KBAR*). Note, however, that the Illinois Freedom to Work Act, which generally governs the enforceability of covenants not to compete in the employer-employee context entered into on or after January 1, 2022, does not by its terms appear to apply to covenants not to compete between a franchisor and franchisee. *See* 820 ILCS 90/5; 820 ILCS 105/3.

---

2. Have the courts articulated the "legitimate interests" of the franchisor that will support enforcement of a covenant against competition in a franchise agreement?

- **If so, what are they (e.g., protection of goodwill, protection of confidential information), and in what contexts did the issue arise?**
- **If not, what interests have been recognized in other contexts (e.g., employment agreements, the sale of business context)?**

Only one Illinois state court decision has directly addressed the "legitimate interests" of the franchisor that will support enforcement of a covenant against competition in a franchise agreement. In *McDonald's System, Inc. v. Sandy's, Inc.*, 45 Ill. App. 2d 57, 195 N.E.2d 22 (1963), where a franchisee copied the restaurant licensed by the franchise agreement, the franchise itself was held to be a valuable property right encompassing a legitimate business interest that justified enforcement of an in-term restrictive covenant. The Illinois Appellate Court found that the franchisees had clearly recognized this valuable property right when they voluntarily executed and accepted the benefits of the franchise agreement. The court noted that the individual franchisees had no experience in the wholesale or retail food business or in the construction or operation of a drive-in restaurant or hamburger stand prior to becoming McDonald's franchisees.

In finding the franchise itself to be a protectable interest, the *McDonald's System* court appears to also have been influenced by the size of the McDonald's system and by the extent to which the franchisees copied the system in a competing restaurant, including the blueprints, menu, equipment, equipment placement, methods and procedures of preparing and serving food and drinks, suggested prices, and purchasing from designated suppliers. The court expressed no concern that these elements did not individually constitute trade secrets. *Id.* at 28–29.

In *In re KBAR, Inc.*, 96 B.R. 158 (Bankr. C.D. Ill. 1988), a fast-food franchisor sought enforcement of a post-term restrictive covenant in a franchise agreement in the Chapter 11 bankruptcy case of its franchisee. The court held that the fast-food franchisor's post-termination restrictive covenant was reasonable as a matter of law to (1) protect confidential marketing and operational information, (2) limit the franchisee's use of the training given and knowledge imparted, (3) allow time for the public association of the former franchisee with the franchise system to dissipate, and (4) allow the franchisor the opportunity to refranchise the areas without competition from the former franchisee. *Id.* at 160.

The court in *Liautaud v. Liautaud*, 221 F.3d 981 (7th Cir. 2000), determined that Jimmy John's interest in protecting the confidentiality of its trade secrets was legitimate, but refused to enforce the covenant not to compete against the recipient of those trade secrets when the covenant contained no temporal limitation and would have effectively prevented the recipient from "expanding anywhere in the world outside of Madison," regardless of whether the recipient was actually using the trade secrets. *Id.* at 987.

"Legitimate interests" have been recognized in other contexts. *See, e.g., U-Haul Company of Central Illinois, Inc. v. Hindahl*, 90 Ill. App. 3d 572, 413 N.E.2d 187 (1980) (enforcing a post-term restrictive covenant in a truck lessor's dealership contract and recognizing the legitimacy of U-Haul's interests in customer contacts). In the licensing context, the Sixth Circuit, applying Illinois law, referred to the "legitimate business interests" of a licensor, "whether deemed confidential information, goodwill, trade secrets or established clientele lists." *In re Talmage*, 758 F.2d 162, 166 (6th Cir. 1985). Confidential information need not be a trade secret to be protectable in Illinois. *See, e.g., Shapiro*, 549 N.E.2d at 796; *Millard Maintenance*, 566 N.E.2d at 385. However, trade secrets are entitled to special statutory protection in Illinois (see the discussion in Question 9 below).

In the context of employment agreements, Illinois courts historically recognized two legitimate interests: (1) near-permanent customer relationships and (2) confidential information or trade secrets. *See, e.g., Appelbaum v. Appelbaum*, 355 Ill. App. 3d 926, 823 N.E.2d 1074, 1081 (2005) (discussing seven-part test for near-permanent relationship); *Emery-Drexel Livery v. Cook-DuPage Transportation Co.*, 40 Ill. App. 3d 937, 353 N.E.2d 182 (1976) (absence of either interest rendered the post-term covenant unenforceable); *see also Mohanty v. St. John Heart Clinic, S.C.*, 225 Ill. 2d 52, 76, 866 N.E.2d 85, 98 (2006) (reviewing alleged near-permanent relationship); *Novamed, Inc. v. Universal Quality Sols., Inc.*, 2016 IL App. (1st) 152673-U, ¶¶ 36-38 (factors that weigh in favor of a near-permanent relationship include exclusivity and the existence of a contract with a customer; customer list information not confidential when it can be obtained from other sources, including by calling the customer); *Office Mates 5, North Shore Inc. v. Hazen*, 234 Ill. App. 3d 557, 599 N.E.2d 1072, 1083 (1992) (a franchisee running an office support personnel placement agency did not meet the near-permanence test with its clients because only half of the clients gave the plaintiff repeat business and only one-third maintained a relationship with the plaintiff for more than two to three years); *Millard Maintenance Service Co. v. Bernero*, 207 Ill. App. 3d 736, 566 N.E.2d 379, 385 (1990) (contractor had protectable interest in pricing formula and customer information); *Shapiro v. Regent Printing Co.*, 192 Ill. App. 3d 1005, 549 N.E.2d 793, 796 (1989) (confidential pricing formula was found not to be a protectable business interest when employer took no steps to treat it as confidential and formula accounted for common cost factors in the industry).

In 2011, the Illinois Supreme Court rejected this formulaic approach and instead held that "whether a legitimate business interest exists is based on the totality of the facts and circumstances of the individual case." *Reliable Fire*, 2011 IL 111871, ¶ 43, 965 N.E.2d 393, 403.

The IFWA, as amended, appears to codify *Reliable Fire*'s "totality of the facts and circumstances" approach and lists the factors relevant to the analysis of a legitimate business interest when evaluating the enforceability of a covenant not to compete or solicit in the context of employment agreements:

> Legitimate business interest of the employer. In determining the legitimate business interest of the employer, the totality of the facts and circumstances of the individual case shall be considered. Factors that may be considered in this analysis include, but are not limited to, the employee's exposure to the employer's customer relationships or other employees, the near-permanence of customer relationships, the employee's acquisition, use, or knowledge of confidential information through the employee's employment, the time restrictions, the place restrictions, and the scope of the activity restrictions. No factor carries any more weight than any other, but rather its importance will depend on the specific facts and circumstances of the individual case. Such factors are only non-conclusive aids in determining the employer's legitimate business interest, which in turn is but one component in the 3-prong rule of reason, grounded in the totality of the circumstances. Each situation must be determined on its own particular facts. Reasonableness is gauged not just by some, but by all of the circumstances. The same identical contract and restraint may be reasonable and valid under one set of circumstances and unreasonable and invalid under another set of circumstances.

820 ILCS 90/7. Under the Act, the covenant must be "no greater than is required for the protection of a legitimate business interest of the employer." 820 ILCS 90/15.

In light of the January 1, 2022, effective date of the amendments to the Illinois Freedom to Work Act, there are no cases as of the date of publication interpreting the statute. However, the statutory criteria are consistent with the Illinois Supreme Court's holding in *Reliable Fire Equipment Co. v. Arredono*, 358 Ill. Dec. 322, 332, 965 N.E. 2d 393, 404 (2011) that there is no "test" for determining the existence of a "legitimate business interest," but rather courts must look to the totality of the facts and circumstances. It remains to be seen whether the historical emphasis on two factors in particular will influence court consideration of restrictive covenants under the new statute and how those changes in the law for employment agreements influence court consideration of covenants in franchise agreements.

---

3. What time limitations have courts recognized as reasonable in the franchise context?

- **If no franchise cases have been decided, what time limitations have been recognized in other contexts?**
- **How have they been related to the interests protected?**

In-term covenants are enforceable during the term of a franchise agreement. In *McDonald's System*, the court said that "as long as appellees seek to avail themselves of the beneficial provisions of that franchise contract, they should not be permitted to disregard or refuse to abide by the several obligations they assumed." *McDonald's System, Inc. v. Sandy's, Inc.*, 45 Ill. App. 2d 57, 195 N.E.2d 22, 31 (1963) (franchisee violated covenant not to engage in similar business during the term of the agreement and a prohibition on duplicating the McDonald's system or using it except at the franchised location).

The reasonableness of post-term time limitations depends on the type of franchise business interest to be protected, as well as the activities prohibited. In *Meineke Discount Muffler Shops, Inc. v. Smith*, Bus. Franchise Guide (CCH) ¶ 9930 (N.D. Ill. 1991), the court enforced a covenant against engaging in any business that is the same as or similar to or competitive with Meineke Discount Muffler Shops for one year following the date of de-identifying with the system. The bankruptcy court in *In re KBAR, Inc.*, 96 B.R. 158, 160 (Bankr. C.D. Ill. 1988), where a fast-food franchisor sought enforcement of a post-term covenant against a bankrupt franchisee, enforced a one-year term, stating that the covenant was enforceable because its impact on competition was minimal and because of its short duration. In *In re Talmage*, 758 F.2d 163, 166 (6th Cir. 1985), the Sixth Circuit found a one-year term reasonable in a license agreement under Illinois law. In *My Favorite Muffin*, an Illinois court enforced a covenant that prohibited the franchisee from operating the same or similar business for two years after the franchise agreement was terminated. 2002 WL 826483, at *1, *4.

In non-franchise contexts, reasonableness determinations vary according to the type of contract or relationship involved and the covenant involved. Illinois courts view restrictive covenants ancillary to a sale of a business more favorably than those ancillary to employment. *See, e.g., Eichmann v. National Hospital & Health Care Services, Inc.*, 308 Ill. App. 3d 337, 719 N.E.2d 1141, 1146 (1999). In the sale-of-business context, Illinois courts seek to protect the goodwill and customer relationships purchased by the buyer. *See Health Pros., Ltd. v. Johnson*, 339 Ill. App. 3d 1021, 1032–34, 791 N.E.2d 1179, 1190–91 (2003) (enforcing three-year covenant that prohibited activity in Illinois and Wisconsin based on history of providing services and marketing efforts).

In the employment context, existing caselaw requires that time restraints be reasonable, and it seems unlikely that will change as courts evaluate covenants through the lens of the Illinois Freedom to Work Act. The first Illinois case to deal with an employment covenant enforced a three-year post-termination covenant against a saloon employee who established a competing saloon. *Old Rose Distilling Co. v. Feuer*, 202 Ill. App. 210 (1916). In *Smithereen Co. v. Renfroe*, 325 Ill. App. 229, 59 N.E.2d 545, 550 (1945), the interest of protecting an employer's confidential information against use by a competing former branch manager supported enforcement of a five-year covenant. In two other cases, the employer's interest in protecting its confidential information supported a three-year covenant against a former employee. *Central Keystone Plating of Illinois, Inc. v. Hutchinson*, 62 Ill. App. 2d 188, 210 N.E.2d 239 (1965) (sales manager); *Wessel Company, Inc. v. Busa*, 28 Ill. App. 3d 686, 329 N.E.2d 414, 418 (1975) (employee had been hired to solicit, procure, and administer the employer's printing business).

After the Illinois Supreme Court's decision in *Reliable Fire*, Illinois courts have focused on the reasonableness of the limitations in the covenant based on the totality of the circumstances, an approach similar to the one outlined in the Illinois Freedom to Work Act. 2011 IL 111871, ¶ 17. For example, in *Zabaneh Franchises, LLC v. Walker*, the court found that a two-year limitation on the former employee's ability to prepare tax returns was reasonable because it only prevented the former employee for preparing tax returns for customers she had previously prepared tax returns for while working for plaintiff. 2012 IL App. (4th) 110215, ¶ 21, 972 N.E.2d 344, 350. The court noted that this limitation "reasonably balances defendant's right to earn a living with plaintiff's right to protect its customer relationships and its investment in developing defendant's skills." *Id.*; *see also InvestRX Corp v.*

IL

DiGiovanni, 2012 IL App. (1st) 120758-U, 2012 WL 6965127 (Aug. 2, 2012) (following *Reliable Fire* and enforcing two-year covenant).

Before *Reliable Fire*, courts focused more on the time needed by the employer to acquire new customers or referral sources, a factor that may still be relevant depending on the case. *See, e.g., Mohanty v. St. John Heart Clinic, S.C.*, 225 Ill. 2d 52, 78, 866 N.E.2d 85, 100 (2006) (five-year restriction reasonably related to the ten years for the employer to establish itself as a successful practice and the three to five years necessary to develop the referral base that supplied physician-employees with nearly all their referrals during their employment); *Midwest Television, Inc. v. Oloffson*, 298 Ill. App. 3d 548, 699 N.E.2d 230, 235 (1998) (12-month restriction reasonably related to the employer's business development needs); *Tyler Enterprises of Elwood, Inc. v. Shafer*, 214 Ill. App. 3d 145, 573 N.E.2d 863 (1991) (three-year non-compete in Stock Option Agreement was enforceable).

Regardless of the test, Illinois courts have often been hostile to covenants that are temporally unlimited. In *Eichmann v. National Hospital & Health Care Services, Inc.*, the court found a temporally unlimited covenant was unreasonable as a matter of law. 308 Ill. App. 3d 337, 719 N.E.2d 1141, 1148 (1999), *appeal denied*, 724 N.E.2d 1267 (Ill. 2000); *see also Johnson v. Country Life Insurance*, 12 Ill. App. 3d 158, 300 N.E.2d 11, 15 (1973) (refusing to enforce temporally unlimited non-competition covenant).

Illinois courts have also addressed time limits in the context of dealer agreements. In *U-Haul Company of Central Illinois, Inc. v. Hindahl*, 90 111. App. 3d 572, 413 N.E.2d 187, 193–94 (1980), the interest to be protected was established customer relations. The court expressed concern over enforcing the covenant against former dealers for one year after the lapse of the current Yellow Pages listing (paid for by U-Haul). Although the trial court did not abuse its discretion in granting preliminary relief in finding the time limit reasonable in order to preserve the status quo, the appellate court suggested that the trial court would reexamine and redetermine the extent of relief necessary after the merits were heard.

---

4. What geographic limitations have courts recognized as reasonable in the franchise context?

- **How have they been related to the interests protected?**
- **Have courts recognized the legitimacy of protecting other franchisees from competition?**

Illinois courts have applied different standards to the reasonableness of geographic limitations with respect to both in-term and post-term covenants. *McDonald's System, Inc. v. Sandy's, Inc.*, 45 Ill. App. 2d 57, 195 N.E.2d 22 (1963), is frequently cited for the proposition that in-term covenants in the franchising context are enforceable without geographic limitation. However, the *McDonald's System* court actually had under review a covenant that contained a geographic limitation, albeit a broad one, of the state where the business was located and all contiguous states. The *McDonald's System* court stated: "[u]nder these and other authorities, the extent of the territorial restriction is a factor that affects the validity of a post-term covenant only." *Id.* at 31. This dicta has been referred to as the "Illinois Rule." For a good discussion of the distinction between in-term and post-term covenants, *see Vendo Co. v. Stoner*, 105 Ill. App. 2d 261, 245 N.E.2d. 263, 273 (1969) (the territory covered by a covenant, otherwise unreasonably broad, will not invalidate the covenant to the extent that it "exists during the term of the employment, lease, franchise agreement, etc."), and the cases cited therein.

Franchise decisions applying Illinois law have used a reasonableness test with respect to geographic limitations on post-term covenants. The Northern District of Illinois in *Meineke Discount Muffler Shops, Inc. v. Smith*, Bus. Franchise Guide (CCH) ¶ 9930 (N.D. Ill. 1991), enjoined competition with any Meineke shop located within a 20-mile radius of the franchisee's former shop. In *In re KBAR, Inc.*, 96 B.R. 158, 160 (Bankr. C.D. Ill. 1988), the bankruptcy court enforced a covenant restricting competition within three miles of its former location or within a one and one-half mile radius of any other Hardee's restaurant.

In the context of a dealer agreement, the appellate court in *U-Haul Company of Central Illinois v. Hindahl*, 90 Ill. App. 3d 572, 413 N.E.2d 187, 192–93 (1980), enforced a county-wide covenant because the former dealers were located in a county seat, phone books were distributed throughout the county, and the dealers derived business throughout the county.

In other contexts, although reasonableness is ultimately the standard by which a geographical restraint is measured, courts may invest reasonableness with a quantifiable physical dimension. The reasonable geographical restraint is often the area that is coextensive with the employer's business territory. *Reliable Fire Equipment Co. v. Arredono*, 358 Ill. Dec. 322, 332, 965 N.E.2d 393, 404 (2011) (holding that the restraint on practice was not greater than necessary to protect the defendant's interests because the restriction was "only within a narrowly circumscribed area of a large metropolitan area"); *Midwest Television, Inc. v. Oloffson*, 298 Ill. App. 3d 548, 699 N.E.2d 230 (1998) (a 100-mile radius from the radio station was reasonable because it matched the station's broadcast radius); *Instrumentalist Co. v. Band, Inc.*, 134 Ill. App. 3d 884, 480 N.E.2d 1273, 1281–82 (1985) (a publication was distributed nationwide so a nationwide geographical restraint was reasonable). Ultimately, however, the restriction must not cause undue hardship to the employee. *Mohanty v. St. John Heart Clinic, S.C.*, 225 Ill. 2d 52, 77, 866 N.E.2d 85, 99 (2006) (a two- and five-mile radius around a medical clinic's office would not cause undue hardship given the heavily populated Chicago metropolitan area).

It seems unlikely that the Illinois Freedom to Work Act will change the Illinois courts' inclination to enforce post-term employment covenants to the extent the geographic limitations are necessary to protect an employer's legitimate business interests. For example, in *Smithereen*, a covenant applicable to the entire city of Chicago was enforced against a former branch manager who had both customer contact and knowledge of the employer's business. *Smithereen Co. v. Renfroe*, 325 Ill. App. 229, 59 N.E.2d 545, 550 (1945). The Sixth Circuit in *In re Talmage*, 758 F.2d 162, 166 (6th Cir. 1985), applying Illinois law, approved a non-solicitation covenant that was geographically unlimited because it restricted the licensee only from continuing to serve any of the licensor's clients. A post-term restriction on competition within a 50-mile radius of two Chicago airports in an agreement relating to the provision of livery services was enforced in *O'Hare-Midway Limousine Service, Inc. v. Quick*, 37 Ill. App. 3d 554, 346 N.E.2d 3 (1976). *But see Emery-Drexel Livery v. Cook-Du Page Transp. Co.*, 40 Ill. App. 3d. 937 (1976) (the post-employment restrictive covenant was not reasonably necessary because the customers voluntarily approached the defendant to expand livery service).

Generally speaking, Illinois courts do not favor contingent geographic restrictions. In *Barrington Trucking Co. v. Casey*, 117 Ill. App. 2d 151, 253 N.E.2d 36 (1969), an employer attempted to enforce a covenant restricting an employee from competing in any area in any state where the employer or its affiliates were engaged in business or soliciting business. The court refused to enforce the covenant, holding that the restraint was irrelevant to the employer's legitimate interest in protecting its customers and imposed an unreasonable burden on the employee. "In order for the defendant to seek employment . . . it seems that he would be required to ascertain from the plaintiff whether it, its subsidiaries or its 'operating affiliates' are either engaged in business in a certain area or actively soliciting such business in such area." 253 N.E.2d at 39. Likewise, in *North American Paper Co. v. Unterberger*, 172 Ill. App. 3d 410, 526 N.E.2d 621, 623–24 (1988), a flexible covenant applicable to a former manager of one of the employer's divisions was interpreted to cover its maximum geographic area, making him virtually unemployable in his field of occupation and other related fields, and thus was voided as unreasonable. *But see Baird & Warner Residential Sales, Inc., v. Mazzone*, 384 Ill. App. 3d 586 (2008) (it was not unreasonable for the employer to put a restraint on a specific geographic location because the restraint only included about 100 agents and did not have the same geographic reach).

An old line of Illinois Supreme Court cases suggests that restraints covering the entire state of Illinois are, on their face, unreasonable and void as against public policy, but later caselaw has called this rationale into question, as with the other bright-line tests in this area. *Dryvit System, Inc. v. Rushing*, 132 Ill. App. 3d 9, 477 N.E.2d 35, 40 (1985) (finding this old line of cases no longer controlling, as the boundaries of states are not those of trade and commerce, and thus in a given situation it may be totally reasonable to both the employer and the employee to have a statewide limitation).

Unlimited geographic restraints, however, may be permissible under certain circumstances. In *Lawter International, Inc. v. Carroll*, 116 Ill. App. 3d 717, 727, 451 N.E.2d 1338 (1983), in upholding the trial court's finding that a covenant containing an unlimited geographic scope was void, the appellate court stated:

> We believe that under current Illinois law the question of the geographical scope of a covenant not to compete is only one of the factors to be considered by a court in determining a covenant's enforceability and not the final test. The factor may be relatively insignificant as in cases where there are special circumstances, such as customer lists, customer contacts, trade secrets or other confidential information to be protected [Citations omitted] . . . or the lack of geographical scope may be determinative as in situations where territorial restrictions as to salesmen or routemen are greater than the area that was served by those employees on behalf of the employer. In the latter situation, the cases almost uniformly hold that excluding service occupations from an entire state by such a covenant is unreasonable.

Another Illinois appellate court has held that "[e]mployees should only be excluded from doing business in the "territorial zone in which relationships with the employer's customers could have been established in ways that could be detrimental in the hands of a competitor." *Cambridge Eng'g, Inc., v. Mercury Partners 90 BI, Inc.*, 378 Ill. App. 3d 47 (2007). Where the covenant is limited to non-solicitation of customers, broader covenants are enforceable. *See, e.g., Wessel Company, Inc. v. Busa*, 28 Ill. App. 3d 686, 329 N.E.2d 414, 417–18 (1985) (250-mile radius from New York City). An unlimited geographic covenant prohibiting contact with former clients where the employer's insurance business was national was also enforced in *Corroon & Black of*

Illinois, Inc. v. Magner, 145 Ill. App. 3d 151, 494 N.E.2d 785 (1986). *But see Riddell, Inc. v. Shawn Stimmel & Bsn Sports*, Case No. 18-C-08062, Civ. No. 18-C-8062, 2019 WL 11505774, at *4 (N.D. Ill. Aug. 9, 2019) (refusing to enforce or rewrite a vague, seemingly nationwide, covenant on the grounds it appeared to be "completely arbitrary").

In *Roberge v. Qualitek International, Inc.*, 2002 U.S. Dist. LEXIS 1217 (N.D. Ill. 2002), a former employee and his new employer filed a declaratory judgment action against a former employer seeking to hold a post-term restrictive covenant void and unenforceable. The covenant contained no geographic limitation and prohibited the former employee from working with a competitor in any capacity for two years. Citing *Eichmann v. National Hospital & Health Care Services*, 308 Ill. App. 3d 337, 719 N.E.2d 1141 (1999), *appeal denied*, 724 N.E.2d 1267 (Ill. 2000), the district court said the lack of a geographical restriction does not automatically invalidate a post-term restraint where the geographical prohibition is qualified by an activity restraint, but a blanket prohibition on competition is prohibited. The court determined the covenant in question was so broad that the former employee would even be prohibited from working as a janitor for a competitor. In holding the covenant void, the court concluded, "There is simply no legitimate business interest of [the former employer] that can justify such a ridiculous result." *Qualitek Int'l, Inc.*, 2002 U.S. Dist. LEXIS at p. 18. *See Oce N. Am., Inc. v. Brazeua*, Case No. 09-C-2381, 2009 U.S. Dist. LEXIS 126626 (N.D. Ill. Sept. 4. 2009) (a restriction that prevents an employee from being associated with a nationwide competitor in any way is not reasonably necessary to protect legitimate business interests).

No court decisions applying Illinois law have addressed whether protecting *other* franchisees from competition is a justification for enforcing a covenant not to compete.

5. What limitations on activities have courts recognized as reasonable in the franchise context?

Unlike a blanket covenant not to compete, an activity restraint that lacks geographical or temporal boundaries is not automatically invalid under Illinois law. *Eichmann v. National Hospital & Health Care Services*, 308 Ill. App. 3d 337, 719 N.E.2d 1141, 1147 (1999), *appeal denied*, 724 N.E.2d 1267 (Ill. 2000) (independent contractor's restraint limited to a particular type of activity, such as solicitation, or a specific customer group). But while geographic and temporal boundaries are not required of activity restraints, "an activity restraint must be reasonably related to the employer's interest in protecting customer relations that its employees developed as a direct result of the employment." *Id.* at 1147; *see also Arpac Corp. v. Murray*, 226 Ill. App. 3d 65, 589 N.E.2d 640, 649 (1992) (an activity covenant designed to protect an employer's relationship with its customers does not require geographic limitations but must be reasonably related to protecting the customer relations that its employee developed while working for the employer).

In the franchising context, the appellate court in *McDonald's System, Inc. v. Sandy's, Inc.*, 45 Ill. App. 2d 57, 195 N.E.2d 22 (1963), where the franchisee duplicated a substantial portion of the McDonald's system, enforced an in-term covenant that precluded operation of any business the same as or similar to McDonald's franchise. In *Meineke Discount Muffler Shops, Inc. v. Smith*, Bus. Franchise Guide (CCH) ¶ 9930 (N.D. Ill. 1991), the district court enjoined a franchisee from engaging in any business the same as, similar to, or competitive with Meineke Muffler Shops. The court in *U-Haul Company of Central Illinois, Inc. v. Hindahl*, 90 Ill. App. 3d 572, 413 N.E.2d 187, 194 (1980), enforced a post-term prohibition against a former dealer engaging in any equipment rental business similar to that operated by U-Haul.

In the employment context, an employer who seeks to prevent a former employee from contacting customers should not proscribe contact with customers that the employee had never before solicited. An otherwise unqualified activity restraint that purports to restrain a former employee from soliciting customers never before contacted by the employee will likely be invalidated as overbroad. *See Christie Clinic, LLC v. Youse*, Case No. 20-CV-2340, 2021 WL 1095332 (C.D. Ill., Jan. 27, 2021) (holding covenant prohibiting the treatment of any patients for 24 months is overbroad, unreasonable, and therefore unenforceable); *Brown & Brown, Inc. v. Ali*, 592 F. Supp. 2d 1009, 1046, 2009 U.S. Dist. LEXIS 10252, at *87 (N.D. Ill. 2009); *Eichmann*, 719 N.E.2d at 1147; *Corroon & Black of Illinois, Inc. v. Magner*, 145 Ill. App. 3d 151, 494 N.E.2d 785, 793 (1986); *McRand, Inc. v. Van Beelen*, 138 Ill. App. 3d 1045, 486 N.E.2d at 1306, 1315 (1985); *Jefco Laboratories, Inc. v. Carroo*, 136 Ill. App. 3d 793, 483 N.E.2d 999, 1003 (1985). Conversely, geographically unlimited activity restraints have been upheld as reasonable where the covenant restrained the former employee from diverting customers with whom he had had direct contact and had "gained special knowledge and familiarity with the customer's requirements." *Eichmann*, 719 N.E.2d at 1147.

Illinois courts will generally give covenants against competition a greater scope of enforceability if the activities restrained are extremely limited. For example, in *World Wide Pharmacal Distributing Co. v. Kolkey*, 5 Ill. App. 2d 201, 125 N.E.2d 309, 312 (1955), a general manager who knew his employer's formula for a pharmaceutical product connected with the enlargement of the female breast was restrained throughout the entire United States for one year from engaging in a competitive business with respect to one specific type of pharmaceutical product. Likewise, in *Corroon & Black of Illinois, Inc. v. Magner*, 145 Ill. App. 3d 151, 494 N.E.2d 785, 793 (1986), the court approved an unlimited geographic covenant that prohibited the employee only from soliciting any client with whom he had contact during his employment.

In *Agrimerica, Inc. v. Mathes*, 170 Ill. App. 3d 1025, 524 N.E.2d 947, 953 (1988), the court suggested that an "activity" covenant related to the employer's interest in protecting customer relations that the employee developed as a direct result of the employment does not require geographic limitation. *But see Prudential Insurance Co. v. Sempetrean*, 171 Ill. App. 3d 810, 525 N.E.2d 1016, 1020 (1988) (court refused to enforce an activity covenant against an insurance agent that was unlimited as to time and geography).

6. Does the state recognize a difference between in-term and post-term covenants?

Illinois has long distinguished between in-term and post-term covenants. *See, e.g., The Vendo Co. v. Stoner*, 105 Ill. App. 2d 261, 245 N.E.2d 263, 274–75 (1969) (*reversed on other grounds*). Under the "Illinois rule" stated in the *McDonald's System* case, the absence of territorial restrictions affects the validity of a post-term covenant only. During the term of the franchise agreement, Illinois courts will enforce in-term covenants not to compete irrespective of their geographic scope. *McDonald's Systems, Inc. v. Sandy's, Inc.*, 45 Ill. App. 2d 57, 195 N.E.2d 22, 31 (1963). In *The Vendo Co.*, the court said, "The territory covered by a covenant against competition, otherwise unreasonably broad, will not invalidate the covenant to the extent that it exists during the term of the employment, lease, franchise agreement, etc."

In a case decided before *Erie Railroad v. Tomkins*, 304 U.S. 64 (1938), and apparently applying federal common law to an Illinois employment contract, the Seventh Circuit said a contract may be considered "in-term" if the party against whom the agreement is enforced is responsible for its termination prior to its expiration. In *Harrison v. Glucose Sugar Refining Co.*, 116 Fed. 304 (7th Cir. 1902), a key employee entered into a five-year employment agreement pursuant to which he agreed not to compete within a radius of 1,500 miles of Chicago, whether or not the employment was in force. The court treated this covenant as an in-term covenant against competition, despite the fact that the employee breached the agreement by working for a competitor. The court stated:

> The extent of the restraint here is only that during the time engaged for he should not enter the service of a rival within the territory occupied by his employer. There is in this agreement, as we conceive, nothing contrary to public policy. If the public be deprived of his supposed skill, it is only because he chose to break his contract, and declines to re-enter the service for which he is engaged and which is still open to him.

Id. at 310.

7. Has the state allowed enforcement of covenants against non-signatories (e.g., family members, newly formed corporations)?

IL

One Illinois case has allowed enforcement of covenants against non-signatories. In *Arwell Division of Orkin Exterminating Co. v. Kendrick*, 131 Ill. App. 2d 632, 267 N.E.2d 352 (1971), the court enforced a restrictive covenant in an employment contract against a non-signatory spouse who opened an extermination business in an area prohibited by the covenant. Although only the husband was the original signatory, the court found that the spouses' concerted actions to evade the covenant justified its enforcement against both of them. The wife was the alter ego of her husband, and her conduct of the competing business "was a thinly veiled subterfuge designed to avoid her husband's obligation under the contract." *Id.* at 634, 267 N.E.2d at 354; *see also In-Kyu Kim v. The Korean News of Chi., Inc.*, No. 17 C 1300, 2017 U.S. Dist. LEXIS 112104, at *13 (N.D. Ill. July 19, 2017) (affirming the holding in *Arwell* that "there are circumstances under which a husband can bind his wife to a contract, if, for example, they are acting in concert in pursuit of a common or joint business enterprise" in sustaining breach of contract claims against wife in non-franchise case).

8. Will the state modify, "blue-pencil," or otherwise reduce a covenant found to be overbroad?

Illinois courts have long wavered as to the extent to which they will "blue-pencil" restrictive covenants, and are often reluctant to do so where the original covenant is too restrictive. That reluctance can be traced back to *House of Vision, Inc. v. Hiyane*, 37 Ill. 2d 32, 225 N.E.2d 21 (1967), where the Illinois Supreme Court addressed the reasonableness of a covenant in an employment contract that restricted competition within a 30-mile radius of any of the employer's offices for an unlimited duration. The appellate court had altered the time limitation. The Illinois Supreme Court reversed, holding the covenant unreasonable as written and refusing to enforce it:

> To stake out unrealistic boundaries in time and space, as the employer did in this case, is to impose upon an employee the risk of proceeding at his peril, or the burden of expensive litigation to ascertain the scope of his obligation. While we do not hold that a court of equity may never modify the restraints embodied in a contract of this type and enforce them as modified, the fairness of the restraint initially imposed is a relevant consideration to a court of equity. We conclude that the restrictions in the employment contract were not reasonably necessary for the protection of the plaintiff.

Id. at 39, 225 N.E.2d at 25.

House of Vision does not stand for the proposition that a court may never reduce a covenant in Illinois, but it does stand for the proposition that a court may refuse to do so if the covenant as written is manifestly unreasonable and onerous.

Following *House of Vision*, Illinois appellate courts have tended to void covenants rather than reduce them. In *Akhter v. Shah*, 119 Ill. App. 3d 131, 456 N.E.2d 232, 235 (Ill. App. 1983), the court held that the fairness of the original restraint was the relevant consideration. The appellate court there denied the plaintiff's request for injunctive relief and declined to modify the covenant because the original restriction neither provided a time limitation nor identified the hospitals in which practice was prohibited: "the restriction, which is too vague and ambiguous, should not be rewritten by a court." *See also Prudential Insurance Co. v. Sempetrean*, 171 Ill. App. 3d 810, 525 N.E.2d 1016, 1020 (1988) (court should not rewrite covenant that has neither a time nor a geographic restriction).

In the case *Dryvit System, Inc. v. Rushing*, 132 Ill. App. 3d 9, 477 N.E.2d 35, 37 (1985), the court, quoting from a law review article, commented that if a party drafting an agreement is confident that the courts will pare down the covenants, the drafters will "fashion truly ominous contracts." Knowing the court will pare down an agreement "could have the potential effect of discouraging the narrow and precise draftsmanship that should be reflected in written agreements." *Lee/O'Keefe Insurance Agency, Inc. v. Ferega*, 163 Ill. App. 3d 997, 516 N.E.2d 1313, 1319 (1987) (modification of this contract "would have been tantamount to drafting a new contract"). *See also AssuredPartners, Inc. v. Schmitt*, 2015 IL App. (1st) 14183 (refusing to modify covenant because it contained several overbroad statements that effectively prevented [the defendant] from practicing his trade); *Arcor, Inc. v. Haas*, 363 Ill. App. 3d 296 (2005) (a court should "refuse to modify an unreasonable restrictive covenant, not merely because it is unreasonable, but where the degree of unreasonableness renders it unfair.").

Even where the restrictive covenant expressly contemplates judicial modification, the court may still void the entire agreement if it finds significant deficiencies. In *Eichmann v. National Hospital & Health Care Services, Inc.*, 308 Ill. App. 3d 337, 719 N.E.2d 1141 (1999), *appeal denied*, 724 N.E.2d 1267 (Ill. 2000), the agreement between the parties contained the following reformation clause:

> If any portion of the foregoing provisions of this covenant not to compete shall be, for any reason, declared invalid or unenforceable, the remaining portion or portions shall nevertheless be valid and enforceable and carried

> into effect to the fullest extent permitted, and the invalid or unenforceable portion shall be reformed, if possible, so as to be valid and enforceable.

Id., 719 N.E.2d at 1144.

Nevertheless, the court in *Eichmann* found the restrictive covenant unreasonably overbroad and unfair in light of the interest the employer sought to protect. Notwithstanding the expressed intent of the parties to reform an unreasonable covenant, the court declined the request to modify:

> Thus, while Illinois law allows a court to modify a restrictive covenant, and even where the parties have incorporated this principle into their agreement through the use of express language allowing modification, a court should refuse to modify an unreasonable restrictive covenant, not merely because it is unreasonable, but where the degree of unreasonableness renders it unfair.

Id., 719 N.E.2d at 1149; *see also Pactiv Corp. v. Menasha Corp.*, 261 F. Supp. 2d 1009 (N.D. Ill. 2003) (despite severability clause, court refused to modify a non-solicitation restriction); *Lawrence & Allen, Inc. v. Cambridge Human Resource Group, Inc.*, 292 Ill. App. 3d 131, 141, 685 N.E.2d 434, 443 (1997) (upholding refusal to make modifications); *Lee/O'Keefe Insurance Agency, Inc. v. Ferega*, 163 Ill. App. 3d 997, 1007, 516 N.E.2d 1313, 1319 (1987) (same).

In *North American Paper Co. v. Unterberger*, 171 Ill. App. 3d 408, 526 N.E.2d 621 (1988), the court flatly refused to modify an allegedly overbroad covenant, stating that the fairness of the restrictions is the relevant consideration in application of blue-penciling. Although this covenant restrained a divisional general manager from competing within a 200-mile radius of where he had conducted business on behalf of the division, the court found no fairness apparent in the covenant, noting that "the Agreement is redolent of the historical past when involuntary servitude was an acceptable practice." *Id.* at 625; *see also Pactiv Corp. v. Menasha Corp.*, 261 F. Supp. 2d 1009 at 1015 ("A court should refuse to modify an unreasonable restrictive covenant where the degree of unreasonableness renders it unfair.") (internal quotations omitted) (citing *Eichmann*, 308 Ill. App. 3d at 347–48); *Grand Vehicle Works Holding Corp. v. Frey*, 2005 U.S. Dist. LEXIS 13629, at *13 (courts applying Illinois law should decline to modify restrictive covenants). In *Roberge v. Qualitek International, Inc.*, 2002 U.S. Dist. LEXIS 1217 (N.D. Ill. 2002), a district court applying Illinois law refused to exercise its discretion to blue-pencil a post-term restrictive covenant that had an unlimited geographic scope and held the covenant unenforceable as a matter of law. "In doing so, we hope to encourage employers to write contracts that are more narrowly tailored to meet their individual needs, rather than overly broad covenants that restrict competition in the marketplace for qualified employees." *Id.* at pp. 20–21; *but see RTC Indus v. Haddon*, 2007 U.S. Dist. LEXIS 67008, at *12, 2007 WL 2743583 (where the court distinguished a blanket prohibition on competition in *Qualitek* from a mere activity restriction in the instant case).

Despite that strong language, however, in other cases, Illinois courts have enforced covenants not to compete as modified. For example, in *Cockerill v. Wilson*, 51 Ill.2d 179, 281 N.E.2d 648 (1972), a case decided only five years after *House of Vision*, the court permitted a plaintiff to seek enforcement of the covenant in only a part of the restricted geographic area even though the complaint seeking lesser enforcement was tantamount to an admission that the covenant was overbroad as drafted. In a 1986 decision, an Illinois appellate court permitted an employer seeking to enforce a geographically limited covenant against an employee's post-term contact of all of the customers of the office in which he was employed to obtain relief only with respect to the employee's actual customers. *Corroon & Black Inc. v. Magner*, 145 Ill. App. 3d 151, 494 N.E.2d 785, 793 (1986) (the covenant stated that the terms were severable and the court is not required to follow the terms of the covenant exactly in issuing an injunction).

Likewise, in *Brown & Brown, Inc. v. Ali*, 592 F. Supp. 2d 1009 (N.D. Ill. 2009), the district court modified a non-solicitation covenant, narrowing the scope of the restriction from all of the former employer's customers to those customers with whom the former employee had direct contact during his employment. *Id.* at 1046 (finding the modified covenant did not impose an undue hardship on the former employee nor harm the public interest). Likewise, in *Wyatt v. Dishong*, 127 Ill. App. 3d 716, 469 N.E.2d 608, 610 (1984), the appellate court affirmed the trial court's reduction of the scope of a geographic restriction in an employment contract. The contract specifically authorized revision of the covenant to reflect the maximum reasonable restrictions allowed under the law of Illinois. *See Anthony Marano Co. v. Passoff*, 2012 IL App. (1st) 112853-U ¶ 29 (where the court recognized that an at-will employment agreement can be modified by an employer as a condition of its continuance).

In *Océ N. Am., Inc. v. Brazeau*, the court emphasized previous rulings recognizing the option to blue pencil, stating the following:

> Under Illinois law, a court may apply the "blue pencil doctrine" to a covenant that is unreasonable on its face. The court can choose to modify or "blue pencil" unreasonable terms of an agreement in order to make it reasonable. A court first should consider the fairness of the restraint initially imposed. "A court should refuse to modify an unreasonable restrictive covenant where 'the degree of unreasonableness renders it unfair." Additionally, a court should consider the severability of the provisions in the agreement: whether the provisions operate independently of each other.

Case No. 09-C-2381, 2009 WL 6056775, at *13 (N.D. Ill. Sept. 4, 2009). Nonetheless, in that case, the court ultimately declined to blue pencil the provision at issue, holding that it did "not believe it is appropriate to rewrite Paragraph 2(b) in the way [plaintiff] suggests because it is tantamount to drafting a brand new provision with no evidence in the record that this was the parties' true intention." *Id.*

The IFWA, which by its terms is limited to certain types of employer-employee covenants, does not appear to clarify the uncertainty present in the common law with regard to blue-penciling. The statute provides that "[e]xtensive judicial reformation . . . may be against the public policy" of Illinois, while also noting that courts have discretion to reform or sever provisions rather than hold the covenant unenforceable. *See* 820 ILCS 90/35.

9. When does a non-compete period begin to run? Will courts equitably extend the term?

Because restrictive covenants are to be strictly construed under Illinois law, a non-compete period will run for the period of time agreed to by the promissee and the promissor in the applicable agreement. *See Marwaha v. Woodridge Clinic, S.C.*, 339 Ill. App. 3d 291, 294, 790 N.E.2d 974, 977 (2003). In *Marwaha*, an employment agreement containing a two-year restrictive covenant terminated by its terms in 1996, but the employee continued to work for the employer until 2001. The covenant contained language that made the provision survive the termination of the agreement. Upon ultimate termination of employment in 2001, the employer sought enforcement of the restrictive covenant, while the employee argued that the covenant ran until June 30, 1998 (two years from the date of termination of the original agreement). *Id.* at 976. The court agreed with the employee, holding that the survival language set out in the covenant could only reasonably be interpreted to mean that the restriction would survive the termination of the original agreement for the stated two-year period. ("[I]t would be strange for parties to an employment contract to provide for a non-compete provision to exist in perpetuity. In our view, the covenant not to compete was triggered only by the termination of the employment under the [original] employment agreement, not by the termination of the subsequent employment under a different agreement."). *Id.* at 977; *see also Virendra S. Bisla, M.D., Ltd v. Parvaiz*, 379 Ill. App. 3d 567, 572, 318 Ill. Dec. 822, 827, 884 N.E.2d 790, 795 (2008) (holding employer could not enforce a non-competition clause five years after the employment agreement expired); *Electronic Support Systems, Inc. v. Schattke*, 70 Ill. App. 3d 469, 470, 388 N.E.2d 787 (1979) (an employment contract containing a covenant not to compete for 18 months after termination of employment began on the date employment was terminated).

Illinois courts have extended the period of a restrictive covenant, but generally do so only when the contract calls for such extension and extension is reasonable under the circumstances. *Citadel Investment Group, LLC v. Teza Technologies LLC*, 398 Ill. App. 3d. 724, 735, 924 N.E.2d 95, 105 (2010) (noting that the agreements at issue did not provide for any extension of an 18-month restrictive period that lapsed two months prior to plaintiff's seeking an injunction, and stating that "relief might be appropriate even after the expiration of the contractual period, but . . . under the circumstances presented, the grant of a preliminary injunction after the expiration of the restrictive covenant would have been an unreasonable restriction of trade"). **IL**

In *Prairie Eye Center, Ltd. v. Butler*, 329 Ill. App. 3d 293, 768 N.E.2d 414 (2002), the appellate court affirmed the enforcement and extension of a restrictive covenant in a situation where the former employee actively violated his covenant during employment, immediately following employment and throughout the trial (despite existence of a preliminary injunction). *Id.* at 418. The court concluded that the monetary damages awarded by the trial court related to the former employer's damages through the time of trial and were "intended to put Prairie in the position it would have been in had the covenant not to compete not been violated," while the lower court's extension of the injunction existed to "enforce the covenant not to compete for which Prairie bargained and did not receive." *Id.* at 424. The court also relied upon the fact that the parties themselves bargained for an extension of the restriction period during any period of non-compliance by including in the employment agreement an express provision: "In the event any violation [of the agreement] is determined, the period of noncompetition shall be extended by a period of time equal to that period beginning when such violation commenced and ending when the activities constituting such violation shall have terminated." *Id.*; *see also Russel Dean, Inc. v. Maher*, No. 17-C-8440, 2018 WL 4679573, at *7 (N.D. Ill. Sept. 28, 2018) (extending period of restrictive covenant in light of defendant's willful violation of the restrictive covenants and other misconduct). *But see Stenstrom Petroleum Services Group, Inc. v. Mesch*, 375 Ill. App. 3d 1077, 1088, 874 N.E.2d 959, 969–70 (2007) (distinguishing *Prairie Eye Center* based on the fact that the employment agreement at issue there contained an express provision to extend the restriction during the period of time of any non-compliance, while the employment agreement at bar contained no such provision).

10. Are there additional nuances or peculiarities of the state's treatment of covenants in the franchising context?

Trade secrets are entitled to special statutory protection in Illinois. Under the Illinois Trade Secrets Act of 1988 (765 ILL. COMP. STAT. 1065/1 *et seq.*), a "trade secret" is defined as:

> Information, including but not limited to, technical or nontechnical data, a formula, pattern, compilation, program, device, method, technique, drawing, process, financial data, or list of actual or potential customers or suppliers, that:
> (1) is sufficiently secret to derive economic value, actual or potential, from not being generally known to other persons who can obtain economic value from its disclosure or use; and
> (2) is the subject of efforts that are reasonable under the circumstances to maintain its secrecy or confidentiality.

765 ILL. COMP. STAT. 1065/2(d).

The Illinois Trade Secrets Act allows actual or threatened misappropriation to be enjoined, damages to be awarded for misappropriation (including exemplary damages in twice the amount of an award if there is willful and malicious misappropriation), and attorney's fees under specified circumstances. The act does not affect contractual remedies, whether or not based on misappropriation, "provided, however, that a contractual or other duty to maintain secrecy or limit use of a trade secret shall not be deemed void or unenforceable solely for lack of durational or geographical limitations on the duty." 765 ILL. COMP. STAT. 1065/8(b)(1).

The enactment of the Illinois Trade Secrets Act appeared to nullify rulings in prior Illinois cases that agreements providing for nondisclosure of trade secrets must be limited as to time and geography. *See, e.g., Disher v. Fulgoni*, 124 Ill. App. 3d 257, 464 N.E.2d 639, 644 (1984); *Cincinnati Tool Steel Co. v. Breed*, 136 Ill. App. 3d 267, 482 N.E.2d 170, 175 (1985). Under the Trade Secrets Act, franchisors who disclose trade secret information, as broadly defined by Illinois law, to their franchisees should be able to prevent the franchisee from using that information in any competitive activity, irrespective of the limitations placed on the enforceability of covenants by Illinois courts.

Nevertheless, some Illinois courts have continued to require that nondisclosure/confidentiality agreements be reasonable in geographical reach and duration. *See Perman v. Arcventures, Inc.*, 196 Ill. App. 3d 758, 554 N.E.2d 982, 986 (1990) (non-disclosure/confidentiality agreement unreasonable and unenforceable given its unlimited geographic and time dimensions).

One Illinois trial court suggested the following rule:

> [w]hether a confidentiality provision requires a temporal or geographic limitation to be enforceable depends on whether the confidentiality provision acts as a restraint on trade. If a confidentiality provision does not act as a restraint on trade, like in *Coady*, the confidentiality provision does not

> require any temporal or geographic limitation to be enforceable. On the other hand, if a confidentiality provision does act as a restraint on trade, like in *AssuredPartners*, *Unterberger*, and *Cincinnati Tool*, by, for example, restricting an employee's ability to work in their chosen career field, the confidentiality provision is unenforceable unless the restraint on trade contains temporal and geographic limitations, and is otherwise reasonable.

First Nat'l Assets Mgmt. v. Garzon, Case No. 2016-CH-06597, 2016 WL 6301871, at *12 (Ill. Cir. Ct.) (Trial Order) (finding confidentiality provision in employment agreement was not restraint of trade and therefore enforceable despite lack of geographic or temporal limitations).

The restriction must also be narrowly tailored to protect only the trade secret information. *Liautaud v. Liautaud*, 221 F.3d 981, 987–88 (7th Cir. 2000) (refusing to enforce a covenant ancillary to the sharing of trade secret information when the restriction would apply "even if [defendant] develop[ed] his own recipes and business strategies").

In *Service Centers of Chicago, Inc. v. Minogue*, 180 Ill. App. 3d 447, 535 N.E.2d 1132 (1989), an employer sought to prevent its salesman from using the employer's confidential information to establish a competing business. The employer contended that the confidential information consisted of a priority system for providing services. The court interpreted the Illinois Trade Secrets Act as having the same definition of trade secret as the *Restatement of Torts*, section 757, which was the Illinois trade secrets law before the enactment of the Trade Secrets Act. *Id.*, 535 N.E.2d at 1135–36. The court found no trade secret, holding:

> By defining confidential information as essentially all of the information provided by [the employer] to [the employee] "concerning or in any way relating" to the services offered by [the employer], the confidentiality agreement amounts in effect to a post-employment covenant not to compete which is completely unrestricted in duration or geographical scope. This type of covenant is unreasonable and will not be enforced.

IL

Id. at 1137. *See generally Archer Daniels Midland Co. v. Sinele*, 2019 IL App. (4th) 180714, ¶ 50, 435 Ill. Dec. 656, 664, 139 N.E. 3d 1036, 1044 (affirming rationale from *Service Centers of Chicago* that an employee will naturally accumulate knowledge and experience while working and these are things an employee is free to take and use in later pursuits); *Alpha Sch. Bus Co. v. Wagner*, 391 Ill. App. 3d 722, 741, 331 Ill. Dec. 378, 297, 910 N.E.2d 1134, 1153 (2009) (rejecting the claim that a customer list of school districts that bus company serviced qualified as a trade secret because that information was publicly available).

In *Strata Marketing, Inc. v. Murphy*, 317 Ill. App. 3d 1054, 740 N.E.2d 1166 (2000), a former employer appealed the dismissal of its claim that a former employee would violate the Illinois Trade Secrets Act if allowed to work for a competitor. The appellate court noted that whether an employment agreement existed or not has no bearing on the issues relevant to a claim under the Trade Secrets Act because a confidentiality agreement is not a prerequisite to recovery. *Id.* at 1175. The court then held that, under the theory of inevitable disclosure, the former employer pled sufficient allegations that the former employee could not operate or function in his new job without relying on the former employer's trade secrets to withstand a motion to dismiss, and remanded the case.

In *Southwest Whey, Inc. v. Nutrition 101, Inc.*, 117 F. Supp. 2d 770 (C.D. Ill. 2000), which involved a dissolved joint venture, the court observed that while a restrictive covenant or confidentiality agreement is not a prerequisite to recovery under the Illinois Trade Secrets Act, some affirmative step must be taken to maintain the trade secret. The district court said the plaintiff there did not establish the existence of a trade secret pursuant to the act because the record did not reveal any affirmative steps taken by the plaintiff to protect its trade secrets. *Id.* at 780. The court in *Standard Mut. Ins. Co. v. Mudron* reiterated that establishing a violation of the Trade Secrets Act requires "a plaintiff to prove that the information at issue was: (1) a trade secret; (2) misappropriated; and (3) used in the defendant's business." 358 Ill. App. 3d 535, 538, 295 Ill. Dec. 118, 121–22, 832 N.E. 2d 269, 272–73 (2005).

While not addressed in the franchise context, it is important to note that Illinois courts generally honor choice-of-law provisions as to substantive matters (as opposed to procedural matters), so long as the provision does not contravene Illinois public policy and there exists some relationship between the chosen forum and the parties to the transaction. *See Emigrant Mortgage Company, Inc. v. Chicago Financial Services, Inc.*, 386 Ill. App. 3d 21, 26, 898 N.E.2d 1069, 1074 (2007) (citing *Belleville Toyota, Inc. v. Toyota Motor Sales, U.S.A., Inc.*, 199 Ill. 2d 325, 351, 770 N.E.2d 177, 194 (Ill. 2002)). So, Illinois courts will refuse to enforce a choice-of-law provision that applies a foreign state's law that is contrary to Illinois law and public policy. *Brown and Brown, Inc. v. Mudron*, 379 Ill. App. 3d 724, 727–28, 887 N.E.2d 437, 439–40 (2008). The agreement in *Brown and Brown* required the application of Florida law. The Illinois Appellate Court found Florida law and Illinois law to be in controversy with respect to the treatment of non-competition covenants in employment agreements. Florida law statutorily prohibits the consideration of the hardship the covenant imposes on the employee, and Illinois law requires that hardship to be considered when determining the enforceability of the covenant. *Id.* The court held that it was a fundamental public policy in Illinois to provide employees with greater protections against noncompetition covenants by requiring consideration of the hardship on the employee. Therefore, because Florida law is contrary to Illinois fundamental public policy, Illinois law must apply. *Id.* (citing to the *Restatement (Second) of Conflict of Laws*, § 187 (1971), which has been adopted by Illinois courts, and which provides that a choice-of-law provision contained in a contract will govern unless (1) the chosen state has no substantial relationship to the parties or the transaction or (2) application of the chosen law would be contrary to a fundamental public policy of a state). The court also noted that Illinois had a greater interest than Florida in the dispute given that the particular insurance agency involved in the dispute was located in Illinois, all of the listed defendants are located in Illinois, the customers allegedly solicited or serviced are located in Illinois, and the actions alleged to be in breach of the agreement took place in Illinois. The fact that the employer was a Florida corporation was not sufficient to require the application of Florida law. *Id.*

Indiana

by Christina L. Fugate*

1. Has the state addressed covenants against competition in the context of franchising?

- **Does the state have a franchising statute or regulations that address covenants against competition?**
- **Does the state have a covenants statute of general applicability that would encompass franchise covenants?**
- **Have the courts addressed covenants in the context of franchising either under a statute or under the state's common law?**

The Indiana Deceptive Franchise Practices Act, Ind. Code § 23-2-2.7-1 *et seq.* (2021), provides that it is unlawful for any franchise agreement to contain a provision requiring a franchisee to covenant not to compete with the franchisor for a period longer than three years or in an area greater than the exclusive area granted by the franchise agreement, or, in the absence of such a provision in the agreement, an area of reasonable size, upon termination of or failure to renew the franchise. Ind. Code § 23-2-2.7-1(9).

Indiana does not have a statute of general applicability governing covenants against competition. Accordingly, the quoted provision, above, is the only statutory provision applicable to covenants in franchise agreements.

In *Tutor Time Learning Centers, LLC v. Larzak, Inc.*, the United States District Court for the Northern District of Indiana found that the scope of a covenant not to compete in a franchise agreement was reasonable because it fell within the specific time and geographic limitations set forth under section 23-2-2.7-1. 2007 WL 2025214, at *10–12 (N.D. Ind. July 6, 2007). Although not directly addressing section 23-2-2.7-1, in *Elder Care Providers of Indiana, Inc. v. Home Instead, Inc.*, the United States District Court for the Southern District of Indiana granted a franchisee's motion for summary judgment finding that the former franchisee did not violate the franchise agreement's covenant not to compete because the activities of the former franchisee were not in direct competition with the franchisor.

*Christina L. Fugate is a partner in the law firm of Ice Miller LLP in Indianapolis, Indiana. She leads the firm's franchise practice.

Other court have addressed covenants not to compete in the context of franchising under Indiana common law. *See South Bend Consumers Club, Inc. v. United Consumers Club, Inc.*, 572 F. Supp. 209 (N.D. Ind. 1983) (granting the franchisee's motion for partial summary judgment on the grounds that the franchise covenant was overly broad in geographic scope); *Hacienda Mexican Restaurant of Kalamazoo Corp. v. Hacienda Franchise Group, Inc.*, 569 N.E.2d 661 (Ind. Ct. App. 1991) (reversing the portion of the trial court's order preliminarily enjoining franchisees from "[o]perating a Mexican restaurant in general"); *McCart v. H&R Block, Inc.*, 470 N.E.2d 756 (Ind. Ct. App. 1984) (affirming enforcement of a covenant prohibiting former franchisee and her husband from engaging in an income tax preparation business within 50 miles of the city in which they operated their franchise for a period of two years).

In determining the reasonableness and enforceability of such covenants, Indiana courts have been guided by legal principles developed in the context of covenants against competition contained in employment contracts. *See, e.g., H&R Block*, 470 N.E.2d at 764 (applying the law of geographic limitations developed in employment contract cases to a franchise case). Although the decisions addressing franchise covenants are discussed below under the appropriate topic headings, readers are cautioned that "in assessing the reasonableness of such restraints time, space and purpose are interrelated and judgment is based upon the whole." *Id.* at 764 n.1 (citing *Frederick v. Professional Building Maintenance Industries, Inc.*, 344 N.E.2d 299, 302 (Ind. Ct. App. 1976)). Accordingly, Indiana courts are more likely to examine the totality of circumstances in enforcing franchise covenants than to apply bright-line rules.

---

2. Have the courts articulated the "legitimate interests" of the franchisor that will support enforcement of a covenant against competition contained in a franchise agreement?

- **If so what are they (e.g., protection of goodwill, protection of confidential information), and in what contexts did the issue arise?**
- **If not, what interests have been recognized in other contexts (e.g., employment agreements, the sale of business context)?**

Three cases have addressed the nature of a franchisor's protectable interest that would support enforcement of a covenant against competition in a franchise agreement. The Indiana Court of Appeals in *McCart v. H&R Block, Inc.*, 470 N.E.2d 756, 763–64 (Ind. Ct. App. 1984), found that H&R Block, a franchisor of income tax return preparation and related services, had a protectable interest in the goodwill associated with its service mark. In that case, the former franchisee and her husband solicited former franchise customers by sending them a packet containing a letter from the former franchisee indicating that she no longer would be affiliated with H&R Block but instead would be assisting her husband in his tax preparation service, and also containing a letter from the franchisee's husband promoting his new tax preparation service and offering it at a 10 percent discount off the price that customers had paid H&R Block the previous year. *Id.* at 759. The couple also instructed the post office to deliver all mail addressed to their new office address even if the mail was addressed to H&R Block. *Id.*

In finding these actions in violation of the covenant against competition contained in the franchise agreement, the court explained that the concept of customer affiliation with the franchisor's service mark is similar to the concept of goodwill in the context of sale of an existing business. *Id.* at 763. The court stated that in both scenarios, "the value of the customers' affiliation with the particular business . . . is part of the bargain sought by the buyer." *Id.* In rejecting the franchisee's argument essentially that the customers at her H&R Block franchise were hers rather than H&R Block's, the court stated that "both parties understood that the bargain for use of the Block service mark was a bargain for customers who would be attracted to the Block name. She cannot now be heard to claim Block has no protectable interest in those customers she gained while offering services under that name." *Id.* at 764. The court then held that the franchisor validly preserved the value of its protectable goodwill by including the covenant not to compete in the franchise agreement. *Id.* at 763.

The U.S. District Court for the Northern District of Indiana in *Tutor Time Learning Centers, LLC v. Larzak, Inc.*, 2007 U.S. Dist. LEXIS 49740 (N.D. Ind. July 6, 2007), found that a franchisor of child-care facilities, Tutor Time, was entitled to protection of the names, addresses, customer requirements, manuals, tutoring requirements, and goodwill established between the tutoring center and its customers (parents of the children attending the tutoring centers) as legitimate business interests. Upon expiration of the franchisee's franchise agreement, the former franchisee opened a competing child-care facility at the same location that was used to occupy the former franchise. *Id.* at *3–5. While the former franchisee installed different computer programs and a new sign was placed outside and on the facility's vans, there was no change made to the staff, telephone number, playground, interior of the building, and color and floor tile schemes, and the former franchisee retained possession of the franchisor's curriculum information manuals, staff meeting manuals, employee handbook, and songbook. *Id.* at *5.

The court found that the franchisee violated the franchise agreement's covenant against competition. The franchisor had established a legitimate, protectable interest in its franchise system, which included its trademarks, methods, materials, and curriculum. *Id.* at *29–31. By signing the franchise agreement, the franchisee agreed and acknowledged the valuable goodwill attached to the "Tutor Time" marks and the franchise system. *Id.*

The U.S. District Court for the Northern District of Indiana also addressed the nature of a franchisor's protectable interest that would support enforcement of a covenant against competition in a franchise agreement under Indiana law. *South Bend Consumers Club, Inc. v. United Consumers Club, Inc.*, 572 F. Supp. 209, 213 (N.D. Ind. 1983). Without engaging in any analysis, the court stated that it would assume that a protectable interest exists in the franchise itself and in other attendant interests, such as customer contacts and goodwill. *Id.* (citations omitted). Though unclear, it seems likely that Indiana courts would find interests other than goodwill to be protectable.

---

3. What time limitations have courts recognized as reasonable in the franchise context?

- **If no franchise cases have been decided, what time limitations have been recognized in other contexts?**
- **How have they been related to interests protected?**

As mentioned above, the Indiana Deceptive Franchise Practices Act provides that it is unlawful for any franchise agreement to contain any provision "[r]equiring a franchisee to covenant not to compete with the franchisor for a period longer than three (3) years." IND. CODE § 23-2-2.7-1(9). In *Tutor Time Learning Centers, LLC v. Larzak, Inc.*, 2007 U.S. Dist. LEXIS 49740, at *32 (N.D. Ind. July 6, 2007), the U.S. District Court for the Northern District of Indiana found that a two-year time restriction fell within the time constraints of section 23-2-2.7-1(9) and was reasonable.

The only other court to address the issue of temporal reasonableness of a covenant against competition in a franchise agreement under Indiana law did so without reference to the statute. In *South Bend Consumers Club, Inc. v. United Consumers Club, Inc.*, 572 F. Supp. 209 (N.D. Ind. 1983), the court concluded that a two-year post-term limitation was reasonable because it corresponded to the length of a customer's membership in the buying club that was the subject of the franchise agreement, and thus presumably protected the franchisor's clientele from being lured to a competitor during the term of the agreement. *Id.* at 214.

---

4. What geographic limitations have courts recognized as reasonable in the franchise context?

> **How have they been related to the interests protected? Have courts recognized the legitimacy of protecting other franchisees from competition?**

The Indiana Deceptive Franchise Practices Act provides that it is unlawful for a franchise agreement to contain a post-term covenant prohibiting a franchisee from competing "in an area greater than the exclusive area granted by the franchise agreement or, in the absence of such a provision in the agreement, an area of reasonable size." IND. CODE § 23-2-2.7-1(9). In the absence of a defined exclusive area, courts determining the reasonableness of geographic limitations generally limit the restricted area to that of the franchisee's former business, though, as explained below, geographic limitations may be treated somewhat more expansively in the franchise context than in the employment context.

In *McCart v. H&R Block, Inc.*, 470 N.E.2d 756, 764 (Ind. Ct. App. 1984), the Indiana Court of Appeals relied on the law of geographic limitations developed in the context of employment contracts in upholding a post-term covenant prohibiting the former franchisee from operating a similar business within a 50-mile radius of the franchise territory, in this case the city of Rochester, Indiana. *Id.* at 765. The franchisee argued that the 50-mile limitation was unreasonable because 22 miles was as far as any customer had traveled for services at the H&R Block office in Rochester. *Id.* In making this argument, she apparently relied on certain employment contract cases in which the courts refused to enforce covenants prohibiting activity "beyond the area within which the employer's protectable interest had been of value to the employee." *Id.* at 764 (citing *Frederick v. Professional Building Maintenance Industries, Inc.*, 344 N.E.2d 299 (Ind. Ct. App. 1976)).

However, the court distinguished the case at bar, in which customers travel to the business location, from employment contract cases in which the enjoined employees would travel to the customers' locations to sell a product or provide a service. *Id.* at 764–65 (distinguishing on this basis *Buanno v. Weinraub*, 81 N.E.2d 600 (Ind. 1948); *4408, Inc. v. Losure*, 373 N.E.2d 899 (Ind. Ct. App. 1978); *Frederick*, 344 N.E.2d at 299). The court explained that in the cited employment cases, the area of the employers' protectable interest was clearly defined by the respective employees' territories; however, in this case, "the customer affiliation is broader and less specific, depending as it must on where the competing office is established." *Id.* The court noted by way of example that the franchisee could open an office 44 miles from its former franchise office and still draw the same customers who previously had traveled 22 miles to the former office. *Id.* Because the franchisor had a protectable interest in those customers as well as the ones in Rochester, the court upheld the covenant. *Id.* This case indicates that geographic limitations may be viewed more expansively in the franchise context than in the employment context, at least in situations in which the nature of the franchise business is such that customers travel to the franchise location.

In *Hacienda Mexican Restaurant of Kalamazoo Corp. v. Hacienda Franchise Group, Inc.*, 569 N.E.2d 661 (Ind. Ct. App. 1991), discussed in detail *infra* under Question 5, the court reversed the portion of the trial court's order preliminarily enjoining the former franchisees from "[o]perating a Mexican restaurant in general." *Id.* at 668. The trial court's order contained no geographic limitation despite the fact that the only covenant in the franchise agreement purporting to restrict the franchisees from operating as a Mexican restaurant in general contained a geographic limitation. *Id.* That covenant provided that the franchisees "shall not, for a period of two (2) years subsequent to [termination of the agreement through default by the franchisees], within a fifty mile radius of any HACIENDA MEXICAN RESTAURANT engage in any similar Mexican restaurant or food business." *Id.* The court stated simply that "[w]e do not need to decide whether this covenant is enforceable because the court's order is not tied to the specific geographic limitations of the covenant." *Id.* Without engaging in any further analysis, it then reversed the portion of the preliminary injunction prohibiting the franchisees from operating as a Mexican restaurant in general. *Id.*

In *Tutor Time*, the court found that a distance restriction of ten miles fell within the distance constraints set forth in section 23-2-2.7-1(9) and was a reasonable restriction. *Tutor Time Learning Centers, LLC v. Larzak*, 2007 U.S. Dist. LEXIS 49740, at *32 (N.D. Ind. July 6, 2007).

On the other hand, in *South Bend Consumers Club, Inc. v. United Consumers Club, Inc.*, the court refused to enforce a covenant prohibiting the former franchisee from operating within an area near any of a franchisor's multiple business outlets. 572 F. Supp. 209, 214 (N.D. Ind. 1983). The franchise agreement at issue in that case contained a post-term covenant prohibiting the franchisee from engaging in the same or substantially similar business "in any area which can be reasonably termed competitive to the franchisor or other franchisees," which, at a minimum, was defined to include a 25-mile radius of the "franchisee's territory or any place of business conducted by the franchisor or any other franchisee of the franchisor." *Id.* at 211. At the time of the decision, the franchisor maintained franchises in 15 states. *Id.* at 214.

The court cited an employment contract case for the proposition that "the extent of the spatial restraint upon the franchise must be limited to the area of the former franchisee's operations," and then found the covenant's geographic restriction to be an overly severe restriction of the franchisee's rights. *Id.* (citing *Donahue v. Permacel Tape Corp.*, 127 N.E.2d 235, 239 (Ind. 1955)). In so holding, the court explained that the franchisee "cannot pose an unreasonable competitive danger in a fifteen state area much greater than the area in which it had formerly operated," and also that the covenant's lack of a defined maximum area could make it impossible for a franchisee "to determine whether a course of action was or was not permissible in view of the language of this covenant." *Id.* After also finding that the covenant could not be modified so as to make it enforceable, discussed *infra* under Question

8, the court granted the franchisee's motion for partial summary judgment on the issue of enforceability of the covenant. *Id.* at 211.

Similarly, in *Wine & Canvas Development LLC v. Weisser*, the court found that a non-competition agreement that did not provide for any limitation to its geographic scope was unenforceable. 2015 WL 1969449, at *11 (S.D. Ind. May 1, 2015).

5. What limitations on activities have courts recognized as reasonable in the franchise context?

In one Indiana case to enforce a franchise covenant against competition, the court upheld as reasonable a covenant prohibiting a former franchisee, whose business was tax return preparation and related services, from competing "directly, indirectly, whether as an owner, stockholder, partner, officer, director or employee, with Block or Block's franchisees in the business of preparing tax returns or performing related services" within a 50-mile radius of the franchise territory. *McCart v. H&R Block, Inc.*, 470 N.E.2d 756, 765 (Ind. Ct. App. 1984). On the other hand, in *Elder Care Providers of Indiana, Inc. v. Home Instead, Inc.*, the United States District Court for the Southern District of Indiana did not enforce a covenant against competition because the court found that a former franchisee's business post-termination was not directly competing with the franchisor. 2017 WL 1106093 (S.D. Ind. Mar. 24, 2017).

No reported cases address the scope of activities, if any, beyond direct competition with the franchisor or its franchisees that may be enforced pursuant to a covenant against competition in the franchise context. However, as Indiana courts have stated in the context of employment contract cases, covenants against competition may proscribe activities only to the extent necessary to protect the party for whose benefit the covenant is granted, and only if reasonable in light of the totality of the circumstances. *See, e.g.*, *Badger Daylighting Corp. v. Palmer*, 2019 WL 4572798 (S.D. Ind. 2019) (finding non-compete preventing employee from working with a competitor in any manner is overbroad); *see also Frederick v. Professional Bldg. Maintenance Industries, Inc.*, 344 N.E.2d 299, 301–02 (Ind. Ct. App. 1976) (citing *Donahue v. Permacel Tape Corp.*, 127 N.E.2d 235 (Ind. 1955); *Wiley v. Baumgardner*, 97 Ind. 66 (1884)).

In *Hacienda Mexican Restaurant of Kalamazoo Corp. v. Hacienda Franchise Group, Inc.*, 569 N.E.2d 661 (Ind. Ct. App. 1991), the court reversed that portion of the trial court's order preliminarily enjoining franchisees from "[o]perating a Mexican restaurant in general." *Id.* at 668. The former franchisees of a Hacienda Mexican Restaurant appealed the trial court's grant of a preliminary injunction prohibiting them from engaging in five separate activities:

1. Operating a Mexican restaurant under the name and style of Hacienda Mexican restaurant.
2. Operating a Mexican restaurant in general.
3. Using or possessing any trademarks or copyrighted materials belonging to Hacienda Franchise Group, Inc.
4. Using or possessing any food or beverage recipes belonging to the [franchisor].
5. Using or possessing any confidential information, signs, symbols, trade dress, advertising or other property bearing the name and style of Hacienda Mexican Restaurants or belonging to the [franchisor].

Id. at 665.

On appeal, the court upheld the preliminary injunction in all respects except the portion prohibiting the franchisees from "[o]perating a Mexican restaurant in general," suggesting that such a proscription is too broad to be enforceable. *Id.* at 668, 671.

The court stated that a preliminary injunction requires a prima facie showing by the movant of a violation of some legal right, that he or she will suffer irreparable harm if the injunction is denied, and lack of an adequate remedy at law. *Id.* at 666 (citations omitted). After reviewing the covenants contained in the franchise agreement, the court determined that they supported the trial court's finding that the "franchisor had a reasonable likelihood of success at trial" with regard to establishing the rights protected by provisions 1, 3, 4, and 5 of the preliminary injunction because those rights were specifically addressed by the covenants. *Id.* at 668.

However, the court found that the trial court had abused its discretion in granting provision 2 of the preliminary injunction because the "franchisor failed to introduce evidence that any legal right would be violated by franchisees 'operating a Mexican restaurant in general.'" *Id.* The only provision in the franchise agreement purporting to restrict the franchisees from operating a Mexican restaurant other than a Hacienda Mexican Restaurant was a covenant providing that the franchisees "shall not, for a period of two (2) years subsequent to [termination of the agreement through default by the franchisees], within a fifty mile radius of any HACIENDA MEXICAN RESTAURANT engage in any *similar* Mexican restaurant or food business." *Id.* (emphasis added). Without further elaboration, the court reversed that portion of the preliminary injunction prohibiting the franchisees from operating a Mexican restaurant in general. *Id.*

The court was obviously reluctant to enforce a broad prohibition against operating a Mexican restaurant in general because the franchise agreement contained no such provision and because there was no evidence that permitting the former franchisee to operate a Mexican restaurant in general would violate a legal right of the franchisor. Although the court did not offer guidance on the types of activities on the part of former franchisees that normally could be prohibited, Indiana courts could be expected to prohibit a former franchisee from operating a "similar" business that might create confusion among consumers and injure the franchisor's legal rights. However, Indiana courts seem unlikely to restrict the activities of former franchisees through the application of broad, categorical proscriptions.

6. Does the state recognize a difference between in-term and post-term covenants?

There are no reported cases addressing this issue under Indiana law.

7. Has the state allowed enforcement of covenants against non-signatories (e.g., family members, newly formed corporations)?

Indiana courts will enforce franchise covenants against persons not parties to a franchise agreement who knowingly participate or aid a signatory in violating the agreement. *See McCart v. H&R Block, Inc.*, 470 N.E.2d 756 (Ind. Ct. App. 1984). In *H&R Block*, the franchisee, June McCart, terminated the franchise agreement with H&R Block for income tax preparation and related services and subsequently began working with her husband's newly formed tax preparation service. *Id.* at 758–59. Though June's husband, Robert, who was a former H&R Block franchisee and district manager, did not sign the franchise agreement, he worked at the franchise location and represented to others that he was involved in the business, though he also engaged in a separate accounting business. *Id.* at 758. The couple's relevant income tax returns reported that most of their income derived from the franchise business, and that both spouses were engaged in the business of "tax preparation under the business name of H&R Block" at the franchise address. *Id.* After June terminated the franchise, the couple solicited former franchise customers by sending them a packet, mailed in an H&R Block envelope with the name blacked out, containing a letter from June indicating that she no longer would be affiliated with H&R Block but instead would be assisting Robert in his tax preparation service. *Id.* at 759. The packet also contained a letter from Robert promoting his new tax preparation service and offering it at a 10 percent discount off the price that customers had paid H&R Block the previous year. *Id.* Additionally, the couple instructed the post office to deliver all mail listing their new office address even if the mail was addressed to H&R Block. *Id.*

In affirming enforcement of the covenant against both the franchisee and her husband, the court stated that "it is not necessary to show Robert's signature on the agreement before enjoining him from assisting the breach of the agreement by June" because the two acted together in perpetrating the breach. *Id.* at 762. The court based its decision not upon the existence of a contractual relationship between Robert and H&R Block, but rather upon the couple's "cooperative conduct," which "amounted to mere subterfuge designed to avoid June's obligation under the contract." *Id.* (citing *Arwell Division of Orkin Exterminating Co. v. Kendrick*, 267 N.E.2d 352 (Ill. Ct. App. 1971)). The court adopted the language of the trial court in explaining the rationale for extending the injunction to cover both June and Robert:

> If this Court were to enjoin June only and allowed Robert to continue the tax preparation trade at the same site and with the same customers the Court would be ignoring the business realities of the situation, frustrating the proper purpose of [the covenant], and affording June McCart indirect competition and benefit in specific violation of the contract terms. The McCarts treated the operation as their joint business (see their personal income tax returns) and held themselves out to the public that way. This Court's order will treat them in the manner they operated.

Id. Accordingly, Indiana courts will enforce franchise covenants against non-signatories who knowingly participate or aid a signatory in violating the agreement.

8. Will the state modify, "blue-pencil," or otherwise reduce a covenant found to be overbroad?

The only court to address the "blue-pencil" doctrine in the context of a franchise covenant under Indiana law is the U.S. District Court for the Northern District of Indiana, which held that although the particular covenant at issue could not be modified, Indiana law would permit franchise covenants to be modified pursuant to the blue-pencil doctrine if the contract terms are divisible. *South Bend Consumers*

Club, Inc. v. United Consumers Club, Inc., 572 F. Supp. 209, 214–15 (N.D. Ind. 1983). The court explained that the process of judicial redaction, also known as "blue-penciling," "may be applied only when the covenant is clearly separated into parts with some parts being reasonable and others clearly not meeting that standard." *Id.* (citing *Licocci v. Cardinal Associates, Inc.*, 445 N.E.2d 556, 561 (Ind. 1983); *Welcome Wagon, Inc. v. Haschert*, 127 N.E.2d 103, 106 (Ind. Ct. App. 1955)). The court stated that although the blue-pencil doctrine may be properly applied to divide separate and independent restrictions so that those that are reasonable may be enforced as written, a single covenant containing an overly broad geographic restriction may not be redacted so as to narrow its geographic scope because such a redaction would be "tantamount to rewriting the contract." *Id.* (citing *Licocci*, 445 N.E.2d at 556; *Frederick v. Professional Building Maintenance Industries, Inc.*, 344 N.E.2d 299 (Ind. Ct. App. 1976)). Accordingly, courts may apply the blue-pencil doctrine to modify overly broad franchise covenants, but only insofar as the reasonable portions of the covenant are separate and distinct from the portion(s) found to be overly broad. Indiana courts' willingness to modify a covenant are limited. Courts will apply the blue-pencil doctrine only to terms that already exist in the agreement. Indiana courts will not add new terms to the covenant. *Heraeus Medical, LLC v. Zimmer, Inc.* (Ind. 2019) (reaffirming Indiana's blue-pencil doctrine that courts cannot add terms to an unenforceable restrictive covenant in a non-competition agreement, even when that agreement contains language purporting to give a court the power to do so).

9. When does a non-compete period begin to run? Will courts equitably extend the term?

The Indiana Deceptive Franchise Practices Act provides that a non-compete period begins to run "upon termination of or failure to renew the franchise." IND. CODE § 23-2-2.7-1(9).

No reported cases have addressed whether Indiana courts will equitably extend the termination period in the franchise context. In other contexts, however, Indiana courts have refused to extend the non-compete period beyond the express terms of the agreement absent appropriate language to that effect. *See, e.g., Franke v. Honeywell, Inc.*, 516 N.E.2d 1090, 1093 (Ind. Ct. App. 1987); *Oxford Financial Group, Ltd. v. Evans*, 795 N.E.2d 1135, 1146 (Ind. Ct. App. 2003). Accordingly, courts will honor a party's explicit agreement to toll the non-compete period or extend it. *See, e.g., Century Personnel, Inc. v. Brummett*, 499 N.E.2d 1160, 1162 (Ind. Ct. App. 1986) (employment agreement contained a clause that tolled the running of the six-month non-compete period during any violation of the restrictive covenant or any other agreements between the parties); *Gleeson v. Preferred Sourcing, LLC*, 883 N.E.2d 164, 169 (Ind. Ct. App. 2008) (employment agreement contained a clause that extended the running of the 18-month non-compete period by the length of any period during which the employee violated the agreement); *Nightingale Home Healthcare, Inc. v. Helmuth*, 15 N.E.3d 1080 (Ind. Ct. App. 2014) (non-compete period began to run from the original date of employee's termination, and a new employment agreement did not reinstate the non-compete).

Further, Indiana courts will not extend the duration of a non-compete through a preliminary injunction as the purpose of a preliminary injunction is to preserve the status quo as it existed before controversy. *Hannum Wagle & Cline Engineering, Inc. v. American Consulting, Inc.*, 64 N.E.3d 863, 882–83 (Ind. Ct. App. 2016).

10. Are there additional nuances or peculiarities of the state's treatment of covenants in the franchising context?

In resolving franchise disputes involving covenants against competition, Indiana courts have looked for guidance in employment contract cases. *See, e.g.*, *McCart v. H&R Block, Inc.*, 470 N.E.2d 756, 764 (Ind. Ct. App. 1984) (applying the law of geographic limitations developed in employment contract cases to a franchise case). Accordingly, a brief review of principles developed in the employment context is instructive to the practitioner faced with a franchise case.

As mentioned in the discussion under Question 1, Indiana law is clear that "[t]he test of validity of a non-competition covenant is dependent not merely upon the covenant itself but upon the entire contract and the situation to which it is related." *Ackerman v. Kimball International, Inc.*, 652 N.E.2d 507, 510 (Ind. 1995) (quoting *Harvest Insurance Agency, Inc. v. Inter-Ocean Insurance Co.*, 492 N.E.2d 686, 688–89 (Ind. 1986) (citing *Jenkins v. King*, 65 N.E.2d 121 (Ind. 1946))). "Covenants not to compete are in restraint of trade and are not favored by law," and accordingly they "are strictly construed against the covenantee and enforced only if reasonable." *Id.* (quoting *Harvest Insurance Agency, Inc.*, 492 N.E.2d at 688–89 (citations omitted)). Covenants must be reasonably necessary to protect the employer, not unreasonably restrictive of the employee, and not contrary to public policy. *Id.* (citing *Harvest Insurance Agency, Inc.*, 492 N.E.2d at 688–89 (citations omitted)).

Although each case is decided based upon the totality of circumstances, an employer wishing to enforce a covenant against a former employee must first establish "a legitimate interest that may be protected by a covenant." *Titus v. Rheitone*, 758 N.E.2d 85, 92 (Ind. Ct. App. 2001). This requires a showing by the employer of "some reason why it would be unfair to allow the employee to compete with the former employer," *id.*, such as "a unique competitive advantage or ability to harm the employer." *Cohoon v. Financial Plans & Strategies, Inc.*, No. 41A04-0102-CV-77, 2001 Ind. App. LEXIS 2227, at *9 (Ind. Ct. App., Dec. 28, 2001) (quoting *Burk v. Heritage Food Service Equipment*, 737 N.E.2d 803, 811 (Ind. Ct. App. 2000) (internal quotation omitted)). In the employment context, protectable interests have included trade secrets, confidential information, and goodwill, the latter category encompassing "'secret or confidential information, such as the names and addresses and requirements of customers and the advantage acquired through representative contact with the trade in the area of their application.'" *Titus*, 758 N.E.2d at 92 (quoting *Burk v. Heritage Food Service Equip.*, 737 N.E.2d 803, 811 (Ind. Ct. App. 2000) (internal quotation omitted)).

After an employer has established a protectable interest, the court then examines "whether the scope of the agreement is reasonable in terms of time, geography, and types of activity prohibited." *Titus*, 758 N.E.2d at 92. To be reasonable, a covenant "must be sufficiently specific in scope to coincide with only the legitimate interests of the employer and to allow the employee a clear understanding of what conduct is prohibited." *Cohoon*, 2001 Ind. App. LEXIS 2227, at *13 (citing *Field v. Alexander & Alexander of Indiana*, 503 N.E.2d 627, 635 (Ind. Ct. App. 1987)).

Indiana courts "have held certain covenants containing lengthy time restriction to be reasonable." *Titus*, 758 N.E.2d at 93 (citations omitted). Few bright-line rules exist, and Indiana courts have enforced covenants lasting up to five years. *Id.* (citing, inter alia, *Pickett v. Pelican Service Associates*, 481 N.E.2d 1113 (Ind. Ct. App. 1985) (finding a five-year covenant to be reasonable)). The franchise statute limitation of three years will control here.

With regard to geographic area, the general rule is that the geographic scope of covenants is limited "to those areas in which the former employee actually worked." *Titus*, 758 N.E.2d at 93 (citing *Cap Gemini America, Inc. v. Judd*, 597 N.E.2d 1272 (Ind. Ct. App. 1995)). An exception exists where "subsequent employment involves the use or divulgence of 'trade secrets' of the former employer that are related to the scope of the latter's business throughout the 'restricted area,'" in which case a covenant without a geographic limitation is not void per se. *Ackerman v. Kimball International, Inc.*, 652 N.E.2d 507, 510 (Ind. 1995) (quoting *Donahue v. Permacel Tape Corp.*, 127 N.E.2d 235 (Ind. 1955)). Additionally, Indiana courts have held that the reasonableness of the elements of geography and types of activity prohibited are related: "'as the specificity of limitation regarding the class of person with whom contact is prohibited increases, the need for limitation expressed in territorial terms decreases' In fact, a covenant not to compete may even be enforced absent a territorial limitation where the covenant sufficiently restricts the class of prohibited contacts." *Cohoon*, 2001 Ind. App. LEXIS 2227, at *13 (quoting *Seach v. Richards, Dieterle & Co.*, 439 N.E.2d 208, 213 (Ind. Ct. App. 1982)). Accordingly, covenants must not cover an area broader than that of the employee's work activities unless the employee possesses knowledge of trade secrets or the covenant sufficiently limits the scope of the prohibited activities. Again, the franchise statute will control.

With regard to the types of activities prohibited, Indiana courts will not enforce covenants protecting an employer's interest in past clients. *Cohoon*, 2001 Ind. App. LEXIS 2227, at *11 (citing *Seach*, 439 N.E.2d at 214). "Past clients" are those with whom the employer had no contact during the employee's tenure. *Id.* (citing *Hahn v. Drees, Perugini & Co.*, 581 N.E.2d 457, 461 n.3 (Ind. Ct. App. 1991)). Additionally, a federal court applying Indiana law refused to enforce a covenant prohibiting competition not only in the business in which the employer did business but also in all of the industries in which the corporate parent and its other subsidiaries did business. *Bridgestone/Firestone, Inc. v. Lockhart*, 5 F. Supp. 2d 667, 683–84 (S.D. Ind. 1998). The same court stated that a prohibition against employment "in any capacity" for a competing company "extends far beyond the employer's legitimate interests and is thus not enforceable." *Id.* at 684. Again, however, the outcome is case-specific and is related to the breadth of the prohibited geographic area.

In summary, Indiana courts addressing the enforceability of covenants against competition in the employment context have required that an employer seeking to enforce such a covenant must first establish a legitimate protectable interest. It must then show that the covenant is reasonable in terms of time, geographic area, and scope of prohibited activities. In all cases, however, the rules are subject to the overriding principle that courts are to examine the totality of circumstances in determining reasonableness and enforceability of covenants. Because of the comparative wealth of cases analyzing covenants against competition in the employment context, courts deciding whether to enforce covenants contained in franchise agreements are likely to continue to look to the principles developed in employment cases for guidance.

Iowa

by Rush Nigut*

1. Has the state addressed covenants against competition in the context of franchising?

- **Does the state have a franchising statute or regulations that address covenants against competition?**
- **Does the state have a covenants statute of general applicability that would encompass franchise covenants?**
- **Have the courts addressed covenants in the context of franchising either under a statute or under the state's common law?**

The Iowa Legislature has passed two statutes regulating franchises that have been codified at Iowa Code Chapter 523H and Iowa Code section 537A.10. The first statute, the Iowa Franchise Act, Iowa Code sections 523H.1 *et seq.*, was enacted in 1992. Section 2 of the Iowa Franchise Act provides that the Act is applicable "to a new or existing franchise that is operated in the state of Iowa." Iowa Code § 523H.2 (1992). However, in *McDonald's Corp. v. Nelson*, 822 F. Supp. 597, 606 (S.D. Iowa 1993), *aff'd, Holiday Inns Franchising, Inc. v. Branstad*, 29 F.3d 383, 385 (8th Cir. 1994), *cert. denied, Iowa v. Holiday Inns Franchising, Inc.*, 513 U.S. 1032 (1994), the United States District Court for the Southern District of Iowa held that application of portions of the Iowa Franchise Act to franchise agreements entered into before the Act's July 1, 1992, effective date substantially impaired franchisors' contractual rights in violation of the Contract Clauses of the United States and Iowa Constitutions. Accordingly, for most purposes, the Iowa Franchise Act is applicable to franchise agreements entered into between July 1, 1992, and June 30, 2000. The second Iowa statute, Iowa Code section 537A.10, governs all franchise agreements entered into on or after July 1, 2000. Iowa Code § 537A.10 (2000). Both statutes are generally referred to as the "Act" or the "Iowa Franchise Act."

For those franchise agreements entered into between July 1, 1992, and June 30, 2000, Iowa Code sections 523H.1 *et seq.* address covenants against competition in several contexts. First, in the context of transferring a franchise, the Act provides:

*Mr. Nigut is a shareholder of the law firm Brick, Gentry Law, P.C. in West Des Moines, Iowa. Allison Steuterman, a shareholder of the same firm, assisted in the preparation of this analysis.

> A franchisor, after a transfer of a franchise, shall not seek to enforce any covenant of the transferred franchise against the transferor which prohibits the transferor from engaging in any lawful occupation or enterprise. However, this subsection does not prohibit the franchisor from enforcing a contractual covenant against the transferor not to exploit the franchisor's trade secrets or intellectual property rights, unless otherwise agreed to by the parties.

IOWA CODE § 523H.5(10).

Second, in the context of nonrenewal of a franchise, the Act provides that a franchisor may refuse to renew a franchise only under certain circumstances, one of which is if the "franchisor completely withdraws from directly or indirectly distributing its products or services in the geographic market served by the franchisee." IOWA CODE § 523H.8(b)(3). However, if the franchisor's grounds for nonrenewal are that it is withdrawing from the franchisee's geographic market, the franchisor must agree "not to seek to enforce any covenant of the nonrenewed franchisee not to compete with the franchisor or franchisees of the franchisor." *Id.*

Finally, Iowa Code section 523H.11 contains a general prohibition against enforcing a post-termination covenant with two alternative exceptions. Section 523H.11 provides, in part:

> REPURCHASE OF ASSETS. A franchisor shall not prohibit a franchisee from, or enforce a prohibition against a franchisee, engaging in any lawful business at any location after a termination or refusal to renew by a franchisor, unless it is one which relies on a substantially similar marketing program as the terminated or nonrenewed franchise or unless the franchisor offers in writing no later than ten business days before expiration of the franchise to purchase the assets of the franchised business for its fair market value as a going concern.

IOWA CODE § 523H.11.

Iowa Code section 537A.10 contains language identical to that set forth in section 523H.8 with respect to nonrenewal of a franchise agreement when a franchisor is withdrawing from a franchisee's geographical market, but both the general prohibition against enforcing post-termination covenants and the prohibition against enforcing covenants in the context of a transfer of a franchise are conspicuously absent from the new statute. Presumably, this indicates a shift in legislative policy and means that for franchise agreements entered into after July 1, 2000, covenants not to compete may be enforceable upon transfer or termination of a franchise. Iowa does not have a general statute governing covenants against competition.

Iowa appellate courts have not addressed covenants against competition in the franchise context and applying the Iowa Franchise Act since it was enacted.[1]

---

1. In *Medicap Pharmacies, Inc. v. Kennedy*, No. 4-98-CV-10031 (S.D. Iowa Feb. 6, 1998), the U.S. District Court for the Southern District of Iowa considered whether a franchisor was likely to succeed in enforcing a non-competition agreement against a former franchisee under Iowa law. The non-competition agreement contained in the parties' franchise agreement precluded the franchisee from operating a competing drug store or pharmacy within two miles of the franchisee's franchise location during the term of the franchise agreement and for a period of two years following its expiration or termination. After comparing the non-competition agreement with others held reasonable by Iowa courts, the court concluded that Iowa courts would find the non-compete reasonable and enforceable. The court did not address the Iowa Franchise Act in its analysis.

In a case decided under the common law, *Casey's General Stores, Inc. v. Campbell Oil Co., Inc.*, 441 N.W.2d 758, 761 (Iowa 1989), the Iowa Supreme Court enforced an in-term covenant in a franchise agreement to prohibit competition by a convenience store franchisee within three miles of the site of any other Casey's General Store franchise.

The franchise agreement between Casey's and its franchisee, Campbell Oil, prohibited the franchisee from engaging "in any business covered by this Agreement at any place other than" the premises specified in the agreement. *Id.* at 759. Campbell Oil initially opened a Casey's General Store in Le Grand, Iowa. Later, Campbell Oil sought to open a second Casey's franchise approximately nine miles from its Le Grand store. *Id.* When Casey's denied the second franchise, Campbell Oil's shareholders, Les and Norma Campbell, bought the property for the proposed store and opened a convenience store on the site under the name "Cissy's." *Id.* The Campbells then opened a second Cissy's store ten blocks from a Casey's store operated by another Casey's franchisee. *Id.*

Casey's brought suit to enforce the non-compete agreement in its franchise agreement with Campbell Oil, alleging that Campbell Oil had breached this covenant by providing the Campbells with the means to open their Cissy's stores and by permitting them to assist in the management and operation of the Cissy's stores. *Id.* at 760. The trial court held that the geographic scope of the covenant was unreasonably broad, but that a radius of three miles from any existing franchise would be reasonable. *Id.* This conclusion, which the Iowa Supreme Court upheld, placed one of the Cissy's stores inside and the other Cissy's store outside the prohibited zone of competition. With respect to the Cissy's store inside the prohibited zone of competition, however, the court held that there was no violation of the covenant not to compete because the acts of the Campbells in running that Cissy's store could not properly be attributed to Campbell Oil, the signatory to the franchise agreement. *Id.*

In *Dairyland, Inc. v. Jenison*, 207 N.W.2d 753, 754 (Iowa 1973), which was also decided prior to enactment of the Iowa Franchise Act, the trial court awarded a franchisor a decree enjoining the defendants, former franchisees, from "engaging in any competitive business with the plaintiff or selling ice cream, ice milk or any other frozen or semi-frozen dairy products" at the location of the former franchise or "at any other location within a radius of ten miles thereof for a period of three years" from the date of the decree. The trial court's decree was not appealed. However, when the defendants later started selling an imitation (nondairy) frozen dessert product at the location of the former franchise, the franchisor sought sanctions for contempt. *Id.* The Iowa Supreme Court ultimately upheld the trial court's finding that the defendants were engaged in competition with plaintiff in violation of the decree: "whether the imitation frozen dessert sold by defendants was a proscribed 'dairy product' is not determinative because the decree also prohibited defendants from directly or indirectly engaging in competition with plaintiff, and defendants' conduct clearly constituted such competition." *Id.* at 755.

The United States District Court for the Northern District of Iowa enforced a franchise agreement that prohibited the franchisee (a financial services advisor) from conducting business in the "same geographic area" for one year following termination. *American Express Financial Advisors, Inc. v. Yantis*, 358 F. Supp. 2d 818, 828–29 (N.D. Iowa 2005). The court found that the restraint was reasonably necessary to protect the franchisor's financial planning business, including customer lists and other trade secrets. *Id.* Although the court discussed Iowa Code Chapter 523H in terms of a choice-of-law clause, it applied Iowa common law in determining the enforceability of the covenant not to compete. *Id.* at 827. In doing so, the court noted that, in Iowa, restrictive covenants are disfavored and only those covenants that are not unreasonably restrictive will be enforced. *Id.* at 829. Covenants not to compete are deemed unreasonably restrictive unless they are tightly limited with regard to both time and geographic area. *Id.* In enforcing the covenant not to compete, the court specifically noted that Iowa has found restrictive covenants enforceable in the franchisor-franchisee context. *Id.*

Although not addressing the ultimate enforceability of the covenant not to compete at issue, the Eighth Circuit Court of Appeals, in *Bandag, Inc. v. Jack's Tire & Oil, Inc.*, 190 F.3d 924, 925–26 (8th Cir. 1999), upheld the U.S. District Court for the Southern District of Iowa's denial of a preliminary injunction enforcing a non-compete found in a franchise agreement. The non-compete was for one year, and it involved prohibiting the defendant from using the "pre-cast or pre-cured tread rubber" method of retreading tires in his franchise territory for that one year. Both courts found that the plaintiff could not establish irreparable harm to justify a preliminary injunction given the wide array of products and services that the defendant offered in addition to retreading, and that the defendant's goodwill was developed before becoming a franchisee. *Id.* In doing so, the court noted that the franchisor had not included covenants not to compete in franchise agreements with other franchisees. This supported the finding that the franchisor would not suffer irreparable damage. *Id.*

2. Have the courts articulated the "legitimate interests" of the franchisor that will support enforcement of a covenant against competition contained in a franchise agreement?

- **If so, what are they (e.g., protection of goodwill, protection of confidential information), and in what contexts did the issue arise?**
- **If not, what interests have been recognized in other contexts (e.g., employment agreements, the sale of business context)?**

In *Casey's General Stores, Inc.*, the court stated that a covenant against competition "should be fairly enforced in view of the objects and purposes of the parties" and that "[n]oncompetition agreements between a franchisor and a franchisee are designed not only to protect the interests of the immediate parties but also to protect other franchisees against competitive activities." *Casey's Gen. Stores, Inc. v. Campbell Oil Co., Inc.*, 441 N.W.2d 758, 761 (Iowa 1989). The *Casey's* court recognized that to the extent that a franchisor exacts agreements from all of its franchisees not to compete with other franchisees, all parties benefit from these reciprocal protections. *Id.* In *American Express Financial Advisors, Inc. v. Yantis*, the court found the covenant not to compete reasonably necessary to protect the franchisor's business and customer goodwill. *Am. Express Fin. Advisors, Inc. v. Yantis*, 358 F. Supp. 2d 818, 828–29 (N.D. Iowa 2005).

Other than in *Casey's* and *American Express*, Iowa state and federal courts have not expressly articulated the "legitimate interests" of the franchisor that will support a covenant against competition in the franchising context. Chapter 523H of the Iowa Franchise Act does expressly permit the enforcement of covenants not to "exploit" the franchisor's trade secrets or intellectual property rights following the transfer of a franchise and permits enforcement of a covenant after termination or nonrenewal if the former franchisee's new business relies on a "substantially similar marketing program." And, as noted above, the general prohibition against enforcement of post-termination and post-transfer covenants against competition in chapter 523H were not carried over to the new franchise statute, section 537A.10.

Iowa state courts have addressed covenants against competition both in the context of employment contracts and independent contractor agreements and in the context of contracts for the sale of a business. Although Iowa courts generally disfavor restraints on competition and trade, they will be enforced if they are tightly limited in time and geographic area, are drafted to reasonably protect the employer's business while not unreasonably restricting the employee's rights, and are not prejudicial to the public interest. *Ag Spectrum Co. v. Elder*, 191 F. Supp. 3d 966, 971 (S.D. Iowa 2016); *Moore Bus. Forms, Inc. v. Wilson*, 953 F. Supp. 1056, 1064 (N.D. Iowa 1996); *Revere Transducers*, 595 N.W.2d 751, 761 (Iowa 1999); *Iowa Glass Depot, Inc., v. Jindrich*, 338 N.W.2d 376, 381 (Iowa 1983); *Rasmussen Heating & Cooling, Inc. v. Idso*, 463 N.W.2d 703, 705 (Iowa Ct. App. 1990).

To be reasonably necessary to protect the employer's business or interest, "[t]here must be some showing that defendant, when he left plaintiff's employment, pirated or had the chance to pirate part of plaintiff's business; took or had the opportunity of taking some part of the good will of plaintiff's business, or it can reasonably be expected some of the patrons or customers he served while in plaintiff's employment will follow him to the new employment." *Moore Bus. Forms, Inc. v. Wilson*, 953 F. Supp. 1056, 1064 (N.D. Iowa 1996) (internal quotations omitted).

Iowa state courts have recognized that an employer may have a legitimate interest in protecting its confidential information and trade secrets and in preventing its employees from unjustly enriching themselves at its expense. In *Dain Bosworth Inc. v. Brandhorst*, 356 N.W.2d 590 (Iowa Ct. App. 1984), for example, the court found that the employer had met its initial burden of proving the covenant was reasonably necessary to protect its business by showing the covenant was intended to protect the company's $20,000 investment in training the employee.

Those same concerns lead a federal district court in Iowa to enforce a franchise agreement that prohibited the franchisee (a financial services advisor) from conducting business in the "same geographic area" for one year following termination. *Am. Express Fin. Advisors, Inc. v. Yantis*, 358 F. Supp. 2d 818, 828–29 (N.D. Iowa 2005). The court found that the restraint was reasonably necessary to protect the franchisor's financial planning business, including customer lists and other trade secrets. *Id.; see also Orkin Exterminating Co., Inc. v. Burnett*, 146 N.W.2d 320, 323 (Iowa 1966) (employee given eight weeks' training in exterminating insects and methods of operation); *Cogley Clinic v. Martini*, 112 N.W.2d 678 (Iowa 1962) (cost to clinic of training new doctor was $10,000); *Federated Mut. Implement & Hardware Ins. Co. v. Erickson*, 110 N.W.2d 264 (Iowa 1961) (insurance agent had intimate knowledge of customer list, policyholders' insurance needs, and policy expiration dates). *Cf. Mut. Loan Co. v. Pierce*, 65 N.W.2d 405, 408, 410 (Iowa 1954) (there is "nothing unique about the personal loan business"; the harm the former employer would suffer "would be no greater than if [the new employer] had hired any other person with 20 months general experience" in the business).

Similarly, a person's close proximity to and knowledge of customers, leading to their ability to divert customers, is a legitimate interest to protect via a covenant not to compete. *Iowa Glass Depot, Inc. v. Jindrich*, 338 N.W.2d 376, 383 (Iowa 1983). The court stated that the nature of the business itself, accessibility to information peculiar to the employer's business, and the nature of the occupation that is restrained are also interests to be considered. *Id.*

Generally, an employee cannot be precluded from exercising the skill and general knowledge that he or she acquired or increased through experience or instruction while employed. *Id.* at 383. Accordingly, Iowa courts look at whether the employer has provided special training or peculiar knowledge to the employee that would allow the employee to unjustly enrich himself at the expense of the employer. *Curtis 1000 Inc. v. Youngblade,* 878 F. Supp. 1224, 1261 (N.D. Iowa 1995). Accordingly, one legitimate interest that may be protected for franchisors is the specialized training and particular knowledge provided to franchisees. Ordinary on-the-job training may not be a sufficient interest of a franchisor to enforce a covenant not to compete. *Ag Spectrum Co. v. Elder*, 865 F.3d 1088, 1092–93 (8th Cir. 2017). In *Ma & Pa, Inc. v. Kelly*, 342 N.W.2d 500, 502 (Iowa 1984), the Iowa Supreme Court focused on a factor "not present in most cases"—the discharge of the employee, as opposed to his voluntary resignation. Although recognizing that under some circumstances termination by the employer would not invalidate the covenant, the court stated that this factor weighs against the grant of an injunction in the employer's favor. *Id.* It is possible that Iowa courts would make a similar distinction in the franchise context if the franchisor were the party terminating the franchise relationship. In the context of independent contractors, covenants not to compete are enforceable, but with even greater restraint than those between employers and employees because the principal in an independent contractor relationship has a less legitimate business interest to protect in an independent contractor relationship than an employer does in an employer/employee relationship. *Ag Spectrum Co. v. Elder*, 865 F.3d 1088, 1092–93 (8th Cir. 2017) (*aff'g Ag Spectrum Co. v. Elder*, 191 F. Supp. 3d 966, 971–93 (S.D. Iowa 2016); *see also Fialkoff v. VGM Group, Inc.*, 2020 WL 10486716, at *4 (N.D. Iowa Aug. 10, 2020) (finding not per se unenforceable but should be viewed with greater scrutiny). Stated another way, the more the relationship leans toward independent contractor and principal rather than employee and employer, the more the customers and knowledge or training are the contractor's and not the principal's. *Id.* As the United States District Court for the Southern District of Iowa stated:

> The independent contractor relationship is traditionally less intimate than the employer-employee relationship. *See* Restatement (Second) of Agency § 220 (Am. Law Inst. 1958). Independent contractors maintain greater control over the manner of their work; engage to a greater extent in a distinct occupation; and work with a less supervision, among other things. *Id.* Because the independent contractor relationship is further separated from an employer's enterprise than is the employment relationship, employers are less likely, for example, to invest in training their independent contractors and less likely to impart trade secret information. Additionally, independent contractors in Iowa do not reap the same benefits from employment as do employees; for example, independent contractors are not protected under Iowa's Wage Payment Collection Act, Iowa Code Chapter 91A, and thus bear greater risk in their dealings with other business entities.

Ag Spectrum Co. v. Elder, 191 F. Supp. 3d at 973.

Both the Eight Circuit Court of Appeals and the United States District Court for the Southern District of Iowa applied Iowa factors, discussed above, for determining the reasonableness of the covenant not to compete and found the covenant not to compete in Elder's independent contractor agreement unenforceable because it was unreasonable. *Ag Spectrum Co. v. Elder*, 865 F.3d at 1092–93; *Ag Spectrum Co. v. Elder*, 191 F. Supp. 3d at 973–75. Elder acted akin to a dealer for Ag Spectrum, purchasing Ag Spectrum products and then selling them to customers. *Id.* Both courts noted that Elder did not benefit from specialized training from Ag Spectrum and most of the customers were the Elder's customers and not Ag Spectrum's customers with Elder developing the relationships and not Ag Spectrum. *Id.* The covenant was not reasonably necessary to protect Ag Spectrum's interests, and Ag Spectrum's benefit from the covenant not to compete was not in proportion to the burden suffered by Elder. *Id.* Accordingly, both courts refused to enforce the covenant not to compete. In the context of contracts for the sale of a business, the contracting parties generally are given more freedom with respect to duration and geographic scope of a non-competition restriction. This is both because the restriction adds to the goodwill and, therefore, the value of the business being sold and because the parties generally are more equal in bargaining power than in the employment context. *Sutton v. Iowa Trenchless, L.C.*, 808 N.W.2d 744, 749 (Iowa Ct. App. 2011); *see also Ehlers v. Iowa Warehouse Co.*, 188 N.W.2d 368, 369 (Iowa 1971); *Baker v. Starkey*, 144 N.W.2d 889, 895–96 (Iowa 1966). The Iowa Supreme Court has expressly recognized that the goodwill of a business is an asset entitled to protection to the extent reasonable. *Kunz v. Bock*, 163 N.W.2d 442, 446 (Iowa 1968); *see also L.H. Henry & Sons v. Rhinesmith*, 260 N.W. 9, 10 (Iowa 1935) (covenant "was reasonably necessary to enable the purchaser to obtain the benefits of his purchase under the contract"); *but see Rasmussen Heating & Cooling, Inc. v. Idso*, 463 N.W.2d 703, 705 (Iowa Ct. App. 1990) (ten-year covenant was not reasonably necessary for the protection of the business, where defendants' competitive activity did not begin until five years after the stock sale).

In *Sutton v. Iowa Trenchless, L.C.*, the court noted that it allows covenants not to compete in purchase agreements to be more restrictive because the goodwill of the business is being sold and because of the equal bargaining powers of the parties. *Sutton v. Iowa Trenchless, L.C.*, 808 N.W.2d at 749. However, the court also stated that tolerance of greater restrictions does not mean all sales of business covenants not to compete were inevitably enforceable and that each situation required analysis to ensure that the restrictions were not overbroad under the circumstances. *Id.* "Even with Purchase Agreements between owners, the true test is whether the restraint is such only as to afford a fair protection to the interest of the party in favor of whom it is given, and not so large as to interfere with the interests of the public. And the restriction must be reasonable, not oppressive, or out of proportion to the benefits which the vendee may, in reason, expect to flow from the restrictive features of the contract." *Id.* at 749–50 (internal citations omitted). Applying these principals,, the court found that the seven year and 350-mile radius was reasonable, valid, and enforceable. *Id.* at 751.

---

3. What time limitations have courts recognized as reasonable in the franchise context? If no franchise cases have been decided, what time limitations have been recognized in other contexts?

➤ How have they been related to the interests protected?

Iowa's state courts have not specifically addressed the issue of what constitutes a reasonable time limitation for a post-termination covenant not to compete in the franchise context. The decision in *Casey's General Stores, Inc. v. Campbell Oil Co., Inc.*, 441 N.W.2d 758, 761 (Iowa 1989) involved a covenant against competition applicable only during the term of the franchise agreement, and therefore the court was not faced with the issue of what constitutes a reasonable duration of a post-term franchise covenant. In *Dairyland, Inc. v. Jenison*, 207 N.W.2d 753, 754 (Iowa 1973), the trial court's decree restrained the former franchisees from engaging in any competitive business within ten miles of their former franchise for a period of three years and the decree was not appealed. In *American Express Financial Advisors, Inc. v. Yantis*, 358 F. Supp. 2d 818, 836 (N.D. Iowa 2005), the court enjoined the former franchisee for one year. *Id.* at 829–30.

In other contexts, Iowa state courts have held that "[c]ovenants not to compete are unreasonably restrictive unless they are tightly limited as to both time and area." *Pathology Consultants v. Gratton*, 343 N.W.2d 428, 434 (Iowa 1984). Generally, courts have found that covenants not to compete for a term of two or three years are reasonable. *Pro Edge, L.P. v. Gue*, 374 F. Supp. 2d 711, 740–41 (N.D. Iowa 2005) (one year); *Tasco Inc. v. Winkel*, 281 N.W.2d 280 (Iowa 1979) (one year); *Iowa Glass Depot, Inc. v. Jindrich*, 338 N.W.2d 376 (Iowa 1983) (three-year covenant; court refused to enforce beyond 11 months); *Ma & Pa Inc. v. Kelly*, 342 N.W.2d 500 (Iowa 1984) (three years); *Farm Bureau Serv. Co. of Maynard v. Kohls*, 203 N.W.2d 209 (Iowa 1972) (two years); *Ehlers v. Iowa Warehouse Co.*, 188 N.W.2d 368 (Iowa 1971) (two years); *Cedar Valley Med. Specialists v. Wright*, 940 N.W.2d 442 (Table), 2019 WL 506325 (Iowa Ct. App. 2019) (two years); *Lucy v. Platinum Servs., Inc.*, 924 N.W.2d 876 (Table), 2018 WL 5840801 (Iowa Ct. App. 2018) (modified to two years); *Phone Connection, Inc. v. Harbst*, 494 N.W.2d 445, 450 (Iowa Ct. App. 1992) (modified to two years); *Rasmussen Heating & Cooling, Inc. v. Idso*, 463 N.W.2d 703, 704–05 (Iowa Ct. App. 1990) (refusing to enforce a ten-year non-compete); *Dental East, P.C. v. Westercamp*, 423 N.W.2d 553 (Iowa Ct. App. 1988) (two years); *Dain Bosworth Inc. v. Brandhorst*, 356 N.W.2d 590 (Iowa Ct. App. 1984) (90 days).

In *Rasmussen*, for example, the court stated that "[a]n examination of recent Iowa cases reveals that our Supreme Court has not enforced a covenant that extended beyond five years [and that] [t]ypically, the duration of a disputed covenant ranges from two years to three years." *Rasmussen*, 463 N.W.2d at 704–05. In *Rasmussen*, the court found that the ten-year covenant in that case was neither tightly time limited nor reasonably necessary for the protection of the business. *Id.* at 705. The court refused to enforce the covenant against the defendants, who had not begun their competitive activity until five years after the sale of their business. The court found that the five years between the sale and the defendants' competitive business activity "allowed the Rasmussens ample time and opportunity to succeed. Any further restrictions would be unduly burdensome." *Id.*; *see also Yantis*, 358 F. Supp. 2d at 829 (enforcing one-year limit on financial advisor franchisee).

In *Phone Connection, Inc. v. Harbst*, 494 N.W.2d 445 (1992), the Iowa Court of Appeals affirmed the district court's modification of a covenant not to compete by restricting the geographical territory to the areas in which the employer had established its business and by decreasing the five-year prohibition to two years. *Id.* at 449–50. Citing *Rasmussen*, the court found that "the restrictive covenant, as modified by the district court, [was] both reasonable and enforceable" in light of the hardship imposed upon Harbst (his livelihood was tied to the telephone business and his large family did not want to move) and the nature of the business in issue. *Id.* at 450.

4. What geographic limitations have courts recognized as reasonable in the franchise context?

- **How have they been related to the interests protected?**
- **Have courts recognized the legitimacy of protecting other franchisees from competition?**

As discussed earlier, the court in *Casey's General Stores, Inc. v. Campbell Oil Co., Inc.*, 441 N.W.2d 758 (Iowa 1989), upheld an order prohibiting competition by the franchisee within three miles of any other Casey's franchise. The court recognized that most of its earlier "decisions establishing geographic zones wherein competition is prohibited have protected locations within a specified radius of some business situs of the covenant obligor" but concluded that, despite that fact, "the district court's attempt to protect the franchisor against competition at all existing franchise sites was proper." *Id.* at 761. In addressing Casey's argument that the zone of protected interest should extend ten miles from existing franchises rather than three miles, the court stated that "any determination of a reasonable geographic limit against competition must be arrived at in a somewhat arbitrary manner." *Id.* The court found that although there was evidence from which the court might conclude that a broader area of geographic protection was warranted, the district court's ultimate finding on the issue was reasonable and should not be disturbed. *Id.*

In recognizing the legitimacy of protecting other franchisees from competition, the Iowa Supreme Court in *Casey's* stated:

> Noncompetition agreements between a franchisor and a franchisee are designed not only to protect the interests of the immediate parties but also to protect other franchisees against competitive activities. Thus, to the extent that such noncompetition agreements are exacted from all franchisees, each franchisee is thereby protected from competition from other franchisees. As a consequence of this reciprocal protection, Campbell Oil, in exchange for the provisions restricting it from competing with other Casey's franchisees, benefits from the protections barring those franchisees from competing against it.

Id. (citing *Armstrong v. Taco Time Int'l, Inc.*, 30 Wash. App. 538, 545, 635 P.2d 1114, 1118 (1981)).

As alluded to in *Casey's*, Iowa courts often limit enforcement of a covenant not to compete in the employment context to an area no greater than that in which the employee actually performed his or her duties. In *Phone Connection, Inc. v. Harbst*, 494 N.W.2d 445 (1992), for example, the court of appeals affirmed the district court's modification of a covenant not to compete in the states of Minnesota and Iowa by restricting the geographical territory to those areas in which the employer had established its business. *Id.* at 450; *see also Farm Bureau Serv. Co. of Maynard v. Kohls*, 203 N.W.2d 209 (Iowa 1972) (two-county area reduced to six townships in which employee actually worked); *Ehlers v. Iowa Warehouse Co.*, 188 N.W.2d 368, 369 (Iowa 1971) (150-mile radius of employer's location narrowed to prohibit solicitation of business only from persons within this area with whom employee had contact while employed by employer); *Orkin Exterminating Co., Inc. v. Burnett*, 146 N.W.2d 320 (Iowa 1966) (ten-mile radius of any location serviced for employer was reasonable); *Baker v. Starkey*, 144 N.W.2d 889 (Iowa 1966) (restrictive covenant must bear some relation to the activities of the employee and must not restrain the employee's activities in a territory into which his former work did not take him).

In *Tasco, Inc. v. Winkel*, 281 N.W.2d 280 (Iowa 1979), however, the court reversed the grant of summary judgment to a former employee on an employer's claim for breach of an employment covenant. The trial court had concluded that the covenant was overbroad and unenforceable as a matter of law, in part because it covered the entire United States. *Id.* at 281. On appeal, the Iowa Supreme Court found that summary judgment was not appropriate because the employer had raised a genuine issue of fact as to whether a nationwide covenant was reasonably necessary to protect its business. *Id.* at 282. Noting that the employer operated nationwide and had a very specialized business, the court remanded for a trial on the merits. *Id.* at 282.

As with time restrictions, Iowa courts seem to be more willing to uphold broad geographical restrictions in cases involving professionals. *See Pro Edge, L.P. v. Gue*, 374 F. Supp. 2d 711, 740–41 (N.D. Iowa 2005) (enforcing noncompete agreement involving a veterinarian with restrictions of 250 miles); *Cogley Clinic v. Martini*, 112 N.W.2d 678 (Iowa 1962) (25 miles around city in which clinic was located was reasonable); *Cedar Valley Medical Specialists v. Wright*, 940 N.W.2d 442 (Table), 2019 WL 5063325, at *1 (Iowa Ct. App. 2019) (involving a physician and a geographical limitation of 35 miles); *Dental East, P.C. v. Westercamp*, 423 N.W.2d 553 (Iowa Ct. App. 1988) (20-mile radius from dental office was reasonable); *Dain Bosworth Inc. v. Brandhorst*, 356 N.W.2d 590 (Iowa Ct. App. 1984) (30-mile radius from brokerage office was reasonable).

5. What limitations on activities have courts recognized as reasonable in the franchise context?

The covenant against competition at issue in *Casey's*, discussed earlier, prohibited the franchisee from engaging in "any business covered by this Agreement at any place other than such premises." *Casey's General Stores, Inc. v. Campbell Oil Co., Inc.*, 441 N.W.2d 758, 759 (Iowa 1989). The court gave no indication that this language might be overbroad and had no trouble concluding that the operation of a Cissy's convenience store fell within the scope of prohibited activity. Although the court concluded that the operation of a Cissy's convenience store within a three-mile radius of any other Casey's store was prohibited by the covenant, it also concluded that the covenant did not preclude the franchisee from supplying petroleum products to Cissy's stores outside the restricted territory. *Id.* at 762 The court stated that it failed to see how that activity had "any bearing on the protected area of retail competition between the franchisor and the franchisee." *Id.*

In *Dairyland, Inc. v. Jenison*, 207 N.W.2d 753 (Iowa 1973), the Iowa Supreme Court upheld a trial court's decree restraining former franchisees from "engaging in any competitive business" with the franchisor. As in *Casey's*, the *Dairyland* court gave no indication that this language might be overbroad and had no trouble concluding that the franchisee should be restrained from selling frozen or semi-frozen dairy desserts as well as similar "nondairy" desserts. *Id.* at 754. In reaching this conclusion, the court recognized that "the public does not distinguish frozen dessert products on the basis [of] whether they contain dairy fat or vegetable fat" and that the franchisees' conduct in selling nondairy desserts clearly constituted competition. *Id.* at 755.

In other contexts, Iowa courts seem more willing to rewrite broad restrictions on competitive activity. In the employment context, for example, courts have held that a restrictive covenant must bear some relation to the activities of the former employee. *Baker v. Starkey*, 144 N.W.2d 889, 895 (Iowa 1966). In *Farm Bureau Services Co. of Maynard v. Kohls*, 203 N.W.2d 209 (Iowa 1972), the court declared that a covenant prohibiting "any business activity competitive to that of [the employer]" was overly broad. The court found that the employer would be amply protected if the former employee were restrained only from those activities he undertook during his employment. *Id.* at 211.

In *Presto-X-Company v. Ewing*, 442 N.W.2d 85 (Iowa 1989), the court considered a covenant not to compete that restricted the former employee from directly or indirectly soliciting or servicing his former employer's customers. The trial court held that the former employee, Ewing, had not violated this covenant by sending notes to some of Presto-X's customers, giving them his home address and telephone number, and advising them that he was no longer employed by the employer and that there could be no violation of the covenant if the customers sought out Ewing's services. On appeal, the Iowa Supreme Court held that the trial court erred in its application of the covenant. The court stated that, "although the note was not worded as an overt solicitation, the implication of it . . . was that Ewing remained available for employment by the Presto-X customers and wanted them to contact him if they desired his services." *Id.* at 88. As such, the court held that the notes were indirect, if not direct, solicitations and were prohibited by the covenant. The court also held that the covenant prohibited "[a]ll servicing of Ewing's former Presto-X customers . . . regardless of who approached whom." *Id.* at 89.

Conversely, deliberately unreasonable and oppressive covenants will be held invalid and covenants not to compete that amount to general restraints on trade, or amount to completely prohibiting an individual to pursue his or her trade, will be deemed invalid and void ab initio. *CRST Expedited, Inc. v. TransAm Trucking, Inc.*, 505 F. Supp. 3d 832, 939 (N.D. Iowa 2020); *Ehlers v. Iowa Warehouse Co.*, 188 N.W.2d 368, 374 (Iowa 1971).

6. Does the state recognize a difference between in-term and post-term covenants?

In *Nelson v. Agro Globe Engineering, Inc.*, 578 N.W.2d 659 (Iowa 1998), the court recognized the difference between in-term and post-term covenants in the employment context. The *Nelson* court held that "covenants not to accept employment with another during the contract should be more broadly enforced than covenants to prevent competition" after termination. *Id.* at 662. The court reasoned that:

> The mischief sought to be prevented by examining the reasonableness of a post-employment covenant not to compete looms less threateningly where the restrictive covenant merely limits an employee from competing with the employer during the term of the contract. The public's interest in competition is not normally endangered by such a covenant. Nor is the employee denied the opportunity to use his or her skills and knowledge to earn a living.

Id. (citations omitted).

The *Nelson* court enforced a covenant that restricted the employee's activities during the term of his employment contract, finding that it was not so broad or long-lasting as to be unduly burdensome to the employee and that the "four-year time period was what [the employer] felt was necessary to give it a chance to become firmly established" in the business. *Id.*

7. Has the state allowed enforcement of covenants against non-signatories (e.g., family members, newly formed corporations)?

In *Casey's General Stores, Inc. v. Campbell Oil Co.*, 441 N.W.2d 758 (Iowa 1989), the court considered whether the covenant not to compete set forth in the franchise agreement was binding upon the Campbells as controlling shareholders of the franchisee corporation, Campbell Oil. The trial court found that the shareholders, Les and Norma Campbell, "were not parties to the agreement and could therefore not be enjoined from personally carrying on the business activities of the Cissy's store" but then ordered the franchisee, Campbell Oil, to remove the Campbells as directors, officers, or employees unless the Campbells terminated their ownership and employment relationships with the Cissy's store. *Id.* at 760. On appeal, the Iowa Supreme Court noted that Casey's had never claimed the Campbells were personally subject to the non-competition agreement and that the relationship between Campbell Oil, as a corporation, and the Campbells "imposes no servitude on the Campbells as individuals." *Id.*

> As controlling shareholders, the Campbells control the actions of the corporation rather than the corporation controlling them. Given this relationship between the Campbells and the corporation which they control, we can discern no basis for concluding that the acts of Les and Norma Campbell in regard to the State Center Cissy's store were the acts of Campbell Oil. We therefore modify the district court's grant of injunctive relief by deleting the requirement that Les and Norma Campbell must elect between continuing as officers and employees of Campbell Oil and maintaining an ownership interest in the State Center Cissy's store.

Id.

In *White Pigeon Agency, Inc. v. Madden*, 2001 WL 855366, at *8 (Iowa Ct. App. 2001), the court issued a permanent injunction against a former employee for violating the non-compete and non-disclosure clauses of her employment agreement with her former insurance agency employer, but refused to impose the injunction against the defendant's new company of which she owned 50 percent (which sold insurance as well). The court found it was unfair to bind the company to the provisions of the individual defendant's contract with White Pigeon as the contract was not between the new company and White Pigeon. *Id.* at 4.

In *Lucy v. Platinum Services, Inc.*, 924 N.W.2d 876 (Table), 2018 WL 5840801, at *1 (Iowa Ct. App. 2018), Lucy entered into a contract with Platinum, his employer, which included a seven-year non-compete. He also entered into a contract with Platinum's majority shareholder, Briggs, for payment under a stock purchase agreement that did not include a non-compete. The court found that, under the plain language of the agreements, they were not part of a single transaction with cross-enforcement provisions and that the contracts were entered into by different parties—one being Platinum and one being Briggs. *Id.* at *3–4. Accordingly, the court refused to extend the terms of the covenant not to compete from the first agreement to the second stock purchase agreement. *Id.* Nothing in the second agreement conditioned payment in the second agreement on the plaintiff's compliance with the covenant not to compete in the first agreement. *Id.*

Iowa courts have enforced non-competition covenants against non-signatories, however, in at least two cases. In *Dental East, P.C. v. Westercamp*, 423 N.W.2d 553, 554 (Iowa Ct. App. 1988), the court held that a covenant prohibiting competition by a professional corporation "and its employees" applied to a dentist, even though the dentist had not signed the agreement in his individual capacity. The court noted that each dentist had signed previous covenants not to compete in his or her individual capacities, which had not been revoked. The new covenant was between the professional corporations because each dentist had formed separate professional corporations in which he or she was respectively employed as the sole dentist. *Id.* at 554. In *L.H. Henry & Sons v. Rhinesmith*, 219 Iowa 1088, 1092, 260 N.W. 9 (Iowa 1935), a case involving the sale of a publishing business, the trial court enjoined a third party from competing with the purchasers by publishing a newspaper in conjunction with the sellers. On appeal, the Iowa Supreme Court upheld the injunction, noting that it did not prohibit the third party from publishing a newspaper on his own, only with the sellers.

8. Will the state modify, "blue-pencil," or otherwise reduce a covenant found to be overbroad?

In *Ehlers v. Iowa Warehouse Co.*, 188 N.W.2d 368 (Iowa 1971), the Iowa Supreme Court overruled an earlier line of cases in which it had adopted an "all or nothing" approach to enforcing non-competition agreements. *See Casey's Gen. Stores, Inc. v. Campbell Oil Co.*, 441 N.W.2d 758, 761 (Iowa 1989). The court in *Ehlers* adopted

> [t]he rule that unless the facts and circumstances indicate bad faith on the part of the employer, we will enforce noncompetitive covenants to the extent they are reasonably necessary to protect his legitimate interests without imposing undue hardship on the employee when the public interest is not adversely affected.

Ehlers, 188 N.W.2d at 370.

The court made it clear that "bad faith" would be found if an employer deliberately imposed an oppressive covenant in the hope that the court would enforce a lesser restriction. *Id.* at 374. In a subsequent case, *Lamp v. American Prosthetics, Inc.*, 379 N.W.2d 909 (Iowa 1986), the court cautioned that it "must necessarily approach the issue of modification with a certain degree of reluctance" and that "while Ehlers allows for modification of such agreements, it does not require a court to do so *sua sponte*." *Id.* at 911. In *Lamp*, the court refused to reduce the scope of the covenant because the issue had not been properly raised in the district court.

Since *Ehlers*, however, Iowa courts have not been reluctant to modify or reduce restrictions in a covenant found to be overbroad. In *Casey's*, the Iowa Supreme Court upheld the trial court's modification of the parties' non-competition agreement by reducing the geographic zone of protection from "any place other than [the franchise] premises" to a zone of three miles around all existing Casey's franchises.

Similarly, in *Phone Connection, Inc. v. Harbst*, 494 N.W.2d 445, 450 (1992), the Iowa Court of Appeals upheld the trial court's modification of a non-competition agreement by reducing the geographical territory from all of Minnesota and Iowa to only those counties in which The Phone Connection had established its business and reducing the time restriction from five years to two years.

9. When does a non-compete period begin to run? Will courts equitably extend the term?

In *Presto-X-Company v. Ewing*, 442 N.W.2d 85, 90 (1989), the Iowa Supreme Court recognized that a covenant not to compete may have little practical value if the time it takes to enforce it approaches or exceeds the covenant's stated duration. *See also Tasco, Inc. v. Winkel*, 281 N.W.2d 280, 282 (Iowa 1979) ("The injunctive part of the requested relief is probably moot by now because more than one year has already passed since the termination of the employment."). In *Presto-X*, the trial court refused to issue an injunction to enforce a two-year post-employment covenant. On appeal, the Iowa Supreme Court held that an injunction should have been granted and that:

> [T]he two-year period of restraint, if measured from the time Ewing was terminated, will end shortly after this appeal is completed. Hence, Presto-X would actually have the benefit of an injunction for only a fraction of the two years specified in the covenant. We think it is necessary in such circumstances to use our equitable powers to extend the restraint period, so as to accomplish full and complete justice between the parties. . . . [W]e hold that the injunction against Ewing shall be effective for one year from the date of this opinion.

Presto-X-Company, 442 N.W.2d at 89–90 (citations omitted).

The court advanced three reasons for its decision to extend the restraint period: (1) to protect the integrity of the judicial process by eliminating the defendant's incentive to delay, (2) to "protect the usefulness of such restrictive covenants," and (3) to give Presto-X "an opportunity to regain the customers it would not have lost had Ewing not violated the covenant." *Id.* at 90.

IA

This same reasoning was applied in the franchise context in the case of *Medicap Pharmacies, Inc. v. Kennedy*, ¶ 11,973 Bus. Franchise Guide (CCH) (S.D. Iowa 2000). In *Medicap*, the franchisor sought to enforce a two-year covenant not to compete against a former franchisee in Iowa after the franchisee terminated its pharmacy franchise and then continued to operate a pharmacy in the location of its former franchise. After the franchisor brought suit in the federal district court in Iowa, the former franchisee filed for bankruptcy and the franchisor's action was stayed pending resolution of the bankruptcy proceedings. Approximately two years later, the bankruptcy court lifted the stay after determining that the franchisor's right to an injunction enforcing the covenant not to compete could not be discharged in bankruptcy. When the franchisor then brought a motion for a preliminary injunction to enforce the covenant against competition, the franchisee argued that the motion was moot because the two-year term had already expired. The federal district court disagreed. *Id.*

Applying Iowa law, the *Medicap* court held that, although the non-compete clause technically had expired, it was in the interest of justice to extend the restraint period for an additional 18 months because it was the franchisee that was primarily responsible for the prolonged litigation and who continued to violate the non-compete clause throughout the majority of the two years following his unilateral termination. The court recognized that refusal to enforce the legal and valid covenant that had yet to be enforced since the action was commenced over two years earlier "would eliminate all force and effect of the covenant." *Id.*

10. Are there additional nuances or peculiarities of the state's treatment of covenants in the franchising context?

In a recent decision, *Kennedy v. Medicap Pharmacies, Inc.*, 267 F.3.d 493 (6th Cir. 2001), the Sixth Circuit Court of Appeals considered the issue of whether a franchisee's obligations under a covenant not to compete contained in a franchise agreement were dischargeable in bankruptcy under Iowa law. The Sixth Circuit affirmed both the bankruptcy court and the district court in holding that under Iowa law, the franchisor's right to equitable relief for the franchisee's breach of the covenant not to compete was not a "claim" dischargeable in bankruptcy. The court held that "[t]he right to equitable relief constitutes a claim only if it is an alternative to a right to payment or if compliance with the equitable order will itself require the payment of money." *Id.* at 497. In determining that the covenant in the *Medicap* case was not dischargeable, the court reasoned that:

> Under Iowa law, damages may be awarded in addition to an injunction for breach of a covenant not to compete. An injunction, however, is designed to avoid irreparable injury and may issue only when the party seeking it has no adequate remedy at law. A review of Iowa cases shows that damages are awarded for specific injuries already incurred, and that an injunction may issue only when damages are inadequate for future injuries. . . . Medicap does not have discretion to choose either damages or equitable relief for future damages. It can only obtain equitable relief if money damages for future injuries are inadequate. Therefore, under Iowa law, equitable relief is not an alternative to a right to payment for future injuries.

Id. at 498 (internal citations omitted).

Additionally, Iowa courts will uphold liquidated damage provisions in covenants not to compete, so long as they do not constitute a penalty. In *Cedar Valley Medical Specialists v. Wright*, 940 N.W.2d 442 (Table), 2019 WL 5063325, at *1 (Iowa Ct. App. 2019), the court found that the liquidated damage clause providing for damages in the amount of $100,000.00, or the compensation paid by CVMS to Wright during the six months immediately preceding the termination of his employment, was reasonable and enforceable. The court reasoned that a liquidated damage provision is reasonable if it compensates the employer for the loss rather than punishing the breach. *Id.* at *6. The factors considered included (1) the anticipated or actual loss caused by the breach and whether the amount fixed is reasonable to the extent it approximates the actual loss and (2) the difficulty of proof of loss. *Id.* Similarly, in *Dental East, PC v. Westercamp*, 423 N.W.2d 553, 555 (Iowa Ct. App. 1988), the court upheld the provision that any breach of the covenant not to compete would result in payment of 40 percent of any amount received from a patient of record for a period of one year.

Kansas

*by Clayton Kaiser and Gary Ayers**

1. Has the state addressed covenants against competition in the context of franchising?

- **Does the state have a franchising statute or regulations that address covenants against competition?**
- **Does the state have a covenants statute of general applicability that would encompass franchise covenants?**
- **Have the courts addressed covenants in the context of franchising either under a statute or under the state's common law?**

Kansas has not enacted statutes or regulations that address covenants against competition in the franchise context, nor has it enacted a general law that encompasses franchise covenants. Kansas courts have, however, addressed covenants against competition generally. They have also addressed covenants against competition in the franchise-specific context in one case, *H&R Block, Inc. v. Lovelace*, 493 P.2d 205 (Kan. 1972).

In *H&R Block*, the covenant between a franchisor and franchisee of an income tax preparation business ran for five years and had no geographic limitation. The court held the entire clause unenforceable for its unlimited geographic reach. *Id.* at 212.

The court reasoned that a covenant against competition is valid if the covenant is ancillary to a lawful contract and (1) is reasonable and (2) does not harm the public welfare. *Id.* at 210. This standard was established in early Kansas cases such as *Foltz v. Struxness*, 168 Kan. 714, 215 P.2d 133 (1950), followed by *H&R Block* and *Eastern Distributing Co. v. Flynn*, 222 Kan. 666, 567 P.2d 1371 (1977). Later, *Weber v. Tillman* became one of the court's leading cases on the four factors necessary to support the restraint of trade created by a covenant not to compete: "(1) Does the covenant protect a legitimate business interest of the employer? (2) Does the covenant create an undue burden on the employee? (3) Is the covenant injurious

*Mr. Kaiser and Mr. Ayers are partners at the law firm Foulston Siefkin LLP.

to the public welfare? (4) Are the time and territorial limitations contained in the covenant reasonable?" 913 P.2d 84, 90 (Kan. 1996). A covenant's reasonableness depends on the rights of the promisee and the promisor, and the reasonableness of the geographic area and time limitations under the facts and circumstances of each particular case. *Id.* Regarding the rights of the promisee and promisor, the court distinguished covenants in employment contracts from covenants in the sale of a business. *H&R Block, Inc. v. Lovelace*, 493 P.2d 205, 211 (Kan. 1972). Covenants between an employer and employee are construed more strictly against the employer because an employee receives no consideration for the covenant other than the employment itself and has pressure to make the covenant to earn a living in the short term. *Id.* Covenants between a seller and buyer of a business, however, are construed neutrally because they are often supported by specific consideration and tend to involve parties with equal bargaining power. *Id.*

The employer-employee and sale-of-business distinction is important in the franchise context because a franchise relationship does not fit neatly into either category. The answer will ordinarily turn on the franchisor's ability to control the franchisee's operations. And in *H&R Block*, the franchisor had a "considerable amount of operational control." 493 P.2d at 212. It could, for example, set office hours and fees, train personnel, and retain title to the franchisee's books and records in the event of the franchisee's breach. *Id.* Thus, the court ruled that the *H&R Block* franchise relationship was "akin to one of employment" and construed the covenant strictly against the franchisor. *Id.* As a result, it refused to enforce the covenant as unreasonable because it had no geographic limit. *Id.*

Notably, the court did not address the covenant's time limitation, nor was it "inclined to write a new contract for the parties." *Id.* Because the trial court also refused to modify the covenant, it sufficed that the geographic reach of the covenant was unreasonable and that made "consideration of other matters . . . unnecessary." *Id.* at 213. Kansas courts will, however, modify covenants against competition, and the court itself has said *H&R Block* "does not stand for non-modification of contracts," and does not "dictate a decision" that a trial court may not modify a covenant against competition. *E. Distrib. Co. v. Flynn*, 567 P.2d 1371, 1379 (Kan. 1977).

2. Have the courts articulated the "legitimate interests" of the franchisor that will support enforcement of a covenant against competition contained in a franchise agreement?

- **If so, what are they (e.g., protection of goodwill, protection of confidential information), and in what contexts did the issue arise?**
- **If not, what interests have been recognized in other contexts (e.g., employment agreements, the sale of business context)?**

The court in *H&R Block, Inc. v. Lovelace* did not identify the legitimate interests that may support enforcement of a covenant against competition. Elsewhere, however, Kansas courts hold that covenants against competition must be supported by a "legitimate interest," and that a party's "mere desire to prevent ordinary competition" is not a legitimate interest. *E. Distrib. Co. v. Flynn*, 567 P.2d 1371, 1376 (Kan. 1977). The legitimate interests Kansas courts have recognized are:

- Customer contacts,[1]
- Trade Secrets,[2]
- Other confidential business information,[3]
- Goodwill and reputation,[4]
- Referral sources,[5] and
- Loss of business.[6]

Kansas courts have also said that they will recognize an employee's specialized training as a legitimate interest. But they view this interest critically because a person leaving employment generally may take "all the skill . . . all the knowledge . . . and all the information" that the employee receives, "so long as nothing is taken that is the property of the employer." *Garst v. Scott*, 220 P. 277, 278 (Kan. 1923). In *Weber v. Tillman*, for example, the Kansas Supreme Court acknowledged with approval that other jurisdictions recognize "special training of employees" as legitimate interests. 913 P.2d 84, 91 (Kan. 1996). Accordingly, to support a legitimate specialized-training interest, a franchisor must point to facts that show the franchisee's training was unique to the franchise or unique to the franchisee. For example, when a specialized-training interest was tested in *Allen, Gibbs & Houlik, L.C. v. Ristow*, the Kansas Court of Appeals ruled that seven years of an employee's "ordinary" and "non-exclusive" training was not a legitimate interest. 94 P.3d 724, 728 (Kan. Ct. App. 2004).

Proof of a business's legitimate interest will depend on factors specific to the interest and the facts of each case. In *E. Distrib. Co. v. Flynn*, for example, the court used four factors to determine whether a liquor distributor had a legitimate customer-contacts interest. 567 P.2d 1371, 1374 (Kan. 1977). They were:

(1) the frequency of the employee's contacts with customers;
(2) whether the employee was the only person who had established such relationships with the former employer's customers;
(3) the location of the interaction between the customers and the employee; and
(4) the nature of the functions performed by the employee.

Id. at 1377. In contrast, to prove a legitimate trade-secret interest, a franchisor must show facts that the franchisee has information meeting the statutory definition of a

KS

1. *E.g.*, *E. Distrib. Co. v. Flynn*, 567 P.2d 1371, 1377 (Kan. 1977); *Caring Hearts Pers. Home Servs., Inc. v. Hobley*, 130 P.3d 1215 (Kan. Ct. App. 2006); *Francis v. Schlotfeldt*, 704 P.2d 381 (Kan. Ct. App. 1985); *SizeWise Rentals, Inc. v. Mediq/PRN Life Support Servs., Inc.*, 87 F. Supp. 2d 1194 (D. Kan. 2000); *Fireworks Spectacular, Inc. v. Premier Pyrotechnics, Inc.*, 86 F. Supp. 2d 1102 (D. Kan. 2000).

2. *E.g.*, *Puritan-Bennett Corp. v. Richter*, 679 P.2d 206 (Kan. 1984); Koch Eng'g Co. v. Faulconer, 610 P.2d 1094, 1104–05 (Kan. 1980); *Mills v. Ressler*, 125 P. 58 (Kan. 1912); *Universal Engraving v. Duarte*, 519 F. Supp. 2d 1140 (D. Kan. 2007); *Heatron v. Shackleford*, 898 F. Supp. 1491, 1500 (D. Kan. 1995).

3. *E.g.*, *Weber v. Tillman*, 913 P.2d 84 (Kan. 1996); *E. Distrib. Co. v. Flynn*, 567 P.2d 1371 (Kan. 1977); *Heatron, Inc. v. Shackleford*, 898 F. Supp. 1491, 1500 (D. Kan. 2000).

4. *E.g.*, *Weber v. Tillman*, 913 P.2d 84 (Kan. 1996); *E. Distrib. Co. v. Flynn*, 567 P.2d 1371 (Kan. 1977).

5. *E.g.*, *Idbeis v. Wichita Surgical Specialists, P.A.*, 279 Kan. 755, 767, 112 P.3d 81, 89 (2005); *Wichita Clinic, P.A. v. Louis*, 185 P.3d 946 (Kan. Ct. App. 2008).

6. *E.g.*, *Varney Bus. Servs., Inc. v. Pottroff*, 59 P.3d 1003 (Kan. 2002).

trade secret under Kansas law. *E.g.*, *Universal Engraving, Inc. v. Duarte*, 519 F. Supp. 2d 1140, 1151 (D. Kan. 2007). That includes information that:

> (i) derives independent economic value, actual or potential, from not being generally known to, and not readily ascertainable by proper means by, other persons who can obtain economic value from its disclosure or use, and
>
> (ii) is the subject of efforts that are reasonable under the circumstances to maintain its secrecy.

Id. (quoting K.S.A. § 60-3320).

Kansas courts have also discussed other legitimate interests that that may support enforcement of restrictive covenants, such as confidential business information (*e.g.*, *Heatron, Inc. v. Shackleford*, 898 F. Supp. 1491 (D. Kan. 1995)), goodwill and reputation (*e.g.*, *Weber v. Tillman*, 913 P.2d 84 (Kan. 1996)), referral sources (*e.g.*, *Wichita Clinic, P.A. v. Louis*, 185 P.3d 946 (Kan. Ct. App. 2008)), and loss of business, (*e.g.*, *Varney Bus. Servs., Inc. v. Pottroff*, 59 P.3d 1003 (Kan. 2002)). Proof necessary to support these interests will depend on the specific facts and circumstances of each case.

Finally, as with all contracts, a covenant against competition must be supported by consideration. *E.g.*, *Puritan-Bennett Corp. v. Richter*, 657 P.2d 589, 591 (Kan. 1983).

---

3. What time limitations have courts recognized as reasonable in the franchise context?

- **If no franchise cases have been decided, what time limitations have been recognized in other contexts?**
- **How have they been related to the interests protected?**

In the only franchise-specific case that addresses covenants against competition in Kansas, *H&R Block, Inc. v Lovelace*, the court did not rule on a covenant's five-year restriction. 493 P.2d 205 (Kan. 1972). It did, however, say that time restrictions must be reasonable under the facts and circumstances of each case, and the trial court in *H&R Block* ruled that the five-year duration was too long. *Id.* at 209–10.

As in *H&R Block*, Kansas courts in other contexts assess the duration of covenants against competition under the facts and circumstances of each case. In general, however, two- and three-year periods associated with professional-services contracts are reasonable. *See, e.g.*, *Weber v. Tillman*, 913 P.2d 84 (Kan. 1996) (enforcing a two-year time restriction in a physician-employment contract); *Wichita Clinic, P.A. v. Louis*, 39 Kan. App. 848, 185 P.3d 946 (2008) (reversing trial court's ruling that at three-year time restriction in a physician-employment contract was unreasonable).

Wichita Clinic typifies the Kansas approach to time restrictions. It reasons that time restrictions are one aspect of the overarching reasonability analysis. Thus, a time restriction's reasonability will also depend on the interest at stake, the burden on the restricted party, and the restriction's relation to the public welfare. 185 P.3d at 952–56. In *Wichita Clinic*, a physician agreed to a three-year restriction with a former employer. In part, because the three-year period was necessary to recruit and train a new physician, the court upheld the restriction. *Id.* Depending on the parties' requirements, Kansas courts have also upheld five- and ten-year restrictions. *See Varney Bus. Servs., Inc. v. Pottroff*, 59 P.3d 1003 (Kan. 2002) (enforcing a provision requiring a departing accountant to compensate its former firm for services that the accountant provided to the firm's clients for five years after departure); *Foltz v. Struxness*, 215 P.2d 133 (Kan. 1950) (enforcing a ten-year restriction in a physician-employment contract but reducing its 100-mile territorial restriction to five miles). The ten-year restriction would undoubtedly not be held to be reasonable today in the physician employee context, where two-year restrictions seem to be the most common. Depending upon the facts and circumstances, five-year restrictions are common in the sale of business context. The reasonableness of a time restriction in a franchise context would likely depend on the size of the franchisor and the franchisee, the economic negotiating positions of the parties, the level of control of the franchisor over the franchisee, and other similar business-specific circumstances.

---

4. What geographic limitations have courts recognized as reasonable in the franchise context?

- **How have they been related to the interests protected?**
- **Have courts recognized the legitimacy of protecting other franchisees from competition?**

In the lone Kansas franchise case, *H&R Block, Inc. v. Lovelace*, the court held that a geographically unlimited covenant against competition was unreasonable and therefore unenforceable. 493 P.2d 205 (1972). Further, though Kansas courts have not assessed the interests of other franchisees, they do demand that a geographic restriction be tailored to protect to the interest at hand.

In *Eastern Distributing Co. v. Flynn*, for example, a covenant restricted a former salesperson from competing for one year after his employment ended within 50 miles of a distributor's sales territory. 567 P.2d 1371 (Kan. 1977). Though the court enforced the one-year term, it reduced the restricted area to counties where the terminated salesperson actually served. *Id.* at 1379. It reasoned that the 50-mile radius was not sufficiently tailored to the customer-contact interest that the employer sought to protect. *Id.* Similarly, in *Foltz v. Struxness*, the court reduced a 100-mile restriction in a physician-employment agreement to five miles. 215 P.2d 133 (Kan. 1950). It agreed with the trial court that a five-mile radius sufficed to protect the employer "in his practice of medicine and surgery." *Id.* at 137.

In contrast, where an employer's business covers a broader area, Kansas courts will uphold broader covenants against competition. Thus, in *Universal Engraving, Inc. v. Duarte*, a Kansas federal district court upheld a worldwide covenant against competition where the employee "perform[ed] his duties world-wide" and "was involved in . . . customer relations world-wide." 519 F. Supp. 2d 1140, 1153 (D. Kan. 2007). Similarly, in *Chem-Trol, Inc. v. Christensen*, the Kansas federal district court upheld a 250-mile covenant against competition. No. 09-2024-EFM, 2009 WL 331625, at *10 (D. Kan. Feb. 10, 2009). Though the court said a 250-mile restriction was "more unusual than that commonly used in Kansas," it reasoned that the employer had customers outside of the 250-mile radius and the employee often traveled more than 250 miles to service customers. *Id.*

5. What limitations on activities have courts recognized as reasonable in the franchise context?

Other than *H&R Block v. Lovelace*, Kansas courts have not addressed limitations on specific activities in the franchising context. 493 P.2d 205 (1972). Ordinarily, the covenant against competition will bar a person from competing against the employer or buyer for a set time in a geographic area. *E.g., Eastern Distributing Co. v. Flynn*, 567 P.2d 1371 (Kan. 1977). But Kansas courts will also analyze other limitations on activities as cases may arise. In *Varney Business Services, Inc. v. Pottroff*, for example, a group of accountants set up a five-year post-termination payment schedule for services that a departing accountant rendered to clients that it retained. 59 P.3d 1003, 1009 (Kan. 2002). Like time and territory restrictions, the court asked whether the covenant was reasonable and whether the covenant was against public policy. *Id.* at 1014–18. And in *Varney*, the court held that the covenant protected the firm's lost-revenue interest and that public policy favored "recognizing provisions that compensate individuals and entities for the loss of a client's business as valid." *Id.* It thus enforced the covenant. *Id.*

6. Does the state recognize a difference between in-term and post-term covenants?

There are currently no cases that discuss any differences between in-term and post-term covenants under Kansas law, although various contractual duties such as the duty of good faith and fair dealing likely provide some protection during the term of an agreement.

7. Has the state allowed enforcement of covenants against non-signatories (e.g., family members, newly formed corporations)?

In the sale-of-business context, yes. In the employer-employee or personal-services context, Kansas courts likely will not.

In *Safelite Glass Corp. v. Fuller*, the Kansas Court of Appeals answered a question of first impression whether a corporate successor could enforce a covenant it was assigned through an asset transfer. 807 P.2d 677 (Kan. Ct. App. 1991). The court held that "in the absence of express language which limits assignability, covenants not to compete which do not involve personal and confidential relations are assignable and may be enforced by a subsequent purchaser of a business as an incident of the business." *Id.* at 683. In reaching that conclusion, the court drew a distinction between the assignability of a covenant in the sale-of-business context and in the employment-contract context. *Id.* at 681. As *H&R Block* reasoned, Kansas courts interpret covenants against competition in employment contracts strictly against the employer. *Id.* In the sale-of-business context, however, Kansas courts interpret covenants against competition neutrally. *See id.* (citing *H&R Block, Inc. v. Lovelace*, 493 P.2d 205 (Kan. 1972)). In *Safelite*, the corporate successor was "essentially the same entity," and the predecessor entity "assigned all its rights" to the successor. *Id.*

at 682–83. Further, because the covenant protected the business's goodwill and the successor entity bargained for that goodwill, the court concluded it should be able to enforce the covenant. *Id.* at 683; *see also Equifax Servs., Inc. v. Hitz*, 905 F.2d 1355, 1361 (10th Cir. 1990) ("In the case of a merger . . . the surviving corporation automatically succeeds to the rights of the merged corporations to enforce employees' covenants not to compete.") (applying Kansas law).

On the other hand, where rights under a covenant are not clearly assigned or transferred, a covenant will not impose rights or obligations on a third party. In *V.C. Video, Inc. v. National Video, Inc.*, a third party purchased some, but not all, of a franchisor's franchisee agreements. 755 F. Supp. 962 (D. Kan. 1990). The result was the third party's existing franchisees had territorial conflicts with some of the seller's left-behind franchisees, which the seller promised to "use[] its best efforts to expeditiously discontinue." *Id.* at 967. When the seller's left-behind franchisees attempted to enforce the covenant in their franchise agreements against the third party, the court refused. *Id.* at 970. It reasoned that the third party did not purchase the seller's left-behind franchisees, and it thus had no responsibility to them. *Id.*

8. Will the state modify, "blue-pencil," or otherwise reduce a covenant found to be overbroad?

Yes. Though the court refused to modify an unreasonable covenant against competition in the franchise context of *H&R Block, Inc. v. Lovelace*, 493 P.2d 205 (1972), it has since said that *H&R Block* "does not stand for non-modification of contracts" and does not "dictate a decision" that a trial court may not modify a covenant against competition. *E. Distrib. Co. v. Flynn*, 567 P.2d 1371, 1379 (Kan. 1977). Rather, the court has said it will "sustain the legality of contracts in whole or in part . . . if reasonably possible to do so[.]" *Weber v. Tillman*, 913 P.2d 84, 96 (Kan. 1996). And "[a]lthough restrictive provisions in contracts . . . must be reasonable and not such as to contravene the public welfare, the paramount public policy is that freedom to contract is not to be interfered with lightly." *Id.*

Indeed, Kansas courts prefer modification of an overly broad covenant over holding a covenant unenforceable in full. *E.g.*, *Bruce D. Graham, M.D., P.A. v. Cirocco*, 69 P.3d 194 (Kan. Ct. App. 2003); *Am. Fidelity Assurance Corp. v. Leonard*, 81 F. Supp. 2d 1115 (D. Kan. 2000). Thus, Kansas courts will readily modify a covenant's time or territory restriction to bring them within the realm of reasonability. *E.g.*, *E. Distrib. Co. v. Flynn*, 567 P.2d 1371 (1977) (affirming trial court's modification of a blanket 50-mile radius to specific counties where a distributor sold products to customers); *Foltz v. Struxness*, 168 Kan. 714, 215 P.2d 133 (1950) (approving trial court's modification of a 100-mile radius to a 5-mile radius from the city in which a physician practiced). In some circumstances, Kansas courts will even expand a covenant's reach. *See Puritan-Bennett Corp. v. Richter*, 679 P.2d 206, 211–12 (Kan. 1984).

Kansas courts will also modify the activity aspect of a covenant. For example, in *Puritan Bennett Corp. v. Richter*, the trial court enjoined a former employee from disclosing an exceptionally broad category of information that extended well beyond the former employer's trade secrets and confidential information. 679 P.2d 206. Because the injunction "virtually bar[red]" the former employee from earning a living, the court limited the injunction to the former employer's "research, development, production or sales techniques." *Id.* at 211.

Courts may also selectively enforce covenants on public-policy grounds. In *Bruce D. Graham, M.D., P.A. v. Cirocco*, for example, the covenant barred a colorectal surgeon from (1) soliciting business for two years within 150 miles of his former office and (2) opening an office for two years within 25 miles of his former office. 69 P.3d 194, 196 (Kan. Ct. App. 2003). The court held the 150-mile solicitation restriction valid but refused to enforce the 25-mile practice restriction. *Id.* at 199–200. It reasoned that the surgeon's "medically necessary subspecialty" was in short supply and the public's interest in obtaining care outweighed the parties' interest in enforcement. *Id.*

9. When does a non-compete period begin to run? Will courts equitably extend the term?

Most covenants against competition in Kansas include a provision that states when the covenant will begin to run—for example, at the termination of the employer-employee relationship or at the closing of a sale. *E.g.*, *Bruce D. Graham, M.D., P.A. v. Cirocco*, 69 P.3d 194, 196 (Kan. Ct. App. 2003) (showing the covenant began running "after leaving . . . employment"). Kansas courts have not addressed a case where the period's beginning is ambiguous or unstated.

Kansas courts will also equitably extend the term of a covenant. In *Puritan-Bennett Corp. v. Richter*, the court equitably extended the term of a covenant where protracted litigation, including multiple appeals, precluded enforcement of the covenant within the covenant's period. 679 P.2d 206, 212 (Kan. Ct. App. 1984). In a similar vein, the court in *Bruce D. Graham, M.D.* held the parties' litigation that outlived the covenant's two-year time period was not moot because it was "capable of repetition, yet evading review." 69 P.3d at 196.

10. Are there additional nuances or peculiarities of the state's treatment of covenants in the franchising context?

When a contract includes a covenant against competition and a valid liquidated-damages clause, Kansas courts will generally allow the defendant to avoid facing an injunction by paying the contract's liquidated damages. In *Idbeis v. Wichita Surgical Specialists, P.A.*, for example, the court said "[t]he remedy for breach of the parties' contract is either an injunction to enforce the contract or a computation of monetary damages." 112 P.3d 81, 92 (Kan. Ct. App. 2005). And because only one of the defendant-surgeons in *Idbeis* had a contract with a liquidated-damages provision, "only he [was] entitled to pay liquidated damages in lieu of ceasing the practice of medicine as provided in his restrictive covenant." *Id.* at 94. Moreover, some trial judges have refused to issue an injunction when the parties have a liquidated-damages provision.

Kentucky

*by Ryan M. Gallagher**

1. Has the state addressed covenants against competition in the context of franchising?

- **Does the state have a franchising statute or regulations that address covenants against competition?**
- **Does the state have a covenants statute of general applicability that would encompass franchise covenants?**
- **Have the courts addressed covenants in the context of franchising either under a statute or under the state's common law?**

Kentucky does not have regulations or a statute that addresses covenants against competition, either in the franchise context or of general applicability.

Kentucky's highest court recognized the validity of a covenant against competition in a franchise agreement and treated it as one restricting employment. *Owen v. Staib*, 307 S.W.2d 758 (Ky. 1957). The franchise contract was terminated in a manner that did not implicate the covenant against competition, so the franchisor was not entitled to damages or enforcement of the five-year non-compete. The appellate court, without further explanation, nevertheless affirmed the trial court's decision, which enjoined the franchisee from soliciting certain business. *Id.* at 760; *see also AmeriSpec, Inc. v. Vornholt, Inc.*, 2008 U.S. Dist. LEXIS 35062 (W.D. Ky. Apr. 29, 2008) (granting a motion for preliminary injunction based on a non-compete clause contained in a franchise agreement, without further analysis, finding that the non-compete was enforceable against franchisee and successor); and *Papa John's Int'l, Inc. v. Pizza Magia Int'l, LLC*, 2001 WL 1789379, at *3–4 (W.D. Ky. May 10, 2001) (describing, in the context of analyzing a franchise agreement non-compete provision, that Kentucky courts give deference to the parties' freedom to contract).

Generally, the law in Kentucky "clearly establishes that covenants not to complete are valid and enforceable." *Kegel v. Tillotson*, 297 S.W.3d 908, 911 (Ky. Ct. App. 2009) (citing *Ceresia v. Mitchell*, 242 S.W.2d 359, 364 (Ky. 1951)); *see also Lareau v. O'Nan*, 355 S.W.2d 679, 681 (Ky. Ct. App. 1962) (acknowledging that Kentucky courts will enforce restrictive covenants unless "very serious inequities would

*Ryan Gallagher is an associate with the law firm of Frost Brown Todd LLC in Louisville, Kentucky.

result"); *Gardner Denver Drum* LLC *v. Goodier*, 2006 WL 1005161, at *4 (W.D. Ky. Apr. 14, 2006) ("Our courts have acknowledged that covenants not to compete play a critical role in business and are favored as long as they are reasonable in geographic scope and duration"); *Advanced Solutions, Inc v. Chamberlin*, 2007 WL 4215654, at *4 (W.D. Ky. 2007) ("Kentucky law has no problem with non-compete agreements per se and in fact sees them as a valuable business tool").

In the employment and sale-of-business contexts, Kentucky courts generally will uphold a non-compete restrictive covenant if valid as a matter of contract interpretation and reasonable. *Louisville Cycle & Supply Company, Inc. v. Baach*, 535 S.W.2d 230 (Ky. 1976); *Ceresia v. Mitchell*, 242 S.W.2d 359 (Ky. 1951); *but see Papa John's Int'l, Inc. v. Rezko*, 2006 WL 1697134, at *3 (N.D. Ill. June 14, 2006) (applying Kentucky law) (noting that Kentucky courts have not yet analyzed and construed non-compete covenants in franchise agreements). Whether a particular non-compete clause is reasonable is highly fact specific. Kentucky courts consider the subject, the nature of the business, the situation of the parties, circumstances of the particular case, and whether the restriction affords fair protection only to the interests of the covenantee and is not so large as to interfere with the public interests or impose undue hardship on the party restricted. *Kegel v. Tillotson*, 297 S.W.3d 908 (Ky. Ct. App. 2009).

---

2. Have the courts articulated the "legitimate interests" of the franchisor that will support enforcement of a covenant against competition contained in a franchise agreement?

- **If so, what are they (e.g., protection of goodwill, protection of confidential information), and in what contexts did the issue arise?**
- **If not, what interests have been recognized in other contexts (e.g., employment agreements, the sale of business context)?**

Kentucky courts have not articulated the legitimate interests of a franchisor that will support a covenant against competition in a franchise agreement. With that being said, Kentucky courts have recognized a number of interests that support upholding restrictive covenants. "To determine reasonableness and consistency with public policy, Kentucky courts consider the scope of a company's business and whether the restrictive covenant is tailored to the company's interests in protecting its information and customer base." *Material Handling Sys., Inc. v. Figueroa Cabrera*, 2021 WL 5236875, at *12 (W.D. Ky. Nov. 10, 2021) (citing *Crowell v. Woodruff*, 245 S.W.2d 447, 449 (Ky. 1951)).

In the context of an employment agreement, Kentucky courts have generally balanced "any substantial rights peculiar to [an employer's] business" against the employee's hardship stemming from enforcement of the non-compete. *Calhoun v. Everman*, 242 S.W.2d 100, 103 (Ky. 1951); *see also Stiles v. Reda*, 228 S.W.2d 445, 456 (Ky. 1950) ("[T]he test of reasonableness is whether the restraint, considering the particular situation and circumstances, is such only as to afford fair protection to the legitimate interests of the [employer] and not so extensive as to interfere with the interests of the public."). *Creative Educational Concepts, Inc. v. Hadzic*, 2017 WL 2573717 (E.D. Ky. June 14, 2017); *but see Borg–Warner Protective Services, Corp. v. Guardsmark, Inc.*, 946 F. Supp. 495, 501 (E.D. Ky. 1996) (distinguishing *Calhoun* by noting that "the more modern cases, including those in Kentucky, place more emphasis on the employer's investment in the employee and have evolved an approach balancing the importance of that factor against the hardship to the employee and the public interest").

Kentucky courts have recognized the legitimate interest of an employer to be protected against unfair competition where the employee obtained knowledge of confidential information or the employer's customers during his or her employment that might be used against the employer. *Thomas W. Briggs Co. v. Mason*, 289 S.W. 295 (Ky. 1926); *see also Gardner Denver Drum LLC v. Goodier*, 2006 WL 1005161, at *9 (W.D. Ky. Apr. 14, 2006). Kentucky courts also recognize the value of the time and money spent to generate goodwill among its customers and the particular vulnerability to solicitation by former employees. *Hammons v. Big Sandy Claims Service, Inc.*, 567 S.W.2d 313 (Ky. Ct. App. 1978). The Kentucky courts also recognize the legitimate interests of employers to protect themselves from unfair competition in a competitive business when they spent considerable time, effort, and money to train their employees. *Davey Tree Expert Co. v. Ackelbein*, 25 S.W.2d 62 (Ky. 1930); *Central Adjustment Bureau, Inc. v. Ingram Associates, Inc.*, 622 S.W.2d 681 (Ky. Ct. App. 1981) (finding that non-competition clauses can be specialized businesses' only protection against employees resigning with the businesses' clients and know-how).

In the sale of a business, Kentucky courts recognize the legitimate interest of a buyer's protection of the value of the goodwill he purchased with the business. *Ceresia v. Mitchell*, 242 S.W.2d 359 (Ky. 1951); *Hodges v. Todd*, 698 S.W.2d 317 (Ky. Ct. App. 1985). Additionally, a buyer has an interest in protecting against the seller's competition that would decrease the value of the business purchased. *Durham v. Lewis*, 21 S.W.2d 1004 (Ky. 1929).

3. What time limitations have courts recognized as reasonable in the franchise context?

- **If no franchise cases have been decided, what time limitations have been recognized in other contexts?**
- **How have they been related to the interests protected?**

Kentucky courts have not decided the extent of reasonable time limitations in the franchise context. Without analyzing the reasonableness of a time limitation and without further explanation, Kentucky's highest court affirmed the trial court's decision to permanently enjoin a franchisee from seeking patients that the franchisee knew had been patients of the franchisor. *Owen v. Staib*, 307 S.W.2d 758 (Ky. 1957).

In general, reasonableness is determined by looking at the character of service to be performed, the relationship of the employee, and whether the restraint imposed on the employee is more comprehensive than is necessary to afford fair protection to the legitimate interests of the employer. *Crowell v. Woodruff*, 245 S.W.2d 447 (Ky. Ct. App. 1978).

In the context of employment agreements, considering the nature of the contract and business, the Kentucky courts have upheld a covenant against competition for six years for a professional services contract in *Bradford v. Billington*, 299 S.W.2d 601 (Ky. 1957); five years in *Lareau v. O'Nan*, 355 S.W.2d 679 (Ky. 1962); three years in *Gardner Denver Drum LLC v. Goodier*, 2006 WL 1005161 (W.D. Ky. Apr. 14, 2006); two years in *Thomas W. Briggs Co. v. Mason*, 289 S.W. 295 (Ky. 1926), *Central Adjustment Bureau, Inc. v. Ingram Associates, Inc.*, 622 S.W.2d 681 (Ky. Ct. App. 1981), and *Material Handling Sys., Inc. v. Figueroa Cabrera*, 2021 WL 5236875 (W.D. Ky. Nov. 10, 2021); and one year in *Hall v. Williard & Woolsey, P.S.C.*, 471 S.W.2d 316 (Ky. 1971). Kentucky courts have found that indefinite restrictions, however, are unreasonable if the protected territory is unreasonable. *Mtn. Comprehensive Health Corp. v. Gibson*, 2015 WL 1194508 (Ky. Ct. App. Mar. 13, 2015) (rejecting a non-compete that contained an indefinite duration with a territory of 50 miles from current and future clinics); *see also Hammons v. Big Sandy Claims Serv., Inc.*, 567 S.W.2d 313, 315 (Ky. Ct. App. 1978) (quoting *Calhoun v. Everman*, 242 S.W.2d 100 (Ky. 1951)) ("Generally contracts in restraint of trade are not enforceable where they are unlimited as to both time and space, or as to where they are unlimited as to space but limited as to time, but where such contracts are unlimited as to time but are confined to a reasonable territory they are enforceable").

In connection with the sale of a business, Kentucky courts have upheld restrictive covenants not to compete for a period as long as ten years in *Durham v. Lewis*, 21 S.W.2d 1004 (Ky. 1929) and *Porter v. Hospital Corporation of America*, 696 S.W.2d 793 (Ky. Ct. App. 1985) and for five years in *Martin v. Ratliff Furniture Co.*, 264 S.W.2d 273 (Ky. 1954). In some older cases, Kentucky courts upheld covenants in which the seller promised not to compete with the buyer in part due to the buyer's promise to continue the purchased business. *Nickell v. Johnson*, 172 S.W. 938 (Ky. 1915); *F.T. Gunther Grocery Co. v. Koll*, 155 S.W. 1145 (Ky. 1913).

---

4. What geographic limitations have courts recognized as reasonable in the franchise context?

- **How have they been related to the interests protected?**
- **Have courts recognized the legitimacy of protecting other franchisees from competition?**

Kentucky courts have not decided the extent of reasonable geographic limitations in the franchise context. In general, the reasonableness of a geographic limitation is determined by considering the subject, nature of the business, situation of the parties, and circumstances of the particular case. *Hammons v. Big Sandy Claims Service, Inc.*, 567 S.W.2d 313 (Ky. Ct. App. 1978).

In the context of an employment contract, the territorial limit is reasonable if it is confined to the territory in which the employer keeps his or her market or carries on his or her business. *Thomas W. Briggs Co. v. Mason*, 289 S.W. 295 (Ky. 1926) (upholding restraint for several cities and states). Kentucky courts have also upheld restraints in the employment context that apply to the entire United States. *Central Adjustment Bureau, Inc. v. Ingram Assocs., Inc.*, 622 S.W.2d 681 (Ky. Ct. App. 1981); *see also Hammons v. Big Sandy Claims Service, Inc.*, 567 S.W.2d 313 (Ky. Ct. App. 1978) (200 miles); *Hall v. Williard & Woolsey, P.S.C.*, 471 S.W.2d 316 (Ky. 1971) (50 miles); *Louisville Cycle & Supply Co., Inc. v. Baach*, 535 S.W.2d 230 (Ky. 1976) (the employee's former sales territory); *Higdon Food Service, Inc. v. Walker & Kesterson Meat Co.*, 641 S.W.2d 751 (Ky. 1982) (the regular route and customers of the employer). The potential expansion of the territory may also factor into its reasonableness. *See Mtn.*

Comprehensive Health Corp. v. Gibson, 2015 WL 1194508 (Ky. Ct. App. Mar. 13, 2015) (rejecting a non-compete with a territory of 50 miles from current and future clinics; however, the court revised the territory).

In connection with the sale of a business, Kentucky courts recognize that covenants against competition may be regarded as necessary to protect the buyer in the enjoyment of the legitimate fruits of his or her purchase and to protect him or her from the unjust use of those fruits by the seller. *Durham v. Lewis*, 21 S.W.2d 1004 (Ky. 1929) (upholding restraint covering four counties). A non-compete has also been upheld in a business sale context for one county in *Martin v. Ratliff Furniture Co.*, 264 S.W.2d 273 (Ky. 1954) and a city and county in *Ceresia v. Mitchell*, 242 S.W.2d 359 (Ky. 1951).

5. What limitations on activities have courts recognized as reasonable in the franchise context?

The Kentucky courts have not discussed the reasonableness of specific limitations on activities in the franchise context. Although deciding that a covenant against competition in the franchise agreement was not enforceable based on the contract's language and without analysis, the Kentucky court nevertheless affirmed a limited form of relief that enjoined the franchisee from seeking patients that the franchisee knew had been patients of the franchisor. *Owen v. Staib*, 307 S.W.2d 758 (Ky. 1957).

In the context of the sale of a business, Kentucky courts will seek to enforce the intentions of the parties at the time of the sale with regard to a covenant not to compete. *Hodges v. Todd*, 698 S.W.2d 317 (Ky. Ct. App. 1985). However, Kentucky has held that a restraint that prohibits the seller from engaging in any kind of business, which extended to his children, was too broad, and thus enjoined the seller only from engaging in competition with the business of the buyers. *Ceresia v. Mitchell*, 242 S.W.2d 359 (Ky. 1951). Typically, a reasonable restriction prohibits the seller from engaging in the same business involved in the sale. *Martin v. Ratliff Furniture Co.*, 264 S.W.2d 273 (Ky. 1954) (seller enjoined from engaging in the furniture business); *Durham v. Lewis*, 21 S.W.2d 1004 (Ky. 1929) (seller prohibited from engaging in the poultry or egg business); *Gropp v. Perkins*, 146 S.W. 389 (Ky. 1912) (seller restrained from engaging in the shoe business); *Hodges v. Todd*, 698 S.W.2d 317 (Ky. Ct. App. 1985) (seller could not build car transport beds or transport trailers).

In the employment context, the employer can limit the dissemination of information concerning its business methods and trade secrets, and thus the restriction may be as broad as the employment or business. *Thomas W. Briggs Co. v. Mason*, 289 S.W. 295 (Ky. 1926). Further, an employer can prohibit a former employee from being employed by, or owning a proprietary interest in, a competing business entity; from divulging or making use of information about the employer's business; and from contacting clients who had been customers of the company while an employee. *Central Adjustment Bureau, Inc. v. Ingram Associates, Inc.*, 622 S.W.2d 681 (Ky. Ct. App. 1981).

Kentucky courts routinely uphold a restriction prohibiting a former employee from engaging in the specific business of his or her former employer. *See, e.g., Davey Tree Expert Co. v. Ackelbein*, 25 S.W.2d 62 (Ky. 1930) (tree surgery); *Kegel v. Tillotson*, 297 S.W.3d 908 (Ky. Ct. App. 2009) (marketing or selling promotional or advertising merchandise); *Daniel Boone Clinic v. Dahhan*, 734 S.W.2d 488 (Ky. Ct. App. 1987) (practicing medicine); *White v. Sullivan*, 667 S.W.2d 385 (Ky. Ct. App. 1983) (public accounting); *Hammons v. Big Sandy Claims Service, Inc.*, 567 S.W.2d 313 (Ky. Ct. App. 1978) (claims service). Other decisions uphold a restriction against engaging in any business that generally competes with the former employer. *See, e.g., Mgmt. Registry, Inc. v. Calvetti*, 2018 WL 1660087 (W.D. Ky. Apr. 5, 2018) (any competition with former employer); *Gardner Denver Drum LLC v. Goodier*, 2006 WL 1005161 (W.D. Ky. Apr. 14, 2006) (any competing business); *Higdon Food Service, Inc. v. Walker & Kesterson Meat Co.*, 641 S.W.2d 751 (Ky. 1982) (may not open a business that would be a competitor); *Louisville Cycle & Supply Co., Inc. v. Baach*, 535 S.W.2d 230 (Ky. 1976) (no competing business); *Hall v. Williard & Woolsey, P.S.C.*, 471 S.W.2d 316 (Ky. 1971) (no competition with employer).

6. Does the state recognize a difference between in-term and post-term covenants?

There are no reported decisions on the difference between in-term and post-term covenants under Kentucky law.

7. Has the state allowed enforcement of covenants against non-signatories (e.g., family members, newly formed corporations)?

Kentucky courts have enforced covenants against competition against non-signatories, such as family members and newly formed corporations. In the franchise context, the Kentucky federal court enforced the non-compete clause against the franchisee's daughter, who had taken over the business and was competing against the franchisor. *AmeriSpec, Inc. v. Vornholt, Inc.*, 2008 U.S. Dist. LEXIS 35062 (W.D. Ky. Apr. 29, 2008). Additionally, a Kentucky federal court, applying Missouri law, enforced the non-compete provision against a non-signatory corporation and its principal on the theory that they were successors to the business of the franchisee. *H&R Block Tax Services v. Sheets*, 2006 U.S. Dist. LEXIS 8437 (E.D. Ky. Mar. 3, 2006).

In other contexts, the restrictive covenant in an employment contract was enforceable against a nonparty who acted as an agent of or was in concert with the restricted employee. *White v. Sullivan*, 667 S.W.2d 385 (Ky. Ct. App. 1983). In the context of the sale of a business, the Kentucky court enforced a restrictive covenant against a newly formed corporation that the seller had organized and in which he was a stockholder, president, and general manager. *Martin v. Ratliff Furniture Co.*, 264 S.W.2d 273 (Ky. 1954).

8. Will the state modify, "blue-pencil," or otherwise reduce a covenant found to be overbroad?

Kentucky courts have adopted the "blue-pencil" rule and will reform or amend restrictions in a non-compete clause if the initial restrictions are overly broad or burdensome. *Kegel v. Tillotson*, 297 S.W.3d 908 (Ky. Ct. App. 2009). In *Kegel*, the appellate court remanded the case to the lower court to determine the appropriate action to take under the "blue-pencil" rule.

In the sale-of-business context, Kentucky courts will enforce a non-competition covenant if the plaintiff establishes a reasonable geographical limitation based on the intention of the parties and equitable considerations. *Hodges v. Todd*, 698 S.W.2d 317 (Ky. Ct. App. 1985). Additionally, in *Ceresia v. Mitchell*, 242 S.W.2d 359 (Ky. 1951), the court affirmed the reformation of a restriction purporting to bar the seller and his children from forever engaging in any business activities in Kentucky to a restriction barring the seller from engaging in the fruit and vegetable business in the county in which the business was located for the period of the 10-year lease. *Id.* at 362.

In an employment agreement, the Kentucky appellate court upheld the lower court's modification of the geographical restriction in a covenant against competition from the area within a radius of 200 miles of any territory being serviced by the employer at the time of the employee's termination to the area within a radius of 200 miles from the employer's office where the employee had worked. *Hammons v. Big Sandy Claims Service, Inc.*, 567 S.W.2d 313, 315 (Ky. Ct. App. 1978). Further, the Kentucky appellate court remanded a case to the trial court, requiring the trial court to apply the "blue-pencil" rule to an indefinite non-compete covenant with a territory of 50 miles from each of the employer's current and future clinic. *Mtn. Comprehensive Health Corp. v. Gibson*, 2015 WL 1194508 (Ky. Ct. App. Mar. 13, 2015). In *Mountain Comprehensive Health*, the court of appeals "[held that] the trial court could have amended the restrictive covenant by removing the overly broad restriction" from a 50-mile radius of any clinic to a less broad restrictive area from the Whitesburg clinic where Gibson had worked. *Id* at *5.

9. When does a non-compete period begin to run? Will courts equitably extend the term?

Kentucky courts have not specifically addressed when a non-compete period will begin or whether they will equitably extend the term. In *Air Relief, Inc. v. Centrifugal Technologies, Inc.*, 2008 WL 4755098 (Ky. Ct. App. Oct. 31, 2008), the Kentucky appellate court found that the appeal was moot based on the expiration of the non-compete period, which had started at the termination of employment. There was no argument regarding an equitable extension or tolling of the agreement. The court, however, noted that injunctive relief is the usual means of addressing a covenant not to compete and would provide a basis for resolution before the non-compete expired.

Further, in *Choate v. Koorsen Protective Servs., Inc.*, 929 S.W.2d 184 (Ky. 1996), the Kentucky Supreme Court dismissed an appeal regarding a temporary restraining order as moot, finding that, by the time the action reached the Kentucky Supreme Court, the defendant was beyond the 12-month non-compete term. The Kentucky court dismissed the appeal, finding that "[a]ny decision by this Court would be meaningless." *Id.*

10. Are there additional nuances or peculiarities of the state's treatment of covenants in the franchising context?

Although not in the franchise context, several Kentucky cases have found that a non-compete covenant was assignable to a successor corporation in the sale of a business. *Gropp v. Perkins*, 148 Ky. 183, 146 S.W. 389 (Ky. 1912); *Kegel v. Tillotson*, 297

S.W.3d 908 (Ky. Ct. App. 2009). Additionally, the covenant in an employment agreement has been upheld as assignable. *Gardner Denver Drum LLC v. Goodier*, 2006 WL 1005161 (W.D. Ky. Apr. 14, 2006); *see also Managed Health Care Assocs., Inc. v. Kethan*, 209 F.3d 923, 928–29 (6th Cir. 2000) (discussing *Choate v. Koorsen Protective Servs., Inc.*, 929 S.W.2d 184 (Ky. 1996) and the assignability of non-compete agreements in Kentucky, finding that the Kentucky Supreme Court would find that non-compete clauses are assignable).

In the franchise context, a Kentucky federal court found that a franchise agreement provision that prohibits the franchisee from challenging the reasonableness of the scope and duration of the non-compete and non-disclosure provisions was not enforceable. *Papa John's Int'l, Inc. v. Pizza Magia Int'l, LLC*, 2001 WL 1789379, at *3–4 (W.D. Ky. May 10, 2001). Rather, whether a covenant is a reasonable restraint of trade is a decision entrusted to the courts and not to the litigants.

Kentucky courts will treat non-solicitation provisions as "inherently more reasonable" than general non-competition provisions, thereby providing greater deference to non-solicitation provisions. *ISCO Inds. Inc. v. Shugart*, 2014 WL 2218116, at * 3 (W.D. Ky. May 28, 2014) (citing *Snider Bolt & Screw, Inc. v. Quality Screw & Nut*, 2009 WL 1657549 (W.D. Ky. June 12, 2009) and *Central Adjustment Bureau, Inc. v. Ingram Associates, Inc.*, 622 S.W.2d 681, 683 (Ky. Ct. App. 1981)).

Additionally, within the context of a franchise agreement, the courts of Kentucky have enforced a liquidated damage provision when one party has breached the covenant against competition. *American Dairy Queen Corporation v. Fortune Street Research & Writing, Inc.*, 753 F. Supp. 2d 675 (W.D. Ky. 2010). Liquidated damages have also been enforced in a non-franchise context. *Gropp v. Perkins*, 148 Ky. 183, 146 S.W. 389 (1912); *Daniel Boone Clinic v. Dahhan*, 734 S.W.2d 488 (Ky. Ct. App. 1987).

Louisiana

*by Amy S. Malish**

1. Has the state addressed covenants against competition in the context of franchising?

- **Does the state have a franchising statute or regulations that address covenants against competition?**
- **Does the state have a covenants statute of general applicability that would encompass franchise covenants?**
- **Have the courts addressed covenants in the context of franchising either under a statute or under the state's common law?**

La. R.S. § 23:921, which was last amended in 2020, expressly governs non-competition covenants in the franchise setting, including those covenants between franchisor and franchisee, as well as those between franchisor and its employees, and the pertinent portion of the statute states:

> § 921. Restraint of business prohibited; restraint on forum prohibited; contracts against engaging in; provisions for:
>
> A. (1) Every contract or agreement, or provision thereof, by which anyone is restrained from exercising a lawful profession, trade, or business of any kind, expect as provided in this Section, shall be null and void. However, every contract or agreement, or provision thereof, which meets the exceptions as provided in this Section, shall be enforceable.
>
> ***
>
> F. (1) Parties to a franchise may agree that:
>
> (a) The franchisor shall refrain from selling, distributing, or granting additional franchises to sell or distribute, within defined geographic territory, those products or services that are subject of the franchise; and

*Amy S. Malish is partner in the law firm Pugh Accardo LLC in New Orleans, Louisiana. Ms. Malish would like to thank Catherine Napolitano for her assistance with preparing this chapter. This chapter incorporates work of the previous author, Joshua K. Trahan.

(b) The franchisee shall:
   (i) During the term of the franchise, refrain from competing with the franchisor or other franchisees of the franchisor or carrying on or engaging in any other business similar to that which is the subject of the franchise.
   (ii) For a period not to exceed two years following the severance of the franchise relationship, refrain from carrying on or engaging in any other business similar to that which is the subject of the franchise and from competing with or soliciting the customers of the franchisor or other franchisees of the franchisor.

(c) The employee if employed by a franchisor shall:
   (i) During the term of his employment by the franchisor, refrain from competing with his employer or any of the franchisees of his employer or carrying on or engaging in any other business similar to that which is the subject of the franchise.
   (ii) For a period not to exceed two years following severance of the employment relationship between the franchisor and the employee, refrain from carrying on or engaging in any other business similar to that which is the subject of the franchise between the franchisor and its franchisees and from competing with or soliciting the customers of his employer or the franchisees of his employer.

***

(4) As used in this Subsection:
   (a) "Franchise" means any continuing commercial relationship created by any arrangement or arrangements as defined in 16 CFR 436.1(h).
   (b) "Franchisee" means any person who participates in a franchise relationship as a franchisee, partner, shareholder with at least a ten percent interest in the franchisee, executive officer of the franchisee, or a person to whom an interest in a franchise is sold, as defined in 16 CFR 436.1(h), provided that no person shall be included in this definition unless he has signed an agreement expressly binding him to the provisions thereof.
   (c) "Franchisor" means any person who participates in a franchise relationship as a franchisor as defined in 16 CFR 436.1(k).

La. R.S. § 23:921(F). Section 23:921(F) modifies a statute that otherwise provides, with limited exceptions, that every agreement to restrain anyone exercising a lawful profession, trade, or business of any kind shall be null and void. The restriction on competition can be structured to apply to either the franchisor or the franchisee, subject to temporal and geographic limits.

In *Smoothie King Franchises, Inc. v. Southside Smoothie & Nutrition Center, Inc.*, 2012 WL1698365 (E.D. La. 5/15/12), the court applied La. R.S. § 23:921 in awarding damages and granting injunctive relief in favor of a franchisor as a result of a former franchisee's breach of its post-term obligations not to compete. While not expressly addressing franchise agreements, there have been several cases where the courts have addressed covenants in various business relationships from which analogies to the franchising context may be drawn. *See, e.g., Southeastrans, Inc. v. Morgan Landry, et al.*, 2021 WL 972098, at *6 (W.D. La. 3/15/21) (non-competition and non-solicitation of customers' covenants unenforceable for geographic limit of "State of Louisiana" was not strictly compliant with La. R.S. § 23:921); *S. E. Auto Dealers Rental Ass'n, Inc. v. EZ Rent To Own, Inc.*, 07-0599, p. 16 (La. App. 4th Cir. 2/27/08); 980 So. 2d 89, 101 (enforcing non-compete covenant between licensor-licensee).

---

2. Have the courts articulated the "legitimate interests" of the franchisor that will support enforcement of a covenant against competition contained in a franchise agreement?

- **If so, what are they (e.g., protection of goodwill, protection of confidential information), and in what contexts did the issue arise?**
- **If not, what interests have been recognized in other contexts (e.g., employment agreements, the sale of business context)?**

In Louisiana, the vast majority of caselaw related to non-compete agreements is based on the employer-employee relationship.

No case has suggested that a franchisor must establish a legitimate interest in order to enforce a covenant against competition. The only express requirements are those of La. R.S. § 23:921(F), which specifically include geographic and temporal limitations. However, when seeking to enforce a non-compete agreement in the franchise context, it may be advisable to explain to the court that, similar to other types of contractual agreements, franchisors have certain legitimate interests that support the enforcement of a non-compete agreement.

For example, caselaw analyzing the statute does recognize that substantial expenses incurred in the training of an employee and/or the advertising of a business are legitimate interests deserving of protection. *See, e.g., SWAT 24 Shreveport Bossier, Inc. v. Bond*, 00-1695 (La. 6/29/01); *Era Helicopters, LLC v. Amegin*, 15-753 (La. App. 3d Cir. 12/9/15); 181 So. 3d 241 (upheld contractual requirement compelling employee to repay cost of training if employment terminated earlier than two years).

In addition to those factors, Louisiana has also recognized that knowledge of trade secrets, financial information, and management techniques all constitute protectable interests. *See Dixie Parking Service, Inc. v. Hargrove*, 96-1929 (La. App. 4th Cir. 3/26/97); 691 So. 2d 1316. La. R.S. § 23:921(B) expressly recognizes, though not specifically in the context of a franchise agreement, the legitimacy of covenants prohibiting competition where the covenant is part of the sale of the goodwill of a business and complies with required temporal and geographic limits. *Cycle Sport, LLC v. Jones*, 2009 WL 3452874 (La. App. 1st Cir. 10/23/09).

3. What time limitations have courts recognized as reasonable in the franchise context?

- **If no franchise cases have been decided, what time limitations have been recognized in other contexts?**
- **How have they been related to the interests protected?**

La. R.S. § 23:921(F)(b)(ii) expressly limits a non-competition agreement in a franchise context to two years following severance of the franchise relationship. Due to Louisiana's long-standing public policy disfavoring agreements not to compete, any agreement restricting competition must strictly comply with the statute, and any ambiguous language in the contract will be construed against the party who drafted it. *SWAT 24 Shreveport Bossier, Inc. v. Bond*, 00-1695 (La. 6/29/01); 808 So. 2d 294; *LaFourche Speech & Language Service, Inc. v. Juckett*, 94-1809 (La. App. 1st Cir. 3/3/95); 652 So. 2d 679; *see also Dixie Parking Service, Inc. v. Hargrove*, 96-1929 (La. App. 4th Cir. 1997); 691 So. 2d 1316.

The strict-compliance requirement reflects Louisiana's strong public policy against non-competition agreements. *Cellular One, Inc. v. Boyd*, 94-1783 (La. App. 1st Cir. 3/3/95); 653 So. 2d 30. Contracts seeking to extend non-competition agreements beyond the two-year statutory limit are null and void. *Id.*; *Allied Bruce Terminix Companies, Inc. v. Ferrier*, 93-0561 (La. App. 1st Cir. 3/11/94); 634 So. 2d 44; *Smith v. Commercial Flooring Gulf Coast, L.L.C.*, 2019 WL 5073582 (La. App. 4th Cir. 10/9/19) (modified lower court's injunction enforcing a non-compete agreement so that the injunctive relief did not extend more than two years from the termination of employment).

4. What geographic limitations have courts recognized as reasonable in the franchise context?

- **How have they been related to the interests protected?**
- **Have courts recognized the legitimacy of protecting other franchisees from competition?**

With regard to franchises, La. R.S. § 23:921(F) states: "Parties to a franchise may agree that . . . the *franchisor* shall refrain from selling, distributing, or granting additional franchises to sell or distribute, *within defined geographic territory*[.]"

In interpreting La. R.S. § 23:921(C), the statutory exception that permits non-compete agreements within the context of employer-employee relationships, a majority of the courts in Louisiana, including the Louisiana Supreme Court, have held that the parish or parishes (counties), municipality or municipalities, or parts thereof must be specified in the non-compete agreement in order for it to be valid. *Yorsch v. Morel*, 16-662 (La. App. 5th Cir. 7/26/17); 223 So. 3d 1274 (geographical provision fails despite a defined term within the agreement listing certain parishes and cities); *Zanella's Wax Bar, LLC v. Trudy's Wax Bar, LLC*, 19-0043, p. 8 (La. App. 1st Cir. 11/7/19); 291 So. 3d 693, 698–99 (description of a non-competition territory radius did not sufficiently identify by listing parishes restricted); *Causin, L.L.C. v. Pace Safety Consultants, LLC*, 2019 WL 385206 (La. App. 4th Cir. 1/30/19) (enforcing listing of restricted parishes and refusing to strike provision permitting expansion on listed parishes that employer does business in at a later date). However, at least one circuit has held that a non-compete clause complied with the statutory geographic limitations even though parishes were not specifically named, based on the conclusion that the parishes were identifiable as a result of the employee's knowledge of the business. *Petroleum Helicopters, Inc. v. Untereker*, 98-1816 (La. App. 3d Cir. 1999); 731 So. 2d 965.

Several federal courts in Louisiana have also made an *Erie* guess on the issue of geographic specificity considering there is no binding precedent under Louisiana law controlling the issue. *Traffic Jam Events, LLC v. Lilley*, 2021 WL 1226409, at *3 (E.D. La. 4/1/21). Those courts have sided with the majority of Louisiana appellate courts, finding failure to specify *any* geographical limit is a fatal flaw and renders such a covenant unenforceable. *Id.*; *Total Safety U.S., Inc. v. Code Red Safety & Rental, LLC*, 423 F. Supp. 3d 309 (E.D. La. 2019); *Waguespack v. Medtronic, Inc.*, 185 F. Supp. 3d 916 (M.D. La. 2016) (failure to list the parishes by name was likely not sufficiently "identifiable"). While not expressly addressing franchisees, courts in Louisiana have recognized the legitimacy of protecting businesses from competitive disadvantage from another who exploits his or her knowledge, skills, or information concerning the business. *Petroleum Helicopters*, 731 So. 2d at 966–67.

Notably, La. R.S. § 23:921(F) does not expressly require that a covenant restricting a franchisee's ability to compete be subject to a geographic limit. Similarly, La. R.S. § 23:921(F), in contrast to other sections of the statute, does not require a geographic scope to a covenant not to compete for employees of the franchisor. Franchisees or the employees of franchisors seeking to avoid their contractual covenants may attempt to argue that a trial court should apply a geographical limit to the scope of the non-competition agreement. No court has addressed whether the requirement of a geographic restriction on a franchisee or an employee of the franchisor can be drawn from elsewhere in the statute. However, the absence of such geographic restrictions from La. R.S. § 23:921(F) indicates a legislative intent to forego such geographic limit.

5. What limitations on activities have courts recognized as reasonable in the franchise context?

La. R.S. § 23:921(F) permits non-competition agreements between parties prohibiting a franchisee "from competing with the franchisor or other franchisees of the franchisor or carrying on or engaging in any other business similar to that which is the subject of the franchise." There are no cases explicitly delineating those restrictions on activities that are reasonable from those that are not. However, it is clear that a court will examine the fairness of the non-competition agreement in a franchise context. *See, e.g., Sentilles v. Kwik-Copy Corp.*, 652 So. 2d 79 (La. App. 4th Cir. 1995) (analyzing whether the non-competition agreement is reciprocal between the parties, and whether other franchisees are subjected to the same restriction on competition).

6. Does the state recognize a difference between in-term and post-term covenants?

Yes. La. R.S. § 23:921(F) specifically recognizes a difference between in-term and post-term agreements. Part (1)(b)(i) describes certain restrictions during the term of the franchise, and part (1)(b)(ii) describes restrictions two years following the severance of the franchise relationship.

7. Has the state allowed enforcement of covenants against non-signatories (e.g., family members, newly formed corporations)?

La. R.S. § 23:921(F)(4)(b) specifically defines a "franchisee" as any person who participates in a franchise relationship as a franchisee, partner, shareholder with at least a 10 percent interest in the franchisee, executive officer of the franchisee, or a person to whom an interest in a franchise is sold, as defined in 16 Code of Federal Regulations 436.1(h). However, the statute further states under this subsection that no person will be considered a "franchisee" under the statute unless he or she is a signatory to the agreement.

No court has addressed the issue regarding enforcement of non-signatories in the franchise context. However, under "alto ego" and "community property" theories, Louisiana courts have allowed enforcement of covenants not to compete against non-signatories. *See, e.g., Lindsrom v. Saer*, 166 So. 636 (La. 1936) (applying alter ego theory to a shareholder who signed a covenant while a member of a corporation); *Muller v. Ramar, Inc.*, 427 So. 2d 625 (La. App. 1983) (wife held to be a "shareholder in community" where her husband sold shares of stock and agreed to a covenant against competition). Accordingly, there is some jurisprudential support for enforcement of covenants not to compete against non-signatories in the franchise context.

8. Will the state modify, "blue-pencil," or otherwise reduce a covenant found to be overbroad?

Louisiana appellate courts have split over whether courts may modify or "blue-pencil" non-compete agreements found to be overbroad if the contract is susceptible to modification based on its language.

Several courts have declined to reform a covenant, citing the statutory requirements for non-compete covenants. *Traffic Jam Events, LLC v. Lilley*, 2021 WL 1226409, at *3 (E.D. La. Apr. 1, 2021) (non-solicitation covenant in independent contractor agreement struck for failure to specify applicable municipality); *Total Safety U.S., Inc. v. Code Red Safety & Rental, LLC*, 423 F. Supp. 3d 309, 315 (E.D. La. 11/06/19) (non-solicitation covenant in employment contract unenforceable for failure to specify applicable municipality).

Yet, other courts have found a distinction between provisions that fail to specify required limits to those that are merely overbroad. In the case of an overbroad geographic limit and with the aid of a severability provision in the agreement, a court may reform the provision and "excise the offending language." *Brock Servs. v. Rogillio*, 936 F.3d 290, 297 (5th Cir. 8/27/19) (quoting *SWAT 24 Shreveport Bossier, Inc. v. Bond*, 00-1695, p. 23 (La. 6/29/01); 808 So. 2d 294, 309, *superseded by statute on other grounds*, La. R.S. § 23:921(D)); *Amcom of Louisiana, Inc. v. Battson*, 96-0319 (La. 3/29/96); 670 So. 2d 1223 (reversed appellate court and reinstated trial court's severance of overbroad geographical provision and leaving compliant provision that specifically identifies restricted municipalities and parish in compliance with § 23:921); *Environmental Safety & Health Consulting Services, Inc. v. Fowler*, 2020 WL 1173587, at *12, n.2 (La. App. 4th Cir. 3/11/20) (upheld despite overbroad geographic restriction identifying parishes where employer did *not* conduct business, suggesting such parishes may be severed from provision); *Heard, McElroy & Vestal, LLC v. Schmidt*, 52,783 (La. App. 2d Cir. 9/25/19); 280 So. 3d 806, 812 (trial court did not abuse its discretion by severing overly broad language in restriction).

9. When does a non-competition period begin to run? Will courts equitably extend the term?

La. R.S. § 23:921(F) contains both in-term and post-term covenants not to compete for franchisees and the employees of franchisor. With respect to post-term covenants not to compete for the franchisee, the statute specifically states that the two-year period begins to run following the severance of the franchise relationship. With respect to employees of the franchisor, the statute specifically states that the two-year period begins to run following the severance of the employment relationship. Accordingly, Louisiana courts have held that the term of the non-compete period is not tolled and contractual provisions to the contrary are null and void. *Delta Fuel Co., Inc. v. Abbott*, 2021 WL 259747, at *3 (W.D. La. 1/25/21) (distinguishing *Sabre Indus. Inc. v. McLaurin*, 2019 WL 3933798, at *4 (W.D. La. 8/19/19) and *Gaylord v. Broadcasting Co. v. Cosmos Broadcasting Co.*, 746 F. 2d 251, 253, n.1 (5th Cir. 1984); *Allied Bruce Terminix v. Ferrier*, 93-0561 (La. App. 1st Cir. 3/11/94); 634 So. 2d 44, 45; *Smith v. Commercial Flooring Gulf Coast, L.L.C.*, 2019 WL 5073582 (La. App. 4th Cir. 10/9/19).

10. Are there additional nuances or peculiarities of the state's treatment of covenants in the franchising context?

La. R.S. § 23:921(H) addresses the right to injunctive relief upon proof of the obligor's breach of a covenant not to compete. The right to injunctive relief is expressly provided for covenants in the franchise context. Importantly, the moving party is entitled to injunctive relief upon presenting evidence of a breach by the obligor without having to demonstrate injunctive relief's typical requirement of the likelihood of irreparable harm. The statute provides in relevant part:

> Any agreement covered by Subsection B, C, E, F, G, J, K, or L of this Section shall be considered an obligation not to do, and failure to perform may entitle the obligee to recover damages for the loss sustained and the profit of which he has been deprived. In addition, upon proof of the obligor's failure to perform, and without the necessity of proving irreparable injury, a court of competition jurisdiction shall order injunctive relief enforcing the terms of the agreement.

La. R.S. § 921(H); *H & E Equip. Servs., Inc. v. Kleinpeter*, 2021 WL 1609250 (La. App. 1st Cir. 4/26/21) (affirmed irreparable injury need not be proven to enjoin under a valid non-compete agreement); *Envtl. Safety & Health Consulting Servs., Inc. v. Fowler*, 19-0813, p. 7 (La. App. 4th Cir. 3/11/20); 302 So. 3d 528 (enjoined former employees from working with competitor considering enforceable non-compete agreements); cf. *J4H, L.L.C. v. Derouen*, 10-0319 (La. App. 1st Cir. 9/10/10); 49 So. 3d 10, 14 (denied injunctive relief for failure to demonstrate independent contractor was performing work "pursuant to a written contract" as completed by La. R.S. § 23:921); *Gaylord v. Broadcasting Co. v. Cosmos Broadcasting Co.*, 746 F. 2d 251, 253, n.1 (5th Cir. 1984) (period of restraint on competition expired such that injunctive relief is no longer appropriate).

Maine

*by Timothy J. Bryant**

1. Has the state addressed covenants against competition in the context of franchising?

- **Does the state have a franchising statute or regulations that address covenants against competition?**
- **Does the state have a covenants statute of general applicability that would encompass franchise covenants?**
- **Have the courts addressed covenants in the context of franchising either under a statute or under the state's common law?**

Maine has not enacted a statute or adopted a regulation that addresses covenants against competition in the franchise context, but it has enacted a statute of general applicability governing covenants against competition. *See* ME. REV. STAT. ANN. tit. 26, § 599. Under Maine law, employers are prohibited from entering into non-competition provisions with employees whose wages are at or below 400% of the federal poverty level. *Id.* at (3). Further, employers must disclose if a non-compete agreement is required "prior to an offer of employment." *Id.* at (4). Specifically, employers "shall notify an employee or prospective employee of a noncompete agreement requirement and provide a copy of the noncompete agreement not less than 3 business days before the employer requires the agreement to be signed." *Id.* Moreover, with the exception of non-compete agreements between employers and physicians, executed non-compete agreements "do not take effect until after one year of the employee's employment with the employer or a period of 6 months from the date the agreement was signed, whichever is later." *Id.* at (5).

Additionally, Maine has addressed restrictive employment agreements, or "no-poach" agreements in the franchise context. *See* ME. REV. STAT. ANN. tit. 26, § 599-B. The statute governs any agreement between two or more employers,

*Timothy J. Bryant is a partner in the law firm of Preti, Flaherty, Beliveau & Pachios, LLP, in Portland, Maine. This chapter incorporates work from the previous edition's chapter authored by Jeffrey M. White.

including through franchise agreements, that "prohibits or restricts one employer from soliciting or hiring another employer's employees or former employees." *Id.* at (1)(A)–(B). Employers are affirmatively prohibited from entering a restrictive employment agreement or enforcing or threatening to enforce a restrictive employment agreement. *Id.* at (2)(A)–(B). The Maine Department of Labor may impose a civil fine of no less than $5,000 per non-compliant agreement. *Id.* at (3).

The Maine Supreme Judicial Court has not yet had the opportunity to interpret section 599-A or section 599-B. The Maine Superior Court found that because section 599-B bars "enforcing or threatening to enforce" restrictive employment agreements, the law applied in equal force to agreements entered into before and after the enactment of the statute. *Page v. Boothbay Region Water Dist.*, 2021 Me. Super. LEXIS 1, at *9 (Mar. 8, 2021). The court further stated that section 599-B is "reasonably related" to a state interest and therefore is not a violation of substantive due process rights. *Id.* at *12–15.The U.S. District Court for the District of Maine also acknowledged the retroactive nature of statute, finding that "[i]t is reasonable to infer that the authors of the bill sought to prevent courts from entering judgments enforcing employment agreements that restrict such free movement, no matter when the underlying complaint was filed." *Woodlands Senior Living, LLC v. MAS Med. Staffing Corp.*, 502 F. Supp. 3d 564, 573 (D. Me. 2020), *opinion vacated on reconsideration*, 2021 WL 2043189 (D. Me. May 21, 2021).

Maine has enacted specific statutes that provide that it is unlawful to directly or indirectly impose unreasonable restrictions through non-competition covenants on motor vehicle dealers or franchisees and personal sports mobile dealers or franchisees. *See* Me. Rev. Stat. Ann. tit. 10, § 1177 (motor vehicle dealers or franchisees); Me. Rev. Stat. Ann. tit. 10, § 1249 (personal sports mobile dealers or franchisees). Provisions in broadcast industry contracts that require an employee to refrain from obtaining employment in a specified geographic area for a specified period of time following the expiration of the contract or upon termination of employment without fault of the employee are presumed to be unreasonable. *See* Me. Rev. Stat. Ann. tit. 26, § 599(2).

While not governing covenants against competition directly, Maine law requires that a manufacturer of recreational vehicles, seeking to establish a new recreational vehicle dealership or relocate an existing one in a market area where the same line is already represented, must notify existing dealers in the market area of its intention to do so. *See* Me. Rev. Stat. Ann. tit 10, § 1435. The statute permits an existing dealer to file a court action protesting the establishment of the additional or relocated dealership and requires the court to determine good cause exists for *not* establishing or relocating the dealership. *Id.* at (2).

The Maine Supreme Judicial Court has considered covenants against competition in both the employment and sale of business contexts. *See, e.g., Sisters of Charity Health System, Inc. v Farrago*, 21 A.3d 110 (Me. 2011) (employment); *Chapman & Drake v. Harrington*, 545 A.2d 645, 647 (Me. 1988); *Lord v. Lord*, 454 A.2d 830, 832 (Me. 1983) (division of interests in insurance agency in divorce proceeding); and *Flaherty v. Libby*, 81 A. 166, 166–67 (Me. 1911) (sale of business). The court has held that restrictive covenants are enforceable "to the extent that they are reasonable and sweep no wider than necessary to protect the business interest in issue." *Chapman & Drake v. Harrington*, 545 A.2d 645, 647 (Me. 1988).

2. Have the courts articulated the "legitimate interests" of the franchisor that will support enforcement of a covenant against competition contained in a franchise agreement?

- If so, what are they (e.g., protection of goodwill, protection of confidential information), and in what contexts did the issue arise?
- If not, what interests have been recognized in other contexts (e.g., employment agreements, the sale of business context)?

There are no reported Maine decisions dealing with covenants against competition in the franchise context. However, Maine courts have addressed non-competition covenants in connection with employment relationships and the sale of a business. In *Roy v. Bolduc*, 34 A.2d 479 (Me. 1943), the Maine Supreme Judicial Court, while refusing to enforce the covenant at issue, recognized that a restrictive covenant can be used to prevent a former employee from utilizing his or her former employer's "trade or business secrets . . . [or] other confidential knowledge gained in the course of employment, and from enticing away old customers." *Id.* at 480–81.

In *Chapman & Drake v. Harrington*, 545 A.2d 645 (Me. 1988), the court recognized an employer's legitimate interests (1) in preventing an employee from taking "for his own benefit the goodwill his employer paid him to develop" and (2) in restricting an employee who has access to "his employer's confidential information, including customer lists, and is in a position to take advantage of that information." *Id.* at 647. *See also Sisters of Charity Health System, Inc. v. Farrago*, 21 A.3d 110 (Me. 2011) (existing patient base and goodwill are protectable interests).

In *Everett J. Prescott, Inc. v. Ross*, 383 F. Supp. 2d 180 (D. Me. 2005), *modified*, 390 F. Supp. 2d 44 and 2005 U.S. Dist. LEXIS 22922, the U.S. District Court for the District of Maine held that Maine law allowed an employer to protect confidential business information ranging from customer lists to proprietary business practices that, if available to a competitor, would likely affect the employer's goodwill. In a case involving a non-disclosure agreement, the Maine Supreme Judicial Court recognized that employers have a legitimate interest in protecting valuable business information even where that information does not rise to the level of a trade secret. *See Bernier v. Merrill Air Engineers*, 770 A.2d 97, 102 (Me. 2001).

In *Flaherty v. Libby*, 81 A. 166 (Me. 1911), the Maine Supreme Judicial Court recognized the legitimate interest of a business buyer in preventing the seller from competing with the business following its sale, noting the need to protect the buyer's interest in acquired goodwill. *Id.* at 167. Since the "goodwill" component of the transaction could be destroyed by the seller's competition, the buyer in *Flaherty* was permitted to restrict the seller from influencing the established customers of the business. *Id.; see also Lord v. Lord*, 454 A.2d 830, 834 (Me. 1983) (covenant against competition imposed by court in division of marital interests in insurance agency).

The U.S. District Court for the District of Maine, applying Michigan law, found no legitimate employer interest and refused to enforce a non-competition agreement where the former employee worked for the new employer in a clerical/administrative role in which she did not solicit any clients or recruit candidates in competition with her former employer. *Kelley Services, Inc. v. Greene*, 535 F. Supp. 2d 180 (D. Me. 2008).

The Maine Superior Court found that the loss of "some clients or business opportunities" caused by an alleged violation of a non-competition portion of a franchise agreement does not independently constitute "irreparable harm" for the purpose of a preliminary injunction. *Coast to Coast Engineering Services v. Stein*, 2006 WL 5218463 (Me. Super. Dec. 12, 2006). Further, injury from the alleged violation was not "irreparable" when the possibility existed the defendant would be ordered to abide by the non-competition clause and damages in the amount of demonstrable lost business could provide an adequate remedy. *Id.* Finally, the court found that "hypothetical injury, even if significant, cannot be the basis for awarding preliminary injunctive relief." *Id.*

3. What time limitations have courts recognized as reasonable in the franchise context?

- **If no franchise cases have been decided, what time limitations have been recognized in other contexts?**
- **How have the time limitations been related to the interests protected?**

There are no reported Maine decisions addressing the issue of reasonable time restrictions in covenants against competition contained in franchise agreements. In other contexts, the Maine Supreme Judicial Court has held that covenants against competition must be limited to a scope that is reasonably necessary to protect the legitimate business interests involved. *See Roy v. Bolduc*, 34 A.2d 479, 480 (Me. 1943). The legitimate scope of any restraint will depend on the nature and value of the asset or interest needing protection. *See, e.g., Lord v. Lord*, 454 A.2d 830, 835 (Me. 1983). Maine law requires the party seeking enforcement of a covenant to establish the reasonableness of its restrictions in light of the interests the party seeks to protect. *See Roy v. Bolduc*, 34 A.2d 479, 480 (Me. 1943); *Flaherty v. Libby*, 81 A. 166, 167 (Me. 1911). In *Chapman & Drake v. Harrington*, 545 A.2d 645 (Me. 1988), the Maine Supreme Judicial Court upheld a five-year covenant entered into by a former employee-insurance agent. *Id.* at 648. The court specifically noted, however, that the covenant prohibited the defendant only from doing business with customers of his former employer and did not prevent him from selling insurance to others. In *Brignull v. Albert*, 666 A.2d 82 (Me. 1995), the court upheld an award of liquidated damages after concluding that the defendant breached his covenant by entering into competition with his former employer 16 months after the termination of the employment relationship. *See id.* at 84. Although the covenant at issue in *Brignull* specified a four-year period of restraint, the court assessed the agreement as the plaintiff sought to apply it and not as written. Accordingly, the court held that a 16-month restriction was reasonable. *See also Sisters of Charity Health System, Inc. v. Farrago*, 21 A.3d 110 (Me. 2011) (two-year duration of non-competition covenant in physician agreement not contested and enforceable).

In *Everett J. Prescott, Inc. v. Ross*, 383 F. Supp. 2d 180 (D. Me. 2005), *modified*, 390 F. Supp. 2d 44 and 2005 U.S. Dist. LEXIS 22922, the U.S. district court found a three-year covenant reasonable because the defendant had knowledge of product pricing that was typically stable over three years, and it took two to four years for a new sales representative to get fully acclimated and reach a desired productivity level. *Id.* at 191. In *Lord v. Lord*, 454 A.2d 830 (Me. 1983), the Maine Supreme Judicial Court held that a court-imposed seven-year term of non-competition was excessive in connection with the division of marital interests in an insurance agency. *Id.* at 835.

In the sale of business context, the Maine Supreme Judicial Court enforced a covenant restricting the seller of a trucking business from engaging in a similar business in the city of Portland for the five-year period following the sale. *See Flaherty v. Libby*, 81 A. 166, 167 (Me. 1911).

---

4. What geographic limitations have courts recognized as reasonable in the franchise context?

- **How have they been related to the interests protected?**
- **Have courts recognized the legitimacy of protecting other franchisees from competition?**

Under Maine law, geographic restrictions in covenants against competition must be reasonable in light of the business interests allegedly requiring protection. *See, e.g., Chapman & Drake v. Harrington*, 545 A.2d 645, 647 (Me. 1988). Maine courts have not applied this rule in the franchise context. In addressing a covenant restricting a former employee from contacting or doing business with his former employer's customers, the Maine Supreme Judicial Court found the covenant reasonable and enforceable despite the absence of an express geographic limitation. *Id.* at 648. The covenant in *Chapman & Drake* prohibited the employee from doing business with insurance customers of his former employer but did not bar him generally from engaging in the insurance business. *Id.* at 646.

In *Flaherty v. Libby*, 81 A. 166 (Me. 1911), the Maine Supreme Judicial Court upheld a covenant prohibiting the seller of a Portland trucking business from engaging "in any similar business in [the city of] Portland, or vicinity, for a term of five years," where the seller became employed by another trucking company, also located in Portland, within nine months of the sale. *Id.* at 166–67. The court's rationale for sustaining an injunction against the seller was that, by engaging in a competing business in the same city and thereby breaching the covenant, the seller would deprive the buyer of the benefit of the goodwill of the business that he had purchased. *Id.* at 167.

In *Brignull v. Albert*, 666 A.2d 82 (Me. 1995), the Maine Supreme Judicial Court upheld an award of liquidated damages for the breach of a covenant prohibiting an optometrist from practicing within 20 miles of the location of his former employer's office for a period of four years. *Id.* at 84. Maine courts assess the reasonableness of restrictive covenants only as plaintiffs seek to apply them and not necessarily as the restrictive covenant "might have been enforced on its terms." *Id.* Therefore, the court upheld the trial court's damage award after concluding that it was reasonable to restrict the ability of the defendant-optometrist to compete within two miles of his former employer's office and within 16 months of ending his tenure with that employer. *Id.* at 84; *see also Sisters of Charity Health System, Inc. v. Farrago*, 21 A.3d 110 (Me 2011) (covenant limiting practice of medicine with competing hospital organization within 25-mile radius enforced).

In *Lord v. Lord*, 454 A.2d 830 (Me. 1983), the Maine Supreme Judicial Court held that a geographic scope of 60 miles for a judicially imposed covenant against competition in connection with the division of marital interests in an insurance agency was not supported by substantial evidence. *Id.* at 835. While it found that a restrictive covenant was appropriate for a fair division of the insurance agency assets because it protected the value of goodwill, the court held that the duration and geographic scope were not based on any specific delineation of the customer pool or market area on which the goodwill was based. *Id.* at 835. Therefore, the court remanded the case for a determination of the nature and components of the business goodwill and the appropriate scope of a covenant reasonably necessary to protect it. *Id.* at 835.

A Maine statute regulating new recreational vehicle dealerships and requiring manufacturers to notify existing dealers of intent to establish additional dealerships establishes as relevant market area zones in a radius of 15 miles around specified cities and otherwise 30 miles around existing dealerships. 10 ME. REV. STAT. ANN. § 1435.

5. What limitations on activities have courts recognized as reasonable in the franchise context?

Although the breadth and nature of the activities that can be properly restricted by a covenant against competition have not been addressed in the franchise context, the Maine Supreme Judicial Court has held that "a former employee may not, absent unusual circumstances, be prevented from entering into the practice of a business that requires no specialized training and does not rely on unique business methods or trade secrets acquired while serving the former employer." *Lord v. Lord*, 454 A.2d 830, 834 (Me. 1983). In the absence of proof that the employee possesses trade secrets or confidential knowledge that could be used to disadvantage the former employer, or that the employee is in a position to interfere with the former employer's customers or exploit its goodwill, enforcement of a covenant against competition is unlikely. *See Roy v. Bolduc*, 34 A.2d 479, 481 (Me. 1943). Without such evidence, enforcement would "unnecessarily interfere with [the employee's] rightful exercise of his skill and knowledge in gaining a livelihood in what is now his . . . trade." *Id.*

In *Wausau Mosinee Paper Corp. v. Magda*, 366 F. Supp. 2d 212 (D. Me. 2005), the U.S. District Court for the District of Maine denied, in part, a preliminary injunction requesting enforcement of a non-competition agreement against a former employee because of the particular injury that the defendant and his family would suffer from discontinuance of his new employment and the manner in which the agreement was first presented to the employee. In balancing relative hardships to the parties, the court noted that (1) the defendant was the sole supporter of his family, (2) his young son was facing surgery, (3) his family had resettled in a new house in another state, (4) the new employer appeared to be the only employer in the defendant's specialty within a reasonable distance, and (5) the non-competition agreement with the plaintiff was not presented to the defendant until after he had accepted employment and committed himself to buying a new home. *Id.* at 223.

6. Does the state recognize a difference between in-term and post-term covenants?

This issue has not been addressed under Maine law.

7. Has the state allowed enforcement of covenants against non-signatories (e.g., family members, newly formed corporations)?

The issue of enforcement of restrictive covenants against non-signatories has not arisen in Maine. The Maine Supreme Judicial Court has noted, however, that the constraints imposed by public policy on covenants against competition would be more demanding where a court-mandated restriction was involved than where the covenant was the result of a consensual agreement. *See Lord v. Lord*, 454 A.2d 830, 834–35 (Me. 1983). This suggests that the court would likely take a limited and conservative approach to enforcing covenants not to compete against non-signatories. While Maine recognizes the tort of interference with contract, it is in the minority of states that require the breach involved to be procured by "fraud or intimidation" to be actionable. *See MacKerron v. Madura*, 445 A.2d 680, 683 (Me. 1982).

8. Will the state modify, "blue-pencil," or otherwise reduce a covenant found to be overbroad?

In *Chapman & Drake v. Harrington*, 545 A.2d 645 (Me. 1988), the Maine Supreme Judicial Court stated, "Since the reasonableness of the non-competition agreement depends upon the specific facts of the case, we assess that agreement only as [the plaintiff seeks] to apply it and not as it might have been enforced on its plain terms." *Id.* at 647 (citations omitted). Thus, it appears that Maine courts will not consider the enforceability of a covenant simply as written if the plaintiff seeks enforcement on a more limited basis. *See Brignull v. Albert*, 666 A.2d 82, 84 (Me. 1995) (citing *Chapman & Drake v. Harrington*, 545 A.2d 645, 647 (Me. 1988) ("Courts assess a non-competition agreement as the employer has sought to apply it and not as it might have been enforced on its terms."). *See also Everett J. Prescott, Inc. v. Ross*, 383 F. Supp. 2d 180 (D. Me. 2005), *modified*, 390 F. Supp. 2d 44 and 2005 U.S. Dist. LEXIS 22922 (same). However, the court in *Prescott* also stated that "the party seeking enforcement cannot leave it to the court to enforce only those provisions that the court deems reasonable. To do so would require the court to redraft the contract." *Id.* at 47. Thus, at the hearing on a motion for a preliminary injunction, the court required the plaintiff to specifically identify the geographic provisions of the non-competition agreement that it was attempting to enforce. *Id.*

9. When does a non-competition period begin to run?

➤ Will courts equitably extend the term?

The Maine Supreme Judicial Court has not directly addressed the issue of whether Maine courts may grant relief beyond the expiration of the term of a non-competition agreement may be granted. However, the Maine Superior Court entered a temporary restraining order, pending a hearing on a preliminary injunction, enjoining defendants from competing with their former employer after the one-year term of the agreement had expired where (1) the employer was not immediately aware of the defendants' breach of the agreements, (2) the defendants did not respond to the employer's letters reminding them of their obligations, (3) the suit was initiated before the expiration of the one-year term, and (4) the employer alleged that the defendants had failed to honor the agreements "from the beginning" after their resignations from employment. *XWave New England Corp. v. Ziegenfus*, No. CV-07-15, 2007 LEXIS 102 (Me. Super. Ct. May 18, 2007) and *XWave New England Corp. v. McLean*, No. CV-07-15, 2007 LEXIS 103 (Me. Super. Ct. May 18, 2007).

10. Are there additional nuances or peculiarities of the state's treatment of covenants in the franchising context?

Since Maine has not addressed covenants not to compete in the franchising context, it is not possible to predict what nuances or peculiarities Maine courts may adopt under Maine law with respect to the treatment of such covenants in franchise agreements.

While reaching different results, the U.S. District Court for the District of Maine and the Maine Superior Court have considered the requirement of irreparable harm for injunctive relief in the context of restrictive covenants in employment contracts for investment advisers. *See, e.g., Merrill Lynch, Pierce, Fenner* & *Smith v. Bishop*, 839 F. Supp. 68, 72–75 (D. Me. 1993); *Merrill Lynch, Pierce, Fenner & Smith v. Bennert*, 980 F. Supp. 73, 75 (D. Me. 1997); *Merrill Lynch, Pierce, Fenner & Smith v. McMahon* (unreported decision of Maine Superior Court, Cumberland County, CV-98-199). These cases all involved provisions prohibiting the disclosure and use of certain confidential information and the solicitation of certain clients of the former employer.

In *Bishop*, the U.S. district court entered an injunction against the use and possession of certain documents containing information about the former employer's clients. *See Merrill Lynch, Pierce, Fenner & Smith v. Bishop*, 839 F. Supp. 68, 72 (D. Me. 1993). The court declined, however, to enter an injunction against the defendant's solicitation of clients, finding that there was an insufficient showing of irreparable harm because relief by way of damages for economic loss was likely to be available. *Id.* at 75. In *Bennert*, the district court followed the *Bishop* rationale, finding insufficient irreparable injury to issue a preliminary injunction. *See Merrill Lynch, Pierce, Fenner & Smith v. Bennert*, 980 F. Supp. 73, 75 (D. Me. 1997). The court also found that the employee's contractual consent to a finding of irreparable injury and entry of injunctive relief were not binding on the court as a matter of public policy. *Id.* at 76. The district court followed *Bishop* and *Bennert* in *American Express Financial Advisors, Inc. v. Temm*, 241 F. Supp. 2d 30 (D. Me. 2003), in which it denied a temporary restraining order on the grounds that money damages for loss of customers could be calculated from consumer account records and expert testimony. *Id.*

In the *McMahon* case, however, the Maine Superior Court noted in its unreported order granting a temporary restraining order that the plaintiff had demonstrated irreparable harm by pointing to the potential use of confidential information and solicitation of clients. Consequently, the court entered a temporary restraining order prohibiting the former employee from soliciting clients of the former employer, accepting business from solicited clients, and using or disclosing information concerning those clients contained in records of the former employer. *Fenner & Smith v. McMahon* (unreported decision of Maine Superior Court, Cumberland County, CV-98-199).

Maryland

*by Allan P. Hillman**

1. Has the state addressed covenants against competition in the context of franchising?

- **Does the state have a franchising statute or regulations that address covenants against competition?**
- **Does the state have a covenants statute of general applicability that would encompass franchise covenants?**
- **Have the courts addressed covenants in the context of franchising under a statute or under the state's common law?**

The Maryland Franchise Registration and Disclosure Law, Md. Code Ann., Bus. Reg. § 14-201 *et seq*., does not address covenants against competition, although the regulations promulgated under the statute require that the franchisor disclose to prospective franchisees any covenant against competition contained in the franchise agreement. There is no other franchising statute or statute of general applicability regarding restrictive covenants.

Under common law, the Maryland courts have addressed covenants against competition, both post-term and in-term, in many cases involving franchises. A leading recent case is *Ledo Pizza System v. Singh*, 983 F. Supp. 2d 632 (D. Md. 2013). The district judge granted a preliminary injunction enforcing a franchisee's post-termination obligations concerning the franchisor's trademark, trade dress, and other contract obligations including not to compete for two years at and within ten miles of the franchisee's location. The court found the scope reasonable, found irreparable harm to the franchisor's goodwill and relationships with its other franchisees if the non-compete was not enforced, found that the balance of hardships favored the franchisor, and found that the public interest favored enforcement of contract obligations. (It also noted the franchisor had tried to help the franchisee avoid failure.)

In *ICENY USA v. M&M's LLC*, 421 F. Supp. 3d 204 (D. Md. 2019), the court granted a preliminary injunction to the franchisor enforcing all post-term requirements including a two-year, five-mile (from any shop) non-compete, but limiting the scope of products restricted to the basic "Thai" ice cream and other "core" products.

*Allan P. Hillman is an attorney at Garcia & Milas. He is admitted to practice in Connecticut and Maryland.

Similarly, in *ATL International, Inc. v. Baradar*, Bus. Franchise Guide (CCH) ¶ 11,345 (D. Md. 1997), the U.S. District Court granted a preliminary injunction under Maryland law (the law chosen in the franchise agreement) to an automotive repair franchisor, finding that the franchisor was likely to succeed on the merits. The court enforced as reasonable a post-term non-compete of two years' duration within ten miles of the former Oregon franchisee's All Tune & Lube location. It found that the franchisor would suffer irreparable harm, holding that (as *Ledo* did later) if a "breakaway" franchisee were allowed to continue operating in violation of the covenant, that would send a signal to other disgruntled franchisees, would damage the franchisor's goodwill, and could unravel the entire franchise system.

There have been a number of other franchise post-term non-compete cases in this century decided under Maryland law. In *Ohio Learning Centers, LLC v. Sylvan Learning, Inc.*, 2012 WL 1067668 (D. Md. Mar. 27, 2012), the court granted summary judgment to the franchisor, enforcing a two-year, five-mile restraint, citing non-franchise cases that had upheld geographic restrictions of 50 miles or of unlimited scope (the latter involving an executive of a national company, however). The court also rejected the contention that the franchisor's alleged breach of the contract was a defense to the non-compete.

In *Sylvan Learning, Inc. v. Learning Solutions, Inc.*, 2011 U.S. Dist. LEXIS 64492 (S.D. Ala., June 17, 2011), the court held that (1) a Maryland choice-of-law clause would not offend Alabama public policy on non-competition agreements; (2) a restriction barring an ex-franchisee from competing for two years within its former territory and within five miles of its border was lawful; (3) the former franchisee's continued use of the Sylvan trademark, telephone number, signs, and violation of other post-term obligations caused irreparable harm through loss of customers and goodwill, and would be preliminarily enjoined; (4) the injury suffered by the former franchisee from a preliminary injunction was self-inflicted because it had breached the franchise agreement; (5) a recitation that the franchisor was entitled to an injunction for violation of certain provisions by the franchisee did not establish entitlement but was "persuasive"; but (6) although a breach of the non-competition covenant caused irreparable harm, that breach did not have to be enjoined because the injunction as to the other obligations "removed" the irreparable harm; and (7) no bond was required of the franchisor as Rule 65 of the FEDERAL RULES OF CIVIL PROCEDURE allows the court discretion to set the bond at zero where there is such a high likelihood of success on the merits.

See also Sylvan Learning, Inc. v. Gulf Coast Education, Inc., Case No 1:10-CV-450-WKW (unreported) (M.D. Ala., Oct. 6, 2010) (preliminary injunction granted under Maryland choice of law, which did not offend Alabama law, enforcing non-compete barring competition for two years and 20 miles from the former franchisee's store and from *any* Sylvan store); *Prosperity Systems, Inc. v. Ali*, 2010 U.S. Dist. LEXIS 132414 (D. Md., Dec. 15, 2010) (while the post-term non-compete of one year and 20 miles from the franchisee's pizza store was likely lawful, the court denied a preliminary injunction, citing a Fourth Circuit case, *Scotts Co. v. United Industries Corp.*, 315 F.3d 264, 284 (4th Cir. 2002), which had held that a court may not give "short shrift" to the harm a party suffers from an injunction even though it is self-inflicted due to the franchisee's own breaches of contract); *The Cleaning Authority v. Neubert*, 739 F. Supp. 2d 804 (D. Md. 2010) (court refused to hold as a matter of law on a motion to dismiss that a two-year, 100-mile covenant was ipso facto overbroad under Maryland law, and ordered factual development of the franchisor's justification); *Naturalawn of America, Inc. v. West Group LLC*, 484 F. Supp. 2d 392 (D. Md.

2007) (granting preliminary injunction to franchisor enforcing non-compete of two years and 20 miles from franchisee's former territory and from *any* territory, finding irreparable harm to the franchisor and its franchisees (the "System" itself) if the injunction were not granted; holding any harm to the enjoined ex-franchisee was self-inflicted and denying it was giving "short shrift" to the harm to the franchisee, discussing at length *Scotts Co. v. United Industry Corp.* (cited earlier in *Prosperity Systems*); and treating "expiration" as also including "termination" even though franchise agreement erred by using only "expiration" in the covenant, where both words were used elsewhere in the franchise agreement); *Wild Bird Centers of North America, Inc. v. Boyce Lee Duer*, Bus. Franchise Guide (CCH) ¶ 14,490 (Cir. Ct. Montgomery Cty. Md., Sept. 2, 2010) (court granted a preliminary injunction).

In *Wild Bird Centers*, the franchisor terminated the agreement after the franchisee abandoned his business and began operating an online business that referred potential customers to competitors of the franchisor. Soon thereafter, the franchisee opened an actual retail storefront less than two miles from his former franchise, selling wild bird–related products. The court held that the non-competition covenant in the franchise agreement that prohibited the franchisee from operating a competing business within 20 miles of the perimeter of the former franchise's territory or from the perimeter of any other franchise territory in the franchisor's system was reasonable and enforceable under Maryland law. The two-year duration of the covenant was held particularly reasonable in light of the parties' fairly lengthy 17-year franchise relationship, to ensure that there would not be a natural flow of customers to a business opened up by the franchisee in violation of the covenant. The geographic scope of the covenant was held reasonable in light of the caselaw and the evidence. The court viewed the scope as also reasonable and necessary to protect the franchisor's interest in preventing a breakaway franchisee from competing directly with the franchisor and its other franchisees after learning the business. Therefore, the covenant protected not only the franchisor but also its other franchisees. Moreover, to prevent harm from the former franchisee's competing online business, the court required him to make it clear to prospective customers who were located within 20 miles from the territory of his former franchise or 20 miles from the territory of any of the franchisor's other franchises that they would not be permitted to purchase services or products from his online business. The court explained that the online business would clearly be accessible by people residing within the territories protected by the covenant; hence, the ex-franchisee necessarily was required to state on his website that his sales and services were not available to those people. *See also The Prudential Real Estate Affiliates, Inc. v. Long & Foster Real Estate, Inc.*, 2000 U.S. App. LEXIS 3394, Bus. Franchise Guide (CCH) ¶ 11,802 (Mar. 6, 2000) (summary judgment for franchisee reversed; while the court did not reach the issue of enforceability of the in-term covenant against competition, it held that even were it unenforceable, such unenforceability would not make the franchise agreement itself unenforceable).

Finally, the U.S. District Court entered a preliminary injunction enforcing a 75-mile, one-year, post-term covenant not to compete against a former cleaning service franchisee in *Merry Maids L.P. v. Kamara*, 33 F. Supp. 2d 443 (D. Md. 1998). While ruling under Tennessee law (the law chosen in the franchise agreement), the court's ruling barred the former franchisee from competing in parts of Maryland, Virginia, and the District of Columbia. The court also held that the franchise relationship was deserving of more non-competition protection than a "mere" employment relationship. *Id.* at 446.

By contrast, in *Budget Rent-A-Car, Inc. v. Raab*, 268 Md. 478, 302 A.2d 11 (1973), the only post-term non-compete case decided in the franchise context before *Baradar*

24 years later, the state court struck down the covenant contained in a car rental franchise agreement. The court held it to be unreasonable, citing the common law applicable to covenants in the employment context, because the franchisee was an unskilled worker who had no trade secrets or customer lists and did not solicit customers. The court did not address expressly whether a different test should be applied in the franchise context. By contrast, as noted, the federal court in *Merry Maids* held the franchise relationship to be more deserving of non-competition protection than a "mere" employment relationship. *Merry Maids*, 33 F. Supp. 2d at 446.

Another franchise case denying a preliminary injunction was *SH Franchising, LLC v. Newlands Homecare*, holding *inter alia* that a restriction of the "similar products and services" was likely overbroad, but principally that the former franchisee was not even competing with the franchisor. 2019 WL 356658 (D. Md. Jan. 29, 2019).

There have been several in-term cases enforcing covenants not to compete. *Horcasitas v. Crown Central Petroleum Corp.*, 649 F. Supp. 1163 (D. Md. 1986), involved a gasoline service station franchise subject to the federal Petroleum Marketing Practices Act (PMPA), 15 U.S.C. § 2801 *et seq.* The court did not apply the common law of Maryland in assessing the validity of the covenant. Instead, it applied the PMPA's test that provisions in a service station franchise agreement be applied in good faith and in the normal course of business. The court held that the covenant met this standard in that the in-term prohibition was "rooted in common sense," was "not unconscionable," and had not been enforced in an arbitrary manner. In *ATL International, Inc. v. Benson*, Bus. Franchise Guide (CCH) ¶ 11,175 (D. Md. 1996), and in *ATL International, Inc. v. Milton*, Bus. Franchise Guide (CCH) ¶ 11,284 (D. Md. 1997), the U.S. District Court, ruling on Maryland law (chosen by the parties in the franchise agreements), enforced by temporary restraining orders in-term covenants not to compete against All Tune & Lube franchisees in South Carolina and Florida, respectively.

2. Have the courts articulated the "legitimate interests" of the franchisor that will support enforcement of a covenant against competition contained in a franchise agreement?

- **If so, what are they (e.g., protection of goodwill, protection of confidential information), and in what contexts did the issue arise?**
- **If not, what interests have been recognized in other contexts (e.g., employment agreements, the sale of business context)?**

The U.S. District Court in Maryland directly addressed the legitimate interests of a franchisor in enforcing covenants against franchisee competition in *ATL v. Baradar*, Bus. Franchise Guide (CCH) ¶ 11,345 (D. Md. 1997). The court held that enforcement of the franchisor's post-term non-compete was necessary because non-enforcement threatened the franchisor's customer goodwill, would send a signal to other disgruntled franchisees, and could cause the destruction of the entire franchise system. *Accord*, *Ledo Pizza*, 983 F. Supp. 2d 632 (D. Md. 2013). The case did not involve protection of trade secrets; therefore, the court did not address that issue.

Sylvan Learning, Inc. v. Learning Solutions, Inc., 2011 U.S. Dist. LEXIS 64492 (S.D. Ala., June 17, 2011) also recognized the franchisor's protectable interest in customer goodwill, as did *Wild Bird Centers of North America, Inc. v. Boyce Lee Duer*, Case No. 326421, Bus. Franchise Guide (CCH) ¶ 14,490 (Cir. Ct. Montgomery Cty. Md., Sept. 2, 2010).

Naturalawn of America, Inc., v. West Group LLC, 484 F. Supp. 2d 392, Bus. Franchise Guide (CCH) ¶ 13,664 (D. Md. 2007) recognized the franchisor's protectable interest in its proprietary information. And, like *ATL International, Inc. v. Baradar*, Bus. Franchise Guide (CCH) ¶ 11,345 (D. Md. 1997), *Sylvan Learning, Inc., v. Gulf Coast Education, Inc.*, Case No 1:10-CV-450-WKW (unreported) (M.D. Ala., Oct. 6, 2010), and *Prosperity Systems, Inc. v. Ali*, 2010 U.S. Dist. LEXIS 132414 (D. Md., Dec. 15, 2010), it recognized the franchisor's protectable interest in preserving the franchise system from breakaway franchises.

In *Budget Rent-A-Car, Inc. v. Raab*, 268 Md. 478, 302 A.2d 11 (1973), the interests of the franchisor in enforcing the covenant were equated with those of an employer. *Cf. Merry Maids, LLC v. Kamara*, 33 F. Supp. 2d 443, 446 (D. Md. 1998) (characterizing the franchisor's interest as more than that of a "mere" employer). The court in *Budget* held that the covenant—a two-year restriction on engaging in a competing business within the city limits of the formerly franchised business—was not necessary to protect the franchisor's interests because (1) the services of the franchisee in renting vehicles were unskilled and not unique; (2) there were no trade secrets, assigned routes, or private customer lists to be protected; and (3) there was no personal contact with customers for the franchisee to exploit.

3. What time limitations have courts recognized as reasonable in the franchise context?

- **If no franchise cases have been decided, what time limitations have been recognized in other contexts?**
- **How have they been related to the interests protected?**

In *ATL International, Inc. v. Baradar*, Bus. Franchise Guide (CCH) ¶ 11,345 (D. Md. 1997), the court enforced a two-year post-term covenant not to compete against a former automotive repair franchisee. The court restrained the Oregonian defendant under Maryland law, the law chosen in the franchise agreement. *Sylvan Learning, Inc. v. Learning Solutions, Inc.*, 2011 U.S. Dist. LEXIS 64492 (S.D. Ala., June 17, 2011) enforced a two-year covenant, as did *Naturalawn of America, Inc, v. West Group LLC*, 484 F. Supp. 2d 392 (D. Md. 2007) and *Wild Bird Centers of North America, Inc. v. Boyce Lee Duer*, Case No. 326421, Bus. Franchise Guide (CCH) ¶ 14,490 (Cir. Ct. Montgomery. Cty. Md., Sept. 2, 2010). The other cases cited in Section 1 all considered maximum two-year covenants and upheld all of them.

4. What geographic limitations have courts recognized as reasonable in the franchise context?

- **How have they been related to the interests protected?**
- **Have courts recognized the legitimacy of protecting other franchises from competition?**

In *ATL International, Inc. v. Baradar*, Bus. Franchise Guide (CCH) ¶ 11,345 (D. Md. 1997), the court enforced the covenant's ban on post-term competition within ten miles of the franchisee's former All Tune & Lube automotive repair shop. The court further recognized that an injunction was necessary to protect other franchisees to prevent the unraveling of the system. In *Merry Maids, LLC v. Kamara*, 33 F. Supp. 2d 443 (D. Md. 1998), the court (ruling under Tennessee law and by implication under Maryland public policy on a restriction affecting a former Maryland franchisee) enforced the agreement's ban on post-term competition within 75 miles of the former franchisee's location.

Other franchise decisions include *Ledo Pizza System, Inc. v. Singh*, 983 F. Supp. 2d 632 (D. Md. 2013) (ten miles from the franchisee's store); *Sylvan Learning, Inc. v. Learning Solutions, Inc.*, 2011 U.S. Dist. LEXIS 64492 (S.D. Ala., June 17, 2011) (enforcing restraint of five miles from border of franchisee's territory and from *any other* territory); *Naturalawn of America, Inc., v. West Group LLC*, 484 F. Supp. 2d 392 (same); *Wild Bird Centers of North America, Inc. v. Boyce Lee Duer*, Case No. 326421, Bus. Franchise Guide (CCH) ¶ 14,490 (Cir. Ct. Montgomery Cty., Md., Sept. 2, 2010) (20 miles); *see also The Cleaning Authority v. Neubert*, 739 F. Supp. 2d 804 (D. Md. 2010) (on motion to dismiss, declining to rule as a matter of law that 100 miles from franchisee's territory was unenforceable and requiring factual development); *see also* the other cases cited in Section 1.

5. What limitations on activities have the courts recognized as reasonable in the franchise context?

The franchise cases cited in Section 1 all enforce a total ban on competition with the franchisor, except *ICENY*, which banned competition only in "core" products of the franchise such as "Thai" ice cream. 425 F. Supp. 2d 204 (D. Md. 2019) *see, e.g., ATL International, Inc. v. Baradar*, Bus. Franchise Guide (CCH) ¶ 11,345 (D. Md. 1997), where the court enforced a total ban on competition with the franchisor's system within ten miles of the ex-franchisee's Oregon location. In *Merry Maids, LLC v. Kamara*, 33 F. Supp. 2d 443 (D. Md. 1998) (Tenn. law), the court enforced a total ban on competition with the franchisor's system within 75 miles of the ex-franchisee's Maryland location.

6. Does the state recognize a difference between in-term and post-term covenants?

Yes, Maryland has enforced in-term covenants in franchise agreements without the need to engage in the reasonableness analysis used in evaluation of post-term covenants. *ATL International, Inc. v. Milton*, Bus. Franchise Guide (CCH) ¶ 11,284 (D. Md. 1997); *ATL International, Inc. v. Benson*, Bus. Franchise Guide (CCH) ¶ 11,175 (D. Md. 1996).

In *Horcasitas v. Crown Central Petroleum Corp.*, 649 F. Supp. 1163 (D. Md. 1986), the U.S. District Court for the District of Maryland upheld an in-term covenant that prohibited a service station franchisee from owning an interest in a competing service station within a five-mile radius of its present location. The court did not apply Maryland's common law of covenants in assessing the covenant. Instead, it held that violation of the covenant was a valid basis for termination under the PMPA, holding that the provision was "rooted in common sense" and "not unconscionable."

7. Has the state allowed enforcement of covenants against non-signatories (e.g., family members, newly formed corporations)?

This issue was raised, but not decided, in *Budget Rent-A-Car, Inc. v. Raab*, 268 Md. 478, 302 A.2d 11 (1973), where the franchisor sought to enforce a covenant signed by the franchisee against the franchisee's wife. The court did not reach the issue because it invalidated the covenant.

Enforcement against third parties has been permitted in the context of the sale of a business. *Checket-Columbia Co. v. Lipman*, 201 Md. 494, 94 A.2d 433 (1953) (covenant signed by an individual enforced against corporation formed and managed by the individual, and against the associates who acted in concert with the covenantor); *Kaliopulus v. Lumm*, 15 Md. 30, 141 A. 440 (1928) (covenant may be enforced against corporation formed by covenantor where corporation was used as the "conscious tool" by which to breach the covenant); *Guerand v. Dandelet*, 32 Md. 561 (1870) (covenant of the father can be enforced against the son where the name of the son was used to conceal the competing activities of the father).

8. Will the state modify, "blue-pencil," or otherwise reduce a covenant found to be overbroad?

Maryland courts have enforced covenants after striking portions found to be unreasonable. The law is unsettled as to whether the only permissible method is this, that is, to "blue-pencil" an overbroad covenant, but in some non-franchise cases Maryland will rewrite covenants to make them reasonable, unless the original covenant is vastly overbroad and overreaching. The most recent franchise case that addressed this was amenable not just to blue-penciling but also to rewriting the covenant to make it enforceable. *See ICENY USA, LLC v. M&M's LLC*, 421 F. Supp. 3d 204 (D. Md. 2019) (rewriting the covenant to restrict competition only to "core products" such as "Thai" ice cream); *but see SH Franchising, LLC v. Newlands Homecare, LLC*, 2019 WL 356658 (D. Md. Jan. 29, 2019) (in dictum observing that a restriction as to "similar products and services" may or may not be enforceable, but declining to grant an injunction where there was no showing the former franchisee was competing as defined in the franchise agreement).

9. When does a non-compete period begin to run? Will courts equitably extend the term?

In *ATL International, Inc. v. Baradar*, Bus. Franchise Guide (CCH) ¶ 11,345 (D. Md. 1997), the covenant began to run at the later of termination or a court order enforcing the covenant, and the court order commenced the time period as of that later date. In *Nationwide Mutual Insurance v. Hart*, 73 Md. App. 406, 534 A.2d 999 (1988), the Maryland Court of Special Appeals held that the time period begins to run at termination, regardless of when actual compliance commences.

10. Are there additional nuances or peculiarities of the state's treatment of covenants in the franchising context?

DAMAGES

In *Ledo Pizza System Inc, v. Singh*, 2014 WL 3810524 (D. Md. July 31, 2014), the court held that damages for violation of the non-compete would be the total lost revenue to the franchisor. The court awarded *all* "lost sales" revenue to Ledo, separately from the award of unpaid royalties and advertising fees, on the basis of the "expectation interest" of the franchisor during the period of the violations.

PUBLIC INTEREST

Enforcing a two-year, ten-mile post-termination covenant against competition, the U.S. District Court held that, as long as the covenant is reasonable, "that is the controlling public interest factor." *ATL International, Inc. v. Baradar*, Bus. Franchise Guide (CCH) 11,345 (D. Md. 1997) at p.30, 336; *accord, Ledo Pizza System Inc, v. Singh*, 983 F. Supp. 2d 632 (D. Md. 2013).

CHOICE OF LAW

In *The Cleaning Authority v. Neubert*, 739 F. Supp. 2d 804 (D. Md. 2010), the court held that a choice-of-law clause would be honored in a non-competition franchise case if the clause met the RESTATEMENT 2D OF CONFLICTS OF LAW § 187 test, including, most significantly, if the forum's rules of enforceability of covenants were not less restrictive than the rules of the contractually chosen state, that is, the forum's public policy was not offended by using the chosen state's law.

CONTRACT PROVISIONS ABOUT HARM AND RIGHT TO INJUNCTIVE RELIEF

In *Sylvan Learning, Inc. v. Learning Solutions, Inc.*, 2011 U.S. Dist. LEXIS 64492 (S.D. Ala., June 17, 2011), the court held that a franchise agreement clause stating that, upon violation of the non-compete by the franchisee, the franchisor had a right to an injunction to prevent irreparable harm was not dispositive, but was "persuasive."

Massachusetts

*by Thomas R. Ayres**

1. Has the state addressed covenants against competition in the context of franchising?

- **Does the state have a franchising statute or regulations that address covenants against competition?**
- **Does the state have a covenants statute of general applicability that would encompass franchise covenants?**
- **Have the courts addressed covenants in the context of franchising either under a statute or under the state's common law?**

Massachusetts does not have a statute regulating franchising generally. Massachusetts enacted a statute covering covenants against competition executed on or after October 1, 2018, but it applies only to employment agreements and does not encompass franchise agreements. *See* MASS. GEN. LAWS ch. 149 § 24L. Franchise lawyers must instead look to the common law for guidance. In *Boulanger v. Dunkin' Donuts Inc.*, 442 Mass. 635 (2004), the state's highest court, the Massachusetts Supreme Judicial Court, directly addressed the enforceability of covenants against competition in franchise agreements in a case of first impression. The case arose when a former Dunkin' Donuts franchisee named Craig Boulanger challenged the enforceability of a covenant against competition contained in multiple franchise agreements he had signed. Specifically, Boulanger sought a declaratory judgment that the covenant restricting him from owning or working for a competing business within five miles of any Dunkin' Donuts establishment for a period of two years after the expiration or termination of the franchise agreements was unenforceable. He also sought monetary damages pursuant to the Massachusetts statute prohibiting unfair and deceptive trade practices.

Boulanger had long been associated with the Dunkin' Donuts system, having worked as an employee at franchised locations in the 1970s, eventually becoming a general manager. He became a franchisee in 1996 when he purchased a franchise unit in upstate New York. He added two more in 1999 and 2000 and was

*Thomas R. Ayres is an attorney in the firm of Witmer Karp Warner & Ryan LLP in Boston. This chapter incorporates work from the third edition written by Eric H. Karp, a partner at the same firm.

represented by counsel in each of these transactions. In February 2002, Boulanger sold his three franchises. In July 2002, he moved to New Hampshire and shortly thereafter contacted Honey Dew Donuts to discuss the possibility of becoming either an employee or franchisee. When Honey Dew Donuts learned of the covenant against competition, it refused to have any further dealings with him. Dunkin' Donuts refused Boulanger's request to waive the covenant, and he sued. *Boulanger*, 422 Mass. at 636–38.

The supreme judicial court first examined whether a covenant against competition in a franchise agreement is more akin to the sale of the business or an employment relationship. The court held that such a covenant is enforceable only if it is (1) necessary to protect a legitimate business interest, (2) reasonably limited in time and space, and (3) consonant with the public interest. Massachusetts courts have historically looked less critically at covenants in the context of the sale of business because they do not implicate a person's right to employment to the same extent as in employment agreements. Moreover, in the sale of business context, courts have been generally less concerned with unequal bargaining power between the parties. The court further pointed out that the franchisee was not the employee of the franchisor, and that he paid for the right to operate the business entity and entered into the covenant with his "eyes wide open." Accordingly, the court determined that the sale of business analogy was more appropriate. *Id.* at 639–40.

Instead of challenging the two-year time period, Boulanger argued that the large number of Dunkin' Donuts locations made the geographic scope of the covenant an effective bar to his employment, especially in the states of Massachusetts and New Hampshire. The court rejected this challenge and held that even if it had analyzed the covenant in the employment context—in which it would have applied a stricter standard—the covenant would still have passed muster. In the context of a sale of business, even the larger geographic restrictions in the covenant would be proper, in part because Boulanger received proceeds from sale. The court pointed out that Boulanger was not barred from employment altogether, as he was free to work at another Dunkin' Donuts location. The purpose of the covenant was to protect the franchise system as a whole; the confidential information he possessed should not be used to the detriment of other franchisees in other locations. The franchise system binds all other franchisees and was part of what Dunkin' Donuts sold and what Boulanger purchased. In this case, it was unreasonable to undermine the value of the franchised business he sold by competing with it. *Id.* at 643–46.

Boulanger has served as a guide to trial and appellate courts applying Massachusetts law on a wide range of cases, especially in cases involving franchising. *See, e.g., Get in Shape Franchise, Inc. v. TFL Fishers, LLC*, 167 F. Supp. 3d 173 (D. Mass. 2016); *7-Eleven, Inc. v. Grewal*, 60 F. Supp. 3d 272 (D. Mass. 2014); *RE/MAX of New England, Inc. v. Prestige Real Estate, Inc.*, 2014 WL 3058295 (D. Mass. July 7, 2014); *Curves Int'l, Inc. v. Fox*, 2013 WL 1946826 (D. Mass. May 9, 2013). In the typical scenario (as with all the cases listed above) where a franchisor seeks a preliminary injunction and/or a temporary restraining order to enforce the covenant against a franchisee, a franchisor must establish that (1) it is likely to succeed on the merits, (2) it is likely to suffer irreparable harm in the absence of preliminary relief, (3) the balance of equities tips in its favor, and (4) an injunction is in the public interest. *See Voice of the Arab World, Inc. v. MDTV Med. News Now, Inc.*, 645 F.3d 26, 32 (1st Cir. 2011); *GTE Prods. Corp. v. Stewart*, 414 Mass. 721, 722 (1993). Federal courts place particular emphasis on the first requirement: the plaintiff's likelihood of success on the merits. *Peoples Fed. Sav. Bank v. People's United Bank*, 672 F.3d 1, 8–9 (1st Cir. 2012).

2. Have the courts articulated "legitimate interests" of the franchisor that will support enforcement of a covenant against competition contained in a franchise agreement?

- If so, what are they (e.g., protection of goodwill, protection of confidential information), and in what contexts did the issue arise?
- If not, what interests have been recognized in other contexts (e.g., employment agreements, the sale of business context)?

The supreme judicial court discussed at length the issue of legitimate business interests in the franchise context in *Boulanger*. It observed that the goodwill in the franchise locations formerly owned by Boulanger was already protected by the covenant against competition granted in favor of his buyer. The court noted that more than goodwill was implicated: Dunkin' Donuts had a legitimate interest in protecting confidential information regarding the entire system, including recipes for coffee and baked goods, financial data, marketing and promotion strategy, new product development, and the location of sites for new stores. Boulanger argued that Dunkin' Donuts had waived the confidentiality of such information because it discussed it in meetings attended by non-franchisees and Dunkin' Donuts employees with access to such information did sign similar covenants. The court found these arguments unavailing, holding that even if Dunkin' Donuts had not done everything possible to guard the secrecy of the information, it was nevertheless confidential. *Boulanger*, 422 Mass. at 642–43. Moreover, if Boulanger were to have worked for a competitor, then information he possessed would likely have been used in ways that would be impossible for Dunkin' Donuts to detect or prove. *Id.* at 643, n.12 (citing *Marcam Corp. v. Orchard*, 885 F. Supp. 294, 297 (D. Mass. 1995) (former employee will inevitably draw on special knowledge acquired during employment even if former employee made "scrupulous efforts" to avoid disclosing confidential information)).

The U.S. District Court for the District of Massachusetts similarly cited protection of "trade secrets, confidential information, and customer goodwill" in granting a fitness franchisor's preliminary injunction against a former franchisee that terminated her franchise agreement and immediately began operating a competing studio. *Get in Shape Franchise, Inc.*, 167 F. Supp. 3d at 199. Although *Boulanger* held that covenants in franchise agreements were more analogous to a sale of business, the court laid out an employment standard for considering the legitimate business interests of the franchisor, Get in Shape for Women (GISFW), as follows:

> Courts will not enforce non-competition agreements meant solely to protect employers from run-of-the-mill business competition. However, the protection of trade secrets, other confidential information, and the good will the employer has acquired through dealings with his customers constitute legitimate business interests. Customer goodwill is a company's positive reputation in the eyes of its customers or potential customers" and is generated by repeat business with existing customers or by referrals to potential customers.

Id. at 199 (internal quotation marks, alterations, and citations omitted). When the franchisee first began operating as a GISFW studio, she received copies of confidential manuals and other training materials about operating a small group fitness studio for women. The franchise agreement acknowledged that she obtained "knowledge of proprietary matters, techniques, and business procedures of Franchisor that are necessary and essential to the operation of the Studio" that were previously unknown to her. *Id.* Moreover, she did not operate a fitness studio at any other location prior to becoming a GISFW franchisee, and she did not move to a different location before beginning to operate as Fit Chicks (the name of her subsequent, non-franchised studio). The franchisee even admitted that the vast majority of the GISFW studio's clients became Fit Chick clients after the transition, at least for some time period. *Id.* at 199–200.

Yet courts do not always accept franchisors' assertions that covenants against competition are protecting their legitimate business interests. In a case involving a real estate agency franchise system, the U.S. District Court for the District of Massachusetts held that there were no trade secrets involved and was skeptical that the former franchisee derived any real benefit from knowing the franchisor's general business strategies. *RE/MAX of New England, Inc.*, 2014 WL 3058295, at *3. In rejecting the franchisor's request for injunctive relief, the court wrote: "Given the nature of the real estate brokerage business, however, there is reason to wonder whether any good will generated by the various offices is due to RE/MAX branding and methods or the work and personal relationships of the agents. At the very least, the record does not convincingly support the former possibility." *Id.*

In a case in which 7-Eleven sought to enforce the post-termination covenant against a franchisee accused of making thousands of fraudulent transactions, the U.S. District Court for the District of Massachusetts denied the franchisor's preliminary injunction because allowing the franchisee to de-identify and continue operating would not cause 7-Eleven's brand to lose any goodwill in the community. *7-Eleven, Inc.*, 60 F. Supp. 3d at 283 ("Customers would have no reason to associate [franchisee's] convenience store with the 7-Eleven brand after 7-Eleven's marks are removed from the premises."). Although the court credited 7-Eleven's argument that it would be hard to salvage the profitability and consumer goodwill of the store if the preliminary injunction were not granted, this potential for increased difficulty still did not outweigh potential harm to the franchisee if the preliminary injunction were granted. The court concluded that it was not clear that delaying enforcement of the non-compete agreement until the trial on the merits would irreparably harm 7–Eleven. The fact that 7-Eleven had 50,000 franchise locations persuaded the court that lost profits associated with one store operating for one or two years would be "miniscule" in comparison to the company's annual profits. The court also found that damages would be measurable and compensable. *Id.* at 283–84.

Similarly, the U.S. District Court for the District of Massachusetts did not accept a manufacturer's conclusory statements about protecting goodwill when it sought enforcement of a covenant against a distributor. *See Rohm & Haas Elec. Materials, LLC v. Electronic Circuit Supplies, Inc.*, 759 F. Supp. 2d 110 (D. Mass. 2010). Citing *Boulanger*, the court concluded that the manufacturer failed to meet its burden to show that the information in the distributor's possession constituted a protected trade secret or confidential trade information. Massachusetts courts have not adopted a uniform rule for determining what constitutes confidential information or trade secrets, and the court listed the following six guiding factors found in the jurisprudence:

(1) the extent to which the information is known outside of the business;
(2) the extent to which it is known by employees and others involved in the business;

(3) the extent of measures taken by the employer to guard the secrecy of the information;
(4) the value of the information to the employer and to his competitors;
(5) the amount of effort or money expended by the employer in developing the information; and
(6) the ease or difficulty with which the information could be properly acquired or duplicated by others.

Id. at 124–25. In addition to "put[ting] the cart before the horse by presuming that the information at issue is confidential," the manufacturer failed to show that there was a "meeting of the minds" that the non-competition provision would continue after an amendment to the distribution agreement. *Id.* at 125.

State and federal courts at the trial and appellate level have approved several measures sufficient for an employer to satisfy its burden of demonstrating that information has been maintained on a confidential basis. Accordingly, a franchisor interested in protecting its confidential information through the enforcement of a covenant against competition is well-advised to:

(1) have its franchisees sign confidentiality agreements;
(2) limit access to material over which it seeks to assert protection to select persons;
(3) keep information worthy of protection out of the view of the general public; and
(4) be prepared to demonstrate how a former franchisee's exposure to confidential information and/or trade secrets will irreparably harm its business by showing:
    (a) direct evidence of disclosure, or
    (b) evidence suggesting that disclosure will be inevitable, even if inadvertent.

See, e.g., National Med. Care, Inc. v. Sharif, 2020 WL 6318922 (Sept. 2, 2020) (enforcing one-year covenant where former high-ranking executive's substantially similar duties and responsibilities at new employer render it unlikely that he will refrain from disclosing and/or using prior employer's confidential information in his new role); *Agero Admin. Serv. Corp. v. Campolo*, 366 F. Supp. 3d 170 (D. Mass. 2019) (enforcing towing company's one-year covenant against employee who had material contact with customers and access to sensitive information); *Aspect Software, Inc. v. Barnett*, 787 F. Supp. 2d 118, 128 (D. Mass. 2011) (enforcing one-year covenant against former high-ranking employee with access to 13 separate categories of trade secrets); *William Gallagher Assocs. Ins. Brokers, Inc. v. Albert Everts*, 2000 WL 1334763 (Mass. Super. Ct. Sept. 6, 2000) (covenant not enforced where no evidence suggesting that employer took measures to protect the secrecy of information or designate it confidential); *Browne v. Merkert Enters., Inc.*, 1998 WL 151253 (Mass. Super. Ct. Mar. 30, 1998) (enforcing six-month covenant where employer kept information in isolated area and limited its review to certain employees).

Although not franchising cases, two recent cases involving anti-raiding covenants are worth mentioning due to the courts' conclusion—similar to the *Boulanger* analysis—that they were more akin to a sale of business than an employment scenario. In *Automile Holdings, LLC v. McGovern*, 483 Mass. 797 (2020), the supreme judicial court upheld a covenant restricting a former high-level executive and minority owner of a closely held corporation from soliciting employees for 18 months after his minority stake was bought out. The court weighed the defendant's bargaining power and legal representation—as well as the covenant's direct connection to his sale of his minority interest and only indirect connection to his prior employment—in concluding that the restrictive covenant was more akin to the sale of a business interest than to an employment relationship. *Id.* at 811. In considering the company's legitimate business interest, the court echoed its concern in *Boulanger* that the defendant not be able to "derogate from the value of the business interest" he sold by competing with it: "[I]n light of McGovern's prior position within [the company], his present position as a competitor well poised to steal [company] employees, and the additional consideration he received in exchange for agreeing to the restrictive covenant, [the company] had a legitimate anti-raiding business interest." *Id.* at 814.

In a decision issued by the influential Business Litigation Session of the Superior Court two weeks later, the court likewise upheld one-year non-solicitation covenants against two management-level employees who worked at a professional staffing company. *Robert Half Int'l, Inc. v. Simon*, 2020 WL 1218988 (Mass. Super. Ct. Jan. 29, 2020). The court nevertheless distinguished between institutional clients served by the employees and clients who had no relationship with the employees:

> Where an employee functions as the exclusive sales representative of a company within a particular area, and as a result that employee makes "repeated attempts to sell to potential customers in the same geographical area," the company may be able to enforce a covenant barring competition within the same area if it can show that the salesperson had essentially become the face of the company to all potential customers in that region.

Id. at *7. Given that franchisors frequently refer to franchisees as being the "face of the brand" within their exclusive territories, courts may apply this language to franchising cases in the future.

---

3. What time limitations have courts recognized as reasonable in the franchise context?

- **If no franchise cases have been decided, what time limitations have been recognized in other contexts?**
- **How have the time limitations been related to interests protected?**

While Boulanger did not challenge the two-year period limiting his ability to compete, the supreme judicial court nevertheless opined that it was reasonable, citing prior landmark rulings with approval. *Boulanger*, 422 Mass. at 643. In franchise cases decided after *Boulanger*, courts have explicitly held that one- and two-year limitation periods are reasonable. In *Get in Shape*, the court upheld a covenant with a two-year limitations period based on its assessment that "[Massachusetts] courts have upheld non-compete terms significantly longer than one year." *Get in Shape Franchise, Inc.*, 167 F. Supp. 3d at 200 (citing *Aspect Software, Inc. v. Barnett*, 787 F. Supp. 2d 118, 128 (D. Mass. 2011); *see Blackwell v. E.M. Helides, Jr., Inc.*, 368 Mass. 225 (1975) (three-year restriction reasonable); *Marine Contractors Co., Inc. v. Hurley*, 365 Mass. 280, 289–90 (1974) (restriction lasting less than three years not excessive); *All Stainless, Inc. v. Colby*, 364 Mass. 773, 779 (1974) (two-year restriction reasonable).

Another franchisor offering fitness and weight-loss services to women, Curves International, sought preliminary injunctive relief to enforce a one-year covenant on a former franchise that decided not to renew her franchise agreement. *Curves Int'l, Inc.*, 2013 WL 1946826. In holding that the covenant was temporally reasonable, the U.S. District Court for the District of Massachusetts noted that the former franchisee acknowledged as much in the franchise agreement. The court then stated: "As the non-compete agreement is necessary to protect Curves' business of selling fitness franchises, it is enforceable." *Id.* at *2. The same court relied on *Curves International* to conclude that 7-Eleven would likely be able to enforce a similar one-year covenant. 60 F. Supp. 3d at 282–83; *see also In re Ward*, 194 B.R. 703 (Bankr. D. Mass. 1996) (two-year covenant in maid service franchise agreement enforceable).

When determining whether the temporal scope of a covenant against competition is reasonable, courts applying Massachusetts law in the employment and sale of business contexts consider the following factors:

(1) the nature of the employer's (or seller's) business;
(2) the character of the employment (or business) involved;
(3) the situation of the parties;
(4) the necessity of the restriction for protecting the employer's (or seller's) business; and
(5) the right of the employee (or seller) to earn a living.

See New England Controls, Inc. v. Pilsbury, 2018 WL 3150223, at *7 (D. Mass. June 27, 2018) (collecting cases and upholding two-year non-solicitation restriction); *see, e.g., Richmond Brothers, Inc. v. Westinghouse Broad Co.*, 357 Mass. 106, 110 (1970); *Alexander & Alexander, Inc. v. Danahy*, 21 Mass. App. Ct. 488 (1986) (upholding five-year restriction covenant against employee who sold his insurance business to employer); *Kroeger v. Stop & Shop Co., Inc.*, 13 Mass. App. Ct. 310 (1982) (affirming reduction of employee's restriction from "so long as he lives" to one year); *Wells v. Wells*, 9 Mass. App. Ct. 321 (1980) (spouse's sale of business with 52-month covenant upheld in part because "concern about unequal bargaining power recedes when the restriction arises in the context of a sale of a business."); *Borden & Remington Corp. v. Barnisch*, 1999 WL 1266161 (Mass. Super. Ct. Oct. 18, 1999) (five-year restriction in connection with employer's purchase of employee's business was reasonable in part because parties were both represented by counsel when entering into agreement).

4. What geographic limitations have courts recognized as reasonable in the franchise context?

- **How have they been related to the interests protected?**
- **Have courts recognized the legitimacy of protecting other franchisees from competition?**

The supreme judicial court discussed at length the reasonableness of the covenant that prevented Boulanger from being employed at a competing location with five miles of any Dunkin' Donuts store. Given that there were approximately 704 and 122 Dunkin' Donuts stores in Massachusetts and New Hampshire at the time, respectively, Boulanger argued that the covenant severely hampered his ability to be employed or own a competing business in these states. Dunkin' Donuts pointed to Boulanger's statement that he would have signed a franchise agreement with Honey Dew Donuts that contained a similar covenant: one year and within three miles of any then-existing Honey Dew Donuts shop. *Boulanger*, 422 Mass. at 643, n.13. In ruling for Dunkin' Donuts, the court stated:

> In these circumstances, we conclude that the five-mile limit is reasonable, not only because a number of our cases have held larger geographic areas to be reasonable, but also because we agree with [Dunkin' Donuts] that what the covenant not to compete was protecting was the [Dunkin' Donuts'] franchise system. The issue is whether confidential information could be used by the plaintiff to harm other franchisees in other locations. The system is reasonable because it binds all other franchisees and is part of what [Dunkin' Donuts] sells. The system is part of what [Boulanger], as a franchisee, purchased and what protected him while he was a franchise owner.

Id. at 645. In a footnote, the court assumed, without deciding, that the franchise agreement was a contract of adhesion, but concluded that it was not unconscionable, did not offend public policy, and was not unfair in the circumstances. *Id.* at 645, n.16.

Post-*Boulanger* franchise decisions by the U.S. District Court for the District of Massachusetts have upheld even more expansive geographic limitations. A one-year restraint on a former franchisee's operation of a fitness facility within ten miles of a Curves location was deemed geographically and temporally reasonable because it was "necessary to protect Curves' business of selling fitness franchises." *Curves Int'l, Inc.*, 2013 WL 1946826, at *2. Likewise, the court upheld GISFW's restriction of within eight miles of the former franchisee's studio location or any other GISFW studio as reasonable, particularly because there was only one other GISFW studio in Indiana, the former franchisee's home state. *Get in Shape Franchise, Inc.*, 167 F. Supp. 3d at 200.

Two pre-*Boulanger* federal court franchise decisions enforced even larger geographic restrictions. In *Diet Center, Inc. v. Day*, 1990 WL 10830131 (D. Mass. Mar. 19, 1990), the court enforced a covenant prohibiting the terminated franchisee from competing with the franchisor within a 30-mile radius of her former territory. The U.S. Bankruptcy Court for the District of Massachusetts enforced a covenant prohibiting a franchisee from entering competition in the franchise business within 50 miles of (1) the area in which the franchisee once had exclusive rights as defined in the agreement or (2) any then-existing franchise. *In re Ward*, 194 B.R. at 705, 708. In approving the agreement, the court implicitly recognized the legitimacy of protecting the franchisor's other franchisees from the competition of former franchisees. *See id.*

5. What limitations on activities have courts recognized as reasonable in the franchise context?

In the franchise context, courts have approved limitations prohibiting competition in the same or similar business. In *Boulanger*, the covenant prohibited competition with the franchisor through employment by or ownership in a business that ". . . sells or offers to sell the same or substantially similar products to those offered by Dunkin' Donuts shops," yet the supreme judicial court did not focus on the covenant's scope as much as its five-mile geographic limitation. 442 Mass. at 637; *see also Curves Int'l, Inc.*, 2013 WL 1946826, at *2 (upholding covenant prohibiting operation of a fitness facility within ten miles of Curves location). Pre-*Boulanger* franchise decisions by federal courts upheld both specific and vague covenants without extensive analysis. *See Diet Center, Inc. v. Day*, 1990 WL 10830131 (D. Mass. Mar. 19, 1990) (covenant (1) prohibited competition with franchisor through (a) sale or delivery of products and services "of the kind sold and distributed" by franchisor and (b) engagement in business similar to that of franchisor; (2) prohibited use of franchisor's proprietary marks; and (3) prohibited use of any confidential methods, techniques, or procedures associated with franchisor); *In re Ward*, 194 B.R. at 705, 709 (upholding less specific covenant prohibiting terminated franchisee from entering into competition with franchisor).

Get in Shape is a post-*Boulanger* franchise case that discussed the broad scope of the limitation imposed by the franchisor's covenant: the franchisee was prohibited from "directly or indirectly" owning, maintaining, operating, engaging in, being employed by, or otherwise having any interest in "any fitness center, health club, personal training studio, or any other business concepts that directly compete with GISFW within an 8 mile radius" of the studio, or any other GISFW location, for two years (i.e., "starting any new business in competition with [GISFW]," "[a]ssisting in starting any new business in competition with [GISFW]," and "[s]oliciting franchisees or clients from [GISFW]"). *Get in Shape Franchise, Inc.*, 167 F. Supp. 3d at 185. When considering whether the former franchisee had breached the covenant, the court noted that she had registered Fit Chicks in her sister's name with the State of Indiana before terminating the franchise agreement with GISFW, sold the studio inventory and equipment to her sister for $1, developed the Fit Chicks workout program, volunteered at the Fit Chicks studio roughly 40 hours per week as a manager, and serviced former GISFW clients. The court held that each of these activities would likely harm GISFW's goodwill and impair its ability to establish another studio in the same town, a factor that supported the granting of a preliminary injunction in favor of the franchisor. *Id.* at 201.

Courts will not necessarily accept covenants that are broad in scope, especially if they can be interpreted in such a way that allows the former franchisee to go about his or her permissible business. For example, in *RE/MAX of New England*, the covenant prevented the former franchisees from directly or indirectly operating, managing, owning, or having any ownership interest in any business "that is a licensee or franchisee of any franchising organization or network that competes with [RE/MAX]." 2014 WL 3058295, at *3. In this case, a multi-unit franchisee operated 13 offices, and when three franchise agreements expired, those three offices began doing business under a separate corporate name (with the same owner). In denying the franchisor's request for a preliminary injunction, the court held that the post-term provision was "aimed at preventing former RE/MAX franchisees from becoming licensees of or franchisees of a 'franchising organization' or a 'franchising network.'" *Id.* Since the new company operating the three offices was neither, there was no violation of the covenant. Another important takeaway from *RE/MAX of New England* is the extent to which courts consider the balancing of the hardships and the public interest when considering whether to grant a preliminary injunction. The court here explicitly referenced evidence that the franchisees had invested over $600,000 in their transition and would have gone out of business—adversely affecting real estate customers, sales agents, and other employees—if they were enjoined. *Id.* at *4.

6. Does the state recognize a difference between in-term and post-term covenants?

The *RE/MAX of New England* case above involved in-term and post-term covenants against competition; however, the court did not enforce either covenant. *Id.* The entity operating all 13 locations (including the three with expired franchise agreements that were operating on a month-to-month-basis) sent a termination letter to the franchisor. For its part, the franchisor insisted that the in-term covenant applied to the ten locations because the multi-unit franchisee had no right to terminate unilaterally. The court simply assumed that the agreements were still in force and decided that the in-term covenant did not apply because they limited only ordinary competition. Since there were no trade secrets involved and the goodwill in the real estate brokerage was more likely generated from personal relationships and legwork (instead of franchisor branding and methods), it denied the franchisor's request for a preliminary injunction. *Id.*

The U.S. District Court for the Eastern District of New York, applying Massachusetts law, deemed an in-term covenant reasonable in a Dunkin' Donuts franchise agreement that prevented the franchisees from owning or operating a competing business. *Dunkin' Donuts, Inc. v. Donut Ring Corp.*, 2008 WL 11429347 (E.D.N.Y. Jan. 31, 2008). Although the court allowed the case to proceed to trial on whether the other restaurants were actually competing and whether the franchisor had waived the covenant, it wrote that "this type of in-term non-compete covenant has been found to be reasonable because it is temporally limited by its very terms—the covenant is relevant and applicable only during the term of the franchise agreement." *Id.* at *7.

7. Has the state allowed enforcement of covenants against non-signatories (e.g., family members, newly formed corporations)?

The one decision directly addressing this issue in the franchise context suggests that courts applying Massachusetts law are reluctant to enforce covenants not to compete against those who did not sign the franchise agreement in their personal capacity. *See Grease Monkey Int'l v. Alco Lubrication Servs., Inc.*, 24 F. Supp. 2d 120, 124–25 (D. Mass. 1998). Here, Robert Lieberman signed a franchise agreement with the franchisor of a fast-service lubrication business on behalf of the franchisee, Alco Lubrication Services, Inc. ("Alco"). Lieberman had formed Alco for the sole purpose of becoming the franchisee and was the corporation's sole officer, director, and shareholder. Lieberman signed a franchise agreement that contained a covenant that prohibited the "franchisee" from engaging in any fast-service lubrication business for two years after the franchise terminated. The express language of the agreement, and the covenant contained in it, identified the "franchisee" as Alco. When the franchise agreement expired, Alco sold its inventory to Road Runner Lube & Co. ("Road Runner"), a limited-liability company whose only members were Lieberman's wife and mother-in-law. Alco then began operating a small used auto sales business, while Road Runner immediately entered the fast-service lubrication market, with Lieberman serving as the store manager. *Id.* at 123.

In denying a preliminary injunction, the U.S. District Court for the District of Massachusetts rejected the franchisor's argument that Lieberman personally was in violation of the covenant, observing that it applied only to the franchisee, which, in this case, referred to Alco and not its officers, directors, or shareholders. *Id.* at 124. In reaching this conclusion, the court relied, in part, on the fact that a later version of the franchisor's current non-competition clause (as opposed to the version Lieberman signed when Alco became a franchisee) had been modified expressly to cover the franchisee's officers and directors in their personal capacities. *See id.* at 124 n.2 (noting that more recent version of agreement required signatory to be "personally liable for the breach of each and every provision in the [franchise] [a]greement . . . [and] be bound by the restrictive covenants . . . contained [therein]"). The court acknowledged that Road Runner and its principals may have been the alter egos of either Lieberman or Alco, and thus may have bound by (and in violation of) the covenant against competition; however, the court could not conclude that the franchisor was likely to prevail on that theory based on the limited evidence before it. *Id.* at 124–26. It is worth mentioning that the court wrote the following when considering the balancing of the equities criterion:

> If [franchisor] ultimately prevails, its alleged harm is compensable. However, Lieberman's ability to earn a living in his chosen field would be extinguished or at least substantially curtailed if he were enjoined. The equities also favor Road Runner. A preliminary injunction would cause Road Runner obvious hardship because it would shut down Road Runner's fast lube operations.

Id. at 125.

More generally, the supreme judicial court has acknowledged six theories under which a signatory may enforce a contract (usually an arbitration agreement) against a non-signatory: (1) incorporation by reference, (2) assumption, (3) agency, (4) veil-piercing/alter ego, (5) equitable estoppel, and (6) third-party beneficiary. *Landry v. Transworld Sys., Inc.*, 485 Mass. 334 (2020) (arbitration agreement not enforceable by non-signatory debt collector under agency and third-party beneficiary theories); *Machado v. System4, LLC*, 471 Mass. 204 (2015) (employees were equitably estopped from avoiding arbitration claims against franchisor and subfranchisors).

8. Will the state modify, "blue-pencil," or otherwise reduce a covenant found to be overboard?

The supreme judicial court recently reaffirmed that if a covenant is found to be too broad "in time, in space or in any other respect," courts will only enforce the agreement "to the extent that is reasonable and to the extent that it is severable for the purposes of enforcement." *Automile Holdings, LLC v. McGovern*, 483 Mass. 797, 808–09 (2020) (quoting *All Stainless, Inc. v. Colby*, 364 Mass. 773, 778 (1974)). There does not appear to be any franchise case in which a court exercised such "blue-pencil" discretion. Indeed, courts rarely reduce the temporal, geographic, or topical scope of covenants, and often do so only at later stages of the litigation after more evidence has been developed. For example, a state superior court reduced three aspects of a covenant protecting an employer that manufactured meter-locking devices sold to utility companies. *Inner-Tite Corp. v. Brozowski*, 27 Mass. L. Rptr. 204, 2010 WL 3038330 (Mass. Super. Ct. Apr. 14, 2010). After a trial on the merits consolidated with the employer's motion for a preliminary injunction, the court

(1) reduced the temporal restriction from two to one year, (2) reduced restricted geographic area from the entire United States to only the southeastern states where the employee had actually worked, and (3) reduced the restricted products to only those to which he had actual responsibility. *See also Genuine Auto Parts Co. v. Auto Parts Int'l, Inc.*, 26 Mass. L. Rptr. 21, 2009 WL 2603163 (Mass. Super. Ct. 2009) (ten-year covenant in agreement to sell business reduced to five years on summary judgment because too limiting on seller's employment opportunities, seller was not fully represented by counsel, and no allocation of specific sum to the covenant); *Tomer v. Hollister Assocs., Inc.*, 2006 WL 4555672 (Mass. Super. Ct. Mar. 6, 2006) (five-year covenant reduced to 18 months on summary judgment because longer time period protected former employer more from ordinary competition than preserving its ability to retain patronage, positive reputation among customers, or generation of repeat business); *American Stop Loss Ins. Brokerage Servs., Inc. v. Prince*, 12 Mass. L. Rptr. 650, 2011 WL 173178 (Mass. Super. Ct. Feb. 15, 2001) (enforcing non-compete against insurance salesman, but permitting him to work for competitor in non-sales capacity); *W.B. Mason Co., Inc. v. Staples, Inc.*, 2001 WL 227855 (Mass. Super. Ct., Jan. 18, 2001) (where covenant provided that employees could not sell office products in defined territory, enforced only insofar as it prohibited employees from selling office products to customers of former employer).

9. When does the non-compete period begin to run? Will courts equitably extend the term?

Without any discussion, when the U.S. District Court of the District of Massachusetts was presented with the choice to begin the period on (1) the day the franchisee purportedly terminated the franchise agreement and informed the franchisor that it was closing (June 24, 2015) or (2) the day the franchisor terminated the franchise agreement (June 30, 2015), the court chose the latter and enforced the two-year covenant until July 1, 2017. *Get in Shape Franchise, Inc.*, 167 F. Supp. 3d at 186, 207. With respect to the question of equitable extension of the term, the supreme judicial court recently observed that "because [noncompetition] agreements serve as a direct restraint on an individual employee's ability to earn a living, we have not allowed the extension of the period of restraint beyond the terms of the agreement." *Automile Holdings, LLC*, 483 Mass. at 816 (citing *All Stainless, Inc. v. Colby*, 364 Mass. 773, 777 (1974) ("because the period of the [restrictive covenant] has expired, [the plaintiff] is left to the recovery of any damages arising from [the violation of the covenant]")); *but see Wells v. Wells*, 9 Mass. App. Ct. 321, 327–28 (1980) (restrictive covenant extended in sale of business where no end date had been present in written contract and one was originally fashioned by trial judge).

10. Are there additional nuances or peculiarities of the state's treatment of covenants in the franchising context?

The author is not aware of any beyond the idiosyncratic facts of the cases cited above.

Michigan

by Mark Burzych *

1. Has the state addressed covenants against competition in the context of franchising?

- **Does the state have a franchising statute or regulations that address covenants against competition?**
- **Does the state have a covenants statute of general applicability that would encompass franchise covenants?**
- **Have the courts addressed covenants in the context of franchising either under a statute or under the state's common law?**

Michigan's statute regulating franchising, the Michigan Franchise Investment Law (MFIL), and the regulations under MFIL do not directly address the enforceability of covenants against competition in the franchising context. *See* MICH. COMP. LAWS ANN. §§ 445.1501–.1546 (West 1984). However, MFIL references covenants against competition in section 27(d), which provides that a provision in a franchise agreement that permits a franchisor to refuse to renew a franchise without fairly compensating the franchisee for the fair market value of certain inventory, supplies, equipment, fixtures, and furnishings is void and unenforceable. *See* MICH. COMP. LAWS ANN. § 445.1527 (West 1984). Section 27(d) only applies if the term of the franchise is less than five years and (1) *the franchisee is prohibited from continuing to conduct substantially the same business in the same area subsequent to the expiration of the franchise* or (2) the franchisee does not receive at least six months' advance notice of the franchisor's intent not to renew the franchise agreement. *Id.*

The Michigan Supreme Court applied the rule of reason to determine the enforceability of covenants against competition even before the enactment of statutes regulating antitrust practices. *See Bristol Windows v. Hoogenstyn*, 650 N.W.2d 670, 677 (Mich. Ct. App. 2002). However, beginning in 1905 and continuing until the enactment of the Michigan Antitrust Reform Act (MARA), *see* MICH. COMP. LAWS ANN. §§ 445.771–.788 (West 1985). Michigan had a statute of general applicability that prohibited covenants

*Mr. Burzych is a member in and President of the law firm of Fahey Schultz Burzych Rhodes, PLC in Okemos, Michigan. The author thanks Hannah Morgan, future associate with Fahey Schultz Burzych Rhodes, PLC, for her excellent and diligent assistance with this chapter. This chapter incorporates work from the previous edition's chapter authored by John A. Forrest.

against competition as restraints of trade, which will be referred to hereinafter as the "pre-MARA statute." *See* Mich. Comp. Laws Ann. § 445.761 (West 1905) (repealed 1985) (hereinafter, pre-MARA statute). The pre-MARA statute read as follows:

> All agreements and contracts in which any person, copartnership or corporation promises or agrees not to engage in any avocation, employment, pursuit, trade, profession or business, whether reasonable or unreasonable, partial or general, limited or unlimited are hereby declared to be against public policy and are illegal and void. *Id.*

Although the MARA statute, by its terms, is limited to employment situations, until 2016 these provisions had been consistently cited in non-employment cases for the proposition that Michigan law expressly provides that covenants not to compete are lawful. *See, e.g., Allegra Network, LLC v. AM Marketing, Inc.*, 2001 WL 37074684 (E.D. Mich. 2001) (finding that Michigan law expressly provides that covenants not to compete are lawful). In 2016, the Michigan Supreme Court reversed course and held that it was an error for Michigan courts rely on the employee-employer framework provided in MARA to evaluate the reasonableness of non-compete agreements in other than employment contexts. Rather, non-compete agreements in other than employment contexts should be evaluated under the rule of reason. *See Innovation Ventures v. Liquid Mfg.*, 885 N.W.2d 861, 864–65 (Mich. 2016) (hereinafter, *Liquid Manufacturing*).

The rule of reason has been articulated by federal courts as:

> [W]hether the restraint imposed is such as merely regulates and perhaps thereby promotes competition or whether it is such as may suppress or even destroy competition. To determine that question the court must ordinarily consider the facts peculiar to the business to which the restraint is applied; its condition before and after the restraint was imposed; the nature of the restraint and its effect, actual or probable. The history of the restraint, the evil believed to exist, the reason for adopting the particular remedy, the purpose or end sought to be attained, are all relevant facts. This is not because a good intention will save an otherwise objectionable regulation or the reverse; but because knowledge of intent may help the court to interpret facts and to predict consequences.

See id. (quoting *Board of Trade of City of Chicago v. United States*, 246 U.S. 231, 238 (1918)).

In *Innovation Ventures, LLC v. Custom Nutrition Laboratories, LLC* (*Innovation Ventures I*), the Sixth Circuit recognized that the Michigan Supreme Court's decision in the 2016 *Liquid Manufacturing* case requires Michigan courts to evaluate non-compete agreements between businesses under the rule of reason rather than by analogy to employment non-compete agreements. 912 F.3d 316, 340 (6th Cir. 2018) (hereinafter, *Innovation Ventures I*). The Sixth Circuit then went on to analyze how the rule of reason should be applied in this context.

Prior to *Liquid Manufacturing*, Michigan law was clear that "[t]he burden of demonstrating the validity of the agreement is on the party seeking enforcement." *Id.* at 341. While the burden of proof likely remains the same in the context of employment non-compete agreements, after *Liquid Manufacturing*, a defendant who contests the enforcement of a non-compete agreement in the business-to-business context on the grounds it is an unreasonable restraint on competition now bears the burden of showing the restraint is unreasonable and therefore invalid. *Id.* (citing *Perceptron, Inc. v. Sensor Adaptive Machines, Inc.*, 221 F.3d 913, 918 (6th Cir. 2000)).

On remand from the Sixth Circuit, the district court was tasked with applying the rule of reason test rather than analogizing to employer non-compete agreements. *Innovation Ventures, LLC v. Custom Nutrition Laboratories, LLC*, 451 F. Supp. 3d 769, 776 (E.D. Mich. 2020) (hereinafter, *Innovation Ventures II*). In determining how to apply the rule of reason test, the court in *Innovation Ventures II* analyzed the "historical roots and development" of the test in Michigan case law. *Id.* at 779. Specifically, the court paid close attention to a standard developed in the 1873 Michigan Supreme Court case, *Hubbard v. Miller*. *Id.* (citing *Hubbard v. Miller*, 27 Mich. 15, 19 (1873)). The standard delineated in *Hubbard* developed over time into what is referred to by Michigan courts as the "common law rule of reason":

> First, the covenant must be for a just and honest purpose. Second, it must be established for the protection of the legitimate interest of the party in whose favor it is imposed. Third, it must be reasonable as between the parties to the contract. Finally, it must not be specially injurious to the public.

See Cardiology Assocs. of Southwestern Michigan, PC v. Zencka, 400 N.W.2d 606, 607–08 (1985).

Based on the district court's understanding of the Michigan Supreme Court's holding in *Liquid Manufacturing*, it concluded that the following factors should be considered when applying the rule of reason test to evaluate challenges to non-compete agreements in contexts other than employment relationships under Michigan law: "(1) whether the restraint is ancillary to the main business purpose of an otherwise lawful contract; (2) whether the restraint protects legitimate property interests, for example, goodwill; (3) whether the restraint's duration, geographic reach, and scope are reasonable considering the nature of the property interest being protected; and (4) whether the restraint suppresses or destroys competition in the relevant market." *Id.* A court must take into account each of these factors to determine whether the restraint is reasonable or void. *Id.* (citing *Hubbard* at 20 ("[I]f reasonable and just, the restriction will be sustained, if not, it will be held void.")).

In evaluating the parties' non-compete agreement under this understanding of the common law rule of reason, the court expressly rejected analogizing to cases cited in the employer-employee context. So, while Michigan courts have a long history of analyzing the reasonableness of a non-compete agreement by analogizing to the employer context, that analysis is no longer recognized under Michigan law. In Michigan, courts will now analyze non-compete agreements under a rule of reason analysis.

---

2. Have the courts articulated the "legitimate interests" of the franchisor that will support enforcement of a covenant against competition contained in a franchise agreement?

- **If so, what are they (e.g., protection of goodwill, protection of confidential information), and in what contexts did the issue arise?**
- **If not, what interests have been recognized in other contexts (e.g., employment agreements, the sale of business context)?**

In *Innovation Ventures II*, the court acknowledged that in its prior findings, the court had already found that the plaintiff had a legitimate business interest in the restrictive covenants, and the defendants had previously conceded that the plaintiff's interest in protecting its goodwill was a legitimate business purpose. *Id.* at 787–89. In its initial determination of whether the plaintiff had legitimate business interests, the district court recognized that "preventing unfair competition through the misuse of a company's goodwill is a legitimate business interest." *See Innovation Ventures, LLC v. Custom Nutrition Laboratories, LLC*, 2015 WL 5679879 (E.D. Mich. Sept. 28, 2015), *rev'd on other grounds, Innovation Ventures, LLC v. Custom Nutrition Laboratories*, LLC, 912 F.3d 316, 340 (6th Cir. 2018).

In *Safeharbor Management Group v. Huston*, the parties entered into an independent contractor agreement under which the defendant, Huston, would solicit and generate insurance business for the plaintiff, Safeharbor, in exchange for compensation in the form of commission. *See Safeharbor Mgmt. Grp., LLC v. Huston*, WL 7641822, at *1 (W.D. Mich. Oct. 26, 2020). After the relationship was terminated, Huston began soliciting business from his former Safeharbor clients, and Safeharbor brought suit against Huston for breach of the non-solicitation clauses contained in their prior agreement. *Id.* The court found that Safeharbor had "a legitimate interest in protecting the goodwill it has cultivated with its clients," so the "protection of its clients via the restrictive covenants" was reasonable. *Id.*

In *Certified Restoration Dry Cleaning Network, LLC v. Tenke Corp.*, the Sixth Circuit enumerated a number of legitimate interests that would support enforcement of a covenant against competition in a franchise agreement. 511 F.3d 535 (6th Cir. 2007). The defendant's franchise was terminated for non-payment. After termination, the defendant continued to service its former restoration dry-cleaning customers. The franchisor brought an action to enforce the non-compete provision in the franchise agreement. The defendant argued that it should not be prevented from continuing to service restoration dry-cleaning customers that it served before entering into the franchise agreement.

Notably, at this time, courts still evaluated non-compete clauses for reasonableness under the employment context by examining the clause's duration and geographic scope and the type of employment prohibited, and Michigan courts also "consider[ed] the reasonableness of the competitive business interests justifying the clause." *Id.* at 546. In this case, the court primarily referenced employment law cases. The court noted that under Michigan law, reasonable covenants not to compete may protect such reasonable interests as trade secrets, confidential information, customers or customer lists, or cost factors and pricing. *Id.* at 547–48 (collecting cases).

The court noted that the franchisor's post-termination non-compete clause was "designed to protect the franchisor . . . from unfair competition by the former franchisee who has knowledge of the franchisor's proprietary Restoration DC System and customer list." *Id.* at 545. The court found that under Michigan law, the franchisor has a reasonable competitive interest in preventing the franchisee from using the confidential information he learned as a franchisee to gain a competitive advantage in the provision of restoration dry-cleaning services. *Id.* at 549.

The court also found that the protection of existing and future franchisees was a legitimate interest that would support the enforcement of a non-compete clause. The court stated that the franchisor had produced evidence to show that the non-competition clause is designed to prevent defendants from having such an unfair advantage over a future franchisee. *Id.* "In short, by prohibiting Defendants from providing any restoration dry cleaning services for two years following termination of the franchise, the non-compete clause prevents Defendants from using their knowledge of Plaintiff's Restoration DC System and the relationships they established as Plaintiff's franchisee to steal customers from Plaintiff's new franchisee." *Id.*

The court in *Tanfran, Inc. v. Aron Alan, LLC* was asked to issue a preliminary injunction to enforce a non-compete provision in a tanning business franchise agreement against persons who were not parties to the franchise agreement. 2007 WL 1796235 (W.D. Mich. 2007). The court found the covenant to be reasonable without specifically discussing the legitimate interests of the franchisor supporting the enforcement of the non-compete. However, in the discussion of the irreparable injury element of the preliminary injunction analysis, the court stated that a "franchisor's inability to enforce a covenant not to compete affects not only the franchisor's ability to maintain control of its reputation and goodwill, but also to refranchise the area." *Id.*

The court in *Little Caesar Enterprises, Inc. v. Little Caesar's VA, Inc.* was asked to issue a preliminary injunction to enforce a non-compete provision in a pizza business franchise agreement. 2009 WL 10459862 (E.D. Va. 2009). The franchisor had terminated the franchise agreement based on a transfer of the business without the franchisor's approval and abandonment of the business by the franchisee of record. The court examined the enforceability of the non-compete clause under Michigan law. Citing *Certified Restoration*, the court noted that courts have held franchisors to have a reasonable competitive interest in preventing former franchisees from using confidential information or business methods that they learned as franchisees to gain a competitive advantage. *Id.*

The court in *Smallbizpros, Inc., v. Court* was asked to issue a preliminary injunction to enforce a non-compete provision in a franchise agreement for a business offering a variety of accounting and business counseling services. 414 F. Supp. 2d 1245 (M.D. Ga. 2006). In this case the former franchisee purported to terminate the franchise agreement, alleging a breach by the franchisor based on the decreasing quality and quantity of support services. The former franchisee continued to operate a similar business under a different name. The court examined the enforceability of the covenant under Michigan law and found the covenant to be reasonable, without specifically discussing the legitimate interests of the franchisor supporting the enforcement of the non-compete. However, in the discussion of the irreparable injury element of the preliminary injunction analysis, the court noted that the franchisor's interests in the non-compete provision included preserving the franchisor's ability to refranchise the franchise territory, retain customers (and the customer's goodwill), and maintain the integrity of the franchise system. *Id.* The court found that each of these purposes would be impaired if the covenant not to compete was not enforced. The court further found that the irreparable harm element was met because it was difficult to determine the monetary value of these injuries, and it may not be possible to undo some of the injuries through monetary damages.

---

3. What time limitations have courts recognized as reasonable in the franchise context?

- **If no franchise cases have been decided, what time limitations have been recognized in other contexts?**
- **How have they been related to interests protected?**

In *Innovation Ventures II*, the federal district court reviewed a number of Michigan cases involving business-to-business non-compete agreements, with durations ranging anywhere from three to twenty years. *See Innovation Ventures II* at 788 (citing *Bristol Window & Door v. Hoogenstyn*, 650 N.W.2d 670, 679 (Mich. Ct. App. 2002) (considering a three-year limitation and remanded for the trial court to determine whether the length was reasonable); *In re Spradlin*, 284 B.R. 830, 836 (E.D. Mich. 2002) (holding that five years was reasonable); *Brillhart v. Danneffel*, 194 N.W.2d 63, 65 (Mich. Ct. App. 1971) (analyzing a covenant not to compete between the buyer and seller of a restaurant under a reasonableness standard and holding that the business-to-business non-compete agreement was reasonable because the defendant understood they were signing a five-year restriction, the defendant's agent wrote the agreement, and they voluntarily signed the contract); *Lieghio v. Loveland Inv.*, 2009 WL 3491620, at *1, *5 (Mich. Ct. App. Oct. 29, 2009) (holding that a twenty-year covenant not to compete in a hotel business was not unreasonable because "the parties' agreement is similar to those upheld in a long line of cases, like *Brillhart*, that have sanctioned covenants not to compete where they are merely a reasonable restraint on a seller's competitive efforts in order to promote the buyer's realization of goodwill in the purchased business."). However, the court further stated that "[t[hese decisions do not provide the Court with much comfort that a business-to-business noncompete agreement lasting 20 years would necessarily be found reasonable under the rule of reason test, but nor do they clearly indicate that a twenty year noncompete agreement with otherwise reasonable terms would automatically be voided under the rule of reason." *Id.* In order to determine the reasonableness of the 20-year non-compete, the court recognized that the defendant knew of the duration when he signed the agreement; however, the plaintiff failed to provide a reasonable justification for the decades-long duration, and the company's interest in protecting its goodwill was not a sufficient justification. *Id.*

In *Safeharbor Management Group v. Huston*, which is discussed in more detail in section 2, the court first considered the reasonableness of a two-year prohibition on soliciting "Vested Clients." *See* Safeharbor Mgmt. Grp., LLC v. Huston, No. 1:20-cv-924, WL 7641822, at *5 (W.D. Mich. Oct. 26, 2020). Safeharbor argued that because it primarily sells insurance products to seniors, the average length of the relationship is only seven years total. *Id.* The court noted that these clients are mainly clients that the defendant, Huston, solicited through his personal relationships, and therefore, to forbid him from servicing these clients for "nearly one-third of the life of the contract ultimately may not be reasonable." *Id.* However, because the defendant understood the contents of the agreement when he signed it, he explicitly agreed to the two-year non-solicitation clause of Safeharbor clients, even those contacts and clients he personally generated. *Id.* Under these circumstances, the court held that the duration of the non-solicitation of "Vested Clients" was reasonable. *Id.* However, the court also held that the indefinite prohibition on contacting "Assigned Clients" was categorically unreasonable. *Id.* (quoting *Wolverine Sign Works v. Powers*, 227 N.W. 669, 670 (Mich. 1929) ("Never is a long time.")).

In *Little Caesar Enterprises, Inc. v. Rooyakker*, the court overturned a lower court decision that held that the franchisor did not have a cause of action because the former franchisee did not breach the two-year non-compete provision in the franchise agreement. 2009 WL 1940563 (Mich. Ct. App. July 7, 2009). The court did not specifically discuss the length of the time limitation, but the court was not troubled by the two-year period.

In *Certified Restoration Dry Cleaning Network, LLC v. Tenke Corp.*, which is discussed in more detail in section 2, the court enforced a non-compete time period of 24 months from the time of expiration or termination of the franchise agreement.

511 F.3d 535 (6th Cir. 2007). In its discussion, the court noted that "[w]ith respect to duration, Michigan courts have not provided any bright-line rules. Rather they 'have upheld non-compete agreements covering time periods of six months to three years.'" *Id.* at 547 (citing *Whirlpool Corp. v. Burns*, 457 F. Supp. 2d 806, 812 (W.D. Mich. 2006)).

In *Tanfran, Inc. v. Aron Alan, LLC*, the court enforced the non-compete period for two years from termination of the agreement. 2007 WL 1796235 (W.D. Mich. 2007). The defendants in that case were disputing whether the non-compete could apply to non-parties to the agreement, and they did not argue that the time period was unreasonable. The court found no reason to conclude that the duration was unreasonable. In *Allegra Network, LLC v. AM Marketing, Inc.*, the court enforced a two-year post-termination covenant not to compete in a printing and copy service business franchise agreement. 2001 WL 37074684 (E.D. Mich. 2001). In *Ohio State Waterproofing, Inc. v. North Coast Waterproofing, Inc.*, the court referenced its earlier order in the case enforcing a two-year post-termination covenant in a basement waterproofing business franchise agreement. 1996 U.S. Dist. LEXIS 16224 (unpublished W.D. Mich. July 16, 1996).

In the sale of business context, longer time limitations have generally been found to be reasonable by Michigan courts. *See, e.g., In re Spradlin*, 284 B.R. 830 (E.D. Mich. 2002) (five years); *Roland v. Kenzie*, 62 N.W.2d 97 (1968) (three years); *Brillhart v. Danneffel*, 194 N.W.2d 63 (1972) (five years not unreasonable in connection with sale of rural restaurant). Despite a vigorous dissent, in *Wolverine Sign Works v. Powers*, the court enforced an agreement in which the seller of a billboard business promised never to sell billboards again within a very large geographic area. 227 N.W. 669 (1929).

---

4. What geographic limitations have courts recognized as reasonable in the franchise context?

- **How have they been related to the interests protected?**
- **Have courts recognized the legitimacy of protecting other franchisees from competition?**

In *Innovation Ventures II*, the court noted that in its prior findings regarding the non-compete agreement between the two parties, the court had found that the geographic locations of the restrictions were reasonable. *See Innovation Ventures II* at 788–89 (citing *Innovation Ventures, LLC v. Custom Nutrition Laboratories, LLC*, 2015 WL 5679879 (E.D. Mich. Sept. 28, 2015), *rev'd on other grounds, Innovation Ventures, LLC v. Custom Nutrition Laboratories, LLC*, 912 F.3d 316, 340 (6th Cir. 2018)). In its previous decision, the court noted that restrictions had "a worldwide geographic limitation," and worldwide geographic limitations "can be reasonable if the employer actually has legitimate business interests throughout the world." *See Innovation Ventures, LLC v. Custom Nutrition Laboratories, LLC*, 2015 WL 5679879, at *24 (E.D. Mich. Sept. 28, 2015), *rev'd on other grounds, Innovation Ventures, LLC v. Custom Nutrition Laboratories, LLC*, 912 F.3d 316, 340 (6th Cir. 2018).

In *Certified Restoration Dry Cleaning Network, LLC v. Tenke Corp.*, which is discussed in more detail in section 2, the court enforced a geographic limitation consisting of (1) the franchisee's territory, (2) the territories of other franchisees as of the date of the termination, and (3) the area contained in a circle having a radius of 25 miles outward from the border of the franchisee's territory. 511 F.3d 535 (6th Cir. 2007). The court found that the geographic limitation in that case was "tailored to serve the legitimate goal of preventing unfair competition with [the franchisor's] future franchisee." *Id.* The defendant had argued that the clause was unreasonable because it prohibited competition in virtually all of Ohio. The court disagreed because "it only extends to a twenty-five mile radius of six of Ohio's eighty-eight counties." The court did not find this "narrowly defined geographic scope" to be patently unreasonable. *Id.* at 550.

In *Tanfran, Inc. v. Aron Alan, LLC*, the court enforced a post-termination non-compete that prohibited competition within 25 miles of the franchisee's location and within 25 miles of any other Mirage Tanning Center retail location. 2007 WL 1796235 (W.D. Mich. 2007). The defendants in that case were disputing whether the non-compete could apply to non-parties to the agreement, and they did not argue that the geographical limitation was unreasonable. The court found no reason to conclude that the geographical limitation was unreasonable.

In *Allegra Network, LLC v. AM Marketing, Inc.*, the court enforced a post-termination covenant in a printing and copy service business franchise agreement that prohibited competition within a ten-mile radius from the site of the franchised business or within five miles from any other Allegra-related operation. 2001 WL 37074684 (E.D. Mich. 2001).

In *Ohio State Waterproofing, Inc. v. North Coast Waterproofing, Inc.*, the court referenced its earlier order in the case enforcing a post-termination covenant in a basement waterproofing business franchise agreement that prohibited competition within 60 miles of any Ever-Dry Waterproofing franchisee's exclusive territory. 1996 U.S. Dist. LEXIS 16224 (W.D. Mich. 1996).

In a case involving a non-competition agreement entered into after MARA in connection with the sale of a furniture distributorship, the Michigan Court of Appeals enforced a two-state geographic limitation (Michigan and Ohio). *See In re* Spradlin, 284 B.R. 830 (E.D. Mich. 2002). In a case involving a non-competition agreement entered into pre-MARA in connection with the sale of a rural restaurant business, the Michigan Court of Appeals enforced a ten-mile geographic limitation. *See Brillhart v. Danneffel*, 36 Mich. App. 359, 364, 194 N.W.2d 63 (1972).

5. What limitations on activities have courts recognized as reasonable in the franchise context?

In *Little Caesar Enterprises, Inc. v. Rooyakker*, the non-compete clause provided that the franchisee must not "either directly or indirectly, for itself or through, on behalf of, or in conjunction with any person, persons, or legal entity, own, maintain, advise, operate, engage in, be employed by, make loans to, or have any interest in or relationship or association with a business which is a quick or fast service restaurant primarily engaged in the sale of pizza, pasta, sandwiches, and/or related products." 2009 WL 1940563 (Mich. Ct. App. July 7, 2009). In this case, the former franchisee had operated multiple franchise restaurants. The former franchisee sold five of the restaurants in an installment sale to an entity owned by the son of the owners of the franchisee. The former franchisee retained two of the restaurants. Without specifically discussing the reasonableness of the limitations on activities, the court of appeals was willing to enforce the contractual limitations contained in the non-compete clause, including the prohibition on making loans to a competing entity.

In *Innovation Ventures II*, the court acknowledged that in its prior findings, the court had already found that the scope of the restrictions was reasonable. *See Innovation Ventures II* at 787–89. In its initial determination as to whether the restrictions were of reasonable scope, the district court noted that "case law makes clear that a limited prohibition from engaging in a part of a market or industry is reasonable." *See Innovation Ventures, LLC v. Custom Nutrition Laboratories, LLC*, 2015 WL 5679879, at *23 (E.D. Mich. Sept. 28, 2015), *rev'd on other grounds, Innovation Ventures, LLC v. Custom Nutrition Laboratories, LLC*, 912 F.3d 316, 340 (6th Cir. 2018).

In *Safeharbor Management Group v. Huston*, which is discussed in greater detail in section 2, the court found that the general scope of the restrictive covenants was reasonable. *See Safeharbor Mgmt. Grp., LLC v. Huston*, WL 7641822, at *1 (W.D. Mich. Oct. 26, 2020). The court noted that the defendant was only prohibited from soliciting Safeharbor's clients; he was not prohibited from beginning a new insurance business, joining a different insurance broker, working with the same insurance companies as Safeharbor, or soliciting new clients and generating new business. *Id.* Because the court found that Safeharbor had a legitimate interest in protecting its goodwill, it held the scope of the restrictive covenants was reasonable. *Id.*

In *Victory Lane Quick Oil Change, Inc. v. Magrid Darwich*, the non-compete clause provided that the franchisee and its owners and guarantors "will not . . . on their own account or as an employee, principal, agent, independent contractor, consultant, affiliate, licensee, partner, officer, director or owner of any other person . . . , own, operate, lease, franchise, conduct, engage in, be connected with, have any interest in or assist any person . . . engaged in any Competitive Business." 2011 WL 2581183 (E.D. Mich. 2011). In this case, the assets of the franchise business were sold to the brother of an owner of the franchisee. The franchisee claimed that it was not operating the competing business. However, the franchisee remained the tenant at the premises because the landlord would not agree to assign the lease to the new owner of the business. Based on this, the court held that the franchisee was arguably "connected with," had an "interest in," or was "assist[ing] any person or Entity engaged in a Competitive Business" in violation of the non-compete clause and the franchisor was likely to prevail on the merits of its breach of contract claim. As with the *Little Caesar Enterprises, Inc. v. Rooyakker* court, without specifically discussing the reasonableness of the limitations on activities, the federal district court was willing to enforce the contractual limitations contained in the non-compete clause and to broadly construe those limitations.

In *Certified Restoration Dry Cleaning Network, LLC v. Tenke Corp.*, which is discussed in more detail in section 2, the court enforced a limitation on engaging in "any restoration dry cleaning business." 511 F.3d 535 (6th Cir. 2007). The court applied this limitation to prohibit the former franchisee from providing any restoration dry-cleaning services, even to customers that the franchisee had before becoming a franchise. The court was not persuaded by the former franchisee's argument that it was not engaging in a restoration dry-cleaning business because restoration dry-cleaning services were not a major part of its business. On remand from the Sixth Circuit, the former franchisee argued that the covenant not to compete should not extend to its preexisting restoration customers because no provision was made, and no consideration was paid or provided by the franchisor to acquire those relationships. *See Certified Restoration Dry Cleaning Network, LLC v.*

Tenke Corp., 2008 WL 2218427 (E.D. Mich. 2008). The federal district court rejected this argument, finding that the unambiguous language of the contract did not provide an exception for prior restoration customers.

In *Allegra Network, LLC v. AM Marketing, Inc.*, the court enforced a post-termination covenant in a printing and copy service business franchise agreement that prohibited the operation of a printing or copy business offering products or services similar to those offered by the franchisor. 2001 WL 37074684 (E.D. Mich. 2001).

In *Ohio State Waterproofing, Inc. v. North Coast Waterproofing, Inc.*, the court referenced its earlier order in the case enforcing a post-termination covenant in a basement waterproofing business franchise agreement that prohibited the operation of a basement waterproofing business, including the solicitation of any customers residing within the restricted area. 1996 U.S. Dist. LEXIS 16224 (W.D. Mich. 1996).

In *Buckingham Tool Corp. v. Evans*, a sale of business case, the court considered one example of what it might mean to "indirectly" engage in a competing business. 192 N.W.2d 362 (Mich. Ct. App. 1971). The buyer of the business in *Buckingham Tool Corp.* claimed that the seller was engaging in a competing business through his son. The seller had lent his son the money necessary to start a competing business. The court found it to be "well settled that a noncompetition agreement is violated where one sets up a competing business in the name of another as a guise to do business for himself. On the other hand, it is not normally a violation of such agreement to merely lend money, extend credit, or the like to a person about to engage in a competing business." *Id.* at 77–78. The *Buckingham Tool Corp.* court found that "the great weight of the evidence indicated that the seller neither participated in the running of the business nor had a financial interest in it" (other than as a creditor), and, therefore, that the seller was not indirectly competing with the buyer. *Id.*

6. Does the state recognize a difference between in-term and post-term covenants?

In 1980, the Michigan attorney general issued an opinion finding that "an in-term covenant restricting a franchisee from engaging in a competing business during the term of the franchise is valid" and that "the franchisor may terminate the franchisee's license if the franchisee violates the covenant by opening a similar business during the life of the franchise and fails to promptly cure such failure to observe the covenant." *See* 5620 Op. Att'y Gen. 531 (1980). The opinion was written while the pre-MARA statute, which appeared to prohibit all franchise covenants against competition, was in effect. In support of his opinion, the attorney general noted that section 27(f) of MFIL (now section 27(d) of MFIL) recognized that a franchise agreement may contain a provision restricting a franchisee from continuing to conduct substantially the same business in the area subsequent to the expiration of the franchise and that MFIL contained no provision prohibiting the franchisee from establishing a similar business during the life of the franchise agreement. The opinion further stated:

> If a franchisor may restrict the activity of a franchisee for a reasonable period of time in the same area subsequent to the expiration of the franchise, in the absence of clear legislative language prohibiting an in-term covenant, there is no reason why a franchisor may not require a prospective franchisee to bind himself to devote his full attention to the operation of the franchise.

> A franchisee who freely contracts with a franchisor to refrain from engaging in a competing similar business during the life of the franchise is not contracting to be engaged in no business or no employment so as to deprive him of the means of earning a livelihood or to deprive the community of his free and unrestricted efforts in his field of pursuit. (citation omitted)
>
> If a prospective franchisee finds such a covenant to be a burden, he is free to decline entering into the franchise agreement. Having entered into the franchise agreement and received the benefits of it, it is untenable to argue that he is deprived of the means of earning the livelihood or that the community will be deprived of his free and unrestricted efforts in the field of activity he has chosen.

Id. It is worth noting that the Michigan attorney general found that certain public policy concerns that might affect the enforceability of post-term covenants (depriving an employee of a means of employment and depriving the community of the employee's efforts in his or her field of pursuit) were not applicable to in-term covenants.

In re Dynamic Enterprises, Inc. v. Fitness World of Jackson, Inc., was also decided under Michigan law while the pre-MARA statute was in effect. 32 B.R. 509, 1983-2 Trade Cas. (CCH) ¶ 65,715 (Bankr. M.D. Tenn. 1983), *abrogated on other grounds by In re SMEC, Inc.*, 160 B.R. 86 (Bankr. M.D. Tenn. 1993). This case involved an action by a franchisor debtor against its franchisee seeking damages for breach of a franchise agreement involving the franchise to operate a fitness center. The franchise agreement at issue included an in-term covenant not to compete prohibiting the franchisee from engaging in the operation of an exercise and fitness establishment during the term of the agreement. The franchisee had opened several other non-franchised fitness centers in violation of the covenant but had not complied with its obligation under the franchise agreement to pay the franchisor monthly service fees determined as a percentage of the gross sales of the other fitness centers. The franchisee challenged the enforceability of the in-term covenant not to compete, citing the pre-MARA statute. The *Dynamic Enterprises, Inc.* court noted the pre-MARA statute's prohibition on covenants, but found that "[r]estrictions on competition during the term of an agreement which are related to the subject matter of the performance of the contract, however, are not within the scope of the antitrust prohibition and are generally enforceable." *Id.* at 520.

7. Has the state allowed enforcement of covenants against non-signatories (e.g., family members, newly formed corporations)?

Courts applying Michigan law have enforced covenants not to compete against non-signatories in some circumstances.

In *Tanfran, Inc. v. Aron Alan, LLC*, the court enforced the covenant against entities that were not signatories to the franchise agreements. 2007 WL 1796235 (W.D. Mich. 2007). In this case, the franchisee owned four Mirage Tanning Center franchises. The non-signatories were a trust (the grantor of the trust was the mother of the owner of the franchisee) and an entity that acquired the assets of the franchisee. The trust had lent money to the franchisee and took security in the assets of the franchisee. The assets of the franchisee were purportedly surrendered to the trust in connection with the security interest of the trust as a result of a default in repaying the loan. The trust then transferred the assets to an entity that continued to operate the businesses as tanning salons under the name "Miracle Tanning." The franchisor brought an action against the trust and Miracle Tanning alleging, in part, that they were violating the non-compete provision in the franchise agreements and requesting injunctive relief against the trust and Miracle Tanning. The court found that the trust and Miracle Tanning had conspired with the franchisee to avoid the effect of the non-competition agreement. The court based this decision on the timing of the surrender (the franchisee had been in default for some time, and the surrender did not occur until after termination of the franchise) and the fact that the trust obtained more than the tangible personal property of the franchisee by continuing to use the phone numbers, customer lists, the franchisor's operations manual, and proprietary software. The court determined that if the trust and Miracle Tanning were allowed to continue the tanning business, it would be tantamount to permitting the franchisee to violate the non-compete agreements. Consequently, a preliminary injunction was issued against the trust and Miracle Tanning. *Id.* at *8.

In *Little Caesar Enterprises, Inc., et al. v. Little Caesar's VA, Inc.*, the court enforced the covenant against an individual who was a partial owner of the franchisee, but who was never known to be an owner or approved as an owner by the franchisor. 2009 WL 10459862 (E.D. Va. 2009). That individual was not a signatory on any of the agreements, and, in fact, the franchisor had refused to allow him to be an owner when the franchisee requested. The court determined that, at least for purposes of issuing a preliminary injunction, the non-signatory should be considered bound by the non-compete agreement. The court based this determination on the fact that the owners of the franchisee had misrepresented the true ownership of the franchise to the franchisor, and the non-signatory individual had actually been in control of the operations of the franchise for a period of time. Consequently, a preliminary injunction was issued against the individual non-signatory.

In *Little Caesar Enterprises, Inc. v. Rooyakker*, the court declined to enforce the covenant not to compete against a non-signatory. 2009 WL 1940563 (Mich. Ct. App. July 7, 2009). In that case, the franchisor took steps to terminate the former franchisee's franchise agreements for seven Little Caesar restaurants and brought a federal lawsuit. The lawsuit settlement agreement required the former franchisee to comply with its post-termination obligations. Subsequently, five of the restaurants were sold to the son of the owners of the former franchisee, and the former franchisee continued to operate two of the restaurants. All of the restaurants were operated under the same trade name. The franchisor brought this action, claiming that the former franchisee and the son's entities were violating the non-compete agreement. The son was not a signatory to the franchise agreements or the settlement agreement. The court found that the settlement agreement was binding on a successor, but that a "buyer of assets" is not a successor. The court also did not accept the franchisor's alternative theory that the son's entities were conspiring to violate the non-compete. *Id.* at 12–13. Consequently, the court upheld the lower court's grant of summary disposition in favor of the son's entity on the grounds that the son's entity was not bound by the settlement agreement. *Id.* at 14.

---

8. Will the state modify, "blue-pencil," or otherwise reduce a covenant found to be overbroad?

Under Michigan law, the court may "blue-pencil" or otherwise reduce a covenant found to be overbroad.

In *Safeharbor Management Group v. Huston*, which is discussed in greater detail in section 2, because the court found that the indefinite prohibition on soliciting "Assigned Clients" was unreasonable, the court limited the duration of the non-solicitation clause for "Assigned Clients" to match the non-solicitation clause for "Vested Clients," the length of which was two years. *See Safeharbor Mgmt. Grp., LLC v. Huston*, WL 7641822, at *5 (W.D. Mich. Oct. 26, 2020); *see also Innovation Ventures, LLC v. Custom Nutrition Laboratories, LLC*, 2015 WL 5679879, at *23 (E.D. Mich. Sept. 28, 2015), *rev'd on other grounds, Innovation Ventures, LLC v. Custom Nutrition Laboratories, LLC*, 912 F.3d 316, 340 (6th Cir. 2018) ("Courts may reform a noncompetition agreement if it is found to be unreasonable.").

In a franchise case, *Smallbizpros, Inc. v. Court*, the court noted in a footnote that the key difference between the non-compete laws of Michigan and those of Georgia is that "Michigan employs the 'blue pencil' rule: an unreasonable agreement may be limited to render it reasonable." 414 F. Supp. 2d 1245 (M.D. Georgia 2006) (citing *Bristol*, 250 Mich. App. 478); *see also Hungry Howie's Pizza & Subs, Inc. v. Ford Blvd. Pizza, Inc.*, 2015 WL 12990682 (E.D. Mich. Nov. 13, 2015) (citing *Follmer, Rudzewicz & Co., PC v. Kosco*, 362 N.W.2d 676, 684 (Mich. 1984) (finding Michigan follows the "blue pencil rule" that allows courts to narrow non-compete agreements so that they are reasonable in determining the enforceability of a non-compete provision in a franchise agreement).

9. When does a non-compete period begin to run?

➤ Will courts equitably extend the term?

Under Michigan law, the term of the non-compete may be extended by the court beyond its stated expiration date as a remedy for breach of the covenant if necessary to avoid injustice, even if that remedy is not expressly provided for in the agreement. *See Thermatool Corporation v. Borzym*, 575 N.W.2d 334 (1998). Also, Michigan courts are willing to enforce the non-compete time period provided in the parties' contract (for example, if the contract provides that the period begins to run from the issuance of an injunction).

In *Little Caesar Enterprises, Inc. v. Rooyakker*, the court noted that the franchisor was seeking equitable relief in the form of an extension of the two-year non-competition covenant, which had expired. 2009 WL 1940563 (Mich. Ct. App. 2009). The court did not reach the issue but cited *Thermatool* in footnote 12 for the rule that "extension of a covenant not to compete may be appropriate where there is 'continuous and systematic activity in violation of the agreement.'" *Id.* at n.12.

In *Certified Restoration Dry Cleaning Network, LLC v. Tenke Corp.*, after remand from the Sixth Circuit, the court found that the franchisor was entitled to a permanent injunction and was faced with the issue of whether the court should extend the term of the covenant not to compete beyond its stated expiration date (24 months after termination) as a remedy for breach of the agreement by the former franchisee. 2008 WL 2218427 (E.D. Mich. 2008). The franchisor argued, relying on *Thermatool*, that since the franchisee refused to abide by the covenant during the stated duration, it was appropriate for the court to extend the term of the injunction so that it expired two years from the date of the preliminary injunction. The court interpreted *Thermatool* as authorizing an extension of a "covenant not to compete beyond its stated expiration date as an appropriate remedy for breach of the agreement only in cases where (1) the breaching party flouted the terms of the covenant not to compete; (2) the breach consisted of continuous and systematic activity, as opposed to an isolated transaction; and (3) it is not possible to determine monetary damages with any degree of certainty." The court did not believe it had sufficient information to make the determination and ordered supplemental briefing by the parties on that issue.

In *Tanfran, Inc. v. Aron Alan, LLC*, without specifically discussing this particular issue, the court ruled that "[b]ecause Tanfran is entitled to the full benefit of the non-compete provision, the two-year period will commence on the date that the Order is entered." 2007 WL 1796235 (W.D. Mich. 2007).

In *Smallbizpros, Inc., dba Padgett Business Services v. James R. Court*, the non-compete period was one year after termination of the agreement. 414 F. Supp. 2d 1245 (M.D. Ga. 2006). The court, without specifically discussing this issue, enjoined the defendants from operating a competing business for a period of one year from the effective date of the injunction.

In *Allegra Network, LLC v. AM Marketing, Inc.*, the non-compete period was "at least two years after termination or entry of an injunction, whichever is later." 2001 WL 37074684 (E.D. Mich. 2001). The court found the non-compete restrictions to be reasonable and enforced the term of the restrictions as stated in the agreement.

10. Are there additional nuances or peculiarities of the state's treatment of covenants in the franchising context?

Under Michigan law, a material breach of the franchise agreement by the franchisor is grounds for rescission of the agreement by the franchisee, which in turn voids a covenant not to compete contained in the franchise agreement. *See P.A.L. Inv. Grp., Inc. v. Staff-Builders, Inc.*, 118 F. Supp. 2d 781, 786–87 (E.D. Mich. 2000). Under Michigan law, in order for a party to rescind the agreement, the material breach must affect a substantial or essential part of the agreement. "In determining whether a breach is material, the court must weigh how the breach impacts the parties' abilities to carry out the rest of the terms of the contract. Where the breach substantially limits the non-breaching party from receiving the benefit of his bargain, the breach is deemed material and the victim of the breach may rescind the deal." *Id.* (citations omitted).

The materiality of a breach of a non-compete clause should not be relevant when determining whether enforcement is appropriate. *See Little Caesar Enterprises, Inc. v. Rooyakker*, 2009 WL 1940563 (Mich. Ct. App. July 7, 2009). "When performance of a duty under a contract is due any non-performance is a breach." *Id.* (citing *Woody v. Tamer*, 405 N.W.2d 213, 216 (1987) (quoting 2 Restatement of Contract, 2d, § 235, p. 211)). However, materiality of the breach may be relevant when the court is determining whether to grant the franchisor equitable relief in the form of an extension of the non-compete period. Also, good faith in attempted performance of the obligations under the non-compete should not be relevant when determining whether enforcement is appropriate. *See Little Caesar Enterprises, Inc. v. Rooyakker*, 2009 WL 1940563 (Mich. Ct. App. July 7, 2009). Poor performance by the franchisor of its obligations under the franchise agreement, without more, does not constitute a sufficient showing of unclean hands to prevent enforcement of a covenant not to compete. *See Smallbizpros, Inc. v. Court*, 414 F. Supp. 2d 1245 (M.D. Ga. 2006).

In *Coates v. Bastian Bros., Inc.*, the Michigan Court of Appeals discussed the "first-breach doctrine" under Michigan law, reasoning that because the employer breached the employment agreement first, the employer cannot enforce the non-competition clause. 741 N.W.2d 539, 546 (Mich. Ct. App. 2007). In this case, the terminated employee argued that the non-competition clause could not be enforced because the employee was terminated without cause in violation of the agreement. The court found that, even if the first-breach doctrine was applicable, the parties contracted out of the doctrine by providing that the employee was barred from competing "regardless of the reasons for the termination of plaintiff's employment." *Id.* at 510. Franchise agreements often provide that a post-termination non-compete will apply on expiration or termination, regardless of the reason. Under the reasoning of the *Coates* case, the non-compete in those agreements would be enforceable even if the franchisor's breach caused termination of the franchise agreement.

At least one federal district court sitting in Michigan has applied Michigan law to determine the enforceability of an employee covenant not to compete where the parties' agreements specified the application of Michigan law, despite arguments by the employee that the law of the state in which the employee is located has a fundamental public policy against enforcement of the covenant not to compete. *See Lowry Computer Products, Inc. v. Head*, 984 F. Supp. 1111, 1113–14 (E.D. Mich. 1997) (The court applied Michigan law and issued a preliminary injunction enforcing the covenant, even though the employee, who was located in California, argued that the covenant would violate a fundamental public policy of California.).

Minnesota

*by Jeffery S. Haff**

1. Has the state addressed covenants against competition in the context of franchising?

- **Does the state have a franchising statute or regulations that address covenants against competition?**
- **Does the state have a covenants statute of general applicability that would encompass franchise covenants?**
- **Have the courts addressed covenants in the context of franchising either under a statute or under the state's common law?**

Minnesota has no general statute regarding covenants against competition. Minnesota also has no regulation that addresses with specificity the enforceability or unenforceability of covenants against competition in the franchising context. There are, however, references to covenants against competition in the regulations relating to the Minnesota Franchise Act, MINN. STAT. § 80C.01–.30 *et seq*.

First, the regulations require that a franchisor's public offering statement set forth "the conditions of any covenant not to compete." *See* MINN. R. 2860.3500, subp. 8 (N) (2011). Second, the regulations clarify that it is an unfair and inequitable practice under the Minnesota Franchise Act for a franchisor to "enforce any unreasonable covenant not to compete after the franchise relationship ceases to exist." *See* MINN. R. 2860.4400, (I) (2011). This regulation is linked to a provision of the Minnesota Franchise Act, MINN. STAT. § 80C.14, which prohibits unfair practices, and MINN. STAT. § 80C.18, which permits the Commissioner of Commerce to promu gate rules. This link has significant consequences because violations of MINN. STAT. § 80C.14 give rise to a private right of action and civil liability under MINN. STAT. § 80C.17(1). The available damages include reasonable attorneys' fees. MINN. STAT. § 80C.17(3). Consequently, it appears from the face of the rules and regulations that a franchisor may violate the Minnesota Franchise Act and incur liability for attorneys' fees by enforcing an "unreasonable" covenant not to compete.

*Jeff Haff is a Partner at Dady & Gardner in Minneapolis, MN.

Given the fact that the Minnesota regulations only discuss "unreasonable" non-competes, with no specific guidance as to what "unreasonable" might be, Minnesota common law is the best guide for analyzing whether a covenant against competition will be deemed unreasonable in the context of franchising. Minnesota courts seem torn between two basic concepts in the area of non-compete law. Nearly all of the cases begin with the concept that non-compete agreements are "disfavored," and some even describe employment non-competes as vestiges of "industrial peonage without redeeming virtue in the American enterprise system." *See* Tanick, *Navigating Non-compete Agreements*, 68 BENCH & B. MINN. 24 (Aug. 2011) citing *Eutectic Welding Alloys Corp. v. West*, 160 N.W.2d 566, 571 (Minn. 1968). Other Minnesota courts begin with the position that non-competes are generally enforceable, so long as the following exist: (1) consideration, (2) a legitimate interest that outweighs the interests of the restricted party, and (3) a reasonable restriction. *Webb Publishing Co. v. Fosshage*, 426 N.W.2d 445, 449–50 (Minn. Ct. App. 1988).

---

2. Have the courts articulated the "legitimate interests" of the franchisor that will support enforcement of a covenant against competition contained in a franchise agreement?

- **If so, what are they (e.g., protection of goodwill, protection of confidential information), and in what contexts did the issue arise?**
- **If not, what interests have been recognized in other contexts (e.g., employment agreements, the sale of business context)?**

Several Minnesota decisions have addressed the legitimate interests of a franchisor that may support enforcement of in-term covenants against competition. In *Adcom Express, Inc. v. EPK, Inc.*, 1996 WL 266412 (Minn. Ct. App. May 21, 1996),[1] the Minnesota Court of Appeals upheld a franchisor's termination of two franchise agreements that was based upon the franchisee's violation of an in-term covenant against competition. In two separate franchise agreements, the franchisee agreed that during the term of the agreement it would not engage in, operate, or participate in any business that was substantially similar to, or reasonably competitive with, the franchisor's business. One of the covenants against competition had no geographic restriction. The other covenant was limited to a 50-mile radius of any other franchised location.

The franchisor terminated both franchise agreements when it learned that the franchisee had assisted a former franchisee in setting up a competing business. The district court declared that the franchisor legally terminated the agreements, and the franchisee appealed. On appeal, the franchisee argued that the covenants against competition were unreasonably vague and overbroad. The Minnesota Court of Appeals rejected that argument. *Id.* at *4. The court applied Minnesota's common-law principles relating to non-compete covenants. Under Minnesota's common law, the court stated that a non-compete covenant is generally valid and will be enforced if it:

1. Citation to unpublished opinions of the Minnesota Court of Appeals is governed by MINN. STAT. § 480A.08(3).

> [i]s for just and honest purpose, for the protection of a legitimate interest of the party in whose favor it is imposed, reasonable as between the parties, and not injurious to the public . . . .

Id. (quoting *Bennett v. Storz Broadcasting Co.*, 134 N.W.2d 892, 898–99 (Minn. 1965)). The prevailing test for determining the reasonableness of a non-compete agreement was also articulated by the *Bennett* court as:

> [w]hether or not the restraint is necessary for the protection of the business or good will of the employer and, if so, whether the stipulation has imposed upon the employee any greater restraint than is reasonably necessary to protect the employer's business . . . .

134 N.W.2d at 899. *See also Kallok v. Medtronic, Inc.*, 573 N.W.2d 356, 361 (Minn. 1998) ("non-compete agreements are enforceable if they serve a legitimate employer interest and are not broader than necessary to protect this interest").

Applying these principles, the *Adcom Express* court enforced the in-term covenant for two reasons:

(1) A franchisor has a legitimate interest in protecting itself or one of its franchisees from the individual competition of another franchisee already operating in a different market; and
(2) The restrictions were reasonable in light of the franchisees' option of ending the contracts (and the restrictions) at any time with advance written notice.

1996 WL 266412, at *4.

Additionally, the court held that the absence of an express territorial limitation did not render the non-compete covenant unenforceable. The court reasoned that the absence of a territorial limitation was permissible because (1) the franchisee had the right to cancel the agreement at will and to pursue another competitive business and (2) the district court had properly exercised its authority to modify the non-compete provision, to limit its enforcement to geographic areas in which another franchise was operating. *Id.*

In *Casey's General Stores, Inc. v. Bowen*, 1983 WL 937214 (D. Minn. 1983), the federal district court granted a gas station/convenience store franchisor's request to enforce an in-term non-compete covenant through a preliminary injunction. The franchise agreement prohibited the franchisee from engaging in "any business which is the same or similar to the business covered by this agreement at any place other than such premises." During the term of the agreement, the franchisee purchased and began operating two gas station/convenience food store franchises under the name of a competing franchisor. The franchisor brought suit claiming that the franchisee's new stores competed with the franchisee's seven existing franchised stores. The franchisee argued that the non-compete covenant was unenforceable because it contained no geographic or time limitation.

In analyzing the non-compete covenant, the Minnesota Federal District Court applied Minnesota's common-law principles to determine whether the non-compete covenants protected a legitimate business interest of the franchisor and whether the terms were reasonable in scope and duration. The *Casey's* court found that the covenant protected a legitimate business interest because it prevented the disclosure of the franchisor's confidential information (i.e., specific procedures, operating manuals, notice of future promotions, and impending changes in gasoline process) to a competitor. The lack of an express geographic restriction did not trouble the court under the circumstances. The court noted that the absence of a geographic restriction was reasonable to protect the franchisor's confidential information because (1) the franchisee purchased stores that operated in a competing franchise system, (2) the franchisee was under a contractual obligation to not disclose any new operating ideas to the competing franchisor, (3) the franchisee hired a single individual to oversee marketing for all of the stores, and (4) the franchisee had intermingled merchandise and equipment among all the stores. Consequently, the court concluded that supervisors of the competing franchisor likely had access to the franchisor's confidential information during inspections of the store. *Id.*

After holding the non-compete covenant to be enforceable, the court concluded that the franchisor had a likelihood of success on its breach of contract claim and would suffer irreparable harm if its confidential information was disclosed to its competitor. The *Casey's* court granted the franchisor's motion for a preliminary injunction and ordered the franchisee to dispose of or transfer its interest in the competing franchised stores within 120 days. *Id.*

In another case involving an in-term non-compete covenant, *Country Kitchen International, Inc. v. P.R. Management*, 1987 WL 1538604 (Anoka Co. Ct. 1987), a franchisor again obtained preliminary injunctive relief to enforce the covenant. In *Country Kitchen*, the franchisee operated five franchised restaurants under five different license agreements, all of which contained the same in-term non-compete covenant. Under the covenant, the franchisee agreed not to affiliate in any manner with any entity engaged in licensing, franchising, or operating restaurants or drive-ins unless previously approved by the franchisor in writing. The franchisee became delinquent on royalty fees for four of its five restaurants, and the franchisor learned that the franchisee was removing the franchisor's marks from those four restaurants, intending to operate them as family-style restaurants under a new name. *Id.*

The franchisor commenced a lawsuit to, among other things, enforce the in-term restrictive covenant. The franchisor requested injunctive relief that would force the franchisee to remove the franchisor's marks from the fifth franchised restaurant as well. *Id.* Applying Minnesota common law, the *Country Kitchen* court analyzed whether the legitimate interests of the franchisor and the scope and duration of the restrictions supported the enforcement of the restrictive covenant. The court found that the non-compete covenant protected a legitimate interest of the franchisor because it protected the franchisor from disclosure of the franchisor's "system" to a competitor. The confidential information making up the franchisor's "system" included, among other things, special menus, methods of operating, purchasing systems, advertising programs, uniforms, restaurant design and layout, and various registered trademarks, service marks, and trade names. *Id.* The court recognized that some of these materials may not constitute trade secrets, but that the information could prove useful to competitors and, thus, were entitled to protection.

After holding the non-compete covenant to be enforceable, the court granted the franchisor's request for injunctive relief. The irreparable harm necessary for the injunction stemmed from the potential disclosure of the franchisor's system to a competitor. The injunction ordered the franchisee to (1) discontinue the use of the franchisor's marks and names on its remaining restaurant; (2) remove all of the franchisor's goods, material, and products from the remaining franchised restaurant; (3) discontinue all advertising that associated the restaurant with the franchisor; and (4) terminate all state and local name registrations using the franchisor's name. *Id.* The relief granted by the court had the effect of terminating the franchise agreement on the remaining restaurant.

In *Anytime Fitness, Inc. v. Family Fitness of Royal, LLC*, 2010 WL 145259 (D. Minn. Jan. 8, 2010), the court refused to enforce an in-term covenant against competition, finding that under Minnesota law, the alleged harm to goodwill, customer relations and franchisee relations were too "speculative." *Id.* at *2. The court also determined that success on the merits (not just injunctive relief) would dissuade other franchisees from ignoring their agreements and competing, making injunctive relief inappropriate. *Id.*; *see also Novus Franchising, Inc. v. Dean*, 2011 WL 1261626, at *3 (D. Minn. Mar. 30, 2011) (rejecting franchisor's argument that "failure to enjoin the [defendants] will cause franchisees around the country to violate their non-compete agreements," noting that "success on the merits of the claim is the proper deterrent for this potential harm, not injunctive relief"). *But see RPC Acquisition Corp. v. J & D World Corp.*, 2013 WL 3338784 (D. Minn. July 2, 2013) (injunction issued after concluding, among other things, that the franchisor would be irreparably harmed without issuance of an injunction since "other franchisees may be emboldened to breach their franchise agreements").

In *Bonus of America, Inc. v. Angel Falls Services, LLC*, 2010 WL 2734218, at *5 n.6 (D. Minn. July 6, 2010), the court applied Texas law but stated that the result under Minnesota law would be "the same" when enforcing an in-term covenant not to compete. The court determined that the franchisee had been using the franchisor's name and confidential information in operating a competing business and, as a result, the franchisor had made an adequate showing of irreparable harm. Therefore, the covenant not to compete was enforceable. *Id.* at *5.

Minnesota also has caselaw regarding post-term covenants not to compete in the franchising context. In *Team Tires Plus, Ltd. v. Heartlein*, 2001 WL 1640068 (D. Minn. Nov. 20, 2001), the federal district court denied a franchisor's request for a preliminary injunction to enforce a post-term covenant against competition. The covenant precluded the franchisee from owning or operating " . . . any retail or wholesale tire and/or battery service center or any other related business . . . that is in any way competitive with or similar to a Tires Plus business within a ten mile radius of the franchised service center," for a period of one year following the effective termination of the franchise agreement. *Id.* at *1. The franchisor terminated the franchise agreement after the franchisee failed to pay the required royalties. When the franchisee failed to de-identify the franchise site and continued to operate an auto service center at the location, the franchisor brought suit to, among other things, enjoin the franchisee's breach of the covenant not to compete.

In connection with the franchisor's motion for injunctive relief, the franchisee informed the court that it had de-identified the store, that it was operating an auto-service center on the site, and that an injunction would ruin him financially. *Id.* at *2. Despite the fact that the franchisee's auto service center appeared to violate the express terms of the covenant against competition, the court denied the injunction. The court wrote that the franchisor failed to show irreparable harm because "[a]ny damage suffered by Tires Plus as a result of the alleged breach is fully compensable by monetary damages." *Id.* The court, however, did not explain or analyze the franchisor's theory for irreparable harm, or explain why the franchisor's showing was insufficient. Moreover, the court did not analyze whether the non-compete covenant would be enforceable as written. *Id.*

A federal district court in Pennsylvania applied both Minnesota and Pennsylvania law to a post-term covenant against competition in the franchising context in *Novus Franchising, Inc. v. Taylor*, 795 F. Supp. 122 (M.D. Pa. 1992). In *Taylor*, a windshield repair franchisor sought to enforce a covenant against competition against a franchisee who continued to repair windshields after three of its four franchise agreements expired and the remaining agreement was terminated. The covenant precluded the franchisee from "engag[ing] in a business that competes with the franchisor for a period of two years in the former franchise territories." *Id.* at 125. The court held that the covenant was enforceable and granted the franchisor's request for a preliminary injunction.

In *Novus Franchising, Inc. v. Dean*, 2010 WL 6421674 (D. Minn. Nov. 29, 2010), a Minnesota court was faced with the argument that a Texas franchisee was violating its two-year post-termination non-compete by operating in its area of primary responsibility after termination of the ten year franchise relationship. While Texas law was applied, the court cited to *Bonus of America, Inc. v. Angel Falls Services, LLC*, 2010 WL 2218574 (D. Minn. May 28, 2010), as persuasive authority. The court in *Bonus of America* had determined that Texas and Minnesota law would yield the same result. Therefore, *Dean* is relevant to how a Minnesota federal court might apply Minnesota non-compete law. In *Dean*, 2010 WL 6421674, at *7, n.4, the franchisor, Novus, cited to the court five cases in which Novus had successfully enforced its two-year post-termination non-compete. The court rejected these authorities either as non binding or as cases won by Novus when the other side failed to show up. *Id.* The court focused its analysis on the reasoning of a 2007 opinion by a Minnesota federal court applying Idaho law — *Novus Franchising, Inc. v. Oksendahl*, 2007 WL 2084143 (D. Minn. July 17, 2007) — in which the court had refused to enforce a post-termination non-compete against a Novus franchisee.

Relying upon the reasoning in *Oksendahl*, the court in *Dean*, 2010 WL 6421674, at *8, refused to enforce the Texas post-termination non-compete because there was no evidence that the Texas franchisee was still using the Novus name or system, and the threat of harm to the franchisor was less than the harm to the franchisee from enforcing the post-termination non-compete through an injunction. *Dean* is also noteworthy because the court considered and rejected three of the reasons for a finding of "irreparable harm" commonly used by franchisors to enforce non-competes, including: (1) loss of customers and goodwill; (2) loss of ability to refranchise the territory; and (3) harm to the integrity of the franchise system. *Id.*, at *11.

In *Novus Franchising, Inc. v. Dawson*, 725 F.3d 885 (8th Cir. 2013), the Eighth Circuit upheld the Minnesota District Court's refusal to enforce a post-termination non-compete clause based on the franchisor's failure to show irreparable harm. Weighing heavily on this determination was the fact that the Franchisor did not seek injunctive relief until seventeen months after the franchisee stopped paying royalties. *Id.* at 895. The court also questioned whether the loss of goodwill the franchisor would allegedly suffer could not be adequately addressed through damages. *Id.* Other courts, however, have held that "[p]otential loss of good will qualifies as irreparable harm." *See Novus Franchising, Inc. v. AZ Glassworks, LLC*, 2012 WL 5057095, at *8 (D. Minn. Sept. 27, 2012), *report and recommendation adopted*, 2012 WL 5072363 (D. Minn. Oct. 18, 2012) (citing *Life Time Fitness, Inc. v. DeCelles*, 854 F. Supp. 2d 690, 695 (D. Minn. 2012) (quotation omitted)).

Courts have also acknowledged, when discussing a franchisor's legitimate interests, that "[i]t is difficult to attract a new franchisee when a former franchisee is improperly competing within the same area." *Novus Franchising, Inc. v. Livengood*, 2012 WL 38580, at *5 (D. Minn. Jan. 9, 2012); *see also Anytime Fitness, Inc. v. Reserve Holdings, LLC*, 2008 WL 5191853, at *6 (D. Minn. Oct. 8, 2008) ("If the preliminary injunction is not granted to enforce AFI's covenant not to compete, its good will will be harmed by a competing business operating at the former Anytime Fitness location, impairing AFI's ability to establish another franchise in that area.").

Outside the context of franchising, there are numerous court decisions that provide guidance on what constitutes a legitimate interest under Minnesota law. *See, e.g., Bennett*, 134 N.W.2d 892 (legitimate to protect against deflection of trade and customers); *Medtronic, Inc. v. Advanced Bionics Corp.*, 630 N.W.2d 438, 452 (Minn. Ct. App. 2001) (legitimate to protect goodwill, including customer relationships and information about customer preferences); *Dynamic Air, Inc. v. Bloch*, 502 N.W.2d 796, 799 (Minn. Ct. App. 1993) (legitimate to protect business and goodwill); *Salitennan v. Finney*, 361 N.W.2d 175, 177 (Minn. Ct. App. 1985) (same); *IDS Life Insurance Co. v. SunAmerica, Inc.*, 958 F. Supp. 1258, 1273 (N.D. Ill. 1997), *aff'd in part, vacated in part sub nom*, 136 F.3d 537 (7th Cir. 1988) (applying Minnesota law, legitimate, interests include goodwill, confidential information, trade secrets, and preventing unfair competition from former employees and agents).

3. What time limitations have courts recognized as reasonable in the franchise context? If no franchise cases have been decided, what time limitations have been recognized in other contexts?

➤ How have they been related to the interests protected?

None of the existing decisions in Minnesota directly address and analyze in detail what period of time constitutes a reasonable time limitation for a post-term covenant against competition in the franchise context. In neither *Team Tires Plus, Ltd. v. Heartlein*, 2001 WL 1640068 (D. Minn. Nov. 20, 2001), nor *Bonus of America, Inc. v. Angel Falls Services, LLC*, 2010 WL 2734218 (D. Minn. July 6, 2010), did the court address the time constraint imposed in the post-termination non-compete at issue. In *Novus Franchising, Inc. v. Gross*, 1994 WL 17092106 (Hennepin County. Dist. Ct. 1994), the court applied Minnesota law and determined that two years was an enforceable non-compete because the non-compete was for only two years and would prevent diminution and damage to the goodwill and marks of Novus. No specific factual finding was made as to exactly why a two-year non-compete was enforceable as written.

Other franchise cases cited in this chapter address in-term covenants against competition that expired upon termination of the franchise agreement and, thus, did not prevent the party from pursuing a competing business afterward. *See Adcom Express, Inc. v. EPK, Inc.*, 1996 WL 266412, at *4 (Minn. Ct. App. May 21, 1996); *Casey's General Stores, Inc. v. Bowen*, 1983 WL 937214 (D. Minn. 1983); *Country Kitchen International, Inc. v. P.R. Management*, 1987 WL 1538604 (Anoka Co. Ct. 1987); *Anytime Fitness, Inc. v. Family Fitness of Royal, LLC*, 2010 WL 145259 (D. Minn. Jan. 8, 2010). As stated above, the results in those cases were mixed, but most tended to enforce the in-term restriction. The court in *Bonus of America*, 2010 WL 2734218, at *5, volunteered that a two-year and 50-mile post-termination non-compete would be enforceable, although the facts of the case at issue dealt only with the in-term portion of the non-compete.

In *Novus Franchising, Inc. v. Dean*, 2010 WL 6421674 (D. Minn. Nov. 29, 2010), the court did not address the length or scope of the non-compete; however, the cases rejected by the court as unpersuasive, including *Novus Franchising, Inc. v. Gross*, 1994 WL 17092106 (Hennepin County Dist. Ct. 1994), found that Novus' two-year post-termination non-compete was enforceable.

A variety of time limitations have been enforced under Minnesota law in the non-franchise context. "In determining the reasonableness of a temporal restriction, courts conduct a fact-specific inquiry seeking to strike a balance between the employer's need to protect its business interests and the employee's need to earn a livelihood." *Yonak v. Hawker Well Works, Inc.*, 2015 WL 1514166, at *4 (Minn. Ct. App. Apr. 6, 2015). Typically, a one-year restrictive covenant is enforceable. *Midwest Sign & Screen Printing Supply Co. v. Dalpe*, 386 F. Supp. 3d 1037, 1046–48 (D. Minn. 2019) ("One-year non-competes are routinely upheld, particularly when the temporal restriction is accompanied by a geographic restriction.") While two-year restrictions are also commonly upheld, *see Medtronic, Inc. v. Advanced Bionics Corp.*, 630 N.W.2d 438, 452 (Minn. Ct. App. 2001) (two-year restriction enforced against former employee), three-year periods are often modified to a shorter period of time. *See, e.g., Dean Van Horn Consulting Assocs., Inc. v. Wold*, 395 N.W.2d 405, 409 (Minn. Ct. App. 1986) (referencing how "the trial court modified the restrictive covenant from a three-year period to a one-year period").

In the context of the sale of a business, the acceptable time restrictions appear to be longer. *See Yonak v. Hawker Well Works, Inc.*, 2015 WL 1514166, at *4 (Minn. Ct. App. Apr. 6, 2015) (five-year non-compete especially reasonable given the business was a start-up and particularly vulnerable to competition); *Lemon v. Gressman*, 2001 WL 290512 (Minn. Ct. App. Mar. 27, 2001) (in sale of business context, court enjoined defendant for five years); *see also Hagen v. Burmeister & Associates, Inc.*, 633 N.W.2d 497, 500 (Minn. 2001) (in connection with sale of business, court enforced ten-year non-compete covenant); *IKON Office Solutions, Inc. v. Dale*, Nos. 01-2667, 2001 WL 1269994 (8th Cir. Oct. 24, 2001) (in sale of business context, three-year term enforced as necessary to protect goodwill). *But see Arizant Holdings Inc. v. Gust*, 668 F. Supp. 2d 1194, 1199 (D. Minn. 2009) (court states in dicta that one-year non-solicitation agreement was overbroad and would need to be blue-penciled).

While these cases do not involve franchises, the factors enunciated in the caselaw are adaptable to the franchise context. For example, courts analyzing a time restriction in the franchise context are likely to focus on the nature of the franchise, the nature of the customer base, the ability of the franchisor to replace and adequately train a new franchisee, and the amount of time that is necessary for the franchisor's customers to become accustomed to the franchisee's replacement.

---

4. What geographic limitations have courts recognized as reasonable in the franchise context?

- **How have they been related to the interests protected?**
- **Have courts recognized the legitimacy of protecting other franchisees from competition?**

The franchise cases addressed above (*see* section 2) provide useful guidance on how Minnesota courts will analyze geographic restrictions in the context of in-term non-compete covenants. Those decisions establish that Minnesota courts recognize the legitimacy of protecting other franchisees from competition. Indeed, in *Adcom Express, Inc. v. EPK, Inc.*, 1996 WL 266412, at *4 (Minn. Ct. App. May 21, 1996), the Minnesota Court of Appeals explicitly acknowledged that a franchisor has "a legitimate interest in protecting itself or one of its franchisees from the individual competition of another franchisee already operating in a different market . . . ." In that case, the court found that a restriction of 50 miles from other franchised locations was reasonable. Similarly, the court in *Bonus of America, Inc. v. Angel Falls Services, LLC*, 2010 WL 2734218, at *5 (D. Minn. July 6, 2010), volunteered when reviewing an in-term non-compete that a 50-mile post-term non-compete would be enforceable. In *Novus Franchising, Inc. v. Gross*, 1994 WL 17092106 (Hennepin County Dist. Ct. 1994), the court determined that a covenant that applied to the "particular geographic area of the franchise agreement" was "valid."

Moreover, in *Casey's General Stores, Inc. v. Bowen*, 1983 WL 937214 (D. Minn. 1983), the Minnesota Federal District Court enforced the covenant not to compete, implicitly recognizing that the disclosure of the franchisor's confidential information to a competing franchisor could also damage other franchisees. The covenant in *Casey's* contained no express geographic restriction but prohibited the franchisee from engaging in "any business that is the same or similar to the business covered by this agreement *at any place other than such premises*." *Id.* (emphasis added). The franchisee bought two stores in a competing franchisor's system. The federal district court enforced the non-compete provision and ordered the franchisee to divest its interest in the stores. The court's primary concern appeared to be that the circumstances strongly suggested that the competing franchisor would be likely to have access to the franchisor's confidential information. (*See supra* at section 2.) Given that the competing franchise stores that were in close proximity to the franchisor's stores were *not* owned by the mutual franchisee, it appears that the court was concerned about protecting other franchisees.

As a general rule in Minnesota, a non-compete covenant is not rendered per se unenforceable if it lacks a territorial limitation. *Dynamic Air, Inc. v. Bloch*, 502 N.W.2d 796, 800 (Minn. Ct. App. 1993). Although "[t]here is no per se rule under Minnesota law that a restriction is unenforceable if it lacks a geographic limitation" (*Nilfisk, Inc. v. Liss*, 17-cv-1902 (WMW/FLN), 2017 WL 7370059, at *5 (D. Minn. June 15, 2017) (citation omitted)), Minnesota courts, in their discretion, have held such limitless provisions render the non-compete unenforceable. *See, e.g., Midwest Sign & Screen Printing Supply Co. v. Dalpe*, 386 F. Supp. 3d 1037, 1046–48 (D. Minn. 2019) ("The Agreement's non-compete covenants (¶¶ 5 and 6), however, have no geographic bounds, and the absence of a territorial limitation renders these terms overbroad and unenforceable.").

5. What limitations on activities have courts recognized as reasonable in the franchise context?

With respect to in-term covenants against competition, Minnesota courts have recognized that a franchisor may reasonably restrict an existing franchisee's right to participate in, operate, or own a competing franchise. In other cases, the courts enforced in-term non-compete provisions against franchisees that either obtained an ownership interest in a competing franchise or assisted a competing franchise. *Adcom Express, Inc. v. EPK, Inc.*, 1996 WL 266412 (Minn. Ct. App. May 21, 1996); *Casey's General Stores, Inc. v. Bowen*, 1983 WL 937214 (D. Minn. 1983); *Country Kitchen International, Inc. v. P.R. Management*, 1987 WL 1538604 (Anoka Co. Ct. 1987). These cases strongly suggest that during the term of a franchise agreement, a Minnesota court will enforce a non-compete provision that precludes a franchisee's involvement with a competing franchise. In two of these decisions, *Casey's* and *Country Kitchen*, the primary reason for enforcement of the non-compete covenant was an identifiable risk that the franchisor's confidential information or its "system" could be used by the franchisee, or by a competing franchisor, to compete against the franchisor.

In the post-termination context, *Novus Franchising, Inc. v. Dean*, 2010 WL 6421674 (D. Minn. Nov. 29, 2010), and *Novus Franchising, Inc. v. Oksendahl*, 2007 WL 2084143 (D. Minn. July 17, 2007), involving the Novus system, appear to focus far more on limiting the use of trade names and trademarks post-termination, rather than simply eliminating all post-termination competition. The *Dean* and *Oksendahl* opinions present a far more difficult standard for proving "irreparable harm," than simply asserting that the former franchisee is now competing with the franchisor.

---

6. Does the state recognize a difference between in-term and post-term covenants?

Minnesota has not specifically addressed whether it will differentiate between in-term and post-term covenants not to compete in the context of franchising. The state and federal courts to date have appeared to apply the exact same legal standards to both post-termination and in-term covenants against competition. For example, in *Anytime Fitness, Inc. v. Family Fitness of Royal, LLC*, 2010 WL 145259 (D. Minn. Jan. 8, 2010), the federal court refused to enforce an in-term covenant against competition and appeared to give no additional deference to the franchisor because the franchisor was enforcing an in-term covenant.

In *Adcom Express, Inc. v. EPK, Inc.*, 1996 WL 266412, at *4 (Minn. Ct. App. May 21, 1996), the Minnesota Court of Appeals did, however, expressly state that it would apply the reasonableness standard articulated in *Bennett v. Storz Broadcasting Co.*, 134 N.W.2d 892, 898–99 (Minn. 1965) (*see supra* at section 2), to both in-term and post-term covenants not to compete. Moreover, the analyses by the courts in *Casey's General Stores, Inc. v. Bowen*, 1983 WL 937214 (D. Minn. 1983) and *Country Kitchen International, Inc. v. P.R. Management*, 1987 WL 1538604 (Anoka Co. Ct. 1987), which apply the *Bennett* reasonableness standard to in-term covenants, are consistent with this approach. There is no indication in *Team Tires Plus, Ltd. v. Heartlein*, 2001 WL 1640068 (D. Minn. Nov. 20, 2001), which involves a post-term covenant in the franchise context, that post-term covenants would be evaluated by a different standard. Indeed, numerous post-term non-compete covenants have been evaluated under the reasonableness standard articulated in *Bennett*. *See, e.g.*, *Davies & Davies Agency, Inc. v. Davies*, 298 N.W.2d 127 (Minn. 1980); *IKON Office Solutions, Inc. v. Dale*, 170 F. Supp. 2d 892, 895 (D. Minn. 2001), *aff'd*, 2001 WL 1269994 (8th Cir. Oct. 24, 2001); *Klick v. Crosstown State Bank of Ham Lake, Inc.*, 372 N.W.2d 85, 88 (Minn. Ct. App. 1985) (analysis of enforcement of post-term restrictive covenant in the employment context).

It bears noting, however, that the absence of a geographic restriction is likely to be less troubling for a court in the context of an in-term covenant than it will be in the context of a post-term covenant. For example, in *Casey's*, the court enforced the in-term covenant not to compete in the absence of a geographic restriction where the evidence showed a strong likelihood that confidential information would be disclosed to a competing franchise system. (*See supra* at section 2). In the context of post-term covenants, courts will generally require that a reasonable geographic restriction be articulated in terms of either a geographic area or some other limitation (i.e., former customers dealt with by the employee). *See, e.g.*, *Dynamic Air, Inc.*

v. Bloch, 502 N.W.2d 796 (Minn. Ct. App. 1993) (absence of geographic restriction does not render non-compete covenant per se invalid); *Davies & Davies Agency, Inc.*, 298 N.W.2d at 131 (50-mile radius of principal cities in which agency operated was too broad for post-term covenant; restriction was limited to solicitation of former agency's customers). Unlike the individual employee in *Medtronic, Inc. v. Hughes*, 2011 WL 134973 (Minn. Ct. App. Jan. 18, 2011), most franchisees do not do business or develop customer relations worldwide.

7. Has the state allowed enforcement of covenants against non-signatories (e.g., family members, newly formed corporations)?

While the issue has not been squarely addressed in the franchise context or in other reported cases, it appears that Minnesota courts would be reluctant to enforce restrictive covenants against non-signatories. First, Minnesota does not generally permit enforcement of contracts against non-parties to the contract. *See, e.g., Lesmeister v. Dilly*, 330 N.W.2d 95, 103 (Minn. 1983). Moreover, "[c]ovenants not to compete are agreements in partial restraint of trade, limiting as they do the right of a party to work and earn a livelihood. Courts . . . look on such contracts with disfavor and scrutinize them with care." *Freeman v. Duluth Clinic, Inc.*, 334 N.W.2d 626, 630 (Minn. 1983); *see also Kallok v. Medtronic, Inc.*, 573 N.W.2d 356, 361 (Minn. 1998) (non-competition covenants "are looked upon with disfavor, cautiously considered, and carefully scrutinized") (quoting *Bennett v. Storz Broadcasting Co.*, 134 N.W.2d 892, 898 (Minn. 1965)). Moreover, in Minnesota, "[p]ublic policy requires that restrictive covenants be strictly construed and not extended beyond the true intent of the parties." *Ecolab, Inc. v. Gartland*, 537 N.W.2d 291, 296 (Minn. Ct. App. 1995) (quoting *Naftalin v. John Wood Co.*, 116 N.W.2d 91, 100 (Minn. 1962)).

One Minnesota court, applying Texas law, granted a preliminary injunction that extended enforcement of a non-compete to non-signatories, a competing corporation and the corporation's sole owner. *Bonus of America, Inc. v. Angel Falls Services, L.L.C.*, 2010 WL 273428, at *6 (D. Minn. July 6, 2010). In *Bonus of America*, the court found sufficient evidence that Hart, who had signed the non-compete, was actively involved in the new competing corporation. Thus, for purposes of a preliminary injunction, the court determined that since the non-signatories were participating in the violation of the non-compete, it was proper for the non-signatories to be bound by the injunction. *Id.*

While Minnesota law is not at all clear on this issue, the primary inquiry used by the Minnesota courts appears to be whether a signatory is violating its non-compete through other entities, not whether the non-signatory is somehow "bound" by a non-compete that it did not sign.

8. Will the state modify, "blue-pencil," or otherwise reduce a covenant found to be overbroad?

Minnesota courts may, at their discretion, modify covenants against competition to the extent necessary to render them reasonable and, thus, enforceable. *See Davies & Davies Agency, Inc. v. Davies*, 298 N.W.2d 127, 131 (Minn. 1980); *Dynamic Air, Inc. v. Bloch*, 502 N.W.2d 796, 800 (Minn. Ct. App. 1993) (court has discretion to modify restrictive covenant); *Klick v. Crosstown State Bank of Ham Lake, Inc.*, 372 N.W.2d 85, 88 (Minn. Ct. App. 1985) (same). "[B]lue-penciling is most appropriate for editing a restrictive covenant's temporal and geographic limitations (or lack thereof), not 'rewrit[ing] the agreement wholesale.'" *Midwest Sign & Screen Printing Supply Co. v. Dalpe*, 386 F. Supp. 3d 1037, 1046–48 (D. Minn. 2019) (citing *Gavaras v. Greenspring Media, LLC*, 994 F. Supp. 2d 1006, 1012 (D. Minn. 2014)).

As the power is discretionary, a party does not have a right to modification of an otherwise overly broad covenant. Indeed, "no cases say that a court must" blue-pencil an otherwise unreasonable restrictive covenant. *See Klick*, 372 N.W.2d at 89 (not abuse of discretion for court to refuse to modify non-compete provision). It does appear, however, that Minnesota courts are more inclined to exercise their power to modify an otherwise overbroad restriction than to invalidate the restriction altogether. *See E.W. Blanch Holdings, Inc. v. Knudson*, 2001 WL 1618165, at *4 (D. Minn. May 10, 2001) ("in Minnesota, courts faced with an overbroad restrictive covenant should not invalidate that covenant, but rather 'blue pencil' it."). *See also Advance Contract Equip. & Design LC v. Lamere*, 2015 WL 5089167, at *5 (Minn. Ct. App. Aug. 31, 2015) ("[I]t is unlikely that a determination that the agreement is unreasonable in temporal or geographic scope would void the entire agreement.").

Importantly, a party relying on a modification should ensure that the court provides an explanation for the modification in case the issue is appealed. *Satellite Indus., Inc. v. Keeling*, 396 N.W.2d 635, 639 (Minn. Ct. App. 1986).

9. When does a non-compete period begin to run? Will courts equitably extend the term?

Minnesota courts have generally stated that "[p]ublic policy requires that restrictive covenants be strictly construed and not extended beyond the true intent of the parties." *Ecolab, Inc. v. Gartland*, 537 N.W.2d 291, 296 (Minn. Ct. App. 1995). Although there are no franchise cases on point, in the non-franchise context, Minnesota courts, when enforcing a non-compete provision, have stated that they will simply enforce the non-compete according to the precise terms of the provision as written. *See Burke v. Fine*, 608 N.W.2d 909 (Minn. Ct. App. 2000) (strictly construing the language of the non-compete provision and holding that the non-compete would begin to run only upon termination of the contract, but the non-compete would not survive the contract's expiration because there was no language in the agreement evidencing the parties' intent for the non-compete to survive the contract's expiration).

However, in rare circumstances, Minnesota courts will equitably extend the term of a non-compete. *See Cherne Industrial, Inc. v. Grounds & Associates, Inc.*, 278 N.W.2d 81, 93 (Minn. 1979) ("there may be situations where injunctive relief extending beyond the expiration of the period established by the covenant is appropriate"); *Overholt Crop Insurance Service Co. v. Travis*, 941 F.2d 1361, 1372 (8th Cir. 1991) (holding that the district court did not err by extending the life of a two-year non-compete when the purpose of the non-compete was to allow Overholt time to hire and train a new sales representative, which did not occur during the running of the non-compete as a result of defendant's actions and the ongoing litigation).

Nevertheless, if the non-compete clause itself contains a tolling provision, a court can extend the term of the non-compete only according to the specific language of the agreement, and cannot extend the term past what is prescribed in the agreement. *Medtronic, Inc. v. Petitti*, 2018 WL 3520858 (Minn. Ct. App. July 23, 2018) (when tolling provision only allowed the duration of the restrictions to be extended by the number of days of non-compliance, the court could not simply extend the non-compete by a year).

10. Are there additional nuances or peculiarities of the state's treatment of covenants in the franchising context?

Minnesota courts have not identified any nuances or peculiarities in their treatment of restrictive covenants in the franchising context. There are, however, a number of issues that should be considered by franchisors and/or franchisees when analyzing covenants against competition governed by Minnesota law.

WHETHER FRANCHISING IS LIKE THE SALE OF A BUSINESS OR AN EMPLOYMENT CONTRACT

Is a franchise agreement closer to the sale of a business or to an employment agreement? The answer can have considerable consequences when it comes to non-compete covenants, because in some jurisdictions non-competition covenants in the employment context are void as a matter of law, but are enforceable when ancillary to the sale of a business. *See, e.g., American Express Financial Advisors, Inc. v. Topel*, 38 F. Supp. 2d 1233, 1238 (D. Colo. 1999) (a covenant against competition in connection with the purchase or sale of a business is exempted from Colorado's ban on covenants against competition). Moreover, courts that address this issue have not been uniform in their outcome. Compare *Budget-Rent-A-Car Corp. of Am. v. Fein*, 342 F.2d 509 (5th Cir. 1965) (courts should examine both sale of business and employment standards), with *Jiffy Lube International, Inc. v. Weiss Bros., Inc.*, 834 F. Supp. 683 (D. N.J. Oct. 1, 1993) (franchise agreement viewed as closer to the sale of a business).

In Minnesota, the courts that have addressed covenants against competition in the franchising context have not attempted to categorize a franchise agreement as a sale of a business or an employment contract. If and when this issue is addressed and resolved by Minnesota courts, it will likely impact the permissible scope of covenants against competition because Minnesota courts distinguish between covenants against competition in the context of an employment agreement versus the context of a business sale. Compare *Bennett v. Storz Broadcasting Co.*, 134 N.W.2d 892, 899–90 (Minn. 1965) (providing a reasonableness standard for employment context), with *Bess v. Bothman*, 257 N.W.2d 791, 795 (Minn. 1977) (providing a broader reasonableness standard in the sale of business context). The reasonableness of an employment covenant is interpreted more narrowly than those covenants made in connection with the sale of a business. *See B & Y Metal Painting, Inc. v. Ball*, 279 N.W.2d 813, 815 (Minn. 1979) (much of the rationale for a strict reasonableness test in the employment context is not present in connection with the sale of a business); *Lemon v. Gressman*, 2001 WL 290512 (Minn. Ct. App. Mar. 27, 2001) (same); *IKON Office Solutions, Inc. v. Dale*, Nos. 01-2667, 2001 WL 1269994 (8th Cir. Oct. 24, 2001) (recognizing that a more lenient standard applies in a transfer of business context). However Minnesota courts resolve this distinction in the future, franchisors and franchisees investigating, drafting, and/or enforcing covenants against competition in Minnesota should be aware that the categorization of franchise agreement will likely affect the permissible scope of covenants against competition.

THE MINNESOTA FRANCHISE ACT'S ANTI-WAIVER CLAUSE

Franchisors and franchisees should also be aware of the anti-waiver provision within the Minnesota Franchise Act and how that may impact the analysis of non-compete covenants. The Minnesota Franchise Act, MINN. STAT. § 80C.21, voids choice-of-law provisions in franchise agreements that waive application of or compliance with the Act for Minnesota franchises. It provides:

> Any condition, stipulation or provision, including any choice of law provision, purporting to bind any person who, at the time of acquiring a franchise is a resident of this state, or, in the case of a partnership or corporation, organized or incorporated under the laws of this state, or purporting to bind a person acquiring any franchise to be operated in this state to waive compliance or which has the effect of waiving compliance with any provision of sections 80C.01 to 80C.22 or any rule or order thereunder is void.

MINN. STAT. § 80C.21 (2021). This amendment became effective May 20, 1989, and courts have held that it does not impact choice-of-law clauses contained in franchise agreements signed prior to that date. *Commercial Property Investments, Inc. v. Quality Inns International, Inc.*, 938 F.2d 870 (8th Cir. 1991).

As noted above (*see* section 1), Minnesota regulations (MINN. R. 2860.4400, (I)) expressly provide that it is an unfair and inequitable practice under the Act for a franchisor to "enforce *any unreasonable* covenant not to compete after the franchise relationship ceases to exist." (emphasis added). The Minnesota Franchise Act and the regulations do not address what constitutes a "reasonable" covenant not to compete. It may be argued that what constitutes a reasonable covenant not to compete should be decided under the law of the state chosen by the parties in the choice-of-law provision. Indeed, Minnesota courts traditionally enforce contractual choice-of-law provisions. *See Hagstrom v. American Circuit Breaker Corp.*, 518 N.W.2d 46, 48 (Minn. Ct. App. 1994). If, however, there is a direct conflict between the law of Minnesota and that of the state chosen in the choice-of-law clause over the reasonableness of the covenant, MINN. STAT. § 80C.21 provides, at a minimum, support for the argument that the Minnesota law must prevail.

HARSH TREATMENT FOR COMPETITORS WHO "INTERFERE" WITH NON-COMPETE AGREEMENTS

One of the most interesting aspects of Minnesota non-compete law is its harsh treatment of competitors who "interfere" with non-compete agreements by hiring employees or others who are subject to non-compete obligations. Generally, absent a contractual fee-shifting provision, a party suing to enforce a non-compete must bear its own attorneys' fees incurred in connection with such a dispute. However, if the party subject to the non-compete has been hired by a third party, under Minnesota law, that third party may be liable for "tortious interference with contract" and the damages for that interference, which, as a matter of law, include the attorneys' fees incurred to enforce the non-compete.

In *Kallok v. Medtronic, Inc.*, 573 N.W.2d 356 (Minn. 1998), the Minnesota Supreme Court laid out this new exception to the "American Rule," stating that the court had always recognized certain exceptions to the American Rule related to torts causing a party to be "thrust into litigation" with another party. When the tort of one party thrusts a second party into litigation with a third party, the tortfeasor must pay the attorneys' fees incurred by the second party. *Id.* at 361. In *Medtronic, Inc.*

v. Hughes, 2011 WL 134973 (Minn. Ct. App. Jan. 18, 2011), the Minnesota Court of Appeals applied *Kallok* in affirming an award of $615,958 in attorneys' fees against an employer who hired the defendant, Mr. Hughes. While the employer argued that it thought the worldwide non-compete was unenforceable, that defense was rejected when Mr. Hughes's new employer refused to present any evidence at trial to support the defense, claiming attorney-client privilege. *Id.* at *8.

Had the defendant in Kallok presented evidence of its consultation with counsel, the court may have ruled differently. "[U]nder *Kallok* . . ., the justification defense to tortious interference with contract may encompass reasonable reliance on advice of counsel." *Sysdyne Corp. v. Rousslang*, 860 N.W.2d 347, 354 (Minn. 2015) (holding "that the trial court did not err in concluding that [defendant] met its burden of proving the justification defense given the evidence supporting [defendant's] reasonable inquiry with outside counsel and honest reliance on counsel's advice that the contract was not enforceable.").

INJUNCTIVE RELIEF

One other nuance or peculiarity of Minnesota law is that there appears to be a growing split between the state and federal courts on how willing a court will be to enforce covenants not to compete through injunctive relief. Since 2007, there have been a number of federal court cases in which the courts have refused to enforce non-competes because the franchisor or employer has not satisfied the court that any great or irreparable harm actually would occur absent an injunction. *See Anytime Fitness, Inc. v. Family Fitness of Royal, LLC*, 2010 WL 145259 (D. Minn. Jan. 8, 2010); *Novus Franchising, Inc. v. Dean*, 2010 WL 6421674 (D. Minn. Nov. 29, 2010); *Novus Franchising, Inc. v. Oksendahl*, 2007 WL 2084143 (D. Minn. July 17, 2007). In the state courts, however, the law seems to be steadily getting worse for those who have signed non-competes and try to defeat requests for injunctive and other relief. *See* Tanick, *Navigating Non-compete Agreements*, 68 Bench & B. Minn. 24 (Aug. 2011), citing recent cases including *Schmidt Towing, Inc. v. Frovik*, 2010 WL 4451572 (Minn. Ct. App. Nov. 9, 2010); *Kallok*, 573 N.W.2d 356, and *Hughes*, 2011 WL 134973.

A recent unpublished opinion issued September 21, 2021, sheds some light on this split. *See Moeschler v. Honkamp Krueger Financial Services, Inc., & Bcor Administrative Services, LLC*, 2021 WL 4273481 (D. Minn. Sept. 21, 2021). Under Minnesota state law, irreparable harm can be inferred from a breach of an enforceable non-compete. *See Medtronic, Inc. v. Gibbons*, 527 F. Supp. 1085, 1091 (D. Minn. 1981), *aff'd*, 684 F.2d 565 (8th Cir. 1982).

"[I]nferring irreparable harm from the breach of a valid restrictive covenant is a *Minnesota* procedural doctrine developed and applied by *Minnesota* courts in deciding whether to grant injunctive relief under the *Minnesota* Rules of Civil Procedure." *Id.* at *9 (emphasis in original). But "a federal court's authority to issue a preliminary injunction is governed by the *Federal* Rules of Civil Procedure and by *federal* case law construing those rules." *Id.* "That authority can neither be expanded nor contracted by the Minnesota courts." *Id.* "In short, when federal law dictates that a likelihood of success and irreparable harm must be established—*actually* established—a state cannot effectively eliminate those requirements by establishing 'presumptions' that bind a federal court." *Id.*

Mississippi

by Benjamin L. Mitchell*

1. Has the state addressed covenants against competition in the context of franchising?

- **Does the state have a franchising statute or regulations that address covenants against competition?**
- **Does the state have a covenants statute of general applicability that would encompass franchise covenants?**
- **Have the courts addressed covenants in the context of franchising either under a statute or under the state's common law?**

Mississippi does not have a franchising statute or franchising regulations addressing covenants against competition.

Section 198 of the Mississippi Constitution directs the legislature to enact laws to prevent all trusts, combinations, contracts, and agreements inimical to the public welfare. Accordingly, section 75-21-1 of Miss. Code Ann. (1972) prohibits, in part, "a combination, contract, understanding or agreement, express or implied, . . . inimical to public welfare and the effect of which would be (a) [t]o restrain trade; . . . [or] (d) [t]o hinder competition in the production, importation, manufacture, transportation, sale or purchase of a commodity."

Section 75-21-3 prohibits, in part, any corporation, individual, partnership, or association, with or without intent, from accomplishing "to a degree inimical to the public welfare," restraint of trade, monopolization, or elimination of competition. Section 75-21-11 provides that such contracts or agreements are void and unenforceable in court.

Courts have held that contracts in restraint of trade are not invalid under Mississippi antitrust law unless they are inimical to the public welfare. *See State* ex rel. *Knox v. Edward Hines Lumber Co.*, 115 So. 598 (Miss. 1928); *Brown v. Staple Cotton Cooperative Association*, 96 So. 849 (Miss. 1923); *Jackson v. Price*, 105 So. 538 (Miss. 1925). In *Wagley v. Colonial Baking Co.*, 45 So. 2d 717, 721, *aff'd*, 46 So. 2d 925 (Miss. 1950), the court held that, if there is proof of one of the acts enumerated in either section 75-21-1 or section 75-21-3, "such act is intrinsically inimical to the public

*Benjamin L. Mitchell is an attorney at Butler Snow LLP in Ridgeland, Mississippi. This chapter incorporates works of the author of the previous edition's chapter, Patrick K. Walls.

welfare without further or special proof of a result beyond the definitions of the statutes, or deduction by the courts that proven violations are or are not inimical to the public welfare."

No Mississippi case has addressed a restrictive covenant in a franchise agreement. In other contexts, Mississippi courts have required that covenants against competition must be ancillary to a lawful contract, reasonable, and consistent with the public interest.

Generally restrictive covenants such as non-competition covenants or agreements are viewed unfavorably by the law. In the context of an employment relationship, the burden of proof will lie with the employer drafting such covenant to show the scope of the employee's permissible business activities after the employment relationship has terminated; the covenant should be reasonable in duration and geographical scope. *Kennedy v. Metropolitan Life Insurance Co.*, 759 So. 2d 362, 368 (Miss. 2000) (the court would not enforce non-competition agreement, as the employer "should bear the burdens of the agreement's ambiguities"). *See also Thames v. Davis & Goulet Insurance*, 420 So. 2d 1041 (Miss. 1982) (where employer failed to offer proof of covenant's reasonableness, necessity, or purpose, injunction not granted). In the context of the sale of a business, the courts are more likely to enforce a non-competition agreement so long as it is "ancillary to the sale" of the business. *LDDS Communications v. Automated Communications*, 35 F.3d 198, 199 (5th Cir. 1994). *See also Cooper v. Glidden*, 515 So. 2d 900 (Miss. 1987).

---

2. Have the courts articulated the "legitimate interests" of the franchisor that will support enforcement of a covenant against competition contained in a franchise agreement?

- **If so, what are they (e.g., protection of goodwill, protection of confidential information), and in what contexts did the issue arise?**
- **If not, what interests have been recognized in other contexts (e.g., employment agreements, the sale of business context)?**

The Mississippi courts have not substantively addressed the enforceability of covenants against competition in the franchise context, but they have articulated the legitimate interest of the vendee of a business or of an employer that may support the enforcement of covenants against competition.

In the employment context, the courts have found that non-competition agreements restrict trade and individual freedom and are not favored by the law. *Frierson v. Sheppard Building Supply Co.*, 154 So. 2d 151, 156 (Miss. 1963); *Texas Road Boring Co. v. Parker*, 194 So. 2d 885, 888 (Miss. 1967). When deciding whether to enforce these agreements, a court will examine three factors: (1) the rights of the employer, (2) the rights of the employee, and (3) the rights of the public. *Id.* In *Redd Pest Control Co., Inc. v. Foster*, 761 So. 2d 967 (Miss. App. 2000), the court enforced a non-competition agreement against ex-employees Foster and Smith. By examining the rights of the employer, employees, and the public, the court found that employer Redd had suffered a sizable economic loss from competition by Smith and Foster, there would be no undue hardship on the part of Smith and Foster in securing other employment, and the public in this area would not suffer from a lack of pest control service. In *Raines v. Bottrell Insurance Agency, Inc.*, 992 So. 2d 642 (Miss. App. 2008), the court enforced a covenant not to compete in Raines's employment contract with Bottrell, as enforcement would not create "a deficiency of service in the insurance industry, and the covenant not to compete was reasonable and the interests of the public are not impaired to the degree necessary to avoid enforcement of the agreement." *Id.* at 646.

Mississippi courts have carefully scrutinized the particular circumstances of each case to maintain a reasonable balance between "unfair competition by an ex-employee" and "reasonable oppression by an employer." One court set forth these considerations as follows:

> A bargain by an employee not to compete with the employer after the employment is terminated . . . [must be] within such territory and during such time as may be reasonably necessary for the protection of the employer, without imposing undue hardship on the employee and provided there is a reasonable basis for the covenant. The validity of such an agreement is dependent upon such considerations as the nature and character of the employment, the size and conditions of the locality to which the prohibition extends and the duration of the prohibition. In short, the evidence must show the reasonableness of the restriction with respect to the nature of the employment, the duration of the period of restraint and the scope and extent of the restriction, territorially.

Donahoe v. Tatum, 134 So. 2d 442, 445 (Miss. 1961) (court enforced restrictive covenant where employee was exposed to employer's business methods, confidential information, and trade secrets, and where enforcement brought no undue hardship to employee).

The court in *Business Communications, Inc. v. Banks*, 2011 WL 590913 (Miss. App. 2011), discussed competition by an ex-employee and whether the competition had to be "unfair," as the *Donahoe* court stated. The court found that "the Supreme Court's decision in *Donahoe* simply cannot be read to require a former employer to prove 'unfair competition' to prevail on a claim to enforce a covenant not to compete. Instead this language reads that the court should look at the restrictions contained in the covenant to determine whether such restrictions need to be reduced." *Id.* at *11. The court went on to find the covenant not to compete that employee Banks signed "valid and enforceable. Such covenants may be used to protect confidential information, trade secrets, proprietary information, customer lists, vendor relationships, business practices, and the employer's investment in training and education of an employee. The employee may not simply take such information to a competitor." *Id.* at *12.

In *Redd Pest Control Co. v. Heatherly*, 157 So. 2d 133 (Miss. 1963), the court noted that post-employment restrictive covenants serve to safeguard the legitimate interest of the employer in protecting its customer base from raids by former employees. In addition, when determining whether to enforce a restrictive covenant, the court took into account that the employer spent large sums to establish his business and to acquire customers. In this case, however, the court reduced the area of the restrictive covenant from the whole state to a 50-mile radius of each city in which the employee had worked, as the employee did not possess trade secrets. *See also Taylor v. Cordis Corp.*, 634 F. Supp. 1242, 1250 (S.D. Miss. 1986) (covenant enforced where corporation would suffer "irreparable harm" if employee were allowed to transfer goodwill he had developed to new employer; threatened injury to corporation outweighed harm to employee); *Bagwell v. H.B. Wellborn & Co.*, 156 So. 2d 739 (Miss.

1963) (covenant enforced against employee with "valuable information" about employer's clients); *Union National Life Insurance Co. v. Tillman*, 143 F. Supp. 2d 638, 646 (N.D. Miss. 2000) (non-competition covenant enforced against ex-employee, as the public would not allow parties to a contract to "unilaterally breach binding contracts and disclose trade secrets"). *But see Empiregas, Inc. v. Bain*, 599 So. 2d 971, 976 (Miss. 1992) (court refused to enforce a non-competition agreement against employee Bain, as his lack of education, physical disability, and lack of employment prospects within reasonable proximity to his home outweighed the employer's rights because the enforcement of the agreement in this case would have a "more oppressive effect" on Bain).

In the context of the sale of a business, the purchaser's interest in maintaining his or her customer base justifies enforcement of a restrictive covenant. In *Cooper v. Gidden*, 515 So. 2d 900, 901 (Miss. 1987), the court enforced a restrictive covenant prohibiting the seller from competition for ten years within a 100-mile radius of the city. In reaching its decision, the court recognized that a substantial amount of the total consideration paid for the business was expressly intended to prevent the seller from competing with the buyer in the future. *See also LDDS Communications v. Automated Communications*, 35 F.3d 198, 199 (5th Cir. 1994) (court enforced a non-competition agreement and a non-solicitation of employee covenant against the seller within the states of Arizona and New Mexico to reasonably protect the assets of the business purchased).

3. What time limitations have courts recognized as reasonable in the franchise context?

- **If no franchise cases have been decided, what time limitations have been recognized in other contexts?**
- **How have they been related to the interests protected?**

No reported decisions address the reasonableness of time limitations in the franchise context.

In the contexts of both the sale of a business and employment, duration of a restrictive covenant must be reasonable in relation to the interest protected. While a wide range of time limitations have been considered valid in these contexts, the courts tend to be more restrictive in employment contracts. *Cooper v. Gidden*, 515 So. 2d 900, 905 (Miss. 1987). However, as a general rule, courts tend to consider a two-year restriction to be reasonable. *Hensley v. E.R. Carpenter Co.*, 633 F.2d 1106 (5th Cir. 1980); *Texas Road Boring Co. v. Parker*, 194 So. 2d 885 (Miss. 1967); *Redd Pest Control Co. v. Heatherly*, 157 So. 2d 133 (Miss. 1963); *Frierson v. Sheppard Building Supply Co.*, 154 So. 2d 151 (Miss. 1963); *Bagwell v. H.B. Wellborn & Co.*, 156 So. 2d 739 (Miss. 1963); *Redd Pest Control Co., Inc. v. Foster*, 761 So. 2d 967 (Miss. App. 2000); *Timber Lake Foods, Inc. v. Estess*, 72 So. 3d 521 (Miss. App. 2011).

Mississippi courts have related the reasonableness of time limitations to the employer's legitimate interests. To the extent that the court recognizes the employer's legitimate interest in preserving its customer base, it will enforce a covenant promoting that end. In *Taylor v. Cordis Corp.*, 634 F. Supp. 1242 (S.D. Miss. 1986), the court enforced two restrictive covenants entered into by the employee, a salesman of heart pacemakers. Due to the special relationship of trust between doctors and hospitals and the company's sales personnel, the manufacturer of the pacemakers relied heavily on its employees for its client base. Accordingly, the court upheld one covenant that prohibited the employee for six months after termination of employment from competing with its employer, as well as a covenant prohibiting the employee for one year following termination from soliciting or contacting any of the employer's clients with whom the employee had had contact during his employment with the company. The one-year restriction was appropriate because it would take the employer a year to train a replacement. *See also Donahoe v. Tatum*, 134 So. 2d 442 (Miss. 1961) (five-year period upheld where employee was exposed to employer's business methods, confidential information, and trade secrets, and had acquaintance with employer's clientele); *Herring Gas Co., Inc. v. Magee*, 813 F. Supp. 1239 (S.D. Miss. 1993), *aff'd*, 22 F.3d 603 (5th Cir. 1994) (six-year non-competition covenant found reasonable where employees had gained valuable knowledge of the business).

In the context of sales of businesses, the courts have generally accepted longer terms for covenants against competition. In *Cooper v. Gidden*, 515 So. 2d 900 (Miss. 1987), the court affirmed the trial court's decision that a ten-year restriction against competition by the seller of a sand business was reasonable. The court based its decision partly on the fact that the vendor had obtained a similar covenant not to compete when he purchased the business and partly on the fact that the patronage and goodwill of the family-owned business consisted mostly of repeat customers. *See also Morgan v. Jacobs*, 200 So. 2d 443 (Miss. 1967) (five-year covenant not to compete entered into upon sale of stock upheld); *Jackson v. Price*, 140 Miss. 249, 105 So. 538 (Miss. 1925) (covenant not to compete in restaurant business enforceable, although it contained no time limitation).

In a situation where the validity of a non-competition clause in a stockholders' agreement was at issue, the court found the clause invalid as to a corporate entity signatory because it was not limited in scope as to duration or geography. *Easy Reach, Inc. v. Hub City Brush, Inc.*, 935 So. 2d 1140 (Miss. App. 2006).

---

4. What geographic limitations have courts recognized as reasonable in the franchise context?

- **How have they been related to the interests protected?**
- **Have courts recognized the legitimacy of protecting other franchisees from competition?**

There are no reported decisions in the franchise context.

In the employment context, Mississippi courts generally limit the geographic scope of a non-competition agreement to those areas in which the ex-employee actually worked or performed services for the employer. *See Union National Life Insurance Co. v. Tillman*, 143 F. Supp. 2d 638 (N.D. Miss. 2000) (non-competition agreement enforced, as geographic scope was limited to the portions of the two counties in which ex-employee had sold insurance for employer); *Redd Pest Control Co., Inc. v. Foster*, 761 So. 2d 967 (Miss. App. 2000) (non-competition agreement enforced, as geographic scope was limited to areas in which ex-employees actually performed pest control services for employer, which in this case was just the city of Brookhaven).

Mississippi courts have related the reasonableness of geographic limitations to an employer's legitimate interests. To the extent that the court recognizes the employer's legitimate interest in preserving its customer base, the court will modify a covenant to accomplish that end. Thus, in *Taylor v. Cordis Corp.*, 634 F. Supp. 1242 (S.D. Miss. 1986), the court enforced a covenant against competition to include only those physicians and their medical groups to whom the employee had sold the employer's products during his employment. The prohibition did not extend to physicians in the state to whom the employee had attempted to sell products unsuccessfully or to prospective customers.

The realities of the world's shrinking geography due to cellular phones, the internet, and technology have not gone unnoticed by the Mississippi courts. In *Timber Lake Foods, Inc. v. Estess*, 72 So. 3d 521 (Miss. App. 2011), employee Stephanie Estess left her employ as a nationwide broker of meat and poultry products for Timber Lake and began working for a direct competitor. Timber Lake sued Estess to enforce the non-compete covenant in her employment agreement, which banned her from working as a meat broker within a 250-mile radius of Tupelo, Mississippi, Timber Lake's headquarters. Estess argued that the 250-mile restriction was arbitrary because her job allowed her to work from anywhere there was a computer and/or telephone. The lower court agreed and found the covenant invalid because its validity would demand a nationwide scope. The court of appeals reversed the lower court, reasoning that "while other jurisdictions have acknowledged that advancements in technology have created a need for such a broad geographic scope in covenants not to compete [footnote omitted], Mississippi law has yet to address the issue." *Id.* at 526. The court went on to write that "since a nationwide geographic restriction would have reasonably protected Timber Lake's interests, we cannot say that Timber Lake's effort to balance Stephanie's interest by reducing that restriction to within a two hundred fifty mile radius of Tupelo was unreasonable." *Id.* at 527.

In the context of sales of businesses, the courts are more likely to enforce greater geographical restrictions. In *Cooper v. Gidden*, 515 So. 2d 900, 905 (Miss. 1987), the vendor of a sand business agreed not to compete with the purchaser within 100 miles of the city where the business was located for a period of ten years. Since gravel was hauled from places 90 miles away and 100 miles was the "trade area," the lower court had determined that the 100-mile radius was de facto justifiable. In addition, the family-owned business was the only enterprise of its kind within the county, and its patronage and goodwill consisted mostly of repeat customers. These factors, as well as a similar covenant obtained by the seller when he purchased the business, led the court to enforce the covenant. *See also LDDS Communications v. Automated Communications*, 35 F.3d 198 (5th Cir. 1994) (court construed disputed language in non-competition agreement to cover entire states of Arizona and New Mexico, as the business assets purchased had been located there); *Morgan v. Jacobs*, 200 So. 2d 433 (Miss. 1967) (old stockholders prohibited from competing against the newly merged newspaper corporation within city and county in which new publication would be published); *Jackson v. Price*, 105 So. 538 (Miss. 1925) (restriction as to municipality in which restaurant was located upheld).

5. What limitations on activities have courts recognized as reasonable in the franchise context?

There are no reported decisions in the franchise context. Generally, contracts are subject to Mississippi statutory prohibitions against restraint of trade or hindrance of competition inimical to the public welfare. Miss. Code Ann. §§ 75-25-1, 3 (1972). Restrictive covenants in other contexts have not been invalidated by these statutes.

In the context of employment contracts or those relating to the sale of a business, any limitation must be shown to be necessary to protect the employer's or the vendee's legitimate interests. *See Thames v. Davis & Goulet Insurance, Inc.*, 420 So. 2d 1041 (Miss. 1982); *Cooper v. Gidden*, 515 So. 2d 900 (Miss. 1987).

6. Does the state recognize a difference between in-term and post-term covenants?

There have been no reported decisions on this issue. In one case, *Taylor v. Cordis Corp.*, 634 F. Supp. 1242 (S.D. Miss. 1986), the manufacturer of heart pacemakers provided for two restrictive covenants. In one, the employee, a salesman of heart pacemakers, covenanted not to compete with the employer during his employment and for six months thereafter. In the second restrictive covenant, the employee agreed not to solicit customers of the employer or to divulge customer information during his employment and for one year thereafter. However, the in-term portions of the covenants were never at issue in the case.

7. Has the state allowed enforcement of covenants against non-signatories (e.g., family members, newly formed corporations)?

This issue does not appear to have been addressed under Mississippi law with respect to activities of family members and closely held entities. However, it has been established by Mississippi courts that, in order to maintain an action to enforce a breach of contract or to recover damages growing out of a breach, a relationship of privity of contract must exist between the party damaged and the party sought to be held liable for the breach. *See Allgood v. Bradford*, 473 So. 2d 402 (Miss. 1985) (no contractual obligation in favor of appellants created by agreement between two other parties). Thus, in *S. Waterworks Supply, Inc. v. Keller*, 2020 WL 8409100 (S.D. Miss. Apr. 16, 2020), a salesman's former employer did not bring a viable cause of action for breach of contract against the branch manager of the salesman's new employer because the branch manager was not a party to the underlying non-compete agreement between the former employer and the salesman.

8. Will the state modify, "blue-pencil," or otherwise reduce a covenant found to be overbroad?

In general, Mississippi courts will modify an unreasonable territorial scope in order to enforce a restrictive covenant. In *Taylor v. Cordis Corp.*, 634 F. Supp. 1242 (S.D. Miss. 1986), the fact that the scope of the territory was not precisely defined was held not to be crucial. The court modified the agreement to cover a reasonable area, that is, the area in which the company could prove the economic justification for the restraint, and excised other areas. *See also LDDS Communications v. Automated Communications*, 35 F.3d 198 (5th Cir. 1994) (in a case involving the sale of a business, the court limited the disputed geographic scope to two states, not the nationwide scope buyer requested); *Hensley v. E.R. Carpenter Co.*, 633 F.2d 1106 (5th Cir. 1980) (court reduced the geographic restriction from the entire continental United States and Canada to 300 miles from Tupelo); *Redd Pest Control Co. v. Heatherly*, 157 So. 2d 133 (Miss. 1963) (statewide restriction reduced to 50-mile radius of city).

No case appears to have addressed the issue of modifying an overbroad temporal limitation.

9. When does a non-compete period begin to run? Will courts equitably extend the term?

Once again, there are no statutes or cases in Mississippi that deal with these issues from a franchising perspective.

In the employment context, Mississippi courts have found that the language of the contract will control. In *HeartSouth, PLLC v. Boyd*, 865 So. 2d 1095 (Miss. 2004), employer HeartSouth argued that an employment agreement containing a covenant not to compete signed by employee Boyd had not expired on March 31, 2001, as the term of the agreement stated, because the agreement renewed due to "the party actions" or as an "implied contract" when Boyd remained an employee after the term of the agreement ended. After looking at a long history of contract law and cases in Mississippi, the court found that it needed to look at the four corners of the document when interpreting it and examine the actual language used. Upon examining the agreement at hand, the court found that "applying these contract principles to the facts leads to the conclusion that the contract between HeartSouth and Boyd was not ambiguous and clearly provided for one year of validity and enforceability," thus finding that the covenant not to compete was no longer enforceable against Boyd after March 31, 2001. *Id.* at 1105.

It does not appear that the Mississippi courts are inclined to equitably extend the term of a covenant not to compete. In *Frierson v. Sheppard Building Supply Co.*, 154 So. 2d 151 (Miss. 1963), the lower court had extended the term of the employee's non-compete covenant by over seven months, finding that the term should run for a period of two years from August 27, 1962 (the date of the Chancellor's final decree), rather than for a period of two years from January 13, 1962, which was the date Frierson was terminated. Sheppard Building Supply argued that the court should equitably extend the term when a delay in getting an injunction was not the employer's fault, while Frierson argued that the court cannot grant relief beyond that contained in the original contract. The court found that "it is the contract the parties themselves made that measures the restriction, both as to scope and to time. Having made the contract limiting the period to two years from the date of termination of employment, the court may not extend the time beyond that date." *Id.* at 156.

10. Are there additional nuances or peculiarities of the state's treatment of covenants in the franchising context?

Although not in the franchising context, two "shopping center" cases are of interest. In *Thornton Brothers v. Gore*, 172 So. 2d 425 (Miss. 1965), a covenant by the lessor of a drugstore to protect the lessee from competition by other lessees in the shopping center was upheld as not being an unlawful restraint of trade. In addition, in *Parker v. Lewis Grocery Co.*, 153 So. 2d 261 (Miss. 1963), an action by the tenants in a shopping center against the landlord to enjoin violation of a restrictive covenant, the court held that the territorial scope of a restrictive covenant may include the reasonable expectation of expansion.

In the employment context, termination of a contract without good cause can affect the enforceability of a non-compete covenant. In *E. Fishing & Rental Tools Co. v. Blaney*, 2012 WL 3154975 (S.D. Miss. Aug. 2, 2012), the court notes that every contract in Mississippi contains an implied covenant of good faith and fair dealing and, while the duty does not alter Mississippi's "at will" employment rule, it can affect the parties' rights under a non-compete agreement. *See also Empiregas, Inc. Of Kosciusko v. Bain*, 599 So. 2d 971 (Miss. 1992) (when employee was terminated without good cause, the employer was not entitled to enforce a non-compete agreement, and the employee was entitled to recover damages, consisting of bonus he would have been paid had he remained with employer).

Under Mississippi law, a non-compete agreement is not enforceable if it is ambiguous, meaning if the contractual provisions are susceptible of two or more reasonable interpretations, directly conflict with one another, or are unclear or of doubtful meaning. In *Advanced Sols. Network, Inc. v. Gill*, 2013 WL 5278201, (S.D. Miss. Sept. 18, 2013), the court found that a five-year non-compete entered into in connection with the sale of a business was not enforceable because the restricted activity of engaging in any "advertising business" was ambiguous and broader than necessary to protect the plaintiff's interests. *See also Scott v. S. Elec. Supply Co.*, 2013 WL 3280276 (N.D. Miss. June 27, 2013) (employee non-competition agreement not ambiguous where language was not susceptible to more than one interpretation).

Missouri

by Jane Cohen *

1. Has the state addressed covenants against competition in the context of franchising?

- **Does the state have a franchising statute or regulations that address covenants against competition?**
- **Does the state have a covenants statute of general applicability that would encompass franchise covenants?**
- **Have the courts addressed covenants in the context of franchising either under a statute or under the state's common law?**

Missouri does not have a franchise statute or regulation that addresses covenants against competition. Missouri does have a statute that prohibits restraint of trade generally that encompasses franchise covenants. Mo. Rev. Stat. § 416.031.

Under Missouri law, generally non-compete agreements are valid and enforceable so long as they are reasonably limited as to time and geographic scope. *Healthcare Svcs. of the Ozarks, Inc. v. Copeland*, 198 S.W.3d 604, 610 (Mo. 2006). They also must be reasonably designed to protect the legitimate business interests of the company. *Id.*; *see also Whelan Sec. Co. v. Kennebrew*, 379 S.W.3d 835, 842 (Mo. 2012).

Missouri courts have addressed covenants against competition in the context of franchising under common law. *See, e.g., Imo's Franchising Inc. v. Kanzoua*, 2020 WL 5534425 (E.D. Mo. Sept. 14, 2020) (granting the franchisor's motion for temporary restraining order prohibiting franchisee, its officers, agents, servants, employees, attorneys, and any other person in active concert or participation with franchisee from engaging in the sale of pizza at its St. Louis location until the hearing on franchisor's motion for preliminary injunction.); *Panera, LLC v. Nettles*, 2016 WL 4124114 (E.D. Mo. Aug. 3, 2016) (granting franchisor's request for temporary restraining order preventing Papa John's (listed as a competitor in employee's non-compete) from employing or using any of Panera's confidential information derived by Papa John's from Panera's ex-employee); *H & R Block Tax Services LLC v. Frias*, 2018 WL 934901 (W.D. Mo. Feb. 16, 2018) (District court granted franchisor's motion for preliminary injunction preventing franchisee and those acting in concert from violating the terms of the franchise agreement, from soliciting any customers

*Jane Cohen owns the firm Law Offices of Jane Cohen LLC based in St. Louis, Missouri.

previously serviced, diverting any business previously served by franchisee during the franchise term, engaging in any tax service business within miles of the franchise territories set forth in the franchise agreements or operating a tax preparation service at its former office. The court denied the relief sought by franchisor against a competing company at which a former employee and the franchisee's wife were then working because the court found the franchisor had not yet established that the franchisee had any control over their work there and even though the franchise agreement defined franchisee's wife and former employee as "Franchise Associates" and held them to the same non-competition and non-solicitation covenants as franchisee, the wife and former franchisee did not sign the agreements and were not parties to the lawsuit.); *H & R Block Enter., LLC v. Taxes Latinos Americanos, LLC*, 2014 WL 12779235 (W.D. Mo. Feb. 19, 2014) (District court enjoined ex-franchisee from violating restrictive covenants in a non-compete they executed pursuant to an agreement under which the franchisee sold their tax preparation business to the franchisor in 2012, and enjoined one of the principals from violating restrictive covenants and terms contained in the employment agreement he signed in conjunction therewith. The court found no proof of violation by the other principal.).

Covenants agreed to as part of a business transaction have been deemed appropriate under Missouri law. *H&R Block Tax Serv. LLC v. Frias*, 2018 WL 934901 (W.D. Mo. Feb. 16, 2018) *citing Orthotic & Prosthetic Lab, Inc. v. Pott*, 851 S.W.2d 633, 643 n.4 (Mo. Ct. App. 1993). Missouri courts distinguish between covenants ancillary to a sale of a business and covenants merely ancillary to an employment contract. Covenants related to the sale of a business are treated more liberally. *Id.*

2. Have the courts articulated the "legitimate interests" of the franchisor that will support enforcement of a covenant against competition contained in a franchise agreement?

- **If so, what are they (e.g., protection of goodwill, protection of confidential information), and in what contexts did the issue arise?**
- **If not, what interests have been recognized in other contexts (e.g., employment agreements, the sale of business context)?**

Missouri courts have recognized a franchisor's reputation, goodwill, and brand recognition as legitimate interests to be protected in enforcing a covenant against competition. *See, e.g., Imo's Franchising Inc. v. Kanzoua*, 2020 WL 5534425 (E.D. Mo. Sept. 14, 2020); *H&R Block Tax Serv. LLC v. Frias*, 2018 WL 934901 (W.D. Mo. Feb. 16, 2018); *H & R Block Enter., LLC v. Ascher*, 2015 WL 12746197 (W.D. Mo. Apr. 3, 2015).

Missouri courts have also recognized that a franchisor has a legitimate interest in preventing a franchisee from unfairly using assets of its franchise business to compete with the franchisor and obtaining an undue advantage for a franchisee's competing business. *See, e.g., H&R Block Tax Serv. LLC v. Frias*, 2018 WL 934901 (W.D. Mo. Feb. 16, 2018); *H & R Block Eastern Enter. Inc. v. Sanks*, 2017 WL 4570803 (W.D. Mo. June 6, 2017) (recognizing franchisor's legitimate interest in protecting client base, client relations, and confidential information); *H &R Block Tax Ser. LLC v. Clayton*, 2016 WL 1247205 (W.D. Mo. Mar. 24, 2016) (franchisor has interest in protecting trade secrets); *but see Sigma-Aldrich Corp. v. Vikin*, 451 S.W.3d 767 (Mo. Ct. App. 2014) (court of appeals affirmed trial court's refusal to enforce non-compete, concluding that information known to former employee was not trade secret or protectable confidential information entitled to protection).

Missouri courts have also found that the public has a valid interest in having covenants against competition enforced in valid contracts. *Imo's Franchising Inc., supra, citing N.I.S. Corp. v. Swindle*, 724 F.2d 707, 710 (8th Cir. 1984); and *Gold v. Holiday Rent-A-Car Int'l, Inc.*, 627 F. Supp. 280, 285 (W.D. Mo. 1985).

Additionally, Missouri has adopted the Uniform Trade Secret Act (MUTSA). The Act defines a trade secret as a method, technique, or process providing economic value. Mo. Rev. Stat. § 417.453(4). Although the franchisor in *Imo's Franchising Inc.* included a count in its complaint for a violation of the MUTSA, no decision on that claim nor any other such claim in a franchise case has been reported in Missouri. While a claim should be included under the MUTSA when a franchisor files suit in Missouri for misappropriation of trade secrets in addition to a contract claim on an agreement not to non-compete, it should not be the sole claim.[1] Client lists and databases are not specifically listed in the definition of "trade secret" found in the MUTSA. This proved fatal in *Cent. Trust & Inv. Co. v Kennedy*, 2013 WL 268687 (Mo. Ct. App. Jan. 24, 2013).

---

3. What time limitations have courts recognized as reasonable in the franchise context?

- **If no franchise cases have been decided, what time limitations have been recognized in other contexts?**
- **How have they been related to the interests protected?**

In the *H & R Block* cases in Missouri, district courts have enforced non-competition agreements for two years within a 25-mile radius of the franchisee's territory as reasonable. *See, e.g., H&R Block Tax Serv. LLC v. Frias*, 2018 WL 934901 (W.D. Mo. Feb. 16, 2018); *H&R Block Tax Servs. LLC v. Clayton*, 2016 WL 1247205, at *3 (W.D. Mo. Mar. 24, 2016); *H&R Block Tax Servs. LLC v. Haworth*, 2015 WL 12747902, at *2 (W.D. Mo. Mar. 26, 2015); *H & R Block Tax Serv. LLC v. Thomas*, 2018 WL 910170 (W.D. Mo. Feb. 15, 2018).

In *H&R Block Enters. LLC v. Ascher*, 2015 WL 12746197, at *2 (W.D. Mo. Apr. 3, 2015), a district court found three- or five-year, 50-mile non-competition and non-solicitation covenants in an asset purchase agreement to be well within restrictions upheld by Missouri. In *Ascher*, the court commented that Missouri courts have allowed similar and broader time and geographical restrictions. *Id., citing, e.g., Champion Sport Ctr., Inc. v. Peters*, 763 S.W.2d 367, 370 (Mo. Ct. App. 1989) (enforcing a restrictive covenant barring the seller of a business from competing with it for eight years in the surrounding three counties); *Long v. Huffman*, 557 S.W.2d 911, 915 (Mo. Ct. App. 1977) (upholding a covenant barring competition for five years within a 60-mile radius of a specified city). The same judge who decided *Ascher* also decided *H & R Block Tax Serv. LLC v. Cardenas*, in which he referenced other examples of broader restrictions. 2020 WL 1031033 (W.D. Mo. Mar. 3, 2020).

---

1. One should also consider filing a claim under the Defend Trade Secrets Act, 18 U.S.C. § 1831 *et. seq.* (2016).

4. What geographic limitations have courts recognized as reasonable in the franchise context?

- **How have they been related to the interests protected?**
- **Have courts recognized the legitimacy of protecting other franchisees from competition?**

Under Missouri law, non-compete agreements are valid and enforceable "so long as they are reasonable." *Healthcare Svcs. of the Ozarks, Inc. v. Copeland*, 198 S.W.3d 604, 610 (Mo. 2006).

In the *H & R Block* cases cited above that involved terminated franchisees, the courts enforced the non-competes as written that included 25 miles surrounding the franchisee's territory. *See, e.g., H & R Block Tax Services LLC v. Cardenas*, 2020 WL 1031033 (Mar. 3, 2020). In the cases in which the franchisee sold his business back to H & R Block, the court enforced the broader non-compete and non-solicitation area of 50 miles from the business as contained within the asset purchase agreement. *See H&R Block Enters. LLC v. Ascher*, 2015 WL 12746197, at *2 (W.D. Mo. Apr. 3, 2015). *H & R Block Enter., LLC v. Texas Latinos Americanos, LLC*, 2014 WL 12779235 (W.D. Mo. Feb. 19, 2014).

In *Gold v. Holiday Rent-A-Car Int'l, Inc.*, 627 F. Supp. 280 (W.D. Mo. 1985), the U.S. District Court for the Western District of Missouri enforced a post-term non-competition covenant contained in a rental car franchise agreement that prohibited competition within 75 miles of the former franchisee's licensed area. In a case involving a business arrangement that was similar to a franchise agreement, the Missouri Court of Appeals upheld a non-competition provision that restricted competition within a ten-mile radius of the business that was formerly operated under the owner's trademark. *Herrington v. Hall*, 624 S.W.2d 148 (Mo. App. W.D. 1981).

Missouri courts have recognized the legitimacy of protecting other franchisees from competition most likely because such protection was contained within the non-compete agreement the franchisor required the franchisee (and possibly others) to sign at the inception of the franchise relationship or as part of an asset purchase agreement. The orders issued in the *H & R Block* cases include such protection.

5. What limitations on activities have courts recognized as reasonable in the franchise context?

Thus far, Missouri courts have generally upheld limitations on activities to which a franchisee contractually agreed in a franchise agreement or in an asset purchase agreement on the sale of the franchised business.

Terminated franchisees have been enjoined from directly or indirectly divulging and using information and knowledge concerning clients, the methods, promotion, advertising, or any other systems or methods of operation of franchised business. *See, e.g., H & R Block Tax Serv. LLC v. Cardenas*, 2020 WL 1031033 (Mar. 3, 2020). They have also been enjoined from retaining or using franchisor's property such as client lists, files, tax returns, computer servers, and all other client data. *Id.* They have been required to transfer their telephone numbers to the franchisor. *Id.*

Missouri courts have also enjoined terminated franchisees from continuing to use the franchisor's trademarks and trade names and required that all articles that display any of franchisor's marks be returned to the franchisor. *Id.*

Missouri courts have also protected the franchisor's customers by enjoining the franchisee from diverting the franchisor's former, existing, and prospective clients away. *Id.* This has included direct or indirect solicitation by mail, telephone, electronically, via the internet, in person, or by other means. *See H & R Block Tax Serv. LLC v. Cardenas*, 2020 WL 1031033 (W.D. Mo. Mar. 3, 2020); *H&R Block Tax Serv. LLC v. Frias*, 2018 WL 934901 (W.D. Mo. Feb. 16, 2018).

Franchisees who sold their franchised businesses to the franchisor have been enjoined from using any of the assets sold including, but not limited to, client lists, client information and client-related assets, telephone numbers, and email addresses. *See, e.g., H & R Block Enter., LLC v. Ascher*, 2015 WL 12746197 (W.D. Mo. Apr. 3, 2015). They have also been enjoined from using the franchisor's trade secrets and confidential information in their possession; from influencing any franchisor's customers to stop doing business with the franchisor; from soliciting franchisor's employees; from leasing to or receiving rents from the former franchised location; and from making false, disparaging, or defamatory comments about the franchisor or otherwise disrupting, damaging, impairing, or interfering with the franchisor's business or that of its affiliates. *Id.*

6. Does the state recognize a difference between in-term and post-term covenants?

No Missouri state or federal court, applying Missouri law, has addressed whether enforcement of in-term non-compete provisions should be judged by different standards from those governing post-term non-compete provisions.

In a case cited in *Herrington v. Hall*, 624 S.W.2d 148 (Mo. App. W.D. 1981), the Illinois Court of Appeals enforced an in-term non-compete provision that prohibited the franchisee from engaging in any business that was the same as or similar to the franchised business. *McDonald's System, Inc. v. Sandy's, Inc.*, 195 N.E.2d 22 (Ill. App. 1963). The court noted that:

> . . . *the extent of the territorial restriction is a factor that affects the validity of a post-term covenant only*. In the instant case the covenant is an in-term, not a post term covenant, and as long as appellees seek to avail themselves of the beneficial provisions of their franchise contract, they should not be permitted to disregard or refuse to abide by the several obligations they assumed.

Id. at 30 (emphasis added).

7. Has the state allowed enforcement of covenants against non-signatories (e.g., family members, newly formed corporations)?

In *Medicine Shoppe International, Inc. v. S.B.S. Pill Dr., Inc.*, 336 F.3d 801 (8th Cir. 2003), the Eighth Circuit affirmed the federal district court's grant of a preliminary injunction enjoining a franchisee's corporate successor from competing with a pharmacy franchisor. *Id.* at 803–05. In applying the test for determining successor liability under Missouri law, the court found that the successor pharmacy was a mere continuation of the former franchisee because it acquired substantially all of its predecessor's assets and "operated the same type of business at the same location as did" its predecessor, including using its phone number, employees, and pharmacist-manager. *Id.* at 804–05.

Further, Missouri courts have enforced covenants against non-signatories in the context of employment agreements and other commercial transactions where the non-signer has knowledge of the breach and actively assists a party to breach the covenant. *See Superior Gearbox Co.*, 869 S.W.2d at 245 n.9 (Mo. App. S.D. 1993) (where "an individual knows about a non-compete agreement and assists a party to that agreement in violating it, the individual may be enjoined from benefiting from the breach") (internal citations omitted); *but see Josten's, Inc. v. Cuquet*, 383 F. Supp. 295 (E.D. Mo. 1974) (court refused to enforce a father's covenant not to compete with his employer against his sons where they did not sign the employment agreement).

8. Will the state modify, "blue-pencil," or otherwise reduce a covenant found to be overbroad?

Missouri Courts recognize that "an unreasonable restriction against competition in a contract may be modified and enforced to the extent that it is reasonable, regardless of the covenant's form of wording." *R.E. Herrington, Inc. v. Frick*, 428 S.W.2d 945 (Mo. App. 1968). *See also Osage Glass, Inc. v. Donovan*, 693 S.W.2d 71, 74 (Mo. 1985) (enforcing a non-compete clause but refusing to enforce it to the extent it was unreasonable). "The ability of courts to modify unreasonable non-compete agreements does not prevent courts from refusing to enforce non-compete agreements that are wholly unreasonable." *Whelan Security Co. v. Kennebrew*, 379 S.W.3d 839 (Mo. 2012).

Cases in which courts have modified the terms of non-competes include *Superior Gearbox Co. v. Edwards*, 869 S.W.2d 239, 247 (Mo. App. S.D. 1993) (the court modified a ten-year covenant and enforced a five-year term); *Orchard Container Corp. v. Orchard*, 601 S.W.2d 299, 303–04 (Mo. App. E.D. 1980) (the geographic scope of a restrictive covenant was reduced from a 200-mile radius to a 125-mile radius); *AEE-EMF, Inc. v. Passmore*, 906 S.W.2d 714, 724 (Mo. App. W.D. 1995) (court reduced temporal scope of nationwide non-competition covenant from five years down to three years).

9. When does a non-compete period begin to run? Will courts equitably extend the term?

"Missouri law recognizes that it is within a court's equitable power to apply tolling to enforce a restrictive covenant for the full agreed-upon period, calculated from the date of an order enforcing it." *H & R Block Eastern Enter. Inc. v. Sanks*, 2017 WL 4570803 (W.D. Mo. June 6, 2017), *quoting Silvers, Asher, Sher & McLaren M.D.s Neurology. P.C. v. Batchu, M.D.*, 16 S.W. 3d 340, 346 (Mo. Ct. App. 2000); *see also H & R Block Tax Serv. LLC v. Fries*, 2018 WL 934901 (W.D. Mo. Feb. 16, 2018); *H & R Block Tax Serv. LLC v. Cardenas*, 2020 WL 1031033 (W.D. Mo. Mar. 3, 2020).

10. Are there additional nuances or peculiarities about the state's treatment of covenants in the franchising context?

As can be seen from the franchise cases discussed above, Missouri courts tend to uphold the written restrictions agreed upon by the franchisee. Further, the Eighth Circuit has held that the breach of a non-compete agreement typically amounts to a per se irreparable injury. *N.I.S. Corp. v. Swindle*, 724 F.2d 707, 710 (8th Cir. 1984); *see also Express Scripts, Inc. v. Lavin*, 2017 WL 2903205, at *8 (E.D. Mo. July 7, 2017).

Covenants not to compete are assignable but may not be enforced unless the assignment is effective. A covenant in an employment agreement that is expressly incorporated into, and made part of, an asset purchase agreement is assignable where the asset purchase agreement provides that it "shall be binding on and inure to the benefit of the parties and their respective heirs, successors, assigns, and legal representatives." *Orthotic & Prosthetic Lab, Inc. Port*, 851 S.W.2d 633, 639 (Mo. Ct. App. E.D. 1993) ("This court has previously held virtually identical language sufficient to support an assignment of a noncompetition covenant in a buy-sell agreement"). However, in *Alldredge v. Twenty-Five Thirty-Two Broadway Corp.*, 509 S.W.2d 744 (Mo. Ct. App. 1974), the court refused to permit the assignee of an employment contract to obtain the benefits of a non-competition provision without the employee's consent. In view of this authority, the drafter of a covenant not to compete is well advised to include language authorizing the assignment of the covenant to avoid disputes about whether the assignment of the covenant is enforceable.

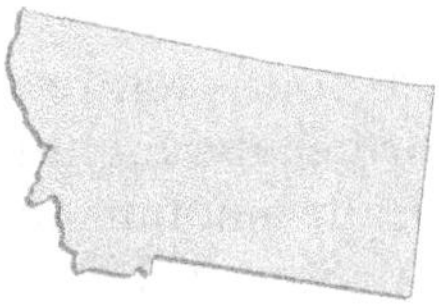

Montana

*by Rodd A. Hamman**

1. Has the state addressed covenants against competition in the context of franchising?

- **Does the state have a franchising statute or regulations that address covenants against competition?**
- **Does the state have a covenants statute of general applicability that would encompass franchise covenants?**
- **Have the courts addressed covenants in the context of franchising either under a statute or under the state's common law?**

Montana has no statute that specifically addresses covenants not to compete in the franchise context. Montana has enacted a statute of general applicability regulating covenants not to compete: "Any contract by which anyone is restrained from exercising a lawful profession, trade, or business of any kind . . . is to that extent void." *See* MONT. CODE ANN. § 28-2-703 *et seq*. The Montana Supreme Court, however, has interpreted this statutory rule to mean that such contract provisions are disfavored, not automatically void. *See Access Organics, Inc. v. Hernandez*, 175 P.3d 899, 902 (2008). Montana has enacted statutory exceptions to this rule for the sale of goodwill of a business and the dissolution of a partnership. *See* MONT. CODE ANN. §§ 28-2-704 and 705. The geographic limitations of both statutory exceptions are expressly limited to: (a) the city where the principal office of the business is located; (b) the county where the principal office of the business is located; (c) a city in any county adjacent to the county in which the principal office of the business is located; (d) any county adjacent to the county in which the principal office of the business is located; or (e) any combination of these areas. MONT. CODE ANN. § 28-2-704(2).

*Rodd A. Hamman practices with the law firm of Calton Hamman & Wolff, P.C. in Billings, Montana. To prepare this analysis, he updated the third edition entry prepared by Gregory G. Pinski with the law firm of Conner, Marr & Pinski in Great Falls, Montana.

2. Have the courts articulated the "legitimate interests" of the franchisor that will support enforcement of a covenant against competition contained in a franchise agreement?

- **If so, what are they (e.g., protection of goodwill, protection of confidential information), and in what contexts did the issue arise?**
- **If not, what interests have been recognized in other contexts (e.g., employment agreements, the sale of business context)?**

The Montana Supreme Court has not addressed the enforceability of a restrictive covenant in the context of a franchise agreement. However, in *H&R Block Tax Service, LLC v. Kutzman*, 681 F. Supp. 2d 1248 (D. Mont. 2010), the Montana federal district court considered the enforceability of non-competition and non-solicitation restrictive covenants in a franchise agreement. In that case, the court held that a franchisor has a legitimate interest in protecting its training, trade name, and business methods, as well as an assurance that the franchisor would not have to compete against another business armed with the same benefits. *See id.* at 1251, 1253 (recognizing that without enforcement of the restrictive covenant, the franchisor could not "readily repair its goodwill, client base, and client relations," while the former franchisee knowingly agreed to the terms of the franchise agreement and enjoyed the fruits of that agreement); *see also American National Property and Casualty Co. v. Camp*, 2011 WL 3348067, at *3 (D. Mont. Aug. 3, 2011). In *Camp, supra*, at *3, the court further recognized that the franchisor's interest in protecting its training, office support, publicity, and assistance in developing new customers was deserving of protection.

3. What time limitations have courts recognized as reasonable in the franchise context?

- **If no franchise cases have been decided, what time limitations have been recognized in other contexts?**
- **How have they been related to the interests protected?**

In *H&R Block Tax Service, LLC v. Kutzman*, 681 F. Supp. 2d 1248 (D. Mont. 2010), and *American National Property and Casualty Co. v. Camp*, 2011 WL 3348067, at *3 (D. Mont. Aug. 3, 2011), the court enforced one-year non-competition restrictive covenants in franchise agreements. In *Kutzman*, the court held that the temporal restriction would provide the franchisor a fair opportunity to retain its goodwill and sell franchises without unfair competition. *See* 681 F. Supp. 2d at 1251.

In other contexts, Montana courts have approved temporal restrictions of longer duration. *See, e.g., Western Media, Inc. v. Merrick*, 224 Mont. 28 (1986) (enforcing a sale of business non-compete provision of 10 years); *Treasure Chemical, Inc. v. Team Laboratory Chemical Corp.*, 609 P.2d 285 (1980) (enforcing a sale of business non-compete provision of three years, while modifying the geographic limitation).

4. What geographic limitations have courts recognized as reasonable in the franchise context?

- **How have they been related to the interests protected?**
- **Have courts recognized the legitimacy of protecting other MT franchisees from competition?**

In *H&R Block Tax Service, LLC v. Kutzman*, 681 F. Supp. 2d 1248, 1251 (D. Mont. 2010), the court enforced a franchise non-compete geographic limitation defined as a 45-mile radius of the franchise territory. In *American National Property and Casualty Co. v. Camp*, 2011 WL 3348067, at *3 (D. Mont. Aug. 3, 2011), the court enforced a franchise non-compete geographic limitation of a 25-mile radius from the franchisee's office.

In upholding the restrictive covenant in a franchise agreement, the court in *Kutzman* held that it was appropriate to look at Montana's law on restrictive covenants in the context of the "sale of goodwill of a business" for guidance on the reasonableness of the challenged restrictions. 681 F. Supp. 2d at 1252 (citing *Wilkinson v. Manpower, Inc.*, 531 F.2d 712 (5th Cir. 1976) (finding no rationale to distinguish a franchise from the sale of a business when analyzing restrictive covenants)). As such, with regard to the geographic restriction, the court held that the 45-mile radius at issue was less than the multiple-county restriction the legislature authorized in the sale of goodwill of a business context under Mont. Code Ann. § 28-2-704(2). The court noted that if it applied the statute, the geographic limitation would be extended to more than 100 miles from the franchise territory, and, therefore, the 45-mile contractual restriction in the franchise agreement was reasonable.

5. What limitations on activities have courts recognized as reasonable in the franchise context?

In *American National Property and Casualty Co. v. Camp*, 2011 WL 3348067, at *3 (D. Mont. Aug. 3, 2011), the court recognized that the restrictive covenant did not prevent the former franchisee from selling insurance products except to former clients of the franchisor. Noting that the franchisor had less than "one percent market share in Montana, meaning [the former franchisee] would be free to sell insurance to 99 percent of the Montana market." In *H&R Block Tax Service, LLC v. Kutzman*, 681 F. Supp. 2d 1248, 1251 (D. Mont. 2010), the court held it was reasonable to restrict the former franchisee's operation of a competing accounting business, which was identical to the business conducted under the franchise agreement.

6. Does the state recognize a difference between in-term and post-term covenants?

There is no reported Montana case dealing with covenants not to compete that differentiates between in-term and post-term covenants. *See infra*, Section 2 (discussing enforcement of post-term restrictive covenants in a franchise agreement). In *Leiman-Scott, Inc. v. Holmes*, 381 P.2d 489 (Mont. 1963), the court found a distributor to have violated an in-term covenant not to compete with an independent dealer.

7. Has the state allowed enforcement of covenants against non-signatories (e.g., family members, newly formed corporations)?

There is no reported Montana case dealing with the enforcement of covenants against non-signatories. Montana has recognized the general rule, however, that a covenant not to compete is assignable and that it need not be expressly assigned. *See Jenson v. Olson*, 395 P.2d 465, 467 (Mont. 1964).

8. Will the state modify, "blue-pencil," or otherwise reduce a covenant found to be overbroad?

In *Dumont v. Tucker*, 822 P.2d 96, 98 (Mont. 1991), the court affirmed a lower court's enforcement of a non-compete provision in the sale of a business, without voiding it entirely. "Under this 'blue-pencil' approach, the district court in the instant case acted correctly in limiting the noncompetition covenant to the contiguous counties as required by Section 28-2-704 of the MCA." *Id.* (citing *Treasure Chemical, Inc. v. Team Laboratory Chemical Corp.*, 609 P.2d 285 (1980)). Thus, modification only consistent with statutory limitations has been approved.

9. When does a non-compete period begin to run? Will courts equitably extend the term?

Although the issue was not directly presented to the court, in *American National Property and Casualty Co. v. Camp*, 2011 WL 3348067, at *3 (D. Mont. Aug. 3, 2011), the court noted that "five months have already passed" and entered the injunction from the date of the franchise termination. The court similarly entered the injunction from the date of the franchise termination in *H&R Block Tax Service, LLC v. Kutzman*, 681 F. Supp. 2d 1248, 1251 (D. Mont. 2010).

10. Are there additional nuances or peculiarities about the state's treatment of covenants in the franchising context?

In *H&R Block Tax Service, LLC v. Kutzman*, 681 F. Supp. 2d 1248, 1251 (D. Mont. 2010), the court made several findings applicable to injunctions in the franchise context. The court rejected the former franchisee's argument that a liquidated damages clause in the franchise agreement precludes a finding of irreparable harm for issuance of a preliminary injunction. The court further held that the enforcement of a covenant not to compete in a franchise agreement served the public interest because the "public has an interest in valid contracts being upheld." *Id.* In enforcing the non-compete provision, the franchisor voluntarily chose to apply more restrictive Montana law, rather than Missouri law, which was specified in the franchise agreement. The court noted that the restrictive covenants were enforceable under either state's law. *Id.* at 1251, n.1. Finally, in entering the injunction, the court required the franchisor to post a $200,000 bond.

Importantly, the Montana Supreme Court has held that MONT. CODE ANN. § 28-2-703 *et seq.*, governing restrictive covenants was modeled after CAL. CIV. CODE § 1673, and, therefore, Montana courts are to be guided by the construction given them by the Supreme Court of California. *See Treasure Chemical, Inc. v. Team Laboratory Chemical Corp.*, 609 P.2d 285, 287 (1980).

In a key decision under MONT. CODE ANN. § 28-2-703, the Montana Supreme Court held in *Mungas v. Great Falls Clinic, LLP*, 221 P.3d 1230 (2009), that a forfeiture provision in a partnership agreement is not void under Montana's statutory scheme prohibiting unreasonable restraints on trade. In that case, the partnership imposed on its partners a forfeiture provision entitled "Competing After Withdrawal or Retirement" that restricted a former partner's practice of medicine in the city of Great Falls for a period of three years, or subjected the former partner to monetary forfeitures under the partnership agreement.

Although not arising in the franchise context, the Montana Supreme Court recently held that continued at-will employment was not sufficient consideration in itself to support an "afterthought" covenant not to compete in the employment context. *See Access Organics, Inc. v. Hernandez*, 175 P.3d 899, 904–05 (2008).

On November 22, 2011, in a case of first impression, the Montana Supreme Court ruled that an employer ordinarily lacks a legitimate business interest in a covenant not to compete when the employer chooses to end the employment relationship with the employee, unless the employer can show that the employee engaged in conduct detrimental to the employer or its clients. *See Wrigg v. Junkermier, Clark, Campanella, Stevens, P.C.*, 2011 MT 290, 265 P.3d 646 (2011) (reversing lower court's decision upholding an employment non-compete provision when employee was terminated by employer). But in a 2016 decision, the court ruled that where the employment agreement expired as opposed to being terminated by the employer, a covenant allowing competition but imposing liquidated damages as compensation was enforceable. *See Junkermier, Clark, Campanella, Stevens, P.C. v. Alborn, Uithoven, Riekenberg, P.C.*, 2016 MT 218, 384 Mont. 464, 380 P.3d 747 (2016). Upon appeal after trial, the court affirmed damages for breach of the covenant. *Junkermier* at 2020 MT 179, 400 Mont. 408, 469 P.3d 111, *reh'g denied* (Aug. 19, 2020).

Nebraska

*by Gary R. Batenhorst**

1. Has the state addressed covenants against competition in the context of franchising?

- **Does the state have a franchising statute or regulations that address covenants against competition?**
- **Does the state have a covenants statute of general applicability that would encompass franchise covenants?**
- **Have the courts addressed covenants in the context of franchising either under a statute or under the state's common law?**

Nebraska's Franchise Practices Act (NFPA) specifically addresses covenants against competition. *See* NEB. REV. STAT. §§ 87-401 to 87-410 (2021). After the decision by the Nebraska Supreme Court invalidating a two-part, post-term covenant not to compete in a franchise agreement in *Unlimited Opportunity, Inc. v. Waadah*, 861 N.W.2d 437 (Neb. 2015), the Nebraska Legislature amended the NFPA in 2018 to specifically permit courts to blue-pencil covenants not to compete in franchise agreements. Accordingly, section 87-404(2) of the NFPA provides, in pertinent part:

> If restrictions in a noncompete agreement are found by an arbitrator or a court to be unreasonable in restraining competition, the arbitrator or court shall reform the terms of the noncompete agreement to the extent necessary to cause the restrictions contained therein to be reasonable and enforceable. The arbitrator or court shall then enforce the noncompete agreement against the franchisee, the guarantor, or any person with a direct or indirect beneficial interest in the franchise in accordance with the reformed terms of the noncompete agreement.

Before this amendment to the NFPA, Nebraska courts consistently refused to blue-pencil non-competes, both in the franchise agreement context and otherwise. Thus, this revision to the NFPA represents a significant change in Nebraska law. The NFPA applies to a franchise that contemplates or requires the franchisee will

*Gary R. Batenhorst practices with the law firm of Cline Williams Wright Johnson & Oldfather, L.L.P., in Omaha, Nebraska. The author wishes to thank Kate Larsen, a Summer Associate at Cline Williams, for her assistance in the research for and preparation of this chapter.

have a place of business in Nebraska with annual gross sales in excess of $35,000 and where more than 20 percent of the franchisee's sales are intended to be from the franchise. NEB. REV. STAT. § 87-403. The revised section 87-404(2) states that the revision also applies to any non-compete agreement "entered into by a franchisor headquartered in the State of Nebraska" unless the franchisor and franchisee otherwise agree. In another indication of the broad scope of this revision, section 87-404(2) applies to non-competes "entered into before, on, or after April 8, 2016."

Several Nebraska statutes of general applicability address restraints on competition. For example, section 59-801 (2021) provides: "[e]very contract, combination in the form of trust or otherwise, or conspiracy in restraint of trade or commerce, within this state, is hereby declared to be illegal." The Nebraska Consumer Protection Act similarly states: "[a]ny contract, combination, in the form of trust or otherwise, or conspiracy in restraint of trade or commerce shall be unlawful," NEB. REV. STAT. § 59-1603 (2021), and that "[u]nfair methods of competition and unfair or deceptive acts or practices in the conduct of any trade or commerce shall be unlawful." NEB. REV. STAT. § 59-1602 (2021). Each of these provisions is subject to interpretation under section 59-829 (2021), which states:

> When any provision of . . . Chapter 59 is the same as or similar to the language of a federal antitrust law, the courts of this state in construing such sections or chapter shall follow the construction given to the federal law by the federal courts.

Accordingly, only restraints of trade that would be held unenforceable under federal antitrust law are illegal under Nebraska law, absent any claims that the restraints violate specific provisions of the Consumer Protection Act or other Nebraska statutes.

None of these statutes specifically preclude non-competition agreements of the type generally found in franchise agreements. Correspondingly, these statutes have not been used to preclude enforcement of non-competition agreements where the agreements meet other enumerated criteria established by Nebraska precedent.

Nebraska courts will enforce reasonable covenants not to compete. Regardless of whether the covenant is related to an employment agreement or is ancillary to the sale of a business, the covenant must be reasonable in the sense that (1) it is not injurious to the public, (2) it is no greater than necessary to protect the employer in a legitimate business interest, and (3) it is not unduly harsh or oppressive on the party against whom it is asserted. *H & R Block Tax Services, Inc. v. Circle A Enterprises, Inc.*, 693 N.W.2d 548, 553–54 (Neb. 2005). Nebraska courts typically apply these three criteria, and cases often stand or fall based on the second criterion.

A covenant ancillary to the sale of a business is not subject to the same heightened scrutiny as a covenant related to an employment agreement and is more broadly enforced. The general rule is that "[p]artial restraints are not unreasonable if they are ancillary to a purchase of property made in good faith and are necessary to afford protection to the purchaser. What is a reasonable restraint depends largely upon the facts of the particular case." *D. W. Trowbridge Ford, Inc. v. Galyen*, 262 N.W.2d 442, 445 (Neb. 1978);*see also Presto-X-Company v. Beller*, 568 N.W.2d 235, 239 (Neb. 1997) (holding a covenant given in connection with the sale of a business is binding if reasonable in time and scope and necessary to protect the buyer's interests).

The Nebraska Supreme Court enforced a post-term non-compete provision in a franchise agreement in *H & R Block Tax Services, Inc. v. Circle A Enterprises, Inc.*, 693 N.W.2d 548 (Neb. 2005). The covenant provided that for one year after termination of the franchise agreement the franchisee would (1) not solicit or divert from H & R

Block or an H & R Block franchisee any person for whom the franchisee prepared a tax return or performed certain other services and (2) not compete directly or indirectly with H & R Block or H & R Block franchisees in preparing tax returns or providing certain other identified services within 45 miles of the franchise territory. *Id.* at 550–51. The trial court construed the two parts of the non-compete provision as an integrated covenant and ruled that the second part of the covenant was unenforceable as it was not limited to former H & R Block clients with whom the franchisee actually did business.

The Nebraska Supreme Court, with two judges dissenting, reversed the lower court and held the non-compete provision to be enforceable. The Supreme Court agreed that the two provisions were an integrated covenant, as they both dealt with post-termination competition, and stated that enforceability turned on whether the covenant not to compete in H & R Block's franchise agreement was more similar to a non-compete provision in the sale of a business or a non-compete provision in an employment agreement.

The Supreme Court reviewed analogous cases from other jurisdictions, including other cases involving H & R Block, one of which upheld the enforceability of an identical covenant. The court noted that the record indicated that H & R Block retained significant control over its franchisees, but "the main purpose of obtaining a franchise from H & R Block is to trade on the reputation and goodwill of its service mark and thereby acquire customers." 693 N.W.2d at 556. The court then concluded that the covenant was more similar to covenants ancillary to the sale of a business and applied Nebraska law to determine the covenant was enforceable. The dissenting judges found franchise agreements more akin to employment contracts, reasoning that a franchisee does not take the goodwill associated with the franchisor's name at the end of the relationship. 693 N.W.2d at 559 (Wright and Connolly, JJ., dissenting).

The Nebraska Supreme Court refused to enforce a two-part, post-term covenant against competition in *Unlimited Opportunity, Inc. v. Waadah*, 861 N.W.2d 437 (Neb. 2015). In *Waadah*, the franchisor terminated a Jani-King franchise agreement after receiving reports the franchisee was attempting to divert customers of the franchised business to the franchisee's separate business. The non-compete covenant in the franchise agreement prohibited the franchisee from operating a business that was the same or similar to the business under the franchise agreement within the franchisee's territory during the term of the franchise agreement and for two years after expiration or termination of the agreement. The non-compete also prohibited competition for one year after expiration or termination of the agreement in any other territory in which a Jani-King franchisee operates.

The trial court concluded that the one-year covenant was unreasonable and did not consider whether the remainder of the covenant was enforceable. In affirming the trial court's decision, the Nebraska Supreme Court reiterated that the court had long held it was not the function of courts to reform non-competes to make them enforceable and that, under Nebraska law, an enforceable portion of a covenant not to compete is not severable from an unenforceable non-compete; thus, the entire covenant was unenforceable.

In reviewing the enforceability of the covenant, the court followed its decision in *H & R Block* in determining the covenant was analogous to a covenant in the sale of a business, and the court noted that Nebraska courts generally are more willing to enforce such covenants than to enforce covenants related to employment contracts. The court noted that, when judging a covenant based on the three factors described above, the covenant must be reasonable as to space and time and no greater than necessary to achieve a legitimate purpose. The court explained that reasonableness depends on the facts of each case but acknowledged that, to be reasonable in space and time, a covenant must normally include a territorial restriction. The court noted that, since Jani-King operates on an international basis, the one-year covenant respecting any other territory in which a Jani-King franchisee operates is analogous to one having no territorial restriction. The court invalidated the one-year covenant, found the two-year covenant inseverable, and held that the entire covenant was unenforceable.

Federal courts in Nebraska have dealt with franchise agreement non-compete issues in two cases in recent years with mixed results. In *Colorado Security Consultants, LLC v. Signal 88 Franchise Group, Inc.*, 2017 WL 1047260 (D. Neb. Mar. 17, 2017), the U.S. District Court for the District of Nebraska declined to issue a preliminary injunction sought by the franchisor to enforce the non-compete provision of a franchise agreement following termination of the franchise agreement. The court stated that, although it recognized the significance of non-compete provisions in franchise agreements, it believed that damages or post-judgment injunctive relief would be sufficient to protect the franchisor's contractual relationships. *Colorado Security Consultants, LLC* involved a Nebraska franchisor and a franchise located in Colorado. Its significance in Nebraska non-compete jurisprudence is limited by the fact that, after applying Nebraska conflicts of law rules, the court applied Colorado law.

In *Complete Nutrition Franchising, LLC v. J. Howell, LLC*, 2018 WL 1174206 (D. Neb. Mar. 6, 2018), the court granted a franchisor's motion for a preliminary injunction enforcing non-compete provisions of a franchise agreement. *Id.* at *2. The court stated that the primary issue was "whether the covenants [were] reasonable in both space and time so that the restraint imposed [was] no greater than necessary to achieve their legitimate purpose." *Id.* at *3. In holding that the franchisor had demonstrated a sufficient likelihood of success on the merits to warrant an injunction, the court compared the case to *H & R Block* and noted that there was no evidence at that point distinguishing the two cases.

---

2. Have the courts articulated the "legitimate interests" of the franchisor that will support enforcement of a covenant against competition contained in a franchise agreement?

- **If so, what are they (e.g., protection of goodwill, protection of confidential information), and in what contexts did the issue arise?**
- **If not, what interests have been recognized in other contexts (e.g., employment agreements, the sale of business context)?**

Nebraska courts have found that a franchisor's goodwill is a legitimate interest that will support enforcement of a non-compete provision. In the sale of a business, Nebraska courts protect the assets purchased, which may include customer lists, trade secrets, general goodwill, and goodwill associated with specific customer accounts.

The Nebraska Supreme Court addressed the legitimate interests of a franchisor with respect to covenants not to compete in *H & R Block Tax Services, Inc. v. Circle A Enterprises, Inc.*, 693 N.W.2d 548 (Neb. 2005). In upholding a post-term covenant not to compete in a franchise agreement, the court identified protection of the franchisor's goodwill as a legitimate interest of the franchisor to be protected. The court noted that the only requirement at issue was whether the covenant was no greater than necessary to protect a franchisor's legitimate business interest.

In deciding whether the non-compete provision in a franchise agreement is more similar to a non-compete provision in an employment agreement or in the sale of a business, the Nebraska Supreme Court quoted from *Jiffy Lube International, Inc. v. Weiss Brothers, Inc.*, 834 F. Supp. 683 (D.N.J. 1993), in which the court held that a franchise agreement non-compete provision was more similar to a non-compete provision in the sale of a business. In discussing the court's rationale in *Weiss Brothers*, the Nebraska Supreme Court stated:

NE

> The court reasoned that a franchisor and a franchisee are in a more equitable bargaining situation than would be found in a typical employer-employee relationship. In addition, it emphasized that the primary characteristic of a franchise is the license given to the franchisee "to trade upon and exploit the franchisor's good will." The court reasoned that when the franchise is terminated, the goodwill is in some sense returned to the franchisor and that thus, a "reasonably crafted" restrictive covenant is necessary to protect the goodwill after its return.

H & R Block, 693 N.W.2d at 554–55 (internal citations omitted).

The Nebraska Supreme Court went on to state that it was "clear that the main purpose of obtaining a franchise from H & R Block is to trade on the reputation and goodwill of its service mark and thereby acquire customers." *Id.* at 556. This ability of the former franchisee to trade on the franchisor's goodwill appeared to be a major factor in the court's determination that the covenant not to compete is more similar to that in the sale of a business.

The emphasis in *H & R Block* on protecting the franchisor's goodwill is consistent with prior Nebraska cases related to covenants not to compete in the sale of a business. In *Presto-X-Company v. Beller*, 568 N.W.2d 235 (Neb. 1997), the Nebraska Supreme Court noted that in a sale of business:

> The use of a covenant not to compete was a reasonable means to protect the value of the assets purchased. However, while a covenant not to compete ancillary to the sale of a business may be utilized to make goodwill a transferable asset, the restraint contained in the covenant must be reasonable in both space and time so that it will be no greater than necessary to achieve its legitimate purpose.

568 N.W.2d at 239.

In *Gaver v. Schneider's O.K. Tire Co.*, 856 N.W.2d 121 (Neb. 2014), the Nebraska Supreme Court cited prior cases noting that the legitimate interests to be protected by a non-compete include trade secrets, confidential information not constituting trade secrets such as a unique business method, an employee's special influence over an employer's customers, contacts developed by the employee during employment, and the employer's development of goodwill.

In *Farm Credit Services of America, FCLA v. Tifft*, 2019 WL 10894030 (D. Neb. Dec. 31, 2019), the U.S. District Court for the District of Nebraska denied summary judgment for a former employee, thereby permitting enforcement of a post-term non-compete provision. The court noted that an employer can have a legitimate interest in enhancing a former employee's pre-existing customer relationships.

3. What time limitations have courts recognized as reasonable in the franchise context?

- **If no franchise cases have been decided, what time limitations have been recognized in other contexts?**
- **How have they been related to the interests protected?**

The Nebraska Supreme Court ties the reasonable time limitation on restrictive covenants to the "useful life" of the protected interest. Accordingly, the court has found a one-year restriction appropriate for a tax-preparation business, as tax returns are prepared annually.

In *H & R Block Tax Services v. Circle A Enterprises*, 693 N.W.2d 548 (Neb. 2005), the Nebraska Supreme Court enforced a post-termination covenant not to compete in a franchise agreement that precluded the franchisee, for a period of one year after termination of the franchise agreement, from (1) directly or indirectly soliciting by phone, mail, or in person or diverting from H & R Block or H & R Block franchisees any person for whom the former franchisee prepared a tax return or performed any related services or additional services and (2) competing directly or indirectly with H & R Block or H & R Block franchisees in the business of preparing tax returns or performing related services or additional services in or within 45 miles of the franchise territory.

In addressing the enforceability of the one-year restraint, the court noted that income tax returns are normally prepared annually so that the one-year restriction kept the former franchisee from "soliciting former H & R Block clients within the restricted area for one tax season." 693 N.W.2d at 556. The court explained that the record in the case established that the one-year restriction was necessary to protect the franchisor's goodwill.

The Nebraska Supreme Court determined in *H & R Block* that the covenant not to compete in a franchise case is analogous to that in the sale of a business. Nebraska law in such cases examines the relationship between the restrictions and the protected interest. One decision cautions that enforcement of a covenant with a particular duration in one case does not mean that a similar duration in another case will be found reasonable. *See Presto-X-Company v. Beller*, 568 N.W.2d 235, 240 (Neb. 1997). In one case, the court upheld a seven-year restrictive covenant, based in part on the parties' acknowledgment that the "useful life" of the customer lists at issue was no more than seven years. *See Chambers-Dobson, Inc. v. Squier*, 472 N.W.2d 391, 401 (Neb. 1991).[1]

In *Unlimited Opportunity, Inc. v. Waadah*, 861 N.W.2d 437 (Neb. 2015), the Nebraska Supreme Court refused to enforce a two-part, post-term covenant not to compete in a franchise agreement. The non-compete prohibited the former franchisee from operating a competing business within the territory granted to the franchisee for two years after termination of the franchise agreement and from operating a competing business for one year after termination in any other territory in which a Jani-King franchisee operates. The court refused to enforce the one-year provision due to its geographic scope and refused to consider the enforceability of the two-year provision because the court found the two parts of the covenant inseverable;

1. The author's firm represented the party seeking to enforce the covenant not to compete in *Chambers-Dobson, Inc. v. Squier*, 472 N.W.2d 391 (Neb. 1991).

thus, the entire covenant was unenforceable. Because the court in *Waadah* was focused on the geographic scope issue, the case provides limited, if any, guidance on the time limitations the Nebraska Supreme Court considers reasonable.

In *Complete Nutrition Franchising, LLC v. J. Howell, LLC*, 2018 WL 1174206 (D. Neb. Mar. 6, 2018), the U.S. District Court for the District of Nebraska granted the franchisor a preliminary injunction enforcing a two-year, post-term non-compete provision in a franchise agreement within a 25-mile radius of each of the franchisee's locations. The court said there was little doubt that the franchisee and its owners breached the non-compete, so the issue was whether it was enforceable under Nebraska law. After discussing *H & R Block Tax Services, Inc. v. Circle A Enterprises, Inc.*, 693 N.W.2d 548 (Neb. 2005), the court said there was no evidence at the time it considered the motion for preliminary injunction to distinguish the case from *H & R Block*. Accordingly, the court granted the preliminary injunction sought by the franchisor.

4. What geographic limitations have courts recognized as reasonable in the franchise context?

- **How have they been related to the interests protected?**
- **Have courts recognized the legitimacy of protecting other franchisees from competition?**

In *H & R Block Tax Services v. Circle A Enterprises*, 693 N.W.2d 548 (Neb. 2005), the Nebraska Supreme Court enforced a post-termination covenant not to compete "in or within 45 miles of the Franchise Territory." 693 N.W.2d at 551. It appears that the franchised territory was the city of Ogallala, Nebraska. In determining that the 45-mile radius was reasonable, the court noted that H & R Block's franchise district manager had testified that the 45-mile radius was necessary to protect H & R Block's service marks and customer relationships. The court noted there were other tax preparers within this 45-mile radius but no H & R Block franchisees. Thus, the court did not discuss the use of a covenant not to compete to protect other franchisees from competition.

In *Unlimited Opportunity, Inc. v. Waadah*, 861 N.W.2d 437 (Neb. 2015), concerns over the reasonableness of the geographic scope of a part of the post-term non-compete in a franchise agreement led the Nebraska Supreme Court to refuse to enforce the entire covenant. The post-term non-compete had two parts: (1) for two years after termination or expiration of the franchise agreement the franchisee could not operate a competing business within the territory granted to the franchisee under the franchise agreement, and (2) for one year after termination or expiration the franchisee could not operate a competing business within the territory of any Jani-King franchisee. This latter component led the trial court to invalidate the entire covenant, a decision the Nebraska Supreme Court affirmed. This decision was consistent with long-standing Nebraska precedent refusing to sever the unenforceable parts of a non-compete from the enforceable parts or to otherwise blue-pencil a covenant to make it enforceable.

As discussed in response to question one above, the Nebraska Legislature amended the Nebraska Franchise Practices Act several years after the *Waadah* decision; the Legislature added NEB. REV. STAT. § 87-404(2), which directs courts and arbitrators to "reform the terms of the noncompete agreement to the extent necessary to cause the restrictions contained therein to be reasonable and enforceable." As a result, franchise agreements that preclude post-term competition within a certain distance of any locations in a franchise system are at risk under Nebraska law, based on the *Waadah* decision, but may be saved by application of the amended statute. There have been no reported decisions to date applying the revised statute to reform a post-term covenant, so it is difficult to predict how Nebraska courts will address future covenants similar to the one-year covenant in *Waadah*, especially in light of Nebraska's longtime prohibition against blue-penciling of covenants not to compete.

Although the court in *O.V. Marketing Associates, Inc. v. Carter*, 766 F. Supp. 960 (D. Kan. 1991) did not enforce the covenant before it under Nebraska law, it did indicate that the presence of other franchisees in the area might be a relevant consideration. The franchisor did not have any franchisees and was not currently seeking any, and the court found this to be a "critical circumstance." *Id.* at 966.

In reviewing the reasonableness of the geographic scope of covenants ancillary to the sale of a business, the Nebraska Supreme Court will examine the facts of a case to determine whether the restraint is reasonable under the circumstances. The Nebraska Supreme Court has upheld a covenant with no specified geographic limitation where it concluded that the important aspect of the covenant was that the seller would not draw customers from specified customer lists. *See Chambers-Dobson, Inc. v. Squier*, 472 N.W.2d 391, 402 (Neb. 1991). The U.S. District Court for the District of Nebraska cited *Squier* in upholding a post-term non-solicitation agreement without a specific geographic limitation where the former employee was prohibited from contacting approximately 100 specific customers. *Farm Credit Servs. of Am., FCLA v. Tifft*, 2019 WL 10894030 (D. Neb. Dec. 31, 2019).

Courts interpreting Nebraska law have been willing to enforce large geographic restrictions when the party seeking enforcement has shown that it was doing business within the claimed area. *See, e.g., RSG, Inc. v. Sidump'r Trailer Co., Inc.*, 2010 WL 428957 (D. Neb. Jan. 29, 2010), in which the court enforced a non-compete ancillary to the sale of a business covering any state or country in North or South America where the party seeking enforcement was doing business.

5. What limitations on activities have courts recognized as reasonable in the franchise context?

In *H & R Block Tax Services v. Circle A Enterprises, Inc.*, 693 N.W.2d 548 (Neb. 2005), the Nebraska Supreme Court enforced a post-term covenant not to compete that prohibited the franchisee from (1) soliciting or diverting from H & R Block or an H & R Block franchisee any person for whom the franchisee had prepared a tax return or performed related services or additional services at any time during the term of the agreement and (2) competing directly or indirectly with H & R Block or H & R Block franchisees in the business of preparing tax returns or performing related services or additional services. The court did not define the terms "related services" or "additional services" in its opinion.

The trial court had refused to enforce the second prong of this non-compete covenant because it was not customer specific, relying on cases in the employment context articulating a customer-specific requirement. But the Nebraska Supreme

Court in *H & R Block* determined that the post-term non-compete covenant in a franchise agreement is more similar to the non-compete covenant connected to the sale of a business than to an employment agreement covenant not to compete; thus, the customer-specific rule did not apply. The court held that a non-compete ancillary to a franchise agreement is enforceable if reasonable in both time and scope. The court noted the annual nature of tax return preparation precluded the former franchisee from soliciting former H & R Block clients for one tax season.

While not applying the strictness found in the employment context, courts interpreting covenants ancillary to the sale of a business still examine the relationship between the scope of prohibited activities and the legitimate interests closely:

> We do not define the permissible scope of a covenant not to compete ancillary to the sale of a business [as] narrowly [as in the context of an employment agreement]. Even where such a sale involves a list of specifically identified customers, as in this case, there may be legitimate reasons why the purchaser must also restrict the seller from competing in a reasonably defined geographic area in order to protect the benefit of his bargain.

Presto-X-Company v. Beller, 568 N.W.2d 235, 241 (Neb. 1997).

In a slightly different situation, a restriction on a seller's solicitation of customers after selling its customer list to another entity was upheld as reasonable, even without a geographic limitation. *See Chambers-Dobson, Inc. v. Squier*, 472 N.W.2d 391, 401 (Neb. 1991). The court in *Chambers-Dobson* discussed the equities in enforcing a covenant not to compete ancillary to the sale of a business:

> It would be more than mild inequity if one sold an item of property, received payment, and, shortly thereafter, were allowed to repossess the property without the purchaser's consent and retain the purchase price paid for the property. Yet, that is exactly what Squier will achieve if he is allowed to pursue an insurance agency that involves the former Squier-McCashland Agency customers.

Id.

---

6. Does the state recognize a difference between in-term and post-term covenants?

No reported Nebraska decisions discuss the difference in enforceability between in-term and post-term covenants not to compete.

---

7. Has the state allowed enforcement of covenants against non-signatories (e.g., family members, newly formed corporations)?

No reported Nebraska decisions applying Nebraska law discuss the enforceability of non-competes in franchise agreements against non-signatories. The U.S. District Court for the District of Nebraska dealt with the enforcement of a post-termination covenant not to compete against a non-signatory in *Merry Maids, L.P. v. WWJD Enterprises, Inc.*, 2006 WL 1720487 (D. Neb. June 20, 2006). The covenant was contained in a Merry Maids franchise agreement with a Nebraska franchisee that provided for application of Tennessee law. The court enforced the covenant against the wife of the owner of the franchisee. While this case applied Tennessee law and says nothing about similarities or differences between Tennessee and Nebraska law on this issue, it still may be instructive regarding how Nebraska courts will deal with this issue.

In *WWJD*, the defendant, James Lovely, owned WWJD, which operated a Merry Maids franchise in Nebraska. Lovely repeatedly failed to acknowledge renewal documents sent to him by Merry Maids, which provided several extensions of the franchise before declaring that it expired on October 17, 2005. James Lovely nevertheless continued to operate the Merry Maids franchise until December of 2005, with assistance from his wife, Stephanie Lovely. In December of 2005, James transferred $10,000 to Stephanie to start a new business—Maids & More, Inc. James transferred certain physical assets to Maids & More, and James and Stephanie retained their Merry Maids list and customer keys.

The court determined that Merry Maids would be irreparably harmed absent an injunction. Stephanie Lovely argued that she could not be enjoined as she had not signed the franchise agreement, but the court rejected the argument as "disingenuous." *Id.* at *11. The court ruled that an injunction against Stephanie was allowed because Fed. R. Civ. P. 65(d) permits enjoining "those persons in active concert or participation" with others enjoined. *Id.* at *11–12 (emphasis removed).

A case decided under Nebraska law, *Adams v. Adams*, 58 N.W.2d 172 (Neb. 1953), may complicate efforts in Nebraska to enforce a covenant not to compete against a non-signatory. Wilson Adams was a partner in Adams Funeral Home with his brother. The partnership agreement prohibited Adams from establishing a new or competitive business, either directly or indirectly, for himself or in association with others, within a specified area for ten years after leaving the partnership. Adams's wife and Kenneth Swanson entered into a partnership to establish the Adams-Swanson Funeral Home within the prohibited area. Adams signed various notes and mortgages to secure financing for his wife's business and provided services to the business without compensation. The Nebraska Supreme Court found that the covenant did not prohibit Wilson Adams from loaning money to others engaged in competition with Adams Funeral Home and that the covenant did not prevent Adams's wife from using her surname in connection with a competing business.

While there was no attempt to enforce the non-compete covenant against Adams's wife in the case, *Adams* is relevant to the issue of what services an individual can perform for the business of another without violating a non-compete provision. The language in this case stating that Adams's wife was free to start her own business and that non-compete covenants are to be strictly construed could be used to argue that a non-compete covenant should not be enforced against non-signatory family members.

---

8. Will the state modify, "blue-pencil," or otherwise reduce a covenant found to be overbroad?

In 2018, the Nebraska Legislature amended the Nebraska Franchise Practices Act (NFPA) to specifically permit courts to blue-pencil covenants not to compete in agreements between a franchisor and a franchisee. Section 87-404(2) of the NFPA states, in relevant part:

> If restrictions in a noncompete agreement are found by an arbitrator or a court to be unreasonable in restraining competition, the arbitrator or court shall reform the terms of the noncompete agreement to the extent necessary to cause the restrictions contained therein to be reasonable and enforceable. The arbitrator or court shall then enforce the noncompete agreement against the franchisee, the guarantor, or any person with a direct or indirect beneficial interest in the franchise in accordance with the reformed terms of the noncompete agreement.

Prior to this amendment to the NFPA, Nebraska followed the minority rule and refused to blue-pencil or otherwise modify covenants not to compete. Thus, this revision to the NFPA represents a significant change in Nebraska law. The NFPA applies to a franchise that contemplates or requires that the franchisee will have a place of business in Nebraska with annual gross sales in excess of $35,000 and where more than 20 percent of the franchisee's sales are intended to be from the franchise. NEB. REV. STAT. § 87-403. The revision to section 87-404(2) states that the revision also applies to any non-compete agreement "entered into by a franchisor headquartered in the State of Nebraska" unless the franchisor and franchisee otherwise agree. Section 87-404(2) applies to non-competes "entered into before, on, or after April 8, 2016."

Before the amendment to the NFPA, Nebraska law was clear that a severability provision would not allow an enforceable portion of a non-compete agreement to be severed from an unenforceable provision. The Nebraska Supreme Court refused to enforce a two-part, post-term covenant against competition in *Unlimited Opportunity, Inc. v. Waadah*, 861 N.W.2d 437 (Neb. 2015). In *Waadah*, the franchisor terminated a Jani-King franchise agreement after receiving reports the franchisee was attempting to divert customers of the franchised business to the franchisee's separate business. The non-compete covenant in the franchise agreement prohibited the franchisee from operating a business that was the same or similar to the business under the franchise agreement within the franchisee's territory during the term of the franchise agreement and for two years after expiration or termination of the agreement. The non-compete also prohibited competition for one year after expiration or termination of the agreement in any other territory in which a Jani-King franchisee operates.

The trial court concluded that the one-year covenant was unreasonable in scope and did not consider whether the remainder of the covenant was enforceable. In affirming the trial court's decision, the Nebraska Supreme Court reiterated that the court had long held it was not the function of courts to reform non-competes to make them enforceable. The court explained that under Nebraska precedent an enforceable portion of a covenant not to compete is not severable from an unenforceable non-compete; thus, the entire covenant was unenforceable.

In the earlier decision of *H & R Block Tax Services, Inc. v. Circle A Enterprises, Inc.*, 693 N.W.2d 548 (Neb. 2005), the Nebraska Supreme Court also stated that Nebraska courts will not modify or blue-pencil an overbroad or otherwise unenforceable covenant. In *H & R Block*, the post-term covenant not to compete in a franchise agreement was found in two subparagraphs in the franchise agreement. The first subparagraph prohibited the franchisee from soliciting for one year after termination of the franchise agreement any person for whom the franchisee prepared a tax return or performed certain other services while an H & R Block franchisee. The second subparagraph prohibited the franchisee from competing with H & R Block or an H & R Block franchisee within 45 miles of the franchise territory for one year. The trial court construed the two subparagraphs as an integrated covenant not to compete after termination of the franchise. The court invalidated the covenant notwithstanding the fact that it believed one part of the covenant would have been valid standing alone. H & R Block argued on appeal that the trial court should have severed the enforceable provision from the unenforceable provision. The Nebraska Supreme Court rejected H & R Block's severability argument, reasoning that the court has long held that it will not reform a non-compete covenant to make it enforceable.

While Nebraska law did not permit severing enforceable and unenforceable covenants, a 2020 federal court decision applied Nebraska law, distinguished *Waadah,* and permitted the confidentiality provisions in an agreement to be severed from the non-compete provisions. In *Signature Style, Inc. v. Roseland,* 2020 WL 58456 (D. Neb. Jan. 6, 2020), the court noted: "*Waadah* did not hold that an invalid covenant not to compete in a contract cannot be severed from otherwise valid provisions . . . *Waadah* is consistent with other cases holding that unenforceable portions of covenants not to compete are inseverable, but still enforcing the broader contracts . . . ." *Id. at* *3.

9. When does a non-compete period begin to run? Will courts equitably extend the term?

There do not appear to be any cases decided by Nebraska courts that discuss issues related to when a non-compete period begins to run. Most Nebraska cases appear to assume that the non-compete period begins with the termination of employment or the completion of the sale of a business. In *H & R Block Tax Services, Inc. v. Circle A Enterprises, Inc.,* 693 N.W.2d 548, 551 (Neb. 2005), the non-compete period began to run on the date the franchise agreement terminated.

There do not appear to be any Nebraska state court cases on the issue of whether under Nebraska law a court may equitably extend the term of a non-compete covenant. In *Agrigenetics, Inc. v. Rose,* 62 F.3d 268 (8th Cir. 1995), the Eighth Circuit considered an appeal from the U.S. District Court for the District of Nebraska's denial of a preliminary injunction to enforce a non-compete covenant against certain former Agrigenetics employees. Agrigenetics filed its appeal after the one-year non-compete term had expired, and the Eighth Circuit found the appeal was moot unless Nebraska law recognized the equitable extension of non-compete terms.

Arguing that Nebraska law recognizes equitable extensions, the former employer cited *Dunning v. Tallman,* 504 N.W.2d 85 (Neb. 1993), a contempt proceeding involving a non-compete provision in a divorce decree. *Agrigenetics,* 62 F.3d at 270. The Eighth Circuit pointed out that the Nebraska Supreme Court had specifically stated it "was *not* deciding 'whether an equity court is empowered to extend a noncompetition provision on breach of the provision'" in *Dunning. Id.* at 270 (quoting *Dunning,* 504 N.W.2d at 93) (emphasis in original). The non-compete provision in *Agrigenetics* provided for one year of non-competition starting from the date the employee departed from the company. 62 F.3d at 271. The Eighth Circuit concluded that because of this language, an equitable extension was unavailable, then dismissed the case based on mootness.

The post-term covenant not to compete in some franchise agreements runs from the later of the expiration or termination of the agreement or the date the franchisee ceases the competitive activity. A 2010 Nebraska Supreme Court case may make it easier to enforce such a covenant. In *Smeal Fire Apparatus Co. v. Kreikemeier*, 782 N.W.2d 848 (Neb. 2010), the Nebraska Supreme Court overruled *Dunning* and held that trial courts may grant equitable relief in contempt proceedings. The *Kreikemeier* opinion devotes two paragraphs to *Dunning*, but the opinion is carefully limited to the context of granting equitable relief in a contempt proceeding. However, the opinion restates dicta from *Dunning* in which the court noted other courts' willingness to extend the duration of a non-competition agreement equal to the duration of the breach.

The new willingness of the Nebraska courts to grant equitable relief in contempt cases may indicate an increased willingness to implement equitable extension as a remedy, but Nebraska has consistently applied strict construction to "covenant[s] restricting competitive freedom." *Agrigenetics*, 62 F.3d at 271. This strongly held policy would likely be used to argue against equitable extension.

10. Are there any additional nuances or peculiarities about the state's treatment of covenants in the franchising context?

There are additional nuances under Nebraska non-compete law, most of which arose in non-franchise cases, of which franchisors and franchisees should be aware.

AMBIGUOUS PROVISIONS IN NON-COMPETE COVENANTS

In *Gary's Implement, Inc. v. Bridgeport Tractor Parts, Inc.*, 702 N.W.2d 355, 368 (Neb. 2005), appeal after new trial at 799 N.W.2d 249 (Neb. 2011), the Nebraska Supreme Court ruled that it was prejudicial error for a trial court to instruct jurors on the meaning of certain provisions of a non-compete covenant related to the sale of a business, because the agreement was ambiguous and thus created a question of fact. This increases the importance of clear and concise drafting, as an ambiguous non-compete covenant will raise factual issues and preclude an attempt to enforce the non-compete covenant by way of summary judgment.

DAMAGES ISSUES

There are several damages issues related to Nebraska non-compete covenants that may impact franchise cases. Nebraska caselaw on whether courts will award damages for a period longer than the term of the non-compete provision is inconsistent. In *Aon Consulting, Inc. v. Midlands Financial Benefits, Inc.*, 748 N.W.2d 626 (Neb. 2008), the Nebraska Supreme Court upheld a trial court ruling that evidence of damages beyond the two-year non-compete period was speculative and irrelevant and therefore inadmissible. *Id.* at 640 (noting defendant was free to solicit business after the two-year restricted period and customers can change brokers whenever they choose). However, in *Gary's Implement, Inc. v. Bridgeport Tractor Parts, Inc.*, 799 N.W.2d 249 (Neb. 2011), the Nebraska Supreme Court stated that there is no legal basis for a jury instruction limiting damages for breach of a covenant not to compete to the five-year non-compete period. The buyer had argued that the breach of the non-compete covenant so impaired the operation of its business that the loss was not fully absorbed by the end of the five-year non-compete period.

Nebraska courts may refuse to grant specific performance of a non-compete provision, even though the plaintiff is otherwise entitled to that relief, where the defendant's conduct shows that further litigation would result from leaving the covenant in place. In *D. W. Trowbridge Ford, Inc. v. Gaylen*, 262 N.W.2d 442, 448 (Neb. 1978), the Nebraska Supreme Court upheld the cancellation of the remaining six years of a 15-year non-compete covenant in return for an award of $5,000 in damages. The defendant in this case sold a car dealership to the plaintiff. The purchase agreement allowed the seller to continue to sell new vehicles for three years, provided he purchased these vehicles from the buyer of his dealership. This action resulted when the buyer alleged that the seller continued to sell new vehicles but did not purchase them from the buyer. In upholding an award of damages rather than enforcing the covenant not to compete, the Nebraska Supreme Court in *Trowbridge* explained that a court may refuse to grant specific performance if the character of performance required would make enforcement unreasonably difficult or would unnecessarily require long, continued supervision by the court.

CONFLICT OF LAWS ISSUES

In *Mertz v. Pharmacists Mutual Insurance Co.*, 625 N.W.2d 197, 202–03 (Neb. 2001), the Nebraska Supreme Court stated that Nebraska follows sections 6 and 196 of the RESTATEMENT (SECOND) OF CONFLICT OF LAWS, which create a presumption that the state where the services are performed is the state with the most significant relationship to the transaction, unless another state has a more significant relationship. The court stated that Nebraska law applied where all of the employee's services were performed in Nebraska. The contract in the case had no choice-of-law clause.

In *Rain & Hail Insurance Service, Inc. v. Casper*, 902 F.2d 699 (8th Cir. 1990), the Eighth Circuit upheld a Nebraska federal district court decision refusing to enforce a two-year, post-term employment non-compete covenant. The contract was entered into in Nebraska but stated that it would be interpreted under Iowa law. The Eighth Circuit upheld the district court's determination that application of Iowa law may be contrary to a fundamental provision of Nebraska law. The employer had argued that applying Iowa law in the case would make a difference, as Iowa law would permit modification of an overly broad non-compete covenant.

In *Colorado Security Consultants, LLC v. Signal 88 Franchise Group, Inc.*, 2017 WL 1047260 (D. Neb. Mar. 17, 2017), a Nebraska franchisor sought to enforce a post-term non-compete against a Colorado franchisee following termination of the franchise agreement. The parties disagreed about whether Nebraska or Colorado law applied. *Id.* at *4. Although the agreement provided that Nebraska law should apply, the court nevertheless concluded Colorado law was applicable. *Id.* In so finding, the court relied on the Eighth Circuit's application of Nebraska conflict-of-law rules in the non-compete case *DCS Sanitation Management, Inc. v. Castillo*, 435 F.3d 892, 895–97 (8th Cir. 2006).

FORFEITURE FOR COMPETITION PROVISIONS

Franchisors occasionally include provisions in franchise termination documents providing that the franchisee will forfeit certain consideration paid in connection with a termination of the franchise if the franchisee breaches a post-term noncompete covenant. In *Brockley v. Lozier Corp.*, 488 N.W.2d 556 (Neb. 1992), the Nebraska Supreme Court considered a forfeiture of a deferred compensation provision in an employment agreement. The court invalidated the provision but explained that such forfeiture clauses will be analyzed in the same manner as non-compete covenants and will be enforced if reasonable.

Nevada

*by Matthew J. Kreutzer**

1. Has the state addressed covenants against competition in the context of franchising?

- **Does the state have a franchising statute or regulations that address covenants against competition?**
- **Does the state have a covenants statute of general applicability that would encompass franchise covenants?**
- **Have the courts addressed covenants in the context of franchising either under a statute or under the state's common law?**

Nevada has no statute or regulation that specifically relates to franchising or franchise agreements. Similarly, Nevada has no statute or regulations addressing covenants against competition in franchise agreements.

The Nevada Unfair Trade Practice Act arguably regulates non-competition covenants generally. NEV. REV. STAT. § 598A.030(2)(a) declares it to be the purpose of the Act to "... prohibit acts in restraint of trade or commerce, except where properly regulated as provided by law." Section 598A.060 enumerates prohibited acts without including covenants not to compete. The Act provides that it "... shall be construed in harmony with prevailing judicial interpretations of the federal antitrust Statutes." *Id.* § 598A.050. The Act specifically exempts restrictive covenants contained in contracts for the sale of businesses and those contained in commercial shopping center leases. *Id.* § 598A.040(5). Section 598A.040(3) also exempts conduct "expressly authorized, regulated, or approved" by statute.

Nevada has a covenants statute of general applicability regarding employees. Section 613.195 permits only reasonable restrictive covenants in the employment context. Under that section, a non-competition covenant is void and unenforceable unless it "(a) is supported by valuable consideration; (b) does not impose any restraint that is greater than is required for the protection of the employer for whose benefit the restraint is imposed; (c) does not impose any undue hardship on the employee; and (d) imposes restrictions that are appropriate in relation to the valuable consideration

*Matthew J. Kreutzer practices with Howard & Howard PLLC in Las Vegas, Nevada. To prepare this analysis, he updated the third edition entry prepared by Randolph L. Howard of Kolesar & Leatham Chtd., Las Vegas and edited by Joy R. Graber.

supporting the noncompetition covenant." NEV. REV. STAT. § 613.195. Nevada courts have not ruled on the treatment of covenants not to compete contained in franchise agreements under this statutory scheme; it appears to be limited to covenants in the context of employment agreements. *Id.* at 6(b) (defining "noncompetition agreement" as "an agreement between an employer and employee").

No reported Nevada decision addresses the enforceability of covenants against competition in the context of franchising.

---

2. Have the courts articulated the "legitimate interests" of the franchisor that will support enforcement of a covenant against competition contained in a franchise agreement?

- **If so, what are they (e.g., protection of goodwill, protection of confidential information), and in what contexts did the issue arise?**
- **If not, what interests have been recognized in other contexts (e.g., employment agreements, the sale of business context)?**

The Nevada courts have not articulated the "legitimate interests" of a franchisor that will support enforcement of a covenant against competition contained in a franchise agreement.

Under Nevada law, "[a] restraint of trade is unreasonable, in the absence of statutory authorization or dominant social or economic justification, if it is greater than is required for the protection of the person for whose benefit the restraint is imposed or imposes undue hardship upon the person restricted.'" *Golden Rd. Motor Inn, Inc. v. Islam*, 132 Nev. 476, 481–82, 376 P.3d 151, 155 (2016), *superseded by statute*, NEV. REV. STAT. § 613.195, as stated in *Paws Up Ranch, LLC v. Martin*, 463 F. Supp. 3d 1160, 1164–65 (D. Nev. 2020). Restrictive covenants that apply to an entire industry as opposed the employees' job duties are less likely to be upheld. *Id.*, 132 Nev. at 482, 376 P.3d at 155 (refusing to enforce covenant that would prohibit former employee "from employment, affiliation, or service with any gaming business or enterprise" because it extended beyond what was necessary to protect the former employer's interests).

In *Hansen v. Edwards*, 83 Nev. 189, 426 P.2d 792 (1967), the court reduced the radius of a non-competition covenant as well as its duration. In upholding the court-modified version of the covenant, the court observed that the employer's ". . . substantial risk of losing patients to an employee is itself an adequate basis for a reasonably designed restraint." *Id.* at 192.

In *Ellis v. McDaniel*, 95 Nev. 455, 596 P.2d 222 (1979), an employment agreement between a medical clinic and an orthopedic surgeon contained a covenant barring the surgeon from practicing medicine within a five-mile radius for a period of two years. The court first noted that the loss of a person's livelihood is very serious and that post-employment, anti-competitive covenants will be scrutinized with greater care than similar covenants incident to the sale of a business. The court acknowledged that "[t]he goodwill and reputation of the clinic are valuable assets and that certain of its orthopedic patients are likely to follow Dr. Ellis." The court continued, "[w]e are nonetheless constrained to agree with Appellant that since none of the doctors at the Elko Clinic are orthopedic specialists, a restraint on Dr. Ellis's practice of his specialty in the Elko area is unreasonable and beyond the scope of any legitimate protectable interest of the Clinic." *Id.* at 459. The court resolved the competing interests by precluding Dr. Ellis from the general practice of medicine during the period set forth in the covenant, but allowing him to practice his specialty, noting the public's need for orthopedic surgeons in the city of Elko.

In *Camco, Inc. v. Baker*, 113 Nev. 512, 936 P.2d 829 (1997), the court recognized that covenants are appropriate if they are limited to the territory where the employer has established customer contacts and goodwill. In that case, the court held that a restrictive covenant covering 50 miles around areas targeted for possible future expansion was unreasonable and void.

In upholding a liquidated damages provision, a Nevada court held that an accounting firm had a legitimate business interest in protecting the "fruits of their labor" and preserving anticipated ongoing revenues from its clients. *Engel v. Ernst*, 102 Nev. 390, 724 P.2d 215 (1986). In *Engel*, the departing accountant who sought to compete with his former employer had signed several agreements providing that he would refrain from serving any of his employer's clients for a two-year period should he choose to leave. The contract had a liquidated damages provision requiring the withdrawing partner to pay "an amount equivalent to the fees that would have been earned by the firm (from the client) during an average one-year period." In upholding the provision under Colorado law, the Nevada court recognized the firm's legitimate interest in the revenues lost from defecting clients.

3. What time limitations have courts recognized as reasonable in the franchise context?

- **If no franchise cases have been decided, what time limitations have been recognized in other contexts?**
- **How have they been related to the interests protected?**

There are no reported decisions discussing the reasonability of time limitations contained in a covenant against competition in the franchise context. There have been several such decisions in the employment context.

In *Hansen v. Edwards*, 83 Nev. 189, 426 P.2d 792 (1967), the court modified a non-competition covenant in an employment contract that contained no time restriction, imposing a one-year limitation in construing the covenant. In *Ellis v. McDaniel*, 95 Nev. 455, 596 P.2d 222 (1979), the court upheld a two-year restriction in an employment contract, while otherwise modifying the non-compete covenant.

In *Las Vegas Novelty, Inc. v. Fernandez*, 105 Nev. 113, 787 P.2d 772 (1990), the court considered a covenant not to compete containing a four-year restriction within a 20-mile radius of the employer's place of business. The trial court had limited the scope of the covenant to one year, with a ten-mile radius. The Nevada Supreme Court reversed on procedural grounds, specifically addressing the reduction in the geographic restriction, while remaining silent on the reduction of the duration of the restriction.

In *Jones v. Deeter*, 112 Nev. 291, 913 P.2d 1272 (1996), the court found a restriction in an employment contract covering a 100-mile radius for five years to be unreasonable per se and unenforceable, without attempting to modify the restrictive covenant. The *Jones* court did not, however, explain why it did not modify the covenant as did the court in *Hansen v. Edwards*. The next year in *Camco, Inc. v. Baker*, 113

Nev. 512, 936 P.2d 829 (1997), the court again found a covenant against competition unreasonable per se based on the breadth of its territorial restriction and refused to modify it, again holding it unenforceable as against public policy without explaining why the covenant would not be modified.

In each case, the Nevada Supreme Court discussed the time limitation without any clear connection to the employer's legitimate interests.

---

4. What geographic limitations have courts recognized as reasonable in the franchise context?

- **How have they been related to the interests protected?**
- **Have courts recognized the legitimacy of protecting other franchisees from competition?**

There are no reported decisions assessing the reasonability of geographic restrictions contained in a covenant against competition in the franchise context. There have been several such decisions in the employment context.

Courts have analyzed the geographic scope of a covenant against competition in an employment agreement in terms of its relation to the protected interests of the employer. In *Hansen v. Edwards*, 83 Nev. 189, 191–92, 426 P.2d 792 (1967), the court reduced a 100-mile restriction to the Reno city limits, stating:

> Where the public interest is not directly involved, the test usually stated for determining the validity of the covenant as written is whether it imposes upon the employee any greater restraint than is reasonably necessary to protect the business and goodwill of the employer. A restraint of trade is unreasonable in the absence of statutory authorization or dominant social or economic justification, if it is greater than is required for the protection of the person for whose benefit the restraint is imposed or imposes undue hardship upon the person restricted.

In *Ellis v. McDaniel*, 95 Nev. 455, 596 P.2d 222 (1979), the court upheld a geographic limitation of five miles from the city limits for an orthopedic surgeon. In *Las Vegas Novelty, Inc. v. Fernandez*, 106 Nev. 113, 787 P.2d 772 (1990), the court reversed the trial court with directions to provide its reasons for reducing a 20-mile restriction around the former employer's premises to only a 10-mile radius. The court expressed concern at the reduction because some of Las Vegas Novelty's important clients were located between 10 and 20 miles away.

At issue in *Sheehan & Sheehan v. Nelson Malley and Co.*, 121 Nev. 481, 117 P.3d 219 (2005), was whether a covenant not to compete that precluded the Sheehans from holding themselves out as accountants within 50 miles of the Las Vegas courthouse had been breached. Whether the 50-mile geographical scope was reasonable was not examined by the court. One of the Sheehan brothers was contacted and hired within 50 miles of the Las Vegas courthouse to perform accounting work for a corporation located in Tucson, Arizona, which was beyond the 50-mile geographic limit. The plaintiff alleged this to have been a breach, but the Nevada Supreme Court disagreed, explaining that the plain language of the covenant not to compete prohibited the Sheehan brothers from performing work within the geographic limit. The court reasoned that just because the party was contacted within the geographical limit does not change the fact that the work was performed beyond the geographical limit, and thus no breach resulted.

In *Shores v. Glob. Experience Specialists, Inc.*, 422 P.3d 1238, 1242 (Nev. 2018), the court held that it was error for the trial court to find a nationwide covenant not to compete reasonable where the plaintiff had made no showing that it had "established customer contacts and goodwill" nationally. The court reiterated that its precedent holding that "a noncompete agreement must be limited to the geographical areas in which an employer has particular business interests" is "no less applicable in instances where the noncompete agreement imposes a nationwide restriction on the former employee."

That said, nationwide covenants are sometimes enforced. In *Accelerated Care Plus Corp. v. Diversicare Mgmt. Servs. Co.*, 2011 WL 3678798 (D. Nev. Aug. 22, 2011), the U.S. District Court for the District of Nevada held that "when an employer's business is national in scope, an unlimited geographical scope may be reasonable so long as the field is sufficiently limited." Citing *Lowry Computer Prods., Inc. v. Head*, 984 F. Supp. 1111, 1116 (E.D. Mich. 1997).

5. What limitations on activities have courts recognized as reasonable in the franchise context?

There are no reported decisions under Nevada law discussing the reasonableness of restricted activities in the franchise context. In *Ellis v. McDaniel*, 95 Nev. 455, 596 P.2d 222 (1979), the court refused to enforce a covenant barring an orthopedic surgeon from any practice of medicine. Instead, the court permitted the surgeon to engage in his specialty, but enforced the covenant as it applied to other areas of medicine. In *Las Vegas Novelty, Inc. v. Fernandez*, 106 Nev. 113, 787 P.2d 772 (1990), the court held a restriction precluding sales of souvenirs "on a wholesale basis" to be reasonable.

Working as an accountant was the activity limited in *Sheehan & Sheehan v. Nelson Malley and Co.*, 121 Nev. 481, 490, 117 P.3d 219 (2005). The conduct that was alleged to have been a breach of the covenant not to compete was accounting work performed for a trust. The clause exempted some trustee work but not accounting work. Though the Nevada Supreme Court agreed this activity amounted to a breach, because a total fee of $300 was received for this service (a fraction of the alleged damages), the breach was determined to be immaterial and did not trigger the liquidated damages clause.

In *Golden Rd. Motor Inn, Inc. v. Islam*, 132 Nev. 476, 481–82, 376 P.3d 151, 155 (2016), superseded by statute, NEV. REV. STAT. § 613.195, as stated in *Paws Up Ranch, LLC v. Martin*, 463 F. Supp. 3d 1160, 1164–65 (D. Nev. 2020), the court refused to enforce against a former employee, a casino host, a restrictive covenant that would have restricted her "from employment, affiliation, or service with any gaming business or enterprise." In that case, the court reasoned that the covenant was too broad because it applied to an entire industry, instead of to the employee's job duties, and would have prohibited the former employee from any casino job whatsoever.

6. Does the state recognize a difference between in-term and post-term covenants?

There are no reported decisions discussing this issue under Nevada law.

7. Has the state allowed enforcement of covenants against non-NV signatories (e.g., family members, newly formed corporations)?

In *Las Vegas Novelty, Inc. v. Fernandez*, 106 Nev. 113, 787 P.2d 772 (1990), the Nevada Supreme Court adopted the majority view that "a party not privy to a covenant not to compete" may be enjoined "if that party breaches that covenant in active concert with the principal party enjoined and with knowledge of the covenant." In so doing, the Nevada court seemingly adopted the federal rule set forth in *Day Cos. v. Patat*, 440 F.2d 1343 (5th Cir. 1971), *cert. denied*, 404 U.S. 830 (1971).

8. Will the state modify, "blue-pencil," or otherwise reduce a covenant found to be overbroad?

There are no reported decisions in Nevada addressing this question in the context of franchise agreements. In employment agreements, Nev. Rev. Stat. § 613.195 requires the court to blue-pencil a covenant where it "finds the covenant is supported by valuable consideration but contains limitations as to time, geographical area or scope of activity to be restrained that are not reasonable, impose a greater restraint than is necessary for the protection of the employer for whose benefit the restraint is imposed and impose[s] undue hardship on the employee."

9. When does a non-compete period begin to run? Will courts equitably extend the term?

There are no reported decisions in Nevada that address these specific issues.

10. Are there additional nuances or peculiarities about the state's treatment of covenants in the franchising context?

There are no reported decisions in the context of franchising.

The enforceability of non-competition covenants does not depend on whether the former employee is employed elsewhere or seeks self-employment. *See Las Vegas Novelty, Inc. v. Fernandez*, 106 Nev. 113, 787 P.2d 772 (1990). Furthermore, "[c]ontinued at-will employment after adoption of the non-compete covenant will be held sufficient consideration to support the covenant." *Camco v. Baker*, 113 Nev. 512, 936 P.2d 829 (1997).

Whether a non-competition covenant survives the sale of a business in Nevada depends on whether the sale is defined as an asset purchase or a merger. In the context of an asset purchase, a covenant not to compete is personal in nature and unassignable absent an express clause permitting assignment, so long as the assignability clause is negotiated at arm's length and supported by additional and separate consideration from that given in exchange for the covenant itself. *Traffic Control Services v. United Rentals*, 120 Nev. 168, 174–75, 87 P.3d 1054 (2004). Subsequent to a merger, Nevada follows the majority of other courts that have concluded that when considering the assignability of a non-competition agreement, the right to enforce it normally vests in the surviving entity of that merger. *HD Supply Facilities v. Bymoen*, 125 Nev. 200, 207, 210 P.3d 183 (2009). *HD Supply* explained the distinction: in an asset purchase, an acquirer does not assume the liabilities of the seller; however, a merger imposes all liabilities on the surviving entity of the entities that were merged. Consequently, *HD Supply* clarified that the *Traffic Control* rule of non-assignability does not apply when a successor entity acquires restrictive employment covenants as a result of a merger.

Finally, covenants not to compete in territories targeted for future expansion have been held unreasonable and will not be enforced. *Camco, Inc. v. Baker*, 113 Nev. 512, 936 P.2d 829 (1997) (holding the covenant to be unreasonable and unenforceable as against public policy, without regard to the court's ability to modify the covenant).

New Hampshire

*by Dan Deane**

1. Has the state addressed covenants against competition in the context of franchising?

- **Does the state have a franchising statute or regulations that address covenants against competition?**
- **Does the state have a covenants statute of general applicability that would encompass franchise covenants?**
- **Have the courts addressed covenants in the context of franchising either under a statute or under the state's common law?**

New Hampshire does not have a franchising statute or regulations that address covenants against competition in franchise agreements, nor does it have a covenants statute of general applicability that encompasses such covenants arising in franchise agreements. Likewise, New Hampshire courts have not addressed covenants in the context of franchising, either under a statute or under the state's common law. However, New Hampshire has enacted a comprehensive statute regulating business practices among motor vehicle manufacturers, distributors, and dealers, N.H. REV. STAT. ANN. § 357-C. The statute provides standards governing when a motor vehicle manufacturer or distributor may appoint a new motor vehicle dealer in the relevant market area of an existing dealer. Furthermore, it is deemed an unfair method of competition and unfair and deceptive practice for any motor vehicle manufacturer, distributor, distributor branch or division, factory branch or division, or any agent thereof to impose unreasonable restrictions on the motor vehicle dealer or motor vehicle franchisee relative to non-competition covenants. *See* N.H. REV. STAT. ANN. § 357-C:3, III(n). The courts have not yet had occasion to determine what would be considered an "unreasonable restriction" in this context.

New Hampshire has in recent years passed a number of statutes regulating non-competes in the health care industry. *See* N.H. REV. STAT. ANN. §§ 326-B:45-a (voiding post-separation non-compete agreements for licensed nurses), 329:31-a (voiding post-separation non-compete agreements for licensed doctors), 315:18

*Dan Deane is an attorney with Nixon Peabody LLP in Manchester, New Hampshire. To prepare this analysis, he updated the third edition entry prepared by Gina M. Norris.

(voiding post-separation non-compete agreements for licensed podiatrists). Additionally, New Hampshire has two statutes that regulate non-competes in the employment context. *See* N.H. Rev. Stat. Ann. §§ 275:70 (voiding employer non-compete agreements to the extent they were not presented to the new employee before the employee accepted the offer of employment), 275:70-a (prohibiting non-compete agreements that restrict "low-wage" employees). *See also High Liner Foods (USA), Inc. v. Groves*, 2020 WL 2048588, at *8 (N.H. Super. Ct. Apr. 12, 2020) (concluding that an informal "napkin memo" at a dinner meeting did not form a contract and therefore disclosure of the non-compete was not required at that time under N.H. Rev. Stat. Ann. § 275:70). While none of these statutes are specific to franchising, the restrictions on non-competes in employment relationships are likely to be relevant to many franchisors and franchisees operating in New Hampshire.

In the employment context, New Hampshire courts will enforce a restrictive covenant if they find, as a matter of law, that the restriction was reasonable at the time the contract was executed, given the circumstances of the case. *Technical Aid Corp. v. Allen*, 134 N.H. 1, 8, 591 A.2d 262, 265–66 (1991). New Hampshire courts employ a three-part test in determining whether a restrictive covenant in an employment contract is reasonable: (1) is the restriction greater than is necessary to protect the legitimate interests of the employer, (2) does the restriction impose an undue hardship on the employee, or (3) is the restriction injurious to the public interest? *Id.* (citing Restatement (Second) of Contracts § 188 (1979)). If any of these questions is answered in the affirmative, the restriction is unreasonable and, thus, unenforceable. The reasonableness of a covenant not to compete is determined as a matter of law. *Id.*

2. Have the courts articulated the "legitimate interests" of the franchisor that will support enforcement of a covenant against competition contained in a franchise agreement?

- **If so, what are they (e.g., protection of goodwill, protection of confidential information), and in what contexts did the issue arise?**
- **If not, what interests have been recognized in other contexts (e.g., employment agreements, the sale of business context)?**

Although the New Hampshire courts have not addressed the "legitimate interests" of a franchisor with respect to covenants against competition, the courts have addressed the "legitimate interests" that will support enforcement of a restrictive covenant in the employment context. Legitimate interests of an employer that may be protected from competition by restrictive covenants include the employer's trade secrets that have been communicated to the employee during the course of employment; confidential information other than trade secrets communicated by the employer to the employee, such as information regarding a unique business method; an employee's special influence over the employer's customers, obtained during the course of employment; contacts developed during the employment; and the employer's development of goodwill and a positive image. *ACAS Acquisitions (Precitech) Inc. v. Hobert*, 155 N.H. 381, 923 A.2d 1076 (2007). *See also Nat'l Employment*

Servs. Corp. v. Olsten Staffing Serv., Inc., 145 N.H. 158, 160, 761 A.2d 401, 405 (2000) (the "legitimate interests" of an employer include the potential for appropriation of confidential information, trade secrets, customer lists, and goodwill).

New Hampshire courts have further clarified that an employer's "legitimate interests" include "trade secrets that have been communicated to the employee during the course of employment" and "confidential information communicated by the employer to the employee, but not involving trade secrets." *Syncom Indus., Inc. v. Wood*, 155 N.H. 73, 920 A.2d 1178, 1185 (2007). Trade secrets, however, are not merely secrets of the trade; they must be secrets known exclusively to the employer. *See Dunfey Realty Co., Inc. v. Enwright*, 101 N.H. 195, 198, 138 A.2d 80, 83 (1957).

The particular circumstances of a given case dictate the scope of these interests. For example, prior to passage of N.H. Rev. Stat. Ann. § 329:31-a, the New Hampshire Supreme Court ruled that a physician could be restricted from treating patients of his former employer for a period of time because the employer possessed a legitimate business interest in prohibiting its employee from competing for existing patients. *Concord Orthopaedics Prof'l Assoc. v. Forbes*, 142 N.H. 440, 443, 702 A.2d 1273, 1276 (N.H. 1997). (As discussed above, New Hampshire statute, N.H. Rev. Stat. Ann. § 329:31-a, now voids, as a matter of public policy, post-separation non-compete agreements for licensed doctors). On the other hand, an agreement that broadly barred an employee from working with *any* client who had transacted business with his employer in the past year was held unenforceable, reasoning that it went "far beyond the defendant's sphere of customer goodwill, and was more restrictive than necessary to protect the plaintiffs' legitimate interests." *Merrimack Valley Wood Prods., Inc. v. Near*, 152 N.H. 192, 199, 876 A.2d 757, 763–64 (2005). *See also Smith, Batchelder & Rugg v. Foster*, 119 N.H. 679, 684, 406 A.2d 1310, 1313 (1979) (despite a restrictive covenant prohibiting an accountant from providing services for any clients of the employer, an accountant leaving a large and financially profitable accounting firm may be permitted to provide services to former clients of the firm).

New Hampshire courts have consistently held that no legitimate interest exists as to new or prospective patients or clients. *See Forbes*, 142 N.H. at 443. The legitimate interests of the employer generally extend only to those areas in which the employee had actual client contact, and because the employee generally cannot have had actual contact with new patients or clients, the employer lacks any legitimate interest in trying to prevent the employee from competing for new patients or clients. *Id. See also Near*, 152 N.H. at 199 (finding that it is generally unreasonable for an employer to prohibit an employee from soliciting customers of the employer with whom he previously had no contact).

A New Hampshire superior court also considered a non-compete agreement in the context of an independent contractor relationship. In *Brian's 1:1 Fitness v. Woodward*, Case No. 2012-CV-00838 (N.H. Super. Ct. Aug. 9, 2013) (unreported), the Merrimack County superior court applied the same three-pronged test to determine whether the restraint was reasonable and focused its inquiry on whether the health club plaintiff had a legitimate interest in restraining the activities of one of its independent fitness trainers. Following a fact-intensive inquiry, the court concluded that the health club did not have a legitimate interest because the independent fitness trainer did not acquire any trade secrets or confidential information, nor did he obtain any special influence with or goodwill of the health club's customers, during the time he worked at the health club.

3. What time limitations have courts recognized as reasonable in the franchise context?

➤ **If no franchise cases have been decided, what limitations have been recognized in other contexts?**

➤ **How have they been related to the interests protected?**

The New Hampshire Supreme Court has not addressed time limitations in the franchise context, although cases in other contexts may be instructive.

In the case of a physician, the New Hampshire Supreme Court upheld a two-year restriction on the physician's right to compete with his former employer. *See Forbes*, 142 N.H. at 444. The court found two years to be a reasonable time to allow a replacement physician to demonstrate his or her effectiveness, and for the public to "disassociate" the former physician from his former employer. *See id.; see also Hobert*, 155 N.H. at 393–94 (finding a two-year restrictive covenant reasonable, based on the employee's intimate knowledge of the employer's customer base and access to all of employer's technical, financial, and customer information).

The court upheld a five-year restriction on a veterinarian's ability to compete with his former employer. *See Moore v. Dover Veterinary Hospital, Inc.*, 116 N.H. 680, 685, 367 A.2d 1044, 1048 (1976). The court reasoned that the employer was closely identified with the veterinarians that it employed and five years was a reasonable period of time for the employer to "extinguish" this identification.

In the context of a salesman in a personnel placement business, the court upheld an 18-month restriction. *See Allen*, 134 N.H. at 8 (holding that the initial development of a rapport with a client may be easier when there is not an alternative supplier who is the beneficiary of the preexisting goodwill of that client).

With respect to contracts for the sale of a business, the New Hampshire Supreme Court has not clearly articulated the standards by which it will judge the reasonableness of a covenant against competition. In the sale of a business case addressing a time limitation, the court found a covenant restricting a seller from competing with a buyer for five years after the sale to be reasonable, but provided little explanation of its reasoning. *See Gosselin v. Archibald*, 121 N.H. 1016, 1021, 437 A.2d 302, 306–07 (1981). Where a non-competition covenant is ancillary to the sale of a business, it may be interpreted more liberally. *Centorr-Vacuum Industries, Inc. v. Lavoie*, 135 N.H. 651, 654, 609 A.2d 1213, 1215 (1992).

4. What geographic limitations have courts recognized as reasonable in the franchise context?

➤ **How have they been related to the interests protected?**

➤ **Have courts recognized the legitimacy of protecting other franchisees from competition?**

The New Hampshire Supreme Court has not addressed geographic limitations in the franchise context and has not addressed the legitimacy of protecting other franchisees from competition.

In the employment context, a geographic restriction must be narrowly tailored to the area in which an employee had client contact, as this area holds the employer's goodwill, which is subject to appropriation by an employee. *See Forbes*, 142 N.H. at 444 (25-mile radius from an orthopedic practice reasonably reflected the practice's normal market); *Moore*, 116 N.H. at 685 (20-mile radius from a former veterinary hospital declared reasonable because animal owners are willing to travel this distance to visit a veterinarian); *Allen*, 134 N.H. at 8 (for salespersons, the geographic scope often corresponds to the territory to which they are assigned to make sales). Where the employer's clientele consists of the general public, it is ordinarily reasonable to devise the geographic restraint in terms of the employer's normal market. *Moore*, 116 N.H. at 685.

In the sale of a business, the New Hampshire Supreme Court upheld a 15-mile non-competition radius, but failed to explain why the scope was reasonable. *See Gosselin*, 121 N.H. at 1021.

5. What limitations on activities have courts recognized as reasonable in the franchise context?

Restrictions on activities have not been addressed in the franchise context in New Hampshire.

In the employment context, the New Hampshire Supreme Court has ruled that a prohibition against "competition" or "competitive activities" is not so vague as to render the prohibition unreasonable per se. *See Allen*, 134 N.H. at 9. As with time and geographical limitations, the court will determine whether an activity restriction is reasonable under the circumstances of a given case. *See id.* at 8, 591 A.2d at 265. In the case of a former agent of a temporary employment agency, the court found it reasonable to prohibit the agent from soliciting or diverting agency personnel and agency customers about which the agent had gained significant knowledge or understanding. *See id.* at 13, 591 A.2d at 269. The court deemed the prohibition reasonable because the agency had a legitimate interest in preventing its former agent from using the knowledge that the agency bestowed upon him to the agency's detriment.

In the sale of a motel business, the court upheld a covenant against competition that prohibited a seller from using a trade name for a new business that would "confuse" the public as to the distinction between the businesses. *See Gosselin*, 121 N.H. at 1021.

6. Does the state recognize a difference between in-term and post-term covenants?

In New Hampshire, a distinction between in-term and post-term covenants can be found only in the employment context. In *Technical Aid Corp. v. Allen*, 134 N.H. 1, 591 A.2d 262 (1991), the New Hampshire Supreme Court expressed greater support for in-term rather than post-term covenants against competition. The court ruled that the legitimate interests of an employer in enforcing a covenant against competition are considerably stronger during the employee's term of employment than subsequent to it because employers are entitled to require "undivided loyalty" from their present employees. *See id.* at 17, 591 A.2d at 271. The court noted that in-term covenants do not impose hardship on employees because the covenants do not prevent employees from working their trade. The court also noted that in-term covenants against competition are not injurious to the public interest.

7. Has the state allowed enforcement of covenants against non-signatories (e.g., family members, newly formed corporations)?

There are no New Hampshire cases addressing the enforcement of covenants against non-signatories in the franchise context. In the context of a sale of a business, the U.S. Bankruptcy Court for the District of New Hampshire has determined that the enforceability of a covenant not to compete can hinge on whether or not the party against whom the covenant would be enforced had executed the agreement in his or her individual capacity. *See In re Clarkeies Market, LLC*, 2004 WL 2745651 (Bankr. D.N.H. Nov. 29, 2004) (unreported opinion) (court allowed summary judgment as to one defendant because none of the agreements containing the non-competition covenants were signed by that defendant in his individual capacity, only as a corporate officer).

8. Will the state modify, "blue-pencil," or otherwise reduce a covenant found to be overbroad?

In New Hampshire, modification of a covenant has been addressed solely in the employment context. In this context, modification or partial enforcement of a covenant against competition may be appropriate if it is in the public interest, so long as the employment contract was executed in good faith. *See Forbes*, 142 N.H. at 445 (trial court properly modified a covenant against competition to permit a departing physician to compete with his former employer in emergency situations, stating that modification or partial enforcement, upon a showing of good faith in the employment contract's execution, may be appropriate if in the public interest). The burden of proving "good faith" rests with the employer seeking to enforce the non-compete and the court will consider "all the relevant circumstances of a particular case." *Solito v. Direct Capital Corp.*, 2018 WL 2283410, at *4 (N.H. Super. Ct. May 17, 2018) (quoting *Maddog Software, Inc. v. Sklader*, 382 F. Supp. 2d 268, 283 (D.N.H. 2005)).

A court's inquiry into "good faith" includes examining the circumstances under which the covenant was obtained and whether the employer has drafted unjustifiably broad provisions. *See Maddog*, 382 F. Supp. 2d at 283 (holding that the absence of proof of bad faith does not equate to proof of good faith for purposes of the good-faith inquiry); *Allen*, 134 N.H. at 18 (employer did not act in good faith in requiring an employee to sign a contract containing a non-competition covenant on the employee's first day of employment, when the employer had previously failed to advise the employee of the contract, and when the employee had already given notice to his former employer); *Foster*, 119 N.H. at 685 (where employees executed their employment agreements after they were hired, in the prior oral negotiations there was no discussion of the employment agreement containing the restrictive covenants, and none of the employees were given any opportunity to understand the restrictive covenants in their agreements, the court declined to reform the restrictive covenants for failure to prove good faith). *See also Solito*, 2018 WL 2283410, at *4 ("An employer who seeks reformation seeks equitable relief, and hoary common law maxims require a person who seeks equitable remedies to have acted equitably.").

9. When does a non-compete period begin to run? Will courts equitably extend the term?

The issue has not been decided in a franchise context. In an employment context, when a covenant not to compete has expired, courts applying New Hampshire law lack the equitable power to extend the covenant's temporal term, despite a defendant's violation of the covenant while it was in effect. *See Maddog*, 382 F. Supp. 2d at 283 (a party seeking to extend the covenant "cannot obtain prospective relief to enforce an expired noncompetition agreement" because a plaintiff has an adequate remedy for breach at law in the form of damages for whatever losses the company can prove that it has suffered as a result).

10. Are there additional nuances or peculiarities about the state's treatment of covenants in the franchising context?

Given the absence of any law addressing restrictive covenants in the franchise context, it is difficult to predict whether New Hampshire will develop any nuances or particularities in this area. In other contexts, however, the New Hampshire Supreme Court has expressly held that the state's public policy encourages free trade and discourages covenants against competition. *See Forbes*, 142 N.H. at 442 (a covenant restricting a physician from competing with his former employer for new patients would not foster the public good). As a result, at least in the employment context, if an employer materially breaches a significant term of an employment contract, the employee may be discharged from his or her legal duty under a restrictive covenant. *See Laconia Clinic, Inc. v. Cullen*, 119 N.H. 804, 807, 408 A.2d 412, 414 (1979) (because providing a physician with financial security was the duty of his employer–health clinic, physician was permitted to seek other employment without being bound by a covenant not to compete when the health clinic failed financially); *Genex Cooperative, Inc. v. Bujnevicie*, 2000 WL 1507319 (D.N.H. July 17, 2000) (applying New Hampshire law, the federal court sitting in diversity held that because an employment agreement implies an obligation on the part of the employer to afford a certain degree of financial stability to a contracting employee, employer materially breached employment agreement by unilaterally and materially reducing an employee's salary).

New Jersey

*by Benjamin A. Levin and David G. Gunther**

1. Has the state addressed covenants against competition in the context of franchising?

- **Does the state have a franchising statute or regulations that address covenants against competition?**
- **Does the state have a covenants statute of general applicability that would encompass franchise covenants?**
- **Have the courts addressed covenants in the context of franchising either under a statute or under the state's common law?**

New Jersey's statute regulating franchising, the New Jersey Franchise Practices Act, N.J. STAT. ANN. § 56:10 *et seq.*, does not address covenants against competition. Likewise, there is no legislation of general applicability in New Jersey that would apply to covenants against competition in the franchising context. Although the New Jersey state courts have not weighed in on this subject, the federal courts have repeatedly addressed the applicability and enforcement of restrictive covenants in the franchising context under New Jersey law. *Jiffy Lube Int'l, Inc. v. Weiss Bros., Inc.*, 834 F. Supp. 683 (D.N.J. 1993) is the seminal case addressing this topic.

In *Weiss Bros.*, the U.S. District Court for the District of New Jersey acknowledged that the New Jersey Supreme Court had not opined on the enforceability of covenants against competition in a franchise context. Having no binding precedent from which to draw, the court first examined whether such a restrictive covenant should be viewed as closer to a covenant executed in connection with an employment contract or a covenant ancillary to the sale of a business. Reasoning that parties to a business transaction, like a franchisor and franchisee, are in a more equitable bargaining position than is found in a typical employer-employee relationship, the court predicted that the New Jersey Supreme Court would liken a restrictive covenant contained in a franchise agreement to a restrictive covenant ancillary to a business sale. In addition, the district court noted that the sale and purchase of a business involves the transfer of inventory, customer information,

*Benjamin Levin and David Gunther are partners at Hyland Levin Shapiro LLP, located in Marlton, New Jersey. The authors would like to thank Michael Greenfield and Opeyemi Akinde for their assistance in preparing this chapter.

and, most importantly, the goodwill established by the seller. The court explained that courts generally are more receptive to restrictive covenants designed to protect consumer goodwill. *Weiss Bros.*, 834 F. Supp. at 691 ("the primary characteristic of a franchise is the license given to the franchisee to trade upon and exploit the franchisor's good will"). *See also Coskey's Television & Radio Sales and Serv., Inc. v. Foti*, 602 A.2d 789, 793 (N.J. Sup. Ct. App. Div. 1992) (holding under New Jersey law that covenants ancillary to the sale of a business "are accorded far more latitude" than covenants ancillary to an employment contract).

The *Weiss Bros.* court then held that a restrictive covenant contained in a franchise agreement is enforceable under New Jersey law only insofar as it meets the three-pronged reasonableness test set forth in *Solari Indus., Inc. v. Malady*, 264 A.2d 53 (N.J. 1970). Under the *Solari* test, (1) the covenant must protect a legitimate interest of the franchisor, (2) the covenant may impose no undue hardship on the franchisee, and (3) the covenant must not impair the public interest. *Weiss Bros.*, 834 F. Supp. at 690. The *Weiss Bros.* court relied on *Solari*, notwithstanding the fact that *Solari* involved the enforceability of a restrictive covenant ancillary to an employment agreement rather than a business agreement. In doing so, the court noted that although *Solari* involved an employment agreement, the *Solari* standard was nonetheless an appropriate standard to apply in the first instance in a franchise context, but should be applied more liberally than in an employment context.

Since the *Weiss Bros.* decision, there have been multiple cases decided by federal courts that have addressed covenants not to compete in a franchising context. These cases have largely relied upon the reasoning laid out in *Weiss Bros. See, e.g.*, *Jackson Hewitt Inc. v. Njoku*, 2021 WL 1827277 (D.N.J. May 6, 2021); *Jackson Hewitt, Inc. v. Dupree-Roberts*, 2013 WL 4039021 (D.N.J. Aug. 7, 2013); *Lawn Doctor, Inc. v. Rizzo*, 2012 WL 6156228 (D.N.J. Dec. 11, 2012); *Jackson Hewitt, Inc. v. Childress*, 2008 WL 199539 (D.N.J. Jan. 15, 2008), *reconsideration denied*, 2008 WL 834386 (D.N.J. Mar. 21, 2008).

---

2. Have the courts articulated the "legitimate interest" of the franchisor that will support enforcement of a covenant against competition contained in a franchise agreement?

- **If so, what are they (e.g., protection of goodwill, protection of confidential information), and in what contexts did the issue arise?**
- **If not, what interests have been recognized in other contexts (e.g., employment agreements, the sale of business context)?**

No New Jersey state court decision has addressed the issue of what constitutes a "legitimate interest" of a franchisor that will support the enforcement of a covenant not to compete in a franchise agreement. The U.S. District Court for the District of New Jersey, however, has held that a franchisor's goodwill, relationship with its customer base, trade secrets, and confidential information all constitute legitimate, protectable interests warranting protection.

The *Weiss Bros.* court emphasized the franchisor's legitimate interest in protecting its own goodwill. "New Jersey courts have emphasized that the primary characteristic of a franchise is the license given to the franchisee to trade upon and exploit the franchisor's goodwill. . . . One can view a franchise agreement, in part, as a conveyance of the franchisors' goodwill to the franchisee for the length of the franchise. When the franchise terminates, the goodwill is, metaphysically, reconveyed to the franchisor. A restrictive covenant, reasonably crafted, is necessary to protect the goodwill after that reconveyance." *Jiffy Lube Int'l, Inc. v. Weiss Bros., Inc.*, 834 F. Supp. 683, 691 (D.N.J. 1993).

Other decisions have held that a franchisor has a legitimate interest in maintaining its existing customer base. In *Jackson Hewitt, Inc. v. Madan*, 83 Fed. Appx. 417 (3d Cir. 2003), the U.S. Court of Appeals for the Third Circuit upheld a covenant against competition, echoing the district court's finding that a franchisor has a right to prevent its clientele from being "diverted" by a former franchisee. *Id.* at 419. In *Jackson Hewitt Inc. v. Childress*, 2008 WL 199539 (D.N.J. Jan. 22, 2008), *reconsideration denied*, 2008 WL 834386 (D.N.J. Mar. 21, 2008), the district court held that "[t]he crux of the covenant not to compete is to provide [franchisor] with an opportunity to transfer former franchisees' customers . . . to alternative . . . franchisees upon the termination of franchise agreements and, thereby, preserve [franchisor's] client base." *Id.* at *7 *See also Jackson Hewitt Inc. v. Njoku*, 2021 WL 1827277, at *9 (D.N.J. May 6, 2021) ("Jackson Hewitt has a legitimate interest in maintaining its customer base after a franchisee has departed from an area.").

The district court has also recognized that a franchisor has a protectable interest in protecting its trade secrets and confidential information. *See Childress*, 2008 WL 834386.

Notably, the district court has held that a franchisor has a legitimate and protectable interest in preserving goodwill and customer relationships even in connection with business lines that it did not offer anywhere near a terminated franchisee's territory. *See Lawn Doctor, Inc. v. Rizzo*, 2012 WL 6156228 (D.N.J. Dec. 11, 2012) (prohibiting a former franchisee from offering irrigation services, notwithstanding the fact that the franchisor had not offered such services within 1,500 miles of the franchisee's territory). Another district court decision, however, has questioned whether the loss of customer relationships would cause a franchisor irreparable harm, justifying a preliminary injunction enforcing a non-compete. *Exec. Home Care Franchising LLC v. Marshall Health Corp.*, 2015 WL 1422133 (D.N.J. Mar. 26, 2015) (refusing to enter a preliminary injunction enforcing a non-compete against a former franchisee who had returned all proprietary information to the franchisor, informed all clients that it was no longer associated with the franchisor, switched locations, and was not using any of the franchisor's marks).

---

3. What time limitations have courts recognized as reasonable in the franchise context?

- **If no franchise cases have been decided, what time limitations have been recognized in other contexts?**
- **How have they been related to the interests protected?**

No New Jersey state court decision has addressed the reasonableness of time limitations in the franchise context, although several federal courts have addressed this issue under New Jersey law. Unfortunately, there is no bright-line rule. Each court has treated the reasonableness of time limitations as a fact-sensitive issue that depends heavily on the specific circumstances of each case.

In *Weiss Bros.*, the U.S. District Court for the District of New Jersey held that a three-year covenant not to compete in a franchise agreement was excessive when measured against the franchisor's protectable interests. The district court, therefore, reduced the duration of the restriction to ten months, the anticipated time that it would require the franchisor to establish a new franchisee in the same area.

Notwithstanding the *Weiss Bros.* decision, subsequent Third Circuit and district court decisions have routinely upheld two-year restrictive covenants in the franchise context. *See Jackson Hewitt Inc. v. Madan*, 83 Fed. Appx. 417 (3d Cir. 2003); *see also Jackson Hewitt Inc. v. Njoku*, 2021 WL 1827277 (D.N.J. May 6, 2021); *Jackson Hewitt Inc. v. Cline*, 2015 WL 6687545 (D.N.J. Oct. 29, 2015).

---

4. What geographic limitations have courts recognized as reasonable in the franchise context?

- **How have they been related to the interests protected?**
- **Have courts recognized the legitimacy of protecting other franchisees from competition?**

No New Jersey state court decision has addressed the reasonableness of geographic limitations in the franchise context. Once again, however, the federal courts have opined on this issue under New Jersey law. Geographic limitations, like temporal limitations, do not permit the easy application of bright-line rules. The reasonableness of a geographic limitation depends heavily on the factual circumstances of the given case.

In *Jiffy Lube Int'l, Inc. v. Weiss Bros., Inc.*, 834 F. Supp. 683 (D.N.J. 1993), the U.S. District Court for the District of New Jersey reduced a ten-mile geographic restriction to five miles. In making its decision, the court held that the ten-mile geographic restriction was excessive in light of the community's relatively small size and the fact that the consumers who sought the franchise brand's services typically did not travel far from their homes to obtain them. Accordingly, the district court held that while the enforcement of a five-mile covenant would preserve the goodwill accumulated at the formerly franchised location, anything more would be synonymous with forbidding the franchisee from competing in what the court deemed to be a "low-technology, routinized business." *Id.* at 692.

In *Jackson Hewitt, Inc. v. Childress*, 2008 WL 199539 (D.N.J. Jan. 15, 2008), however, the district court upheld a geographic restriction extending ten miles from the zip codes in which the former franchisee had exclusive rights. In doing so, the district court noted that customers could still easily access the former franchisee's services outside of the protected area. In *Jackson Hewitt Inc. v. Njoku*, 2021 WL 1827277 (D.N.J. May 6, 2021), the district court followed the reasoning in *Childress* to uphold a ten-mile geographic restriction. The district court ruled that a ten-mile restriction did not impose undue hardship on the former franchisee, as he continued to serve numerous out-of-state clients (for whom his geographic location was irrelevant) and was able to retain 60 percent of his former clients after moving his office location eight miles. The court also ruled that a ten-mile restriction did not reduce the availability or increase the cost of tax preparation services for the general public, noting that there were 50 other Jackson Hewitt locations within ten miles of the former franchisee's location.

The district court has even upheld a geographic restriction that extended 50 miles from the franchisee's former territory and the territory of any other franchisee. *Lawn Doctor, Inc. v. Rizzo*, 2012 WL 6156228 (D.N.J. Dec. 11, 2012).

5. What limitations on activities have courts recognized as reasonable in the franchise context?

No New Jersey state court decision has addressed what limitations on activities are reasonable in a franchise context. The U.S. District Court for the District of New Jersey, however, has examined this issue. In general, it appears that the district court is willing to enforce broad restrictions under New Jersey law.

In *Jackson Hewitt, Inc. v. Childress*, 2008 WL 199539 (D.N.J. Jan. 15, 2008), the district court upheld a broad restriction under which a franchisee agreed that he would not "directly or indirectly prepare or electronically file individual tax returns, teach tax courses, offer Bank Products, or own, engage in, operate, [or] manage . . . a Competing Tax Business . . . ." Similarly, in *Athlete's Foot Mktg. Assocs., LLC v. FL Consulting Inc.*, 2007 WL 1321199 (D.N.J. May 2, 2007), the district court upheld an activity restriction that prohibited the franchisee from "operating a store that sells athletic footwear and other related products . . . ."

In *Lawn Doctor v. Rizzo*, 2012 WL 6156228 (D.N.J. Dec. 11, 2012), the court interpreted a restrictive covenant as prohibiting a former franchisee from offering irrigation services, despite the fact that the franchisor had not offered such irrigation services within 1,500 miles of the former franchisee's territory. In *Rizzo*, the relevant covenant prohibited the former franchisee from operating "a business for the establishment, care and conditioning of lawns or other vegetation or any related or ancillary services, including, but not limited to, trees, shrubbery and other plant life." The court held that "irrigation services" clearly fell within this definition and noted that the covenant was not restricted to "lawn care and conditioning services actually provided by [franchisor]." *Id.* at *10. Thus, the fact that the franchisor did not offer such services within 1,500 miles of the franchisee's territory was deemed irrelevant.

6. Does the state recognize a difference between in-term and post-term covenants?

There are no New Jersey state court decisions that address the difference between in-term and post-term covenants. Likewise, the federal courts have not substantively addressed how the issue might be handled under New Jersey law.

In the employment context, however, there is a well-developed body of law that draws a distinction between in-term and post-term covenants against competition. Under the common law of New Jersey, an employee has a duty not to compete with his or her employer during the course of his or her employment (i.e., "in-term"). *Lamorte Burns & Co., Inc. v. Walters*, 770 A.2d 1158 (N.J. 2001) (holding that an employee owes an undivided duty of loyalty to his or her employer and has a duty not to compete with his or her employer). In contrast to this extremely broad in-term restriction, a contractual post-term covenant against competition is enforceable only to the extent that the covenant complies with the reasonableness factors set forth in *Solari Indus., Inc. v. Malady*, 264 A.2d 53 (N.J. 1970).

7. Has the state allowed enforcement of covenants against non-signatories (e.g., family members, newly formed corporations)?

The New Jersey state courts have not addressed whether restrictive covenants may be enforced against non-signatories. In *Jackson Hewitt, Inc. v. Barnes*, 2011 WL 181431 (D.N.J. Jan. 18, 2011), however, the U.S. District Court for the District of New Jersey enforced a restrictive covenant against a non-signatory. In *Barnes*, the district court upheld a restrictive covenant not only against a franchisee but also against the franchisee's "employees, agents, independent contractors, and all those who act in concert or participation with them."

In *Barnes*, the franchisor alleged that the former franchisee was planning on using his father to operate 15 competing tax-preparation businesses in circumvention of a covenant against competition. The franchisor, therefore, sought injunctive relief not only against the franchisee/signatory but also potentially against the signatory's father. The court agreed to enforce the restrictive covenant against the defendants, as well as their "'affiliates, shareholders, partners, members or other parties who have a direct or indirect legal or beneficial interest in' from the prohibited activities." In justifying this approach, the court noted that "[a]lthough injunctions are an extraordinary measure, and not ordinarily applicable to third parties, the New Jersey Superior Court's Appellate Division held in *Horizon Health Ctr. v. Felicissimo*, 722 A.2d 611, 613 (N.J. Super. Ct. App. Div. 1999) that 'injunctions of this nature are generally broad enough to encompass nonparties, who are bound provided they have actual notice of its substance and contents. The reason is to avoid nullification of a decree by unnamed aiders and abettors who carry out the prohibited acts.'"

8. Will the state modify, "blue-pencil," or otherwise reduce a covenant found to be overbroad?

Solari Indus., Inc. v. Malady, 264 A.2d 53 (N.J. 1970), and its progeny provide courts with the authority to reduce the geographic area, temporal period of enforcement, and scope of prohibited activity contained in a covenant against competition in order to render it reasonable under the circumstances. The U.S. District Court for the District of New Jersey has explicitly recognized that this authority extends to the franchise context. *See Jiffy Lube Int'l, Inc. v. Weiss Bros., Inc.*, 834 F. Supp. 683, 691 (D.N.J. 1993).

9. When does a non-compete period begin to run?

➢ **Will courts equitably extend the term?**

The specific terms of a covenant against competition govern when the non-compete period commences. That said, restrictive covenants generally begin to run upon termination of the franchise.

The U.S. District Court for the District of New Jersey has been willing to equitably extend the term of a covenant if a former franchisee does not abide by the covenant and the franchisor is therefore forced to initiate litigation. In such cases, the covenant will typically run from when the franchisee begins complying with its obligations or when the court enters injunctive relief. In *Jackson Hewitt, Inc. v. Childress*, 2008 WL 199539 (D.N.J. Jan. 15, 2008), the district court equitably extended a non-compete period that had expired during the course of litigation such that it ran from the date of the franchisee's compliance with the covenant. *See also Jackson Hewitt, Inc. v. DJSG Utah Tax Serv., LLC*, 2013 WL 2459887 (D.N.J. June 5, 2013) (extending a covenant for two years from the entry of injunctive relief). In *Jackson Hewitt, Inc. v. Barnes Enters.*, 2012 WL 1600572 (D.N.J. May 7, 2012), however, the district court refused to restart the term of a restrictive covenant from the date injunctive relief was entered because there was not sufficient evidence that the former franchisee had been violating the covenant in the interim.

10. Are there additional nuances or peculiarities about the state's treatment of covenants in the franchising context?

In general, courts applying New Jersey law have equated covenants against competition in the franchise context to covenants contained in agreements ancillary to the sale of a business. Accordingly, the courts have applied a liberal approach in enforcing such covenants because of, among other things, the nature of the franchise relationship and the existence of identifiable goodwill. *See Weiss Bros.*, 834 F. Supp. at 691.

New Mexico

*by Sally Dahlstrom**

1. Has the state addressed covenants against competition in the context of franchising?

- **Does the state have a franchising statute or regulations that address covenants against competition?**
- **Does the state have a covenants statute of general applicability that would encompass franchise covenants?**
- **Have the courts addressed covenants in the context of franchising either under a statute or under the state's common law?**

The New Mexico legislature has not enacted any statute or regulations applicable specifically to franchising that address covenants not to compete. New Mexico, moreover, does not have a general non-competition statute that would encompass franchise covenants. In determining whether to issue injunctive relief to enforce a post-termination covenant not to compete contained in a franchise agreement, a New Mexico federal district court has held that "the public has an interest in enforcing covenants not to compete contained within valid contracts as long as the covenant is reasonably limited in scope, duration, and geographic region." *Dunkin' Donuts Inc. v. Sharif, Inc.*, 2003 WL 24128052, at *4 (D.N.M. Nov. 20, 2003).

Although New Mexico does not have a specific statute outlining the requirements for a covenant not to compete, New Mexico's Antitrust Act, N.M. Stat. § 57-1-1 *et seq.* (the Act), includes statutory provisions affecting restrictive covenants. The Act regulates anti-competitive conduct in New Mexico. Section 57-1-1 provides that "[e]very contract, agreement, combination, or conspiracy in restraint of trade or commerce, any part of which trade or commerce is within this state, is unlawful." The New Mexico legislature has held that the Act is to be "construed in harmony" with federal antitrust laws, N.M. Stat. § 57-1-15, including the Sherman Act, 15 U.S.C. § 1, which only prohibits "unreasonable" restraints on trade. *See, e.g., Johnson v. Blue Cross/Blue Shield of New Mexico*, 677 F. Supp. 1112, 1117 (D.N.M. 1987) ("the question is not whether the challenged conduct restrained trade, but whether it constituted an unreasonable restraint on trade"). Accordingly, as the *Dunkin'*

*Sally Dahlstrom practices in the Dallas, Texas, office of Haynes and Boone, LLP.

Donuts court held, covenants not to compete will be enforced in New Mexico if the scope, duration, and geographic region are reasonably limited.

However, covenants not to compete are no longer generally enforceable in all employment agreements. In 2017, New Mexico outlawed the enforcement of covenants not to compete for employment agreements with certain health care practitioners. N.M. Stat. Ann. § 24-1I-2 (West 2017). The statute is not generally applicable, but instead only applies to health care practitioners, or (1) a dentist, (2) an osteopathic physician, (3) a physician, (4) a podiatrist, (5) a certified registered nurse anesthetist, (6) a certified nurse practitioner, and (7) a certified nurse-midwife. N.M. Stat. Ann. § 24-1I-1 (West 2017). Specifically, the statute prohibits the use of a non-compete provision to restrict a health care practitioner's right to provide clinical health services in New Mexico upon the termination of (1) the agreement, (2) a renewal or extension of the agreement, or (3) a health care practitioner's employment with a party seeking to enforce the agreement. N.M. Stat. Ann. § 24-1I-2. Therefore, for health care practitioners, the statute overrides the general enforceability of non-competes, governed by N.M. Stat. § 57-1-1, regardless of the reasonability of the covenant's scope, duration, and geographic restrictions. *Id.*

In New Mexico, two areas in which covenants not to compete are prevalent and often litigated are (1) the sale of a business and (2) employment contracts. Although New Mexico courts have not issued many opinions analyzing non-compete covenants in the franchise context, the courts' scrutiny of such covenants in other contexts is instructive.

In *Campbell v. Millennium Ventures, LLC*, 55 P.3d 429, 435 (N.M. Ct. App. 2002), a New Mexico appellate court opined on the value of a covenant not to compete in relation to the sale of a business. Just as goodwill is generally an interest that a court considers when determining whether to enforce a covenant not to compete, the *Campbell* court observed that "a buyer often seeks to purchase a covenant not to compete in order to preserve the goodwill of the business being purchased." *Campbell*, 55 P.3d at 435 (citing *Mitchell v. Mitchell*, 104 N.M. 205, 719 P.2d 432, 438 (N.M. Ct. App. 1986)). Goodwill has been characterized as being "of great importance" and a "valuable asset of the business." *Id.*

Likewise, in the employment context, New Mexico courts have held that covenants not to compete are enforceable and will be enforced to give effect to the parties' intent. In *Manuel Lujan Insurance, Inc. v. Jordan*, 673 P.2d 1306 (N.M. 1983), the New Mexico Supreme Court broadly construed a covenant not to compete so that the restriction prohibited not only solicitation but also acceptance of customers. In *Manuel Lujan Ins.*, Jordan began working as a manager for an insurance company's bond department. A contract was not executed between the parties at the start of Jordan's employment because Jordan was involved in litigation pertaining to a covenant not to compete in the employment contract with his previous employer. After that litigation concluded, Jordan and Lujan executed an employment contract. The post-termination covenant in the contract prohibited Jordan from soliciting the company's customers (policyholders). The covenant further stated that its purpose was that Jordan "not in any manner directly or indirectly enter into competition with the company." Although Jordan argued that the covenant only prohibited him from soliciting the company's customers (and thus he could accept non-solicited customers), the New Mexico Supreme Court held that the parties "contemplated a comprehensive ban on acceptance, not merely a narrow promise not to solicit." *Id.* at 1309; *compare with Resource Associates Grant Writing and Evaluation Services, LLC v. Maberry*, 2009 WL 1232133, at *11 (D.N.M. Apr. 23, 2009) (employee was permitted to accept business from former employer's clients and providers as long as she did not approach them within the two-year non-solicitation period); *Insure New Mexico, LLC v. McGonigle*, 995 P. 2d 1053, 1059 (N.M. Ct. App. 2000) (although the court held that "noncompetition covenants are ordinarily enforceable as long as a court deems them reasonable," the court did not conclude that the non-solicitation provision expanded to prohibit competition). As demonstrated in caselaw, New Mexico courts require that the covenant expressly prohibit "competition," and courts will not redraft the covenant to include additional language if the prohibition is limited to solicitation.

As illustrated in the employment context, the parties should ensure that the contractual grounds to enforce a covenant not to compete are satisfied. A court will forgo determining whether the common-law elements to enforce a non-competition covenant are satisfied if the contractual terms required to invoke the covenant are not met. In *Danzer v. Professional Insurors, Inc.*, 679 P.2d 1276, 1280–81 (N.M. 1984), the New Mexico Supreme Court affirmed that a covenant not to compete was not enforceable because the employee was terminated without good cause. Although "good cause" was not a precondition to either party's termination of the employment agreement in *Danzer*, the contract provided that if the employee were terminated without good cause, then the employee would not be bound by the covenant not to compete.

Generally, New Mexico caselaw suggests that if the covenant contains the necessary reasonable requisites, courts favor enforcement of covenants not to compete. New Mexico's earlier caselaw clearly set forth that non-competition covenants are enforceable if they are reasonable. *See Lovelace Clinic v. Murphy*, 417 P.2d 450, 453 (N.M. 1966). In responding to an argument that a covenant not to compete was invalid because its purpose was to eliminate or restrict competition, the New Mexico Supreme Court held that:

> [T]his court does take the view that restrictive covenants in employment contracts, wherein the restraints imposed are reasonable, create legally enforceable rights and duties apart from the rights and duties that would be so enforced [sic] in the absence of such covenants . . . . There is no doubt that this type of covenant tends to some extent to eliminate or restrict competition, and in many instances may operate as some compulsion on the part of the employee to remain in the employ of the employer. These are usually the main purposes of such covenants, and these are legitimate purposes, so long as the restrictions are reasonable . . . . The public has an interest in seeing that competition is not unreasonably limited or restricted, but it also has an interest in protecting the freedom of persons to contract, and in enforcing contractual rights and obligations.

Id. The New Mexico Supreme Court expanded its discussion of the reasonableness requirement governing covenants not to compete in *Bowen v. Carlsbad Insurance & Real Estate, Inc.*, 724 P.2d 223 (N.M. 1986). In *Bowen*, as an initial matter, the supreme court stated the well-settled rule in New Mexico: a restrictive covenant is valid if it includes reasonable limits of time and space and is ancillary to an otherwise enforceable agreement (i.e., a sale agreement for a business). The supreme court further noted that "courts are more reluctant to disturb restrictive covenants in buy-sell agreements than those in employment contracts." *Id.* at 225. Evaluating reasonableness of a covenant not to compete is a fact-based exercise. In the context of the sale of a business, courts consider factors such as the "nature of the business, its location, the parties involved, the purchase price, and the main object of the restriction." *Id.* The *Bowen* court defined the central question posed to determine the reasonableness of a covenant not to compete, which is applicable even in the franchise context: Is the covenant limited such that its purpose is to protect the business's legitimate interests and to secure the business's goodwill? The New Mexico Supreme Court explained not only why the covenant was reasonable but also why the covenant was not void as a restraint on trade:

> It is limited as to time and space and is subsidiary to the main purpose of disposing of an established business. Furthermore, there was no bad faith in negotiating the contract between the parties as evidenced by the reciprocal provision contained in the covenant. The covenant should be enforced as written; it being entered into voluntarily and for consideration. It is as much a matter of public concern to see that valid engagements are observed as it is to frustrate oppressive ones.

Bowen, 724 P.2d at 226. This language is applicable to all covenants not to compete, particularly covenants sought to be enforced in the context of franchise agreements and in general.

2. Have the courts articulated the "legitimate interests" of the franchisor that will support enforcement of a covenant against competition contained in a franchise agreement?

- **If so, what are they (e.g., protection of goodwill, protection of confidential information), and in what contexts did the issue arise?**
- **If not, what interests have been recognized in other contexts (e.g., employment agreements, the sale of business context)?**

New Mexico courts have not articulated the legitimate interests of a franchisor that will support enforcement of a covenant against competition contained in a franchise agreement. Nevertheless, cases in other contexts are instructive and indicate that a court would consider the protection of goodwill, among other interests, as a legitimate interest that would support the enforcement of a covenant against competition contained in a franchise agreement.

While New Mexico courts do indicate that interests such as the protection of goodwill are a valid reason to uphold a covenant not to compete, New Mexico courts do not appear to consistently require a party to prove that a covenant not to compete is necessary to protect its legitimate business interests in order for such a covenant to be enforceable. In the employment context, in *Lovelace Clinic v. Murphy*, 417 P.2d 450 (N.M. 1966), the court upheld a covenant not to compete under which a dermatologist was prohibited from practicing medicine for three years in the county where the medical practice with which he formerly practiced was located. The court's opinion reflects that it viewed the accumulated goodwill as belonging to the employer. The dermatologist terminated his employment with the medical practice prior to the expiration of an employment contract that contained the three-year post-termination covenant not to compete. He argued that the covenant was invalid because it was not necessary to protect the legitimate interests of the medical practice. The court rejected his arguments, finding that the reasonableness and enforceability of the covenant not to compete were not contingent upon "the existence of a legally enforceable right or duty independent of the rights and duties created by the contract of employment or association." *Lovelace Clinic*, 417 P.2d 453. That is, the party enforcing the covenant not to compete did not have to prove a reason existed beyond the agreement itself. The court found, however, that "[t]here is no doubt that this type of covenant tends to . . . restrict competition, and . . . may operate as some compulsion on the part of the employee to remain in the employ of the employer. These are usually the main purposes of such covenants, and these are legitimate purposes." *Id.* (citing *Granger v. Craven*, 159 Minn. 296, 199 N.W. 10 (1924) (finding that goodwill belonged to the employer)).

New Mexico courts have recognized that a buyer of a business will often seek a covenant not to compete to preserve the goodwill of a business. *Campbell v. Millennium Ventures, LLC*, 55 P.3d 429 (N.M. 2002) (citing *Mitchell v. Mitchell*, 719 P.2d 432, 438 (N.M. Ct. App. 1986)). In the context of the sale of a business, New Mexico courts have recognized the value of the business's goodwill in upholding reasonable covenants not to compete. *See Gonzales v. Reynolds*, 275 P. 922, 922–23 (N.M. 1929) (finding that a large part of the value paid for a business consisted of the protection afforded by a covenant not to compete and that the covenant was no broader than necessary to protect the goodwill of the business sold). In *Bowen v. Carlsbad Insurance & Real Estate*, 724 P.2d 223 (N.M. 1986), the court began its assessment of a 15-year covenant not to compete following the sale of a business with the general premise that "[a]greements in partial restraint of trade ancillary to the sale of a business appear to be sanctioned because of the value of the goodwill purchased" (citing *Palumbo v. Piccioni*, 103 A. 815 (N.J. 1918)). The seller of the business alleged that the covenant not to compete was broader than necessary to protect the buyer's legitimate interests and to secure the goodwill of the business. The court disagreed and found that the covenant was supported by a need to protect the goodwill of the business, as if the former owner were allowed to solicit business during the term of the covenant not to compete, the goodwill of the business that he sold would be destroyed.

---

3. What time limitations have courts recognized as reasonable in the franchise context?

➤ **If no franchise cases have been decided, what time limitations have been recognized in other contexts?**

➤ **How have they been related to the interests protected?**

Dunkin' Donuts Inc. v. Sharif, Inc., 2003 WL 24128052, at *4 (D.N.M. Nov. 20, 2003) is one of the few franchise cases in New Mexico in which a post-termination covenant not to compete was enforced. In its opinion, however, the district court did not state the duration of the restriction in the 1986 franchise agreement.

In other contexts, New Mexico courts have upheld post-termination covenants not to compete for various time limitations, *e.g.*, *Manuel Lujan Insurance, Inc. v. Jordan*, 673 P.2d 1306, 1310 (N.M. 1983) (two years; insurance employment context); *Rapid Temps, Inc. v. Lamon*, 192 P.3d 799, 802–03 (N.M. Ct. App. 2008) (three years from date of termination; staffing employment context); *Campbell v. Millennium*

Ventures, LLC, 55 P. 3d 429, 430 (N.M. Ct. App. 2002) (three years; sale of business and employment context); *Lovelace Clinic v. Murphy*, 417 P.2d 450, 454 (N.M. 1966) (three years from employment termination date); *Bowen v. Carlsbad Insurance & Real Estate, Inc.*, 724 P.2d 223, 226 (N.M. 1986) (15 years; sale of business).

Post-termination restrictive covenants are generally upheld for two to three years. The appellant did challenge the length of the 15-year covenant in *Bowen*. In upholding the covenant, the supreme court noted that the covenant was based upon the 15-year amortized payout of the purchase price. *Bowen*, 724 P.2d at 226. As reflected in *Bowen*, the purchase price is one of the settled factors that a court may consider when deciding whether to enforce a covenant not to compete. Based on this, the supreme court held that "substantial evidence" reasonably supported the trial court's finding. *Id.*

4. What geographic limitations have courts recognized as reasonable in the franchise context?

- **How have they been related to the interests protected?**
- **Have courts recognized the legitimacy of protecting other franchisees from competition?**

New Mexico courts have not addressed what geographic limitations would be reasonable in the franchise context, nor have there been any cases that address the legitimacy of protecting other franchisees from competition, but cases in other contexts are instructive. In such cases, restrictions to the immediate geographic area (such as a town or county) have been upheld.

In the context of real estate leases, the New Mexico Supreme Court has stated that "[r]adius restrictions serve a legitimate purpose," *Winrock Entertainment v. House of Fabrics of New Mexico*, 579 P.2d 787, 789 (N.M. 1978), namely protecting the landlord and other tenants. *See generally LensCrafters, Inc. v. Kehoe*, 282 P.3d 758, 765 (N.M. 2012) (holding that when a non-compete provision of a lease is previously terminated by the lessor's non-renewal letter, the non-compete is no longer enforceable). The radius restriction in question was two miles, which the court upheld. The radius restriction in *Winrock* related directly to the interest that the landlord sought to protect—that is, sales by its tenants. Similar to a case in the franchise context in which a court might find that a geographic limitation is warranted to protect the interests of other franchisees, the court's opinion in *Winrock* suggests that it considered not only the interests of the landlord but also the interests of the other shopping center tenants.

In the context of the sale of a business, the New Mexico Supreme Court, in *Bowen v. Carlsbad Insurance & Real Estate*, 724 P.2d 223 (N.M. 1986), upheld a covenant not to compete that restricted competitive activity "within a 15-mile radius of Carlsbad, New Mexico." In so concluding, the court articulated that the covenant was reasonable to protect the goodwill of the business sold. In the context of employment, courts have upheld city-wide and county-wide restrictions. *Nichols v. Anderson*, 92 P.2d 781 (N.M. 1939); *Lovelace Clinic v. Murphy*, 417 P.2d 450 (N.M. 1966). In *Lovelace*, the court also indicated that the restriction was necessary to protect the goodwill of the employer.

5. What limitations on activities have courts recognized as reasonable in the franchise context?

In *Dunkin' Donuts Inc. v. Sharif, Inc.*, 2003 WL 24128052, at *5 (D.N.M. Nov. 20, 2003), the court granted a preliminary injunction that restricted a terminated Dunkin' Donuts franchisee from any further use of the franchisor's trademarks, proprietary marks, system, and operating manuals, and "from competing in any business which sells products of the type offered by Dunkin' Donuts shops." In *Dunkin' Donuts*, the franchisee did not dispute whether the scope of activities in the covenant not to compete was unreasonable or too broad. In fact, the franchisee did not deny that it had failed to comply with the franchise agreement's post-termination obligations. As such, the only statement that the district court made related to the scope of the covenant's activities is that Dunkin' Donuts had an interest in having the commitment of all its franchisees not to compete with other franchisees in the system. Presumably, because the products were limited to those sold or offered by other Dunkin' Donuts franchisees, the district court held that the limitations on the covenant's activities were reasonable. No further guidance is available in New Mexico to indicate the courts' recognition of reasonable limitations on activities in the franchise context.

6. Does the state recognize a difference between in-term and post-term covenants?

This issue does not appear to have been addressed under New Mexico law.

7. Has the state allowed enforcement of covenants against non-signatories (e.g., family members, newly formed corporations)?

Little guidance is available to instruct on whether a New Mexico court would permit the enforcement of a covenant not to compete against a non-signatory, such as a family member or a newly formed entity.

In *Gallup Electric Light Co. v. Pacific Improvement Co.*, 113 P. 848 (N.M. 1911), the court found that non-signatories were not bound by a restrictive covenant where there was no evidence that they knew of a covenant. Further, the court in *Gallup* found that the signatory of the restrictive covenant was not precluded from loaning money to others, even if the recipient of the loan may use it to engage in competition that would be precluded by the covenant.

The Tenth Circuit, in *Hedrick v. Perry*, 102 F.2d 802 (10th Cir. 1939), found both a signatory and non-signatory of a restrictive covenant to be liable in the case of a sale of a business where the seller conspired with a third party to transfer the seller's customers to the third party in violation of the restrictive covenant. However, it is not apparent from the court's opinion that it applied New Mexico law in reaching this conclusion.

8. Will the state modify, "red-pencil," or otherwise reduce a covenant found to be overbroad?

The New Mexico Court of Appeals, in *KidsKare, P.C. v. Mann*, 350 P.3d 1228 (N.M. Ct. App. 2015), recently addressed the legality of the "red-pencil" doctrine (as it is known in New Mexico), or the modification of certain non-compete restrictions deemed to be unreasonable by the court.[1] In *KidsKare*, the court of appeals was asked to determine whether the district court's decision to reform the geographic restriction of KidsKare's non-competition clause from 100 miles to 30 miles was permissible. Before addressing the reasonability of the reformed distance restriction, the court addressed the broader question of the legality of the red-pencil doctrine in New Mexico. Due to *KidsKare*'s status as a case of first impression, the court explicitly limited its holding. Rather than allow for a broad application of the decision to the permissibility of the red-pencil doctrine in all cases, the court explicitly detailed the factors in the instant case that allowed the district court to modify KidsKare's covenant language. Specifically, the court looked at the language of the employment agreement itself, which provided that all provisions not found to be "invalid, illegal, or unenforceable, in whole or in part" were to remain intact and enforceable. *KidsKare*, at 1232. The court determined that this contract language makes it clear that the parties previously agreed that the covenant not to compete could still be enforced even if one of its provisions was found to be unreasonable through the type of reformation process used by the district court. *Id.* Relying on this language, the court of appeals limited its endorsement of the red-pencil doctrine to situations where the agreement similarly allows for a court's modification of a covenant not to compete.

NM

Once the court determined that the district court's use of the red-pencil doctrine was permissible, the analysis shifted to the acceptability of the reformed geographic restriction. Relying on the New Mexico Supreme Court's decision in *Lovelace*, the court of appeals looked at whether a covenant not to compete within a 30-mile radius after the termination of the employment agreement is reasonable and enforceable. This analysis led to the reaffirmation of the New Mexico Supreme Court's holding that "covenants not to compete with reasonable restraints will be enforced when 'they are not against public policy, and any detriment to the public interest in the possible loss of the services of the covenantor is more than offset by the public benefit arising out of the preservation of the freedom of contract.' *Lovelace*, at 450." *KidsKare*, at 1231. Accordingly, the court of appeals' decision in *KidsKare* stands for the legality of the red-pencil doctrine in specific situations, while simultaneously reasserting the enforceability of covenants not to compete when they are reasonable and not against public policy.

1. The court in *KidsKare* did not use the term "red-pencil" or "blue-pencil," and it is still unclear the extent to which New Mexico law allows red penciling (nullification of the whole non-compete agreement), blue penciling (removal of text), or reformation (addition or modification of text) absent contractual provisions allowing those practices.

9. When does a non-compete period begin to run? Will courts equitably extend the term?

In the employment context, a New Mexico court has found that the term of a non-compete period began to run on termination of employment. *Lovelace Clinic v. Murphy*, 417 P.2d 450 (N.M. 1966). Similarly, covenants not to compete following the sale of a business commence on such a sale. *See, e.g., Bowen v. Carlsbad Insurance & Real Estate, Inc.*, 724 P.2d 223 (N.M. 1986). There is no indication that a New Mexico court would equitably extend the term of a covenant not to compete if such covenant were violated.

10. Are there additional nuances or peculiarities about the state's treatment of covenants in the franchising context?

New Mexico courts have long found that an agreement not to compete must be ancillary to another transaction (i.e., a "naked" agreement not to compete will not suffice). *See Nichols v. Anderson*, 92 P.2d 781 (N.M. 1939); *accord Gross, Kelly & Co. v. Bibo*, 145 P. 480 (N.M. 1914).

In *Bowen v. Carlsbad Insurance & Real Estate, Inc.*, 724 P.2d 223, 226 (N.M. 1986), the court rejected Bowen's contention that he had the "option to pay liquidated damages and then engage in the [prohibited] business" in violation of a covenant not to compete. The court concluded that while parties may make their contract such that the parties have the option to pay damages or to perform the contract, the parties in *Bowen* did not intend for the liquidated damages to serve as a "payable privilege to engage in conduct forbidden by the contract." *Id.* (citation omitted). In *Bowen*, the court rejected Carlsbad's claim for liquidated damages because Bowen ceased the prohibited conduct immediately upon the trial court's finding that a 15-year covenant not to compete was enforceable and, thus, Carlsbad did not suffer substantial damages. Therefore, while liquidated damages are permissible in New Mexico in the event of the breach of a covenant not to compete, the party seeking such damages must prove its losses. Moreover, the adverse party cannot avoid the application of a covenant not to compete simply by paying the liquidated damages.

New York

*by Michael Einbinder**

1. Has the state addressed covenants against competition in the context of franchising?

- **Does the state have a franchising statute or regulations that address covenants against competition?**
- **Does the state have a covenants statute of general applicability that would encompass franchise covenants?**
- **Have the courts addressed covenants in the context of franchising either under a statute or under the state's common law?**

The New York Franchise Act, Article 33 of the N.Y. GEN. BUS. LAW §§ 680–95 (McKinney 1996), does not address covenants against competition. Further, New York does not have a statute of general applicability that would encompass covenants against competition in the franchise context. Some litigants have argued that restrictive covenants are not enforceable under New York's Donnelly Act, Article 22 of N.Y. GEN. BUS. LAW § 340 (McKinney 1999). The Donnelly Act specifically provides, in relevant part, that "[e]very contract, agreement, arrangement or combination whereby a monopoly in the conduct of any business, trade, or commerce . . . or whereby competition or the free exercise of any activity in the conduct of any business, trade, or commerce . . . is or may be restrained . . . is hereby declared to be against public policy, illegal and void." The Donnelly Act is "modeled after the Sherman Act . . . ." *Venture Technology Inc. v. National Fuel Gas Co.*, 685 F.2d 41, 42 (2d Cir. 1982), *cert. denied*, 459 U.S. 1007, 103 S. Ct. 362, 74 L. Ed. 2d 398 (1982). Like the Sherman Act, the Donnelly Act proscribes only unreasonable restraints of trade. *Business Foods Service, Inc. v. Food Concepts Corp.*, 533 F. Supp. 992, 996 (E.D.N.Y. 1982). Under both the Sherman Act and the Donnelly Act, restrictive covenants are valid if they are reasonably related to legitimate interests of one of the parties. This test is known as the rule of reason approach. *Savings Bank of Yonkers, N.Y. v. County Dollar Corp.*, 43 A.D.2d 327, 351 N.Y.S.2d 157 (2d Dept. 1974).

In theory, the Donnelly Act could be applied in a franchise context. However, no reported franchise case exists in which a litigant was successful in arguing that enforcement of a restrictive covenant would violate the Donnelly Act. *See Carvel*

*Michael Einbinder is a member of Einbinder & Dunn, LLP, in New York, New York.

Corp. v. Eisenberg, 692 F. Supp. 182 (S.D.N.Y. 1988) (court found that the Donnelly Act did not apply). However, the Donnelly Act has been relied upon to reject restrictive covenants in New York in non-franchise contexts. *See Triple D&E, Inc. v. Van Buren*, 72 Misc. 2d 569, 339 N.Y.S.2d 821 (N.Y. Sup. Ct. 1972) (non-competition provision in licensing agreement with driver was not enforceable by industrial catering company because, among other factors, the knowledge acquired by the drivers during the license agreement was not a trade secret and the caterer's dealings with the drivers were so one-sided that the agreement was rendered unconscionable) and *Paramount Pad Co. v. Baumrind*, 4 N.Y.2d 393, 175 N.Y.S.2d 809, 151 N.E.2d 609 (1958) (the court of appeals, the highest court in New York, decided that the restrictive covenant exceeded the employer's legitimate interests and unreasonably prevented employee-salesman from pursuing employment where employer would not be harmed). Compare *Triple D&E* and *Paramount Pad, supra,* with *Baker's Aid, a Division of Raubvogel Co., Inc. v. Hussman Foodservice Company*, 730 F. Supp. 1209 (E.D.N.Y. 1990) (restrictive covenant, as reformed by the court, was a reasonable restraint on trade permissible under the Sherman Act and the Donnelly Act). In *Baker's Aid*, 730 F. Supp. 1209, the defendant (an oven supplier) was prohibited for a ten-year period from soliciting, selling, and distributing to Baker's Aid's customers any rack type or deck oven based on Baker's Aid's specifications.

Rather than relying on statutory law, New York courts analyze the issue of enforceability of covenants against competition under New York's common law. The court in *Bradford v. The New York Times Co.*, 501 F.2d 51 (2d Cir. 1974), indicated that while the appellant urged that the agreement violates the Donnelly Act, it is well understood that the New York statutory prohibition is no broader than the common law and that it adds no further strictures on otherwise reasonable restraints. *See Matter of Davies*, 168 N.Y. 89, 61 N.E. 118 (1901); *Matter of Jackson*, 57 Misc. 1, 107 N.Y.S. 799 (Sup. Ct. 1907). Under the common law, courts have recognized covenants against competition in three distinct categories: (1) purchase of a business with accompanying goodwill, (2) employment relations, and (3) ordinary commercial contracts. Under New York law, the enforceability of a restrictive covenant depends in part upon the nature of the underlying contract. *See DAR & Associates, Inc. v. Uniforce Services, Inc.*, 37 F. Supp. 2d 192, 195 (E.D.N.Y. 1999).

Enforceability in the context of a purchase of a business rests on the premise that a buyer of a business should be permitted to restrict his or her seller's freedom of trade so as to prevent the latter from recapturing and utilizing, by competition, the goodwill of the very business that he or she transferred for value. *Purchasing Associates, Inc. v. Weitz*, 13 N.Y.2d 267, 246 N.Y.S.2d 600, 196 N.E.2d 245 (1963). In fact, a seller of a business has a legal duty to refrain from acting to impair the "goodwill" transferred to the purchaser in exchange for part of the purchase price. *Hyde Park Products Corp. v. Maximilian Lerner Corp.*, 65 N.Y.2d 316, 321, 491 N.Y.S.2d 302, 305, 480 N.E.2d 1084, 1087 (1985). In such cases, courts will enforce restrictive covenants barring the seller from competing with the purchaser and from soliciting former customers. However, such restrictive covenants are evaluated pursuant to a different (and somewhat less strict) standard from that applicable to employment contracts. The sole limitation on the enforceability of such a covenant is that its duration and scope be reasonably necessary to protect the buyer's legitimate interest in the purchased asset. *Hadari v. Leshchinsky*, 242 A.D.2d 557, 558, 662 N.Y.S.2d 85, 86 (1997); *Mohawk Maintenance Co., Inc. v. Kessler*, 52 N.Y.2d 276, 473 N.Y.S.2d 646, 419 N.E.2d 324 (1981).

Courts treat restrictive covenants in employment agreements differently than they do covenants in the context of a purchase of a business. Because enforcement of employee restrictive covenants may result in the loss of an individual's livelihood, such covenants are "rigorously examined." *American Institute of Chemical Engineers v. Reber-Friel Co.*, 682 F.2d 382, 387 (2d Cir. 1982). New York has adopted the modern, prevailing common-law three-prong test to determine the reasonableness of an employee restrictive covenant. This prevailing test provides that a restraint is reasonable only if it (1) is no greater than is required for the protection of the legitimate interest of the employer, (2) does not impose undue hardship on the employee, and (3) is not injurious to the public. *BDO Siedman v. Hirshberg*, 93 N.Y.2d 382, 388–89, 690 N.Y.S.2d 854, 712 N.E.2d 1220 (1999). A violation of any prong renders the covenant invalid. However, as noted in section 8, *infra*, a court may reform a restrictive covenant so that the restrictive covenant may be enforceable.

With agreements not to compete between professionals, courts have given greater weight to the interests of the employer in restricting competition within a confined geographical area. In *Gelder Medical Group v. Webber*, 41 N.Y.2d 680, 394 N.Y.S.2d 867, 363 N.E.2d 573 (1977), and *Karpinski v. Ingrasci*, 28 N.Y.2d 45, 320 N.Y.S.2d 1, 268 N.E.2d 751 (N.Y. 1971), restraints on competition were enforced in limited rural areas (permanently in *Karpinski* and for five years in *Gelder*). The rationale for the different application of the common-law rule stems from the fact that professionals are deemed to provide "unique or extraordinary" services. *BDO Siedman*, 93 N.Y.2d 382, 389, 690 N.Y.S.2d 854, 712 N.E.2d 1220, citing *Reed, Roberts Associates, Inc. v. Strauman*, 40 N.Y.2d 303, 308, 386 N.Y.S.2d 677, 680, 353 N.E.2d 590, 593 (1976).

New York courts have recognized an employee choice doctrine exception to the general disfavor against enforcing non-compete provisions in employment contexts. The exception applies in cases where an employer conditions receipt of post-employment benefits upon compliance with a restrictive covenant. *Morris v. Schroder Capital Management International*, 7 N.Y.3d 616, 619–21, 825 N.Y.S.2d 697, 859 N.E.2d 503 (2006), citing *Post v. Merrill Lynch, Pierce, Fenner & Smith*, 48 N.Y.2d 84, 421 N.Y.S.2d 847, 397 N.E.2d 358 (1979). The exception rests on the premise that if the employee is given the choice of preserving his or her rights under his or her contract (by refraining from competition) or risking forfeiture of such rights by exercising his or her right to compete, there is no unreasonable restraint upon an employee's liberty to earn a living. *Id.* at 621, 825 NY.S.2d 697, 859 N.E.2d 503, citing *Kristt v. Whelan*, 4 A.D.2d 195, 199, 164 N.Y.S.2d 239 (1st Dept. 1957), *aff'd without op.* 5 N.Y.2d 807, 181 N.Y.S.2d 205, 155 N.E.2d 116 (1958). The exception assumes that an employee who leaves his or her employer makes an informed choice between forfeiting his or her benefit or retaining the benefit by avoiding competitive employment. *Id.*, citing *Kristt*, 4 A.D.2d at 199, 164 N.Y.S.2d 239.

The third category of cases deal with restrictive covenants agreed to as part of ordinary commercial contracts, such as franchise agreements and license agreements. In these cases, courts will apply a simple rule of reason test, balancing the competing public policies in favor of robust competition and freedom to contract. *Baker's Aid*, 730 F. Supp. 1209, 1214; *Winston Franchise Corp. v. Williams*, 1992 WL 7843 at 6 (S.D.N.Y. Jan. 10, 1992). New York courts will look at the totality of the circumstance when determining if a restrictive covenant in a commercial agreement is enforceable. *Crye Precision LLC v. Duro Textiles, LLC*, 689 Fed. Appx. 104, 106 (2d Cir. 2017). The following factors have been considered in applying the rule of reason test: (1) whether the plaintiff has demonstrated a legitimate business interest that warrants the enforcement of the restrictive covenants, (2) the reasonableness of the covenants with respect to geographic scope and temporal duration, and

(3) the degree of hardship that enforcing these covenants would inflict upon the defendants, bearing in mind the degree to which they consciously agreed to bear the risk of such hardship when they entered into the agreements. *See Carvel Corp. v. DePaola*, 2001 WL 528203 (Conn. Apr. 24, 2001) (decided under New York law); *DAR & Assoc.*, 37 F. Supp. 2d 192.

In *ServiceMaster Residential/Commercial Services, L.P. v. Westchester Cleaning Services, Inc.*, 2001 WL 396520 (S.D.N.Y. Apr. 19, 2001), a disaster restoration and cleaning services franchisor brought an application for preliminary injunction against defendant-franchisee to enforce a non-compete clause contained within the franchise agreement. The non-compete clause provided that for a period of one year after the franchise's termination, defendant was prohibited from owning or engaging in any business within defendant's former territory that performed any of the services licensed by ServiceMaster. Defendant argued that the non-compete clause should not be enforced because the clause was unreasonable given the circumstances. Defendant argued that ServiceMaster's technology was not unique and that because three other ServiceMaster franchises were already operating in the territory, ServiceMaster's interests in protecting its know-how and ability to place another franchise in the territory were outweighed by the harm to the defendant if the defendant were prohibited from establishing another cleaning business for one year. The court was not persuaded by the defendant's arguments and found in favor of ServiceMaster. The court found that the franchisor provided the franchisee with training, confidential manuals, knowledge, and ability to launch a restoration cleaning business and that the defendant used those tools to operate its business for 15 years. Hence, the court reasoned that ServiceMaster's technology and know-how must have possessed sufficient value. The court also rejected the defendant's argument concerning the number of franchises operating within the territory. The court noted that the fact that three other franchises operated within the same territory does not mean that the franchisor lacked a legitimate interest in placing another franchise in the territory, because it appeared to the court that there was enough business to support four franchises.

The defendant also argued that a residential and commercial cleaning business differed from a retail store (e.g., ice cream store) because the chances of consumer confusion and damage to the franchisor's goodwill were less likely, but the court was not persuaded by this argument either. Rather, the court noted that many of the franchisor's clients were obtained through referrals from the insurance industry and that there was a danger to the franchisor if the defendant attempted to capitalize on relationships built with such entities. The court recognized that such actions by the defendant could harm the franchisor's goodwill and jeopardize its ability to place a new franchise in the territory. Accordingly, the court granted the franchisor's application for preliminary injunction enjoining the defendant from engaging in the type of cleaning services offered by ServiceMaster within the defendant's former territory.

In *DAR & Assoc.*, 37 F. Supp. 2d 192, Uniforce, a supplemental-staffing service franchisor selling franchises that provide temporary employees to businesses and governmental agencies, sought to enforce a non-compete provision in its licensing agreement. The license agreement provided that for a period of one year after termination or the date DAR ceased to operate a Uniforce temporary personnel service business, whichever is later, DAR and its principals would not have any direct or indirect interest (1) in any business offering temporary personnel services operating within a radius of 50 miles of DAR's former place of business or (2) any entity that is granting or licensing businesses offering temporary personnel services. Additionally, DAR and its principals agreed that for two years after termination, they would not solicit or accept temporary personnel service business from any former DAR client or solicit for employment or employ any person employed by Uniforce and placed by DAR within one year prior to the effective date of termination or the date DAR ceased to operate a Uniforce temporary personnel service business, whichever is later.

Uniforce argued that through its operating manual, training tapes, training sessions, and consultations, it imparted to DAR confidential information pertaining to developing and selling Uniforce product lines; training managers; techniques on how to recruit, retain, reactivate, and acquire referrals; sales presentations to prospective clients; billing rates; and advertising and cross-selling techniques. Persuaded by Uniforce's arguments, the court found that DAR took advantage of Uniforce's unique system pertaining to the management, training, marketing, and general operations of a supplemental staffing office. The court also found that Uniforce established a vast client base and temporary employee applicant pool during the nearly ten years that DAR had been a Uniforce licensee. The court indicated its concern that if DAR were permitted to use the know-how and proprietary information it acquired while operating as a Uniforce licensee as well as the goodwill it developed, DAR could unfairly divert business away from Uniforce.

In determining whether the restrictive covenants were reasonable, the *DAR & Assoc.* court made several observations: (1) the non-compete and non-solicitation clauses were specifically negotiated by sophisticated businessmen and businesswomen; (2) in exchange for them, Uniforce made significant financial concessions to DAR, including a waiver of its licensing fee and a two-year reduction of its share of the profits; (3) enforcement of the restrictive covenants would not create an undue hardship for DAR; (4) DAR was represented by counsel at the time the license agreement was entered into; and (5) there was no evidence that DAR was coerced into entering into the transaction or that the restrictive covenants were anything other than negotiated provisions in exchange for which DAR received valuable consideration. Thus, the court found that the hardship DAR faced was mitigated by the fact that DAR and its principals specifically agreed to bear the risk of that hardship and that they were paid fairly to do so, in that DAR received the benefit of the bargain by its use of the Uniforce trade name and proprietary information over ten years. *See also Carvel Corp. v. DePaola*, 2001 WL 528203 (no evidence that the covenants not to compete were anything other than negotiated provisions in exchange for which the defendants received valuable consideration. Any hardship that the defendants faced was mitigated by the fact that the defendants agreed to bear the risk of that hardship. The defendants received the benefit of their bargain by their use of the Carvel trade name, proprietary information, and goodwill over the course of ten years).

Accordingly, the court granted summary judgment in favor of Uniforce, finding the non-compete and non-solicitation covenants reasonable in both geographic scope and duration. Further, the court found the covenants were reasonably related to Uniforce's interests in protecting its goodwill, know-how, and other proprietary information as well as Uniforce's legitimate desire to install a franchise in the market. *Id.* at 199, citing *Carvel Corp. v. Eisenberg*, 692 F. Supp. 182, 186.

In *Carvel Corp. v. Rait*, 117 A.D.2d 485, 503 N.Y.S.2d 406 (2d Dept. 1986), Carvel, a franchisor of ice cream stores, sought to enforce a restrictive covenant against a former franchise whose franchise agreement expired. After expiration of the franchise agreement, the defendant-franchisee continued to operate a retail ice cream store at the same location. The franchise agreement contained a restrictive covenant providing that in the event the agreement was terminated for any reason except for franchisor's breach, then for a period of three years, the franchisee would not directly or indirectly engage in the production, distribution, or sale of ice cream or other frozen deserts within a radius of two miles of the site of the Carvel store. The supreme court, appellate division, affirmed the supreme court's grant of summary judgment in favor of Carvel, concluding that the restrictive covenant was intended by the parties to apply in the event that the agreement was terminated by reason of expiration of its term as well as by any other form of termination and also concluding, without discussion, that the defendant failed to show the covenant was unreasonable with respect to either geographical scope or temporal duration so as to give rise to the possibility of unconscionability.

In *Carvel Corp. v. Eisenberg*, 692 F. Supp. 182, 186, the court upheld the same restrictive covenant at issue in *Carvel v. Rait*, 117 A.D.2d 485, 503 N.Y.S.2d 406. The defendant in *Eisenberg* argued that the restrictive covenant should not apply because the franchise agreement expired by its terms rather than by being terminated. The court found that the parties intended the provision to apply in the event of termination by expiration as well as by any other form of termination. As in *Carvel Corp v. Rait*, 117 A.D.2d 485, 503 N.Y.S.2d 406, by continuing to operate the ice cream store at the same location after the expiration of the contract, the defendants violated the restrictive covenants. Applying standards applicable to analyzing employment-related restrictive covenants (i.e., serving legitimate business purposes), the court found that the restrictive covenants in this instance were not unreasonable in length or geographic scope. The same restrictive covenant was also upheld in *Carvel Corp. v. Piacente*, 162 A.D.2d 168, 556 N.Y.S.2d 301 (1st Dept. 1990), where the franchisor terminated the franchisee for using non–Carvel-approved products under the Carvel logo, despite allegations by the franchisee that the franchisor breached the franchise agreement.

In *Winston Franchise*, 1992 WL 7843, the plaintiff, a franchisor of employment agencies specializing in the retail food, drug, and food-manufacturing industries, moved for a preliminary injunction compelling compliance by the defendant, Williams, with a restrictive covenant contained in the franchise agreement. The defendant terminated the franchise agreement and began operating a competing employment agency specializing in placing individuals in the beverage industry. The restrictive covenant provided that for a period of three years following termination, the franchisee would not directly or indirectly engage in any competitive business in the United States, enter the employment of or render services to a company engaging in a competitive business in the United States, or divulge information concerning client lists, employment applicants, and employment offerings that were acquired as a result of the franchisee's agreement with the franchisor. In contrast to the franchise cases noted above, the court refused to enforce the three-year restrictive covenant.

The court observed that because Williams specialized exclusively in the beverage industry, a subset of the food industry, and that all of his present expertise and contacts are limited to that industry, Williams would be required to start a new business from scratch if the restrictive covenants were enforced. In analyzing this case, the court distinguished cases decided under the "sale of business" rule and cases decided under the more stringent criteria for employment contracts, as well as the standard applied in *Carvel Corp. v. Eisenberg*, 692 F. Supp. 182, 186, which had been previously decided by the same court. In distinguishing *Carvel Corp. v. Eisenberg*, 692 F. Supp. 182, the court noted that Winston had not shown any technical know-how comparable to that of Carvel or offered any proof of its intention to establish another franchise in the market. *Winston Franchise*, 1992 WL 7843 at 7. Applying the rule of reason governing the enforceability of restrictive covenants in ordinary contracts, the court found that much of what Winston sought to protect was not protectable. However, the court found that names of applicants for employment are not publicly available and, as such, may not be appropriated by Williams to compete in the same business. Accordingly, the court pared down the restrictions and imposed an injunction enjoining Williams's use of applicant information generated during the existence of the franchise agreement and further ordered Williams to return certain information to Winston.

2. Have the courts articulated the "legitimate interests" of the franchisor that will support enforcement of a covenant against competition contained in a franchise agreement?

- **If so, what are they (e.g., protection of goodwill, protection of confidential information), and in what contexts did the issue arise?**
- **If not, what interests have been recognized in other contexts (e.g., employment agreements, the sale of business context)?**

New York courts will enforce a non-compete clause between business entities only where it protects a legitimate business interest and where its terms are reasonable both in time and geographic scope. *See DAR & Associates, Inc. v. Uniforce Services, Inc.*, 37 F. Supp. 2d 192, 196–98 (E.D.N.Y. 1999); *Carvel Corp. v. Eisenberg*, 692 F. Supp. 182, 185–86 (S.D.N.Y. 1988); and *Westbury Donuts, Inc., Donut Queen, Ltd. v. Dunkin' Donuts of America, Inc.*, 1983 WL 937202 (DC N.Y. Eastern Dist. Mar. 15, 1983). In the franchise context, courts have recognized several factors that will support enforcement of a covenant against competition, including a franchisor's interest in protecting its goodwill, know-how, confidential information, trade secrets, the integrity of the franchise system, customer and referral relationships, and the franchisor's desire to refranchise the market. *See DAR & Assoc.*, 37 F. Supp. 2d 192; *Carvel Corp. v. DePaola*, 2001 WL 528203 (Conn. Apr. 24, 2001); *ServiceMaster Residential/Commercial Services, L.P. v. Westchester Cleaning Services, Inc.*, 2001 WL 396520 (S.D.N.Y. Apr. 19, 2001); and *RESCUECOMM Corp. v. Matthews*, 2006 WL 1742073 (N.D.N.Y. June 20, 2006) (enjoining a former franchisee during pendency of the action from soliciting business from or providing computer-related sales and services to any of the franchisor's current or former customers).

In *ServiceMaster*, 2001 WL 396520, at *4, the court enforced a restrictive covenant against a former franchisee, prohibiting the franchisee for one year from owning or engaging in a competitive business within defendant's former territory. In doing so, the court recognized the franchisor's legitimate interests in protecting (1) its technology, confidential information, and know-how, all of which was provided to franchisee; (2) the goodwill generated from its customer and referral relationships; and (3) its ability to place another franchise in the territory. In *DAR & Assoc.*, 37 F. Supp. 2d 192, 199, the court concluded that Uniforce possessed legitimate business interests in protecting its know-how, goodwill, client base, pool of temporary employees, and ability to secure another franchise in the market that warranted protection through restrictive covenants. The court noted further that if DAR were permitted to compete in its present territory directly against a new Uniforce franchise, DAR could use the know-how and proprietary information it acquired while operating under the Uniforce trade name, as well as the goodwill it developed as a Uniforce licensee, to divert business away from Uniforce.

In *Carvel Corp. v. DePaola*, 2001 WL 528203, at *11, the court observed that Carvel has a legitimate interest in protecting its know-how, trade secrets, and goodwill as well as limiting the franchisee's ability to operate a substantially similar, if not identical, ice cream shop offering substantially similar, if not identical, ice cream products in the same location as the former Carvel shops. Furthermore, the court noted that the franchisee's continued use of Carvel's proprietary information in a competing operation, without paying the franchise fees and other fees provided for by the agreements, tended to undermine the integrity of the franchise system. *See also Carvel Corp. v. Eisenberg*, 692 F. Supp. 182, 185 (the court observed that the restrictive covenants were reasonably related to Carvel's interests in protecting its know-how and its ability to install another franchise in the market).

In *Singas Famous Pizza Brands Corp. v. New York Advertising LLC*, 2011 WL 497978 (S.D.N.Y. Feb. 10, 2011), *aff'd* 2012 WL 899231 (2d Cir. Mar. 19, 2012), the court granted the franchisor's motion for preliminary injunction prohibiting the franchisee and a third party from operating pizza restaurants (located at the franchise's former location as well as at a location approximately seven miles from the franchise's former location) in violation of the post-termination restrictive covenants contained within the franchise agreement. The court in *Singas*, 2011 WL 497978, at *7, noted that "[t]here is a recognized danger that former franchisees will use the knowledge that they have gained from the franchisor to serve its former customers, and that continued operation under a different name may confuse customers and thereby damage the good-will of the franchisor." *Id.* at 8, citing *ServiceMaster*, 2001 WL 396520, at *3. Moreover, the court found that the existence of a renegade franchisee operating a competing pizza restaurant in the same location would inhibit the franchisor's ability to convince a new franchisee to open in that area. Further, the *Singas* court noted that other courts have reasoned that the franchise system itself is endangered if a franchisee is permitted to avoid its reasonable non-compete obligations. *Id.*, citing *ServiceMaster*, 2001 WL 396520, at *4.

In *Winston Franchise Corp. v. Williams*, 1992 WL 7843 (S.D.N.Y. Jan. 10, 1992), the court applied the rule of reason test and found that the franchisor did not show that the franchisee possessed any technical know-how comparable to that shown in *Carvel Corp. v. Eisenberg*, 192 F. Supp. 182, nor offered any proof that the franchisor intended to establish another franchise in the market. In considering whether the franchisor demonstrated legitimate business interests, the court noted that legitimate business interests include protection of trade secrets and prevention of unfair competition. *Winston Franchise*, 1992 WL 7843, at *8. The court found that much of what the franchisor sought to protect by enforcing the restrictive covenants was not protectable (e.g., names, addresses, and detailed information of customers in the beverage industry are not confidential because they are readily available from other sources; and the methodology used by the franchisor is not a trade secret because other employment agencies operate nationwide franchise systems, conduct seminar and training sessions, and exchange information). The court noted that "knowledge of the intricacies of plaintiff's business operation . . . does not qualify for protection as a trade secret." *Id. See also Reed, Roberts Associates, Inc. v. Strauman*, 40 N.Y.2d 303,

309, 386 N.Y.S.2d 677, 680, 353 N.E.2d 590, 593 (1976). On the other hand, where an employment agency amassed a list of job applicants whose names are not publicly ascertainable, a former employee could not appropriate those names in order to compete in the same business. *See Ecolab, Inc. v. Paolo*, 753 F. Supp. 1100 (E.D.N.Y. 1991). The court concluded that Williams's possession of applicant files generated during the existence of the license agreement was the sole area in which the franchisor had shown a likelihood of success in enforcing the restrictive covenant. *Winston Franchise*, 1992 WL 7843, at *11. The court reasoned that the franchisor was entitled to preliminary injunction but not in the form requested by the franchisor, because what was requested would put Williams out of business entirely for three years and would deny him the ability to earn a livelihood placing personnel in the beverage industry, his field of specialization, and would deny him access to corporate customers whose names are publicly ascertainable and hence not protectable by the franchisor.

The court in *Reed, Roberts*, 40 N.Y.2d 303, 309, 386 N.Y.S.2d 677, 353 N.E.2d 590, set forth a two-part test for determining whether a restrictive covenant serves the employer's legitimate interests. The court held that restrictive covenants will be enforceable only (1) to the extent necessary to prevent disclosure or use of trade secrets or confidential information or (2) where an employee's services are unique or extraordinary. Courts have generally held that an employee's services are unique enough to support a post-employment non-compete agreement only in jobs where the employer's services depend on an employee's special talents, such as with musicians, professional athletes, and actors. *See Ticor Title Insurance Co. v. Cohen*, 173 F.3d 63, 70 (2d Cir. 1963). In order to justify a restrictive covenant, an employer must show more than simply that the employee excels at his or her work or that his or her services are of high value to the employer; an employer must show that an employee's services are of such character as to make his or her replacement impossible or that the loss of such services would cause the employer irreparable injury. *American Institute of Chemical Engineers v. Reber-Friel Co.*, 682 F.2d 382, 390 (2d Cir. 1982) (quoting *Purchasing Assoc.*, 13 N.Y.2d 272, 274, 246 N.Y.S.2d 600, 196 N.E.2d 245). Additional justifications for imposing an employee non-compete covenant have been found to include forestalling unfair competition and protecting the "goodwill" that an employee develops with the employer's clients in the course of employment. *See BDO Seidman v. Hirshberg*, 93 N.Y.2d 382, 389, 690 N.Y.S.2d 854, 712 N.E.2d 1220 (1999); *Columbia Ribbon*, 42 N.Y.2d 496, 398 N.Y.S.2d 1004, 369 N.E.2d 4; and *Purchasing Assoc.*, 13 N.Y.2d 272, 274, 246 N.Y.S.2d 600, 196 N.E.2d 245.

Generally, covenants against competition will be enforced to the extent necessary to protect the employer from unfair competition stemming from the employee's use or disclosure of trade secrets or confidential customer lists. *See IVI Environmental, Inc. v. McGovern*, 269 A.D.2d 497, 707 N.Y.S.2d 107 (2d Dept. 2000); *Columbia Ribbon*, 42 N.Y.2d 496, 499, 398 N.Y.S.2d 1004, 369 N.E.2d 4; *Reed, Roberts*, 40 N.Y.2d 303, 307–08, 386 N.Y.S.2d 677, 353 N.E.2d 590. In the absence of a showing that an employee has used or disclosed trade secrets or confidential customer lists, or that his or her services are special, unique, or extraordinary, a covenant that prohibits an employee from pursuing a similar vocation after termination of employment is unenforceable. *Independent Metal Strap v. Cohen*, 96 A.D.2d 830, 465 N.Y.S.2d 579 (2d Dept. 1983), citing *Columbia Ribbon*, 42 N.Y.2d 496, 398 N.Y.S.2d 1004, 369 N.E.2d 4; *Reed, Roberts*, 40 N.Y.2d 303, 386 N.Y.S.2d 677, 353 N.E.2d 590.

New York courts evaluate the enforceability of covenants not to compete accompanying the sale of a business under a more lenient standard than those made as part of an employment contract. *N.W. Ayer & Son, Inc. v. Deare*, 1998 WL 811873, at *2 (S.D.N.Y. Nov. 18, 1998); *Purchasing Assoc.*, 13 N.Y.2d 267, 271, 246 N.Y.S.2d 600, 196 N.E.2d 245. "A covenant that accompanies a sale of a business must be reasonable—not more extensive, in terms of the time and space, than is reasonably necessary to the buyer for the protection of his legitimate interest in the enjoyment of the asset bought." *Id.* In *N.W. Ayer*, the court ruled that the restrictive covenants against competition and solicitation of clients were made as an inducement to the buyer to enter into the agreement and were reasonably necessary to protect the buyer's investment. The *DAR & Assoc.* court noted that enforcement of a restrictive covenant is necessary to prevent the seller from recapturing and utilizing, by competition, the goodwill it sold. *DAR & Assoc.*, 37 F. Supp. 2d 192, 196 citing *Purchasing Assoc.*, 13 N.Y.2d 267, 271, 246 N.Y.S.2d 600, 196 N.E.2d

In upholding restrictive covenants against competition and solicitation, the court noted that the seller has a legal duty to refrain from acting to impair the goodwill it transferred to the plaintiff in connection with the sale of the business. *Mohawk Maintenance Co., Inc. v. Kessler*, 52 N.Y.2d 276, 279, 473 N.Y.S.2d 646, 419 N.E.2d 324 (1981); *Town Line Repairs, Inc. v. Anderson*, 90 A.D.2d 517, 455 N.Y.S.2d 28 (2d Dept. 1982). When the seller solicits former customers, he is, in effect, directly impairing the very asset that he has purported to transfer, namely the "goodwill" of his former business. The duty to refrain from impairing the goodwill sold exists independent from any additional obligation expressed in the restrictive covenants contained in the contract of sale. The covenant not to solicit former customers should also apply to the transfer of ownership by a minority owner. *Kraft Agency, Inc. v. Delmonico*, 110 A.D.2d 177, 494 N.Y.S.2d 77 (4th Dept. 1985); *Von Bremen v. MacMonnies*, 200 N.Y. 41, 93 N.E. 186 (1910) (irrespective of the percentage being transferred, the same underlying rationale applies that a "man may not derogate from his own grant.").

In the context of other commercial contracts, a restrictive covenant may be enforceable provided that it protects the covenantee from unfair competition. Under New York law, unfair competition is a malleable tort that includes any "misappropriation for commercial advantage of a benefit or property right belonging to another." *Baker's Aid, a Division of Raubvogel Co., Inc. v. Hussman Foodservice Company*, 730 F. Supp. 1209, 1215 (E.D.N.Y. 1990), citing *Marcraft Recreation Corp. v. Frances Devlin Co., Inc.*, 459 F. Supp. 195, 199 (S.D.N.Y. 1978). In *Baker's Aid*, 730 F. Supp. 1209, the court reasoned that in situations not involving employment relationships or the sale of a business, the court must balance the competing public policies in favor of robust competition and freedom of contract in order to determine whether to enforce a non-competition agreement.

3. What time limitations have courts recognized as reasonable in the franchise context?

- **If no franchise cases have been decided, what time limitations have been recognized in other contexts?**
- **How have they been related to the interests protected?**

In the franchise context, courts have enforced covenants against competition with varying time limitations. As noted above, covenants against competition will be enforced provided that they satisfy the rule of reason test and protect a legitimate interest of the franchisor. In *Westbury Donuts, Inc. v. Dunkin' Donuts of America, Inc.*, 1982 WL 1019129 (E.D.N.Y. July 12, 1982), a restrictive covenant prohibiting the operation of a business competitive to a donut shop for 18 months was upheld. There, the court found that the post-term covenant was reasonably necessary to protect the legitimate interest of the franchisor and did not prevent the franchisee from maintaining a livelihood, in that the franchisee was free to operate a different type of restaurant, rather than a donut shop.

In *DAR & Associates, Inc. v. Uniforce Services, Inc.*, 37 F. Supp. 2d 192 (E.D.N.Y. 1999), the court upheld covenants restricting ownership of any direct or indirect interest in a competing business for one year and solicitation of business from former clients for two years. In both *ServiceMaster Residential/Commercial Services, L.P. v. Westchester Cleaning Services, Inc.*, 2001 WL 396520 (S.D.N.Y. Apr. 19, 2001), and *TKO Fleet Enterprises, Inc. v. Elite Limousine Plus, Inc.*, 184 Misc. 2d 460, 708 N.Y.S.2d 593 (N.Y. Sup. Ct. 2000), a one-year restrictive covenant enjoining the franchisee from owning or operating a competing business was upheld. In three separate but similar cases, the courts have upheld a restrictive covenant that prohibited an ice cream shop franchisee for a period of three years from directly or indirectly engaging in a competing business, noting that such restriction was sufficiently limited in duration to protect the franchisor's business interests. *See Carvel Corp. v. DePaola*, 2001 WL 528203 (Conn. Apr. 24, 2001); *Carvel Corp. v. Rait*, 117 A.D.2d 485, 503 N.Y.S.2d 406 (2d Dept. 1986); and *Carvel Corp. v. Eisenberg*, 692 F. Supp. 182 (S.D.N.Y. 1988).

NY

In an employment context, New York has also generally enforced covenants against competition of varying durations, provided that the time and geographic scope of the covenant are reasonable and the restrictive covenant was necessary to protect a legitimate interest of the employer. *See Service Systems Corp. v. Harris*, 41 A.D.2d 20, 341 N.Y.S.2d 702 (E.D.N.Y. 1997) (three years); *Mallory Factor, Inc. v. Schwartz*, 146 A.D.2d 465, 536 N.Y.S.2d 752 (1st Dept. 1989), *aff'd* by *Mallory Factor, Inc. v. Jicka*, 168 A.D.2d 344 (1st Dept. 1990) (two years); *Giller v. Harcourt Brace & Company*, 166 Misc. 2d 599, 634 N.Y.S.2d 646 (N.Y. Sup. Ct. 1995) (two years); *BDO Siedman v. Hirshberg*, 93 N.Y.2d 382, 690 N.Y.S.2d 854, 712 N.E.2d 1220 (1999) (18 months); *J.H. Goldberg Co., Inc. v. Stern*, 53 A.D.2d 246, 385 N.Y.S.2d 427 (4th Dept. 1976) (one year). Compare this against *EarthWeb, Inc. v. Schlack*, 71 F. Supp. 2d 299 (S.D.N.Y. 1999), where the court shortened a one-year restrictive covenant to six months given the dynamic nature of the industry (information technology).

In the sale of businesses context, courts will uphold restrictive covenants provided that the covenants are reasonable with respect to time, scope, and area and not broader than necessary to protect the buyer's interests. *Purchasing Associates, Inc. v. Weitz*, 13 N.Y.2d 267, 271, 246 N.Y.S.2d 600, 196 N.E.2d 245 (1963). In *Mohawk Maintenance, Co., Inc. v. Kessler*, 52 N.Y.2d 276, 281, 437 N.Y.S.2d 646, 419 N.E.2d 324 (1981), the court upheld a restrictive covenant for two years, prohibiting the seller from engaging in a competitive business in New York, Connecticut, and any other state where the business was actively doing business on the closing date of the sale. In *Town Line Repairs, Inc. v. Anderson*, 90 A.D.2d 517, 518, 455 N.Y.S.2d 28 (2d Dept. 1982), the court held that a restrictive covenant preventing the seller from operating an automobile repair shop located within two and one-half miles from purchaser's automobile repair facility for an unlimited duration should not be declared invalid merely because it lacked a durational limit. Rather, the court remanded the case for a hearing on the issue of what was a reasonable time in view of the particulars of the business. In *Brintec Corp. v. Akzo, N.V.*, 129 A.D.2d 447, 514 N.Y.S.2d 18 (1st Dept.

1987), the court upheld a restrictive covenant preventing the seller from engaging in a competitive business for a period of five years. Additionally, in cases where a seller transfers the goodwill of a business, courts will enforce an implied covenant for an unlimited period of time prohibiting the seller from soliciting its former customers. *See Mohawk Maintenance*, 52 N.Y.2d 276, 437 N.Y.S.2d 646, 419 N.E.2d 324.

In the context of restrictive covenants in ordinary contracts, the court in *Baker's Aid, a Division of Raubvogel Co., Inc. v. Hussman Foodservice Company*, 730 F. Supp. 1209 (E.D.N.Y. 1990), upheld a ten-year restrictive covenant barring the defendant from soliciting, distributing, manufacturing, or selling to Baker's Aid's customers any rack-type oven or a deck oven based on the specifications or any reasonable facsimile. In that instance, the *Baker's Aid* court likened the specifications to trade secrets and found that those specifications should be protected so as to prevent Baker's Aid from facing unfair competition.

---

4. What geographic limitations have courts recognized in the franchise context?

- **How have they been related to the interests protected?**
- **Have courts recognized the legitimacy of protecting other franchisees from competition?**

New York courts have upheld restrictive covenants in franchising contexts, provided that the covenants are geographically reasonable to protect the franchisor's legitimate business interests. In *DAR & Associates, Inc. v. Uniforce Services, Inc.*, 37 F. Supp. 2d 192, 199 (E.D.N.Y. 1999), the court upheld a provision restricting a former licensee from competing within 50 miles of its former place of business for one year, because the court found that the restrictive covenant was related to the franchisor's interests in protecting its goodwill, know-how, and other proprietary information, as well as its legitimate desire to install a new franchisee in the market. In *TKO Fleet Enterprises, Inc. v. Elite Limousine Plus, Inc.*, 184 Misc. 2d 460, 708 N.Y.S.2d 593 (N.Y. Sup. Ct. 2000), the court upheld a restrictive covenant that prevented a franchisee from owning a competitive business within a 50-mile radius of Times Square for one year. Apparently, the court determined that the restrictive covenant was reasonable because the restrictive covenant was not intended to prevent the franchisee from working as a chauffeur in the luxury car business, but only to restrict the franchisee from acting as a principal, director, officer, or stockholder of a competitive business. Compare *DAR & Assoc.*, 37 F. Supp. 2d 1992, and *TKO Fleet Enterprises, supra*, to *Maxon v. Franklin Traffic Service, Inc.*, 261 A.D.2d 830, 689 N.Y.S.2d 559 (4th Dept. 1999), where the court concluded that a restrictive covenant prohibiting a shipping and freight management franchisee from engaging in a similar business for a period of five years within 300 miles of any office operated by the franchisor to be unreasonable as to time, scope, and area and to be unduly burdensome. *See also Westbury Donuts, Inc., Donut Queen, Ltd. v. Dunkin' Donuts of America, Inc.*, 1983 WL 937202 (E.D.N.Y. Mar. 15, 1983), in which the court found that a two-mile radius from any other Dunkin' Donuts shop was not unreasonable because the franchise competed to some extent with another franchise at a distance greater than two miles. In the three *Carvel Corp.* cases, the respective courts found that the restrictive covenants barring the defendant franchisees from directly or indirectly engaging in whole or in part in the production, distribution, or sale of ice cream or other frozen desserts whether as a proprietor, employee, officer, director, agent, joint venturer, partner, or other capacity whatsoever, at the location of the defendants' respective Carvel store or within a radius of two miles of the site of the defendants' respective Carvel store, was reasonable and sufficiently limited in geographic scope to protect the franchisor's legitimate business interests. *Carvel Corp. v. DePaola*, 2001 WL 528203 (Conn. Apr. 24, 2001), *Carvel Corp. v. Rait*, 117 A.D.2d 485, 503 N.Y.S.2d 406 (2d Dept. 1986), and *Carvel Corp. v. Eisenberg*, 692 F. Supp. 182 (S.D.N.Y. 1988). Similarly, the *Singas* court granted a preliminary injunction prohibiting the defendant franchisee from operating an Italian restaurant at the franchise's former location as well as within ten miles of the location of its former franchise restaurant, basing its decision on the concern that the franchisee's continued operation would confuse customers, thereby damaging the franchisor's goodwill and the entire franchise system. *Singas Famous Pizza Brands Corp. v. New York Advertising LLC*, 2011 WL 497978 (S.D.N.Y. Feb. 10, 2011), *aff'd* 2012 WL 899231 (2d Cir. Mar. 19, 2012).

In *Mister Softee, Inc. v. Tsirkos*, 2014 WL 2535114, at *8 (S.D.N.Y. June 5, 2014) the plaintiff franchisor sought to enjoin a former franchisee from competing in his former territories and those of any other franchisee for two years pursuant to the non-competition covenants in his franchise agreements. The restrictive covenants, as written, barred the defendant from competing in the ice cream business—retail and wholesale, mobile and fixed—for two years anywhere in six counties (comprising four boroughs of New York City and all of Long Island). The court took judicial notice that the area for which the plaintiff sought protection was well over 100 miles in length and included the homes and businesses of millions of people. The court found that the plaintiff had demonstrated a likelihood of success in showing the reasonableness of the covenant insofar as it applied to retail operations in the defendant's former territories and areas proximate thereto. The court found credible the plaintiff's evidence that recruiting a new franchise holder for the former territories would be far more difficult if the former franchisee were operating in the same area. The court further found credible that because of the short selling season in the ice cream industry, it would take two years to establish a replacement franchisee. The court noted that customer goodwill and business methods are legitimate spheres of protection with respect to former franchisee competition. However, the court found that the non-compete was overbroad in two respects: in its restraint on the defendant's ability to compete in wholesale ice cream and supply operations, and in its geographic reach. The court enforced it only to the extent of enjoining retail ice cream sales in defendant's former territories and in other franchisees' territories within a five-mile radius of his former territories. As narrowed, the court found that the non-compete was reasonable in time and geographic scope, and would not be oppressive in its operation as to the defendant's business and was thus enforceable, citing *Eisenberg*, 692 F. Supp. 182, 186 and *Golden Krust Patties, Inc. v. Bullock*, 957 F. Supp. 2d 186, 199 (E.D.N.Y. 2013).

5. What limitations on activities have courts recognized as reasonable in the franchise context?

New York courts have not discussed reasonable limitations on activities in the franchise context to the same extent that they have discussed reasonable limitations in duration and geographic scope. In considering limitations on activities, some courts have factored in the franchisee's ability to maintain a living if the restrictive covenants were enforced. *See Winston Franchise Corp. v. Williams*, 1992 WL 7843 (S.D.N.Y. Jan. 10, 1992), and *Westbury Donuts, Inc., Donut Queen, Ltd. v. Dunkin' Donuts of America, Inc.*, 1983 WL 937202 (E.D.N.Y. Mar. 15, 1983). Nonetheless, New York courts have applied the rule of reason test to uphold various limitations, including prohibitions against engaging in a competitive business (either directly or indirectly), soliciting former and current customers, and using the franchisor's confidential information. *See DAR & Associates, Inc. v. Uniforce Services, Inc.*, 37 F. Supp. 2d 192, 195 (E.D.N.Y. 1999) (prohibited former franchisee from operating a competing temporary personnel service business within the area and from soliciting former employees and temporary personnel service business from former clients); *Singas Famous Pizza Brands Corp. v. New York Advertising LLC*, 2011 WL 497978 (S.D.N.Y. Feb. 10, 2011), *aff'd* 2012 WL 899231 (2d Cir. Mar. 19, 2012) (preliminary injunction granted enjoining former franchisee from operating a competing pizza restaurant from the location of the former franchised restaurant and from a location within ten miles of the location of the former franchised restaurant); *Westbury Donuts, Inc., supra* (former franchisee enjoined from operating a competing donut store within two miles of the former franchised location); *Carvel Corp. v. Eisenberg*, 692 F. Supp. 182 (S.D.N.Y. 1988) (barred former franchisee from operating a competing ice cream store within two miles of the former franchised location); *ServiceMaster Residential/Commercial Services, L.P. v. Westchester Cleaning Services, Inc.*, 2001 WL 396520 (S.D.N.Y. Apr. 19, 2001) (preliminary injunction granted enjoining former franchisee from operating a competing cleaning service within the territory); and *RESCUECOMM Corp. v. Matthews*, 2006 WL 1742073 (N.D.N.Y. June 20, 2006) (enjoined the former franchisee from soliciting customers because the franchisor provided the former franchisee with training and manuals pertaining to the best methods for operating a successful computer sales and service, business skills that the former franchisee did not previously have and that the former franchisee used to establish his own business). In *Winston Franchise*, 1992 WL 7843, the court required a former franchisee to return to the franchisor applicant information that had been generated during the term of the franchise agreement and barred the former franchisee from using that information to solicit those applicants.

6. Does the state recognize a difference between in-term and post-term covenants?

No New York court has made a significant effort to analyze differences between in-term and post-term restrictive covenants in the franchise context. Without a discussion concerning the merits of the in-term restrictive covenant, in *Westbury Donuts, Inc., Donut Queen, Ltd. v. Dunkin' Donuts of America, Inc.*, 1983 WL 937202 (E.D.N.Y. Mar. 15, 1983), the court held that the franchisee's covenant not to operate any business substantially similar to the donut-shop franchise during the term of the franchise agreement was reasonable and enforceable. The court noted that the franchisee violated the in-term covenant by operating an independent donut shop in a nearby town and by distributing coupons at its Dunkin' Donuts store "under the name and style of Dunkin' Donuts," inviting customers to "visit our other donut shop." *Id.* Similarly, the *Singas* court found that the franchisor properly terminated a franchise agreement because of the franchisee's violation of its in-term restrictive covenant by assisting a third party in the operation of a competitive pizza restaurant. *Singas Famous Pizza Brands Corp. v. New York Advertising LLC*, 2011 WL 497978 (S.D.N.Y. Feb. 10, 2011), *aff'd* 2012 WL 899231 (2d Cir. Mar. 19, 2012). However, the *Singas* court did not discuss the merits of the in-term restrictive covenant or proffer any rationale for analyzing the reasonableness of in-term covenants in general.

In an employment context, the court in *Bradford v. The New York Times Co.*, 501 F.2d 51, 58 (2d Cir. 1974), noted that there is more flexibility in determining whether an in-term covenant is reasonable as opposed to a post-term covenant because the employee is receiving some consideration for the in-term covenant, in that his or her salary is being paid. The *Bradford* court observed that post-term covenants are scrutinized more closely because the former employee may lose his or her opportunity to make a living and become a public charge. In *N.W. Ayer & Son, Inc. v. Deare*, 1998 WL 811873 at 2 (S.D.N.Y. Nov. 18, 1998), the court granted a preliminary injunction upholding a post-term restrictive covenant barring competition with the plaintiff, an advertising company, but refused to grant a preliminary injunction with respect to the defendants servicing a Starbucks account solicited while under employment with the plaintiff, in violation of the in-term restrictive covenants. The *N.W. Ayer* court refused to enjoin the defendants from servicing Starbucks because the plaintiff could not represent Starbucks themselves without creating internal conflict with another advertising account. In that instance, the court noted that because the plaintiff suffered no loss of business, loss of profit, or loss of goodwill with respect to the Starbucks account, preliminary injunctive relief enjoining the defendants from competing with the plaintiff should not include the Starbucks account.

7. Has the state allowed enforcement of covenants against non-signatories (e.g., family members, newly formed corporations)?

The general rule is that if a person does not sign in his or her individual capacity, he or she is not to be bound. *See National Survival Game of New York, Inc. v. NSG of LI Corp.*, 169 A.D.2d 760, 565 N.Y.S.2d 127 (2d Dept. 1991) (court upheld restrictive covenant prohibiting NSG of LI Corp. and Michael Cuocco from competing with plaintiff for two years following termination, but not John Cuocco and his corporation, American Air Gun Games, Inc., because they were not parties to the agreement). In *ATC Healthcare v. Nurses Staffing*, 2000 WL 36695824 (E.D.N.Y. Feb. 16, 2000), the court ruled that the franchisee officer was not individually bound by the terms of the franchise agreement, including non-competition provisions, because he did not sign the agreement in his individual capacity and no proof was offered that he intended to be bound by the agreement. The court noted further that because the franchise agreement, a form document, provided that if the franchisee were going to be personally liable, a separate document would be executed. Because the franchisor never requested to have a separate document executed by the franchisee officer, nor asked him to be personally obligated to the restrictive covenants, the court found that no restrictive covenant was enforceable against the franchisee officer personally.

However, in certain instances, a court will enforce a restrictive covenant against a non-signatory. In *Singas Famous Pizza Brands Corp. v. New York Advertising LLC*,

2011 WL 497978 (S.D.N.Y. Feb. 10, 2011), *aff'd* 2012 WL 899231 (2d Cir. Mar. 19, 2012), the court granted a preliminary injunction against a non-franchisee entity alleged to be wholly owned by the husband of the franchisee's principal. The court also noted that the franchisee was at least indirectly involved in the operation of the non-franchised restaurant. There, the court noted that the non-franchisee entity restaurant owned by the franchisee's husband tried to "trade on a relationship with Singas when it has none." *Id.* at 9. The court further noted that advertisements listed the franchised restaurant and the non-franchised restaurant together, a former employee from the franchised restaurant was brought over to make pizza at the non-franchised restaurant, equipment from the franchised restaurant was used at the non-franchised restaurant, menus for the two restaurants were nearly identical, and the principals of the two entities met with the franchisor's representative simultaneously to explain how the two entities could use income, training, and resources from the non-franchised restaurant to assist the franchised restaurant. For all of the above reasons, the court granted an injunction enjoining the franchisee and the owner of the non-franchised restaurant from operating, directly or indirectly, the non-franchised restaurant.

In *Golden Krust Patties, Inc. v. Bullock*, 957 F. Supp. 2d 186 (E.D.N.Y. 2013), the court issued a preliminary injunction enforcing a non-compete agreement preventing a fast-food restaurant franchise owner from operating a similarly themed restaurant at the franchise location following termination of the franchise agreement. The court found that the preliminary injunction applied equally to the franchise owner's son who managed the restaurant, where it was undisputed that the son was an agent of the franchise owner, and the owner was precluded from having any interest in such a restaurant, even through an agency relationship.

Courts have also enforced restrictive covenants against non-signatories in employment relationship contexts. In *Ecolab, Inc. v. Paolo*, 753 F. Supp. 1100 (E.D.N.Y. 1991), the court ruled that a competitor wrongfully interfered with its employees' contractual obligations to their former employer. There, the court observed that the competitor was aware that restrictive covenants prohibited its employees for one year from soliciting accounts previously serviced during the course of their former employment. Despite its knowledge, the competitor induced its employees to solicit their former accounts in violation of the restrictive covenants. Accordingly, the court enjoined the competitor during the pendency of the action from (1) servicing, selling, soliciting the sale, or accepting orders for products or services competitive with Ecolab and (2) disclosing or using any confidential information belonging to Ecolab. In *Churchill Communications Corp. v. Demyanovich*, 668 F. Supp. 207, 215 (S.D.N.Y. 1987), the court enforced a restrictive covenant against Demyanovich (a former employee) and a non-signatory corporation, of which Demyanovich owned 90 percent of its shares, from soliciting, either directly or indirectly, any customer of the former employer.

8. Will the state modify, "blue-pencil," or otherwise reduce a covenant found to be overbroad?

New York courts have reformed restrictive covenants to shorten the duration and narrow the geographic scope of the covenant as well as tailor the scope of the prohibited activities to ensure that the restrictive covenant is reasonable as reformed. In a franchise context, the court in *Winston Franchise* reformed a restrictive covenant that prohibited a former franchisee from competing with the franchisor for three years. *Winston Franchise Corp. v. Williams*, 1992 WL 7843 (S.D.N.Y. Jan. 10, 1992). Instead, the *Winston Franchise* court barred the former franchisee from soliciting business using applicant information he obtained during the term of his franchise relationship. In *Baker's Aid*, the court held that where a restrictive covenant contains both reasonable and overbroad provisions, the court may "make use of the tool of severance, paring an unreasonable restraint down to appropriate size and enforcing it." *Baker's Aid, a Division of Raubvogel Co., Inc. v. Hussman Foodservice Company*, 730 F. Supp. 1209, 1216 (E.D.N.Y. 1990), citing *Karpinski v. Ingrasci*, 28 N.Y.2d 45, 52, 320 N.Y.S.2d 1, 7, 268 N.E.2d 751, 757 (N.Y. 1971). The court in *Baker's Aid* severed the proscription of competition in the rack-oven markets of the United States and Canada, ultimately holding that the covenant, as reformed, was enforceable. In *Karpinski*, 28 N.Y.2d, 45, 51–52, 320 N.Y.S.2d 1, 268 N.E.2d 751, the court expressly recognized and applied the judicial power to sever and granted partial enforcement of an overbroad employee restrictive covenant. The *Karpinski* court refused to give effect to the portion of the covenant that barred the practice of general dentistry, but enforced the portion of the covenant concerning the practice of oral surgery because the employer specialized in oral surgery as opposed to general dentistry. In *BDO Siedman v. Hirshberg*, 93 N.Y.2d 382, 394–95, 690 N.Y.S.2d 854, 712 N.E.2d 1220 (1999), the court also provided for severability and partial enforcement of non-compete covenants to the extent that such covenants protect an employer's legitimate interest rather than refusing to enforce overly broad restrictive covenants in their entirety. There, the *BDO Siedman* court enforced the restrictive covenant, but limited it to the extent that it reached clients that did not belong to the employee. In *Doubleclick, Inc. v. Henderson*, 1997 WL 731413 (N.Y. Sup. Ct. Nov. 7, 1997), the court refused to enforce a restrictive covenant prohibiting defendants for a period of at least 12 months from launching a competitive business or from working for a direct competitor. Instead, the *Doubleclick* court shortened the restrictive covenant to enjoin defendants from competing with the plaintiff for a period of six months.

However, where restrictive covenants are not reasonably tailored to protect the legitimate interests of the party seeking their enforcement, courts have refused to reform the restrictive covenant and have held such restrictive covenants to be unenforceable for being unreasonable and overbroad. Where an employer made no showing that the former employee possessed confidential information, provided anything but commonplace services, a loss of business, customers, or other damage, the court in *Columbia Ribbon & Carbon Manufacturing Co., Inc. v. A-1-A Corp.*, 42 N.Y.2d 496, 398 N.Y.S.2d 1004, 369 N.E.2d 4 (1977), perceived no basis on which to grant equitable relief and refused to reform the restrictive covenant. The court in *Jay's Custom Stringing* declined to exercise its discretion to "blue-pencil" the restrictive covenant, noting that the dynamic, relationship-based nature of the tennis racket–customizing industry and its lack of geographical boundaries strongly militates against a judicially crafted restrictive covenant. *Jay's Custom Stringing, Inc. v. Yu*, 2001 WL 761067, at *7 (S.D.N.Y. July 6, 2001).

9. When does a non-compete period begin to run? Will courts equitably extend the term?

Generally, the term of a non-competition provision will begin to run from the date the underlying relationship terminates, but courts may, but rarely do, extend the term of the restrictive covenant. In employment contexts, the restrictive covenant will run from the date of termination. *See Mallory Factor, Inc. v. Schwartz*, 146 A.D.2d 465, 536 N.Y.S.2d 752 (1st Dept. 1989), *aff'd* by *Mallory Factor, Inc. v. Jicka*, 168 A.D.2d 344 (1st Dept. 1990) (injunction will run from time of termination); *National Survival Game of New York, Inc. v. NSG of LI Corp.*, 169 A.D.2d 760, 565 N.Y.S.2d 127 (2d Dept. 1991) (by the terms of the agreement, an individual was barred from competing for two years following termination, and because that agreement was terminated on October 28, 1985, the right to an injunction under the terms of the agreement expired on October 28, 1987).

In *New York Real Est. Inst., Inc. v. Edelman*, 42 A.D.3d 321, 321–22, 839 N.Y.S.2d 488, 489–90 (2007), the First Department extended a two-year non-compete. In connection with the defendant's sale of his real estate school to the plaintiff, he entered into an agreement not to compete on Long Island for two years. The New York Supreme Court denied the plaintiff's request for a preliminary injunction because it did not seek an injunction to enforce the restrictive covenant for 16 months after it became aware of facts underling the defendant's alleged breach. The First Department, however, found that despite the plaintiff's delay in seeking injunctive relief, the defendant has not claimed or shown that he changed his position or would be prejudiced as a consequence of the plaintiff's delay. *Id.* at 322. The First Department also noted that the defendant had hidden his ownership interest in the competing school for the entire two-year duration of the non-compete agreement. The First Department held that where a party unilaterally breaches an agreement not to compete and the time period during which competition was precluded has since expired, such time period may be extended for the length of time that the offending party was in violation of the agreement

In *Sutherland Global Services, Inc. v. Crowley*, 21 Misc. 3d 344, 867 N.Y.S.2d 874 (N.Y. Sup. Ct. 2008), the court, distinguishing *Edelman*, refused to extend a restrictive covenant from one year from the date the employment was terminated to one year from the date the preliminary injunction was issued prior to trial. However, the *Sutherland Global* court left the door open to extend the term of the restrictive covenant by noting that a court should decline "to extend a restrictive covenant's term until, after discovery, a fuller record is developed or expiration of that term is rapidly approaching." *Id.* at 348, 867 N.Y.S.2d 874. The court in *Doubleclick, Inc. v. Henderson*, 1997 WL 731413 (N.Y. Sup. Ct. Nov. 7, 1997), held that the restrictive covenant would be enforced against the defendants for six months after the date the preliminary injunction was issued, as opposed to from the date the defendants' employment with the plaintiff terminated. The court reasoned that the defendants had knowledge of Doubleclick's trade secrets and the defendants' cavalier attitude toward their duties to Doubleclick suggested that it was likely that the defendants would use those trade secrets in competition with Doubleclick. Accordingly, the court determined that Doubleclick's motion for preliminary injunction should be granted and that six months was an appropriate period for Doubleclick's trade secrets pertaining to internet advertising, which the court noted changes at great speed.

10. Are there additional nuances or peculiarities of the state's treatment of covenants in the franchising context?

New York courts recognize the right of contracting parties to select which state's laws will apply to their contract. *See State-Wide Capital Corp. v. Superior Bank FSB*,

1999 WL 258268 (S.D.N.Y. Apr. 29, 1999). New York courts used to analyze significant contacts, interest in the litigation, and the public policy of the foreign jurisdiction, even when faced with a contract with a New York choice-of-law provision. *See, e.g., Estee Lauder Cos. v. Batra*, 430 F. Supp. 2d 158, 170–74 (S.D.N.Y. 2006). In 2012, however, the New York Court of Appeals held that "the need for a conflict-of-laws analysis is obviated by the terms of the parties' agreement" if there was an express choice of New York law in a contract meeting the requirements of General Obligations Law § 5-1401. *IRB-Brasil Resseguros, S.A. v. Inepar Invs., S.A.*, 20 N.Y.3d 310, 315, 982 N.E.2d 609, 612 (2012). Three years later, the court held more broadly that "'New York courts should not engage in any conflicts analysis where the parties include a choice-of-law provision in their contract, even if the contract is one that does not fall within General Obligations Law § 5-1401.'" *Willis Re Inc. v. Herriott*, 2021 WL 3204764, at *15 (S.D.N.Y. July 22, 2021) (quoting *Ministers & Missionaries Benefit Bd. v. Snow*, 26 N.Y.3d 466, 474, 25 N.Y.S.3d 21, 45 N.E.3d 917 (2015).

In the franchising context, a New York court has enforced a non-compete covenant subject to and enforceable under the laws of another state because enforcement of the covenant comported with the laws of New York. New York courts have not been presented with a case in which a court had to determine the enforceability of a non-compete covenant that conflicted with the laws of New York. The only New York case that addressed enforcement of a non-compete covenant in a franchise context under the laws of another state is *ServiceMaster Residential/Commercial Services, L.P. v. Westchester Cleaning Services, Inc.*, 2001 WL 396520 (S.D.N.Y. Apr. 19, 2001). There, the franchise agreement contained a choice-of-law provision requiring the application of Tennessee law. Under New York's choice-of-law rules, courts will honor a contractual choice-of-law provision if it bears a reasonable relationship to the dispute. The *ServiceMaster* court found that Tennessee law applied to the dispute because the franchisor's principal place of business was located in Tennessee. The *ServiceMaster* court was comfortable in applying Tennessee law to the subject matter because the court noted that the standards governing non-compete covenants applied by Tennessee and New York are substantially similar.

North Carolina

*by Joseph "Jack" Santaniello**

1. Has the state addressed covenants against competition in the context of franchising?

- **Does the state have a franchising statute or regulations that address covenants against competition?**
- **Does the state have a covenant statute of general applicability that would encompass franchise covenants?**
- **Have the courts addressed covenants in the context of franchising either under a statute or under the state's common law?**

North Carolina does not have a statute or regulation directly addressing covenants against competition in the franchising context. Restraints on trade in general are covered by N.C. GEN. STAT. § 75-1, which states that "[e]very contract, combination in the form of trust or otherwise, or conspiracy in restraint of trade or commerce in the State of North Carolina is hereby declared to be illegal."

Section 75-4 requires that all contracts that would lawfully attempt to restrict competition be in writing. Specifically, section 75-4 states that "[n]o contract or agreement hereafter made, limiting the rights of any person to do business anywhere in the State of North Carolina shall be enforceable unless such agreement is in writing duly signed by the party who agrees not to enter into any such business within such territory."

North Carolina also has a Business Opportunity Sales Act (*see* N.C. GEN. STAT. § 66-94 (2021) *et seq.*), which includes the sales of franchise opportunities and exceptions to state registration. However, this statute does not address covenants against competition.

Generally speaking, non-competition covenants are contracts "in restraint of trade" and, as such, are "carefully scrutinized" by North Carolina courts. *Chemi-Metals Processing, Inc. v. McEneny*, 476 S.E.2d 374, 376 (N.C. Ct. App. 1996) (citing *United Labs., Inc. v. Kuykendall*, 322 N.C. 643, 649–50, 370 S.E.2d 375, 380 (N.C. 1988)). This applies in both the employment context and the sale of business context. However, "[a]ccording to well-established North Carolina law, non-competition agreements contained in an employment contract are more closely scrutinized than

*Joseph "Jack" Santaniello is a partner at Shumaker in Charlotte, North Carolina.

those contained in a contract for the sale of a business." *Outdoor Lighting Perspectives Franchising, Inc. v. Harders*, 747 S.E.2d 256, 262 (N.C. Ct. App. 2013) (citing *Keith v. Day*, 81 N.C. App. 185, 193, 343 S.E.2d 562, 567 (N.C. Ct. App. 1986)).

In the employment context, to be enforceable, such restraints must be (1) in writing, (2) part of the contract of employment or sale of the business, (3) based on valuable consideration, (4) reasonably necessary for the protection of the promisee's interest, and (5) reasonable as to time and territory. *ChemiMetals*, 476 S.E.2d at 376. (citing *Pro. Liab. Consultants v. Todd*, 122 N.C. App. 212, 215, 468 S.E.2d 578, 580 (N.C. Ct. App. 1996)). In the sale of business context, "when one sells a trade or business and, as an incident of the sale, covenants not to engage in the same business in competition with the purchaser, the covenant is valid and enforceable (1) if it is reasonably necessary to protect the legitimate interest of the purchaser; (2) if it is reasonable with respect to both time and territory; and (3) if it does not interfere with the interest of the public." *Outdoor Lighting*, 747 S.E.2d at 262 (citing *Jewel Box Stores Corp. v. Morrow*, 272 N.C. 659, 662–63, 158 S.E.2d 840, 843 (N.C. 1968)).

The *Outdoor Lighting* court further stated that the "practical differences between the typical employer-employee arrangement and the typical buyer-seller arrangement render it illogical to conclude that the rules typically governing either arrangement should be applied with unbending rigidity," and "[a]s a result, in light of this determination, we conclude that elements of the tests utilized in both the employee-employer and the business sale context are relevant." *Id.* at 263. Therefore, the enforceability of covenants not to compete between franchisors and franchisees is evaluated using the test of enforceability for covenants in the employment context as well as the test of enforceability for covenants in the sale of business context.

The *Outdoor Lighting* court concluded that in this case where the franchisor was seeking enforcement of the franchisee's post-termination obligations, the court should consider (1) the area, or scope, of the restriction, (2) the area assigned to the franchisee, (3) the area in which the franchisee actually worked or was subject to work, (4) the area in which the franchisor operated, (5) the nature of the business involved, and (6) the nature of the franchisee's duty and his knowledge of the franchisor's business operation. *Id.* at 262.

2. Have the courts articulated the "legitimate interests" of the franchisor that will support enforcement of a covenant against competition contained in a franchise agreement?

- **If so, what are they (e.g., protection of goodwill, protection of confidential information), and in what contexts did the issue arise?**
- **If not, what interests have been recognized in other contexts (e.g., employment agreements, the sale of business context)?**

In *Maaco Franchising, LLC v. Boensch*, 2016 WL 4746215, at *11 (W.D.N.C. Sept. 12, 2016), the court found that the franchisor was entitled to a preliminary injunction based on the former franchisee's breach of a non-competition provision. In that case, the franchisor terminated the franchise agreement with the franchisee for failing to comply with the franchise agreement and the former franchisee continued to operate its business in violation of the franchise agreement's non-compete obligations. *Id.* Here the court found the covenant not to compete was necessary to protect the franchisor's valid and legitimate business interests. *Id.* Specifically, the non-competition covenant was specifically designed to protect Maaco's proprietary operating system, its confidential information, and the goodwill associated with its trademarks, service marks, trade name, and trade dress developed through the investment of a substantial amount of time, money, and effort. *Id.*

Similarly, in *Meineke Car Care Centers, Inc. v. Bica*, 2011 WL 4829420, at *6 (W.D.N.C. Oct. 12, 2011), the court held that enforcement of the covenant not to compete was necessary to protect the legitimate business interests of the franchisor and proceeded to articulate those business interests as follows: "Meineke had expended substantial resources developing its processes, manuals, advertising materials, and on building goodwill and obtaining a national reputation as a provider of automotive services." The court further acknowledged that the defendants received training, assistance, and a protected territory in which to build a successful automotive business. *Id.* By signing the franchise agreement, the defendants recognized and took advantage of the value of the confidential and proprietary information Meineke gave them. *Id.* The court then stated, "[i]f the [c]ourt allows Defendants to continue operating their store in violation of the covenant not to compete, Defendants will be able to use the confidential and proprietary information they acquired from Meineke to take business away from it." *Id.* The same court in *Outdoor Lighting Perspectives Franchising, Inc. v. Home Amenities, Inc.*, 2012 WL 137808, at *3 (W.D.N.C. Jan. 18, 2012), expanded on *Bica* by recognizing that the franchisor has "a legitimate interest in preserving the integrity of its franchise system." The court held that if the non-compete provisions are not enforced, the franchise system "is placed in jeopardy as franchisees may ignore their agreements and begin operating as a competing business knowing that the non-compete provisions may be disregarded at will and provide no protection to other franchisees." *Id.*

Interestingly, the *Boensch* court also held that a defendant's agreement to the time and scope of the non-competition provision also strongly supports the reasonableness of those time and scope provisions. *Boensch*, 2016 WL 4746215, at *6 (citing *Kuykendall*, 322 N.C. at 649, 370 S.E.2d at 380). As the North Carolina Supreme Court stated, "by enforcing the restrictions [a] court is only requiring the defendants to do what they agreed to do." *Id.*

In *Meineke Car Care Centers, Inc. v. Quinones*, 2006 WL 1549708, at *4 (W.D.N.C. 2006), the court granted a franchisor's motion for a preliminary injunction, concluding that allowing former franchisees to operate a competing business in violation of the covenant not to compete would cause irreparable harm to the franchisor by depriving the franchisor of the customers and the market that it established over the course of the franchise relationship and by making it difficult for the franchisor to re-establish an authorized franchise in the area. Moreover, allowing former franchisees to violate the covenant not to compete gives them an unfair competitive advantage over legitimate franchisees in the area because "they are able to offer their services for a lower price than the franchisees since they do not have to pay [franchisor's] royalty or advertising contributions." *Id.*

Protectable legitimate interests also include protection of "customer relationships and goodwill against misappropriation by departing employees." *Window Gang Ventures, Corp. v. Salinas*, 2019 WL 1471073, at *7 (N.C. Super. Ct. Apr. 2, 2019) (citing *Kuykendall*, 322 N.C. at 651, 370 S.E.2d at 381). Nevertheless, the restriction "must be no wider in scope than is necessary to protect the business of the employer." *Id.* (citing *VisionAIR, Inc. v. James*, 167 N.C. App. 504, 508, 606 S.E.2d

359, 362 (N.C. Ct. App. 2004)). Our courts routinely hold that non-competition covenants are overbroad, and therefore unenforceable, when they "prohibit the employee from engaging in future work that is distinct from the duties actually performed by the employee." *Id.* (citing *Medical Staffing Network v. Ridgeway*, 670 S.E.2d 321, 327 (N.C. Ct. App. 2009)). In this case, the covenant prohibited businesses that are "the same" or "similar" to the franchisor and not simply those that are "competitive" to the franchisor, and the court held the covenant was overbroad and unenforceable.

Furthermore, the court in *Laboratory Corp. of America Holdings v. Kearns*, 84 F. Supp. 3d 447, 459 (M.D.N.C. 2015), outlined "the contours of an employer's legitimate interests in its goodwill and customer relationships" as follows: "[P]rotection of customer relationships and goodwill against misappropriation by departing employees is well recognized as a legitimate protectable interest of the employer. The greater the employee's opportunity to engage in personal contact with the employer's customer, the greater the need for the employer to protect these customer relationships. This theory, which is often referred to as the 'customer contact' theory, is most applicable where the employee is the sole or primary contact between the customer and the employer." *Id.* (citing *Kuykendall*, 322 N.C. at 651, 370 S.E.2d at 381).

3. What time limitations have courts recognized as reasonable in the franchise context?

> **If no franchise cases have been decided, what time limitations have been recognized in other contexts?**

> **How have they been related to the interests protected?**

In evaluating reasonableness as to time and territory restrictions, North Carolina courts must consider these elements in tandem, as the two requirements are neither independent nor unrelated. Time and territory restrictions standing alone may be reasonable. However, the combined effect of the two may be unreasonable. *MJM Investigations, Inc. v. Sjostedt*, 698 S.E.2d 202 (N.C. Ct. App. 2010) (citing *Farr Associates, Inc. v. Baskin*, 138 N.C. App. 276, 280, 530 S.E.2d 878, 881 (N.C. Ct. App. 2000)). A longer period of time is acceptable where the geographic restriction is smaller, and vice versa. *Akzo Nobel Coatings, Inc. v. Rogers*, 2011 WL 5316772, at *12 (N.C. Super. Ct. Nov. 3, 2011) (citing *Farr Associates*, 138 N.C. App. at 280, 530 S.E.2d at 881).

The leading franchise case in North Carolina similarly held that restrictive covenants must be reasonable with respect to both place and time. *Boensch*, 2016 WL 4746215, at *6 . In this case, the court found that the term, which was for one year, was well within the range of time regularly upheld as reasonable in North Carolina. *Id.* (citing *Bica*, 2011 WL 4829420, at *4). Specifically, this amount of time was a reasonable period to permit a franchisor the opportunity to retain the goodwill in the market area without any erosion arising from the former franchisee's provision of goods and services that do not meet the franchisor's standards. *See Meineke Car Care Centers, Inc. v. RLB Holdings, LLC*, 423 F. App'x 274, 286 (4th Cir. 2011).

A time limitation of two years has similarly been well recognized as reasonable. *See Lockhart v. Home-Grown Industries of Georgia, Inc.*, 2007 WL 2688551, at *5 (W.D.N.C. Sept. 10, 2007); *Triangle Leasing Co. v. McMahon*, 327 N.C. 224, 227, 393

S.E.2d 854, 856 (N.C. 1990); *Keith*, 81 N.C. App. at 194–95, 343 S.E.2d at 567–68; *National League of Junior Cotillions, Inc. v. Porter*, 2007 WL 2316823, at *1 (W.D.N.C. Aug. 9, 2007) (license case).

However, in *AMV Holdings, LLC v. American Vapes, Inc.*, 2019 WL 3406315, at *11 (W.D.N.C. July 26, 2019), the court held the franchisor was not entitled to a preliminary injunction based on the franchisor and franchisee's two-year post-termination covenant not to compete. In that case, a franchisee continued to operate a vape store in violation of the covenant not to compete in the franchise agreement and the franchisor sought a preliminary injunction. *Id.* The covenant not to compete prohibited the franchisee from engaging in any competitive business "for a period of two years," "in the same state . . . as the franchised locations or any [of franchisor's] franchised business or development territory." *Id.* The court found the covenant not to compete was overbroad—not because of the two-year period, but rather because of the broad geographical restriction which extended to the entire state, with a population of millions—in comparison to the franchisee's territory of approximately 15,000. *Id.*

Beyond the one- to two-year range, North Carolina courts have allowed a five-year time restriction as the "outer boundary" of reasonableness for non-competes that are ancillary to employment, although five-year restrictions are not favored. *Keith*, 81 N.C. App. at 194, 343 S.E.2d at 567. Note, however, that when North Carolina courts have reviewed restrictions on competition resulting from the sale of a business, they have upheld restrictive covenants containing limitations of 10, 15, and 20 years, as well as limitations for the life of one of the parties. *Jewel Box Stores*, 272 N.C. at 663, 158 S.E.2d at 843.

North Carolina law also supports equitable tolling. That is, the length of any period in which the employee is found to be in violation of the non-compete agreement is added to the length of the restriction. In *Philips Electronics North America Corp. v. Hope*, 631 F. Supp. 2d 705, 718 (M.D.N.C. 2009), the two-year period of an employee's non-competition agreement was tolled from the date that the employee commenced his competitive activities, as the agreement provided that "periods of protection shall not be reduced by any period of time during which [employee is] not in compliance therewith."

---

4. What geographic limitations have courts recognized as reasonable in the franchise context?

- **How have they been related to the interests protected?**
- **Have courts recognized the legitimacy of protecting other franchisees from competition?**

The North Carolina Appeals Court, in *Hartman v. W.H. Odell & Assocs., Inc.*, 117 N.C. App. 307, 312, 450 S.E.2d 912, 917 (N.C. Ct. App. 1994), set out a six-part test to determine whether the geographic scope of a covenant not to compete is reasonable. The six factors are (1) the area or scope of the restriction, (2) the area assigned to the employee, (3) the area where the employee actually worked, (4) the area in which the employer operated, (5) the nature of the business involved, and (6) the nature of the employee's duty and his knowledge of the employer's business operation. *Id.*

In *Boensch*, 2016 WL 4746215, at *6, the court held the restrictive covenant as reasonable as to territorial restriction because, among other reasons, the territorial restriction was limited to ten miles from the franchised location and any other

Maaco centers. The court further held that such a radius is reasonable because it protects a franchisor, such as Maaco, from a former franchisee diluting its goodwill and reputation in the relevant trade area. *See Outdoor Lighting Perspectives Franchising, Inc. v. OLP-Pittsburgh, Inc.*, 2012 WL 1313251, at *2 (W.D.N.C. Apr. 17, 2012). It also permits Maaco the opportunity to protect authorized franchisees and/or secure other franchisees in that trade area. *See Bica*, 2011 WL 4829420, at *5 (noting that allowing a former franchisee to continue operations would unfairly burden other franchisees in the area).

In *Home Amenities*, 2012 WL 137808, at *3, the court reviewed a two-year post-termination restrictive covenant related to any "Competitive Business within 100 miles of the Territory or any other franchisee's territory." The court blue-penciled (removed) "100 miles of" from the restrictive covenant language. *Id.* The court stated that the restriction, in this modified format, protects the franchisor's legitimate business interests and is reasonable. *Id.*

In *ACS Partners, LLC v. Americon Group, Inc.*, 2010 WL 883663, at *6 (W.D.N.C. Mar. 5, 2010), the court stated that North Carolina courts generally uphold national territory restrictions in covenants not to compete when the plaintiff company does business nationally. *See also Harwell Entertainment, Inc. v. Heim*, 276 N.C. 475, 481, 173 S.E.2d 316, 320 (N.C. 1970) (North Carolina Supreme Court found that nationwide protection would appear to be reasonable and proper for a company engaged in nationwide activities), and *Triangle Leasing*, 327 N.C. at 229, 393 S.E.2d at 858 (finding the territorial restriction in the non-competition clause of the parties' contract reasonable and enforceable because defendant's access to customer lists, price sheets, and policies affecting company business outside of the Wilmington area would warrant a contractual prohibition against solicitation of plaintiff's customers regardless of their location).

North Carolina courts also recognize customer-based restrictions in lieu of territorial restrictions. "[C]ustomers developed by a salesperson are the property of the employer and may be protected by a contract under which the salesperson is forbidden from soliciting those customers for a reasonable time after leaving his or her employment." *Whittaker Gen. Med. Corp. v. Daniel*, 324 N.C. 523, 525 379 S.E.2d 824, 826 (N.C. 1989). In *Wachovia Insurance Services, Inc. v. McGuirt*, 2006 WL 3720430, at *2 (N.C. Super. Ct. Dec. 19, 2006), the court reviewed a two-year non-compete related to customers of the employer. The court stated that a covenant with a client-based restriction in lieu of specific territorial restrictions and a two-year restrictive period has been accepted under North Carolina law. *Id.* at 10 (citing *Triangle Leasing*, 327 N.C. at 229–30, 393 S.E.2d at 858); *Wade S. Dunbar Insurance Agency, Inc. v. Barber*, 147 N.C. App. 463, 469, 556 S.E.2d 331, 335–36 (N.C. Ct. App. 2001). However, a client-based limitation cannot extend beyond the contacts made by the employee during the period of the employee's employment. *American Rentals, LLC v. Pomponio*, 2008 WL 496131, at *7 (N.Y. Sup. Ct. Feb. 25, 2008) (New York federal district court case interpreting North Carolina law and citing *Hartman*, 117 N.C. App. 307).

5. What limitations on activities have courts recognized as reasonable in the franchise context?

In *Bica*, 2011 WL 4829420, at *6, the court granted Meineke's motion for a preliminary injunction enforcing a non-compete that prohibited defendants, for a period of one year after termination, from "directly or indirectly . . . own[ing] a legal or beneficial interest in, manag[ing], operat[ing], or consult[ing] with: (a) any Competitive Business located at the Premises [of Defendants' former Meineke Center]; (b) any Competitive Business located within a radius of [six] miles of [the Premises]; (c) any Competitive Business located within a radius of [six] miles of any Meineke Center in operation on the effective date of termination or expiration." *Id.*

In *Boensch*, 2016 WL 4746215, at *2, Maaco sought to have the court enforce (and that court did enforce) the franchisee's post-termination obligations as set forth in the franchise agreement and under the law. Specifically, Maaco demanded, among other things, that the defendants (1) stop operating the center in violation of the franchise agreement's non-competition provision, (2) stop use of the Maaco System, (3) stop use and display of the Maaco Marks, (4) stop accepting new customers using Maaco's forms and paperwork, (5) modify and/or alter the center to disassociate itself from Maaco, and (6) return the operations manual and all other records, files, instructions, correspondence, and material related to the defendants' operation of the center. *Id.* It should be noted that in this case, the franchisor also sought the issuance of a preliminary injunction for trade dress infringement and trademark infringement, which were also granted. *Id.*

6. Does the state recognize a difference between in-term and post-term covenants?

No reported decisions have directly addressed this issue under North Carolina law. However, the court in *Grow Biz International, Inc. v. MNO, Inc.*, 2002 WL 113849, at *6 (D. Minn. Jan. 25, 2002), a Minnesota federal district court case applying North Carolina law, considered the defendant's argument that the court should consider the in-term and post-term anti-competition covenants separately. The defendants contended that the court should not consider the post-term covenant at all because the in-term covenants, if found to be valid, had post-term restrictive consequences. *Id.* The court declined to consider the distinction between the in-term and post-term covenants, stating that the court's task was to determine whether the defendants' conduct of operating the business violated their contractual obligations. *Id.* Therefore, the court held it needed to find that only one of the covenants was valid and breached because either covenant would provide an equal and independent basis for the injunction sought by the franchisor. *Id.*

7. Has the state allowed enforcement of covenants against non-signatories (e.g., family members, newly formed corporations)?

In *Rauch Industries, Inc. v. Radko*, 2007 WL 3124647, at *5 (W.D.N.C. Oct. 25, 2007), the court stated that a non-competition agreement generally cannot be enforced against a non-signatory to the agreement based on N.C. Gen. Stat. § 75-4. In that case, however, the defendant's employment agreement specifically prohibited the defendant from offering certain products to certain customers or competing against the employer on his own or in conjunction with others. *Id.* The court further stated that strangers can be enjoined who knowingly aid in violation of the non-compete. *Id.* Therefore, the court enjoined the customer from acting in concert or participation with the defendant. *Id.*

In *Philips Electronics*, 631 F. Supp. 2d at 713, the defendant contended that the plaintiff lacked standing to enforce the non-competition agreement because, to the extent the defendant bargained for it, he did so with the plaintiff's predecessor in interest, not the plaintiff. Under North Carolina law, a corporation generally may enforce a non-competition agreement executed by an employee of its predecessor in interest. *Id.* That court also held that "[a] covenant not to compete with a business is assignable" "as part of an asset purchase agreement." *Id.* (citing *Reynolds & Reynolds Co. v. Tart*, 955 F. Supp. 547, 556 (W.D.N.C. 1997)). Although the *Reynolds* case (and those others cited in *Philips Electronics*) specifically addressed asset purchase agreements, it indicates that a non-competition agreement is enforceable by an entity acquiring the agreement through a stock purchase. *Id.* North Carolina law also provides that, in the event of a merger, the surviving corporation succeeds to "all real estate and other property owned by each merging corporation" by operation of law, without the need for an express assignment. *Id.* (citing N.C. GEN. STAT. § 55-11-06(a)(2)).

8. Will the state modify, "blue-pencil," or otherwise reduce a covenant found to be overbroad?

North Carolina does allow for modification, or "blue-penciling," but such power is very limited. The North Carolina blue-pencil rule "severely limits what the court may do to alter the covenant." *Window Gang Ventures*, 2019 WL 1471073, at *8 (citing *Hartman*, 117 N.C. App. at 312, 450 S.E.2d at 917). As a general rule, "[t]he courts will not rewrite a contract if it is too broad but will simply not enforce it." *Whittaker Gen. Med.*, 324 N.C. at 528, 379 S.E.2d at 828; *see also Beverage Sys. of the Carolinas, LLC v. Associated Beverage Repair, LLC*, 368 N.C. 693, 699, 784 S.E.2d 457, 461 (N.C. 2016) ("[W]hen an agreement not to compete is found to be unreasonable, we have held that the court is powerless unilaterally to amend the terms of the contract."). "A court at most may choose not to enforce a distinctly separable part of a covenant in order to render the provision reasonable. It may not otherwise revise or rewrite the covenant." *Window Gang Ventures*, 2019 WL 1471073, at *9 (citing *Hartman*, 117 N.C. App. at 317, 450 S.E.2d at 920). In particular, the court "may not resurrect, in whole cloth, a covenant not to compete by erasing and replacing offending, but key, portions of a contract." *Pro. Liab. Consultants*, 122 N.C. App. at 221, 468 S.E.2d at 584. If an overbroad covenant is not separable into distinct parts, it may be "unsalvageable." *Beverage Sys. of the Carolinas*, 784 S.E.2d at 461. For example, in *RLM Communications, Inc. v. Tuschen*, 831 F.3d 190 (4th Cir. 2016), the court found overbroad, and refused to modify the scope of restricted activity of, a covenant purporting to prohibit a former employee from directly or indirectly participating "in a business that is similar to a business now or later operated" by the employer. *Id.* at 196–99.

9. When does a non-compete begin to run?

➤ Will courts equitably extend the term?

A non-compete period typically begins to run at the time specified in the contract. *Philips Electronics*, 631 F. Supp. 2d at 718. In that case, the non-competition agreement specifically provided that the two-year non-compete period was triggered by "the expiration or termination of . . . employment . . . irrespective of the manner or cause of such termination." *Id.* The court stated that North Carolina law recognizes equitable tolling. *Id.* That is, any period in which the employee is found to be in violation of the non-compete agreement is added to the length of the restriction. *Id.* In that case, the two-year period of the employee's non-competition agreement was tolled from the date the employee commenced his competitive activities, as the agreement provided that "periods of protection shall not be reduced by any period of time during which [employee is] not in compliance therewith." *Id.*

10. Are there additional nuances or peculiarities of the state's treatment of covenants in the franchising context?

Not particular to the franchising context, but more generally applicable, is the timing of the signing of a covenant not to compete. It is a general rule that if restrictive covenants are contained in the initial employment contract, then they are founded upon adequate legal consideration, as the mutual promises of employer and employee provide valuable considerations each to the other for the contract. *Safety Equip. Sales & Serv. v. Williams*, 22 N.C. App. 410, 412, 206 S.E.2d 745, 748 (N.C. Ct. App. 1974). Relatedly, where a covenant not to compete is part of the original verbal employment contract, it is supported by consideration—despite the fact that the contract is not actually signed until sometime after employment has begun. *Barber*, 556 S.E.2d at 335. However, "the terms of a verbal covenant which is later reduced to writing must have been agreed upon at the time of employment in order for the later written covenant to be valid and enforceable" without additional consideration. *Young v. Mastrom, Inc.*, 99 N.C. App. 120, 123, 392 S.E.2d 446, 448 (N.C. Ct. App. 1990) (citing *Stevenson v. Parsons*, 96 N.C. App. 93, 97, 384 S.E.2d 291, 293 (N.C. Ct. App. 1989)). Furthermore, "[a] covenant entered into after an employment relationship already exists must be supported by new consideration, such as a raise in pay or a new job assignment." *Reynolds*, 955 F. Supp. at 553.

North Dakota

*by William Sentell**

1. Has the state addressed covenants against competition in the context of franchising?

- **Does the state have a franchising statute or regulations that address covenants against competition?**
- **Does the state have a covenants statute of general applicability that would encompass franchise covenants?**
- **Have the courts addressed covenants in the context of franchising either under a statute or under the state's common law?**

North Dakota's Franchise Investment Law, N.D. CENT. CODE § 51-19-06 (22), provides that a franchisor's application for registration in the state must include "[a] statement explaining the terms and effects of any covenant not to compete which is or will be included in the franchise or other agreement to be executed by the franchisee." The North Dakota Franchise Investment Law does not otherwise address covenants against competition. However, North Dakota does have a statute of general applicability with regard to covenants against competition. Section 9-08-06 of the N.D. CENT. CODE (West 2022) provides:

> A contract by which anyone is restrained from exercising a lawful profession, trade, or business of any kind is to that extent void, except:
>
> 1. A person that sells the goodwill of a business and the person's partners, members, or shareholders may agree with the buyer to refrain from carrying on a similar business within a reasonable geographic area and for a reasonable length of time, if the buyer or any person deriving title to the goodwill from the buyer carries on a like business in that area.
> 2. Partners, members, or shareholders, upon or in anticipation of a dissolution of a partnership, limited liability company, or corporation; upon or in anticipation of a dissociation of a partner or member; or as part of an agreement addressing the dissociation or sale of a part-

*William Sentell is a partner at Akerman LLP. To prepare this analysis, he updated the third edition entry prepared by Peter W. Zuger.

> ner, member, or shareholder's ownership interest, may agree that all or any number of them will not carry on a similar business within a reasonable geographic area where the partnership, limited liability company, or corporation business has been transacted, or within a specified part of the area.

Section 9-08-06 was amended in 2019. As a result of the amendment, some of the concepts in the statute were broadened. For example, a person selling the goodwill of a business and agreeing with a buyer to refrain from carrying a similar business may also include as bound parties "the person's partners, members, or shareholders." The geographic restraints in subsection (1) are no longer limited to a "specified county, city, or a part of either" and now simply apply in a "reasonable geographic area and for a reasonable length of time if the buyer or any person deriving title to the goodwill from the buyer carries on a like business in that area." Similarly, the geographic restraints in subsection (2) had been limited to "the same city" and now apply within "a reasonable geographic area where the partnership, limited liability company, or corporation business has been transacted, or within a specified part." By its literal terms, subsection (2) had also been limited to partnerships and now also refers to the dissolution of limited liability companies and corporations.

Section 9-08-06 has not yet been applied in any reported decision involving a franchise, nor are there any reported decisions addressing covenants against competition in the franchise context under North Dakota common law. However, the North Dakota Securities Commissioner has held that franchise disclosure documents that disclose the existence of covenants restricting competition that are contrary to section 9-08-06, without further disclosing that such covenants will be subject to the statute, are unfair, unjust, or inequitable. Thus, it is likely that section 9-08-06 is applicable in the franchise context.

While there is no caselaw in North Dakota addressing covenants not to compete in the franchise context, there are a number of reported decisions in North Dakota applying section 9-08-06 in the employment context. North Dakota courts have held that section 9-08-06 invalidates covenants in employment agreements that bar an employee from competing with a former employer or working for a competitor after termination of the employment relationship.

For example, in *Osborne v. Brown & Saenger, Inc.*, 904 N.W.2d 34 (N.D. 2017), the North Dakota Supreme Court declined to enforce a non-compete covenant contained in an employment contract, citing North Dakota's strong public policy against non-compete agreements. The employment contract purported to require application of South Dakota law, and specified that any dispute would be resolved in state court in South Dakota. In declining to enforce the non-compete, the court noted that section 9-08-06 "represents one of the oldest and most continuous application of public policy in contract law." *Id.* at 38, quoting *Earthworks, Inc. v. Sehn*, 553 N.W.2d 490, 496 (N.D. 1996).

In *Werlinger v. Mutual Service Casualty Insurance Co.*, 496 N.W.2d 26 (N.D. 1993), the North Dakota Supreme Court held that a provision in an employment contract prohibiting an employee from working for a competitor after completion of his employment, or imposing a penalty if he did so, was void because it violated section 9-08-06. Similarly, in *Warner and Company v. Solberg*, 634 N.W.2d 65 (N.D. 2001), the North Dakota Supreme Court held that provisions in an insurance producer's employment contract that prohibited the producer from attempting "to affect the discontinuance of any of the Agency's insurance business" and from accepting or writing "any policy of insurance in replacement of any policy issued by the Agency" after termination of employment were void because they violated section 9-08-06. *Id.* at 71–73. Most recent, in *Kelly v. Kelly*, 806 N.W.2d 133 (N.D. 2011), the North Dakota Supreme Court applied section 9-08-06 in a divorce. The court stated that while section 9-08-06 is not directly applicable to property distributions in a divorce decree, the public policy under section 9-08-06, in addition to legal consistency, warranted the district court's determination to "distribute marital property in conformity with limitations imposed on contracting parties in N.D.C.C. Section 9–08–06." *Id.* As such, the court prohibited the wife from interfering with the husband's insurance business, so that the goodwill of the business would be protected in accordance with section 9-08-06.

Section 9-08-06 does provide for two exceptions to the general prohibition of covenants against competition: situations involving the dissolution of an entity and situations involving the sale of a business. North Dakota courts have narrowly construed these exceptions, however, as permissible only in the one city or county in which the business was located. *See Earthworks, Inc. v. Sehn*, 553 N.W.2d 490 (N.D. 1996); *Lire, Inc. v. North Dakota Bob's Pizza Inn Restaurants, Inc.*, 541 N.W.2d 432 (N.D. 1995); *Igoe v. Atlas Ready-Mix, Inc.*, 134 N.W.2d 511 (N.D. 1965); *Pruco Securities Corp. v. Montgomery*, 264 F. Supp. 2d 862 (D.N.D. 2003). Under the 2019 amendment to section 9-08-06, it appears a court would have more flexibility to permit enforcement of a non-compete in a broader area, provided that the area was reasonable.

---

2. Have the courts articulated the "legitimate interests" of the franchisor that will support enforcement of a covenant against competition contained in a franchise agreement?

- **If so, what are they (e.g., protection of goodwill, protection of confidential information), and in what contexts did the issue arise?**
- **If not, what interests have been recognized in other contexts (e.g., employment agreements, the sale of a business context)?**

North Dakota courts have not articulated the "legitimate interests" of a franchisor that would support enforcement of a covenant against competition in a franchise agreement. In construing section 9-08-06, however, the North Dakota Supreme Court has declared that the statute's primary purpose is to protect "the public's access to the services" and not necessarily to protect the interests of the contracting parties. *See Warner and Company v. Solberg*, 634 N.W.2d 65, 70 (N.D. 2001); *Earthworks, Inc. v. Sehn*, 553 N.W.2d 490 (N.D. 1996) (the purpose of section 9-08-06 is to "promote commercial activity by restricting the ability of individuals to form agreements not to compete."); *CDI Energy Services v. West River Pumps, Inc.*, 567 F.3d 398 (8th Cir. 2009) ("North Dakota deems the public's access to services to be a more pressing policy concern than the details of the relationship between a particular employee and employer.").

There is a second policy factor that exists in North Dakota. In *CDI Energy Services*, 567 F.3d at 404, the Eighth Circuit Court of Appeals noted that in North Dakota, employee loyalty is in the public's interest. As such, employees are prohibited from soliciting away customers while they are still working for their employer. This policy factor is limited in scope to the duration of the employment relationship. Given the clear mandate of section 9-08-06 to generally prohibit covenants against competition, restraints on solicitation are likewise not enforceable after employment ceases. *Warner and Company v. Solberg*, 634 N.W.2d 65, 73 (N.D. 2001).

3. What time limitations have courts recognized as reasonable in the franchise context?

- **If no franchise cases have been decided, what time limitations have been recognized in other contexts?**
- **How have they been related to the interests protected?**

North Dakota courts have not addressed the reasonableness of the duration of a restrictive covenant in the franchising context nor in any other context. As discussed earlier, section 9-08-06 generally prohibits covenants against competition of any duration, except in situations involving the sale of the goodwill of a business or the dissolution of a partnership, limited liability company, or corporation. In the context of the sale of goodwill, the statute was amended in 2019 to specify that the restriction must be "for a reasonable length of time." That language does not appear in subsection (2), which deals with the dissolution of an entity.

In cases in which a covenant against competition was permissible under section 9-08-06, the North Dakota Supreme Court has enforced lengthy covenants without addressing whether the time restrictions were reasonable. In *Herman v. Newman Signs, Inc.*, 417 N.W.2d 179 (N.D. 1987), and *Igoe v. Atlas Ready-Mix, Inc.*, 134 N.W.2d 511 (N.D. 1965), both of which involved sales of businesses, the North Dakota Supreme Court upheld restrictive covenants lasting ten years. Similarly, in *Hawkins Chemical, Inc. v. McNea*, 321 N.W.2d 918 (N.D. 1982), which also involved the sale of a business, the North Dakota Supreme Court held that a restrictive covenant lasting nine years was enforceable. In *Lire, Inc. v. Bob's Pizza Inn Restaurants, Inc.*, 541 N.W.2d 432 (N.D. 1995), the court upheld a covenant not to sell Italian-type foods for a period of five years following the sale of a restaurant. In *Kelly v. Kelly*, 806 N.W.2d 133 (N.D. 2011), the court upheld the district court's determination to restrain the business owner's ex-wife from interfering with the operation of the ex-husband's business for five years.

4. What geographic limitations have courts recognized as reasonable in the franchise context?

- **How have they been related to the interests protected?**
- **Have courts recognized the legitimacy of protecting other franchises from competition?**

Section 9-08-06 expressly provides some geographic limitations on the enforcement of covenants not to compete in situations involving the sale of a business and the dissolution of an entity. In cases involving the sale of a business, a covenant against competition is enforceable only "within a reasonable geographic area and for a reasonable length of time, if the buyer or any person deriving title to the goodwill from the buyer carries on a like business in that area." In cases involving the dissolution of a partnership, limited liability company, or corporation, the covenant is enforceable only "within a reasonable geographic area where the partnership, limited liability company, or corporation business has been transacted, or within a specified part of the area."

Prior to the 2019 amendment, North Dakota courts had strictly construed the geographical limitations set forth in section 9-08-06. For example, in *Earthworks,*

Inc. v. Sehn, 553 N.W.2d 490 (N.D. 1996), the North Dakota Supreme Court held that a covenant against competition encompassing the "state of North Dakota" was enforceable only in Burleigh County, the county in which the buyer's business was located. *Id.* at 494. In *Lire, Inc. v. Bob's Pizza Inn Restaurants, Inc.*, 541 N.W.2d 432 (N.D. 1995), the court limited the geographical territory of a non-compete agreement from "within a radius of 60 miles of Rugby" to simply "the city of Rugby." *Id.* at 435. Under the 2019 amendment to section 9-08-06, it appears a court would have more flexibility to permit enforcement of a non-compete in a broader area, provided that the area was reasonable.

5. What limitations on activities have courts recognized as reasonable in the franchise context?

There are no reported North Dakota cases dealing with the reasonableness of limitations on activities in the franchising context. As set forth above, section 9-08-06 permits covenants against competition only in situations involving the sale of the goodwill of a business and the dissolution of a partnership, limited liability company, or corporation.

6. Does the state recognize a difference between in-term and post-term covenants?

In *Warner and Company v. Solberg*, 634 N.W.2d 65 (N.D. 2001), the North Dakota Supreme Court recognized that while section 9-08-06 prohibits an employer from restraining an employee's right to solicit the employer's clients after the termination of the employment relationship, an employee may not solicit an employer's clients for the employee during the employment relationship. The court stated that "soliciting the employer's clients for one's self, without the employer's consent, is contrary to the purpose of N.D.C.C. Section 34-02-14. Such activity, even in the absence of an agreement, constitutes a breach of loyalty entitling [the employer] to 'equitable protection against unfair competition.'" *Id.* at 72.

7. Has the state allowed enforcement of covenants against non-signatories (e.g., family members, newly formed corporations)?

Section 9-08-06 was amended in 2019. As a result of the amendment, a person selling the goodwill of a business and agreeing with a buyer to refrain from carrying a similar business may also include as bound parties "the person's partners, members, or shareholders." It is unclear whether that statute would permit enforcement against non-signatories, but it does appear to make enforcement easier.

In *Kelly v. Kelly*, 806 N.W.2d 133 (N.D. 2011), a covenant not to compete was not directly at issue. However, the court prohibited the wife from competing with the former husband's business under section 9-08-06 as part of the divorce decree. The court concluded that the district court had authority to restrain the former wife's interference with the former husband's business to protect the goodwill of the company. Thus, while the former wife did not sign a covenant not to compete, the court still restrained the former wife from competing with the former husband's insurance business.

8. Will the state modify, "blue-pencil," or otherwise reduce a covenant found to be overbroad?

North Dakota courts will modify covenants in order to enforce compliance with the geographic limitations of section 9-08-06. As set forth above, when a restrictive covenant is enforceable under the statute, a party can be required to refrain from carrying on a similar business within a "reasonable geographic area." Where the restrictive covenant, by its terms, restricts a party in a larger geographic area, the court will modify, but not void, the covenant. *See Earthworks, Inc. v. Sehn*, 553 N.W.2d 490 (N.D. 1996) (covenant modified to restrict seller's activities to single county); *Lire, Inc. v. Bob's Pizza Inn Restaurants, Inc.*, 541 N.W.2d 432 (N.D. 1995) (covenant modified to restrict seller's activities in city of Rugby); *Herman v. Newman Signs, Inc.*, 417 N.W.2d 179 (N.D. 1987) (covenant modified to restrict seller's activities in the county of its principal place of business); *Hawkins Chemical Inc. v. McNea*, 321 N.W.2d 918 (N.D. 1982) (covenant modified to restrict seller's activities in county where its real estate was located); *see also Kelly v. Kelly*, 806 N.W.2d 133 (N.D. 2011) (public policy and legal consistency warranted the district court exercising its authority to distribute marital property in conformity with limitations imposed on contracting parties under section 9-08-06(1), and thus the case was remanded to apply the geographic limitations of section 9-08-06(1) to the restraining order).

9. When does a non-compete period begin to run? Will courts equitably extend the term?

North Dakota does not have any caselaw in the franchise context or in any other context that indicates when the non-compete period begins to run.

10. Are there additional nuances or peculiarities about the state's treatment of covenants in the franchising context?

If the franchise agreement provides that it is to be controlled by the laws of a state other than North Dakota, a North Dakota court may nevertheless apply section 9-08-06 (1987) to limit the effectiveness of a restrictive covenant. *See Osborne v. Brown & Saenger, Inc.*, 904 N.W.2d 34 (N.D. 2017); *Forney Industries v. Andre*, 246 F. Supp. 333 (D.N.D. 1965). Accordingly, if a franchisor is able, while complying with the requirements of jurisdiction and venue, to initiate an action to enforce a restrictive covenant in a state other than North Dakota, it should do so in an attempt to avoid the possible application of the North Dakota statute.

Ohio

*by Judith L. Marsh and Herbert A. Hedden**

1. Has the state addressed covenants against competition in the context of franchising?

- **Does the state have a franchising statute or regulations that address covenants against competition?**
- **Does the state have a covenants statute of general applicability that would encompass franchise covenants?**
- **Have the courts addressed covenants in the context of franchising either under a statute or under the state's common law?**

Ohio has no statute addressing covenants against competition in the franchising context. As a result, Ohio courts have looked to Ohio common law when ruling on the validity of such covenants.

Ohio's antitrust statutes contain the only statutory provisions affecting restrictive covenants. Ohio Rev. Code Ann. §§ 1331.01–1331.14 (West 2017). These statutes, known as the "Valentine Act," prohibit unreasonable restraints of trade and have been applied to restrictive covenants on the grounds that such covenants can be so restrictive that they are unreasonable restraints. The Valentine Act states that a trust, as defined by the Act, is unlawful and void, and defines *trust*, in pertinent part, as:

> a combination of capital, skill, or acts by two or more persons for any of the following purposes:
>
> (a) To create or carry out restrictions in trade or commerce;
>
> (b) To limit or reduce the production, or increase or reduce the price of merchandise or a commodity;
>
> (c) To prevent competition in . . . sale, or purchase of merchandise, produce, or a commodity; . . .
>
> (e) To make, enter into, execute, or carry out contracts, obligations, or agreements of any kind . . . by which they agree to pool, combine, or

*Judith L. Marsh and Herbert A. Hedden are partners in the law firm of Vorys, Sater, Seymour, and Pease LLP in Columbus, Ohio.

> directly or indirectly unite any interests which they have connected with the sale . . . of such article or commodity, that its price might in any manner be affected. . . .

OHIO REV. CODE ANN. § 1331.01(C) (West 2017).

Ohio's Valentine Act was patterned after the Sherman Antitrust Act, and as a consequence, Ohio interprets the Valentine Act in light of the federal construction of the Sherman Act. Although the plain language of Ohio's Valentine Act prohibits any agreement or combination that would "create or carry out restrictions in trade or commerce," Ohio courts follow the "rule of reason," adopted by the federal courts construing the Sherman Act, in interpreting the Valentine Act. *C.K. & J.K., Inc. v. Fairview Shopping Center Corp.*, 63 Ohio St. 2d 201, 205, 407 N.E.2d 507, 508–09 (1980). "When such contracts are incident and ancillary to some lawful business and are not unreasonable in their scope and operation, they are not illegal." *List v. Burley Tobacco Growers' Cooperative Association*, 114 Ohio St. 361, 363, 151 N.E. 471, syllabus (¶ 4) (1926).

There are no reported cases holding that covenants against competition in franchise agreements violate Ohio's Valentine Act. However, an Ohio court has addressed the statute's potential application to covenants against competition in franchise agreements stating, in dicta, "[g]enerally, a covenant not to compete that is ancillary to a business franchise agreement is valid and enforceable and does not constitute an unlawful restraint of trade under R.C. 1331 (Ohio's Valentine Act) only if it is reasonable under the facts and circumstances of the case. The principles applicable to the validity of anti-competitive covenants in general are also applicable to covenants incident to business franchise agreements." *Convenient Food Mart, Inc. v. Con. Inc.*, 1996 WL 635848, at *6 (Ohio Ct. App. Sept. 30, 1996) (citations omitted).[1] In *Interstate Automatic Transmission Co., Inc. v. W. H. McAlpine Co., Inc.*, 1981 WL 2193 (N.D. Ohio June 17, 1981), the U.S. District Court for the Northern District of Ohio, applying Ohio law, stated: "A franchise agreement has some similarities with employment agreements and some similarities with sale of business agreements. Agreements not to compete, entered into in conjunction with termination of employment or sale of the business, are not per se illegal or otherwise unreasonable within the meaning of Section 1 of the Sherman Act if they are reasonable in duration and geographical limitations."

---

1. Under the Ohio Supreme Court Rules for the Reporting of Opinions, all opinions of the courts of appeals issued after May 1, 2002, may be "cited as legal authority and weighted as deemed appropriate by the courts without regard to whether the opinion was published or in what form it was published." Rep. Op. R. 3.4. Although unpublished cases decided prior to May 1, 2002, are not controlling law in Ohio, Ohio courts still find those unpublished cases to be persuasive. *See Cleveland Botanical Garden v. Drewien*, 2020-Ohio-1278, ¶ 47, 153 N.E.3d 700, 712 (Ohio Ct. App. Apr. 2, 2020); *Watson v. Neff*, 2009 WL 1175168, ¶ 16 (Ohio Ct. App. Apr. 29, 2009); *In re B.L.*, 2016 WL 2853575, 2016-Ohio-2982, ¶ 11 (Ohio Ct. App. May 16, 2016).

2. Have the courts articulated the "legitimate interests" of the franchisor that will support enforcement of a covenant against competition contained in a franchise agreement?

- **If so, what are they (e.g., protection of goodwill, protection of confidential information), and in what contexts did the issue arise?**
- **If not, what interests have been recognized in other contexts (e.g., employment agreements, the sale of business context)?**

Ohio courts have held that the following interests of the franchisor will support enforcement of a covenant against competition: "the need to preserve goodwill associated with [the franchisor's] registered names and marks and to protect against unfair competition" (*Matco Tools Corp. v. Urquhart*, 435 F. Supp. 3d 802, 810 (N.D. Ohio 2019)); protection of goodwill developed under a licensed mark and avoidance of customer confusion, the potential damage that may result to the franchisor's trade name and reputation (*Economou v. Physicians Weight Loss Centers of America*, 756 F. Supp. 1024, 1032 (N.D. Ohio 1991)); protection of a competitive advantage arising from the use of a franchisor's methods of operations, even though those methods may not amount to trade secrets (existence of a trade secret is not a prerequisite for a showing that a legitimate interest exists in protecting a franchisor's method of operation, *Discount Muffler Shops, Inc. v. Seely*, 1983 WL 6849, at *2 (Ohio Ct. App. July 1, 1983), court stating, "Although the evidence is insufficient to establish that appellant's method of operation constituted a trade secret, the evidence does indicate that appellant's operations were sufficiently different from those of other muffler installers to provide appellant with a significant competitive edge."); avoiding the difficulties for the franchisor in selling other franchises within that market area and resulting in lost revenue if the former franchisee were permitted to breach the franchise agreement's non-competition provisions without consequence (*ITS Fin., L.L.C. v. Gebre*, 2014 WL 2169606 (Ohio Ct. App. May 23, 2014); and protection against use of a similar name (*Discount Muffler Shops, Inc. v. Seely*, 1983 WL 6849 (Ohio App. Lucas County July 1, 1983)).

OH

In *Discount Muffler Shops, Inc. v. Seely*, 1983 WL 6849, at *2–3 (Ohio Ct. App. July 1, 1983), a former Discount Muffler franchisee was enjoined from operating a competing muffler shop for one year from the date of entry of the court's judgment, and within 25 miles of Toledo, where the franchised shop had been located. The former franchisee was also enjoined by the court from using the name "Viscount Muffler" because of its similarity to the franchisor's "Discount Muffler" trademark. The court stated its view that the former franchisee's use of the name "Viscount Muffler," along with the franchisee's continued operation in the same location as the franchised business, constituted "an attempt to capitalize on the good will created under the Discount Muffler franchise." 1983 WL 6849, at *2–3 (the trial court had denied the franchisor's request for injunctive relief; appellate court modified the franchise agreement's post-termination non-competition provision's time limitation (three years) and geographic limitation (75 miles) to one year and 25 miles).

Ohio law also recognizes a franchisor's legitimate business interest in enforcement of non-competition covenants as protecting the survival of the franchisor's business itself. In *Economou v. Physicians Weight Loss Centers of America*, 756 F. Supp. 1024 (N.D. Ohio 1991), franchisees operating weight-loss centers in four locations in New Jersey sought a preliminary injunction to prevent the franchisor from enforcing the covenant not to compete contained within the franchise agreement. The district court, applying Ohio law, noted that the most important business interest at stake was the "survival of the business itself" and quoted testimony of the franchisor's executive vice president regarding the importance of the enforceability of the franchise agreement's covenant against competition to the survival of the franchise system. *Id.* at 1032–33. *See also H.H. Franchising Sys., Inc. v. Aronson*, 2015 WL 401343 (S.D. Ohio 2015).

The existence of an actual threat to a franchisor's ability to compete in the market area at issue may be a prerequisite to an Ohio court's enforcement of a covenant against competition. In *Physicians Weight Loss Centers of America v. Creighton*, 1992 WL 176992 (N.D. Ohio Mar. 30, 1992), the court, applying Ohio law, stated that "[a]s a threshold matter, we believe it sound to require the existence of an actual threat to *existing* competition before a non-compete covenant may be enforced." *Id.* at 24,517. In *Creighton*, the franchisor had no centers in operation within the area in New Hampshire covered by the covenant against competition at the time the franchisor was seeking enforcement of the covenant. The court rejected the franchisor's argument that the lack of existing competition was due to the franchisee's wrongful acts, explaining that for the court "to uphold the reasonableness of the noncompetition clause based upon a conjecture that the franchisor *might* have been able to compete but for certain behavior of the franchisee would be an unwarranted exercise in judicial guesswork. . . ." *Id.* at 24,517–18. In granting partial summary judgment dismissing the franchisor's request for injunctive relief to enforce the non-competition covenant against the franchisee, the *Creighton* court held that "in all cases the existence of an actual, real threat to competition" is required before the reasonableness of a non-compete covenant can be upheld. *Id.* at 24,518.

3. What time limitations have courts recognized as reasonable in the franchise context?

- **If no franchise cases have been decided, what time limitations have been recognized in other contexts?**
- **How have they been related to the interests protected?**

In *Stoner v. Salon Lofts, L.L.C.*, 2012 WL 2928671 (Ohio Ct. App. July 19, 2012), the court affirmed the judgment of the trial court in enforcing the terms of an "Agreement of Owners of Franchise" against the franchisee providing for a non-competition period of two years and blocking the franchisee from opening competing businesses within a territory consisting of 11 specified counties.

A non-competition covenant in a franchise agreement having a time limitation of two years was found by a federal district court to be reasonable as a matter of law in *Petland, Inc. v. Hendrix*, 2004 WL 3406089 (S.D. Ohio Sept. 14, 2004).

In *Discount Muffler Shops, Inc. v. Seely*, 1983 WL 6849, at *3 (Ohio Ct. App. July 1, 1983), the court enforced a modified one-year post-termination covenant against competition with a 25-mile geographic limitation, commencing upon the date of the judgment, against a franchisee who wrongfully terminated his agreement with his franchisor, stating that it found "that some restrictions prohibiting [the franchisee] from competing with [the franchisor] is [sic] reasonably necessary to protect [the franchisor's] legitimate interests." *Id.* The original covenant prohibited the franchisee from competing with the franchisor within a 75-mile radius of Toledo for a period of three years after termination of the franchise agreement. In finding that enforcing the non-competition covenant was reasonably necessary to protect the franchisor's legitimate interests, the court cited the following: (1) the franchisor had provided the franchisee with initial financing for the business and offered continuing assistance with building the business, (2) the franchisor's operating system was sufficiently different from those of competitors to provide a significant competitive edge, and (3) the franchisee had sole direct contact with customers of the business. The court justified its reductions in the duration and geographic limitation, citing the balancing of the interests of the franchisor and franchisee.

A federal district court applying Ohio law to non-competition covenants in the franchise context refused to enforce two covenants against competition containing temporal restrictions of one year and two years based on the franchisor's inability to show the reasonableness of the time or area of the restrictions. *American Nursing Care of Toledo, Inc. v. Leisure*, 609 F. Supp. 419 (N.D. Ohio 1984). The court found that covenants restricting the business of providing temporary nursing services were unreasonable in light of the undue hardship imposed on the franchisees and undue interference with the franchisees' right to make a living. The court noted that the franchisor's competing nursing facilities were not existing enterprises in the markets of the franchised businesses until after the franchisees had breached the agreement.

Other Ohio decisions in the franchise context indicate that when the franchisor's legitimate interests are found to merit protection, one-year time restrictions are reasonable. In *Interstate Automatic Transmission Co., Inc. v. W.H. McAlpine Co., Inc.*, 1981 WL 746483 (N.D. Ohio June 17, 1981), the U.S. District Court for the Northern District of Ohio, applying Ohio law, found a one-year restriction to be reasonable in the context of a franchise agreement, although the court did not enforce the covenant not to compete, in part because the geographical restrictions were found to be greater than necessary to protect the franchisor's interests. The franchisor in this case had no operations at the time of the termination within the restricted Toledo market with which the former franchisee would be in competition, and the court, strictly construing the non-competition covenant, stated that "[a]t the time of termination the covenant was incapable of enforcement because there was no violation of the clear terms of the covenant." *See H.H. Franchising Sys., Inc. v. Aronson*, 2015 WL 401343 (S.D. Ohio Jan. 28, 2015) (enjoining the franchisee for one year from competing with the franchisor within the franchisee's territory); *Relo Franchise Serv., Inc., v. Gilman*, 2018 WL 7288084 (S.D. Ohio 2018) (granting in favor of franchisor a preliminary injunction for one year following termination of the franchise).

Economou v. Physicians Weight Loss Centers of America, 756 F. Supp. 1024 (N.D. Ohio 1991), involved covenants against competition contained in two franchise agreements, one with a one-year duration and another with a three-year duration. The court found the one-year duration to be reasonable and applied it to both of the covenants, stating that no evidence was presented to support the longer three-year restriction for one of the two locations, and that the one-year durational limit for covenants against competition has often been upheld in Ohio in the employment context. The court wrote that the franchisor was protecting a legitimate business interest—survival of the business of the franchisor—in seeking to enforce the non-competition covenant. The court justified its modification of the time limitation in one of the franchise agreements from three years to one year by citing the balancing of interests of the franchisor and franchisee and stating that it could "ascertain no reason for the three-year limit." *Id.* at 1033–34.

Many of the decisions by Ohio courts dealing with covenants against competition have been in the employment context, and these decisions are frequently cited by Ohio courts dealing with covenants in the franchise context. In *Briggs v. Butler*, 140 Ohio St. 499, 511, 45 N.E.2d 757, 763 (1942) (overruled on other grounds),[2] the Ohio Supreme Court reversed the court of appeals and found a five-year restriction imposed by a covenant against competition in the employment context to be enforceable. *See Hamilton Insurance Services, Inc. v. Nationwide Insurance Companies*, 86 Ohio St. 3d 270, 274–75, 714 N.E.2d 898, 901–02 (1999) (Ohio Supreme Court reversed court of appeals' decision and enforced a covenant against competition in a corporate agency agreement between an employee/insurance agent and an employer/insurance company that prohibited competition by the employee within one year of termination).

As a general matter, time restrictions imposed by covenants against competition are reviewed by Ohio courts on a case-by-case basis, and decisions are often based upon factual distinctions. *See Extine v. Williamson Midwest, Inc.*, 176 Ohio St. 403, 405, 200 N.E.2d 297, syllabus (¶ 1) (1964) (overruled on other grounds)[3] ("In determining the validity of a covenant or agreement in restraint of trade, each case must be decided on its own facts, and a reasonable balance must be maintained among the interests of employers, employees, and the public."); *Briggs v. Butler*, 140 Ohio St. 499, 510, 45 N.E.2d 757, 762 (1942) ("[u]nquestionably the decision of every case of this nature turns upon and in great measure is governed by its own peculiar facts.").

---

4. What geographic limitations have courts recognized as reasonable in the franchise context?

- **How have they been related to the interests protected?**
- **Have courts recognized the legitimacy of protecting other franchisees from competition?**

In *Stoner v. Salon Lofts, L.L.C.*, 2012 WL 2928671 (Ohio Ct. App. July 19, 2012), the court affirmed the judgment of the trial court in enforcing the terms of an "Agreement of Owners of Franchise" against the franchisee opening competing businesses within a territory consisting of 11 specified counties during a non-competition period of two years.

In *H.H. Franchising Sys., Inc. v. Aronson*, 2015 WL 401343 (S.D. Ohio 2015), the federal district court granted the franchisor's motion for summary judgment against the defendant franchisee, enjoining the franchisee for one year from competing with the franchisor within the area including seven postal zip codes that constituted the franchise territories.

In *Discount Muffler Shops, Inc. v. Seely*, 1983 WL 6849 (Ohio Ct. App. July 1, 1983), the court reduced a geographic restriction contained in a non-competition covenant in a franchise agreement from the area within 75 miles of Toledo to the area within 25 miles of Toledo. The *Discount Muffler Shops* court cited the reasoning of the Ohio Supreme Court in *Raimonde v. Van Vlerah*, 42 Ohio St. 2d 21, 26, 325 N.E.2d 544, 545 (1975), a case in the employment context in which the court held

---

2. In *Briggs* and *Extine*, the Ohio Supreme Court applied the "blue-pencil" test to construe an employment agreement. As discussed in section 8 of this chapter, the court in *Raimonde v. Van Vlerah*, 42 Ohio St. 2d. 21, 325 N.E.2d 544 (1975), abandoned the "blue-pencil" test in favor of a "rule of reasonableness."

3. *See* note 2, *supra*.

that "a covenant not to compete which imposes unreasonable restrictions upon an employee will be enforced to the extent necessary to protect the employer's legitimate interests." Such a restraint is reasonable if "[it] is no greater than is required for the protection of the employer, does not impose an undue hardship on the employee, and is not injurious to the public." *Id.* The *Discount Muffler Shops* court stated that it was balancing the interests of the franchisor with those of the franchisee in reducing the area subject to the geographic restriction. 1983 WL 6849, at *3 (Ohio Ct. App. July 1, 1983)

In *Interstate Automatic Transmission Co., Inc. v. W.H. McAlpine Co., Inc.*, 1981 WL 2193 (N.D. Ohio June 17, 1981), the court noted that other cases had upheld much greater territorial restrictions and found that the prohibition of competition by the former franchisee within a ten-mile radius of the franchisee's former location was not an unreasonable geographic restriction. However, the court strictly construed the language of the covenant (providing that the franchisee would not "compete" in the area) to require the franchisor or its other franchisees to be operating within the area restricted by the covenant at the time of the termination in order for the covenant to be operative. Because neither the franchisor nor any of its other franchisees operated businesses within the portion of the Toledo market to which the non-competition provision applied at the time of the termination, the court found that there was no violation of the covenant. The court rejected the franchisor's argument that if an Interstate Automatic Transmission shop were subsequently opened within the restricted area, the covenant would then come into force, requiring the former franchisee to close its doors. The court also found that it would be unreasonable to enforce a further restriction against competition by the former franchisee within a ten-mile radius of other businesses operated by the franchisor or its franchisees in markets other than the Toledo market.

In general, Ohio courts have limited the geographic scope of a covenant not to compete to the area in which the former franchisee or former employee carried on business activities, or in which the former franchisor or former employer continued to operate. *See Interstate Automatic Transmission*, at 12,707.

A non-competition covenant in a franchising agreement providing a geographic limitation within a radius of 15 miles of the outer boundaries of the franchisee's exclusive territory was found by a federal district court to be reasonable as a matter of law in *Petland, Inc. v. Hendrix*, 2004 WL 3406089 (S.D. Ohio Sept. 14, 2004).

Similarly, in *Economou v. Physician's Weight Loss Centers of America*, 756 F. Supp. 1024, 1034 (N.D. Ohio 1991), the court found that a 50-mile geographic restriction (centered upon the location of the franchised business) contained in a franchise agreement was reasonable, while noting that there was no testimony by either the franchisor or the franchisee on the issue of the reasonableness of the restriction.

Cases involving the refusal by a court to enforce geographic restrictions in non-competition covenants include *Convenient Food Mart, Inc. v. Con. Inc.*, 1996 WL 635848 (Ohio Ct. App. Sept. 30, 1996), in which the court declined to enforce a restriction preventing the former franchisee from establishing a competing business within a two-and-a-half-mile distance from the formerly franchised business, citing severe hardships to the former franchisee and the public, as well as the court's determination that the franchisor was undeserving of the court's equitable relief, and *American Nursing Care of Toledo, Inc. v. Leisure*, 609 F. Supp. 419, 432 (N.D. Ohio 1984), in which a federal district court applying Ohio law held that geographic limitations of 10 miles and 100 miles, in separate franchise agreements, were unreasonable restrictions imposing an undue hardship upon the franchisee and undue interference with the franchisee's right to make a living.

5. What limitations on activities have courts recognized as reasonable in the franchise context?

Ohio courts have upheld restrictions prohibiting a former franchisee from engaging in a competing business. *Dealer Specialties, Inc. v. Car Data 24/7, Inc.*, 2016 WL 5341797 (S.D. Ohio 2016) (court granting injunction against franchisee from competing with franchisor within the franchisee's territory, or within 20 miles of the franchisee's territory, or within 20 miles of the territory granted to other franchisees or the territory of franchisor or its affiliates selling similar products or services); *Discount Muffler Shops, Inc. v. Seely*, 1983 WL 6849 (Ohio Ct. App. July 1, 1983); *Economou v. Physicians Weight Loss Centers*, 756 F. Supp. 1024 (N.D. Ohio 1991).

Restrictions prohibiting the adoption of a deceptively similar name by a former franchisee have also been upheld. *Discount Muffler Shops, Inc. v. Seely*, 1983 WL 6849 (Ohio App. Lucas County July 1, 1983) (franchisee could not use the name "Viscount Muffler," as it amounted to capitalizing on the franchisor's goodwill created under the "Discount Muffler" name).

6. Does the state recognize a difference between in-term and post-term covenants?

Ohio has not addressed this issue in the franchise context.

7. Has the state allowed enforcement of covenants against non-signatories (e.g., family members, newly formed corporations)?

An Ohio court may grant relief if the non-signatory to a covenant against competition acts in concert with the signatory to the covenant and the party that is the intended beneficiary of the covenant is harmed by the resulting unfair competition. *Standard Oil Co. v. Landmark Farm Bureau Cooperative*, 52 Ohio App. 2d 225, 263, 369 N.E.2d 785, 792 (1976). In *Standard Oil Co.*, a post-term non-competition covenant was contained in an agreement for the distribution of heating oil and other Sohio petroleum products. An injunction against dealing with the distributor's former customers for Sohio products was granted against one of the distributor's former employees (the distributor's son), as well as against the company distributing petroleum products in competition with the distributor that subsequently hired the distributor's son.

8. Will the state modify, "blue-pencil," or otherwise reduce a covenant found to be overbroad?

Raimonde v. Van Vlerah, 42 Ohio St. 2d. 21, 325 N.E.2d 544 (1975), is the seminal case with respect to the modification of covenants against competition in Ohio. The Ohio Supreme Court in *Raimonde* held that "a covenant not to compete which imposes unreasonable restrictions upon an employee will be enforced to the extent necessary to protect the employer's legitimate interests." *Id.* at 25–26, 325 N.E.2d at 547; *see also Lake Land Employment Group of Akron, LLC v. Columber*, 101 Ohio St. 3d 242, 248, 804 N.E.2d 27, 33 (2004) (employment case reaffirming *Raimonde*). The *Raimonde* decision empowers Ohio courts to modify or amend agreements in order to fashion restrictions that would be reasonable between the parties and enables the courts to evaluate all the factors comprising "reasonableness" in the context of employee covenants. The Ohio Supreme Court followed *Raimonde* in *Rogers v. Runfola & Associates Inc.*, 57 Ohio St. 3d 5, 565 N.E.2d 540 (1991), a case involving a covenant against competition in the employment context in which the court modified both the timing and geographic limitations in the covenant. Regarding the evaluation of "reasonableness," the federal district court in *Physicians Weight Loss Centers of America v. Creighton*, 1992 WL 176992 (N.D. Ohio Mar. 30, 1992), wrote that "a court reviewing the covenant should keep in mind the fact-specific, case-by-case nature of the issue regarding the covenant's reasonableness."

Prior to the Ohio Supreme Court's decision in *Raimonde*, Ohio courts utilized the "blue-pencil" test to construe covenants against competition. The "blue-pencil" test provided that if unreasonable provisions existed in a contract, they might be stricken if divisible, but not amended or modified. *Raimonde*, 325 N.E.2d at 546. Further, the "blue-pencil" test provided that if restrictions were unreasonable and indivisible, the entire contract must fail. *See also Briggs v. Butler*, 140 Ohio St. 499, 45 N.E.2d 757 (1942); *Extine v. Williamson Midwest, Inc.*, 176 Ohio St. 403, 200 N.E.2d 297 (1964). In its *Raimonde* opinion, the Ohio Supreme Court abandoned the "blue-pencil" test in favor of a "rule of reasonableness," which permits courts to determine, on the basis of all available evidence, the restrictions that would be reasonable between the parties. *Raimonde*, 325 N.E.2d at 547.

In the franchise context, other courts have followed the Ohio Supreme Court's decision in *Raimonde* in numerous decisions, including *Economou v. Physicians Weight Loss Centers of America*, 756 F. Supp 1024, 1031 (N.D. Ohio 1991); *Discount Muffler Shops, Inc. v. Seely*, 1983 WL 6849, at *2 (Ohio Ct. App. July 1, 1983); *Physicians Weight Loss Centers of America v. Creighton*, 1992 WL 176992 (N.D. Ohio Mar. 30, 1992); *Convenient Food Mart, Inc. v. Con. Inc.*, 1996 WL 635848 (Ohio Ct. App. Sept. 30, 1996); and *Interstate Automatic Transmission Co, Inc. v. W.H. McAlpine Co., Inc.*, 1981 WL 2193 (N.D. Ohio June 17, 1981).

9. When does a non-compete period begin to run? Will courts equitably extend the term?

In the employment context and in the franchising context, Ohio courts will often deprive the party failing to comply with a covenant against competition of the advantages resulting from delay inherent in the litigation process, and will grant an injunction for the full term stated in the covenant, or for the modified period deemed reasonable by the court, effective from the date of judgment.

In *Rogers v. Runfola & Associates, Inc.*, 57 Ohio St. 3d 5, 565 N.E.2d 540 (1991), both the trial and appellate courts had ruled that the covenants against competition applicable to the employees were unenforceable and, accordingly, refused to issue an injunction. The Supreme Court of Ohio, following *Raimonde v. Van Vlerah*, 42 Ohio St. 21, 325 N.E.2d 544 (1975), after modifying the temporal and geographic limitations of the covenants, issued an injunction for a one-year period to take effect 60 days after the court's order, notwithstanding the expiration during the course of the litigation of the period stated in the covenant provision. *Rogers*, 57 Ohio St. 3d 5, at 9. The Ohio Supreme Court remanded the case to the trial court for a determination of the damages, if any, caused by the employees by disregarding the covenants not to compete, as modified.

In *Raimonde*, although the former employer sought injunctive relief for three years from the date of the employee's termination, the trial court enjoined the employee for three years from the date of the trial court's order. The Ohio Supreme Court found such a result to be entirely proper. 42 Ohio St. 2d. at 28. *See also Economou v. Physicians Weight Loss Centers of America*, 756 F. Supp. 1024 (N.D. Ohio 1991) (court reduced a three-year post-term covenant against competition to one year in granting a preliminary injunction in favor of the franchisor); *Discount Muffler Shops, Inc. v. Seely*, 1983 WL 6849 (Ohio Ct. App. July 1, 1983) (the injunction and time limitation was for a period of one year from the date of entry of the appellate court's judgment).

---

10. Are there additional nuances or peculiarities about the state's treatment of covenants in the franchising context?

Under Ohio law, "the party seeking enforcement of the covenant [against competition] bears the burden of establishing its reasonableness by clear and convincing evidence." *Physicians Weight Loss Centers of America v. Creighton*, 1992 WL 176992 (N.D. Ohio Mar. 30, 1992) (citing *Levine v. Beckman*, 48 Ohio App. 3d 24, 27 (Ohio Ct. App. 1988)).

Covenants against competition are to be strictly construed by Ohio courts. *Physicians Weight Loss Centers of America v. Creighton*, 1992 WL 176992 (N.D. Ohio Mar. 30, 1992). *See also Interstate Automatic Transmission Co., Inc. v. W. H. McAlpine Co., Inc.*, 1981 WL 746483 (N.D. Ohio June 17, 1981) (the court, strictly construing the non-competition provision, stated that "[a]t the time of termination the covenant was incapable of enforcement because there was no violation of the clear terms of the covenant.").

In *D.P. Dough Franchising, LLC v. Southworth*, 2017 WL 4315013 (S.D. Ohio 2017), an Ohio federal district court considered a franchise agreement that included both a non-competition covenant as well as a provision prohibiting the diversion of business by the franchisee. The court stated that under Ohio law a non-diversion provision is akin to other restrictive covenants and would analyze both provisions under the standards set forth in the *Raimonde* and *Rogers* opinions. The non-diversion provision restricted the franchisee from diverting or attempting to divert any business or customer from any D.P. Dough restaurant during the three years after termination of the franchise. The court found that the non-diversion provision was unclear regarding whether it applied only to restaurants open at the time that the franchise was terminated or also applied to restaurants opened during the three-year restrictive period. With regard to the ambiguous provision, the court decided that it applied only to restaurants operating before the franchisee began operating its competing business.

A federal district court, applying Ohio law, held that a restaurant franchisor that was a third-party beneficiary of a franchise agreement executed by its terminated subfranchisor and a subfranchisee could enforce the non-competition covenant (as well as other provisions of the franchise agreement) against the subfranchisee.

Kitchen Investment Group Inc. v. Buchtel Food, Inc., 2004 WL 7204389 (N.D. Ohio Jan. 8, 2004). The court found that the express language of the covenant demonstrated that the non-competition provisions were meant to benefit the franchisor, notwithstanding that the franchisor was not a party to the franchise agreement.

Finally, it has long been the rule in Ohio that a plaintiff in equity must come to the court with clean hands. Thus, a franchisor desiring to enforce a covenant against competition and seeking equitable relief against a franchisee "must be deserving of such relief, and a court sitting in equity will not issue an injunction to aide a wrongdoer . . . or allow a party to exploit his own negligence." *Convenient Food Mart, Inc. v. Con. Inc.*, 1996 WL 635848, at *7 (Ohio Ct. App. Sept. 30, 1996).

Oklahoma

By Donald A. Burleson*

1. Has the state addressed covenants against competition in the context of franchising?

- **Does the state have a franchising statute or regulations that address covenants against competition?**
- **Does the state have a covenants statute of general applicability that would encompass franchise covenants?**
- **Have the courts addressed covenants in the context of franchising either under a statute or under the state's common law?**

Oklahoma does not have a franchising statute or franchise regulations, and therefore has no law or regulation specifically addressing covenants against competition in the context of franchising.

The Oklahoma legislature has adopted statutory provisions addressing contracts in restraint of trade, which have been applied in the context of covenants against competition. As part of its general antitrust statutory law, Oklahoma statutes provide:

> Every act, agreement, contract, or combination in the form of a trust, or otherwise, or conspiracy in restraint of trade or commerce within this state is hereby declared to be against public policy and illegal.

OKLA. STAT. tit. 79, § 203 (effective July 1, 1998).

This provision was part of the Oklahoma Antitrust Reform Act and replaced certain repealed antitrust provisions previously found at section 1 of the same title. The language of both the new and repealed sections is virtually identical (and therefore has been applicable since before Oklahoma statehood), so pre-1998 caselaw is instructive. On its face section 203 might seem to prohibit all contracts that restrain trade in any way. However, the provision it replaced was interpreted by Oklahoma courts, following applicable precedent interpreting antitrust statutes under a "rule of reason," to prohibit only *unreasonable* restraints of trade. *See, e.g., Crown Paint Co. v. Bankston*, 1981 OK 4, 640 P.2d 948 (Okla. 1981), *cert. denied*, 455 U.S. 946 (1982).

*Mr. Burleson is a licensed Texas lawyer, member of the Texas Bar Association, and President of Burleson Consulting, LLC. This chapter was prepared incorporating previous works of the author and the previous edition of this publication, including portions authored by Nancy Glisan Gourley.

In addition to the provisions in Title 79, Oklahoma statutes regarding unlawful contracts contain a section in Title 15 entitled "Restraint of Trade Void." This section provides:

> Every contract by which any one [sic] is restrained from exercising a lawful profession, trade or business of any kind, otherwise than as provided by Sections 218 and 219 of this title, or otherwise than as provided by [a new Section 219A, added in 2001], is to that extent void.

OKLA. STAT. tit. 15, § 217 (as amended effective June 4, 2001).

Section 218 provides an exception to the provisions of section 217 for covenants ancillary to the sale of goodwill of a business. *See* OKLA. STAT. tit. 15, § 218 (as amended effective June 3, 1989). It states that a seller of the goodwill of a business may agree with the buyer "to refrain from carrying on a similar business within a specified county and any county or counties contiguous thereto, or a specified city or town or any part thereof, so long as the buyer, or any person deriving title to the goodwill from him carries on a like business therein." *Id.* It goes on to specifically permit "blue-penciling" of overly broad territorial restrictions. *Id.* Section 218 has been interpreted by courts applying Oklahoma law in the franchise context.

Section 219 provides an exception to the provisions of section 217 in relation to the dissolution of a partnership. *See* OKLA. STAT. tit. 15, § 219 (as amended effective June 3, 1989). It has not been interpreted by courts applying Oklahoma law in the franchise context.

Section 219A relates to non-compete provisions in employment contracts, providing:

> A person who makes an agreement with an employer, whether in writing or verbally, not to compete with the employer after the employment relationship has been terminated, shall be permitted to engage in the same business as that conducted by the former employer or in a similar business as that conducted by the former employer as long as the former employee does not directly solicit the sale of goods, services or a combination of goods and services from the established customers of the former employer.
>
> Any provision in a contract between an employer and an employee in conflict with the provisions of this section shall be void and unenforceable.

OKLA. STAT. tit. 15, § 219A (added effective June 4, 2001).

Section 219B relates to non-solicitation of employees provisions, providing:

> A contract or contractual provision which prohibits an employee or independent contractor of a person or business from soliciting, directly or indirectly, actively or inactively, the employees or independent contractors of that person or business to become employees or independent contractors of another person or business shall not be construed as a restraint from exercising a lawful profession, trade or business of any kind. Sections 217, 218, 219 and 219A of Title 15 of the Oklahoma Statutes shall not apply to such contracts or contractual provisions.

OKLA. STAT. tit. 15, § 219B (added effective Nov. 1, 2013).

As with the antitrust statutes, Oklahoma courts have interpreted the provisions of section 217 more narrowly than its bare wording, holding that only unreasonable restraints are prohibited. *See, e.g., Bayly, Martin & Fay, Inc. v. Pickard*, 1989 OK 122,

780 P.2d 1168 (Okla. 1989); *Crown Paint*, 640 P.2d 948; *Tatum v. Colonial Life & Accident Insurance Co. of America*, 1970 OK 27, 465 P. 2d 448 (Okla. 1970); *Cardiovascular Surgical Specialists, Corporation v. Mammana*, 2002 OK 27, 61 P.3d 210 (Okla. 2002), *rehearing denied* 2003; *Loewen Group Acquisition Corporation v. Matthews*, 2000 OK Civ. App. 109, 12 P. 3d 977 (Okla. Civ. App. 2000), *released for publication, and cases cited therein; Oliver v. Omnicare, Inc.*, 2004 OK Civ. App. 93, 103 P.3d 626 (Okla. Civ. App. 2004) *released for publication; Vanguard Environmental, Inc. v. Curler*, 2008 OK Civ. App. 57, 190 P.3d 1158 (Okla. Civ. App. 2008), *released for publication, as corrected.*

There are no reported decisions from Oklahoma courts addressing covenants against competition in the franchise context. In the dealership context, the Oklahoma Supreme Court upheld an in-term covenant prohibiting a manufacturer from competing in a dealer's exclusive territory. *Crown Paint*, 640 P.2d at 951.

Two different federal courts applying Oklahoma law have upheld covenants against competition in the franchise context. The federal district court in *Domino's Pizza, Inc. v. El-Tan, Inc., et al.*, 1995 WL 367893 (N.D. Okla. Apr. 28, 1995) interpreted the "goodwill" exception of section 218 to apply to franchise contracts. By entering a preliminary injunction, it enforced a one-year post-term covenant prohibiting direct or indirect involvement in any carryout or delivery pizza store business within ten miles of the premises of the terminated franchise location. In so doing, the court determined that it was likely that Oklahoma courts would find the covenant valid under section 218. The court also determined that the provisions would be valid under section 217. A different federal court declined to apply the reasoning of *Domino's Pizza* related to section 218. *See Express Services, Inc. v. Averette*, 2007 WL 1888652 (W.D. Okla. June 29, 2007). That court found that in the absence of any decision by an Oklahoma court applying it in this context, section 218 should be strictly construed. *Id.* at *6. The court looked to a literal reading of the statute to find that section 218 applied only to restrictions on sellers of goodwill (such as the franchisor) but not to buyers of goodwill (such as the franchisee). *Id.* at *5. Instead, the court applied the general provisions of section 217 to grant in part a motion for summary judgment by the franchisor seeking enforcement of the covenants. *Id.* In the *Express Services* case, the franchisee started a new competing temporary employment business using individuals who had applied with or worked for the franchised location and placing them for temporary employment with customers of the former franchised location. *Id.* at *3. The federal district court granted summary judgment in part, approving an in-term restriction on a former temporary employment service franchisee as written and blue-penciling an overly broad post-term restriction. *See id.* at *4–5. The court reasoned that the in-term restriction that prohibited the franchisee from engaging in any business that competed with the franchisor protected the franchisor against unfair competition by prohibiting the franchisee from "using his position and/or knowledge to assist a competing business while in association with [franchisor]" and was thus "in harmony with Oklahoma law." *Id.* at *4. However, it found the post-term covenant's restrictions on "indirect" solicitation and accepting voluntary, unsolicited contact from former associates, as well as the geographic restriction, overly broad. *Id.* at *4–5. It thus struck the offending provisions. The surviving modified provision prohibited the franchisee, for 18 months from the date of termination or expiration of the franchise agreement, from "directly soliciting former clients, associates, or job applicants" within the geographic area previously assigned to franchisee. *Id.* at *5.

The section 217 reasoning of the court in *Express Services* was consistent with decisions of Oklahoma courts when applying section 217 in the employment context. Although the particular restrictions in section 219A might require a slightly different analysis in post-2001 contracts in the employment context, the general treatment of covenants against competition in employment cases under section 217 is instructive. In that context, Oklahoma courts, at least prior to the enactment of section 219A, have generally found that "reasonable restraints that protect against *unfair* competition will be enforced." *Loewen Group, supra* at 980. A "reasonable" restraint is one that "(1) is no greater than is required for the employer's protection from unfair competition; (2) does not impose undue hardship on the employee; and, (3) is not injurious to the public." *Id.* In *Key Temporary Personnel, Inc. v. Cox*, 1994 OK Civ. App. 123, 884 P.2d 1213 (Okla. Civ. App. 1994), *released for publication*, the Oklahoma Court of Civil Appeals applied the "reasonableness" test to uphold a provision prohibiting a former employee from "directly or indirectly" soliciting, diverting, or attempting to solicit or divert "any client of the Company." *Id.* at 1214.

Another division of the Oklahoma Court of Civil Appeals upheld a provision in which an employee agreed "not to contract with, for or by any group, agency, client and/or entity contracting with or served by [Hedges] for a period of two (2) years after termination of employment with [Hedges]." *Thane A. Hedges Regional Speech and Hearing Center, Inc. v. Baughman*, 1998 OK Civ. App. 122, 996 P.2d 939, 940 (Okla. Civ. App. 1998), *released for publication*.

The Oklahoma Supreme Court utilized a reasonableness test in applying section 217 to an employment agreement in *Cardiovascular Surgical Specialists, supra.* The court upheld a one-year non-solicitation restriction that permitted patients to self-select the former employee, but struck down a two-year ban on practice in the same specialty in a 20-mile radius of the employer's offices and a nine-month ban on accepting referrals from other physicians. *See Cardiovascular Surgical Specialists*, 61 P.3d at 215. In striking down the two restrictions, the court did not rely on the mere fact that the employee was a physician, but in striking down the practice restriction, it did reason that, due to the distance to the nearest alternative hospital, the employee would effectively be required to change specialties in order to remain in practice. The court found this unreasonable. *Id.* at 214. In addition, in analyzing the ban on accepting referrals, the court recognized that within the medical profession, doctors make referrals to other doctors, not to corporations, based upon the reputation of the doctor to whom the patient is being referred. Applying this rationale, the court found that the former employer had no legitimate interest in the former employee's referral base and the restriction on referrals was therefore unreasonable. *Id.*

---

2. Have the courts articulated the "legitimate interests" of the franchisor that will support enforcement of a covenant against competition contained in a franchise agreement?

- **If so, what are they (e.g., protection of goodwill, protection of confidential information), and in what contexts did the issue arise?**
- **If not, what interests have been recognized in other contexts (e.g., employment agreements, the sale of business context)?**

The interests of a franchisor that will support enforcement of a covenant against competition contained in a franchise agreement were addressed by two federal district courts sitting in diversity in unpublished opinions applying Oklahoma law. In

Domino's Pizza, Inc. v. El-Tan, Inc., et al., 1995 WL 367893 (N.D. Okla. Apr. 28, 1995), the court upheld a covenant against competition based on the franchisor's interest in its goodwill. The court applied Okla. Stat. tit. 15, § 218, finding as a matter of fact that "the franchise agreements constitute a sale of Domino's goodwill for the duration of the franchise agreements." *Id.* at *2. The court acknowledged that other states, including California, have reached other conclusions, but found that split of authority unpersuasive. *Id.* at *9. The court described Domino's goodwill as having accrued over its history of operating or franchising approximately 5,000 pizza carryout or delivery stores worldwide and extensively advertising the company's brand. *Id.* at *2. The court held that section 218 specifically permitted restrictions against competition in connection with the sale of goodwill (*Id.* at *9) and that an Oklahoma court would likely find the covenant not to compete valid under section 218. *Id.* at *10. It also held that, even if the covenant were not considered connected with a sale of goodwill, it would be valid under Okla. Stat. tit. § 217 and the cases decided thereunder as a reasonable restriction on the exercise of a lawful profession. *Id.*

More recently, a different federal district court declined to find section 218 applicable to a franchise agreement, but nonetheless upheld a modified version of a post-term covenant against competition in a franchise agreement by applying section 217. *Express Services, Inc. v. Averette*, 2007 WL 1888652 (W.D. Okla. June 29, 2007). In that case, a worldwide temporary personnel services franchisor was granted protection against direct solicitation by the former franchisee of former clients, associates, or job applicants, in order to protect the franchisor's interest in preventing "unfair competition" through "direct inducement" of business to a competitor. *Id.* at *4. In striking down restrictions on "indirect inducements," the court intended to protect the interests of third parties who might wish to voluntarily do business with the former franchisee. *Id.* at *5.

In *Smoot v. B & J Restoration Services, Inc.*, 2012 OK Civ. App. 58, 279 P.3d 805 (Okla. Civ. App. 2012), officers of a ServPro franchisee were determined to be personally liable for breach of a non-compete provision contained in a purchase agreement under section 218, despite the fact that such officers executed the purchase agreement at issue in only their corporate capacity. In so holding, the court recognized the obligation not to compete, as set forth in the purchase agreement, also extended to each officer, director, and shareholder or other owner or partner of the ServPro franchisee. *Id.*

Outside the franchise context, in interpreting the general restrictions of section 217 and the exceptions to it found in sections 218, 219, and 219A, to protect against unfair competition and give the employer the benefit of relationships with customers built up over the years, Oklahoma courts and federal courts applying Oklahoma law have enforced "hands off" covenants in employment-related agreements, protecting specific types of activity in which the employer is engaged, specific geographic areas in which the employer actually operates, goodwill of the employer, and specific clients or customers of the employer, or some combination of these categories. *See, e.g., Tatum v. Colonial Life & Accident Insurance Co. of America*, 1970 OK 27, 465 P.2d 448 (Okla. 1970); *Key Temporary Personnel, Inc. v. Cox*, 1994 OK Civ. App. 123, 884 P.2d 1213 (Okla. Civ. App. 1994); *Inergy Propane LLC v. Lundy*, 2009 OK Civ. App. 8, 219 P.3d 547 (2008), *reh'g denied* 2008; *cert. denied 2009; released for publication.*

Autry v. Acosta, Inc. represents yet another cautionary decision indicating that Oklahoma courts will require strict compliance with section 219A, in order to enforce any non-solicitation provision against an Oklahoma resident. 2018 OK CIV APP 8, ¶ 31, 410 P.3d 1017, 1023–24. In *Autry*, an Oklahoma appellate court noted that Acosta's contract prohibited both direct *and indirect* solicitation, which was broader than Oklahoma law (i.e., which limits such activities to direct solicitation only). *Id.* The court reasoned that because the agreement, as written, would prohibit Autry from soliciting clients she had worked with at Acosta, but who were not current clients and had not been clients for some time, it was not limited to preventing solicitation of "established customers." *Id.* Similarly, Acosta's contract prohibited Autry from engaging in the "business of selling, soliciting, promoting sale of . . . ," which was broader than Oklahoma law on the subject (i.e., that addresses the solicitation of the sale of goods or services or a combination thereof). Thus, the court invalidated the entire non-solicitation provision. *Id.*

3. What time limitations have courts recognized as reasonable in the franchise context? If no franchise cases have been decided, what time limitations have been recognized in other contexts?

➤ **How have they been related to the interests protected?**

In *Domino's Pizza, Inc. v. El-Tan, Inc., et al.*, 1995 WL 367893 (N.D. Okla. Apr. 28, 1995), the federal district court upheld a one-year post-term restriction on operating competing businesses in a specified geographic area. In *Express Services, Inc. v. Averette*, 2007 WL 1888652 (W.D. Okla. June 29, 2007), the federal district court upheld an 18-month post-term ban on diverting clients, associates, or job applicants to a competitor by direct inducement.

Outside the franchise context, Okla. Stat. tit. 15, § 217 and the exceptions thereto in sections 218, 219, and 219A provide the framework for analysis of appropriate time limitations. When applying section 217 to employment agreements, Oklahoma courts and federal courts applying Oklahoma law have enforced covenants against competition ranging in duration from nine months to two years after termination of employment. In *Cardiovascular Surgical Specialists Corporation v. Mammana*, 2002 OK 27, 61 P.3d 210 (Okla. 2002), *reh'g denied*, the Oklahoma Supreme Court upheld a one-year ban on a doctor's solicitation of patients of his former employer, while preserving the rights of the patients to seek him out. The court also struck down a requirement that the former employee not practice his specialty for two years within 20 miles of his former employer, finding that the distance to the next closest hospital effectively barred him from such practice within 100 miles. *Id.* In *Key Temporary Personnel, Inc. v. Cox*, 1994 OK Civ. App. 123, 884 P.2d 1213 (Okla. Civ. App. 1994), a nine-month restriction on soliciting or diverting clients of a temporary personnel agency was upheld. The court in *Thane A. Hedges Regional Speech and Hearing Center, Inc. v. Baughman*, 1998 OK Civ. App. 122, 996 P.2d 939, 940 (Okla. Civ. App. 1998), *released for publication*, upheld a two-year post-employment restriction on working for entities contracting with or served by Hedges. *See also Tatum v. Colonial Life & Accident Insurance Co. of America*, 1970 OK 27, 465 P.2d 448 (Okla. 1970) (two-year "hands-off" provision enforced).

Covenants in the employment context containing restrictions longer than two years have not found favor with Oklahoma courts or with federal courts applying Oklahoma law. In *Bayly, Martin & Fay, Inc. v. Pickard*, 1989 OK 122, 780 P. 2d 1168 (Okla. 1989), the Oklahoma Supreme Court declined to enforce a covenant that included a three-year restriction on the activities of a former employee. *See also Loewen Group Acquisition Corporation v. Matthews*, 2000 OK Civ. App. 109, 12 P.3d 977

OK

(Okla. Civ. App. 2000), *released for publication* (three-year restriction not enforced); *Cohen Realty, Inc. v. Marinick*, 1991 OK Civ. App. 71, 817 P.2d 747 (Okla. Civ. App. 1991) (ten-year restriction not enforced).

Since the enactment of OKLA. STAT. tit. 15, § 219A, any employment agreements entered into after June 4, 2001, that contain covenants by the employee not to compete with the employer must permit the employee to "engage in the same business as that conducted by the former employer or a similar business as that conducted by the former employer as long as the former employee does not directly solicit the sale of goods, services or a combination of goods and services from established customers of the former employer." *Id.* Courts applying this section have upheld 2-year restrictions against such direct solicitation. *See, e.g., Inergy Propane v. Lundy*, 2009 OK Civ. App. 8, 219 P.3d 547 (Okla. Civ. App. 2009), *reh'g denied; cert. denied; Drummond American LLC v. Share Corporation*, 2009 WL 240190 (W.D. Okla. Aug. 3, 2009). In *Inergy Propane*, the court applied a "reasonableness" test to section 219A, even though that section, on its face, contains no such restriction. *Inergy Propane*, 219 P. 3d at 55. The court upheld a 2-year restriction on direct solicitation of the former employer's customers. *Id.* at 560.

Covenants in connection with the sale of goodwill are considered under OKLA. STAT. tit. 15, § 218. Section 218 permits such covenants to endure "within a specified county and any county or counties contiguous thereto, or a specified city or town or any part thereof, so long as the buyer, or any person deriving title to the goodwill from him carries on a like business." This provision has been applied to affirm the appropriateness of a restriction extending to the longer of three years after the sale of the business or one year after the last payment pursuant to the agreement. *See Southwest Stainless, L.P., et al v. Sappington*, 2008 WL 3013548 (N.D. Okla. Aug. 1, 2008), *aff'd* 582 F.3d 1176 (10th Cir. 2009). Two courts that otherwise struck down on other grounds covenants in connection with sales of goodwill of a business nevertheless recognized that such covenants having a duration of five years from the sale of the business were consistent with Oklahoma law. *See Vanguard Environmental, Inc. v. Cutler*, 2008 OK Civ. App. 57, 190 P.3d 1158 (Okla. Civ. App. 2008), *released for publication; Eakle v. Grinnell Corporation*, 272 F. Supp. 2d 1304 (E.D. Okla. 2003). In *Inergy Propane*, the Oklahoma Court of Civil Appeals applied the reasonableness test to the non-compete provision in the contract for sale and found that a 15-year restriction after the sale was valid, because it was bargained for and it was not unlimited. *See Inergy Propane*, 219 P. 3d at 555. Notwithstanding the absence of a geographic limitation in section 218, it is likely that a court would nonetheless engage in a "reasonableness" analysis and impose one if it is absent or blue-pencil one that is overly broad.

---

4. What geographic limitations have courts recognized as reasonable in the franchise context?

- **How have they been related to the interests protected?**
- **Have courts recognized the legitimacy of protecting other franchisees from competition?**

The federal district court in *Domino's Pizza, Inc. v. El-Tan, Inc., et al.*, 1995 WL 367893 (N.D. Okla. Apr. 28, 1995), recognized a one-year limitation in a ten-mile radius extending from the premises of the franchisee and entered a preliminary injunction enforcing the limitation. In so doing, the court noted that "Domino's would suffer irreparable harm due to its inability to attract new franchisees to the area. . . ." *Id.*

at *10. In *Express Services, Inc. v. Averette*, 2007 WL 1888652 (W.D. Okla. June 29, 2007), the federal district court blue-penciled the restrictions to limit them to the geographic area assigned to the former franchisee in the franchise agreement. For covenants falling within the statutory "goodwill" and "partnership" exceptions to OKLA. STAT. tit 15, § 217, sections 218 and 219 of title 15 provide geographic limitations of "a specified county and any county or counties contiguous thereto, or a specified city or town or any part thereof." *See* OKLA. STAT. tit 15, §§ 218, 219. Provisions that otherwise comply with these sections but are overly broad geographically can be reformed to include only the county of the primary place of the conduct of the subject business and contiguous counties. *Id. See, e.g., Southwest Stainless, L.P., et al v. Sappington*, 2008 WL 3013548 (N.D. Okla. Aug. 1, 2008), *aff'd* 582 F.3d 1176 (10th Cir. 2009) (reforming a geographic area encompassing Arkansas and Oklahoma to encompass only Tulsa County and the surrounding counties).

In other employment cases decided under section 217, among the geographic restrictions *not* enforced were a limit of 15 miles from each of three locations (which effectively eliminated an entire metropolitan area) in *Loewen Group Acquisition Corporation v. Matthews*, 2000 OK Civ. App. 109, 12 P.3d 977 (Okla. Civ. App. 2000), *released for publication*; a restriction on activity within Texas, Oklahoma, New Mexico, and Arkansas, where the employee had been stationed exclusively in Oklahoma in *Herchman v. Sun Medical, Inc.*, 751 F. Supp. 942 (N.D. Okla. 1990); a covenant with no geographical limits in *Cohen Realty, Inc. v. Marinick*, 1991 OK Civ. App. 71, 817 P.2d 747 (Okla. Civ. App. 1991); and a 20-mile area surrounding the employer's medical offices, where the nearest hospital outside the 20-mile radius was 100 miles away in *Cardiovascular Surgical Specialists Corporation v. Mammana*, 2002 OK 27, 61 P.3d 210 (Okla. 2002) *reh'g denied.*

OKLA. STAT. tit 15, § 219A permits agreements restricting the ability of former employees to compete with employers. Such agreements must permit former employees to engage in the same business as conducted by the former employer or a similar business, but may prohibit the former employee from "directly soliciting the sale of goods, services or a combination of goods and services from the established customers of the former employer." *Id.* Section 219A does not on its face include a geographic limit. However, it is likely that a court would nonetheless conduct a "reasonableness" analysis and impose one. For example, the Oklahoma Court of Civil Appeals, in a case involving both a non-compete agreement in connection with a sale of a business and a related but separate employment agreement, reasoned that section 219A does not supplant the requirement for the reasonableness analysis required by section 217. *See Inergy Propane v. Lundy*, 2009 OK Civ. App. 8, 219 P.3d 547, 556 (Okla. Civ. App. 2009), *reh'g denied; cert. denied.* Applying its analysis to the geographic limitations provisions of the non-compete provision of the employment agreement, the court upheld a 50 mile radius of the former employee's assigned place of work, finding that there were no geographic limits in section 219A (only limits on the types of activities) so the subject provision is less restrictive than the statute permits. *Id.* at 560–61.

5. What limitations on activities have courts recognized as reasonable in the franchise context?

The federal district court in *Domino's Pizza, Inc. v. El-Tan, Inc., et al.*, 1995 WL 367893 (N.D. Okla. Apr. 28, 1995) upheld a covenant in a franchise agreement stating that a former pizza store franchisee could not for a period of one year "directly or indirectly for the benefit of you or your owners, or through or on behalf of or in conjunction with any other person, partnership or corporation, own, engage in, be employed by, advise, assist, invest in, franchise, make loans to, or have any other interest, whether financial or otherwise in any carry-out or delivery pizza store business located at the premises of the Store or within 10 miles of the Store." 1995 WL 367893, at *2. In *Express Services, Inc. v. Averette*, 2007 WL 1888652 (W.D. Okla. June 29, 2007), the federal district court approved of an in-term restriction on a former temporary employment service franchisee "engaging in any business that is a competitor of [franchisor]." 2007 WL 1888652, at *4. The court blue-penciled a broad post-term restriction, limiting it to prohibit the franchisee (for 18 months after the franchise terminated) "from directly soliciting former clients, associates or job applicants" of the franchisor. *Id.* at *5.

In the employment context, courts will find covenants in any employment agreements covered by OKLA. STAT. tit 15, § 219A to be limited to restrictions on direct solicitation of the sale of goods or services or a combination of the two to established customers of the former employer. Caselaw interpreting section 217 in the employment context for contracts entered into prior to 2001 is generally consistent with this language. For example, the Oklahoma Supreme Court did not enforce a restriction on a physician accepting referrals from other doctors or a requirement that he practice a different specialty for two years, but upheld a ban on direct solicitation of patients of the former employer. *Cardiovascular Surgical Specialists, Corporation v. Mammana*, 2002 OK 27, 61 P.3d 210 (Okla. 2002), *reh'g denied*. Similarly, the Oklahoma Court of Civil Appeals struck down a covenant that contained broad limits on general marketing activity, contacts with former clients of the former employer, and contacts with suppliers in the same industry. *Vanguard Environmental, Inc. v. Cutler*, 2008 OK Civ. App. 57, 190 P.3d 1158 (Okla. Civ. App. 2008), *released for publication.*

6. Does the state recognize a difference between in-term and post-term covenants?

Virtually all caselaw related to enforcement of covenants under Oklahoma law involves post-term covenants. However, in the franchise context a federal court sitting in diversity has specifically upheld a broad covenant against engaging in the same business as the franchisor during the term of the franchise agreement. *Express Services, Inc. v. Averette*, 2007 WL 1888652 (W.D. Okla. June 29, 2007). The court reasoned that prohibiting a franchisee from "using his position and/or knowledge to assist a competing business while in association with [the franchisor] . . . protects [franchisor] from unfair competition and is therefore in harmony with Oklahoma law." *Id.* at *4.

7. Has the state allowed enforcement of covenants against non-signatories (e.g., family members, newly formed corporations)?

No Oklahoma court or federal court applying Oklahoma law has allowed enforcement of covenants against non-signatories such as family members or newly formed corporations. However, these courts have specifically declined to enforce covenants against signatories if the effect is to improperly affect the rights of third parties, such as patients or referring physicians (*Cardiovascular Surgical Specialists, Corporation v. Mammana*, 2002 OK 27, 61 P.3d 210 (Okla. 2002), *reh'g denied.*); potential customers who were not customers of the previous employer (*Vanguard Environmental, Inc. v. Cutler*, 2008 OK Civ. App. 57, 190 P.3d 1158 (Okla. Civ. App. 2008), *released for publication*); or employment applicants (*Express Services, Inc. v. Averette*, 2007 WL 1888652 (W.D. Okla. June 29, 2007)).

8. Will the state modify, "blue-pencil," or otherwise reduce a covenant found to be overbroad?

Under the statutory provisions of title 15, courts are specifically permitted to reform or "blue-pencil" employment contracts that are overly broad geographically. OKLA. STAT. tit. 15, §§ 218, 219. Both sections 218 and 219 permit a covenant that is otherwise lawful but that exceeds the territorial restrictions of those sections to be reformed to include only the county where the primary activity of the subject business or partnership was conducted and the contiguous counties. *Id.*

Caselaw permits courts to reform other overly broad provisions, but not if the reformation would require the court to supply essential terms of the contract. *See, e.g., Bayly, Martin & Fay, Inc. v. Pickard*, 1989 OK 122, 780 P.2d 1168, 1174 (Okla. 1989) (the Oklahoma Supreme Court held that the prohibition was too broad to be judicially reformed because it also covered prospective clients and all lines of insurance, including those that the employee had not sold for the previous employer). If the covenant is flawed in several respects and the court would be required to materially alter it, the covenant will be voided instead. *See, e.g., Howard v. Nitro-Lift Technologies, L.L.C.*, 2011 WL 5865068 (Okla. Nov. 22, 2011), *not released for publication in official reporter* (covenant went so far beyond the provisions of section 219A that the court declined to reform it; court held that it could not determine whether the contract's reference to "present customers" was equivalent to the "established customers" language in the statute); *Vanguard Environmental, Inc. v. Cutler*, 2008 OK Civ. App. 57, 190 P.3d 1158 (Okla. Civ. App. 2008), *released for publication* (court would have had to completely rewrite the covenant); *Loewen Group Acquisition Corporation v. Matthews*, 2000 OK Civ. App. 109, 12 P.3d 977 (Okla. Civ. App. 2000), *released for publication* (court would have had to reform geographic, time, and scope provisions); *Herchman v. Sun Medical, Inc.*, 751 F. Supp. 942 (N.D. Okla. 1990) (covenant was overly broad in several respects and lacked clear definitions of the essential terms "customer" and "business").

In *Autry v. Acosta, Inc.*, the appellate court ruled it would not rewrite the non-solicitation agreement at issue to define the term "established customers," as that would have been tantamount to supplying a material term to the original contract. 2018 OK Civ. App. 8, ¶ 31, 410 P.3d 1017, 1023–24. In following Oklahoma Supreme Court precedent, the appellate court thus refused to "blue-pencil" the agreement and, instead, invalidated the entire non-solicitation provision. *Id.*

A federal court applying Oklahoma law to a covenant in a franchise agreement upheld an in-term prohibition against direct solicitation of former clients, associates, or job applicants and modified a post-term covenant to limit the restrictions to direct inducement of business to a competitor. *Express Services, Inc. v. Averette*, 2007

WL 1888652 (W.D. Okla. June 29, 2007). In that case, reasoning that courts should not enforce covenants that keep a former franchisee from engaging in a business or that improperly affect the rights of third parties, the court struck down restrictions against doing business with former clients who inadvertently view advertising of the new business or anyone who voluntarily contacts the former franchisee, as well as a prohibition on taking job applications from third parties, but left intact the post-term restriction on direct solicitation. *Id.* In a case outside the franchise context, the Oklahoma Supreme Court, evaluating a covenant under section 217, struck two offending provisions of a covenant (a two-year ban on practicing the same specialty within a 20-mile geographic limit, too broad under the facts of the case, and a ban on accepting referrals or direct patient contact, an unreasonable restriction on third parties), but left intact an enforceable provision against direct solicitation. *Cardiovascular Surgical Specialists, Corporation v. Mammana*, 2002 OK 27, 61 P.3d 210 (Okla. 2002), *reh'g denied.*

In the employment context, a federal court applying section 218 blue-penciled a geographic restriction to reduce it from an impermissible seven-state area to an area encompassing the county in which the business was conducted and contiguous counties. *Southwest Stainless, L.P., et al v. Sappington*, 2008 WL 3013548 (N.D. Okla. Aug. 1, 2008), *aff'd* 582 F.3d 1176 (10th Cir. 2009).

9. When does a non-compete period begin to run? Will courts equitably extend the term?

Cases interpreting covenants under Oklahoma law generally involve non-compete periods that commence upon termination of the relationship. However, a federal court applying Okla. Stat. tit. 15, § 218 to a covenant related to the sale of a business upheld a one-year covenant that began to run on the date that the seller received its last compensation under the agreement. *Southwest Stainless, L.P., et al v. Sappington*, 2008 WL 3013548 (N.D. Okla. Aug. 1, 2008), *aff'd* 582 F.3d 1176 (10th Cir. 2009). The court further found that the time period of the covenant was extended by any period of breach, as provided in the non-competition agreement, so the injunction ran for one year from judgment. *Id.* at *30.

10. What are the additional nuances or peculiarities of the state's treatment of covenants in the franchising context?

Oklahoma courts will look beyond contractual provisions to analyze covenants against competition under Oklahoma law in two contexts: agreements to arbitrate and choice of law. There are no cases related to this approach in the franchise context.

In *Express Services, Inc. v. King*, 2017WL3741555 (W.D. Okla. 2017), the court examined the applicability of the discovery rule, as well as the continuous-accrual doctrine and the continuing-wrong theory, as same related to the statute of limitations applying to a franchisee's alleged breach of a covenant not to compete. Noting the Oklahoma Supreme Court had never discussed the discovery rule as an element of contract law, as opposed to a feature of tort law, the federal court held the discovery rule does not apply breach of contract claims. *Id.* The court likewise noted that the Oklahoma Supreme Court had never acknowledged the continuing wrong theory in connection with a breach of contract action. Conversely, however, Oklahoma courts had recognized the concept of the continuous-accrual doctrine, which treats each breach of contract as an independently actionable wrong with its own time limit for recovery, meaning that it supports recovery only for damages arising from those breaches falling within the limitations period. *Id.*

Using similar reasoning, Courts interpreting Oklahoma law have applied Oklahoma law to determine the enforceability of non-competition agreements where the agreement designated another state's law to apply to the contract. In an employment-related case in which the parties had agreed to apply Ohio law to the contract, the Oklahoma Court of Civil Appeals found that Ohio law "may only be used to govern this agreement if it does not violate the provisions of Oklahoma law with respect to contracts in restraint of trade." *Oliver v. Omnicare, Inc.*, 2004 OK Civ. App. 93, 103 P.3d 626, 629 (Okla. Civ. App. 2004), *released for publication*. In reversing a summary judgment and remanding the case for further proceedings, the court limited the application of Oklahoma law to the covenant and not to the broader transaction of which the covenant was a part. *Id.* A federal court applying Oklahoma law has also found that Oklahoma law would determine enforceability of a non-compete provision despite a choice of Florida law to apply to the agreement. *Southwest Stainless, L.P., et al v. Sappington*, 2008 WL 3013548 (N.D. Okla. Aug. 1, 2008), *aff'd* 582 F.3d 1176 (10th Cir. 2009). In granting partial summary judgment, the court found that Florida law would uphold the covenant as written. *Southwest Stainless, L.P., et al v. Sappington*, 2008 WL 918706, at *5 (N.D. Okla. Apr. 1, 2008). The court went on to find that "Oklahoma law governs the interpretation of the Noncompete Provisions because the parties' choice of law 'violate[s] the provisions of Oklahoma law with respect to contracts in restraint of trade.'" *Id.* at *6 (citing *Oliver v Omnicare, Inc., supra*). Applying Oklahoma law to the covenant, the court reformed the covenant to limit its geographic applicability but otherwise left the covenant intact as complying with Okla. Stat. tit. 15, § 218.

Oregon

*by Leslie S. Johnson**

1. Has the state addressed covenants against competition in the context of franchising?

- **Does the state have a franchising statute or regulations that address covenants against competition?**
- **Does the state have a covenants statute of general applicability that would encompass franchise covenants?**
- **Have the courts addressed covenants in the context of franchising either under a statute or under the state's common law?**

Oregon has no statute addressing covenants against competition in the franchise setting. Oregon's only statute addressing restrictive covenants is limited to such agreements between employers and employees. That state law, at ORS 653.295, limits the circumstances under which a non-compete may be required by an employer, notably imposing on the employer a duty to provide substantial pre-employment notice to prospective employees of a requirement for a non-compete and restricting such agreements to employees that fit specific criteria, including a minimum salary and certain administrative, executive, or professional jobs (as described in ORS 653.020(3)). Updates to ORS 653.295 in the 2020 and 2021 legislative sessions imposed new procedural requirements, the failure of which may void any attempted restriction by contract. The statute places no restrictions on non-solicitation agreements. Franchise transactions in Oregon are governed by ORS Chapter 650 and the rules and regulations promulgated thereunder. Trade secret protection is separately addressed at ORS 646.461–.475.

While there is a substantial body of Oregon caselaw discussing the validity of covenants against competition, as of the publication date there are no decisions from Oregon's appellate courts specifically discussing such a covenant in the context of the franchise relationship, apart from review of a traditional purchasing/sourcing restriction described in section 5 below. A reported decision from the federal trial court does discuss a restraint entered into in a franchise relationship. In *Stephenson v. Great Frame Up Systems, Inc.*, 184 F. Supp. 2d 1048 (D. Or. 2002), the

*Leslie S. Johnson is Of Counsel to the firm of Samuels Yoelin Kantor, LLP in Portland, Oregon.

court declined to enforce the restraint because the franchisor was no longer present in the territory sought to be protected, and there was no evidence the party seeking enforcement suffered any damages from the alleged violation.

Franchise agreements, including any competitive restraints they contain, are subject to traditional principles and precedents under contract law, restraints of trade, and the statutory and common law covering the protection of trade secrets. With respect to other contract relationships, Oregon courts have been adamant that a complete restraint of trade will never be enforceable. The threshold questions of validity will always be (1) whether the restraint was supported by consideration at the time it was made and (2) whether the time and geographic limits are reasonable in relation to the interests of the party seeking to enforce and the interests of the public. The test for reasonableness under Oregon law is that the restraint may only be so broad as to afford "fair protection" to the interests of the enforcing party without interfering with the interests of the public. *Eldridge v. Johnston*, 195 Or. 379, 403, 245 P.2d 239, 250 (1952).

---

2. Have the courts articulated the "legitimate interests" of the franchisor that will support enforcement of a covenant against competition contained in a franchise agreement?

- **If so, what are they (e.g., protection of goodwill, protection of confidential information), and in what contexts did the issue arise?**
- **If not, what interests have been recognized in other contexts (e.g., employment agreements, the sale of business context)?**

Oregon courts have not discussed "legitimate interests" specific to the franchise relationship but have affirmed that proof of a protectable interest is required to support restraints in settings other than employment contracts, *Universal Ideas Corp. v. Esty*, 84 Or. App. 541, 545 734 P.2d 408, 410 (1987), and have discussed the "legitimate interests" or "protectable interests" of a party that will support the enforcement of a non-compete in a variety of contexts. Always, protectable interests must be more than general knowledge, skill, facility, or on-the-job experience, even if gained at the employer's expense. *See, e.g., Rem Metals Corp. v. Logan*, 278 Or. 715, 720–21, 565 P.2d 1080, 1083 (1977) (employer failed to prove protectable interest). Legitimate interests include valuable customer or supplier contacts (*North Pacific Lumber v. Moore*, 275 Or. 359, 364–65, 551 P.2d 431, 434–35 (1976)); customer lists or specialized customer information (*Volt Services Group. Division of Volt Management Corp. v. Adecco Employment Services, Inc.*, 178 Or. App. 121, 126–27, 35 P.3d 329, 334 (2001)); supplier names and requirements (*North Pacific Lumber, supra*); trade secrets (*Nike, Inc. v. McCarthy*, 379 F.3d 576 (9th Cir. 2004)); and goodwill (*Eldridge v. Johnston*, 195 Or. 379, 404–05, 245 P.2d 239, 251 (1952)).

Restraints that are not supported at least by a transfer of goodwill fail for lack of consideration. *See, e.g., Hemstreet v. Warlick*, 281 Or. 579, 576 P.2d 1 (1978) (court refused to enforce competitive restraint that was executed between partners in a settlement agreement and divorced from any transfer of goodwill or interest in business); and *Donohue v. Peterson*, 161 Or. 65, 87 P.2d 770 (1939) (court refused to enforce non-compete against dentist where non-compete appeared in lease between plaintiff and defendant, there was no evidence that plaintiff was practicing dentistry when agreement was made, and plaintiff terminated lease before entering new dentistry practice).

3. What time limitations have courts recognized as reasonable in the franchise context? If no franchise cases have been decided, what time limitations have been recognized in other contexts?

- **How have they been related to the interests protected?**

There are no such decisions from the Oregon courts based on franchise relationships. In other contexts, Oregon courts routinely affirm contractual time limits of one to five years. In *Farmers Insurance Exchange v. Fraley*, 80 Or. App. 117, 119, 720 P.2d 770, 771 (1986), for example, a one-year term was deemed "fair" and enforced against insurance company's former agent given the defendant's access to confidential information while employed and the plaintiff's legitimate interest in limiting his solicitation of their policy holders. In *Cascade Exchange, Inc. v. Reed*, 278 Or. 749, 751, 565 P.2d 1095, 1096 (1977), a two-year term was enforced against former employees of a trucking company who attempted to set up a competing company. That court held the equities clearly lay with the employer for enforcement of the express terms given the specialized knowledge of the former employees of their employer's customer contacts and requirements, and the employees' conduct in setting up another business with "callous indifference to the contractual undertakings" in their original non-competes. A five-year term was enforced against a former sales employee in *Western Medical Consultants, Inc. v. Johnson*, 835 F. Supp. 554 (D. Or. 1993), *aff'd* 80 F.3d 1331 (9th Cir. 1996). In *Eldridge v. Johnston*, 195 Or. 379, 411, 245 P.2d 239, 254 (1952), a ten-year limitation period was affirmed without any discussion while the geographic limit against former partners in a meatpacking business was reduced to coincide with the scope of the plaintiff's remaining active business. Citing *Eldridge*, a later court, in *McCallum v. Asbury*, 238 Or. 257, 393 P.2d 774 (1964), enforced a ten-year term against a former partner in a medical partnership, noting the partner had entered the partnership with full knowledge of the restriction, he had gained substantial benefits from the partnership, the other partners had made substantial investments in the partnership that they were entitled to protect, and there was no evidence the public would suffer from a lack of access to care.

4. What geographic limitations have courts recognized as reasonable in the franchise context?

- **How have they been related to the interests protected?**
- **Have courts recognized the legitimacy of protecting other franchisees from competition?**

As noted above, there is no decision from an Oregon appellate court specific to the franchise relationship. When a geographic limit is challenged as unreasonable, Oregon courts will look for the proposed geographic limit to coincide with the reach of the business that is being protected. So, in *Eldridge v. Johnston*, 195 Or. 379, 245 P.2d 239 (1952), the contractual restraint was written to exclude defendants from two states; when the evidence established that the plaintiff's business was only present in four counties, the court modified the geographic limit to conform. *See also Cascade Exchange, Inc. v. Reed and Parker*, 278 Or. 749, 565 P.2d 1095 (1977) (court affirmed restriction for entire state of Oregon based on reach of plaintiff-employer). Modification may also be based on the balance between the interest of the party seeking enforcement and the public's interest in access to the product or service. For example, in *Pacific Kidney & Hypertension, LLC v. Kassakian*, 156 F. Supp. 3d 1219 (2016), on a motion for a temporary restraining order, the court allowed a physician to continue her practice within the area restricted by the parties' agreement in order to avoid disruption of treatment of her existing patients, but enjoined her from soliciting new patients pending further proceedings. The defendant in *McCallum v. Asbury*, 238 Or. 257, 393 P.2d 774 (1964), challenged a restriction measured by a 30-mile radius from his former medical practice, though without persuading the court that the distance would unreasonably interfere with the public's interest.

5. What limitations on activities have courts recognized as reasonable in the franchise context?

ORS Chapter 650 does impose reasonableness requirements on purchasing restrictions and similar terms typical of franchise systems. In *Harold Butler Enterprises No. 97, Inc. v. Vanlandingham*, 264 Or. 414, 505 P.2d 1149 (1973), the Oregon Supreme Court held that the franchisor's requirement that the franchisee purchase from the franchisor or its designees, even at higher prices than available from other suppliers, was deemed valid and enforceable. The defendant-franchisee resisted the plaintiff-franchisor's collection action, in part, by challenging the franchisor's addition of a management fee to the cost of food and supplies required to be purchased from the franchisor. The arrangement survived scrutiny under contract and antitrust law.

Outside the franchise context, as the cases cited throughout this chapter reflect, courts routinely enforce confidentiality and non-disclosure agreements, restrictions on contact with customers or employees of the enforcing party, and order return of valuable intellectual property wrongfully obtained, upon proof of a legitimate interest in protecting such information, relationships, or property.

6. Does the state recognize a difference between in-term and post-term covenants?

No Oregon case has discussed this issue directly. It is true, though, that the courts react negatively to evidence that a party started getting ready to compete before the end of the employment because that is a breach of the employee's common law duty of loyalty. *See, e.g., Kelite Products, Inc. v. Brandt*, 206 Or. 636, 294 P.2d 320 (1956) (court strictly enforced express terms of non-compete against former employees who made plans to take business with them to new employer while still employed).

7. Has the state allowed enforcement of covenants against non-signatories (e.g., family members, newly formed corporations)?

Yes. Oregon courts routinely extend enforcement of covenants to new employers who knowingly employ defendants in violation of non-competes and/or to business organizations organized and employed in wrongful conduct. That being said, the express authority for including non-signatories in judgments enforcing non-competes is found in Oregon's Uniform Trade Secrets Act, ORS 646.461(2)(a) and (d), rather than the non-compete statute. Because violation of non-competes often includes wrongful use of trade secrets, the courts extend enforcement to persons or entities that, by virtue of the contracting party's conduct, have unlawfully come into possession of trade secrets and other proprietary information. *See, e.g., Lamb-Weston, Inc. v. McCain Foods, Ltd.*, 941 F.2d 970 (9th Cir. 1991) (affirming award of injunctive relief to ensure defendants, including new business, not unjustly enriched by unlawful use of confidential information).

8. Will the state modify, "blue-pencil," or otherwise reduce a covenant found to be overbroad?

Yes. Oregon courts may modify a covenant determined to be unreasonably broad in its original form in order to preserve as enforceable an otherwise invalid agreement. In *Eldridge v. Johnston*, 195 Or. 379, 245 P.2d 239 (1952), for example, the Oregon Supreme Court modified the original two-state restriction to the four-county area in which the parties actually competed. Occasionally, the court will insert a limit when the provision had no limit rather than rendering covenant invalid. *See Kelite Products, Inc. v. Brandt*, 206 Or. 636, 654–56, 294 P.2d 320, 328–29 (1956) (because the contract's restraint was reasonable and lawful in other respects, the court inserted a reasonable time limit despite the absence of one in the subject agreement). *But see Konecranes, Inc. v. Scott Sinclair*, 340 F. Supp. 2d 1126, 1131 (D. Or. 2004) (declaring unreasonable provision void and expressing reluctance to rewrite any overly broad restriction in order not to encourage employers to overreach in their drafting).

9. When does a non-compete period begin to run? Will courts equitably extend the term?

No Oregon decisions suggest any common law basis for construing a non-compete to commence on any date other than that provided in the contract—typically, at the end of the contract relationship. Similarly, there is no Oregon precedent for equitable extension of a term of a restriction. To the contrary, Oregon courts have held that once the express period of a restrictive covenant has expired, a claim for injunctive relief may be moot. *See Profiessional Business Svcs., Inc. v. Gustafson*, 285 Or. 307 (1979). The best chance for extension of a time limit is contract language extending the covenant for the period of a proven violation or relying on traditional common-law bases for preliminary or permanent injunctive relief.

10. What are the additional nuances or peculiarities of the state's treatment of covenants in the franchising context?

In Oregon, the trend continues toward limiting the use of competitive restraints in the employment context. The statutory limits at ORS 653.295—on an employer's right to require such a restraint, on the allowable scope of the restraint, and on imposing specific procedural requirements—have been narrowed in the last two legislative sessions. The statutory limits do not presently apply to franchise agreements and other business-to-business arrangements.

Pennsylvania

*by Constantine T. Fournaris**

1. Has the state addressed covenants against competition in the context of franchising?

- **Does the state have a franchising statute or regulations that address covenants against competition?**
- **Does the state have a covenants statute of general applicability that would encompass franchise covenants?**
- **Have the courts addressed covenants in the context of franchising either under a statute or under the state's common law?**

Pennsylvania does not have a franchising statute, franchising regulations, or a statute of general applicability addressing covenants against competition. However, numerous federal and state courts have applied Pennsylvania common law in reviewing covenants against competition in the franchise context.

The Pennsylvania Supreme Court has addressed covenants against competition in the context of franchising under the state's common law. The standard for the enforcement of a covenant against competition contained in a franchise agreement was set out by the Pennsylvania Supreme Court in *Piercing Pagoda, Inc. v. Hoffner*, 465 Pa. 500, 351 A.2d 207 (1976). In *Piercing Pagoda*, the plaintiff was a franchisor of a retail business opportunity featuring earrings and ear piercing. The franchise agreement at issue provided: "the franchisee will not own, operate or participate in any business employing ear piercing for three years within 30 miles of any existing Piercing Pagoda or for one year where the business had been operated and terminated." *Id.* at 505, 351 A.2d at 209. After terminating the franchise agreement, the franchisees continued to operate businesses similar to the franchised business at their formerly franchised locations.

After determining that the franchisor had protectable, legitimate interests, the Pennsylvania Supreme Court enforced the covenant. In doing so, the court stated:

*Mr. Fournaris is a partner in Wiggin and Dana LLP in Philadelphia, Pennsylvania. Mr. Fournaris and Wiggin and Dana LLP served as counsel for the franchisor Maaco Franchising, Inc. in the case *Maaco Franchising, Inc. v. Augustin*, 2010 WL 1644278 (E.D. Pa. Apr. 20, 2010). Mr. Fournaris and Wiggin and Dana LLP served as counsel for the franchisor Goddard Systems, Inc. in the case *Goddard Systems, Inc. v. Gondal*, 2018 WL 1566570 (D. Del. Mar. 29, 2018).

"our courts will permit the equitable enforcement of a covenant not to compete included in a franchise agreement where the restrictions are reasonably necessary for the protection of the franchisor without imposing undue hardship on the franchisee and the restrictions are reasonably limited as to duration of time and geographical extent." *Id.* at 511, 351 A.2d at 212. *Accord*, *Pittsburgh Logistics Systems, Inc. v. Beemac Trucking, LLC*, 2021 WL 1676399, at *14 (Pa. Apr. 29, 2021) (non-franchise context); *Maaco Enterprises, Inc. v. O'Brien*, 1991 U.S. Dist. LEXIS 1348 (E.D. Pa. Feb. 6, 1991); *Rita's Water Ice Franchise Corp. v. DBI Investment Corp.*, 1996 WL 165518 (E.D. Pa. Apr. 8, 1996); *Maaco Enterprises, Inc. v. Bremner*, 1998 WL 669936 (E.D. Pa. Sept. 29, 1998); *Soft Pretzel Franchise Systems, Inc. v. Taralli, Inc.*, 2013 WL 5525015, at *8 (E.D. Pa. Oct. 4, 2013); *Cottman Transmissions Systems, LLC v. Gano*, 2013 WL 842709, at *7 (E.D. Pa. Mar. 7, 2013); *Tantopia Franchising Co., LLC v. West Coast Tans of PA, LLC*, 918 F. Supp. 2d 407, 414–15 (E.D. Pa. 2013); *Jade Group, Inc. v. Cottman Transmission Centers, LLC*, 2016 WL 3763024, at *12 (E.D. Pa. July 13, 2016).

---

2. Have the courts articulated the "legitimate interests" of the franchisor that will support enforcement of a covenant against competition contained in a franchise agreement?

- **If so, what are they (e.g., protection of goodwill, protection of confidential information), and in what contexts did the issue arise?**
- **If not, what interests have been recognized in other contexts (e.g., employment agreements, the sale of business context)?**

In *Piercing Pagoda, Inc. v. Hoffner*, 465 Pa. 500, 351 A.2d 207 (1976), the Pennsylvania Supreme Court stated that an "existing franchise is a legitimate business interest and therefore protectable." *Id.* at 509, 351 A.2d at 211. The court first noted that the franchisee had executed the covenant not to compete in order to secure the "benefits of the franchise," benefits that were identified to include training, use of the registered trademark of the franchisor, and the right to sell the franchisor's product. The court then concluded that, because the franchisee had received those benefits, all of which the court considered substantial, "continued operation of the [franchisee's] stores subsequent to the termination of the agreement would adversely affect the ability of the franchisor to secure another franchisee in the same territory. This is a legitimate interest . . . ." *Id.* at 509–10, 351 A.2d at 211–12.

Since the Pennsylvania Supreme Court's decision in *Piercing Pagoda*, other courts have made clear that protecting the value and goodwill built up under the franchisor's name and method of operation also is a legitimate interest. *See, e.g.*, *Rita's Water Ice Franchise Corp. v. DBI Investment Corp.*, 1996 WL 165518 (E.D. Pa. Apr. 8, 1996); *Novus Franchising, Inc. v. Taylor*, 795 F. Supp. 122, 128 (M.D. Pa. 1992); *Rita's Water Ice Franchise Co., LLC v. S.A. Smith Enterprises, LLC*, 2011 WL 101694, at *8 (E.D. Pa. Jan. 11, 2011); *AAMCO Transmissions, Inc. v. Singh*, 2012 WL 4510928, at *5 (E.D. Pa. Oct. 1, 2012); *Soft Pretzel Franchise Systems, Inc. v. Taralli, Inc.*, 2013 WL 5525015, at *10 (E.D. Pa. Oct. 4, 2013) (purpose of restrictive covenant is to protect against loss of reputation, damage to goodwill, and customer confusion; use of valuable training, knowledge, and experience gained from the franchisor to compete would harm goodwill and franchisor's ability to effectively compete); and *Tantopia Franchising Co., LLC v. West Coast Tans of PA, LLC*, 918 F. Supp. 2d 407,

415, 417–19 (E.D. Pa. 2013) (the court granted a preliminary injunction enforcing the non-compete covenant, concluding continued operation of a competing salon would cause irreparable harm due to injury to goodwill, reduction in the value of the mark to a potential new franchisee, likelihood of interference with customer relationships, and the poor precedent permitting former franchisees to violate their franchise agreement, including the non-compete covenant).

Moreover, courts have routinely held that the enforcement of a former franchisee's restrictive covenants is in the public interest. *Novus Franchising, Inc. v. Taylor*, 795 F. Supp. 122, 132 (M.D. Pa. 1992). *Accord Maaco Enterprises, Inc. v. Bremner*, 1998 WL 669936, at *5 (enforcement of former franchisee's non-competition is in the public interest); *Rita's Water Ice Franchise Corp. v. DBI Investment Corp.*, 1996 WL 165518, at *5 (E.D. Pa. Apr. 8, 1996) ("the public interest supports contractual enforcement by preventing competition in violation of a valid restrictive covenant"); *Tantopia Franchising Co., LLC v. West Coast Tans of PA, LLC*, 918 F. Supp. 2d 407, 420 (E.D. Pa. 2013) (same).

In Pennsylvania, restrictive covenants are enforceable only if they are ancillary to a contract for the sale of a business (the sale of goodwill or other subject property) or an employment contract. *Piercing Pagoda*, 465 Pa. at 506–08, 351 A.2d at 210–11. Covenants not to compete in a franchise agreement are enforceable because they have been deemed to be analogous to covenants in an employment contract. *Pittsburgh Logistics Systems, Inc. v. Beemac Trucking, LLC*, 2021 WL 1676399, at *13 (Pa. Apr. 29, 2021) (non-franchise context) (*citing Piercing Pagoda*, 465 Pa. at 510–12, 351 A.2d at 212).

---

3. What time limitations have courts recognized as reasonable in the franchise context? If no franchise cases have been decided, what time limitations have been recognized in other contexts?

➤ How have they been related to the interests protected?

The standard by which the *Piercing Pagoda* reasonableness criterion is determined is whether the covenant against competition imposes restrictions broader than necessary to protect the covenantee's interest in the sale of its franchise to the covenantor. *Piercing Pagoda, Inc. v. Hoffner*, 465 Pa. 500, 511–13, 351 A.2d 207, 212–13 (1976). *See also Bell Fuel Corp. v. Cattolico*, 375 Pa. Super. Ct. 238, 251, 544 A.2d 450, 459 (1988) (non-franchise context). Thus, under *Piercing Pagoda*, the overall temporal and geographic reasonableness of the restrictive covenant is the test, considered in the context of the franchisor's needs and the impact on the franchisee.

In *Piercing Pagoda*, the court upheld the enforcement of a post-termination covenant against competition that prohibited the franchisees from competing for a period of three years within 30 miles of any operating Piercing Pagoda store and for one year at the franchisee's formerly franchised location. In doing so, the court stated: "[t]he covenant in this case is reasonably limited since it is within such territory and during such time as may be reasonably necessary for the protection of the franchisor without imposing undue hardship on the franchisee." *Id.* at 512, 351 A.2d at 212–13. *See also Maaco Franchising, Inc. v. Augustin*, 2010 WL 1644278, at *3 (E.D. Pa. Apr. 20, 2010) ("Given the time needed to bring a franchise up to speed and to protect the franchisor's interests, I find the one-year term to be reasonable");

Maaco Enterprises, Inc. v. O'Brien, 1991 U.S. Dist. LEXIS 1348 (E.D. Pa. Feb. 6, 1991) (one-year prohibition on the operation of a substantially similar business within a ten-mile radius of the formerly franchised business deemed reasonable under Pennsylvania law); *Maaco Enterprises, Inc. v. Bremner*, 1998 WL 669936 (E.D. Pa. Sept. 29, 1998) (same); *Rita's Water Ice Franchise Co., LLC v. S.A. Smith Enterprises, LLC*, 2011 WL 101694, at *7 (E.D. Pa. Jan. 11, 2011) (two-year covenant reasonable to give franchisor the opportunity to establish a new franchise); *Tantopia Franchising Co., LLC v. West Coast Tans of PA, LLC*, 918 F. Supp. 2d 407, 415 n.7 (E.D. Pa. 2013) (two-year prohibition on ownership of or assistance to businesses offering the same or similar products or services within the protected territory of the formerly franchised business, its county, or municipality, a radius of five miles of the formerly franchised business, or a radius of ten miles of any other business operating under the franchisor's marks deemed reasonable; the court cited a collection of cases in which two-year and three-year time restrictions and ten-mile, thirty-mile and fifty-mile radius geographic restrictions deemed reasonable).

---

4. What geographic limitations have courts recognized as reasonable in the franchise context?

- **How have they been related to the interests protected?**
- **Have courts recognized the legitimacy of protecting other franchisees from competition?**

The post-termination covenant enforced by the Pennsylvania Supreme Court in *Piercing Pagoda, Inc. v. Hoffner*, 465 Pa. 500, 351 A.2d 207 (1976) contained restrictions in two geographic areas. The first restriction applied to the area in which the franchisee's previously franchised store had operated. The court enforced a restriction on competition in this area for one year after termination of the franchise agreement. The second restriction applied to an area covering a radius of 30 miles from any existing store in the franchise system. The court enforced a restriction on competition in this area for three years after termination of the franchise agreement. In relating the geographic scope of the covenant to the franchisor's interest, the court stated:

> By its terms, the covenant recognizes that the [franchisor] has a greater interest in those areas where [the franchisor] actually operates a store than in those areas where his franchisees alone are in operation. This construction affords adequate protection to the business interest of the [franchisor] without undue hardship to the [franchisee].

Id. at 511–12, 351 A.2d at 212.

In *Piercing Pagoda*, all of the other stores in the franchise system were owned by the franchisor. Thus, the question of protecting other franchisees from competition was not addressed.

Since *Piercing Pagoda* was decided, Pennsylvania courts have consistently upheld as reasonable post-termination restrictive covenants limited to a franchisee's former territories. *See Novus Franchising, Inc. v. Taylor*, 795 F. Supp. 122, 128 (M.D. Pa. 1992). *See also Maaco Franchising, Inc. v. Augustin*, 2010 WL 1644278, at *3 (E.D. Pa. Apr. 20, 2010) (ten-mile radius from location of franchisee's location

PA

reasonable in geographic scope because the business at the location could draw customers from up to ten miles away); *Maaco Enterprises, Inc. v. O'Brien*, 1991 U.S. Dist. LEXIS 1348 (E.D. Pa. Feb. 6, 1991) (one-year prohibition on the operation of a substantially similar business within a ten-mile radius of the formerly franchised business deemed reasonable under Pennsylvania law); *Maaco Enterprises, Inc. v. Bremner*, 1998 WL 669936 (E.D. Pa. Sept. 29, 1998) (same).

Pennsylvania courts have reached different conclusions whether a nationwide restriction limited to a radius of any operating unit of the franchisor is enforceable, with the result sometimes dependent on the particular facts or the stage of the case. In *AAMCO Transmissions, Inc. v. Romano*, 42 F. Supp. 3d 700, 711–12 (E.D. Pa. 2014), the court in denying the former franchisee's motion to dismiss held that it could not conclude at the motion to dismiss stage that a covenant prohibiting the former franchisee from engaging in the transmission repair business within a radius of ten miles of the franchisee's former center or any other AAMCO center is unreasonable. The court noted the Third Circuit's statement that "[i]n this Information Age, a *per se* rule against broad geographic restrictions would seem hopelessly antiquated, and, indeed, Pennsylvania courts (and federal district courts applying Pennsylvania law) have found broad geographic restrictions reasonable so long as they are roughly consonant with the scope of the employee's duties." *Id.* at 711 (citations omitted). In *AAMCO Transmissions v. Romano*, 2016 WL 792498, at *7 (E.D. Pa. Mar. 1, 2016), *vacated as moot*, No. 13-5747 (E.D. Pa. June 27, 2016) (no controversy because defendant closed their business), following a bench trial in the same action, the court modified the geographic scope of the covenant and denied the grant of a permanent injunction because the covenant as modified was not violated. In discussing a collection of cases interpreting similar AAMCO covenants with different outcomes concerning the reasonableness of the geographic scope, the court stated: "[a] restrictive covenant found to be reasonable in one case may be unreasonable in others. *Insulation Corp. of Am. v. Brobston*, 667 A.2d 729, 734 (Pa. Super. Ct. 1995)." (internal quotation mark omitted). *Id.* at *7 n.10. *See also Dunkin' Donuts Franchising, LLC v. Claudi A I, LLC*, 2014 WL 5343724, at *11 (E.D. Pa. Oct. 20, 2014) (enforcing non-compete clause that forbade franchisee from operating for 24 months within five miles of the formerly franchised business or any other store under the franchisor's marks that is open or under development after stating that the geographic scope "does give me some hesitation").

5. What limitations on activities have the courts recognized as reasonable in the franchise context?

In *Piercing Pagoda, Inc. v. Hoffner*, 465 Pa. 500, 351 A.2d 207 (1976), the franchised business was a retailer of earrings that also provided an ear-piercing service. The covenant against competition restricted the former franchisee from owning, operating, or participating in "any business employing ear piercing." *Id.* at 505, 351 A.2d at 209. In enforcing the restrictive covenant, the court did not address the scope of the activities covered under the restriction.

Since the Pennsylvania Supreme Court's decision in *Piercing Pagoda*, several other courts have made clear that a prohibition against operating the same or a substantially similar business as the formerly franchised business is reasonable. *See Rita's Water Ice Franchise Corp. v. DBI Investment Corp.*, 1996 WL 165518 (E.D. Pa.

Apr. 8, 1996); *see also Maaco Enterprises, Inc. v. O'Brien*, 1991 U.S. Dist. LEXIS 1348 (E.D. Pa. Feb. 6, 1991); *Maaco Enterprises, Inc. v. Bremner*, 1998 WL 669936 (E.D. Pa. Sept. 29, 1998). In *Tantopia Franchising Co., LLC v. West Coast Tans of PA, LLC*, 918 F. Supp. 2d 407, 419–20 (E.D. Pa. 2013), the court held that the former franchisee could offer massage and anti-aging services and products not offered under the franchise system.

6. Does the state recognize a difference between in-term and post-term covenants?

Pennsylvania courts have not to date differentiated between in-term and post-term covenants. *Piercing Pagoda, Inc. v. Hoffner*, 465 Pa. 500, 351 A.2d 207 (1976), and its progeny under Pennsylvania law involved post-term covenants. No published Pennsylvania case has discussed the enforceability under Pennsylvania law of an in-term covenant contained in a franchise agreement.

7. Has the state allowed the enforcement of covenants against non-signatories (e.g., family members, newly formed corporations)?

In *Tantopia Franchising Co., LLC v. West Coast Tans of PA, LLC*, 918 F. Supp. 2d 407, 416–17 (E.D. Pa. 2013), the court found that an individual with a long-standing strong bond with the covenantors and an entity that owned the competing business were "a mere continuation of, or straw man for," the covenantors and were bound by the covenant. In enforcing the covenant, the court in *Tantopia* held that "[i]t is well-established that a non-covenantor who benefits from the covenantor's relationship with a competing business must abide by the same restrictive covenant agreed to by the covenantor." *Id., citing Suburban Oil Services, Inc. v. Parker*, 63 Pa. D. & C.2d 91, 93 (Luzerne County 1973) ("[W]here a husband is enjoined from establishing a second business after covenanting not to compete, a wife should not be allowed to obtain the benefit of the proceeds of said covenant and then defiantly, in her name, establish a like business.") (other non-Pennsylvania citations omitted). *See also AAMCO Transmissions, Inc. v. Romano*, 42 F. Supp. 3d 700, 710–11 (E.D. Pa. 2014) (non-competition covenant may also apply to covenantor's wife who is alleged to co-own and co-operate the competing business as the covenantor's agent) (*citing Tantopia* and *Suburban Oil Services*) (internal citation omitted).

In *Goddard Systems, Inc. v. Gondal*, 2018 WL 1566570 (D. Del. Mar. 29, 2018) (applying Pennsylvania law), the court held that it could not enjoin non-party intervenors who were operating a business at the site of the former franchised location. The court explained that while a successor-in-interest may be able to be bound by an injunction that has already issued, "it is not clear that a successor-in-interest non-party may, in the first instance, be enjoined instead of a party." *Id.* at 29. Relying on cases decided by the Federal Circuit, the court further explained that it could not enjoin a non-party, although once an injunction has issued under FEDERAL RULE OF CIVIL PROCEDURE 65 against a party, it could hold a non-party in contempt if the non-party abets the defendant in violating the injunction or is legally identified with the defendant. *Id.* at 30–32.

8. Will the state modify, "blue-pencil," or otherwise reduce a covenant found to be overbroad?

There have been several reported cases decided under Pennsylvania law involving the judicial modification of a covenant against competition in the franchise context. In *AAMCO Transmissions v. Romano*, 2016 WL 792498 (E.D. Pa. Mar. 1, 2016), *vacated as moot*, No. 13-5747 (E.D. Pa. June 27, 2016) (no controversy because defendant closed their business), the court modified the geographic scope of a non-competition covenant that restricted the former franchisees from operating a center within a ten-mile radius from any AAMCO center located anywhere in the United States or Canada to a ten-mile radius of any AAMCO center in the county where the franchisees' former franchise was located. In doing so, the court stated: "Pennsylvania courts will modify, or blue pencil, non-compete agreements if the restriction is too broad but the franchisor is entitled to some protection." *Id.* at *7–8 (citations omitted). *See, e.g., AAMCO Transmissions, Inc. v. Graham*, 1990 WL 118050, at *3 (E.D. Pa. Aug. 9, 1990) ("In the instant case we find that the terms of the restrictive covenant are unduly burdensome on the [franchisees] in only one respect. The covenant restricts them from operating a center anywhere that Aamco has an existing center. We find that this geographic restriction is overly broad. We, therefore, will limit its application to the [franchisee's former] metropolitan areas."). *See also Cottman Transmissions Systems, LLC v. Gano*, 2013 WL 842709, at *8 (E.D. Pa. Mar. 7, 2013) (same). *But see AAMCO Transmissions, Inc. v. Singh*, 2012 WL 4510928, at *3 (E.D. Pa. Oct. 1, 2012) and *Otiogiakhi v. AAMCO Transmissions, Inc.*, 2011 WL 5825953, at *1–2 (D.N.J. Nov. 17, 2011) (enforcing similar AAMCO non-compete provisions as written).

9. When does a non-compete period begin to run? Will courts equitably extend the term?

Under Pennsylvania law, a non-compete is a creation of contract and therefore begins to run as specified by its terms. Accordingly, the violation of a covenant not to compete by itself does not extend the period of a covenant. *Hayes v. Altman*, 438 Pa. 451, 455, 266 A.2d 269, 271 (1970). If a franchisor wants to enjoy the protection afforded by a tolling provision pending a franchisee's compliance with a covenant, the franchisor should include language extending the covenant in the event it is violated. *See Maaco Franchising, Inc. v. Augustin*, 2010 WL 1644278, at *4 (E.D. Pa. Apr. 20, 2010). Pennsylvania courts have found a provision extending a covenant not to compete if it were violated to be enforceable. *See, e.g., Worldwide Auditing Services, Inc.* v. *Richter*, 402 Pa. Super. Ct. 584, 592, 587 A.2d 772, 776–77 (1991) (non-franchise context); *Chromalox, Inc. v. Crombie*, 2021 WL 2659523, at *7 (W.D. Pa. June 29, 2021) (non-franchise context).

In an appropriate case, an equitable extension of a non-compete period might be granted under Pennsylvania law. "Pennsylvania follows the traditional common law rule of strictly construing covenants not to compete; it does so because such covenants constitute partial restraints of trade, and, therefore, always clash, in some measure, with the common law's policy of encouraging free competition." *Westec Security Services, Inc. v. Westinghouse Electric Corp.*, 538 F. Supp. 108, 121 (E.D. Pa. 1982) (*citing Hayes v. Altman*, 438 Pa. 451, 455, 266 A.2d 269, 271 (1970); *Morgan's Home Equipment Corp. v. Martucci*, 390 Pa. 618, 136 A.2d 838, 844 (1953)). At the same time, however, it is a well-known axiom that "[t]he authorities are uniformly to the effect, that where performance is prevented by either party no advantage can be taken by the party causing the failure." *Bloshinski v. Falaz*, 168 Pa. Super. Ct. 565, 569 (1951) (*quoting Vankirk v. Patterson*, 201 Pa. 90, 50 A. 966 (1902)). "Where a party who insists upon exact time has himself been the cause of delay, specific performance will be decreed." *Unatin 7-Up Company, Inc. v. Solomon*, 350 Pa. 632, 636, 39 A.2d. 835 (1944).

One intermediate Pennsylvania court disapproved of any extension of a covenant not to compete after the restrictive period had expired except by the covenant's own terms. *See Davis v. Buckham*, 280 Pa. Super. Ct. 106, 114, 421 A.2d 427, 431 (1980). (Distinguishing cases in which extensions were granted following expiration of the term as involving sales contracts, the court stated: "[s]ince covenants not to compete must be strictly construed, see *Hayes v. Altman*, supra, 438 Pa. at 454, 266 A.2d at 271, it is questionable whether in any case a chancellor would be justified in extending the period of the restriction.") Nevertheless, in *Hayes v. Altman*, the Pennsylvania Supreme Court, when faced with the issue, had indicated it might allow for an extension if the covenantor's fraud or unnecessary delay caused unjustly permitted the covenant to expire and not be enforced. *Hayes v. Altman*, 438 Pa. at 456, 266 A.2d at 272. Where a franchisor can establish that the misconduct of a franchisee during the litigation directly caused delay in enforcement of the covenant, an equitable extension should be available and granted. *See, e.g., TYCO Fire Products, L.P. v. Fuchs*, 2017 WL 5509889, at *6 (Pa. Super. Ct. Nov. 17, 2017) (non-franchise context) (court extended period of non-competition covenant where restrictive covenant had not expired at time injunction was ordered and covenantor had caused unnecessary delay in the litigation of the validity and enforceability of the covenant).

10. Are there additional nuances or peculiarities of the state's treatment of covenants in the franchising context?

Under Pennsylvania law, the party seeking to avoid enforcement of the covenant has the burden of proving that the covenant is unenforceable. *See AAMCO Transmissions, Inc. v. Romano*, 42 F. Supp. 3d 700, 711 (E.D. Pa. 2014) ("Unreasonableness of the geographic scope of a non-compete is an affirmative defense on which the [defendants] bear the burden of proof."); *Our Town v. Rousseau*, 2017 WL 34698, at *6 (M.D. Pa. Jan. 3, 2017); *see also John G. Bryant Co., Inc. v. Sling Testing & Repair*, 471 Pa. 1, 8, 369 A.2d 1164, 1169 (Pa. 1977).

Under Pennsylvania law, the franchise contract as written plays a central role in the adjudication of a franchise dispute. In *LJL Transportation, Inc. v. Pilot Air Freight Corp.*, 599 Pa. 546, 559–60, 962 A.2d 639 (2009), the Pennsylvania Supreme Court explained "a franchise agreement is a contract to be interpreted under contract principles." *Id.* at 647 (citing *Mace v. Atlantic Refining Marketing Corp.*, 567 Pa. 71, 80, 785 A.2d 491, 496 (2001)). These principles include that "[w]hen the words of an agreement are clear and unambiguous, the intent of the parties is to be ascertained from the language used in the agreement, *Steuart v. McChesney*, 498 Pa. 45, 49, 444 A.2d 659, 661 (1982), which will be given its commonly accepted and plain meaning, *J.K. Willison, Jr. v. Consol Coal Co.*, 536 Pa. 49, 54, 637 A.2d 979, 982 (1994)." *Id. Accord, Goddard Systems, Inc. v. Gondal*, 2018 WL 1566570, at *13 (D. Del. Mar. 29, 2018).

"Pennsylvania law dictates that 'because restrictive covenants are a partial restraint upon the free exercise of trade' they should be 'strictly construed[.]'" *Goddard Systems, Inc. v. Gondal*, at *13 (citations omitted). Sometimes, as in *LJL Transportation, Inc. v. Pilot Air Freight Corp.*, courts construe a franchise agreement strictly against franchisees, particularly when the facts support an inference of deliberate wrongdoing by the franchisee. Of course, the opportunity for a court to construe a franchise agreement strictly against a franchisor, particularly when the facts support an inference of deliberate wrongdoing by the franchisor, equally exists.

There are no additional nuances or peculiarities that have been identified under Pennsylvania law with respect to the treatment of covenants against competition in the franchise context.

Puerto Rico

*by Rossell Barrios Esq. **

1. Has the state addressed covenants against competition in the context of franchising?

- **Does the state have a franchising statute or regulations that address covenants against competition?**
- **Does the state have a covenant statute of general applicability that would encompass franchise covenants?**
- **Have the courts addressed covenants in the context of franchising either under a statute or under the state's common law?**

Puerto Rico[1] has distribution, franchise, and sales representation legislation intended to protect distributors, franchisees, and sales representatives from unjustified actions by their principals or grantors. *See* Dealers' Contracts Act, also known as Law No. 75 of June 24, 1964, 10 P.R. LAWS ANN. §§ 278–78e (hereinafter the Dealers' Act or Law 75); and Sales Representatives' Contracts Act, also known as Law No. 21 of December 10, 1991, 10 P.R. LAWS ANN. §§ 279–79h (hereinafter Law 21). A "distributor" is defined in the statute as a "person actually interested in a dealer's contract because of his having effectively in his charge in Puerto Rico the distribution, agency, concession or representation of a given merchandise or service." 10 L.P.R.A. § 278(a). A "dealer's contract," in turn, is defined as a "relationship established between a dealer and a principal or grantor whereby and irrespectively of the manner in which the parties may call, characterize or execute

*Mr. Rossell Barrios is a capital member of in the Trial Practice Department Goldman Antonetti & Córdova, LLC located in San Juan, Puerto Rico, and a member of the bars of Puerto Rico and the District of Columbia. A member of the Goldman Antonetti & Cordova law firm was counsel of record in *Arthur Young & Co. v. Vega III*, 136 P.R. Dec. 157 (1994), discussed *infra.*

1. Puerto Rico is an unincorporated territory of the United States after the United States wrested Puerto Rico and other colonies from Spain during the Spanish American War of 1898. Since then, the territory of Puerto Rico has undergone some political and name changes. It is now known as the "Commonwealth of Puerto Rico." For all relevant purposes herein, Puerto Rico is legally treated as if it were a state of the union with a dual court system. Puerto Ricans were invested, by a law of Congress, with the U.S. citizenship in 1917. The final political destiny of Puerto Rico remains to be determined. Puerto Rico's population has traditionally been extremely fragmented about that question.

such relationship, the former actually and effectively takes charge of the distribution of a merchandise, or of the rendering of a service, by concession or franchise, on the market of Puerto Rico." 10 L.P.R.A. § 278(b). A "distribution contract," as defined in Law 75, includes a franchise relationship. Law 75 protects a "distributor" from the termination, impairment, or refusal to renew a "distribution contract" without just cause. *See* 10 P.R. LAWS ANN. § 278(a), (b), (d). Under Act 75, Puerto Rico is an evergreen jurisdiction, in that contract expiration dates are automatically extended by legislative fiat unless there is just cause. Law 21, in turn, protects an "independent entrepreneur who establishes a sales representation contract of an *exclusive* nature, with a principal or grantor, and who is assigned a specific territory or market, within the Commonwealth of Puerto Rico." It includes the figure known as "manufacturer's representative." 10 L.P.R.A. § 279(a). Law 21 affords exclusive sales representatives very similar protection to that provided by Law 75 to distributors and franchisees. Puerto Rico lacks a franchise disclosure statute.

Puerto Rico's statutes governing relationships with distributors, franchisees, and sales representatives do not specifically address covenants against competition, and there is no statute of general applicability that would separately cover franchise agreements. Although the Supreme Court of Puerto Rico had previously considered related issues—*see General Gases & Supplies Corp. v. Shoring & Forming Systems, Inc.*, 153 D.P.R. 861 (2001) (validity of a covenant not to compete among competitors is subject to the rule of reason embodied in Puerto Rico's antitrust laws); *see also Arthur Young & Co. v. Vega III*, 136 D.P.R. 157 (1994) (validating covenants not to compete in the employment context under criteria based on reasonableness of term, geographic extension, and compensation)—there were no reported Puerto Rico court decisions directly addressing the issues raised by covenants against competition in franchise agreements until 2010. In *Franquicias Martin's BBQ, Inc. v. García de Gracia*, 178 D.P.R. 978 (2010), the court analyzed a clause forbidding competition for two years with a geographic extension of ten miles from any other restaurant in the system and the same or similar food product that was the subject of the system. *See* 178 D.P.R. at 982–83.

Before *Franquicias Martin's BBQ*, the court had ruled in the employment context that a covenant not to compete in Puerto Rico was enforceable if it complied with a six-part test: (1) the employer has a legitimate interest in the agreement, (2) the duration of the prohibition corresponds with the employer's interest but does not exceed 12 months, (3) the employer provides consideration other than mere job tenure in exchange for the employee signing the non-competition covenant, (4) the contract is valid (i.e., the product of an offer, acceptance, and consideration), (5) the agreement is in writing, and (6) reasonableness of any geographic or customer-oriented limitations imposed by the covenant. *See Arthur Young & Co. v. Vega III*, 136 D.P.R. 157, 175–76 (1994) (establishing the six-part test and declaring null and void a covenant not to compete because the duration of the restriction exceeded 12 months); *Aconi Telecomm., Inc. v. Noa*, 136 D.P.R. 579 (1994) (declaring valid a covenant not to compete contained in an employment agreement after applying the six-part test); *CCPR Serv. Inc. v. Pretti-Alicea*, P.R. App. No. KLAN9501194, 1996 P.R. App. LEXIS 585, at *4–11 (TA PR Apr. 24, 1996) (applying *Arthur Young & Co.* retroactively); *Lucas–Insertco Pharm. Printing Co. of Maryland LLC v. Salzano*, 124 F. Supp. 2d 27, 29–31 (D.P.R. 2000) (applying Puerto Rico law, as established in *Arthur Young & Co.*, to uphold a covenant not to compete in an employment agreement); *Smarte Carte, Inc. v. Colón*, 47 F. Supp. 2d 183, 188 (D.P.R. 1999) (applying criteria in *Arthur Young & Co.* in the context of a covenant not to compete in an agreement to provide management and maintenance services and declaring covenant invalid for lack of consideration and for exceeding the time limitation. *See also Santiago-Sepulveda v. Esso Standard Oil Co. (P.R.), Inc.*, 638 F. Supp. 2d 193, 201 (D.P.R. 2009); *Phillips v. Willis Re Inc.*, 2021 WL 1554260 (D.P.R. Apr. 19, 2021).

2. Have the courts articulated the "legitimate interests" of the franchisor that will support enforcement of a covenant against competition contained in a franchise agreement?

- **If so, what are they (e.g., protection of goodwill, protection of confidential information), and in what contexts did the issue arise?**
- **If not, what interests have been recognized in other contexts (e.g., employment agreements, the sale of business context)?**

While Puerto Rico lacks a statute of general applicability to such covenants, the general rule under the Civil Code is that contracting parties may establish any agreements, covenants, and terms and conditions that are not contrary to "law, morals, or public policy." *See* 31 P.R. Laws Ann. § 3372. The Supreme Court of Puerto Rico reiterated this general rule in *Franquicias Martin's BBQ, Inc v. García de Gracia*, 178 D.P.R. 978 (2010). The court compared the treatment the covenants have received in other U.S. and European jurisdictions that consider the clause to be licit if the terms are reasonable. However, as there is no uniformity in their treatment, the court found it appropriate to announce that the restrictions in the clauses regarding time limitations, geographic area, and activities concerning the business must be reasonable to protect the franchisor's legitimate interest without causing damage to the franchisee. In *Franquicias Martin's BBQ, Inc.*, the court gave examples of legitimate interests that a franchisor might have: a unique method or system of doing business, confidential information, business secrets, intellectual property, and a relationship with customers, among others. The court also warned that the franchisee can also have legitimate interests, especially if it invests all its resources in the business and assumes financial or credit risks.[2]

In *R.W. Int'l Corp. v. Welch Foods, Inc.*, 88 F.3d 49 (1st Cir. 1996), the United States Court of Appeals for the First Circuit held that a manufacturer had not violated Law 75 when it refused to modify an agreement to permit a distributor to handle competing product lines during the duration of the relationship. *See id.* at 53–54. In *R.W. Int'l*, the court held that a manufacturer's desire to (1) increase sales, (2) avoid conflicts of interests in the distribution of its products, and (3) stimulate the distributor to devote full marketing priority, support, and promotion to the manufacturer's products constituted legitimate business interests sufficient to support a covenant not to compete at least *during the period in which the franchise agreement was in effect*. *See id.* In the employment context, Puerto Rico commonwealth and federal courts have recognized the legitimacy of an employer's interests in (1) protecting its relationships with customers, (2) maintaining its customer base, (3) avoiding substantial adverse effects to its business, and (4) preserving the confidentiality of its business operations or sensitive information of clients. *See Arthur Young & Co.*, 136

2. With respect to geographic and functional scope of covenants not to compete, see response to question number 4 below.

D.P.R. 157, 178–79 (1994); *Aconi Telecomm. v. Noa*, 136 D.P.R. 579, 582 (1994); *Salzano*, 124 F. Supp. 2d at 29–30; *Casco Sales Co. v. Maruyama U.S., Inc.*, 901 F. Supp. 2d 311, 317 (D.P.R. 2012). It appears reasonable that these considerations are applicable by analogy to other types of relationships or contexts including a franchise.

---

3. What time limitations have courts recognized as reasonable in the franchise context? If no franchise cases have been decided, what time limitations have been recognized in other contexts?

➤ **How have they been related to the interests protected?**

Before *Franquicias Martin's BBQ, Inc v. García de Gracia*, 178 D.P.R. 978 (2010), Puerto Rico courts had not considered the validity of time limitations in the franchise context. In the employment context, for a covenant not to compete to be enforceable, it may not exceed a period of 12 months from the end of the employment relationship. *See Arthur Young & Co. v. Vega III*, 136 D.P.R. 157, 175 (1994).

In *Franquicias Martin's BBQ Inc.* the court concluded that a two-year term of non-competition, and the restriction from selling the same or similar products to those of the franchise, was reasonable. The non-competition clause did not prohibit the possibility of running another restaurant in the same location within the next two years, so long as the franchisee ceased using confidential information and techniques, as well as the franchisor's distinctive structural and design features such as colors and menu.

In *Arthur Young & Co.*, the court held that the legitimate interests of the employer, an accounting firm, could not justify "the two-year restriction in the employment agreement, when generally the audit and tax counseling services are provided annually, in intervals of less time, or continuously." *Arthur Young & Co.*, 136 D.P.R. at 182 (translation ours). The court also reasoned that an accounting firm is generally capable of replacing the former employee with another who can learn the client's operations in six weeks or less, and a term of one year is reasonable to restore any confidence lost by the client. *See id.* Similarly, in *Smarte Carte v. Colón*, 47 F. Supp. 2d 183 (D.P.R. 1999), the United States District Court for the District of Puerto Rico invalidated a non-competition clause in an agreement to provide maintenance and management services because it exceeded the 12-month restriction in *Arthur Young & Co. See Smarte Carte*, 47 F. Supp. 2d at 188–89. The district court did not expressly consider whether the time limitation set forth in *Arthur Young & Co.* applied beyond the employment context.

In *General Gases & Supplies Corp. v. Shoring & Forming Systems, Inc.*, 153 D.P.R. 861 (2001), a case alleging unlawful restraint of trade under Puerto Rico law, the Supreme Court of Puerto Rico held that one factor considered in testing the legality of a non-compete agreement under the rule of reason analysis is the duration of the restriction. *See id.* The court, however, did not decide whether the criteria in *Arthur Young & Co.* would be dispositive of that issue.

Thus, whether a franchise covenant not to compete for a term that exceeds 12 months would be enforceable if the franchisor adduced legitimate business justifications for that restriction remained an open question. Puerto Rico law also did not foreclose an argument by a franchisor that legitimate business interests may justify the reasonableness of a time restriction exceeding 12 months. Because the trend, however, was not to apply the criteria in *Arthur Young & Co.* to commercial disputes, and because the consequence of failing to meet any of the six requirements in *Arthur Young & Co.* is non-enforcement of the covenant not to compete without the possibility of modification by the court, it had been a risky proposition for a franchisor to contractually require a time restriction exceeding 12 months.

4. What geographic limitations have courts recognized as reasonable in the franchise context?

- **How have they been related to the interests protected?**
- **Have courts recognized the legitimacy of protecting other franchisees from competition?**

Until *Franquicias Martin's BBQ, Inc v. García de Gracia*, 178 D.P.R. 978 (2010), no Puerto Rico authority had addressed the geographic limitations that would be enforceable in a covenant not to compete in the franchise context. In the employment context, the reach of the prohibition must correspond to the interest of the employer, in terms of the object, duration, and place of restriction or affected clients. *Arthur Young & Co v. Vega III*, 136 D.P.R. 157, 175 (1994). The prohibition must specify the geographic boundaries or the affected clients. *See id.*

If the drafter of the covenant chooses a territorial restriction, it should be limited to that area strictly necessary to avoid actual competition between the employer and the employee. *Salzano*, 124 F. Supp. 2d at 30 (quoting *Arthur Young & Co.*, 136 D.P.R. at 175–76). The geographic limitation may extend to territories where the employee maintained relationships with the employer's customers. *Salzano*, 124 F. Supp. 2d at 30–31 (D.P.R. 2000) (upholding geographic limitation that restricted competition in states where the employer provided services to customers and where the employee's relationships extended to all of the employer's customers); *but see CCPR Serv., Inc.*, P.R. App. No. KLAN9501194, 1996 P.R. App. LEXIS 585, at *4–11 (TA PR, Apr. 24, 1996) (geographic restriction covering both the entire Puerto Rico territory and all clients of employer was unreasonable given the scope of the employee's job as a salesman).

PR

In *Franquicias Martin's BBQ Inc.*, when analyzing the clause's geographic restrictions, the court concluded that the ten miles of required distance from any other restaurant franchised by the plaintiff (franchisor) was too broad, given that the actual operating reach area of the franchise was two miles. As a result of the disapproval of the clause's territorial extension restriction, the court declared the clause unreasonable and unenforceable, and refused to impose its own criteria and substitute the "parties' contracting will."

As a result of its evaluation of the interests of both parties in *Franquicias Martin's BBQ Inc.*, the Supreme Court of Puerto Rico refused to establish specific standards that would apply to all franchise agreements containing covenants against competition. Instead, the court ruled that it is necessary to pay close attention to the particular nature of the business and the interest of both parties to determine the time and other limits that might be reasonable for the clause to be valid. Regarding the territorial extension of the clause, the court ruled that the territorial reach of the clause should be limited to the area of operation of the franchise in controversy, unless the franchisor can show a specific and legitimate interest that demands more territorial protection. Furthermore, the court concluded that the restricted activities should be limited to those that would place the franchisor at a disadvantage if the former franchisee were allowed to continue using the franchisor's method and information within a certain geographic area or regarding certain clientele and during a certain period of time using the information and advantage of having been a franchisee.

5. What limitations on activities have courts recognized as reasonable in the franchise context?

Puerto Rico courts had not addressed the scope of restrictions on activities that would be considered reasonable in the franchising context before *Franquicias Martin's BBQ, Inc. v. García de Gracia*, 178 D.P.R. 978 (2010). The court there ruled that restricted activities should be limited to those that would place the franchisor in a disadvantageous position if the franchisee continued to use the franchisor's methods and information. In *Franquicias Martin's BBQ, Inc.*, the fast-food restaurant Martin's BBQ sold roasted chicken "rotisserie" style using a particular recipe with a variety of side orders. The court understood that protecting the franchise system was reasonable, as well as the recipes and the way of conducting the franchised business. The court also concluded that the franchisee had gained certain expertise and market acceptance using the franchisor's name, the methods, and recipes in the same locale and same format of the franchise.

In employment agreements, the object of the prohibition must be limited to activities similar to those carried out by the employer; it is not necessary that it be limited to the specific duties or functions of the employee. *Arthur Young & Co. v. Vega III*, 136 D.P.R. 157, 175 (1994). When the covenant seeks to restrict an employee's contacts with company clients, it should refer only to those clients the employee personally serviced during a reasonable period of time before resigning and that at the time of the resignation or for a period immediately before were still clients of the employer. *Id.* at 176. The reasonableness of the scope of a limitation on a former employee's client-related activities depends on the nature of the relevant industry and any public interests at stake. *See id.*

6. Does the state recognize a difference between in-term and post-term covenants?

Puerto Rico courts have not distinguished between in-term and post-term covenants not to compete. The Puerto Rico Supreme Court cases that have considered covenants not to compete, even in the employment context, have addressed only post-term restrictions. A federal case that considered an agreement with both in-term and post-term restrictions invalidated the covenant for a violation of the post-term time limitation. *See Smarte Carte, Inc.*, 47 F. Supp. 2d at 185; *see also Arthur Young & Co. v. Vega III*, 136 D.P.R. 157, 172–73 (1994) (noting that Spanish civil law validates a covenant not to compete during the employment relationship but restricts post-term restrictions). It stands to reason that the test established for post-term covenants would not be a good fit for in-term covenants. The reason is that the public policy behind the judicial doctrine established in the cited caselaw is to protect the livelihoods of the franchisees or employees, as the case might be. In-term covenants normally do not threaten their livelihoods. In fact, distributors routinely agree to exclusively distribute the manufacturer's products during the term of the distribution contract. This would have the same effect as a covenant not to compete in the business format franchise context. In any event, it would be best to draft the post-term and in-term covenants in separate sections of the contract because Puerto Rico courts will not blue-pencil unenforceable covenants not to compete.

7. Has the state allowed enforcement of covenants against non-signatories (e.g., family members, newly formed corporations)?

There are no reported Puerto Rico cases that address claims arising from an alleged breach of a covenant not to compete by someone other than the contracting party. Also, while Puerto Rico courts have recognized an action for tortious interference with contractual relations, no reported case has decided whether non-parties would be contractually bound by a covenant or liable for tortious interference with such a covenant. *Cf. Smarte Carte, Inc.*, 47 F. Supp. at 189 (contracting party's son could not have breached any warranties in a separate contract because the covenant not to compete in the contract with his father, which provided the basis of the claim, was unenforceable). It stands to reason that a person under the control or associated with the contracting party could be a surrogate for such contracting party. In such a case, a tenable argument could be made that the covenant has been deceitfully breached by the contracting party.

8. Will the state modify, "blue-pencil," or otherwise reduce a covenant found to be overbroad?

PR

Under Puerto Rico law, covenants against competition that are overbroad as written or fail to meet any of the legal requirements set forth in *Franquicias Martin's BBQ, Inc v. García de Gracia*, 178 D.P.R. 978 (2010), cannot be modified by a court and have been declared null and void for being unreasonable, invalid, contrary to contractual good faith, and against public policy. *See id.* at 1002. The court cited the following with approval:

> "Courts that refuse to reform an unreasonable covenant recognize such a covenant's *in terrorem* potential. The refusal to rectify is based on a policy of preventing franchisor aggrandizement. If courts held otherwise, franchisors could fashion overbroad covenants with the confidence that most franchisees would respect their contractual obligations—no matter how burdensome—and that, if one or two franchisees ever violated the covenants, the judiciary still would modify and then enforce these covenants."

See id. at 992, n.11 (citing R.W. Emerson, *Franchising Covenants against Competition*, 80 Iowa L. Rev. 1049, 1057 (1995)).

See also Smarte Carte, Inc., 47 F. Supp. 2d at 189 ([the] invalidation is strictly enforced, and courts are instructed not to apply the common law rule of reasonableness in order to modify the provision).

9. When does a non-compete period begin to run? Will courts equitably extend the term?

The court in *Franquicias Martin's BBQ, Inc v. García de Gracia*, 178 D.P.R. 978 (2010), considered a post-term covenant. It did not address the issue of when the period began to run, taking it as a given that it began at the time of the termination of the franchise. There was no indication that the court would be willing to either modify or equitably extend the term of the covenant during the period of its breach. The court rejected any attempt to modify the will of the parties reflected in a covenant not to compete that does not comply with all of the reasonableness criteria. *See id.* at 1002. However, if the post-term covenant is valid and is being breached, it would be reasonable to argue that the limited period of the covenant begins to run after the breach ceases.

10. What are the additional nuances or peculiarities of the state's treatment of covenants in the franchising context?

A Puerto Rico court would invalidate a covenant not to compete, in the employment context, where the employer has not given the employee adequate consideration for the restriction or where the employee has been pressured or deceived or has otherwise entered into the agreement unwillingly or unknowingly. *Cf. Aconi Telecomm., Inc. v. Noa*, 136 D.P.R. 579, 584 (1994) (employer's representation that employee would "fall behind in the company" if he declined to sign the covenant did not constitute coercion or undue influence). However, the court in *Franquicias Martin's BBQ, Inc. v. García de Gracia*, 178 D.P.R. 978 (2010), did not mention the same requirement of adequate, additional consideration.

Puerto Rico is a civil law jurisdiction. *See Arthur Young & Co. v. Vega III*, 136 D.P.R. 157, 169 (1994). Federal courts with jurisdiction over matters arising in Puerto Rico have ruled that reliance on common law sources for persuasive value is permissible when Puerto Rico's Supreme Court has not decided a precise issue of law. *See Acosta-Mestre v. Hilton Int'l of Puerto Rico, Inc.*, 156 F.3d 49, 54 (1st Cir. 1998); *Smarte Carte*, 47 F. Supp. 2d at 187.

Puerto Rico's Dealers' Act expressly forbids including a choice-of-law clause in a distribution or franchise agreement on public policy grounds. 10 L.P.R.A. § 278b-2 (1978). This section has been judicially enforced. *Caribbean Wholesale & Service Corp. v. US JVC Corp.*, 855 F. Supp. 627 (S.D.N.Y. 1994) (Leisure, J.); *see also Pan Am. Computer Corp. v. Data General Corp.*, 467 F. Supp. 969, 970 (D.P.R. 1979); *Southern International Sales Co. v. Potter & Brumfield Div. of AMF Inc.*, 410 F. Supp. 1339, 1342 (S.D.N.Y. 1976) (Weinfeld, J.) (applying New York choice of law rules, Law 75 held to govern despite choice-of-law clause specifying Indiana law). In the context of employment cases, Puerto Rico courts will not honor a choice-of-law provision, on public policy grounds, where the law of the specified jurisdiction is more restrictive of an employee's freedom to contract. *See Smarte Carte, Inc.*, 47 F. Supp. 2d at 187–88 (validity of covenant not to compete governed by Puerto Rico law despite a choice-of-law provision that specified Minnesota law); *Salzano*, 124 F. Supp. 2d at 29.

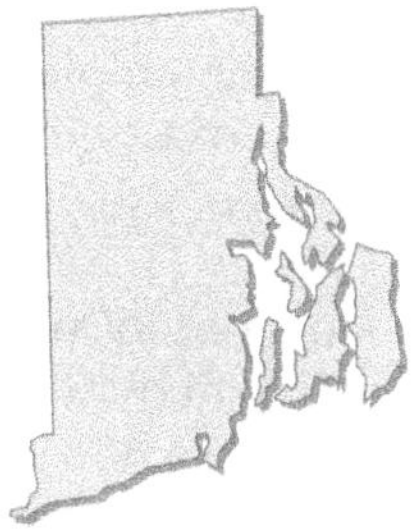

Rhode Island

*by Elizabeth M. Myers**

1. Has the state addressed covenants against competition in the context of franchising?

- **Does the state have a franchising statute or regulations that address covenants against competition?**
- **Does the state have a covenants statute of general applicability that would encompass franchise covenants?**
- **Have the courts addressed covenants in the context of franchising either under a statute or under the state's common law?**

In 1993, the Rhode Island legislature enacted the Franchise Investment Act. 19 R.I. GEN. LAWS §§ 19-28-1–19-28-30. The legislature enacted this statute in light of its findings that suggested that many franchisees, lacking sufficient bargaining power, purchase franchises despite being unfamiliar with the business involved and with industry practices specific to franchising. Accordingly, the statute seeks to ensure that a potential franchisee receives the information necessary to "make an informed decision about the offered franchise." *Id.* To date, the Rhode Island Supreme Court has not addressed the statute's effect on covenants not to compete contained in franchise agreements. Likewise, there are no reported decisions addressing Rhode Island common law with respect to restrictive covenants contained in franchise agreements.

While Rhode Island does not have a comprehensive franchise statute that specifically addresses covenants against competition, it does have a statute of limited applicability. 31 R.I. GEN. LAWS §§ 31-5-1–31-5-7, entitled Restrictions on Dealerships, states that it is unlawful to impose unreasonable restrictions on a motor dealer or franchise, relative to, among other things, non-competition agreements. However, the Rhode Island legislature more recently passed a statute of general applicability that could potentially apply to franchise agreements. On January 15, 2020, the Rhode Island legislature enacted the Rhode Island Noncompetition Agreement Act, 28 R.I. GEN. LAWS §§ 28-59-1–28-59-3. The Act limits the enforceability of certain restrictive covenants that are contained in a non-competition agreement. A "noncompetition

*Ms. Myers is a partner with the firm of Verrill Dana, LLP in Providence, Rhode Island.

agreement" is defined as "an agreement between an employer and an employee, or otherwise arising out of an existing or anticipated employment relationship, under which an employee or expected employee agrees that he or she will not engage in certain specified activities competitive with his or her employer after the employment relationship has ended." 28 R.I. GEN. LAWS § 28-59-2. The question of whether a franchisee, whether an individual or a corporate entity, is an employee, as some franchisees have suggested, has not been litigated.

When addressing the enforceability of post-employment covenants not to compete, Rhode Island courts have required that the party seeking enforcement demonstrate (1) that the covenant is ancillary to an otherwise valid agreement (such as an employment contract, a contract for the purchase and sale of a business, or a settlement agreement), (2) that the covenant is supported by adequate consideration, and (3) that there exists a legitimate interest that the covenant is designed to protect. *See R.J. Carbone Co. v. Regan*, 582 F. Supp. 2d 220, 224 (D.R.I. 2008) citing *Durapin, Inc. v. American Products, Inc.*, 559 A.2d 1051, 1053 (R.I. 1989) (outlining requirements); *Allen v. Creative Services, Inc.*, 1992 WL 813643 (R.I. Super. Ct. Jul 6, 1992) (same); *see also CVS Pharmacy, Inc. v. Lavin*, 384 F. Supp. 3d 227, 236 (D.R.I. 2019).

Rhode Island courts have addressed covenants not to compete executed ancillary to the sale of a business, settlement agreements, distributor and supply agreements, and, most frequently, those arising in the context of an employment relationship. *See, e.g., Nestle Food Company v. Miller*, 836 F. Supp. 69 (D.R.I. 1993) (employment); *Block v. Vetcor*, 2000 WL 1634784 (R.I. Super. Ct. May 19, 2000) (employment); *Narragansett Coated Paper Corp. v. Lapierre*, 1998 WL 388400 (R.I. Super. Ct. June 25, 1998) (employment); *Aim High Academy, Inc. v. Jessen*, 2008 WL 5325586 (R.I. Super. Ct. Dec. 10, 2008) (employment); *R.J. Carbone Co. v. Regan*, 582 F. Supp. 2d 220 (D.R.I. 2008) (employment); *Astro-Med, Inc. v. Nihon Kohden America, Inc.*, 591 F.3d 1 (1st Cir. 2009) (employment); *In re Givens*, 251 B.R. 11 (Bkrtcy. D.R.I. 2000) (business sale); *Durapin, Inc. v. American Products, Inc.*, 559 A.2d 1051, 1057 (R.I. 1989) (distributorship); *Home Gas Corporation of Massachusetts, Inc. v. DeBlois Oil Company*, 691 F. Supp. 567 (D.R.I. 1987) (distributorship); *Max Garelick, Inc. v. Leonardo*, 250 A.2d 354 (R.I. 1969) (supply agreement).

Rhode Island courts have not addressed whether the signing of a covenant not to compete in the context of a franchise agreement provides sufficient consideration to support the covenant. In the context of an employment relationship, the Rhode Island Supreme Court has not decided whether continued employment provides sufficient consideration to support a covenant not to compete. *See Nestle Food Company v. Miller*, 836 F. Supp. 69, 77, n.32 (D.R.I. 1993), in which the court enforced the covenant citing authority from other jurisdictions. In *Aim High Academy, Inc. v. Jessen*, 2008 WL 5325586 (R.I. Super Ct. Dec. 10, 2008), the Rhode Island Superior Court held that continued employment does provide adequate consideration to support the restrictive covenant.

After establishing the threshold requirements, Rhode Island courts consider whether the restriction is reasonable. "Reasonableness" is determined by ascertaining whether the restriction (1) is limited to protect only the legitimate interest at issue; (2) is limited in duration, geographic coverage, and activity; (3) places an undue burden on the promisor that is not outweighed by the promisee's legitimate interest; and (4) is likely to injure the public. *R.J. Carbone Co. v. Regan*, 582 F. Supp. 2d 220 (D.R.I. 2008). *See CVS Pharmacy, Inc. v. Lavin*, 384 F. Supp. 3d 227, 236 (D.R.I. 2019); *Nestle Food Company v. Miller*, 836 F. Supp. 69, 73 (D.R.I. 1993); *Durapin, Inc. v. American Products, Inc.*, 559 A.2d 1051, 1053 (R.I. 1989).

Whether a restrictive covenant is reasonable is a question of law to be decided by the court. *See Durapin, Inc. v. American Products, Inc.*, 559 A.2d 1051 (R.I. 1989); *Allen v. Creative Services, Inc.*, 1992 WL 813643 (R.I. Super. Ct. July 6, 1992). Courts making this determination generally require the party seeking enforcement to show that the restriction embodied in the non-competition provision is reasonably limited in time, geographic area, and activity. *See Aim High Academy, Inc. v. Jessen*, 2008 WL 5325586 (R.I. Super. Ct. Dec. 10, 2008); *Home Gas Corporation of Massachusetts, Inc. v. DeBlois Oil Company*, 691 F. Supp. 567, 573 (D.R.I. 1987); *Nestle Food Company v. Miller*, 836 F. Supp. 69, 75 (D.R.I. 1993); *Max Garelick Inc. v. Leonardo*, 250 A.2d 354, 356 (R.I. 1969). Courts also consider the hardship that a given restriction exerts on the restricted party and on the public. *See Nestle Food Company v. Miller*, 836 F. Supp. 69 (D.R.I. 1993); *Home Gas Corporation of Massachusetts, Inc. v. DeBlois Oil Company*, 691 F. Supp. 567 (D.R.I. 1987) (same); *In re Givens*, 251 B.R. 11 (Bkrtcy. D.R.I. 2000); *Durapin, Inc. v. American Products, Inc.*, 559 A.2d 1051, 1057 (R.I. 1989); *Allen v. Creative Services, Inc.*, No. 92-0726, 1992 WL 813643 (R.I. Super. Ct. July 6, 1992).

Most of these cases are discussed in greater detail below.

---

2. Have courts articulated the "legitimate interests" of the franchisor that will support enforcement of a covenant against competition contained in a franchise agreement?

- **If so, what are they (e.g., protection of goodwill, protection of confidential information), and in what contexts did the issue arise?**
- **If not, what interests have been recognized in other contexts (e.g., employment agreements, the sale of business context)?**

Because no Rhode Island court has addressed covenants not to compete in the franchise context, it is unclear what "legitimate interests" would be found to support the enforcement of a covenant against competition contained in a franchise agreement.

Where a non-competition provision is contained in an employment, settlement, or distributorship agreement, or where it is ancillary to the sale of a business, courts have held that the protection of confidential information or the maintenance of goodwill is sufficient to support enforcement. Courts have recognized two types of confidential information: (1) customer lists and (2) customer information, business methods, and materials. *See R.J. Carbone Co. v. Regan*, 582 F. Supp. 2d 220 (D.R.I. 2008) (goodwill and confidential information); *Aim High Academy, Inc. v. Jessen*, 2008 WL 5325586 (R.I. Super. Ct. Dec. 10, 2008) (customer confidential information); *Home Gas Corporation of Massachusetts, Inc. v. DeBlois Oil Company*, 691 F. Supp. 567, 574 (D.R.I. 1987) (confidential customer list); *Nestle Food Company v. Miller*, 836 F. Supp. 69 (D.R.I. 1993) (confidential information and goodwill); *Dial Media, Inc. v. Schiff*, 612 F. Supp. 1483 (D.R.I. 1985) (goodwill and trade secrets); *Durapin, Inc. v. American Products, Inc.*, 559 A.2d 1051 (R.I. 1989) (confidential customer list; also noting at 559 A.2d at 1057 that protectible nature of customer list is a question of law); *Allen v. Creative Services, Inc.*, 1992 WL 813643 (R.I. Super. Ct. July 6, 1992) (proprietary information such as training manuals, investigative techniques, lists of confidential sources, and client files); *Narragansett Coated Paper Corp. v. Lapierre*, 1998 WL 388400 (R.I. Super. Ct. June 25, 1998) (manufacturing processes and materials). In the absence of such interests, courts will not enforce a covenant not to compete because such a covenant would constitute an unfair restraint on competition. *See Dial Media, Inc. v. Schiff*, 612 F. Supp. 1483 (D.R.I. 1985). It is well settled that the desire to be free from ordinary competition will not support the enforcement of a non-competition provision. *Id.* at 1489; *Durapin, Inc. v. American Products, Inc.*, 559 A.2d 1051, 1057 (R.I. 1989); *Max Garelick, Inc. v. Leonardo*, 250 A.2d 354 (R.I. 1969).

CUSTOMER LISTS

Courts have recognized a customer list as deserving protection where it is confidential in nature. *Compare Nestle Food Company v. Miller*, 836 F. Supp. 69 (D.R.I. 1993) (finding a protectable interest in a customer list after concluding that it was confidential in nature) with *Chemart Company v. Nixon*, 1992 WL 813516 (R.I. Super. Ct. Feb. 21, 1992) (concluding, in misappropriation case, that customer list was not confidential because there was no evidence suggesting that the identities of the plaintiff's customers were difficult to ascertain). Whether a customer list is confidential in nature depends upon how easily one conducting an independent investigation could ascertain the information contained on that list. *See Nestle Food Company v. Miller*, 836 F. Supp. 69, 73–74 (D.R.I. 1993); *Home Gas Corporation of Massachusetts, Inc. v. DeBlois Oil Company*, 691 F. Supp. 567, 573 (D.R.I. 1987).

Where the identities of customers included in an allegedly confidential customer list can be obtained using ordinary business channels or trade directories, a court will not consider that list confidential. For instance, customer lists were deemed not confidential in *Durapin, Inc. v. American Products, Inc.*, 559 A.2d 1051, 1057 (R.I. 1989) (identity of customers was "common knowledge"); *Chemart Company v. Nixon*, 1992 WL 813516 (R.I. Super. Ct. Feb. 21, 1992) (identities of the customers could be ascertained through ordinary means); *Callahan v. Rhode Island Oil Co.*, 240 A.2d 411 (R.I. 1968) (customers disclosed their need for certain products publicly); *cf. Abbey Medical/Abbey Rents, Inc. v. Mignacca*, 471 A.2d 189 (R.I. 1984) (noting, in misappropriation case, that a customer list will not be considered confidential where one can obtain customer identities through ordinary business channels or trade directories; concluding, however, that the list under consideration was confidential). On the other hand, where a list can be compiled only through the expenditure of time, effort, and money, and where the customers included in it are not discoverable through the use of any public source, such a list may be accorded confidential status. This was the case in, for example, *Aim High Academy, Inc. v Jessen*, 2008 WL 5325586 152 (R.I. Super. Ct. Dec. 10, 2008) (student customer list not readily ascertainable, hence confidential); *Nestle Food Company v. Miller*, 836 F. Supp. 69 (D.R.I. 1993) (customer database generated by employer with significant effort over many years of sifting through a universe of some 2,500 potential purchasers was confidential); *Home Gas Corporation of Massachusetts, Inc. v. DeBlois Oil Company*, 691 F. Supp. 567 (D.R.I. 1987) (customer list that included trade information about each customer, such as specialized requirements, contact persons, pricing policies, and credit histories, was confidential); *Abbey Medical/Abbey Rents, Inc. v. Mignacca*, 471 A.2d 189 (R.I. 1984) (customer list confidential where defendant admitted customer names were not readily ascertainable from public sources). Even where the identities of the customers on a list are readily ascertainable, the list may still be deemed confidential if it contains additional, more detailed information concerning the customers' particular needs. *See, e.g., Home Gas Corporation of Massachusetts, Inc. v. DeBlois Oil Company*, 691 F. Supp. 567 (D.R.I. 1987) (customer list included specific information regarding customer needs, credit, and so on); *Rego Displays, Inc. v. Fournier*, 379 A.2d 1098, 1101 (R.I. 1977) (identities of employer's customers, coupled with employee's knowledge of their specific needs, "took on the attributes of a trade secret when it was appropriated for [the employee's] private use.").

The decision of the federal district court in *Home Gas Corporation of Massachusetts, Inc. v. DeBlois Oil Company*, 691 F. Supp. 567 (D.R.I. 1987), provides an illustrative example of how Rhode Island courts (and federal courts interpreting Rhode Island law) determine whether a customer list has sufficient confidential attributes that it would support the enforcement of a covenant against competition. The plaintiff in *Home Gas* was a retailer of liquid propane gas who engaged the services of the defendant, DeBlois Oil, to distribute the gas to the plaintiff's customers. The arrangement called for the plaintiff-retailer to transfer to DeBlois Oil more than 4,000 customer accounts and liquid propane gas cylinders marked "Home Gas." DeBlois Oil was to support and maintain these accounts and cylinders. The agreement memorializing this arrangement included a covenant prohibiting DeBlois Oil, the distributor, from engaging in "the business . . . of selling, marketing, bottling or otherwise dealing in" liquid propane gas for two years after the termination of the parties' relationship. 691 F. Supp. at 570.

After the parties decided not to renew their distributorship agreement, DeBlois Oil began servicing the plaintiff's old customers, prompting the plaintiff to seek enforcement of the covenant not to compete. In response, DeBlois Oil argued that the plaintiff's customer list was not confidential (and therefore not sufficient to support the covenant) because the information contained in it was readily ascertainable by someone driving by the plaintiff's customers' places of business and identifying cylinders marked "Home Gas." The court rejected this contention, noting that DeBlois Oil had access to trade information such as the names and addresses of the plaintiff's customers and that it knew the volume of liquid propane gas used by each customer, the prices being charged to a particular customer, the credit histories of each customer, and the supply needs of each customer. The court noted that such detailed information could not be gleaned through any public source or by "looking into backyards." 691 F. Supp. at 575. The court concluded that the customer list was confidential.

Similarly, in *Nestle Food Company v. Miller*, 836 F. Supp. 69 (D.R.I. 1993), the federal district court concluded that the plaintiff-employer's customer list was confidential and, therefore, constituted a legitimate interest worthy of protection. The defendant-salesman in *Nestle Food*, after signing a covenant against competition, left the employ of the plaintiff, went to work for a competitor, and quickly began soliciting his former employer's customers. These customers were all listed on a database that the plaintiff had compiled over a number of years using data collected by the plaintiff's salespeople in response to "direct mailings, customer calls . . . , and other types of customer referrals . . . ." 836 F. Supp. at 71. The court concluded that the customer-related information contained on the database was not readily ascertainable through ordinary business channels. Specifically, the court noted that the plaintiff had "expended significant effort over many years to sift through a universe of some 2,500 potential purchasers to create a database of the names of organizations" that would have a consistent need for the plaintiff's product. *Id.* at 74. Moreover, the database contained other information such as the names of contact persons, the time of year when the customer would be expected to make purchases, and the amount of product that the customer could be counted on to buy each year. Even the defendant-employee conceded that such information was "sometimes . . . difficult to obtain." *Id.*

CUSTOMER INFORMATION, BUSINESS METHODS, AND MATERIALS

Rhode Island courts have also recognized that certain business methods and materials can constitute confidential information sufficient to support a covenant not to compete. *See R.J. Carbone Co. v. Regan*, 582 F. Supp. 2d 220 (D.R.I. 2008) (customer preference, unique patterns, and ordering history); *Aim High Academy, Inc. v Jessen*, 2008 WL 5325586 (R.I. Super. Ct. Dec. 10, 2008) (customer credit information, proprietary company programs, coaching and training methods). *But see Chelo's of Woonsocket, Inc., et al. v. Chelo*, 2004 WL 603417 (R.I. Super. Mar. 4, 2004) (plaintiff had no legitimate interest in protecting menu items, price structure, and restaurant's look and feel).

Although this type of information is not deemed confidential as often as customer lists, the Rhode Island District Court and several state superior courts have found it to be worthy of the protection afforded by a non-competition provision. In *R. J. Carbone Co. v. Regan*, 582 F. Supp. 2d 220 (D.R.I. 2008), the plaintiff's former employer, a Rhode Island wholesale floral distributor, sought to enforce a one-year non-competition restriction contained in the employment agreement of its former employee. The former employee challenged the validity of the restriction, claiming that the information in his possession—customer preferences, patterns, and ordering history—was not confidential and, therefore, his former employer did not have a legitimate interest in protecting this information. The court disagreed, stating that while "customer related information is generally not protectable unless it is confidential and proprietary . . . [t]estimony by Thomas Carbone and Regan revealed knowledge of something more than simply a list of florists from the phonebook. For example, Regan testified that learning whether a customer is 'worth it' often requires spending time with the customer and continuously going to retail locations. Regan's approximately 250 customers were identified over time as worthwhile based on their purchasing history, consistent sales volume, good credit and accessible locations." 582 F. Supp. at 225.

In *Allen v. Creative Services, Inc.*, 1992 WL 813643 (R.I. Super. Ct. July 6, 1992), the defendant-employer, an investigative and security consulting firm, moved for a preliminary injunction seeking to enforce covenants against competition between it and two of its former employees. The court concluded that the employer possessed a legitimate interest in proprietary information such as training manuals, lists of confidential sources, and certain investigative techniques. In reaching this result, the court also acknowledged that a business interest need not rise to the level of a trade secret in order to be entitled to protection. *See id.* at *2, *4 (granting a preliminary injunction and enforcing 18-month and one-year restrictions on competition).

Likewise, in *Narragansett Coated Paper Corp. v. Lapierre*, 1998 WL 388400 (R.I. Super. Ct. June 25, 1998), the superior court found that the plaintiff-employer had established the existence of confidential information sufficient to support the enforcement of a covenant against competition by pointing to proprietary information other than a customer list. Specifically, the court noted that the defendant-former employee had acquired special knowledge of the plaintiff-employer's manufacturing methods, such as information concerning (1) how it manufactured its unique, recently developed product; (2) what raw materials it used to manufacture its product; (3) what suppliers the employer obtained its materials from; and (4) the special machinery ("unique to the industry") that the employer used in its production process. *See id.* at *2. Based on these findings, the court was satisfied that the plaintiff had met its burden of showing that it had a legitimate interest worthy of protection; however, the employer's failure to protect itself from post-employment disclosure of this confidential information by other employees, who were "far more knowledgeable" than the defendant-employee, militated against enforcing the covenant against competition.

Additional, albeit indirect, support for the recognition of this type of confidential information as a legitimate interest can be found in decisions addressing customer lists. *E.g, Home Gas Corporation of Massachusetts, Inc. v. DeBlois Oil Company*, 691 F. Supp. 567 (D.R.I. 1987), and *Nestle Food Company v. Miller*, 836 F. Supp. 69 (D.R.I. 1993), both discussed earlier.

GOODWILL

The Rhode Island Supreme Court has long recognized that the goodwill implicit in the sale of a business constitutes a legitimate interest worthy of the protection afforded by a covenant not to compete. *See French v. Parker*, 14 A. 870 (R.I. 1888); *Koppers Products Co. v. Readio*, 197 A. 441 (R.I. 1938); *Mento v. Lanni*, 262 A.2d 839 (R.I. 1970).

In re Givens, 251 B.R. 11 (Bkrtcy. D.R.I. 2000), provides a helpful example concerning how and why the goodwill transferred in the sale of a business is entitled to the protection of a covenant not to compete. The defendant-seller in that case invented and sold buoy-stabilized rafts for decades and, after experiencing years of success in that market, decided to sell his business to the plaintiff-purchaser. As part of the transaction, the seller agreed not to re-enter the raft business. Shortly after the sale, however, the seller did just that and continued to sell rafts. Analyzing whether a protectable interest was present, the federal bankruptcy court observed that the post-sale covenant was "clearly intended to protect for [the purchaser] the positive goodwill that [the seller] had developed over several decades of manufacturing, selling and servicing the [r]aft, and the name recognition associated with the [seller's] name." 251 B.R. at 14. By contacting former customers, the seller had damaged the favorable reputation associated with the product, which reputation the defendant-seller had sold to the plaintiff-purchaser. The court granted the plaintiff's motion for a preliminary injunction, enforcing a six-year, worldwide covenant not to compete against the defendant-seller.

In the employment context, courts have acknowledged that the goodwill inherent in the "special relationship" that an employee develops with customers on behalf of his or her employer can serve as a legitimate interest sufficient to support the enforcement of a covenant against competition. *E.g., R.J. Carbone Co. v. Regan*, 582 F. Supp. 2d 220 (D.R.I. 2008); *Nestle Food Company v. Miller*, 836 F. Supp. 69 (D.R.I. 1993); *Allen v. Creative Services, Inc.*, 1992 WL 813643, at *2 (R.I. Super. Ct. July 6, 1992); *Block v. Vetcor of Warwick, LLC*, 2000 WL 1634784 (R.I. Super. Ct. May 19, 2000). In *Nestle*, the federal district court for the district of Rhode Island specifically addressed the concept of goodwill as a legitimate interest in the employment context. There, the defendant-salesman, while subject to a one-year covenant not to compete, left the plaintiff-employer and went to work for one of its chief competitors. The court looked at the confidential information that the salesman possessed, but concluded that such information was "less important" than the plaintiff's interest in protecting its "goodwill." 836 F. Supp. at 75. The court described "goodwill" as "the special relationship that its salesmen [had] developed with customers on behalf of [the plaintiff]." The goodwill in this instance clearly belonged to the employer, despite the salesperson's role in generating it. *Id.* at 71 n.6, 75.

3. What time limitations have courts recognized as reasonable in the franchise context? If no franchise cases have been decided, what time limitations have been recognized in other contexts?

➤ How have the time limitations been related to the interests protected?

Rhode Island courts have not addressed the time restrictions that would be considered reasonable in a covenant not to compete contained in a franchise agreement. In other contexts, courts have upheld covenants, unlimited in duration, where such a restriction is reasonable in light of the legitimate interest protected.

As discussed at the outset, Rhode Island courts will enforce covenants not to compete only if they are reasonable in view of the interests they are designed to protect. If the time restraint extends longer than what is reasonably required to protect the covenantee's legitimate interests, a court will deem the restrictive covenant unreasonable. *See Home Gas Corporation of Massachusetts, Inc. v. DeBlois Oil Company*, 691 F. Supp. 567, 575 (D.R.I. 1987) (*citing* RESTATEMENT (SECOND) OF CONTRACTS § 188 cmt. d (1981)). Because the reasonableness of a given restriction depends on the legitimate interest for which protection is sought, whether a given time restriction is upheld is dependent upon the specific conditions of each case. *See Max Garelick, Inc. v. Leonardo*, 250 A.2d 354, 356–57 (R.I. 1969) ("[C]ontracts in restraint of trade are not necessarily void by reason of universality of time . . . nor of space; but they depend upon the reasonableness of the restrictions under the conditions of each case.").

Where courts have found that the legitimate interest so warranted, they have upheld covenants with no time limitations at all. *See F. Saia Restaurants v. Pat's Italian Food to Go, Inc.*, 2012 WL 2133511 (R.I. Super. Ct. June 5, 2012). Early decisions indicate that the goodwill transferred in the sale of a business represents one such interest. *E.g., Koppers Products Co. v. Readio*, 197 A. 441 (R.I. 1938); *Tillinghast v. Boothby*, 37 A. 344, 344 (R.I. 1897); *French v. Parker*, 14 A. 870 (R.I. 1888). At the same time, courts have refused to enforce covenants with time restrictions as short as two years where the legitimate interest under consideration could be adequately protected with a restrictive period of shorter duration. *E.g., Narragansett Coated Paper Corp. v. Lapierre*, 1998 WL 388400 (R.I. Super. Ct. June 25, 1998).

Between these wide parameters, Rhode Island courts have upheld temporal restrictions ranging from one to seven years in duration. One year restrictions were upheld in *Aim High Academy, Inc. v. Jessen*, 2008 WL 5325586 (R.I. Super. Ct. Dec. 10, 2008); *R.J. Carbone Co. v. Regan*, 582 F. Supp. 2d 220 (D.R.I. 2008); *Astro-Med, Inc. v. Nihon Kohden America, Inc.*, 591 F.3d 1 (1st Cir. 2009); *Allen v. Creative Services, Inc.*, No. 92-0726, 1992 WL 813643, at *3 (R.I. Super. Ct. July 6, 1992) (one-year and 18-month covenants preliminarily enforced); and *Nestle Food Company v. Miller*, 836 F. Supp. 69 (D.R.I. 1993). Lengthier durations were approved in *Home Gas Corporation of Massachusetts, Inc. v. DeBlois Oil Company*, 691 F. Supp. 567 (D.R.I. 1987) (two years); *Block v. Vetcor of Warwick, LLC*, 2000 WL 1634784 (R.I. Super. Ct. May 19, 2000) (two years); *Griggs and Browne Co., Inc. v. Healy*, 453 A.2d 761 (R.I. 1982) (three years); *Oakdale Manufacturing Company v. Garst*, 28 A. 973 (R.I. 1899) (five years); *In re Givens*, 251 B.R. 11 (Bkrtcy. D.R.I. 2000) (six years reasonable where the business purchaser required sufficient time to (1) get business up and running without competing against the seller, who possessed inside knowledge; (2) develop its own sales force; (3) overcome negative comments and marketplace confusion;

and (4) develop new business in view of negative impact resulting from seller's misrepresentations); *North Shore Dye House, Inc. v. Rosenfield*, 166 A. 346 (R.I. 1933) (seven years). *But see Max Garelick, Inc. v. Leonardo*, 250 A.2d 354 (R.I. 1969) (holding that a five-year restraint prohibiting the defendant from purchasing grain from the plaintiff's supplier was unreasonable and unenforceable because there was no legitimate interest requiring protection).

The general rule reflected in these decisions is that courts will uphold time restrictions that go no further than what is necessary to protect the legitimate interest at issue. *E.g., Block v. Vetcor of Warwick, LLC*, 2000 WL 1634784 (R.I. Super. Ct. May 19, 2000). In that case, the plaintiffs, two veterinarians, executed two-year covenants not to compete that prohibited them from engaging in a business competitive with the defendant clinic within ten miles of the clinic's offices. After the relationship between the parties deteriorated, the defendant clinic terminated the veterinarians, who subsequently brought suit seeking judgment declaring the covenants unenforceable as against public policy. On defendant clinic's motion for a preliminary injunction, the court had little trouble identifying goodwill as the legitimate interest requiring protection. *Id.* at *6 ("Noncompetes are customary to protect goodwill at stake in service-oriented businesses where employees must build a client base . . ."). The court tied the temporal limitation to the legitimate interest, reasoning that two years was necessary for replacement veterinarians to demonstrate their effectiveness, and for the public to disassociate the veterinarians and the clinic, and noted that, in passing on time limitations, a court should "consider the time necessary to 'obliterate in the minds of the public' the association between the identity of the physician with his employer's practice." *Id.*

4. What geographic limitations have courts recognized as reasonable in the franchise context?

- **How have the geographic limitations been related to the interests protected?**
- **Have courts recognized the legitimacy of protecting other franchisees from competition?**

RI

Rhode Island courts have not addressed the reasonableness of a covenant's geographic restriction in the context of a franchise agreement. In other contexts, when determining the reasonableness of a geographic restriction in a covenant not to compete, Rhode Island courts focus on the breadth of restriction that is necessary to protect the legitimate interest at stake. *See, e.g., Home Gas Corporation of Massachusetts, Inc. v. DeBlois Oil Company*, 691 F. Supp. 567, 570 (D.R.I. 1987) ("If [a restrictive covenant] covers a geographic area more extensive . . . than is required to protect the [p]laintiff's interests the restrictive covenant is unreasonable."); *Koppers Products Company v. Readio*, 197 A. 441 (R.I. 1938) (noting that, in general, restrictive covenants are enforced only when the restrictions do not extend beyond what is necessary for the protection of those in whose favor they are made). Where a geographic limitation extends beyond what is necessary to safeguard the interest identified, a court will strike the covenant or, at the very least, modify it so that it is confined to the limited area necessary to protect the legitimate interest of the party seeking enforcement. *E.g., see North Shore Dye House, Inc. v. Rosenfield*, 166 A. 346 (R.I. 1933); *Koppers Products Company v. Readio*, 197 A. 441 (R.I. 1938).

In many instances, this approach has led Rhode Island courts to uphold or modify covenants to extend the geographic restrictions to the territory that a former employee (or the seller of a business) covered prior to leaving a plaintiff-employer (or selling his or her business to the plaintiff-purchaser). *See Astro-Med, Inc. v. Nihon Kohden America, Inc.*, 591 F.3d 1 (1st Cir. 2009) (enforcing a one-year restrictive covenant but modifying the scope of the geographic coverage from North America and Europe to Florida, which was the former employee's territory at the time of the termination); *R.J. Carbone Co. v. Regan*, 582 F. Supp. 2d 220 (D.R.I. 2008) (geographic restriction covering an area within a 100-mile radius of Hartford modified to extend only to territory where those customers with whom former employee actually worked reside); *Aim High Academy, Inc. v. Jessen*, 2008 WL 5325586 (R.I. Super. Ct. Dec. 10, 2008) (geographic restriction covering the entire state of Rhode Island modified and limited to a 15-mile radius of the Aim High facility in East Greenwich, Rhode Island); *Allen v. Creative Services, Inc.*, 1992 WL 813643 (R.I. Super. Ct. July 6, 1992) (where no geographic scope was specified in the agreement, the court limited the geographic scope to the area where the employees had previously performed services for the employer); *Nestle Food Company v. Miller*, 836 F. Supp. 69 (D.R.I. 1993) (upholding a one-year covenant that prohibited an employee from working for a competitor in the territory assigned to the employee at the time of the termination of his employment).

Decisions like the one issued by the federal bankruptcy court in *In re Givens*, 251 B.R. 11 (Bkrtcy. D.R.I. 2000), demonstrate that courts interpreting Rhode Island law are willing to enforce a covenant with a wide-ranging geographic scope so long as it is supported by the legitimate interest under consideration. The covenant at issue lacked a defined geographic scope. After a hearing in which the plaintiff offered evidence suggesting that the market for its product was worldwide, the court enforced the covenant and its corresponding worldwide scope, reasoning that the broad sweep was necessary to protect the plaintiff's legitimate interests. *See also Allen v. Creative Services, Inc.*, 1992 WL 813643 (R.I. Super. Ct. July 6, 1992) (where employees performed services in three states, the broad scope was necessary to protect the employer's goodwill in those areas).

Addressing covenants with more specific terms, Rhode Island courts have adhered to the practice of focusing on the legitimate interest and whether or not the geographic restriction was reasonably necessary to protect that interest. This approach has resulted in the approval of restrictions covering specific counties and radii of 75 miles, 40 miles, and ten miles. *E.g., Tillinghast v. Boothby*, 37 A. 344, 344 (R.I. 1897) (county-wide); *Griggs and Browne Co., Inc. v. Healy*, 453 A.2d 761 (R.I. 1982) (75-mile radius of plaintiff's office); *Home Gas Corporation of Massachusetts, Inc. v. DeBlois Oil Company*, 691 F. Supp. 567 (D.R.I. 1987) (40-mile radius of distributor's place of business); *Block v. Vetcor of Warwick, LLC*, 2000 WL 1634784 (R.I. Super. Ct. May 19, 2000) (ten-mile radius of plaintiff's veterinary clinic). Where covenantee's interest could be protected by less burdensome restraints, courts have stricken restrictions ranging more widely. *E.g., Herreshoff v. Boutineau*, 19 A. 712, 713 (R.I. 1890) (state-wide restriction not overly broad); *Mento v. Lanni*, 262 A.2d 839 (R.I. 1970) (two-mile restriction unreasonable). Again, the determination of what is reasonable depends on the facts of each case.

5. What limitations on activities have courts recognized as reasonable in the franchise context?

Rhode Island courts have not addressed the scope of restrictions on activities that would be considered reasonable in the franchising context. In other contexts, when addressing the reasonableness of a covenant not to compete, courts consider the range of activities that a covenant seeks to restrict in light of the enforcing party's legitimate interests. *E.g., Nestle Food Company v. Miller*, 836 F. Supp. 69, 76 (D.R.I. 1993) (upholding a one-year covenant not to compete but only prohibiting the former employee from soliciting customers of the employer, reasoning that the employer's legitimate interests could be adequately protected by "less draconian means"); *Koppers Products Co. v. Readio*, 197 A. 441, 445 (R.I. 1938) (enforcement of non-competes should "go no further than is reasonably necessary in order to enforce the rights of the employer and protect its business.").

While not expressly addressing the reasonableness of specific activity restrictions, courts have upheld covenants containing broadly worded restrictions concerning what a covenantee can, and cannot, do. For instance, in affirming a trial court's decision to grant a preliminary injunction and enforce a three-year covenant, the Rhode Island Supreme Court upheld a sweeping provision that prohibited a defendant-former employee from engaging in "any business—as an employee, partner, stockholder, or otherwise—which was competitive with the [exterminating] business conducted by plaintiff." *Griggs and Browne Co., Inc. v. Healy*, 453 A.2d 761, 762 (R.I. 1982). *See also North Shore Dye House, Inc. v. Rosenfield*, 166 A. 346, 350 (R.I. 1933) (enforcing a covenant that prohibited the defendant, the seller of a cleansing and dyeing business, from "engag[ing] directly or indirectly in the cleansing, dyeing, or laundry business in any capacity"); *Block v. Vetcor of Warwick, LLC*, 2000 WL 1634784, at *6 (R.I. Super. Ct. May 19, 2000) (upholding a covenant that prohibited the plaintiff-employees from engaging in "any specialty group practice . . . which is competitive with the veterinary business of [the defendant clinic] or any of the other members of the [group including the defendant clinic].").

Rhode Island courts appear tolerant of covenants that are narrowly tailored in their restraint of activities to restrict only those activities harmful to the legitimate interests at issue. As the court explained in *Home Gas Corporation of Massachusetts, Inc. v. DeBlois Oil Company*, 691 F. Supp. 567, 576 (D.R.I. 1987), "A restraint that limits one field of many available to the promis[or] and limits the solicitation of former customers rather than eliminates competition is easier to justify." (citing RESTATEMENT (SECOND) OF CONTRACTS § 188 cmt. g (1981)). Accordingly, courts have not hesitated to scale back activity restrictions where they reach beyond what is necessary to protect the interests of the party seeking enforcement. *E.g., Durapin, Inc. v. American Products, Inc.*, 559 A.2d 1051 (R.I. 1989) (adopting a rule of partial enforcement, which permits unreasonable restraints to be modified by the court and then enforced); *see also* section 8 *infra*. In *Nestle Food Company v. Miller*, 836 F. Supp. 69 (D.R.I. 1993), for instance, the federal district court for the district of Rhode Island addressed a covenant that prohibited the defendant, who sold candy products to fundraising organizations, from engaging or in any way assisting "any sales or similar related [sic] work or services for any third-party fundraising company or third-party fundraising products of any kind." 836 F. Supp. at 72–73. Although

RI

concluding that the geographic and temporal scopes of the covenant were reasonable, the court held that the employer had not demonstrated the necessity of going to the "extreme of prohibiting former employees from working for a competitor." *Id.* at 75–76. The court concluded that the plaintiff's legitimate interests could be protected through "less draconian means." *Id.* Accordingly, the court enforced a narrower set of restrictions that prohibited the employee from disclosing confidential information and soliciting the plaintiff-employer's customers. *See also Narragansett Coated Paper Corp. v. Lapierre*, 1998 WL 388400 (R.I. Super. Ct. June 25, 1998) (narrowing scope of activities restrained).

6. Does the state recognize a difference between in-term and post-term covenants?

Rhode Island courts have not directly addressed the issue of whether, in the franchise context or otherwise, in-term covenants are treated differently from post-term covenants. In *Griggs and Browne Co., Inc. v. Healy*, 453 A.2d 761 (R.I. 1982), the state's highest court had occasion to rule upon a hybrid covenant that included both in-term and post-term periods of non-competition. While upholding the trial court's decision to issue an injunction based on a post-term violation of that covenant, the court declined to discuss whether the enforceability of covenants operative during the term of a contractual relationship is determined using the same standards applicable to post-term covenants. Two federal courts interpreting state law similarly declined to undertake such an analysis: *Nestle Food Company v. Miller*, 836 F. Supp. 69 (D.R.I. 1993) and *Home Gas Corporation of Massachusetts, Inc. v. DeBlois Oil Company*, 691 F. Supp. 567 (D.R.I. 1987).

7. Has the state allowed enforcement of covenants against non-signatories (e.g., family members, newly formed corporations)?

There are no reported Rhode Island cases addressing the enforcement of covenants against competition against non-signatories in a franchise context. In other contexts, one federal district court interpreting Rhode Island law concluded that one could enforce a covenant not to compete against a non-signatory where the non-signatory was the alter ego or instrumentality of the restrained party. In *Home Gas Corporation of Massachusetts, Inc. v. DeBlois Oil Company*, 691 F. Supp. 567 (D.R.I. 1987), the court acknowledged that "[a] covenant not to compete is enforceable against a person or company, not parties to the contract, but the alter ego or instrumentality of the covenantor who is a party to the contract." 691 F. Supp. at 576. After determining that the defendant-distributor dominated the second company and was sufficiently intertwined in the business of the second company, the court concluded that it would not recognize their separate corporate identities. Accordingly, the court enforced the covenant, as modified to prohibit only solicitation of the plaintiff-retailer's former customers, against the defendant-distributor as well as the second company. The court also noted in dicta that a company that hires an individual subject to a covenant against competition can be enjoined based on that covenant despite the fact that the company was not a party to its terms. *Id.*

8. Will the state modify, "blue-pencil," or otherwise reduce a covenant found to be overbroad?

In *Durapin, Inc. v. American Products, Inc.*, 559 A.2d 1051 (R.I. 1989), the Rhode Island Supreme Court put an end to years of uncertainty over how a court should deal with unreasonable restrictive covenants when it adopted the rule of "partial enforcement." 599 A.2d at 1058–59 (addressing the partial enforcement rule in the context of a covenant contained in a distributorship agreement). Under this doctrine, an unreasonable covenant will be modified and enforced to the extent it is reasonably necessary to protect the legitimate interest of the party in whose favor it runs, so long as that party has not demonstrated any "bad faith or deliberate overreaching" in seeking and obtaining the agreement in the first place. *Id.* at 1058. In choosing this approach, the court rejected the "all or nothing" rule, which mandated that an unreasonable covenant be stricken in its entirety. The court also rejected the more restrictive "blue-pencil" approach that had been partially embraced in the court's earlier decision in *Max Garelick, Inc. v. Leonardo*, 250 A.2d 354 (R.I. 1969). Under the blue-pencil rule, a court would enforce an unreasonable covenant only if it "remained grammatically meaningful after striking out any offending provisions." 250 A.2d at 357. In deciding to adopt the partial enforcement rule over the blue-pencil approach, the court noted that the RESTATEMENT (SECOND) OF CONTRACTS had rejected the latter approach because of its emphasis on form over substance. *See also Ferrofluidics Corp. v. Advanced Vacuum Components, Inc.*, 968 F.2d 1463, 1469 (1st Cir. 1992) citing *Durapin Inc. v. American Products, Inc.*, 559 A.2d 1051, 1058 (R.I. 1989).

Although the decision in *Durapin* dealt with a covenant arising in a distributorship agreement between a manufacturer and a distributor, state and federal trial courts have employed its reasoning when addressing unreasonable covenants arising in the contexts of employment, settlement, and sale of business agreements, including the following: *In re Givens*, 251 B.R. 11 (Bkrtcy. D.R.I. 2000) (reducing the duration of an unlimited covenant to six years, but declining to change the unlimited geographic scope); *Nestle Food Company v. Miller*, 836 F. Supp. 69 (D.R.I. 1993) (modifying the covenant so that it only prohibited the former employee from disclosing confidential information or soliciting customers of his former employer); *Home Gas Corporation of Massachusetts, Inc. v. DeBlois Oil Company*, 691 F. Supp. 567 (D.R.I. 1987) (narrowing the covenant to enjoin a defendant-distributor from soliciting the plaintiff's former customers); *Narragansett Coated Paper Corp. v. Lapierre*, No. 97-2842, 1998 WL 388400 (R.I. Super. Ct. June 25, 1998) (modifying the scope of relief so that the defendant-employee was precluded only from disclosing confidential information and soliciting customers of the plaintiff-employer); *Allen v. Creative Services, Inc.*, 1992 WL 813643 (R.I. Super. Ct. July 6, 1992) (reducing a covenant's unlimited geographic scope to the area in which the plaintiff-former employee had performed services for the defendant-employer); *R.J. Carbone Co. v. Regan*, 582 F. Supp. 2d 220 (D.R.I. 2008) (rejecting a 100-mile radius of Hartford, Connecticut, and limiting the territory to the area that contained those customers with whom the former employee worked and had been invoiced by the company within the 24-month period prior to the employee's termination); and *Aim High Academy, Inc. v. Jessen*, 2008 WL 5325586 (R.I. Super. Ct. Dec. 10, 2008) (modifying a geographic restriction covering the entire state of Rhode Island to an area within a 15-mile radius of the plaintiff's facility).

The United States Court of Appeals for the First Circuit applied the *Durapin* rationale in *Astro-Med, Inc. v. Nihon Kohden America, Inc.*, 591 F.3d 1 (1st Cir. 2009) and held that a non-competition covenant with an overly broad geographic restriction could be partially enforced to reduce the scope of the geographic coverage from North America and Europe to Florida and a subset of Astro-Med's customers. In the district court, a verdict was entered for plaintiff, and the scope of the non-compete was limited to the state of Florida and a subset of the plaintiff's customers. Appealing the verdict, the defendant argued that the non-competition provision was unenforceable until it was judicially modified; hence, the damage award should be vacated. The appellate court rejected the defendant's novel argument stating: "Their logic would give the promisor in a non-competition agreement one free breach, requiring a prior judicial order before the provision could be said to have been violated. Such a proposition, the validity of which is without authority, would eviscerate all but the most narrowly tailored non-competition agreements since a modification of any term of the provision would justify a breach of all of its terms" *Id.* at 15.

In a case applying Rhode Island law, the United States District Court for the Northern District of Illinois ruled that a finding of good faith on the part of the party seeking to enforce a non-competition covenant is required before the court will partially modify such a provision. In *Saban v. Caremark Rx, LLC*, 780 F. Supp. 2d 700 (N.D. Ill. 2010), the court was asked to determine the enforceability of a one-year non-competition covenant with a broadly defined description of prohibited activities, including prohibitions against the former employee engaging in any activity for a competitor of Caremark, in addition to a non-disclosure clause that contained a broadly written restriction on activities and geographic area. In 2009, defendant Saban signed an employment agreement with Caremark that was governed by Rhode Island law. The agreement contained a non-disclosure provision and a broadly written non-competition provision that prohibited Saban from engaging in any activity for a competitor of Caremark. The court determined that the non-competition covenant was unenforceable as it was overly broad. In considering whether to partially enforce the non-competition clause, the court concluded that Caremark acted in bad faith when it intentionally drafted the overly broad restriction. The court examined the particularities of the employment relationship, the former employee's position with the current employer, competition between the current and former employers, and the broad language of the contract, and concluded that the covenant was overly broad. The court explained that good faith on the part of the drafter was a necessary prerequisite to partial enforcement of a non-competition covenant, citing 4 Williston on Contracts § 13:26 (1981): "The need for good faith, as articulated by Williston, is that upholding deliberately unreasonable covenants tends to encourage employers and purchasers possessing superior bargaining power over that of their employees and vendors to insist upon unreasonable and excessive restrictions, secure in the knowledge that the promise may be upheld in part, if not in full." The court noted that "a court will not aid a party who has taken advantage of his dominant bargaining power to extract from the other party a promise that is clearly so broad as to offend public policy by redrafting the agreement." Restatement (Second) of Contracts § 184. The non-competition restriction was drafted "in total disregard for the requirement that it not extend beyond Caremark's legitimate business interests" and was unenforceable.

9. When does a non-compete period begin to run? Will courts equitably extend the term?

Courts applying Rhode Island law have issued conflicting decisions concerning whether a court will measure the restrictive period of a covenant from the date of termination or the date of the court order granting the injunction.

Parties seeking to enforce non-competition agreements can be deprived of the benefit of a covenant, deemed reasonable by a court, where the litigation aimed at accomplishing enforcement concludes after the expiration of the temporal restriction. *See, e.g., Eastern Container Corp. v. Craine*, 624 A.2d 833 (R.I. 1993) (affirming the trial court's enforcement of a two-year covenant from the date of the employee's termination, as opposed to the date—two months later—on which the trial judge issued an injunction). One way around this "mootness" problem is for courts enforcing such agreements to measure the restrictive period from the date the injunction issues.

Courts in Rhode Island have taken divergent approaches to this issue. Two federal district court decisions take the view that the time should run from the date of the order enforcing the covenant. In *Nestle Food Company v. Miller*, 836 F. Supp. 69 (D.R.I. 1993), the employer included language in its covenant providing that, if the employer was required to institute legal action to enforce the covenant following the employee's termination, the one-year time limitation would "begin on the date of termination . . . and extend to the date that is one year from the date the court grants [the employer's] request for . . . relief." 836 F. Supp. at 73. While not explicitly relying on this language, the court in *Nestle Food* issued a preliminary injunction restraining the defendant-employee for one year from the date the order was issued. Likewise, in *Home Gas Corporation of Massachusetts, Inc. v. DeBlois Oil Company*, 691 F. Supp. 567 (D.R.I. 1987), after concluding that the modified covenant at issue was enforceable, the court noted that it would be "an idle gesture" to grant an injunction enforcing a two-year time restriction when that injunction, measured from the date of the contract's termination, would expire seven months from the court's order. 691 F. Supp. at 578. To rectify this problem, the court extended the injunction so that it covered a period of two years from the date of the court's entry of judgment.

In contrast, the Rhode Island Supreme Court, in *Eastern Container Corp. v. Craine*, 624 A.2d 833 (1st Cir. 1993), affirmed a ruling by a trial court that measured the restricted time period from the date of the breaching employee's termination. The employee in *Eastern Container* had left the plaintiff-employer on March 4, 1991. In response, the plaintiff moved for, and obtained, a preliminary injunction two months later on June 28, 1991; however, the injunction only enjoined the employee until March 6, 1993, two years from the date of the defendant-employee's resignation. The defendant-employee appealed, arguing that the restraint was greater in scope than necessary, but the court refused to entertain this argument, noting that the time for the restrictive injunction expired by its own terms on March 6, 1993, two months prior to the supreme court's May 10, 1993, ruling. 624 A.2d at 835 ("The question of whether the injunction should have been issued in the first place is therefore moot, because there is no relief this court could grant.").

10. Are there additional nuances or peculiarities of the state's treatment of covenants in the franchising context?

Rhode Island courts have not considered the treatment of covenants in a franchising context. However, it is important to note that the question of whether continued employment represents adequate consideration for a covenant signed after the commencement of employment has not been definitively decided in Rhode Island.

As with every contract, an agreement not to compete must be supported by consideration if it is to be enforced. *See Durapin, Inc. v. American Products, Inc.*, 559 A.2d 1051, 1053 (R.I. 1989) ("A party seeking to enforce a noncompetition provision must show that . . . the provision is supported by adequate consideration."). When an employee signs a covenant at the inception of employment, his or her salary often represents the requisite consideration. Similarly, if an employee is asked to execute a covenant after the commencement of his or her employment and the employer, at that time, provides him or her with some benefit in exchange, the requirement of consideration is satisfied. *See Block v. Vetcor of Warwick, LLC*, 2000 WL 1634784 (R.I. Super. Ct. May 19, 2000) (noting that where employer offered employee equity in the employer's business and a bonus program, such was consideration for the agreement containing the non-compete). Where, however, an employee signs a covenant not to compete following his or her start date, and the employer provides no benefit other than continued employment, some jurisdictions conclude that the agreement fails for lack of consideration. *See Dial Media, Inc. v. Schiff*, 612 F. Supp. 1483 (D.R.I. 1985) (noting a split in jurisdictions concerning whether continuation of an employment relationship constitutes sufficient consideration for a restrictive covenant signed after the commencement of employment).

State courts in Rhode Island have declined to resolve the issue of whether continued employment constitutes sufficient consideration. *See Dial Media, Inc. v. Schiff*, 612 F. Supp. 1483 (D.R.I. 1985) (acknowledging a lack of Rhode Island caselaw on point and declining to address the issue). The decision by the federal district court in *Nestle Food Company v. Miller*, 836 F. Supp. 69 (D.R.I. 1993), however, provides some guidance. There, recognizing that the employee had executed the subject covenant after commencing employment, the court, presumably fulfilling its obligation to predict how the Rhode Island Supreme Court would decide the issue, held as follows: "Even if there was no consideration other than allowing [the defendant employee] to continue as an employee with all of the . . . benefits associated therewith, such continuation of employment constitutes adequate consideration." 836 F. Supp. at 77. The court referenced caselaw from other jurisdictions, noting that it provided "ample support" for the result reached. *Id.* at 77 n.32.

The one court addressing the enforceability of forum selection clauses contained in covenants against competition concluded that they are enforceable. In *Microfibres, Inc. v. McDevitt-Askew*, 20 F. Supp. 2d 316 (D.R.I. 1998), the federal district court for the district of Rhode Island upheld a forum selection clause contained in a covenant against competition in which the employee agreed to submit to the jurisdiction and venue of Rhode Island courts in order to resolve any claims arising out of the agreement. Although employed by a company headquartered in Rhode Island, the employee in *Microfibres* resided in North Carolina, performed her primary job duties within North Carolina, and had traveled to Rhode Island on only three occasions before leaving to work for a competitor. These facts notwithstanding, the district court refused to grant the employee's motion to dismiss for lack of personal jurisdiction, holding that she had waived her right to challenge jurisdiction through her acceptance of the forum selection clause included in the non-competition agreement. The employee's motion to transfer the action to North Carolina met a similar fate, as the court rejected various arguments aimed at challenging the enforceability of the clause, including (1) the unequal bargaining power between the employer and the employee and (2) the fact that the clause was in boilerplate language. The court's decision was based, in part, on the fact that the agreement was presented to the employee well in advance of her start date and that she did not object to any of its terms. Had the contract been imposed on the employee in mid-employment or in such a way that she could not negotiate any of its terms, the court noted, "then its adhesive nature might be deemed unreasonable or unfair and cause the clause to be unenforceable." 20 F. Supp. 2d at 325.

South Carolina

*by Natalma (Tami) McKnew**

1. Has the state addressed covenants against competition in the context of franchising?

- **Does the state have a franchising statute or regulations that address covenants against competition?**
- **Does the state have a covenants statute of general applicability that would encompass franchise covenants?**
- **Have the courts addressed covenants in the context of franchising either under a statute or under the state's common law?**

South Carolina lacks a statute that specifically addresses franchising. The state's Business Opportunity Sales Act (SC CODE § 39-57-10 *et seq.*) and special industry statutes do not reach the issue of restrictive covenants. Nor has any reported South Carolina case squarely addressed the merits of a covenant against competition in a franchise agreement. The only franchise case involving a restrictive covenant, *Spill The Beans, Inc. v. Sweetreats, Inc.*, 2009 WL 4110313 (D.S.C. Nov. 24, 2009), enforced a restrictive covenant on a rule to show cause but did not address its legal merits. The covenant prohibited competition for a period of 24 months within 15 miles of the former franchisee's location and within 15 miles of any other franchised location. However, a federal district court in the state addressed this issue in the context of a distribution agreement in *International Safety Access Corp. v. Integrity Worldwide, Inc.*, 2010 WL 11552932 (D.S.C. Oct. 27, 2010). Analogizing the distributor agreement at issue in the case to a franchise, the court marshalled franchise cases from several jurisdictions and concluded that "[a]ll such restraints on trade in a franchise agreement, . . . must be reasonable as to time, scope and territorial limitation" (citation omitted). *Id.* at *4.

---

*Ms. McKnew is a partner in the firm of Fox Rothschild, LLP in Greenville, South Carolina. Fox Rothschild or its predecessors Smith Moore Leatherwood LLP or Leatherwood Walker Todd and Mann, P.C. were involved in the following cases cited herein: *Spill The Beans, Inc. v. Sweetreats, Inc.*, 2009 WL 4110313 (D.S.C. Nov. 24, 2009); *Reidman Corp. v. Jarosh*, 290 S.C. 252, 349 S.E.2d 404 (S.C. 1986); *Sermons v. Caine & Estes Insurance Agency, Inc.*, 275 S.C. 506, 27 S.E.2d 338 (1980); *Standard Register Co. v. Kerrigan*, 238 S.C. 54, 119 S.E.2d 533 (S.C. 1961); and *Reidman Corp. v. Jarosh*, 290 S.C. 252, 349 S.E.2d 404 (S.C. 1986).

As in other jurisdictions, competitive concerns underpin limitations on restrictive covenants. Thus, in the early 20th century, the South Carolina Supreme Court posed the concern as a monopolization issue, ultimately deciding in *Walter A. Wood Mowing and Reaping Co. v. Greenwood Hardware Co.*, 75 S.C. 378, 55 S.E. 378 (S.C. 1906) that restricting competition by the seller of the business was not monopolistic. The court there concluded that "contracts in partial restraint of trade are valid if reasonable and founded upon a valuable consideration." 55 S.E. at 386.

No South Carolina court has announced whether a restrictive covenant in a franchise agreement should be analogized to such a restriction in an employment agreement or in connection with the sale of a business. *International Safety Access Corp. v. Integrity Worldwide, Inc.*, 2010 WL 11552932 (D.S.C. Oct. 27, 2010) focused on a restrictive covenant in a distributor agreement. The court explained that the covenant would be strictly construed against the enforcer and could be enforced against the former distributor only if reasonable under prevailing South Carolina jurisprudence. Applying employment-related case authority, the court found the covenant unenforceable. In *Preferred Research, Inc. v. Reeve*, 292 S.C. 545, 357 S.E.2d 489 (S.C. App. 1987), the South Carolina Court of Appeals described the license agreement at issue as similar to a franchise agreement and observed that because a franchise agreement "inherently involves parties of unequal bargaining power, it is more closely analogous to an employment agreement than an agreement relating to the sale of a business . . . ." Significantly, however, the license was governed by Georgia law, and the court upheld the covenant based on Georgia law. While these two cases suggest that the rationale applied to non-compete provisions in employment agreements would be applied to such covenants in franchise agreements, no South Carolina case clearly reaches that conclusion.

Covenants against competition in employment agreements are viewed with disfavor by South Carolina courts, will be strictly construed, and will be enforced only if reasonable. *Oxman v. Sherman*, 239 S.C. 218, 122 S.E.2d 559 (S.C. 1961). The well-established indicia of enforceability in South Carolina are whether the covenant (1) is necessary to protect the legitimate interests of the employer, (2) is reasonably limited in duration and scope, (3) is not unduly harsh on the employee's opportunities for future employment, (4) is supported by valuable consideration, and (5) does not offend public policy. A raft of cases stand for this long-standing proposition. *See, e.g., Rental Uniform Service of Florence, Inc. v. Dudley*, 278 S.C. 674, 301 S.E.2d 142 (S.C. 1983); *Stringer v. Herron*, 309 S.C. 529, 424 S.E.2d 547 (S.C. App. 1992); *Poole v. Incentives Unlimited, Inc.*, 345 S.C. 378, 548 S.E.2d 207 (S.C. 2001); *Lampman v. DeWolff Boberg & Assoc.*, 319 Fed. Appx. 293 (4th Cir. 2009). As the court noted in *Stringer v. Herron, supra*, the analysis of enforceability depends on the particular facts of each case.

Non-compete covenants arising from "the sale of a business between two sophisticated parties . . . should be scrutinized at a more relaxed level than non-compete covenants executed in connection with employment contracts." *Palmetto Mortuary Transport, Inc. v. Knight Systems*, 424 S.C. 444, 456, 818 S.E.2d 724, 731 (S.C. 2018). The indicia of enforcement nevertheless mirror those of employment restrictions. A restrictive covenant ancillary to the sale of a business will be upheld if it (1) is necessary to protect the buyer's legitimate interests, (2) is reasonably limited in time and scope, (3) is supported by valuable consideration, and (4) is reasonable in terms of public policy. *Id.* The burden of proof on enforceability rests with the party attempting enforcement. *Delmar Studios of the Carolinas v. Kinsey*, 233 S.C. 313, 104 S.E.2d 338 (S.C. 1958).

2. Have the courts articulated the "legitimate interests" of the franchisor that will support enforcement of a covenant against competition contained in a franchise agreement?

- **If so, what are they (e.g., protection of goodwill, protection of confidential information), and in what contexts did the issue arise?**
- **If not, what interests have been recognized in other contexts (e.g., employment agreements, the sale of business context)?**

The only reported franchise restriction case in South Carolina, *Spill The Beans, Inc. v. Sweetreats, Inc.*, 2009 WL 4110313 (D.S.C. Nov. 24, 2009), before the district court on a rule to show cause, did not address the franchisor's legitimate interests.

In the absence of a franchise case, *Rockford Manufacturing, Ltd. v. Bennet*, 296 F. Supp. 2d 681 (D.S.C. 2003) may be instructive. The district court in that case acknowledged an employer's legitimate interest in protecting its existing dealer network from solicitation by former employees. South Carolina courts have also acknowledged an employer's legitimate interest in protecting its:

- Goodwill: *Almers v. The South Carolina National Bank of Charleston*, 265 S.C. 48, 217 S.E.2d 135 (S.C. 1975); *Baugh v. Columbia Heart Clinic, P.A.*, 402 S.C. 1, 738 S.E.2d 480 (S.C. App. 2013).
- Existing customers: *Standard Register Co. v. Kerrigan*, 238 S.C. 54, 119 S.E.2d 533, 538 (S.C. 1961) (amusingly borrowing a quote from *Arthur Murray Dance Studios of Cleveland, Inc. v. Witter*, 62 Ohio L. Abs. 17, 105 N.E.2d 685: "Just as one has to consider the difference between tossing a tiger or a pet cat into a cage with a human being, so here, in determining whether an ex-employee is a threatening menace, one has to consider the very nature of the actor"); *Almers v. The South Carolina National Bank of Charleston, supra; Stringer v. Herron*, 309 S.C. 529, 424 S.E.2d 547 (S.C. App. 1992); *Collins Music Co., Inc. v. Parent*, 288 S.C. 91, 340 S.E.2d 794 (S.C. App. 1986); *Baugh v. Columbia Heart Clinic, P.A., supra* (patients and referral sources).
- Inventions: *Milliken & Co. v. Morin*, 399 S.C. 23, 731 S.E.2d 288 (S.C. 2012).
- Trade secrets: *Rockford Manufacturing, Ltd. v. Bennet, supra; Milliken & Co. v. Morin, supra.*

Similar interests have been acknowledged as legitimate to the buyer in restrictive covenants ancillary to the purchase of a business. In *Reeves v. Sargeant*, 200 S.C. 494, 21 S.E.2d 184, 187 (S.C. 1942), the court acknowledged the buyer's right to "fair and full protection of the business, good will and trade name which the vendee has purchased and paid for . . . ." Thus, South Carolina courts have recognized a business buyer's legitimate interest in protecting:

- Goodwill and clientele: *Sermons v. Caine & Estes Insurance Agency, Inc.*, 275 S.C. 506, 273 S.E.2d 338 (S.C. 1980); *Palmetto Mortuary Transport, Inc. v. Knight Systems, Inc*, 424 S.C. 444, 818 S.E.2d 724 (S.C. 2018).
- Trade secrets, proprietary information, and business contacts: *Hagemeyer North America, Inc. v. Thompson*, 2006 WL 516733 (D.S.C. Mar. 1, 2006).
- The acquired entity's employees: *Café Associates, Ltd. v. Gerngross*, 305 S.C. 6, 406 S.E.2d 162 (S.C. 1991).

A promisee is never entitled to protection from competition per se, however. *Almers v. The South Carolina National Bank of Charleston, supra; Carolina Chemical Equipment Co., Inc. v. Muckenfuss*, 322 S.C. 289, 471 S.E.2d 721 (S.C. App. 1996).

3. What time limitations have courts recognized as reasonable in the franchise context? If no franchise cases have been decided, what limitations have been recognized in other contexts?

➤ **How have they been related to the interests protected?**

In *Spill the Beans, Inc. v. Sweetreats, Inc.*, 2009 WL 4110313 (D.S.C. Nov. 29, 2009), the court enforced, without discussion, a 24-month post-termination franchise non-compete.

In general, South Carolina courts require restrictive covenants to contain a reasonable time limitation. In *Standard Register Co. v. Kerrigan*, 238 S.C. 54, 69, 119 S.E.2d 533 (S.C. 1961), the South Carolina Supreme Court explained that the duration of the restriction "renders a restraint unreasonable if the period of time is so long as to interfere with [the] interest of the general public by depriving it of the employee's industry and service." *See also Sermons v. Caine & Estes Insurance Agency, Inc.*, 275 S.C. 506, 273 S.E.2d 338 (S.C. 1980) (referring to the "right of a person to use his talents to earn a living"); *Milliken & Co. v. Morin*, 399 S.C. 23, 731 S.E.2d 288 (S.C. 2012) (assessing impact on ex-employee).

A two- or three-year covenant against competition has been routinely approved in South Carolina. *E.g., Standard Register Co. v. Kerrigan, supra* (two years); *Rental Uniform Service of Florence, Inc. v. Dudley*, 278 S.C. 674, 301 S.E.2d 142 (S.C. 1983) (three years); *Moser v. Gosnell*, 334 S.C. 425, 513 S.E.2d 123 (S.C. App. 1999) (three years, business sale); *Caine & Estes Insurance Agency, Inc. v. Watts*, 278 S.C. 207, 293 S.E.2d 859 (S.C. 1982) (three years); *Rockford Manufacturing, Ltd. v. Bennet*, 296 F. Supp. 2d 681 (D.S.C. 2003) (two years); *Furman v. United States*, 602 F. Supp. 444 (D.S.C. 1984) (three years).

Restrictive periods of five years were upheld in two cases involving the sale of businesses: *Café Associates, Ltd. v. Gerngross*, 305 S.C. 6, 406 S.E.2d 162 (S.C. 1991), and *Metts v. Wenberg*, 158 S.C. 411, 155 S.E. 734 (S.C. 1930).

The South Carolina Supreme Court characterized a restriction of expressed unlimited duration as unnecessary, unreasonable, and unenforceable in *Sermons v. Caine & Estes Insurance Agency, Inc., supra*. However, in *Reeves v. Sargeant*, 200 S.C. 494, 21 S.E.2d 184 (S.C. 1942), the court allowed enforcement of a restriction unlimited in time where "the restrictive covenant [is] incidental to another lawful contract of sale involving some interest requiring the protection of the restraint." 200 S.C. at 502. The facts of the *Reeves* case were unusual and perhaps contributed to the court's willingness to reverse the lower court and enforce a perpetual restriction. After selling his photography business, Mr. Sargeant evidently experienced seller's remorse and "commenced a systematic effort to drive the plaintiff out of business," *id.* at 497–98, and "in direct and flagrant breach of his contract," *id.* at 498, continued in the photography business within the restricted area.

4. What geographic limitations have courts recognized as reasonable in the franchise context?

➤ **How have they been related to the interests protected?**

➤ **Have the courts recognized the legitimacy of protecting other franchisees from competition?**

No South Carolina court has directly discussed the geographic scope of a covenant against competition in a franchise agreement. In other contexts, South Carolina courts have generally compared the geographic scope of the restriction to the territory in which the employee actually operated (*Standard Register Co. v. Kerrigan*, 238 S.C. 54, 119 S.E.2d 533 (S.C. 1961)) or, in a business sale, the area actually served by the business (*Stringer v. Herron*, 309 S.C. 529, 424 S.E.2d 547 (S.C. App. 1992)).

In the employment context, the court in *Standard Register Co. v. Kerrigan*, 119 S.E.2d at 553, explained that a restriction on competition in the area actually worked by the employee, or in which the employee had established contacts with the employer's customers, was "necessary for the protection of the employer." *See also Eastern Business Forms, Inc. v. Kistler*, 258 S.C. 429, 189 S.E.2d 22 (S.C. 1972); *Sermons v. Caine & Estes Insurance Agency, Inc.*, 275 S.C. 506, 273 S.E.2d 338 (S.C. 1980) (entire state too broad); *Team IA, Inc. v. Lucas*, 395 S.C. 237, 717 S.E.2d 103 (S.C. App. 2011) (nationwide coverage too broad).

A non-compete agreement lacking any geographic limitation is usually unenforceable (*Lampman v. DeWolff Boberg & Assoc.*, 319 Fed. Appx. 293 (4th Cir. 2009); *International Safety Access Corp. v. Integrity Worldwide*, 2020 WL 11552932 (D.S.C. Oct. 27, 2010)). However, South Carolina courts have held that a customer limitation may substitute for a geographic limitation, *Caine & Estes Insurance Agency, Inc. v. Watts*, 278 S.C. 207, 293 S.E.2d 859 (S.C. 1982), under the rationale that a restriction so limited is reasonably necessary to protect the employer's business. To the same effect are *Rockford Manufacturing, Ltd. v. Bennet*, 296 F. Supp. 2d 681 (D.S.C. 2003); *Vessel Medical, Inc. v. Elliott*, 2015 WL 5437173 (D.S.C. Sept. 15, 2015); *Pearl Insurance Group, LLC v. Baker*, 2018 WL 4103333 (D.S.C. Aug. 29, 2018); and *Synthes USA, Inc. v. Davis*, 2017 WL 5972705 (D.S.C. Dec. 1, 2017). Such a limitation, however, must be specific and is subject to the same enforceability analysis as other non-competes. *Café Associates, Inc. v. Gerngross*, 305 S.C. 6, 406 S.E.2d 162 (S.C. 1991). A restrictive covenant prohibiting an ex-employee generally from soliciting or accepting business from any client with whom he or she worked, or that was a client of the ex-employer, was condemned in *Fournil v. Turbeville Insurance Agency, Inc.*, 2008 WL 11349821 (D.S.C. Dec. 30, 2008). The ex-employee, the court noted in *Fournil*, could breach the restriction without ever knowing it. By contrast, in *Collins Music Co., Inc. v. Parent*, 288 S.C. 91, 340 S.E.2d 794 (S.C. App. 1986), the names of specific customers were included in the covenant against competition, a client limitation that provided an acceptable substitute for a geographic limitation.

Geographic restrictions in connection with the sale of a business are subject to the same expressed limitations, occasionally with an overlay of concern for potential effects on competition. The court in *Somerset v. Reyner*, 233 S.C. 324, 104 S.E.2d 344 (S.C. 1958), invalidated a post-transaction restrictive covenant on the seller that embraced far more territory than had been served by the seller's "comparatively small retail store." Enforcement of the broad restriction, the court noted, would "constitute a restraint upon trade . . . ." 104 S.E.2d at 347. In *Stringer v. Herron, supra*, the South Carolina Court of Appeals invalidated a covenant against competition in a business sales agreement based on an overly broad geographic restriction. Evidence demonstrated that 84 percent of the veterinary clinic's patients lived within ten miles of the clinic, rendering a 15-mile restriction that reached into four additional South Carolina counties and into Georgia unreasonable. Applying the same rationale, but reaching a different conclusion, the court upheld a 20-mile restriction in *Baugh v. Columbia Heart Clinic, P.A.*, 402 S.C. 1, 738 S.E.2d 480 (S.C. App. 2013).

Sermons v. Caine & Estes Insurance Agency, Inc., supra; Poynter Investments, Inc. v. Century Builders of Piedmont, Inc., 387 S.C. 583, 694 S.E.2d 15 (S.C. 2010); and *Hagemeyer North America, Inc. v. Thompson*, 2006 WL 516733 (D.S.C. Mar. 1, 2006) involved hybrid agreements. Each of the defendants had sold their business to the plaintiffs, and then signed employment agreements with the new purchaser. To the covenants in the post-sale agreements, the courts echoed the standards applicable in employment agreements. In *Sermons* and *Poynter* the court invalidated the covenants, while in *Hagemeyer* the scope was deemed reasonable. Although echoing the same reasonableness standards as in employment cases, the court in *Hagemeyer* acknowledged that covenants against competition "are given greater deference in the context of a sale of business than in the employment context." 2006 WL 516733, at *10.

The South Carolina Supreme Court reiterated the *Stringer* analysis in *Palmetto Mortuary Transport, Inc. v. Knight Systems, Inc.*, 424 S.C. 444, 818 S.E.2d 724 (S.C. 2018), which involved a different sort of hybrid agreement. As a part of the sales transaction, the parties entered into a ten-year non-exclusive supply agreement, pursuant to which the business seller would supply certain products to the buyer. While reiterating the *Stringer* analysis, the court upheld a 150-mile restricted area despite the business' usual three or four county service area, citing the "ameliorating effects" of the supply agreement and the buyer's intent to expand its service area as facts supporting enforcement.

5. What limitations on activities have courts recognized as reasonable in the franchise context?

The sole South Carolina case involving a franchise, *Spill the Beans, Inc. v. Sweetreats, Inc.*, 2009 WL 4110313 (D.S.C. Nov. 24, 2009), was on a rule to show cause that enforced a covenant restricting the covenantor from engaging in a business similar to the franchised business. Perhaps due to the posture of the case, no rationale for the court's order appears in the published opinion.

Milliken & Co. v. Morin, 399 S.C. 23, 731 S.E.2d 288 (S.C. 2012) addresses the enforcement of confidentiality and invention assignment clauses in an employment agreement. As related in section 10 below, such restrictions are subject to the similar limiting considerations as covenants against competition; if overly broad in scope, they will not be enforced. The particular clauses under consideration in *Milliken* were a grantback (invention assignment) and non-disclosure of proprietary work of the employer. Excluded from the restrictive provisions were any inventions or work by the defendant, a PhD physicist, not involving the employer's business, supplies, facility, equipment, or proprietary information. The provisions were enforceable, the court concluded, because they were expressly limited to matters in which Milliken had a direct and legitimate interest. The former employee was otherwise free to continue employment in his chosen field.

In other contexts, covenants satisfying the applicable standards of enforcement and preventing the following activities have been approved in South Carolina:

- Becoming employed by or engaging in a business similar to the promisee's
    - *Standard Register Co. v. Kerrigan*, 238 S.C. 94, 119 S.E.2d 533 (S.C. 1961)
    - *Oxman v. Sherman*, 239 S.C. 218, 122 S.E.2d 559 (S.C. 1961)

- *Delmar Studios of the Carolinas v. Kinsey*, 233 S.C. 313, 104 S.E.2d 338 (S.C. 1958)
- *Hagemeyer North America, Inc. v. Thompson*, 2006 WL 516733 (D.S.C. Mar. 1, 2006)
- *Somerset v. Reyner*, 233 S.C. 324, 104 S.E.2d 344 (S.C. 1958)
- *Café Associates, Inc. v. Gerngross*, 305 S.C. 6, 406 S.E.2d 162 (S.C. 1991)
- *Palmetto Mortuary Transport, Inc. v. Knight Systems, Inc.*, 424 S.C. 444, 818 S.E.2d 724 (S.C. 2018)

- Soliciting customers
  - *Rockford Manufacturing, Ltd. v. Bennet*, 296 F. Supp. 2d 681 (D.S.C. 2003)
  - *Caine & Estes Insurance Agency, Inc. v. Watts*, 278 S.C. 207, 293 S.E.2d 859 (S.C. 1982)
  - *Collins Music Co., Inc. v. Parent*, 288 S.C. 91, 340 S.E.2d 794 (S.C. App. 1986)
  - *Wolff v. Colonial Life and Accident Ins. Co.*, 309 S.C. 100, 420 S.E.2d 217 (S.C. App. 1992)
  - *Pearl Ins. Co. v. Baker*, 2018 WL 4103333 (D.S.C. Aug. 29, 2018)
- Soliciting the promisee's employees
  - *Café Associates, Inc. v. Gerngross, supra*
- Soliciting the promisee's dealers
  - *Rockford Manufacturing, Ltd. v. Bennet, supra*
- Assisting others to engage in competition with the promisee
  - *Baugh v. Columbia Heart Clinic, P.A.*, 402 S.C. 1, 738 S.E.2d 480 (S.C. App. 2013)

6. Does the state recognize a difference between in-term and post-term covenants?

The U.S. District Court addressed this issue in the context of a distribution agreement in *International Safety Access Corp. v. Integrity Worldwide, Inc.*, 2010 WL 11552932 (D.S.C. Oct. 27, 2010). Analogizing the distributor agreement at issue in the case to a franchise, the court marshalled franchise cases from several jurisdictions and concluded that "[a]ll such restraints on trade in a franchise agreement, regardless as to when they are in effect, must be reasonable as to time, scope and territorial limitation" (citation omitted). 2010 WL 11552932, at *4. "*To be enforceable, the restriction must be reasonable 'without regard to whether they are in-term or post-term covenants'*" (citation omitted). *Id.* at *3 (emphasis in original).

7. Has the state allowed enforcement of covenants against non-signatories (e.g., family members, newly formed corporations)?

No published South Carolina case has expressed an opinion on this issue, except in the context of injunctive relief. For instance, in *Spill the Beans, Inc. v. Sweetreats, Inc.*, 2009 WL 4110313 (D.S.C. Nov. 24, 2009), the court enforced by injunction a non-compete against transferees of the original franchisee, unfortunately without analysis. In a non-franchise context, *see, e.g., Rental Service Corp. v. Nunamaker*, 2006

WL 1677152 (D.S.C. June 14, 2006), the court granted the plaintiff's motion for preliminary injunctive relief, enjoining the defendant "and any person or entity acting in concert with him."

8. Will the state modify, "blue-pencil," or otherwise reduce a covenant found to be overbroad?

Although not in the franchise context, South Carolina courts have expressly and repeatedly rejected any notion that a court may "blue-pencil" or otherwise amend a covenant against competition and thereby transform an unenforceable covenant into an enforceable one. A restrictive covenant must be enforceable as written, or it cannot be enforced at all. *Eastern Business Forms, Inc. v. Kistler*, 258 S.C. 429, 189 S.E.2d 22 (S.C. 1972); *Somerset v. Reyner*, 233 S.C. 324, 104 S.E.2d 344 (S.C. 1958). In *Stonhard, Inc. v. Carolina Flooring Specialists, Inc.*, 366 S.C. 156, 160, 621 S.E.2d 352, 354 (S.C. 2005), the South Carolina Supreme Court explained that "[t]o add and enforce [a curative] term requires this Court to bind these parties to a term that does not reflect the parties' original intention." The policy is so robust that South Carolina courts have refused to enforce an agreement of the parties during litigation to narrow the restriction, as evident in *Poynter Investments, Inc. v. Century Builders of Piedmont, Inc.*, 387 S.C. 583, 588, 694 S.E.2d 15, 18 (S.C. 2010): "[R]estrictions in a non-compete clause cannot be rewritten by a court or limited by the parties' agreement, but must stand or fall on their own terms." A plaintiff employer's willingness to stipulate to a narrower restriction was similarly rejected in *Faces Boutique, Ltd. v. Gibbs*, 318 S.C. 39, 455 S.E.2d 707 (S.C. App. 1995).

Despite South Carolina courts' distaste for altering written agreements, however, the courts may excise unenforceable covenant provisions from enforceable ones if the covenant is severable or divisible. As the district court explained in *Rockford Manufacturing, Ltd. v. Bennet*, 296 F. Supp. 2d 681 (D.S.C. 2003), severability depends upon the specific wording of the covenant or agreement, for example, whether restrictions are separately expressed or whether the agreement includes a provision allowing severance. An otherwise unenforceable "indivisible covenant may not be enforced even to a reasonable extent." *Id.* at 687. The employee's agreement in *Team IA, Inc. v. Lucas*, 395 S.C. 237, 717 S.E.2d 103 (S.C. 2012) included two different forms of restrictive covenants, a non-compete and a non-solicitation. The non-compete provision was unenforceable because it purported to apply nationally and could not be judicially rewritten. However, the court concluded that the non-solicitation provision, extending to the employees' customers in multiple states, might be enforceable.

9. When does a non-compete period begin to run? Will courts equitably extend the term?

Onset of the non-compete period is determined by contract. South Carolina courts will not equitably extend a covenant against competition, as the South Carolina Supreme Court directly held in *Stonhard, Inc. v. Carolina Flooring Specialists, Inc.*, 366 S.C. 156, 621 S.E.2d 352 (S.C. 2005) and *Mailsource, LLC v. M.A. Bailey & Assoc., Inc.*, 356 S.C. 363, 588 S.E.2d 635 (S.C. App. 2003) (non-compete in shareholder agreement).

10. What are the additional nuances or peculiarities of the state's treatment of covenants in the franchising context?

NON-DISCLOSURE AND CONFIDENTIALITY AGREEMENTS

South Carolina courts have applied the standards of reasonableness to non-disclosure and confidentiality agreements, as the court of appeals did in *Carolina Chemical Equipment Co. v. Muckenfuss*, 322 S.C. 289, 471 S.E.2d 721 (S.C. App. 1996). The non-disclosure provision in that case was subjected to a reasonableness analysis and found deficient. As the court explained, in this context "courts impose no presumptions against employers and do not subject the employee's promise or covenant not to disclose to a rigid test or analysis." *Id.* at 302. Despite the somewhat relaxed scrutiny, the court invalidated the non-disclosure, explaining that it was so broad that it substantially prevented the ex-employee from using his general skills and knowledge and thus operated as a non-compete.

In an apparent effort to protect trade secrets from the taint of *Muckenfuss*, in 1997 the South Carolina Trade Secrets Act, S.C. Code § 39-8-10 *et seq.*, was amended to include, at section 39-8-30(D), the following: "A contractual duty not to disclose or divulge a trade secret, to maintain the secrecy of a trade secret, or to limit the use of a trade secret must not be considered void or unenforceable or against public policy for lack of a durational or geographical limitation." It is important to note, however, that the statute applies only to "trade secrets," not to confidential or proprietary information generally. Despite the amendment to the Trade Secrets Act, courts continue to subject broad non-disclosure and secrecy agreements to close scrutiny. *See, e.g., Fay v. Total Quality Logistics*, 419 S.C. 622, 799 S.E.2d 319 (S.C. App. 2017), certiorari granted Feb. 1, 2018.

In apparent tension with *Muckenfuss* is the South Carolina Supreme Court's decision in *Milliken & Company v. Morin*, 399 S.C. 23, 731 S.E.2d 288 (S.C. App. 2012), in which the court refused to characterize a grantback or holdover clause in an employment agreement as a non-compete. The employee, a PhD chemist, had granted ownership rights to Milliken in all inventions, during employment or within one year of its end, except those that did not use Milliken resources, were developed on the employee's own time, did not relate to any anticipated business of Milliken, or were not the result of any work performed for Milliken. The agreement also included a non-disclosure clause. Applying the relaxed analytical standard set forth in *Muckenfuss*, the court held that both the non-disclosure and the holdover clauses were enforceable: "[T]hey do not operate in restraint of the employee's trade but merely vest ownership of an invention with the entity which ought to have it." 731 S.E.2d at 292. The federal district court in South Carolina extended the *Milliken v. Morin* relaxed analysis to confidential information in *Williams v. Unum Group*, 2017 WL 10756823 (D.S.C. Oct. 18, 2017).

FORFEITURE CLAUSES AND LIQUIDATED DAMAGES

Forfeiture clauses have occasionally rescued restrictive covenants from application of a reasonableness analysis. *J.W. Hunt & Co. v. Davis*, 313 S.C. 352, 437 S.E.2d 557 (S.C. App. 1993), concerned a restrictive covenant in a partnership agreement that allowed a withdrawing partner to continue his accounting practice and keep his clients, upon payment of liquidated damages to the partnership. The defendant's attempt to characterize the payment as a forfeiture clause did not sway the court.

Because the provision prohibited the withdrawing partner from neither continuing in the profession nor retaining his clients, it was not a non-compete and not subject to a reasonableness analysis.

The restrictive covenants at issue in *Baugh v. Columbia Heart Clinic, P.A.*, 402 S.C. 1, 738 S.E.2d 480 (S.C. App. 2013) appeared in employment agreements, distinguishing the case from *J.W. Hunt*, which the court held must be subjected to a reasonableness analysis. An ex-employee of the clinic was required to forfeit payments to which he was entitled post-employment in the event he entered into competition with his ex-employer. "Forfeiture clauses are generally subject to reasonableness review, and none of our courts have declined to apply a reasonableness analysis to forfeitures." 738 S.E.2d at 488. This conclusion is in harmony with *Almers v. The South Carolina National Bank of Charleston*, 265 S.C. 48, 217 S.E.2d 135 (S.C. 1975), in which the court held that a clause by which the employee forfeited payments from his profit-sharing plan was an unenforceable forfeiture.

CONSIDERATION

A covenant against competition must be supported by valuable consideration, defined as "some right, interest, profit, or benefit accruing to one party or some forbearance, detriment, loss or responsibility given, suffered or undertaken by the other." *Prestwick Golf Club, Inc. v. Prestwick Ltd. Partnership*, 331 S.C. 385, 389, 503 S.E.2d 184, 186 (S.C. App. 1998). In the employment context, hiring always fulfills the consideration requirement, *Reidman Corp. v. Jarosh*, 290 S.C. 252, 349 S.E.2d 404 (S.C. 1986), but continued employment alone does not, *Poole v. Incentives Unlimited, Inc.*, 345 S.C. 378, 548 S.E.2d 207 (S.C. 2001). A change in an employee's contractual relationship may also constitute consideration, as the court held in *Baugh v. Columbia Heart Clinic, P.A.*, 402 S.C. 1, 738 S.E.2d 480 (S.C. App. 2013). Although the new employment agreements at issue in that case did not change the existing compensation system, the parameters of the non-compete in the new agreements were stricter and the liquidated damages clause was added. These changes satisfied the requirement for new consideration.

In the absence of applicable franchise precedent in South Carolina, one might be on solid ground predicting that the initiation of a franchise relationship constitutes valuable consideration capable of supporting a covenant against competition. However, the South Carolina position on continued employment may cast doubt upon the continuation of a franchise relationship (e.g., renewal) as satisfying the consideration requirement.

COVENANTS SUBJECT TO FOREIGN LAW

That a restrictive covenant by its terms is subject to and complies with the law of another state (or even a foreign country) does not guarantee its enforcement in South Carolina. If the covenant offends South Carolina's strict limitations on restrictions, a South Carolina court will refuse to enforce it. *E.g., Stonhard, Inc. v. Carolina Flooring Specialists, Inc.*, 366 S.C. 156, 621 S.E.2d 352 (S.C. 2005) (blue-penciling refused, although consistent with applicable New Jersey law, because contrary to South Carolina public policy), and *Herring v. LaPolla Industries, Inc.*, 2013 WL 12148771 (D.S.C. Nov. 26, 2013) (same).

South Dakota

*by Jeffrey S. Haff**

1. Has the state addressed covenants against competition in the context of franchising?

- **Does the state have a franchising statute or regulations that address covenants against competition?**
- **Does the state have a covenants statute of general applicability that would encompass franchise covenants?**
- **Have the courts addressed covenants in the context of franchising either under a statute or under the state's common law?**

South Dakota's franchise laws address a franchisor's obligations regarding registration, disclosure, and prohibitions against fraudulent statements, but those laws do not address covenants against competition. South Dakota Codified Laws § 37-5A-1 *et seq.* South Dakota does have a statute of general applicability providing that covenants against competition are void unless the covenant falls within one of four enumerated exceptions. South Dakota Codified Laws section 53-9-8 states:

> **Contracts in restraint of trade, void, exceptions.**
>
> Every contract restraining exercise of a lawful profession, trade, or business is void to that extent, except as provided by §§ 53-9-9 to 53-9-11, inclusive, and § 53-9-12.

South Dakota's statute represents "a legislative expression of public policy" disfavoring restraints of trade. *Farm Bureau Life Ins. Co. v. Dolly*, 910 N.W.2d 196, 201 (S.D. 2018). Indeed, in *Lindskov v. Lindskov*, 800 N.W.2d 715, 718 (S.D. 2011), the South Dakota Supreme Court reiterated the general state of South Dakota law by holding "[i]n South Dakota, contracts in restraint of trade are generally void as against public policy . . . ." The plaintiff in the *Lindskov* case had attempted to stretch a non-disparagement clause to include a prohibition on competition. The contractual non-disparagement clause was included in a stock purchase agreement between two feuding shareholders. The relevant section of the stock purchase agreement, captioned "Confidentiality and Non-disparagement," provided:

*Mr. Haff practices with the law firm of Dady& Gardner, P.A. in Minneapolis, Minnesota.

> In addition, Seller and Buyer agree that they shall not hereinafter engage in any form of conduct, or make any statements or representations, that will disparage or otherwise harm the reputation, goodwill, or commercial interests of the other party.

Id at 717.

After the selling shareholder opened a competing business, the buyer sought to have the court interpret the provision "[n]ot hereinafter engage in any form of conduct . . . that will . . . harm the reputation, goodwill, or commercial interests of the other party" as a covenant against competition. The South Dakota Supreme Court affirmed the lower court and refused to accept that interpretation. Had the provision been properly drafted, it would likely have been enforceable as an exception to section 53-9-8. The court reiterated that "[t]here must be a distinct agreement creating a covenant in restraint of trade." *Id.* at 718.

South Dakota law does not favor non-competition provisions, and even where permitted, the provisions are strictly construed against enforcement. Sections 53-9-9 to 53-9-12 of the South Dakota Codified Laws contain exceptions from general rule of section 53-9-8 captioned the "sale of goodwill," "dissolution of partnership," "employment contract," and "captive agents" (insurance agents). These statutory exceptions, however, are nevertheless "construed narrowly so as to promote the prohibition against contracts in restraint of trade." *Miller v. Honkamp Krueger Fin. Servs., Inc.*, 9 F.4th 1011, 1017 (8th Cir. 2021) (citing *Communication Technical System, Inc. v. Densmore*, 583 N.W.2d 125 (S.D. 1998)).

It would seem at first glance that non-competition covenants in franchise agreements do not fall within any of these statutory exceptions because, arguably, franchise agreements (1) do not provide for the franchisee's sale of the goodwill of the franchisee's business to the franchisor, (2) do not involve the dissolution of a partnership between the franchisor and the franchisee, and (3) are not employment contracts; additionally, franchisees are not insurance agents. There are no reported cases in South Dakota analyzing whether any of the statutory exceptions contained in sections 53-9-9 through 53-9-12 apply to franchise agreements.

From 1993 to July 2001, the South Dakota Division of Securities required that an addendum be attached to every franchise agreement distributed in South Dakota, stating:

> Covenants not to compete upon termination or expiration of the franchise agreement are generally unenforceable in the State of South Dakota, except in certain instances as provided by law.

BUS. FRANCHISE GUIDE (CCH) ¶ 5410.01.

SD

The division required that this language be set forth in all franchise registration documents incorporating covenants against competition. *Id.* This requirement was reflective of the division's policy to protect franchisees from unfair covenants against competition. However, in its statement of policy issued on July 24, 2001, the division appeared to have either (1) softened its position or (2) chosen to reduce the degree to which it regulates franchise transactions, as it has eliminated the previously required addendum. "The [D]ivision no longer requires any state addendum to the franchise agreement." BUS. FRANCHISE GUIDE (CCH) ¶ 5410.01.

The United States District Court, in *Hot Stuff Foods, LLC v. Mean Gene's Enterprises, Inc.*, 468 F. Supp. 2d 1078 (D.S.D. 2006), reviewed sections 53-9-8 and 53-9-11 to analyze a non-competition provision in an employment contract. The district court there acknowledged a distinction in South Dakota law that recognizes that "[a]n agreement not to disclose information or solicit, unlike a covenant not to compete, is free from challenge as a general restraint on trade. However, such covenants are strictly construed and enforced only to the extent reasonably necessary to protect the employer's interest in confidential information." The district court held that the non-competition provisions in the employment agreement were enforceable and consistent with South Dakota law.

---

2. Have the courts articulated the "legitimate interests" of the franchisor that will support the enforcement of a covenant against competition contained in a franchise agreement?

- **If so, what are they (e.g., protection of goodwill, protection of confidential information), and in what contexts did the issue arise?**
- **If not, what interests have been recognized in other contexts (e.g., employment agreements, the sale of business context)?**

There are no reported franchise cases. However, South Dakota has articulated "legitimate interests" that will support enforcement of a covenant against competition. One of these interests is codified by the statutory exception contained in section 53-9-9 of the South Dakota Codified Laws regarding the sale of goodwill. South Dakota has also recognized a party's legitimate interest in the protection of trade secrets and confidential information.

PROTECTION OF GOODWILL

Whether a franchisee's business is successful depends, in large part, on the goodwill that the franchisor and the franchisee are able to establish for the individual business. Thus, courts could construe the sale of a franchise as the "sale of goodwill" and subject to the exception contained in section 53-9-9. *See Arnott v. American Oil Co.*, 609 F.2d 873, 882 (8th Cir. 1979) ("A franchisee . . . builds the goodwill of his own business and the goodwill of the franchisor."). Covenants against competition involving the sale of goodwill have been upheld as long as they comply with section 53-9-9, which provides:

> Any person who sells the goodwill of a business may agree with the buyer to refrain from carrying on a similar business within a specified county, city, or other specified area, as long as the buyer or person deriving title to the goodwill from the seller carries on a like business within the specified geographical area.

In *Franklin v. Forever Venture, Inc.*, 696 N.W.2d 545, 551–53 (S.D. 2005), the South Dakota Supreme Court had occasion to define the meaning of "similar business" as referenced in section 53-9-9. The case involved the sale of a restaurant business in which a specified portion of the purchase price was allocated to goodwill and a covenant not to compete. The seller later became employed with another food service business. Even though there were significant differences in the operational methods of the two businesses, the supreme court concluded that the seller's employment with the other business could be enjoined. In making its analysis, the court stated, "[w]e conclude that a determination of what constitutes 'carrying on a similar business' in SDCL 53-9-9 should not include businesses or activities that are isolated, insubstantial, or non-detrimental. Whether the business actually detrimentally competes will depend on the facts of a particular case." *Id.* at 551. Years later, upon further opportunity to define the phrase "similar business" as used in section 53-9-9, the supreme court simply reaffirmed the fact-specific nature of the inquiry described in *Franklin*. *See JAS Enterprises, Inc. v. BBS Enterprises, Inc.*, 835 N.W.2d 117 (S.D. 2013) (noting that the determination as to whether defendant engaged in a "similar business" was a question of fact for the jury).

In *Simpson v. C&R Supply, Inc.*, 598 N.W.2d 914, 919 (S.D. 1999), a non-franchise case, the South Dakota Supreme Court invalidated a clause prohibiting a seller of goodwill from competing with the buyer "within all counties within any of the United States of America." The *Simpson* court found this restriction to be overbroad, but modified the covenant to restrict competition within the city of Sioux Falls. Similarly, in *Ward v. Midcom, Inc.*, 575 N.W.2d 233 (S.D. 1998), the South Dakota Supreme Court enforced a covenant against competition in a stock option repurchase agreement. The court applied section 53-9-9 to the stock repurchase agreement, finding that the sale of stock is analogous to the sale of goodwill. However, as the covenant against competition contained no territorial limitation, the court modified the covenant to include only the county in which business was located.

PROTECTION OF TRADE SECRETS AND CONFIDENTIAL INFORMATION

South Dakota has also recognized an interest in protecting trade secrets and confidential information. However, these interests are protected by non-disclosure agreements as opposed to covenants against competition. A non-disclosure agreement differs from a non-competition agreement, and "is not subject to the same restrictions as a non-compete agreement." *Sterling Computers Corp. v. Fling*, 2019 WL 5104013, at *4 (D.S.D. Oct. 11, 2019). *See also First American Systems, Inc. v. Rezatto*, 311 N.W.2d 51, 56 (S.D. 1981).

A non-competition agreement restricts competition for a specified period of time and over a designated geographical area. *Central Monitoring Service v. Zakinski*, 553 N.W.2d 513, 516 (S.D. 1996). By contrast, non-disclosure clauses typically protect against dissemination of trade secrets, confidential business practices, and marketing strategies unique to a business. "Because a non-disclosure clause, unlike a non-compete clause, is not a *general restraint on trade* in South Dakota, it is not held to the same strict standard as a non-compete clause if the language is too broad." *Billion v. Oxford*, 2016 WL 3976636, at *4 (D.S.D. July 22, 2016) (emphasis added). *See also Hot Stuff Foods, LLC v. Mean Gene's Enterprises, Inc.*, 468 F. Supp. 2d 1078 (D.S.D. 2006), to the same effect.

In *First American Systems v. Rezatto*, *supra*, an insurance agent opened his own insurance agency using the confidential customer information of his former employer. During the agent's employment with First American, he had signed an employment agreement that contained a non-disclosure provision, wherein the agent agreed not to reveal confidential customer information such as policy terms or expiration dates for a term of ten years. In determining whether the information sought to be protected was a trade secret, the court focused on the parties' intent to create a confidential relationship and found that the employee was put on notice by the employment contract that the customer information was secret and that the "[employer] intended to seek remedial action to prevent a disclosure." *Id.* at 58. The court further found that even though the separate elements of the customer information (i.e., expiration and renewal dates, personal customer data, and addresses) did not rise to the level of a trade secret, the information, "taken together and construed in light of the contract's express creation of confidentiality comprise a trade secret." *Id.* at 57.

Similarly, in *Overholt Crop Insurance Service Co. v. Travis*, 941 F.2d 1361, 1367 (8th Cir. 1991), the court found that a former sales representative of an insurance agency had breached the non-disclosure clause of his employment agreement with the agency. The non-disclosure clause prevented the former sales representative from soliciting the agency's customers or exploiting confidential customer information. During the representative's employment with the agency, he began soliciting customers from the agency for a competing agency and sharing commissions with the competing agency. The *Overholt* court held that the non-disclosure clauses were "legally enforceable under South Dakota law." *Id.* at 1369. Like *Rezatto*, the *Overholt* court focused on the parties' intent to create a confidential relationship: "[The sales representative] appears to have been fully cognizant of [the agency's] intention to create a confidential relationship. The terms of his employment contract clearly announce this intent. . . . Our decision in this case is controlled by *Rezatto's* holding that information that might not otherwise qualify as trade secrets is elevated to this status when construed in light of the contract's creation of a confidential relationship." *Id.* at 1368. The addition of section 53-9-12 to the South Dakota Codified Laws in 2005 appears to validate the court's decision in *Overholt*. *See also Walling Chemical Co. v. Bigner*, 349 N.W.2d 647, 650 (S.D. 1984) (finding that non-disclosure provision in employment agreement that referred to territorial limitations of the sales representative's authority and confidential customer information was a reasonable restriction); *Mid-America Marketing Corp. v. Dakota Industries*, 281 N.W.2d 419, 423 (S.D. 1979) *on rehearing*, 289 N.W.2d 797 (S.D. 1980) (allowing non-disclosure agreement to protect written customer lists).

Based upon the above analysis regarding trade secrets and confidential information, it appears that despite the uncertainty about the enforceability of franchise covenants not to compete in South Dakota, a non-disclosure clause may be enforced. The relationship between a franchisee and a franchisor is generally considered a confidential relationship, and operational procedures such as recipes or product manufacturing procedures are usually classified as trade secrets. *See*, for instance, *Uncle B's Bakery, Inc. v. O'Rourke*, 920 F. Supp. 1405, 1425 (N.D. Iowa 1996) (finding bagel manufacturer's recipes and manufacturing and packaging processes for its refrigerated bagels were likely to be trade secrets). Thus, a franchisee who opens a competing business using operational procedures, confidential customer information, or any other information that, taken together and construed in light of the franchise agreement's intent to create a confidential relationship, may well be subject to the enforcement of a non-disclosure clause in the franchise agreement.

THE EMPLOYMENT CONTRACTS EXCEPTION

Section 53-9-11 of the South Dakota Codified Laws provides:

> An employee may agree with an employer at the time of employment or at any time during his employment not to engage directly or indirectly in the same business or profession as that of his employer for any period not

> exceeding two years from the date of termination of the agreement and not to solicit existing customers of the employer within a specified county, first or second class municipality or other specified area for any period not exceeding two years from the date of termination of the agreement, if the employer continues to carry on a like business therein.

South Dakota distinguishes between an employee who voluntarily quits and an employee who is fired in determining the validity of covenants against competition. When an employee voluntarily quits, the court will enforce a non-competition agreement so long as the agreement complies with section 53-9-11. *See Central Monitoring Service, Inc. v. Zakinski*, 553 N.W.2d 513, 520 (S.D. 1996) ("We hold that if an employee voluntarily quits his employment or is fired for good cause . . . no further showing of reasonableness will be necessary as long as the non-compete or non-disclosure agreement complies with SDCL 53-9-11."); *Centrol, Inc. v. Morrow*, 489 N.W.2d 890, 893 (S.D. 1992) (no further showing of reasonableness is necessary if the non-compete agreement complies with section 53-9-11). However, if an employer fires an employee without good cause or through no fault of the employee, the court "must engage in a balancing test." *Zakinski*, 489 N.W.2d 893. *See First American Systems, Inc. v. Rezatto*, 311 N.W.2d 51 (S.D. 1981); *Hot Stuff Foods, LLC v. Mean Gene's Enterprises, Inc.*, 468 F. Supp. 2d 1078 (D.S.D. 2006).

The distinction between employees who voluntarily quit and employees who are fired may be important in the franchising context. If the policy of the South Dakota employment exception were applied to franchising, one could argue that a franchisee who voluntarily left its franchisor's system would be bound by the restrictions of its covenant not to compete, while a franchisee who was terminated through no fault of its own would be entitled to a balancing or "reasonableness" analysis in determining the enforceability of its covenant.

---

3. What time limitations have courts recognized as reasonable in the franchise context? If no franchise cases have been decided, what time limitations have been recognized in other contexts?

➤ How have they been related to the interests protected?

South Dakota courts have not addressed the reasonableness of the duration of a covenant not to compete in the franchising context. This is not surprising since, until 2001, the Division of Securities appeared to regard all such covenants as unenforceable. See the discussion at section 1 preceding. However, sections 53-9-9 and 53-9-11 of the South Dakota Codified Laws contain time limitations for covenants against competition in contracts for the sale of goods and employment contracts. Section 53-9-9 permits a buyer of a business to prevent the seller from carrying on a similar business "as long as the buyer or person deriving title to the goodwill from the seller carries on a like business." Section 53-9-11 permits a covenant against competition in an employment contract "for any period not exceeding two years from the date of termination of the agreement," and section 53-9-12 (enacted in 2005) permits a similar two-year restraint on captive insurance agents.

SD

Covenants against competition in sale of business agreements, employment contracts, and insurance agents that comply with the time limitations in sections 53-9-9, 53-9-11 and 53-9-12 are presumptively valid without further proof. *American*

Rim & Brake v. Zoellner, 382 N.W.2d 421, 424 (S.D. 1984) (finding that covenants against competition that comport with the statutory language of section 53-9-9 are valid without a further showing of reasonableness). However, non-disclosure agreements that fall outside the parameters of these exemptions are subjected to a test of reasonableness.

A three-prong test for reasonableness was established in *First American Systems, Inc. v. Rezatto*, 311 N.W.2d 51 (S.D. 1981). As discussed above, in *Rezatto*, an insurance agent, covenanted not to reveal confidential customer information. The court, after having found that the confidential customer information qualified as a trade secret, employed a three-part test to determine the reasonableness of the non-disclosure covenant. The court held that a non-disclosure covenant is reasonable if it (1) is no greater than required for the protection of the employer, (2) does not impose undue hardship on the employee, and (3) is not injurious to the public. This three-prong test is known as the *Rezatto* test. In applying this test, the court found that the ten-year term of the non-disclosure agreement raised a factual question for determination by the trial court on remand.

In *Overholt v. Travis*, 941 F.2d 1361 (8th Cir. 1991), the court relied on the reasoning in *Rezatto* to determine the validity of a two-year restrictive covenant. As discussed previously, in *Overholt*, the court examined the reasonableness of a non-disclosure and non-solicitation clause that prevented employees from soliciting their former employer's customers or exploiting confidential customer information for two years. Relying on the fact that the *Rezatto* court "noted with approval restrictive covenants with durations of two and three years," the *Overholt* court found that a two-year restrictive covenant was "legally enforceable under South Dakota law." *Id.* at 1368. Both *Rezatto* and *Overholt* were decided prior to enactment of South Dakota Codified Laws section 53-9-12, which established a specified, permitted exemption for non-competition agreements of two years or less signed by captive insurance agents. Even after the enactment of section 53-9-12, the three-part *Rezatto* test is still used by the courts in determining whether a non-compete clause constitutes an unlawful restraint on trade. *See Aqreva, LLC v. Eide Bailly, LLP*, 950 N.W.2d 774, 783–84 (S.D. 2020).

4. What geographic limitations have courts recognized as reasonable in the franchise context?

- **How have they been related to the interests protected?**
- **Have courts recognized the legitimacy of protecting other franchisees from competition?**

South Dakota courts have not addressed the reasonableness of a geographic restriction contained in a covenant against competition in the franchising context. However, sections 53-9-9 to 53-9-12 of the South Dakota Codified Laws contain geographic limitations that are enforced in other contexts. Section 53-9-10 permits partners to agree not to carry on a similar business "within the same municipality where the partnership business has been transacted or within a specified part thereof." Section 53-9-11 permits an employer to require that a former employee "not [] solicit existing customers of the employer within a specified county, first or second class municipality or other specified area" if the employer continues to carry on a like business therein. Section 53-9-12 (enacted in 2005) permits a restriction against a captive insurance agent "within a specified county, first or second class municipality, or other specified area. . . ."

Section 53-9-9 was amended in 1997. The current version permits a buyer of a business to prevent the seller from carrying on a similar business "within a specified county, city, or other specified area." The previous version restricted the seller from carrying on a similar business "within a specified county, city, or part thereof." South Dakota has had few opportunities to address the validity of covenants against competition under the current version (or cases construing the similar language of section 53-9-12), but the decisions in reported cases applying the statute do not hinge on, and therefore provide little insight on, the significance of the scope of the geographic restriction. *See JAS Enterprises, Inc. v. BBS Enterprises, Inc.*, 835 N.W.2d 117 (S.D. 2013) (no discussion of the geographic restriction described as a "(100) mile radius of Rapid City, South Dakota."); *Aqreva, LLC v. Eide Bailly, LLP*, 950 N.W.2d 774, 783–84 (S.D. 2020) (non-compete was unenforceable based on lack of employment status, obviating discussion on the world-wide geographic limitation in the non-compete).

In *Simpson v. C&R Supply, Inc.*, 598 N.W.2d 914 (S.D. 1999), the court considered the validity of a covenant against competition that restricted a seller from operating: "(i) within a radius of 25 miles of Sioux Falls, South Dakota; (ii) within a radius of 250 miles of Sioux Falls, South Dakota; and (iii) within all counties within any of the United States of America." *Id.* at 920. The *Simpson* court found that the clause "within all counties within any of the United States" violated the prior version of section 53-9-9 in that it "g[ave] no specific 'county, city, or part thereof' in which the [seller] was to restrain from operating." *Id.* The court then modified or "blue-penciled" the agreement "to comport with the statute by reducing the boundaries to include only those markets within the city limits of Sioux Falls, the only legal benchmark provided in the covenant." *Id.* at 921.

In *Ward v. Midcom, Inc.*, 575 N.W.2d 233 (S.D. 1998), the court considered the validity of a covenant against competition that contained no territorial limitation. Analyzing the clause under the prior version of section 53-9-9, the court found that the covenant was invalid. "[T]he applicable version of the statute expressly limits non-competition agreements to 'a specified county, city, or part thereof' and we are bound by the statute's provisions in effect when the contract was executed." *Id.* at 239. The *Ward* court noted, however, that "a global limitation may be permissible" under the current version of section 53-9-9. The court then modified the covenant so that it was enforceable within the county in which the business was located.

5. What limitations on activities have courts recognized as reasonable in the franchise context?

There are no reported South Dakota cases dealing with the reasonableness of restrictions on activities in the franchising context. As discussed above, sections 53-9-8 through 53-9-12 of the South Dakota Codified Laws permit covenants against competition only in situations regarding the sale of goodwill, the dissolution of a partnership, employment contracts, and captive insurance agents.

6. Does the state recognize a difference between in-term and post-term covenants?

There are no reported South Dakota cases that discuss any difference in the enforceability of in-term and post-term covenants in the franchising context. However, in *Communication Technical System v. Densmore*, 583 N.W.2d 125 (S.D. 1998), the court considered the validity of an "Agreement Not to Recruit" that contained both in-term and post-term restrictions. In *Densmore*, a programming company agreed to provide programming services to a computer company, Gateway. The two companies entered into an "Agreement Not to Recruit" the other's employees "during the time [the programming company] was providing services for Gateway and for a period of one year following the termination of such services." *Id.* at 126. The court did not analyze the difference between the in-term and post-term restrictions of the "Agreement Not to Recruit," but rather held that the entire agreement was unenforceable because it did not comport with any of the then-extant statutory exceptions of South Dakota Codified Laws sections 53-9-8 through 53-9-11.

7. Has the state allowed enforcement of covenants against non-signatories (e.g., family members, newly formed corporations)?

There are no reported South Dakota cases dealing with whether a covenant against competition may be enforced against non-signatories in the franchising context. There is, however, some dicta suggesting that courts would be reluctant to enforce non-competes against non-signatories. *See Commc'n Tech. Sys., Inc. v. Densmore*, 583 N.W.2d 125, 133 (S.D. 1998) (Miller, C.J., concurring) (noting that former employees could not be prevented from "accepting" their former employer's clients "*because the[] clients are not parties to the contract* and should be allowed to choose who they would like to do business with.") (emphasis added). *See also Aqreva, LLC v. Eide Bailly, LLP*, 950 N.W.2d 774, 783–84 (S.D. 2020) (non-compete provision in purchase agreement was not necessarily enforceable against principal of the purchased business, when he was not individually identified in the purchase agreement).

8. Will the state modify, "blue-pencil," or otherwise reduce a covenant found to be overbroad?

"[I]f a non-compete clause is too broad, South Dakota has allowed for partial enforcement in certain instances." *Billion v. Oxford*, 2016 WL 3976636, at *4 (D.S.D. July 22, 2016). Indeed, South Dakota courts have "'blue lined' . . . covenants since 1969." *First American Systems, Inc. v. Rezatto*, 311 N.W.2d 51 (S.D. 1981), referring to *Loescher v. Policky*, 173 N.W.2d 50 (S.D. 1969), in which the court modified a non-competition agreement restricting a veterinarian from practicing for ten years from the termination of his employment to comport with the then current statute allowing a restriction for ten years from the date of the agreement.

In *Simpson v. C&R Supply, Inc.*, 598 N.W.2d 914 (S.D. 1999), the court modified a covenant against competition that restricted competition within any county in the United States, reducing its application to the city limits of Sioux Falls. Similarly, in *Ward v. Midcom, Inc.*, 575 N.W.2d 233 (S.D. 1998), the court modified a covenant against competition that contained no territorial restriction, reducing its application to the specific county in which the business was located.

9. When does a non-compete period begin to run? Will courts equitably extend the term?

Under South Dakota law, courts construe the duration of the non-compete period strictly according to the terms of the agreement or the statutory exceptions.

In *Expansion Cap. Grp., LLC v. Patterson*, 514 F. Supp. 3d 1095, 1119–20 (D.S.D. 2021), the parties disputed the date from which the non-compete period would run. The debate centered around the fact that the former employee was formally terminated from his position as CEO on June 24, 2016, but continued to be involved with the company in other capacities (e.g., as a board member) until January 25, 2017. Because the former employee never signed a new non-compete agreement after his initial termination, the court held that, per the terms of the non-compete, the one-year non-compete could not be enforced past June 24, 2017. *Id.* at 1120.

In *McKie Ford Lincoln, Inc. v. Hanna*, 907 N.W.2d 795 (S.D. 2018), the non-compete clause at issue stated that it would run: "for a period of one year subsequent to such termination [of employment], *not to include any period of violation or period of time required for litigation to enforce the covenants.*" (emphasis added). Two months after the end of the employee's employment, the employer sued the employee for breach of the non-compete. *Id.* at 798. The litigation lasted two years, and after it concluded the employer argued there were ten months remaining on the one-year non-compete. The court disagreed based on the plain language of South Dakota Codified Laws section 53-9-11, which only permits an agreement between an employee and employer for a period "not exceeding two years from the date of termination of the agreement." The *Hanna* court pointed out that the statute does not allow for tolling in the event of litigation and would need to be construed narrowly. *Id.* at 799. Because, however, the litigation brought by the employer was unsuccessful, the court ruled the tolling provision in the agreement itself, which only included a "period of time required for litigation to *enforce* the covenants," did not apply and it was ultimately "unnecessary to discuss whether a contractual tolling provision can toll the two-year limitation period for a non-compete under SDCL 53-9-11." *Id.* at 800.

10. Are there additional nuances or peculiarities of the state's treatment of covenants in the franchising context?

There are no reported South Dakota cases dealing with covenants against competition in the franchising context. However, as discussed above, covenants against competition are enforceable in employment contracts subject to the restrictions contained in section 53-9-11 of the South Dakota Codified Laws. An employee may agree to a covenant against competition at any time during his or her employment. South Dakota Codified Law § 53-9-11. If an employee enters into a covenant against competition when he or she begins employment, no additional consideration is necessary as long as the agreement comports with section 53-9-11. *Central Monitoring Service, Inc. v. Zakinski*, 553 N.W.2d 513, 517 (S.D. 1996). However, if an employee enters into a covenant against competition after his or her employment has begun, the court must consider whether the covenant is a completely new covenant or merely an alteration of the existing employment contract. If the covenant is an alteration of the existing covenant, that is, "not a 'stand-alone' agreement, but part and parcel of the [original] employment agreement, no additional consideration is necessary." *Id.* at 518. In contrast, if the covenant "is a completely new contract, new consideration is required." *Id.* at 517.

Tennessee

by Kelli L. Thompson *

1. Has the state addressed covenants against competition in the context of franchising?

- **Does the state have a franchising statute or regulations that address covenants against competition?**
- **Does the state have a covenants statute of general applicability that would encompass franchise covenants?**
- **Have the courts addressed covenants in the context of franchising either under a statute or under the state's common law?**

There is no Tennessee franchise statute or covenants statute of general applicability that is applicable to covenants against competition in the franchising context. However, both the Tennessee Court of Appeals and the United States District Court for the Middle District of Tennessee have found covenants against competition in franchise agreements to be valid and enforceable. Likewise, the United States District Court for the Southern District of New York and the United States District Court for the District of Nebraska, both applying Tennessee law, have held post-termination non-competition clauses contained in franchise agreements enforceable.

In *Servpro Industries, Inc. v. Pizzillo*, 2001 WL 120731, at *1 (Tenn. Ct. App. Feb. 14, 2001), the Tennessee Court of Appeals considered a covenant against competition contained in a franchise agreement relative to a restoration business. The franchise agreement granted the franchisee the right to operate a Servpro business providing professional cleaning, damage restoration, and related services to residential and commercial customers within a non-exclusive territory located in Fort Lauderdale, Florida. The covenant provided that the franchisee would not divert or attempt to divert any Servpro customer to any competitor and that the franchisee would not engage in the same or similar business or otherwise compete with Servpro or its other franchisees. The covenant was applicable within the franchisee's territory and within a 25-mile radius of the territory for a period of two years following

*Ms. Thompson practices law in Oak Ridge, Tennessee. Ms. Thompson was counsel of record for the defendants/appellants in *Package Express Center, Inc. v. Maund et al.*, 2001 WL 579051 (Tenn. App. 2001).

termination of the franchise agreement. The clause provided that the two-year term would be extended for any period of non-compliance.

In *Servpro Indus., Inc.*, the dispute arose out of alleged violations of the franchisor's territorial policies by a franchisee whose territory was adjacent to the defendant franchisee's territory. The defendant franchisee complained to Servpro, and Servpro reprimanded the other franchisee, but took no legal action against it. Subsequently, the defendant franchisee ceased making royalty payments and allowed the franchise agreement to expire. The defendant franchisee's wife then formed a new corporation and began operating a business within the defendant franchisee's former territory. The new business provided essentially the same services provided by the formerly franchised business, and the defendant franchisee began working for the new company. Servpro filed suit to collect royalty payments and to enforce the non-competition covenant. The defendant franchisee counterclaimed, asserting that Servpro had first breached the agreement by failing to enforce its territorial policies, and therefore, it could not pursue a claim for a subsequent alleged breach of the same agreement.

After the trial court found for Servpro on all claims, the defendant franchisee appealed. In affirming the trial court's enforcement of the covenant against competition, the Tennessee Court of Appeals recognized that Servpro had a legitimate business interest to protect—the value of the franchise that it was offering to prospective franchisees. The court stated that it was apparent that Servpro would have a more difficult time finding a new franchisee in the territory if the former franchisee were performing the same services within that territory and soliciting the same customers that the former franchisee had previously solicited under the Servpro name. As a result, the court found that Servpro should be able to protect the value of its franchises by preventing its former franchisees from competing against it for a reasonable time and within a limited geographic area.

In *Total Car Franchising Corp. v. L&S Paint Works, Inc.*, 981 F. Supp. 1079 (M.D. Tenn. 1997), a Tennessee federal district court granted injunctive relief to enforce a covenant against competition in a franchise agreement. Total Car Franchising Corporation, a franchisor of vehicle appearance technology franchises, brought an action against a terminated franchisee and sought injunctive relief to enforce a non-competition agreement.

The covenant at issue in *Total Car* provided that for two years after termination of the franchise agreement, the franchisee would not engage in any business offering the same or similar services within the franchisee's former territory, metropolitan Nashville. The provision also prohibited the franchisee from engaging in, assisting, or having any financial or management interest, directly or indirectly, in any other mobile or fixed-location paint restoration business in the metropolitan Nashville area for a period of two years following termination of the franchise agreement. Further, the franchisee was prohibited for two years following termination from soliciting, inducing, or attempting to divert any customer that it served while a franchisee.

Following the termination of the franchise agreement by Total Car, the owner of the former franchisee corporation continued to provide on-site paint restoration services through a new corporation and under a different trade name, using the same vehicle. Total Car sought injunctive relief to enforce the former franchisee's covenant against competition pending arbitration, and the court found that injunctive relief was appropriate. In reaching its decision, the court looked to another Tennessee decision that evaluated the enforceability of non-competition covenants in the employment context.

Although there is no inflexible formula for determining reasonableness of a restrictive covenant, the Tennessee Supreme Court has laid out several factors to be considered, namely (1) the consideration supporting the agreement, (2) the legitimacy of the business interest to be protected, (3) the economic hardship imposed on the employee, and (4) whether such a covenant would be inimical to the public interest. *Total Car*, at 1081 (citing *Allright v. Auto Parks, Inc.*, 219 Tenn. 280, 409 S.W.2d 361, 363 (Tenn. 1966)). The court found that both the territorial scope and the duration of the covenant against competition were reasonable under Tennessee law. It therefore ruled that Total Car was likely to succeed in proving that the defendant-franchisee had breached the covenant and granted injunctive relief.

The Federal District Court for the Southern District of New York, applying Tennessee law, also enforced a covenant against competition in the franchise context. *ServiceMaster Residential/Commercial Services, L.P. et al. v. Westchester Cleaning Services, Inc. et al.*, 2001WL 396520, at *1 (S.D.N.Y. Apr. 19, 2001). In this case, the court enforced a non-competition clause that, for a period of one year after the termination of the franchise agreement, prohibited the former franchisee from owning or engaging in any business within the former franchisee's territory that performed any of the services that had been licensed to the former franchisee by the franchisor. In granting the franchisor's request for preliminary injunction to enforce the non-competition provision, the court stated: "[i]n the franchise post-termination context, such covenants have been enforced where their scope is reasonably related to the protection of the franchisor's know-how and its ability to place new franchisees in the same territory." *Id.* at *9.

Courts have continued to follow these requirements established under Tennessee law and enforce non-competes in the franchise context. In 2018, the Western District of Tennessee evaluated the enforceability of a non-compete in *Amerispec, LLC. v. Omni Enterprises, Inc. et al.*, 2018 WL 2248459 (W.D. Tenn. 2018). In *Amerispec*, the terminated franchisees argued that the noncompete in an expired Franchise Agreement was not enforceable because the parties continued to operate after the expiration of the Franchise Agreement. *Id.* at *2. The former franchisee continued to operate after the expiration of the Franchise Agreement and before the franchisor notified them the Franchise Agreement had been terminated. However, AmeriSpec was attempting to negotiate a new agreement with the franchisee. The franchisee ceased operation of its AmeriSpec and began operation as "American Property Inspection Services." *Id.* at *3. At that point, the franchisor notified the franchisees to cease operating a competing business. The former franchisees argued that since the franchise agreement had expired, the noncompete provisions were no longer enforceable. *Id.* at *5.

Evaluating the former franchisee's argument, the Western District of Tennessee (citing the Tennessee Supreme Court) found that "when the parties continue to perform the same services after a contract for a definite term has expired, it is presumed that they are operating under a new contract having the same terms and conditions as the original one." *Id. BSG. LLC. v. Check Velocity, Inc.*, 395 S.W.3d 90, 94 (Tenn. 2012 (quoting *Delzell v. Pope*, 200 Tenn. 641, 194 S.W.2d 690, 694 (1956)). The court found that the former franchisees accepted the benefits of the franchise status and traded on the goodwill of AmeriSpec until they abruptly changed the name of the business. *Id.* at *5 (citing *ServiceMaster Residential/Commercial Servs., L.P. v. Westchester Cleaning Servs., Inc.*, 2001 WL 396520, at *3). Accordingly, the court found there was an implied contract in fact under the terms of the expired franchise agreement. *Id.* at *6.

Next, the court evaluated the enforceability of the non-compete under the factors established by *Servpro Indus., Inc. v. Pizzillo*, namely the reasonableness of the duration and geographic scope of the restrictions, as well as balancing one party's right to earn a living and to practice his trade against the other's right to be free from unfair competition. *Id.* at *6. The court found that AmeriSpec had shown through the facts and caselaw that if the former franchisees were not enjoined from operating a competing business in the territories covered by the franchise agreements, their conduct would pose a substantial threat of irreparable harm to AmeriSpec's franchise business. *Id.*

The standards set out in the cases discussed above are consistent with Tennessee's criteria for the enforcement of covenants not to compete generally. Although covenants not to compete are disfavored, they may be enforced if they are deemed to be reasonable under the circumstances. *Murfreesboro Medical Clinic, P.A. v. Udom*, 166 S.W.3d 674, 678 (Tenn. 2005); *Allright Auto Parks, Inc. v. Berry*, 219 Tenn. 280, 409 S.W.2d 361 (Tenn. 1966); *Hasty v. Rent-A-Driver, Inc.*, 671 S.W.2d 471 (Tenn. 1984); *Central Adjustment Bureau, Inc. v. Ingram*, 678 S.W.2d 28 (Tenn. 1984); *Vantage Technology, LLC v. Cross*, 17 S.W.3d 637 (Tenn. Ct. App. 1999). The question of what is reasonable is defined by the duration of the restriction and its geographic scope as well as other factors that balance one person's right to earn a living and practice a trade against the other person's need to be protected from the dangers of unfair competition. *Dabora, Inc. v. Kline*, 884 S.W.2d 475 (Tenn. Ct. App. 1994).

In *Udom*, the trial court entered an injunction enforcing a covenant not to compete between a physician and his former practice. On appeal, the court of appeals reversed the grant of the injunction, but found that the covenant not to compete was enforceable. *Murfreesboro Medical*, at 675. However, the Tennessee Supreme Court reversed the court of appeals and found that except for those specifically proscribed by statute, a covenant not to compete for a physician is unenforceable and void. *Id.* The court reiterated the holdings of *Allright Auto Parks*, but also found that covenants not to compete that implicate important public policy issues are even more strictly construed. *Id.* at 676. Much like restrictive covenants in the practice of law, restrictive covenants in the medical profession raise concerns regarding the public good. Having a greater number of physicians practicing in a community benefits the public by providing greater access to health care, improves the quality of care, and keeps costs affordable. In addition, a person has the right to choose his or her physician and to continue an ongoing relationship with that physician. *Id.* at 676. Although the physician-patient relationship is typically different from a franchisor-franchisee relationship, the analysis used by the court in *Udom* could prove useful in certain franchisor-franchisee relationships as well.

Non-competes are enforceable if they are reasonable under the circumstances. *Allright Auto Parks*, 409 S.W.2d at 363. The method for determining the enforceability of these agreements is flexible, and "each case must stand or fall on its own facts." *Id.* The factors to be examined are the following: (1) the consideration supporting the non-compete, (2) the threatened danger to the employer if the agreement is not enforced, (3) the economic hardship that the non-compete would impose on the employee, and (4) whether enforcement of the contract would be against the public interest.

Tennessee courts have long held that "employment, even for an indefinite period of time, subject to termination at the option of the employer is sufficient consideration" to support a non-compete. *Ramsey v. Mutual Supply Co.*, 427 S.W.2d 849, 852 (Tenn. Ct. App. 1968) (citing *Di-Deeland, Inc. v. Colvin*, 347 S.W.2d 483,

485–86 (Tenn. 1961)). Most Tennessee courts do not provide examples of consideration other than "continued employment" when examining employment contracts. However, they have held that a non-compete "signed prior to, contemporaneously with or shortly after employment begins is part of the original agreement, and . . . is supported by consideration." *Central Adjustment Bureau*, 678 S.W.2d 28, 33 (Tenn. 1984). Whether "continued employment" satisfies the consideration requirement depends on the facts of the case. For example, in *Central Adjustment Bureau*, the court stated, "It is possible . . . that employment for only a short period of time would be insufficient consideration." *Id.* at 35 (citing *Frierson v. Sheppard Building Supply Co.*, 154 So. 2d 151, 154 (1963) (stating that "[i]f appellant had been discharged shortly after signing the agreement, this court would probably hold the agreement was not supported by consideration")).

In *Central Adjustment Bureau*, the court examined an agreement between a debt collection corporation and its employees. The employees argued that because they were not presented with the non-compete until the first day of employment or shortly thereafter, it was "not the subject of free bargaining" and therefore was not supported by consideration. 678 S.W.2d at 30, 33. The court stated that the employees' argument, if successful, would not allow employers and employees who were already working to enter into agreements with one another. The court held that the employees' argument was invalid and that the non-compete at issue was supported by consideration. As a result of the holding in *Central Adjustment Bureau*, it appears that Tennessee courts will find that employment is sufficient consideration for an agreement where the non-compete is part of the original employment contract.

---

2. Have the courts articulated the "legitimate interests" of the franchisor that will support enforcement of a covenant against competition contained in a franchise agreement?

- **If so, what are they (e.g., protection of goodwill, protection of confidential information), and in what contexts did the issue arise?**
- **If not, what interests have been recognized in other contexts (e.g., employment agreements, the sale of business context)?**

Courts applying Tennessee law have addressed specifically the interests of a franchisor that support enforcement of a covenant against competition in a franchise agreement. Likewise, Tennessee distinguishes the protection of a franchisor versus the protection of a business in the enforcement of a non-compete against a former employee.

The Tennessee Court of Appeals in *Servpro Industries, Inc. v. Pizzillo*, 2001 WL 120731, at *1 (Tenn. Ct. App. Feb. 14, 2001), found that a covenant against competition in a franchise agreement protects not only the franchisor's information and goodwill, but also the product the franchisor sells—the franchise itself (citing *Shakey's Inc. v. Martin*, 430 P.2d 504 (Idaho 1967)). The *Servpro Indus., Inc.* court found it apparent that Servpro would have a more difficult time locating a new franchisee for the former franchisee's territory if the former franchisee were providing the same services within that same territory, soliciting the same customers that the former franchisee had previously serviced as a Servpro franchisee. In enforcing the covenant against competition, the court stated:

> While we have no wish to unduly restrict Mr. Pizzillo in the exercise of his trade, we believe Servpro should be able to protect the value of its franchises by preventing its former franchisees from competing against it for a reasonable time and within a limited geographic area. By signing the franchise agreement, Mr. Pizzillo agreed to be bound by the non-competition agreement, and we believe the trial court was correct in finding it enforceable against him.

Id. at *22.

In *ServiceMaster Residential/Commercial Services, L.P. et al. v. Westchester Cleaning Services, Inc. et al.*, 2001 WL 396520, at *1 (S.D.N.Y. Apr. 19, 2001), the court, applying Tennessee law, also recognized the plaintiff franchisor's interest in its goodwill with its customers, its interest in refranchising the market left vacant by termination of the former franchisee, and its interest in avoiding the danger to the franchise system itself if a franchisee were permitted to avoid its reasonable non-competition obligations.

In *Total Car Franchising Corp. v. L&S Paint Works, Inc.*, 981 F. Supp. 1079 (M.D. Tenn. 1977), the United States District Court for the Middle District of Tennessee recognized the interest of a franchisor in protecting its franchise in the post-termination period. The court found that the former franchisee received confidential proprietary information from Total Car and had served as a franchisee in the Nashville area for two years. "Now, he is the sole proprietor of ProTouch Auto Services, Inc., which provides precisely the same services that L&S [the former franchised entity] did. Consequently, the record is not 'bereft of any facts of the type ordinarily used to attempt to justify a non-competition clause.'" *Id.* at 1083.

In the franchise context, there are no reported Tennessee decisions finding that a non-competition covenant was unenforceable due to an insufficient interest on the part of the franchisor. However, some limitations on protectable interests have been articulated by the courts in the non-franchise context. The Tennessee Supreme Court has imposed a limitation upon the enforceability of post-employment non-competition provisions by requiring that the restriction should be no greater than reasonably necessary to protect the legitimate business interests of the former employer. In *Hasty v. Rent-a-Driver, Inc.*, 671 S.W.2d 471 (Tenn. 1984), the court refused to enforce a covenant not to compete imposed in an employment contract of a driver of one of the tractor-trailer units leased to a corporate customer on the basis that the driver played no role in obtaining the business or negotiating the contracts and that the employer had not "shown a need for the restrictive covenant that could justify it in the face of the resulting restraint and hardship on the employee." *Id.* at 474.

For an employer to be entitled to the protection of a non-compete (i.e., have a protectable interest), it must show facts over and above ordinary competition. *Vantage Technology, LLC v. Cross*, 17 S.W.3d 637, 644 (Tenn. Ct. App. 1999) (quoting *Hasty*, 671 S.W.2d at 473). The facts must be "such that, without the [contract], the employee would gain an unfair advantage in future competition with the employer." *Id.* Courts have generally recognized the following three categories of protectable interests: (1) where the employer provided the employee with specialized training, (2) where the employer gave the employee access to trade secrets or other confidential business information, and (3) where the employer's business was of the type that customers tend to associate the business with its employees. *Id.; see also Cam International, L.P. v. Turner*, 1992 WL 74567 (Tenn. App. Apr. 15, 1992).

An employer has a protectable interest where the employer provides the employee with specialized training. *Hasty v. Rent-A-Driver, Inc.*, 671 S.W.2d 471, 473 (Tenn. 1984); *see also Vantage Technology*, 17 S.W.3d at 645. In *Hasty*, the court stated that general skill and knowledge acquired through training are not protectable interests. *Hasty*, 671 S.W.2d at 473. Furthermore, this rule applies to both knowledge brought into the employment relationship and knowledge acquired during the employment relationship. *Vantage Tech.*, 17 S.W.3d at 645. However, training "in conjunction with other factors," such as the training being specialized, is a protectable interest. *Hasty*, 671 S.W.2d at 473.

In *Selox, Inc. v. Ford*, the court stressed the importance of distinguishing between general skills or knowledge of a trade and information that is "peculiar to [an] employer's business." *Selox, Inc. v. Ford*, 675 S.W.2d 474, 476 (Tenn. 1984). In *Selox*, the employee's duties involved selling industrial gases and welding supplies for Selox. The employee was initially trained by being sent on a sales route with another salesperson and being required to attend weekly sales meetings. The court found that the employee had not received "additional or specialized training and that the particular work done by [the employee] could have been performed by any other employee of average competence." *Id.* at 475. The employer failed to show that it was entitled to enforcement of the non-compete.

Some courts focus on the amount of money expended by the employer to prepare the employee for the job when deciding whether the employer has a protectable interest. *See* generally *Koehler v. Cummings*, 380 F. Supp. 1294, 1306 (M.D. Tenn. 1971); *William B. Tanner v. Taylor*, 530 S.W.2d 517, 522 (Tenn. Ct. App. 1974). In *William B. Tanner*, the court noted, "[The employee] was hired and trained to become sales manager at considerable expense to his employer." Additionally, in *Koehler*, the court pointed out that the company had invested approximately $30,000 in developing the ideas of the employee. The court stated, "The danger to the employer has already been seen. [The company] has one valuable asset, the ideas of the [employee]. . . . The threatened danger to the employer . . . lay in experiencing competition from its own former idea man." 380 F. Supp. at 1306–07. In both cases, the courts found that the employer had invested a sufficient amount of resources to establish a protectable interest.

An employer may also have a protectable interest where an employer provides an employee with access to trade secrets or other confidential business information. *Vantage Technology*, 17 S.W.3d at 645. The terms "trade secret" and "confidential information" are used synonymously in Tennessee. *Hickory Specialties, Inc. v. Forest Flavors International, Inc.*, 26 F. Supp. 2d 1029 (M.D. Tenn. 1998) (citing *Heyer-Jordan & Associates, Inc. v. Jordan*, 801 S.W.2d 814, 821 (Tenn. Ct. App. 1990)). In *Vantage Technology*, the employer was a "mobile service provider" of medical equipment to hospitals. 17 S.W.3d at 641. The company also provided technicians who would assist the physicians during surgery. The court held that the employer had a protectable interest because the employees were "made privy to surgeon preferences . . . and had a degree of knowledge of [the Company's] other customers and the prices [the Company] charged for its services." *Id.* at 646.

In *Thompson, Breeding, Dunn, Creswell & Sparks v. Bowlin*, 765 S.W.2d 743 (Tenn. Ct. App. 1987), the court held that client lists containing the names of "present customers" are a protectable interest of the employer. This holding seemed to suggest that "present customer" lists qualify as confidential business information. However, this holding has been slightly limited by decisions that have followed. For example, where the identity of potential customers can be determined by a mere examination of the Yellow Pages or a study of the industry, the customer names do not qualify as confidential business information. *Amarr Company, Inc. v. Depew*, 1996WL 600330, at *4 (Tenn. App. 1996). In *Amarr Company, Inc.*, the employer was a wholesale manufacturer and seller of garage doors. The court determined that the employer's customers could be determined from a general study of the industry and by looking at the Yellow Pages. The court also stated that price lists were available to any customer and therefore were not confidential information.

The court in *Selox, Inc.* came to a similar conclusion when it held that a seller of industrial gases and welding products did not have a protectable interest. The court stated that the identity of people in the market for welding supplies could be determined by looking at the Yellow Pages. However, in *Baker v. Hooper*, the court came to the opposite conclusion where the employer owned and operated a nail salon. *Baker v. Hooper*, 1998 WL 608285 (Tenn. App. Aug. 6, 1998). The court explained that customers in the nail industry who seek out nail services could not be ascertained by looking in the phone book or studying the industry. Simply put, customer information that is "readily ascertainable from public sources is not entitled to protection." *Cam Int'l*, 1992 WL 745671, at *4.

An employer also may have a protectable interest where customers tend to associate the employer's business with the employees. *Hasty*, 671 S.W.2d at 473. Another way to view it is that an employer has an interest in the relationships between its employees and customers. *Vantage Tech.*, 17 S.W.3d at 645. In *Hasty*, the court determined that while the employee "had personal contact with [the customer] . . . he had no influence on [the customer's] decision regarding its use of the services of [the employer]." 671 S.W.2d at 473. Therefore, the employer did not have a protectable interest.

In *Vantage Technology*, the court determined that the employer had a protectable interest because of the company's special customer relationships. 17 S.W.3d at 646. The employer in *Vantage Technology* provided medical equipment services to hospitals and provided technicians to assist physicians during surgery. The relationships that grew between the employees and the physicians were initiated by the company and built the goodwill of the company. The relationships involved direct mailings, face-to-face demonstrations wherein the employees sold the products, and the use of entertainment expense accounts on which the employees purchased meals and gifts for the physicians. The court determined that the employer had an interest in its customers sufficient to invoke the protection of a non-compete. In a similar case, the court examined an agreement between an insurance company and its former employee, an insurance salesclerk. *Powell v. McDonnell Insurance Co.*, 1997 WL 589232, at *5 (Tenn. Ct. App. Sept. 24, 1997). The record indicated that the company had encouraged its employees to build relationships with their customers. Additionally, the company invested many resources in fostering these relationships. As in *Vantage Technology*, the court determined that the company had established a protectable interest.

In some instances, an employer might have a protectable interest where an employee is able to use contacts obtained while working for the employer to benefit one of the employer's competitors. In *Dabora, Inc. v. Kline*, 884 S.W.2d 475, 478 (Tenn. Ct. App. 1994), the court examined a non-compete between a highly specialized equestrian periodical and one of its former employees. The court stated, "By virtue of [the employee's] association with [the employer], [the employee] was able to quickly develop close personal relationships with many of the major players in the . . . industry." *Id.* at 478. The court further explained that the employee's use of these contacts for the benefit of the employer's competition would rise to the level of unfair competition. The court made no mention of whether the "contacts" could be ascertained through public information but instead focused on the unfair advantage the employer would have if the employee used the information to benefit one of the employer's competitors.

3. What time limitations have courts recognized as reasonable in the franchise context? If no franchise cases have been decided, what time limitations have been recognized in other contexts?

➤ **How have they been related to the interests protected?**

Courts applying Tennessee law have held two-year post-termination non-competition covenants to be reasonable and enforceable in the franchise context. *Servpro Industries, Inc. v. Pizzillo*, 2001 WL 120731, at *1 (Tenn. App. Feb. 14, 2001); *Total Car Franchising Corp. v. L&S Paint Works, Inc.*, 981 F. Supp. 1079, 1082 (M.D. Tenn. 1997). A one-year restriction in a covenant against competition was found reasonable under Tennessee law by the federal district courts for the Southern District of New York and the District of Nebraska. *ServiceMaster Residential/Commercial Services, L.P. et al. v. Westchester Cleaning Services, Inc. et al.*, 2001 WL 396520, at *1 (S.D.N.Y. Apr. 19, 2001). In each of these cases, the courts involved found the respective covenants not to compete enforceable because they were reasonable under the circumstances. The courts found that the time restrictions were reasonable and that the franchisors were protecting their legitimate business interests—their goodwill and their products. The courts did not ignore the restrictions on the franchisees that would result from the enforcement of the non-competition covenants, but instead balanced those interests against those of the franchisors. In the end, the courts found that the franchisors were within their rights in protecting the value of their franchises by restricting former franchisees from competition for a reasonable time.

In evaluating the reasonableness of time restrictions outside the franchise context and in the employment setting, courts have found that the time and territorial limits of a non-compete can be no more restrictive than is necessary to protect the employer's interests. *Allright Auto Parks, Inc. v. Berry*, 219 Tenn. 280, 409 S.W.2d 361, 363 (Tenn. 1966). Few decisions have addressed the issue of time restrictions in detail. As with territorial limitations, the important issue is whether the restrictions are greater than necessary to protect the employer's interests. *Allright Auto Parks*, 409 S.W.2d at 286–87. In *Central Adjustment Bureau v. Ingram*, 678 S.W.2d 28, 36 (Tenn. 1984), the court examined the nature of the employer's industry, debt collection, to determine whether a two-year limitation was unreasonably broad. The court held that the limitation was too broad when it stated, "[W]hen clients of a collection agency change agencies in order to maintain a relationship with a former employee, they do so immediately." *Id.* On the other hand, in *Harvey v. Appalachian Claims Services, Inc.*, 1995 WL 140746 (Tenn. App. 1995), the court held that a three-year time limitation was not too restrictive because the company was trying to establish itself.

Generally, non-competes are strictly construed in favor of the employee. *Allright Auto Parks*, 409 S.W.2d at 365; *see also Hasty*, 671 S.W.2d at 472. Furthermore, the drafter of the agreement (usually the employer) must take responsibility for ambiguous terms because ambiguities are construed against the drafter. *B & L Corp. v. Thomas & Thorngren, Inc.*, 917 S.W.2d 674 (Tenn. Ct. App. 1995). The court accounted for these propositions when it modified a non-compete to state that the 50-mile restriction represented the employee's driving distance. *Id.* at 648.

A variety of time limitations have been upheld in other contexts. *See Greene County Tire & Supply, Inc. v. Spurlin*, 207 Tenn. 189, 338 S.W.2d 597 (Tenn. 1960) (five-year, 100-mile restriction in connection with the sale of assets of a tire business enforced); *Federated Mutual Implement and Hardware Insurance Co. v. Anderson*, 351 S.W.2d 411 (Tenn. Ct. App. 1961) (two-year, six-county restriction on insurance salesman employee upheld); *Di-Deeland, Inc. v. Colvin*, 347 S.W.2d 483 (Tenn. 1961) (six-month, 45-mile restriction on laundry employee enforced).

---

4. What geographic limitations have courts recognized as reasonable in the franchise context?

- **How have they been related to the interests protected?**
- **Have courts recognized the legitimacy of protecting other franchisees from competition?**

In *Servpro Industries, Inc. v. Pizzillo*, 2001 WL 120731, at *1, *15–22 (Tenn. App. Feb. 14, 2001), the court found a geographic restriction including the franchisee's former franchised territory, as well as a 25-mile radius around that territory, to be reasonable and enforceable in the franchise context. The court reasoned that the franchisor's interest is in protecting the value of the basic product it has to sell, which is its franchisees. Therefore, although the court was mindful of Pizzillo's ability to exercise his trade, they found Servpro should be able to protect the value of its franchises by preventing its former franchisees from competing against it for a reasonable time and within a limited geographic scope. Likewise, a geographic restriction that prohibited a former franchisee from competing within the metropolitan Nashville area (the area within which he operated as a franchisee) was found reasonable by the court in *Total Car Franchising Corp. v. L&S Paint Works, Inc.*, 981 F. Supp. 1079, 1082 (M.D. Tenn. 1997). In *ServiceMaster Residential/Commercial Services, L.P. et al. v. Westchester Cleaning Services, Inc. et al.*, 2001 WL 396520 7, at *1, *12–13 (S.D.N.Y. Apr. 19, 2001), the court, construing Tennessee law, upheld a geographic restriction that prohibited the former franchisee from competing within its former franchised territory (Westchester County, New York). In each of these cases, the courts found the geographic restrictions in the covenants not to compete enforceable because they were reasonable under the circumstances.

Outside of the franchise context, courts tend to limit the geographical limitations to that which is reasonable to protect the employer without placing an undue burden on a former employee's ability to earn a living. An agreement is unreasonable and unenforceable where it embraces territory in which the employee never performed services for his or her employer, unless the contract is intended to protect a trade secret. In *Allright Auto Parks*, the employee's non-compete prohibited her from providing services in 46 cities, but she had only worked in six. *Allright Auto Parks, Inc. v. Berry*, 219 Tenn. 280, 409 S.W.2d 361, 363 (Tenn. 1966). The court stated that the agreement was too restrictive. In another decision, the court upheld a non-compete that prohibited the employee from working in any of his former territories, which included several cities in Tennessee, Kentucky, Virginia, West Virginia, and North Carolina. *Standard Forms Co. v. Nave*, 422 F. Supp. 619, 623–24 (E.D. Tenn. 1976). In contrast, the court struck down a contract where it prohibited the employee from "being associated with any like business anywhere the [employer] ha[d] customers, undisputed to be in some thirty-six states" regardless of whether the employee had worked with the customers. *Delta Corp. of America v. Sebrite Corp.*, 391 F. Supp. 638, 640 (E.D. Tenn. 1974).

In *Koehler v. Cummings*, the court cited the general rule from *Allright Auto Parks* that non-competes cannot exclude employees from territory in which they had never worked. *Koehler v. Cummings*, 380 F. Supp. 1294, 1308 (M.D. Tenn. 1971). However, the *Koehler* court reached a different result. In *Koehler*, the employer hired the employee to invent and exhibit specialized and novel safety equipment in a number of cities across the country. The court concluded that the 30-state territory limitation was reasonable because the field was highly specialized. The court reasoned that the restriction was necessary to protect the investment that the company had made in the product. In a similar case, the court found a non-compete that covered the entire country was reasonable because the employer's industry (the equestrian newspaper industry) was limited to only six or seven publications. *Dabora, Inc. v. Kline*, 884 S.W.2d 475, 478 (Tenn. App. 1994). Furthermore, the non-compete at issue only prohibited the employee from working for certain publications. The court noted that the agreement was only as restrictive as necessary to protect the employer's interest.

In yet another Tennessee decision, the court held that a non-compete prohibiting an employee from working in a territory in which the employee had no contact at the time of the contract is reasonable if it "could be reasonably anticipated that such territory might be within [the employee's] coverage at some period during employment." *Ramsey v. Mutual Supply Co.*, 427 S.W.2d 849, 853 (Tenn. App. 1968). In *Ramsey*, the employee was one of two salespeople working for the company. Both employees had a designated area in which they sold. The court determined that, at the time the contract was made, it could be reasonably anticipated that one salesperson would have to work in the other salesperson's territory. Therefore, the territory limitation was reasonable although it reached outside the area in which the employee had worked and into another employee's territory. In another decision, the court seemed to look favorably upon a non-compete that did not have any territorial limitations. *See Thompson, Breeding, Dunn, Creswell & Sparks v. Bowlin*, 765 S.W.2d 743, 745–46 (Tenn. App. 1987). The court noted that the employee was only prohibited from soliciting the business of certain clients, which left him more "freedom to practice his profession in the same area as the [Company]." *Id.*

5. What limitations on activities have courts recognized as reasonable in the franchise context?

Tennessee courts have found it reasonable for a franchisor to limit the ability of a former franchisee to engage in competition against its franchisor for a limited period of time and within a limited geographic area. *Servpro Industries, Inc. v. Pizzillo*, 2001 WL 120731, at *1, *22 (Tenn. Ct. App. Feb. 14, 2001); *Total Car Franchising Corp. v. L&S Paint Works, Inc.*, 981 F. Supp. 1079, 1082 (M.D. Tenn. 1997). In *Servpro*, the court found that Servpro had an interest to protect, and that interest was what it sells, franchises to franchisees. Specifically, the court found that Servo should be able to protect the value of its franchises by preventing its former franchisees from competing against it for a reasonable time within a limited geographic area. In so finding, the court upheld the enforceability of a non-compete that prohibited the franchisee from competing within its territory and within a 25-mile radius thereof for a period of two years following termination of the franchise. In *Total Car Franchising*, the district court also found a non-compete enforceable that was limited to the franchisee's geographic territory for a period of two years using the same reasoning.

6. Does the state recognize a difference between in-term and post-term covenants?

There are no decisions under Tennessee law distinguishing between in-term and post-term covenants against competition in the franchise context.

7. Has the state allowed enforcement of covenants against non-signatories (e.g., family members, newly formed corporations)?

In *Total Car Franchising Corp. v. L&S Paint Works, Inc.*, 981 F. Supp. 1079, 1082 (M.D. Tenn. 1997), the court granted a franchisor's motion for injunctive relief pending arbitration and issued an order prohibiting a former franchisee corporate entity, its officers, partners, agents, employees, and attorneys, and all persons in active concert or participation with the former franchisee corporate entity from continuing to violate the covenants against competition contained in the franchise agreement pending the final determination of the issue in arbitration. The court found that the owner of the former franchisee corporation had, after termination of the franchise agreement, formed a new corporation and continued to operate an automotive paint restoration service business in violation of the restrictive covenants in the franchise agreement. Citing *National Medical Care, Inc. v. Gardiner*, 1986 WL 3157, at *2 (Tenn. Ct. App. Mar. 12, 1986) (enjoining not only director of dialysis center but also his "servants or agents and those acting in collusion or combination" with him), the court held that the more recently formed corporation was also bound by the restrictive covenants in the franchise agreement entered into by the former franchisee corporate entity.

Likewise, in *Amerispec, LLC. v. Sutko Real Estate Services, Inc.*, 2020 WL 3913584 (W.D. Tenn. July 10, 2020), the franchisee and the franchisor entered into a post-termination agreement whereby the franchisee agreed to be bound by the post-termination non-compete obligations of the franchise agreement. *Id.* at *2. However, the franchisee principal's son, who was employed by the franchisee as vice president, formed a separate entity and began to provide identical services under a newly formed entity, using the same location and same employees. Although the new entity changed its name and location just prior to the injunction hearing, the defendants argued that the non-compete should not be enforced as to the son and the new entity because they were not signatories to the non-compete provision. *Id.* at *5. The court disagreed and enforced the non-compete provisions against the non-signatories.

The defendants asserted that AmeriSpec knew that the son was involved in the franchised business, yet it did not require the son to sign a non-compete. *Id.* at *8. The defendants also claimed that the father took active steps to cease his involvement of the operations and sell them to his son, and all of the steps the father took were in furtherance of complying with his post-termination obligations. However, the court was not convinced, and it found that the son and his company were likewise enjoined from competing against AmeriSpec in the territory covered by the non-compete and for its duration. In doing so, the court looked to the actual relationship between the person enjoined and the person thought to be bound by the injunction. *Id.* at *9. In other words, the son and his company were acting in concert or participation with the franchisee when he acted counter to his contractual obligations not to compete citing Fed. R. Civ. P. 65(d)(2)(C). As a result, the court enjoined not only the franchisee and its principal but also the principal's son and a new entity created to continue operating the same business in the protected territory. *Id.* at *12.

8. Will the state modify, "blue-pencil," or otherwise reduce a covenant found to be overbroad?

Tennessee courts may modify or reduce a covenant that is found to be overbroad. In *Central Adjustment Bureau, Inc. v. Ingram*, 678 S.W.2d 28 (Tenn. 1984), the Tennessee Supreme Court considered the question of whether future employment of an at-will employee who signed an employment contract after having been employed for a period of time that contained a covenant against competition was sufficient consideration to support the enforcement of that agreement. In the case, the court also found it to be appropriate that judicial modification of overly broad covenants against competition be allowed in Tennessee, especially when the covenant itself specifically provided for modification.

The court considered whether it should follow the "blue-pencil" rule as opposed to a rule of reasonableness:

> Courts have taken one of two approaches in modifying restrictive covenants. The "blue pencil" rule provides that an unreasonable restriction against competition may be modified and enforced to the extent that a grammatically meaningful reasonable restriction remains after the words making the restriction unreasonable are stricken. . . . The blue pencil rule has the advantage of simplicity and prevents a court from actually rewriting private agreements. On the other hand, the contract still fails if the offending provision cannot be stricken. Often a divisible term contains an integral part of the agreement so that "blue penciling" the provision emasculates the contract. . . . The rule has been criticized as emphasizing form over substance. . . . It has been rejected as against the weight of authority. . . .
>
> The most recent trend, therefore, has been to abandon the "blue pencil" rule in favor of a rule of reasonableness. . . . This rule provides that unless the circumstances indicate bad faith on the part of the employer, a court will enforce covenants not to compete to the extent that they are reasonably necessary to protect the employer's interest "without imposing

> undue hardship on the employee when the public interest is not adversely affected."
>
> We are persuaded that the rule of reasonableness is the better rule.

Id. at 36–37 (citations omitted).

The covenant not to compete in *Central Adjustment Bureau, Inc.*, executed by employees of a debt collection agency, prohibited direct and indirect competition for two years following termination of employment in *any* area within the United States and prohibited contact during this period by the former employees with any customer of the employer who was a client of the employer during any part of the employee's employment. The Tennessee Supreme Court upheld the lower court's judicial modification of the covenant to one year within the actual area in which the employees had previously worked and its reduction of the covenant's applicability to only those customers who were the employer's clients during the two months prior to the employees' resignations. The court stated that, if there were credible evidence to support a finding that the contract was deliberately unreasonable and oppressive, then it could be found to be invalid. Thus, based upon *Central Adjustment Bureau, Inc.*, Tennessee follows the rule of reasonableness and allows judicial modification of the restrictions of covenants against competition.

9. When does a non-compete period begin to run? Will courts equitably extend the term?

Non-competes or covenants against competition time periods begin to run when the agreement in which they are included is terminated. For example, if there is a non-compete in a franchise agreement, the time period set forth in the non-competition provision will begin to run at the time the franchise agreement terminates. The franchisor cannot sit by and allow the non-compete period to expire, and then request that the court issue prospective injunctive relief.

In *Package Express Center, Inc. v. Maund et al.*, the Tennessee Court of Appeals rejected the chancery court's issuance of prospective injunctive relief. *Package Express Center, Inc. v. Maund et al.*, 2001 WL 579051 (Tenn. App. 2001). In this action, Package Express entered into agreements with local drug stores, in this case, Athens Pharmacy in Athens, Alabama, to provide materials and supplies, so that customers of the pharmacy could ship packages from the store. Mr. Maund terminated the agreement in February of 1995, and a month later, Package Express filed suit seeking injunctive relief, damages and attorneys' fees. Package Express never pursued a temporary restraining order or preliminary injunction during the 18-month period following termination of the agreement, and the case was tried in March of 2000. At trial, the court awarded both prospective injunctive relief for 18 months and damages for $2,478.00 for shipping fees for the period from February 1995 through December 1999, as well as attorneys' fees in excess of $10,000.

On appeal, the court of appeals found that although the parties' agreement was titled "lease agreement," the relationship between them was closer to that of a franchise agreement. *Id.* at *6. The court of appeals proceeded to find that the non-compete was enforceable because Package Express had a "protectable interest" because "customers were drawn to Athens Pharmacy by the name recognition and goodwill of Athens Pharmacy, not Package Express." *Id.* at *9–10. Judge Sussano filed a dissenting opinion, finding that the majority's finding was precisely why

Package Express did not have a protectable interest in Athens Pharmacy's business relationships with its customers.

Once the majority found that Package Express had a protectable interest, it considered the trial court's award of prospective injunctive relief, in addition to damages. The court of appeals noted that while the complaint sought both injunctive relief and damages, there was no indication that Package Express ever attempted to obtain a temporary restraining order or injunction under Rule 65, TENN. R. CIV. P. Finding the equitable maxim "equity aids the vigilant, not those who sleep upon their rights" applicable, the court found that because Package Express did not attempt to obtain an injunction during the 18-month time period, it was error for the trial court to issue prospective injunctive relief.

In *Amerispec, LLC. v. Omni Enterprises, Inc. et al.*, 2018 WL 2248459 (W.D. Tenn. 2018), the court did find that the duration of the one-year non-compete would run from the date of the effective termination of the franchise agreement rather than one year from the date the court issued the preliminary injunction as argued by AmeriSpec. *Id.* at *8.

10. Are there additional nuances or peculiarities of the state's treatment of covenants in the franchising context?

There are no additional nuances or peculiarities of Tennessee's treatment of covenants against competition in the franchising context.

Texas

*by Will K. Woods**

1. Has the state addressed covenants against competition in the context of franchising?

- **Does the state have a franchising statute or regulations that address covenants against competition?**
- **Does the state have a covenants statute of general applicability that would encompass franchise covenants?**
- **Have the courts addressed covenants in the context of franchising either under a statute or under the state's common law?**

Texas has no franchising statute or regulation that addresses covenants against competition. Sections 15.50 and 15.51 of the Texas Business and Commerce Code, effective August 28, 1989, address the enforceability of covenants not to compete generally as follows:

> **§ 15.50. Criteria for Enforceability of Covenants Not to Compete**
>
> Notwithstanding Section 15.05 of this code, and subject to any applicable provision of Subsection (b), a covenant not to compete is enforceable if it is ancillary to or part of an otherwise enforceable agreement at the time the agreement is made to the extent that it contains limitations as to time, geographical area, and scope of activity to be restrained that are reasonable and do not impose a greater restraint than is necessary to protect the goodwill or other business interest of the promisee.
>
> **§ 15.51. Procedures and Remedies in Actions to Enforce Covenants Not to Compete**
>
> (a) Except as provided in Subsection (c) of this section, a court may award the promisee under a covenant not to compete damages, injunctive relief,

*Mr. Woods is a partner in the law firm of Baker McKenzie in Dallas, Texas, and is a member of the Texas bar. This chapter was prepared incorporating previous works of the author and the previous edition of this publication, including portions authored by Mr. Woods's retired partner, Ann Hurwitz. Mr. Woods wishes to acknowledge Rocio Deitz, an Associate in the franchise practice group at Baker McKenzie in Dallas, for her contributions to this update.

> or both damages and injunctive relief for a breach by the promisor of the covenant.
>
> If the primary purpose of the agreement to which the covenant is ancillary is to obligate the promisor to render personal services, for a term or at will, the promisee has the burden of establishing that the covenant meets the criteria specified by Section 15.50 of this code. If the agreement has a different primary purpose, the promisor has the burden of establishing that the covenant does not meet those criteria. For the purposes of this subsection, the "burden of establishing" a fact means the burden of persuading the triers of fact that the existence of the fact is more probable than its nonexistence.
>
> If the covenant is found to be ancillary to or part of an otherwise enforceable agreement but contains limitations as to time, geographical area, or scope of activity to be restrained that are not reasonable and impose a greater restraint than is necessary to protect the goodwill or other business interest of the promisee, the court shall reform the covenant to the extent necessary to cause the limitations contained in the covenant as to time, geographical area, and scope of activity to be restrained to be reasonable and to impose a restraint that is not greater than necessary to protect the goodwill or other business interest of the promisee and enforce the covenant as reformed, except that the court may not award the promisee damages for a breach of the covenant before its reformation and the relief granted to the promisee shall be limited to injunctive relief. If the primary purpose of the agreement to which the covenant is ancillary is to obligate the promisor to render personal services, the promisor establishes that the promisee knew at the time of the execution of the agreement that the covenant did not contain limitations as to time, geographical area, and scope of activity to be restrained that were reasonable and the limitations imposed a greater restraint than necessary to protect the goodwill or other business interest of the promisee, and the promisee sought to enforce the covenant to a greater extent than was necessary to protect the goodwill or other business interest of the promisee, the court may award the promisor the costs, including reasonable attorney's fees, actually and reasonably incurred by the promisor in defending the action to enforce the covenant.

TEX. BUS. & COM. CODE §§ 15.50–.51 (Supp. 2002).

The Texas legislature further provided that these provisions apply to covenants entered into "before, on, or after" the effective date of the amendment. The reference to "Section 15.05 of this code" is to the section that includes the provision that "[e]very contract, combination, or conspiracy in restraint of trade or commerce is unlawful."

Finally, in 1993, in an effort to clarify the preemptive effect of sections 15.50–.51, the legislature provided:

> **§ 15.52. Preemption of Other Law**
>
> The criteria for enforceability of a covenant not to compete provided by Section 15.50 of this code and the procedures and remedies in an action to enforce a covenant not to compete provided by Section 15.51 of this code are exclusive and preempt any other criteria for enforceability of a covenant not to compete or procedures and remedies in an action to enforce a covenant not to compete under common law or otherwise.

TEX. BUS. & COM. CODE § 15.52 (Supp. 2002).

The purpose of sections 15.50–.52 was to return Texas law regarding covenants against competition to the common law of Texas as it existed prior to 1987. In early 1987, the Texas Supreme Court applied Texas common law with respect to covenants against competition for the first time in the context of a franchise agreement. In *Hill v. Mobile Auto Trim, Inc.*, 725 S.W.2d 168 (Tex. 1987), the Texas Supreme Court set out four criteria that a covenant not to compete must meet to qualify as reasonable:

> it must be necessary for the protection of a legitimate interest of the promisee, such as protecting business goodwill or trade secrets;
>
> it must not be oppressive to the promisor; that is, the time, territory, and activities prohibited must be reasonable;
>
> it must not be injurious to the public; and
>
> it must be supported by valuable consideration.

By themselves, these criteria would not have signaled a change in the law. The court's application of them in *Hill*, however, departed dramatically from prior cases.

The court noted that special training or knowledge acquired by an employee through his or her employer would constitute valuable consideration sufficient to support a covenant not to compete, and that allowing the use or sale of such valuable training or knowledge after termination of employment would create a disincentive for employers to train or educate their employees. Because Mobile Auto Trim had not shown it had provided any such training or knowledge to Hill, however, the court held that there was no consideration to support the covenant. The court gave no value to the grant of the franchise. *Id.* at 171.

The *Hill* court went on to hold that a covenant not to compete that restrained the right of an individual to engage in a "common calling" was void as against public policy and would not be enforced. The court did not define "common calling," but most of the Texas cases discussing the "common calling" test construed this term broadly. *Id.* at 172.

In response to *Hill*, the Texas legislature largely supplanted the Texas common law relating to the enforcement of covenants not to compete by enacting (and subsequently amending) sections 15.50, 15.51, and 15.52 of the Texas Business and Commerce Code (the Covenants Not to Compete Act). That act essentially returned the law to its pre-*Hill*, common-law state. The Covenants Not to Compete Act, as amended, discards the "common calling" test and provides that the only consideration that is required is that the covenant be "ancillary to an otherwise enforceable agreement at the time the agreement is made." *See DeSantis v. Wackenhut Corporation*, 793 S.W.2d 670 (Tex. 1990), *cert. denied*, 498 U.S. 1048 (1991); *Oliver et al. v. Rogers et al.*, 976 S.W.2d 792 (Tex. App.–Houston [1st Dist.] 1998, *pet. denied*).

In *Light v. Centel Cellular Company of Texas*, 883 S.W.2d 642 (Tex. 1994), the Texas Supreme Court confirmed the essential preemption of the field by the Covenants Not to Compete Act and addressed the issue of consideration by analyzing whether a covenant not to compete entered into by an at-will employee was "ancillary to an otherwise enforceable agreement." Although not a franchise case, this case has relevance in the franchise context. Ms. Light was a salesperson employed to sell pagers and other communications devices. The employment arrangement contemplated that Light would receive training (including confidential and proprietary information with respect to the operation of the business), much like a franchisee or distributor would receive.

The court noted that because Light was an at-will employee, by definition, there could not be an "otherwise enforceable agreement" (i.e., one that is not illusory) with respect to components of the employment relationship such as duration of employment, compensation, and so on. However, an at-will employment relationship does not preclude the formation of other contracts between an employee and employer to which a covenant not to compete could be "ancillary." *Id.* at 644–45.

Although there was an "otherwise enforceable agreement" between the parties—Light promised to give 14 days' notice before terminating her employment and to return to Centel product inventory she had in her possession—the court held that the covenant not to compete was not "ancillary" to that agreement. *Id.* at 647. Although Centel's promise to provide training could have involved confidential and proprietary information, "the covenant not to compete was not designed to enforce any of Light's return promises in the otherwise enforceable agreement." *Id.* Therefore, the covenant was unenforceable due to the absence of sufficient consideration. If Light had promised not to disclose any confidential or proprietary information given to her by Centel in an otherwise enforceable agreement, the covenant would have been "ancillary" to that otherwise enforceable agreement resulting in sufficient consideration having been given. *Id.* at 648. *See also Olander v. Compass Bank et al.*, 172 F. Supp. 2d 846 (S.D. Tex. 2001).

In *Amerispec, Inc. v. Metro Inspection Services, Inc. et al.*, 2001 WL 770999 (N.D. Tex. July 3, 2001), the U.S. District Court for the Northern District of Texas partially upheld a covenant not to compete that was ancillary to a franchise agreement. (*See* section 4 *infra.*) In that case, the court noted that sufficient consideration was exchanged: proprietary information and training in exchange for the franchisee's promise not to disclose it or use it competitively.

Hill made a significant distinction between covenants not to compete that were entered into in the context of the sale of a business and those entered into in connection with an employment relationship. The distinction between employment and sale of business covenants not to compete appears now to be limited by the Covenants Not to Compete Act to determining which party has the burden of proof regarding the enforceability of the covenant. The Covenants Not to Compete Act provides that "if the primary purpose of the agreement to which the covenant [not to compete] is ancillary is to obligate the promisor to render personal services, for a term or at will, the promisee has the burden of establishing that the covenant meets the [enforceability] criteria . . . ." Tex. Bus. & Com. Code § 15.51(b). "If the agreement has a different primary purpose, the promisor has the burden of establishing that the covenant does not meet those criteria." *Id.*

Since the enactment of the Covenants Not to Compete Act in its current form, the Texas Supreme Court has not directly addressed which party has the burden of proof in an action to enforce a covenant not to compete that is ancillary to a franchise agreement. However, the U.S. District Court for the Northern District of Texas held in *Amerispec, Inc.* that a franchise agreement is *not* a personal services contract, and, therefore, the franchisee had the burden to establish that the criteria for enforceability of a covenant not to compete were not met. 2001 WL 770999, at *3. Additionally, in *Butts Retail, Inc. v. Diversifoods, Inc.*, 840 S.W.2d 770 (Tex. App.–Beaumont 1992, *writ denied*), the court held that the franchisee had the burden to prove that the covenant at issue was unenforceable. *See also Meineke Discount Muffler v. Jaynes*, 999 F.2d 120 (5th Cir. 1993) (a franchise agreement is not a personal services contract, and, therefore, the franchisee has the burden of proof to show that the covenant not to compete was unreasonable).

Because the Covenants Not to Compete Act was intended to return the law to its pre-*Hill* state, the approach taken by Texas courts for many years prior to *Hill* is instructive. In the seminal case of *Weatherford Oil Tool Co. v. Campbell*, 340 S.W.2d 950 (Tex. 1960), an employer sought to enforce an employment contract containing a covenant not to compete. *Weatherford* held that the covenant had to be reasonable to be enforceable, and that it would be unreasonable if it were of greater scope than necessary to protect the business and goodwill of the employer, or imposed undue hardship on the person restricted. *Id.* at 951–52.

Weatherford involved three former employees, two salesmen and an office worker, who had signed non-competition agreements at the start of their employment. They had been trained in the methods and techniques for the use and installation of Weatherford's products. After they terminated their employment, they organized ⊠ company and began selling items similar to those manufactured by their former employer. When Weatherford sought to enforce the non-competition covenant, the former employees claimed it was void because it unreasonably restricted their future employment. The court found that the covenant amounted to an undertaking not to compete for one year, without territorial limitation, and that there was no reason why such broad coverage was required to protect Weatherford's business or goodwill. *Id.* at 952.

In 2006, in another case involving a covenant not to compete between an employer and an employee, the Texas Supreme Court revisited a footnote in *Light* that held that a "unilateral contract, since it could be accepted only by future performance, could not support a covenant not to compete [because] it was not an 'otherwise enforceable agreement at the time the agreement is made' as required by § 15.50 [of the Covenants Not to Compete Act]." *Alex Sheshunoff Management Services, L.P. v. Johnson*, 209 S.W.3d 644 (Tex. 2006). In *Sheshunoff*, an employee signed an at-will employment agreement containing a covenant not to compete in which the employer promised to provide the employee access to confidential information, and the employee promised not to disclose the confidential information. Although the employer did not immediately provide the employee access to confidential information at the time the employment agreement was signed, it did provide the employee access to the confidential information over time.

Disagreeing with the *Light* court's interpretation of section 15.50 of the Covenants Not to Compete Act, the *Sheshunoff* court held that a covenant not to compete is not invalid solely because the employer's promise is illusory at the time the agreement is made. The court held that the covenant not to compete must simply be "ancillary to or part of the agreement at the time the agreement is made," as opposed to the *Light* court's interpretation that the agreement must be enforceable at the time the agreement is made. *Id.* at 651. "[A] unilateral contract formed when the employer performs a promise that was illusory when made can satisfy the requirements of the Act." *Id.* Although the employer's promise to provide the employee access to the confidential information was illusory at the time the employment agreement was signed, the employer formed a unilateral contract, and the requirements of the Covenants Not to Compete Act were met, when the employer ultimately provided the employee access to the confidential information. *Id.*

Furthermore, the *Sheshunoff* court admonished that a court's examination of the enforceability of a covenant not to compete should not be focused on the "overly technical disputes" concerning whether a covenant is "ancillary to an otherwise enforceable agreement." Rather, the court stated that the focus should be on whether the covenant's restraints as to time, geographical area, and scope of activity are reasonable and "do not impose a greater restraint than is necessary to protect the goodwill or other business interest of the promisee." *Id.* at 655 (quoting TEX. BUS. & COM. CODE § 15.50(a)).

Finally, in 2009, the Texas Supreme Court held in another employer-employee case that a covenant not to compete can be enforceable even where one party expressly promises not to disclose confidential information but the other party does not expressly promise to provide the confidential information, so long as the nature of the employment for which the employee was hired *reasonably requires* the employer to disclose confidential information to the employee. *Mann Frankfort Stein & Lipp v. Fielding*, 289 S.W.3d 844, 845–46 (Tex. 2009). Building on *Sheshunoff*, the court held that the employer's implied promise to convey confidential information and its eventual bestowal of that confidential information constituted the consideration necessary to make the covenant not to compete enforceable.

---

2. Have the courts articulated the "legitimate interests" of the franchisor that will support enforcement of a covenant against competition contained in a franchise agreement?

- **If so, what are they (e.g., protection of goodwill, protection of confidential information), and in what contexts did the issue arise?**
- **If not, what interests have been recognized in other contexts (e.g., employment agreements, the sale of business context)?**

Under *Hill v. Mobile Auto Trim, Inc.*, 725 S.W.2d 168, 172 (Tex. 1987), the only interests likely to support a covenant not to compete in a franchise agreement were the protection of the franchisor's trade secrets and the protection of specialized training or knowledge (to the extent that may be different from trade secrets) acquired by the franchisee in connection with his operation of the franchise business under the franchise agreement. *See also Martin v. Credit Protection Association, Inc.*, 793 S.W.2d 667 (Tex. 1990); *Alphagraphics Franchising, Inc. v. Babbitt*, 1989 Tex. App. LEXIS 89 (Tex. App.–Houston [1st Dist.] Jan. 18, 1989). Prior to *Hill*, both business and employee/franchisee goodwill inured to the benefit of the franchisor or employer and were interests the franchisor or employer was entitled to protect. *See Henshaw v. Kroenecke*, 656 S.W.2d 416 (Tex. 1983) (employer has a legitimate interest to protect in retaining clients that would be taken by employee).

The Covenants Not to Compete Act broadly states that "goodwill and other legitimate business interests of the promisee" are worthy of protection. Texas cases have discussed and accepted specialized knowledge or training and trade secrets as protectable interests in employment and franchise agreement covenants. In *Amerispec, Inc. v. Metro Inspection Services, Inc. et al.*, 2001 Westlaw 770999 (N.D. Tex. 2001), the court held that "proprietary information" was a protectable interest. And in *Butts Retail, Inc. v. Diversifoods, Inc.*, 840 S.W.2d 770 (Tex. App.–Beaumont 1992, *writ denied*), the Texas Court of Appeals for the 9th District of Texas held that a franchisor's "business goodwill, trade secrets, or other confidential or proprietary information" are legitimate interests that support the enforcement of a covenant not to compete ancillary to or in a franchise agreement. However, the Covenants Not to

Compete Act and recent caselaw have rejected the more specific *Hill* requirement that some "special training or knowledge" had to be imparted to the promisor in order to support a covenant not to compete. *See Curtis v. Ziff Energy Group, Ltd.*, 12 S.W.3d 114, 118 (Tex. App.–Houston [14th Dist.] 1999, *no writ*) (holding that only one non-illusory promise to which the covenant not to compete is ancillary is needed to establish consideration). *See also Amerispec, Inc., supra.*

In *DeSantis v. Wackenhut Corporation*, 793 S.W.2d 670 (Tex. 1990), *cert. denied*, 498 U.S. 1048 (1991), the court held that a jury finding of no irreparable harm to Wackenhut was equivalent to a failure to find that Wackenhut had a protectable interest to support the covenant. In *DeSantis*, the employee had not been shown to have received any special training or information while employed. The failure to find any protectable interest of the promisee proved to be all that was necessary to hold that the covenant was unreasonable and thus unenforceable. *Id.* at 685.

On the same day *DeSantis* was decided, the Texas Supreme Court decided *Martin v. Credit Protection Association, Inc.*, 793 S.W.2d 667 (Tex. 1990). Martin had started as a salesman for Credit Protection Association (CPA) in 1980, eventually working up to the position of vice president. In 1983, Martin had been required to sign a covenant not to compete as a condition of his continued employment. The lower court had held that Martin had received special training in the sale of debt collection services, an area in which he had no prior experience. Under facts similar to the *Light* case, the Texas Supreme Court held that because Martin was an employee-at-will when he signed the non-competition covenant, and because there was no employment agreement other than the covenant not to compete, the covenant was not ancillary to an employment agreement as a matter of law. *Id.* at 669–70. That is, the covenant not to compete was not supported by independent consideration and was, therefore, void in all respects. *Id.*

In *Peat Marwick Main & Co. v. Haass*, 818 S.W.2d 381, 388 (Tex. 1991), the court held that even though the contract provisions at issue dealt with the sale of an accounting practice and required only the reimbursement to the buyer of its out-of-pocket costs of acquiring clients whose business the departing seller continued to service, they restricted the right of the seller to render personal services and had to be viewed as covenants not to compete. The court found the provisions to be unenforceable as an unreasonable restraint on the seller and reversed the lower appellate court's award of damages to the buyer. *Id.* at 387–88. Although Texas law provides that damages cannot be recovered for breach of an overly broad covenant not to compete prior to its reformation, the result seems especially harsh in this case.

Notwithstanding *Haass*, there has never been any real dispute that the sale of a business and its associated goodwill provides a protectable interest sufficient to support an ancillary covenant not to compete. In *Hospital Consultants, Inc. v. Potyka*, 531 S.W.2d 657, 663 (Tex. App.–San Antonio 1975, *writ ref'd n.r.e.*), the court stated:

> It is true that there are cases, such as those involving sale of a business or goodwill, where a restrictive covenant has been enforced although its sole objective is the elimination of competition. But a restrictive covenant in connection with the sale of a business or goodwill is quite different from a post-employment restriction. A transfer of goodwill cannot be accomplished effectively unless the transferror agrees not to diminish the value of the thing transferred by refraining from competing with his transferee. Such a restraint is necessary in order to insure that the transferee will receive the full value of the thing that he is acquiring. . . . The transfer of

a business or goodwill of itself furnished, by its very nature, the special circumstances that make the transferror's agreement not to compete reasonable and enforceable.

Chandler v. Mastercraft Dental Corp., 739 S.W.2d 460 (Tex. App.–Fort Worth 1987, *writ denied*), dealt with the enforcement of a covenant not to compete incident to the sale of a dental equipment manufacturing and sales business. The trial court had issued an injunction upholding the terms of the covenant not to compete. In its consideration of the case, the appellate court held the covenants were necessary to protect Mastercraft's goodwill and trade secrets that were incident to the sale. *Id.* at 464–65.

M.R.S. Datascope, Inc. v. Exchange Data Corp., 745 S.W.2d 542 (Tex. App.–Houston [1st Dist.] 1988, *no writ*), also dealt with the sale of a business. M.R.S. was engaged in the medical records service business. The defendants, former employees of M.R.S., went to work for a direct competitor, Exchange Data Corporation. The individual defendants, Houghton and Woolf, each had previously owned and ultimately sold their own medical records service businesses to M.R.S. When Woolf sold her business to M.R.S., she entered into a written employment contract ancillary to the sale of her business containing a covenant not to compete for three years in the seven counties surrounding Houston after the termination of her employment.

In holding Woolf's covenant enforceable, the court looked at the business interest that M.R.S. sought to protect and found that Woolf's covenant was both incident to the sale of her business and part of her employment contract. *Id.* at 545. As M.R.S. had a legitimate interest in protecting the business goodwill that it acquired by purchasing Woolf's company, Woolf's promise not to compete with M.R.S. increased the value of the business. As demonstrated by both *Chandler* and *M.R.S.*, Texas courts readily recognize the existence of a legitimate business interest in a covenant not to compete that is ancillary to the sale of a business.

---

3. What time limitations have courts recognized as reasonable in the franchise context? If no franchise cases have been decided, what time limitations have been recognized in other contexts?

➤ How have they been related to the interests protected?

The Covenants Not to Compete Act provides that the time restrictions in covenants not to compete must be reasonable considering the business interests at issue, and Texas common law is consistent with this approach. Although no Texas courts have specifically analyzed the issue of reasonable time restrictions in a franchise non-competition agreement, the court in *Butts Retail, Inc. v. Diversifoods, Inc.*, 840 S.W.2d 770 (Tex. App.–Beaumont 1992, *writ denied*), upheld a covenant not to compete that provided that the franchisee would not operate a similar business in the mall in which the franchised unit was located for two years after termination or expiration of the franchise agreement. Several post-employment covenants containing two-year non-competition terms have been enforced where enforcement was limited to protecting the former employer from solicitation of its customers. *See, e.g.*, *Bertotti v. C.E. Shepherd Co.*, 752 S.W.2d 648 (Tex. App.–Houston [14th Dist.] 1988, *no writ*) (prohibition on the sale of competitive products to customers of a former employer with worldwide scope; confidential information protected). In another post-employment covenant case, an 18-month term was found reasonable for a former employee who had "performed a sophisticated management function" for the former employer. *B. Cantrell Oil Co. v. Hino Gas Sales, Inc.*, 756 S.W.2d 781 (Tex. App.–Corpus Christi 1988, *no writ*) (18-month term was limited to one county and had run by the time of the appellate decision). *See also Unitel Corp v. Decker*, 731 S.W.2d 636 (Tex. App.–Houston [14th Dist.] 1987, *no writ*) (one-year covenant upheld to protect training and confidential sales leads).

As one might expect, longer terms have been held reasonable in sale of business cases. A five-year restriction was upheld in *Chandler v. Mastercraft Dental Corp.*, 739 S.W.2d 460 (Tex. App.–Fort Worth 1987, *writ denied*) (business goodwill was the "key asset" purchased; trade secrets also were entitled to protection). *See also Farmer v. Holley*, 237 S.W.3d 758 (Tex. App.–Waco 2007, *pet. denied*).

The reasonableness of a time restriction in a covenant not to compete is a question of law. In determining the reasonableness of the duration of a covenant, Texas courts look to a wide range of factors and have considerable discretion. *Bob Pagan Ford, Inc. v. Smith*, 638 S.W.2d 176, 178 (Tex. App.–Houston [1st Dist.] 1982, *no writ*). These include the time remaining in the restriction at the time of trial, payments to the covenantor, and the covenantor's ability to earn a living.

There is no simple test or rule by which a court can determine whether the duration of a covenant is unreasonable. The court must make this determination on the facts of the particular case before it. *See Justin Belt Co. v. Yost*, 502 S.W.2d 681 (Tex. 1973) (approving trial court reformation of covenant of seven years); *York v. Dotson*, 271 S.W.2d 347, 348 (Tex. Civ. App.–Fort Worth 1954, *writ ref'd n.r.e.*) (one may lawfully agree not to compete in a particular business, in a reasonably limited territory, during the remainder of his or her life); *Greenstein v. Simpson*, 660 S.W.2d 155 (Tex. App.–Waco 1983, *writ ref'd n.r.e.*) (a person may agree, in connection with the sale of his or her business, not to re-enter a similar competitive business for the remainder of his or her life).

In determining the reasonableness of time restrictions, courts will take into account the underlying agreement, looking in particular at whether the covenant against competition arose in an employment context or in connection with the sale of a business. The test in either case is reasonableness, but what is reasonable with respect to the sale of a business will differ from what is reasonable in the employment context.

4. What geographic limitations have courts recognized as reasonable in the franchise context?

- **How have they been related to the interests protected?**
- **Have courts recognized the legitimacy of protecting other franchisees from competition?**

Geographic restrictions on competition are analyzed in a manner similar to time restrictions. The Covenants Not to Compete Act provides that the geographical area to which a covenant not to compete applies must be reasonable. The restrictive covenant must be supported by the business interests sought to be protected by the franchisor and may extend only as far as necessary to protect those interests.

In *Butts Retail, Inc. v. Diversifoods, Inc.*, 840 S.W.2d 770 (Tex. App.–Beaumont 1992, *writ denied*), a franchise agreement, under which a franchisee opened a store in the "Parkdale Mall" in Beaumont, Texas, included an in-term covenant not to compete that prohibited the franchisee from operating another similar business within the "metropolitan area of the Parkdale Mall store" in Beaumont, Texas. During the term of the franchise agreement, the franchisee opened a similar store under a different name in the "Central Mall" in Port Arthur, Texas, which is relatively close to Beaumont, Texas, and the franchisor sued to enforce the covenant not to compete. The court held that because the "metropolitan area of the Parkdale Mall" was not sufficiently definite as to geographic scope, the in-term covenant not to compete was unenforceable. *Id.* at 774.

In *Amerispec, Inc. v. Metro Inspection Services, Inc.*, 2001 Westlaw 770999 (N.D. Tex. July 3, 2001), the covenant not to compete provided that the franchisee could not own or operate a business similar to its Amerispec building inspection business for one year after the termination or expiration of the franchise agreement (1) within the franchise territory designated by the franchise agreement, (2) within a ten-mile radius of that franchise territory, or (3) within a ten-mile radius of the office of any other Amerispec franchise in existence at the time of the termination or expiration. The court upheld the covenant (and granted Amerispec a preliminary injunction) as it related to the franchise territory and the area within a ten-mile radius of the franchise territory, but refused to grant Amerispec injunctive relief with respect to that portion of the covenant related to areas within ten miles of any other Amerispec franchise office because Amerispec failed to produce sufficient evidence that the "remote" portion of the covenant was necessary to protect a legitimate business interest. However, the court noted that the "holding is limited to the preliminary injunction ruling. It is not a final decision—which can only be reached after full consideration of the merits (by pretrial motion or trial)—that [the remote portion of] the noncompete covenant is unreasonable, and therefore partly unenforceable, in its geographical scope." *See also Meineke Discount Muffler v. Jaynes*, 999 F.2d 120 (5th Cir. 1993) (a one-year/20-mile radius restriction in a franchise agreement held not unreasonable as a matter of law).

Outside the franchise context, in *Weatherford Oil Tool Co. v. Campbell*, 340 S.W.2d 950 (Tex. 1960), the Texas Supreme Court held that a restrictive covenant must bear some relation to the activities of the employer. The geographic coverage may be only as extensive as necessary to protect the interest of the former employer. *See* 5 Restatement (Second) of Contracts § 188, cmt.

The breadth of territorial restrictions in non-competition covenants may vary with the nature and extent of the employer's business operations. *See Matlock v. Data Processing Security, Inc.*, 618 S.W.2d 327 (Tex. 1981). In determining the reasonableness of territorial restraints, courts balance "the interests of the employer, the employee, and the public while being 'mindful of the basic policies of individual liberty, freedom of contract, freedom of trade, protection of business, encouragement of competition and discouragement of monopoly.'" *Id.* at 329 (quoting *Fidelity Union Life Ins. Co. v. Protective Life Insurance Co.*, 356 F. Supp. 1199, 1203 (N.D. Tex. 1972), *aff'd mem.*, 477 F.2d 594 (5th Cir. 1973)). *See also Frankiewicz v. National Comp Associates*, 633 S.W.2d 505, 507 (Tex. 1982); *Justin Belt Co. v. Yost*, 502 S.W.2d 681 (Tex. 1973).

In *Bertotti v. C.E. Shepherd Co.*, 752 S.W.2d 648 (Tex. App.–Houston [14th Dist.] 1988, *no writ*), the court upheld as reasonable an agreement that limited competition throughout the United States and numerous foreign countries. The court held that the evidence supported the employer's claim that it conducted business in all 50 states and in certain foreign countries and, under the circumstances of the case, the covenant was not unreasonable. *Id.* at 654.

In *Vais Arms Inc. v. George Vais*, 383 F.3d 287 (5th Cir. 2004), the court upheld a covenant not to compete throughout the United States. The court reasoned that the geographic limitation sensibly comported with the national character of the business the promisor had sold to the promisee because the record showed that the promisor had advertised the business via nationally distributed trade publications, mail order catalogues, and the internet. The court further concluded that "restrict[ing] the geographic limits of the covenant to just those states in which [the promisor] had actually consummated one or more sales, while disregarding the nationwide scope of his marketing efforts, would be legally absurd." *Id.* at 296.

In *Wilson v. Chemco Chemical Co.*, 711 S.W.2d 265 (Tex. App.–Dallas 1986, *no writ*), the court looked at the potential injury that the party bargaining for the covenant would suffer—that is, what were the protectable interests—when determining what was reasonable. *Wilson* involved an action against an independent contractor for breach of a covenant not to compete. The covenantee alleged potential loss of goodwill and customers; no claims were made involving trade secrets. The court held that where the potential loss consists of goodwill and customers, then the reasonable area of restraint is that area where the covenantor worked for the former business and established customers. *Id.* at 267. This position has been regarded as well established in Texas. *See, e.g., Cross v. Chem-Air South, Inc.*, 648 S.W.2d 754, 757 (Tex. App.–Beaumont 1983, *no writ*) ("the test for reasonableness as to territorial restraint is whether or not the injunction is confined to territory actually covered by the former employee in his work for the employer"); *Cawse-Morgan v. Murray*, 633 S.W.2d 348, 350 (Tex. App.–Corpus Christi 1982, *no writ*); *Martin v. Kidde Sales & Service, Inc.*, 496 S.W.2d 714, 718–29 (Tex. Civ. App.–Waco 1973, *no writ*) (largely unskilled labor and little training "confine injunction of the former employee to the area where the employee has worked for his former employer"); *Weber v. Hesse Envelope Co.*, 342 S.W.2d 652, 655 (Tex. Civ. App.–Dallas 1960, *no writ*) (to prevent a former employee from raiding customers of his former employer, injunction limited to the area actually covered by the employee in his work for his employer); *Krueger, Hutchinson & Overton Clinic v. Lewis*, 266 S.W.2d 885, 889 (Tex. Civ. App.–Lubbock), *aff'd*, 269 S.W.2d 798 (Tex. 1954) ("the rule with reference to space limitations, as often announced by the courts, is usually determined by the territory served professionally in such cases").

5. What limitations on activities have courts recognized as reasonable in the franchise context?

As with temporal and territorial restrictions, under the Covenants Not to Compete Act restrictions as to activity must be reasonable and may be only as broad as necessary to protect the legitimate business interests of the covenantee. The rejection of the "common calling" test in *Hill v. Mobile Auto Trim, Inc.*, 725 S.W.2d 168 (Tex. 1987), has clarified that a relatively wide range of activities related to the business may be prohibited.

For example, in *Butts Retail, Inc. v. Diversifoods, Inc.*, 840 S.W.2d 770 (Tex. App.–Beaumont 1992, *writ denied*), the court upheld a covenant not to compete that prohibited the franchisee from "operating a business selling fruit and nuts" in a mall for a two-year period after the expiration or termination of the franchise agreement. In *Amerispec, Inc. v. Metro Inspection Services, Inc. et al.*, 2001 WL 770999, at *2 (N.D. Tex. July 3, 2001), the covenant not to compete prohibited the franchisee from "directly or indirectly operating, owning, being employed by, or consulting with any business that conducts residential building inspections or providing business inspection services" for one year after the termination or expiration of the franchise agreement in a certain area. The defendant argued that the interests worthy of protection were limited to Amerispec's trademark, and that they should be required only to cease using the name and to return material that contained the marks. The court rejected the franchisee's challenge to the scope of the activity to be restrained and held that the broad restriction on the franchisee's activities was reasonable. *Id.* at *5.

6. Does the state recognize a difference between in-term and post-term covenants?

Neither the Covenants Not to Compete Act nor the few decisions analyzing in-term covenants not to compete in the franchise relationship appear to distinguish between in-term and post-term covenants. *See, e.g., Butts Retail, Inc. v. Diversifoods, Inc.*, 840 S.W.2d 770 (Tex. App.–Beaumont 1992, *writ denied*). However, because covenants not to compete must be reasonable *considering the interests to be protected*, a court may find much broader in-term covenants reasonable.

7. Has the state allowed enforcement of covenants against non-signatories (e.g., family members, newly formed corporations)?

In the franchising context, no case has been found that addresses the enforceability of covenants not to compete against non-signatories under Texas law.

In the sale of a business context, in *Henson Patriot Ltd. Co. v. Medina*, 2014 WL 4546973 (W.D. Tex. Sept. 11, 2014), the U.S. District Court for the Western District of Texas upheld a five-year covenant not to compete against a non-signatory because it was necessary to protect the purchaser's goodwill. The court explained that a Texas court may extend a non-compete to a non-signatory when "an entity is created by a signatory for the purpose of competing to circumvent, or perpetuate a 'fraud' on, the non-compete" or "a signatory significantly aids, abets, consults, or advise[s] another entity or person's competition with the buyer when the non-compete forbids aiding, abetting, consulting or advising." *Id.* at *7.

8. Will the state modify, "blue-pencil," or otherwise reduce a covenant found to be overbroad?

The Covenants Not to Compete Act provides for reforming, and the long-standing practice of Texas courts has been to reform, covenants not to compete when found to be overbroad and to enforce those covenants as so reformed. That is, if the covenant is ancillary to an otherwise enforceable agreement, it may be reformed to make reasonable its restrictions as to time, geographic area, and/or scope of activities. If it is necessary to reform the covenant, however, no damages may be awarded for a breach that occurred before the reformation. *See* TEX. BUS. & COM. CODE § 15.51(c).

In *Butts Retail, Inc. v. Diversifoods, Inc.*, 840 S.W.2d 770 (Tex. App.–Beaumont 1992, *writ denied*), as discussed previously, the franchisor sought to enforce a covenant not to compete against a franchisee, which provided that (1) for a period of two years after the expiration or termination of the franchise agreement, the franchisee could not operate a similar business in the mall in which the franchised unit had been located (the Parkdale Mall) and (2) during the term of the franchise agreement, the franchisee could not operate another similar business at the Parkdale Mall or within the "metropolitan area of the Parkdale Mall store in Beaumont, Texas." *Id.* at 772. The appellate court held that the second portion of the covenant was unenforceable and unreasonable because it did not sufficiently identify an appropriately limited area as to the territory and geography covered. *Id.* at 774–75. Yet rather than holding that the entire covenant was unenforceable, the court struck the second portion of the covenant only and upheld that first portion prohibiting the franchisee from operating a similar business at the Parkdale Mall. *Id.* at 773–74.

Outside the franchise context, in *Weatherford Oil Tool Co. v. Campbell*, 340 S.W.2d 950 (Tex. 1960), the court held that where a covenant not to compete was unreasonable with respect to time, scope, or geography, the court had the freedom to reform the covenant and would enforce it by granting an injunction restraining the defendant from competing for a time and within an area that are reasonable under the circumstances. *Weatherford* held that reformation of a covenant was appropriate only where injunctive relief was sought. If a party seeking to enforce a covenant not to compete also seeks damages, the covenant "must stand or fall on the contract as written." *Id.* at 953. *See also Matlock v. Data Processing Security, Inc.*, 618 S.W.2d 327, 329 (Tex. 1981) (overbroad injunction modified); *Justin Belt Co. v. Yost*, 502 S.W.2d 681, 684 (Tex. 1973) (where the covenant of an employee is found to be unreasonable in time or in area, the court may reform the contract so as to create reasonable restrictions).

---

9. When does a non-compete period begin to run? Will courts equitably extend the term?

Outside of the franchising context, while Texas courts do not deny themselves the ability to equitably extend non-compete periods in limited circumstances, recent caselaw shows a reluctance by the courts to do so. In 2006, a Texas appellate court considered an appellant's argument that the trial court erred in refusing to equitably extend the non-compete period beyond its original one-year term. *RenewData Corp. v. Strickler*, 2006 WL 504998 (Tex. App.–Austin Mar. 3, 2006, *no pet.*). The court examined the appellant's behavior, including the appellant's failure to expeditiously file suit to enjoin the defendant from violating its covenant not to compete and then twice moving for continuances after filing suit, and found that the delays in enforcing the covenant not to compete were not "simply inherent to litigation but were attributable to" the appellant. *Id.* at *5. Although the court acknowledged Fifth Circuit authority for equitably extending a non-compete period (citing *Guy Carpenter & Co. v. Provenzale*, 334 F.3d 459, 464 (5th Cir.2003)), the court held that because the appellant did not diligently pursue its remedies under the non-competition covenant, the trial court did not abuse its discretion in refusing to equitably extend the non-compete period. *Id.*

In 2007, a second Texas appellate court also refused to equitably extend the non-compete period. *Farmer v. Holley*, 237 S.W.3d 758 (Tex. App.–Waco 2007, *pet. denied*). In *Farmer*, a dance instructor sold her dance studio and entered into a covenant not to compete for a period of five years. Following the sale, the purchaser filed suit against the seller, alleging violations of the covenant not to compete. The trial court granted the purchaser's motion for summary judgment and equitably delayed the non-compete period so that the five-year period began on the date of summary judgment rather than the date of the purchase agreement. Like the *Strickler* court, the appellate court acknowledged Fifth Circuit authority for equitably extending a non-compete period (citing *Guy Carpenter & Co. v. Provenzale*, 334 F.3d 459, 464 (5th Cir. 2003) and *Premier Industries Corp. v. Texas Industries Fastener Co.*, 450 F.2d 444, 448 (5th Cir. 1971)), but the court held that because the seller's violations of the covenant not to compete were not "continuous and persistent," the trial court abused its discretion by equitably delaying the start of the non-compete period. *Id.* at 761.

However, in appropriate cases, courts have equitably extended non-compete periods. In *Rimkus Consulting Group, Inc. v. Budinger*, 2001 WL 619067, at *4 (Tex. App–Houston June 7, 2001, *no pet.*), an employer sought to enforce a covenant not to compete after the employee violated the covenant by joining a competing consulting group. The court affirmed the trial court's equitable extension of the covenant not to compete, holding that because the plaintiff "moved diligently to protect its rights[,] it would therefore be inequitable to allow litigation to deprive it of the benefit of injunctive relief." *Id.* (citing *Premier Industries Corp. v. Texas Industries Fastener Co.*, 450 F.2d 444, 448 (5th Cir. 1971)).

10. Are there additional nuances or peculiarities of the state's treatment of covenants in the franchising context?

As discussed above, a covenant not to compete must be "ancillary" to an otherwise enforceable agreement and must be reasonable as to time, geographic reach, and activity restrained. These are obviously subjective determinations that could lead to inconsistent results, but the Covenants Not to Compete Act has brought some clarity and relative certainty to the area.

Outside the franchise context, in *Weatherford Oil Tool Co. v. Campbell*, 340 S.W.2d 950, 953 (Tex. 1960), the Texas Supreme Court ruled that if a court modifies a covenant not to compete due to an unreasonable limitation with respect to time, scope, or geography, no money damages can be recovered for any acts done before the covenant was modified. *See also* TEX. BUS. & COM. CODE ANN. § 15.51(c) (Vernon Supp. 2000) (monetary damages or attorney's fees are not permitted when a covenant not to compete must be reformed).

In the employer-employee context, Texas courts have weighed the extent to which choice-of-law and forum selection clauses will be enforced. In *DeSantis v. Wackenhut Corp.*, 793 S.W.2d 670 (Tex. 1990), the Texas Supreme Court held that enforcement of non-competition covenants was a matter of fundamental Texas public policy and should be governed by Texas law. In *DeSantis*, an employment agreement between a Florida corporation and a Texas employee included a choice-of-law provision designating Florida law as governing disputes under the parties' non-compete agreement. The court held that because "the law governing enforcement of non-competition agreements is fundamental policy in Texas . . . to apply the law of another state to determine the enforceability of such an agreement . . . would be contrary to that policy." *Id.* at 681.

In *In re AutoNation, Inc.*, 228 S.W.3d 663 (Tex. 2007), however, the Texas Supreme Court held that a forum selection clause requiring a dispute concerning a covenant not to compete to be heard in a Florida court was enforceable. Not unlike the facts in *DeSantis*, the dispute involved a Texas employee, an automobile dealership general manager, and a Florida corporation. The parties' non-competition agreement stated that all disputes concerning the agreement would be heard in Florida court and would be governed by Florida law. The court rejected the defendant's argument that the *DeSantis* ruling on governing law compelled a similar ruling on forum selection clauses and held that, under principles of interstate comity and on the basis that the parties freely negotiated the agreement, a Texas court could not prevent a party from asking a Florida court to honor the express terms of the non-competition agreement. *Id.* at 669–70.

U.S. Virgin Islands

*by James A. Meaney**

1. Has the state addressed covenants against competition in the context of franchising?

- **Does the state have a franchising statute or regulations that address covenants against competition?**
- **Does the state have a covenants statute of general applicability that would encompass franchise covenants?**
- **Have the courts addressed covenants in the context of franchising either under a statute or under the state's common law?**

The U.S. Virgin Islands does not have a franchising statute or regulations addressing covenants against competition. The territory does have a franchise relationship law that focuses on the requirement of "good-faith" grounds for termination. *See* 12A V.I. CODE ANN. § 130 *et seq.* The U.S. Virgin Islands franchise relationship statute does not address covenants against competition, nor has it spawned any caselaw touching on covenants against competition in franchise arrangements.

There is no U.S. Virgin Islands statute governing covenants against competition generally that would encompass franchise covenants. While the U.S. Virgin Islands does not have a statute of general applicability focusing on covenants against competition, it has adopted an Antimonopoly Law (11 V.I. CODE ANN. § 1501 *et seq.*) that arguably applies to an employment covenant.

The Antimonopoly Law provides that it is a violation to "make any contract with, . . . any other person who is, *or but for a prior agreement would be,* a competitor of such person: (b) . . . limiting . . . the sale or supply of any service, for the purpose or with the effect of [fixing, controlling, or maintaining the price or rate charged for any commodity sold or bought by the parties thereto, or the fee charged or paid for any service performed or received by the parties thereto]." *But see Williamson v. Hess,* 16 V.I. 284, 291, 1979 WL 447866 (Terr. Ct. May 19, 1979) (rejecting the argument that the Antimonopoly Law applied to a covenant against competition contained in an employment agreement and emphasizing that the law "addresses itself to contracts among competitors which restrain trade because of monopolistic

*James A. Meaney is a partner with the law firm of Zaino Law Group, LPA, in Dublin, Ohio.

or oligarchic practices." *Id.* at 291.). For a broader discussion of the application of the U.S. Virgin Islands Antimonopoly Law, *see Sea Air Shuttle Corporation d/b/a VISS and Sea Air Shuttle Corporation of the Virgin Islands v. The Virgin Islands Port Authority and Caribbean Air-boats, Inc.*, 782 F. Supp. 1070 (D.V.I. 1991), and *Sunny Isle Shopping Center, Inc. v. Xtra Super Food Centers, Inc., d/b/a Pueblo and Kmart Corporation*, 237 F. Supp. 2d 606 (D.V.I. 2002) (involving a restrictive covenant contained in a shopping center lease).

Prior to 2011, the RESTATEMENTS OF LAW as adopted by the American Law Institute was applied in the U.S. Virgin Islands in the absence of any local law to the contrary.[1] V.I. CODE ANN. § 4. Two reported U.S. Virgin Islands cases applied the RESTATEMENT (SECOND) OF CONTRACTS, reaching disparate results: *Williamson v. Hess, supra* (after reviewing the five factors set out in RESTATEMENT (SECOND) OF CONTRACTS section 515 as relevant in determining the reasonableness of a covenant against competition, the court concluded that the agreement was reasonable because the established veterinarian-covenantee had a limited local clientele and the junior veterinarian–covenantor had a number of alternative employment options); and *Virgin Islands Diving School/Supplies v. Dixon, et al.*, 20 V.I. 54, 1983 WL 889860 (Terr. Ct. Oct. 19, 1983) (relying upon RESTATEMENT (SECOND) OF CONTRACTS section 118(2)(b), the court voided a non-competition covenant as one of adhesion "since it was prepared by a party with excessive bargaining power"). For additional background on the treatment of adhesion contracts in the territory, *see Trailer Marine Transportation Corporation A/K/A Interisland Intermodal Lines, Inc. v. Charley's Trucking, Inc., et al.*, 20 V.I. 282; 1984 V.I. LEXIS 16 (Terr. Ct., Mar. 15, 1984).

In 2011, however, the Virgin Islands Supreme Court held in *Banks v. International Rental and Leasing Corp.*, 55 V.I. 967, 2011 WL 6299025 (Dec. 15, 2011), that 1 V.I. CODE ANN. § 4 was implicitly overruled when the legislature adopted 4 V.I. CODE ANN. § 21, observing that the legislature intended to "develop the common law [of the Virgin Islands] through judicial precedent." *Id.* at 977.

The Virgin Islands Superior Court interpreted the instructions of the supreme court in *Banks* in *Arvidson v. Buchar*, 71 V.I. 277, 2019 WL 4307580 (V.I. Super. Sept. 10, 2019), a non-compete case, ultimately concluding that the restriction on competition between business principals and an employed manager was unenforceable. In a thoughtful and detailed opinion, the court in *Arvidson* reviewed the analytical framework applied by various states, rejected the RESTATEMENT framework (although noting that the common law approach is substantially similar), and defined a common law analysis that begins with determining whether the covenant is supported by consideration and accommodates the promisor's right to work, the right to contract, and the public's right to competition. The covenant must not impose an undue burden on the promisor. "Accordingly, in the Virgin Islands, a contract which is only in partial restraint of trade may be valid and enforceable when it (1) is ancillary to the main purpose of a valid contract or transaction, (2) is supported by valid consideration, (3) passes a three-pronged test assessing whether the covenant safeguards a protectable business interest of the promisee, and (4) is reasonable with regard to its duration, geographic area covered, and manner or scope of activities restricted when protecting the legitimate interests of the promisee." 71 V.I. at 311. The court observed that the relationship between the parties to the covenant was essentially one of employment and strictly scrutinized

1. The U.S. Virgin Islands is a territory, not a state.

the covenant. Absent provisions limiting the duration or describing an applicable geographic scope, the covenant was invalid and unenforceable.

As indicated in the discussion below, despite the departure from the analytical framework established by the RESTATEMENT, the few cases decided under the prior RESTATEMENT standard may yet be useful precedent. For instance, *Williamson v. Hess*, 16 V.I. 284, 1979 WL 447866 (Terr. Ct. May 19, 1979), includes a useful example of analyzing the impact of a restraint on the promisor. Finding that the veterinarian employee had no prior "roots" in the Virgin Islands, was young, possessed adequate financial resources, and could easily establish himself outside of the geographical scope of the covenant (the islands of St. Thomas and St. John), the court concluded that enforcement would not impose an undue hardship.

---

2. Have the courts articulated the "legitimate interests" of the franchisor that will support enforcement of a covenant against competition contained in a franchise agreement?

- **If so, what are they (e.g., protection of goodwill, protection of confidential information), and in what contexts did the issue arise?**
- **If not, what interests have been recognized in other contexts (e.g., employment agreements, the sale of business context)?**

The U.S. Virgin Islands courts have not articulated the "legitimate interests" of a franchisor that will support the enforcement of a covenant against competition contained in a franchise agreement. In a non-franchise context, the court in *Arvidson v. Buchar, supra,* cited *V.I. Diving School/Supplies v. Dixon*, 20 V.I. 54, 60 (V.I. Terr. Ct. 1979) in support of the requirement that a promisee must have a protectable, legitimate business interest. *Arvidson, supra,* at 301. In the *V.I. Diving* case, trade secrets, unique services provided by the promisee, and confidential information related to the promisee's business were mentioned as protectable interests.

The court in *Arvidson v. Buchar, supra,* further opined that goodwill is a protectable interest in the sale of a business, and that in an employment context protectable interests include "trade secrets, business secrets, confidential information regarding product development, internally-generated customer lists which are not readily ascertained from public sources, clients and customers in situations in which 'the employee closely associates or has repeated contact with the employer's customers so that the customer tends to associate the employer's business with the employee;' and competition from an employee who has developed an ability to offer services that are unique or extraordinary in nature." 71 V.I. Super. at 318.

---

3. What time limitations have courts recognized as reasonable in the franchise context?

- **If no franchise cases have been decided, what time limitations have been recognized in other contexts?**
- **How have they been related to the interests protected?**

No reported U.S. Virgin Islands decision has directly addressed which time restrictions are reasonable in a franchise context. In pre-2011 decisions, in an employment context, a restriction of three years was upheld as reasonable. *Williamson v. Hess*, 16 V.I. 284, 293, 1979 WL 447866 (Terr. Ct. May 19, 1979). The court in *Arvidson v. Buchar, supra*, noted that the absence of a time limitation may not be fatal to enforcement if the covenant is limited geographically. Generally, however, the covenant may not extend "for a longer period of time than necessary to protect the promisee." 71 V.I. Super. at 322. Lacking both a time and a geographic limitation, the covenant at issue in the case was found to be unenforceable.

---

4. What geographic limitations have courts recognized as reasonable in the franchise context?

- **How have they been related to the interests protected?**
- **Have courts recognized the legitimacy of protecting other franchisees from competition?**

No reported U.S. Virgin Islands decision addresses the issue of geographic reasonableness of a covenant against competition in a franchise context. However, because geography plays no small part in the analysis of most covenants against competition, the location of the U.S. Virgin Islands may influence court decisions more than any other single factor. The U.S. Virgin Islands lie in the Caribbean Sea, 1,100 miles southeast of Miami and just 45 miles to the east of Puerto Rico. The U.S. Virgin Islands consist of four separate and distinct main islands—St. Thomas, St. John, St. Croix, and Water Island. In a pre-2011 decision in the employment context, a restriction limited to St. Thomas and St. John has been upheld as reasonable. *Williamson v. Hess*, 16 V.I. 284, 293, 1979 WL 447866 (Terr. Ct. May 19, 1979).

The court in *Arvidson v. Buchar, supra*, addressed the geographic limitation generally, explaining that "the geographic scope of a covenant to not compete must be no larger than is fairly required for the promisee's protection, a determination that 'depend(s) on the nature and extent of the [promisee's] business and the degree of the promisor's involvement in that business.'" 71 V.I. Super. at 323. Lacking both a time and a geographic limitation, the covenant at issue in the case was unenforceable.

---

5. What limitations on activities have courts recognized as reasonable in the franchise context?

The U.S. Virgin Islands courts have not addressed the scope of restrictions on activities that would be considered reasonable in the franchise context.

---

6. Does the state recognize a difference between in-term and post-term covenants?

No reported U.S. Virgin Islands case has addressed this issue.

7. Has the state allowed enforcement of covenants against non-signatories (e.g., family members, newly formed corporations)?

No reported U.S. Virgin Islands case has addressed this issue.

8. Will the state modify, "blue-pencil," or otherwise reduce a covenant found to be overbroad?

No reported U.S. Virgin Islands case has addressed this issue in a franchise context. In a pre-2011 context, the court in *Sunny Isle Shopping Center, Inc. v. Xtra Super Food Centers, Inc., d/b/a Pueblo and Kmart Corporation*, 237 F. Supp. 2d 606 (D.V.I. 2002), after a thorough review of section 7.2 of the RESTATEMENT (SECOND) OF PROPERTY, LANDLORD AND TENANT and relevant caselaw, applied a "blue pencil" to a restrictive covenant in a shopping center lease, reducing the geographic scope from a five-mile radius to the boundaries of the shopping center.

The court in *Arvidson v. Buchar, supra*, addressed the issue of revising otherwise unreasonable covenants to their reasonable limits. After undertaking a thorough review of the common law approaches to the issue, the court rejected a strict "no blue pencil" rule and adopted an equitable reformation approach. "Equitable modification . . . [is] more consistent with the inherent concerns of a court of equity—fairness and reasonableness . . . and allows a court to escape the rule of arbitrary refusal to enforce a covenant which, while unreasonable or indefinite in some of its terms nevertheless serves to protect a legitimate interest of the parties or the public" (internal quotations omitted). 71 V.I. Super. at 331. The covenant at issue was completely lacking time or geographic limitations. In that event, the court declared that because durational, geographic, and scope limitations were completely absent from the covenant as written, the court would need to supply all these essential terms. While the court possesses the inherent power to supply such terms, the court noted, "That power should not reward employers who have everything to gain from writing overbroad covenants." The court refused to supply the absent terms.

9. When does a non-compete period begin to run? Will courts equitably extend the term?

No reported U.S. Virgin Islands case has addressed this issue.

10. Are there additional nuances or peculiarities about the state's treatment of covenants in the franchising context?

The U.S. Virgin Islands is a truly unique forum for the enforcement of restrictive covenants. Beyond the geographical issues identified above, a court's treatment of a covenant may be further influenced by (1) a local, insular culture that frequently exhibits a protectionist attitude; (2) a small economic base with limited employment opportunities; and (3) two separate economic zones because of St. Croix's distant location, which is approximately 35 miles to the south of the other islands. In particular, practitioners should be cognizant that the U.S. Virgin Islands courts and juries have been known to reflect a fairly prevalent protectionist attitude in matters involving "state-siders" versus "locals."

There are no additional nuances or peculiarities that have been identified under U.S. Virgin Islands law with respect to enforcement of franchise covenants against competition.

Utah

*by Daniel Purdie, Karen Taylor DelPriore, and Annemarie Garrett**

1. Has the state addressed covenants against competition in the context of franchising?

- **Does the state have a franchising statute or regulations that address covenants against competition?**
- **Does the state have a covenants statute of general applicability that would encompass franchise covenants?**
- **Have the courts addressed covenants in the context of franchising either under a statute or under the state's common law?**

There are no Utah statutes or regulations addressing covenants against competition in franchising.

Two cases have directly addressed the enforceability of a covenant against competition in the context of franchising. In *Bad Ass Coffee Company of Hawaii, Inc. v. JH Nterprises, L.L.C.*, 636 F. Supp. 2d 1237, 1247 (D. Utah 2009), the district court enforced a provision of the franchise agreement prohibiting the franchisee, its family, and its "members owners, partners, managers, officers or directors" from participating in any way or having any interest in any business "engaged in the sale or offering of products the same or similar to [the franchisor's]" for two years after the termination or expiration of the agreement. The prohibition was limited to franchisee's designated territory or a distance of three miles from any other existing franchise.

Similarly, the Utah Supreme Court enforced a covenant against competition that extended one year past the franchise term in *Pelton's Spudnuts, Inc. v. Doane*, 234 P.2d 852 (Utah 1951). In that case, the prohibition was limited to a geographic area of approximately 20 miles by 15 miles.

*Lee A. Wright, author of this chapter in the third edition, Karen Taylor DelPriore, and Daniel Purdie are Shareholders with Kirton McConkie focusing their legal practices on domestic and international franchising, licensing, manufacturing, and distribution, including disclosure and compliance. Annemarie Garrett is an associate with Kirton McConkie focusing on commercial and intellectual property litigation.

One other Utah case recognized the validity of a non-competition covenant but refused to enforce it based on a prior breach by the franchisor. *Holbrook v. Master Protection Corp.*, 883 P.2d 295 (Utah Ct. App. 1994). Although the court may have accepted the non-competition covenant as valid, it ultimately ruled that "due to [franchisor's] material breach of the franchise agreements [the franchisor] was barred from enforcing the [non-competition] provisions of the franchise agreements." *Id.* at 300.

More generally, Utah law provides that a court must enforce a non-compete agreement if "(1) the agreement is 'supported by consideration,' (2) there was no 'bad faith' in contract negotiations, (3) the agreement is 'necessary to protect the goodwill of the business' and (4) it is 'reasonable in its restrictions in terms of time and geographic area.'" *Bad Ass Coffee Co.*, 636 F. Supp. 2d at 1246 (citing *Kasco Services Corp. v. Benson*, 831 P.2d 86, 88 n.1 (Utah 1992)).

---

2. Have the courts articulated the "legitimate interests" of the franchisor that will support enforcement of a covenant against competition contained in a franchise agreement?

- **If so, what are they (e.g., protection of goodwill, protection of confidential information), and in what contexts did the issue arise?**
- **If not, what interests have been recognized in other contexts (e.g., employment agreements, the sale of business context)?**

In a 2009 case ruling on the enforceability of a non-competition covenant in a franchise agreement, *Bad Ass Coffee Company of Hawaii, Inc. v. JH Nterprises, L.L.C.*, 636 F. Supp. 2d 1237, 1247 (D. Utah 2009), the Utah District Court upheld a two-year post-term prohibition against competition, citing the protection of a franchising company's goodwill as a legitimate interest. *Id.* at 1246. Specifically, the court cited the fact that the defendant switched its location "overnight" from the franchised brand to another coffee shop with a similar logo and several identical menu items. The court reasoned that this sudden switch could "signal to potential BACH customers that the [franchisee] lost faith in the BACH brand" or "set an example [to other franchisees] that they can leave the BACH franchise and immediately start competing if they are unhappy with BACH." *Id.*

The Utah District Court more recently reiterated the legitimate interests described above in the context of a franchise agreement. The court listed the protection of a company's "goodwill, reputation, and franchise system" as legitimate interests justifying enforcement of a non-competition covenant. *Property Management Business Solutions v. Averitte*, 2018 WL 4327922, at *6 (D. Utah Sept. 10, 2018).

In other contexts, Utah courts have discussed additional "legitimate interests" that support the enforcement of a covenant against competition. In the employment and business sale context, the Utah Supreme Court enforced a covenant against competition based on goodwill. In *TruGreen v. Mower Bros., Inc.*, 199 P.3d 929 (Utah 2008), an employee resigned from TruGreen and began working for a competing lawn care company within a few weeks. The court did not address the issue of whether there had been a breach, but in discussing the proper measure of damages for breach of a non-compete, it recognized goodwill as a legitimate interest, holding that "such covenants are enforceable as long as they are . . . necessary to protect a company's good will." *Id.* at 932. The court also upheld goodwill as a legitimate interest in *Valley Mortuary v. Fairbanks*, 225 P.2d 739 (Utah 1950), a case involving the sale of mortuary property, including real property, furniture, fixtures, a hearse, and caskets. The sale agreement contained a clause preventing the buyer from "operat[ing] a mortuary or funeral business" in two counties for a period of 25 years. The issue at hand was not whether the restriction was unreasonable or unenforceable, but whether the buyer's business was a "mortuary or funeral business." *Id.* at 740–41.

The Utah Supreme Court further discussed goodwill as a legitimate interest in *Allen v. Rose Park Pharmacy*, 237 P.2d 823 (Utah 1951). *See also Scenic Aviation v. Blick*, No. 2:02-CV-01201 PGC, 2003 WL 26060445, at *5 (D. Utah Aug. 4, 2003) (discussing the enforceability of a restrictive covenant where it is needed to protect goodwill). In *Rose Park Pharmacy*, Osbourne Allen was hired as a drug store manager and entered into an employment contract with Rose Park Pharmacy that contained a non-competition clause stating that in the event of the contract's termination, Osbourne would not "directly or indirectly compete, as an employee or principal in the operation of a drug store or pharmacy within a radius of two miles of this drug store" for five years after the termination. *Id.* at 824. The court discussed restrictive covenants generally, stating that "restrictive covenants are generally upheld by the courts where they are necessary for the protection of the business for the benefit of which the covenant was made and no greater restraint is imposed than is reasonably necessary to secure such protection." *Id.* at 826. The court ultimately based its decision on the protection of trade secrets and goodwill, holding that "an employer is . . . entitled to the goodwill created by his employee, as is the purchaser of an establishment which includes the goodwill of the business." *Id.* at 827. It went on to reason that "when the individual responsible for creating the goodwill and the business to which it attaches, become separated, it is necessary to preserve that goodwill to the business by a covenant on the part of the individual that he will not compete in an area where his personal reputation will detach the old customers from the old business." *Id.*

The Utah Supreme Court has recognized legitimate interests, including an employer's investment in its employees, even in cases where goodwill is not at issue. In *Robbins v. Finlay*, 645 P.2d 623 (Utah 1982), another case involving an employment agreement, the court refused to enforce the non-competition covenant, but it did discuss several legitimate interests:

> The reasonableness of a covenant depends upon several factors, including its geographical extent; the duration of the limitation; the nature of the employee's duties; and the nature of the interest which the employer seeks to protect such as trade secrets, the goodwill of his business, or an extraordinary investment in the training or education of the employee. . . . Covenants not to compete which are primarily designed to limit competition or restrain the right to engage in a common calling are not enforceable.

Id. at 627.

However, in *Robbins*, the court found that the particular employee in question, a hearing aid salesman, was not responsible for the employer's goodwill and did not have knowledge of trade secrets. The court suggested that an employee with special skills or who performed special services would support enforcing the covenant when it found that, in the case at hand, the employee's services were not "special, unique or extraordinary, even if their value to his employer was high." *Id.* at 628.

In a later case also involving an employment contract, the Utah Supreme Court upheld the non-competition covenant, finding both that the covenant was necessary to protect the goodwill of the business and that the services rendered were "special, unique or extraordinary." *System Concepts v. Dixon*, 669 P.2d 421, 426 (Utah 1983) (citing *Robbins v. Finlay*, *supra* at 627–28). In that case, the employee was a "national sales manager" who signed a restrictive covenant preventing her from providing services to competitors within two years of her termination.

In *J & K Computer Systems v. Parrish*, 642 P.2d 732 (Utah 1982), the Utah Supreme Court recognized the protection of trade secrets as a legitimate interest when it upheld the enforceability of a restrictive covenant in an employment agreement. In this case the restriction was in place for one year and prohibited a computer programmer from becoming employed with a competing company or a current customer or from being self-employed in competition with the employer. The court relied on the "well recognized principal" of protecting "the inventor of a special process or trade secret" in upholding the covenant as it pertained to current customers. *Id.* at 735.

---

3. What time limitations have courts recognized as reasonable in the franchise context? If no franchise cases have been decided, what time limitations have been recognized in other contexts?

➤ **How have they been related to the interests protected?**

Utah courts have not discussed the reasonableness of time limitations in covenants against competition contained in franchise agreements, although two reported cases enforced covenants with time restrictions generally. In *Bad Ass Coffee Company of Hawaii, Inc. v. JH Nterprises, L.L.C.*, 636 F. Supp. 2d 1237, 1247 (D. Utah 2009), the Utah Federal District Court enforced a covenant containing a two-year post-term prohibition against competition, and in *Pelton's Spudnuts, Inc. v. Doane*, 234 P.2d 852 (Utah 1951), the Utah Supreme Court enforced a one-year post-term restriction on competition.

In *Bad Ass Coffee*, the court specifically recognized that a covenant against competition must be "'reasonable in its restrictions in terms of time and geographic area,'" but did not further discuss the parameters of the reasonableness standard, since the time and geography restrictions in the covenant were not at issue. *Bad Ass Coffee Co.*, 636 F. Supp. 2d at 1246 (citing *Kasco Servs. Corp. v. Benson*, 831 P.2d 86, 88 n.1 (Utah 1992)).

Further, in the unreported case *Prop. Mgmt. Bus. Sols. v. Averitte*, 2018 WL 4327922, at *5–6 (D. Utah Sept. 10, 2018), a franchisor argued that the two-year non-competition covenant at issue was reasonable because "the two-year period is necessary to give current and potential [franchise] customers time to stop identifying [the former franchisee] with the [franchise] brand" and "to allow it time to locate and train a replacement franchisee." In relation to granting a preliminary injunction, the court stated that it was "persuaded" that the franchisor was "likely to show the two-year restriction is reasonable." *Id.*

With respect to covenants against competition in employment relationships, section 34-51-201 of the Utah Code limits any "post-employment restrictive covenant entered into on or after May 10, 2016" to a period of one year "from the day on which the employee is no longer employed by the employer." In a case involving the sale of a business, however, the court upheld a 25-year non-competition covenant in the sales contract. *See Valley Mortuary v. Fairbanks, supra.* In that case, neither party seemed to dispute the length of time, and the court did not provide reasoning for finding it reasonable.

---

4. What geographic limitations have courts recognized as reasonable in the franchise context?

- **How have they been related to the interests protected?**
- **Have courts recognized the legitimacy of protecting other franchisees from competition?**

In *Prop. Mgmt. Bus. Sols. v. Averitte*, 2018 WL 4327922, at *5–6 (D. Utah Sept. 10, 2018), the Utah District Court discussed reasonable geographic limitations for a covenant against competition contained in a franchise agreement. The court indicated that "[a] restrictive covenant is generally enforceable if it 'specifies an area no greater than that to which the business extends.'" *Id.* at 6 (citing *Elec. Distributors, Inc. v. SFR, Inc.*, 166 F.3d 1074, 1085 (10th Cir. 1999). The franchisee conceded that it had no intention of operating outside of Arizona, so in limiting the analysis to the state where the franchisee operated, the court then determined that the franchisor was likely to succeed in showing that a geographic restriction preventing the former franchisee from competing within 50 miles of any franchise location in the state was reasonable. *Id.* at 5–6.

Other than this unreported case, Utah courts have not discussed the reasonableness of geographic limitations in covenants against competition contained in franchise agreements, although two reported cases have enforced covenants with geographic restrictions. In *Bad Ass Coffee Company of Hawaii, Inc. v. JH Nterprises, L.L.C.*, 636 F. Supp. 2d 1237, 1247 (D. Utah 2009), the Utah Federal District Court enforced a limitation of a three-mile radius from the franchisor's other locations, and in *Pelton's Spudnuts, Inc. v. Doane*, 234 P.2d 852 (Utah 1951) the Utah Supreme Court enforced geographic limitation covering three local communities serviced by the franchisor with a geographic area of approximately 15 miles by 20 miles.

In *Bad Ass Coffee*, the court specifically recognized that a covenant against competition must be "'reasonable in its restrictions in terms of time and geographic area'" but did not further discuss the parameters of the reasonableness standard since the time and geography restrictions in the covenant were not at issue. *Bad Ass Coffee Co.*, 636 F. Supp. 2d at 1246 (citing *Kasco Servs. Corp. v. Benson*, 831 P.2d 86, 88 n.1 (Utah 1992)). The court also noted that the original agreement contained a ten-mile radius limitation, but because the franchisor specifically limited the relief sought to a radius of three miles, the court did not discuss the reasonableness or enforceability of the ten-mile radius. *Id.*

Outside the franchise context, Utah courts have recognized geographic limitations ranging from a two-mile radius, *Allen v. Rose Park Pharmacy*, 237 P.2d 823 (Utah 1951) (employment contract) to a 25-mile radius, *Valley Mortuary v. Fairbanks*, 225 P.2d 739 (Utah 1950) (sale of business). The courts seem to base their determination of reasonableness on a combination of time and geography, as seen in *Rose Park Pharmacy*, where a relatively small two-mile geographic limitation was taken into consideration in determining that the five-year time limitation was reasonable. *Rose Park Pharmacy*, 237 P.2d at 827.

5. What limitations on activities have courts recognized as reasonable in the franchise context?

The Utah District Court addressed limitations on activities in the franchise context in *Prop. Mgmt. Bus. Sols. v. Averitte*, 2018 WL 4327922, at *6 (D. Utah Sept. 10, 2018). Because the court was addressing a motion for a preliminary injunction, it was hampered by an incomplete factual record and limited its finding to the specific activities provided as examples of a competitive business. The court indicated that the franchisor could likely show that the activity restrictions were "not overbroad, but rather 'carefully drawn to protect only [franchisor's] legitimate interests.'" *Id.* (citing *Robbins v. Finlay*, 645 P.2d 623, 627 (Utah 1982)).

Limitations on activities were not specifically addressed in either Utah case ruling directly on the enforceability of a covenant in a franchise agreement. *See Bad Ass Coffee Company of Hawaii, Inc. v. JH Nterprises, L.L.C.*, 636 F. Supp. 2d 1237 (D. Utah 2009); *Pelton's Spudnuts, Inc. v. Doane*, 234 P.2d 852 (Utah 1951). The court in *Bad Ass Coffee*, relying on reasoning from *System Concepts, Inc. v. Dixon*, 669 P.2d 421 (Utah 1983), did state that, in the context of limitations in a covenant for noncompetition, "'reasonableness of the restraints in a restrictive covenant is determined on a case-by-case basis, taking into account the particular facts and circumstances surrounding the case and the subject covenant.'" *Bad Ass Coffee Co.*, 636 F. Supp. 2d 1237 at 1247 (citing *System Concepts*, 669 P.2d at 427).

Outside the context of franchise agreements, Utah courts seem to suggest that specific limitations on activities may be required to render a covenant enforceable. In particular, in *Robbins v. Finlay*, 645 P.2d 623 (Utah 1982), the court held that "covenants not to compete which are primarily designed to limit competition or restrain the right to engage in a common calling are not enforceable." *Id.* at 627.

6. Does the state recognize a difference between in-term and post-term covenants?

Utah courts have not yet recognized any difference in the enforceability of in-term and post-term covenants.

7. Has the state allowed enforcement of covenants against non-signatories (e.g., family members, newly formed corporations)?

Utah courts have not addressed the enforcement of covenants against non-signatories in the context of franchise agreements. However, *Kasco Services Corp. v. Benson*, 831 P.2d 86 (Utah 1992), involved the employment agreement of a salesman of butcher supplies with a non-competition clause providing that the salesman could not compete in the butcher supply business for 18 months. The defendant and his wife opened their own butcher supply business within a few months of terminating his employment. After the trial court refused to enjoin the wife because she was not in privity of contract, the Utah Supreme Court held that if a non-signatory has knowledge of a restrictive covenant and still helps a signatory in violating that covenant, the non-signatory may be enjoined.

8. Will the state modify, "blue-pencil," or otherwise reduce a covenant found to be over broad?

Utah courts have not specifically adopted a "blue-pencil" rule, but the Utah Supreme Court seems willing, in at least two cases, to reduce a covenant found to be overbroad. In *System Concepts, Inc. v. Dixon*, 669 P.2d 421, 426 (Utah 1983), the court suggested that a limitation would be reasonable if the contract did not contain specific language restricting geography. In *J & K Computer Systems v. Parrish*, 642 P.2d 732 (Utah 1982), the court found that a provision restricting an employee from accepting employment "with a competing company, a current customer, or on his or her own account in competition with the Employer . . . " was overbroad. Rather than finding the covenant unenforceable, the court instead decided to enforce the covenant as it related to current customers. *Id.* at 736.

In contrast, the Utah District Court has indicated that where modifying a provision alters it beyond its fundamental nature, unconscionable non-competition provisions will not be rewritten so as to be rendered enforceable. In *First Am. Title Ins. Co. v. Nw. Title Ins. Agency, LLC*, 2016 WL 6902473, at *21–22 (D. Utah Nov. 23, 2016), the court states that, rather than "blue penciling words in the [agreement] to render it consistent with Utah law, the offensive provisions will not be enforced."

9. When does a non-compete period begin to run? Will courts equitably extend the term?

Utah courts have not specifically addressed the time when a non-compete period begins to run. However, in context it appears the courts allow the contractual provision of the agreement between the parties to determine when the non-compete period will begin to run. In *Bad Ass Coffee Company of Hawaii, Inc. v. JH Nterprises, L.L.C.*, 636 F. Supp. 2d 1237, 1247 (D. Utah 2009), for example, the district court enforced a non-compete provision of the franchise agreement which time period began to run "after the termination or expiration of the Agreement." While the court did not specifically discuss the timing when the non-compete period began to run, it did enforce the provision of the agreement that set out the time the parties contractually agreed it would begin to run. Utah courts have not specifically addressed whether non-compete periods may be equitably extended.

10. What are the additional nuances or peculiarities of the state's treatment of covenants in the franchising context?

There are no additional nuances or peculiarities of the treatment by Utah courts of covenants in the franchising context.

Vermont

*by Wanda I. Otero**

1. Has the state addressed covenants against competition in the context of franchising?

- **Does the state have a franchising statute or regulations that address covenants against competition?**
- **Does the state have a covenants statute of general applicability that would encompass franchise covenants?**
- **Have the courts addressed covenants in the context of franchising either under a statute or under the state's common law?**

Vermont has no statute or regulation addressing covenants against competition. Furthermore, no court appears to have addressed the common law of Vermont as applied to restrictive covenants in the franchising context.

2. Have the courts articulated the "legitimate interests" of the franchisor that will support enforcement of a covenant against competition contained in a franchise agreement?

- **If so, what are they (e.g., protection of goodwill, protection of confidential information), and in what contexts did the issue arise?**
- **If not, what interests have been recognized in other contexts (e.g., employment agreements, the sale of business context)?**

Vermont courts have not discussed the interests of a franchisor that would support a covenant against competition in a franchise agreement. The Vermont courts have, however, identified legitimate interests of employers that can support enforcement of a covenant against competition contained in an employment contract. In *Vermont Electric Supply Company v. Andrus*, 132 Vt. 195, 315 A.2d 456 (1974), *appeal after remand*, 133 Vt. 422, 340 A.2d 77 (1975) (affirming damages award), *supplemented by* 135 Vt. 190, 373 A.2d 531 (1977), the Vermont Supreme Court held that employers

*Ms. Otero serves as General Counsel for Vermont-NEA in Montpelier, Vermont.

may restrict the competitive activities of former employees where necessary to prevent potential misuse of the employer's confidential business information and customer relationships, stating:

> [The former employee's] expertise and reputation in the kitchen installation business arose through special training and experience furnished by the plaintiff. His relationship with builders and contractors in the area, the prime source of business, were the product of plaintiff's initial sponsorship. He had been entrusted with intimate knowledge of the plaintiff's cost and profit factors, as well as its techniques of presentation and bidding. The potential for harm to the plaintiff's business was certainly established, and the restrictions agreed to were not unreasonable under the circumstances.

315 A.2d at 458.

The test for enforceability of an employment non-competition covenant is the reasonableness of the restriction in light of the interest of the employer sought to be protected. *Vermont Elec. Supply*, 132 Vt. at 198, 315 A.2d at 458; *see Roy's Orthopedic, Inc. v. Lavigne*, 142 Vt. 347, 350, 454 A.2d 1242, 1244 (1982), *appeal after remand*, 145 Vt. 324, 487 A.2d 173 (1985). In general, restrictive covenants in employment agreements will be enforced under Vermont law "unless the agreement is found to be contrary to public policy, unnecessary for the protection of the employer, or unnecessarily restrictive of the rights of the employee, with due regard being given to the subject matter of the contract and the circumstances and conditions under which it is to be performed." *Id.* (quoting *Vermont Elec. Supply Co.*, 132 Vt. at 198, 315 A.2d at 458). Under this approach, inquiries regarding duration and geographic scope of the restrictions are crucial to determining whether a covenant not to compete unduly restricts the rights of the covenantor. *See Fine Foods, Inc. v. Dahlin*, 147 Vt. 599, 523 A.2d 1228, 1231 (1986).

In *Systems & Software, Inc. v. Barnes*, the Vermont Supreme Court further clarified that non-competition agreements may protect a variety of employer interests beyond trade secrets or confidential customer information, which are often protected by other laws even in the absence of such agreements. 178 Vt. 389, 391–92, 886 A.2d 762, 764–65 (2005) (citing 15 G. Giesel, Corbin on Contracts § 80.16, at 141–42 (rev. ed. 2003); 9 V.S.A. §§ 4601–09 (Cum. Supp. 2004)). The court also referenced the draft of the THIRD RESTATEMENT on employment law for the proposition that "non-competition agreements may protect legitimate employer interests such as customer relationships and employee-specific goodwill that are 'significantly broader' than proprietary information such as trade secrets and confidential customer information." *Id.* (quoting RESTATEMENT (THIRD) OF EMPLOYMENT LAW § 6.05 cmt. b ("[Section] 6.05 sometimes allows an employer contractually to prevent all competition by a former employee, even competition that does not make use of the employer's proprietary information.")).

The court found it "not necessary" however, to establish the full "range of employer interests" that could be protected and affirmed the trial court's decision on the ground that "during his employment with plaintiff, defendant had acquired inside knowledge about the strengths and weaknesses of plaintiff's products—knowledge that he could use to compete against plaintiff." *Sys. & Software*, 178 Vt. at 392, 886 A.2d at 765.

The Vermont courts have not articulated the interests of the purchaser of a business that support enforcement of a covenant against competition in the sale of business context. Nonetheless, the Supreme Court of Vermont has upheld such a restriction citing employment termination cases. *Id.*

3. What time limitations have courts of the state recognized as reasonable in the franchise context? If no franchise cases have been decided, what time limitations have been recognized in other contexts?

➤ **How have they been related to the interest protected?**

There are no reported cases in the franchise context. The court in *Vermont Electric Supply Company v. Andrus*, 132 Vt. 195, 315 A.2d 456 (1974), *appeal after remand*, 133 Vt. 422, 340 A.2d 77 (1975) (affirming damages award), *supplemented by* 135 Vt. 190, 373 A.2d 531 (1977), enforced a covenant forbidding a former employee from competing with his former employer for five years in one Vermont county, where the employee had been entrusted with intimate knowledge of the employer's business and the employee's current business contacts flowed from the employer's initial sponsorship of the employee.

Although the court did not directly address the length of the restriction, in finding the restriction reasonable, it emphasized the following:

> [T]his case deals with an employee who voluntarily left his employer for the very purpose of going into business competitively in the same special field. He was not placed in the double bind of being both fired and subject to five years of employment restraint. His expertise and reputation in the kitchen installation business arose through special training and experience furnished by the plaintiff. His relationship with builders and contractors in the area, the prime source of business, were the product of plaintiff's initial sponsorship. He had been entrusted with intimate knowledge of the plaintiff's cost and profit factors, as well as its techniques of presentation and bidding. The potential for harm to the plaintiff's business was certainly established, and the restrictions agreed to were not unreasonable under the circumstances.

132 Vt. at 199, 315 A.2d at 458.

In *Fine Foods, Inc. v. Dahlin*, 147 Vt. 599, 523 A.2d 1228 (1986), a restrictive covenant forbidding the seller of a business from competing for five years within 25 miles of the business sold was found to be enforceable. While acknowledging that "[i]nquiries regarding time and place restrictions are crucial to a determination of whether a covenant not to compete unduly restricts the rights of an individual," the court merely stated that "[w]ith respect to time, this Court has approved a covenant containing a five-year restriction of competitive employment." 147 Vt. at 604, 523 A.2d at 1231 (citing *Vermont Elec. Supply*, 132 Vt. at 199, 315 A.2d at 458).

In *A.N. Deringer, Inc. v. Strough*, 103 F.3d 243 (2d Cir. 1996) the United States Court of Appeals for the Second Circuit determined that a 90-day restriction against competitive employment by a former salesperson was enforceable under Vermont law.

4. What geographic limitations have courts recognized as reasonable in the franchise context?

➤ **How have they been related to the interests protected?**

➤ **Have courts recognized the legitimacy of protecting other franchises from competition?**

There are no reported cases in the franchise context. In *Vermont Electric Supply Company v. Andrus*, 132 Vt. 195, 315 A.2d 456 (1974), *appeal after remand*, 133 Vt. 422, 340 A.2d 77 (1975) (affirming damages award), *supplemented by* 135 Vt. 190, 373 A.2d 531 (1977), the court upheld a restriction on competition within the principal county in which the former employee had represented the employer. In *Fine Foods, Inc. v. Dahlin*, 147 Vt. 599, 523 A.2d 1228 (1986), the court upheld a geographic restriction of 25 miles from the site of the seller's former business. In *A.N. Deringer, Inc. v. Strough*, 103 F.3d 243 (2d Cir. 1996), the United States Court of Appeals for the Second Circuit held that a covenant prohibiting competitive employment within 100 miles of any of the employer's 30 places of business was unreasonable based on geographic proximity because the employer needed protection only within the employee's former sales territory, which encompassed a much smaller geographical range.

The Vermont Supreme Court has emphasized that due consideration must be given to the factual circumstances of each case. In *Systems & Software, Inc. v. Barnes*, 178 Vt. 389, 886 A.2d 762 (2005), the court noted that both the former employer and the third party entity for whom the former employee was providing services "served a small market of customers; thus, the loss of even a single contract could deprive plaintiff of revenue for many years, especially considering the need for service and software updates." 178 Vt. at 392, 886 A.2d at 765.

5. What limitations on activities have courts recognized as reasonable in the franchise context?

This issue does not appear to have been addressed under Vermont law in the franchise context. In other contexts however, the courts have found relatively broad contractual restrictions to be reasonable. The Vermont Supreme Court has pointed out that "[a]lthough a restraint on competition is easier to justify if the restraint is limited to the taking of the former employer's customers as contrasted with competition in general," employers "may seek to protect the good will of the business with [either] a general covenant not to compete or with a specific prohibition on contact with customers." *Systems & Software, Inc. v. Barnes*, 178 Vt. 389, 392, 886 A.2d 762, 764–65 (2005) (quoting Restatement (Second) of Contracts § 188 cmt. g). The court reasoned:

> Determining which restraints are reasonable has not been an exact science. The reasonableness of the restrictions will vary by industry and will depend highly on the nature of the interest justifying the restrictive covenant. Generally, courts will uphold a contractual ban on an employee's post-employment competition if it would be difficult for an employer to determine when an employee is soliciting its customers.

Id. citing Restatement (Second) of Contracts §§ 6.05 cmt. c, 6.06 cmt. c ("Because it is essentially impossible to monitor an employee's 'use' of goodwill, this interest will support a complete ban on competition as long as it is reasonably limited temporally and geographically.").

6. Does the state recognize a difference between in-term and post-term covenants?

This issue does not appear to have been addressed under Vermont law.

7. Has the state allowed enforcement of covenants against non-signatories (e.g., family members, newly formed corporations)?

This issue does not appear to have been directly addressed under Vermont law. In the context of determining whether an employer took adequate steps to maintain the confidentiality of certain proprietary information to be afforded protection under the Vermont Trade Secret Act, the Supreme Court of Vermont refused to imply the existence of a covenant against competition. *See Dicks v. Jensen*, 172 Vt. 43, 51, 768 A.2d 1279, 1285 (2001). Emphasizing the restraint the court utilizes in enforcing explicit covenants not to compete, the court indicated that it will not enforce a covenant against competition where there is not a signed agreement.

8. Will the state modify, "blue-pencil," or otherwise reduce a covenant found to be overbroad?

Although earlier cases suggested that the Vermont Supreme Court would not modify the terms of a non-competition agreement, *see Roy's Orthopedic, Inc. v. Lavigne*, 142 Vt. 347, 454 A.2d 1242 (1982), *appeal after remand*, 145 Vt. 324, 487 A.2d 173 (1985) (court will not extend duration of covenant even if delay in enforcement was caused by delay in the judicial process), more recent cases indicate otherwise. In *A.N. Deringer, Inc. v. Strough*, 103 F.3d 243, 247–48 (2d Cir. 1996), the Second Circuit Court of Appeals opined that Vermont law would permit the reformation and enforcement of an overly broad covenant against competition. The restrictive covenant in *A.N. Deringer, Inc.* prohibited competitive employment within a 100-mile radius of any of the employer's 30 offices, and the court determined that this geographic restriction was unreasonably broad. Based on the fact that the Supreme Court of Vermont regularly relied upon the RESTATEMENT (SECOND) OF CONTRACTS, the Second Circuit concluded that a Vermont court would do so with reference to the question of whether a covenant against competition could be reformed, and accordingly held that Vermont courts would "permit enforcement of a defective restrictive covenant to the limit of its validity." *Id.* at 247. Based on this conclusion the Second Circuit judicially reformed the covenant to apply only to the employee's former sales territory.

Subsequently, in *Summits 7, Inc. v. Kelly*, 178 Vt. 396, 406, 886 A.2d 365, 374 (2005), the Vermont Supreme Court agreed with the Second Circuit and specifically rejected the all-or-nothing rule for enforcement of restrictive covenants, explaining:

> Most modern courts agree that a trial court can enforce restrictive covenants to the extent that they are reasonable. Corbin on Contracts, § 80.26, at 189 (rev. ed. 2003)("The rule for partial enforcement is the better rule, and courts should apply it in any case in which nothing is wrong with the agreement except that the parties have agreed upon a restraint that is somewhat in excess of what protection of the good will or other protectable interest requires."); *see A.N. Deringer, Inc. v. Strough*, 103 F.3d 243, 247-48 (2d Cir. 1996) (noting "modern trend" away from all-or-nothing rule and predicting that Vermont would permit enforcement of defective restrictive covenant to limit of its validity); *Hopper v. All Pet Animal Clinic, Inc.*, 861

P.2d 531, 545-46 (Wyo. 1993) (noting that "[i]n the best considered modern cases," courts have enforced covenants not to compete against defendants whose breach occurred within plainly reasonable restricted area, even though terms of agreement imposed larger and unreasonable restraint).

Based on the foregoing, the court declined the former employee's request that the case be reversed and remanded so that the lower court could examine the geographic scope of the agreement. Since the employee's new job was located within a short geographic distance of the former employer, the court affirmed the lower court's enforcement of the restriction, stating that it was "not . . . necessary for a court to determine the exact limiting boundary of a restriction so long as the employer can show that the employee breached a reasonable restriction." *Summits 7*, 178 Vt. at 407, 886 A.2d at 374 (citing CORBIN ON CONTRACTS, *supra*, § 80.26, at 182–83).

9. When does a non-compete period begin to run? Will courts equitably extend the term?

The effective period of a non-compete is governed by the contract. Although Vermont courts will give effect to an express tolling provision contained in a non-competition agreement, they will not extend the duration of the restriction on equitable grounds.

In *Roy's Orthopedic Inc. v. Lavigne*, 145 Vt. 324, 487 A.2d 173 (1985), a former employee violated a covenant not to compete for a period of three years following the termination of his employment. Although the former employer obtained an injunction to enforce the agreement in the superior court, the injunction was stayed during appeal and the three-year period expired during the litigation. Acknowledging that the result was "harsh," the court nonetheless suspended the implementation of the plaintiff's remedy but not the running of the three-year-period of the covenant, even though this left the former employer with no remedy at all. The court emphasized that "the possible consequences of the delays inherent in litigation based on a breach of the non-competition clause might have been provided for [in the contract]," *id.* at 328, 487 A.2d at 176, meaning that the parties could have included a tolling provision.

10. Are there additional nuances or peculiarities of the state's treatment of covenants in the franchising context?

In a couple of respects, the approach Vermont law has taken to the enforcement of covenants against competition varies from that taken in many other states:

1. While Vermont's approach to the enforceability of restrictive covenants is similar to that taken in many other states (i.e., covenants against competition are scrutinized to determine their reasonableness), Vermont courts place the burden of proving *unreasonableness* on the party against whom enforcement is sought. *See Vermont Electric Supply Company v. Andrus*, 132

Vt. 195, 315 A.2d 456 (1974), *appeal after remand*, 133 Vt. 422, 340 A.2d 77 (1975) (affirming damages award), *supplemented by* 135 Vt. 190, 373 A.2d 531 (1977); *Fine Foods, Inc. v. Dahlin*, 147 Vt. 599, 523 A.2d 1228 (1986).

2. Vermont courts have indicated that they may scrutinize the application of a covenant more closely where an employee was involuntarily terminated than when he or she voluntarily resigned to go into competition with his or her employer. *See, e.g.*, *Vermont Elec. Supply Co.*, 132 Vt. at 197, 315 A.2d at 458.

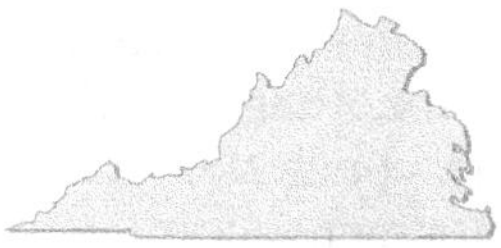

Virginia

*by Justin L. Sallis**

1. Has the state addressed covenants against competition in the context of franchising?

- **Does the state have a franchising statute or regulations that address covenants against competition?**
- **Does the state have a covenants statute of general applicability that would encompass franchise covenants?**
- **Have the courts addressed covenants in the context of franchising either under a statute or under the state's common law?**

Virginia has a statute that regulates franchising (Retail Franchising Act, VA. CODE ANN. § 13.1-557 *et seq.* (West 2021)), but that statute does not address covenants against competition, and there is no general covenants statute in Virginia that would cover covenants contained in franchise agreements.

In the employment context, Virginia recently passed a law, effective July 1, 2020, prohibiting employers from entering into, enforcing, or threatening to enforce a covenant against competition with any "low-wage employee," as the term is defined in the statute. VA. CODE ANN. § 40.1-28.7:8 (West 2021). The law also provides that a covenant "shall not restrict an employee from providing a service to a customer or client of the employer if the employee does not initiate contact with or solicit the customer or client." *Id.* It does not, however, prohibit employers from entering into or enforcing agreements intended to prevent the misappropriation or sharing of an employer's trade secrets or other proprietary or confidential information. *Id.* At this time, there is little reason to believe the law could or would be applied to a franchise relationship.

In *Brenco Enterprises, Inc. v. Takeout Taxi Franchising Systems, Inc.*, Chancery No. 177164, 2003 WL 21659422 (Va. Cir. Ct. May 2, 2003), a Virginia Circuit Court considered, in an extensive opinion, the enforceability of a covenant against competition contained in a franchise agreement. The franchisees urged the court to

---

*Mr. Sallis is a Partner in the Washington, D.C., office of Lathrop GPM LLP. He was assisted in the preparation of this analysis by Cameron Johnson, an associate in Lathrop GPM's Washington, D.C., office, and is indebted to Peter J. Klarfeld, also of Lathrop GPM, for laying the foundations of this analysis.

apply the standard used to analyze covenants against competition in employment agreements. The franchisor argued that the covenant should be analyzed under the more lenient reasonableness standard applied to a covenant against competition ancillary to the sale of a business. The court discussed the similarities between a franchise agreement and an employment agreement, on the one hand, and an agreement for the sale of a business, on the other hand, and concluded that a "franchise relationship is arguably incomparable to either employment contracts or contracts of sale." *Id.* at *58–59. Ultimately, the court decided that use of the more lenient reasonableness standard applicable to covenants ancillary to the sale of a business was appropriate.

The court in *Brenco* identified several facets of the franchise relationship that, taken together, distinguish it from either the employment or sale of business model. First, the court observed that, in contrast to an employment relationship, a franchise relationship involves the association of the franchisee with the franchisor's goodwill. Second, the franchise relationship involves the franchisee's use of the franchisor's trademarks and trade secrets, whereas an employment agreement does not usually involve these proprietary materials. Third, unlike most employees, a franchisee may lose a significant capital investment when the franchise relationship terminates. Fourth, a competitive business run by a former franchisee may directly and negatively impact the economic interests of current franchisees. On the other hand, *Brenco* also observed that, unlike an agreement to sell a business, a franchise agreement creates a long-term relationship in which the franchisor retains some control over the franchisee's operations. Finally, unlike the seller of a business, a franchisee typically does not receive compensation for the value of its business when the franchise relationship ends.

The *Brenco* court followed the established Virginia rule that the party seeking to enforce a covenant against competition must demonstrate that the restraint is no greater than necessary to protect a legitimate business interest, is not unduly harsh or oppressive, and is reasonable in light of sound public policy. With regard to the reasonableness prong, which the *Brenco* court assessed under the more lenient standard applied to the sale of a business, the court stated:

> In determining the reasonableness of a restrictive covenant, it is relevant to consider the parties involved, their respective positions, and the circumstances of the transaction. Specifically, courts assess (i) the geographic scope of the restraint, (ii) the temporal scope of the restraint; and (iii) the scope of the restricted activities.

Id. at *61 (quotations omitted). Applying this approach, the court found enforceable a covenant that prevented the franchisee from engaging in the same or a substantially similar business, within a five- or ten-mile (in urban areas) or 50-mile (in rural areas) radius of the franchisee's territory, for a one-year time period. In structure, this approach follows the well-established standard applied to covenants against competition in employment agreements, which "will be enforced if the contract is narrowly drawn to protect the employer's legitimate business interest, is not unduly burdensome on the employee's ability to earn a living, and is not against public policy." *Omniplex World Servs. Corp. v. US Investigations Servs., Inc.*, 618 S.E.2d 340, 342 (Va. 2005).

Several federal cases applying Virginia law have also upheld post-termination covenants against competition contained in franchise agreements. *See JTH Tax, Inc. v. Lee*, 514 F. Supp. 2d 818 (E.D. Va. 2007) (granting an injunction to enforce a two-year restriction in a 25-mile radius of the franchisee's former territory without discussing which reasonableness standard it applied); *JTH Tax, Inc. v. Donofrio*, No. 2:06cv47, 2006 WL 2796841 (E.D. Va. Sept. 26, 2006) (same); *Jackson Hewitt, Inc. v. Greene*, 865 F. Supp. 1199 (E.D. Va. 1994) (applying, without discussing the issue, the reasonableness standard used to evaluate covenants against competition in employment agreements and upholding a one-year restriction in a ten-mile radius of the franchisee's former territory).

Depending on the language of the agreement, a post-termination covenant against competition may not apply when the agreement reaches the end of its term naturally. In *Hamden v. Total Car Franchising Corp.*, 548 Fed. Appx. 842 (4th Cir. Nov. 22, 2013), the Fourth Circuit affirmed a district court's holding that "'termination' as used in the restrictive covenants did not encompass an 'expiration'[.]" *Hamden*, 548 Fed. Appx. at 845. The *Hamden* court applied general principles of contract interpretation and reviewed the contract as a whole to find that the agreement's use of the word "termination" contemplated an affirmative action—such as a default—causing the end of the parties' relationship before the natural end of the agreement's term. Because the franchise agreement at issue had expired, the post-termination covenants triggered by solely "termination" did not apply. *Id.* at 849–50.

---

2. Have the courts articulated the "legitimate interests" of the franchisor that will support enforcement of a covenant against competition contained in a franchise agreement?

- **If so, what are they (e.g., protection of goodwill, protection of confidential information), and in what contexts did the issue arise?**
- **If not, what interests have been recognized in other contexts (e.g., employment agreements, the sale of business context)?**

In *Brenco Enterprises, Inc. v. Takeout Taxi Franchising Systems, Inc.*, Chancery No. 177164, 2003 WL 21659422 (Va. Cir. Ct. May 2, 2003), the court identified several legitimate interests of the franchisor that it viewed as warranting protection through enforcement of a covenant against competition. First, the court considered the goodwill of the franchised business. As stated by the court, "a franchise agreement is a conveyance of the franchisor's good will [sic] to the franchisee for the length of the franchise. When the franchise terminates, the good will is transferred back to the franchisor. Given this exchange of good will, a covenant not to compete may be necessary to protect a franchisor's good will after the reconveyance." *Id.* at *93 (citations omitted). Since a franchise agreement contemplates that the franchisee will become associated with the franchisor's goodwill, the franchisor bargains for the covenant to protect itself and its other franchisees from the injury that would result if a departing franchisee retained that goodwill when the franchise agreement ended.

Brenco also recognized the franchisor's interest in controlling the proprietary and confidential information disclosed to franchisees in the course of the franchise relationship, such as the business systems, methods of operation, proprietary software, customer databases, advertising, and promotional materials used by the franchised system. Finally, the court recognized the franchisor's interest in preventing customer confusion, which could result from the former franchisees' continued use of the franchisor's proprietary business system (in this case, the use of menu guides).

The *Brenco* court declined to accept the franchisees' contention that the franchisor had no protectable interests. The franchisees argued that because the franchisor was not registered to sell franchises in any state, was insolvent and had little value, did not operate in some of the franchisees' former territories, and stopped providing key services to the franchisees, the franchisor no longer had any legitimate business interests to protect. However, the court held that a franchisor need not be in the business of selling franchises at the time in order to claim a protectable interest. It then found that the franchisees had not provided any evidence that the franchisor was insolvent, and that the fact that the system was currently faltering did not mean it lacked value. The court held that the fact that the franchisor did not operate in some of the franchisees' former territories did not mean it could not protect its interests in those territories, because the franchisor provided evidence of its intent and ability to provide service in those territories in the future. Finally, the court found no material breaches by the franchisor, despite the franchisees' contention that the franchisor failed to provide services.

The United States District Court for the Eastern District of Virginia has identified franchisor interests that warranted enforcing a covenant contained in a franchise agreement for a tax preparation business. The court noted that absent enforcement, the franchisee would continue to operate the same business in the same area, presenting the franchisor with a high likelihood of permanent loss of former and potential customers. *JTH Tax, Inc. v. Lee*, 514 F. Supp. 2d 818 (E.D. Va. 2007); *JTH Tax, Inc. v. Donofrio*, No. 2:06cv47, 2006 WL 2796841 (E.D. Va. Sept. 26, 2006). In addition, the court stated that the loss of goodwill could provide the threat of irreparable harm necessary to support injunctive relief. *Donofrio*, 2006 WL 2796841, at *14. Finally, the court found that enforcing a valid agreement not to compete served the public interest in preventing consumer confusion. *Lee*, 514 F. Supp. 2d at 826.

In the employment context, Virginia law recognizes the legitimacy of protecting confidential records, business methods, and customer lists. *See Roanoke Eng'g Sales Co. v. Rosenbaum*, 290 S.E.2d 882 (Va. 1992). It also recognizes the employer's interest in protecting customer contacts, even when the employees had not actually acquired or possessed confidential information. *Blue Ridge Anesthesia & Critical Care, Inc. v. Gidick*, 389 S.E.2d 467 (Va. 1990). The protection of trade secrets and sensitive information is also recognized as warranted. *Hair Club for Men, LLC v. Ehson*, No. 1:16cv236, 2016 WL 4577019 (E.D. Va. Aug. 31, 2016); *Lanmark Tech., Inc. v. Canales*, 454 F. Supp. 2d 524 (E.D. Va. 2006).

---

3. What time limitations have courts recognized as reasonable in the franchise context? If no franchise cases have been decided, what time limitations have been recognized in other contexts?

➤ How have they been related to the interests protected?

In *Brenco Enterprises, Inc. v. Takeout Taxi Franchising Systems, Inc.*, Chancery No. 177164, 2003 WL 21659422, at *70 (Va. Cir. Ct. May 2, 2003), the parties did not dispute the reasonableness of the covenant's one-year restriction, and the court found that duration "sufficiently tailored and reasonable under the circumstances." The court in *Jackson Hewitt, Inc. v. Greene*, 865 F. Supp. 1199, 1208 (E.D. Va. 1994), also upheld a one-year restriction, finding it was "not unduly harsh or oppressive to [the franchisee's] ability to earn a living." The Eastern District of Virginia has also upheld two-year restrictions, with little or no discussion of the relationship of the time period to the interests protected. *JTH Tax, Inc. v. Callahan*, No. 2:12cv691, 2013 WL 12146520 (E.D. Va. Aug. 27, 2013) ("[A]lthough a preliminary injunction will restrain Defendant from earning a living through a tax preparation business, such limitation is short-term (2 years) and covers a limited geographical region." (citation omitted)); *JTH Tax, Inc. v. Lee*, 514 F. Supp. 2d 818 (E.D. Va. 2007); *JTH Tax, Inc. v. Donofrio*, No. 2:06cv47, 2006 WL 2796841 (E.D. Va. Sept. 26, 2006).

The Virginia Supreme Court has generally upheld covenants of two to three years in the employment context. *See Roanoke Eng'g Sales Co. v. Rosenbaum*, 290 S.E.2d 882 (Va. 1992) (three years); *Blue Ridge Anesthesia & Critical Care, Inc. v. Gidick*, 389 S.E.2d 467 (Va. 1990) (three years); *Paramount Termite Control Co. v. Rector*, 380 S.E.2d 922 (Va. 1989), *overruled on other grounds, Home Paramount Pest Control Cos. v. Shaffer*, 718 S.E.2d 762 (Va. 2011) (two years). *But see Simmons v. Miller*, 544 S.E.2d 666 (Va. 2001) (refusing to uphold a three-year covenant because the length, combined with the expansive restriction on activities and lack of geographic limitation, rendered the covenant overbroad). Covenants lasting five years in agreements for the sale of a business have been upheld. *Centennial Broad. LLC v. Burns*, No. 6:06cv006, 2006 WL 2850640 (W.D. Va. Sept. 29, 2006) (five years); *Meissel v. Finley*, 95 S.E.2d 186 (Va. 1956) (upholding a five-year restriction because it was related to the business); *see also Nat'l Homes Corp. v. Lester Indus., Inc.*, 404 F.2d 225 (4th Cir. 1968) (affirming enforcement of a covenant in an employment agreement ancillary to the purchase of a business that would last from the date of termination through the remainder of the ten-year employment agreement).

---

4. What geographic limitations have courts recognized as reasonable in the franchise context?

- **How have they been related to the interests protected?**
- **Have courts recognized the legitimacy of protecting other franchisees from competition?**

In *Brenco Enterprises, Inc. v. Takeout Taxi Franchising Systems, Inc.*, Chancery No. 177164, 2003 WL 21659422 (Va. Cir. Ct. May 2, 2003), the court upheld a restriction that covered, in rural areas, a 50-mile radius from the franchisee's former territory or any other franchised business, and a five- or ten-mile radius in urban areas. The franchisees argued that this area was uncertain and overly broad because it depended on the existence and location of other franchises at the end of the franchise term, a circumstance that a franchisee could not predict when entering into the agreement. *Brenco* noted that other courts had upheld similar covenants and that the number of franchises had actually declined since the agreements were executed. The court held that under the more lenient standard applied in the franchise context, the geographic restriction was reasonable.

The court in *Jackson Hewitt, Inc. v. Greene*, 865 F. Supp. 1199 (E.D. Va. 1994), upheld a restriction that covered a ten-mile radius from the former franchisee's territory as not unduly harsh or oppressive (in connection with a one-year time limit). The Eastern District of Virginia has also upheld restrictions on competition within 25 miles of the franchisee's former territory with little or no discussion of the reasonableness of the geographic scope. *JTH Tax, Inc. v. Callahan*, No. 2:12cv691, 2013 WL 12146520 (E.D. Va. Aug. 27, 2013); *JTH Tax, Inc. v. Lee*, 514 F. Supp. 2d 818 (E.D. Va. 2007); *JTH Tax, Inc. v. Donofrio*, No. 2:06cv47, 2006 WL 2796841 (E.D. Va. Sept. 26, 2006).

In the employment context, the Virginia Supreme Court has upheld covenants that prevent competition in a former employee's territory, or contact with a former employee's customers. *Advanced Marine Enters., Inc. v. PRC Inc.*, 501 S.E.2d 148 (Va. 1998) (upholding a restriction preventing competition within 50 miles of any of the employer's offices); *Roanoke Eng'g Sales Co. v. Rosenbaum*, 290 S.E.2d 882 (Va. 1992) (upholding covenant prohibiting a former executive from competing in any territory in which any of the company's branches did business, because he had access to confidential and operational information from all of the company's branches); *Blue Ridge Anesthesia & Critical Care, Inc. v. Gidick*, 389 S.E.2d 467 (Va. 1990) (former territory). The lack of a geographic limitation to a covenant's scope is not necessarily "fatal" to the covenant, as long as it is otherwise narrowly tailored in function and duration. *Preferred Sys. Sols., Inc. v. GP Consulting, LLC*, 732 S.E.2d 676, 682 (Va. 2012); *O'Sullivan Films, Inc. v. Neaves*, 352 F. Supp. 3d 617 (W.D. Va. 2018); *MeadWestvaco Corp. v. Bates*, 91 Va. Cir. 509 (Va. Cir. Ct. 2013) (observing restriction against competing anywhere in the world where former employer does business "not geographically unlimited").

5. What limitations on activities have courts recognized as reasonable in the franchise context?

In addressing franchise covenants, Virginia courts have upheld prohibitions on engaging or having an interest in a business that is substantially similar to the franchised business. For example, the covenant at issue in *Brenco Enterprises, Inc. v. Takeout Taxi Franchising Systems, Inc.*, Chancery No. 177164, 2003 WL 21659422 (Va. Cir. Ct. May 2, 2003), stated that a terminated franchisee could not "either directly or indirectly . . . own, maintain, engage in, be employed by, advise, assist, invest in, franchise, make loans to, or have any interest in any business which is the same as or substantially similar to the Franchised Business." The court upheld this covenant, reasoning that "the covenant does not *generally* preclude the franchisees from working for a competitor, but rather *specifically* prohibits the franchisees for a period of one year from seeking employment in 'any business that is the same or substantially similar to' the restaurant delivery service business." *Id.* at *70.

Similarly, in *JTH Tax, Inc. v. Lee*, 514 F. Supp. 2d 818 (E.D. Va. 2007), the court noted that the former franchisee was free to operate any other kind of business or to operate a competing tax business outside of the specified territory. The covenant in *Lee* required that the terminated franchisee not, "either directly or indirectly, 'be employed by, work with, be engaged in, be interested in or advise, invest or contribute money to, lend money to or guarantee the debts or obligations of, any person or entity engaged in tax return preparation, electronic filing, or Bank Products.'" *Id.* at 822. Although the court recognized this would restrict the former franchisee's ability to work in the tax preparation business in a specified territory for a specified time period, the court stated that it was doing nothing more than enforcing the former franchisee's contractual obligations. *See also JTH Tax, Inc. v.*

Donofrio, No. 2:06cv47, 2006 WL 2796841 (E.D. Va. Sept. 26, 2006) (enforcing the same covenant). In the *Lee* and *Donofrio* cases, the courts also upheld restrictions on solicitations of former customers. *Lee*, 514 F. Supp. 2d at 823, 825; *Donofrio*, 2006 WL 2796841, at *9, *14 (upholding a provision requiring that a former franchisee not "directly or indirectly, solicit the patronage of any person or entity served by any of [his] prior [JTH] offices in the last 12 months.").

In the employment context, the Virginia Supreme Court has enforced covenants that prohibit activity that "is of the same type as that actually engaged in by the former employer." *Home Paramount Pest Control Cos. v. Shaffer*, 718 S.E.2d 762, 764 (Va. 2011). However, a covenant that prevents a former employee from engaging in a competitive business "in any manner whatsoever" is overbroad and unenforceable. *Id.* at 765. In reaching that holding, the Virginia Supreme Court overruled its 1989 opinion upholding the same covenant in *Paramount Termite Control Co. v. Rector*, 380 S.E.2d 922 (Va. 1989), explaining that it had "incrementally clarified" the law and "gradually refined its application" in the intervening years. *Home Paramount*, 718 S.E.2d at 766. *See also Omniplex World Servs. Corp. v. US Investigations Servs., Inc.*, 618 S.E.2d 340 (Va. 2005) (finding the covenant overbroad in the scope of employment prohibited, and unenforceable); *Motion Control Sys., Inc. v. East*, 546 S.E.2d 424 (Va. 2001) (same); *Simmons v. Miller*, 544 S.E.2d 666 (Va. 2001) (same).

Given the fact that covenants in agreements for the sale of a business and franchise agreements are treated more leniently with respect to the reasonableness prong, it is not clear that covenants in those types of agreements that prevented the covenantor from engaging in a competitive business "in any manner whatsoever" would also be considered overbroad and unenforceable. *See Thomas v. Owens*, 27 Va. Cir. 367, 370 (Va. Cir. Ct. 1992) (upholding a covenant ancillary to the sale of a business that prevented the seller from competing "directly or indirectly . . . either as an owner, employee or stockholder of a competing business"). Indeed, the lower court franchise cases discussed above suggest that covenants contained in franchise agreements would receive more lenient treatment. However, an opinion from a Virginia Circuit Court demonstrates that issue is not settled. In *United Marketing Solutions, Inc. v. Goldberg*, Letter Op., No. 00065117-00, 2012 WL 7985729 (Va. Cir. Ct. (Loudoun Cty.) Feb. 27, 2012), a franchise case, the court applied *Home Paramount* and determined that the non-competition provisions were unenforceable. It stated, "[t]he right of the defendants to engage in employment activities is not dependent upon their future conflicts arising from singular employment with another competing franchisor." *Id.* at *2.

6. Does the state recognize a difference between in-term and post-term covenants?

No Virginia state court decision appears to have discussed whether the enforceability of in-term and post-term covenants should be analyzed under different standards. One case, *Redden v. Liptau*, No. CH-2005-4914 & CL-2008-13395, 2010 WL 931016 (Va. Cir. Ct. Feb. 16, 2010), considered an in-term covenant in an employment agreement using the standard in *Omniplex World Services Corp. v. US Investigation Services, Inc.*, 618 S.E. 2d 340 (Va. 2005), for post-term covenants without distinguishing between post-term and in-term enforcement.

A federal case interpreting Virginia law held that an in-term covenant in a distributorship agreement should receive greater latitude than a post-term covenant. *Major v. Orthopedic Equipment Co.*, 496 F. Supp. 604, 615 (E.D. Va. 1980). The court relied on the fact that during the term of the agreement, Major received employment security from the very contract he was challenging, so the normal public policy concern that covenants restrict a person's ability to earn a living was not present.

7. Has the state allowed enforcement of covenants against non-signatories (e.g., family members, newly formed corporations)?

There are no reported Virginia state court cases that deal with enforcement of covenants against non-signatories in the franchise context. However, the United States District Court for the Eastern District of Virginia has enforced covenants against non-signatory family members who were working in active concert with the defendant to violate the covenant. In *JTH v. Lee*, 540 F. Supp. 2d 642 (E.D. Va. 2007) (later opinion, *JTH Tax, Inc. v. Lee*, 514 F. Supp. 2d 818 (E.D. Va. 2007)), the court found that a franchisee's wife was violating the court's injunction, and held her in contempt. The court did so even though the defendant's wife was not a party to the case and was not specifically mentioned in the injunction. Since the wife had actual knowledge of the terms of the injunction, and the competing business was set up in her name, the court found that she was "in active concert" with Lee, and thus the injunction could be enforced against her as well. *Id.* at 648.

The Virginia Supreme Court has held that claims for conspiracy to induce the breach of a covenant against competition could also warrant an injunction against non-signatories of the contract. *Catercorp. Inc. v. Catering Concepts, Inc.*, 431 S.E.2d 277 (Va. 1993).

8. Will the state modify, "blue-pencil," or otherwise reduce a covenant found to be overbroad?

The law in Virginia has been well-settled that courts will not blue-pencil or reform the scope of a covenant that is overly broad. As one Virginia Circuit Court noted, "'it is clear from the restrictive covenant jurisprudence in Virginia that judicial reformation of such agreements is discouraged.'" *Daston Corp. v. MiCore Sols., Inc.*, 80 Va. Cir. 611, 618 (Va. Cir. Ct. 2010) (quoting *Lasership, Inc. v. Watson*, 79 Va. Cir. 205, 216 (Va. Cir. Ct. 2009)) (employment agreement). Moreover, Virginia courts have declined to give effect to the subjective intent of the parties and instead will strictly construe the covenant as drafted. *Linville v. Servisoft of Va., Inc.*, 174 S.E.2d 785 (Va. 1970); *see also Jennings v. Pomeroy*, 8 Va. Cir. 111 (Va. Cir. Ct. 1984) (declining to modify a non-competition provision in an agreement for the sale of a business); *Richardson v. Paxton Co.*, 127 S.E.2d 113 (Va. 1962) (holding that a restraint that was too broad could not be enforced because the covenant must be strictly construed).

Virginia courts have also declined to give effect to contractual provisions giving a court authority to reduce the scope of a covenant in order to make it enforceable. *Lasership*, 79 Va. Cir. at 217; *see also BB&T Ins. Servs., Inc. v. Thomas Rutherfoord, Inc.*, 80 Va. Cir. 174, 181 (Va. Cir. Ct. 2010) (declining to follow a contract provision that allowed for "blue penciling"). The *Lasership* court explained that the decision not to modify restrictive covenants stemmed from a desire to prevent prospective employees from having to try to predict the extent to which an overbroad covenant would be enforced before deciding whether to accept a job, and held that giving a court the authority to reduce the scope of a covenant did not relieve that burden. *Id.* at 217.

Federal courts applying Virginia law have reached the same conclusion. *Alston Studios, Inc. v. Gress & Assocs.*, 492 F.2d 279 (4th Cir. 1974); *Darton Envtl., Inc. v. FJUVO Collections, LLC*, 332 F. Supp. 3d 1022 (W.D. Va. 2018); *Lanmark Tech., Inc. v. Canales*, 454 F. Supp. 2d 524 (E.D. Va. 2006); *Roto-Die Co. v. Lesser*, 899 F. Supp. 1515 (W.D. Va. 1995).

9. When does a non-compete period begin to run? Will courts equitably extend the term?

Courts in Virginia have demonstrated a willingness to equitably extend the term of a covenant. In *Brenco Enterprises, Inc. v. Takeout Taxi Franchising Systems, Inc.*, Chancery No. 177164, 2003 WL 21659422, at *101 (Va. Cir. Ct. May 2, 2003), the court enforced a one-year covenant, stating that the restriction would run from "either the expiration date of the respective agreements or . . . the date of the end of this litigation, whichever occurs later." In *JTH Tax, Inc. v. Boone*, No. 2:09cv69, 2009 WL 10689518, at *6 (E.D. Va. May 7, 2009), the court enforced a two-year covenant from the date of the judgment, to prevent a former franchisee from benefiting from violating the covenant during the pendency of the litigation. *See also JTH Tax, Inc. v. Harlan C. Hanson Enters., Inc.*, No. 2:12cv625, 2013 WL 12097424 (E.D. Va. Mar. 25, 2013) (same).

Similarly, in the employment context, the Supreme Court of Virginia has authorized enforcement of a covenant beginning with the date of the final decision upholding the covenant and continuing for the duration provided for in the contract. For instance, in *Roanoke Engineering Sales Company v. Rosenbaum*, 290 S.E.2d 882 (Va. 1992), the court noted that the flexibility of equitable relief supported a result that would not allow the party violating the covenant to benefit from delays in judicial administration that the parties cannot control. *Roanoke* enforced the three-year covenant for two and a half years following the resolution of the lawsuit, deducting six months for the company's delay in filing a lawsuit. Other cases have reached a similar result. *See Paws With A Cause, Inc. v. Crumpler*, No. 94-1968, 1996 WL 1796 (4th Cir. Jan. 3, 1996) (per curiam) (applying Virginia law and affirming the district court's decision to begin enforcement of the three-year covenant on the date the preliminary relief was ordered); *Hair Club for Men, LLC v. Ehson*, No. 1:16cv236, 2016 WL 6780310 (E.D. Va. Nov. 14, 2016) (enforcing two-year covenant from date of jury verdict and noting public interest in "discourag[ing] the use of the court system as a means to mitigate the duration of contractual provisions."); *Consol. Indust. Roofing, Inc. v. Williams*, 17 Va. Cir. 341 (Va. Cir. Ct. 1989) (enforcing a two-year covenant beginning on the date of entry of the order, and noting that the case was timely filed within several weeks of the defendant's departure from the plaintiff company).

10. Are there additional nuances or peculiarities of the state's treatment of covenants in the franchising context?

At least in the context of employment agreements, Virginia courts strictly construe ambiguities in a covenant against competition against the drafter. *See Combined Ins. Co. of Am. v. Wiest*, 578 F. Supp. 2d 822 (W.D. Va. 2008); *Omniplex World Servs. Corp. v.*

US Investigations Servs., Inc., 618 S.E.2d 340 (Va. 2005); *Simmons v. Miller*, 544 S.E.2d 666 (Va. 2001).

On the other hand, Virginia courts will apply the parties' choice-of-law provision, absent unusual circumstances. *Hitachi Credit Am. Corp. v. Signet Bank*, 166 F.3d 614 (4th Cir. 1999); *Settlement Funding, LLC v. Von Neumann-Lillie*, 645 S.E.2d 436, 438 (Va. 2007) ("If a contract specifies that the substantive law of another jurisdiction governs its interpretation or application, the parties' choice of substantive law should be applied." (citation omitted)). "Unusual circumstances exist where there is 'no reasonable basis' for the choice-of-law provision, or where a party agreed to the provision due to improper means such as fraud or misrepresentation." *Run Them Sweet, LLC v. CPA Glob. Ltd.*, 224 F. Supp. 3d 462, 466 n.2 (E.D. Va. 2016) (citations omitted).

Washington

*by Howard R. Morrill**

1. Has the state addressed covenants against competition in the context of franchising?

- **Does the state have a franchising statute or regulations that address covenants against competition?**
- **Does the state have a covenants statute of general applicability that would encompass franchise covenants?**
- **Have the courts addressed covenants in the context of franchising either under a statute or under the state's common law?**

WASH. REV. CODE § 49.62.005 *et seq.* declares any non-competition agreement "void and unenforceable against an independent contractor unless the independent contractor's earnings from the party seeking enforcement exceed two hundred fifty thousand dollars per year." WASH. REV. CODE § 49.62.030. The statute, however, excludes non-competition agreements contained in franchise agreements, provided the franchise offering was compliant with Washington's franchise registration provisions. WASH. REV. CODE § 49.62.010(4)(e); *see JTH Tax LLC v. McHugh*, WL 1689731 (W.D. Wash. 2020) (finding no violation of WASH. REV. CODE § 49.62.005 *et seq.* was likely where the franchise in question was sold under a statutory exemption from registration). Therefore, while franchises that were legally offered and sold appear to be unaffected, the fact that a franchise was sold illegally in the distant past could suddenly become outcome determinative in a franchise dispute arising many years later.

The Washington Franchise Investment Protection Act, WASH. REV. CODE § 19.100.010 *et seq.*, does provide that a franchisor must agree in writing not to enforce a covenant not to compete against a non-renewed franchisee, and provide one year's notice of non-renewal, in order to avoid compensating that franchisee for its goodwill. *See* WASH. REV. CODE § 19.100.180(2)(i).

WASH. REV. CODE § 19.86.030 generally declares that a contract "in restraint of trade or commerce" is unlawful. And WASH. REV. CODE § 49.62.060 explicitly prohibits a franchisor from restricting, restraining, or prohibiting a franchisee from (1) soliciting or hiring any employee of a franchisee of the same franchisor or (2) soliciting or hiring any employee of the franchisor.

*Howard R. Morrill is a sole practitioner in Seattle, licensed in the State of Washington since 1987.

The only published Washington case specifically addressing a covenant not to compete in a franchising context is *Armstrong v. Taco Time International, Inc.*, 30 Wash. App. 538, 635 P.2d 1114 (1981). The case pre-dates the enactment of WASH. REV. CODE § 49.62.005 *et seq.*, but the statute does not explicitly or implicitly reverse or modify it. *Armstrong* is discussed below.

---

2. Have the courts articulated the "legitimate interests" of the franchisor that will support enforcement of a covenant against competition contained in a franchise agreement?

- **If so, what are they (e.g., protection of goodwill, protection of confidential information), and in what contexts did the issue arise?**
- **If not, what interests have been recognized in other contexts (e.g., employment agreements, the sale of business context)?**

In *Armstrong v. Taco Time International, Inc.*, 30 Wash. App. 538, 635 P.2d 1114, 1119 (1981), the Washington Court of Appeals apparently agreed with the trial court that a franchisor's legitimate interests include protecting its ability to sell new franchises and protecting its franchisees from competition by a fellow franchisee, which presumably refers to competition for customers. *See Perry v. Moran*, 109 Wash. 2d 691, 748 P.2d 224, 229 (1987) (specifically linking the time constraint against competition in an employment contract to the retention of the employer's clients). The *Armstrong* court recognized that each of the franchised locations had some reasonably identifiable trade area that could be protected, leaving open the possibility that mileage might not always be the most reasonable way for a court to express a geographic prohibition. The trial court had explicitly found the franchise rights to be "very valuable." *Armstrong*, 635 P.2d at 1118.

The *Armstrong* court held that a franchise agreement is "akin to an employment contract." *Id.* at 1117. The phrase "akin to" is significant, especially given the subsequent enactment of WASH. REV. CODE § 49.62.005 *et seq.* expressing the Washington legislature's obvious hostility toward non-competition covenants in employment agreements particularly. As discussed above, provided a franchise offering was compliant with Washington's registration provisions, the franchise agreement involved is explicitly excluded from the statute's reach. *See* WASH. REV. CODE § 49.62.010(4)(e). However, given the *Armstrong* court's explicit likening of the franchise agreement to an employment contract, the franchisee resisting enforcement of a non-competition covenant is likely to point to the statute as a statement of public policy disfavoring specific enforcement of franchise covenants' non-compete as well.

Traditionally, in Washington, a covenant against competition in an employment agreement has been deemed reasonable, and therefore upheld, if it is necessary for the protection of the business or goodwill of the owner, and if it does not impose an undue hardship on the former employee. *Perry*, 748 P.2d 229. Further, an employment relationship can be a confidential one, giving rise to a duty not to use the employer's confidential information and trade secrets in competition with that employer, even in the absence of any written covenant. *Ed Nowogroski Insurance, Inc. v. Rucker*, 137 Wash. 2d 427, 971 P.2d 936, 940–43 (1999).

3. What time limitations have courts recognized as reasonable in the franchise context? If no franchise cases have been decided, what time limitations have been recognized in other contexts?

➤ **How have they been related to the interests protected?**

In *Armstrong v. Taco Time International, Inc.*, 30 Wash. App. 538, 635 P.2d 1114, 1118–19 (1981), the Washington Court of Appeals affirmed the trial court's reduction of a franchise agreement's five-year post-termination covenant not to compete to two-and-a-half years. The court found this modified time limit to be reasonable as a matter of law, agreeing that the original five-year restriction was overbroad. This was in accord with the decision of the Washington Supreme Court in *Wood v. May*, 73 Wash. 2d 307, 438 P.2d 587 (1968), an employment case cited by the *Armstrong* court. In *Wood*, the Washington Supreme Court stated that a five-year post-term restriction was "probably unreasonable" and granted a new trial. *Wood*, 438 P.2d at 590. However, while *Wood* makes it clear that the reasonableness of a time limitation depends upon the facts of the case, it provides no explanation of how the determination of reasonableness would vary with those facts, refusing to limit the trial court "to any given formula for determining reasonable restrictions." *Id.*

The interests being protected in *Armstrong* were not directly linked to the time limitation of the covenant. The *Armstrong* court briefly mentioned that the legitimately protected interests included the franchisor's ability to sell franchises and its interest in the existing franchisees' ability to operate without competition from a fellow franchisee. *Armstrong*, 635 P.2d at 1119. To the extent this relates to the time limitations at all, it appears to be in the implicit recognition that many of the former franchisee's customers will develop new shopping habits and loyalties if it is prevented from operating for a period of time.

It is perhaps worth noting that Wash. Rev. Code § 49.62.005 *et seq.* imposes a rebuttable presumption that a restrictive period in excess of 18 months is unreasonable with respect to an employee. Wash. Rev. Code § 49.62.020(2). No similar presumption is provided for with respect to independent contractors. *See* Wash. Rev. Code § 49.62.030. Franchise agreements almost uniformly describe franchisees as independent contractors, yet *Armstrong* analogizes a franchise agreement to an employment agreement. Obviously, *Armstrong* could be used to construct an argument that a franchise non-competition covenant in excess of 18 months is presumptively unreasonable.

4. What geographic limitations have courts recognized as reasonable in the franchise context?

➤ **How have they been related to the interests protected?**

➤ **Have courts recognized the legitimacy of protecting other franchisees from competition?**

In *Armstrong v. Taco Time International, Inc.*, 30 Wash. App. 538, 635 P.2d 1114 (1981), the trial court reduced a franchise agreement's restriction against competition within the continental United States to a 25-mile radius from any existing franchised restaurant. The court of appeals apparently approved the trial court's rejection of the original territorial restriction, but found that the decision to use a one-size-fits-all mileage restriction was not in keeping with the purpose to protect the existing franchisees from competition, concluding that the court needed to look at the agreed "buffer zone" the franchisor had promised each individual franchisee. *Armstrong*, 635 P.2d at 1118. Clearly in this case the court of appeals explicitly related the geographical restriction to its intended purpose—the protection of the other franchisees. The *Armstrong* court's treatment of the geographical restriction may not have broad application however; the court noted that the parties had agreed that the need for protection could not be fairly expressed by a uniform mileage restriction.

Washington courts seem to recognize the difficulty in using bright-line mileage restrictions in the analogous employment context as well. The issue and the protectable interest of the employer is really its clientele. Thus, the court in *Wood v. May*, 73 Wash. 2d 307, 438 P.2d 587 (1968), while ruling that the trial court had been correct in finding a 100-mile radius too restrictive, obliquely suggested that it might be proper for a court to express the restrictions on the former employee in terms of the customers he had served during his employment instead of using distance. *Wood*, 438 P.2d at 590; *see also Knight, Vale and Gregory v. McDaniel*, 37 Wash. App. 366, 680 P.2d 448, 452 (1984) (holding it was reasonable for a time to prohibit former employee accountants from seeking the work of employer's clients with whom the former employees came into contact as a result of their employment).

---

5. What limitations on activities have courts recognized as reasonable in the franchise context?

Armstrong v. Taco Time International, Inc., 30 Wash. App. 538, 635 P.2d 1114 (1981), is the only reported decision of a Washington court dealing with non-competition agreements in franchising. The decision provides little guidance on what limitations on competing activities will be deemed reasonable, tautologically concluding that operating a competing restaurant is competing and therefore prohibited. The appellate court did reverse the trial court's determination that the franchisee in question could not sell his restaurants without obtaining the purchaser's agreement not to operate a Mexican themed restaurant on the premises, but only because the parties' contract did not contain such a provision. *Id.* at 1120. The *Armstrong* court did not suggest that such a requirement would have been unenforceable had it been included in the franchise agreement.

Turning again to the employment context that *Armstrong* described as analogous to franchising, it seems clear that prohibiting a former employee from working for a competitor in any capacity is going too far. *See Copier Specialists, Inc. v. Gillen*, 76 Wash. App. 771, 887 P.2d 919 (1995) (copier repairman would not be enjoined from working for a competing service merely because his employer had trained him, where he was not required to use any confidential information and had little if any customer contact in his new position). However, a limitation on seeking the business of a former employer's customers with whom the employee came into contact because of that former employment has been upheld. *See, e.g., Knight, Vale and Gregory v. McDaniel*, 37 Wash. App. 366, 680 P.2d 448 (1984). Analogizing to these employment cases, presumably a former restaurant franchisee could not be prevented from working as a line chef in the kitchen of a nearby, competing restaurant, but he or she might well be prohibited from serving as its marketing director or its maitre'd.

6. Does the state recognize a difference between in-term and post-term covenants?

The *Armstrong v. Taco Time International, Inc.*, 30 Wash. App. 538, 635 P.2d 1114 (1981) case explicitly declined to recognize any difference between in-term and post-term covenants in a franchise context. Both the in-term and post-term covenants were held to be overly broad as written and were modified in exactly the same fashion.

7. Has the state allowed enforcement of covenants against non-signatories (e.g., family members, newly formed corporations)?

There is no specific guidance on this question in any Washington published decision. Although in *Armstrong v. Taco Time International, Inc.*, 30 Wash. App. 538, 635 P.2d 1114 (1981), there were other defendants affiliated with the franchisee, the case contains no discussion of the enforcement of the covenants against non-signatories. There do not appear to be any helpful authorities from any non-franchise context either.

8. Will the state modify, "blue-pencil," or otherwise reduce a covenant found to be overbroad?

In Washington, a court will modify an overly broad covenant against competition to reflect a reasonable restriction, at least as to time and geography. *See, e.g., Wood v. May*, 73 Wash. 2d 307, 438 P.2d 587 (1968); *Emerick v. Cardiac Study Center, Inc.*, 189 Wash. App. 711, 357 P. 3d 696 (2015); *Armstrong v. Taco Time International, Inc.*, 30 Wash. App. 538, 635 P.2d 1114 (1981). *Wood* and *Armstrong* are discussed above; *Emerick* is discussed below.

9. When does a non-compete period begin to run? Will courts equitably extend the term?

When a non-compete period begins to run is presumably governed exclusively by the contract, as covenants against competition are creatures of contract only. *See Ed Nowogroski Insurance, Inc. v. Rucker*, 137 Wash. 2d 427, 971 P.2d 936, 941 (1999) ("As a general rule, an employee who has not signed an agreement not to compete is free, upon leaving employment, to engage in competitive employment."); *see also Riverview Floral, Ltd. v. Watkins*, 51 Wash. App. 658, 754 P.2d 1055, 1058 (1988) (court narrowly construed language of the non-compete agreement).

The Washington Court of Appeals approved and affirmed a trial court's equitable tolling of a covenant against competition in *Emerick v. Cardiac Study Center, Inc.*,

189 Wash. App. 711, 357 P.3d 696 (2015). The only apparent limitation upon doing so is that any injunction must issue before the expiration of the original restricted period. *Id.*, 357 P.3d at 706.

10. Are there additional nuances or peculiarities of the state's treatment of covenants in the franchising context?

As mentioned earlier, the Washington Franchise Investment Protection Act, WASH. REV. CODE § 19.100.010 *et seq.*, provides that a franchisor may be required to agree not to enforce a covenant not to compete in the narrow context of a franchisee's non-renewal. WASH. REV. CODE § 19.100.180(2)(i). Whether a wrongful termination or other violation of the Franchise Investment Protection Act should render a covenant not to compete unenforceable is a question that has not been addressed in any published opinion of the Washington court and is not directly answered by the statute's text.

Although there are no published Washington cases invalidating non-compete agreements enforceable in another state, a contractual choice of law provision should be disregarded if (1) without the provision, Washington law would apply; (2) the chosen state's law violates a fundamental public policy of Washington; and (3) Washington's interest in the determination of the issue materially outweighs the chosen state's interest. *McKee v. AT&T Corporation*, 164 Wash. 2d 372, 191 P.3d 845, 851 (2008). If these tests were met, there is every reason to believe Washington would invalidate a covenant against competition.

West Virginia

*By Natalma (Tami) McKnew**

1. Has the state addressed covenants against competition in the context of franchising?

- **Does the state have a franchising statute or regulations that address covenants against competition?**
- **Does the state have a covenants statute of general applicability that would encompass franchise covenants?**
- **Have the courts addressed covenants in the context of franchising either under a statute or under the state's common law?**

West Virginia has not adopted a franchise statute or promulgated any regulations affecting franchising, nor has West Virginia enacted any statutes specifically directed to covenants against competition in a general context. However, there are two statutes that may apply to covenants against competition. West Virginia has enacted the Uniform Trade Secrets Act (codified as W. Va. Code § 47-22-1 *et seq.*) (the Trade Secrets Act), which has general applicability and may be used, in appropriate circumstances to bar current or former employees from utilizing trade secrets in subsequent employment. West Virginia Code section 47-22-1(d) defines a trade secret as

> [I]nformation, including but not limited, a formula, pattern, compilation, program, device, method, technique or process, that:
>
> (1) Derives independent economic value, actual or potential, from not being generally known to, and not being readily ascertainable by property means by, other persons who can obtain economic value from its disclosure or use; and
>
> (2) Is the subject of efforts that are reasonable under the circumstances to maintain its secrecy.

The Trade Secrets Act could be used to protect any information derived from franchise agreements and business models that various franchises utilize in

*Natalma (Tami) McKnew is a partner at Fox Rothschild, LLP. Kenneth J. Barton Jr. authored the West Virginia entry for the third edition of this book, upon which this entry is based.

developing and continuing their business, and to restrict former employees accordingly. *McGough v. Nalco Co.*, 203 Fed. Appx. 450 (4th Cir. 2006) (applying West Virginia law).

While the West Virginia Antitrust Act (the Antitrust Act) may theoretically apply to restrictive covenants in franchise agreements, the West Virginia Supreme Court of Appeals rejected that approach in *Reddy v. Community Health Foundation of Man*, 171 W. Va. 368, 298 S.E.2d 906 (1982), commenting, "Franchise agreements, agreements to buy or sell certain commodity at specified time and price, employments agreements, agreements between management and unions-all operate as limitations on unrestricted trade without being unlawful restraints." *Id.*, 171 W. Va. at 372, 298 S.E.2d at 909.

As reflected below, the West Virginia courts do not hesitate to enforce covenants not to compete, *Huntington Eye Associates, Inc., v. LoCascio*, 210 W. Va. 76, 553 S.E.2d 773 (2001), or to reject them, *Cook v. Robinson*, 2011 WL 4708855 (N.D. W. Va. Oct. 4, 2011) based on established legal principles.

---

2. Have the courts articulated the "legitimate interests" of the franchisor that will support enforcement of a covenant against competition contained in a franchise agreement?

- **If so, what are they (e.g., protection of goodwill, protection of confidential information), and in what contexts did the issue arise?**
- **If not, what interests have been recognized in other contexts (e.g., employment agreements, the sale of business context)?**

Neither the state nor federal courts in West Virginia have considered covenants against competition in the franchise context. However, in both employment agreements and the sale of businesses, multiple protectable interests have been identified. Courts in West Virginia are more likely to enforce a restrictive covenant in the context of a sale of business than in an employment agreement, as the two types of restrictions have different purposes. As the federal district court stated in *Cook v. Robinson*, 2011 WL 4608855, at *5 (N.D. W. Va. Oct. 4, 2011):

> [a] restriction imposed on the seller of a business ensures that the seller received the highest possible price for the business and the buyer will not risk losing what was purchased should the seller become a competitor. The objective of the covenant not to compete, ancillary to the employment contract, on the other hand, "prevent[s] the competitive use, for a defined period of time, of information, skills or relationships which are distinctive to the employer and which the employee acquired . . . in the course of employment. (internal citations omitted).

Covenants against competition are narrowly construed and must be carefully drafted in order to provide the desired protection. For example, in *Huddleston v. Mariotti*, 143 W. Va. 419, 102 S.E.2d 527 (1958), the Huddlestons purchased a motel from the Mariottis. Included in the sale documents was a covenant that the Mariottis would "not engage in the motel business within a radius of 10 miles of the Bel-Air Motel for a period of 10 years following the date of th[e] sale." *Id.*, 143 W. Va. at 421, 102 S.E.2d at 528. Shortly after the closing Mariotti began the construction of a larger motel less than a mile from the Bel-Air Motel, intending to sell the new property to a third party. The trial court enjoined Mariotti's project, but the West Virginia Supreme Court of Appeals reversed, concluding that the post-sale restriction did not prohibit constructing and selling another motel: "That language, to us, can have only the meaning or effect of precluding the Mariottis from engaging in, that is, conducting or operating, directly or indirectly, a motel business. It has no relation to the construction or sale of any competing motel." *Id.*, 143 W. Va. at 423, 102 S.E.2d at 529.

In *Helms Boys, Inc. v. Brady*, 177 W. Va. 66, 67, 297 S.E.2d 840, 842 (1982), the West Virginia Supreme Court of Appeals acknowledged that it had not previously had occasion to define a protectable employer interest, but had previously enforced restrictive covenants to protect an employer's interest in unique or confidential information, such as a trade secret or customer list. The employer in *Helms* did not rely on confidential information, but simply sought to restrict a management employee from undertaking similar employment within five years and 100 miles of the employer's store. The court refused to enforce the restrictive covenant. The skills and information acquired by the employee were of a general managerial nature—including supervising, merchandising, purchasing, and advertising—and were not protectable employer interests.

A month following the *Helms* decision, the West Virginia Supreme Court issued its opinion in *Reddy v. Community Health Foundation of Man*, 171 W.Va. 368, 298 S.E.2d 906 (1982). In *Reddy*, an emergency room physician had entered into an independent contractor agreement that included a restrictive covenant that he would not practice medicine within 30 air miles of Man, West Virginia, for a period of three years after the termination of his agreement with the employer. The court articulated three protectable employer interests: (1) special information imparted to the employee during the employment relationship, (2) goodwill of customers to whom an employee was exposed while working for the employer, and (3) any particular skills that the employee specifically acquired during the period of employment. *Id.*, 171 W. Va. at 374, 298 S.E.2d at 912. The non-compete at issue lacked any business purpose, the court concluded. Although Dr. Reddy was a physician, the health foundation with which he contracted did not provide medical service, and the doctor and the foundation were not in competition.

The court in *Reddy* further articulated the three-factor inquiry to determine whether a covenant not to compete in an employment agreement was reasonable. First, a reviewing court must determine, usually as a matter of law, that the covenant is reasonable on its face; if the court cannot determine reasonableness from the face of the document, the burden is upon the employer to prove that the covenant is reasonable. Second, the employer must prove that the covenant protects a legitimate interest. Third, once those two elements are established, the covenant is presumptively enforceable in its entirety, and the burden then shifts to the employee who then must demonstrate the factual absence of a protectable interest or that enforcement of the covenant in its entirety "would result in a limitation of his freedom that is unnecessary to protect the legitimate interests of the employer." *Id.*, 171 W. Va. at 383, 298 S.E.2d at 921.

An employer's protectable business interests, as defined by West Virginia courts, include (1) confidential information, (2) confidential information obtained during employment, and (3) particularized skills obtained during employment. *O. Hommel Co. v. Fink*, 115 W. Va. 686, 177 S.E. 619 (1934) (confidential information); *Gant v. Hygeia Facilities Foundation, Inc.*, 181 W. Va. 805, 384 S.E.2d 842 (1989) (confidential information obtained during employment); *Special Services Bureau, Inc. v. Friend*, 2019 WL 4257185 (W. Va. Sept. 9, 2019) (particularized skills obtained during employment); *Cook*, 2011 WL 4708855, at *8 (same); *Helms*, 177 W. Va. 66, 297 S.E.2d 840 (same); and *Appalachian Laboratories, Inc. v. Bostic*, 178 W. Va. 386, 359 S.E.2d 614 (1987) (same). By contrast, the court in *Corky Wells Electric, Inc. v. Pratt*, 2019 WL 10056967, at *12 (N.D. W. Va. Dec. 5, 2019) concluded that the employer lacked a protectable interest in barring an employee from the "general engineering business." It is important to note that the interest an employer is seeking to protect must be articulated, and the failure to do so will likely doom enforcement. *Cook*, 2011 WL 4708855, at *8; *Voorhees v. Guyan Machine Co.*, 191 W. Va. 450, 446 S.E.2d 672 (1994).

West Virginia courts will also enforce "non-piracy" or non-solicitation provisions contained in employment agreements. In *Wood v. Accordia of West Virginia, Inc.*, 217 W.Va. 406, 413, 618 S.E.2d 415, 422 (2005), the West Virginia Supreme Court upheld Accordia's restriction of its former employees from using its current and prospective customer accounts and information contained therein for a period of two years following the cessation of employment. Importantly, the employer allowed the former employees to remain working in the insurance industry and compete with Accordia for customers. The court recognized and approved of these types of covenants as being less restrictive on the employees and on economic forces in the marketplace.

Notwithstanding the result in *Huddleston, supra*, West Virginia courts are more likely to enforce restrictive covenants in the business sales context. *See, e.g., Axford v. Price*, 134 W. Va. 725, 61 S.E.2d 637 (1950) (upholding post-sale restriction). The court explained in *Weaver v. Ritchie*, 197 W. Va. 690, 694, 478 S.E.2d 363, 367 (1996), that the "rule of reason" is applied with lesser scrutiny in the sales contract than the covenant as applied in an employment agreement. Reinforcing *Reddy*, the court held that "[a] covenant not to compete ancillary to a sale of business is reasonable only if it (1) is no greater than is required for the protection of the buyer; (2) does not impose an undue hardship upon the seller, and (3) is not injurious to the public." *Id.*, 197 W. Va. at 697, 478 S.E.2d at 370.

3. What time limitations have courts recognized as reasonable in the franchise context? If no franchise cases have been decided, what time limitations have been recognized in other contexts?

➤ How have they been related to the interests protected?

There are no decisions from the West Virginia courts addressing the reasonableness of time limitations in the franchise context. However, reasonable time limitations have been addressed in both employment and business sales cases. As with terms related to scope of the agreement and interests to be protected, courts will enforce the extent and duration only "to the extent necessary to protect the rights of the parties and the interest of the public therein, if any." *Axford v. Price*, 134 W. Va. 725, 731, 61 S.E.2d 637, 640 (1950). "An employee covenant is unreasonable on its face if its time or area limitations are excessively broad, or where the covenant appears designed to intimidate employees rather that to protect the employer's business. . . ." *Cook v. Robinson*, 2011 WL 4708855, at *5 (N.D. W. Va. Oct. 4, 2011) (citing *Reddy v. Community Health Foundation of Man*, 171 W. Va. 368, 298 S.E.2d 906 (1982)).

Generally speaking, West Virginia courts allow more extended limitation periods when businesses are being sold. *E.g., Weaver v. Ritchie*, 197 W. Va. 690, 478 S.E.2d 363 (1996) (15 years); *Huddleston v. Mariotti*, 143 W. Va. 419, 102 S.E.2d 527 (1958) (ten years); and *Axford*, 134 W. Va. 725, 61 S.E.2d 637 (unlimited duration interpreted as to the extent necessary to protect the purchaser). In *Axford*, the sellers too cleverly attempted to circumvent the non-compete provision in the sales agreement by using its former employees as the conduit to breach the agreement. They sold meats at wholesale to drivers whom they had formerly employed; the drivers in turn sold to the same stores they served as they had during their employment with the sellers. On appeal, the court found the covenant enforceable and rejected the argument that the sellers were not in breach because they did not employ the drivers.

In the employment context, courts narrow the time limitations more often than in the sale of businesses. In *Pancake Realty Co. v. Harber*, 137 W. Va. 605, 73 S.E.2d 438 (1952), a restriction of unlimited duration was found void as being unreasonable, but the court modified the restriction to one year, which it had determined to be reasonable. By contrast, the court in *Cook v. Robinson*, 2011 WL 4708855 (N.D. W. Va. Oct. 4, 2011), rejected and refused to judicially alter a ten-year non-compete. While a covenant not to compete for a period of five years was rejected on other grounds, the court made no comment about the period of time being unacceptable in *Appalachian Laboratories, Inc. v. Bostic*, 178 W. Va. 386, 359 S.E.2d 614 (1987).

Based upon the opinions rendered to date, it appears that covenants of up to three years are acceptable. *E.g., Gant v. Hygeia Facilities Foundation, Inc.*, 181 W. Va. 805, 384, S.E.2d 842 (1989); *O. Hommel Co. v. Fink*, 115 W. Va. 686, 117 S.E.2d 618 (1934); *Wood v. Accordia of West Virginia, Inc.*, 217 W. Va. 406, 618 S.E.2d 415 (2005); *Huntington Eye Associates, Inc. v. LoCascio*, 210 W. Va. 76, 553 S.E.2d 773 (2001); *Voorhees v. Guyan Machinery Co.*, 191 W. Va. 450, 446 S.E.2d 672 (1994); *Torbett v. Wheeling Dollar Sav. & Trust Co.*, 178 W. Va. 210, 314 S.E.2d 166 (1983); *PEMCO Corp. v. Rose*, 163 W. Va. 420, 257 S.E.2d 363 (1979); and *Wyckoff v. Painter*, 145 W. Va. 310, 115 S.E.2d 80 (1960).

---

4. What geographic limitations have courts recognized as reasonable in the franchise context?

- **How have they been related to the interests protected?**
- **Have courts recognized the legitimacy of protecting other franchisees from competition?**

There are no cases in West Virginia addressing geographic limitations of covenants not to compete in franchise contracts, although courts have addressed these issues in the context of both employment contracts and business sales agreements. West Virginia courts will enforce restrictions "to the extent necessary to protect the rights of the parties and the interest of the public therein, if any." *Axford v. Price*, 134 W. Va. 725, 731, 61 S.E.2d 637, 640 (1950). "An employee covenant is unreasonable on its face if its time or area limitations are excessively broad, or where the covenant appears designed to intimidate employees rather that to protect the employer's business." *Cook v. Robinson*, 2011 WL 4708855, at *5 (N.D. W. Va. Oct. 4, 2011) (citing *Reddy v. Community Health Foundation of Man*, 171 W. Va. 368, 298 S.E.2d 906 (1982).

In the employment context, if there is no geographic limitation, or an ill-defined one, restrictive covenants likely will not be enforced. *Pancake Realty Co. v. Harber*, 137 W. Va. 605, 73 S.E.2d 438 (1952) (rejecting a restrictive covenant with no territorial limitation); *Corky Wells Electric, Inc. v. Pratt*, 2019 WL 10056067, at *13 (N.D. W. Va. Dec. 5, 2019) (rejecting a vaguely defined territory defined as all areas in which the employer "has been, is currently being, and . . . in which [it] has conducted business"). In *Gant v. Hygeia Facilities Foundation, Inc.*, 181 W. Va. 805, 809, 384 S.E.2d 842, 846 (1989), the West Virginia Supreme Court of Appeals concluded that a 30-air-mile radius was reasonable, while in *Wyckoff v. Painter*, 145 W. Va. 310, 115 S.E.2d 80 (1960), a restriction encompassing the entire state was upheld.

A reasonable geographic area is determined, in part, by the scope of the employee's work, as the court signaled in *Costanzo v. EMS USA, Inc.*, 2017 WL 4215952 (N.D. W. Va. Sept. 21, 2017). The court in that case did not reject out of hand a 100-mile radius, explaining that it needed additional evidence of the area served by the ex-employee. However, mileage is not always a decisive issue. For instance, a 30-mile restriction was deemed unreasonable by the court in *JAK Productions, Inc. v. Bayer*, 94 F. Supp. 3d 777 (S.D. W. Va. 2015), *aff'd* 616 Fed. Appx. 94 (4th Cir. 2015), thus invalidating the non-compete provision. The court reasoned that the "covenant's geographical restriction is not reasonable given the industry at issue," 94 F. Supp. 3d at 784, observing that "[N]ot all businesses today rely upon the natural patronage of a physical neighborhood." *Id.* at 785. The plaintiff's call center, for which the defendant made calls throughout a wide geographic area comprising several states, was one such business. The geographic scope of the non-compete was unrelated to the extensive area within which the employee made calls; thus, the restriction was unreasonable.

Where the restriction is in a contract for a sale of business, the territorial limit will be relaxed. *Axford*, 134 W. Va. at 731, 61 S.E.2d at 640 (limited to any area where the purchaser was in business). For instance, the West Virginia Supreme Court of Appeals upheld a 50-mile restriction in *Weaver v. Ritchie*, 197 W. Va. 690, 478 S.E.2d 363 (1996).

5. What limitations on activities have courts recognized as reasonable in the franchise context?

There are no cases in West Virginia addressing activities limited by covenants not to compete in franchise contracts, although the issue has been addressed in the context of employment and business sales.

In the employment context, the scope of prohibited activities depends on the nature of the ex-employee's work and the nature of the information and training (formal and informal) provided by the employer. In *Moore Business Forms, Inc. v. Foppiano*, 181 W. Va. 305, 307–08, 382 S.E.2d 499, 501–02 (1989), for instance, the court rejected any restriction upon a sales representative, finding that the company had not provided any specialized or unique training during the course of employment. *See also Helms Boys, Inc. v. Brady*, 177 W. Va. 66, 297 S.E.2d 840 (1982) (salesman did not receive specialized sales training that could not be acquired at any business), and *Voorhees v. Guyan Machinery Co.*, 191 W. Va. 450, 446 S.E.2d 672 (1994) (skills of a general supervisory nature, such as supervising, merchandising, purchasing, and advertising, were not protectable activities).

In the sale of business context, courts will typically restrict the seller from engaging in a competing business similar to that which had been sold. *See, e.g.*,

Weaver v. Ritchie, 197 W. Va. 690, 478 S.E.2d 363 (1996) (optometry practice); *Huddleston v. Mariotti*, 143 W. Va. 419, 102 S.E.2d 527 (1958) (motel); *Axford v. Price*, 134 W. Va. 725, 61 S.E.2d 637 (1950) (wholesale meat business).

6. Does the state recognize a difference between in-term and post-term covenants?

West Virginia courts have not addressed the issue. However, since courts have approved of franchise agreements as a reasonable restraint on trade, at least in dicta, *Reddy v. Community Health Foundation of Man*, 171 W. Va. 368, 298 S.E.2d 906 (1982), enforcement of both in-term and post-term covenants seems likely.

7. Has the state allowed enforcement of covenants against non-signatories (e.g., family members, newly formed corporations)?

West Virginia courts have not addressed the issue.

8. Will the state modify, "blue-pencil," or otherwise reduce a covenant found to be overbroad?

There are no decisions in West Virginia squarely addressing the ability of a court to "blue-pencil" an overly broad non-compete in a franchise agreement or otherwise, and extant jurisprudence is mixed. Several cases reflect courts' refusal to blue-pencil facially unreasonably restrictive covenants in employment agreements. *E.g.*, *McGough v. Nalco Co.*, 203 Fed. Appx. 450 (4th Cir. 2006) (applying West Virginia law); *Reddy v. Community Health Foundation of Man*, 171 W. Va. 368, 298 S.E.2d 906 (1982); *Pancake Realty Co. v. Harber*, 137 W. Va. 605, 73 S.E.2d 438 (1952).

By contrast, the covenant in *O. Hommel Co. v. Fink*, 115 W. Va. 686, 117 S.E.2d 618 (1934) was deemed generally reasonable, and the court narrowed a three-year restrictive covenant encompassing Canada and the eastern United States to the areas in which the employee actually did business. Interestingly, there appears to be inherent conflict between *Pancake* and *O. Hommel*. There are two possible distinctions between the "no blue-pencil" outcome of the *Pancake* case and the decision in *O. Hommel*. The covenant at issue in *Pancake* lacked any geographic limitation, while that in *O. Hommel* was overly broad. The second distinction is that the covenant in *Pancake* was found to be invalid on its face, while that in *O. Hommel* was not.

9. When does a non-compete period begin to run? Will courts equitably extend the term?

The courts in West Virginia will look to the agreement to determine when the non-compete period begins to run. There is no authority to suggest that courts will equitably extend the term.

10. Are there additional nuances or peculiarities of the state's treatment of covenants in the franchising context?

West Virginia lacks authority addressing restrictive covenants in franchise agreements. However, issues of consideration, choice of law provisions, and the burden of proof can present themselves in the context of restrictive covenants generally and are worthy of discussion.

CONSIDERATION

Consideration supporting a covenant not to compete is a precondition to validity, *Cook v. Robinson*, 2011 WL 4708855, at *9 (W.D. W. Va. Oct. 4, 2011). In that case, payment of $20,000 specifically for the non-compete satisfied the consideration requirement. The employment at issue in *Costanzo v. EMS USA, Inc.*, 2017 WL 4215952, at *3 (N.D. W. Va. Sept. 21, 2017) was at-will, but the employee's access to confidential information in the course of his employment satisfied the requirement for consideration. The execution of a new contract, affording the continuing employee 120 days' prior notice of termination, was deemed sufficient consideration in *Corky Wells Electric, Inc. v. Pratt*, 2019 WL 10056967, at *10 (N.D. W. Va. Dec. 5, 2019).

The ex-employee in *Audiology Distribution, LLC v. Hawkins*, 2014 WL 6775599 (N.D. W. Va. Dec. 2, 2014) executed an employment agreement and a separate non-compete agreement, both two days after she had actually started working. She argued that the non-compete was void for lack of consideration, but the court disagreed. She had been informed prior to beginning employment that a non-compete would be required. The "covenant not to compete was clearly part of the contract formation process before she began her employment." *Id.* at *10. The non-compete and the employment agreement thus would be "construed together and considered to constitute one transaction." *Id.* at *9. Employment was consideration for the non-compete.

CHOICE OF LAW

Despite a contractual choice of law, West Virginia courts will be slow to apply the law of a forum that appears to have little contact to the transaction. In *General Electric Company v. Keyser*, 166 W. Va. 456, 275 S.E.2d 289 (1981), a commercial guaranty in a California loan transaction specified New York, G.E.'s state of incorporation, as governing law. Keyser, a West Virginia resident, guaranteed payment of a promissory note to G.E. by a California corporation. When the borrower defaulted, G.E. sued Keyser in a West Virginia court. Keyser defended on the basis that under California law, the debt was usurious. Concluding that California rather than New York law applied, the guaranty the court stated:

> We hold, therefore, that a choice of law provision in a contract will not be given effect when the contract bears no substantial relationship with the jurisdiction whose laws the parties have chosen to govern the agreement, or when the application of that law would offend the public policy of this state.

Keyser, 166 W. Va. at 470, 275 S.E.2d at 297.

Application of this principle is reflected in *Corky Wells Electric, Inc. v. Pratt*, 2019 WL 10056967, at *10 (N.D. W. Va. Dec. 5, 2019), in which the court considered a restrictive covenant in an employment agreement. Although the choice of law provision selected Kentucky law, the court applied West Virginia law. Kentucky failed both prongs of the test described in *General Electric Company v. Keyser, supra;* the dispute lacked any association with Kentucky, and application of Kentucky law would offend the public policy of West Virginia.

BURDEN OF PROOF

While there are no West Virginia cases dealing with the burden of proof in enforcing a restrictive covenant in a franchise agreement, the principle has been addressed in both sales of businesses and employment contracts.

In *Reddy v. Community Health Foundation of Man*, 171 W. Va. 368, 298 S.E.2d 906 (1982), the court articulated the burden of proof in a non-compete dispute in the employment context, identifying three analytical principles: First, a reviewing court must determine, usually as a matter of law, that the covenant is reasonable on its face and falls within one of the legitimate interests to be protected. If the court cannot determine reasonableness from the face of the document, the burden is upon the employer to prove that the covenant is reasonable. Second, the employer must prove that the covenant is protecting a legitimate interest. Once those two elements are established, the covenant is presumptively enforceable in its entirety, and the burden shifts to the employee who then must prove non-breach or that enforcement of the covenant in its entirety "would result in a limitation of [the employee's] freedom that is unnecessary to protect the legitimate interests of the employer." *Reddy*, 171 W. Va. at 383, 298 S.E.2d at 921.

Wisconsin

*by Roberta F. Howell**

1. Has the state addressed covenants against competition in the context of franchising?

- **Does the state have a franchising statute or regulations that address covenants against competition?**
- **Does the state have a covenants statute of general applicability that would encompass franchise covenants?**
- **Have the courts addressed covenants in the context of franchising either under a statute or under the state's common law?**

Wisconsin does not have a statute or regulation specifically addressing covenants against competition in franchise agreements. However, the Wisconsin Fair Dealership Law (WFDL), WIS. STAT. Ch. 135, applies to most, if not all, franchise agreements. The law prevents substantial change to the competitive circumstances, or termination, of a dealership relationship without good cause and proper notice. The WFDL definition of "good cause" requires that the reasons for a termination or substantial change in competitive circumstances of a dealership agreement be "essential and reasonable." WIS. STAT. § 135.02(4)(a). Therefore, with regard to dealership agreements, enforcement of an in-term restrictive covenant may be subject to close scrutiny. *But cf., Deutchland Enterprises, Ltd. v. Burger King Corp.*, 957 F.2d 449 (7th Cir. 1992) (in-term restrictive covenant found to be "essential and reasonable" under WFDL). In addition, "good cause" within the meaning of the WFDL requires that the restrictive covenant be applied in a non-discriminatory manner between similarly situated franchisees. WIS. STAT. § 135.02(4)(a).

No Wisconsin case has addressed the impact of the WFDL on a post-term restrictive covenant. The WFDL does not expressly prohibit a restrictive covenant.

Wisconsin also has a covenant not to compete statute applicable to employment agreements that could be construed to encompass such covenants in franchise agreements. That statute provides:

> A covenant by an assistant, servant or agent not to compete with his or her employer or principal during the term of the employment or agency, or after

*Ms. Howell is a partner with the law firm of Foley & Lardner LLP in Madison, Wisconsin, and a member of the Wisconsin bar.

> the termination of that employment or agency, within a specified territory and during a specified time is lawful and enforceable only if the restrictions imposed are reasonably necessary for the protection of the employer or principal. Any covenant, described in this subsection, imposing an unreasonable restraint is illegal, void and unenforceable even as to any part of the covenant or performance that would be a reasonable restraint.

WIS. STAT. § 103.465.

However, the United States Court of Appeals for the Fifth Circuit held that this statute does not apply to a franchise agreement, *Wilkinson v. Manpower, Inc.*, 531 F.2d 712 (5th Cir. 1976), as has a Wisconsin circuit court in an unreported decision. *See also H&R Block Eastern Tax Services, Inc. v. Vorpahl*, 255 F. Supp. 2d 930 (E.D. Wis. 2003) (citing *Wilkinson*). Similarly, the United States District Court for the Eastern District of Wisconsin held that cases interpreting this statute were "not dispositive" in the franchise context. *Deutchland Enterprises*, Bus. Franchise Guide (CCH) ¶ 9609. The Wisconsin Supreme Court held that this statute applied to a restrictive covenant in a lease agreement involving the rental of a lunch wagon and route. *Chuck Wagon Catering, Inc. v. Raduege*, 88 Wis. 2d 740, 277 N.W.2d 787 (1979); *cf. Farm Credit Services of North Central Wisconsin, ACA v. Wysocki*, 2001 WI 51, 243 Wis. 2d 305, 627 N.W.2d 444 (2001). The Wisconsin Supreme Court held that the criteria of Wisconsin Statute section 103.465 are the same as Wisconsin common law for employment agreement covenants. *Streiff v. American Family Mut. Ins. Co.*, 118 Wis. 2d 602, 348 N.W.2d 505 (1984).

---

2. Have the courts articulated the "legitimate interests" of the franchisor that will support enforcement of a covenant against competition contained in a franchise agreement?

- **If so, what are they (e.g., protection of goodwill, protection of confidential information), and in what contexts did the issue arise?**
- **If not, what interests have been recognized in other contexts (e.g., employment agreements, the sale of business context)?**

The Seventh Circuit has held that the franchisor's interest in the franchisee's loyalty and best efforts, advance notice of the franchisor's marketing strategies, and access to its operating methods and policies were sufficient to support enforcement of an in-term covenant. The court also found that the violation of the covenant was "good cause" for termination under the WFDL, WIS. STAT. Ch. 135. *Deutchland Enterprises, Ltd. v. Burger King Corp.*, 957 F.2d at 453. A Wisconsin circuit court and one Wisconsin appellate court have held that the interests supporting a franchise covenant against competition are the same as would support a sale of a business or employment covenant. The rule of reason applies. *H&R Block v. Otto*, No. 80-C V-7409 (Wis. Cir. Ct. Dane County 1982); *Buchholz Insurance Agency, Inc. v. Ziegler*, 188 Wis. 2d 603, 526 N.W.2d 279 (Ct. App. 1994). *See also Wilkinson v. Manpower, Inc.*, 531 F.2d 712 (5th Cir. 1976) (analogizing the franchise covenant against competition to one involved in the sale of a business).

Wisconsin Statute section 103.465 requires that there be a protectable interest in an employment agreement's restrictive covenant. *Lakeside Oil Co. v. Slutsky*, 8

Wis. 2d 157, 98 N.W.2d 415 (1959). Protected interests in employment agreements include preventing the use of trade secrets or lists of customers or services of the employee that are of a unique character. *Behnke v. Hertz Corp.*, 70 Wis. 2d 818, 235 N.W.2d 690 (1975); *Pollack v. Calimag*, 157 Wis. 2d 222, 458 N.W.2d 591 (Ct. App. 1990). Wisconsin also recognizes that an employer has a protectable interest in preventing competition by a former employee who developed a special relationship with customers as a route sales clerk. *Farm Credit Services of North Central Wisconsin, ACA v. Wysocki*, 2001 WI 51, 243 Wis. 2d 305, 627 N.W.2d 444 (2001); *Chuck Wagon Catering, Inc. v. Raduege*, 88 Wis. 2d 740, 277 N.W.2d 787 (1979); *Abbott Laboratories. v. Norse Chemical Corp.*, 33 Wis. 2d 445, 147 N.W.2d 529 (1967). Wisconsin will protect confidential business information in situations involving high-level management personnel. *Rollins Burdick Hunter of Wisconsin, Inc. v. Hamilton*, 101 Wis. 2d 460, 304 N.W.2d 752 (1981); *Pollack v. Calimag*, 157 Wis. 2d 222, 458 N.W.2d 591 (Ct. App. 1990). Wisconsin will also protect an employer where a limited customer base closely identifies a key employee with an employer's business. *Fields Foundation, Ltd. v. Christensen*, 103 Wis. 2d 465, 309 N.W.2d 125 (Ct. App. 1981); *Geocaris v. Surgical Consultants, Ltd.*, 100 Wis. 2d 387, 302 N.W.2d 76 (Ct. App. 1981).

Wisconsin courts recognize the legitimacy of restrictive covenants in the sale of a business agreement if they are reasonably necessary to protect a legitimate interest. Protection is legitimate where key personnel were hired by a competing business, and where those personnel had sufficient capability and opportunity to cause harm. *Reiman Associates, Inc. v. R/A Advertising, Inc.*, 102 Wis. 2d 305, 306 N.W.2d 292 (Ct. App. 1981). Wisconsin courts recognize protection of property interests and goodwill for covenants not to compete in the sale of a business or components of business. *George M. Danke Co. v. Marten*, 207 Wis. 290, 241 N.W. 359 (1932). Wisconsin allows a much greater scope of restraint in contracts between vendor and vendee than between employer and employee. *Fullerton Lumber Co. v. Torborg*, 270 Wis. 133, 70 N.W.2d 585 (1955), *superseded by statute on other grounds as recognized in General Medical Corp. v. Kobs*, 179 Wis. 2d 422, 507 N.W.2d 381 (Ct. App. 1993). Outside the employment agreement context, the test is the reasonableness of the restrictive covenant. *Id.*; *Madson v. Johnson*, 164 Wis. 612, 160 N.W. 1085 (1917); *Wilkinson*, 531 F.2d 717. To be considered reasonable, a covenant incident to the sale of a business must be (1) reasonably necessary for the protection of the beneficiary; (2) reasonable as between the parties, and particularly as to the party restrained, considering time, space, purpose, and scope; and (3) not specifically injurious to the public. *Reiman Associates*, 102 Wis. 2d at 309, 306 N.W.2d at 295.

3. What time limitations have courts recognized as reasonable in the franchise context? If no franchise cases have been decided, what time limitations have been recognized in other contexts?

➤ How have they been related to the interests protected?

One Wisconsin appellate court and one Wisconsin circuit court found two-year post-term limitations reasonable in a franchise agreement not to compete. *Buchholz*

Insurance Agency, Inc. v. Ziegler, 188 Wis. 2d 603, 526 N.W.2d 279 (Ct. App. 1994); *H&R Block v. Otto*, No. 80-CV-7409 (Wis. Cir. Ct. Dane County 1982). The United States Court of Appeals for the Fifth Circuit found that a two-year post-term restraint in a franchise agreement restrictive covenant is reasonable under Wisconsin law. *Wilkinson v. Manpower, Inc.*, 531 F.2d 712 (5th Cir. 1976).

Under section 103.465, a covenant must provide a time limitation. A reasonable time limitation will not be read into an agreement. *Streiff v. American Family Mut. Ins. Co.*, 118 Wis. 2d 602, 348 N.W.2d 505 (1984). Time limitations in the employment agreement context are scrutinized for reasonableness in relation to the employer's interest to be protected. *Rollins Burdick Hunter of Wisconsin, Inc. v. Hamilton*, 101 Wis. 2d 460, 304 N.W.2d 752 (1981) (enforcing covenant against an insurance agent from competing against his former employer by soliciting insurance business for a period of the lesser of two years or the employee's period of employment with the agency). The time limitation is a factor in determining whether the covenant is oppressive and harsh on the employee or injurious to the interests of the general public. *Lakeside Oil Co. v. Slutsky*, 8 Wis. 2d 157, 98 N.W.2d 415 (1959) (upholding a two-year limitation in the employment agreement of a heating oil salesman who had only seasonal contact with customers, and noting that a shorter period may be necessary where customer contacts are more frequent). In the context of employment agreements, the courts have found two-year restrictions reasonable. *Id.*; *Eureka Laundry Co. v. Long*, 146 Wis. 205, 131 N.W. 412 (1911) (enforcing a two-year post-termination non-compete provision in the employment agreement of a laundry wagon driver for a route in the city of Milwaukee prohibiting the post-termination solicitation of any customers serviced on the route by the laundry wagon driver during the term of his employment); *Fields Foundation, Ltd. v. Christensen*, 103 Wis. 2d 465, 309 N.W.2d 125 (Ct. App. 1981) (upholding a two-year post-termination restriction in the employment agreement for a specialized medical center director, citing the medical communities' close identification of the director with the specialized medical center); *Chuck Wagon Catering, Inc. v. Raduege*, 88 Wis. 2d 740, 277 N.W.2d 787 (1979) (finding a one-year post-termination restriction reasonable to protect the plaintiff catering company's customer contacts by prohibiting the former lunch wagon driver from soliciting former customers on his lunch wagon route until new drivers had an opportunity to become acquainted with the former driver's customers, but noting that a two-year limitation is generally considered reasonable); *Pollack v. Calimag*, 157 Wis. 2d 222, 458 N.W.2d 591 (Ct. App. 1990) (enforcing a post-termination covenant in a pain clinic physician's employment agreement prohibiting the physician from engaging in a competing business for one year, and also prohibiting him from soliciting the pain clinic's patients for two years, citing the fact that the pain clinic's patients received relatively long-term therapy and rehabilitation).

In the sale of a business context, covenants not to compete are not subject to exacting scrutiny of reasonableness in relationship to the interest protected. *Reiman Associates, Inc. v. R/A Advertising, Inc.*, 102 Wis. 2d 305, 306 N.W.2d 292 (Ct. App. 1981). In the context of the sale of a business, Wisconsin courts allow restrictive covenants without time limitation for specified localities in the sale of business. *Madson v. Johnson*, 164 Wis. 612, 160 N.W. 1085 (1917); *Reiman Associates*, 102 Wis. 2d 305, 306 N.W.2d 292 (recognizing unlimited time rule, finding six-year limitation valid in that case).

4. What geographic limitations have courts recognized as reasonable in the franchise context?

- **How have they been related to the interests protected?**
- **Have courts recognized the legitimacy of protecting other franchisees from competition?**

The Eastern District of Wisconsin upheld a 45-mile post-term restrictive covenant against a franchisee in *H&R Block Eastern Tax Services, Inc. v. Vorpahl*, 255 F. Supp. 2d 930 (E.D. Wis. 2003). A Wisconsin circuit court found a 50-mile restriction unreasonable in a franchise agreement, where other competing franchisees were located within 13 miles; the court reduced the radius to 12 miles. *H&R Block v. Otto*, No. 80-CV-7409 (Wis. Cir. Ct. Dane County 1982). The United States Court of Appeals for the Fifth Circuit, applying Wisconsin law, held that a covenant not to compete in a franchise agreement preventing competition in the six counties served by the franchisee was reasonable under Wisconsin law. It also noted that the covenant would even be enforceable under the more demanding standard in section 103.465 applicable to employment contracts and that Wisconsin had adopted the RESTATEMENT rule that greater restrictions are more reasonable in sale of business contracts than in employment contracts. *Wilkinson v. Manpower, Inc.*, 531 F.2d 712, 716 (5th Cir. 1976). The U.S. District Court for the Eastern District of Wisconsin enforced a geographically unlimited in-term covenant in a franchise agreement stating, in part, that it was not convinced that the provisions of section 103.465 should be applied to a franchise agreement. In any event, it seemed reasonable that more restrictions would be allowed during the term of the agreement than after termination of the agreement. *Deutchland Enterprises, Ltd. v. Burger King Corp.*, Bus. Franchise Guide (CCH) ¶ 9609 (E.D. Wis. 1990).

In the employment agreement context, Wisconsin strictly enforces the rule that geographic limitation must be co-extensive with an employee's territory during employment. *Behnke v. Hertz Corp.*, 70 Wis. 2d 818, 235 N.W.2d 690 (1975). A covenant restricting the solicitation of former customers was held to satisfy the geographic area requirement. *Rollins Burdick Hunter of Wisconsin, Inc. v. Hamilton*, 101 Wis. 2d 460, 304 N.W.2d 752 (1981). The Wisconsin Court of Appeals has reaffirmed that an employment covenant's "geographic restraint is reasonable if it is limited to the area actually served." *Pollack v. Calimag*, 157 Wis. 2d at 238, 458 N.W.2d at 599 (Ct. App. 1990) (20-mile restraint upheld). Geographic limitations in the employment agreement context are scrutinized for reasonable and direct relationship to the employer's protected interests. *Behnke*, 70 Wis. 2d 818, 235 N.W.2d 690. "[L]imitation expressed in terms of particular clients or customers more closely approximates the area of the employer's vulnerability to unfair competition by a former employee and does not deprive the employee of legitimate competitive opportunities to which he is entitled." *Rollins Burdick Hunter*, 101 Wis. 2d at 466, 304 N.W.2d at 755.

The reasonableness of covenants in the sale of a business depends on the intent of the parties and whether the geographic restriction relates to the interest protected. *George M. Danke Co. v. Marten*, 207 Wis. 290, 241 N.W. 359 (1932) (new trial granted to consider the circumstances under which the agreement was executed, facts and customs relating to the business involved, and the practical construction of the agreement by the parties in order to ascertain the interest to be protected).

In the sale of a business context, the courts have upheld a covenant prohibiting a veterinarian from practicing veterinary medicine in the city and in the vicinity of the veterinary business sold by the veterinarian. *Madson v. Johnson*, 164 Wis. 612, 160 N.W. 1085 (1917).

5. What limitations on activities have courts recognized as reasonable in the franchise context?

No decision construing Wisconsin law has specifically addressed the scope of activity that may be encompassed by a covenant against competition in the franchise context.

6. Does the state recognize a difference between in-term and post-term covenants?

In *Deutchland Enterprises., Ltd. v. Burger King Corp.*, Bus. Franchise Guide (CCH) ¶ 9609 (E.D. Wis. 1990), the court held that the limitations of time and geographical scope set forth in section 103.465, which is most often applied in post-term employment cases, were not dispositive in an in-term franchise covenant. The court stated, "[i]t also seems reasonable that more restrictions would be allowed during the term of an agreement than after the termination of an agreement." *Id.* The court enforced the in-term covenant contained in the franchise agreement against a Wisconsin Burger King franchisee that had become a Hardee's franchisee in Michigan.

7. Has the state allowed enforcement of covenants against non-signatories (e.g., family members, newly formed corporations)?

Although the Wisconsin courts have not addressed this issue, an analogous issue arose in *Deutchland Enterprises, Ltd. v. Burger King Corp.*, Bus. Franchise Guide (CCH) ¶ 9609 (E.D. Wis. 1990). There, a Burger King franchisee obtained Hardee's franchise rights in violation of his Burger King franchise agreement, which contained an in-term non-compete provision. Burger King sought to terminate based on the violation. The franchisee attempted to cure the violation by a number of transactions that, ultimately, resulted in the Hardee's franchises being owned by a corporation nominally owned by a third party but whose obligations were guaranteed by the franchisee's owner, who paid rent to the franchisee's owner and, generally, was viewed by the court as a mere "shell" in a "shell game." Thus, while the non-compete was not enforced by preventing the franchisee or its owner from entering into a competitive business, it was considered good cause supporting the termination.

Although focusing on the enforcement of an arbitration agreement against a non-signatory, the Seventh Circuit, in *Everett v. Paul Davis Restoration, Inc.*, 771 F.3d 38 (2014), confirmed an arbitration award enforcing a restrictive covenant against the co-owner of a limited liability company formed to operate a franchise business even though she never signed an agreement because she received direct benefits from a franchise agreement, and thus was bound under doctrine of direct benefits estoppel to submit dispute regarding enforceability of post-termination non-compete provision to arbitration pursuant to franchise agreement. The franchise agreement was signed by her husband and co-owner, and she received the same benefits as her husband (including benefiting from trading upon the name, goodwill, reputation and other direct contractual benefits of the franchise agreement; the franchise agreement required her husband to form the LLC to operate the franchise; the wife was actively involved in operating the franchise during the term, and she and her husband colluded to avoid the franchise agreement's restrictive covenant).

8. Will the state modify, or "blue-pencil," or otherwise reduce a covenant found to be overbroad?

Wisconsin courts will not "blue-pencil" an employment agreement's restrictive covenant. Wis. Stat. § 103.465; *Streiff v. American Family Mutual Ins. Co.*, 118 Wis. 2d 602, 608, 348 N.W.2d 505, 509 (1984). Wisconsin courts will "blue line" a covenant in the sale of a business situation and enforce it to the extent necessary and reasonable under the circumstances. *Fullerton Lumber Co. v. Torborg*, 270 Wis. 133, 70 N.W.2d 585 (1955); *Streiff*, 118 Wis. 2d at 608, 348 N.W.2d at 509 (Wis. Stat. § 103.465 was enacted in response to the *Fullerton* holding, but the rule still applies to agreements incident to the sale of a business); *Reiman Associates, Inc. v. R/A Advertising, Inc.*, 102 Wis. 2d 305, 306 N.W.2d 292 (Ct. App. 1981).

A Wisconsin circuit court found a franchise agreement's restrictive covenant would be enforced to the extent necessary and reasonable under the circumstances. *H&R Block v. Otto*, No. 80-CV-7409 (Wis. Cir. Ct. Dane County 1982) (citing *Reiman Associates*, 102 Wis. 2d 305, 306 N.W.2d 292) (50-mile non-compete radius reduced to 12 miles based on court's conclusion that it was highly doubtful that a potential customer of tax preparation services would travel 50 miles for assistance). *See also H&R Block Eastern Tax Services, Inc. v. Vorpahl*, 255 F. Supp. 2d 930 (E.D. Wis. 2003) (rejecting applicability of Wis. Stat. § 103.465 to franchise agreement and finding that, accordingly, restrictive covenant would be enforceable to the extent reasonable; citing *Reiman*).

9. When does a non-compete period begin to run? Will courts equitably extend the term?

No decision construing Wisconsin law has specifically addressed when a non-compete period begins to run. While there are no decisions directly addressing whether a court will equitably extend the term, it has been held that under section 103.465, a provision extending the period in both the non-competition and non-solicitation clauses for the period of pre-enforcement non-compliance was unreasonable and consequently rendered the two-year time period in each clause unreasonable, void, and unenforceable, even if each clause were otherwise reasonable. *H&R Block Eastern Enterprises, Inc. v. Swenson*, 307 Wis. 2d 390, 745 N.W.2d 421 (Wis. App. 2008).

10. Are there additional nuances or peculiarities of the state's treatment of covenants in the franchising context?

The Wisconsin Fair Dealership Law may have a significant impact on the enforcement of restrictive covenants within Wisconsin franchise agreements. The existence of a restrictive covenant in a franchise or other distribution agreement increases the likelihood that the agreement will be classified as a "dealership agreement" protected by the WFDL. A restrictive covenant may help establish the "community of interest" element of the definition of "dealership." The restrictive covenant eliminates the franchisee's ability to maintain companion lines or products, and thus increases the franchisor's percentage of the franchisee's business, and demonstrates significant control by the franchisor over the conduct of the franchisee's business. *See generally Ziegler Co. v. Rexnord, Inc.*, 139 Wis. 2d 593, 407 N.W.2d 873 (1987); *Kenosha Liquor Co. v. Heublein, Inc.*, 895 F.2d 418 (7th Cir. 1990).

Restrictive covenants are not prohibited by the WFDL. However, their enforcement under the WFDL is subject to the strict notice and cure provisions and may be prohibited by injunction or an award of damages if it is determined that the restrictive covenant is not "essential and reasonable" or has been applied to the franchisee in a discriminatory manner, and thus contrary to the statutory good cause requirement for termination. *See* Wis. Stat. §§ 135.02(4)(a), .03, .04, and .06.

A restrictive covenant could itself be a substantial change in competitive circumstances if, for example, a franchisor attempted to impose the restriction after the initial franchise or dealership had been negotiated and/or partially performed, or otherwise attempted to impose a restriction that had not been part of the "dealership agreement." In that situation, the franchisor must impose the covenant only upon proper notice, and it must be reasonable, essential and non-discriminatory.

Wyoming

*by Lee R. Dickinson**

1. Has the state addressed covenants against competition in the context of franchising?

- **Does the state have a franchising statute or regulations that address covenants against competition?**
- **Does the state have a covenants statute of general applicability that would encompass franchise covenants?**
- **Have the courts addressed covenants in the context of franchising either under a statute or under the state's common law?**

Wyoming has not addressed covenants against competition in the context of franchising. Wyoming has no comprehensive franchise disclosure or registration statutes. Wyoming does have, however, a motor vehicle franchise act (Wyo. Stat. Ann. § 31-16-101 *et seq.*), a farm equipment fair dealership act (Wyo. Stat. Ann. § 40-20-101 *et seq.*), and a malt beverage distributor and manufacturer relationship law (Wyo. Stat. Ann. § 12-9-101 *et seq.*). Although the statutes do not address covenants against competition, the motor vehicle franchise act does prohibit a licensed manufacturer from unfairly competing with a dealer who is operating under an agreement or franchise from the manufacturer (Wyo. Stat. Ann. § 31-16-108(c)(vii)); the farm equipment fair dealership act prohibits suppliers from coercing a dealer into refusing to purchase equipment manufactured by another supplier (Wyo. Stat. Ann. § 40-20-114(a)(iii)); and the malt beverage distributor and manufacturer relationship law prohibits a manufacturer, or his or her agent or representative, from discriminating in price, programs, or terms offered to different franchisees, where the effect may substantially lessen competition (Wyo. Stat. Ann. § 12-9-104(a)(v)). Wyoming does not have a statute or regulation of general application addressing covenants against competition.

*Mr. Dickinson is the founder of Dickinson Law, P.C. in Cheyenne, Wyoming. He is also Of Counsel to Hathaway & Kunz, LLP in Cheyenne.

2. Have the courts articulated the "legitimate interests" of the franchisor that will support enforcement of a covenant against competition contained in a franchise agreement?

- **If so, what are they (e.g., protection of goodwill, protection of confidential information), and in what contexts did the issue arise?**
- **If not, what interests have been recognized in other contexts (e.g., employment agreements, the sale of business context)?**

Wyoming has not addressed non-competition agreements in the context of a franchise agreement, and consequently, the legitimate interests of a franchisor in the enforcement of covenants against competition have not been articulated. However, Wyoming courts have addressed the legitimate interests that would support the enforcement of covenants against competition in the context of employment agreements and the sale of a business.

The Wyoming Supreme Court has identified certain factors to consider when evaluating the reasonableness of a covenant not to compete in an employment context, including:

- the degree of inequality in bargaining power;
- the risk of the covenantee losing customers;
- the extent of respective participation by the parties in securing and retaining customers;
- the good faith of the covenantee;
- the existence of sources or general knowledge pertaining to the identity of customers;
- the nature and extent of the business position held by the covenantor;
- the covenantor's training, health, and education, and needs of his or her family;
- the current conditions of employment;
- the necessity of the covenantor changing his or her calling or residence; and
- the correspondence of the restraint with the need for protecting the legitimate interests of the covenantee.

See, e.g., Hopper v. All Pet Animal Clinic, Inc., 861 P.2d 531, 540 (Wyo. 1993).

In *Hopper v. All Pet Animal Clinic, Inc.*, the Supreme Court of Wyoming enforced a covenant not to compete against a former employee. Following graduation from college, the defendant relocated from Colorado to Laramie, Wyoming, to accept a position in plaintiff's veterinarian clinic. The parties entered into a written employment agreement that contained a provision whereby the defendant agreed that upon termination of her employment, she would not practice small animal medicine for a period of three years from the date of termination within five miles of the corporate limits of Laramie, Wyoming. When the defendant later left the employ of plaintiff, she purchased a veterinary clinic within the city of Laramie with a practice including large and small animals.

The district court determined that the covenant not to compete was enforceable as a matter of law and contained reasonable geographic and durational limits necessary to protect plaintiff's special interests. The special interests found by the district court included:[special influence over and direct contact with plaintiff's clients; access to client files; access to pricing policies; and instruction in practice development. Defendant was enjoined from practicing small animal medicine within five miles of the corporate limits of Laramie for a period of three years. The district court further found that the damages suffered by plaintiff were speculative and not proven by a preponderance of the evidence.

On appeal to the Wyoming Supreme Court, the judgment was affirmed but modified to reduce the durational limit of the covenant to a one-year period. In its opinion, the supreme court examined the special interests of the employer that would support the enforcement of the covenant in this case. The plaintiff, a veterinary clinic that specialized in a small animal practice, was entitled to protect its business from the detrimental impact of competition by employees who, but for their employment, would not have been able to gain a special influence over clients or customers. The defendant had relocated to Laramie upon completion of her degree to work for the plaintiff and had no significant professional contact with the community prior to that time. The defendant's exposure to clients, and the knowledge of clinic operations that her employer shared with her, had a monetary value. In addition, her employer was entitled to reasonable protection from irreparable harm. Further, the loss of clients to the defendant's practice sufficiently demonstrated actual harm from unfair competition.

The Wyoming Supreme Court also viewed the covenant in relation to other competing special interests and found that the covenant did not create a restraint of trade issue because the public would not suffer injury from enforcement of the covenant. The short-term unavailability of the defendant resulting from enforcement of the covenant was unlikely, as a matter of law, to injure the public since her services were neither unique nor uncommon and were available at several other veterinary clinics within Laramie.

Although criticized and clarified in *Hopper*, the following two cases remain informative. In *Ridley v. Krout*, 180 P.2d 124 (Wyo. 1947), the Wyoming Supreme Court refused to enforce a covenant against a former employee where the court found that the primary purpose of the covenant was to prevent the employee from quitting his present employment rather than to protect the employer's trade secrets. Similarly, in *Tench v. Weaver*, 374 P.2d 27 (Wyo. 1962), the Wyoming Supreme Court refused to enforce a covenant in an employment agreement, holding that for a restraint to be reasonable it must afford only fair protection to the interests of the party in whose favor it is given, and not be so broad as to interfere with the interests of the public.

In *CBM Geosolutions, Inc. v. Gas Sensing Technology Corp.*, 2009 WY 113, ¶ 10, 215 P.3d 1054, 1058 (2009), the Wyoming Supreme Court upheld a preliminary injunction issued by a district court, where there was a finding that the employer would "suffer immediate, great and irreparable harm and damage in the event that Defendants . . . are allowed to compete with [employer] in violation of the covenants-not-to-compete . . . ." The underlying interests considered by the court were:

- [defendants] had been trained by [plaintiff] in the innovative technology now used by [plaintiff] to provide services to its customers;
- the innovative technology used by the [plaintiff] company is essential to its competitive edge in the marketplace and that only a few companies provide similar services in the market;
- the services offered by [defendants] involved disclosing information on the process to customers, which would cause permanent

> loss of those customers because they would no longer require the services of a company like [plaintiff].

The *CBM* court also recited those factors identified by *Hopper* when determining the reasonableness of a covenant not to compete. *Id.* at ¶ 13.

The Wyoming Supreme Court has recognized a difference between the considerations of an employer-employee covenant not to compete and those of the purchase of a business. In *Holland v. Holland*, 2001 WY 113, ¶ 7, 35 P.3d 409, 411 (Wyo. 2001), the court dealt with a non-competition agreement associated with the division of marital property in a divorce action. The court stated, "courts are less disposed to sustain an agreement which forms part of a contract for employment, than where similar agreements are attached to a contract of sale. The reason for that difference is that in a case such as this [sale of a business], there is less likely to be hardship to the promissor and less chance of any injury to the public. An important part of our analysis must include a weighing of the right to contract with the public policy to the effect that, in some circumstances, such covenants are not favored." *Id.* at ¶ 12. The court also noted, "the most useful rule of thumb to be used in this case is that 'each case must turn on its own facts, with the courts seeking to divine the intent of the parties with respect to the dependency of particular promises, and to reach fair and reasonable results.' In addition, where it is clear that the covenant not to compete is at the heart of the agreement between the parties, so that it can be said that the parties would not have entered into that agreement without the covenant, then the agreement may be enforceable." *Id.* at ¶ 13.

In *WSP, Inc. v. Wyoming Steel Fabricators & Erectors, Inc.*, 2007 WY 80, 158 P.3d 651 (Wyo. 2007), the Wyoming Supreme Court upheld the finding of breach of a non-compete covenant in the context of a sale of business, where the party selling the business would not remove a sign containing the business name that hung in front of a competing business to that of the purchasing party. This act was held in violation because of the goodwill that had been purchased with the sale of the business. The *WSP, Inc.* case involved a selling party that entered into a non-compete agreement that included a prohibition on the use of the name "Wyoming Steel Products" in any manner that directly competed with the covenantee's business. *Id.* at ¶ 5. The selling party refused to remove a sign containing the name "Wyoming Steel Products" that hung in front of a building that he leased to a competitor of the purchasing party. The court held that "[i]n addition to refraining from direct competition in a general sense, WSP expressly promised not to use the 'Wyoming Steel Products' name 'in any manner that directly competes' with WSFE's business." *Id.* at ¶ 13. The court reasoned that "The goodwill of the business is often a more important aspect of the purchase of a business than the physical assets. An agreement by the seller to refrain from competition with the buyer can be critical to the transfer of goodwill. A transfer of goodwill cannot be effectively accomplished without an enforceable agreement by the transferor not to act so unreasonably to diminish the value of that which he is selling." *Id.* at ¶ 14.

---

3. What time limitations have courts recognized as reasonable in the franchise context? If no franchise cases have been decided, what time limitations have been recognized in other contexts?

➤ **How have they been related to the interests protected?**

The Wyoming Supreme Court has made the following statement with regard to time limitations on covenants not to compete:

> A durational limitation should be reasonably related to the legitimate interest which the employer is seeking to protect. Rest. (Second) of Contracts, *supra*, § 188 cmt. b. In determining whether a restraint extends for a longer period of time than necessary to protect the employer, the court must determine how much time is needed for the risk of injury to be reasonably moderated. When the restraint is for the purpose of protecting customer relationships, its duration is reasonable only if it is no longer than necessary for the employer to put a new [individual] on the job and for the new employee to have a reasonable opportunity to demonstrate his [or her] effectiveness to the customers. If a restraint on this ground is justifiable at all, it seems that a period of several months would usually be reasonable. If the selling or servicing relationship is relatively complex, a longer period may be called for. Courts seldom criticize restraints of six months or a year on the grounds of duration as such, and even longer restraints are often enforced.

Hopper v. All Pet Animal Clinic, 861 P.2d 531, 544–45 (Wyo. 1993) (citations omitted).

In *Hopper v. All Pet Animal Clinic, Inc., supra*, the Wyoming Supreme Court, addressing a covenant not to compete in an employment situation, reduced the three-year time restriction on competition to a one-year restriction, because it was unable to find a reasonable relationship between the three-year durational requirement and protection of the plaintiff's special interests. In evaluating whether a restraint extends for a longer period than necessary to protect the employer, the court must determine how much time is required for the risk of injury to be reasonably moderated. Based on the frequency of client visits, the court reasoned that a replacement veterinarian at the plaintiff's clinic would be able to demonstrate his or her own professionalism to virtually all of the clinic's clients in a one-year period. The court thus held, as a matter of law, that enforcement of a one-year durational limit was reasonable and sufficiently protected the interests of the plaintiff without violating public policy.

Similarly, in *Ridley v. Krout*, 180 P.2d 124 (Wyo. 1947), the Wyoming Supreme Court specifically noted that for a restrictive covenant to be reasonable, it must satisfy restrictions as to time and territory. There, the defendant had covenanted that he would not engage in a competitive business for a period of seven years after termination of his services. The court held that the covenant seemed designed to prevent the defendant from quitting the services of the plaintiff, and not primarily to prevent him from divulging secrets of the plaintiff. The court applied rationale from other cited cases, wherein the covenant would have required the defendant to essentially change his occupation, or move to a different community, which burden would be harsh. The court concluded that this time period was too long, thus upholding the trial court's holding that the period was unreasonable.

In *Holland v. Holland*, 2001 WY 113, ¶ 7, 35 P.3d 409, 412 (Wyo. 2001), the Wyoming Supreme Court, analogizing the situation to the sale of a business, upheld a lifetime covenant not to compete where the parties, in the disposition of the parties' marital estate upon divorce, agreed that the wife would receive the family dry-cleaning business, and the husband agreed that he would not compete in Albany County with the business for the remainder of his life. The husband challenged enforcement and asked that the restriction be reduced to no more than a two-year period. The *Holland* court stated that the husband must clearly demonstrate that the covenant not to compete was unreasonable with respect to the lifetime duration provision. The court ultimately held that "under the unique circumstances of this case, Husband has failed to demonstrate that the lifetime covenant not to compete is unreasonable. Husband voluntarily agreed to the covenant as part of arm's length negotiations and without coercion from the district court, he received in excess of $300,000.00 as consideration for his agreement (as well as receiving all of the parties' real property, much of which was income producing), and Husband had evinced a desire to drive Wife out of business through direct competition (and he had the financial means to do so)." *Id.* at ¶ 20, 415.

4. What geographic limitations have courts recognized as reasonable in the franchise context?

- **How have they been related to the interests protected?**
- **Have courts recognized the legitimacy of protecting other franchisees from competition?**

Wyoming Courts have not addressed the geographic limitations on non-competition agreements in the franchise context. However, Wyoming has addressed geographical limitations on covenants not to compete in relation to employment. In *Hopper v. All Pet Animal Clinic, Inc.*, 861 P.2d 531 (Wyo. 1993), the Wyoming Supreme Court found that a restriction restraining the defendant from conducting business within a five-mile radius of Laramie, Wyoming, was reasonable. Reasonable geographic restraints are generally limited to the area in which the former employee actually worked or from which clients were drawn. The evidence in *Hopper* indicated that clients of the plaintiff were located throughout the county surrounding Laramie. The court stated that, despite Wyoming's rural nature, the five-mile restriction effectively limited unfair competition without presenting an undue hardship and that the defendant could have opened a practice at other locations within the county.

In *Ridley v. Krout*, 180 P.2d 124 (Wyo. 1947), the Wyoming Supreme Court found that a restriction restraining the defendant from conducting business in Sheridan County, Johnson County, and Campbell County, Wyoming, was unreasonable as to territory. The court noted that the case did not deal with a salesperson or customers in a special line of business, but with repair work on various mechanical devices necessary for numerous inhabitants in each county identified in the covenant. It was impractical to expect the citizens of the city of Gillette to travel a distance of over 100 miles to have bicycles, lawnmowers, or other mechanical devices repaired or to have keys made or safes opened. This type of geographic restraint would be contrary to public interest, depriving the citizens of a particular city of the opportunity of having the defendant present at a place where work could be performed in a prompt and reasonable fashion.

In *CBM Geosolutions, Inc. v. Gas Sensing Technology Corp.*, 2009 WY 113, ¶ 13, 215 P.3d 1054, 1059 (Wyo. 2009), the Wyoming Supreme Court upheld a district court preliminary injunction where there was sufficient evidence that a covenant not to compete existed in writing, the document was signed ancillary to a legitimate employment relationship that constituted reasonable consideration, and a party presented evidence that "could lead the court to conclude that a restriction that was national in nature but narrowly tailored to one aspect of the industry was reasonable under the circumstances."

Recently, in *Brown v. Best Home Health & Hospice*, 2021 WY 83, 491 P.3d 1021 (Wyo. 2021), the Wyoming Supreme Court held that the trial court abused its discretion by granting a temporary restraining order against three nurses and enforcing a 50-mile-radius agreement not to compete. In reversing the temporary injunction and remanding to the trial court, the court held that the employer had not provided sufficient evidence that it was likely to succeed on the merits of its claims because there had been no analysis of the public policy impact of enforcing the non-compete covenant on the availability of nursing services in the impacted area (as well as a lack of sufficient consideration for already-employed nurses in granting the covenant).

5. What limitations on activities have courts recognized as reasonable in the franchise context?

The Wyoming courts have not addressed what restrictions on activities would be deemed reasonable in the franchising context. Wyoming would likely restrict certain activities based upon the legitimate interests sought to be protected. For instance, in the employment context, the Wyoming Supreme Court stated that "[e]mployers are entitled to protect their business from the detrimental impact of competition by employees who, but for their employment, would have had the ability to gain a special influence over clients or customers." *Hopper v. All Pet Animal Clinic*, 861 P.2d 531, 542 (Wyo. 1993). The court also stated, "Wyoming has previously recognized that the legitimate interests of the employer, covenantee, which may be protected from competition include: (a) the employer's trade secrets which have been communicated to the employee during the course of employment; (b) onfidential information communicated by the employer to the employee, but not involving trade secrets, such as information on a unique business method; and (c) special influence by the employee obtained during the course of employment over the employer's customers." *Id.* at 540.

The *Hopper* court discussed the special interests of the employer and determined that the employee's introduction to the employer's clients, client files, pricing policies, and practice development techniques provided information that exceeded the skills that the employee brought with her to her employment and that the proven loss of 187 of the employer's clients demonstrated actual harm from unfair competition. The *Hopper* court ultimately held that the non-compete was violated based upon the interests of the employer that the non-compete sought to protect.

6. Does the state recognize a difference between in-term and post-term covenants?

The Wyoming courts have not addressed any differences in enforcement that may be appropriate between in-term and post-term covenants.

7. Has the state allowed enforcement of covenants against non-signatories (e.g., family members, newly formed corporations)?

Wyoming has not yet directly addressed this issue. However, the federal district court for the District of Wyoming has addressed the issue of enforcement of non-competition covenants against family members, declined to enforce the covenant against those persons who were not parties to the agreement, and held that the latter were therefore not bound by the covenant's provisions. In *Keller v. California Liquid Gas Corp.*, 363 F. Supp. 123 (D. Wyo. 1973), the sellers of a liquid petroleum gas appliance business agreed that for a period of ten years they would not engage in a competing business within certain designated areas of Montana. In exchange for the covenant, the sellers received $100,000 to be disbursed in ten yearly installments of $10,000.

The sellers died before receiving the first installment. Payments were made for three additional years following their deaths and then were terminated by the buyer prior to the expiration of the ten-year period. The *Keller* plaintiffs, heirs of the sellers, sued for the balance owed under the non-competition agreement. The purchaser counterclaimed, alleging in the alternative that the plaintiffs had violated the covenant by engaging in the liquified petroleum business, or that the covenant not to compete was personal, terminating upon the death of the covenantors. The United States District Court found that the heirs at law of the sellers were not signatories to the purchase agreement covenant and were not bound by its provisions. The covenant not to compete was found to be personal in nature and ceased upon the death of the covenantors. No monies were due from purchaser to the heirs subsequent to the death of the covenantors, and the purchaser was entitled to recover the money paid after the sellers' deaths.

8. Will the state modify, "blue-pencil" or otherwise reduce a covenant found to be overbroad?

This is unlikely. In February 2022, the Wyoming Supreme Court expressly abandoned the "blue-pencil" rule, at least in the employment context, holding that "it is no longer tenable for courts to use the blue pencil rule to modify unreasonable noncompete agreements." *Hassler v. Circle C Resources*, 2022 WY 8, ¶ 1, ___ P.3d ___. Charlene Hassler, a certified nursing assistant, was employed by Circle C Resources to provide home health care services to its patients. Ms. Hassler worked with one patient in particular who required full-time habilitation care. Ms. Hassler left the employ of Circle C and went to work for another health care provider but continued to perform full-time habilitation care for the same patient. Circle C sued Ms. Hassler for breach of the covenant not to compete, which required that Ms. Hassler, for a period of 24 months after her employment ceased, not perform any competitive services in any geographic area in which Circle C has marketed its services in the preceding year. The covenant not to compete also contained its own, express "blue-pencil" provision under the heading "Maximum Restrictions of Time, Scope, and Geographic Area Intended."

After holding that the restrictions contained in the covenant not to compete were unreasonable, the court held that the

> blue pencil rule adopted in *Hopper* is contrary to traditional contract law, has worked an injustice on employees, and has contributed to uncertainty in business relationships by encouraging employers to draft overly broad, unreasonable restraints on trade. . . . We, therefore, overrule *Hopper*'s adoption of the liberal blue pencil rule. Returning to our roots, a noncompete agreement which includes unreasonable restrictions on trade violates public policy and is invalid.

Id. at ¶ 29.

In reaching its holding, the Wyoming Supreme Court went to great lengths to point out disparities in the relationship between Ms. Hassler, as employee, and Circle C, as employer. For example, the court noted that "Circle C was paid $121,142.10 per year through Medicaid waiver programs[, and] . . . in turn, paid Ms. Hassler approximately $26,400 per year, resulting in an annual net profit to Circle C of $94,742.10." *Id.* at ¶ 8. The court also noted that Ms. Hassler was paid "significantly more" by her new employer. *Id.* at ¶ 6. The court then stated that the "blue pencil rule was intended to be a tool to prevent *former employees* from unfairly competing with *employers* . . . [but] in practice, the rule places an unfair burden on *employees* and creates uncertainty in *business relationships*." *Id.* at ¶ 22 (emphasis added). The court reasoned that, "[b]y rejecting the liberal blue pencil rule, we encourage *employers* to incorporate only reasonable trade restraints into their *employment* contracts and to assure such restraints are reasonably tied to legitimate interests requiring protection." *Id.* at ¶ 28 (emphasis added).

For additional reading, *see also Skaf v. Wyoming Cardiopulmonary Services*, 2021 WY 105, 495 P.3d 887, which foretold of the holding in *Hassler*. In a special concurring opinion, Justice Davis stated, "I write separately because I believe the blue pencil rule is antithetical to our principles of contract enforcement and our recognized goals of fair competition and certainty in business. . . . [I]n an appropriate case, I would go farther than the majority opinion and eliminate the [blue pencil] rule." *Hassler*, 2022 WY at ¶ 51. As the court stated in direct response to Justice Davis's special concurrence, "This is an appropriate case." *Hassler* at ¶ 21.

While the facts of the *Hassler* case are squarely in the employment context, it is likely that the "all-or-nothing" rule of construction of covenants not to compete would be extended to franchise relationships, particularly in the presence of disparities in bargaining power between franchisee and franchisor; it is less clear whether and how these new principles would be extended to arm's length business purchases that contain covenants not to compete. There are certainly distinguishable facts, however, between the *Hassler* and *Skaf* cases and most franchise relationships.

9. When does a non-compete period begin to run? Will courts equitably extend the term?

The Wyoming Supreme Court has not addressed when a non-compete period begins to run. However, the court has dealt with a typical employment situation in which a non-compete period begins to run upon the occurrence of a triggering event, such as where an employment contract specifies the period of non-competition that begins on termination of employment. Even when the court has modified the period of non-competition to a lesser period than contemplated under the non-competition agreement, the court held that the modified period began on the date of termination. *Hopper v. All Pet Animal Clinic*, 861 P.2d 531, 547 (Wyo. 1993).

Thus far, the Wyoming Supreme Court has not equitably extended a non-compete period, nor does it appear to have been addressed. It is unlikely, however, that Wyoming would extend a non-compete period beyond the terms agreed to by the parties. Wyoming has taken the position adopted in the RESTATEMENT (SECOND) OF CONTRACTS, section 184, which does not permit the court to add to the terms of the covenant. "Sometimes a term is unenforceable on grounds of public policy because it is too broad, even though a narrower term would be enforceable. In such a situation, under Subsection (2), the court may refuse to enforce only part of the term, while enforcing the other part of the term as well as the rest of the agreement. The court's power in such a case is not a power of reformation, however, and it will not, in the course of determining what part of the term to enforce, add to the scope of the term in any way." *Hopper*, 861 P.2d at 546 (citing RESTATEMENT (SECOND) OF CONTRACTS § 184 cmt. b).

10. Are there additional nuances or peculiarities of the state's treatment of covenants in the franchising context?

An additional item of note that has been addressed by the Wyoming Supreme Court was the recognition of a five-part test to determine whether a covenant not to compete is valid within the employment context. The court said, "A valid and enforceable covenant not to compete requires a showing that the covenant is: (1) in writing; (2) part of a contract of employment; (3) based on reasonable consideration; (4) reasonable in durational and geographical limitations; and (5) not against public policy." *Hopper v. All Pet Animal Clinic*, 861 P.2d 531, 540 (Wyo. 1993). In the context of a sale of business, a Wyoming court will similarly look at public policy and the reasonableness of the covenant; however, in the sale of a business, Wyoming courts are less likely to set aside the covenant not to compete. *See Holland v. Holland*, 2001 WY 113, ¶¶ 12–13, 35 P.3d 409, 413 (Wyo. 2001) ("The reason for that difference is that in a case such as this [sale of a business], there is less likely to be hardship to the promissor and less chance of any injury to the public. An important part of our analysis must include a weighing of the right to contract with the public policy to the effect that, in some circumstances, such covenants are not favored . . . . In addition, where it is clear that the covenant not to compete is at the heart of the agreement between the parties, so that it can be said that the parties would not have entered into that agreement without the covenant, then the agreement may be enforceable."). *But see Brown*, 2021 WY 83, ¶ 36, 491 P.3d 1021, 1033 (reversing temporary injunction against employee nurses because employer made "insufficient showing of probable success" on the basis of public policy impact on the availability of nursing services within the restricted geographic area).

Wyoming has addressed the burden of proof when addressing covenants not to compete, stating, "[t]he initial burden is on the employer to prove the covenant is reasonable and has a fair relation to, and is necessary for, the business interests for which protection is sought." *Hopper*, 861 P.2d at 539 (citing *Tench v. Weaver*, 374 P.2d 27, 29 (Wyo. 1962)). Once that burden is met, "[t]he employee is then given the chance to rebut the presumptive enforceability of the covenant by showing either that he has no company trade assets to abuse, or that the assets made available to him properly belong to him, or that the interests asserted by the employer may be protected by a partial enforcement of the covenant. If the employee prevails in this latter regard then the covenant may be tailored by the court to comport with the equities of the case." *Id.* at 547. The opposite is true in the circumstance of the sale of a business, where the burden is placed on the one challenging the covenant not to compete. *Holland v. Holland*, 2001 WY 113, ¶ 10, 35 P.3d 409, 413 (Wyo. 2001).

Another item of note came from the Bankruptcy Court for the District of Wyoming, which held that money received for granting a covenant not to compete constitutes ordinary income to the covenantor and may be amortized over the life of the covenant by the purchasers. *In re Turner*, 147 B.R. 989, 995 (Bankr. D. Wyo. 1992). Additionally, the court stated that when "there is no agreement between a buyer and seller to allocate any part of a purchase price to a non-compete covenant, the seller may treat all proceeds as capital gain." *Id.*

Bankruptcy Issues

*by Craig Tractenberg**

1. When a franchisee files bankruptcy, can the franchise agreement be rejected, thereby eliminating any obligation not to compete?

Upon filing bankruptcy, creditors are enjoined from terminating and generally enforcing the franchise agreement absent court approval. A bankruptcy court may grant relief from the automatic stay imposed by 11 U.S.C. § 362. *In re Mainous*, 610 B.R. 916 (Bankr. S.D. Ala. 2019) (relief from stay to enforce post-term non-compete).

A party filing bankruptcy, the "debtor," is granted the opportunity under the Bankruptcy Code to assume, assign, or reject executory contracts. The term "executory contract" is not defined by the Bankruptcy Code but "generally includes contracts on which performance remains due to some extent on both sides." H.R. Rep. No. 595, 95th Cong., 1st Sess., 340, 347 (1977). Most courts have adopted Professor Countryman's definition: "a contract under which the obligation of both the bankrupt and the other party to the contract are so far unperformed that the failure of either to complete performance would constitute a material breach excusing the performance of the other." Countryman, *Executory Contracts in Bankruptcy, Part I*, 57 Minn. L. Rev. 439, 460 (1973). Franchise agreements are routinely held to be executory contracts. *See, e.g., Moody v. Amoco Oil Co.*, 734 F.2d 1200 (7th Cir.), *cert. denied*, 496 U.S. 982 (1984). Where a franchise agreement is assumed, the franchisee is obligated to assume all of the obligations, including the covenant not to compete. The debtor may not assign its franchise agreement without first assuming its obligations. *See* 11 U.S.C. § 365(b) and (c).

The debtor may also choose to "reject" the franchise agreement and its obligations as part of the statutory scheme of the Bankruptcy Code to permit rehabilitation. Court permission to reject the contract permits a bankruptcy court to allow the debtor to breach the franchise agreement and substitute future performances with a damage claim.

Modern cases hold that a covenant not to compete may be enforced even if the franchise agreement, or other agreement containing such a covenant not to compete, is rejected. Modern caselaw supports the proposition that rejection of

*Craig Tractenberg is a partner in the law firm of Fox Rothschild LLP resident in the New York and Pennsylvania offices and is a member of the bars of Florida, New Jersey, New York, and Pennsylvania. In the previous edition, he was assisted by Christopher Desidero and Robert Christmas, of the law firm of Nixon Peabody LLP.

an executory contract is not the cancellation but rather a breach of the contract, and therefore, available remedies may include enforcement of a covenant against competition. *Don & Lin Trucking Co., Inc.*, 110 B.R. 562 (Bankr. N.D. Ala. 1990); *In re Thomas*, 133 B.R. 92 (Bankr. N.D. Ohio, 1991); *In re Printronics*, 189 B.R. 995 (Bankr. N.D. Fla. 1995); *In re Steaks to Go*, 226 B.R. 35 (Bankr. E.D. Mo. 1998); *In re Klein*, 218 B.R. 787 (Bankr. W.D. Pa. 1998) (". . . very purpose of the covenant is to govern the relationship between the parties *after* the demise of the underlying contract, even though the covenant is not an executory contract in and of itself"); *In re Sir Speedy*, 256 B.R. 657 (D. Mass. 2000); *see also In re Annabel*, 263 B.R. 19, 28 (Bankr. N.D.N.Y. 2001) ("in the context of a Chapter 7 bankruptcy, the discharge injunction will not affect the enforcement of a party's injunctive breach remedy on a debtor's covenant not to compete where compliance requires simple abstention from conduct and does not give rise to monetary payment"); *In re Alongi*, 272 B.R. 148, 155 (Bankr. D. Md. 2001) ("The enforceability of a covenant not to compete against a debtor does not turn on whether the contract containing the covenant is rejected, because rejection does not terminate the contract.") (quoting *Executory Contracts Revisited: A Reply to Professor Westbrook*, 62 U. Colo. L. Rev. 1, 18 (1991)); *Cinicola v. Scharffenberger*, 248 F.3d 110, 119 (3d Cir. 2001) (non-competition covenant contained in an employment agreement that was rejected is continued in effect because it remained enforceable under state law); *Freedom Medical, Inc. v. Janssens (In re Janssens)*, 449 B.R. 42, 61 (Bankr. D. Md. 2010) (covenant not to compete enforceable even after a contract is rejected by operation of law); *Top Rank, Inc. v. Ortiz (In re Ortiz)*, 400 B.R. 755, 769 (C.D. Cal. 2009) (rejection of a contract does not affect a covenant not to compete if it is otherwise enforceable under state law); *Abboud v. Ground Round, Inc. (In re Ground Round, Inc.)*, 335 B.R. 253, 263 (B.A.P. 1st Cir. 2005) (covenant not to compete did not give rise to a "claim" and therefore was not subject to discharge).

These modern cases are supported by the decision of the United States Supreme Court in *Mission Products Holdings v. Tempnology (In re Tempnology)*, 587 US. ___, 139 S. Ct. 1652 (2019), holding that the rejection of a trademark license is to be treated as a breach of contract under common law.

Although not explicitly overruled by *In re Tempnology*, some cases granted relief from the non-compete on policy grounds that enforcement of any portion of the rejected contract would hinder the fresh start intended by the Bankruptcy Code. *See, e.g., Burger King Corp. v. Rovine Corp. (In re Rovine Corp.)*, 6 B.R. 661 (Bankr. W.D. Tenn. 1980) (rejection of franchise included rejection of covenant); *Silk Plants, Etc., Franchise Systems, Inc. v. Register (In re Register)*, 95 B.R. 73, 74 (Bankr. M.D. Tenn.), *aff'd*, 100 B.R. 360 (M.D. Tenn. 1989) (covenant is rejected with franchise agreement because no evidence exists that covenant is a separate contract); *JRT, Inc. v. TCBY Systems, Inc. (In re JRT, Inc.)*, 121 B.R. 314 (Bankr. W.D. Mich. 1990) (covenant is an "integral, nondivisible part of the executory franchise agreement: therefore . . . may be rejected").

2. Does the franchisee's obligation under a covenant not to compete qualify as a "debt" that is dischargeable in bankruptcy?

If the franchise agreement is not rejected, the next question is whether a franchisee's discharge under the Bankruptcy Code prevents a franchisor from enforcing the non-competition provision. The Bankruptcy Code's goal is to give debtors a "fresh start." *See, e.g., Grogan v. Garner*, 498 U.S. 279, 286 (1991). One of the ways in which that goal is accomplished is by granting the debtor a complete discharge for all "debts" existing as of the time of the bankruptcy. 11 U.S.C. §§ 727(b) and 1141(d). A "debt" is a "liability on a claim." 11 U.S.C. § 101(12). A "claim" includes a "right to payment." 11 U.S.C. § 101(5)(A). Thus, a bankruptcy typically will result in the discharge of all claims for monetary damages that existed at the time of the bankruptcy.

In addition to a "right to payment," a dischargeable "claim" also includes a "right to an *equitable* remedy for breach of performance if such breach gives rise to a right of payment, whether or not such right to an equitable remedy is reduced to judgment, fixed, contingent, matured, unmatured, disputed, undisputed, secured, or unsecured . . . ." 11 U.S.C. § 101(5)(B) (emphasis added). As a result, when a creditor seeks an equitable remedy, such a request may or may not qualify as a "claim." Although the precise analysis varies, the majority of courts have held that a franchisor's request for an injunction to enforce a covenant not to compete does *not* come within the definition of a "claim" and therefore is not discharged by the franchisee's filing for bankruptcy.

Under section 101(5)(B) of the Bankruptcy Code, a dischargeable "claim" includes a right to an equitable remedy for breach "if such breach gives rise to a right of payment." The starting point for interpreting this language is the Supreme Court's decision in *Ohio v. Kovacs*, 469 U.S. 274 (1985). In that case, a lower court had issued an injunction requiring the debtor to clean up environmental contamination. The debtor then declared bankruptcy, and the state of Ohio sought his assets to pay for the unfinished environmental work. In determining whether enforcement of an injunction was a "claim" for bankruptcy purposes, *Kovacs* focused on the fact that the only way for the debtor to comply with the injunction was to pay a third party to perform the required cleanup. *Id.* at 282. Because enforcement of the injunction would require an expenditure of money by the debtor, the Court held that the request for enforcement did qualify as a "claim" and was dischargeable in bankruptcy.

Since *Kovacs*, most courts have held that a franchisor's request for injunctive relief to enforce a covenant not to compete does not qualify as a "claim" and therefore is not dischargeable in bankruptcy. The case of *Udell v. Standard Carpetland USA, Inc.*, 18 F.3d 403 (7th Cir. 1994), involved an employee who had a three-year post-termination covenant not to compete. The *Udell* court examined *Kovacs* and the legislative history of section 101(5)(B). The court held that "a right to an equitable remedy for breach of performance is a 'claim' if the same breach also gives rise to a right to a payment 'with respect to' the equitable remedy. If the right to payment is an 'alternative' to the right to an equitable remedy, the necessary relationship clearly exists, for the two remedies would be substitutes for one another." *Id.* at 408. The court therefore looked to the governing substantive law and observed that "Indiana law permits the award of an injunction in addition to liquidated damages." *Id.* Thus, because an injunction and an award of damages were "cumulative and not alternative," the request for injunctive relief was not a "claim" and was not discharged as part of the bankruptcy. *Id.* at 409.

The U.S. Court of Appeals for the Sixth Circuit became the first federal appellate court to address the enforceability of a covenant against competition subsequent to a bankruptcy filing in the franchise context. In *Kennedy v. Medicap Pharmacies, Inc.*, 267 F.3d 493 (6th Cir. 2001), two franchisees of a nationwide pharmacy chain purported to terminate their franchise agreement, but continued to operate their pharmacy at the same location in violation of the two-year post-termination non-competition provision contained in the franchise agreement. The franchisor commenced an action to enforce the covenant, and the franchisees filed for bankruptcy. The *Kennedy* court quoted the holding in *Udell*, agreed with it, and then set out its own holding as follows: "The right to equitable relief constitutes a claim only if it is an alternative to a right to payment or if compliance with the equitable order will itself require the payment of money." *Id.* at 497. Thus, under this analysis, there are two questions that must be answered in determining whether a franchisor will be able to enforce a covenant against competition against a franchisee who has filed bankruptcy: (1) under the applicable state law, would an injunction be "an alternative to a right to payment"? and (2) would compliance with an injunction enforcing the covenant against competition require the franchisee to pay money? Only if both questions are answered in the negative can the franchisor enforce its covenant against competition after a franchisee's bankruptcy filing.

The *Kennedy* court noted first that "compliance with an injunction would not require the expenditure of money. The Kennedys would simply be required to cease operating the pharmacy in violation of the franchise agreement." *Id.* The court concluded that under Iowa law, an injunction was not an "alternative to a right to payment for future injuries." *Id.* Because both portions of the two-part inquiry were answered in the negative, the Sixth Circuit held that the franchisor's request for an injunction was not discharged by the franchisee's bankruptcy filing.

Other cases concluding that a covenant against competition is not dischargeable in bankruptcy include *Sir Speedy, Inc. v. Morse*, 256 B.R. 657 (D. Mass. 2000); *In re Reppond*, 238 B.R. 442 (Bankr. E.D. Ark. 1999); *Kwik-Kopy Corp. v. Klein*, 218 B.R. 787 (Bankr. W.D. Pa. 1998); *In re Printronics, Inc.*, 189 B.R. 995 (Bankr. N.D. Fla. 1995); *In re Nyren*, 187 B.R. 424 (Bankr. D. Conn. 1995); *In re Hughes*, 166 B.R. 103 (Bankr. S.D. Ohio 1994); *In re May*, 141 B.R. 940 (Bankr. S.D. Ohio 1992); *In re Thomas*, 133 B.R. 92 (Bankr. N.D. Ohio 1991); *In re Oseen*, 133 B.R. 527 (Bankr. D. Idaho 1991); *In re Noco, Inc.*, 76 B.R. 839 (Bankr. N.D. Fla. 1987); *In re Cooper*, 47 B.R. 842 (Bankr. W.D. Mo. 1985); *In re Peitz*, 53 B.R. 336 (Bankr. M.D. Fla. 1985); and *In re Cox*, 53 B.R. 829 (Bankr. M.D. Fla. 1985); *In re Annabel*, 263 B.R. 19 (Bankr. N.D.N.Y. 2001). *See also Tantopia Franchising Co., LLC v. West Coast Tans of PA, LLC*, 918 F. Supp. 2d 407 (E.D. PA 2013) (post-term non-compete enforced after bankruptcy where debtor did not disclose in bankruptcy) and *In re Roberts*, 607 B.R. 635 (Bankr. N.D. Ill. 2019) (injunction denied on the merits).

A minority of courts, however, have held that an obligation under a covenant against competition is dischargeable relying on an interpretation of state law. In *Maids International, Inc. v. Ward*, 194 B.R. 703 (Bankr. D. Mass. 1996), a former franchisee, while admittedly in breach of its covenant against competition, filed bankruptcy. The court framed the issue as follows: "Do the nondebtor's injunctive rights constitute a 'claim' so as to be subject to discharge?" *Id.* at 708. The *Maids Int'l* court answered this question in the affirmative. The viability of *Maids Int'l* was called into some doubt by the subsequent opinion in *Sir Speedy, Inc. v. Morse*, 256 B.R. at 658 (2000). In that case, as in *Maids Int'l*, the bankruptcy judge had held that the franchisor's right to enforce the covenant against competition was a dischargeable "claim." *Id.* In *Sir Speedy*, however, the franchisor appealed the bankruptcy court's decision to the U.S. District Court for the District of Massachusetts, which reversed and held that "the breach of a noncompete agreement does not give rise to a right to payment and thus is not a 'claim' under § 101(5)(B)." *Id.*

In re Kilpatrick, 160 B.R. 560 (Bankr. E.D. Mich. 1993), involved a contract for the sale of business assets and the seller's subsequent breach of the contractual provision prohibiting competition after the sale. The *Kilpatrick* court held that the buyer-creditor's request for injunctive relief was discharged by the seller-debtor's bankruptcy unless the buyer could prove that the breach of the covenant "would not entitle it to monetary damages under Michigan law." *Id.* at 565. After examining the evidence, the court determined that the buyer-creditor had failed to prove that "the breach of the covenant would result in damages too difficult to estimate, and that specific performance/injunctive relief would therefore be its only viable remedy." *Id.* at 566. The difference between *Kilpatrick* and the other cases discussed above is that the *Kilpatrick* court determined the propriety and availability of injunctive relief to enforce the covenant against competition. Normally, the bankruptcy courts simply hold that the request for injunctive relief is not automatically discharged as part of the bankruptcy, leaving it to the state or federal courts to decide whether an injunction would actually be issued.

In re Silk Plants, Etc. Franchise Systems, Inc., 100 B.R. 360 (M.D. Tenn. 1989), is another case in which a franchisor sought to enjoin its insolvent former franchisee from violating its covenant not to compete. The *Silk Plants* court affirmed the bankruptcy court's holding that the franchisor was not entitled to the requested injunction. *Id.* at 362–63. As in *Kilpatrick*, this result was based on the fact that the bankruptcy court "found that it could reduce the injury suffered by the [franchisor] to a dollar-amount." *Id.* at 362. Because monetary damages were sufficient to protect the franchisor's interests, it was entitled to assert such a claim for damages as part of the bankruptcy proceedings, but was not granted an injunction against future breaches of the covenant not to compete. *Id.* at 362–63.

3. What is the effect on a covenant against competition if the franchisor files for bankruptcy?

➤ If a franchisor is liquidated, can the purchaser of its assets enforce a covenant against competition contained in a franchise agreement?

Although this precise question has not been adjudicated, the issues are a mixture of state and bankruptcy law. As a matter of state law, most jurisdictions hold that covenants not to compete are assignable. *See, e.g., J.H. Renarde, Inc. v. Sims*, 711 A.2d 410 (N.J. Super. Ct. Ch. Div. 1998) (rejecting the defendant's argument that a noncompetition agreement was not enforceable by a successor employer); *A. Fink & Sons v. Goldberg*, 139 A. 408 (N.J. Ch. 1927) ("upon the sale of a business, a restrictive covenant made in connection with such sale is assignable without express words to that effect, and passes as an incident of the business sold"). Some jurisdictions do not permit assignment absent express authority to assign. *E.g., All-Pak, Inc. v. Johnston*, 694 A.2d 347 (Pa. Super. Ct. 1997).

Under section 363(e) of the Bankruptcy Code, assets may be sold under conditions imposed by the bankruptcy court, and any party with an interest in the assets sold may request that the sale be conditioned on the assignability and enforcement or nonenforcement of the covenant not to compete. If a potential bidder for the assets were unsure regarding the assignability or enforceability of the assets, this insecurity could chill bidding or rehabilitation of the debtor; accordingly, it may well be within the province of the bankruptcy court to determine these disputes when authorizing sale or disposition of the assets. *In the matter of Annabel*, 235 B.R. 19 (Bankr. N.D.N.Y. 2001) (discussing considerations in reorganization cases where covenants not to compete may be enforced).

4. If a franchisor reorganizes under Chapter 11, does it lose the right to enforce non-competition provisions in its franchise agreements?

The goal of Chapter 11 bankruptcy is for the debtor to file a plan of reorganization that will be approved by the creditors and confirmed by the bankruptcy court. Once a Chapter 11 plan is confirmed, the plan is in essence a new contract between the debtor and its creditors. Chapter 11 plans can be liquidating plans, such as when the debtor company sells its assets in an orderly fashion, or rehabilitative plans, where the debtor company reorganizes its financial affairs as a going concern. In the present context, the question is whether a franchisor, by virtue of reorganizing under Chapter 11, loses the right to enforce non-competition provisions contained in its franchise agreements.

If the franchise agreement was terminated pre-petition, the franchisor's Chapter 11 filing does not affect the enforceability of a covenant not to compete.

A simple scenario occurs when a franchise agreement contains a post-termination non-competition obligation, the agreement is terminated by either party, and the franchisor subsequently files for bankruptcy protection under Chapter 11. Under those circumstances, the bankruptcy filing should not affect the franchisor's ability to enforce the non-competition provision.

Generally, when a debtor files for bankruptcy, all property owned by the debtor at the time of the filing becomes property of the estate. 11 U.S.C. § 541(a)(1). This includes "all legal or equitable interests of the debtor in property as of the commencement of the case," (*id.*) a category that is broad enough to include all causes of action for breach of contract that accrued prior to the bankruptcy filing. *See, e.g., In re Ryerson*, 739 F.2d 1423, 1425 (9th Cir. 1984). Thus, if a franchisee breaches a post-termination non-competition obligation prior to the franchisor's Chapter 11 filing, the franchisor's claim for that breach of contract simply becomes part of the bankruptcy estate to be pursued by the trustee like any other contract claim. If the franchise agreement was not terminated pre-petition, the effect of the Chapter 11 filing depends on whether the franchisor assumes or rejects the franchise agreement.

It is not as simple if the franchise agreement is still in existence when the franchisor files for protection under Chapter 11. In this case, whether the covenant against competition may be enforced depends on whether the franchise agreement in question is assumed or rejected during the course of the bankruptcy proceedings.

In general, any executory contract may be assumed or rejected by the bankruptcy trustee. 11 U.S.C. § 365(a). A contract must be assumed in its entirety, however; "a debtor may not assume the favorable aspects . . . and reject the unfavorable aspects of the same contract." *U.S. v. Carolina Parachute Corp.*, 907 F.2d 1469, 1472 (4th Cir. 1990). In a Chapter 11 case, the decision to assume or reject a contract may occur at any time up until the reorganization plan is confirmed by the bankruptcy court, unless the court orders the debtor to assume or reject within another specified period of time.

It should be noted that, even if a franchisor decides to assume a particular agreement, assumption does not occur automatically. The debtor must obtain bankruptcy court approval in order to assume a contract. 11 U.S.C. § 365(a). If a contract is assumed, then the parties retain their rights under state law. *See, e.g., Wainer v. A.J. Equities, Ltd.*, 984 F.2d 679, 683 (5th Cir. 1993). Accordingly, when a franchise agreement is successfully assumed during a Chapter 11 proceeding, the franchisor's contractual rights are unaffected, and a non-competition provision should be enforceable, absent some independent state law basis to invalidate the covenant.

A franchisor filing Chapter 11 bankruptcy may decide to reject one or more of its existing franchise agreements. Rejection of an executory contract also requires bankruptcy court approval. 11 U.S.C. § 365(a). In general, the rejection of an executory contract constitutes a breach of that contract, and the breach is deemed to have occurred immediately before the filing of the bankruptcy petition. 11 U.S.C. § 365(g)(1). *In re Tempnology, supra*. Such a breach gives the non-breaching party (i.e., the creditor-franchisee) a right to assert a claim for damages as part of the bankruptcy estate. *See, e.g., In re Murphy*, 694 F.2d 172, 174 (8th Cir. 1982). Beyond the creditor's right to assert a claim for damages, there is disagreement concerning whether rejection constitutes an actual termination of the agreement. This is a question that was not answered by the Supreme Court in the *Tempnology* case. Regardless of whether the agreement is deemed terminated, however, a franchisor that rejects a franchise agreement is likely to lose the ability to enforce any provision of the agreement. Therefore, the importance to the franchisor of the non-competition provision will often be a significant factor in the decision to assume or reject a franchise agreement.

Canadian Province Analysis

Alberta

*by Tamara Prince and Alyshea Surani**

1. Has the province addressed covenants against competition in the context of franchising?

- **Does the province have a franchising statute or regulations that address covenants against competition?**
- **Does the province have a covenants statute of general applicability that would encompass franchise covenants?**
- **Have the courts addressed covenants in the context of franchising either under a statute or the province's common law?**

Alberta's franchising statue and regulation, the Alberta *Franchises Act*, R.S.A. 2000 c. F-23 (Can. Alta) (the Act), and regulations, *Franchises Regulation*, AR 240/95 (the Regulation), do not address covenants against competition. The Act does impose a mutual duty of fair dealing on all parties to a franchise agreement in the performance and enforcement of the franchise agreement (section 7 of the Act), which could affect the manner in which a covenant against competition would be required to be performed or enforced. It is an open question as to whether this is at all distinguishable from such obligations at common law. Alberta does not have a covenants statute of general applicability that would encompass franchise covenants.

The Alberta Court of Queen's bench addressed the enforceability of a covenant against competition in a franchise agreement in *Mapleleaf Franchise Concepts, Inc. v. Nassus Frameworks Ltd.*, 2011 ABQB 594 (Can. Alta. Q.B.). A franchisee of a picture framing business defeated an attempt by the franchisor to enjoin the franchisee from continuing to carry on a competing business after the expiry of the term of a franchise agreement. The decision did not analyze the reasonableness of any of the elements of the covenant relating to legitimate interests, duration, geographical area, or scope. Rather, the decision was based on a significant difference between the summary of the covenant against competition in the franchisor's disclosure document and a covenant contained in the franchise agreement. The disclosure

*Tamara Prince and Alyshea Surani are in the law firm of Cassels Brock & Blackwell LLP in Calgary, Alberta, Canada; Daniel Zalmanowitz Q.C., Ellery Lew, and Susan Clapp of Witten LLP in Edmonton, Alberta, Canada, authored the Alberta entry in the third edition of this book.

document summarized the covenant as being for two years within three kilometers of another franchisee, but the covenant in the agreement restrained competition for two years within ten kilometers of any other franchisee.

---

2. Have the courts articulated the "legitimate interests" of the franchisor that will support enforcement of a covenant against competition contained in a franchise agreement?

- **If so, what are they (e.g., protection of goodwill, protection of confidential information), and in what contexts did the issue arise?**
- **If not, what interests have been recognized in other contexts (e.g., employment agreements, the sale of business context)?**

Alberta courts have not addressed the legitimate interests of the franchisor in relation to covenants against competition in the franchise agreement context. There are a number of Alberta cases in the context of employment agreements and in the context of agreements relating to the sale of a business that have addressed the legitimate interests of the employer or the seller. The principles in these cases may be applied differently in the franchise context.

The foundation of the law in Alberta in relation to covenants in restraint of trade has been interpreted by Alberta courts as a balance among (1) the legitimate interests of the party imposing the limitation, (2) the party under imposition, and (3) the public interest in a healthy competitive economic environment. Alberta courts have been guided by decisions of the Supreme Court of Canada (SCC) (*Maguire v. Northland Drug Co.*, [1935] S.C.R. 412 (Can.); *Elsley v. J.G. Collins Insurance Agencies Ltd.*, [1978] 2 S.C.R. 916 (Can.); *Doerner v. Bliss & Laughlin Industries Inc.*, [1980] 2 S.C.R. 865 (Can.); and *Shafron v. KRG Insurance Brokers (Western) Inc.*, [2009] 1 S.C.R. 157 (Can.)).

The general principles established by these SCC decisions include, inter alia, that (1) covenants in restraint of trade are generally considered unenforceable but can be rebutted based on specific facts of each case (e.g., in the contexts of the sale of business and employment agreements), (2) a restraint of trade must be reasonable and not go further than necessary to protect the rights the employer is entitled to protect, and (3) to determine if a restraint of trade is reasonable; the courts must determine if the restraint is a fair compromise between the two competing interests.

In *Elsley*, the factors to consider when assessing a covenant against competition include (1) whether the employer has a legitimate proprietary interest entitled to protection, (2) whether the geographic or time scope of the covenant is too broad, and (3) whether the covenant is unenforceable as being simply against competition and not limited to proscribing solicitation of clients of the former employer. In addition, restrictive covenants in employment agreements should be given less latitude than similar covenants in a business sale agreement because of the inequality of bargaining power that underlies the employment relationship as distinguished from the sale of business or other similar commercial transactions.

These general principles are echoed in the Alberta Court of Queen's Bench *Ensign Drilling Inc. v. Lundle*, 2007 ABQB 357 (Can. Alta. Q.B.), at paragraph 66, where the court cites *Elsley* for authority that the validity of a covenant against competition should depend on the facts of each case and the circumstances surrounding the contract. At paragraph 66, the court wrote that the courts must "resist the inclination to lift a restrictive covenant out of an employment agreement and examine it in a disembodied manner, as if it were some strange scientific specimen under microscopic scrutiny"

Alberta courts have applied the "legitimate interests" principles in a number of decisions in the employment context where the court examines the competing interests of both the employer and employee. The court assesses the relationship between the employer and employee, where there can be a fiduciary relationship or where there is a proprietary interest in the clients, and therefore imposes an implied restrictive convent into an employment agreement (*Physique Health Club Ltd. v. Carlsen*, [1997] 4 W.W.R. 609 (Can. Alta. C.A.) and *Human Resource Capital Group Inc. (c.o.b. Spherion) v. Reis*, 2009 ABQB 159 (Can. Alta. Q.B.), the Alberta Court of Queen's Bench).

In the case of a sale of business and a restrictive covenant in a sale agreement in Alberta, in his concurring reasons, J.A. O'Ferrall cites *Shafron* in *Goska J. Nowak Professional Corp. v. Robinson*, 2016 ABCA 240, where the court recognized that where a sale of business occurs, both parties have a legitimate interest in the enforceability of a restraint of trade, since this could be the only avenue for the seller to effectively transfer the goodwill of their business. The court opined, at paragraph 71, that the public has an interest to ensure that the "restraint of trade doctrine does not unnecessarily restrict the purchase and sale of businesses."

3. What time limitations have courts recognized as reasonable in the franchise context? If no franchise cases have been decided, what time limitations have been recognized in other contexts?

➤ How have they been related to the interests protected?

Alberta courts have not specifically analyzed the issue of reasonable time restrictions in relation to covenants against competition in franchise agreements. In other contexts, the Alberta courts have held that whether a time limitation can be upheld by a court depends on whether the time restriction is reasonable as between the parties and whether it goes any further than necessary to protect the legitimate interests involved. Reasonableness is assessed at the time the contract is entered into (*Yellowhead Petroleum Products Ltd. v. United Farmers of Alberta Co-Operative Ltd.*, 2004 ABQB 665 (Can. Alta. Q.B.)).

Where two freely contracting parties are aware and understand the nature of the time limitation clause, the court should not interfere (*Shalimar Physiotherapy Ltd. v. Deans*, [1989] A.J. No. 663 (Can. Alta. Q.B.)). The court in Alberta has upheld time limitation clauses in the context of an employment agreement up to five years in duration: (1) in *Shalimar Physiotherapy*, the court found that a four-year time restriction against the employee providing services to any of the plaintiff's patients or former patients was reasonable and enforceable; (2) in *Garbutt Business College Limited v. Henderson and Henderson Secretarial School Limited*, [1939] A.J. No. 33 (Can. Alta. Sup. Ct.), the court upheld a non-competition agreement in an employment agreement that provided for a five-year time limitation from the date the agreement terminated (The defendant was a long-time employee of the plaintiff and then became the principal of the plaintiff's college in Calgary. The employment agreement for the new position was negotiated to include a five-year time limitation. The defendant used the success of students he taught while employed with the plaintiff to advertise for students at his new school, which influenced prospective students for four or five years into the future.); and (3) in *961945 Alberta Ltd (Servicemaster of Edmonton Disaster Restoration) v. Meyer*, 2018 ABQB 564, where there was evidence that the parties themselves agreed that the time limitation was reasonable, and the court upheld a two-year time restriction.

On the other hand, the courts in Alberta have struck time limitation clauses in the employment context, regardless of time restriction duration, where the employee had an entry-level position or where the employees were not key to management and were just ordinary employees (*Travel Co. v. Keeling*, 2009 ABQB 399 (Can. Alta. Q.B.) and *Innersolutions Ltd. v. Hooper*, 2015 ABQB 258)).

The courts have applied a more liberal application of the reasonableness standard in relation to the sale of a business, as the party agreeing to the restriction is obtaining value for his or her business, and the transaction usually involves negotiation between two parties where the sale price includes a component for the covenant against competition. The rationale is that it is in the public interest that parties be free to sell businesses at prices bargained for, knowing that the courts will uphold reasonable restrictions. The court in Alberta has upheld restrictive covenants with two- and ten-year time restrictions in relation to the sale of a business, where the plaintiff has a proprietary business interest that is reasonable for it to protect (*Canwest Propane, Inc. v. Steele*, [1990] A.J. No. 903 (Can. Alta. Q.B.); *Ensign Drilling Inc. v. Lundle*, 2007 ABQB 357 (Can. Alta. Q.B.); and *Fluorescent Sales & Service Ltd. v. Bastien*, (1958) 39 W.W.R. 659 (Can. Alta. C.A.)).

The courts in Alberta have also examined time-restrictive covenants where the duration of limitation varied depending on the context.

In the context of an independent contractor relationship, the Alberta Court of Queen's Bench in *Community Credit Union Ltd. v. Ast*, 2007 ABQB 46 (Can. Alta. Q.B.), held that a fair and reasonable time restriction would have been one year following the financial advisor's departure. The restrictive covenant in this situation was a "ladder" provision that contained various time restrictions in decreasing amounts. The court struck the parts of the restrictive covenant that included time restrictions of greater than one year. The court found that a financial advisor is in a position where there is a high degree of personal loyalty between the clients and the financial advisor, and the clients place a significant degree of trust in the financial advisor (for clarity, the financial advisor in this case was found to be an independent contractor and not an employee).

In the context of a real estate agent and a real estate brokerage firm, the Alberta Court of Queen's Bench, in *Smode v. Deveaux*, 1997 CarswellAlta 1075 (Can. Alta. Q.B.), held that a two-year time restriction on the real estate agent was reasonable and binding.

In the context of a sales representative agreement, the Alberta Court of Appeal, in *Herff Jones Canada Inc. v. Todd* (1996), 181 A.R. 236 (Can. Alta. C.A.), affirmed the lower decision of the Alberta Court of Queen's Bench that a non-competition agreement that restricted a sales representative for a period of four years from soliciting or contacting directly or indirectly any of those schools and accounts who were customers of the respondent, as of a specified date, was reasonable and enforceable. The salesperson had created special relationships with the customers that the employer had a proprietary interest to protect, where the salesperson would be entitled to split commissions for three years after he left the employer.

In the context of a shareholder's agreement that included a non-competition agreement relating to a company that provided drilling services to the oil and gas industry, the Alberta Court of Queen's Bench, in *Senos v. Pacesetter Performance Drilling Ltd.*, 2010 ABQB 533 (Can. Alta. Q.B.), upheld a one-year restriction. This case is discussed in further detail in section 4 below.

The principles noted above in relation to time limitations in restrictive covenants may be applied differently in the franchise context. Although franchise agreements involve a greater degree of disclosure of system methods and other intellectual property than in an employment relationship, in many situations the franchisor and the franchisee do not have equal bargaining power when entering into the franchise agreement. Accordingly, it may be that restrictive covenants in franchise agreements would be held to the higher level of scrutiny than the courts apply to restrictive covenants in employment agreements.

4. What geographic limitations have courts recognized as reasonable in the franchise context?

- **How have they been related to the interests protected?**
- **Have the courts recognized the legitimacy of protecting other franchisees from competition?**

The Alberta courts have not specifically analyzed the issue of geographic limitations in relation to covenants against competition in franchise agreements. However, the issue has been analyzed in other contexts where the court emphasizes that the geographic limitation must be reasonable as between the parties and in relation to public policy.

In *Yellowhead*, the Alberta Court of Queen's Bench confirmed that a geographic limitation will not be upheld if it is broader "than reasonably necessary to protect the legitimate interest involved. Reasonableness is to be assessed at the time when the contract was entered into." In order to be reasonable, the geographic limitation could not be larger than was adequate for its intended purpose. In *Yellowhead*, where one corporation was acting as agent for another corporation and supplying services to the customers of the second corporation, the court upheld a restricted area defined as the territory the agent had worked in for the plaintiff, and an additional 30-kilometer radius from the boundary of that territory.

In the context of an independent contractor (a financial advisor in this case), the court in *Community Credit Union*, found that a fair and reasonable geographical restriction would be to limit the financial planner's ability to work as a financial planner for any of his previous employer's customers within a 20-mile radius of any branch of the previous employer to whose members the financial advisor had provided services.

In *Enerflow Industries Inc. v. Surefire*, 2013 ABQB 196, the non-compete covenant contained no geographic restriction and purported to prevent the employee from competing with the employer anywhere in the world. The court concluded that this was onerous, unreasonable, and unnecessary to protect the employee's interests. This was later echoed in *Jacobs v. PHAT Training Inc.*, 2014 ABQB 100, where the non-competition clause in a consultant contract did not address a geographical limit and the court found that it was unreasonable and unenforceable.

In the context of the sale of a business there are several cases in which restrictive covenants with geographic limitations have been considered. Generally, the courts have upheld a geographic limitation where the geographic scope was reasonable in the context of the particular business (e.g., oil drilling business, insurance business, etc.), or where the geographic limitation was negotiated between the parties and their lawyers (*Ensign Drilling Inc. v. Lundle*, 2007 ABQB 357 (Can. Alta. Q.B.), *Dale and Company Ltd. v. Land et al*, (1987) 84 A.R. 52 (Can. Alta. C.A.), and *Senos v. Pacesetter Performance Drilling Ltd.*, 2010 ABQB 533 (Can. Alta. Q.B.)). In *1059028 Alberta Ltd. v. Capio Oilfield Services Ltd.*, 2016 ABQB 234, the court considered the entire agreement and the intent of the parties to a business sale agreement, and enforced a restrictive covenant where the geographic scope was not drafted clearly and a "blank" was to be filled in.

The principles noted above in relation to geographical limitations may be applied differently in the franchise context, for the same reasons outlined above regarding time restrictions—namely, that often franchisor and franchisee are seen to not have equal bargaining power. Restrictive covenants in franchise agreements are more likely to be held to a higher level of scrutiny than the courts apply to restrictive covenants in employment agreements and sale agreements.

5. What limitations on activities have courts recognized as reasonable in the franchise context?

While there are no Alberta decisions where the court has limited activities in the franchise context, the court in *Jamani v. Subway Franchise Systems of Canada, Ltd.*, 2008 ABQB 677 (Can. Alta. Q.B.) reviewed a decision of the arbitrator enforcing an in-term covenant against competition that prohibited a Subway franchisee from owning, operating, or assisting another person to own or operate any other identical or similar business anywhere, directly or indirectly, during the term of the franchise agreement. Subway was successful in the arbitration. The arbitrator found a breach of the covenant and ordered termination of the two Subway franchise agreements and financial remedies against the franchisee. The franchisee appealed the decision to the court. Subway prevailed on appeal, as the judge found no error of law. The case establishes that whether limitations on activities are reasonable in the franchise context is a mixed question of fact and law.

Although not in a franchise context, there is authority in Alberta that a restricted activity must be as detailed as possible and not overly broad. As with geographic and temporal restrictions, the courts have held that a restriction on activities will not be enforced if it is broader than needed to adequately protect the party in whose favour it is imposed. For example, in the employment context, the court in *Gold In the Net Hockey School Inc. v. Netpower Inc.*, 2007 ABQB 520 (Can. Alta. Q.B.), held that the restriction to ". . . not start up any hockey school or become involved in personally training any other goaltenders or make any contact with Gold students and suppliers . . ." was too broad. The court held that the legitimate proprietary interest that the plaintiff was entitled to protect was limited to goaltending schools. The restricted activity in this case was broad enough to catch all hockey schools generally and therefore was unreasonable and unenforceable.

In the context of the sale of a business the court in *Ensign Drilling* upheld a covenant restricting the activity of "contract drilling business." The court considered that four of the five companies involved were engaged in the business of contract drilling for oil and natural gas. The fifth company rented out ancillary equipment used in that process. In that context, the court found that it was clear that the parties understood and agreed that the prohibition in the restrictive covenant related to the contract drilling business for oil and natural gas.

In the context of one corporation acting as agent for another, in *Yellowhead* the court upheld a covenant in which the covenantor agreed not to ". . . carry on, or be engaged in or involved in or connected with, any business that markets, sells or otherwise deals in any product similar to any combustion engine fuel Product or any lubricant Product which is at any time sold by us through you while this Agreement is in effect" (paragraph 23).

6. Does the province recognize a difference between in-term and post-term covenants?

There is no clear authority in Alberta that recognizes a difference between in-term and post-term covenants in franchise agreements. The *Jamani* decision addressed and upheld an in-term restrictive covenant in a franchise agreement, but only in arbitration. Prior caselaw, discussed earlier in further detail in section 2, involved post-term covenants, not in-term covenants, but it does not appear that the court in any of these cases considered this distinction. Rather than surmising that the same tests would not apply to in-term and post-term covenants, it could be that legitimate interests, and therefore the reasonableness of the covenant, may differ depending on whether the franchise agreement has expired.

7. Has the province allowed enforcement of covenants against non-signatories (e.g., family members, newly formed corporations)?

Although there is no reported decision in Alberta in which a court has found a non-signatory to be bound by covenants in a franchise agreement, the court in *Canwest Propane, Inc.* found an employer to be vicariously liable for the acts of an employee who breached a restrictive covenant in an agreement the employee had made with a third party, because the employer benefited from the employee's breaches. The employer was not aware nor a signatory to that agreement.

The courts of Alberta have pierced the corporate veil of a corporation that was a party to an agreement to find the individual shareholder liable, even though the individual had not signed the agreement in his personal capacity. In *Phillips v. 707739 Alberta Ltd.*, 2000 ABQB 139 (Can. Alta. Q.B.), the court discussed the applicable considerations when deciding whether to pierce the corporate veil. The court considered whether (1) the corporation was incorporated to do a wrongful act, (2) the corporation was directed by the individual to do wrongful things, (3) there was fraud involved in the agreement, (4) there was a de facto agency by the corporation on behalf of the individual, (5) the corporation was incorporated for a single enterprise, and (6) the corporation was the "alter ego" of the individual.

However, the court in *Winget v. Safeguard Business Systems Ltd.*, [1993] A.J. No. 346 (Can. Alta. Q.B.), did not enforce the covenants against the non-signatories, son and widow, where the father signed a distributorship agreement with Safeguard

Business Systems. The father passed away, and after some failed negotiations with Safeguard, the son started up his own distributorship, representing competitive products. It appeared that the father's wife gave the son some information from the deceased father's business. The court wrote, "if [Safeguard] wanted to stop the son from going into business for himself and soliciting customers of [Safeguard] it should have contracted for that with the son." The court also declined to find any personal liability on the part of the widow because she had not signed the agreement in her personal capacity, and any liability of the estate of father relating to the acts of the son as an employee of the father ended upon his death, at which point the son was no longer an employee.

8. Will the province modify, "blue-pencil," or otherwise reduce a covenant found to be overbroad?

There is no Alberta caselaw dealing with "blue-pencil" or other severance theories in the franchise context, and while generally a "blue-pencil" rule will not be applied, some recent decisions may be seen to have left the door slightly open, especially in the context between vendor and purchaser and public interest. Accordingly, this issue is not fully settled in Alberta.

Alberta law at one time recognized the principle of reading down a covenant in restraint of trade if it was found to be overly broad. This had been described as the application of the "blue pencil" or "notional severance," in which the court could strike out unreasonable or objectionable portions of a clause, leaving the balance standing and enforceable. In accordance with recent decisions, that is no longer the case. The Alberta Court of Appeal in *Globex Foreign Exchange Corp. v. Kelcher*, 2005 ABCA 419 (Can. Alta. C.A.), reviewed severance in the context of a post-employment restriction and reasoned that an employer cannot prepare unreasonably broad restrictive covenants and then expect the court to rewrite them.

This reasoning was followed in *Travel Co.* at paragraph 50, where the court quotes *Shafron* for the proposition, stating:

> . . . two previously established tools to address unlawful restrictive covenants, (1) striking out only the offensive words or phrases and attempting to preserve the balance of the covenant, or (2) reading the entire contract down to make that which was overly broad more palatable, would no longer be the law in Canada, at least as it related to restrictive covenants found in employment contracts.

This statement of law is restricted to employment contracts, leaving some uncertainty about severance in the franchise context. In *Travel Co.* at paragraph 57, the court observed that there remains uncertainty in the law as to whether a court may write down the contract if the contract contains a clause permitting it. However, in the same breath the court commented that similar considerations would mitigate against upholding such a clause.

Another decision that leaves open the possibility of the court using the "blue-pencil" or "notional severance approach" is the 2007 decision of the Albert Court of Queen's Bench in the *Community Credit Union*, which dealt with a ladder-type restrictive covenant. The covenant contained five different geographic restrictions and five different time restrictions and specifically provided that each covenant was separate and distinct, and if one was found to be void or unenforceable, the remaining ones would survive. The court confirmed the principle that the courts will not rewrite an unreasonably broad covenant against competition so as to make it enforceable, but questioned whether that principle applied in this situation where there were separate and distinct covenants of decreasing scale. The court distinguished this situation from one in which the court would substitute its own restrictive covenant for what was drafted; instead, the court here would sever the overly broad provisions in order to give effect to the clear objective intention of the parties. This decision begs the question of how this employee could have known what restrictions applied without advice from the court. Therefore, this decision has left open the possibility of severance in relation to non-competition agreements in employment agreements and potentially in other types of agreements. There has been no consideration in Alberta as to whether a court might use the statutory duty of fair dealing contained in section 9.7 of the Alberta *Franchises Act*, R.S.A. 2000 c. F-23 (Can. Alta.), in relation to a franchise agreement that includes a "ladder type" restrictive covenant, so this argument is potentially open.

The Alberta Court of Appeal decision in *City Wide Towing and Recovery Service Ltd. v. Poole*, 2020 ABCA 305, deals with an overly broad and ultimately unreasonable geographical scope non-competition covenant in the context of a sale of assets. The court distinguished between commercial cases and employment cases and concluded that blue-pencil severance was warranted in the former. The court clarified at paragraph 46 that "the reason that blue pencil severance is so limited in application is the imbalance in the relationship between employer and employee, with public policy favoring the employees' rights to freely carry on [their] occupation over that of the employer to restrict it unreasonable." On the other hand, the court identified authority in Canada and England in which blue-pencil severance was deemed acceptable depending on the context, one between vendor and purchaser.

In the context of a real estate agent and a real estate brokerage firm, the Alberta Court of Queen's Bench in *Smode* found that the geographical restriction in the non-competition covenant limited to the geographical area of Grande Cache was reasonable and binding. Even though the covenant in question did not expressly provide that the non-competition covenant was limited to Grande Cache, the court implied such a limit into the covenant.

In relation to partners in a medical practitioner's office, the Alberta Court of Appeal, in *Baker v. Lintott*, (1981) 4 W.W.R. 766 (Can. Alta. C.A.), reversed the trial decision and found that a covenant against competition for a two-year period within a 25-mile radius of Medicine Hat was valid and enforceable. There were 17 family doctors in the area, all of whom were associated with only five clinics. The trial judge opined that greater public access to and choice of medical services (i.e., services that the public requires) was in the public interest and concluded that five clinics offered insufficient choice for the public. In his view, the choice was already limited, and it was not in the public interest to restrict further the public's choice of medical practitioners. The Alberta Court of Appeal disagreed and upheld the restriction since it was reasonable as between the parties.

9. When does a non-compete period begin to run? Will courts equitably extend the term?

In *Ensign Drilling, Inc. v. Lundle*, 2007 ABQB 357 (Can. Alta. Q.B.), and *Dreco Energy Services Ltd. v. Wenzel*, 2008 ABQB 112 (Can. Alta. Q.B.), it was argued that for equitable reasons, in the employment and independent contractor contexts, the term of a restrictive covenant should be extended to take into account prior periods of unrestrained breach. This argument was rejected in both cases. Specifically, in *Dreco Energy*, the court was faced with the expiry of a five-year covenant prior to trial and a request from the plaintiff to continue the pre-trial injunction until at least the trial. The justice reviewed this request in the context of the test for an interlocutory injunction. There was some uncertainty as to the date of the covenant's expiry, but even that did not convince the justice, who reasoned that to resolve that uncertainty in favor of the plaintiff would be to grant the plaintiff its trial remedy prior to a trial. This decision was upheld appeal on appeal (2008 ABCA 290 (Can. Alta. C.A.)).

In *Goska*, the associate agreement specified that the dentist who sold the practice was to work for the dentist buyer for five years followed by a two-year non-compete period. Accordingly, the overall duration of the restraint of trade was seven years. The dentist who sold the practice worked for the dentist buyer for seven years, and the court decided that was not reasonable to extend the two-year restrictive covenant, resulting in a restraint of trade of nine years, even though the non-compete clause was characterized as being in support of the sale of the dental practice. Since the parties did not expressly address (in the associate agreement) that the non-compete would extend further if the seller dentist extended his work period, the extension was not reasonable. The non-compete ended at the seven-year mark.

There are certain contexts and facts where the court has extended a restrictive covenant. For example, in *Community Credit Union*, the court held that the one-year restriction, which was to commence on termination of the contract between the employer and the financial advisor, was reasonable and binding. The financial advisor's contract with the employer had been terminated on October 15, 2003, but the court held that because it took several months for all of the files to be transferred from the employer to the financial advisor (the files in question being the source of the financial advisor's breach), the one-year restriction was extended for an additional two and a half months.

10. Are there additional nuances or peculiarities of the province's treatment of covenants in the franchising context?

APPLICABLE LAW, VENUE AND CONFLICTS

The Act contains sections that may affect the application of provisions in a franchise agreement relating to applicable law and venue unenforceable. Sections 16 and 17 of the Act state:

> 16. Alberta law. – The law of Alberta applies to franchise agreements.
>
> 17. Limit on jurisdictional choice. – Any provision in a franchise agreement restricting the application of the law of Alberta or restricting the jurisdiction or venue to any form outside Alberta is void with respect to a claim otherwise enforceable under this Act in Alberta.

Although it would appear that a franchisor seeking to enforce a covenant against a franchisee in Alberta or obtain damages as a result of a breach of such a covenant would be forced to take action in an Alberta court, the Alberta courts have interpreted section 17 of the Act so that this will not always be the case. In *Bad Ass Coffee Co. of Hawaii v. Bad Ass Enterprises Inc.*, 2008 ABQB 404 (Can. Alta. Q.B.), the court affirmed the decision of the master that allowed a Utah judgment obtained by the U.S. franchisor against the franchisee and the guarantor to be enforced in Alberta. The franchisor had moved in Utah for an order compelling arbitration of the claim by the franchisor that the franchisee and the guarantor had breached the franchise agreements. The Alberta lawyer for the franchisee and the guarantor objected to the arbitration in Utah. The Utah lawyer for the franchisee and the guarantor appeared at the application to argue that pursuant to the Act, the court lacked jurisdiction, and venue in Utah was inappropriate. The Alberta Court of Queen's Bench found that by their lawyer appearing at the application, the franchisee and the guarantor attorned to the courts of Utah. The court held that the contractual choice of Utah law, while contrary to the requirement of section 16 of the Act, did not render the contractual choices of Utah law and of a Utah venue void under section 17 of the Act, because the claim being made by the franchisor was not a "claim otherwise enforceable under" the Act. The court also cited section 15 of the Act, which states:

> 15. Other remedies. – The rights of action conferred by this Act are in addition to and do not derogate from any other right the franchisee or the franchisor may have at law.

If a litigant attempts to use sections 16 and 17 to overcome a foreign choice of law and choice of venue in a franchise agreement, it should consider framing the claim or defense in the context of specific requirements of the Act. For example, a franchisee defending an action relating to a covenant against competition in Alberta could attempt to circumvent a foreign choice of law and choice of venue in a contract and have Alberta law apply by framing its defense in the context of the covenant to deal fairly in section 7 of the Act, which would, perhaps, make the claim otherwise enforceable under the Act.

GUARANTEES ACKNOWLEDGEMENT ACT

Alberta has a statute called the *Guarantees Acknowledgement Act*, R.S.A. 2000, c. G-11 (Can. Alta.) (the GAA), which is unique in Canada. In order for a personal guarantee to be enforceable, there must be a certificate of notary public in a form prescribed by the GAA and the related regulations, pursuant to which a notary public must confirm that the guarantor appeared before him or her and that the notary public was satisfied that the guarantor understood the nature of the guarantee. Failure to comply with the GAA may render a personal guarantee, including an individual guarantee of a non-compete, unenforceable. The courts have not considered whether personal covenants by an individual guarantor of a franchise agreement not to compete contained in a guarantee would be enforceable against the individual guarantor if the GAA were not satisfied.

Also, in *Bad Ass Coffee*, the guarantor in defending the claim against him personally argued that the foreign judgment should not be enforced because it would be against public policy in Alberta since the GAA was not satisfied. The court referred to the guarantor's testimony confirming that he had signed the guarantees in Alberta in front of his Alberta lawyer and that he understood the nature of what he was signing. Accordingly, the court said there was no public policy against enforcing the guarantee.

NON-COMPETITION CLAUSES VS. NON-SOLICITATION CLAUSES

The Alberta courts draw a distinction between non-competition clauses and non-solicitation clauses; however, the courts apply the same tests of reasonableness but less stringently in non-solicitation covenants.

In *Evans v. Sports Corp.*, 2011 ABQB 244 (Can. Alta. Q.B.), the court held that while a non-competition covenant must be reasonable in terms of geography and duration, a non-solicitation covenant did not need to be limited by geography because it is already naturally limited by reference to customers. The court thus upheld a non-solicitation clause that had no geographical limitation.

In *Globex*, the Court of Appeal overturned the chambers judge's decision to uphold the non-competition covenant but granted an injunction enforcing the non-solicitation covenant.

CONSIDERATION

A significant issue in the Alberta caselaw affecting the enforceability of a restrictive covenant focuses on whether there was consideration for the covenant. This was the most significant issue in *Globex*, and the primary basis for the failure of the covenants in an employment context. It is not a new issue, and *Globex* draws on reasoning going back at least to *Maguire*. In *Globex* the employees entered into both non-competition and non-solicitation covenants after they had been employed for a period of time. Prior caselaw suggested that consideration was required to impose such an onerous covenant where it was imposed during the employment relationship and also suggested that continuation of employment can be adequate consideration.

In *Community Credit Union*, the issue of consideration was briefly reviewed. In this case, the non-competition agreement was entered into at the same time as the contract for the work, so the above issue did not apply. The agreement in this case called for $10 in consideration to be paid to the financial advisor, which the financial advisor alleged was never paid. The Alberta Court of Queen's Bench held that to the extent the $10 was never paid, it remains due and owing, but the financial planner had never asked for it. The court held at paragraph 35 that "both parties got something for value out of the contract and the non-competition agreement does not fail for want of consideration."

Practically, except in the case of covenants entered into between the franchisee/franchisor and its employees after employment commenced, this issue will not usually arise in the franchise context where covenants are contained in the franchise agreement entered into at the beginning of the relationship.

WRONGFUL DISMISSAL, FUNDAMENTAL BREACH

In *Windship Aviation Ltd. v. deMeulles*, 2002 ABQB 669 (Can. Alta. Q.B.), the court, relying primarily on Ontario authorities, concluded that wrongful termination of employment represents a repudiation of the employment agreement, freeing the employee from his contractual obligations and precluding enforcement of a non-competition covenant. The *Globex* case, in obiter, appears to confirm this approach.

This was also reinforced in the Alberta Court of Queen's Bench case *961945 Alberta Ltd.*, which held that even where there was evidence that did not support an imbalance of bargaining power, the more rigorous approach of interpreting a restrictive covenant was warranted within a share purchase agreement arising from an employment relationship. The employee also became a party to the franchise agreement that contained a non-competition covenant and was also scrutinized by the court according to the standard applied in an employment agreement. While the restrictive covenants were valid, the court found that the employer and franchisor were unable to establish a strong prima facie case showing that the employee was dismissed for cause, therefore also failing to demonstrate that the restrictive covenants were enforceable.

If the same principle were to be applied in a franchise context, a franchisor that wrongfully terminates a franchise agreement may not be able to enforce the restrictive covenant contained in that franchise agreement against the franchisee.

WAIVER

In the *Community Credit Union* case, the non-competition covenant at issue included a clause whereby the financial advisor waived any defenses as to the reasonableness of the covenants in the agreement, including duration and scope; confirmed the covenants were reasonable and valid; and waived all defenses to the strict enforcement thereof. The Alberta Court of Queen's Bench held that clauses such as this could be severed from the agreement to give effect to the intention of the parties, which was clearly to have the court review the covenants and determine the appropriate scope of the restrictive covenant. The court also stated at paragraph 52, although in obiter, that the court had "some misgivings that such a clause would ever be enforceable when it purports to waive defences to an agreement in restraint of trade, when those defences have always been grounded in public policy."

British Columbia

*by Geoffrey B. Shaw and Danielle DiPardo**

1. Has the province addressed covenants against competition in the context of franchising?

- **Does the province have a franchising statute or regulations that address covenants against competition?**
- **Does the province have a covenants statute of general applicability that would encompass franchise covenants?**
- **Have the courts addressed covenants in the context of franchising either under a statute or under the province's common law?**

British Columbia's *Franchises Act*, SBC 2015, ch. 35 and Franchise Regulation came into force on February 1, 2017. Neither the *Franchises Act* nor the Franchise Regulations address covenants against competition. Further, British Columbia does not have any covenants legislation of general applicability that encompasses franchise covenants. In British Columbia, the courts address covenants contained in franchise agreements via the common law and the doctrine of precedent.

Generally stated, the law in British Columbia recognizes a distinction between restrictive covenants contained in employment contracts and those embodied in contracts for the purchase of a business. The former tend to be void and unenforceable as an undue restraint of trade, whereas the latter are typically generally presumed to be enforceable as a legitimate protection of the purchaser's investment in the goodwill of the business. This point is emphasized in the case of *Burgess v. Industrial Frictions and Supply Co. Ltd.*, [1987] B.C.J. No. 273 (Can. B.C.C.A.):

> In determining whether a covenant in restraint of trade is enforceable, a covenant exacted by a purchaser from a vendor on a sale of the goodwill of the business stands on a different footing than an employment contract. Contracts of employment in restraint of trade are viewed by the law as prima facie offensive and are liable not to be enforced, in the absence

*Geoffrey B. Shaw and Danielle DiPardo practice at Cassels, Brock & Blackwell LLP. Shaw and DiPardo have updated the British Columbia chapter of the third edition of *Covenants Against Competition in Franchise Agreements* originally prepared by Judy A. Rost, who practices at Alexander Holburn Beaudin & Lang LLP.

> of special circumstances such as a close personal relationship between the employee and the employer's customers. . . . The opposite approach applies to contracts for the sale of the goodwill of a business. It is the policy of the law and in the public interest that a contract for the sale of a business fully entered into should prima facie be enforced. . . . It is reasonable that a vendor would seek to protect a business against the competition of an outgoing partner. . . . The remaining partner's livelihood depends substantially on the goodwill created an on the extent to which he or she is able to preserve it. It is, in short, a proper matter for protection.

Whether a restrictive covenant will be enforced is matter of public policy in British Columbia. There are many aspects of a restrictive covenant that may make it enforceable or not. Specifically, a court will weigh the reasonableness of a covenant's geographic and temporal application—a restrictive covenant cannot restrict activities any more than is *necessary* (as is contextually determined) to protect a franchisor's proprietary interests.

---

2. Have the courts articulated the "legitimate interests" of the franchisor that will support enforcement of a covenant against competition contained in a franchise agreement?

- **If so, what are they (e.g., protection of goodwill, protection of confidential information), and in what contexts did the issue arise?**
- **If not, what interests have been recognized in other contexts (e.g., employment agreements, the sale of business context)?**

The British Columbia courts have recognized that a franchise is attractive to people who want to run their own business. It offers less risk as the business model has typically been proven in the marketplace. Further, it offers training, support, and contacts that would not otherwise have been available to the franchisee. In *Pacific N.W. Cruiseshipcenters v. Super Cruise World (Delta) Inc.* (1991), 38 C.P.R. (3d) 528 (Can. B.C. Sup. Ct. in Chambers) at p. 3, the court identified the benefits of franchising as follows:

> The franchisor provides the franchisee with the benefit of its accumulated knowledge, its contacts, its system of doing business. It provides the franchisee with the tools to earn an income (hopefully) and tools for a competitive edge in the marketplace.

In exchange for these advantages the franchisee agrees, among other things, not to compete with the franchisor during the term and for a period of time following termination.

In *BMR Bath Master Reglazing Ltd. v. Watson*, 2010 BCSC 1170, [2010] B.C.J. No. 1633 (Can. B.C. Sup. Ct.) (*Watson*), which concerned a franchisor's attempt to enforce the terms of several restrictive covenants against a former franchisee, the British Columbia Supreme Court stated:

> In appropriate circumstances, protection is given to trade secrets, confidential information or trade connections. Courts recognize a proprietary interest in confidential information. Clauses prohibiting the solicitation

of customers are more readily enforced than clauses which prevent competition. The former recognizes a business's interest in existing trade connections. Non-competition clauses have been described as a more drastic weapon enforceable only in exceptional circumstances, and limited in time and space, since they are attempts to keep a person out of business.

At the core of assessing legitimate interests is whether the clauses included to protect them in franchise agreements are considered reasonable. Are they what is required—not more nor less—to protect legitimate interests without unfairly restraining trade? The validity of a restrictive covenant can only be determined in its overall context (*953947 B.C. Ltd. v. Source Office Furniture & Systems Ltd.*, 2016 BCSC 2233, 274 A.C.W.S. (3d) 94 (Can. B.C. Sup. Ct.) (*Source Office Furniture*)). Courts in British Columbia have indicated that the reasonableness of a restrictive covenant in terms of its area and duration is to be measured by the reasonable mutual expectations of the parties at the time of making the contract (*TMI Turf Management Inc. v. R. De Noble Enterprises Ltd.*, (1994), 52 C.P.R. (3d) 129, 5 C.C.E.L (2d) 165 (Can. B.C. Sup. Ct.)).

---

3. What time limitations have courts recognized as reasonable in the franchise context? If no franchise cases have been decided, what time limitations have been recognized in other contexts?

➤ **How have they been related to the interests protected?**

The time limitations that will be recognized as reasonable by the courts tend to vary depending on the context, but typically a period of two years is held to be a reasonable restraint on trade: *TMI Turf Management*; see also *Source Office Furniture*. In determining what is reasonable, courts are always conscious of the tension between the freedom to contract and the public policy considerations against restraint of trade. Two years has been upheld in British Columbia as an appropriate balance between the franchisor's need to replace lost customers and protect its business interests and the former franchisee's need to be allowed to pursue new business opportunities with the knowledge and skills it legitimately gained over the course of the agreement.

In *TMI Turf Management*, the British Columbia Supreme Court ruled that a restrictive covenant imposing a non-compete period of two years was reasonable and enforceable. Turf Management Inc. was a franchisor who licensed the Weed Man lawn-maintenance system. In its franchise agreement with De Noble Enterprises, the franchisee committed not to compete against TMI Turf in the two years following termination of the agreement:

> 10.01 Neither the Licensee, including any of its director, officers and shareholders, shall [sic] at any time within the term of the licence granted herein *or the period of two (2) years following the termination of such licence*, either individually or in partnership or jointly or in conjunction with any person or persons, firm, corporation , association, syndicate or company, as principal, agent, shareholder or in any other manner whatsoever, carry on or be engaged in or concerned with or interested in, or advise, lend money to, guarantee the debts or obligations of, or permit his name or any part thereof

> to be used or employed by or associated with, any person or persons, firm, association, syndicate company or corporation engaged in or concerned with or interested in, any business the same as or similar to the lawn-care business of the Licensee within: [goes on to describe geographical area].

TMI Turf Management, at para. 4 (emphasis added).

In 1993, the franchisee purported to terminate the agreement and at the same time, the owner incorporated a new company, Island Green Management Systems Inc., to which he transferred all or most of the franchisee's assets. The new company also provided lawn-maintenance services to many of the customers the franchisee had acquired under the franchise agreement. TMI Turf was granted an injunction to restrain Island Green Management Systems Inc. from competing against it during the prohibited period. The court stated:

> It would be bound to be very prejudicial to TMI if he were allowed to close down his Weed Man business one day and open up the next day in the same business but no longer under the aegis of Turf's assignee TMI. The geographic scope and duration of the restraint, measured by the reasonable mutual expectations of the parties at the time the contract was entered into, both come within what I find to be legally permissible time limits.

TMI Turf Management, at para. 21.

In *Super Cruise*, the plaintiff/franchisor successfully enforced a restrictive covenant prohibiting its former franchisee from competing against it within a defined territory. Under the franchise agreement, the franchisee had the exclusive right to market holidays through the Cruiseshipcenter retail outlet in Delta, British Columbia, which was specifically defined by particular postal codes. During the term of the franchise agreement, and without the franchisee's knowledge, the franchisor permitted a third party to open a Cruiseshipcenter retail outlet in Surrey, a neighboring municipality. The franchisee claimed it had been granted a right of first refusal for any nearby Cruiseshipcenter retail outlets in an oral agreement after the initial agreement had been entered into. Relations between the parties soured as a result. The franchisee terminated the agreement, incorporated a new company providing exactly the same travel services, in the same location, even using the same telephone number, and went into business competing against the franchisor. On these facts the court held there was a fair question to be tried and that the interlocutory injunction was warranted in the meantime, as the contract provided that the franchisee would not compete against the franchisor for a year following termination of the agreement and within a radius of five miles of a Cruiseshipcenter franchise.

---

4. What geographic limitations have courts recognized as reasonable in the franchise context?

- **How have they been related to the interests protected?**
- **Have courts recognized the legitimacy of protecting other franchisees from competition?**

Non-competition covenants will generally set out the geographic area in which a franchisee may not compete with the franchised system. In upholding geographic provisions in restrictive covenants, courts have recognized the legitimacy of protecting the interests of the general franchise system, which would include the interests of other franchisees. The question to be determined is whether the restraint of trade can be justified as reasonable in the interests of the parties.

As with temporal limitations, whether a geographic limitation is reasonable will depend on context. For example, in the pizza delivery context, franchisees often have protected geographical areas consistent with their defined delivery and service areas (*362041 B.C. Ltd v. Domino's Pizza of Canada*, 2006 BCSC 792, 2006 Carswell BC 1221 (Can. B.C. Sup. Ct.).

In *TMI Turf Management*, the British Columbia Supreme Court granted an injunction against a franchisee who was found to have breached the terms of a restrictive covenant that defined a specific geographical area relating to the prior service area that was "off limits" for a period of two years following the end of the agreement. Interestingly, in that case, the particular clause (10.01) forbade the franchisee from carrying on a lawn-care business within:

i) the licensed territory;
ii) the Province of Ontario;
iii) the Provinces of Ontario and Quebec;
iv) Canada; and
v) Canada and the United States.

But in its application, the franchisor sought only to enforce section "i) the licensed territory." The clause immediately following clause 10.01 declared each section in clause 10.01 to be a separate and distinct covenant. This strategy meant the franchisor avoided having to ask the court to "blue-pencil" the agreement into an acceptable form. As discussed earlier in section 3, the court held that the geographic scope was a reasonable reflection of the mutual expectations of the parties at the time of contracting and legally enforceable (*TMI Turf Management*, at para. 21).

5. What limitations on activities have courts recognized as reasonable in the franchise context?

Whether a limitation on activities is reasonable will depend on such factors as how similar the activity is to the activity prohibited in the agreement and whether there are other extenuating circumstances (such as the confidential information having become available in the public domain). Where the prohibited activity is the same as the activity carried on by the franchisor, a clause prohibiting a former franchisee from carrying on the same activity is more likely to be upheld as reasonable, but where a clause is overly broad in prohibiting activity beyond the business of the franchise, it will likely be rendered void.

For example, in *Watson*, the franchise agreement prohibited the franchisee from competing against the franchisor's "bathtub, sink, tile and related residential and commercial fixture and appliance reglazing and refinishing/resurfacing and bathtub liner and bathtub wall installation service business." The agreement also forbade solicitation, trading in Bathmaster's trademark, or using the trade connections the franchisee acquired while in Kamloops (where the franchise was located). In finding the former franchisee had breached none of these covenants, the court held that the defendant/franchisee was providing remodeling rather than refinishing or resurfacing surfaces as contemplated by the agreement (i.e., that the business was similar, but not the same). The court also held that there was no evidence to support the assertion that the franchisee was using confidential information, and the confidential information at issue was not protected by the clause in any event as it was within the public domain.

Kynas v. Zippy Print Franchise Ltd., [1985] B.C.J. No. 1291, 1985 Carswell BC 2257 (Can. B.C. Sup. Ct.), concerned a term in a franchise agreement that prohibited the franchisee from carrying on "the business of printing" for a period of 18 months following the end of the agreement. This language was found to be ambiguous, as it could be interpreted as prohibiting either carrying on the franchise printing business specifically or any printing business in general. As a result, the plaintiff/franchisor's request for an interim injunction was denied.

Two other British Columbia cases indicate that the more similar the new business is to the old franchise, the more likely a court will be willing to uphold restrictive covenants against competition. In *Super Cruise*, the former franchisee incorporated a new business that provided exactly the same services, operated out of the same office, and used the same telephone number as the former franchise. The restrictive covenant in the franchise agreement that prohibited competition was upheld. In *TMI Turf Management*, the court upheld the restrictive covenant where the former franchisee terminated the agreement, transferred its assets into a new company, engaged in the precise business that was at the core of the original franchise, and secured many, if not most, of the former franchise's customers.

6. Does the province recognize a difference between in-term and post-term covenants?

British Columbia recognizes no particular difference between in-term and post-term restrictive covenants—both are a restraint on trade and presumptively unenforceable unless they can be shown to be unambiguous and reasonable. This is consistent with how restrictive covenants are characterized under general principles of common law; nevertheless, as most disputes arise following the termination of a business or employment relationship, litigation in the area is usually in the post-term context.

7. Has the province allowed enforcement of covenants against non-signatories (e.g., family members, newly formed corporations)?

The issue of enforcing covenants against non-signatories has yet to be addressed by British Columbia courts, but it is reasonable to assume they would apply basic contractual principles (privity of contract) to bar any party to a franchise agreement from attempting to enforce its terms against a non-signatory, such as family members, with the possible exception of non-arm's length companies.

For instance, in *Bhangoo v. Soon*, 2010 BCSC 826, [2010] B.C.W.L.D. 7591 (Can. B.C. Sup. Ct.), the British Columbia Supreme Court dismissed a claim against defendants who had been in control of the day-to-day operations of a company on the basis that the plaintiff failed to establish that the defendant undertook personal responsibility under the contract. As the defendants were not personal signatories to the contract, the dispute was properly between the plaintiff and the corporation. The fact that the defendants were in de facto control of the corporation was not sufficient to hold them personally responsible.

8. Will the province modify, "blue-pencil," or otherwise reduce a covenant found to be overbroad?

In franchise agreement disputes, whether a court in British Columbia will modify, "blue-pencil," or otherwise reduce an overbroad covenant, depends greatly on the context in which it arises. Overall, the judicial trend in Canada seems to be that courts are moving away from imposing their own interpretation of the parties' intent by rewriting a clause in order to render it valid.

The Supreme Court of Canada stated in *Shafron v. KRG Insurance Brokers (Western) Inc.*, 2009 SCC 6, [2009] 1 S.C.R. 157 (Can.), at paragraph 36:

> I am of the opinion that blue pencil severance may be resorted to sparingly and only in cases where the part being removed is clearly severable, trivial and not part of the main purport of the restrictive covenant. However, the general rule must be that a restrictive covenant in an employment contract found to be ambiguous or unreasonable in its terms will be void and unenforceable.

In that case, a term in a restrictive covenant that prevented a departing employee from competing against its former employer in the "Metropolitan area of Greater Vancouver" was held to be ambiguous and therefore barred the enforcement of the entire covenant. However, that was an employment case, and the court cautioned at paragraphs 18 and 19:

> It is important at this juncture to differentiate between a contract for the sale of a business and an employment contract.
>
> [19] In *Nordenfelt*, Lord Macnaghten pointed out that there is greater freedom to contract between buyer and seller than between employer and employee. At p. 566, he wrote:
>
>> To a certain extent, different considerations must apply in cases of apprenticeship and cases of that sort, on the one hand, and cases of the sale of a business or dissolution of partnership on the other. A man is bound an apprentice because he wishes to learn a trade and to practice it. A man may sell because he is getting too old for the strain and worry of business, or because he wishes for some other reason to retire from business altogether. Then there is obviously more freedom of contract between buyer and seller than between master and servant or between an employer and a person seeking employment.
>
> Although the comments of Lord Macnaghten focus on apprenticeship, the same concept has been extended and applied to contracts between employers and employees.

In the sale of a business context, courts will more readily enforce a restrictive covenant. In *Blunt v. De Palma et al.*, 2005 BCSC 992, [2005] B.C.W.L.D. 5337 (Can. B.C. Sup. Ct.), the Supreme Court of British Columbia upheld a restrictive covenant in relation to the sale of a denturist business. In support of its decision in the *Blunt* case, the court quoted from the Supreme Court of Canada decision *J.G. Collins Insurance Agencies Ltd. v. Elsley*, 1978 CNLII 7 (SCC), [1978] 2 S.C.R. 916, at page 923 as follows:

> The distinction made in the cases between a restrictive covenant contained in an agreement for the sale of a business and one contained in a contract of employment is well-conceived and responsive to practical considerations. A person seeking to sell his business might find himself with an unsaleable commodity if denied the right to assure the purchaser that he, the vendor, would not later enter into competition. Difficulty lies in definition of the time during which, and the area within which, the non-competitive covenant is to operate, but if these are reasonable, the courts will normally give effect to the covenant.

As a franchise agreement falls into the no-man's land between "sale of business" and "employment contract," there remain some questions as the applicability of the rationale from *Shafron* in the franchising context. To date, in British Columbia, only one case has applied *Shafron* to a franchise dispute.

Watson concerned an application by a plaintiff/franchisor for an interim injunction against the defendant/former franchisee. The franchisor alleged, among other things, that the franchisee had breached the terms of a non-compete clause in the original franchise agreement. The clause prohibited the franchisee from competing against the franchisor in any area where another franchise was carrying on business for at least two years after the end of the agreement. The franchisor alleged that the franchisee was competing against the franchisor in "Victoria"; this was held to be ambiguous and therefore unenforceable. However, in applying *Shafron* to the franchising context, the B.C. Supreme Court was careful to note:

> In determining the enforceability of a restrictive covenant, the courts will have regard to all of the circumstances between the parties. Hence the approach to reasonableness in the context of the sale of the business is somewhat different from the approach between an employer and an employee. Courts are apparently more willing to protect a new business owner from competition in the same market place by the former principal of that very business than they are to prevent an employee from competing against a former employer, providing that he or she does not make use of proprietary information or trade secrets in doing so . . . the facts of this case do not involve a former franchisee competing against the franchise he previously held . . . . In my opinion, in these circumstances, the principles as they have been articulated in the context of employer/employee cases offer significant guidance to the resolution of the matter before me.

On this reasoning it appears that courts in British Columbia will make a case-by-case determination of whether the franchise at issue aligns more closely with a sale of business or an employer/employee relationship. In the former, courts may be less likely to apply *Shafron*, and there may be some room to "blue-pencil" the offending covenant into an acceptable form. However, where the context aligns more with the latter, courts will likely refuse to sever any part of the covenant, relying on the reasoning in *Shafron*.

9. When does a non-compete period begin to run? Will courts equitably extend the term?

A non-compete period begins to run on termination of the franchise agreement. To date there is no indication that courts in British Columbia will equitably extend this term. It seems quite unlikely a court would take this step given that courts have expressed a reluctance to enforce restrictive covenants at all, unless it can be shown they are both unambiguous and reasonable (see *Shafron*, previous page). Given the underlying principle that restrictive covenants are a restraint on trade and valid only where parties have freely contracted into them, it is difficult to conceive of an argument, equitable or otherwise, that would convince a court to extend the time period already bargained for and agreed to on set terms by the parties.

10. Are there additional nuances or peculiarities of the province's treatment of covenants in the franchising context?

INTERIM INJUNCTIONS IN BRITISH COLUMBIA

The first remedy sought when a franchisee breaches a non-compete clause in a franchise agreement is an interim injunction. In order to satisfy a court that an interim injunction is warranted, a party must demonstrate:

1) that there is a serious question to be tried;
2) that irreparable harm will occur to the party seeking the injunction if it is not granted; and
3) that the balance of convenience favours granting an injunction;

RJR MacDonald Inc. v. Canada (Attorney General), [1994] 1 S.C.R. 311 (Can.).

Although non-competition clauses are enforced in British Columbia, it is difficult for franchisors to satisfy the interim injunction test.

First, unless the entire franchise system is at risk, a court may conclude that damages are an adequate remedy and therefore there is no irreparable harm (as required under the second arm of the test) if the non-compete clause is not enforced. Second, the franchisee will argue that its ability to make a living is at risk, or that the business it has set up and money it has invested in that business will be lost if the injunction is granted (which goes to both the second and third arms of the test, irreparable harm and whether the balance of convenience favors granting the injunction). The practical result is that, on an interim basis, it can be difficult for franchisors to enforce non-competition clauses.

This was the case in *Wine Kitz Franchise Corp. v. Pritchard*, 2002 BCSC 1819 (Can. B.C. Sup. Ct.). The franchisor alleged, among other things, that the franchisee had contravened a non-compete clause when on termination of the agreement, it went into substantially the same business within the geographically restricted territory and within a prohibited 12-month time-period. The defendant owned a single franchise among many. The court held there was a serious issue to be tried.

In assessing "irreparable harm" to the franchisor, the court determined there would be more harm to the franchisee than the franchisor were an injunction to be granted, stating at paragraph 20, "Clearly, the claim then of that plaintiff [franchisor] can be dealt with as a question of damages." In assessing "irreparable harm," the court sided with the franchisee, stating:

> I have no hesitation in finding that the defendants would suffer greater harm if they were now forced to discontinue their present operations, and become again franchisees of the Wine Kitz materials.
>
> . . .
>
> On the other hand, as I've said, the discontinuance of a franchise store will have less harmful effects on the plaintiffs. They have already taken steps to encourage customers of the defendants to take their business to Abbotsford and the Wine Kitz store there. There is evidence that they should, without too much difficulty, be able to start up a Wine Art operated store in Chilliwack, if they choose to do so.

Wine Kitz at paras. 24–26.

In weighing the balance of convenience, the court was particularly influenced by the franchisees' assertion that they were likely to lose their business along with their home if the non-compete clause were enforced, whereas the damage that would accrue to the franchisor by maintaining the status quo pending the outcome of a trial on the merits was substantially less. In the end, the court determined the "balance of convenience" favored dismissing the application for an interim injunction. The court was also influenced by the argument that the non-compete clause was overbroad and therefore potentially unenforceable.

BC

DUTY OF GOOD FAITH

Section 3(1) of the *Franchises Act* imposes a duty of fair dealing on both franchisor and franchisee in the performance and enforcement of franchise agreements, including exercising rights under franchise agreements. Additionally, courts in British Columbia have accepted that there is a common law duty of good faith imposed on dealings between franchisors and franchisees. Further, they have demonstrated a willingness to enforce this duty that may impact the enforcement of restrictive covenants, although to date, this has occurred only within other contexts.

In *Domino's Pizza*, the franchisee applied for an interim injunction restraining the franchisor from opening another franchise within the boundaries of the franchisee's service area. Under the franchise agreement, the franchisor had discretion to modify the boundaries, but in granting the injunction, the court held there was a fair question to be tried regarding whether the franchisor's unilateral revision of the boundaries without consulting the franchisee had met the requisite standard of good faith, fair dealing, and reasonableness.

This development is somewhat at odds with earlier authority that did not extend the duty of good faith so far. In *Sultani v. Blenz the Canadian Coffee Co.*, 2005 BCSC 571, 2005 Carswell BC 877 (Can. B.C. Sup. Ct.), *aff'd on appeal* 2005 BCCA 578 (Can. B.C. Ct. of Appeal) the plaintiff/franchisee claimed the defendant/franchisor had breached a duty of good faith and fair dealing when it refused to allow the franchisee to exercise what the franchisee alleged was a right to renew the lease. Instead, the franchisor allowed the lease to lapse and, on its expiry, terminated the franchise agreement. In finding no such duty had been breached, the court noted at paragraph 16 that "neither the franchise agreement nor the sublease contains either a right or an option to renew" and that no evidence was led to demonstrate the existence of an oral agreement to renew. The court held (at para. 25):

> In all the circumstances, it also cannot be said that Blenz acted dishonestly, unreasonably, or unfairly so to have acted in bad faith. . . . The plaintiff read the documents and was not rushed into signing by the defendants. Finally the duty of fair dealing does not compel a party to renew an expiring relationship when it is not considered commercially reasonable to do so. Here, Blenz explained that it had a new commercial programme to introduce at this downtown location and that it wanted to do so on its own, not through a franchisee.

Overall, the duty of good faith appears to be developing as a tool that British Columbia courts may engage to go beyond the four corners of a franchise agreement. This may result in an analysis of the conduct of the franchisor prior to enforcing restrictive covenants.

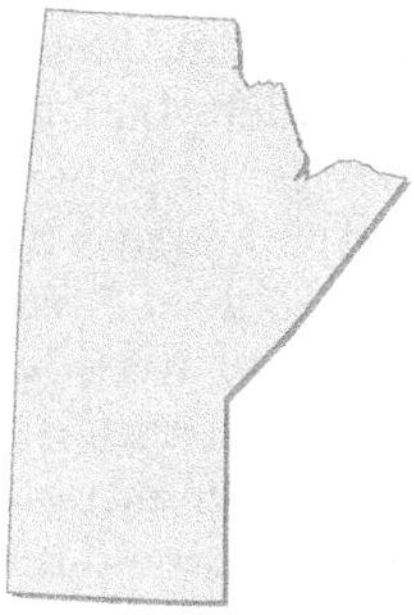

Manitoba

*by Geoffrey B. Shaw and Danielle DiPardo**

1. Has the province addressed covenants against competition in the context of franchising?

- **Does the province have a franchising statute or regulations that address covenants against competition?**
- **Does the province have a covenants statute of general applicability that would encompass franchise covenants?**
- **Have the courts addressed covenants in the context of franchising either under a statute or under the province's common law?**

Manitoba passed the Franchises Act, S.M. 2010, c.13 (Can. Man.) (the MFA) on June 17, 2010. The Franchise Regulation was proclaimed in March of 2012, and the MFA came into force on October 1, 2012. The MFA is primarily disclosure legislation. It seeks to provide franchisees extra protection since franchisors will be required to provide potential franchisees with disclosure documents containing prescribed information, not less than 14 days before the franchisees sign any franchise agreement or pay any consideration to the franchisor. The MFA and the proposed regulations do not contain any provisions that address covenants against competition in franchise agreements.

Manitoba does not have a covenants statute of general applicability that addresses restrictive covenants. In Manitoba, the law regarding restrictive covenants is governed by the common law, and few cases have dealt with the issue in the context of franchise agreements.

In Manitoba, the leading case on the enforceability of restrictive covenants is *Elsley v. J.G. Collins Insurance Agencies*, [1978] 2 S.C.R. 916 (Can.). Even though the case deals with the enforceability of restrictive covenants in an employment context, Dickson J., writing for the majority of the Supreme Court of Canada, made several general comments regarding restrictive covenants that would likely apply to their use in franchise agreements. The respondent purchased Elsley's insurance company and subsequently employed him. Elsley's employment contract contained a

*Geoffrey B. Shaw and Danielle DiPardo practice at Cassels, Brock & Blackwell LLP. Shaw and DiPardo have updated the Manitoba chapter of the third edition of *Covenants against Competition in Franchise Agreements* originally prepared by Andrew D.M. Ogaranko, Q.C., who practiced with Pitblado LLP in Winnipeg, Manitoba, Canada.

restriction prohibiting Elsley from engaging in the general insurance agent business while employed by the respondent, or for a five-year period after the termination of his employment. The respondent employed Elsley for 17 years before he left and began his own insurance business. During the course of his employment, Elsley dealt extensively with the respondent's clients, and most policyholders had no contact with anyone else. In fact, a significant number of the respondent's policyholders transferred their business to Elsley's new company. The test articulated by the court in *Elsley* to determine whether a restrictive covenant is reasonable is three-pronged. First, the court must determine if the party seeking to enforce the covenant has a proprietary or legitimate interest entitled to be protected. Second, the court must examine the temporal and spatial features of the covenant to determine if they are reasonable or too broad in scope. Finally, the court must determine if the covenant is intended to prevent competition generally, and, if so, whether such a restriction is necessary to protect the covenantee's interests in the circumstances. A restrictive covenant in an employment contract will be subjected to more scrutiny than a restrictive covenant found in a sale of business agreement.

The Supreme Court of Canada found in *Elsley* that to be enforceable, a restrictive covenant must be reasonable given the public interest and circumstances of the particular situation. Restrictive covenants are generally not in the public's interest since they discourage competition and place restraints on trade. However, parties have the right to contract among themselves, especially when there is equality in bargaining power.

In an employment situation, the dynamics of the relationship must be carefully analyzed to determine whether there was an imbalance in the bargaining power of the parties when the contract was entered into. Typically, complete restrictions on competition are unenforceable. However, in *Elsley*, the court clarified that where the restrictive covenant protects trade secrets, confidential information, and/or trade connections of the employer, the covenant may be enforceable. It also held that an employer cannot have a proprietary interest in potential clients. However, with respect to actual clients, the court stated (at page 926):

> Nevertheless, in exceptional cases, of which I think this is one, the nature of the employment may justify a covenant prohibiting an employee not only from soliciting customers, but also from establishing his own business or working for others so as to be likely to appropriate the employer's trade connection through his acquaintance with the employer's customers. This may indeed be the only effective covenant to protect the proprietary interest of the employer. A simple non-solicitation clause would not suffice.

The court observed that a broad restrictive covenant will be enforceable in an employment situation where the employee has formed close personal relationships with the clients of the business. A restrictive covenant may be necessary to prevent such an employee from using "the intimacies and knowledge which he had acquired in the course of his employment in order to create a practice of his own in that same place and by doing so undermine the business and connection of the employer" *Elsley* (p. 926). Taking the close connection that Elsley had with clients into consideration, as well as the fact that there was no suggestion that customers would suffer from the loss of Elsley's business services, as there were multiple other insurance agents in the area, the restrictive covenant was enforced.

Rapid-Med Plus Franchise Corp. v. Elliot, [1991] M.J. No. 322 (Can. Man. C.A.), was an appeal from an interlocutory order restraining the defendants Elliot and

2446049 Manitoba Ltd. (244) from competing with the plaintiff franchisor in contravention of the franchise agreement. The interlocutory order also prohibited the co-defendants, Quality and Bodimetric, from inducing a breach of contract. The facts are as follows. The franchisor provided services to insurance companies by facilitating the medical examination and assessment of prospective clients. The defendant, Elliot, was an employee of the plaintiff franchisor. She left her employment with the plaintiff to enter into a franchise agreement with Quality and Bodimetric on behalf of herself and the other co-defendant, 244. The effect of the agreement was to grant 244 the exclusive right and franchise to carry on the franchisor's business in Manitoba. A number of restrictive covenants were contained in the franchise agreement, namely that Elliot and 244 would not disclose the plaintiff's trade secrets to others, compete with the plaintiff's business anywhere during the term of the agreement, and compete with the plaintiff for a period of three years following the termination of the agreement in Manitoba or within the exclusive territory of any other franchised dealer. The plaintiff discovered that Quality and Bodimetric were actively trying to recruit Elliot to work for them. The plaintiff also obtained evidence that Elliot had begun introducing large clients of the plaintiff to Quality and Bodimetric in an effort to get their business. The plaintiffs sought an injunction to enforce the restrictive covenant in the franchise agreement. The defendants argued that the covenant was unreasonable in terms of both territory and time.

The court in *Rapid-Med Plus* looked at the purpose of the covenant and stated that the prohibition against competition in Manitoba was included to prevent Elliot from taking advantage of the relationships she had developed with the plaintiff's clients. The court relied on Dickson J.'s comments in *Elsley*, in which it was held that a restrictive covenant may be reasonable in an employment situation where the employee is in a position to develop close relationships with the employer's clients. Applying those comments to the case at hand, the court found that the very nature of the insurance business involves the formation of close relationships between the agent and the clients or, in this case, between the franchisee and the franchisor's insurance clients. Therefore,

> It is entirely reasonable that, in putting Elliot in a position where she might develop these relationships, the plaintiff should require her and her numbered company not to compete with it for a period of three years in the area where the contact with those customers would occur.

The Manitoba Court of Appeal found that the covenant was reasonable with respect to its restriction on competitive actions within Manitoba. However, the prohibition against all other territories was severed and excluded from the interlocutory injunction order.

Nutter's Bulk & Natural Foods Ltd. v. G.S. Kelcon Ltd., [2000] M.J. No. 114 (Can. Man. C.A.), dealt with an appeal from the decision of a motions judge, denying the grant of an interim injunction to enforce a restrictive covenant. The operation of the covenant would have had the effect of closing the defendant's business pending trial. The defendant was the franchisee of the plaintiff, and sold a variety of bulk and health foods. The restrictive covenant in the franchise agreement read as follows:

> 5.04 (b) Upon termination of the Franchise Agreement for any reason whatsoever . . . , the Franchisee may not have any interest in any business which is a retailer or wholesaler of foods or any other organization which is similar to the business of "Nutter's Fruit & Nut Co." within a radius of

Ten (10) miles of his former retail or wholesale food franchise, for a period of Five (5) years, provided that:

(i) If the geographic area encompassed by the foregoing covenant is at any time determined to be unreasonable by a Court of competent jurisdiction and adjudicating upon the validity of the covenant, then the geographic area shall be reduced mile by mile to a geographic area determined by such Court to be reasonable;

(ii) If the Five (5) year time limit as set forth in the foregoing covenant is at any time determined to be unreasonable by a Court of competent jurisdiction and adjudicating upon the validity of the covenant, then such time limitation shall be reduced by Six (6) month periods to the time determined by such Court as reasonable.

The defendants decided not to renew the franchise agreement at the expiration of its term. However, they continued to carry on business at the same location, selling the same products. Only the store's name had changed. Since the wording of the covenant was vague, the Manitoba Court of Appeal carefully examined whether the intent of the provision was to restrict the defendants from engaging in the wholesale food business in its entirety or whether it was restricted to the type of business that the plaintiff was in. Even though the "clause containing the restrictive covenant is not a model of drafting competence," it was held that the intent of the covenant was to prohibit the defendants from engaging in a similar business to the plaintiffs business, which was the retail sale of bulk groceries. The court deferred to the trial judge to determine if the covenant was enforceable. Huband J.A., however, made the following observation:

> The business of the franchise as described in the agreement—bulk grocery items—might be such a broad category as to make the time and area restrictions unreasonable. It is one thing to impose severe restrictions where the business in question is of a specialized, scientific, or technical nature, while such restraints may be unreasonable in a business as competitive and commonplace as retailing bulk groceries.

In order to obtain an interim injunction, the plaintiff must prove the following (*RJR MacDonald Inc. v. Canada (Attorney General)*, [1994] 1 S.C.R. 311 (Can.):

1. it has a strong prima facie case (i.e., there is some probability of success at trial) or there is a serious question to be tried;
2. it will suffer irreparable harm if the injunction is not granted; and
3. the balance of convenience lies with the plaintiff.

Huband J.A., in *Nutter's Bulk & Natural Foods*, remarked that the enforceability of the restrictive covenant was not clear and obvious, but rather "simply arguable"; the court analyzed whether irreparable harm would be suffered and whether the balance of convenience lies with the plaintiff. The court held that the plaintiff would not suffer irreparable harm if the injunction were not granted since there would be a record of the defendant's gross sales, making it relatively straightforward to determine the plaintiff's potential damages. Furthermore, the balance of convenience favored the defendant. Two years had passed since the expiration of the franchise agreement, and since the parties had moved relatively quickly through the litigation process, it was likely that a trial date was not far away. The court also noted that when the defendants first began operating the franchised business, it floundered. In response, the defendants began selling health foods. Even though the plaintiff initially was opposed to the incorporation of health foods in its product lineup, it was adopted by the franchise as a whole, and at the time of trial, it comprised 30 percent of the franchise's sales. In addition, the franchise agreement terminated naturally and was not breached by the defendants. In light of the foregoing, the court held that this was not a case where irreparable harm could be assumed. As a result, the interim injunction was denied. Prior to trial, the case was settled so the enforceability of the restrictive covenant was never adjudicated.

Imasco Retail Inc. (c.o.b. Shoppers Drug Mart) v. Blanaru, [1995] M.J. No. 332 (Can. Man. Q.B.), was an action for damages for breach of a franchise agreement. The plaintiff and defendant had entered into an agreement to expand their existing franchise business to include the sale of drugs to nursing homes. Subsequent to the extension of the franchise agreement, the defendant set up a separate business and sold drugs to other parties, which he did not disclose to the plaintiff franchisor. The plaintiff brought an action for damages alleging that the defendant had fraudulently withheld profits owing under the franchise agreement and sought an accounting of monies owed. Wright J. found that the defendant fraudulently withheld monies from the plaintiff, resulting in a financial loss to the plaintiff. In arriving at his decision, the court considered the provisions of the franchise agreement that required the defendant to devote his "entire time, labour, skill, effort and attention to the franchised business and the management, conduct and operation thereof." He interpreted the provision to be an unequivocal restrictive covenant prohibiting the defendant from carrying on a separate business during the duration of the franchise agreement. Therefore, the business that the defendant had set up on the side clearly violated the provisions of the franchise agreement.

MB

In *Winnipeg Livestock Sales Ltd. v. Plewman*, 2000 MBCA 60 (Can. Man. C.A.), the Manitoba Court of Appeal considered the application of the principles enunciated in *Elsley* to restrictive covenants in employment contracts. Since this case deals with restrictive covenants in employment contracts, its application to franchise cases is unclear. The plaintiff, Winnipeg Livestock Sales Ltd., was a large livestock auction market in Manitoba. The defendant, Desmond Plewman, was an independent contractor of the plaintiff who provided auctioneering services. The employment contract stated that Plewman was not to solicit or provide livestock auctioneering services to any person in Manitoba "who is or is likely to be in competition with the Business" for 18 months after the termination of his services. After Plewman terminated his contract with Winnipeg Livestock, he purchased an interest in the co-defendant, Grunthal Livestock Auction Mart Limited, a business directly in competition with the plaintiff. The plaintiff brought an application for an interim injunction to enforce the restrictive covenant contained in the employment contract. The motions judge granted the interim injunction, and Plewman appealed. The court first noted that "[i]t is settled law that a restrictive covenant is a contract in restraint of trade which is prima facie contrary to public policy and hence void. Such a covenant is enforceable *only it if it is reasonable and in the public* interest" (emphasis added), which requires an analysis of the restrictive covenant. The court then further clarified that in determining whether an employer has a proprietary interest in clients, the degree of loyalty that the clientele demonstrates is a significant factor in determining whether a general non-competition clause or a specific and limited non-solicitation clause is most appropriate in the circumstances. The court listed a number of factors that are relevant in determining whether a restrictive covenant is reasonable in the circumstance (at para. 41):

- length of time with the employer;
- amount of personal service to the clients;
- whether the employee dealt with clients exclusively or on a sustained and recurring basis;
- whether the knowledge about the client which the employee gained was of a confidential nature, or involved an intimate knowledge of the client's particular needs, preferences or idiosyncrasies;
- whether the nature of the employee's work meant that the employee had influence over clients in the sense that the clients relied upon the employee's advice, or trusted the employee;
- if competition by the employee has already occurred, whether there is evidence that clients have switched their business to him, especially without direct solicitation;
- the nature of the business with respect to customer loyalty, how clients are "won" and kept, and whether the clientele is recurring; and
- the community involved and whether there were clientele yet to be exploited.

Analyzing the facts of the case, the Manitoba Court of Appeal found that the restrictive covenant was unreasonable and unenforceable because it prohibited Plewman from engaging in auctioneering. Winnipeg Livestock was unable to adduce evidence showing that Plewman had a close relationship with clients or that clients requested "him and only him to do their auctioneering." There was also no evidence indicating customer loyalty or how clients were acquired or retained. The appeal was, therefore, allowed.

The Manitoba Court of Queen's Bench addressed the unenforceability of restrictive covenants in employment agreements in *One Insurance Group Ltd. v. Roy et al.*, 2018 MBQB 190 (Can. Man. Q.B.). In that case, the defendant employee entered into a non-competition and a non-solicitation agreement with his employer in 2005. Under the non-solicitation agreement, the defendant agreed that, should he cease to be employed by his employer, he would not solicit business from any client of the corporation "at any time." The non-competition agreement provided that the defendant was restricted from engaging with any competing business, for a period of five years, within the limits of the employer's town and municipality. Pursuant to a later corporate reorganization in 2012, the defendant entered into an additional non-solicitation agreement that restricted the defendant from soliciting or transacting business with any customer of his employer for one year after his employment ends. The defendant subsequently sold his ownership in the employer to the plaintiff, under the terms of which he entered into an additional agreement in 2015 affirming that the 2005 non-competition and non-solicitation agreements were still valid and binding. The defendant retired briefly before being approached by a competing insurance company that, in light of the agreements, assured the defendant he would not be operating within the town or municipality, and would not be solicitating his former clients from the plaintiff. Following the defendant commencing his employment with his new employer, the plaintiff brought an action seeking to enforce the agreements. Addressing the enforceability of the restrictive covenants, the court first observed that this analysis requires an examination of whether the restrictive covenant is ambiguous; if it is ambiguous as to the parameters of the prohibition on activity, time, or geography, it is prima facie unreasonable and enforceable. The court held that the non-competition agreement could be upheld and enforced, as it contained both spatial and temporal features that limited the extent of the prohibited activities. Noting that the term of five years is likely outside the range of what could be considered reasonable, the agreement was nevertheless upheld as it was not unreasonable for the parties to have agreed to such a term while aware of the consequences and importance of this agreement. Dealing with the non-solicitation agreements, the first non-solicitation agreement, restraining the defendant from soliciting business from the clients of the plaintiff "at any time," was deemed to be overly broad due to the lack of a temporal limitation. Comparatively, the 2012 non-solicitation agreement was held to be reasonable as it contained both temporal and spatial limitations that were consistent with protecting the plaintiff's investment in the insurance business.

---

2. Have the courts articulated the "legitimate interests" of the franchisor that will support enforcement of a covenant against competition contained in a franchise agreement?

- **If so, what are they (e.g., protection of goodwill, protection of confidential information), and in what contexts did the issue arise?**
- **If not, what interests have been recognized in other contexts (e.g., employment agreements, the sale of business context)?**

As the Supreme Court of Canada enunciated in *Elsley*, in order for a restrictive covenant to be reasonable and enforceable, the party enforcing the covenant must be able to identify the proprietary interest that is being protected. One interest that the courts have consistently upheld as legitimately in need of protection is the franchisor's trade connections. A franchisor does not have a proprietary interest in potential customers. However, where a franchisee has worked closely with clients, has developed a personal relationship with them, and has developed an intimate knowledge of their needs so as to give the franchisee a competitive advantage, such trade connections have been deemed worthy of protection by the courts. Based on the cases discussed above, the importance of trade connections and the protection of clientele mainly arise in franchise situations where personal services are being provided to the customers. However, a lack of loyalty among the franchise's customers will militate against a finding of a legitimate proprietary interest (*Winnipeg Livestock Sales*; *Steinke v. Barrett*, 2012 MBQB 49 at para 52).

In *Friesen v. McKague* (1992), 81 Man. R. (2d) 290 (Can. Man. C.A.), the Manitoba Court of Appeal further commented on the legitimate business interests worthy of protection (at page 8):

> While the relationship between the parties in *Rapid-Med Plus* was that of franchisor and franchisee, the dicta applies with equal force to the circumstances of this case where the defendant was able to develop direct and personal relationships with customers because the plaintiffs had put him into the position where those relationships would develop. There was no inequality of bargaining power between the parties in this case. The defendant was a professional and in receipt of legal advice at all stages of the proceedings. Given the nature of the specific area of practice assigned to the defendant and of the community involved, it was entirely appropriate

that there be a general restriction because of the close personal relationship that undoubtedly developed between the defendant and the clinic's customers. This was indeed the only effective way to protect the plaintiff's legitimate business interests.

The protection of confidential information and trade secrets has also been identified by the courts as a legitimate proprietary interest of franchisors (see *Rapid-Med Plus; Sun Life Financial Distributors (Canada) Inc. v. Sanche*, 2008 MBQB 99 at para. 58).

Imperial Oil Ltd. v. Westlake Fuel Ltd., 2001 MBCA 130 (Can. Man. C.A.) dealt with the enforceability of a restrictive covenant in an agency agreement. Even though it does not deal directly with a franchise situation, the Manitoba Court of Appeal's analysis is applicable to franchise agreements. The defendants in *Imperial* appealed the lower court's ruling granting an interim injunction against the defendants in favor of the plaintiff, essentially shutting down the defendants' operations. The plaintiffs had appointed the defendant, Westlake Fuel Ltd., as its agent for the sale and delivery of fuel and products to its customers in Manitoba. The personal defendants, Kevin and Kimberley Johnson, the sole directors and officers of the defendant Westlake, had provided personal guarantees to fulfill all covenants under the agreement. The agency agreement contained the following restrictive covenant (at para. 11):

> Agent agrees that he will not for a period of twelve (12) months after the expiration or other termination of this Agreement, directly or indirectly, as principal, agent, partner, employee or otherwise howsoever, solicit orders for or supply within the market area any products then being sold by IMPERIAL within the market area, to any person, firm or corporation who purchased such products within the market area either as an assigned or as an unassigned customer within the period of twelve (12) months preceding the date of expiration or termination of this Agreement.

After the agreement was terminated by the plaintiff for an alleged breach by the defendants, Kevin registered the business name Westshore Fuel and Oil and began delivering oil products in Manitoba. The plaintiff sought to enforce the restrictive covenant contained in the agency agreement. Relying on the recent judgment of the Manitoba Court of Appeal in *Winnipeg Livestock Sales*, Philp J.A. re-articulated the test for assessing the reasonableness of a restrictive covenant:

1. Does the party seeking to enforce the covenant have a proprietary or legitimate interest entitled to protection?
2. Are the temporal and spatial features of the covenant reasonable, or too broad?
3. Does the covenant prevent competition generally, and if so, is this restriction reasonably required for the protection of the covenantee in the circumstances?

The defendants argued that the covenant was not enforceable because the plaintiff had no proprietary interest to protect. However, the Manitoba Court of Appeal disagreed with the defendants because there was evidence that the plaintiff had provided Kevin Johnson and the other defendants with an established list of customers. The plaintiff had a proprietary interest in protecting its trade connection, since it was reasonable to assume that the defendants may obtain a personal knowledge of and influence over the plaintiff's customers that would be harmful to the plaintiff's business if the defendants were allowed to compete. The court further noted that the covenant was not a general restraint on trade since it did not seek to prohibit the defendants from competing with the plaintiff or from supplying customers that were not related to the plaintiff. Given the restrictive nature of the covenant, it did not seek to extend beyond the "legitimate proprietary interest that arose from the nature of the relationship that was contemplated by the agency agreement." Therefore, the restrictive covenant was enforceable. However, when determining whether an interim injunction should be granted, Philp J.A. was not convinced that the plaintiff would suffer any irreparable harm that would justify the injunction. Furthermore, the defendants would suffer more harm if the injunction were in place since it would impair their ability to earn a living. Therefore, the injunction was not granted. The case was settled before it proceeded to trial.

3. What time limitations have the courts recognized as reasonable in the franchise context? If no franchise cases have been decided, what time limitations have been recognized in other contexts?

➤ **How have they been related to the interests protected?**

The Manitoba courts have recognized the validity of restrictive covenants in effect during the duration of the franchise agreement (see *Rapid-Med Plus* and *Imasco Retail*). The courts have also recognized that a three-year limitation following termination of the franchise agreement was reasonable (see *Rapid-Med Plus*). Furthermore, there was no time limitation expressed in *Rapid-Med Plus* with respect to the prohibition against disclosing the franchisor's trade secrets and confidences to others. In *Nutter's Bulk & Natural Foods*, the Manitoba Court of Appeal stated that the enforceability of a restrictive covenant prohibiting competition for five years following the termination of the franchise agreement was "simply arguable." However, in the court's view, it was not the time limitation that made the enforceability of the covenant questionable. Rather, the uncertainty was over whether the interest that sought to be protected by the covenant was legitimate.

It is clear that the enforceability of restrictive covenants during the term of the franchise agreement is intended to protect the proprietary interests of the franchisor. Following the termination of the franchise, the three- to five-year time limitation is meant to protect the trade connections of the franchisor, so that the franchisee does not obtain a competitive advantage through the connections that it had established during the course of the franchise arrangement.

4. What geographic limitations have courts recognized as reasonable in the franchise context?

➤ **How have they been related to the interests protected?**

➤ **Have the courts recognized the legitimacy of protecting other franchisees from competition?**

With respect to restrictive covenants that are operable during the term of the franchise agreement, franchisees are generally prohibited from competing with the franchisor's business anywhere. This has not been identified by the courts to be unreasonable (see *Rapid-Med Plus* and *Imasco Retail*).

With respect to post-term covenants, the Manitoba Court of Appeal stated that a restriction against competing with the franchisor in Manitoba was reasonable in *Rapid-Med Plus.* The court declined to comment on whether the geographical limitation prohibiting the franchisee from competing in any "exclusive territory of any other franchised dealer" was reasonable. However, the court did recognize the justification for such a restriction.

In *Nutter's Bulk & Natural Foods,* the franchisee was prohibited from competing with the franchisor within ten miles of the former franchise location. As previously stated, the court commented that it was not "clear and obvious" that the restrictive covenant was reasonable, but the problems with the covenant did not appear to stem from the geographical limitations imposed.

The Manitoba courts have not yet recognized the legitimacy of protecting franchisees outside of the province from competition. In *Rapid-Med Plus,* the franchisee was prohibited from competing with the franchisor for a period of three years after the termination of the agreement "within the exclusive territory of any other franchised dealer." The Manitoba Court of Appeal held that the restriction pertaining to the territory of other franchised dealers was meant to protect the plaintiff's other franchisees from the wrongful use of information and trade secrets that the franchisee had obtained during the course of the arrangement. However, in deciding whether to grant an interlocutory injunction, the court held that the injunction order was to be amended to enforce the Manitoba portion of the covenant only. This was done with the consent of the franchisor. As the case settled before trial, there is no further judicial interpretation of the covenant.

5. What limitations on activities have courts recognized as reasonable in the franchise context?

Generally, in the franchise context, covenants have restricted the franchisee's right to engage in business similar or identical to the franchisor's business, in a specific geographical region, for a defined period of time. The purpose of the covenants has generally been identified as protection of the franchisor's trade connections. Specifically, the courts have recognized the following limitations on activities in the franchise context:

- Upon termination of the franchise relationship, the franchisee is prohibited from engaging in a business similar to that of the franchisor for a specified time in a certain geographical region (see *Rapid-Med Plus* and *Imasco Retail*);
- The franchisee will not disclose the franchisor's "trade secrets, know-how, or confidences to others" (see *Rapid-Med Plus*);
- The franchisee will not compete with the franchisor's business during the duration of the franchise arrangement anywhere (see *Rapid-Med Plus*); and
- The franchisee must devote his "entire time, labour, skill, effort and attention to the franchised business and the management, conduct and operation thereof" (see *Imasco Retail*).

It is important for a franchisor to restrict the limitations on competition as much as possible, so the covenant does not have the effect of being overly broad. In *Nutter's Bulk & Natural Foods,* the restrictive covenant was drafted in such a way that it prohibited the franchisee from engaging in the retailing of bulk groceries. The court found the category of bulk grocery retail to be extremely broad as to make the restrictive covenant possibly unenforceable. Where the business is as "competitive and commonplace" as the retail sale of bulk groceries is, such a restriction may be unenforceable. This is in contrast to a very specialized, scientific, or technical business where a blanket restriction may be appropriate. It should be noted that the Manitoba Court of Appeal stated that the enforceability of the restrictive covenant was a matter for the trial judge to determine, but the case did not proceed to trial.

6. Does the province recognize a difference between in-term and post-term covenants?

In the context of franchise cases, the courts have not explicitly recognized a difference between in-term and post-term covenants. However, in both the *Rapid-Med Plus* and *Imasco Retail* decisions, the courts dealt with franchise agreements that contained non-compete clauses both during the duration of the agreements and after termination.

In both cases, the in-term covenants prohibiting competition during the terms of the franchises were not stringently analyzed and were found to be reasonable in the circumstances. Given the nature of a franchise relationship, it would be reasonable that the parties would agree to a covenant restricting competition in a similar business or industry. There appears to be a high emphasis on the protection of the franchisor during the term of the franchise arrangement. Post-term covenants are more contentious, however, because they restrict the ability of the franchisee to compete after the franchise relationship has been terminated. Based on the *Rapid-Med* and *Imasco* cases, courts appear to be more stringent in their application of the principles to post-term covenants than in-term covenants in franchise situations.

7. Has the province allowed enforcement of covenants against non-signatories (e.g., family members, newly formed corporations)?

Whether a restrictive covenant will be enforceable against non-signatories to the franchise agreement is dependent on the actual franchise agreement itself. The Manitoba Court of Appeal addressed this very issue, albeit in the context of an agency agreement, in *Imperial*. The defendants, Kevin and Kimberley Johnson, had provided personal guarantees to the plaintiff, promising to observe and perform all covenants under the agency agreement. The court held that the personal guarantees did not have the effect of binding Kevin and Kimberley Johnson to the restrictive covenant.

The court's finding in *Imperial* that a general personal guarantee to be bound by the covenants contained in the master agreement is not sufficient to bind non-signatories to the overarching agreement demonstrates that collateral non-compete agreements must be entered into. The courts will not bind non-signatories to a restrictive covenant unless the parties have specifically contracted to be bound by the restriction.

8. Will the province modify, "blue-pencil," or otherwise reduce a covenant found to be overbroad?

The defendants argued that the restrictive covenant at issue in *Rapid-Med Plus* was overly broad because it restricted the defendants from competing with the franchisor for a period of three years from the termination of the franchise agreement within Manitoba or within the exclusive territory of any other franchised dealer. At the appeal, the plaintiff stated that it had no objection to the amendment of the injunction so that it only applied to the activities of the defendants within Manitoba. Twaddle J.A. commented that the injunction could only be amended if the restrictive covenant were drafted in such a way that the two geographic areas could be severed from one another. In this particular case, each geographic area was clearly defined in the contract and was included to protect the franchisor's legitimate business interests in each of the areas. The purpose of the covenant against competition in Manitoba was to prevent the defendants from taking advantage of the franchisor's trade connections. The covenant against competition in the territories of other franchise holders was meant to preclude the defendants from the wrongful use of the franchisor's trade secrets. The court did not comment on whether the different geographical restrictions were reasonable or enforceable. The covenant was read down by the court, and the injunction order was amended to restrict the competitive actions of the defendants in Manitoba only.

In *Steinbach Credit Union et al. v. Hardman et al.*, 2007 MBCA 25 (Can. Man. C.A.), it was clarified that there is indeed a precedent in Manitoba law to sever a restrictive covenant that might otherwise be unenforceable. However, the Manitoba Court of Appeal stated that whether severance is appropriate in the circumstances is an issue that should be addressed at trial.

The Manitoba Court of Appeal in *Nutter's Bulk & Natural Foods* dealt with a restrictive covenant that was found to be overly broad. To recap, the franchise agreement contained a non-compete clause that restricted competition by geographic location and time: the franchisee was not permitted to compete with the franchisor within a ten-mile radius of the former retail franchise for a period of five years. The covenant further provided that if a court determined that the clause was unreasonable with respect to the geographical area, then the geographical region "shall be reduced mile by mile to the geographic area determined by such Court to be reasonable." If the five-year time limitation were determined to be unreasonable, then "such time limitation shall be reduced by Six (6) month periods to the time determined by such Court as reasonable." Huband J.A. made the following comments about the write-down provisions (at para. 18):

> I am also conscious that the restrictive covenant contains provisions for reducing the limitations as to time and area to what a court of law finds reasonable. Do these provisions meet the requirements as to certainty of contract? And do these clauses potentially involve the court in rewriting the contract for the parties? Whether these provisions are valid are matters for the trial court to decide.

It is clear from Huband J.A.'s comments that there are fundamental problems with such write-down provisions, as they engage the courts in rewriting the contract between the parties, which courts are typically hesitant to do because it violates the freedom of parties to contract.

In *Shafron v. KRG Insurance Brokers (Western) Inc.*, 2009 SCC 6 (Can.), the Supreme Court of Canada dealt with whether the doctrine of severance could be used to enforce a restrictive covenant in an employment contract that would otherwise be rendered unreasonable because of ambiguity. The court differentiated between two types of severance: notional severance, meaning a reading down of the contractual provision to make it legal and enforceable, and blue-pencil severance, which involves the removal of part of the offending contractual provision. The court held that notional severance should not be used to cure a defective restrictive covenant in employment contracts. Blue-pencil severance may only be used in the rarest of cases, where the part being removed is trivial and not a main aspect of the covenant. Rothstein J. further stated (at para. 41):

> Not only would the use of notional severance change the terms of the covenant from the parties' initial agreement to what the court thinks they should have agreed to, it would also change the risks assumed by the parties. The restrictive covenant is sought by the employer. The obligation is on the employee. Having regard to the generally accepted imbalance of power between employers and employees, to introduce the doctrine of notional severance to read down an unreasonable restrictive covenant to what is reasonable provides no inducement to an employer to ensure the reasonableness of the covenant and inappropriately increases the risk that the employee will be forced to abide by an unreasonable covenant.

MB

The court did not comment on the use to cure defective restrictive covenants in sale of business situations. Since there is presumably less power imbalance between the parties in that situation, the courts may be more willing to use severance techniques to cure defects.

The plaintiff employer in *One Insurance Group* sought to apply the principles of severance from *Shafron*, the court therein dealing with the enforceability of a non-solicitation agreement that was held to be overly broad due to a lack of spatial and temporal features to its restriction. The relevant provision required the covenantor to "not at any time solicit business from any client of the corporation *at any time*" (at para 61, emphasis added). Citing *Shafron* and the principles of notional and blue-pencil severance, the court noted that both types of severance apply in limited circumstances to "remove illegal features of a contract so as to render the contract in conformity with the law"; the court is not in a position to rewrite an agreement to give effect to the intention of the parties. The court refused to invoke either principle of severance to remedy the defective provision, holding rather that it was overly broad and unenforceable.

In *People Corporation v. Mansbridge*, 2021 MBQB 170 (Can. Man. Q.B.), the court referenced *Shafron* in its decision of whether a non-solicitation provision in a contract was enforceable, and where held to be unenforceable, whether the principles of severance could be used to remedy any deficiencies in the provision. The relevant provision restricted the defendant employee from soliciting clients of the plaintiff employer. The court held that the term "client" was overly broad, as it could be interpreted to include all clients the employer ever had or will have, and thus the restrictive covenant was unreasonable and unenforceable. The court further rejected the plaintiff employer's argument that the principle of severance could be used to remedy the provision, noting that the principles of severance do not apply to employment contracts, and that even if they did, the changes the plaintiff sought would amount to a rewrite of the provision, well beyond blue-pencil severance (at paras. 42–43).

It remains to be seen whether the Manitoba courts will follow other jurisdictions in Canada and expressly recognize a distinction between restrictive covenants contained in employment contracts and those embodied in contracts for the purchase of a business.

9. When does a non-compete period begin to run? Will courts equitably extend the term?

Based on the jurisprudence, there are two time periods from which non-compete clauses typically run. The first is a general non-compete clause prohibiting the franchisee from competing with the franchised business during the term of the franchise agreement. Such a covenant was determined to be enforceable in *Imasco Retail*. The second period begins to run after the franchise agreement has expired, whereby the franchisee agrees not to compete with the franchisor for a period of time after the franchise arrangement has ended.

There are no reported cases whereby the courts have extended the term of the non-compete. It is arguable that the court would not equitably extend the term because it would have the effect of rewriting the contract for the parties involved.

10. Are there additional nuances or peculiarities of the province's treatment of covenants in the franchising context?

The majority of the jurisprudence relating to the enforceability of restrictive covenants has arisen in the context of motions for interlocutory injunctions to enforce the provisions of the covenant. In such scenarios, it is not necessary for the moving party to prove that the covenant is enforceable. All that is required is that they show they have a strong prima facie case. This has been interpreted to mean that the plaintiff must prove that there is some probability of success at trial. If the enforceability of the covenant is not "clear and obvious," as Twaddle J.A. commented in *Nutter's Bulk & Natural Foods*, it is highly unlikely that an interim injunction will be granted.

It is also significant to note that in Manitoba, the majority of the restrictive covenants focus on the protection of the franchisor's clients. In determining whether the franchisor has a legitimate proprietary interest that is worthy of protection, the nature of the clientele is a significant factor that the courts take into consideration. Where there is a high degree of loyalty among the clientele, the courts are more inclined to find that the restrictive covenant is enforceable. This is especially so where the franchisee provides personal services and is likely to develop a close relationship with clients. However, if the franchisee can prove that the nature of the clientele is transitory with little loyalty, then it is less likely that the courts will find that the restrictive covenant is reasonable in the circumstances.

New Brunswick

*By Ashley Arbour**

1. Has the province addressed covenants against competition in the context of franchising?

- **Does the province have a franchising statute or regulations that address covenants against competition?**
- **Does the province have a covenants statute of general applicability that would encompass franchise covenants?**
- **Have the courts addressed covenants in the context of franchising either under a statute or under the province's common law?**

The courts in New Brunswick have not addressed covenants against competition in the context of franchise agreements. Until 2011, franchise agreements in force in New Brunswick were regulated by the common law or, in certain circumstances, by the legislation applicable in the franchise agreement's governing jurisdiction. In 2011, New Brunswick saw the first codification of legislation proper to franchise agreements in the *Franchises Act*, S.N.B. 2007, c. F-23.5 (the 2011 Act), which sought to establish a more cohesive standard by codifying and clarifying the requirements, limitations, and minimum standards applicable to franchise agreements in New Brunswick.

The 2011 Act was repealed in February 2014, at which time the *Franchises Act*, RSNB 2014, c. 111 (the Act) was proclaimed. The Act came into force on February 9, 2015, and was consolidated on January 1, 2020. The Act continues to mirror many provisions found in provinces such as Ontario, Alberta, and Prince Edward Island. One key distinction adopted by the Government of New Brunswick is the explicit duty of good faith and fair dealing extending to the performance and enforcement of franchise agreements in New Brunswick, which is expressly provided in the *Disclosure Document Regulation* of the Act.

Despite the codification of certain rights and restrictions, the Act was drafted broadly and remains silent on a number of important points, one being the applicability of covenants against competition in franchise agreements. The closest

*Ashley Arbour is an attorney in the Fredricton office of Cox & Palmer.

provision relating to covenants against competition can be found at section 10 of the Act, which provides for no derogation of other rights, setting out:

> The rights conferred by or under this Act are in addition to and do not derogate from any other right or remedy any party to a franchise agreement may have at law.

As a result of the statutory silence in terms of covenants against competition, affected parties seeking to determine matters relating to non-competition provisions and covenants in franchise agreements applicable in New Brunswick must continue to rely on the common law. Affected parties have traditionally also relied on additional covenants contained in the franchise agreements, which oftentimes establish that the applicable law is that of the governing jurisdiction in which the franchisor is located. These exterior governing jurisdictions have traditionally been found to have more comprehensive and detailed statutory requirements, which guide or regulate covenants against competition in a much more detailed fashion than is statutorily available in New Brunswick. Despite this reliance upon the statutes and regulations available outside of New Brunswick, the Act does caution against explicitly limiting the applicability of provincial law. At subsection 11(1), the Act sets out:

> A provision in a franchise agreement purporting to restrict the application of the law of New Brunswick or to restrict jurisdiction or venue to a forum outside New Brunswick is void with respect to a claim otherwise enforceable under this Act in New Brunswick.

Subsection 11(1) of the Act supports the conclusion that, as the Act does not address covenants against competition, franchisors and franchisees will be required to rely on the common law and reported decisions from other jurisdictions to settle any claims relating to the validity and enforceability of non-competition covenants in franchise agreements applicable in New Brunswick. Since the Act's enactment in 2011, there have been no reported cases in the province of New Brunswick that relate to covenants against competition in the franchise agreement context.

---

2. Have the courts articulated the "legitimate interests" of the franchisor that will support enforcement of a covenant against competition contained in a franchise agreement?

- **If so, what are they (e.g., protection of goodwill, protection of confidential information), and in what contexts did the issue arise?**
- **If not, what interests have been recognized in other contexts (e.g., employment agreements, the sale of business context)?**

Courts in New Brunswick have defined the basic approach to assessing the enforceability of non-competes in differing contexts. The courts have recognized that employers and purchasers of businesses have legitimate interests in the protection of their trade secrets, such as confidential information, procedure manuals, customer lists, and the use of corporate names, for example. In exchange for access to and the use of this information, employees and vendors of businesses must typically sign covenants against competition with the employer or purchaser of the business for a set period of time and within a specific geographic location following the termination of their employment or the closing of the sale of the business. Whether a covenant against competition is "reasonable" requires consideration of the following:

1. Is it within the public interest?
2. Does it protect a legitimate proprietary interest?
3. Was it reasonable at the time the parties entered into the agreement?
4. Is it reasonable with respect to the restricted geographic area?

Geoffrey England, *Employment- Restrictive Covenants*, in HALSBURY'S LAWS OF CANADA (Lexis Nexis, 2010) (QL). Similar arguments can be made for the relationship between the vendor and purchaser of a business, and we expect they could be paralleled in respect to the franchise law context in New Brunswick.

Despite the lack of reported caselaw relating to covenants against competition in the franchise context, the general principles of franchise law in New Brunswick have been addressed in various circumstances. In *Thrifty Canada Ltd. v. A & H Enterprises Ltd.* (1988), 85 NBR (2d) 55, NBJ No. 15 (NBQB) , the defendant franchisee, A & H Enterprises Ltd. (A & H), ran a Thrifty Canada Ltd. franchise at the Moncton Airport. After termination of the franchise agreement by A & H, it entered into business with another car rental franchisor, Hertz Rent-a-Car, which operated in direct competition with Thrifty. The original franchise agreement included a clause that the franchisee would not compete with Thrifty for a period of two years within the greater-Moncton area, following the termination of the franchise agreement. Landry J. for the New Brunswick Court of Queen's Bench applied the test for reasonableness as outlined in *Bard Transport v. Bard*, [1978] 23 NBR (2d) 304, 44 APR 304 (NBQB), by Dickson J. at p. 309:

> The general doctrine in this regard is that covenants in restraint of trade are prima facie unenforceable at common law and are enforceable only if they are reasonable with reference to the interests of the parties concerned and of the public. The onus of establishing that a covenant is no more than reasonable in the interests of the parties is on the person who seeks to rely upon it. If he establishes that it is no more than reasonable in the interests of the parties, the onus of proving that it is contrary to public interest lies on the party attacking it.

Landry J. held that the time and geographic restrictions on trade were reasonable under the circumstances.

Although the courts in New Brunswick have not assessed the "legitimate interests" of a franchisor in the context of a covenant against competition, there are reported cases that address the general principles of franchise law in New Brunswick. In *Saint Cinnamon Bakery Ltd v. Cimat Recycle Inc*, 2006 NBQB 420, the plaintiff franchisor, Saint Cinnamon Bakery (SCBL), entered into a franchise agreement with the defendant franchisee, Cimat Recycle Inc. and two shareholders of the defendant. The franchise agreement contained a restrictive covenant not to compete following the expiration or termination of the agreement. The terms of the non-competition clause included both timing and geographic restrictions, namely two years and within two miles of the franchise location. SCBL later terminated the agreement, alleging a number of violations of the franchise agreement, including an allegation that the defendants opened a competing business in the former SCBL premises in breach of the restrictive covenant. The court in *Saint Cinnamon* was not required to determine whether the defendants breached the non-competition covenant because the owner of the competing new business was a third party and was not bound by the terms of the franchise agreement. However, the court commented on the importance of the non-compete clause to SCBL's business at paragraphs 71–73:

> SCBL is an international franchising company and relies on its agreements to maintain and protect its system. It argues that if a party is able to gain the benefits afforded to it under a Franchise Agreement and then simply disregard its own obligations, the whole SCBL franchising system will be negatively affected. The strength of its franchise contracts would become seriously weakened. It argues that if the Court did not enforce restrictive clauses such as section 20.01, there is a real fear that other franchisees will view such a precedent as an opportunity to follow the actions taken by the defendants in this case, and SCBL would be placed in a very precarious financial position. SCBL submits that such a negative effect on the SCBL company would continue into the future and that the damage suffered would not be quantifiable and that monetary compensation would not satisfy the damages suffered.
>
> SCBL argues that it will suffer irreparable harm unless the temporary injunction is granted, not only against Cimat Recycle Inc., Rejean St-Onge and Guilda Nittolo, but also against, the Numbered Company doing business as *Resto Chez Mat*, and Angelo Nittolo.
>
> I agree with these arguments as far as the defendants are concerned. However, this does not apply to the third parties. They are not franchisees of SCBL.

Except for *Saint Cinnamon Bakery*, the courts in New Brunswick have not had the opportunity to specifically address the "legitimate interests" of franchisors within the context of franchisor/franchisee relationships. Courts have, however, addressed "legitimate interests" in the context of the sale of a business and in employment circumstances. While the following caselaw does not involve franchises, the argument can be made that covenants against competition in the sale of a business or termination of employment have the same underlying concerns as covenants against competition in the franchise relationship.

In *Capital Safe & Lock Service Ltd v. Steeves*, 2000 NBCA 1, the New Brunswick Court of Appeal addressed the issue of non-competition provisions in the context of employment and the sale of a business. Drapeau J.A., held that the trial judge did not err in concluding that a restrictive covenant restraining a former manager of Capital Safe & Lock from trade for a ten-year time period within a 100-mile radius of the City of Fredericton was reasonable. Given the facts of the particular case, Capital Safe had an interest in protecting its business from competition from the defendant as a result of his breadth of experience and knowledge in the industry (*Capital Safe* at ¶ 36). Drapeau J.A. held that the non-competition covenant was enforceable.

In the trial decision of *Imperial Oil v. H.H.L. Fuels Ltd*, 2004 NBQB 370, involving an agency agreement, Rideout J. reviewed some of the key cases in Canada dealing with non-competition clauses in an employment law context. He stated at paragraph 35 that while the "considerations [he] outlined related to an employment situation, many of the considerations [were] applicable to the present case." Beginning at paragraph 31, Rideout J. discussed a number of considerations with respect to the validity of non-competition clauses, including the length of service with the employer, the amount of personal service to clients, whether the employee dealt with clients exclusively, whether the knowledge gained by the employee was confidential or of an intimate knowledge of the client, whether the employee had influence over the client, whether clients had followed the employee, the nature of the business with respect to customer loyalty, the community involved, and whether there were clientele yet to be exploited. These could be considered legitimate interests. Affirming the trial decision, the New Brunswick Court of Appeal in *Imperial Oil*, 2006 NBCA 1 found a 12-month time limitation to be reasonable and therefore enforceable: Mr. Herman had 30 years' experience in the field, he was known in the community, and he had gained knowledge of Imperial Oil's operations and inner workings.

The courts have generally not provided detailed explanations regarding their decisions to find covenants against competition enforceable. In the employment context, Glennie J. stated in *Brunswick News Inc v. Langdon*, 2007 NBQB 423 at paragraph 50, that "free competition should trump any restraint on . . . [an employee] to freely pursue meaningful employment and to earn a livelihood, without restriction, except with respect to the use of confidential information." Thus, courts in New Brunswick have upheld restrictive covenants that are sufficiently specific to accomplish the goal of protecting an employer's interests, without compromising the ability of the employee to eventually pursue a new career in a similar field. Thus, non-competition covenants, whether founded in franchise agreements, statute, or other settings, are deemed to be valid if they are reasonable, both between the parties and in the public interest. To be deemed reasonable, the covenant must protect a proprietary interest of the franchisor but must not be broader in geographical area, time, or scope than is necessary to protect these interests. As demonstrated in the above-noted cases, these general guiding principles apply in the context of franchise law in New Brunswick. In all of the above-noted cases, it has been found that legitimate interests include protection of confidential business information, such as client lists and methods of doing business that may be later used in competition against the employer. It has been predominantly employed in the context of protecting a business's proprietary rights in their client lists. It is expected that the same type of confidential information stemming from the operation of a franchise would also receive protection and that a retired franchisee would be precluded from using such information in order to compete with the franchisor. The above-noted cases also illustrate the fact that the enforceability of a restrictive covenant, whether in the context of a sale of business or in an employment or franchise relationship, must be decided on the facts of each case.

3. What time limitations have courts recognized as reasonable in the franchise context? If no franchise cases have been decided, what time limitations have been recognized in other contexts?

➤ **How have they been related to the interests protected?**

New Brunswick courts have recognized limitations regarding competition within a specific period of time and geographic location as reasonable in the franchise context. A two-year time period has been upheld as a reasonable restraint on trade in *Thrifty Canada Ltd*. However, all cases are decided on their facts, as in any other case relating to franchise law.

As we have seen in *Imperial Oil v. H.H.L. Fuels Ltd*, 2004 NBQB 370, Rideout J. outlined various criteria to be assessed in determining whether particular restrictive covenants will be deemed exceptional and therefore reasonable. While the assessment is within an agency context, many of the criteria may be relevant with respect to restrictive covenants in a franchise agreement. The New Brunswick Court of Appeal in *Imperial Oil* found a 12-month time limitation to be reasonable. Although not in the franchise context, similar analysis should be applicable. Generally the time limitations begin to run instantaneously at the expiration or termination of the franchise agreement, as outlined in paragraph 22:

> In determining that section 9.08 was enforceable, thus reasonable and in the public interest, the trial judge found by inference in response to his analysis that: (1) Imperial had a proprietary or legitimate interest entitled to protection, (2) the temporal and spatial features of the covenant were reasonable, or not too broad, and (3) any restriction for the prevention of competition was reasonably required for the protection of Imperial in the circumstances.

---

4. What geographic limitations have courts recognized as reasonable in the franchise context?

- **How have they been related to the interests protected?**
- **Have courts recognized the legitimacy of protecting other franchisees from competition?**

This question needs to be considered in tandem with question 3. In New Brunswick, the courts have yet to establish a set of rules or proper parameters as to what restrictive covenants are deemed reasonable in a franchisor/franchisee context. In any reported cases pertaining to covenants against competition generally, the reasonableness of each covenant has been considered on a case-by-case basis, depending on the fact pattern of each specific matter.

In *Bardeaux St-Hilaire Inc v. Bonenfant*, 2002 NBCA 50, the New Brunswick Court of Appeal set aside a non-competition clause as the parties had failed to include a territorial limit. With respect to territory, the clause simply stated that "all of the territory served by the corporation." This was ambiguous and insufficient, and the court set the covenant aside for failure to include an adequate territorial limit.

In the trial decision of *Capital Safe & Lock Service Ltd v. Steeves*, 1999 Carswell NB 378, the court addressed the issue of non-competition provisions in the context of employment and the sale of a business, upholding a covenant restricting a former manager of Capital Safe & Lock from trade for a ten-year time period within a 100-mile radius of the City of Fredericton, and found that such was reasonable. On appeal, *Capital Safe & Lock Service Ltd v. Steeves*, 2000 NBCA 1, the decision was affirmed. The court rejected the argument that the 100-mile radius was overly vague because it failed to identify the boundaries and further failed to clearly define the scope of the restriction on the former employee's activities. The appellate court applied a contextual interpretation of the geographical restriction and reviewed the preamble of the employment agreement prior to concluding that the geographical restriction in the covenant against competition was not so vague as to render it void.

In *Spielo Manufacturing Inc v. Estey*, [2000] NBJ No 486, the New Brunswick Court of Queen's Bench upheld a rather exceptional geographic radius in the parties' employment contract. Based on exceptional circumstances established, the defendant was not permitted to work for any business involved in creating, developing, marketing, distributing, or servicing video lottery equipment anywhere in Canada or the United States of America for a period of two years. In finding that the employer otherwise would suffer irreparable harm, the court cited, inter alia, actual competition between the employee's former and current employer, the nature of the employee's work, the small universe of customers for the competing employers in the gaming industry, confidential and proprietary information of the business, and contract language.

Spielo was pled in *Dent Wizard Canada Ltd. v. Day*, 2007 NBQB 197, when the plaintiff sought to enforce a covenant against competition setting out a two-year, 150-mile radius and two-year non-compete clause, to support the former employer's claim that irreparable harm would occur in the absence of the restriction. The court, however, refused to enforce covenant, factually distinguishing the nature of Speilo's business from that in the instant case.

What will be considered reasonable in terms of specific conditions in a covenant against competition will therefore be heavily fact-dependant.

5. What limitations on activities have courts recognized as reasonable in the franchise context?

The issue of limitations on activities in the franchise context has not yet been addressed by New Brunswick courts.

6. Does the province recognize a difference between in-term and post-term covenants?

The Act does not explicitly recognize a difference between in-term and post-term covenants. However, section 3 of the Act refers to fair dealing obligations in the franchise context:

> 3(1) Every franchise agreement imposes on each party a duty of fair dealing in the performance and enforcement of the franchise agreement.
>
> 3(2) A party to a franchise agreement has a right of action for damages against another party to the franchise agreement who breaches the duty of fair dealing.
>
> 3(3) For the purposes of this section,
>
> (*a*) the duty of fair dealing includes the duty to act in good faith and in accordance with reasonable commercial standards, and
>
> (*b*) the performance and enforcement of the franchise agreement includes the exercise of a right under the agreement.

A breach of an in-term covenant may therefore be considered a breach of the duty of fair dealing.

In *Turf Management Systems Inc. v. Anmar Associates Ltd.* (1995), 169 NBR (2d) 287, NBJ No. 523 (NBQB), the court allowed a motion for an interlocutory injunction restraining the respondent, Anmar Associates Ltd. (and its director, Michael Ross), from operating a lawn mowing business while still a franchisee for Weed Man, contrary to the terms of the franchise agreement. In reviewing the application for interlocutory injunction in favor of Turf Management, Larlee J. stated as follows at paragraph 13:

> I think that there is a potential loss of customers in this case and I am convinced that that potential loss of customers could cause irreparable harm which could not be compensated for by damages.

Canadian law of restraint of trade holds that a non-competition covenant cannot be so broad as to restrain a former employee from participating in any kind of business after the franchise relationship comes to an end. In *Imperial Sheet Metal Ltd v. Landry*, 2007 NBCA 51, the court J.A. discussed the difference between in-term and post-term covenants in the employment context. While not a franchise case, the court's comments at paragraphs 34–35 are nonetheless relevant in the franchise context:

> [34] In employment law, the common law and equitable obligations of an employee are cast in terms of a duty to act in good faith, a duty of fidelity and the equitable duty not to breach confidences. A non-fiduciary employee owes the employer a general duty of good faith and fidelity during the currency of the employment relationship. This translates into a duty not to compete with the employer, either directly or indirectly, during the currency of the employment relationship. It also translates into a duty not to disclose "trade secrets" and other "confidential information".
>
> [35] Leaving aside the employee's duty to keep confidences, it has to be asked whether there are any common law restrictions preventing an employee from establishing a competitive business or from working for a competitor of the former employer. On this point, the law has long been settled. During the course of their employment, employees are not permitted to compete, directly or indirectly, with their employers. As a general observation, employees who surreptitiously set about to establish a competitive business while continuing to work for their soon-to-be former employer often find it difficult to establish that the duty of fidelity has not been breached. Those who wait until the employment relationship has terminated are more successful in defending a law suit for breaches of the duty of good faith and fidelity. Once the employment relationship ends, the non-fiduciary employee is permitted to engage in fair competition with a former employer.

7. Has the province allowed enforcement of covenants against non-signatories (e.g., family members, newly formed corporations)?

There are no specific provisions in the Act relating to non-signatories. Few reported cases address this issue within the franchise context, and therefore we are often left to turn to reported cases pertaining to the enforcement of non-competition covenants in the employment context, or in other jurisdictions.

In *Kent Building Supplies v. Magasin du Ridge Ltée*, 2004 NBQB 152, the court determined that a signatory to a non-competition agreement was prohibited from selling real property to a third party whom he knew would then be in competition with the plaintiff, noting that the third party was aware of the non-competition agreement. Accordingly, the court found that such restrictive covenants could be enforceable against the party to the agreement, especially if substantial consideration were received in exchange for executing this covenant, and that such restrictive covenants could have the net effect of binding a third party that was fully aware of the existence of such covenants with the view of prohibiting their breach.

In *Saint Cinnamon Bakery*, a franchisee, GN, was party to a franchise agreement when she incorporated a numbered company and was listed as a director. The franchisor obtained an interim injunction against GN and the numbered company for breaching the franchise agreement and competing within the protected territory as defined in the franchise agreement. A year later, GN no longer appeared as the director of the numbered company, and GN's father was listed as the sole director of the numbered company. The franchisor applied for an order that the injunction apply to GN's father, as well as the numbered company, who were non-parties to the main action. The franchisor argued that the numbered company had been created by the franchisee GN and in conjunction with GN's father for the purpose of frustrating the franchisor's enforcement of rights under the franchise agreement, and that GN's father and the numbered company should be subject to the injunction. The court found, however, that there was insufficient evidence to establish that the numbered company had been created for the purpose of defeating the non-competition obligations under the franchise agreement. The court further concluded that the franchise agreement did not prevent any other entity, including GN's father, from opening a similar business selling similar products, in the exact same location. The court ultimately concluded that the third parties, specifically GN's father and the numbered company, were not signatories to the franchise agreement and therefore could not be bound by it.

Similarly, in *Imperial Oil v. H.H.L. Fuels Ltd*, 2004 NBQB 370, the court held that while a non-competition and non-solicitation provision in an agency agreement was valid and enforceable, it did not apply to the defendant company, as this company was not a party to the agreement. Rather, the company was incorporated by the agent's son after Imperial Oil had terminated the agency agreement containing the restrictive covenant.

8. Will the province modify, "blue-pencil," or otherwise reduce a covenant found to be overbroad?

There are no legislative provisions in New Brunswick that would apply to modify, "blue-pencil," or reduce a covenant found to be overly broad. Franchisors and franchisees must rely on the common law for any remedies regarding non-competition covenants.

The Supreme Court of Canada case *Transport North American Express Inc v. New Solutions Financial Corp*, 2004 SCC 7, addressed the issue of "blue-penciling" or severing non-competition covenants, albeit in the context of employment, stating at paragraph 57:

Under the blue-pencil test, severance is only possible if the judge can strike out, by drawing a line through, the portion of the contract they want to remove, leaving the portions that are not tainted by illegality, without affecting the meaning of the part remaining. In other words, the offending provision must constitute a separate promise, and one that is not part of the main purport and substance of the contract.

Consequently, courts in New Brunswick are not entitled to "blue-pencil" non-competition covenants, unless doing so will not affect the main substance of the contract. In addition, ambiguous non-competition covenants may be struck entirely from an agreement. *See KRG Insurance Brokers (Western) Inc v. Shafron*, 2009 SCC 6.

9. When does a non-compete period begin to run? Will courts equitably extend the term?

There is no caselaw in New Brunswick addressing this issue. However, it is recognized that a non-competition covenant will generally begin to run in-term as soon as the franchise relationship begins, and will continue to run after termination of the franchise agreement as outlined therein. We have not been able to find any instances where courts have equitably extended the term of the non-competition covenant; however, demonstrating a material change in circumstances might justify extending such restrictive provision, based on an equitable relief basis.

10. What are the additional nuances or peculiarities of the province's treatment of covenants in the franchising context?

The franchise legislation in New Brunswick that came into force in 2015 has not yet been assessed by the courts. However, every franchisor should be aware of the fair dealing provisions contained in the Act and ensure it has complied with such obligations prior to taking any enforcement proceedings, namely those that may be aimed at enforcing restrictive covenants.

Newfoundland and Labrador

*by Megan Taylor**

1. Has the province addressed covenants against competition in the context of franchising?

- **Does the province have a franchising statute or regulations that address covenants against competition?**
- **Does the province have a covenants statute of general applicability that would encompass franchise covenants?**
- **Have the courts addressed covenants in the context of franchising either under a statute or under the province's common law?**

Newfoundland and Labrador does not have a franchising statute or regulations specifically addressing covenants against competition in the franchising context, nor has it enacted any statute of general applicability governing franchising or covenants against competition. Covenants against competition are dealt with under the common law.

MTY Tiki Enterprises v. Azmy Enterprises Inc, 2018 NLSC 169 (Can. Nfld. Sup. Ct.) is the only reported Newfoundland and Labrador decision involving covenants against competition in the context of franchising. This case was an interlocutory application for injunctive relief to stop a former franchisee from operating a business allegedly in competition with the franchise. The court did not specifically address the enforceability of the covenant at issue. The extent of the court's comments on the restrictive covenant were made during its analysis to determine if injunctive relief was appropriate. The court commented briefly (para. 62) that while sections of the franchise agreement contained general acknowledgments that there was goodwill associated with the "Franchise Marks and Franchise System" used in the franchises, there was no evidence provided to identify how the operation of a restaurant selling products commonly sold in other restaurants would adversely impact MTY's proprietary interests.

*Megan Taylor is a partner with the law firm of Cox & Palmer in St. John's, Newfoundland. Kaylyn Anthony, an articled clerk with the law firm of Cox & Palmer in St. John's, Newfoundland, assisted in the preparation of this chapter.

Newfoundland and Labrador courts have addressed non-competition agreements more extensively in the employment and other commercial contexts and are commonly referred to as covenants in restraint of trade. The courts have held that the common law is governed by the holding of the Supreme Court of Canada in *J.G. Collins Insurance Agencies v. Elsley* (1978), 83 D.L.R. (3d) 1 (Can. S.C.C.). This is evident in *Scale Shop (1985) Ltd. v. Kinsella* (1985), 107 Nfld. & P.E.I.R. 216 (Can. Nfld. S.C. (T.D.)), where the court, in considering covenants in restraint of trade, quoted *J.G. Collins* as follows at paragraph 8:

> The contractual restrictions are commonly referred to as covenants in restraint of trade. The question is whether they are valid. In *J.G. Collins Insurance Agencies v. Elsley* (1978), 83 D.L.R. (3d) 1 (S.C.C.) at p. 5, Dickson J., for the Court, said:
>
>> A covenant in restraint of trade is enforceable only if it is reasonable between the parties and with reference to the public interest. As in many of the cases that come before the Courts, competing demands must be weighed. There is an important public interest in discouraging restraints on trade, and maintaining free and open competition unencumbered by the fetters of restrictive covenants. On the other hand, the Courts have been disinclined to restrict the right to contract, particularly when that right has been exercised by knowledgeable persons of equal bargaining power. In assessing the opposing interests, the word one finds repeated throughout the cases is the word "reasonable". The test of reasonableness can be applied, however, only in the peculiar circumstances of the particular case.

Thus, it can be expected that courts will require a franchisor to prove the reasonableness of the covenants before they will consider enforcing them.

More recently, the Newfoundland and Labrador Supreme Court in *WM Tapper Ltd v. Valero Energy Inc*, 2017 NLTD(G) 63 (Can. Nfld. Sup. Ct.), considered a restrictive covenant in an agency agreement. The court in *Tapper* relied on the *J.G. Collins* factors in assessing reasonableness at paragraph 76 of its decision: (1) Is there a proprietary interest to be protected? (2) Are the temporal or spatial features of the clause too broad? (3) Is the covenant unenforceable as being against competition generally, and not limited to proscribing solicitation of clients of the former employer? The court found that a one-year period prohibiting the agent from soliciting clients within the market area served by them was reasonable. However, the agent was also prohibited from undertaking a wide range of activities, which was determined to be overbroad and therefore the clause as a whole was determined to be unreasonable.

---

2. Have the courts articulated the "legitimate interests" of the franchisor that will support enforcement of a covenant against competition contained in a franchise agreement?

- **If so, what are they (e.g., protection of goodwill, protection of confidential information), and in what contexts did the issue arise?**
- **If not, what interests have been recognized in other contexts (e.g., employment agreements, the sale of business context)?**

As noted previously, there are no reported Newfoundland and Labrador decisions that expressly address the enforceability of covenants against competition in the context of franchising. While the court in *MTY Tiki Enterprises v. Azmy Enterprises Inc*, 2018 NLSC 169 (Can. Nfld. Sup. Ct.), commented briefly on the goodwill associated with the system used in the Extreme Pita franchises, the court did not make an express ruling on whether this would constitute a legitimate interest of a franchisor that would support enforcement of a covenant against competition. The court held that there was no evidence presented in the case to support the argument that the operation of the business at issue would adversely impact any proprietary interest one had in the goodwill associated with franchise marks and franchise systems. This implies that the court may be willing to find such a proprietary interest in other cases if proved based on the facts.

In Newfoundland and Labrador, determinative caselaw in this area has been limited to non-competition agreements in the employment and other commercial contexts. In these cases, it has been found that legitimate interests include protection of confidential business information, such as client lists and methods of doing business that may be later used in competition against the employer. The concept of "legitimate interests" has been predominantly employed in the context of protecting a business's proprietary rights in their client lists.

In *Target Marketing & Communications v. MacDonald*, [1998] N.J. No. 287 (Can. Nfld. Sup. Ct.), Target, a marketing and advertising company, claimed that it had shared confidential information with MacDonald, its former employee, including client identities and services provided to its clients, product design, pricing and sales policies, and names of key personnel within its clients' organizations. MacDonald's contract of employment included a restrictive covenant. She agreed not to disclose confidential information on leaving Target or work on accounts held by Target within one year of leaving. She also agreed not to work for any competitor located in St. John's or perform work east of Hamilton, Ontario, for six months. After three years with Target, MacDonald commenced work with a direct competitor. Target brought an action for breach of contract, seeking an interlocutory injunction enforcing the restrictive covenant.

NF

The application was dismissed. The restriction against working for a competitor located in St. John's and the six-month time were found to be reasonable. However, the restrictions were not designed to protect a legitimate interest in confidential information held by Target. MacDonald acquired information about Target and its clients generally in the course of her employment. The information was not acquired through direct contact with clients. Target failed to show that MacDonald had to use or used the confidential information in the course of her new employment, and there was no presumption that MacDonald would act unethically. The restriction could not be rewritten or read down in order to achieve a level of reasonableness.

In *Reed Stenhouse Companies Ltd. v. Learning* (1990), 83 Nfld. & P.E.I.R. 322 (Can. Nfld. Sup. Ct.), the court enforced a restrictive covenant against contacting an ex-employer's clients. The covenant and injunction were against contacting clients with whom the ex-employee had had contact. The employer had been in business for many years and had built up its client list, with which the defendant became familiar as a result of his employment. The plaintiff wished to protect the client list, and the defendant agreed. The court recognized the client list as a legitimate business interest justifying the granting of the injunction.

In *Simoni v. Sugarman*, [2000] N.J. No. 128 (Can. Nfld. Sup. Ct.), the court again recognized the legitimate business interest involved in the protection of proprietary rights in a client base. The court partially upheld a covenant restraining a podiatrist from soliciting business from potential customers whom he would not have known without his previous employment.

The legitimate interest of protecting a client base was also recognized in the earlier case of *Dynamex Canada Inc. v. Miller, et al.* (1997), 158 Nfld. & P.E.I.R. 142 (Can. Nfld. Sup. Ct.), affirmed (1998), 161 Nfld. & P.E.I.R. 97 (Can. Nfld. C.A.). The court viewed as legitimate that a defendant was prevented from soliciting business from customers of the plaintiff whom he had formerly serviced during his employment with them in a courier service.

The Newfoundland and Labrador Supreme Court continued this trend in *WM Tapper Ltd v. Valero Energy Inc*, 2017 NLTD(G) 63 (Can. Nfld. Sup. Ct.), where Ultramar, a principal to an agency agreement, was found to have an interest in protecting its customer base currently being served by the agents to the agreement.

In *Co-operators General Insurance Co. v. Stoyles*, [2000] N.J. No. 124 (Can. Nfld. Sup. Ct.), an application to enforce a non-competition provision was dismissed. Stoyles had been in the industry for 16 years prior to his employment with Co-operators. The court held that, in the year that Stoyles worked for them, Co-operators did not acquire any proprietary interest in his files or former customers and could not prevent Stoyles from using his skill and judgment and personal recollection of those people.

---

3. What time limitations have courts recognized as reasonable in the franchise context? If no franchise cases have been decided, what time limitations have been recognized in other contexts?

> **How have they been related to the interests protected?**

There are no reported Newfoundland and Labrador decisions addressing the issue of reasonable time restrictions in covenants against competition contained in franchise agreements. In other contexts, it has been held that covenants against competition must be limited to a scope that is reasonably necessary to protect the legitimate business interests involved. The time limit must be reasonable in light of the interest entitled to protection.

In *Target Marketing & Communications v. MacDonald*, [1998] N.J. No. 287 (Can. Nfld. Sup. Ct.), a restriction against working for a competitor located in St. John's (the city of the employee's previous employment with Target) for a six-month time period was reasonable.

In *Simoni v. Sugarman*, [2000] N.J. No. 128 (Can. Nfld. Sup. Ct.), the Newfoundland and Labrador Supreme Court granted an injunction to restrict Dr. Sugarman, former employee of Dr. Simoni's podiatric clinic, from diagnosing or treating individuals whose names were contained on a client list Sugarman brought with him from the clinic. He was also restricted from diagnosing or treating former clients of the Simoni clinic for two years. Sugarman had been brought to the province by Simoni and had been instructed by Simoni to write to 1,500 to 2,000 current and former clients of Simoni to advise them of his availability to service them at the Simoni clinic. He would not have known of these potential customers without his employment with Simoni. The two-year time limit was reasonable given the circumstances of this case.

In *Dynamex Canada Inc. v. Miller, et al.* (1997), 158 Nfld. & P.E.I.R. 142 (Can. Nfld. Sup. Ct.), affirmed (1998), 161 Nfld. & P.E.I.R. 97 (Can. Nfld. C.A.), the court upheld a covenant restricting the defendant for 12 months from soliciting business from those customers of the plaintiff who he had formerly serviced during his employment with them in a courier service. The court held that the defendant was not subject to an imbalance of power when he agreed to this restriction, and the one-year period was a reasonable length. The plaintiff was entitled to protect its business by preventing the defendant from soliciting its customers.

Co-operators General Insurance Co. v. Stoyles, [2000] N.J. No. 124 (Can. Nfld. Sup. Ct.), was an application for an interlocutory injunction to enjoin Stoyles and his company from competing with Co-operators. Stoyles had 16 years of experience in the insurance industry before entering an agreement with Co-operators to sell exclusively for them. The restrictive covenant in the agreement provided that, for one year following termination, Stoyles was not to contract or otherwise deal with any person who acquired Co-operators' products through his agency. On termination, Co-operators collected from Stoyles all of its computers and insurance manuals, but it did not request his paper files. As of the application date, he had not solicited any existing or former Co-operators' clients.

The application was dismissed. Co-operators did not acquire any proprietary interest in Stoyles' files or former customers. It could not prevent him from using his skill and judgment and personal recollection of those people. It had unequal bargaining power over him. The covenant was too broad, without any restriction to the time it covered prior to termination or on whether the potential clients still had to be Co-operators' clients. Neither did the agreement indicate whether the potential clients were not to be solicited by Stoyles.

More recently, in *WM Tapper Ltd v. Valero Energy Inc*, 2017 NLTD(G) 63 (Can. Nfld. Sup. Ct.), the Newfoundland and Labrador Supreme Court found a one-year period following the termination of an agency agreement, during which time the agent was prohibited from soliciting clients within the market area served by them, to be reasonable. The temporal limitation was also applicable to a broad restriction on activities that the agent could engage in following the termination of the agreement. This activity aspect of the restrictive covenant was ultimately found to be unreasonable.

4. What geographic limitations have courts recognized as reasonable in the franchise context?

- **How have they been related to the interests protected?**
- **Have courts recognized the legitimacy of protecting other franchisees from competition?**

There is no Newfoundland and Labrador case dealing with these issues in the context of a franchise agreement. Courts generally look at the nature of the protectable interest in determining the reasonableness of the geographic coverage of covenants not to compete in the employment and other commercial contexts.

In *Target Marketing & Communications v. MacDonald*, [1998] N.J. No. 287 (Can. Nfld. Sup. Ct.), the geographic restriction was limited to the city of the employee's previous employment. This geographic restriction, which was in place for a period of six months, was viewed as reasonable.

In *Simoni v. Sugarman*, [2000] N.J. No. 128 (Can. Nfld. Sup. Ct.), the restriction was also limited to the city of the previous employer, and this was found to be a reasonable restriction for a two-year period.

In *Dynamex Canada Inc. v. Miller, et al.* (1997), 158 Nfld. & P.E.I.R. 142 (Can. Nfld. Sup. Ct.), affirmed (1998), 161 Nfld. & P.E.I.R. 97 (Can. Nfld. C.A.), the court considered the spatial reasonableness of a non-competition clause in an employment contract. There was no express geographical limitation to the restriction; however, the nature of the restriction contained within it an inherent spatial limitation. The clause related to "customers of the company" at the time of termination or within a period of 12 months prior thereto. The restriction was therefore limited to the area of the employer's operations and, as a result, would not extend beyond what would be considered a legitimate interest for Dynamex to protect. This also was found to be reasonable.

In *WM Tapper Ltd v. Valero Energy Inc*, 2017 NLTD(G) 63 (Can. Nfld. Sup. Ct.), the restriction was limited to the metro St. John's area; this being the area that the agent to the agreement in question served on behalf of Ultramar. This spatial limitation was agreed to be reasonable by the agent, and the court concurred, finding the geographic limitation reasonable.

5. What limitations on activities have courts recognized as reasonable in the franchise context?

In *WM Tapper Ltd v. Valero Energy Inc*, 2017 NLTD(G) 63 (Can. Nfld. Sup. Ct.), the court considered a year-long restrictive covenant in an agency contract. Tapper was an agent of Ultramar for the purpose of selling and delivering heating fuel, among other products, in a defined market area within the St. John's area. The covenant purported to restrict the agent, unless otherwise agreed to by the principal, from engaging in businesses that handled or used petroleum products, as well as preventing the agent from having anything to do with petroleum products, whether or not it had to do with the principal's customers, or the heating delivery business, which was the subject of the contract.[1] The court held that the restricted activities would have extended the restrictions to most of the agent's other businesses, which included a gas station and convenience store, and would have had a significant impact on the agent's activities that were unrelated to the contract with Ultramar. The court was unable to sever the restrictions on activities from the covenant without having to rewrite the entire clause, and therefore it declared the entire clause to be unreasonable and thus unenforceable.

In the employment context, a former employee was restricted from "soliciting business" from past customers for a period of one year in *Dynamex Canada Inc. v. Miller, et al.* (1997), 158 Nfld. & P.E.I.R. 142 (Can. Nfld. Sup. Ct.), affirmed (1998), 161 Nfld. & P.E.I.R. 97 (Can. Nfld. C.A.), and a former partner in a podiatry business was prevented from "diagnosing or treating" individuals who had been patients of the partnership for a period of two years following the termination of their business relationship in *Simoni v. Sugarman*, [2000] N.J. No. 128 (Can. Nfld. Sup. Ct.). Both periods were found to be reasonable. In *Target Marketing & Communications v.*

1. At paras. 81–82.

MacDonald, [1998] N.J. No. 287 (Can. Nfld. Sup. Ct.), a restriction against "working for a competitor" located in the city of the employee's previous employment for a six-month time period was reasonable.

6. Does the province recognize a difference between in-term and post-term covenants?

Courts in Newfoundland and Labrador have not addressed whether recognition of a difference in enforceability between in-term and post-term covenants would be appropriate.

7. Has the province allowed enforcement of covenants against non-signatories (e.g., family members, newly formed corporations)?

There are no Newfoundland and Labrador cases addressing covenants not to compete against non-signatories. However, there is one case that addresses the granting of injunctive relief that would have had a significant impact on a non-signatory to a restrictive covenant.

In *Podiatry Associates Inc v. Sugarman*, 2011 NLTD 168 (Can. Nfld. Sup. Ct.), the court refused to grant injunctive relief to enjoin Sugarman from soliciting current and former clients of the plaintiff, Simoni's, podiatry clinic and employing a former employee, Cramm. Simoni argued that Cramm held specialized knowledge in the method of fabrication of orthotics that, if she were to continue to be employed by Sugarman, created an unfair advantage and unfair competition. Cramm, who was not a party to the restrictive covenant at issue, nor a party to the originating action and not otherwise restricted from working for a competing business, was hired by Sugarman after resigning from her employment with Simoni. The court refused to grant the requested injunction on the basis that it would not be appropriate to make Cramm, a non-signatory to the restrictive covenant at issue, bear the full burden of the injunction given that it would result in her employment being terminated.

8. Will the province modify, "blue-pencil," or otherwise reduce a covenant found to be overbroad?

In the past, Newfoundland and Labrador courts have enforced covenants after striking portions found to be unreasonable, unless the restrictive covenant is vastly overbroad and overreaching. In *Target Marketing & Communications v. MacDonald*, [1998] N.J. No. 287 (Can. Nfld. Sup. Ct.), the court stated as follows, at paragraph 27:

> The courts apply a "blue pencil" rule of severance, where they will sever, if possible, offending provisions of a contract, which go too far in restricting trade and competition, and enforce the remaining, reasonable restrictions. However, if the offending parts cannot be clearly removed, the agreement as a whole will fall. The gist of the blue pencil rule is that the courts will strike out words but not add anything.

The clause in that case was too broad and could not be saved by the blue pencil rule.

In *Simoni v. Sugarman*, [2000] N.J. No. 128 (Can. Nfld. Sup. Ct.) the court used the blue pencil rule to partially enforce the covenant in question, striking down part of the covenant on the ground that it was too broad and unduly restrictive of competition. Certain portions of the covenant were severed because they were deemed unenforceable. The covenant purported, for a period of two years from termination of employment, to prohibit the defendant, either directly or indirectly, as an employee or otherwise, from having any interest in a podiatric business which "solicit[s] or compete[s] for the patients who attend at the [plaintiff's] Facilities and/or carry out podiatric checkups and all other podiatric care."

In *Co-operators General Insurance Co. v. Stoyles*, [2000] N.J. No. 124 (Can. Nfld. Sup. Ct.), it was decided that a simple severance of the offending words would not solve the problem. To save the clause, the court would have to virtually rewrite the covenant for the parties. The restriction was overreaching because it was not confined to current customers or even those who had been customers in the previous 12 months but extended to any person who had purchased a Co-operators policy during the currency of the employment agreement (i.e. about five years) and even those who may have cancelled a policy shortly after the agreement began and had had no contact with Co-operators since that time. The court found, at paragraph 54, that:

> Indeed, if one were to extend the wording of this clause to its logical conclusion, if the contract had lasted for 15 or 20 years, rather than just 5, the defendants would be restricted from soliciting a person who perhaps some 20 years earlier had had a policy with the plaintiffs but has had no dealings with them since that time. This is far too sweeping a restriction to be described as a simple protection of any legitimate proprietary interest the plaintiffs have in their customers. It is aimed mainly at restricting competition by the defendants with the plaintiffs upon the termination of the agency agreement: a restriction which is contrary to public policy.

On this basis, the entire clause was found unenforceable as being in restraint of trade.

More recently, the Supreme Court of Canada has expressly stated its position in relation to severance and restrictive covenants in *KRG Insurance Brokers (Western) Inc v. Shafron*, 2009 SCC 6. There are two types of severance when permitted: "notional" severance, which involves reading down a contractual provision so as to make it legal and enforceable, and "blue-pencil" severance, which involves removing part of a contractual provision. The Supreme Court of Canada ruled that notional severance is not an appropriate mechanism to cure a defective restrictive covenant, and that the "blue-pencil" method may only be resorted to in rare cases where the part being removed is trivial and not part of the main purport of the restrictive covenant.

The Newfoundland and Labrador Supreme Court adopted this position at paragraph 106 of its decision in *WM Tapper Ltd v. Valero Energy Inc*, 2017 NLTD(G) 63, establishing that "blue-pencil" severance, or the removal of an offending portion of a restrictive covenant, may only be used in rare circumstances where the portion is clearly severable and if it is of little importance to the meaning of the overall clause. The court ultimately refused to apply "blue-pencil" severance in this case as the unreasonable portions of the clause, these being the restrictions placed on activities the agent could perform upon termination of the agreement, were not severable or trivial, and dealing with same would require a complete redrafting of the clause.

9. When does a non-compete period begin to run? Will courts equitably extend the term?

There are no Newfoundland and Labrador cases addressing the issue of when a non-compete period will begin to run or whether the term will be equitably extended.

10. Are there additional nuances or peculiarities of the province's treatment of covenants in the franchising context?

In Newfoundland and Labrador, the majority of caselaw on non-compete covenants has arisen in the context of employment agreements. Regardless of the context, it has been suggested that the predominant factor in the assessment of the clause is the relative bargaining power of the parties. The greater the imbalance of bargaining power, the more willing a court will be to find that a covenant is unreasonable. Therefore, it can be inferred that restrictive covenants in the franchising context may be interpreted slightly less strictly than in previous employment agreement cases in this province, because a franchise owner will arguably have greater bargaining power than an employee. Of course, this will depend on all the circumstances of the situation present when the franchise agreement was entered.

The predominant importance of the relative bargaining strength of the parties is illustrated in *Dynamex Canada Inc. v. Miller, et al.* (1997), 158 Nfld. & P.E.I.R. 142 (Can. Nfld. Sup. Ct.), *affirmed* (1998), 161 Nfld. & P.E.I.R. 97 (Can. Nfld. C.A.). In that case, a courier business was sold to Dynamex. Miller, a senior courier with the former business, signed a new employment agreement that purported to restrain him from competing with Dynamex for a period of one year after leaving its employment. Six months later Miller left and began soliciting customers whom he had serviced while employed. Dynamex sought an order restraining Miller from soliciting business from its customers. The court determined that the relevant consideration is the relative inequality in bargaining strength between the parties. It was argued there that the more restrictive approach that is often taken in employment situations due to an imbalance in bargaining power should not apply, given the fact that the relationship was not of employer-employee but one of principal and independent contractor. These distinctions were not accepted by the court. Irrespective of whether Miller was an employee or an independent contractor, he was, in the circumstances, a person who faced an imbalance of bargaining power, and the policy of protecting against an imbalance of bargaining power thus applied in this context.

In addition, the Supreme Court of Canada has made it clear in its decisions *KRG Insurance Brokers (Western) Inc v. Shafron*, 2009 SCC 6, and *Guay Inc c. Payette*, 2013 SCC 45, that a distinction should be made between covenants against competition when included in an employment contract, when the covenants are to be scrutinized more rigorously, and other commercial contracts, where the reasonableness analysis is to be applied more generously.

These Supreme Court of Canada decisions were adopted in *WM Tapper Ltd v. Valero Energy Inc*, 2017 NLTD(G) 63, where the court reiterated that one of the key issues in determining the reasonableness of a restrictive covenant is whether there is a power imbalance between the parties. The court found that, based on the evidence before it, the agency agreement between Tapper and Ultramar was a contract of adhesion, and Tapper had no choice but to accept the terms as they were. Therefore, the rules were strictly applied.

Nova Scotia

*by Geoff Breen **

1. Has the province addressed covenants against competition in the context of franchising?

- **Does the province have a franchising statute or regulations that address covenants against competition?**
- **Does the province have a covenants statute of general applicability that would encompass franchise covenants?**
- **Have the courts addressed covenants in the context of franchising either under a statute or under the province's common law?**

Nova Scotia does not have any statutes or regulations that address covenants against competition, or any statutes that would encompass these issues. As a result, these issues are assessed based on common law court decisions, both local to Nova Scotia and supplemented by other relevant Canadian legal decisions. As a general principle, a restrictive covenant must be reasonable in the context so that it does not restrict a party more than necessary to protect legitimate interests (*Atlantic Business Interiors Ltd. v. Hipson*, 2005 NSCA 16 (Can. N.S.C.A.); *Jorna & Craig Inc. v. Chiasson*, 2020 NSCA 42 (Can. N.S.C.A.)).

Regarding franchise disputes specifically, Nova Scotia decisions considering restrictive covenants have primarily been addressed in interlocutory injunctions. Interlocutory injunctions are generally sought at the outset of a legal proceeding for an order to enforce restrictive covenants, pending final disposition of the matter.

An interlocutory injunction does not constitute a final decision on the merits of a case. Rather, in seeking an interlocutory injunction, a party must generally establish the following three criteria: (1) that their case raises a serious issue or, if the interlocutory injunction will effectively constitute a final disposition of the dispute, that they have prima facie case (*Groupe Restaurants Imvescor Inc. v. Zliv Creations Inc.*, 2017 NSSC 31 (Can. N.S. Sup. Ct.)), (2) that they will suffer irreparable harm if the injunction is not granted, and (3) that the balance of convenience favors granting of the injunction (*MEDIchair v. I.M.P.*, 2005 NSSC 72 (Can. N.S. Sup. Ct.)). While this test is followed in Nova Scotia, note that Nova Scotia's *Judicature Act* also provides

*Geoff Breen is a Partner with the law firm of Cox & Palmer in Halifax, Nova Scotia. Geoff thanks Sarah Gray, articled clerk, for her assistance.

that a court may grant an injunction on such terms deemed appropriate where it appears to the court to be "just and convenient" (*Judicature Act*, R.S.N.S. 1989, c. 240 s. 49(3)).

In practice, an interlocutory injunction is treated as "exceptional relief" (*MEDIchair v. I.M.P.*, 2005 NSSC 72 (Can. N.S. Sup. Ct.)) and, in Nova Scotia, franchisors have had limited success in enforcing restrictive covenants in this context. In particular, franchisors are often unable to demonstrate that they are suffering irreparable harm that cannot be compensated by way of damages (*MEDIchair v. I.M.P.*, 2005 NSSC 72 (Can. N.S. Sup. Ct.)) and/or to satisfy the court that the "balance of convenience" favors the injunction when considering the harm that will be caused in restraining the former franchisee from carrying on their business (*Uniglobe Travel (Atlantic) Inc. v. Fundy Travel Ltd.*, 113 N.S.R. (2d) 340 (Can. N.S. Sup. Ct.); 21227449 *Nova Scotia Ltd. v. Donna's Seashore Investments Ltd*, 162 N.S.R. (2d) 74 (Can. N.S. Sup. Ct.); *Groupe Restaurants Imvescor Inc. v. Zliv Creations Inc.*, 2017 NSSC 31 (Can. N.S. Sup. Ct.)).

The fact that franchisors have not generally been successful in interlocutory injunctions should not be taken to mean that Nova Scotia courts are unwilling to enforce restrictive covenants where the evidence is sufficient. In *Groupe Restaurants Imvescor Inc. v. Zliv Creations Inc.*, 2017 NSSC 31 (Can. N.S. Sup. Ct.), a franchisor sought an interlocutory injunction against a franchisee and other business partners to prevent them from opening a competing business. In this case, the court did not grant an injunction against the business partners as the evidence regarding their involvement with the franchise agreement was unclear, and it was apparent that preventing them from establishing their new business would be economically devastating to at least one of the partners. As for the franchisee, however, he admitted to being in breach of the franchise agreement and therefore consented to an injunction against himself, which the court endorsed, noting that the franchisor had a strong prima facie case against him. The court also suggested that, if a franchisor can make out a strong prima facie case that there is a breach of a restrictive covenant, it should not be precluded from obtaining an injunction even if it cannot demonstrate irreparable harm, stating:

> A person bound by an enforceable non-competition provision should not be able to avoid injunctive relief by claiming that the loss to the franchisor is compensable by an award of damages. Where there is a prima facie case that the defendant is bound by that agreement other principles are at stake. The three parts of the test for an injunction relate to each other in some significant ways. Here, if the case involves the economic torts, the case needs only to be established to a low threshold level, but the anticipated damages would be of a kind that could be compensated by an award of damages. If the case involves the enforcement of a restraint of trade, the irreparability of the harm should not stand in the way of the injunction, but the case runs into problems with the higher standard of proof.

In *2703203 Manitoba Inc. v. Parks, 2002 NSSC 265* (Can. N.S. Sup. Ct.), the court refused to grant an interlocutory injunction against the alleged controlling parties of a franchisee that had "flipped" the franchise into a competing business. However, following trial on the merits and then an appeal, the franchisor was ultimately granted an injunction and was also awarded $70,500 in damages, including for lost franchise fees, together with $40,000 in punitive damages (*Manitoba Inc. v. Parks*, 2007 NSCA 36 (Can. N.S.C.A.)). These sanctions were not based directly upon a breach of specific restrictive covenants, but instead were based on the defendants' actions in causing the franchisee to breach its obligations under franchise agreement, among other things.

---

2. Have the courts articulated the "legitimate interests" of the franchisor that will support enforcement of a covenant against competition contained in a franchise agreement?

- **If so, what are they (e.g., protection of goodwill, protection of confidential information), and in what contexts did the issue arise?**
- **If not, what interests have been recognized in other contexts (e.g., employment agreements, the sale of business context)?**

Where Nova Scotia courts have addressed restrictive covenants in the franchise context, they have recognized that interests associated with loss of goodwill, protection of proprietary information, and even the financial ability of the franchisor to survive may all be legitimate interests. *21227449 Nova Scotia Ltd. v. Donna's Seashore Investments Ltd*, (1997) 162 N.S.R. (2d) 74 (Can. N.S. Sup. Ct.); *Groupe Restaurants Imvescor Inc. v. Zliv Creations Inc.*, 2017 NSSC 31.

Outside the franchise context, Nova Scotia courts have recognized the strong inherent interests that a purchaser of a business will have in enforcing restrictive covenants against a seller. In *Jorna & Craig Inc. v. Chiasson*, 2020 NSCA 42 (Can. N.S.C.A.), the Nova Scotia Court of Appeal considered a restrictive covenant that prevented the vendor of a pharmacy from competing with the buyer. In this case, the court held that restrictive covenants provide the purchaser with protection from competition by the former owner who knew the business and its customers and, in the absence of providing this protection, an owner might not be able to sell its business.

NS

Restrictive covenants have also been considered in the employment context. In this context, the courts have been more hesitant to enforce restrictive covenants, particularly due to the power imbalance between employer and employee and a general view that it is unfair to limit an individual from exploiting their own knowledge and skills to earn a living (*J.G. Collins Insurance Agencies v. Elsley*, [1978] S.C.J. No. 47 (S.C.C.); *Keltic Transportation Inc. v. Montgomery*, 2014 NSSC 414 (Can. N.S. Sup. Ct.)).

In *Atlantic Business Interiors Ltd. v. Hipson*, 2005 NSCA 16 (Can. N.S.C.A.), an employee had signed an employment contract containing a restrictive covenant preventing him from joining a competitor or soliciting clients for a period of 12 months. He was responsible for all contact with one major client. Immediately after he terminated his employment contract and joined another firm, the major client followed him to that firm. While the employer was ultimately unsuccessful in this case, the court recognized that the employer had a legitimate interest in protecting its trade connection with the client, and also recognized that trade secrets and other confidential information constitute legitimate interests to be protected.

Accordingly, there are numerous interests that the courts have recognized as legitimate bases for restrictive covenants, but, as is discussed further ahead, it will likely be necessary for franchisors to demonstrate that their restrictive covenants are appropriately drafted to protect only those legitimate interests.

3. What time limitations have courts recognized as reasonable in the franchise context? If no franchise cases have been decided, what time limitations have been recognized in other contexts?

- **How have they been related to the interests protected?**

There is limited direct insight in Nova Scotia as to what temporal limit may be considered in the franchise context. In *Groupe Restaurants Imvescor Inc. v. Zliv Creations Inc.*, 2017 NSSC 31 (Can. N.S. Sup. Ct.), the court approved a consent interlocutory injunction against a franchisee in respect of a two-year non-competition clause. While the court found the franchisor had a strong prima facie case, however, it is important to note that no final decision on the enforceability of this clause was rendered.

Within the context of employment decisions, the reasonableness of the length of a restrictive covenant will be assessed based on the individual circumstances. However, courts have accepted that periods between six months (*Keltic Transportation Inc. v. Montgomery*, 2014 NSSC 414 (Can. N.S. Sup. Ct.)) and 12 months (*Atlantic Business Interiors Ltd. v. Hipson*, 2005 NSCA 16 (Can. N.S.C.A.)) are reasonable and have not necessarily ruled out that longer periods may be appropriate in certain cases, such as those involving particularly key employees. However, in *MacQuarrie's Drugs Ltd. v. Salsman*, 2012 NSSC 234 (Can. N.S. Sup. Ct.), the Nova Scotia court did find that a five-year non-competition clause for an employee was prima facie unreasonable.

In sale of business cases, the courts have again been more lenient with time periods as compared to the employment context, upholding restrictive periods in excess of two years and up to seven years (*Greening Industries Ltd. et al. v. Penny et al.*, [1965] N.S.J. No. 16 (Can. N.S. Sup. Ct.); *S. & D. Smith Central Supplies Ltd. v. Robson*, [1988] N.S.J. No. 129 (Can. N.S. Sup. Ct.); *Jorna & Craig Inc. v. Chiasson*, 2020 NSCA 42 (Can. N.S.C.A.)).

4. What geographic limitations have courts recognized as reasonable in the franchise context?

- **How have they been related to the interests protected?**
- **Have courts recognized the legitimacy of protecting other franchisees from competition?**

No Nova Scotia franchise decisions have specifically addressed reasonableness of geographic scope. Accordingly, it is necessary to look to other contexts.

In the employment context, the court in *Atlantic Business Interiors Ltd. v. Hipson*, 2005 NSCA 16 (Can. N.S.C.A.) found that a geographic limit of mainland Nova Scotia, which was tied into the employer's main dealer territory for key products, was reasonable.

In *MacQuarrie's Drugs Ltd. v. Salsman*, 2012 NSSC 234 (Can. N.S. Sup. Ct.), the court briefly considered geographic limitations when considering the balance of convenience on an interlocutory injunction being sought against a former pharmacy employee. In rejecting the injunction, the court expressed concern that requiring a former employee not to start a pharmacy in his own town would require him to work outside the community where he'd lived his whole life.

Within the context of the sale of a business, the court in *Jorna & Craig Inc. v. Chiasson*, 2020 NSCA 42 (Can. N.S.C.A.) upheld a non-competition clause that prevented a pharmacy vendor from competing in Halifax peninsula, as this was where the pharmacy and its customer base were located.

In *S. & D. Smith Central Supplies Ltd. v. Robson*, [1988] N.S.J. No. 129 (Can. N.S. Sup. Ct.), the restrictive covenant prevented business vendors in the city of Sydney. The court found that the covenants were not excessive in terms of area, given the nature of the market and the small size of the town.

As with temporal limitations, therefore, the caselaw demonstrates that geographic scope must generally be reasonable and go no further than necessary to protect the legitimate interests of the protected party. Accordingly, the specific location of a franchisee business and its customer base will likely be particularly relevant in assessing the reasonableness of the geographic scope of a restrictive covenant.

5. What limitations on activities have courts recognized as reasonable in the franchise context?

In *Groupe Restaurants Imvescor Inc. v. Zliv Creations Inc.*, 2017 NSSC 31 (Can. N.S. Sup. Ct.), the court approved a consent interlocutory injunction on a non-competition provision that restricted the franchisee of a pizza and pasta restaurant from being engaged in any restaurant business. Again, while the court did not render a final decision on the enforceability of this provision, it did find that the franchisor had a strong prima facie case against the franchisee.

In the context of a business sale, non-competition provisions are routinely used and have been upheld. In *S. & D. Smith Central Supplies Ltd. v. Robson*, [1988] N.S.J. No. 129 (Can. N.S. Sup. Ct.), the court upheld a restrictive covenant that prevented the vendor of a kitchen business from selling kitchen products.

NS

In *Jorna & Craig Inc. v. Chiasson*, 2020 NSCA 42 (Can. N.S.C.A.), the Nova Scotia Court of Appeal upheld a non-competition agreement against a pharmacy vendor that prohibited him from participating in a pharmacy company or company in a "related industry," rejecting arguments that the non-competition provision was overly broad in the context.

Contrast the sale of business cases with the employment context, where non-competition provisions are more rarely upheld, particularly if less restrictive covenants would have adequately protected the employer's legitimate interests. In *Atlantic Business Interiors Ltd. v. Hipson*, 2005 NSCA 16 (Can. N.S.C.A.), the court held that the non-competition clause was unenforceable, as a simple non-solicitation clause preventing the employee from interacting with customers would have sufficed to meet the employer's needs.

6. Does the province recognize a difference between in-term and post-term covenants?

Nova Scotia cases have not specifically addressed the distinction between in-term and post-term covenants. However, given that court concerns over restrictive covenants largely arise from the fact that they prevent a party from applying their skills and knowledge to earn a living, it is likely that, all other factors being equal, in-term covenants would generally be viewed as more reasonable than post-term covenants.

7. Has the province allowed enforcement of covenants against non-signatories (e.g., family members, newly formed corporations)?

While Nova Scotia courts have generally respected principles of privity of contract, in the context of franchise disputes the Nova Scotia courts have not ruled out enforcement of covenants against non-signatories to a franchise agreement but have ultimately rejected interlocutory injunctions in these cases (*Groupe Restaurants Imvescor Inc. v. Zliv Creations Inc.*, 2017 NSSC 31 (Can. N.S. Sup. Ct.); *MEDIchair v. I.M.P.*, 2005 NSSC 72 (Can. N.S. Sup. Ct.)).

In rejecting an interlocutory injunction sought against certain senior officials with a franchisee in *MEDIchair v. I.M.P.*, 2005 NSSC 72 (Can. N.S. Sup. Ct.), the court noted specifically that the franchisor had failed to secure a signed copy of the franchise agreement schedule that was intended to bind those defendants to the restrictive covenants.

Even if restrictive covenants cannot be enforced against non-signatories, a franchisor may still have tort claims against these parties where they intentionally interfere with the franchisor-franchisee contractual relationship. As discussed above, in *Manitoba Inc. v. Parks*, 2007 NSCA 36 (Can. N.S.C.A.), the franchisor was granted an injunction and damages against parties, including non-signatories to the franchise agreement, who the court found had been heavily involved in the franchise and had, among other things, engaged in intentional interference with the franchisor's contractual relations.

8. Will the province modify, "blue-pencil," or otherwise reduce a covenant found to be overbroad?

This issue has not been addressed in the context of franchise disputes in Nova Scotia.

In the employment context, courts have been resistant to writing down or modifying overly broad or vague restrictive covenants. As discussed above, in *Atlantic Business Interiors Ltd. v. Hipson*, 2005 NSCA 16 (Can. N.S.C.A.), the court found that a non-solicitation provision would have been appropriate but declined to save the restrictive covenant by writing down the non-competition provision to a non-solicitation provision.

In *Shafron v. KRG Insurance Brokers (Western) Inc.*, 2009 SCC 6 (S.C.C.), the Supreme Court of Canada held that the concept of "notional severance," effectively rewriting a restrictive covenant to make it enforceable, does not apply to employment contracts. The Supreme Court of Canada did, however, indicate that "blue-pencil" severance of an unenforceable section of a restrictive covenant may be available in limited cases where the part being removed is clearly severable, trivial, and not part of the main purport of the restrictive covenant.

In the context of the sale of a business, the courts have demonstrated some more willingness to modify an otherwise unenforceable restrictive covenant. In *Greening Industries Ltd. et al. v. Penny et al.*, [1965] N.S.J. No. 16 (Can. N.S. Sup. Ct.), the court considered an action for damages and an injunction as a result of a breach of restrictive covenant following the sale of a business. The covenant provided that the vendors would not directly or indirectly engage in the manufacture of synthetic rope for five years in all of Canada, or similar work. The court severed from the covenant the references to "similar work" and also replaced the reference to "Canada" with the Maritime Provinces.

9. When does a non-compete period begin to run? Will courts equitably extend the term?

There are no published cases that suggest a unique analysis to the commencement of a non-compete period. The start of a non-compete period must of course be assessed based on the wording of the franchise agreement.

There is no precedent for an equitable extension to a non-compete period in Nova Scotia.

10. Are there additional nuances or peculiarities of the province's treatment of covenants in the franchising context?

There are no other unique issues of note in this context.

Ontario

*by Geoffrey B. Shaw and Colin Pendrith**

1. Has the province addressed covenants against competition in the context of franchising?

- **Does the province have a franchising statute or regulations that address covenants against competition?**
- **Does the province have a covenants statute of general applicability that would encompass franchise covenants?**
- **Have the courts addressed covenants in the context of franchising either under a statute or under the province's common law?**

Ontario's franchising statute, the *Arthur Wishart Act (Franchise Disclosure) 2000*, S.O. 2000, c. 3, does not specifically address covenants against competition. However, section 3 of the *Arthur Wishart Act* does impose a duty of fair dealing on both the franchisor and franchisee, pursuant to which the parties are required to act in good faith regarding the performance and enforcement of the franchise agreement. This duty will act as an undertone to the courts' interpretation of covenants against competition.

Ontario does not have any covenants statutes of general applicability that encompass franchise covenants.

Covenants against competition are addressed under Ontario's common law, which has largely developed in the context of employment agreements. The leading case on the enforceability of restrictive covenants in employment agreements is the Supreme Court of Canada's decision in *Elsley et al. v. J. G. Collins Insurance Agencies Ltd.* (1978), 83 D.L.R. (3d) 1 (S.C.C.), which holds that a covenant in restraint of trade is enforceable only if it is reasonable as between the parties and with reference to the public interest. The Supreme Court of Canada stated that the validity of a restrictive covenant will generally be assessed by reference to three questions. First, is there a proprietary interest entitled to protection? Second, are the temporal or spatial features of the covenant too broad? And third, is the covenant unenforceable as being against competition generally?

*Geoffrey B. Shaw and Colin Pendrith are partners in Cassels Brock & Blackwell LLP's advocacy department and practice within the Franchise Law Group.

As explained by the Supreme Court of Canada in *Shafron v. KRG Insurance Brokers (Western) Inc.*, 2009 SCC 6, an ambiguous restrictive covenant will be *prima facie* unenforceable because the party seeking enforcement will be unable to demonstrate reasonableness in the face of an ambiguity.

As the party that will be seeking to enforce a restrictive covenant, the franchisor will have the onus to establish the reasonableness of the covenant (*Bark & Fitz Inc. v. 2139138 Ontario Inc.*, [2010] O.J. No. 1428 (S.C.J.)).

The assessment of the reasonableness of a covenant is contextual. In *Payette v. Guay*, 2013 SCC 45, the Supreme Court of Canada reiterated that the level of scrutiny applicable to the reasonableness of a restrictive covenant will differ depending on whether the covenant in question is tied to the sale of a business or an employment agreement, with a higher level of scrutiny being applied in the employment context.

This issue was further considered in the franchise context in *MEDIchair LP v. DME Medequip Inc.*, 2016 ONCA 168. However, in that decision, the Court of Appeal for Ontario did not resolve the question of the appropriate degree of scrutiny to be applied to restrictive covenants in the franchise context, leaving the issue in need of further appellate consideration. The Court of Appeal for Ontario explained:

> Although this case involves a restrictive covenant in a franchise agreement, I do not need to decide what level of scrutiny properly applies, because the focus of the inquiry is not the reasonableness of the extent of the temporal or territorial restrictions. Instead, it is whether there is a legitimate interest of the franchisor in this case that is entitled to the protection of the covenant. The requirement of a legitimate protectable interest is common to both levels of scrutiny.

In Ontario, the enforceability of a restrictive covenant is typically considered holistically and not in isolation. In *Elsley*, the Supreme Court explained that the validity of a restrictive covenant can only be determined by an overall assessment of the clause, the agreement and all of the surrounding circumstances. In the franchise case of *Invescor Restaurants Inc. v. 3574423 Canada Inc.* [2011] O.J. No. 1412, Justice Wilton-Siegel noted that this principle from *Elsley* is equally applicable to a restrictive covenant in a franchise agreement. On appeal, in *Imvescor Restaurants Inc. v. 3574423 Canada Inc.*, 2012 ONCA 387, the Court of Appeal for Ontario upheld the Superior Court decision, declining to find the restrictive covenant to be ambiguous (and therefore unenforceable) as a pure question of law. Instead, the Court suggested that an analysis of ambiguity would benefit from a full factual record.

---

2. Have the courts articulated the "legitimate interests" of the franchisors that will support enforcement of a covenant against competition contained in a franchise agreement?

- **If so, what are they?**
- **If not, what interests have been recognized in other contexts?**

Although not a franchise case, in *Elsley et al. v. J. G. Collins Insurance Agencies Ltd.* (1978), 83 D.L.R. (3d) 1 (S.C.C.), the Supreme Court of Canada recognized a legitimate interest in the "reasonable protection to trade secrets, confidential information, and trade connections of the employer." Similar legitimate interests are recognized in franchise cases.

In *Allegra of North America, Inc. v. Wayne Zapfe et al.* (1 October 2001), Milton 01-CV-212994 (Ont. S.C.J.), the court recognized that if the franchisees were allowed to carry on a "shadow business" within a five-mile limit without demonstrating any significant change in their work or customer base, the "character of the franchisor's business will be changed. It will be carrying on a training business, not a franchise business. The core of the franchise system will be destroyed." These comments recognize that the franchise system as a whole constitutes a legitimate interest.

More recently in *MEDIchair LP v. DME Medequip Inc.*, 2016 ONCA 168, the Court of Appeal for Ontario explained:

> The respondent has a legitimate or proprietary interest to protect in the goodwill in its MEDIchair system, including the trade secrets, method of operation, contacts and other benefits that are obtained by a franchisee. However, the purpose of the restrictive covenant is to protect that interest only for a limited time and within a defined territory. After the specified period, that interest is no longer protected by the covenant. Similarly, during the period, that interest is only protected within the defined territory.

In *Quizno's Canada Restaurant Corporation v. 1450987 Ontario Corp.* [2009] O.J. No. 1743 (S.C.J.), Justice Perell held that "the irreparable harm suffered by the franchisor goes to its goodwill, its reputation and its responsibility to the franchisees of the chain to maintain the integrity of the franchise system". In the same decision, Justice Perell noted that the "most precious possession of a franchisor is its trademark and systems. The practice is to protect those interests in the terms of contracts with the franchisees for the benefit of the franchisor and other franchisees." Implicit to these comments is the recognition that the integrity of the franchise system and its trademarks constitute legitimate interests that are worthy of protection.

In *Quizno's* Justice Perell referred to the Quebec decision of *Second Cup Ltd v. Ahsam*, [2001] Q.J. No. 1763 (Q.S.C.), in which Justice Zerbisias held:

> Where a member of the franchise chain fails to uphold the policies, standards and operating methods and system to which all of the franchisees have subscribed by executing their franchise agreement, and upon which they rely to advance their mutual interests, it is incumbent upon the franchisor to take measures against the infringing party to force it to cease from tarnishing the reputation of the chain and from diminishing the value of the trademark and the banner. The franchisor must act to protect the integrity of the chain

---

3. What time limitations have courts recognized as reasonable in the franchise context? If no franchise cases have been decided, what time limitations have been recognized in other contexts?

➤ How have they been related to the interests protected?

The time limitation that will be reasonable will vary from one factual scenario to another, but should not be broader than required to protect the franchisor's interests. Historically, covenants lasting for two years, and occasionally more, have been found to be reasonable; however, there is no rule of thumb. The reasonableness of the temporal restriction will depend on the nature of the interest being protected, as well as the on the scope of the restricted activity and the geographic limits in the covenant.

In *Quizno's Canada Restaurant Corporation v. 1450987 Ontario Corp.*, [2009] O.J. No. 1743 (S.C.J.) the franchise agreement restricted the franchisee from competing within a defined eight-kilometer radius of the franchise location for two years. Although the court did not specifically comment on the reasonability of the two-year limitation, it did grant the injunction sought by the franchisor.

In *Color Your World Inc. v. Schaus*, [1987] O.J. No. 1300 (S.C.) an interlocutory injunction was granted, enforcing a two-year covenant against competition within a ten-mile geographical radius. The franchisor, a paint store, was seeking to prevent the franchisee's owner from using the intimacies and knowledge which he had acquired in the course of his employment in order to open his own business and undermine the franchisor's business. Justice Misener stated, "Given the impossibility of precision in human affairs, and the impossibility of gauging in advance the strength of the personal loyalty that any particular manager or franchisee might be able to cultivate, I cannot think that any court would declare a two year restriction upon competition as other than reasonable."

In *Enco Seat Covers Ltd. v. Enco Auto Trim and Glass (Newmarket) Ltd.*, [1993] O.J. No. 88 (Ont. Gen. Div.) it was held that a three-year non-competition clause was reasonable and was not more than required to protect the plaintiff's interest. The franchisor in this case was in the business of repairing upholstery in cars, installing automobile seat covers and auto glass.

In *1460904 Ontario Inc. (c.o.b. MDG Computers Scarborough) v. MDG Computers Canada Inc.*, [2006] O.J. No. 4390 (S.C.J.) the franchise agreement included a restrictive covenant prohibiting a terminated franchisee from competing with MDG within a ten-mile radius of the franchisee's store site for five years following upon termination. Although not the main issue in the motion, the court held that the franchise agreement arguably had overreaching provisions, including the asserted restrictive covenant.

In *1598631 Ontario Inc. v. Imvescor Restaurant Group Inc.*, 2015 ONSC 1888, a five-year restriction was found to be reasonable, keeping in mind the long-term contractual relationship between the parties and the fact that the restricted activity was very specific. The covenant in question only restricted the former franchisee from using the same recipes at a competing restaurant, not from competing more generally. This highlights the courts' inclination to enforce covenants of greater duration where the restricted activity is more tailored.

In *MTY TIKI MING Enterprises v. Boundris*, 2016 ONSC 3290 a two-year restrictive covenant was enforced; however, no argument was advanced concerning the overbreadth of the temporal restriction.

If a non-competition clause has no temporal limitation, it will almost certainly be found to be overbroad and unenforceable. In *Yesac Creative Foods Inc. v. Hohnjec*, [1985] O.J. No. 519 (H.C.J.), the court held that the plaintiff had failed to demonstrate that the covenants were no wider than required to protect its legitimate business interests. The franchise agreement provided that the franchisee would not engage "in any other business which in anyway is competing with the franchisor or its franchisees or which are related to the food, beverage or restaurant business." The restriction was apparently of unlimited duration. The court found this covenant overly broad, unreasonable, and unenforceable. It further held that the covenant was a mere attempt to prevent competition per se and was not tailored or narrowed to demonstrate it did not extend beyond what was required to protect the legitimate commercial interest of the covenantee.

Unsurprisingly, and as noted in *1598631 Ontario Inc. v. Imvescor Restaurant Group Inc.*, 2015 ONSC 1888, courts in Ontario do not consider the reasonableness of temporal restrictions in isolation, but will consider the reasonableness of the restrictive covenant as a whole, including the geographic limitation.

---

4. What geographic limitations have the courts recognized as reasonable in the franchise context?

- **How have they been related to the interests protected?**
- **Have courts recognized the legitimacy of protecting other franchisees from competition?**

As with temporal limitations, what is considered to be a reasonable geographic limitation will vary from case to case. The underlying principle is that the geographical limitation must not be broader than is required to protect the franchisor's business interests. Where the franchise agreement contains a defined area of exclusivity or a delivery zone, that area is a logical proxy for a reasonable geographic restriction in a restrictive covenant. In *Cashmoney v. 1035216 Ontario Inc.* (2 October 2003), Toronto 03-CV-248970CM1 (Ont. S.C.J.), the court upheld a covenant restricting competition in the "franchised area."

In *MEDIchair LP v. DME Medequip Inc.*, 2016 ONCA 168, the Court of Appeal for Ontario refused to enforce a restrictive covenant where the franchisor did not intend to re-franchise the area covered by the covenant. The court reasoned that the franchisor had legitimate or proprietary interest to protect in areas where it was operating, but not within the now abandoned area of the covenant. Accordingly, continued operations by the franchisor in the area covered by the restricted covenant are highly relevant to whether the covenant will be enforced. A franchisor without active business in a particular region will be challenged to enforce a restrictive covenant within it.

While there is no universal rule, an eight-kilometer (approximately five mile) geographic limitation has frequently been held to be reasonable. In *Quizno's Canada Restaurant Corporation v. 1450987 Ontario Corp.*, [2009] O.J. No. 1743 (S.C.J.) the court granted an injunction to prevent the franchisee from competing within a defined eight-kilometer radius. In *Allegra of North America, Inc. v. Wayne Zapfe et al.* (1 October 2001), Milton 01-CV-212994 (Ont. S.C.J.) an injunction was granted within a five-mile limit.

Larger geographic restrictions have been enforced in certain circumstances. In *Cash Converters Canada Inc. v. 1167430 Ontario Inc.*, [2001] O.J. No. 5860 (S.C.J.), the reasonableness of the geographic limitation was not explicitly discussed; however, the court granted an injunction preventing the franchisee from having any direct or indirect interest as a disclosed or beneficial owner in a competitive business operating within 30 kilometers of a specific Cash Converter store, or within 15 kilometers of any other Cash Converter store.

In *Pet Valu Canada Inc. v. 1381114 Ontario Limited*, 2013 ONSC 5361, a covenant restricting competition within 20 kilometers of any Pet Valu store was enforced; however, the decision did not discuss the reasonableness of the covenant.

In *1598631 Ontario Inc. v. Imvescor Restaurant Group Inc.*, 2015 ONSC 1888, a covenant restricting competition within ten kilometers of any Bâton Rouge restaurant was found to be reasonable, notwithstanding that the franchisee's protected area was only two kilometers. In addition to considering the highly tailored scope of restricted activities (discussed earlier in section 3), Justice Glustein gave some guidance on the reasonableness of covenants in the restaurant industry:

> The temporal, geographic, and scope restrictions of Section 16.3 are reasonable. Section 16.3 has a very limited scope, which only restricts a former franchisee from using the same recipes for most of the products sold at their competing restaurant. Consequently, a 5-year, 10-kilometre restriction is reasonable "in a fully competitive industry such as the restaurant industry which is characterized by limited barriers to entry" "to allow a franchisor to enjoy the fruits of its efforts in developing a particular concept and to provide an opportunity to prospective franchisees who consider that an investment in a franchise of an operating chain with a recognized name, décor and menu reduces the franchisee's investment risk"

In *Pizza Pizza Ltd. v. Gatto*, [1996] O.J. No. 4087, Justice Wilkins expressed serious doubt about the reasonableness of geographical limits of the non-competition clause. The clause prohibited the franchisee from "competing with any Pizza Pizza store within any regional municipality, city, town or village within which any one of the franchised outlets is located at the date of termination of the contract." Justice Wilkins held that "In effect, on the basis of the evidence before me, if the clause were implemented literally, Gatto would be prohibited from operating an Italian restaurant in Costa Rica and Panama." When considering the reasonableness of the geographic restriction, courts in Ontario will consider the franchisor's interest in protecting other franchisees. In *Pizza Pizza Ltd. v. Gatto*, Justice Wilkins stated, "It would appear that the only interest the plaintiff has in the enforcement of the restraint of trade covenants in issue is that of protecting the rights of the one store within the municipal boundaries of Richmond Hill, and that store is not a party to these proceedings." Although Justice Wilkins declined to grant an injunction, his comments recognize the franchisor's interest in protecting other franchisees, specifically the Richmond Hill franchise.

In *Invescor Restaurants Inc. v. 3574423 Canada Inc.*, [2011] O.J. No. 1412 (S.C.J.), Justice Wilton-Siegal's analysis of a geographic limitation considered the intentions of the parties at the time of the negotiation and execution of the franchise agreement. The franchisee argued that the restrictive covenant should have been drafted to limit the geographic scope to those provinces in which the franchisor had a reasonable expectation of expansion over the term of the franchise agreement. Justice Wilton-Siegal held that the franchisee failed to demonstrate that the covenant did not accord with the intention or reasonable expectations of the parties at the time of execution of the franchise agreement. Justice Wilton-Siegel stated:

> Given their right of first refusal to obtain the franchise for the second individual Bâton Rouge restaurant in the Greater Toronto Area agreed to in the Addendum and their expectation of a general opportunity to participate in the growth of the franchise in Ontario, the Canada-wide scope of the restrictive covenant was not an issue for them at such time.

More recently, the Court of Appeal for Ontario confirmed that reasonableness of a covenant is assessed at the time that it is granted and based on their anticipated activities. In *MEDIchair LP v. DME Medequip Inc.*, 2016 ONCA 168, the court held:

As the reasonableness of the covenant will be interpreted based on the parties' anticipated expansion of the business when they entered into their agreement, it should similarly be interpreted to take account of the parties' expectations at that time with respect to the future continued operation of the franchise in the territory. In this case, the clause was reasonable on the assumption and understanding that MEDIchair would want to continue to operate in the protected Peterborough area, but not if it did not. In *Allegra of North America and Allegra Corp. of Canada v. Russell Sugimura*, (August 26, 2008), Milton, CV-08-21790-00 (Ont. S.C.), where the franchisor did not intend to open another franchise location within the territory covered by the restrictive covenant, the court effectively applied the same principle. It refused to enforce the covenant where Allegra had nothing left to protect within the geographic area.

A complete restriction without any geographical limitation will almost certainly be found to be unenforceable. Although not a franchise case, in *H.L. Staebler Co. v. Allan*, [2008] O.J. No. 3048 (C.A.), the Court of Appeal for Ontario held that "the absence of a geographical limit combined with the blanket prohibition on conducting business renders the Restrictive Covenant 'overbroad' and unenforceable."

5. What limitations on activities have courts recognized as reasonable in the franchise context?

The more tailored the restricted activity in the covenant, the more likely a court will be to enforce it. Specificity serves two purposes. First, it reduces ambiguity as to the scope of the covenant, and second, it rebuts the argument that the covenant is overbroad.

Covenants that prevent franchisees from using a franchisor's trade secrets, customer lists, or other confidential information are generally considered reasonable. Blanket prohibitions on competition, while often permitted, leave room for a franchisee to argue that the restraint goes too far.

If the restrictive covenant does not precisely define the restricted business, it will be left to the court to interpret whether the new business is sufficiently similar to the franchised business so as to be reasonably captured by the restrictive covenant. This arrangement can be risky to franchisors. For example, in *Dynamex Canada Franchise Holdings Inc. v. P&D Investments Ltd. (Knight Courier Service PDI)*, [2009] O.J. No. 2048 (S.C.J.), the restrictive covenant prevented the franchisee from carrying on "any business competitive with or similar to that of the Franchised Business." The court declined to enforce the covenant, finding that a same-day courier service was not the same or similar to an overnight courier service. Had the restrictive covenant specifically stated that the franchisee could not carry on a "courier business," the result may well have been different. This cautionary case illustrates a pitfall that can arise from imprecise drafting in the franchise agreement.

In contrast, in *Ontario Duct Cleaning v. Wiles*, [2001] O.J. No. 5150 (S.C.J.), Justice Rivard granted an injunction preventing the franchisee from carrying on "any business which consists primarily of the provision of cleaning services for air ducts or forced air heating or cooling systems." In this case, the covenant against competition contained a high degree of specificity that allowed the court to grant an injunction.

In *MEDIchair LP v. DME Medequip Inc.*, 2016 ONCA 168, one of the issues before the Court of Appeal for Ontario was whether the use of the words "similar to" created ambiguity in the description of the prohibited business. The court rejected the argument that the words were ambiguous or otherwise made the covenant unenforceable:

> The application judge dealt with this argument. He found that the respondent has "a method of operation, goodwill, products, and services that it has a legitimate interest in protecting from similar operations specializing in the sale or rental of home medical equipment." In other words, the similarity is found by comparing not only the product line, but also the method of operation, including whether the appellant was trading on the goodwill of the MEDIchair operation from which it had benefitted over the years.

6. Does the province recognize a difference between in-term and post-term covenants?

It is more common that franchisees will be in violation of post-term covenants than in-term covenants; however, there is no categorical distinction between in-term and post-term covenants concerning the covenant's validity in law. Courts are willing to uphold the validity of covenants in both cases, provided that the test in *Elsley et al. v. J. G. Collins Insurance Agencies Ltd.*, (1978), 83 D.L.R. (3d) 1 (S.C.C.) is met. However, courts seem to recognize that an in-term covenant carries a certain degree of inherent reasonability. As Justice Wilton-Siegel noted in the franchise case of *Invescor Restaurants Inc. v. 3574423 Canada Inc.*, [2011] O.J. No. 1412 (S.C.J.) "[s]o long as the franchisee is receiving the benefit of the Franchise Agreement, the franchisee should not be able to undermine the value of the franchise."

ON

In *Greco Franchising Inc. v. Franco Milito et al.*, 2021 ONSC 3950, Justice Hackland adopted Justice Wilton-Siegel's above-noted comments concerning the reasonableness of in-term covenants. While the covenant in question was determined to be reasonable, Justice Hackland declined to grant an injunction because there was some doubt as to whether the franchisor had fundamentally breached the franchise agreement such that the entire agreement was unenforceable. On that basis, Justice Hackland found that a strong prima facie case had not been established.

Although there has yet to be judicial consideration of the issue, in the context of in-term covenants, it may be that a franchisee who is in breach of an in-term covenant will also be in breach of the duty of fair dealing, good faith, and reasonable commercial practice imposed by section 3 of the *Arthur Wishart Act (Franchise Disclosure) 2000*, S.O. 2000 c. 3. Under section 3, a party to a franchise agreement has a right of action for damages against another party to the franchise agreement who breaches the duty of fair dealing in the performance or enforcement of the franchise agreement.

7. Has the province allowed enforcement of covenants against non-signatories?

In Ontario, courts have been willing to grant injunctive relief against non-signatories. For example, in *Bark & Fitz Inc. v. 2139138 Ontario Inc.*, [2010] O.J. No. 1428 (S.C.J.), Justice Karakatsanis, as she then was, held:

> The franchisor is asserting a claim that as principals of the franchisees, they are not entitled to operate in breach of the non-competition provisions of the contract. Counsel did not provide any case law in support of their position. Nevertheless, I find that this raises a serious issue to be tried. If the non-competition clause did not bind the principal of the corporate franchisee, that clause would be effectively meaningless: the principal could simply start a new corporation.

Although not a final determination of whether the non-signatory was bound, the court was willing to grant an injunction, which in many cases has the same practical effect as a final judgment.

Similarly, in *Ontario Duct Cleaning Ltd. v. Wiles*, [2001] O.J. No. 5150 (S.C.J.), it was held that "[t]he evidence presented on this motion also supports the proposition that Advanced Air Quality Inc. was incorporated for the purpose of defeating the non-competition obligations of Mr. Wiles. It is appropriate to include the relief sought against that company because the company was formed for the purpose of enabling Mr. Wiles, under this corporate cloak, to compete with the plaintiff when Mr. Wiles had undertaken not to do so."

In *Bulk Barn Foods Ltd v. Faber*, [2003] O.J. No. 5553 (S.C.J.), Justice Matlow enjoined the wife of the franchisee although she did not sign the franchise agreement. In this case, a clause in the franchise agreement had required all shareholders of the franchisee's corporation to be bound by the non-competition clause. Because the franchisor's wife did not disclose that she was a shareholder of the corporation, she did not sign. In the circumstances, Justice Matlow held that the franchisee's wife should be viewed as if she had signed it.

In *Pet Valu Canada Inc. v. 1381114 Ontario Limited*, 2013 ONSC 5361, Justice Backhouse found that the operation of a competing business, ostensibly by a franchisee's husband, was in fact a "transparent effort" to assist the franchisee in avoiding the effect of the restrictive covenant. In this case, there was a finding that the franchisee was involved in the operation of the competing business. In the result, the competing business was enjoined.

In certain cases, judges are unwilling to enforce covenants against non-signatories. For example, in *Print Three Franchising Corp. v. Mitchinson Investments Corp.*, [1997] O.J. No. 1880 (Ont. Gen. Div.), the court declined to enjoin two individuals, one of whom was the directing mind of the corporate franchisee but was not a signatory. The court noted the lack of a clause in that agreement that was binding upon officers, directors, and/or employees of the franchise holder.

8. Will the province modify, "blue-pencil" or otherwise reduce a covenant found to be overbroad?

Courts in Ontario have rarely applied blue-pencil severance or otherwise reduced the scope of a restrictive covenant in a franchise agreement. In *Cashmoney v. 1035216 Ontario Inc.*, (2 October 2003), Toronto 03-CV-248970CM1 (Ont. S.C.J.), the court severed part of a restrictive covenant that prohibited the operation of a competing business "within the Franchised Area or otherwise within any Province in Canada wherein Cashplan Financial Centres operate" by striking all but the words "franchised area."

Despite the decision in *Cashmoney, supra*, the use of "blue-pencil" severance is the exception rather than the norm. In *KRG Insurance Brokers (Western) Inc. v. Shafron*, [2009] 1 S.C.R. 157 (S.C.C.) the Supreme Court of Canada cautioned against the use of blue-pencil severance. The Supreme Court of Canada held "As for blue-pencil severance, it may only be resorted to in rare cases where the part being removed is trivial, and not part of the main purport of the restrictive covenant."

In some non-franchise commercial cases, and particularly where sophisticated parties are involved, blue-pencil severance has been used more liberally. For example, in GDL *Solutions Inc. v. Walker*, 2012 ONSC 4378, Justice Brown explained:

> The instant case is in the context of the sale of a business rather than in the employment context. Therefore, the cautions regarding severance are less applicable. However, I find that only "blue line" severance is appropriate. This case involved two sophisticated parties who were both represented by counsel, and who engaged in many months of negotiation. It would not be appropriate to rewrite their contract for them. However, where individual terms are found to be unreasonable, they can certainly be severed.

Despite these developments in these commercial context, blue-pencil and other forms of severance are anticipated to remain rare in the franchise context.

9. When does a non-compete period begin to run? Will courts equitably extend the term?

A post-termination non-compete period typically begins to run when the franchise agreement ends. In *Ziebart Canada Inc. v. Enkin*, [2005] O.J. No. 5415 (S.C.J.), the franchise agreement expired; however, the franchisor allowed the franchisee to continue using its trademarks for three years afterward to allow the franchisee to sell the business. The non-competition clause prevented competition for a period of two years.

ON

In *Ziebert*, the court held that prior to the expiry of the franchise agreement, it was open to the franchisor to require that any continuing business between the parties would extend the term of the contract for all purposes, including the non-competition provisions; however, the franchisor did not do so. The court held that the non-competition issue never presented itself to the minds of the parties, whilst these dealings continued after termination of the contract on its terms. Accordingly, the court refused to extend the non-compete period and grant an injunction.

Given the general rule that restrictive covenants should be no longer than necessary to protect the interests of the franchisor, it seems unlikely that such a period would be extended absent exceptional circumstances.

10. Are there additional nuances or peculiarities of the province's treatment of covenants in the franchising context?

THE DUTY OF GOOD FAITH

Section 3 of the *Arthur Wishart Act (Franchise Disclosure) 2000*, S.O. 2000, c. 3, places a duty of fair dealing on both parties to a franchise agreement. The duty of fair dealing includes the duty to act in good faith and in accordance with reasonable commercial standards. The duty has often been described as a standard that is less than a fiduciary duty.

In *Shelanu Inc. v. Print Three Franchising Corp.* (2003), 64 O.R. (3d) (C.A.), the Court of Appeal for Ontario explained that "'Good faith,' while permitting a party to act self-interestedly, nonetheless qualifies this by positively requiring that party, in his decision and action, to have regard to the legitimate interests therein of the other. The 'fiduciary' standard for its part enjoins one party to act in the interests of the other—to act selflessly and with undivided loyalty." The breach of the duty of good faith is an independent actionable wrong, for which damages may be sought.

Recent jurisprudence from the Supreme Court of Canada has expanded the application of the common law duty of good faith, which overlaps with the statutory duty contained in the *Arthur Wishart Act (Franchise Disclosure) 2000*, S.O. 2000, c. 3. In *Bhasin v. Hrynew*, 2014 SCC 71, the Supreme Court of Canada recognized that good faith contractual performance is a general organizing principle of Canadian common law, and that parties to a contract are under a duty to act honestly in the performance of their contractual obligations.

The duties of good faith and honest performance have been further developed by the Supreme Court of Canada in *C.M. Callow Inc. v. Zollinger*, 2020 SCC 45 and *Wastech Services Ltd. v. Greater Vancouver Sewerage and Drainage District*, 2021 SCC 7.

Although no jurisprudence in Ontario has considered the issue, on its face, the breach by a franchisee of an in-term covenant against competition would also constitute a breach of the duty of good faith and/or the duty of honest performance. The duty of honesty may be uniquely engaged where the franchisee's competing business is being concealed from the franchisor.

As the duty of good faith is reciprocal, a franchisor who competes with its own franchisee may also be held to be in breach of its duty of good faith, even in the absence of a non-compete provision. In the lower court decision of *Shelanu Inc. v. Print Three Franchising Corp.*, [2000] O.J. No. 4129 (S.C.J.), the trial judge made a finding to this effect:

> It seems to me to be intrinsically troublesome for a franchisor to develop a concept for a new franchise operation that will operate in competition with its existing franchise operation. Even though Le Print Express franchisees were directed at a specific segment of the industry, I am satisfied that they not only would, but did, take work and customers from existing Print Three franchisees. As a consequence, in my view, the establishment of such an enterprise by the very person who owned and controlled the defendant was fundamentally at odds with the defendant's obligations, including the obligation to deal in good faith, to its franchisees.

On appeal, the Court of Appeal for Ontario found as a fact that Le Print Express was not competing with Shelanu's franchise; however, the court did not challenge the lower court's finding that a franchisor that competes with its own franchisees is acting in violation of its duty of fair dealing and good faith.

Because a breach of the duty of good faith and fair dealing confers a right of action for damages under the *Arthur Wishart Act* and at common law, the absence of a covenant against competition in a franchise agreement does not mean that a franchisee may engage in a competing business with impunity.

INTERLOCUTORY INJUNCTIONS

Most often, covenants against competition in franchise agreements are considered in the context of interlocutory injunctions. Although not a final determination on the merits, an interlocutory injunction is often functionally equivalent to a final judgment because the term of the covenant may expire before a trial on the merits can occur. The Supreme Court of Canada set out the general test for interlocutory relief in *RJR-MacDonald v. Canada (Atty. Gen.)*, [1994] 1 S.C.R. 311 (S.C.C.). The party seeking the injunction must establish that:

i. there is a serious issue to be tried;
ii. it will suffer irreparable harm if the injunction is not granted; and
iii. the balance of convenience favours granting the injunction.

In certain cases, the "serious issue to be tried" standard has been elevated by the courts to a "strong *prima facie* case." While the "serious issue to be tried" standard sets a lower threshold, the "strong *prima facie* case" standard involves a more intensive examination of the merits. In the franchise case of *Quizno's Canada Restaurant Corporation v. 1450987 Ontario Corp.*, [2009] O.J. No. 1743 (S.C.J.), Justice Perell described the strong prima facie standard as "a strong case with a high although not absolutely assured likelihood of success based on the material presently before the court." Justice Perell held that "the strong *prima facie* test standard is the measure used for determining whether it is appropriate to enforce a restrictive covenant by an injunction that would restrain an individual's cherished ability to make a living and to use his or her knowledge and skills obtained during employment." In Ontario, when franchisors seek to enforce a covenant against competition through an injunction, this higher standard may be applied.

Some older Ontario cases suggested that a clear breach of a negative covenant should lead to the granting injunctive relief without proof of irreparable harm or consideration of the balance of convenience. *E.g.*, *Cashmoney v. 1035216 Ontario Inc.*, (2 October 2003), Toronto 03-CV-248970CM1 (S.C.J.), *Ontario Duct Cleaning v. Wiles*, [2001] O.J. No. 5150 (S.C.J.), and *Pet Valu Canada Inc. v. 1381114 Ontario Ltd.*, 2013 ONSC 53. ON

However, the principle emerging from these cases has been questioned. In *Telesis Technologies, Inc. v. Sure Controls Systems Inc.*, [2010] O.J. No. 4875 (S.C.J.), Justice Roberts held:

> The presence of a negative covenant does not divest the court of its discretion in injunctive matters. As also noted by the court in *Van Wagner Communications Co.*, the court may still consider the factors of irreparable harm and balance of convenience, although they will have less weight in the face of the strength of the plaintiff's case and the defendant's admitted breach of the non-competition clause.

In *Weston Gardens Retirement Inc. v. 2540250 Ontario Ltd.*, 2019 ONSC 2663, Justice Nishikawa explained:

> However, in *Stop'N Cash 1000 Inc. v. 1553785 Ontario Ltd*, [2006] 332 O.A.C. 392, 2006 CarswellOnt 11652 (Div. Ct.) at para. 9, the Divisional Court stated: "[u]ntil the Supreme Court has spoken again, we must follow the RJR criteria faithfully." See also, *MD Management Ltd. v. Campbell*, 2010 ONSC 6373 (Div. Ct.) at para. 5. Weston Gardens must provide clear evidence of irreparable harm.

Similar statements were made by Justice Boswell in *MTY TIKI MING Enterprises v. Boundris*, 2016 ONSC 3290.

Although the jurisprudence is somewhat conflicted, the more recent trend requires consideration of both irreparable harm and the balance of convenience, even where a clear breach of the covenant is established.

Irreparable harm, as contemplated by the injunctive test, is harm that is not compensable by damages. In the franchise context, damage to a franchisor's goodwill is often cited as the type of harm that justifies injunctive relief. In *Kardish Food Franchising Corp. v. 874073 Ontario Inc.*, [1995] O.J. No. 2849, the court stated:

> The success of the plaintiff's franchise business depends in large measure on the goodwill associated with its name and its customer connections. To allow franchisees to take the benefit of such goodwill, set up their business and then unilaterally terminate the agreement and continue on their own two feet in complete disregard of their obligations to the franchisor when they feel they are able to do so is unfair. The plaintiff should not be confined to its remedy in damages.

Prince Edward Island

*by Jordan K. M. Brown**

1. Has the province addressed covenants against competition in the context of franchising?

- **Does the province have a franchising statute or regulations that address covenants against competition?**
- **Does the province have a covenants statute of general applicability that would encompass franchise covenants?**
- **Have the courts addressed covenants in the context of franchising either under a statute or under the province's common law?**

Prince Edward Island's general franchising statute, the *Franchises Act*, R.S.P.E.I. 1988, c. F-14 (Can. P.E.I.) (the Act), does not specifically deal with covenants against competition. However, the Act states at section 10:

> The rights conferred by or under this Act are in addition to and do not derogate from any other right or remedy any party to a franchise agreement may have at law.

Consequently, issues of non-competition covenants would be addressed by reference to the common law. It should also be noted that franchise agreements often provide that the law of the jurisdiction where the franchisor is located is the governing jurisdiction. The Act addresses attempts to avoid the laws of Prince Edward Island in franchise agreements by stating in section 11:

> Any provision in a franchise agreement purporting to restrict the application of the law of Prince Edward Island or to restrict jurisdiction or venue to a forum outside Prince Edward Island is void with respect to a claim otherwise enforceable under this Act in Prince Edward Island.

This section of the Act supports the conclusion that, as the Act does not address covenants against competition, a franchisor and franchisee will be required to rely on the common law in Prince Edward Island to settle any claims seeking to enforce non-competition covenants.

*Jordan K. M. Brown practices with the law firm of Cox & Palmer in Charlottetown, Prince Edward Island. Sasha Perry, of the same firm, assisted Mr. Brown in the preparation of this analysis.

In addition, section 5(1) of the Franchises Act requires a franchisor to make certain disclosures to a prospective franchisee. Such disclosures, which are set out in section 15 of *Franchises Act Regulations*, P.E.I. Reg. EC232/06 (Can. P.E.I.), include, "a concise summary of all the provisions in the franchise agreement that deal with the termination of the agreement, the renewal of the agreement and the transfer of the franchise and a list of where these provisions are found in the agreement." Covenants against competition would likely fall within the ambit of provisions that deal with the termination of the agreement, and thus may be part of the information that is required to be summarized and provided to a prospective franchisee.

Prince Edward Island does not have a covenants statute of general applicability.

Courts in Prince Edward Island look to the common law to determine the enforceability of restrictive covenants. Prince Edward Island's only decision that addresses covenants in the context of franchising is *D.L.T. Holdings Inc. v. Grow Biz International Inc.*, 2001 PESCTD 27 (Can. P.E.I. Sup. Ct.). In this case, the court upheld an arbitration award enforcing the provisions of a franchise agreement. The franchise agreement contained a non-competition clause stating that the franchisee would not operate a children's clothing store within a six-mile radius of the franchise for a period of one year after termination of the agreement. The franchisee submitted that the entire agreement should not be enforced on the ground of public policy due to the inequality of bargaining power between the parties. Although not specifically addressed in the decision, the court ultimately decided that if there had been any inequality of bargaining power, it was very slight and it did not affect the covenant's enforceability. The court commented that the nature of the franchise relationship dictates that onerous terms are often required. The franchise agreement was enforced, along with the one-year non-competition covenant.

The Prince Edward Island courts have addressed the enforceability of restrictive covenants in the employment context as well. In *Island Glass Limited v. O'Connor*, [1980] P.E.I.J. No. 88 (Can. P.E.I Sup. Ct.), the court enforced a non-solicitation clause relating to employees and clients, as well as a three-mile non-competition covenant, each for a period of three years. In this case, Mr. O'Connor established a competitive glass business a few hundred meters from his former employer's business location, shortly after tendering his resignation. The court stated that covenants against competition are enforceable, if they are reasonable in relation to the interests of the parties, and the interests of the public.

In *Dream Weavers Wedding Consultants & Co-ordinators Inc. v. Astley*, [2000] P.E.I.J. No. 36 (Can. P.E.I. Sup. Ct.), the court confirmed that restrictive covenants must be directed at protecting the legitimate proprietary interests of the employer. Restrictive covenants directed solely at preventing competition will not be enforced. The court commented that it takes a far stricter and less favorable view of covenants entered into between master and servant than it does of similar covenants between vendor and purchaser, or in partnership agreements.

---

2. Have the courts articulated the "legitimate interests" of the franchisor that will support enforcement of a covenant against competition contained in a franchise agreement?

➤ **If so, what are they (e.g., protection of goodwill, protection of confidential information), and in what contexts did the issue arise?**

➤ If not, what interests have been recognized in other contexts (e.g., employment agreements, the sale of business context)?

Prince Edward Island courts have not articulated which interests of the franchisor are sufficiently important to warrant the protection of a covenant against competition. In the employment context, Prince Edward Island courts have enforced covenants protecting legitimate interests such as the employer's labour force, clients, and business site area, so long as the restrictions are reasonable and not contrary to the public interest.

In *Island Glass Limited v. O'Connor*, [1980] P.E.I.J. No. 88 (Can. P.E.I. Sup. Ct.), the court enforced a non-solicitation clause relating to employees and clients, as well as a three-mile non-competition covenant, each for a period of three years. The court held that it was reasonable and not injurious to the public interest for the employer to protect its interest in its labor force, to protect interests in customer clientele, and to protect the business site it had established. In particular, the court found that the covenants were not contrary to the public interest, as auto glass customers in this area were well-served by numerous businesses.

In *Spike v. Rocca Group Ltd. and Muise*, [1980] P.E.I.J. No. 66 (Can. P.E.I. Sup. Ct.), the court addressed non-competition clauses in the context of a lease agreement. Two hair salons, located in the same shopping plaza, agreed to non-competition covenants limiting the type of services they could offer. (Muise was restricted to the styling of men's hair, while Spike was restricted to the styling of women's hair.) Muise vacated the shopping plaza and became employed with a nearby hair salon. Spike, who remained in the shopping plaza, sought an injunction on the basis that Muise was in breach of the non-competition covenant. The covenant restricted competition within a two-mile radius. The court declined to enforce the covenant on the basis that the covenant died upon the termination of the tenancy; however, the court went on to consider the reasonableness of the covenant. It was found that the landlord had an interest in protecting the marketability of his shopping plaza; the non-competition clause served as an inducement for prospective tenants. The lessees had an interest in a reasonable degree of non-competition within the confines of the shopping plaza. However, the covenant was found to be in restraint of trade as it unreasonably restricted competition within Prince Edward Island's capital city and was thus prima facie void.

PE

---

3. What time limitations have courts recognized as reasonable in the franchise context? If no franchise cases have been decided, what time limitations have been recognized in other contexts?

➤ How have they been related to the interests protected?

The only Prince Edward Island case addressing the reasonableness of time limitations of covenants against competition in the context of franchising is *D.L.T. Holdings Inc. v. Grow Biz International Inc.*, 2001 PESCTD 27 (Can. P.E.I. Sup. Ct.). A non-competition clause of one year was found to be enforceable; however, there was no specific discussion on the relationship of this clause with the legitimate interest of the franchisor.

In an employment or sale of business context, courts have not articulated the relationship between the duration of a non-competition covenant and the interest it purports to protect. In *Island Glass Limited v. O'Connor*, [1980] P.E.I.J. No. 88 (Can.

P.E.I. Sup. Ct.), a three-year non-competition clause in an employment agreement was enforced; however, the duration of the covenant was not mentioned in the court's assessment of enforceability.

---

4. What geographic limitations have courts recognized as reasonable in the franchise context?

- **How have they been related to the interests protected?**
- **Have courts recognized the legitimacy of protecting other franchisees from competition?**

There are no reported Prince Edward Island decisions that address the reasonableness of geographic limitations in the franchise context. The court in *D.L.T. Holdings Inc. v. Grow Biz International Inc.*, 2001 PESCTD 27 (Can. P.E.I. Sup. Ct.), enforced a six-mile restriction on competition within a franchise agreement, but the court did not discuss its reasons for determining it to be reasonable. The court found that the franchising agreement and its provisions were not unconscionable, and thus the entire agreement was enforceable.

In an employment context, Prince Edward Island courts determine the reasonableness of geographic restrictions on competition based on the nature of the business and the relationship between the parties. *Spike v. Rocca Group Ltd. and Muise,* [1980] P.E.I.J. No. 66 (Can. P.E.I. Sup. Ct.), involved a commercial lease agreement between a barber and a landlord. The court addressed a non-competition clause with a two-mile restriction and found it to be unreasonable because it effectively deprived the barber from earning a living at his trade within Prince Edward Island's capital city, Charlottetown. The court noted that the covenant might have been justified in a large metropolitan area, but not in this case.

Island Glass Limited v. O'Connor, [1980] P.E.I.J. No. 88 (Can. P.E.I. Sup. Ct.), was decided shortly after *Spike*. However, the court in *Island Glass* distinguished the two cases and reached a different result in terms of what constitutes a reasonable geographic restriction. The employer in *Island Glass* operated an auto glass business. His key employee resigned and started a competing auto glass business within a few hundred feet of his former employer. The court enforced three-mile restriction on competition. This case was distinguished from *Spike* on its facts, and specifically due to the differences in relationships between the parties (i.e., the lessee/lessor relationship versus employee/employer relationship). The court noted that with modern methods of communication and transportation it would have been "no hardship" for the former employee to locate outside the three-mile radius.

In *Dream Weavers Wedding Consultants & Co-ordinators Inc. v. Astley,* [2000] P.E.I.J. No. 36 (Can. P.E.I. Sup. Ct.), the court decided not to enforce a non-competition covenant because it was not confined to a particular geographic area.

---

5. What limitations on activities have courts recognized as reasonable in the franchise context?

Prince Edward Island courts have not addressed the scope of restrictions on activities that would be considered reasonable in the franchise context. Furthermore, there are no Prince Edward Island cases addressing the reasonableness of restrictions on activities in the employment or sale of business context. In *Dream Weavers Wedding Consultants & Co-ordinators Inc. v. Astley*, [2000] P.E.I.J. No. 36 (Can. P.E.I. Sup. Ct.), a two-year, non-competition covenant in an employment agreement prevented the employee from creating or being directly or indirectly part of any business or venture that "is the same as, or similar to, or competes with that of [the Plaintiff]"; however, the scope of the restricted activities was not mentioned in the court's assessment of enforceability.

6. Does the province recognize a difference between in-term and post-term covenants?

Prince Edward Island courts have not addressed whether recognition of a difference in enforceability between in-term and post-term covenants would be appropriate.

7. Has the province allowed enforcement of covenants against non-signatories (e.g., family members, newly formed corporations)?

There are no Prince Edward Island cases addressing the enforcement of covenants not to compete against non-signatories.

8. Will the province modify, "blue-pencil," or otherwise reduce a covenant found to be overbroad?

PE

This issue has been dealt with by Prince Edward Island courts in two decisions. In both decisions, the courts held that they were not permitted to modify or otherwise redraft a covenant that was found to be overbroad so as to make it enforceable.

In *Dream Weavers Wedding Consultants & Co-ordinators Inc. v. Astley*, [2000] P.E.I.J. No. 36 (Can. P.E.I. Sup. Ct.), this issue was discussed and the Prince Edward Island Supreme Court stated as follows at paragraphs 13 and 14:

> **13** The second ground for denying an injunction in the present case is based on the conclusion that the clause is unenforceable owing to overly broad terms of its drafting. In particular, I note that the scope of the anti-competition clause was not confined to a particular geographic area, and so, at the very least, it was ambiguous on the face of its terms. While it was precise as to the scope of its duration, it was lacking clarity as to its proper geographic scope.
>
> **14** Where a court finds the terms of a restrictive covenant to be overly broad, it is not compelled to "read-in" a more precise or more reasonable interpretation, particularly if the material clause is found to be wanting in some respect. I do not find a clear line of authority for the proposition that a court may sever the offending aspect of a problematic clause with the idea of making the agreement suitable for the purpose of granting an injunction. As a case on point I would refer to the recent decision of Justice

Low in *Phytoderm Inc. v. Urwin*, [1999] O.J. No. 383 (Ont. Gen. Div.) where he observed at para. 22:

> Evidence has been adduced that Quebec courts have held, in respect of Article 2089, [pertaining to restrictive covenants] that where the temporal duration of a covenant is longer than is necessary to protect the legitimate interests of the employer, the court may "write down" the duration of the covenant. No evidence was led, however, to suggest that where a covenant is so broad and overreaching as to exceed what is necessary to protect the employer's interests, that the court will in effect redraft the covenant so as to make it enforceable. To the contrary, the Quebec courts have adopted the same view as have Ontario courts in this respect, namely that a covenant is either valid or not, and the court will not re-write the agreement.

A similar rationale can be advanced to meet the assertion that the clause as drafted is not so much overly broad as it is vague. Shortly put, the court is not obliged to clarify the construction of an agreement that has been formed between two contracting parties. Specifically addressing the issue of ambiguous drafting in the context of a restrictive covenant, I would refer to *Halsbury's Laws of England*, 4th ed., Vol. 47 (London: Butterworths, 1994) at para. 58, where it states:

> 58. Certainty. The agreement in restraint of trade must not be too vague, and the parties cannot leave it to the court to frame their agreement to meet a particular breach.

This issue was also dealt with by the Prince Edward Island Supreme Court in *Spike v. Rocca Group Ltd. and Muise*, [1980] P.E.I.J. No. 66 (Can. P.E.I. Sup. Ct.). In that case the court held that a non-compete covenant that restricted the plaintiff from opening a similar business within two miles of the defendant's was overly broad and unenforceable. Concerning the court's ability to correct the deficiencies in the covenant, C.R. McQuaid, J. stated at paragraph 18:

> The clause, as worded, might possibly find justification in a large metropolitan area, such as Toronto or Montreal, depending upon the individual circumstances, but certainly not in the instant case. It may well be that the defendants' present location is offensive to the plaintiff and within a radius of distance to which some restrictive covenant could be reasonably considered to apply, if properly worded, but it is not for this, or any court, to correct such deficiencies, but rather must it take the covenant as it finds it.

This paragraph was referenced with approval at paragraph 42 in *Island Glass Limited v. O'Connor*, [1980] P.E.I.J. No. 88 (Can. P.E.I. Sup. Ct.).

Given the foregoing, it is unlikely that covenants that are found to be overbroad would be modified or otherwise reduced in Prince Edward Island courts.

---

9. When does a non-compete period begin to run? Will courts equitably extend the term?

There are no Prince Edward Island cases addressing the issue of when a non-compete period will begin to run or whether the term will be equitably extended.

10. Are there additional nuances or peculiarities of the province's treatment of covenants in the franchising context?

Prince Edward Island's general franchising statute, the *Franchises Act*, R.S.P.E.I. 1988, c. F-14 (Can. P.E.I.), at section 3, does impose upon each party to a franchise agreement a duty of good faith and fair dealing:

> 3. (1) Every franchise agreement imposes on each party a duty of fair dealing in the performance and enforcement of the agreement, including in the exercise of a right under the agreement.
>
> (2) A party to a franchise agreement has a right of action for damages against another party to the franchise agreement who breaches the duty of fair dealing.
>
> (3) For the purpose of this section, the duty of fair dealing includes the duty to act in good faith and in accordance with reasonable commercial standards. 2005, c.36, s.3.

It also provides for an award of damages in respect of a breach of this duty. In certain circumstances, this could be relevant in respect of covenants dealing with competition.

Québec

by Myriam Brixi*

1. Has the province addressed covenants against competition in the context of franchising?

- **Does the province have a franchising statute or regulations that address covenants against competition?**
- **Does the province have a covenant statute of general applicability that would encompass franchise covenants?**
- **Have the courts addressed covenants in the context of franchising, either under a statute or under the province's common law?**

The province of Québec does not have franchise laws or regulations that deal specifically with this area of business and there is no specific law, with respect to restrictive covenants, that would be of general application to franchise agreements' non-competition covenants.

The province of Québec falls under civil law jurisdiction, which is governed by the *Civil Code of Québec* (chapter CCQ-1991) (hereinafter the Civil Code or C.C.Q.). Thus, common law is not applicable in civil matters and precedents are not binding, but nevertheless it serves as a guide to the court for the interpretation of franchise agreements as well as its covenants. Franchise agreements have been qualified by Québec courts as "sui generis," subject to the general rules of the Civil Code.

Due to the nature of franchise agreements, the courts have been applying the rules of interpretation specific to employment contracts or agreements for the sale of a business, considering the context in which these agreements are concluded. The Civil Code does not contain express sections dealing with non-compete covenants in a commercial or franchise setting. However, it does contain an article that deals specifically with covenants against competition, in the context of employment contracts, which reads as follows:

> **2089.** The parties may stipulate in writing and in express terms that, even after the termination of the contract, the employee may neither compete

*Myriam Brixi was assisted by Stéphanie Destrempes in the preparation of this chapter. They are partners at Lavery, de Billy, LLP. Myriam Brixi practices in the Litigation and Dispute Resolution Group, and Stéphanie Destrempes in the Franchise and Distribution Group.

with his employer nor participate in any capacity whatsoever in an enterprise which would compete with him.

However, the stipulation shall be limited as to time, place and type of employment, to what is necessary for the protection of the legitimate interests of the employer.

The burden of proof that the stipulation is valid is on the employer.

In the context of franchising in Québec, the courts have dealt with non-competition covenants under the applicable contract law in the province, which was developed in a civil law environment. Thus, non-competition covenants in franchise agreements must not be (1) against the public order, (2) unreasonable in relation to the legitimate interests of both parties, or (3) too vague or ambiguous. *Les Restaurants Pacini Inc. v. Les Mets Gour-Bec Ltée*, (C.S., 1993-08-03) SOQUIJ AZ-93021605 (Can. Que. Sup. Ct.); *Groupe Vap Inc. v. Gestion Hugo Devin Inc.*, 2017 QCCS 542 (Can. Que. Sup. Ct.). These covenants are therefore interpreted restrictively by the courts since, in various cases, their impact was tantamount to a restriction of the right to work. *9169-3556 Québec Inc. v. Gestions René Simoneau ltée*, 2009 QCCS 3890 (Can. Que. Sup. Ct.).

Concretely, non-competition covenants in franchise agreements must be limited in scope based on three considerations: (1) duration, (2) territory, and (3) nature of the activity for which protection is sought. A well-know statement on the issue in Québec can be found in *Copiscope Inc. v. TRM Copy Centers (Canada) Ltd*, 1998 CanLII 12603 (Can. Que. C.A.):

> The validity of the Noncompetition Covenant must be determined on the basis of well settled principles set out in the jurisprudence.
>
> 1) Undertakings in restraint of trade are generally against public order;
>
> 2) there may, within reasonable limits, be contractual restrictions on the freedom to conduct a specified commercial activity;
>
> 3) the validity of such restrictions is dependant on their being reasonable, particularly regarding the length of time that they are to apply and the territory where they are to be applicable;
>
> 4) furthermore, it must be shown that the restrictions are necessary for the reasonable protection of the interests of the party in whose favor they are granted;
>
> 5) if the restrictions do not meet the test of reasonability they will be struck down as being contrary to public order.

In other words, franchisors should keep in mind that the essence of the criteria developed to assess the reasonableness of a non-competition clause is primarily based on the employee's (or franchisee's or business seller's) future employment and business opportunities, which are restricted by a non-competition clause applicable after the termination of his or her employment (or termination of the franchise agreement or by the terms of an agreement for the sale of a business). Such criteria are considered in light of the public order principle that the right to work and trade may not be unreasonably restricted. Therefore, the assessment of a non-competition clause in these circumstances is likely to vary from one case to another, depending on the facts of a specific situation.

Thus, it is now well-accepted that non-competition clauses in franchise agreements should not be more onerous than necessary in terms of duration, territory, and nature of the activity for which protection is sought. Otherwise, they may be declared illegal by the courts. *Restaurants Pacini inc. v. Mets Gour-bec ltée.*, (1993) AZ-95021564 (Can. Que. Sup. Ct.).

---

2. Have the courts articulated the "legitimate interests" of the franchisor that will support enforcement of a covenant against competition contained in a franchise agreement?

- **If so, what are they (e.g., protection of goodwill, protection of confidential information), and in what context did the issue arise?**
- **If not, what interests have been recognized in other contexts (e.g., employment agreements, the sale of business context)?**

Québec jurisprudence on restrictive non-competition covenants in a commercial context, including franchising, has established that the party seeking to benefit from such a covenant must prove not only that the covenant exists contractually, but also that it is reasonable in that it aims to protect the legitimate interests of the party seeking to benefit from it. *Copiscope Inc. v. TRM Copy Centers (Canada) Ltd*, 1998 CanLII 12603 (Can. Que. C.A.); *Les Restaurants Pacini inc. v. Mets Gour-bec ltée.*, (1993) AZ-95021564 (Can. Que. Sup. Ct.); *9169-3556 Québec Inc. v. Gestions René Simoneau ltée*, 2009 QCCS 3890 (Can. Que. Sup. Ct.); *Payette v. Guay Inc.* [2013] 3 SCR 95 (Can. Que., Can Supr. Ct.); *Provigo Distribution inc. v. Complexe Commercial de l'Île Inc.*, 2020 QCCA 970 (Can. Que. C.A.). This assessment of reasonableness, in a commercial context, is made with regard to the legitimate interests of the party benefiting from such a non-competition covenant and the specific nature of the parties' business relationship. These "legitimate interests" are defined based on the three criteria that must be proven in order to conclude that the covenant is reasonable: limited scope as to (1) duration, (2) territory, and (3) nature of protected activity. *Provigo Distribution inc. v. Complexe commercial de l'Île Inc.*, 2020 QCCA 970 (Can. Que. C.A.).

In *Les Restaurants Pacini inc. v. Mets Gour-bec ltée.* (1993), AZ-95021564 (Can. Que. Sup. Ct.), while the court determined that the scope of the clause in question was reasonable in terms of its duration and territory, it found that it was overbroad in terms of the type of activity it sought to protect (i.e., the operation of any type of restaurant within the temporal and territorial limits of the clause).

In the case of *9169-3556 Québec Inc. v. Gestions René Simoneau ltée*, 2009 QCCS 3890 (Can. Que. Sup. Ct.), also in a franchise context, the court found that the franchisor had failed to demonstrate its legitimate interests in seeking a two-year temporal limitation along with a 20-kilometer territorial limitation around the geographical limits of the city of Montreal. No evidence or justification was provided by the franchisor in order to support its legitimate interests in such temporal and geographic limitations. The franchisor argued that transportation in the lawn care business was mainly done by truck, thus justifying the geographical limitations sought. However, this argument was not accepted by the court.

Generally, the "legitimate interests" of the franchisor include the protection of an existing clientele, goodwill, trademarks, and other like items. In *Voyages Héritage A. & G. Inc. v. 9041-2784 Québec Inc.*, 2003 CanLII 4989 (Can. Que. Sup. Ct.), a case where the non-competition covenant was enforced by the court, the primary interest being protected was the existing clientele (see also, at the interlocutory injunction step, *9045-6740 Québec Inc. v. 9049-6902 Québec Inc.*, REJB 2003-49605 (Can. Que. C.A.); and *H&R Block Canada Inc. v. Gilbert Trucheon*, REJB 2000-19345 (Can. Que. C.A.)). In *Nettoyeurs Michel Forget Ltée v. Nettoyeur Josée Goupil Inc.*, EYB 1989-76537 (Can. Que. Sup. Ct.), where the franchise agreement was for the operation of a dry-cleaning business, the court recognized a one-year time limitation period intended to protect the franchisor's interest in the trademarks, colors, and the "look and feel," as well as the existing clientele. In this case, it was proven that even though the ex-franchisee's new business, situated in the same location as the old franchise, changed the name appearing on the front signage, the colors and layout of the dry-cleaning operation stayed the same.

3. What time limitations have courts recognized as reasonable in the franchise context? If no franchise cases have been decided, what time limitations have been recognized in other contexts?

➤ How have they been related to the interests protected?

The courts have not determined a specific time limitation that is generally accepted in a franchise context. Therefore, it is not possible to define a general rule as to a reasonable time limitation of a non-compete covenant in a franchise agreement. Each case must be determined on its own merit and analyzed according to various factors, such as the length of the contractual relation between the parties, the franchisor's legitimate interests, and the type of activity being protected. For example, in *Les Restaurants Pacini inc. v. Mets Gour-bec ltée.* (1993), AZ-95021564 (Can. Que. Sup. Ct.), a case in which the type of activity being protected was the operation of a "restaurant" type of business, the court found that a two-year limitation was reasonable in the circumstances (the covenant was deemed invalid for other reasons). Likewise, in *Boutique Médiévale La Table Ronde Inc. v. Distribution Obytech Nord Inc.*, 2002 CanLII 30540 (Can. Que. Sup. Ct.), a case in which the activity protected was retail shops specializing in medieval fashion and accessories, a two-year limitation period was found to be reasonable (the court does not justify this decision; it simply applies the non-compete covenant as is). In *H&R Block Canada Inc. v. Gilbert Trucheon*, REJB 2000-19345 (Can. Que. Sup. Ct.), a case in which a tax preparation and accounting business was being protected, a two-year limitation period was found to be reasonable (the reasonableness of the two-year limitation period was not disputed by the defendants). In *Ménage-Poly inc. v. Abdelali*, 2015 QCCS 2072 (Can. Que. Sup. Ct.), a case in which the type of activity protected was a residential, commercial, and industrial cleaning service, the court, in granting a permanent injunction, found that a three-year limitation was reasonable. The court did not provide justification in this regard but considered (1) that the parties agreed on the reasonableness of the non-compete disposition within the franchise agreement and (2) the findings in *Payette v. Guay*, [2013] 3 SCR 95 (Can. Supr. Ct.). Thus, in several cases, non-competition covenants with a limited duration of two years were deemed reasonable by the courts.

Conversely, in *9169-3556 Québec Inc. v. Gestions René Simoneau ltée*, 2009 QCCS 3890 (Can. Que. Sup. Ct.), where the type of activity protected was "lawn care," a two-year limitation was found to be unreasonable, considering that the type of work is seasonal in nature. In *Jiu-Jitsu Cyr inc. v. Duchesneau*, J.E.98-1653 (Can. Que. Sup. Ct.), a five-year limitation was considered unreasonable. In this case, the non-compete covenant clause was for the benefit of the franchisee. The franchise agreement was entered into for an unlimited period of time and provided that, following the termination of the franchise agreement, the franchisee would refrain from opening a Jiu-Jitsu club within a five-kilometer radius for a five-year period. Since the contract was for an unlimited period and the only consideration paid by the franchisee when entering the franchise agreement was $5,000.00 plus the liability for the lease, the court considered the non-competition clause unreasonable. In *169914 Canada Inc. v. 2638-9833 Québec inc. et als* (1992), AZ-92021476 (Can. Que. Sup. Ct.), a five-year limitation period was also considered unreasonable given that the franchisor was unable to demonstrate its legitimate interests in justifying such a period.

In *Provigo Distribution inc. v. Complexe commercial de l'Île inc.*, 2020 QCCA 970 (Can. Que. C.A.), the court concluded that the non-competition clause found in the commercial sale agreement was reasonable, and therefore valid, since its duration was not contrary to the public order and was limited to what was necessary to protect the legitimate interests of the parties in the context of their business relationship. In this case, the restrictive covenant had an indefinite term, and although the clause did not have a specific maturity date, the clause remained in effect as long as the operation of the business continued on the remaining land.

Caselaw has reiterated that the time limitation scope of the non-compete clause must be assessed in light of the type of business being operated. *9169-3556 Québec inc. v. Gestions René Simoneau ltée*, 2009 QCCS 3890 (Can. Que. Sup. Ct.). This clarification is essential as the court must analyze the context of each situation to assess the reasonableness of the non-competition clause. Therefore, the tendency of courts to rely exclusively on past decisions to determine the reasonableness of the scope of the non-compete covenant must be avoided.

4. What geographic limitations have courts recognized as reasonable in the franchise context?

- **How have they been related to the interests protected?**
- **Have courts recognized the legitimacy of protecting other franchisees from competition?**

Non-competition clauses in franchise agreements provide franchisors with two types of protection. On one hand, they protect them from competition from a former franchisee in the territory in which they operated. On the other hand, they protect the territories adjacent to other current franchisees of the network against competition from a former franchisee. *Joe Loue Tout inc. v. Jubinville*, 1997 CanLII 9035 (QCCS) (Can. Que. Sup. Ct.); *135871 Canada inc. v. R.X. Soleil en forme inc.*, EYB 1991-58829 (Can. Que. Sup. Ct.).

Generally, a territorial limitation that encompasses too large a territory would be deemed illegal and against the public order. This said, it is also impossible to determine a general rule as to the territorial limitations that courts have deemed acceptable in a franchising context. The courts are reluctant to find a non-compete covenant reasonable when the protected territory is broader than the one defined in the scope of the franchise agreement. However, in a situation where a party is not bound by an exclusive territory, the reasonableness of the territory is often determined by the demographics of the clientele.

Each case must be determined on its own merit, and the territorial limitation must be analyzed within the context of the type of activity being protected. For example, in *Les Restaurants Pacini inc. v. Mets Gour-bec ltée.* (1993), AZ-95021564 (Can. Que. Sup. Ct.), a case where the type of activity protected was the operation of a "restaurant" type of business, the court found that a limitation of ten kilometers around the franchised restaurant, and five kilometers around any other franchised restaurant, was reasonable in the circumstances, because the franchisor was trying to protect the "concept" behind the Pacini restaurants (the covenant was deemed invalid for other reasons). In contrast, in *9169-3556 Québec Inc. v. Gestions René Simoneau ltée*, 2009 QCCS 3890 (Can. Que. Sup. Ct.), the type of activity being protected was lawn care, and a limit of 20 kilometers around the geographical limits of the city of Montreal was deemed to be unreasonable, given the type of seasonal work involved and the fact that such a large area would encompass the majority of the province's population. In *H&R Block Canada Inc. v. Gilbert Trucheon*, REJB 2000-19345 (Can. Que. C.A.), a territorial limitation of 50 miles around the former franchise location was deemed reasonable in the circumstances.

Another example can be found in *Boutique Médiévale La Table Ronde Inc. v. Distribution Obytech Nord Inc.*, 2002 CanLII 30540 (Can. Que. Sup. Ct.), where the court enforced a territorial limitation encompassing the entire province of Québec. The court did not provide justifications for this, but simply applied the non-compete covenant as is. In *Multi-marque inc. v. Giroux*, J.E. 98-1573 (Can. Que. Sup. Ct.), the court enforced a territorial limitation of approximately 30 kilometers (the clause was described in terms of municipalities), based on the nature of the business of the franchisor, which was a bread delivery business. In this case, the geographical limitation was found to be reasonable because it did not prevent the former franchisee from developing a new territory within a reasonable distance of his residence.

In *135871 Canada inc. v. R.X. Soleil en forme inc.*, JE 91-313 (Can. Que. Sup. Ct.), the court recognized the legitimacy of the franchisor's intention to protect other franchisees from the competition of an ex-franchisee, as well as the legitimacy of the franchisor's interest in protecting its "concept" (an artificial suntanning business and related look and feel). The court found that a territorial limitation of five miles around any existing franchise was valid. On the contrary, in *Joe Loue Tout inc. v. Jubinville*, 1997 CanLII 9035 (QCCS) (Can. Que. Sup. Ct.), the court refused to apply the restrictive covenant as it restrained the possibility to operate a similar business within a ten-kilometer radius of the place of operation of the franchise and the premises of any other franchisee, when there were at least 59 in the province of Québec. The court held that the covenant was too broad.

In *Nettoyeur Michel Forget v. Nettoyeur Josée Goupil inc.*, EYB 1989-76537 (C.S.), it was established that a five-kilometer territory was reasonable, taking into consideration the nature of the franchise network, in relation to the correlative obligation of the franchisor to grant territorial exclusivity to the franchisee.

In *Groupe Vap Inc. v. Gestion Hugo Devin inc.*, 2017 QCCS 542 (Can. Que. Sup. Ct.), although this was not a decision on merit, the court reiterated that the non-competition disposition in a franchise context must not be too vague (by being ambiguous) with regards to the scope of limitation of the duration, territory, and nature of the activity that is sought to be protected. In this case, the existence of two distinct non-compete dispositions within the same franchise agreement contributed to the ambiguity of the interpretation of the covenants.

In essence, non-competition clauses of two, five, and ten kilometers around each location were found to be reasonable in a franchise context.

5. What limitations on activities have courts recognized as reasonable in the franchise context?

In general, the nature of the activities protected must not exceed a reasonable protection of the franchisor, *9169-3556 Québec Inc. v. Gestions René Simoneau ltée*, 2009 QCCS 3890 (Can. Que. Sup. Ct.), meaning that these clauses must avoid including activities that are not related to those of the franchisor. Therefore, the restriction imposed should not exceed the franchisor's main field of activity to avoid jeopardizing its validity. *9169-3556 Québec Inc. v. Groupe Nutripro*, J.E. 2008-1967, EYB 2008-146609 (S.C.) (Can. Que. Sup. Ct).

The limitations on activities must be narrowly defined and not overly broad as to encompass ordinary activities, such as mowing lawns, *9169-3556 Québec Inc. v. Gestions René Simoneau ltée*, 2009 QCCS 3890 (Can. Que. Sup. Ct.), or the exploitation of any type of restaurant, *Les Restaurants Pacini inc. v. Mets Gour-bec ltée*, (1993), AZ-95021564 (Can. Que. Sup. Ct.). In both cases, the courts found that the activity that was sought to be protected was overly broad in connection with the type of clientele that is sought to be retained and the trademarks that are sought to be protected. In *Restaurant Chez Gérard Patates frites ltée v. Gestion Paulimar inc.*, 2009 QCCS 276 (Can. Que. Sup. Ct.), although the validity of the non-competition clause is not examined on the merits, the court's comments are interesting as to the activity covered by the clause. The court refused to enforce the non-compete covenant (even though it found it to be otherwise valid) since the new restaurant was not similar in kind to the previous franchised restaurant. The new restaurant was a full-service restaurant, seven times bigger than the previous franchise, with four times the revenue and with the capacity to seat 240 clients, while the previous franchise was a "snack-bar" type establishment. The court concluded that a non-compete covenant must be interpreted in the context of the specific activity sought to be protected (in this case a snack-bar), and that it did not prohibit the sale of ordinary and widespread products such as French fries and hamburgers.

At first glance, the words or expressions used to describe the prohibited activity in a non-compete disposition of a franchise agreement may seem vague or ambiguous. Thus, the courts will seek to interpret this clause to determine whether there is any real ambiguity. In the case of a franchise agreement qualified as an adhesion contract under the Civil Code, doubts as to the interpretation of a non-competition covenant must be interpreted in favor of the franchisee. In these circumstances, it is common for a non-competition covenant to prevent the operation of a business offering "similar activities" to those of the franchisor. In such cases, the franchise agreement must clearly and precisely describe the business being operated, and it will then be up to the courts to determine what constitutes a similar business based on the factual situation, and to conclude whether there has been a breach.

In interpreting the scope of "similar activities," the court must conduct an overall analysis of the business operated. In addition, it must consider the franchisee's authorized activities at the time of signing the agreement, but also what is subsequently added. Therefore, a non-competition covenant that accurately refers to the franchisor's operations and activities may be fully valid and enforceable.

6. Does the province recognize a difference between in-term and post-term covenants?

In Québec, the jurisprudence does not distinguish between clauses being in force during the term or at the end of the term of the franchise agreement, for any reason whatsoever. In any event, such clauses must be unambiguous and reasonable. For example, in *Rogers Cantel inc. v. Elbanna Sales inc*, J.E. 2003-449 (Can. Que. C.A.), the Court of Appeal confirmed the right of the cellular phones and service provider to terminate the contract with its agent based on the violation of an exclusivity clause, which did not provide territorial restriction. It strictly provided that the agent should not enter an agent contract with a competitor of Cantel.

7. Has the province allowed enforcement of covenants against non-signatories (e.g., family members, newly formed corporations)?

In some circumstances, Québec courts have allowed the enforcement of covenants against non-signatories, for example, at the interlocutory injunction stage. *9045-6740 Québec Inc. v. 9049-6902 Québec Inc.*, REJB 2003-49605 (Can. Que. C.A.), where the court ordered that the non-compete covenant be respected by the specific defendants, as well as their officers, directors, agents, and employees. Usually, in such circumstances, the non-compete covenants are drafted to include wording such as "the franchisee, its principals, managers, and any other shareholders covenant personally, jointly and severally, on behalf of or in association with any other person, partnership, association or corporation, not to directly or indirectly operate, license, franchise, possess, maintain, become involved with, carry on, engaged in or be concerned with, or have an interest or advise, of any nature whatsoever, or permit their names or any part thereof to be used or employed in any business in connection with the operation of," and so on or similar wording or variations thereof. The most common example is when an ex-franchisee goes into business, either as an employee or in a self-employed capacity, in a similar field as the franchisor, but through either another existing corporation or a newly formed corporation.

Another example can be seen in *Boutique Médiévale La Table Inc. v. Distribution Obytech Nord Inc.*, 2001 CanLII 30540 (Can. Que. Sup. Ct.), where the court ordered that the corporate franchisee, along with its officers, representatives, directors, agents, and employees, refrain from operating a business similar in nature to the franchisor's. The court has also granted injunction remedies against the new distributor and franchisor in order to protect the goodwill and clientele of the franchisor. *E.g., A. Poupart et cie v. Desgroseillers*, [1964] R.P. 80 (Can. Que. Sup. Ct.); *Rotisserie St-Hubert Ltée v. Perfico Sport inc.*, J.E. 2002-490 (Can. Que. Sup. Ct.).

However, and unless it was expressly provided for in the franchise agreement, the courts will be reluctant to enforce a non-competition clause against a person related to the franchisee (such as his or her spouse) who was not involved in the operations of the franchise business and not a party to the initial agreement.

8. Will the province modify, "blue-pencil," or otherwise reduce a covenant found to be overbroad?

In Québec, and contrary to common law caselaw, Québec courts will refuse to modify, "blue-pencil," or otherwise reduce a covenant found to be overbroad; the non-competition covenant is either valid or not. When a non-competition disposition is declared abusive, it becomes null and void and will not be rectified. If the covenant is not valid in any one of its components (limitation as to the time period, territory, or nature of the activity protected), the entire covenant falls. *Les Restaurants Pacini inc. v. Mets Gour-bec ltée*, (1993), AZ-95021564 (Can. Que. Sup. Ct.); *Pauzé v. Descôteaux et al.*, (1986), AZ-86011267 (Can. Que. C.A.); *Office Overload inc. v. Trencaroff*, (1973), AZ-73011195 (Can. Que. C.A.); *169914 Canada inc. v. 2638-9833 Québec inc. et als.*, (1992), AZ-92021476 (Can. Que. Sup. Ct.); *Restaurant Chez Doc inc. v. 9061-7481 Québec inc.*, 2006 QCCA 55 (Can. Que. C.A.); *9169-3556 Québec Inc. v. Gestions René Simoneau ltée*, 2009 QCCS 3890 (Can. Que. Sup. Ct.).

In certain isolated cases, such as *Nettoyeurs Michel Forget Ltée. v. Vidéoflex inc.*, EYB 1993-58943 (Can. Que. C.A.) and *Distribution Yves Paquette Inc. v. Le Club International Video Film CIVF (1987) Inc.*, SOQUIJ AZ-92021419 (Can. Que. Sup. Ct.), courts have modified otherwise overbroad non-compete clauses, but only when such clauses expressly allowed the court to exercise such power. This said, despite these two cases, the courts' ability to modify overbroad non-compete covenants is far from being accepted in Québec. It is not the responsibility of the court to correct the agreements that the parties have drafted. Contractual provisions stipulating that it is up to the court to rectify a non-competition covenant in a way that would allow it to be "reasonable" are not binding in the courts and would have the effect of leaving the parties in limbo until a final judgment is rendered, thereby undermining the stability of contracts. *9169-3556 Québec Inc. v. Gestions René Simoneau ltée*, 2009 QCCS 3890 (Can. Que. Sup. Ct.); *169914 Canada Inc. v. 2638-9833 Québec inc.*, EYB 1992-75045 (C.S.) (Can. Que. Sup. Ct.).

Furthermore, in *Groupe Vap Inc. v. Gestion Hugo Devin inc.*, 2017 QCCS 542 (Can. Que. Sup. Ct.), the court was presented with two distinct non-compete dispositions within the same franchise agreement, each of which were deemed clear when taken separately (but not necessarily legal), but the cumulations of both were proven to be vague and ambiguous. The court concluded that inviting the court to choose one clause of the franchise agreement over the other is equivalent to trying to divide the non-competition covenant to keep what is claimed to be valid and dismiss what is not. The court cannot engage in an exercise of dissecting such a covenant. It is not the courts' role to rectify an agreement drafted by one party, and to come to the rescue of this same party imposing an inadequate restrictive covenant. *9169-3556 Québec Inc. v. Gestions René Simoneau ltée*, 2009 QCCS 3890 (Can. Que. Sup. Ct.); *Restaurant chez Doc Inc. v. 9061-7481 Québec inc.*, 2006 QCCA 55 (Can. Que. C.A.).

9. When does a non-compete period begin to run? Will courts equitably extend the term?

A post-term non-compete period begins only at the expiry of the term of the franchise agreement, or as otherwise provided in the agreement, upon its termination for any reason whatsoever. However, in *Billards Dooly's Inc. v. Enterprise Prébour ltée*, 2011 QCCS 3944 (Can. Que. Sup. Ct.), the court held that a Dooly's Billiards franchise was never actually open despite the signing of the franchise contract. Accordingly, the term of the contract never started and therefore, neither the in-term non-compete covenant nor the one-year post-term non-compete covenant was enforceable.

In *Bandag Inc. v. St-Paul Bandag*, J.E. 2001-7 (Can. Que. Sup. Ct.), the court decided that since the franchisee operated on a verbal agreement for six years after the termination of the franchise agreement, the franchisor could not rely on the covenant clause contained in the franchise agreement terminated six years prior.

Consequently, some franchisors will include in their standard form of franchise agreement a disposition stipulating that, despite the end of the term of the agreement, should the parties remain in business with one another as if the agreement were still in force, then the application of the post-term non-competition clause will begin as soon as the business relationship between the parties ends.

10. Are there additional nuances or peculiarities of the province's treatment of covenants in the franchising context?

Québec caselaw on non-competition covenants can be divided into two broad categories: (1) caselaw regarding employment contracts and (2) caselaw regarding commercial matters. According to each of these categories, the interpretation of these covenants requires the application of distinct rules. *Payette v. Guay Inc.*, [2013] 3 SCR 95 (Can. Supr. Ct.).

Caselaw concerning non-compete covenants, in the context of an employment contract, is rendered based on the above-mentioned article 2089 C.C.Q. In this case, Québec courts have taken a firm position regarding the enforceability of such covenants. In the employment context, covenants are very narrowly construed and deemed illegal and unenforceable or against the public order more readily than in a strictly commercial matter.

This strict interpretation of employment matters can be explained by the disproportionate bargaining power between the employer and the employee. This imbalance is very often present in the relationship between a franchisor and a franchisee, both at the time of negotiation of the franchise agreement and at the time of its renewal. The imbalance results in a contract of adhesion between the parties. The franchise agreement by its nature is often characterized as a contract of adhesion. *9169-3556 Québec inc. v. Gestions René Simoneau ltée*, 2009 QCCS 3890 (Can. Que. Sup. Ct.); *Distribution Stéréo Plus inc. v. Télévision J.M. Beaudoin inc.*, 2007 CanLII 5105 (QC C.S.) (Can. Que. Sup. Ct.). In the case of a franchise agreement qualified as a contract of adhesion, the imbalance of power justifies a stricter interpretation as to the enforceability of non-compete covenants, of the nature found in employment contracts. *See, e.g., Aliments Humpty Dumpty Ltee v. Gagnon*, [1988] R.J.Q. 1840 (Can. Que. Sup. Ct.); *Les Restaurants Pacini Inc. v. Les Mets Gour-Bec Ltée*, (C.S., 1993-08-03) SOQUIJ AZ-93021605 (Can. Que. Sup. Ct.); and *9169-3556 Québec Inc. v. Gestions René Simoneau ltée*, 2009 QCCS 3890 (Can. Que. Sup. Ct.).

As for the franchise agreements falling into the second category somewhere between those found in commercial contracts (i.e., sale of business agreements), for which the franchisee has had the opportunity to negotiate essential terms with the franchisor, the rules of interpretation of a non-competition covenant will be more generous and the courts will allow more leeway in the construction or enforcement of non-compete covenants. In commercial matters, a restrictive covenant of non-competition is legal unless it is shown by a preponderance of evidence that it is unreasonable in its scope. In such a context, the validity of a non-competition clause will depend on the circumstances in which the contract was concluded, as well as various other factors such as the nature of the business's activities, the parties' experience and expertise, or the fact that the parties had access to legal counsel or other professionals. *Payette v. Guay*, [2013] 3 SCR 95 (Can. Supr. Ct.); *Provigo Distribution inc. v. Complexe commercial de l'Île inc.*, 2020 QCCA 970 (Can. Que. C.A.).

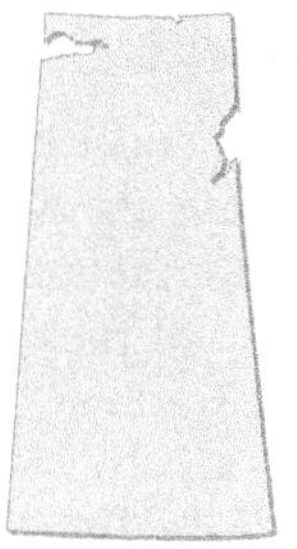

Saskatchewan

*By Conrad Hadubiak, Q.C. **

1. Has the province addressed covenants against competition in the context of franchising?

- **Does the province have a franchising statute or regulations that address covenants against competition?**
- **Does the province have a covenants statute of general applicability that would encompass franchise covenants?**
- **Have the courts addressed covenants in the context of franchising either under a statute or under the province's common law?**

There is no specific franchise legislation in Saskatchewan, which means that covenants against competition in the franchising context are dealt with as a matter of contract law. Nor does Saskatchewan have a covenants statute of general applicability that would encompass franchise covenants. Generally, however, in order for a covenant against competition to be found reasonable and enforced, courts will consider whether the plaintiff has a legitimate *proprietary* interest that warrants protection, the reasonableness of the geographic area the restrictive covenant is intended to cover, the reasonableness of the arrangement between the parties, and the extent to which the restrictive covenant fetters competition or constitutes an unreasonable restraint on trade. There are few cases in Saskatchewan that deal with the non-competition covenants specifically in the franchising context. For this reason, we have examined judicial interpretation of non-competition covenants in the employment context to supplement our understanding of such covenants in the franchising context.

Covenants against competition are dealt with under Saskatchewan's common law and are narrowly construed. *Thienes v. Godenir*, 2011 SKQB 271 (Can. Sask. Q.B.) at para. 37 summarizes a widely used four-prong test in Saskatchewan to assess the reasonableness and enforceability of a restrictive covenant:

> In summary, to assess the reasonableness of a restrictive covenant to determine whether the Court should enforce it, the following questions must be addressed:

*Conrad Hadubiak practices in the Regina office of MLT Aikins LLP. Aziz Aboudheir, also in the Regina office of MLT Aikins, LLP, assisted in the preparation of this chapter.

1. Does the plaintiff have a proprietary interest to protect?
2. Are the spatial and temporal features of the clause too broad?
3. Is the non-competition clause reasonable as between the parties?
4. Is the clause unenforceable as being against competition generally?

In *Pillar to Post Inc. v. Hudon*, 2001 SKQB 369 (Can. Sask. Q.B.), the court dismissed an application that would prevent a franchisee from operating its new home inspecting business after the termination of the parties' franchise agreement. The court held that where an injunction is likely to resolve a substantial part of the dispute between the parties, a strong prima facie case is required, stating: "In Saskatchewan the courts have over the years concluded that where a breach of a restrictive covenant is at issue and there is a likelihood that the whole dispute between the parties will be substantially decided or likely to be resolved by the outcome of the interim injunction application, then the plaintiff must establish a strong prima facie case in order to succeed." The court held that the affidavit evidence may be insufficient to assess the reasonableness of the restrictive covenant and was concerned that closing down the defendants' business without a full trial of the issues in dispute would take away their livelihood.

In *Roblan Distributors Ltd. v. Theofan* (1993), 107 Sask. R. 268 (Can. Sask. Q.B.), a clause that prohibited the defendant from operating or working at a record store business within a 25-mile radius of any of plaintiff's stores throughout Canada for a three-year period was found to be too restrictive and was void. Justice Barclay held:

> In the case at bar as there are Sam the Record Man outlets in every province of Canada and given that the restriction is for a period of three years, the provision, in my view, is so restrictive as to its terms and geography as to be treated as prima facie void. The authorities are to the effect that Roblan must therefore justify or establish that the clause is reasonable in the circumstances. In this case Roblan has not advanced any reason or presented any evidence as to why it is necessary to restrain competition for a period of three years and should extend throughout the whole of the country. (citation omitted)

Justice Barclay held further that "The law appears to be well settled that in the absence of a legitimate proprietary interest requiring protection, a restrictive covenant is contrary to public policy and void."

---

2. Have the courts articulated the "legitimate interests" of the franchisor that will support enforcement of a covenant against competition contained in a franchise agreement?

➤ **If so, what are they (e.g., protection of goodwill, protection of confidential information), and in what contexts did the issue arise?**

➤ **If not, what interests have been recognized in other contexts (e.g., employment agreements, the sale of business context)?**

The court in *Roblan Distributors Ltd. v. Theofan* (1993), 107 Sask. R. 268 (Can. Sask. Q.B.) has stated that a "legitimate proprietary interest requiring protection" is required. The court did not specifically define what those interests might be;

however, the court did find that there was no legitimate proprietary interest requiring protection in that case. Core to the court's decision appears to be the fact that the franchisor did not have any outlets in Saskatchewan.

In *Ergonic Resources Inc. v. Waker et al.*, [1982] 19 Sask. R. 128 (Can. Sask. Q.B.), the court declined to grant an injunction against an ex-franchisee who began operating a competing computer store. In this decision, the court recognized that a franchise system and confidential information such as customer lists are legitimate interests of a franchisor, and that an injunction could not by justified because the ex-franchisee no longer had the benefit of that information. Justice Gerein held at para. 14:

> Should I be in error as to any of the foregoing I would still decline to grant the interim injunction for the reason that I am not satisfied that the plaintiff would suffer irreparable harm. The defendants are operating out of one location in a rather large urban centre. They no longer will have the benefit of the plaintiff's franchise system or assistance. They, as best as I can make out, are not possessed of any unique or confidential information such as customer lists. They will simply be operating a retail store.

In *Turtle v. Valvoline Canadian Franchising Corp*, 2021 SKCA 46, the Saskatchewan Court of Appeal stayed an interlocutory injunction enjoining an ex-franchisee from operating a competing oil change business. The chambers judge who granted the injunction found that the franchisor would suffer irreparable harm in part because the ex-franchisee continued to accept the franchisor's coupons and use its trademarks. Despite the injunction having been stayed, it is clear that trademarks constitute a legitimate business interest of a franchisor. There was, however, recognition by the court of the franchisor's legitimate interests; the court lifted the stay on the condition that the director of the ex-franchisee resign from her directorship and abstain from being involved in the competing oil change business pending determination of the appeal.

Another legitimate interest was recognized in the employment/independent contractor context when the court decided in *Fonkalsrud v. Boxall*, 2014 SKQB 134 (Can. Sask. Q.B.), that the owner of a massage therapy business had a legitimate proprietary interest in the client base and corporate relationships she had developed over the years. Although the restrictive covenant in question ultimately was not enforced on account that it was overbroad and a non-solicitation clause would have sufficed, this decision indicates that a business owner's built-up client base and corporate relationships are legitimate interests that can be relied on, at least in part, to enforce covenants against competition, so long as the scope of the covenant is reasonable. SK

Outside of the franchise context, the Saskatchewan courts considered the application of a non-competition agreement in *Cantelo (c.o.b. Drillers Tattoos) v. Paton*, 2011 SKPC 186 (Can. Sask. Prov. Ct.). *Cantelo* concerned the application of a restrictive covenant in the context of a one-year apprenticeship agreement, which had extended beyond its initial term. Paton was a tattoo artist who had agreed to rent a chair from Cantelo, the proprietor of a tattoo business. The agreement contained the following restrictive covenant:

> Adam Paton agrees that in event of the termination of this agreement by either party and after the term hereof has expired that he will not engage in tattooing for gain nor will he be a proprietor of, nor employee, servant

> or contractor of any person or corporation engaged in the operation of a tattooing business within a 200 mile (320 km) radius of the City of Yorkton for a period of 3 years commencing the final date at Drillers Tattoos.

The court held that the restrictive covenant was aimed at eliminating competition, as opposed to protecting a legitimate proprietary interest, and was therefore against public policy.

---

3. What time limitations have courts recognized as reasonable in the franchise context?

- **How have they been related to the interests protected?**

The Saskatchewan courts have held restrictive covenants arising from franchise agreements to be unreasonable at durations of two and three years. In *Pillar to Post Inc. v. Hudon*, 2001 SKQB 369 (Can. Sask. Q.B.), the court held that it would consider geographic distance and time limits in assessing the reasonableness of a restrictive covenant; however, the impact of a two-year time limit on the defendants' livelihood could not be determined on affidavit evidence alone. Yet, on the balance of convenience, the defendants were not enjoined from continuing their home inspection business, the effect of which was to invalidate, or at least postpone until resolution at trial, the two-year time period the agreement had contemplated. In *Roblan Distributors Ltd. v. Theofan* (1993), 107 Sask. R. 268 (Can. Sask. Q.B.), the court held that a three-year time limitation was unreasonable. The applicant failed to offer reasons or evidence as to why a restraint on competition was necessary for a three-year period.

These cases are consistent with the earlier holding in *Tradeland Agencies Ltd. v. MacKinnon and MacKinnon Holdings Ltd.*, [1979] 5 Sask. R. 438 (Can. Sask. Q.B.), in which the court noted that the time and area contemplated by a covenant, in order to be enforceable, must not be "excessive, having regard to the circumstances of the case." Although *Tradeland* was not a franchising case, in light of this holding, a necessarily fact-specific inquiry would determine the reasonableness of a time limit. For example, in *Rawlco Radio Ltd. v. Lozinski*, 2012 SKQB 460 (Can. Sask. Q.B.), the court, analyzing the facts in detail, found a time limit of six months on employment to be reasonable.

---

4. What geographic limitations have courts recognized as reasonable in the franchise context?

- **How have they been related to the interests protected?**
- **Have courts recognized the legitimacy of protecting other franchisees from competition?**

In *Pillar to Post Inc. v. Hudon*, 2001 SKQB 369 (Can. Sask. Q.B.), the court held that the impact of a twenty-mile geographic limitation on the defendants' livelihood could not be determined on affidavit evidence alone, which lends to an inference that a 20-mile limitation could potentially be reasonable. By contrast, in *Roblan*

Distributors Ltd v. Theofan, [1993] 107 Sask. R. 268 (Can. Sask. Q.B.), a nationwide geographical prohibition on operating within 25 miles of another franchise was considered unreasonable in a franchising context.

In another case outside of the franchise context, *Rawlco Radio Ltd. v. Lozinski*, 2012 SKQB 460 (Can. Sask. Q.B.), the court found a geographic restriction of "the City of Saskatoon and a 100-kilometer radius thereof" to be reasonable. The court reasoned that upholding the restrictive covenant would in no way lessen competition in the marketplace and that the former employee would not be unduly restricted from pursuing his career within television, newspaper, and the internet in other places in Saskatchewan. The court found that "many of the restrictive covenants upheld in other cases before this Court have been for two years, with some of them for an area including all of Saskatchewan. The current restriction is much more reasonable." Thus, it can be inferred that by reducing geographic restrictions to include a single marketplace, these covenants are more likely to be found reasonable and upheld.

With respect to the question of protecting other franchisees from competition, the court considered such a matter in *Ergonic Resources Inc. v. Waker*, [1982] 19 Sask. R. 128 (Can. Sask. Q.B.). The facts of the case were that a franchisee was carrying on business in the same area as another franchisee. However, the franchisee had stopped operating as a franchise, despite still being within the term of the franchise agreement. The court held at para. 17 that "the fact that the defendants are in competition to a franchise outlet does not concern me for the reason that when that outlet commenced business it knew competition would exist. The only difference now is that the competition is not another franchisee." The restrictive covenant in question prevented the franchisee from carrying on a similar business to the franchise in the "current authorized locations, and any other area in which we have granted a franchise." The application judge found the latter portion relating to the area unreasonable because, as stated at para. 11, it could include "all of Saskatchewan, all of Canada, or for that matter, even wider areas." Based on the *Ergonic* decision, it can be concluded that, as of yet, Saskatchewan has not recognized a legitimate interest in protecting other franchisees from competition.

5. What limitations on activities have courts recognized as reasonable in the franchise context?

There are few Saskatchewan cases in which the scope of a non-compete was held to be reasonable. As a result, given that the courts are reluctant to uphold non-competition agreements, it is prudent for a practitioner to draft agreements as narrowly as the circumstances will permit so as to increase the likelihood of withstanding judicial scrutiny.

The decision in *Aquifer Distribution Ltd. v. McMurtry*, 2008 SKQB 456 (Can. Sask. Q.B.), provides some guidance on what a proprietary interest might reasonably be. For instance, with respect to clients, a reasonable proprietary interest might include earned goodwill and actual customer lists, but not potential clients who were once solicited but declined to do business. The proprietary interest in clientele and business contacts was affirmed in an employment context in *Fonkalsrud v. Boxall*, 2014 SKQB 134 (Can. Sask. Q.B.).

The court in *Aquifer* found a "one-year restraint" on a former employee's activities in Saskatchewan, given the former managerial roles held by the employee throughout

Saskatchewan, was prima facie reasonable in scope; however, the court ultimately held the impugned covenant to be directed at restraining an individual from carrying on his or her occupation, which is contrary to public policy and therefore unreasonable.

6. Does the province recognize a difference between in-term and post-term covenants?

In *Turtle v. Valvoline Canadian Franchising Corp*, 2021 SKCA 46 (Can. Sask. C.A.), the applicant was successful in obtaining a stay of enforcement of an injunction granted by the chambers judge that would prevent the applicant from operating a competing oil change business. In this case, the applicant was party to two franchise agreements for two different oil change locations. One agreement had ostensibly expired while the other continued to be in effect. The chambers judge and the Saskatchewan Court of Appeal made no distinction in their analysis between the in-term restrictive covenant still in effect under one franchise agreement and the post-term restrictive covenant under the ostensibly expired franchise agreement. Based on these decisions, it can be inferred that there is little, if any, difference in how in-term and post-term restrictive covenants are treated in Saskatchewan. However, as these decisions did not turn on the issue of in-term or post-term covenants, the conclusion based on *Valvoline* may be subject to sudden change.

7. Has the province allowed enforcement of covenants against non-signatories (e.g., family members, newly formed corporations)?

Turtle v. Valvoline Canadian Franchising Corp, 2021 SKCA 76 (Can. Sask. C.A.) touched upon the enforcement of covenants against non-signatories. Valvoline, a franchisor, sued two former franchises as well as their sole director, seeking an injunction enjoining the operation of an oil change business. The impugned oil change business used to be a franchisee of Valvoline; however, following the expiry of the franchise agreement, the business instead began offering oil changes under the name of a separate business that was incorporated by the sole director. Valvoline alleged that since the sole director signed the franchise agreement on behalf of the corporations, she was personally bound to the agreements and the non-competition covenants contained in them. Although the signatory was the sole director of the ex-franchisee, the court held that the established principles of separate corporate personality, in conjunction with the finding that a principal may bind the corporation but not the reverse, meant that the non-compete was not enforceable as against the sole director of the ex-franchisee. As such, with respect to the enforceability of non-competition covenants, the court found that these covenants are not enforceable against non-signatories.

8. Will the province modify, "blue-pencil," or otherwise reduce a covenant found to be overbroad?

Although not a franchise case, in *Direct Integrated Transportation Inc. v. Haryett*, 2005 SKQB 55 (Can. Sask. Q.B.), the court held that it would be inappropriate for the court to rewrite an overly broad non-competition covenant. The court specifically stated that "[g]iven the broad language employed in the instant non-competition covenant, and the absence of any evidence of what Dasher, Haryett, and Westberg intended at the time the Service Contracts were executed, it would be inappropriate for this Court to rewrite the Covenant by adding words thereto limiting the geographical area to which it applies." In this respect, Saskatchewan is similar to other Canadian provinces in exhibiting a reluctance to rewrite contracts.

In *Garda Canada Security Corp v. Ramirez*, 2011 SKQB 294 (Can. Sask. Q.B.), the court considered an employment contract that contained a restrictive covenant against the solicitation of "any person, firm or corporation that was a customer of [the employer] during the period of time that the Employee was employed by [the employer]." The lack of express geographic restriction in the employment agreement, the overall length of the employee's employment, and that fact that the scope of the employer's clientele "extend[ed] well beyond the reaches of Saskatchewan" led the trial judge to conclude that the spatial limitation on the restrictive covenant was unreasonable and could not be upheld. Despite this conclusion, the trial judge was able to justify the breadth of the restrictive covenant based on public policy. Although the trial judge did not choose to limit the covenant, her willingness to do so may be inferred from her analysis. Absent the public policy justification for the covenant, it is possible that the trial judge may have agreed with the respondent to "read down" the covenant to be limited to just the Saskatchewan marketplace.

9. When does a non-compete period begin to run? Will courts equitably extend the term?

In *Culligan Canada Ltd. v. Fettes*, 2010 SKQB 339 (Can. Sask. Q.B.), at para. 9, the court held that the "weight of judicial authority is that injunctions are not granted if they will effectively extend the contractual term of a restrictive covenant, thus giving the plaintiff a further competition free period." This case suggests that the courts in Saskatchewan will not equitably extend the term of the non-compete period.

10. Are there additional nuances or peculiarities of the province's treatment of covenants in the franchising context?

As in other Canadian provinces, in Saskatchewan, restrictive covenants are often enforced by way of interlocutory injunction. The legal test for interlocutory injunctions in Saskatchewan is described in *Deloitte, Haskins & Sells v. Brooker* (1983), 20 B.L.R. 252, 23 Sask. R. 58 (Can. Sask. Q.B.), at para. 9, as follows:

> The following principles determine whether or not an interlocutory injunction will be granted:
>
> > (1) An interlocutory injunction will only be granted where the right to relief is clear.
> >
> > (2) The plaintiff in asserting that right must show a strong prima facie case, in support of the right which he asserts and a strong possibility that he will succeed at trial.

> (3) The plaintiff must be able to show that an injunction until the hearing, is necessary to protect him against irreparable damage and loss, mere inconvenience is not enough.
>
> (4) Where any doubt exists as to the plaintiff's right or if his right is not disputed, but if violation is denied, the court should determine on the balance of convenience to the parties the nature, of the injury which the defendant on the one hand would suffer if the injunction was granted and he should turn out to be right and that the plaintiff on the other hand might sustain if the injunction was refused and he should ultimately turn out to be right. The burden of proof that the inconvenience which the plaintiff will suffer by the refusal of the injunction is greater that [sic] which the defendant will suffer lies on the plaintiff. (*Halsbury's Laws of England*) (3d Ed.), vol. 21, p. 364).

This test, as articulated in *Deloitte*, has been cited many times and was applied in a franchising context in *Roblan Distributors Ltd. v. Theofan* (1993), 107 Sask. R. 268 (Can. Sask. Q.B.) and *Pillar to Post Inc v. Hudon*, 2001 SKQB 369 (Can. Sask. Q.B.).

Mexico Analysis

Mexico

*by Jorge Mondragón, Lucia Fernández, and Patricio Martinez**

1. Has the country addressed covenants against competition in the context of franchising?

- **Does the country have a franchising statute or regulations that address covenants against competition?**
- **Does the country have a covenants statute of general applicability that would encompass franchise covenants?**
- **Have the courts addressed covenants in the context of franchising either under a statute or under the country's common law?**

There are no statutes or regulations that specifically address covenants against competition in the context of franchising. Mexican federal courts have also not addressed covenants against competition in the context of franchising.[1] Since no statute directly regulates covenants against competition, they are equivalent to any other negative covenant and, therefore, regulated by articles 2027 and 2028 of the Federal Civil Code and article 6 Bis of the Commerce Code.

There are, however, several factors that differentiate covenants against competition from other negative covenants, especially within the context of franchising. First, a covenant against competition could violate employment rights if the covenant applies to individuals. Second, the covenant could be an anticompetitive restriction. Third, a franchisee that breaches a non-competition covenant could incur a sanction if the acts performed by the franchisee are considered "unfair competition" under the Federal Law for the Protection of Industrial Property (*Ley Federal de Protección a la Propiedad Industrial* ("LFPPI")).

*Jorge Mondragon is a partner and Lucia Fernandez and Patricio Martinez are counsels in the law firm of Gonzalez Calvillo, S.C. Associates Deborah Luengo and Daniel González also contributed to this article.

1. The judicial system in Mexico is divided into federal and state (local) courts. The Federal Law for the Protection of Industrial Property (*Ley Federal de Protección a la Propiedad Industrial*), which regulates franchises, states that Mexican federal courts have jurisdiction over infractions regulated by such law, as well as any civil or mercantile controversies that result from its application. Likewise, industrial property and mercantile matters are governed by federal law.

VALIDITY AND LIMITATIONS

Civil and Mercantile Federal Law

Under Mexican law, contracts and their provisions must be lawful to be valid, which means that the terms must not contravene public policy and "accepted practices" (*buenas costumbres*). The latter is not a concept defined by law. There is no universally accepted definition, but "accepted practices" are generally considered repeated practices typically taken as a moral obligation in an organized social, economic, and political community, which are essential means for achieving a general and individual well-being.[2]

Covenants against competition should be, a priori, enforced under Mexican contractual law just as any other negative covenant, with specific liquidated damages agreed upon by the parties or, in the absence of such agreement, seeking damages and lost profits to be determined by the competent court. In the latter case, the affected party files a claim in civil courts. A judge would determine and estimate the appropriate award. Notwithstanding the foregoing, in the context of franchising, the LFPPI could have precedence in regulating breaches of covenants against competition, as explained below.

Constitutional Law

Article 5 of the Mexican Constitution guarantees the right to pursue a livelihood, stating that no one shall be prevented from exercising the profession, industry, or commerce he or she chooses, provided that such employment is lawful.

It also provides that the State shall not allow the enforcement of any contract, covenant, or agreement that pretends to diminish a person's liberty to carry out an activity. The Mexican Constitution prohibits arrangements where individuals agree to renounce, temporarily or permanently, their right to exercise a profession, industry, or commerce.

Execution and enforcement of covenants against competition in franchise agreements are generally complicated when the franchisee is an individual and significantly more if they ultimately prevent the individual's ability to work in a specific industry within the entire Mexican territory. Some nuances could help the application of non-compete covenants, such as limiting the territory, activity, and period of application, so the covenant is not an absolute prohibition of exercising a specific profession.

Proving that the franchisee has access to trade secrets and that letting him compete for a specific time with the franchisor would give him an unfair competitive advantage is also an accepted restriction. A circuit court decision followed similar reasoning, although it was related to non-compete covenants in the context of a business's sale. This decision is further described in the answer to section 2 below.

Mexican Antitrust Statue

The Federal Competition Commission (*Comisión Federal de Competencia Económica* ("Cofece")) is the agency in charge of guaranteeing free market access and economic competition, as well as preventing, investigating, and prosecuting anticompetitive conducts in all markets, except telecommunications and broadcasting, which fall

2. Thesis number 165500 of the Fourth Collegiate Civil Court of the First Circuit, published in *Seminario Judicial de la Federación y su Gaceta XXXI*, January 2010, civil law, p. 2171, ninth period.

under the authority of the Federal Telecommunications Institute (*Instituto Federal de Telecomunicaciones*). Therefore, unless a franchise is telecom-related, it is likely that Cofece will be the authority with jurisdiction over competition matters involving the franchise.

Under the Mexican Antitrust Statue (*Ley Federal de Competencia Económica* ("LFCE")), "concentrations" are mergers, acquisitions of control, or any act through which companies, associations, shares, quota parts, trusts, or assets in general are accumulated by competitors, suppliers, clients, or any other economic agent.

The LFCE requires that economic agents involved in concentrations that meet specific criteria are mandated to seek approval from Cofece before closing. Cofece will review the transaction to confirm if it should approve or block it and will have up to 60 business days once the file is complete to issue its decision.

One of the elements that Cofece considers for the authorization of concentrations is the inclusion of non-compete and non-solicitation covenants as part of the terms and conditions of the transaction. Cofece's Merger Guidelines[3] include a description of such covenants and the generally accepted parameters for such kinds of covenants. Although the Merger Guidelines are not binding, they reflect Cofece's standards and how it may address these types of covenants.

Limitations

The Merger Guidelines describe non-compete covenants in the context of mergers and acquisitions as those agreements by which one of the parties (generally the selling party) assumes the obligation not to compete, directly or indirectly, with the acquiring party for a specific period, in the business that is the subject matter of the transaction and in those areas where the target company is active.

Additionally, the Merger Guidelines describe non-solicitation covenants as agreements by which one of the parties (generally the seller or both) assumes the obligation not to actively seek to hire those individuals who already work or render their professional services in the target company. Notwithstanding the foregoing, Cofece only rules on non-solicitation covenants when they are equivalent to non-compete covenants and assesses them following the criteria provided for this type of provision.

Cofece only approves non-competition clauses in the context of a merger or acquisition but may also review them in abuse of dominance cases (referred to as relative monopolistic practices).

When reviewing covenants against competition, Cofece does so on a case-by-case basis, analyzing the justification of the inclusion of non-compete covenants in certain transactions. For its analysis, it considers (1) parties subject to the restriction, (2) product or service coverage, (3) geographical coverage, and (4) duration. Such elements are further described below:

(i) Parties subject to the restriction – Limited to the seller(s) and the entities of its economic group; it may include the special purpose vehicle (SPV) through which the parties implemented the transaction and remain part of the seller's group.

MX

3. *Merger Guidelines (Guía para la Notificación de Concentraciones)*, Cofece, 2021, https://www.cofece.mx/wp-content/uploads/2021/04/DOF-08abril2021-01.pdf.

(ii) Product or service coverage – Limited to the products and services offered by the target of the transaction.[4]
(iii) Geographical coverage – Limited to the areas where the target was active or in advanced stages to enter a specific market.
(iv) Duration – Generally limited to three years after closing or the end of the joint venture; more extended periods may be acceptable under specific market circumstances.

Although not all transactions include non-compete or non-solicitation covenants, Cofece addresses this type of covenant frequently. According to Cofece's 2020 Report on Concentrations, from the 128 concentrations resolved during 2020, only 35 (27.3 percent) included non-compete covenants.

When a non-compete clause fails to meet Cofece's criteria, it is expected that the parties will voluntarily amend its terms to avoid having their pre-merger filing conditioned or blocked. In the franchising context, in April 2021, Cofece conditioned the transaction between G500 SAPI, G500 Corporation, and G500 Network, by which they planned to vertically integrate through a franchise agreement with several gas stations. The transaction was conditioned because the non-compete covenant did not comply with Cofece's criteria. Cofece considered that through this agreement, the G500 Network would be able to recommend prices and service standards that could diminish competition by coordinating competing gas stations.[5]

Violations

If a breach of a covenant not to compete in a franchising context is considered unfair competition in terms of the LFPPI, the authorities may sanction the breaching conduct. Performing actions against accepted customs or practices in the industry, commerce, and services that imply an unfair competition, which relates to matters regulated under such law, could be considered administrative infractions under said law.

The Federal Courts stated that the breach of non-compete covenants could be regarded as unfair competition. In a 1959 case, the Third Chamber of the Supreme Court of Justice stated that loss related to breach of a non-competition covenant should be related to the benefit, profits, or gain caused by such unfair competition.[6]

Administrative infractions are determined in an administrative proceeding before the Mexican Institute of Industrial Property ("Institute"). Following the administrative proceeding, the Institute issues a resolution that contains its findings, including, if appropriate, sanctions for administrative infractions. Per the provisions of the LFPPI, possible sanctions are:

1. Fines of up to 250,000 units of measure and update in Mexico (approximately $1,120,000 U.S. dollars).

---

4. In transactions that are carried out abroad and involve products and/or services manufactured in multiple jurisdictions, the non-competition covenant may be negotiated at a global level. In this case, it may include all the products and/or services offered by the target of the transaction worldwide, even if in Mexico the seller's activities are limited to only some of them.

5. G500 SAPI, G500 Corporation and G500 Network, File CNT-022-2020, Cofece (April 22, 2021), https://www.cofece.mx/CFCResoluciones/docs/Concentraciones/V6074/3/5417961.pdf.

6. Thesis No. 271744 of the Third Chamber of the Supreme Court of Justice of the Nation, published in the SEMINARIO JUDICIAL DE LA FEDERACIÓN, fourth part, XXVIII, October 1959, civil law, p. 224, sixth period.

2. Additional fines of up to 1,000 units of measure and update in Mexico (approximately $4,480 U.S. dollars) per day if the infraction persists.
3. Temporary closure for up to 90 days.
4. Definitive closure.

In addition to the foregoing, the LFPPI allows the damaged party to seek damages and losses either before the Institute or in a civil court, which should never be lower than 40 percent of the indicator of the legitimate value suffered by the affected holder of the industrial property right.

An important issue in cases involving a breach of a non-competition covenant used to be whether a party could demand the payment of damages and losses in a civil court without first obtaining a resolution from the Institute declaring that the breach constitutes an unfair practice. The Supreme Court addressed the issue, stating in a now-binding precedent that a decision from the Institute is necessary before a complaint for damages and losses can be filed in the civil courts.[7]

---

2. Have the courts articulated the "legitimate interests" of the franchisor that will support enforcement of a covenant against competition contained in a franchise agreement?

- **If so, what are they (e.g., protection of goodwill, protection of confidential information), and in what contexts did the issue arise?**
- **If not, what interests have been recognized in other contexts (e.g., employment agreements, the sale of business context)?**

Mexican courts have not yet addressed the issue of non-compete covenants in the franchise context and, therefore, have not addressed the "legitimate interests" of franchisors.

Despite the above, the Civil Circuit Court has addressed non-compete covenants in the business transaction context.[8] The court concluded that said covenants do not breach the law nor the public policy or accepted practices since the protection of competition in the commercial sphere is crucial.

The court also stated that non-compete covenants do not necessarily violate the employment rights or freedom of activities established in article 5 of the Mexican Constitution, provided they do not go beyond the necessary limits to prevent unfair competition. These limits are assessed on a case-by-case basis to ensure that its objective is to prevent unlawful competition.

The court established that there must be limits regarding the restricted parties, product or services coverage, geographical coverage, and duration of the non-compete covenant. On this note, the court stated that unlimited non-compete covenants are unlawful because they go against accepted commercial practices.

---

7. Jurisprudence no. 181491 of the First Chamber of the Supreme Court of Justice of the Nation, published in the SEMINARIO JUDICIAL DE LA FEDERACIÓN Y SU GACETA XIX, May 2004, civil law, p. 356, ninth period.

8. Thesis number 165500 of the Fourth Collegiate Civil Court of the First Circuit, published in the SEMINARIO JUDICIAL DE LA FEDERACIÓN Y SU GACETA XXXI, January 2010, civil law, p. 2171, ninth period.

The court further established that non-compete covenants could be applicable even in the absence of an agreement, as such covenants would be a natural consequence of the business sale, based on article 1796 of the Mexican Civil Federal Code, which states that an agreement compels the parties to comply with not only what is expressly agreed but also the consequences related to good faith, customs, and statutes.

Please note that this issue has been addressed in only one case by a federal court in a judicial decision. Under Mexican law, judicial decisions are considered isolated theses and do not constitute per se a mandatory precedent.

3. What time limitations have courts recognized as reasonable in the franchise context?

- **If no franchise cases have been decided, what time limitations have been recognized in other contexts?**
- **How have they been related to the interests protected?**

Federal courts have not recognized specific time limitations as reasonable in the franchise context or any other.

From an antitrust perspective, the Merger Guidelines establish that non-compete covenants will be limited to three years after the transaction's closing (i.e., once authorized by Cofece and the transaction has been implemented), and the duration is duly justified. More extended post-term restrictions may be acceptable to Cofece if certain market characteristics and circumstances are present, in the understanding that these exceptions tend to be scarce.

In business transactions, the duration of a non-compete covenant should be no longer than necessary to protect a legitimate interest. The Merger Guidelines establish that the first element in determining whether a non-compete covenant is justified is to verify whether the transaction involves transferring assets that lack property rights or regulatory protection and, therefore, should be protected by the non-compete covenant. In such case, the four elements (parties subject to the restriction, product or service coverage, geographical coverage, and duration) are assessed to determine if they are pro- or anticompetitive.

4. What geographic limitations have courts recognized as reasonable in the franchise context?

- **How have they been related to the interests protected?**
- **Have courts recognized the legitimacy of protecting other franchisees from competition?**

While federal courts have not recognized specific geographic limitations as reasonable in the franchise context, under antitrust law, geographic limitations imposed to franchisees would be assessed following a rule of reason approach. They could be deemed illegal if franchisors impose them with market power and they result in anticompetitive foreclosure.

5. What limitations on activities have courts recognized as reasonable in the franchise context?

Federal courts have not recognized specific limitations on activities as reasonable in the franchise context.

In business transactions, the Merger Guidelines do not address limitations of activities regarding non-compete covenants. Nevertheless, they address goods and services limitations, stating that the scope of such clauses should be limited to those goods and services that are subject to the transaction. In the case of franchises, this must refer to the franchised products/services.

6. Does the country recognize a difference between in-term and post-term covenants?

From an antitrust perspective, in-term covenants must comply with the requirements related to the identity of the restricted parties and the scope of the restriction (product/service and geographical), and can be valid for as long as the franchise agreement is in place.

Post-term covenants would additionally be subject to the general three-year term previously discussed.

7. Has the country allowed enforcement of covenants against non-signatories (e.g., family members, newly formed corporations)?

In the sale of a business, the Merger Guidelines state that legitimate non-compete covenants should apply only to the seller and the entities that form part of its economic group, since they transfer the assets and could take advantage of its knowledge of the market and technology, disturbing the efficiency of the asset transfer. Thus, depending on the scope of the language used in a non-compete clause, while non-signatories would not be legally bound to comply with such covenant, their actions could trigger a breach of such covenant for which the signatory would be liable.

8. Will the country modify, "blue-pencil," or otherwise reduce a covenant found to be overbroad?

Considering that Mexico is a civil-law country where freedom of contract is one of the essential principles of contract law, courts could consider the non-compete covenants either enforceable, as per the terms agreed by the parties, or unenforceable due to violating conditions in the contract formation.

Notwithstanding the foregoing, in the context of antitrust legislation, Cofece may order to reduce the scope of a non-compete covenant to issue its authorization in connection with concentrations or as a result of an investigation for abuse of dominance.

9. When does a non-compete period begin to run? Will courts equitably extend the term?

The non-compete period may run from the date of the franchise agreement and for the agreed-upon period after its termination. No equitable extension exists, given that Mexico is a civil-law country.

10. Are there additional nuances or peculiarities of the country's treatment of covenants in the franchising context?

We have not identified any additional nuances or peculiarities that may be relevant in the franchising context.